Twentieth-Century Literary Criticism

Guide to Gale Literary Criticism Series

For criticism on	Consult these Gale series
Authors now living or who died after December 31, 1959	***CONTEMPORARY LITERARY CRITICISM (CLC)***
Authors who died between 1900 and 1959	***TWENTIETH-CENTURY LITERARY CRITICISM (TCLC)***
Authors who died between 1800 and 1899	***NINETEENTH-CENTURY LITERATURE CRITICISM (NCLC)***
Authors who died between 1400 and 1799	***LITERATURE CRITICISM FROM 1400 TO 1800 (LC)*** ***SHAKESPEAREAN CRITICISM (SC)***
Authors who died before 1400	***CLASSICAL AND MEDIEVAL LITERATURE CRITICISM (CMLC)***
Black writers of the past two hundred years	***BLACK LITERATURE CRITICISM (BLC)***
Authors of books for children and young adults	***CHILDREN'S LITERATURE REVIEW (CLR)***
Dramatists	***DRAMA CRITICISM (DC)***
Hispanic writers of the late nineteenth and twentieth centuries	***HISPANIC LITERATURE CRITICISM (HLC)***
Native North American writers and orators of the eighteenth, nineteenth, and twentieth centuries	***NATIVE NORTH AMERICAN LITERATURE (NNAL)***
Poets	***POETRY CRITICISM (PC)***
Short story writers	***SHORT STORY CRITICISM (SSC)***
Major authors from the Renaissance to the present	***WORLD LITERATURE CRITICISM, 1500 TO THE PRESENT (WLC)***

ISSN 0276-8178

Volume 66

Twentieth-Century Literary Criticism

Excerpts from Criticism of the Works of Novelists, Poets, Playwrights, Short Story Writers, and Other Creative Writers Who Lived between 1900 and 1960, from the First Published Critical Appraisals to Current Evaluations

Nancy Dziedzic
Scot Peacock
Editors

Thomas Ligotti
Associate Editor

GALE

DETROIT • NEW YORK • TORONTO • LONDON

STAFF

Nancy Dziedzic, Scot Peacock, *Editors*

Kathleen J. Edgar, Thomas Ligotti,
Associate Editors

Marlene S. Hurst, *Permissions Manager*
Margaret A. Chamberlain, Maria Franklin, Kimberly F. Smilay, *Permissions Specialists*

Diane Cooper, Edna Hedblad, Michele Lonoconus, Maureen Puhl, Shalice Shah,
Permissions Associates
Sarah Chesney, Jeffrey Hermann, *Permissions Assistants*

Victoria B. Cariappa, *Research Manager*
Laura C. Bissey, Julia C. Daniel, Tamara C. Nott, Michele P. Pica,
Research Associates
Alfred A. Gardner, I, *Research Assistant*

Mary Beth Trimper, *Production Director*
Deborah L. Milliken, *Production Assistant*

Sherrell Hobbs, *Macintosh Artist*
Randy Bassett, *Image Database Supervisor*
Robert Duncan, *Imaging Specialist*
Pamela Hayes, *Photography Coordinator*

The paper used in this publication meets the minimum requirements of American National Standard for Information Sciences—Permanence Paper for Printed Library Materials, ANSI Z39.48-1984. ∞™

Library of Congress Catalog Card Number 76-46132
ISBN 0-7876-1164-6
ISSN 0276-8178

Printed in the United States of America
10 9 8 7 6 5 4 3 2 1

Contents

Preface

Since its inception more than fifteen years ago, *Twentieth-Century Literary Criticism* has been purchased and used by nearly 10,000 school, public, and college or university libraries. *TCLC* has covered more than 500 authors, representing 58 nationalities, and over 25,000 titles. No other reference source has surveyed the critical response to twentieth-century authors and literature as thoroughly as *TCLC*. In the words of one reviewer, "there is nothing comparable available." *TCLC* "is a gold mine of information—dates, pseudonyms, biographical information, and criticism from books and periodicals—which many libraries would have difficulty assembling on their own."

Scope of the Series

TCLC is designed to serve as an introduction to authors who died between 1900 and 1960 and to the most significant interpretations of these author's works. The great poets, novelists, short story writers, playwrights, and philosophers of this period are frequently studied in high school and college literature courses. In organizing and excerpting the vast amount of critical material written on these authors, *TCLC* helps students develop valuable insight into literary history, promotes a better understanding of the texts, and sparks ideas for papers and assignments. Each entry in *TCLC* presents a comprehensive survey of an author's career or an individual work of literature and provides the user with a multiplicity of interpretations and assessments. Such variety allows students to pursue their own interests; furthermore, it fosters an awareness that literature is dynamic and responsive to many different opinions.

Every fourth volume of *TCLC* is devoted to literary topics. These topic entries widen the focus of the series from individual authors to such broader subjects as literary movements, prominent themes in twentieth-century literature, literary reaction to political and historical events, significant eras in literary history, prominent literary anniversaries, and the literatures of cultures that are often overlooked by English-speaking readers.

TCLC is designed as a companion series to Gale's *Contemporary Literary Criticism,* which reprints commentary on authors now living or who have died since 1960. Because of the different periods under consideration, there is no duplication of material between *CLC* and *TCLC*. For additional information about *CLC* and Gale's other criticism titles, users should consult the Guide to Gale Literary Criticism Series preceding the title page in this volume.

Coverage

Each volume of *TCLC* is carefully compiled to present:

- criticism of authors, or literary topics, representing a variety of genres and nationalities
- both major and lesser-known writers and literary works of the period
- 6-12 authors or 3-6 topics per volume
- individual entries that survey critical response to each author's work or each topic in literary history, including early criticism to reflect initial reactions; later criticism to represent any rise or decline in reputation; and current retrospective analyses.

Organization of This Book

An author entry consists of the following elements: author heading, biographical and critical introduction, list of principal works, excerpts of criticism (each preceded by an annotation and a bibliographic citation), and a bibliography of further reading.

- The **Author Heading** consists of the name under which the author most commonly wrote, followed by birth and death dates. If an author wrote consistently under a pseudonym, the pseudonym will be listed in the author heading and the real name given in parentheses on the first line of the biographical and critical introduction. Also located at the beginning of the introduction to the author entry are any name variations under which an author wrote, including transliterated forms for authors whose languages use nonroman alphabets.

- The **Biographical and Critical Introduction** outlines the author's life and career, as well as the critical issues surrounding his or her work. References to past volumes of *TCLC* are provided at the beginning of the introduction. Additional sources of information in other biographical and critical reference series published by Gale, including *Short Story Criticism, Children's Literature Review, Contemporary Authors, Dictionary of Literary Biography,* and *Something about the Author,* are listed in a box at the end of the entry.

- Some *TCLC* entries include **Portraits** of the author. Entries also may contain reproductions of materials pertinent to an author's career, including manuscript pages, title pages, dust jackets, letters, and drawings, as well as photographs of important people, places, and events in an author's life.

- The **List of Principal Works** is chronological by date of first book publication and identifies the genre of each work. In the case of foreign authors with both foreign-language publications and English translations, the title and date of the first English-language edition are given in brackets. Unless otherwise indicated, dramas are dated by first performance, not first publication.

- Critical excerpts are prefaced by **Annotations** providing the reader with information about both the critic and the criticism that follows. Included are the critic's reputation, individual approach to literary criticism, and particular expertise in an author's works. Also noted are the relative importance of a work of criticism, the scope of the excerpt, and the growth of critical controversy or changes in critical trends regarding an author. In some cases, these annotations cross-reference excerpts by critics who discuss each other's commentary.

- A complete **Bibliographic Citation** designed to facilitate location of the original essay or book precedes each piece of criticism.

- **Criticism** is arranged chronologically in each author entry to provide a perspective on changes in critical evaluation over the years. All titles of works by the author featured in the entry are printed in boldface type to enable the user to easily locate discussion of particular works. Also for purposes of easier identification, the critic's name and the publication date of the essay are given at the beginning of each piece of criticism. Unsigned criticism is preceded by the title of the journal in which it appeared. Some of the excerpts in *TCLC* also contain translated material. Unless otherwise noted, translations in brackets are by the editors; translations in parentheses or continuous with the text are by the critic. Publication information (such as footnotes or page and line references to specific editions of works) have been deleted at the editor's discretion to provide smoother reading of the text.

- An annotated list of **Further Reading** appearing at the end of each author entry suggests secondary sources on the author. In some cases it includes essays for which the editors could not obtain reprint rights.

Cumulative Indexes

- Each volume of *TCLC* contains a cumulative **Author Index** listing all authors who have appeared in Gale's Literary Criticism Series, along with cross references to such biographical series as *Contemporary Authors* and *Dictionary of Literary Biography.* For readers' convenience, a complete list of Gale titles included appears on the first page of the author index. Useful for locating authors within the various series, this index is particularly valuable for those authors who are identified by a certain period but who, because of their death dates, are placed in another, or for those authors whose careers span two periods. For example, F. Scott Fitzgerald is found in *TCLC,* yet a writer often associated with him, Ernest Hemingway, is found in *CLC.*

- Each *TCLC* volume includes a cumulative **Nationality Index** which lists all authors who have appeared in *TCLC* volumes, arranged alphabetically under their respective nationalities, as well as Topics volume entries devoted to particular national literatures.

- Each new volume in Gale's Literary Criticism Series includes a cumulative **Topic Index,** which lists all literary topics treated in *NCLC, TCLC, LC 1400-1800,* and the *CLC* yearbook.

- Each new volume of *TCLC,* with the exception of the Topics volumes, includes a **Title Index** listing the titles of all literary works discussed in the volume. In response to numerous suggestions from librarians, Gale has also produced a **Special Paperbound Edition** of the *TCLC* title index. This annual cumulation lists all titles discussed in the series since its inception and is issued with the first volume of *TCLC* published each year. Additional copies of the index are available on request. Librarians and patrons will welcome this separate index; it saves shelf space, is easy to use, and is recyclable upon receipt of the following year's cumulation. Titles discussed in the Topics volume entries are not included *TCLC* cumulative index.

Citing *Twentieth-Century Literary Criticism*

When writing papers, students who quote directly from any volume in Gale's literary Criticism Series may use the following general forms to footnote reprinted criticism. The first example pertains to materials drawn from periodicals, the second to material reprinted from books.

[1]William H. Slavick, "Going to School to DuBose Heyward," *The Harlem Renaissance Re-examined,* (AMS Press, 1987); excerpted and reprinted in *Twentieth-Century Literary Criticism,* Vol. 59, ed. Jennifer Gariepy (Detroit: Gale Research, 1995), pp. 94-105.

[2]George Orwell, "Reflections on Gandhi," *Partisan Review,* 6 (Winter 1949), pp. 85-92; excerpted and reprinted in *Twentieth-Century Literary Criticism,* Vol. 59, ed. Jennifer Gariepy (Detroit: Gale Research, 1995), pp. 40-3.

Suggestions Are Welcome

In response to suggestions, several features have been added to *TCLC* since the series began, including annotations to excerpted criticism, a cumulative index to authors in all Gale literary criticism series, entries devoted to criticism on a single work by a major author, more extensive illustrations, and a title index listing all literary works discussed in the series since its inception.

Readers who wish to suggest authors or topics to appear in future volumes, or who have other suggestions, are cordially invited to write the editors.

Acknowledgments

The editors wish to thank the copyright holders of the excerpted criticism included in this volume and the permissions managers of many book and magazine publishing companies for assisting us in securing reprint rights. We are also grateful to the staffs of the Detroit Public Library, the Library of Congress, the University of Detroit Mercy Library, Wayne State University Purdy/Kresge Library Complex, and the University of Michigan Libraries for making their resources available to us. Following is a list of the copyright holders who have granted us permission to reprint material in this volume of ***TCLC.*** Every effort has been made to trace copyright, but if omissions have been made, please let us know.

COPYRIGHTED EXCERPTS IN *TCLC,* VOLUME 66, WERE REPRINTED FROM THE FOLLOWING PERIODICALS:

A Review of English Literature, v. 3, January, 1962 for "Fiction and Illness" by Oliver Jelly. © Longmans, Green & Co. Ltd. 1962. Reproduced by permission of the publisher.—***American Quarterly,*** v. XVI, Fall, 1964 for "The Love Comics and American Popular Culture" by A. W. Sadler. Copyright 1964, renewed 1992, American Studies Association. Reproduced by permission of the publisher.—***Asian Theatre Journal,*** v. 9, Spring, 1992. © by the University of Hawaii Press. All rights reserved. Reproduced by permission.— ***Comparative Literature Studies,*** v. 19, March, 1982. Copyright © 1982 by The Pennsylvania State University. Reproduced by permission of The Pennsylvania State University Press.— ***Criticism,*** v. XXXIV, Winter, 1992 for "Plagues and Publication: Ballads and the Representation of Disease in the English Renaissance" by Sharon Achinstein. Copyright, 1992, Wayne State University Press. Reproduced by permission of the publisher and the author.— ***Encounter,*** v. LXXII, May, 1989 for "Visionary Gleams" by Yasunari Takahashi. © 1989 by the author. Reproduced by permission of the author.— ***History Today,*** v. 44, July, 1994. © History Today Limited 1994. Reproduced by permission.— ***The Humanist,*** v. 54, March-April 1994. Copyright 1994 by the American Humanist Association. Reproduced by permission of the author.— ***Journal of American Culture,*** v. 15, Summer, 1992; v. 16, Spring, 1993. Copyright © 1992, 1993 by Ray B. Browne. Both reproduced by permission.— ***Journal of Popular Culture,*** v. VIII, Spring, 1975; v. XII, Spring, 1979; v. 17, Summer, 1983. Copyright © 1975, 1979, 1983 by Ray B. Browne. All reproduced by permission.— ***Literature East and West,*** v. XIX, January-December, 1975. © Literature East and West Inc. Reproduced by permission.— ***MLN,*** v. 105, December, 1990. © copyright 1990 by The Johns Hopkins University Press. All rights reserved. Reproduced by permission.— ***Modern Drama,*** v. 35, March, 1992. Copyright 1992 Modern Drama, University of Toronto. Reproduced by permission.— ***Modern Language Quarterly,*** v. 48, September, 1987. © 1989 University of Washington. Reproduced by permission of Duke University Press.— ***The New Republic,*** v. 196, June 22, 1987. © 1987 The New Republic, Inc. Reproduced by permission.— ***The New York Times Magazine,*** May 2, 1971 for "Shazam! Here Comes Captain Relevant" by Saul Braun. Copyright © 1971 by Saul Braun. Reproduced by permission of William Morris Agency, Inc. on behalf of the author.—***Psychology Today,*** v. 18, February, 1984. Copyright © 1984 Sussex Publishers, Inc. Reproduced with permission from ***Psychology Today Magazine.*— *Studies in Short Fiction,*** v. 30, Fall, 1993. Copyright 1993 by Newberry College. Reproduced by permission.— ***Utne Reader,*** n. 59, Sept.-Oct., 1993. Copyright © 1993 by LENS Publishing Co. All rights reserved. Reproduced by permission.— ***Victorian Studies,*** v. XIX, June, 1976 for "Brain Fever in Nineteenth-Century Literature: Fact and Fiction" by Audrey C. Peterson. Reproduced by permission of the Trustees of Indiana University and the author.— ***World Literature Today,*** v. 62, Summer, 1988. Copyright 1988 by the University of Oklahoma. Reproduced by permission.

COPYRIGHTED EXCERPTS IN *TCLC,* VOLUME 66, WERE REPRINTED FROM THE FOLLOWING BOOKS:

Abel, Bob. From "Up from the Underground: Notes on the New Comix," in ***Mass Culture Revisited.*** Edited by

Bernard Rosenberg and David Manning White. Van Nostrand Reinhold Company, 1971. Copyright © 1971 by Litton Educational Publishing, Inc. All rights reserved. Reproduced by permission.— Barker, Martin. From ***A Haunt of Fears: The Strange History of the British Horror Comics Campaign.*** Pluto Press, 1984. Copyright © Martin Barker, 1984. Reproduced by permission.— Biasin, Gian-Paolo. From ***Literary Diseases: Theme and Metaphor in the Italian Novel.*** University of Texas Press, 1975. Copyright © 1975 by Gian-Paolo Biasin. All rights reserved. Reproduced by permission of the publisher and the author.— Daniels, Les. From ***Comix: A History of Comic Books in America.*** Bonanza Books, 1971. Copyright © MCMLXXI by Les Daniels and Mad Peck Studios. All rights reserved. Reproduced by permission of the author.— Denneny, Michael. From "AIDS Writing and the Creation of a Gay Culture," in ***Confronting AIDS Through Literature: The Responsibilities of Representation.*** Edited by Judith Laurence Pastore. University of Illinois Press, 1993. © 1993 by the Board of Trustees of the University of Illinois. Reproduced by permission of the author.— Dewey, Joseph. From "The Music for a Closing: Responses to AIDS in Three American Novels," in ***AIDS: The Literary Response.*** Edited by Emmanuel S. Nelson. Twayne Publishers, 1992. Copyright © 1992 by Twayne Publishers. All rights reserved. Reproduced with the permission of Twayne Publishers, an imprint of Simon & Schuster Macmillan.— Dorfman, Ariel and Armand Mattelart. From ***How to Read Donald Duck: Imperialist Ideology in the Disney Comic.*** Translated by David Kunzle. International General, 1975. Copyright © Ariel Dorfman and Armand Mattelart 1971. English translation copyright © I.G. Editions, Inc., 1975. All rights reserved. Reproduced by permission.— Feiffer, Jules. From an introduction and afterword in ***The Great Comic Book Heroes.*** Edited by Jules Feiffer. The Dial Press, 1965. Copyright © 1965, renewed 1965 by The Dial Press. All rights reserved. Reproduced by permission of Doubleday, a division of Bantam Doubleday Dell Publishing Group, Inc.— Fiedler, Leslie. From ***The Collected Essays of Leslie Fiedler, Vol. II.*** Stein and Day, 1971. Copyright © 1971 by Leslie A. Fiedler. Reproduced with permission of the author.—Gessel, Van C. From "Postoccupation Literary Movements and Developments in Japan," in ***Legacies and Ambiguities: Postwar Fiction and Culture in West Germany and Japan.*** Edited by Ernestine Schlant and J. Thomas Rimer. The Johns Hopkins University Press, 1991. © 1991 by The Woodrow Wilson International Center for Scholars. Reproduced by permission of The Johns Hopkins University Press.— Hajime, Kijima. From "On Postwar Japanese Poetry," in ***The Poetry of Postwar Japan.*** Edited by Kijima Hajime. University of Iowa Press, 1975. © 1975 by The University of Iowa. All rights reserved. Reproduced by permission of the author.— Herndl, Diane Price. From ***Invalid Women: Figuring Feminine Illness in American Fiction and Culture, 1840-1940.*** The University of North Carolina Press, 1993. © 1993 by the University of North Carolina Press. All rights reserved. Reproduced by permission of the publisher.— Hijiya-Kirschnereit, Irmela. From ***Post-World War II Literature: The Intellectual Climate in Japan, 1945-1985, in Legacies and Ambiguities: Postwar Fiction and Culture in West Germany and Japan.*** Edited by Ernestine Schlant and J. Thomas Rimer. The Johns Hopkins University Press, 1991. © 1991 by The Woodrow Wilson International Center for Scholars. Reproduced by permission of The Johns Hopkins University Press.— Huxley, David. From "The Real Thing: New Images of Vietnam in American Comic Books," in ***Vietnam Images: War and Representation.*** Edited by Jeffrey Walsh and James Aulich. Macmillan Press, 1989. © Editorial Board, Lumiere (Co-operative) Press Ltd. 1989. All rights reserved. Reproduced by permission.— Keene, Donald. From ***Landscapes and Portraits: Appreciation of Japanese Culture.*** Kodansha International Ltd., 1971. Copyright in Japan, 1971, by Kodansha International Ltd. All rights reserved. Reproduced by permission.— Levy, Barbara Fass. From ***To Blight with Plague: Studies in a Literary Theme.*** New York University Press, 1992. Reproduced by permission.— Levy, Barbara Fass. From ***To Blight with Plague: Studies in a Literary Theme.*** New York University Press, 1992. Reproduced by permission.—Lippit, Noriko Mizuta. From ***Reality and Fiction in Modern Japanese Literature.*** Sharpe, 1980. Copyright © 1980 by M. E. Sharpe, Inc. All rights reserved. Reproduced by permission.— Lippit, Noriko Mizuta. From ***Reality and Fiction in Modern Japanese Literature.*** Sharpe, 1980. Copyright © 1980 by M. E. Sharpe, Inc. All rights reserved. Reproduced by permission.— McCue, Greg S., with Clive Bloom. From ***Dark Knights: The New Comics in Context.*** Pluto Press, 1993. Copyright © Lumiere (Co-operative) Press Ltd., 1993. Reproduced by permission.— Meyers, Jeffrey. From ***Disease and the Novel, 1880-1960.*** The Macmillan Press Ltd., 1985. © Jeffrey Meyers 1985. All rights reserved. Reproduced by permission of Macmillan, London and Basingstoke.— Reitberger, Reinhold and Wolfgang Fuchs. From ***Comics: Anatomy of a Mass Medium.*** Translated by Nadia Fowler. Little, Brown and Company, 1972. Copyright © 1972 Reinhold Reitberger and Wolfgang Fuchs; translation copyright © 1972 by Studio Vista Publishers. All rights reserved. Reproduced by permission.— Rimer, J. Thomas. From ***Pilgrimages: Aspects of Japanese Literature and Culture.*** University of Hawaii Press, 1988. © 1988 J. Thomas Rimer. All rights reserved. Reproduced by permission.— Savage, William W., Jr. From ***Comic Books and America, 1945-1954.*** University of Oklahoma Press, 1990. Copyright © 1990 by the University of Oklahoma Press,

Norman, Publishing Division of the University. All rights reserved. Reproduced by permission.— White, Ted. From "The Spawn of M. C. Gaines," in ***All in Color For A Dime.*** Edited by Dick Lupoff and Don Thompson. Arlington House, 1970. Copyright © 1970 by Richard A. Lupoff and Don Thompson. All rights reserved. Reproduced by permission of Richard A. Lupoff and Ted White.— Witek, Joseph. From ***Comic Books as History: The Narrative Art of Jack Jackson, Art Spiegelman, and Harvey Pekar.*** University Press of Mississippi, 1989. Copyright © 1989 by the University Press of Mississippi. All rights reserved. Reproduced by permission.— Won, Ko. From ***Buddhist Elements in Dada: A Comparison of Tristan Tzara, Takahashi Shinkichi, and Their Fellow Poets.*** New York University Press, 1977. Copyright © 1977 by New York University. Reproduced by permission.— Woolf, Virginia. From ***The Moment and Other Essays.*** Hogarth Press, 1947, Harcourt Brace Jovanovich, 1948. Copyright 1948, renewed 1976 by Harcourt Brace Jovanovich, Inc. Reproduced by permission of Harcourt Brace & Company. In Canada by the Literary Estate of Virginia Woolf and The Hogarth Press.

Comic Books

INTRODUCTION

Once regarded as one of the lower forms of mass entertainment, comic books are today widely considered to be potentially capable of complex and profound expression as both literary and visual art forms. Whereas Dr. Fredric Wertham's 1956 diatribe *Seduction of the Innocent* warned parents against the mind-warping influence of comics on children, many commentators now study the modern myth of the hero as found in *Superman*, while others are looking to *Donald Duck* and *Uncle Scrooge* comics for messages promoting global capitalism. Taking into account the psychological impact of gestures, visual styles, and montage effects possible with sequential art, critical inquiries also address the visual aspect of comic books, especially the adaptation of Hollywood film techniques to the panel-by-panel language of comics.

While most comic books are composed of formulaic stories drawn from various genres, including superhero, science fiction, western, war, horror, romance, and humor, some creators have exploited this mass-medium to bring socially-relevant tales to their audience. For example, the comics *Two-Fisted Tales, Shock SuspensStories,* and *Weird Science,* all produced during the 1950s by EC Publications, featured stories that dealt seriously with issues of racism, bigotry, and war. Another EC comic, *Mad,* ushered in a new era of satire through parodies of popular American culture. As an example of the social-consciousness of the early 1970s, writer Denny O'Neil and artist Neal Adams broached the subject of teenage drug abuse through a *Green Lantern/Green Arrow* storyline.

In step with the sexual and political revolutions of the 1960s, underground artists—many inspired by the EC comics of their childhood—used the comic book as a forum for frank depictions of changing lifestyles. R. Crumb, creator of Fritz the Cat and one of the founders of the psychedelic-inspired *Zap,* was a prolific contributor to undergrounds and continues to draw autobiographical stories that often render, in clinical detail, his unconventional sexual obsessions. During the 1980s *Raw* magazine editor Art Spiegelman aspired to bring comics to a new level of sophistication by publishing avantegarde works by European and art-school-trained cartoonists. Spiegelman's own *Maus,* which was inspired by his father's Holocaust experiences, won a Pulitzer Prize in 1992, and proved to critics that comics could be a viable medium for serious literature.

REPRESENTATIVE WORKS

Matt Baker
: *Phantom Lady* 17 (superhero) 1948

Carl Barks
: *Donald Duck Four Color* 9 (humor) 1942

C. C. Beck
: *Whiz Comics* 2 (superhero; debut of Captain Marvel) 1940

Jack Cole
: *Plastic Man* 1 (superhero) 1943

R. Crumb
: *Zap Comics* (underground) 1967-

Will Eisner
: *Spirit* (detective) 1940-52

Bill Everett
: *Marvel Comics* 1 (superhero; debut of Submariner) 1939

M. C. Gaines
: *Famous Funnies* 1 (first monthly color comic book; humor) 1934

William Gaines and Al Feldstein
: *Haunt of Fear* (horror) 1950-54
: *Shock SuspenStories* (suspense) 1952-55
: *Weird Science* (science fiction) 1950-53

Gilbert and Jaime Hernandez
: *Love and Rockets* (adult) 1982-96

Bob Kane
: *Detective Comics* 27 (superhero; debut of Batman) 1939

Walt Kelly
: *Animal Comics* (humor) 1942-47
: *Pogo Possum* (humor) 1949-54

Jack Kirby and Joe Simon
: *Captain America Comics* 1 (superhero; debut of Captain America) 1941-47

Harvey Kurtzman
: *Mad* (satire) 1952-55
: *Two-Fisted Tales* (war) 1950-55

Stan Lee and Jack Kirby
: *Fantastic Four* 1 (superhero; debut of Fantastic Four) 1961
: *Amazing Fantasy* 15 (superhero; debut of Spiderman) 1962

William Moulton Marston
: *All Star Comics* 8 (superhero; debut of Wonder Woman) 1941

Frank Miller
: *Batman: The Dark Knight Returns* (superhero; graphic novel) 1986

Jerome Siegel and Joe Shuster
: *Action Comics* 1 (superhero; debut of Superman) 1938

Art Spiegelman
Maus, A Survivor's Tale: My Father Bleeds History (graphic novel) 1986
Maus, A Survivor's Tale: And Here My Troubles Began (graphic novel) 1991
John Stanley
Little Lulu Four Color 74 (humor) 1945

HISTORICAL AND CRITICAL PERSPECTIVES

Ted White

SOURCE: "The Spawn of M. C. Gaines," in *All in Color for a Dime*, edited by Dick Lupoff and Don Thompson, Arlington House, 1970, pp. 21-43.

[*In the following essay, White profiles an early history of comic books, culminating in the creation of Superman and Batman.*]

It's a story which has grown into modern myth—a myth which in some respects equals and parallels the myth of Superman himself—the story of how two boys, Jerome Siegel and Joe Shuster, fresh out of high school, sold their dream comic strip and achieved world fame.

As science fiction fans, Siegel and Shuster had published an early science fiction fan magazine, the title of which was, not so surprisingly, *Science Fiction*. It was a mimeographed publication and appeared in the early 1930s. In many respects, including the poor paper on which it was published, it resembled more closely fan magazines being published by s.f. and comics fans now than it did most of its contemporaries. Most of the material was written by Siegel, and all the illustrations were by Shuster.

As the myth has it, while still in high school, science fiction fans Siegel and Shuster dreamed up their science fictional superman: a man come to Earth from another planet, metabolically adapted for a greater gravity and far harsher environmental pressures than ours. Here on Earth, the superman would find his powers vastly multiplied, just as we would find ours greater on, for instance, the Moon.

According to the story, sample art and scripts for *Superman* were drawn and prepared for submission as early as 1935. M. C. Gaines remembered seeing it while he was associated with the Dell line of comics, but could not find a place for either the original concept or the crude rendering, in books that were then given over entirely to Sunday comics reprints.

The tale of *Superman*'s round of rejections is very much like the story of the best seller rejected by 26 publishers before finding its home with the 27th—perhaps not entirely true, but certainly too colorful to ignore in the retelling. In any case, the team of Siegel & Shuster had sold some half dozen other original strips before finding a home for their baby *Superman*.

Let's backtrack for a minute, though. To understand the peculiar success story of *Superman*, one must have some understanding of comics publishing in the 1930s.

Newspaper comics were born around the turn of the century, and it was inevitable that someone, sooner or later, would begin collecting the daily and Sunday newspaper strips into book and booklet form. This began in the 1920s, with a variety of nonstandardized sizes and formats. On my shelf of oddities there is a five-by-seven "book" of *Little Orphan Annie* sitting next to a ten-by-ten collection of *Mutt & Jeff*, both products of the late twenties, and both printed in black and white.

In the early thirties, while young Siegel and Shuster were day-dreaming in math or science class over their *Superman* or their fan magazine, a man named M. C. Gaines created the comic book.

It was called *Funnies on Parade*, and it was the prototype for the successful *Famous Funnies*: it measured (approximately) seven by ten inches, was printed in color on newsprint, and was devoted exclusively to reprints of the popular Sunday comics features of the time, usually reprinting a complete Sunday feature on each page.

Gaines has simply taken the dimensions in which the Sunday comics were printed, and proportionately reduced them so that his book could be printed on the same color presses and use material prepared for Sunday comics publication. It was less a master stroke than eminent common sense.

Funnies on Parade was a trial balloon. It was followed by *Century of Comics* (so named because it contained 100 pages; it was a dime-store giveaway and had no price on it), and one or two other one-shots, including *Famous Funnies*. Apparently both idea and format were a success, because soon *Famous Funnies* was a continuing title and other publishers were coming out with imitations. (*Famous Funnies* outlasted its competition and survived into the mid-fifties, long after the other reprint titles had given up.)

At that time comics were published by newspaper syndicates, by pulp publishers (like Dell), and by distributors. One such distributor was the Independent News Co., whose trademark was an inconspicuous "IND" on the cover of many comics and magazines for a number of years. Independent owned Detective Comics, Inc., the publisher of *Detective Comics* (not surprisingly), *More Fun Comics* and *Adventure Comics*.

I have found it difficult to pin down M. C. Gaines's movements from company to company in those early years. One might almost suspect he was the Johnny Appleseed of comic books, because he seemed to go from company to company, launching comic book lines at each new place. It appears that he did not stay long with the *Famous Funnies* people, and by 1935 he was with Dell, in time as I mentioned, to see and to reject Superman. By 1938 he was associated with Detective Comics, Inc., although apparently as a publishing partner with a line of his own.

I am not being totally frivolous calling Gaines the Johnny Appleseed of comic books. Gaines was dedicated, *in principle,* to the comic book concept. His fervor was almost religious. At this time, remember, comics as such were not specifically juvenile. Comics were spawned in the newspapers, and presumably were read by the whole family. They were easy to grasp, and yet capable of conveying a considerable quantity of information. "A picture is worth a thousand words" must have been one of Gaines's favorite maxims. It was in this same period that the mass media as a whole were undergoing an entire revolution toward the visual, the pictorial. The year 1936 had witnessed the birth of *Life* magazine and "photo-journalism." Perhaps the linkage of words and pictures represented a new democratic ideal for the time. In any case, Gaines was more than a fast-buck artist looking for an easy way to millions. He was a dedicated man—as we'll see later.

But we are still setting the stage. Gaines had invented the *reprint* comic book: what about the original-material comic?

It's hard to pin down the origins of the "all-new" comics. I suspect the reason was a simple one: in a short time the reprint material was used up and there was nothing left for new titles. Some enterprising publisher made the decision to buy new material, written and drawn especially for the comic books, at first to pad out his reprints (still the headline attractions), and then, later, to replace them.

The early comic book originals were, for the most part, awful. They set out to imitate the reprints, and often a six-page story would have a running head on each page, in imitating of the Sunday reprints, each page of which *required* a running head originally. But surely the artists and writers who produced the new material were far more poorly paid—even if they received the same amount which the creator of reprints were paid. The reprints were earning their big money from newspaper syndication; the new material made what little it did solely from comic book publication. Standards quickly fell, and I think it is significant that even now they have not been entirely regained. Today, in most cases, the comic book is no more than a training ground for newspaper-strip artists.

It must also be said that comic book publishers were, all in all, a thieving, grasping lot. Not to dwell too long upon the point, they were crooks. In many instances, they were men with a good deal of money, recently earned during Prohibition, who were seeking legitimate businesses into which they might safely move. Comics—and pulp magazines—seemed like a good bet. These men had learned their so-called business ethics in a rough school. They applied them across the board in their new businesses.

The first rule was, *Do it cheap.* Find cheap labor, pay cheap prices. Low overhead. Tie up as little money as possible. Take out as much money as possible. The results were predictable—in a few short years the bad drove out the good.

Put in simple terms, most of the work being done for comic books by 1940 was being done by teenage boys, some still in high school, some dropouts. Many were enormously talented, but most came from lower-class backgrounds, were willing to work cheap (the Depression was still being felt), and were easily exploited.

The publishers became millionaires—no comic book writer, editor or artist ever did.

By 1936, Siegel and Shuster were selling strips to *Detective, More Fun* and *Adventure Comics.* These included "Dr. Occult," "Federal Men," and "Radio Squad." Later strips included "Slam Bradley." The art on the early strips was crude. Shuster's work had none of the finesse or quality of an Alex Raymond or a Hal Foster. It was, to speak plainly, amateurish. Siegel's scripts were little better. The plots were rudimentary, the dialogue and captions were in basic English and barely functional at that. Had they never produced *Superman,* I doubt whether anyone would remember them today.

Meanwhile, *Superman* was growing tattered in his trips through editorial offices. Conceived as a comic book original, he had been cut apart, redrawn, repasted, and redone as a daily strip for possible syndication. When, in 1938, M. C. Gaines heard that the publisher of *Detective Comics* wanted to start another title, he recommended *Superman* for it, and the daily strips were again recut, repasted, and reworked back into comic book pages.

The publisher bought it. *Superman* was launched in the first issue of *Action Comics.*

The first four Superman stories in *Action Comics* were later reprinted in *Superman* #1. In either form it is easy to detect the lines where pasteups occur, to see where panels were extended or added, and even to find different styles of art in adjacent panels. (Later stories, reprinted a year or so later from *published* newspaper strips, still carried their ben-day shading over from the black & white medium.)

Judged by current standards, the stories were rudimentary and the art crude. Indeed, National Comics will today not reprint the oldest *Superman* stories in their present reprint titles because they fall below acceptable standards. Nevertheless they were full of a raw kind of power which made them an instant success. They were, after all, stories about a *super*-man.

It was 1938, and the country was shuddering its way out from the crippling blow to its economy in 1929. The air was full of talk of war in Europe, and of the mad clown named Hitler. Technocracy was preaching that science could rule the world and end all Man's problems, while the Communists were seeking One World under socialism in a dictatorship of the proletariat. It was a time of idealism and of shattered ideals. We were down but not out. Our world had crumbled, but we knew we could build a better one.

We hadn't grown up yet.

Enter Superman.

Born on the planet Krypton, and sent to Earth in a rocket by his father shortly before that planet exploded, Superman landed on Earth while still a baby, was adopted by the Kents, and grew into a super-healthy young man.

But he could not fly. He was vulnerable to gas, to oxygen starvation, and to some rays. His skin was tough, but not so tough it couldn't be pierced by "a bursting shell." In his first story, he was described in this fashion:

> As the lad grew older, he learned to his delight that he could hurdle skyscrapers . . . Leap an eighth of a mile . . . Raise tremendous weights . . . Run faster than a streamline train [which is to say, faster than eighty miles an hour]—And nothing less than a bursting shell could penetrate his skin!

That last piece of description was over a panel which showed a doctor saying, "What th'—? This is the sixth hypodermic needle I've broken on your skin!" To which Kent replies with a grin, "Try again, Doc!"

> The passing away of his foster parents greatly grieved Clark Kent. But it strengthened a determination that had been growing in his mind. Clark decided he must turn his titanic strength into channels that would benefit mankind.
>
> And so was created—
>
> SUPERMAN—champion of the oppressed, the physical marvel who had sworn to devote his existence to helping those in need!

You'll note that Superman was a little more human in those days. Although he could not fly, he could leap "an eighth of a mile," or over a skyscraper, and this was in itself no small novelty in the world of 1938. He could race trains or lift a car, and bullets and knives bounced harmlessly from his skin. It was enough.

(When that page was reprinted in 1960 in the *Giant Superman Annual* #2, billed as "rare, out-of-print scenes from the very first Superman story!", the editors couldn't keep their hands off it. The art appears intact, but the blurb about Superman's skin has been altered to read, ". . . *And not even* a bursting shell could penetrate his skin!" Thus is history rewritten.)

For a man who was setting out to "help those in need," Superman had a remarkably pedestrian mind. For the most part he did not occupy himself with sweeping social change; instead he battled crooks and racketeers, uncovering corruption in low places. One of his favorite tactics was to race ahead of a fleeing car of crooks, and then stop dead in front of it. The car would slam to a stop against Superman's body as if he were a brick wall.

When the crooks came tumbling out of the car, half-stunned, Superman would grab the ringleader and leap into the air with him. There he might simply swing the terrified man about with acrobatic ease. Or he might leave the man clutching fearfully to the top of a telephone pole or the peak of a roof. The object was to frighten the man into subjection. (I'm afraid the Supreme Court would today take a dim view of any confession extracted by these means.) Quite often, as Superman and his captive were falling back to earth, the man would be screaming, "You're gonna kill us!" or something like that.

It's fortunate for Superman that neither Siegel nor Shuster had absorbed much from their high-school science classes, or, for that matter, from the science fiction of that time. Had the laws of inertia been in force while Superman was standing steadfast before a speeding car, the outcome might often have been quite different. And if Superman had actually had sufficient internal mass to stop a speeding car, I hate to think of the holes he would have kicked in the sidewalks with each of his aerial leaps.

But those were simpler times. And if the comic book had not originally been aimed at a specific age group, it had certainly found one: the kids. How many kids knew the science that would debunk Superman? *How many kids,* knowing it, *would have cared?*

Superman was a myth-figure: he was our dreams personified, even as he must have been Siegel and Shuster's. Superman was, almost literally, the perfect Boy Scout. We still believed in Boy Scouts then.

Most of the Superman myth was established within the first year of Superman's publication. (He appeared monthly in *Action Comics* as the lead story.) As Clark Kent, he went to work for the *Daily Star* (soon to be the *Daily Planet*) as a reporter. Perry White became his editor, and he quickly found a rival in fellow reporter Lois Lane.

Most of those early stories dwelled, with what I can only describe as a magnificent sense of wonder, upon Superman's physical attributes. (These soon broadened to include an early version of his x-ray vision.) The pages in which Superman did little but outrace trains or cars, leap buildings, or toss crooks around ("Look! The bullets bounce right offa him!") probably outnumbered those in which the plot (if there was one) was materially advanced.

Superman was a myth-figure: he was our dreams personified, even as he must have been Siegel and Shuster's. Superman was, almost literally, the perfect Boy Scout. We still believed in Boy Scouts then.

—Ted White

But war was coming. Everyone could see it. In several 1939 and 1940 stories Superman found himself in mythical European countries fighting off invasions of one sort or another. In one of these stories an evil, world-conquering scientist was introduced. His name was Luthor, and he had red hair. The plot of the story in question was probably borrowed from Flash Gordon. Usually Superman, as Clark Kent, would find himself a war correspondent on the scene. When danger threatened, the mufti was doffed and Superman made quick work of the enemy's squadron of airplanes, fleet of tanks, and small army of soldiers. Yeah! Just as we Americans could mop up any *real* trouble.

Then came 1941.

Suddenly, we *were* at war. It must have thrown Superman's publishers into a tizzy. Here was this marvelous man, this superman, who had already demonstrated his ability to handle almost any size war—what were we going to do with him? If he went to war against Hitler, how could we explain the fact that America had not instantly won?

The solution was ingenious. As Clark Kent, Superman went down to his local draft board to enlist. But in his nervous desire to get into the Army, he accidentally employed his x-ray vision during the eye test. Instead of reading the chart before him, he read the one in the room beyond! He was flunked out as a 4-F. The shame—!

Why this should keep Superman *as Superman* out of the war they never explained, but it at least solved the real-life problem. While Captain America, Sub-Mariner, and a host of other superheroes or quasi-super-heroes in the comics went off to war, Superman stayed home to deal with fifth-column saboteurs and war profiteers, and to continue helping little old ladies safely across the streets.

As time went on, Superman lost his early fragility. Rays, gasses, and even bursting shells no longer bothered him. Although he continued to leap into the air in his peculiarly characteristic way, resembling a leap-frog in motion, somehow he had found the power of sustained flight. His relationship with Lois Lane mellowed somewhat, and indeed led briefly to marriage.

(The episode in which Superman and Lois Lane married is one of the most hushed-up in the history of comics. It occurred in the daily Superman newspaper strip, shortly after the war.

The marriage was intended, by the writer and artist on the strip, to be real, and it lasted for a period of weeks, until someone over at the comic book end happened to discover it. Since the comic book publishers controlled the strip—a reversal of the usual procedure—they dictated an abrupt change. It was explained that it wasn't the same Lois Lane, and that it was all happening on an alien, but parallel, planet, and the marriage was therefore a fraud.

Since then, Superman and Lois Lane have "married" a number of times, but always in what the editors of the comic books have charmingly called "Imaginary Stories"—stories outside the true, real, mythos—"what-if" stories. But more of these later.)

By the mid-forties Superman was Big Business. Within a year of his first publication, he was selling over a million copies of the titles he appeared in, and he revolutionized the comics industry as a whole. Very quickly everyone was imitating him, usually poorly. Detective Comics, Inc. became Superman-D.C., and sued the first imitator, Will Eisner's *Wonder Man* (a Fox Features comic), out of business. But soon the flood was beyond control, and Superman-D.C. (now National) was reserving its legal guns only for the biggest game. It was ultimately National's lawsuit which drove Fawcett to drop *Captain Marvel,* although I suspect drooping sales were an equal factor.

If Superman was such a hit, surely spin-offs of Superman would do equally well, or so the publishers reasoned. Thus, *Superboy—the Adventures of Superman when he was a Boy.* Although this required considerable revision of the mythos, *Superboy* was introduced soon after the war in *More Fun Comics,* and soon transferred to *Adventure Comics* (*More Fun* was dropped), where he remains today (as part of a "Legion of Super-Heroes").

Early "Superboy" stories tried to be faithful in their fashion. The young Clark Kent wore a miniature Superman costume, but he was concerned with boyish pursuits. One cover showed him shooting marbles with his awed pals; a story in another issue of *Adventure* concerned soap-box racers—a plot closer at heart to those in the boys' books than to comic book superheroes. If Superman was a young man in 1938, then his boyhood must have occurred in the late twenties and early thirties. The earlier artists and writers remembered this; later it was forgotten.

By the mid-fifties, Superboy seemed to live in the present (the cars were all modern, and clothes and plots equally so—every home had television), coexisting with his older self.

By the late fifties, he had time-travel completely under control, and was spending most of his time in the future with that Legion of Super Heroes (about which the less said the better), and had established a high-school enmity with the youthful Luthor (long Superman's nemesis) who had already lost his hair in an unfortunate experiment.

Of course, by then Superman himself was hardly recognizable. He was, we were told, totally invulnerable to *anything* except Kryptonite and—get this!—*magic*.

Kryptonite was introduced in the mid-forties (on his radio program, I believe) because Superman was, even then, becoming too powerful to be easily dealt with by his writers and artists. There was no excitement in a story about a man capable of doing anything required (including travelling in time) to right whatever was wrong within the first two pages of any story. It was decided, therefore, that if gas, rays, or automobiles no longer affected him, perhaps bits of radioactive material from the core of his exploded home planet, Krypton, might diminish his strength.

The early Kryptonite was green. Sometimes its radiation seemed only to strip Superman of his extraordinary powers; on other occasions it seemed to be able to kill him through a cumulative weakening process. In any case, it was always there when Superman was in danger of getting out of his creators' control. Sometime around 1950, Luthor learned to synthesize it, and for a while Kryptonite was as common as old comics under the bed.

In the late fifties Kryptonite mutated into a whole spectrum of materials: Red Kryptonite, Gold Kryptonite, etc., each with its own special powers over Superman. The authors of Superman stories have since gained a good deal of mileage from these convenient new forms.

In addition, they have given us Supergirl (another survivor of Krypton), Superdog, Supercat, and even Superhorse. They have provided a Phantom Zone full of old Kryptonian criminals; a miniaturized Kryptonian city, Kandor, in a bottle (a large-ish bottle, it must be admitted); and even a Fortress of Solitude in the North for Superman's home away from home (this was stolen directly from *Doc Savage* without so much as a by-your-leave). The mythos has become cluttered.

Indeed, if one wants to write a Superman story today, he will find little if anything of the original Siegel-Shuster Superman has survived. His story must fit within the ever more constrictive net woven by the interlocking mythos of Superman, Superboy, Supergirl, the stories in *Superman's Girl-Friend, Lois Lane,* and the stories in *Superman's Pal, Jimmy Olsen,* to say nothing of the shared Superman-Batman adventures in *World's Finest Comics*.

It is not altogether surprising that the best stories published in the last six to eight years have been the *Imaginary Stories*. In these stories the author can depart from the mythos. He can pretend Superman *has* married Lois Lane, and go on from there to see what might happen next. (For a while there was a parallel mythos building around Superman's children by Lois Lane in a series of *Imaginary Stories*.) One of the best of all the stories was "The Day Superman Died." In it, he really did die. Clearly, an "Imaginary Story."

But, what nonsense, really! The proprietors of Superman have virtually painted themselves into a corner with their overwhelming mythos of sub-characters and sub-plot situations. Detail has been piled upon detail until the character and quality of Superman which so endeared him to us have been totally submerged.

Siegel and Shuster are long gone. Shuster apparently stopped drawing Superman in 1939 or 1940. Larry Ivie, a most scholarly Superman-phile, says that he has found the work of at least six other artists in the stories published in that period, and by 1941 or 1942 the style was recognizably different.

The principal artist on these stories was Shuster's assistant, Wayne Boring. Boring drew many of the comic book stories and most of the syndicated newspaper strips throughout the forties and fifties, and still does a story once in a while today.

Shuster did some of the work on the earliest Superboy stories, and pencilled for various substandard horror and crime comics in the early fifties. Rumors are that he has lost much of his sight, and his work on the syndicated *Funnyman* (with Siegel, in the late forties) was the last to show his style or carry his name.

Siegel continued to write many of the features that had been started before *Superman,* and to write the early *Spectre* stories for Bernard Baily. But his writing seemed to lose its fire when divorced from *Superman,* and on the other stories he was only a competent hack. In the mid-forties Siegel decided that, although National owned all rights to Superman, and was paying him a comfortable royalty, he had been cheated. He approached M. C. Gaines, and briefly enlisted his support in a legal battle against National. It was at this time that the familiar Siegel & Shuster by-line balloon, which had appeared largely as a courtesy on the *Superman* stories, was dropped. *Funnyman* was to be a comeback for the team, after they lost their lawsuit, but despite a promising start with both newspaper syndication and comic book publication, it failed. Since then Siegel has continued writing comic book stories, some of them, ironically, for *Superman;* others, for lesser features for other publishers. A collection of his stories for the *Archie* comic group's superheroes was issued several years ago as a paperback book titled *High Camp Super Heroes*. In addition he continues developing new comic series concepts, hoping once more to make the kind of hit he did thirty years ago.

And what of M. C. Gaines?

Although Gaines certainly was responsible for *Superman*'s ultimate appearance in print as well as for the very medium in which Superman was published, he was not *Superman*'s publisher. He began his own line of superhero comics, also bearing the Superman-DC imprint, but none of them won him as much success as *Superman* brought his partners. (The best known of Gaines's superheroes were Flash, Green Lantern and Wonder Woman. All are being published today by National.)

In 1941, Gaines, convinced of the importance of comic books, and of the need to fashion the right products for their youthful readership, began publishing *Picture Stories from the Bible*. In 1945 he sold his other titles (the superheroes) to National, and began his own firm, Educational Comics, Inc. There he continued *Picture Stories from the Bible,* adding *Picture Stories of Science, Picture Stories from American History,* and *Picture Stories from World History*.

These "good" comics may have been what Gaines thought the customers *ought* to want, but as has happened so many times in the popular media, they weren't what the customers bought. None made money, and when Gaines was killed in a boating accident a few years later, his business manager quietly folded them. Another Gaines comic, *Fat and Slat* (an imitation of Mutt & Jeff done by Ed Wheelan of *Minute Movies* fame), was converted into *International Crime Patrol,* and EC floundered about among the third-, fourth-, and fifth-rate comics until M. C.'s son, William Gaines, took an interest in the company and launched "New Trend" comics in the early fifties, the best-written and best-illustrated comic books ever produced. This line of comics led to Harvey Kurtzman's brilliant *Mad,* and ultimately to the magazine *Mad* of today. William Gaines sold his company to a Wall Street holding company in the early sixties for a reputedly large sum of money, remained as publisher of *Mad* in the bargain, and has since watched the holding company sell his company (which now publishes only *Mad*) to National in a bizarre sort of full circle. Today, in turn, the Kinney System owns National. . . .

If Superman was the product of youthful dreaming, his partner, Batman, is the product of sharp contrivance. Unlike Siegel & Shuster's *Superman,* Bob Kane's *Batman* was put together in 1939 to meet a need—it was National's own answer to *Superman*'s success, and it is significant that *Batman* shared the honors with *Wonder Man* as the second superhero published.

As I mentioned, National quickly sued *Wonder Man* out of existence; both *Wonder Man* and *Batman* first appeared on the stands the same month.

Bob Kane was a second-rate cartoonist whose sole claim to fame before *Batman* was a series of single-page "funnies" and a poorly drawn adventure strip. (Most of the stories in the new material comic books were adventure strips of varying sorts.)

Batman was not Kane's idea; it was dreamed up in an editorial session. Kane did not write the first story; it was written by either Gardner F. Fox or Bill Finger (reports vary). If Kane even drew the early stories, it was with considerable help from artists like Jack Cole (*Plastic Man*), Jerry Robinson and Bob Wood (*Daredevil*). By the time of its early success, the stories were being drawn by Robinson and his friends. Although Kane's name appeared on every story until the mid-sixties (and the birth of the "New Look" Batman), his sole function was to subcontract the inking and the pencilling to other artists—and the subdivision of payments seemed to guarantee substandard art.

Nevertheless, *Batman* was in most respects a better strip than *Superman,* and was a better-conceived character, as well.

In these days of pop art, camp trivia, and lingering memories of the *Batman* television program, it is a little difficult to remember that Batman was originally something of an innovation, and certainly one of the best-realized of the early-forties comics characters.

Properly speaking, Batman was not (and is not) a superhero. He wears a costume, but he is only an ordinary human being: he has no super powers. As such, he was not the first in comics. National was publishing The Crimson Avenger (in *Detective Comics*) before either Superman or Batman first saw print. But The Crimson Avenger was basically a copy of The Shadow, an already famous pulp and radio character, as was also The Sandman (*Adventure Comics*), and the other masked crime-fighters of the period.

But Batman was of a new genre—the *costumed* comic-book hero. Like Superman, he not only had two identities, but when in costume he *appeared* as an awesome figure, quite transcendent over mundane humanity. Masked, his cape spread over his shoulders like two great bat-wings, his costume all greys and blacks, he must have been one of the most potentially frightening heroes in comics.

And this is how he often appeared—avenger-like in the night, sometimes in menacing silhouette, or with his shadow cast before him, twice life size. He *did* things with that cape of his. Superman's flapped behind him like a red bath towel, but Batman's blue-black ribbed cape enfolded him like a cloak, often hiding his muscled body from view.

Batman, like Superman, was an orphan, but his parents were normal Earth humans. The Waynes were coming home from a night out when a crook named Joey Chill shot and killed them. Their son, Bruce, somehow survived and vowed vengence when he was grown. He studied law, criminology, and forensic science, and he trained his body. He also either inherited a great deal of money or earned a lot fast.

Finally, clad in his smoking jacket, pipe in hand (the very picture of what comic book artists might aspire to be), he speculated on the way in which he would Strike Terror Into The Hearts of the Underworld. A bat flew in the open window, and inspiration struck—he would become The Batman.

And so he did. A pair of grey flannel longjohns, black boots, black gloves, a cowl, mask, and the long, ribbed cape, and he was indeed The Batman.

I have my doubts about the terror such an outfit would strike in the hearts of the underworld, but no doubts at all that for a boy poring over a Batman adventure in *Detective Comics,* this was exciting stuff indeed.

Part of it was in the drawing. After the early awkward illustrations (perhaps actually by Kane), the style evolved into sombre, night-tinged moodiness, replete with great shadows and an implacably stern-visaged Batman. Batman did not toss crooks into the air to frighten them; occasionally he shot them, (He did not, however, often carry a gun. Very few costume heroes in the comics have ever carried guns of the normal, lethal variety.) More often, he found himself in a fight, usually with the odds against him. Sometimes he won; sometimes he did not. (He usually lost in the earlier pages and won in the later pages of a story; it balanced out.)

The writing was important. Not for the actual prose in which the stories were told, but for the use that was made of plots and situations. Batman didn't have Superman's superabundance of muscle—occasionally he had to use his brains. Batman was much more of a detective. (Superman appeared in *Action Comics;* Batman in *Detective Comics*; somehow that did not seem entirely coincidental.) As a result, Batman seemed more at home fighting common hoods, sticking up for the corner shoeshine boy, or the shopkeeper who wouldn't pay protection. When the war began, you didn't *expect* him to hop the first plane to Europe to put a quick finish to the whole mess.

Batman was human.

It is my firm conviction that the years 1940-46 were *Batman*'s best—in terms of both art and stories. I believe my judgment is unclouded by nostalgia, since I began reading *Batman* comics in the late forties and encountered the earlier stories only much later.

Actually, by the time I became acquainted with The Batman, he had already lost the definite article and was simple, familiar Batman, and had embarked upon a series of science-fictional adventures which were jarringly out of place in his own nocturnal milieu. The slide downhill into the fifties was a quick one. The art deteriorated noticeably, the old plots were replaced by visitors from the future, or aliens from other planets, etc. Even the one "legitimate" use of time travel, Batman's voyages back in time through hypnosis (were they dreams, or were they real?) was abandoned. By the early sixties, alien menaces were Batman's stock in trade.

Then the "New Look" Batman was introduced, not long before he made his TV debut. The titles (*Detective, Batman*) were transferred to another editor, and Carmine Infantino (one of National's major artists at that time) was not only assigned Batman stories, but allowed to sign his name to them. The only costuming change was to place a yellow bulls-eye around the bat symbol on his chest, and, truthfully, for all the change in art I don't think that the stories were that much better. But the alien menaces *were* shelved, and if Batman had not yet recaptured his old menace and mystery, he was at least functioning as a detective once again.

I've ignored Batman's sidekick thus far, because he deserves treatment on his own.

Robin ("The Boy Wonder") was one of the first—if not *the* first—costumed sidekick, in comics. Ostensibly a boy aerialist with a circus troop, Dick Grayson was orphaned in mysterious circumstances, adopted by Bruce Wayne and trained to be his assistant. (In many respects this "origin" parallels the way in which the Human Torch picked up *his* sidekick, Toro—ah, but it's a small world!)

The notion of giving a superhero a boy sidekick was probably born of a desire to give the comics' youthful readers someone they could identify with. As such, it was a mistake. Boys don't identify with *boys* in mystery-adventure stories; they identify with *men*—especially when one is the real hero of the story. Robin was often excess baggage in Batman's stories, just as were Captain America's Bucky, Green Arrow's Speedy, Aquaman's Aqualad, et al. But for a while, during the first wave of the superhero boom (1940-43), you could hardly find a comic book without a costumed boy sidekick in it. Blame Batman—he started it.

He also caused himself a little extra trouble when Dr. Wertham stated, in *Seduction of the Innocent,* that the relationship between Batman and Robin (which is to say, between Bruce Wayne and his ward, Dick Grayson) was sexually unhealthy. Dr. Wertham was of the certain notion, which became well publicized, that not only was the relationship homosexual, *it was obviously homosexual to the comics' youthful readers!* One shudders to think what the good doctor would have made of the Boy Scout Handbook, with its wholesome enthusiasm for exactly the same sort of "comradeship" between the boy scouts and their counsellors.

It's fashionable today to sneer a little and to chuckle at the Boy Scout image, at the goody-two-shoes approach.

It's fashionable to see rampaging homosexual lust in every man's hand on a boy's shoulder, but I wonder if in our cynicism we aren't cutting ourselves off from a part of the innocence of childhood.

I'm certain that Dr. Wertham must have had no knowledge of the ideals and conditioning we had as boys and Boy Scouts. These ideals have permeated boys' books of the last four generations, and their reflection in Batman's fatherly comradeship with Robin was not only innocent, but touchingly inspiring. No boy I ever knew read more than that into Batman's relationship with Robin, and I doubt anything more was intended.

It seems inevitable that if a comic book feature becomes successful, its lead character will accumulate additional supporting characters. Batman also had a butler, Alfred, who began as a roly-poly sort of man, but soon slimmed down into the dignified prototype of an English servant. Alfred shared the knowledge of Batman's and Robin's civilian identities. (He was also Bruce Wayne's butler.) Alfred was popular enough in the mid-forties to warrant his own featurette in *Batman,* but it lasted only a few years. More recently, the "New Look" killed Alfred off, but, because of demands made by the TV producers, he was brought back to life in a bizarre fashion (he was possessed by an alien spirit).

Another long-time supporting player is Commissioner Gordon. His role has been unswerving—he has served throughout the years as Batman's liaison with the police force, and has personally manned the giant searchlight which for years flashed the Batsignal on the heavens to summon Batman. (In recent years, post-"New Look," a "hotline" phone has taken over this function. One wonders how a line was strung into Bruce Wayne's home without tipping off his identity as Batman. . . .)

There have been a number of girls, none of them lasting more than a few years, despite the valiant attempts of each to become Batman's Lois Lane. Considering what a pest Lois has been to Superman for all these many years, perhaps that's just as well.

But the most memorable supporting characters in Batman's life have been the villains.

He met the Joker in 1940. A fantastic harlequin figure, face chalk-white and rouged like a clown's, the Joker was originally a contract killer, and he and Batman played for keeps with each other. Since the initiation of the Comics Code Authority, however, the Joker has become more of a clown and less of a menace. Like Batman, his best setting was the nocturnal mystery of the 1940s stories.

The second most memorable figure would undoubtedly be the Penguin. A fat figure of a man (and most splendidly portrayed on television by Burgess Meredith), his crimes usually involved birds or umbrellas, or both. He has changed very little through the years, coming on stage in the mid-forties; he now seems to be in semi-retirement.

The Catwoman was originally known only as The Cat, but as she developed during the forties she became Batman's most intriguing opponent. Ruthless and a gang leader, she was also beautiful and romantically intrigued by Batman's square jaw. She reformed in the early fifties, and subsequent adventures have not been quite the same.

The list at this point degenerates into recent repeat villains. Only a few remain from the older days. The best was Two-Face, a demented ex-DA, scarred on one side of his face by acid thrown at him in court, who pitched a half-defaced coin to decide if he would commit a crime. If the defaced side landed upright, he became a criminal; if the clean side turned up, he would refrain from the crime. It was a classic case of split personality, and ultimately he was cured and his face restored by plastic surgery.

The Riddler, exhumed by television to good effect, had appeared only twice, in 1948, in two consecutive issues of *Detective Comics,* before his quite recent revival. I think I can safely say that (in the pages of contemporary comics at least) he would have been better left alone.

In the late fifties and early sixties, Batman, apparently doomed forever to play second fiddle to Superman, had the entire Superman Syndrome wished upon him: a Batdog, a Batwoman, a Batgirl, even an alien pixy, Bat-Mite. "The New Look" scuttled all that, and rightly so, along with a series of "Imaginary Stories" supposedly written by Alfred the butler about the Batman of the future, the grown-up Robin, and Batman's son.

There is something about the Superman and Batman stories of the early forties which, for all their technical crudity, puts them head and shoulders above the slick but empty products of today. Part of it was freshness, newness. Part of it was the youthfulness of the men who created them. And part of it was simply a product of the times. The books were crude, but vital; less realistically rendered, but far more faithful to the idealizations which each character represented. Superman and Batman gave comic books—those which printed new material—their first real commercial viability, and pointed the way for almost three decades of sometimes chancy publishing in the field.

Until 1938, the best comics, and the comics which sold the best, were the reprint publications. Their material was better, and produced to higher standards. Quality, despite the iron-mongers and beer salesmen who publish the comics, has always been what sold comic books.

Superman and Batman changed all that. Each in his own way set standards as yet unexcelled for the field. Each was prototypal. Each also set sales records. Publishers never argue with sales records.

They also set comic books solidly as children's fare: locked the seven-by-ten color-printed newsprint format Gaines devised into a rigid style aimed solely at teenagers and children. So far, all experiments to publish comic books in this format or any similar format for adults have failed. The biggest reason they have failed is public opinion.

The public seems to feel that comics—once the direct competitor of the now-gone adult-oriented pulp magazine—are for kids . . . no matter how many adults sneak-read them. What intelligent, self-respecting man would admit to reading about men who run about in colored tights and capes, Fighting Crime and Righting Wrongs?

Only kids still believe it might be possible.

Perhaps M. C. Gaines would have been happy for at least that much.

Jules Feiffer

SOURCE: An introduction and afterword in *The Great Comic Book Heroes*, edited by Jules Feiffer, The Dial Press, 1965, pp. 11-45, 185-89.

[*In the following excerpt, Feiffer offers opinions about the comic strips of his childhood, their artists and publishers, and the controversies they inspired during the 1930s and 1940s.*]

I

Comic books, World War II, the depression, and I all got going at roughly the same time. I was eight. *Detective Comics* was on the stands, Hitler was in Spain, and the middle class (by whose employment record we gauge depressions) was, after short gains, again out of work. I mention these items in tandem, not only to give color to the period, but as a sly historic survey to those in our own time who, of the items cited, only know of comic books.

Eight was a bad age for me. Only a year earlier I had won a gold medal in the John Wanamaker Art Contest for a crayon drawing on oak tag paper of Tom Mix jailing an outlaw. So at seven I was a winner—and didn't know how to handle it. Not that triumph isn't at any age hard to handle, but the younger you are the more of a shock it is to learn that it simply doesn't change anything. Grownups still wielded all the power, still could not be talked back to, still were always right however many times they contradicted themselves. By eight I had become a politician of the grownup, indexing his mysterious ways and hiding underground my lust for getting even until I was old enough, big enough, and important enough to make a bid for it. That bid was to come by way of a career—(I knew I'd never grow big enough to beat up everybody; my hope was to, somehow, get to own everything and fire everybody). The career I chose, the only one that seemed to fit the skills I was then sure of—a mild reading ability mixed with a mild drawing ability—was comics.

So I came to the field with more serious intent than my opiate-minded contemporaries. While they, in those pre-super days were eating up *Cosmo, Phantom of Disguise*; *Speed Saunders*; and *Bart Regan, Spy,* I was counting how many frames there were to a page, how many pages there were to a story—learning how to form, for my own use, phrases like: @X#?!; marking for future reference which comic book hero was swiped from which radio hero: Buck Marshall from Tom Mix; the Crimson Avenger from the Green Hornet—

There were, at the time, striking similarities between radio and comic books. The heroes were the same (often with the same names: Don Winslow, Mandrake, Tom Mix—); the villains were the same: oriental spies, primordial monsters, cattle rustlers—but the experience was different. As an apprentice pro I found comic books the more tangible outlet for fantasy. One could put something down on paper—hard-lined panels and balloons, done the way the big boys did it. Far more satisfying than the radio serial game: that of making up programs at night in bed, getting the voices right, the footsteps and door slams right, the rumbling organ background right—and doing it all in soft enough undertones so as to escape being caught by that grownup reading Lanny Budd in the next room who at any moment might give his spirit shattering cry: *"For the last time stop talking to yourself and go to sleep!"* Radio was too damn public.

My interest in comics began on the most sophisticated of levels, the daily newspaper strip, and thereafter proceeded downhill. My father used to come home after work, when there was work, with two papers: the *New York Times* (a total loss), and the *World-Telegram*. The *Telegram* had *Joe Jinks* (later called *Dynamite Dunn*), *Our Boarding House, Out Our Way, Little Mary Mixup, Alley Oop*—and my favorite at the time: *Wash Tubbs,* whose soldier of fortune hero, Captain Easy, set a standard whose high point in one field was Pat Ryan and, in another, any role Clark Gable ever played.

For awhile the *Telegram* ran an anemic four-page color supplement that came out on Saturdays—an embarrassing day for color supplements. They so obviously belonged to Sunday. So except for the loss of Captain Easy, I felt no real grief when my father abandoned the *Telegram* to follow his hero, Heywood Broun to the *New York Evening Post*. The *Post* had *Dixie Dugan, The Bungle Family, Dinky Dinkerton, Secret Agent 67/8, Nancy* (then called *Fritzi-Ritz*), and that masterpiece of sentimental naturalism: *Abbie an' Slats*. I studied that strip—its Sturges-like characters, its Saroyanesque plots, its uniquely cadenced dialogue. No strip other than Will Eisner's *Spirit* rivalled it in structure. No strip, except Caniffs' *Terry,* rivalled it in atmosphere.

There were, of course, good strips, *very* good ones in those papers that my father did not let into the house.

The *Hearst* papers. The *Daily News*. Cartoons from the outlawed press were not to be seen on weekdays, but on Sundays, one casually dropped in on Hearst-oriented homes (never very clean, as I remember), and read *Puck, The Comic Weekly,* skipping quickly over *Bringing Up Father* to pounce succulently on page two: *Jungle Jim* and *Flash Gordon.* Too beautiful to be believed. When *Prince Valiant* began a few years later, I burned with the temptation of the damned: I begged my father to sell out to Hearst. He never did. My Hearst friends and I drifted apart. My cause lost its urgency; my attention switched to *Terry and the Pirates*—in the *Daily News*—more hated in my house than even Hearst. Why, I must have wondered in kind, was it my lot to be a Capulet when the best strips were Montagues?

It should have been a relief, then, when the first regularly scheduled comic book came out. It was called *Famous Funnies* and, in sixty-four pages of color, minutely reprinted many of my favorites in the enemy camp. Instead, my reaction was that of a movie purist when first confronted with sound: this was not the way it was done. Greatness in order to remain great must stay true to its form. This new form, so jumbled together, so erratically edited and badly colored, was demeaning to that art—basic black and white and four panels across—that I was determined to make my life's work. I read them, yes I read them: *Famous Funnies* first, then *Popular Comics,* then *King*—but with always a sense of being cheated. I was not getting top performance for my dime.

Not until March, 1937, when the first issue of *Detective Comics* came out. Original material had previously been used in comic books, but almost all of its was in the shape and style of then existing newspaper strips. *Detective Comics* was the first of the originals to be devoted to a single theme—crime fighting. And it looked different. Crime was fought in larger panels, fewer to a page. Most stories were complete in that issue (no more of the accursed: "to be continued . . ."). And a lot less shilly shallying before getting down to the action. A strange new world: unfamiliar heroes, unfamiliar drawing styles (if style is the word)—and written (if written is the word), in language not very different from that of a primer:

> In every large city there are G-Men. In every large seaport there are G-Men known as Harbor Police. 'Speed' Cyril Saunders is a special operative in a unit of the river patrol.

So began story one, issue one of *Detective Comics*.

The typical comic book circa 1937-38 measured about 7¼ by 10¼, averaged sixty-four pages in length, was glisteningly processed in four colors on the cover and flatly and indifferently colored on the inside, if colored at all. (For in the early days some stories were still in black and white; others in tones of sickly red on one page, sickly blue on another, so that it was quite possible for a character to have a white face and blue clothing for the first two pages of a story and a pink face and red clothing for the rest.) They didn't have the class of the daily strips but, to me, this enhanced their value. The daily strips, by their sleek professionalism held an aloof quality which comic books, being not quite professional, easily avoided. They were closer to home, more comfortable to live with, less like grownups.

The heroes were mostly detectives of one kind or another; or soldiers of fortune; here and there, even a magician. Whatever they were, they were tall, but not too tall—space limitations, you see; they were dark (blonde heroes were an exception, possibly because most movie heroes were dark; possibly because it was a chance for the artist to stick in a blob of black and call it hair. The blonde heroes, in every case, were curly-haired. The dark heroes, when full color came in, turned blue); they were handsome—well, symbolically handsome. The world of comics was a form of visual shorthand, so that the average hero need not have been handsome in fact, so long as his face was held to the required arrangement of lines that readers had been taught to be the accepted sign of handsome: sharp, slanting eyebrows, thick at the ends, thinning out toward the nose, of which in three-quarter view there was hardly any—just a small V placed slightly above the mouth, casting the faintest knick of a shadow. One never saw a nose full view. There was never a full view. They were too hard to draw. Eyes were usually ball-less, two thin slits. Mouths were always thick, quick single lines—never double. Mouths for some reason, were rarely shown open. Dialogue, theoretically, was spoken from the nose. Heroes' faces were square-jawed; in some cases, all-jawed. Often there was a cleft in the chin. Most heroes, whatever magazine they came from, looked like members of one of two families: Pat Ryan's or Flash Gordon's. Except for the magicians, all of whom looked like Mandrake. The three mythic archetypes.

That first *Detective Comics,* aside from its ground-breaking role, is memorable for the debut of Creig Flessel, not then a good illustrator, but within the first half-dozen issues, to become one of the best in the business—a master of the suspense cover. And another debut: that of Jerry Siegel and Joe Shuster, then in their pre-*Superman* days, weighing in with a slam-bang, hell for leather cross between Victor McLaglen and Captain Easy (with a Flash Gordon jaw), appropriately named *Slam Bradley,* because slamming was what he did most of the time. Always, of course, against bad guys—and always having a wonderful time. It was this action-filled rawness, this world of lusty hoodlumism, of Saturday movie serials seven days a week that made the new comic books, from their first day of publication, the principal reading matter in my life. That, plus the pragmatic insight that here, in a field where they hardly knew how to draw at all, I could make my earliest gains.

I studied styles. There was Tom Hickey who lettered with disconcerting open W's; who used an awful lot of dialogue ("printing," was the hated word for it in my neighborhood) to tell a painfully slow-moving story, full of heroes named Ian. Too thin-blooded. Too English. . . .

The problem in pre-super days was that, with few exceptions, heroes were not very interesting. And by any realistic appraisal, certainly no match for the villains who were bigger, stronger, smarter (as who wasn't?), and, even worse, were notorious scene stealers. Who cared about Speed Saunders, Larry Steele, Bruce Nelson, et. al. when there were oriental villains around? Tong warriors lurking in shadows, with trident beards, pointy fingernails, and skin the color of ripe lemons. With narrow, missile-like eyes slantingly aimed at the nose; a nose aged and curdled with corrupt wisdom, shrivelled in high expectancy of the coming tortures on the next page. How they toyed with those drab ofay heroes: trap set, trap sprung, into the pit, up comes the water, down comes the pendulum, out from the side come the walls. Through an unconvincing mixture of dumb-luck and general science 1, the hero escaped, just barely; caught and beat up the villain: that wizened ancient who, in toe to toe combat was, of course, no match for the younger man. And readers were supposed to cheer? Hardly! The following month it all happened again. Same hero, different oriental, slight variance in the torture.

Villains, whatever fate befell them in the obligatory last panel, were infinitely better equipped than those silly, hapless heroes. Not only comics, but life taught us that. Those of us raised in ghetto neighborhoods were being asked to believe that crime didn't pay? Tell that to the butcher! Nice guys finished last; landlords, first. Villains by their simple appointment to the role were miles ahead. It was not to be believed that any ordinary human could combat them. More was required. Someone with a call. When *Superman* at last appeared, he brought with him the deep satisfaction of all underground truths: our reaction was less, "How original!" than, "But, of course!"

II

The advent of the super-hero was a bizarre comeuppance for the American dream. Horatio Alger could no longer make it on his own. He needed "Shazam!" Here was fantasy with a cynically realistic base: once the odds were appraised honestly it was apparent you had to be super to get on in this world.

The particular brilliance of Superman lay not only in the fact that he was the first of the super-heroes, but in the concept of his alter ego. What made Superman different from the legion of imitators to follow was not that when he took off his clothes he could beat up everybody—they all did that. What made Superman extraordinary was his point of origin: Clark Kent.

Remember, Kent was not Superman's true identity as Bruce Wayne was the Batman's or (on radio) Lamont Cranston, the Shadow's. Just the opposite. Clark Kent was the fiction. Previous heroes, the Shadow, the Green Hornet, The Lone Ranger were not only more vulnerable, they were fakes. I don't mean to criticize, it's just a statement of fact. The Shadow had to cloud men's minds to be in business. The Green Hornet had to go through the fetishist fol-de-rol of donning costume, floppy hat, black mask, gas gun, menacing automobile, and insect sound effects before he was even ready to go out in the street. The Lone Ranger needed an accoutremental white horse, an Indian, and an establishing cry of Hi-Yo Silver to separate him from all those other masked men running around the West in days of yesteryear.

But Superman had only to wake up in the morning to be Superman. In his case, Clark Kent was the put on. The fellow with the eyeglasses and the acne and the walk girls laughed at wasn't real, didn't exist, was a sacrificial disguise, an act of discreet martyrdom. *Had they but known!*

And for what purpose? Did Superman become Clark Kent in order to lead a normal life, have friends, be known as a nice guy, meet girls? Hardly. There's too much of the hair shirt in the role, too much devotion to the imprimatur of impotence—an insight, perhaps, into the fantasy life of the Man of Steel. Superman as a secret masochist? Field for study there. For if it was otherwise, if the point, the only point, was to lead a "normal life," why not a more typical identity? How can one be a cowardly star reporter, subject to fainting spells in time of crisis, and not expect to raise serious questions?

The truth may be that Kent existed not for the purposes of the story but the reader. He is Superman's opinion of the rest of us, a pointed caricature of what we, the non-criminal element, were really like. His fake identity was our real one. That's why we loved him so. For if that wasn't really us; if there were no Clark Kents, only lots of glasses and cheap suits which, when removed, revealed all of us in our true identities—what a hell of an improved world it would have been!

In drawing style, both in figure and costume, Superman was a simplified parody of Flash Gordon. But if Alex Raymond was the Dior for Superman, Joe Shuster set the fashion from then on. Everybody elses super-costumes were copies from his shop. Shuster represented the best of old-style comic book drawing. His work was direct, unprettied—crude and vigorous; as easy to read as a diagram. No creamy lines, no glossy illustrative effects, no touch of that bloodless prefabrication that passes for professionalism these days. Slickness, thank God, was beyond his means. He could not draw well, but he drew single-mindedly—no one could ghost that style. It was the man. When assistants began "improving" the appearance of the strip it promptly went downhill. It looked like it was being drawn in a bank.

But, oh, those early drawings! Superman running up the sides of dams, leaping over anything that stood in his way (no one drew skyscrapers like Shuster. Impressionistic shafts, Superman poised over them, his leaping leg tucked under his ass, his landing leg tautly pointed earthward), cleaning and jerking two-ton get-away cars and pounding them into the sides of cliffs—and all this done lightly, unportentiously, still with that early Slam Bradley exuberance. What matter that the stories quickly lost interest; that once you've made a man super you've plotted him out of believable conflicts; that even super-villains, super-mad scientists and, yes, super-orientals were dull and lifeless next to the overwhelming image of that which Clark Kent became when he took off his clothes. So what if the stories were boring, the villains blah? This was the Superman Show—a touring road company backing up a great star. Everything was a stage wait until he came on. Then it was all worth-while.

Besides, for the alert reader there were other fields of interest. It seems that among Lois Lane, Clark Kent, and Superman there existed a schizoid and chaste *menage a' trois*. Clark Kent loved but felt abashed with Lois Lane; Superman saved Lois Lane when she was in trouble, found her a pest the rest of the time. Since Superman and Clark Kent were the same person this behavior demands explanation. It can't be that Kent wanted Lois to respect him for himself, since himself was Superman. Then, it appears, he wanted Lois to respect him for his fake self, to love him when he acted the coward, to be there when he pretended he needed her. She never was—so, of course, he loved her. A typical American romance. Superman never needed her, never needed anybody—in any event, Lois chased *him*—so, of course, he didn't love her. He had contempt for her. Another typical American romance.

Love is really the pursuit of a desired object, not pursuit by it. Once you've caught the object there is no longer any reason to love it, to have it hanging around. There must be other desirable objects out there, somewhere. So Clark Kent acted as the control for Superman. What Kent wanted was just that which Superman didn't want to be bothered with. Kent wanted Lois, Superman didn't: thus marking the difference between a sissy and a man. A sissy wanted girls who scorned him; a man scorned girls who wanted him. Our cultural opposite of the man who didn't make out with women has never been the man who did—but rather, the man who could if he wanted to, but still didn't. The ideal of masculine strength, whether Gary Cooper's, Lil Abner's, or Superman's, was for one to be so virile and handsome, to be in such a position of strength that he need never go near girls. Except to help them. And then get the hell out. Real rapport was not for women. It was for villains. That's why they got hit so hard.

III

The problem with other super-heroes was that the most convenient way of becoming one had already been taken. Superman was from another planet. One of the self-denigrating laws of all science fiction is that every other planet is better than ours. Other planets may have funny looking people but they think better, know more languages (including English), and are much further along in the business of rocketry and destruction. So, by definition, Superman had to be super: no outer-space weakling had ever been let in. The immediate and enormous success of Superman called for the creation of a tribe of successors—but where were they to come from? Not from other planets; Superman had all other planets tied up legally. Those one or two super-heroes who defied the ban were taken apart by lawyers—(nothing is as super as a writ).

The answer, then, rested with science. That strange bubbly world of test tubes and gobbledy-gook which had, in the past, done such great work in bringing the dead back to life in the form of monsters—why couldn't it also make men super? Thus Joe Higgins went into his laboratory and came out as the Shield; and John Sterling went into his laboratory and came out as Steel Sterling; and Steve Rogers went into the laboratory of kindly Professor Reinstein and came out as Captain America; and kindly Professor Horton went into his laboratory and came out with a synthetic man, named, illogically, the Human Torch. Science had run amok!

And not only science. With business booming comic book titles, too, ran amok: *Whiz, Startling, Astounding, Top Notch, Blue Ribbon, Zip, Silver Streak, Mystery Men, Wonder World, Mystic, Military, National, Police, Big Shot, Marvel-Mystery, Jackpot, Target, Pep, Champion, Master, Daredevil, Star-Spangled, All-American, All-Star, All-Flash, Sensation, Blue Bolt, Crash, Smash,* and *Hit Comics*. Setting loose a menagerie of flying men, webbed men, robot men, ghost men, miniscule men, flexible-sized men—men of all shapes and costume blackening the comic book skies like locusts in drag.

Skyman, Sky Chief, The Face, The Sub Mariner, The Angel, The Comet, The Hangman, Mr. Justice, Uncle Sam, The Web, The Doll Man, Plastic Man, The White Streak—all scrambling for a piece of the market. Their magazines were competitively dated months ahead, so that if Big-Shot released an issue in January and dated it March, in reprisal All-American would date its February issue August. Aficionadoes began to check: comic books not dated a minimum of four months in advance were deemed shabby. One was hesitant to be seen with them.

Understandably, this Pandora's box of men-of-steel was viewed gravely by Superman. One story of the time, denied by everyone, but for years a legend in the business, and reported as such, was that rival impresarios worried lest the Superman people bring legal or marketing reprisals (their distributive arm circulated not only their own, but most other comic books) volunteered certain major concessions. Such as capes. It was granted that Superman, being the *premiere danseuse* of superheroes, was the only one entitled to wear a cape. All others were, with appropriate ceremony, circumsized. (One could imagine the scene: The Shield, G-Man Extraordinary, standing in a field, his modest emblem, the

American Flag, plucked from his burly shoulders, folded in half, then in quarters—neatly—so that no part touched the ground. Buried in Arlington, a choked up marine playing taps; J. Edgar Hoover, a prominent character in the strip, standing alongside. Rumor had it that he sent flowers).

The most savage reprisals in comic books were, just as in revolutions, saved not for one's enemies but for one's own kind. If, for a moment, Superman may be described as the Lenin of super-heroes, Captain Marvel must be his Trotsky. Ideologically of the same bent, who could have predicted that within months the two would be at each others throats—or that, in time, Captain Marvel would present the only serious threat to the power of the man without whom he could not have existed?

From the beginning Captain Marvel possessed certain advantages in the struggle. In terms of reader identification, Superman was far too puritanical: if you didn't come from his planet you couldn't ever be super—that was that. But the more liberal Captain Marvel left the door open. His method of becoming super was the simplest of all—no solar systems or test tubes involved—all that was needed was a magic word: "Shazam!"

"Pie in the sky!" retorted the pro-Superman bloc, but millions of readers wondered. If all it took was a magic word then all that was required was the finding of it. Small surprise that for awhile Captain Marvel caught and passed the austere patriarch of the super-movement.

More than that, Captain Marvel was gifted with the light touch. Billy Batson, the newsboy, who Captain Marvel truly was, was drawn by artist C. C. Beck as an oval faced, dot eyed, squigly-haired boy familiar to any child who ever sent for a how-to-draw-heads course. The magic for readers in Captain Marvel was that not only did it appear easy to become him, it looked easy to draw him. Deceptively so. Captain Marvel was better drawn, really, than Superman. C. C. Beck followed in the tradition of Roy Crane's *Wash Tubbs,* drawing with a virginal simplicity that at times was almost stick like—but still there was style. Villains ranged from mad scientist, Dr. Sivana (the best in the business), who uncannily resembled Donald Duck, to Mr. Mind, a worm who talked and wore glasses, to Tawky Tawny, a tiger who talked and wore a business suit. A Disneyland of happy violence. The Captain himself came out dumber than the average super-hero—or perhaps, less was expected of him. A friendly fullback of a fellow with apple cheeks and dimples, one could imagine him being a buddy rather than a hero, an overgrown boy who chased villains as if they were squirrels. A perfect fantasy figure for, say, Charlie Brown. His future seemed assured. What a shock, then, the day Superman took him to court.

Happily, I did not learn of the Superman versus Captain Marvel law suit until years later. It would have done me no good to discover two of my idols, staunch believers in direct action, bent over, hands cupped to lips, whispering in the ears of their lawyers. No one should have to grow up that fast.

The Superman people said that Captain Marvel was a direct steal. The Captain Marvel people said what do you mean; sheer coincidence; isn't there room for the small businessman; we don't know what you're talking about. It went on that way for years, but the outcome was clear from the start. Captain Marvel fought hard but he was a paper tiger. One wondered whether he was beginning to drink. He was losing his lean, Fred MacMurray look, fleshing out fast in the face, in the gut, in the hips, moving onward and outward to Jack Oakie.

Then too there was great disappointment in the word "Shazam!" As it turned out it didn't work for readers. Other magic words were tried. They didn't work either. There are just so many magic words until one feels he's been made a fool of. How easy it became to hate "Shazam! Shazam! Shazam!" That taunting cry that worked fine for Captain Marvel but didn't do a damn thing for the rest of us.

I had the vague feeling that Captain Marvel was making fun of me. More and more his adventures took on the tone of parodies—item: Billy Batson being turned into a baby by mad scientist Dr. Sivana and thus not being able to say the magic word, it coming out "Tha-Tham!" I was not prepared for frivolousness on the part of my super-heroes! When the *Captain Marvel* people finally settled the case and went out of business, I couldn't have cared less.

IV

Batman trailed Superman by a year and was obviously intended as an offshoot, but his lineage—the school of rich idlers who put on masks—dates back to the Scarlet Pimpernel and includes Zorro, and The Green Hornet, with whom Batman bears the closest as well as most contemporaneous resemblance. Both the Green Hornet and Batman were wealthy, both dabbled in chemistry, both had super-vehicles, and both costumed themselves with a view toward striking terror into the hearts of evildoers. The Green Hornet buzzed; the Batman flapped—that was the essential difference.

Not that there weren't innovations: Batman popularized in comic books the strange idea, first used by the Phantom in newspapers, that when you put on your mask, your eyes disappeared. Two white slits showed—that was all. If that didn't strike terror into the hearts of evildoers, nothing would.

Batman, apparently, was in better physical shape than the Green Hornet; less dependent on the creature comforts of super-vehicles, or the rich man's use of nonlethal gas warfare. Batman got more meaningfully into the fray and, in consequence, was more clobbered. Though a good deal was made of his extraordinary stamina much of it, as it turns out, was for punishment—another innovation for super heroes: there was some reason to believe he had a glass jaw.

But Batman was not a super-hero in its truest sense (however we may have liked to think of him). If you pricked him, he bled—buckets. Superman's superiority lay in the offense, Batman's lay in the rebound. Whatever was done to him: whatever trap laid, wound opened, skull fractured, all he had to show for it was a discreet patch of band-aid on his right shoulder. With Superman we won; with Batman we held our own. Individual preferences were based on the ambitions and arrogance of one's fantasies.

The Batman school preferred a vulnerable hero to an invulnerable one; preferred a hero who was able to take punishment and triumph in the end to a hero who took comparatively little punishment, just dished it out. I suspect the Batman school of having healthier egoes. In my own case the concept of triumph over adversity was never very convincing. My own observations led me to believe that the only triumph most people eked out of adversity was to manage to stay alive as it swept by. With me, I didn't think it would be any different. I preferred to play it safe and be Superman.

Another point: I couldn't have been Batman even if I wanted to. If I were ever to be trapped in a steel vault with the walls closing in on all sides, I was obviously going to have to break out with my fists because it was clear from my earliest school grades that I was never going to have the know-how to invent an explosive in my underground laboratory that would blow me to safety. I was lousy at science. And I found the thought of having an underground laboratory chilling. My idea of a super-hero was some guy, bad with his hands, who came from an advanced planet so that he didn't have to go to gym to be strong or go to school to be smart. The sort of super-hero I admired had to be primarily passive, but invulnerable.

What made Batman interesting then, was not his strength but his story line. Batman, as a feature, was infinitely better plotted, better villained, and better looking than Superman. Batman inhabited a world where no one, no matter the time of day, cast anything but long shadows—seen from weird perspectives. Batman's world was scarey; Superman's, never. Bob Kane, Batman's creator, combined *Terry and the Pirates*-style drawing with *Dick Tracy*-style villains, e.g., The Joker, The Penguin, The Cat Woman, The Scarecrow, The Riddler, Clay-Face, Two-Face, Dr. Death, Hugo Strange.

Kane's early drawings, pretentious and stiff, coordinated perfectly with his early writing technique—a form of florid pre-literacy so typical of comic books of that day. . . . [An] example from a Kane feature of that time [Clip Carson, *Action Comics*]:

> Africa—the dark continent whose jungles teem with insects, beasts, fever, and wild natives. A land of terrible secrets no man can read . . . up the river to the shore of Kenye, Clip Carson, vagabond adventurer, paddles his canoe.

Despite it all, I remember Clip Carson warmly—and who, having once noted Batman smart-assing his way through a fist fight, has not forever been taken with him? Kane's strength, as did Shuster's, lay not in his draftsmanship (which was never quite believable), but in his total involvement in what he was doing (which made everything believable). However badly drawn and crudely written, Batman's world took control of the reader. If Kane said so, men *did* pose stroking their chins whenever they weren't fighting, running, or shooting in such a way that hand and chin never quite made contact; if Kane said so gangsters *did* wear those peculiar styled hats and suits—bought off the rack from a line nobody in the world had ever seen before; if Kane said so heads were not egg shaped, but rectangular; chins occupied not the bottom sixth of a face but the bottom half—because Kane's was an authentic fantasy, a genuine vision, so that however one might nit-pick the components, the end product remained an impregnable whole: gripping and original. Kane, more than any other comic book man (except Will Eisner who will be discussed later), set and made believable the terms offered to the reader.

Batman's world was more cinematic than Superman's. Kane was one of the early experimenters with angle shots and though he was not as compulsively avant grade in his use of the worms eye, the birds eye, the shot through the wineglass, as others in the field he was the only one of the *Detective, Adventure, Action Comics* line who managed to get that Warner Brother's fog-infested look.

For just as the movie studios had their individual trademarks, their way of lighting, their special approach to subject matter by which they could be identified even if one came in at the middle, so did comic books. National who produced the D.C. line, was the MGM of the field. It had the great stars, the crisp-brittle lighting, the elder statesman touch—smoothly exciting, eschewing the more boisterous effects of its less wealthy competitors. Superman was the best, but the most humorless of the super heroes (befitting his position); Batman was the best, but the most wooden of the masked heroes (a bit of early Robert Taylor there)—neither was quite touchable. They were State Department White Papers of the mind. And National, who issued them, was the government in power.

The opposite extreme was Fox—the Monogram Studios of the industry. Fox had the best covers and the worst insides. The covers were rendered in a modified pulp style: well-drawn, exotically muscled, half-undressed heroes rescuing well-drawn, exotically muscled, half-undressed maidens. The settings, often as not, were in the conventional oriental-mad scientist's laboratory—hissing test tubes going off everywhere; a hulking multiracial lab assistant at the ready to violate the girl; the masked hero crashing through a sky light, guns, aimed at nobody, flaming in each hand; the girl, strapped to an operating table screaming fetchingly—not yet aware that the crisis was passed.

Since the covers of Fox books were drawn by good men and the insides drawn by bad men, the hero on the cover could only be connected to his facsimile on the inside by the design of his leotards. Fox, like Monogram, had few stars and a deeply felt plot shortage. It pushed hard on the Green Mask, a slender, inadequate looking hero who beat up slender, inadequate looking criminals. While this business of fighting crime within one's weight division had something to recommend it, The Green Mask, somehow, never caught on.

To recoup, Fox made a star of the Blue Beetle, another Green Hornet derivative (in this case, a cop in real life), who, in order to fight criminals outside the reach of the law liked to dress as a beetle, this being his idea of a symbol that would strike terror into the hearts of evildoers—(not the first cop to work outside the law, but one of the few who had the decency to take off his uniform while doing it). As it turned out—and unpredictably—evil-doers were impressed with the Blue Beetle. His sign—the shadow of a great beetle projected into the evildoer's line of vision struck terror into their hearts. He wore a Phantom-type uniform, with scales—rather unpleasant looking without being impressive. He was a great favorite for a far longer time than he deserved.

Fox titles included *Mystery Men Comics, Wonder World Comics, Science Comics, Fantastic Comics*—all of them washed out, never looking quite alive or quite finished—existing in a mechanical limbo. The good men working for Fox soon moved elsewhere. Fiction House, a better outfit by inches, was often the place. As Republic was to Monogram, Fiction House was to Fox. Its one lasting contribution: *Sheena, Queen of the Jungle,* signed by W. Morgan Thomas (a pseudonym), drawn and very likely written by S. R. Powell who was later to do the best of the magician strips (not excepting Mandrake): Mr. Mystic.

Sheena was a voluptuous Tarzan who laid waste to wild beasts, savages, and evil white men in the jungle of her day, always assisted by her boy friend, Bob, a neat, young fellow in boots and jodpers who mainly stayed free of harms way while Sheena, manfully, cleaned out the trouble spots. Not as unfair a division of labor as you might think once you saw the two of them back to back, for while the boyfriend was supposed to be taller and more muscular, it was Sheena who gave the impression of size. Standing proud in the foreground, challenging an overmatched lion to hand to hand combat while her admiring young man stood in the tree shadows, holding her spear.

Sheena was the star of *Jungle Comics,* a book I looked at only when there were nothing but novels to read around the house. Beating up lions did not particularly interest me; my problem was with people. Nor did the people Sheena laid out interest me very much: they were the usual crop of white hunters in search of the elephant's graveyard, a strip of land so devout in its implications to jungle book fanciers that one could only assume the elephants took instruction in the church before dying.

Fiction House books had a boxed, constipated look. Balloons were rectangular, restricted looking. Anybody knew—or should have known—that good balloons were scalloped bubbles floating light as air on the tops of panels. Free and imaginative. Rectangular balloons were depressants—something architectural looking about them; something textbooky. They were no more to be trusted than those cartoons that gave up balloons entirely and ran an open narrative across the bottom of the panels—cartoons trying their damnedest not to look or sound like cartoons—set in the past tense, full of he saids and she saids. The past tense was a violation of comic book decorum—(and newspaper strips too). Comics were too immediate an experience to subjugate the reader to a past tense. Written narratives posed a deliberate similarity to *real books:* those wordy enclosures that threatened knowledge, threatened advance, threatened a hold on one's soul so that he could not keep it to mark time with, but must move ahead; learn; grow—all dubious outside values. (Prince Valiant too, was guilty of that bookish style but it was set in King Arthur's day. So I learned to live with it. But I couldn't put up with it in Tarzan and I could barely tolerate it in Flash Gordon. And I didn't like it anywhere else).

V

Fiction House put out *Fight Comics, Planet Comics, Wing Comics;* its one attempt at innovation was an outsized black and white book called *Jumbo Comics*—an unworkable hybrid of conventional comic book material and conventional newspaper material. Its single feature of interest was *Hawk of the Seas,* signed by Willis Rensie (Eisner spelled backwards). Hawk was a pirate feature, notable only as a trial run for *The Spirit,* full of the baroque angle shots that Eisner introduced to the business. Eisner had come to my attention a few years earlier doing a one shot, black and white feature called *'Muss 'Em Up' Donovan* in a comic book with the flop-oriented title of *Centaur Funny Pages*. 'Muss 'Em Up' Donovan was a detective, fired from the force on charges of police brutality (his victims, evidently, were white). Donovan is called back to action by a city administration overly harassed by crime who feel it is time for an approach that circumvents the legalistic niceties of due process. Such administrations were in vogue in all comic books of the thirties and forties. The heroes they culled out of the darkness operated, masked or not, outside the reach of the law. Their job: to catch criminals operating outside the reach of the law. In theory, one would think a difficult identity problem—but as it turned out in practice, not really.

Heroes and readers jointly conspired to believe that the police were honest, but inept; well-meaning, but dumb—except for good cops like Donovan, who were vicious. Arraignment was for sissies; a he-man wanted gore. Operating within the reach of the law a hero could get busted for that. So heroes, with the oblique consent of the power structure ("If you get into trouble, we can't vouch for you"), wandered outside the reach of the law, pummelled everyone in sight, killed a slew of people—and brought honor back to Central City, back to Metropolis, back to Gotham.

'Muss 'Em Up' Donovan was one such vigilante, a hawk-nosed, trench-coated primitive, bitter over his expulsion from office, but avid to answer the bell when duty once again called. Pages of violence: 'Muss 'Em Up' beating the truth out of a snivelling progression of stoolies; 'Muss 'Em Up' kicking in doors; 'Muss 'Em Up' shooting and getting shot at—a one man guerrilla war on crime. A grateful citizenery responded with vigor. 'Muss 'Em Up' was reinstated—allowed to 'Muss 'Em Up' in uniform once again. In those pre-civil rights days, we thought of that as a happy ending.

Will Eisner was an early master of the German expressionist approach in comic books—the Fritz Lang school. 'Muss 'Em Up' was full of dark shadows, creepy angle shots, graphic close-ups of violence and terror. Eisner's world seemed more real than the world of other comic book men because it looked that much more like a movie. The underground terror of RKO prison pictures, of convicts rioting, of armored car robberies, of Paul Muni or Henry Fonda not being allowed to go straight. The further films dug into the black fantasies of a depression generation the more they were labelled realism. Eisner retooled this mythic realism to his own uses: black fantasies on paper. Just as with the movies, it was labelled realism. Eisner's line had weight. Clothing sat on his characters heavily; when they bent an arm, deep folds sprang into action everywhere. When one Eisner character slugged another, a real fist hit real flesh. Violence was no externalized plot exercise, it was the gut of his style. Massive and indigestible, it curdled, lava-like, from the page.

Eisner moved on from Fiction House to land, finally, with the Quality Comic Group—the Warner Brothers of the business—creating the tone for their entire line: *The Doll Man, Black Hawk, Uncle Sam, The Black Condor, The Ray, Espionage—starring Black-X*—Eisner creations all. He'd draw a few episodes and abandon the characters—bequeath them to Lou Fine, Reed Crandall, others. No matter. The Quality books bore his look, his layout, his way of telling a story. For Eisner did just about all of his own writing—a rarity in comic book men. His stories carried the same weight as his line, involving a reader, setting the terms, making the most unlikely of plot twists credible.

His high point was *The Spirit,* a comic book section created as a Sunday supplement for newspapers. It began in 1939 and ran, weekly, until 1942, when Eisner went into the army and had to surrender the strip to (the joke is unavoidable), a ghost.

Sartorially the Spirit was miles apart from other masked heroes. He didn't wear tights, just a baggy blue business suit, a wide-brimmed blue hat that needed blocking, and, for a disguise, a matching blue eye mask, drawn as if it were a skin graft. For some reason, he rarely wore socks—or if he did they were flesh colored. I often wondered about that.

Just as Milton Caniff's characters were identifiable by their perennial WASPish, upper middle-class look, so were Eisner's identifiable by that look of just having got off the boat. The Spirit reeked of lower middle-class: his nose may have turned up, but we all knew he was Jewish.

What's more, he had a sense of humor. Very few comic book characters did. Superman was strait-laced; Batman wisecracked, but was basically rigid; Captain Marvel had a touch of Lil Abner, but that was parody, not humor. Alone among mystery men the Spirit operated (for comic books), in a relatively mature world in which one took stands somewhat more complex than hitting or not hitting people. Violent it was: this was to remain Eisner's stock in trade—but the Spirit's violence often turned in on itself, proved nothing, became, simply, an existential exercise; part of somebody else's game. The Spirit could even suffer defeat in the end: be outfoxed by a woman foe—stand there, his tongue making a dent in his cheek—charming in his boyish, Dennis O'Keefe way; a comment on the ultimate ineffectuality of even superheroes. But, of course, once a hero turns that vulnerable he loses interest to both author and readers. The Spirit, through the years, became a figurehead, the chairman of the board, presiding over eight pages of other people's stories. An inessential do-gooder, doing a walk-on on page 8, to tie up loose strings. A masked Mary Worth.

Not that he wasn't virile. Much of the Spirit's charm lay in his response to intense physical punishment. Hoodlums could slug him, shoot him, bend pipes over his head. The Spirit merely stuck his tongue in his cheek and beat the crap out of them; a more rational response than Batman's, for all his preening. For Batman had to take off his rich idler's street clothes, put on his Batshirt, his Batshorts, his Battights, his Batboots; buckle on his Batbelt full of secret potions and chemical explosives; tie on his Batcape; slip on his Batmask; climb in his Batmobile and go fight the Joker who in one punch (defensively described by the author as maniacal), would knock him silly. Not so with the Spirit. It took a mob to pin him down and no maniacal punch ever took him out of a fight. Eisner was too good a writer for that sort of nonsense.

Eventually Eisner developed story lines that are perhaps best described as documentary fables—seemingly authentic when one reads them, but impossible, after the fact. There was the one about Hitler walking around in a Willy Lomanish middle world: subways rolling, Bronx girls chattering, street bums kicking him around. His purpose in coming to America: to explain himself, to be accepted as a nice guy, to be liked. Silly when you thought of it, but for eight pages, grimly convincing.

Or the man who was a million years old—whose exploits are being read about by two young archeologists of the future who discover, in mountain ruins, the tattered remains of an old Spirit pamphlet, which details his story: the story of the oldest man in the world, cursed to live forever for being evil, until on the top of a mountain, in combat with the Spirit, he plunges into the ocean and drowns. "Ridiculous story," say these archeologists of the future as they finish the last page; these being their final words, for coming up behind them is that very old man; his staff raised high to crush their skulls, to toss them over the mountain edge into the ocean, and to then dance away, singing.

I collected Eisners and studied them fastidiously. And I wasn't the only one. Alone among comic book men, Eisner was a cartoonist other cartoonists swiped from.

VI

I created a *Spirit* swipe (*The Eel*) and a *Flash* swipe (*The Streak*) a *Lone Ranger* swipe (*The Masked Caballero*) a *Hawkman* swipe (*The Vulture*) and even a *Clip Carson* swipe (*Gunner Dixon*: "Gunner Dixon is not meant to be a bold super athletic math genius who with his super powers turns to do good in this war-torn world—NO! He's just an ordinary guy, he's no mental giant, he can't lick an army with his bare fist, but he can hold his own in any fight. All he is, is an *American*").

VII

Though I may have pirated the super-heroes I never went near their boy companions. I couldn't stand boy companions. If the theory behind Robin the Boy Wonder, Roy the Superboy, The Sandman's Sandy, The Shield's Rusty, The Human Torch's Toro, The Green Arrow's Speedy was to give young readers a character with whom to identify it failed dismally in my case. The super *grownups* were the ones I identified with. They were versions of me in the future. There was still time to prepare. But Robin the Boy Wonder was my own age. One need only look at him to see he could fight better, swing from a rope better, play ball better, eat better, and live better—for while I lived in the east Bronx, Robin lived in a mansion, and while I was trying, somehow, to please my mother—and getting it all wrong, Robin was rescuing Batman and getting the gold medals. He didn't even have to live with his mother.

Robin wasn't skinny. He had the build of a middleweight, the legs of a wrestler. He was obviously an "A" student, the center of every circle, the one picked for greatness in the crowd—God, how I hated him. You can imagine how pleased I was when, years later, I heard he was a fag.

In *Seduction of the Innocent,* psychiatrist Fredric Wertham writes of the relationship between Batman and Robin:

> They constantly rescue each other from violent attacks by an unending number of enemies. The feeling is conveyed that we men must stick together because there are so many villainous creatures who have to be exterminated. . . . Sometimes Batman ends up in bed injured and young Robin is shown sitting next to him. At home they lead an idyllic life. They are Bruce Wayne and 'Dick' Grayson. Bruce Wayne is described as a 'socialite' and the official relationship is that Dick is Bruce's ward. They live in sumptuous quarters, with beautiful flowers in large vases. . . . Batman is sometimes shown in a dressing gown. . . . It is like a wish dream of two homosexuals living together.

For the personal reasons previously listed I'd be delighted to think Wertham right in his conjectures (at least in Robin's case; Batman might have been duped), but conscience dictates otherwise: Batman and Robin were no more or less queer than were their youngish readers, many of whom palled around together, didn't trust girls, played games that had lots of bodily contact, and from similar surface evidence were more or less queer. But this sort of case-building is much too restrictive. In our society it is not only homosexuals who don't like women. Almost no one does. Batman and Robin are merely a legitimate continuation of that misanthropic maleness than runs, unvaryingly, through every branch of American entertainment, high or low: literature, movies, comic books, or party jokes. The broad tone of our mass media has always been inbred, narcissistic, reactionary. Mocking Jews because most of the writers weren't; mocking Negroes because all of the writers weren't; denigrating women because all of the writers were either married or had mothers. Mass entertainment being engineered by men, it was natural that a primary target be women: who were fighting harder for their rights, evening the score, unsettling the traditional balance between the sexes. In a depression they were often able to find work where their men could not. They were clearly the enemy.

Wertham cites testimony taken from homosexuals to prove the secret kicks received from the knowledge that Batman and Robin were living together, going out together, adventuring together. But so were the Green Hornet and Kato (hmm—an oriental . . .) and the Lone Ranger and Tonto (Christ! An Indian!)—and so, for that matter, did Fred Astaire and Ginger Rogers hang around together an awful lot, but, God knows, I saw everyone of their movies and it never occurred to me they were sleeping with each other. If homosexual fads were certain proof of that which will turn our young queer, then we should long ago have burned not just Batman books, but all Bette Davis, Joan Crawford, and Judy Garland movies.

Wertham goes on to point to *Wonder Woman* as the lesbian counterpart to Batman:

> For boys, Wonder Woman is a frightening image. For girls she is a morbid ideal. Where Batman is antifeminine, the attractive Wonder Woman and her counterparts are definitely antimasculine.

Well, I can't comment on the image girls had of Wonder Woman. I never knew they read her—or any comic book. That *girls* had a preference for my brand of literature would have been more of a frightening image to me than any number of men being beaten up by Wonder Woman.

Whether Wonder Woman was a lesbian's dream I do not know, but I know for a fact she was every Jewish boy's unfantasied picture of the world as it really was. You mean men weren't wicked and weak? You mean women weren't badly taken advantage of? You mean women didn't have to be *stronger* than men to survive in this world? Not in *my* house!

My problem with Wonder Woman was that I could never get myself to believe she was that good. For if she was as strong as they said, why wasn't she tougher looking? Why wasn't she bigger? Why was she so flat-chested? And why did I always feel that, whatever her vaunted Amazon power, she wouldn't have lasted a round with Sheena, Queen of the Jungle?

No, Wonder Woman seemed like too much of a put up job, a fixed comic strip—a product of group thinking rather than the individual inspiration that created Superman. It was obvious from the start that a bunch of men got together in a smoke-filled room and brain stormed themselves a Super Lady. But nobody's heart was in it. It was choppily written and dully drawn. I see now that my objection is just the opposite of Wertham's: Wonder Woman wasn't dykey enough. Her violence was too immaculate, never once boiling over into a little fantasmal sadism. Had they given us a Wonder Woman with balls—that would have been something for Dr. Wertham and the rest of us to wrestle with!

. . . . .

In the years since Dr. Wertham and his supporters launched their attacks, comic books have toned down considerably, almost antiseptically. Publishers in fear of their lives wrote a code, set up a review board, and volunteered themselves into censorship rather than have it imposed from the outside. Dr. Wertham scorns self-regulation as misleading. Old time fans scorn it as having brought on the death of comic books as they once knew and loved them: for surprisingly, there *are* old comic book fans. A small army of them. Men in their thirties and early forties wearing school ties and tweeds, teaching in universities, writing ad copy, writing for chic-magazines, writing novels—who continue to be addicts; who save old comic books, buy them, trade them, and will, many of them, pay up to fifty dollars for the first issues of *Superman* or *Batman;* who publish and mail to each other mimeographed "fanzines"—strange little publications deifying what is looked back on as "the golden age of comic books." Ruined by Wertham. Ruined by growing up.

So Dr. Wertham is wrong in his contention . . . that no one matures remembering the things.

His other charges against comic books: that they were a participating factor in juvenile delinquency and, in some cases, juvenile suicide, that they inspired experiments, ala Superman, in free-fall flight which could only end badly, that they were, in general, a corrupting influence, glorifying crime and depravity can only, in all fairness, be answered: "But of course. Why else read them?"

Comic books, first of all are junk. To accuse them of being what they are is to make no accusation at all: there is no such thing as *uncorrupt* junk or *moral* junk or *educational* junk—though attempts at the latter have, from time to time, been foisted on us. But education is not the purpose of junk (which is one reason why *True Comics* and *Classic Comics* and other half-hearted attempts to bring reality or literature into the field invariably looked embarrassing). Junk is there to entertain on the basest, most compromised of levels. It finds the lowest fantasmal common denominator and proceeds from there. Its choice of tone is dependent on its choice of audience, so that women's magazines will make a pretense at veneer scorned by movie-fan magazines, but both are, unarguably, junk. If not to their publishers, certainly to a good many of their readers who, when challenged, will say defiantly: "I know it's junk, but I like it." Which is the whole point about junk. It is there to be nothing else but liked. Junk is a second-class citizen of the arts; a status of which we and it are constantly aware. There are certain inherent privileges in second-class citizenship. Irresponsibility is one. Not being taken seriously is another. Junk, like the drunk at the wedding, can get away with doing or saying anything because, by its very appearance, it is already in disgrace. It has no one's respect to lose; no image to endanger. It's values are the least middle class of all the mass media. That's why it is needed so.

The success of the best junk lies in its ability to come close, but not too close; to titillate without touching us. To arouse without giving satisfaction. Junk is a tease; and in the years when the most we need is teasing we cherish it—in later years when teasing no longer satisfies we graduate—hopefully, into better things or haplessly, into pathetic, and sometimes violent attempts to make the teasing come true.

It is this antisocial side of junk that Dr. Wertham scorns in his attack on comic books. What he dismisses—perhaps, because the case was made badly—is the more positive side of junk. (The entire debate on comic books was, in my opinion, poorly handled. The attack was strident and spotty; the defense, smug and spotty—proving, perhaps, that even when grownups correctly verbalize a point about children, they manage to miss it: so that a child expert can talk about how important fantasies of aggression are for children, thereby destroying forever the value of fantasies of aggression. Once a child is told: "Go on, darling. I'm watching. Fantasize," he no longer has a reason.) Still, there is a positive side to comic books that more than makes up for their much publicized antisocial influence. That is: their *underground* antisocial influence.

Adult have their defense against time: it is called "responsibility," and once one assumes it he can form his life into a set of routines which will account for all those hours when he is fresh, and justifies escape during all those hours when he is stale or tired. It is not size or age or childishness that separate children from adults. It is "responsibility." Adults come in all sizes, ages, and differing varieties of childishness, but as long as they have "responsibility" we recognize, often by the light gone out of their eyes, that they are what we call grownup. When grownups cope with "responsibility" for enough number of years they are retired from it. They are given, in exchange, a "leisure problem." They sit around with their "leisure problem" and try to figure out what to do with it. Sometimes they go crazy. Sometimes they get other jobs. Sometimes it gets too much for them and they die. They have been handed an undetermined future of nonresponsible time and they don't know what to do about it.

And that is precisely the way it is with children. Time is the ever-present factor in their lives. It passes slowly or fast, always against their best interests: good time is over in a minute; bad time takes forever. Short on "responsibility," they are confronted with a "leisure problem." That infamous question: "What am I going to do with myself?" correctly rephrased should read: "What am I going to do to get away from myself?"

And then, dear God, there's school! Nobody really knows why he's going to school. Even if one likes it, it is still, in the best light, an authoritarian restriction of freedom: where one has to obey and be subservient to people not even his parents. Where one has to learn concurrently, book rules and social rules, few of which are taught in a way to broaden horizons. So books become enemies and society becomes a hostile force that one had best put off encountering until the last moment possible.

Children, hungry for reasons, are seldom given convincing ones. They are bombarded with hard work, labelled education—not seen therefore as child labor. They rise for school at the same time or earlier than their fathers, start work without office chatter, go till noon without coffee breaks, have waxed milk for lunch instead of dry martinis, then back at the desk till three o'clock. Facing greater threats and riskier decisions than their fathers have had to meet since *their* day in school. And always at someone else's convenience. Someone else dictates when to rise, what's to be good for breakfast, what's to be learned in school, what's to be good for lunch, what're to be play hours, what're to be homework hours, what's to be delicious for dinner and what's to be, suddenly, bedtime. This goes on until summer—when there is, once again, a "leisure problem." "What," the child asks, "am I going to do with myself?" Millions of things, as it turns out, but no sooner have they been discovered then it is time to go back to school.

It should come as no surprise then, that within this shifting hodgepodge of external pressures, a child, simply to save his sanity, must go underground. Have a place to hide where he cannot be got at by grownups. A place that implies, if only obliquely, that *they're* not so much; that *they* don't know everything; that *they* can't fly the way some people can, or let bullets bounce harmlessly off their chests, or beat up whomever picks on them, or—oh, joy of joys!—even become invisible! A no-man's land. A relief zone. And the basic sustenance for this relief was, in my day, comic books.

With them we were able to roam free, disguised in costume, committing the greatest of feats—and the worst of sins. And, in every instance, getting away with them. For a little while, at least, it was our show. For a little while, at least, we were the bosses. Psychically renewed, we could then return above ground and put up with another couple of days of victimization. Comic books were our booze.

Just as in earlier days for other children it was pulps, and *Nick Carter,* and penny dreadfuls—all junk in their own right, but less disapproved of latterly because they were less violent. But, predictably, as the ante on violence rose in the culture, so too did it rise in the junk.

Comic books, which had few public (as opposed to professional) defenders in the days that Dr. Wertham was attacking them, are now looked back on by an increasing number of my generation as samples of our youthful innocence instead of our youthful corruption. A sign, perhaps, of the potency of that corruption. A corruption—a lie, really—that put us in charge, however temporarily, of the world in which we lived; and gave us the means, however arbitrary, of defining right from wrong, good from bad, hero from villain. It is something for which old fans can understandably pine—almost as if having become overly conscious of the imposition of junk on our adult values: on our architecture, our highways, our advertising, our mass media, our politics—and even in the air we breathe, flying black chunks of it—we have staged a retreat to a better remembered brand of junk. A junk that knew its place was underground where it had no power and thus only titillated, rather than above ground where it truly has power—and thus, only depresses.

Ronald Schmitt

SOURCE: "Deconstructive Comics," in *Journal of Popular Culture*, Vol. 25, No. 4, Spring, 1992, pp. 153-61.

[*In the following essay, Schmitt analyzes comic books as a mixed medium of word balloons and illustrations, and discusses their relationship to linguistic development.*]

Comic books have been and continue to be one of the most marginalized of art forms. The assumption that the "reading" of comics is a frivolous and inferior activity seems a given even among those who do not see them as a threat. But in fact, those conservative educators who do see the effects of comic books as a threat are probably more correct in their assumptions than those who dismiss this very influential and powerful art medium of the 20th century as frivolous. The effects of comic books on youngsters are quite subversive but not in the moral, behavioral sense which conservative educators perceive but rather in their effects on traditional, hierarchical modes of reading and on the entire notion of literacy.

In the academic community, little has been written about comic books. What little research has been done centers almost exclusively on issues of content rather than analyses of form and while it is impossible to abstract one concept from the other it is interesting that in an intellectual climate where the interest in "deconstructing" paternalistic hierarchies is so strong, few scholars are interested in the deconstructive effect of the comic book and other media forms on the traditional mode of the signifier: the linear, print-block text. It is no accident that the proliferation of comic books and comic book reading occurred when it did and has now somewhat receded as a social phenomenon for it has a clear link with a media revolution which is still in the process of numerous transformations, yielding new art forms and demanding new perceptions of language and literacy.

It will be my endeavor in this analysis to show how comics are an important deconstructive and revolutionary medium in the 20th century cultural transference from the hierarchical domination of the printed book as the exclusive medium of literacy to an inclusion of the concept of audio-visual (television and film) "literacy." The notion of the page of written text as the most effective and "preferred" conduit to ideas, information and ultimately "intelligence" and literacy is still a firmly entrenched hierarchy in all levels of education but especially in higher education. The revolution which the usurpation of the print medium's preferred status in education would cause in terms of "retooling" schools for a new standard of literacy would be nothing less than catastrophic to entrenched, traditionally trained instructors. It is not surprising then that the resistance to accepting the growing effect of these new forms of media can often take distinctly paranoid and angry forms. Comic books are indeed an "attack" on traditional values, one which contains within its seemingly inconsequential and frivolous facade, the deconstructive seeds of a revolution in perception, likely to leave no stone of traditional educative practice unturned.

While the incorporation of pictorial text with written text is as old as the illuminated manuscript, it is clear that the comic book as pop cultural industry is a distinctively 20th century, American phenomenon. And as with so many American industries, it produces a disposable product. As McLuhan points out, just as the highly popular, pre-Gutenberg *Biblia Pauperum,* woodcut printed bibles for the poor, were despised by the learned and not preserved, so it is with the comic book. Printed on cheap, pulp paper with low quality color and graphic resolution, the comic book publisher's primary interest is in keeping cost low enough to provide for maximum distribution at minimum cost.

But while comics and so many other mass media products are marketed as non-serious, inconsequential and disposable distractions for the "non-literary" public, they often produce extremely serious and concerned responses from authority figures. Martin Barker observes that the suppression of pop culture can be traced historically from the time of the Industrial Revolution, with far less interest in it prior to that time. Clearly this is due to the acknowledgement by conservative institutions of the tremendous power now available in the proliferation of various mass-media "texts." This can be observed dramatically in the cartoon broadsides, posters and pamphlets of the Nazi propaganda machine in the 1930s & 1940s, dates which are interestingly concurrent with the "birth" of important U.S. comic book mythic figures like Superman.

Yet, despite its academic dismissal as inconsequential, it is undeniable that ideology and mass media products like comic books are inseparable concepts. Tracing the history of the comic book reveals its intimate connection with U.S. political and ideological "savoir," and its evolution into increasingly marginalized and subversive forms.

Arthur Asa Berger's analysis of comic books and strips, *The Comic Stripped American,* outlines the progression and development of some of the most familiar and influential comics. It becomes immediately evident in such a survey that comic book characters reveal essential myths and ideologies of the cultures in which they are produced, but their popularity clearly stems from the fact that they offer alternatives to and escape from the ideology of the status quo. Far from being a watered-down, inferior substitute of "high" cultural art, they are distinct, alternative visions which reveal more about the fears, neuroses and power struggles of the populous than high art does. Berger makes the important insight that the "high" literary perspective (existentialist, absurd, cynical) is primarily a European import that did not fit pervasive pre-World War II American attitudes. What he calls the First Generation Comics (Mutt & Jeff, Katzenjammer Kids, Krazy Kat, etc.) show the innocence, naivete and optimism of early 20th century America, virtually untouched by the radical political and social upheavals occurring in Europe. The Second Generation, the age of the first superheroes Dick Tracy and Buck Rogers, show an America requiring fantasies of superhuman power to overcome the devastatingly dehumanizing forces associated with Fascism and the Second World War. By the Third Generation Comics (The Marvel Comics Group, Eroticomics and Underground Comics) the Fall is complete and comics are overtly political, sexual and even radical, insisting on a "relevance" in which even the most escapist comics involve themselves with social issues, often issues which are not "acceptable" to older generations who are used to the more innocent comics of previous years.

Both Berger and Saul Braun raise the extremely provocative and interesting question of whether a generation influenced by the Third Generation comics, confronting the corrupt, military-industrial complex of a generation influenced by the Second Generation comics, brought about the student activism which shook universities in the 1960s.

> It is not irrelevant to note that the Vietnamese war developed without hindrance—with some few exceptions—from a generation of men flying around the world on a fantasy power trip, and was resisted in the main by their sons, the generation that began rejecting the comic books of the fifties with their sanitized, censored, surreal images of the world. . . .

But comics have always had a strong tradition of being satirical, erotic and a medium which has used its marginality to celebrate that which is unacceptable in "serious" discourse. When the discourse of the political status quo becomes tyrannical and suffocating, then pop culture must choose between falling lockstep into repressive patterns (a position quite alien to all forms of humor and fantasy) or reacting to the repressive status quo with equal vehemence and, perhaps, paranoia.

One of the most striking and bizarre collisions of cultural ideology occurred in the 1950s when a number of educators, parents and teacher's groups, spearheaded by the influential book *Seduction of the Innocent* by Fredric Wertham, mobilized an aggressive campaign to rigidly control the content of comic books in the U.S. It is an extraordinary social phenomenon, virtually ignored by social historians, that comic book sales reached an all time high in the 1950s, with cases documented by Wertham of children "reading" as many as 50-75 comic books a week. Interest in school work and traditional reading all but disappeared as, to the horror of social theorists, children revealed over and over again their fascination with the sensational violence, semi-nudity, and defiance of authority in comics, while expressing unapologetic boredom with school work and socially approved pastimes. Wertham himself confoundedly admits that comics aroused "their interest, their mental participation and their passions and their sympathies" far more than the teachings of the home, school or church. In addition, Wertham, in interviews with youngsters, discovered that children found the crimes, brutality and sexuality in comics far more intriguing than the moralizing endings, meant to pass off these titillating comics as socially redeemable products.

The comic book mania in the late 1950s was a case of giving the public, even an immature public, what it wanted and needed. The 1950s child's fascination—indeed compulsion—with comics was linked to the Peyton Place promiscuity, domestic violence and decadence which seethed in the suburbs of America, glossed over by a *Leave It To Beaver* facade. Children have always had a delightful habit of cutting directly to the heart of a situation and laying bare its hypocrisies and pretensions. Wertham, far from being a paranoid old man, was reading the signs correctly. Comics were a threat to the status quo's facade of order and proper conduct. Wertham was reaching into the skeleton-filled closets of a repressive, paranoid culture when he explored the comic book in depth. It is no wonder he got scared.

The comic book mania in the late 1950s was a case of giving the public, even an immature public, what it wanted and needed. The 1950s child's fascination—indeed compulsion—with comics was linked to the Peyton Place promiscuity, domestic violence and decadence which seethed in the suburbs of America, glossed over by a *Leave It To Beaver* facade.

—Ronald Schmitt

The idea that the highly impressionable young mind must necessarily mimic that which it sees has been the major assumption which has backed most of the attacks on the content of children's media. Martin Barker persuasively rejects the entire notion of "identification" as a form of paternalism which assumes that people must be saved from their own base instincts, and that titillating stimuli like comic books and television are like drugs which must be carefully controlled or we will all become addicts. Thus, as Barker points out, identification becomes a focal point of worry by patriarchal ideologies about the behavior of the masses.

It is not my intention to suggest that no restraints in children's conduct or interests are necessary in our society; on the contrary, such restraints define a culture's morality as surely as its adult laws do. But Wertham reveals a lot when he says:

> Murder, crime and drug traffic are offered to children in a literature which the defenders of comic

> books call the modern version of the stories of the Brothers Grimm, Hans Christian Anderson or Mother Goose. But are there heroin addicts in Grimm, marihuana smokers in Anderson or dope peddlers in Mother Goose?

Indeed, there aren't, which says far more about adult's conduct than children's. Wertham's entire campaign was the horror of a society forced to look at its own sins, and wondering if the disease in them would spread to their young. It was a classic case of psychological projection (as is the entire notion of identification); the refusal to see within oneself, that which one so readily sees in another.

But far more interesting than the adult's fears of the content of comics, with all of the repressed fantasies of sexuality and violence which lie barely beneath the surface of their own cultural skins, is the effect which Wertham notes that comics have on the process of reading itself. He stresses that, as a result of his research, it is clear to him that though comics do contain words, the emphasis is on the visual image, as opposed to what he calls the "proper" word. Hence, he asserts that comic reading is an inadequate experience, not contributing to (in fact damaging) the educational process, which he claims must be "useful."

Again, while the ideological basis of his statements is strikingly transparent, there is an important grain of truth in what Wertham says. Probably the most significant statement in his book is this one:

> This kind of picture reading is not actually a form of reading, nor is it a pre-stage of real reading. *It is an evasion of reading and almost its opposite.* Habitual picture readers are severely handicapped in the task of becoming readers of books later, for the habit of picture reading interferes with the acquisition of well-developed reading habits. (Emphasis mine.)

Indeed, the skills involved in comic book "reading" in no way prepare a youngster for print-block text literacy. As Wertham observes, the left-to-right eye coordination of conventional reading is not improved by comic reading, for an entirely different eye coordination is employed in scanning the pictures and speech balloons. Two separate techniques must be employed by youngsters; two separate literacies. Unfortunately for Wertham and others who wish to maintain the primacy of reading the print-block text, comic reading actively deconstructs traditional ways of reading, creating a different literacy in which pictorial and word texts continually exchange emphasis, effectively eradicating the primacy of either.

The relationship between the words and pictures in a comic book, rather than being the collision of dialectical opposites which Wertham sees, is more akin to Derrida's concept of "différance." Since it is impossible to "see" both picture and words simultaneously, the presence of the one necessitates the absence of the other creating a continual, unresolvable play of difference between the two textual forms. In addition, signification and stable meaning is continually deferred as the eye, instead of scanning left to right in even, linear patterns, jumps between words and pictures, spiraling, zig-zagging and often interrupting the entire process to re-scan the information in a new way. Rather than two "stable" texts (words and pictures) juxtaposed, the comic book is a form of self-inflicted "double-writing," collapsing traditional strategies for reading word and picture texts.

In this regard, the difference between the comic book and comic strip must be stressed. The pattern of yuppie, political comic strips like *Doonesbury*, and especially "intellectual" comics like *The Far Side*, is more in keeping with the illustrated book. There are often large, single blocks of word text above or below the pictures, with the characters involved in little action other than talking. If extensive action or a sight gag is employed, it is often presented without a word balloon. The effect is to read the entire word text, then look at the picture, as with an illustrated book.

But in most modern comic books, especially those from innovators like Stan Lee of Marvel Comics, the speech balloons are broken into small parts and dispersed asymmetrically throughout the framed image; "chopping it up." The layout of the separate framed images on the page is often non-linear as well, with diagonal, circular and single configurations instead of the left-to-right, top-to-bottom configuration of early comic books, which mimicked one long comic strip, laid out in book form. The words themselves in comic books violate traditional roles in signification and are employed in ways which challenge the boundaries generally accorded to the printed word. As Derrida points out in his critique of Saussure's "phonocentrism" in *Of Grammatology*:

> If one considers the now recognized fragility of the notions of pictogram, ideogram, etc., and the uncertainty of the frontiers between so-called pictographic, ideographic, and phonetic texts, one realizes not only the unwiseness of the Saussurian limitation but the need for general linguistics to abandon the entire family of concepts inherited from metaphysics—often through the intermediary of a psychology—and clustering around the concept of arbitrariness.

The "uncertainty of the frontiers between so-called pictographic, ideographic and phonetic scripts" is underscored in comic book typeface.

As Barker observes, there is a complex system of conventions in the typeface of comics which relates to audio rather than graphic representation. Bold print is meant to indicate loudness while small print is a whisper. Jagged print is meant to suggest scratchy or shaky sounds and voices. The different shapes of balloons indicate the source of the "sound": speech, thought, radio transmission, etc. The sanctity of standard written English as inviolable discourse is further eroded in comics by the continual use of intentionally misspelled words, generally spelled so as to be more phonetically accurate than the correct spelling, or to emphasize some letter or syllable for oral pronunciation.

I would add that modern comic books go well beyond these familiar conventions, to erode the entire sense of the distinction between word and picture as well as word and sound. Sound effects are expressed in monosyllabic "invented" words which are themselves art works (colorful graphic shapes rather than black letters on a light background). These words are not in balloons but are superimposed over the pictures, "violating" the space of the visual image like graffiti. The title letters of comic books often blur the distinction between letter and picture by dripping like blood, or forming lightning bolts, or incorporating some iconic detail of a character's costume or persona—a shield or horns for example.

In addition, comic books often casually cross narrative boundaries by including boxes at the bottom of many frames which directly address the reader with quips, insights and expository details the editor/artist feels are necessary. This self-conscious narrative intrusion, considered such a radical technique in post-modern literature, has always been a standard part of modern comic book convention.

Thus, the relationship between word and picture in the comic book is a continual tension between presence and absence—the word text alternating as symbol, sound and pure image, the pictorial text continually chopped-up by words supposedly indispensable for grasping the "meaning" of the story. The word text and the pictorial text are continually deconstructing each other, allowing the reader no solid pattern or strategy with which to quiet the continual play between them. It is word and picture alternating as the term "sous rature." Any attempt to privilege one textual form over the other, as Wertham tries to do, only forces the other to emerge.

Clearly these conventions of comic book art represent an important interplay between the traditional written text, the printed picture and another form of media from which the comic book borrows many of its conventions—television. The words in a comic book, speaking in reductionist terms, "replace" the audio, as well as the titles and slogans, on a television show, with louder and softer volumes, vocal emphasis, superimposed sound effects, even an intrusive announcer's voice telling us what we missed last week or can expect to see next week. But because of the nature of written word texts and the visual exclusivity they demand, their use as "supplements" to a pictorial text is impossible. The comic book reader's eye must be continually diverted from the words to process the information in the "other" text. Unlike TV, one cannot listen to the words and look at the pictures at the same time.

Similarly, comic book visual artists found it impossible to create complex narratives with pictures alone, so they incorporated words, perhaps believing that they could, as Wertham suggests, co-opt the written word under the weighty effect of the visual image. But again, the eye is continually drawn away from the picture to read the words.

But the comic book's relationship with television literacy goes far beyond an awkward and unsuccessful sense of mimicking another medium's conventions. Two of the pillars of Western art, the printed book and the static, framed picture, are actively fragmented and "televisionized." The printed word, as shown, is altered to make it function as an audio and, at times, a pictorial signifier. The pictorial image (itself a two-dimensional matrix of colored dots) is broken up into fragments, not only by the speech balloons, but through a serialized patterning of images which defies the static sense of a framed picture. By varying perspective continually with the equivalent of different camera angles (close-ups, high and low angles, cropped framing, etc.), by employing such conventions as the familiar blurred outline or trailing lines behind a quickly moving character, and, of course, by employing a continuing series of frames, the comic book visual image has, built into its form, a much stronger sense of movement than a single painting or sketch.

Thus, the comic book occupies a curious and unique position in the 20th century electronic media revolution. It represents a transitional medium that directly transforms the printed word and the framed picture, paving the way for a new type of literacy which combines these and other traditional texts (spoken word, music) in the ultimate of intertextual media forms: television. The function of the picture and the word is no longer conceived of as separate, or supplementary in a hierarchical sense. Both signifying forms exist in an interplay which blurs any clear boundaries between them and fragments any sense of formal unity they presume to represent.

Leslie Fiedler

SOURCE: "The Middle Against Both Ends," in *The Collected Essays of Leslie Fiedler*, Vol. II, Stein and Day, 1971, pp. 415-28.

[*In the following essay, Fiedler dismisses the worry over comic books as a weakness of culturally intolerant middlebrows.*]

I am surely one of the few people pretending to intellectual respectability who can boast that he has read more comic books than attacks on comic books. I do not mean that I have consulted or studied the comics—I have read them, often with some pleasure. Nephews and nieces, my own children, and the children of neighbors have brought them to me to share their enjoyment. An old lady on a ferry boat in Puget Sound once dropped two in my lap in wordless sympathy: I was wearing, at the time, a sailor's uniform.

I have somewhat more difficulty in getting through the books that attack them. I am put off, to begin with, by inaccuracies of fact. When Mr. Geoffrey Wanger in his *Parade of Pleasure* calls Superboy "Superman's brother" (he is, of course, Superman himself as a child), I am made suspicious. Actually, Mr. Wagner's book is one of the least painful on the subject; confused, to be sure, but quite lively and not in the least smug; though it propounds the preposterous theory that the whole of "popular literature" is a conspiracy on the part of the "plutos" to corrupt an innocent American people. Such easy melodrama can only satisfy someone prepared to believe, as Mr. Wagner apparently does, that the young girls of Harlem are being led astray by the *double-entendres* of blues records!

Mr. Wagner's notions are at least more varied and subtle than Mr. Gershon Legman's, who cries out in his *Love and Death* that it is simply our sexual frustrations which breed a popular literature dedicated to violence. But Mr. Legman's theory explains too much: not only comic books but Hemingway, war, Luce, Faulkner, the status of women—and, I should suppose, Mr. Legman's own shrill hyperboles. At that, Mr. Legman seems more to the point in his search for some deeply underlying cause than Fredric Wertham, in *Seduction of the Innocent,* with his contention that the pulps and comics in themselves are schools for murder. That the undefined aggressiveness of disturbed children can be given a shape by comic books, I do not doubt; and one could make a good case for the contention that such literature standardizes crime woefully or inhibits imagination in violence, but I find it hard to consider so obvious a symptom a prime cause of anything. Perhaps I am a little sensitive on this score, having heard the charge this week that the recent suicide of one of our college freshmen was caused by his having read (in a course of which I am in charge) Goethe, Dostoevski, and *Death of a Salesman.* Damn it, he *had* read them, and he *did* kill himself!

In none of the books on comics I have looked into, and in none of the reports of ladies' clubs, protests of legislators, or statements of moral indignation by pastors, have I come on any real attempt to understand comic books: to define the form, midway between icon and story; to distinguish the subtypes: animal, adolescent, crime, Western, etc.; or even to separate out, from the dead-pan varieties, tongue-in-cheek sports like *Pogo,* frank satire like *Mad,* or semisurrealist variations like *Plastic Man.* It would not take someone with the talents of an Aristotle, but merely with his method, to ask the rewarding questions about this kind of literature that he asked once about an equally popular and bloody genre: what are its causes and its natural form?

A cursory examination would show that the superhero comic (*Superman, Captain Marvel, Wonder Woman,* etc.) is the final form; it is statistically the most popular with the most avid readers, and it provides the only new legendary material invented along with the form rather than adapted to it.

Next, one would have to abstract the most general pattern of the myth of the superhero and deduce its significance: the urban setting, the threatened universal catastrophe, the hero who never uses arms, who returns to weakness and obscurity, who must keep his identity secret, who is impotent, etc. Not until then could one ask with any hope of an answer: what end do the comics serve? Why have they gained an immense body of readers precisely in the past fifteen or twenty years? Why must they be disguised as children's literature though read by men and women of all ages? And having answered these, one could pose the most dangerous question of all: why the constant, virulent attacks on the comics, and, indeed, on the whole of popular culture of which they are especially flagrant examples?

Strategically, if not logically, the last question should be asked first. Why the attacks? Such assaults by scientists and laymen are as characteristic of our age as puritanical diatribes against the stage of the Elizabethan Era, and pious protests against novel reading in the later eighteenth century. I suspect that a study of such conventional reactions reveals at least as much about the nature of a period as an examination of the forms to which they respond. The most fascinating and suspicious aspect of the opposition to popular narrative is its unanimity; everyone from the members of the Montana State Legislature to the ladies of the Parent Teachers Association of Boston, Massachusetts, from British M.P.'s to the wilder post-Freudians of two continents agree on this, though they may agree on nothing else. What they have in common is, I am afraid, the sense that they are all, according to their lights, righteous. And their protests represent only one more example (though an unlikely one) of the notorious failure of righteousness in matters involving art.

Just what is it with which vulgar literature is charged by various guardians of morality or sanity? With everything: encouraging crime, destroying literacy, expressing sexual frustration, unleashing sadism, spreading antidemocratic ideas, and, of course, corrupting youth. To understand the grounds of such charges, their justification and their bias, we must understand something of the nature of the subart with which we are dealing.

Perhaps it is most illuminating to begin by saying that it is a peculiarly American phenomenon, an unexpected by-product of an attempt, not only to extend literacy universally, but to delegate taste to majority suffrage. I do not mean, of course, that it is found only in the United States, but that wherever it is found, it comes first from us, and is still to be discovered in fully developed form only among us. Our experience along these lines is, in this sense, a preview for the rest of the world of what must follow the inevitable dissolution of the older aristocratic cultures.

One has only to examine certain Continental imitations of picture magazines like *Look* or *Life* or Disney-inspired cartoon books to be aware at once of the debt to

American examples and of the failure of the imitations. For a true "popular literature" demands a more than ordinary slickness, the sort of high finish possible only to a machine-produced commodity in an economy of maximum prosperity. Contemporary popular culture, which is a function of an industrialized society, is distinguished from older folk art by its refusal to be shabby or second-rate in appearance, by a refusal to know its place. It is a product of the same impulse which has made available the sort of ready-made clothing which aims at destroying the possibility of knowing a lady by her dress.

Yet the articles of popular culture are made, not to be treasured, but to be thrown away; a paperback book is like a disposable diaper or a paper milk container. For all its competent finish, it cannot be preserved on dusty shelves like the calf-bound volumes of another day; indeed, its very mode of existence challenges the concept of a library, private or public. The sort of conspicuous waste once reserved for an elite is now available to anyone; and this is inconceivable without an absurdly high standard of living, just as it is unimaginable without a degree of mechanical efficiency that permits industry to replace nature, and invents—among other disposable synthetics—one for literature.

Just as the production of popular narrative demands industrial conditions most favorably developed in the United States, its distribution requires the peculiar conditions of our market places: the mass or democratized market. Subbooks and subarts are not distributed primarily through the traditional institutions: museums, libraries, and schools, which remain firmly in the hands of those who deplore mass culture. It is in drugstores and supermarkets and airline terminals that this kind of literature mingles without condescension with chocolate bars and soap flakes. We have reached the end of a long process, begun, let us say, with Samuel Richardson, in which the work of art has approached closer and closer to the status of a commodity. Even the comic book is a last descendant of *Pamela,* the final consequence of letting the tastes (or more precisely, the buying power) of a class unpledged to maintaining the traditional genres determine literary success or failure.

Those who cry out now that the work of a Mickey Spillane or *The Adventures of Superman* travesty the novel forget that the novel was long accused of travestying literature. What seems to offend us most is not the further downgrading of literary standards so much as the fact that the medium, the very notion and shape of a book, is being parodied by the comics. Jazz or the movies, which are also popular urban arts, depending for their distribution and acceptance on developments in technology (for jazz the gramophone), really upset us much less.

It is the final, though camouflaged, rejection of literacy implicit in these new forms which is the most legitimate source of distress; but all arts so universally consumed have been for illiterates, even stained glass windows and the plays of Shakespeare. What is new in our present situation, and hence especially upsetting, is that this is the first art for *post*-literates, i.e., for those who have refused the benefit for which they were presumed to have sighed in their long exclusion. Besides, modern popular narrative is disconcertingly not oral; it will not surrender the benefits of the printing press as a machine, however indifferent it may be to that press as the perpetrator of techniques devised first for pen or quill. Everything that the press can provide—except matter to be really read—is demanded: picture, typography, even in many cases the illusion of reading along with the relaxed pleasure of illiteracy. Yet the new popular forms remain somehow prose narrative or pictographic substitutes for the novel; even the cognate form of the movies is notoriously more like a novel than a play in its handling of time, space and narrative progression.

From the folk literature of the past, which ever since the triumph of the machine we have been trying sentimentally to recapture, popular literature differs in its rejection of the picturesque. Rooted in prose rather than in verse, secular rather than religious in origin, defining itself against the city rather than the world of outdoor nature, a by-product of the factory rather than agriculture, present-day popular literature defeats romantic expectations of peasants in their embroidered blouses chanting or plucking balalaikas for the approval of their betters. The haters of our own popular art love to condescend to the folk; and on records or in fashionable night clubs in recent years, we have had entertainers who have earned enviable livings producing commercial imitations of folk songs. But contemporary vulgar culture is brutal and disturbing: the quasi-spontaneous expression of the uprooted and culturally dispossessed inhabitants of anonymous cities, contriving mythologies which reduce to manageable form the threat of science, the horror of unlimited war, the general spread of corruption in a world where the social bases of old loyalties and heroisms have long been destroyed. That such an art is exploited for profit in a commercial society, mass-produced by nameless collaborators, standardized and debased, is of secondary importance. It is the patented nightmare of us all, a packaged way of coming to terms with one's environment sold for a dime to all those who have rejected the unasked-for gift of literacy.

Thought of in this light, the comic books with their legends of the eternally threatened metropolis eternally protected by immaculate and modest heroes (who shrink back after each exploit into the image of the crippled newsboy, the impotent and cowardly reporter) are seen as inheritors, for all their superficial differences, of the *inner* impulses of traditional folk art. Their gross drawing, their poverty of language, cannot disguise their heritage of aboriginal violence, their exploitation of the ancient conflict of black magic and white. Beneath their journalistic commentary on A-bomb and communism, they touch archetypal material: those shared figures of our lower minds more like the patterns of dream than fact. In a world where men threaten to dissolve into their most superficial and mechanical techniques, to become their borrowed newspaper platitudes, they remain close to the impulsive, subliminal life. They are our not quite machine-subdued Grimm, though the Black Forest has become, as it must, the City; the Wizard, the Scientist; and Simple Hans, Captain Marvel. In a society which thinks of itself as "scientific"—and of the Marvelous as childish—such a literature must seem primarily children's literature, though, of course, it is ready by people of all ages.

We are now in a position to begin to answer the question: what do the righteous really have against comic books? In some parts of the world, simply the fact that they are American is sufficient, and certain homegrown self-contemners follow this line even in the United States. But it is really a minor argument, lent a certain temporary importance by passing political exigencies. To declare oneself against "the Americanization of culture" is meaningless unless one is set resolutely against industrialization and mass education.

More to the point is the attack on mass culture for its betrayal of literacy itself. In a very few cases, this charge is made seriously and with full realization of its import; but most often it amounts to nothing but an accusation of "bad grammar" or "slang" on the part of some schoolmarm to whom the spread of "different than" seems to threaten the future of civilized discourse. What should set us on guard in this case is that it is not the fully literate, the intellectuals and serious writers, who lead the attack, but the insecure semiliterate. In America, there is something a little absurd about the indignant delegation from the Parent Teachers Association (themselves clutching the latest issue of *Life*) crying out in defense of literature. Asked for suggestions, such critics are likely to propose *The Readers Digest* as required reading in high school—or to urge more comic book versions of the "classics": emasculated Melville, expurgated Hawthorne, or a child's version of something "uplifting" like "The Fall of the House of Usher." In other countries, corresponding counterparts are not hard to find.

As a matter of fact, this charge is scarcely ever urged with much conviction. It is really the portrayal of crime and horror (and less usually sex) that the enlightened censors deplore. It has been charged against vulgar art that it is sadistic, fetishistic, brutal, full of terror; that it pictures women with exaggeratedly full breasts and rumps, portrays death on the printed page, is often covertly homosexual, etc., etc. About these charges, there are two obvious things to say. First, by and large, they are true. Second, they are also true about much of the most serious art of our time, especially that produced in America.

There is no count of sadism and brutality which could not be equally proved against Hemingway or Faulkner or Paul Bowles—or, for that matter, Edgar Allan Poe. There are certain more literate critics who are victims of their own confusion in this regard; and who will condemn a Class B movie for its images of flagellation or bloodshed only to praise in the next breath such an orgy of high-minded sadism as *Le Salaire de la Peur*. The politics of the French picture may be preferable, or its photography; but this cannot redeem the scene in which a mud-and-oil-soaked truck driver crawls from a pit of sludge to reveal the protruding white bones of the multiple fracture of the thigh. This is as much horror-pornography as *Scarface* or *Little Caesar*. You cannot condemn *Superman* for the exploitation of violence, and praise the existentialist-homosexual-sadist shockers of Paul Bowles. It is possible to murmur by way of explanation something vague about art or catharsis; but no one is ready to advocate the suppression of anything merely because it is aesthetically bad. In this age of conflicting standards, we would all soon suppress each other.

You cannot condemn *Superman* for the exploitation of violence, and praise the existentialist-homosexual-sadist shockers of Paul Bowles.

—Leslie Fiedler

An occasional Savonarola is, of course, ready to make the total rejection; and secretly or openly, the run-of-the-mill condemner of mass culture does condemn, on precisely the same grounds, most contemporary literature of distinction. Historically, one can make quite a convincing case to prove that our highest and lowest arts come from a common antibourgeois source. Edgar Allan Poe, who lived the image of the Dandy that has been haunting high art ever since, also, one remembers, invented the popular detective story; and there is a direct line from Hemingway to O'Hara to Dashiell Hammett to Raymond Chandler to Mickey Spillane to Richard S. Prather.

Of both lines of descent from Poe, one can say that they tell a black and distressing truth (we are creatures of dark impulse in a threatened and guilty world), and that they challenge the more genteel versions of "good taste." Behind the opposition to vulgar literature, there is at work the same fear of the archetypal and the unconscious itself that motivated similar attacks on Elizabethan drama and on the eighteenth-century novel. We always judge Gosson a fool in terms of Shakespeare; but this is not the point—he was just as wrong in his attack on the worst written, the most outrageously bloody and bawdy plays of his time. I should hate my argument to be understood as a defense of what is banal and mechanical and dull (there is, of course, a great deal!) in mass culture; it is merely a counterattack against those who are aiming through that banality and dullness at what moves all literature of worth. Anyone at all sensitive to the life of the imagination would surely prefer his kids to read the coarsest fables of Black and White contending for the City of Man, rather than have them spell out, "Oh, see, Jane. Funny, funny Jane," or read to themselves hygienic accounts of the operation of supermarkets or manureless farms. Yet most school-board members are on the side of mental hygiene; and it is they who lead the charge against mass culture.

Anyone old enough to have seen, say, *Rain* is on guard against those who in the guise of wanting to destroy savagery and ignorance wage war on spontaneity and richness. But we are likely to think of such possibilities purely in sexual terms; the new righteous themselves have been touched lightly by Freud and are firm believers in frankness and "sex education." But in the midst of their selfcongratulation at their emancipation, they have become victims of a new and ferocious prudery. One who would be ashamed to lecture his masturbating son on the dangers of insanity, is quite prepared (especially if he has been reading Wertham) to predict the electric chair for the young scoundrel with a bootlegged comic. Superman is our Sadie Thompson. We live in an age when the child who is exposed to the "facts of life" is protected from "the facts of death." In the United States, for instance a certain Doctor Spock has produced an enlightened guide to child care for modern mothers—a paperback book which sold, I would guess, millions of copies. Tell the child all about sex, the good doctor advises, but on the subject of death—hush!

By more "advanced" consultants, the taboo is advanced further toward absurdity: no blood-soaked Grimm, no terrifying Andersen, no childhood verses about cradles that fall—for fear breeds insecurity; insecurity, aggression; aggression, war. There is even a "happy," that is to say, expurgated, Mother Goose in which the three blind mice have become "kind mice"—and the farmer's wife no longer hacks off their tails, but "cuts them some cheese with a carving knife." Everywhere the fear of fear is endemic, the fear of the very names of fear; those who have most ardently desired to end warfare and personal cruelty in the world around them, and are therefore most frustrated by their persistence, conspire to stamp out violence on the nursery bookshelf. This much they can do anyhow. If they can't hold up the weather, at least they can break the bloody glass.

This same fear of the instinctual and the dark, this denial of death and guilt by the enlightened genteel, motivates their distrust of serious literature, too. Faulkner is snubbed and the comic books are banned, not in the interests of the classics or even of Robert Louis Stevenson, as the attackers claim, but in the name of a literature of the middle ground which finds its fictitious vision of a kindly and congenial world attacked from above and below. I speak now not of the few intellectual converts to the cause of censorship, but of the main body of genteel book-banners, whose idol is Lloyd Douglas or even A. J. Cronin. When a critic like Mr. Wagner is led to applaud what he sees as a "trend" toward making doctors, lawyers, etc. the heroes of certain magazine stories, he has fallen into the trap of regarding middling fiction as a transmission belt from the vulgar to the high. There is no question, however, of a slow climb from the level of literature which celebrates newspaper reporters, newsboys, radio commentators (who are also superheroes in tightfitting uniforms with insignia), through one which centers around prosperous professionals, to the heights of serious literature, whose protagonists are suicides full of incestuous longings, lady lushes with clipped hair, bootleggers, gangsters, and broken-down pugs. To try to state the progression is to reveal its absurdity.

The conception of such a "trend" is nothing more than the standard attitude of a standard kind of literature, the literature of slick-paper ladies' magazines, which prefers the stereotype to the archetype, loves poetic justice, sentimentality, and gentility, and is peopled by characters who bathe frequently, live in the suburbs, and are professionals. Such literature circles mindlessly inside the trap of its two themes: unconsummated adultery and the consummated pure romance. There can be little doubt about which kind of persons and which sort of fables best typify our plight, which tell the truth—or better: a truth in the language of those to whom they speak.

In the last phrase, there is a rub. The notion that there is more than one language of art, or rather, that there is something not quite art, which performs art's function for most men in our society, is disquieting enough for anyone, and completely unacceptable to the sentimental egalitarian, who had dreamed of universal literacy leading directly to a universal culture. It is here that we begin to see that there is a politics as well as a pathology involved in the bourgeois hostility to popular culture. I do not refer only to the explicit political ideas embodied in the comics or in the literature of the cultural élite; but certainly each of these arts has a characteristic attitude: populist-authoritarian on the one hand, and aristocratic-authoritarian on the other.

It is notorious how few of the eminent novelists or poets of our time have shared the political ideals we (most readers of this magazine and I) would agree are the most noble available to us. The flirtations of Yeats and Lawrence with fascism, Pound's weird amalgam of Confucianism, Jeffersonianism, and Social Credit, the modified Dixiecrat principles of Faulkner—all make the point with terrible reiteration. Between the best art and poetry of our age and the critical liberal reader there can be no bond of shared belief; at best we have the ironic confrontation of the skeptical mind and the believing imagination. It is this division which has, I suppose, led us to define more and more narrowly the "aesthetic experience," to attempt to isolate a quality of seeing and saying that has a moral value quite independent of *what* is seen or heard.

> Time that with this strange excuse
> Pardoned Kipling and his views,
> And will pardon Paul Claudel,
> Pardons him for writing well.

But the genteel middling mind which turns to art for entertainment and uplift, finds this point of view reprehensible, and cries out in rage against those who give Ezra Pound a prize and who claim that "to permit other considerations than that of poetic achievement to sway the decision world . . . deny the validity of that objective perception of value on which any civilized society must rest." We live in the midst of a strange two-front class war: the readers of the slicks battling the subscribers to the "little reviews" and the consumers of pulps; the sentimental-egalitarian conscience against the ironical-aristocratic sensibility on the one hand and the brutal-populist mentality on the other. The joke, of course, is that it is the "democratic" center which calls here and now for suppression of its rivals; while the elite advocate a condescending tolerance, and the vulgar ask only to be let alone.

It is disconcerting to find cultural repression flourishing at the point where middling culture meets a kindly, if not vigorously thought-out, liberalism. The sort of right-thinking citizen who subsidizes trips to America for Japanese girls scarred by the Hiroshima bombing and deplores McCarthy in the public press also deplores, and would censor, the comics. In one sense, this is fair enough; for beneath the veneer of slogans that "crime doesn't pay" and the superficial praise of law and order, the comics do reflect that dark populist faith which Senator McCarthy has exploited. There is a kind of "black socialism" of the American masses which underlies formal allegiances to one party or another: the sense that there is always a conspiracy at the centers of political and financial power; the notion that the official defenders of the commonwealth are "bought" more often than not; an impatience with moral scruples and a distrust of intelligence, especially in the expert and scientist; a willingness to identify the enemy, the dark projection of everything most feared in the self, with some journalistically-defined political opponent of the moment.

This is not quite the "fascism" it is sometimes called. There is, for instance, no European anti-Semitism involved, despite the conventional hooked nose of the scientist-villain. (The inventors and chief producers of comic books have been, as it happens, Jews.) There is also no adulation of a dictator figure on the model of Hitler or Stalin; though one of the archetypes of the Deliverer in the comics is called Superman, he is quite unlike the Nietzschean figure—it is the image of Cincinnatus which persists in him, an archetype that has possessed the American imagination since the time of Washington: the leader who enlists for the duration and retires unrewarded to obscurity.

It would be absurd to ask the consumer of such art to admire in the place of images that project his own impotence and longing for civil peace some hero of middling culture—say, the good boy of Arthur Miller's *Death of a Salesman,* who, because he has studied hard in school, has become a lawyer who argues cases before the Supreme Court and has friends who own their own tennis courts. As absurd as to ask the general populace to worship Stephen Dedalus or Captain Ahab! But the high-minded petty-bourgeois cannot understand or forgive the rejection of his own dream, which he considers as nothing less than the final dream of humanity. The very existence of a kind of art based on allegiances and values other than his challenges an article of his political faith; and when such an art is "popular," that is, more read, more liked, more bought than his own, he feels his *raison d'être,* his basic life defense, imperiled. The failure of the petty bourgeoisie to achieve cultural hegemony threatens their dream of a truly classless society; for they believe, with some justification, that such a society can afford only a single culture. And they see, in the persistence of a high art and a low art on either side of their average own, symptoms of the re-emergence of classes in a quarter where no one had troubled to stand guard.

The problem posed by popular culture is finally, then, a problem of class distinction in a democratic society. What is at stake is the refusal of cultural equality by a large part of the population. It is misleading to think of popular culture as the product of a conspiracy of profiteers against the rest of us. This venerable notion of an eternally oppressed and deprived but innocent people is precisely what the rise of mass culture challenges. Much of what upper-class egalitarians dreamed for him, the ordinary man does not want—especially literacy. The situation is bewildering and complex, for the people have not rejected completely the notion of cultural equality; rather, they desire its symbol but not its fact. At the very moment when half of the population of the United States reads no *hardcover* book in a year, more than half of all high school graduates are entering universities and colleges; in twenty-five years almost all Americans will at least begin a higher education. It is clear that what is demanded is a B.A. for everyone, with the stipulation that no one be forced to read to get it. And this the colleges, with "objective tests" and "visual aids," are doing their reluctant best to satisfy.

One of the more exasperating aspects of the cultural defeat of the egalitarians is that it followed a seeming victory. For a while (in the Anglo-Saxon world at least) it appeared as if the spread of literacy, the rise of the bourgeoisie, and the emergence of the novel as a reigning form would succeed in destroying both traditional folk art and an aristocratic literature still pledged to epic, ode, and verse tragedy. But the novel itself (in the hands of Lawrence, Proust, Kafka, etc.) soon passed beyond the comprehension of those for whom it was originally contrived; and the retrograde derivations from it—various steps in a retreat toward wordless narrative: digests, pulp fiction, movies, picture magazines—revealed that middling literature was not in fact the legitimate heir of either folk art or high art, much less the successor of both, but a *tertium quid* of uncertain status and value.

The middlebrow reacts with equal fury to an art that baffles his understanding and to one which refuses to aspire to his level. The first reminds him that he has not yet, after all, *arrived* (and, indeed, may never make it); the second suggests to him a condition to which he might easily relapse, one perhaps that might have made him happier with less effort (and here exacerbated puritanism is joined to baffled egalitarianism)—even suggests what his state may appear like to those a notch above. Since he cannot on his own terms explain to himself why anyone should choose any level but the highest (that is, his own), the failure of the vulgar seems to him the product of mere ignorance and laziness—a crime! And the rejection by the advanced artist of his canons strikes him as a finicking excess, a pointless and unforgivable snobbism. Both, that is, suggest the intolerable notion of a hierarchy of taste, a hierarchy of values, the possibility of cultural classes in a democratic state; and before this, puzzled and enraged, he can only call a cop. The fear of the vulgar is the obverse of the fear of excellence, and both are aspects of the fear of difference: symptoms of a drive for conformity on the level of the timid, sentimental, mindless-bodiless genteel.

Saul Braun

SOURCE: "Shazam! Here Comes Captain Relevant," in *Popular Culture and the Expanding Consciousness*, edited by Ray B. Browne, John Wiley & Sons, Inc., 1973, pp. 81-98.

[*In the following essay, Braun takes stock of the impact comic book artists have had on other media, such as cinema, and outlines the early 1970s trend in socially relevant comics characters.*]

Envision a scene in a comic book:

In Panel 1, two New York City policemen are pointing skyward with their jaws hanging open and one is saying, "Wha . . . ?" They are looking at four or five men and women, shown in Panel 2 plummeting through the air feet first, as though riding surfboards. The dominant figure has a black long coat thrown over his shoulders, wears a peaked, flat-brim hat and carries a cane. As the group lands on the street and enters the "Vision Building," Panel 3, a hairy hip figure on the sidewalk observes to a friend: "Fellini's in town."

In Panel 4, an office interior, the man with the cape is saying to the secretary, "I am Federico Fellini, come to pay his respects to . . ." Turn the page and there is the Fellini figure in the background finishing his balloon: ". . . the amazing Stan Lee." In the foreground is a tall, skinny man with a black D. H. Lawrence beard, wearing bathing trunks, longsleeved turtleneck sweater and misshapen sailor hat. Stan Lee stands alongside a table that has been piled on another table, and on top of that is a typewriter with a manuscript page inserted in it that reads: "The Amazing Spiderman. In the Grip of the Goblin! It's happening again. As we saw last. . . ."

This visit, in more mundane fashion, actually took place. Stan Lee has been writing comic books for 30 years and is now editor-in-chief of the Marvel Comics line. His reputation with *cognoscenti* is very, very high.

Alain Resnais is also a Lee fan and the two are now working together on a movie. Lee has succeeded so well with his art that he has spent a good deal of his time traveling around the country speaking at colleges. In his office at home—which is currently a Manhattan apartment in the East 60's—he has several shelves filled with tapes of his college talks. An Ivy League student was once quoted as telling him, "We think of Marvel Comics as the 20th century mythology and you as this generation's Homer."

Lee's comic antiheroes (Spiderman, Fantastic Four, Submariner, Thor, Captain America) have revolutionized an industry that took a beating from its critics and from TV in the nineteen-fifties. For decades, comic book writers and artists were considered little more than production workers, virtually interchangeable. Now Lee and his former collaborator, artist Jack Kirby of National Comics, Marvel's principal rival, are considered superstars—and their work reflects a growing sophistication in the industry that has attracted both young and old readers.

"We're in a renaissance," says Carmine Infantino, editorial director at National Comics, and he offers as proof the fact that at Brown University in Providence, R.I., they have a course, proposed by the students, called "Comparative Comics." A prospectus for the course sets out the case for comic books as Native Art:

> Comics, long scorned by parents, educators, psychologists, lawmakers, American Legionnaires, moral crusaders, civic groups and J. Edgar Hoover, have developed into a new and interesting art form. Combining 'new journalism' with greater illustrative realism, comics are a reflection of both real society and personal fantasy. No longer restricted to simple, good vs. evil plot lines and unimaginative, sticklike figures, comics can now be read at several different levels by various age groups. There are still heroes for the younger readers, but now the heroes are different—they ponder moral questions, have emotional differences, and are just as neurotic as real people. Captain America openly sympathizes with campus radicals, the Black Widow fights side by side with the Young Lords, Lois Lane apes John Howard Griffin and turns herself black to study racism, and everybody battles to save the environment.

As for Fellini, his interest in American comic books, and Stan Lee's work in particular, is no passing fancy. For an introduction to Jim Steranko's *History of the Comics,* he wrote the following lines:

> Not satisfied being heroes, but becoming even more heroic, the characters in the Marvel group know how to laugh at themselves. Their adventures are offered publicly like a larger-than-life spectacle,

> each searching masochistically within himself to find a sort of maturity, yet the results are nothing to be avoided: it is a brilliant tale, aggressive and retaliatory, a tale that continues to be reborn for eternity, without fear of obstacles or paradoxes. We cannot die from obstacles and paradoxes, if we face them with laughter. Only of boredom might we perish. And from boredom, fortunately, the comics keep a distance.

For an industry that wields considerable influence, comic-book publishing has only a small fraternity of workers. There are something like 200 million comic books sold each year, a volume produced by less than 200 people, including writers, artists and letterers. The artists fall into two categories, pencilers and inkers. Pencilers are slightly more highly reputed than inkers but, with few exceptions, nobody in the business has much of a public reputation, and most are poorly compensated. Most are freelancers, paid at a page rate that the various publishers prefer not to divulge. A rate of $15 a page, however, is said to be not uncommon.

> This is a fiercely competitive business [says Infantino]. After Superman clicked in 1935 everybody jumped in; there were millions of outfits. Then one by one they all slipped away. When World War II ended, then came survival of the fittest and, boom, they died by the wayside.

As in other industries, power gradually became concentrated during the nineteen-fifties and sixties, and now the industry consists of perhaps half a dozen companies with annual sales of about 200 million. National, the leader, sells about 70 million. Marvel sells 40 million, Archie 35 million, and the next three firms—Charlton (Yogi Bear, Beetle Bailey, Flintstones), Gold Key (Bugs Bunny, Donald Duck, Mickey Mouse) and Harvey (Casper the Friendly Ghost, Richie Rich, Sad Sack) each sell about 25 million. That is a great many copies, but doesn't necessarily reflect profitability. The index of profit and loss is not sales but the percentage of published copies that are returned unsold from the store racks. A book that suffers returns of more than 50 per cent is in trouble.

Martin Goodman, president of the Magazine Management Company, which puts out the Marvel line, recalls that the golden age of comics was the war years and immediately afterwards. By the late forties, he says: everything began to collapse. TV was kicking the hell out of a great number of comics. A book like Donald Duck went from 2¼ million monthly sale to about 200,000. You couldn't give the animated stuff away, the Disney stuff, because of TV. TV murdered it. Because if a kid spends Saturday morning looking at the stuff, what parent is going to give the kid another couple of dimes to buy the same thing again?

> Industrywide . . . the volume is not going up. I think the comic-book field suffers from the same thing TV does. After a few years, an erosion sets in. You still maintain loyal readers, but you lose a lot more readers than you're picking up. That's why we have so many superhero characters, and run superheroes together. Even if you take two characters that are weak sellers and run them together in the same book, somehow, psychologically, the reader feels he's getting more. You get the Avenger follower and the Submariner follower. Often you see a new title do great on the first issue and then it begins to slide off . . .

Goodman recalls with avuncular diffidence the arrival of Stan Lee at Marvel, then called Timely Comics:

> Stan started as a kid here; he's my wife's cousin. That was in 1941, something like that. He came in as an apprentice, to learn the business. He had a talent for writing. I think when Stan developed the Marvel superheroes he did a very good job, and he got a lot of college kids reading us. They make up a segment of our readership, but when you play it to them you lose the very young kids who just can't follow the whole damn thing. We try to keep a balance. Because I read some stories sometimes and I can't even understand them. I really can't!

Today's superhero is about as much like his predecessors as today's child is like his parents. My recollection of the typical pre-World War II child (me) is of a sensitive, lonely kid full of fantasies of power and experiencing, at the same time, a life of endless frustration and powerlessness. Nobody knew, of course, about the hidden power, the supermuscles rippling beneath the coarse woolen suits I had to wear that itched like crazy. How I longed to rip off that suit. Shaz . . .

Comic book buffs will not need to be reminded that Shazam is the magic name of a mysterious bald gentleman with a white beard down to his waist, which, when spoken by newsboy Billy Batson, turns Billy into Captain Marvel. The book didn't last long, due to the swift, self-righteous reprisals of National Comics, which took Captain Marvel to court for impersonating Superman. It lasted long enough to impress upon my memory, however, that "S" stood for Solomon's wisdom, "H" for Hercules's strength, "A" for Atlas's stamina, "Z" for Zeus's power, "A" for Achilles's courage and "M" for Mercury's speed. I always had trouble remembering the last two; like many another man, I have gone through life saying "Shaz" to myself and getting nowhere.

So my childhood was one of repressed anger and sullen obedience and scratching all winter long, together with an iron will that kept me from lifting my all-powerful fist and destroying those who threatened me: Nazis, Japs, Polish kids (mostly at Easter time), older kids, teachers and parents. My personal favorite was Submariner. He hated everybody.

Actually, all of the early comic-book heroes perfectly mirrored my own condition, and even provided pertinent psychological details. The parents of superheroes were always being killed by bad men or cataclysmic upheavals over which the heroes—let me make this one thing perfectly clear—had absolutely no control. However, they then embarked on a guilty, relentless, lifelong pursuit of evildoers. So many villains in so many bizarre guises only attested to the elusiveness and prevalence of—and persistence of—superhero complicity.

Secretly powerful people, like the superheroes and me, always assumed the guise of meekness; yet even the "real" identities were only symbols. All-powerful Superman equaled all-powerful father. Batman's costume disguise, like the typical parental bluster of the time, was intended to "strike terror into their hearts." For "their" read not only criminal but child.

Infantino, whose National Comics publishes, among others, the long-run superhit of the comic-book industry, Superman, believes that power is the industry's main motif:

> The theme of comic books is power. The villain wants power. He wants to take over the world. Take over the other person's mind. There's something about sitting in the car with the motorcycles flanking you back and front and the world at your feet. It motivates all of us.

For three decades, the social setting was an America more or less continuously at war. At war with poverty in the thirties, with Fascism in the early forties, and with the International Red Conspiracy in the late forties and in the fifties. During these years there existed simultaneously, if uneasily, in our consciousness the belief that we were uniquely strong and that nothing would avail except the unrelenting exercise of that strength. From wanting or being forced to take the law into our own hands during the thirties, we moved swiftly towards believing that our security depended on taking the whole world into our hands. That carried us from the Depression to Korea and, eventually, in the sixties, to a confused war in which it was impossible to tell whether we were strong or weak, in which irresponsible complacency existed comfortably with political and social atrocities that could spring only from secret weakness masquerading as strength.

It is not irrelevant to note that the Vietnamese war developed without hindrance—with some few exceptions—from a generation of men flying around the world on a fantasy-power trip, and was resisted in the main by their sons, the generation that began rejecting the comic books of the fifties with their sanitized, censored, surreal images of the world: a world in which "we" were good and "they" were bad, in which lawlessness masqueraded as heroism, in which blacks were invisible, in which, according to a survey taken in 1953 by University of California professors, men led "active lives" but women were interested mainly in "romantic love" and only villainous women "try to gain power and status." A world in which no superhero, whatever his excesses, ever doubted that he was using his powers wisely and morally.

During this time the industry was adopting a self-censorship code of ethics in response to the hue and cry raised by a Congressional look into the industry's excesses of gore and by the appearance of *Seduction of the Innocent,* a shrill piece of psycho-criticism by a psychiatrist named Fredric Wertham, who supported his view that the comics were a pernicious influence on children with stories like: "A boy of 13 committed a 'lust murder' of a girl of 6. Arrested and jailed, he asked only for comic books."

While it is true some publishers were printing stories with grisly and violent elements, I must confess that I to this day find myself unable to believe that the worst comic books could have corrupted the child's mind as much as the knowledge that in his own world, the world he was being educated to join, 6 million men, women and children had only recently been killed in gas ovens for no very good reason, and large numbers of others had died at Hiroshima and Dresden, for only slightly better reasons. Two of my own strongest memories of the time are of my father, who owned a candy store, denying me the treasure trove of comics ("They'll ruin your mind"), and of my father, after receiving a telegram telling him that his family had been wiped out in some concentration camp somewhere, turning ashen and falling to his knees. So, Superman, where were you when we needed you? My mind was corrupted, yes, and so were those of countless other children of the forties and fifties.

During this time, the only comic that held its own commercially was none other than William M. Gaines's *MAD.* Gaines's defense of one of his horror comics was the high point at hearings of the Senate subcommittee on juvenile delinquency. The cover, depicting the severed head of a blonde, said Gaines, would have been in bad taste "if the head were held a little higher so the neck would show the blood dripping out."

The industry response was the comics code, including provisions forbidding horror, excessive bloodshed, gory or gruesome crimes, depravity, lust, sadism and masochism; an authority to administer the code was created, with power to deny the industry seal of approval to any comic book violating its provisions. This satisfied parents and educators, but only intensified the sales slide for seal-of-approval comic books. The turnabout came in 1961, when Stan Lee metamorphosed the Marvel line and very likely saved comic books from an untimely death. [Lee recalls:]

> Our competitors couldn't understand why our stuff was selling. They would have a superhero see a monster in the street and he'd say, "Oh, a creature, I must destroy him before he crushes the world." And they'd have another superhero in another book see a monster and he'd say, "Oh, a creature, I must destroy him before he crushes the world." It was so formularized. I said to my writers, "Is that what you'd say in real life? If you saw a monster coming down the street, you'd say, 'Gee, there must be a masquerade party going on.'"

> Because sales were down and out of sheer boredom, I changed the whole line around. New ways of talking, hangups, introspection and brooding. I brought out a new magazine called *The Fantastic Four,* in 1961. Goodman came to me with sales figures. The competitors were doing well with a superhero team. Well, I didn't want to do anything like what they were doing, so I talked to Jack Kirby about it. I said, "Let's let them not always get along well; let's let them have arguments. Let's make them talk like real people and react like real people. Why should they all get superpowers that make them beautiful? Let's get a guy who becomes very ugly." That was The Thing. I hate heroes anyway. Just 'cause a guy has superpowers, why couldn't he be a *nebbish,* have sinus trouble and athlete's foot?

The most successful of the Stan Lee antiheroes was one Spiderman, an immediate hit and still the top of the Marvel line. Spidey, as he is known to his fans, is actually Peter Parker, a teenager who has "the proportionate strength of a spider," whatever that means, and yet, in Lee's words, "can still lose a fight, make dumb mistakes, have acne, have trouble with girls and have not too much money."

In Parker's world, nobody says, "Oh, a creature." In an early story, Spiderman apprehends three criminals robbing a store, and the following dialogue ensues:

> *Spidey:* If you're thinking of putting up a fight, brother, let me warn you . . .
>
> *Crook:* A fight? The only fight I'll put up is in court. I'm suin' you for assault and battery, and I got witnesses to prove it.
>
> *Second crook:* Yeah, that's right.

If it is not already perfectly clear that the last vestiges of the nineteen-forties have fallen away from the world that Spiderman inhabits, it becomes so two panels later when one crook says, right to his face, "Don't you feel like a jerk paradin' around in public in that get-up?"

After overhearing a conversation in another episode between two men who also apparently consider him a kook, Parker goes home and, unlike any superhero before him, does some soul-searching. "Can they be right? Am I really some sort of crackpot wasting my time seeking fame and glory? Why do I do it? Why don't I give the whole thing up?"

The 48-year-old Lee may very well have asked precisely these questions at some point in his career. He's been in the business since 1938 when, as a 16-year-old high school graduate, he held some odd jobs (delivery boy, theater usher, office boy). Then he came to Timely Comics with some scripts and was hired by editors Joe Simon and Jack Kirby.

For the next 20 years, he labored professionally, but without any special devotion, to what he thought of as a temporary job. When Simon and Kirby left, Lee took over as editor as well as writer, and all during the forties and fifties, mass-produced comic books, 40 or 45 different titles a month.

> The top sellers varied from month to month, in cycles. Romance books, mystery books. We followed the trend. When war books were big, we put out war books. Then one day my wife came to me and said, "You've got to stop kidding yourself. This is your work. You've got to put yourself into it." So I did. Joanie is the one you really ought to interview. She's beautiful and talented. And my daughter, Joanie, who's 21, she's also beautiful and talented. I'm a very lucky guy.

His wife, he says, is exactly the dream girl he'd always wanted, and he decided to marry her the first time he saw her. At the time she was married to another man, but that hardly deterred him. For something like 25 years, the Lees lived a quiet domestic life in Hewlett Harbor, L. I., before recently moving back into town. Lee is nothing if not a devoted family man. Among his other self-evident qualities: he enjoys talking about his work. He is in the office Tuesdays and Thursdays, editing, and at home the other five days of the week, writing.

> I'm the least temperamental writer you'll ever know . . . I write a minimum of four comic books a month. Writing is easy. The thing is characterization. That takes time. The thing I hate most is writing plots. My scripts are full of X-outs [crossed-out words]. I read them out loud while writing, including sound effects. "*Pttuuuu.* Take that, you rat!" I get carried away.

The comic industry has treated Lee very well. He is now, he says, in the 50 to 60 per cent income tax bracket, and he has a very high-paying, five-year contract with Cadence Industries, which bought Magazine Management Company from Goodman some 2½ years ago. When the contract expires, he says, he's not sure what he'll do. He has the vague discontent of a man looking for new fields to conquer, or, to use another simile, the look of a superhero adrift in a world that no longer wants him to solve its problems.

Last year he solved a recurring problem for industry workers by helping to form the Academy of Comic Book Artists:

> I felt that the publishers themselves weren't doing anything to improve the image of the comic books, so I thought, why don't *we* do it? Also I wanted to leave it as a legacy to the industry that has supported me over 30 years.

The academy now has as members about 80 writers, artists and letterers. I attended one of their recent meetings, held at the Statler-Hilton Hotel in the Petit Cafe, a barren, pastel-blue and mirrored room with about 200 gray metal folding chairs with glass ashtrays on them, and a gray metal long table with glass ashtrays and a lined yellow pad on it.

Around the room, leaning on gray folding chairs, were "story boards" from comic books that have been nominated for this year's awards, which are to be called Shazams.

Sketches of the proposed designs for the Shazams were being passed around, most of them serious renderings of the jagged bolt of lightning that accompanied Billy Batson's transformation. One, however, represented a side of comic book artistry that the fans rarely see: A naked young woman, bent forward at the waist, stands upon the pedestal, while the airborne Shazam lightning bolt strikes her in the rear. She has a look of unanticipated delight upon her face.

There were about 30 men present, and one or two young women. Among the artists and writers I spoke to, there was general agreement that working in the comic-book industry was not all magic transformations of unworthy flesh. Problems mentioned as organic included the lack of economic security, the inability of the artists to keep control over their material, insufficient prestige and a catch-all category that is apparently the source of abiding resentment: publishers who do not treat them as serious artists.

As for the censorship of the Comics Code Authority, virtually everybody agreed they wanted more freedom. Younger writers, in fact, are bringing fresh ideas into the field. But, as 33-year-old Archie Goodwin, who writes "Creepy Comics" for Jim Warren Publishers, wryly observes, the real problem is self-censorship: "The truth is, maybe half the people here wouldn't do their work any different if they didn't have censorship."

It did seem to me as I observed the crowd that there was perhaps more than a random sample of serious-purposed people who spoke haltingly, with tendentious meekness. The meeting began with nominations for A.C.B.A. officers for the coming year. I gleefully anticipated some earth-shaking confrontations between good and evil, but none developed. Nobody slipped off to a telephone booth to change. The two nominations for president, Neal Adams and Dick Giordano, by coincidence, jointly draw the *Green Lantern-Green Arrow* book for National. Lantern and Arrow have been squabbling lately, but Adams and Giordano were not at all disputatious.

In the entire group I was able to uncover only a single secret life.

"This is my secret life," Roy Thomas admitted. "Or rather it was, when I was a teacher at Fox High School in Arnold, Mo." Thomas, a bespectacled 30-year-old who wears his corn-silk hair straight down almost to the shoulders, edits at Marvel. "After school hours, I was publishing a comics fanzine called *Alter Ego*. I spent all my time at night working on *Alter Ego*."

"The people in this business," Lee said to me after the meeting, "are sincere, honorable, really decent guys. We're all dedicated, we love comics. The work we do is very important to the readers. I get mail that closes with, 'God bless you.' Most of us, we're like little kids, who, if you pat us on the head, we're happy."

All in all, add a little touch of resentment, discontent and a pinch of paranoia to Lee's description and you have the modern-day comic book superhero. Lee himself has only one frustration in a long, satisfying career:

> For years the big things on campus have been McLuhan and Tolkien, and Stan Lee and Marvel, and everybody knew about McLuhan and Tolkien, but nobody knew about Marvel. Now our competitor is coming out with 'relevant' comics and he has big public relations people, so he's been easing in on our publicity.

Relevance is currently such a lure that even industry classics like Archie are having a stab at it. John Goldwater, president of Archie Comics, says that Archie definitely keeps up with the times, and offers as evidence Xerox copies of a silver print, which is an engraver's photographic proof of an original drawing. It was of a recent six-page Archie story entitled, "Weigh Out Scene."

> This is a civil-rights story. . . . It's done subtly. It has to do with a fat boy who comes to town who can't fit into the mainstream with the teenagers in town. Because of his obesity, he's taunted and humiliated. You know how kids are. Then one night Archie has a dream. And in this dream he is obese and fat and everybody is taunting him and ridiculing him and now he finally realizes what happened to this poor kid. So then there is a complete turnaround. But we don't say, remember, this kid is black. We don't say that. But the subtlety is there.

Goldwater, who is also president of the Comics Code Authority, is convinced that "comics don't ruin your mind." He says: "I wouldn't be in this business unless it had some value, some educational value. If you can get a kid today to read, it's quite some victory—instead of him looking at the boob tube, you know?"

Recently there were some ruffled feelings in the industry when Marvel issued a comic book without the authority seal, which was denied because the subject of drugs was alluded to in one story that showed a stoned black kid tottering on a rooftop. Goldwater felt that hinted a bit of sensationalism, and Infantino believes the subject calls for a more thorough and responsible treatment. Lee scoffs. Black kids getting stoned isn't exactly a biannual occurrence, he suggests. Goodman calls the fuss a tempest in a teapot. Goldwater, at any rate, is not inclined to be harsh:

> Goodman came before the publishers and promised not to do it again. So we're satisfied. Anybody with 15 solid years of high standards of publishing comic books with the seal is entitled to one mistake.

Subsequently the publishers agreed to give themselves permission to deal with the subject. "Narcotics addiction," says the new guideline, "shall not be presented except as a vicious habit."

Goodman is not so sure relevance will continue to sustain sales, but Infantino is elated at National's success with social issues.

National turned toward relevance and social commentary for the same reasons Marvel had a decade earlier. [Says Infantino]:

> I'd like to say I had a great dream, but it didn't happen that way. Green Lantern was dying. The whole superhero line was dying. Everything was sagging, everything. When your sales don't work, they're telling you something. The front office told me, get rid of the book, but I said, let me try something, just for three issues. We started interviewing groups of kids around the country. The one thing they kept repeating: they want to know the truth. Suddenly the light bulb goes on: Wow, we've been missing the boat here!

In the first of National's relevant books, which came out in the fall of 1970, Green Lantern comes to the aid of a respectable citizen, besieged by a crowd, who turns out to be a slum landlord badly in need of a thrashing. Lantern is confused to discover his pal Green Arrow actually siding with The People. "You mean you're . . . defending . . . these . . . ANARCHISTS?" he says.

Following a tour of the ghetto, Green Lantern is finally brought face to face with reality by an old black man who says:

> I been readin' about you, how you work for the Blue Skins, and how on a planet someplace you helped out the Orange Skins . . . and you done considerable for the Purple Skins. Only there's Skins you never bothered with. The Black Skins. I want to know . . . how come? Answer me that, Mr. Green Lantern.

This story, written by 28-year-old Denny O'Neil, is one of the nominees for the writing Shazam, and the consensus of opinion, even among rival nominees, is that he'll win it. In the following months, O'Neil had the superheroes on the road discovering America and taking up such provocative current issues as the Manson family, the mistreatment of American Indians, the Chicago Seven trial, and, finally, in a forth-coming issue, the style and substance of the President and Vice President.

Mr. Agnew appears as Grandy, a simpering but vicious private-school cook whose ward is a certain ski-nosed child-witch named Sybil. A mere gaze from Sybil can cause great pain; one look from her and even Arrow and Lantern double over in agony. That certainly is making things clear. Grandy is constantly justifying his nastiness: "Old Grandy doesn't kill. I simply do my duty. Punish those who can't respect order. You may die. But that won't be my fault." [Says Infantino]:

> What we're saying here is, there can be troubles with your Government unless you have the right leaders. Sure, we expect flak from the Administration, but we feel the kids have a right to know, and they want to know. The kids are more sophisticated than anyone imagines, and we feel the doors are so wide open here that we're going in many directions.
>
> You wouldn't believe whom I'm talking to. Big-name writers—and they're interested. We have innovations in mind for older audiences, and in graphics we're going to take it such a step forward, it'll blow the mind.

He was so excited during our talk that he stood up. "We're akin to a young lady pregnant and having her first baby." He grinned shyly.

The artist who has produced the most innovative work for Infantino is 53-year-old Jack Kirby, about whom Stan Lee says:

> He is one of the giants, a real titan. He's had tremendous influence in the field. His art work has great power and drama and tells a story beautifully. No matter what he draws it looks exciting, and that's the name of the game.

Unlike the "relevant" comic books, Kirby's new line eschews self-conscious liberal rhetoric about social issues and returns to the basic function of comic books: to describe in an exciting, imaginative way how power operates in the world, the struggle to attain it by those who lack it and the uses to which it is put by those who have it.

Kirby began to conceive his new comic books when he was still at Marvel, but felt he might not get enough editorial autonomy. He left his $35,000-a-year job at Marvel and took his new books to National. He also moved from New York to Southern California, where he edits, writes and draws the books.

His new heroes are the Forever People, whom he describes as "the other side of the gap—the under-30 group. I'm over 50. I've had no personal experience of the counterculture. It's all from the imagination."

The Forever People arrive on earth through a "boom tube," which is an attempt to offer approximate coordinates for an experiential conjunction of media wash and psychedelic trip. They are said to be "In Search of a Dream." There are five of them: one is a relaxed, self-assured, young black man who, probably not by accident, carries the group's power source, known as the "mother box"; another is a shaggy-bearded giant who overwhelms his small-minded taunters with a loving, crushing bear hug; the third, a beautiful saintly flower child named Serafin is called a "sensitive"; the fourth, a combination rock star-football hero transmogrified into one Mark Moonrider; and the fifth, a girl named Beautiful Dreamer.

The mother box, which warns them of impending danger, also transforms them—not into five distinct, ego-involved superheroes but into a single all-powerful Infinity Man, who comes from a place where "all of natural law shifts, and bends, and changes. Where the answer to gravity is antigravity—and simply done."

These new heroes, unlike the characters of the sixties, are brash, confident youngsters whose superpower lies in their ability to unify. They are also, says Kirby, "basically nonviolent."

Infantino has been asked up to Yale to talk about Kirby's new books, and to Brown, for the new course in Comparative Comics. Students in Comp. Com. I will doubtless relish Kirby's toying with words like "gravity" (and other mild Joycean puns sprinkled elsewhere) to suggest elements of his parable of culture vs. counterculture. Suffice it to say here that the Forever People are from New Genesis, where the land is eternally green and children frolic in joy, and their enemy is Darkseid, who serves "holocaust and death."

The story of New Genesis is also told in another new Kirby book called *New Gods*. When the old gods died, the story goes, the New Gods rose on New Genesis, where the High-Father, who alone has access to The Source, bows to the young, saying, "They are the carriers of life. They must remain free. Life flowers in freedom."

Opposed to New Genesis is its "dark shadow," Apokolips, the home of evil Darkseid and his rotten minions. Darkseid's planet "is a dismal, unclean place of great ugly houses sheltering uglier machines." Apokolips is an armed camp where those who live with weapons rule the wretches who built them. Life is the evil here. And death the great goal. All that New Genesis stands for is reversed on Apokolips.

Darkseid has not, of course, been content to rule on Apokolips. He wants to duplicate that horror on, of all places, Earth, and he can do this if he manages somehow to acquire the "antilife equation." With it, he will be able to "snuff out all life on Earth—with a word."

Thus is the battle drawn, and the Forever People, notably, are not going to waste their time hassling with raucous hardhats who don't understand the crisis. When a hostile, paranoid, Middle-America type confronts them, they arrange it so that he sees them just about the way he remembers kids to have been in his own childhood: Beautiful Dreamer wearing a sensible frilly dress down to her knees, the cosmic-sensitive Serafin wearing a high-school sweater and beanie, Moonrider with hat and tie and close-cropped hair.

> "What's going on here? You kids look so different—and yet so familiar."
>
> "Why sure," says Beautiful Dreamer soothingly. "You used to know lots of kids like us. Remember? We never passed without saying hello."

In the titanic struggle against Darkseid, the Forever People have lots of help, and they are beginning to populate four different comic books: *Forever People*, *New Gods*, *Mister Miracle* and *Superman's Pal Jimmy Olsen.* Both Superman and Jimmy Olsen are being altered to fit the evolution of Kirby's Faulknerian saga of the difficult days leading to Armageddon. Already identified in the Kirby iconography on the side of the good are the newly revived and updated Newsboy Legion, so popular in the nineteen-forties; various dropout tribes living in "The Wild Area" and "experimenting with life" after harnessing the DNA molecule; and a tribe of technologically sophisticated youths called "Hairies," who live in a mobile "Mountain of Judgment" as protection against those who would destroy them. "You know our story," says one Hairy. "We seek only to be left alone—to use our talents, to develop fully."

On the other side, in support of Darkseid are middle managers and technocrats of the Establishment, like Morgan Edge, a media baron who treats his new employee Clark Kent—now a TV newscaster—abominably.

Darkseid's lousy band also includes an assortment of grotesque supervillains. Among them are DeSaad and his terrifying "Fear Machine," and a handsome toothy character named Glorious Godfrey, a revivalist. Godfrey is drawn to look like an actor playing Billy Graham in a Hollywood film biography of Richard Nixon starring George Hamilton.

"I hear you right thinkers," Godfrey says to his grim, eyeless audience of true believers, "You're shouting antilife—the positive belief."

In the background acolytes carry signs: "Life has pitfalls! Antilife is protection!" And, "You can justify anything with antilife!" And, "Life will make you doubt! Antilife will make you right!" [Kirby admits:]

> I have no final answers. I have no end in mind. This is like a continuing novel. My feeling about these times is that they're hopeful but full of danger. Any time you have silos buried around the country there's danger. In the forties when I created Captain America, that was my feeling then, that patriotism. Comics are definitely a native American art. They always have been. And I'm feeling very good about this. My mail has been about 90 per cent positive, and sales are good.

Infantino adds:

> The kids at Yale think Kirby's new books are more tuned in to them than any other media. They're reading transcripts from *New Gods* over their radio station. The Kirby books are a conscious attempt to show what things look like when you're out where the kids are. The collages, the influence of

> the drug culture. We're showing them basically what they're seeing. We're turning into what they're experiencing.

If that is true—and I am not so sure it isn't—then perhaps the rest of us had better begin choosing sides. New Genesis anyone?

Martin Barker

SOURCE: "The Genre of Horror," in *A Haunt of Fears: The Strange History of the British Horror Comics Campaign*, Pluto Press, 1984, pp. 112-39.

[*In the following essay, Barker praises the censored horror comics of the 1950s as meditations on doubt and subjective identification.*]

In 1964 Ballantine Books produced a series of reprints in pocket-book size of some of EC's classic horror tales. The back cover of one of these, a reprinting from *Tales from the Crypt,* exactly caught something important about these strips and their relations with their readers. Readers were being invited in with a wicked grin. 'Come in if you dare,' was the echoing chuckle. This is a very important clue to the nature of these comics. We are *dared* to come in and test, by reading the tales, the limits of our courage and endurance. The form of the dare in the first instance is to see if we can stomach this awful fare. In the EC range there were even horror-guides: the Old Witch, the Crypt-Keeper and the Vault-Keeper. Each experience, they promised, would be more shocking, more revolting, than the last. Dare we go on?

The analogy with children's dares is helpful. True, we can chicken out; but think of the feeling of failure if we do. True, different to the playground, there is none but ourselves to laugh if we fail. The point is that we will not understand the logic of this kind of 'terror-tales' unless we understand them as starting from a dare-relationship. *The horror comics proffer a social relationship with their readers based on the logic of testing our limits.*

How does this work? Having put forward a strong thesis, I will plunge in at the deep end and take a 'typically foul' example. 'Foul' is not here intended as a simple evaluative term, since the publishers themselves would have tended to use it of their publications. After all, a horror comic that is not horrid would warrant prosecution under the Trades Description Act! So consider from *Seduction of the Innocent* one of the frames that decorated its middle pages. Wertham did not give the source of this frame. It actually appears in a strip called 'The Way to a Man's Heart'.

The story concerns Diane Ford's troubles with her husband Frank, who won't take any notice of her, even though she is beautiful (and 'with plenty to offer'—hence that frame Wertham disingenously abstracted). Frank loves only his food. After desperate attempts to win his affection back, Diane does what all the advice books urge—she telephones mum. Mum suggests taking him out for a slap-up meal to get him in a good humour. She tries it, but she knows she's failed when he shows no interest at another man making insulting passes at her. He couldn't care less. Things go from bad to worse when he neglects their anniversary to meet his business partner—at a restaurant. Mum steps in again, and offers to prepare the ultimate meal for him at home—only they will say that Diane made it. They'll win his heart back through appealing to his greed. So there it is. The table is laid to perfection, they await his verdict expectantly. Has it worked? 'Mmmm . . . not bad at all Of course I've *tasted better,* but it was all right!' That did it—he has insulted mum-in-law's cooking. Seizing the carving knife, she goes for Frank—to Diane's horror. 'Well,' says mum, 'you wanted my advice, didn't you! And I gave it to you . . . the only way to a man's heart is through his stomach! Here, take it!' And she holds out Frank's heart, neatly cut out.

What a pun! And what a way of embodying a pun! Notice that the strip had opened with our horror-guide preparing us: leading us up to that title. Diane has a problem, she calls mum, and mum gets insulted and finds a very novel way to a man's heart. She subverts the mother-in-lawish adage. So the *mechanism* of the story is a grisly revamping of that saying: a story-pun. But what is the *lesson* of the story? Can it be said to suggest anything to us? Should mother-in-law be kept out of domestic disputes? Did he get what was coming to him? Should we be careful of metaphorical sentences? It leaves you thinking a bit, doesn't it?

And that is just the point that I want to make. Such a story, using a horror-pun, works on us by upsetting our expectations. The pun is the mechanism. It has to be set up at the beginning, the problem had to be set out for us by the horro-guide, in order that we should be able to make any sense of the end at all. Imagine that instead of the return to the pun in the last frame, mum had said 'I'm not going to sit there and let him insult my cooking.' With just that change, the whole story changes in kind. But if the pun is our point of engagement with the story, it is not the point of the story itself. So what is the story's point? We don't know, only that when we think about it—even if just for a moment—it suggests several issues: literal meanings and their odd uses, greedy and unkind husbands who take their wives for granted, outsiders who interfere in marital relationships, mothers-in-law and their image. It shocks us into a momentary awareness, without in any way telling us what in particular to think.

Not every such strip works equally well. I would not find it hard to show strips which struggle miserably to achieve even a pun. But to know that some do not succeed is to acknowledge that there is a pattern they are striving to achieve. 'The Way to a Man's Heart' nicely illustrates what this pattern is. Looking at it, we can see that it is very spare, with just enough story development for the force of the pun to be maximised. There is not much in the way of character development for mum-in-law so that it cannot become an exercise in her motivation, with our sympathies directed for or against. The only moral conclusion already implicit in the story-telling prior to the end is that Frank deserves *something* done to him—but not this. The ending, as a summation of the story-line, is achieved through the pun, not through particular pressures on mum, or through particular exploration of her psychology. The very tightness and spare unity of the story is what leaves us with a small gasp, and a touch of uncertainty. There is, in other words, an inbuilt ambiguity, and our thought-responses are unguided. The most that can come from such a strip and its jolt to us is an area for thinking.

I think, in the light of this, we need to pause over the question of horror itself. It is clearly not nice to present a woman with a carved-out piece of her husband. (There are plenty of equivalent examples, where other bits of anatomy reached the dinner table.) Critics have very commonly expressed the view that things like this present a view of the world which is essentially foul. But this can mean either a worry that regular encounters with such foulness will leave readers with a complacent attitude towards such evils in *real* form; or that these regular encounters will leave readers disturbed and thus harmed by the stench. It is important to distinguish these, since different psychological mechanisms are being suggested in each case, and different replies are required.

I find the first complaint nonsensical in the case of 'The Way to a Man's Heart'. For it depends for its meaning on the reader recognising that what the mother-in-law does is, in truth, horrible. It is not simply the awful glee on her face. It is that the pun can only jolt us, and therefore the strip can only be meaningful if we have been struck by the dreadful rewriting of the old saying: 'The way to a man's heart is through his stomach.' Otherwise we couldn't see why the things are there. If you doubt this, try rethinking the story with a different title, say, 'The Neglectful Husband', and have the mother-in-law say in the last frame: 'Well, you wanted my advice, didn't you . . . ?' Well, what? The temptation is to round it off with another pun. What about: 'I told you to cut out if you couldn't stomach it any longer'? It is poor by comparison, but it is trying to serve the same purpose of giving a completed meaning to the story. Something that is without meaning or sense to the reader is hardly likely to be a source of major influence on the fantasy-life or the moral sense, since it will have no toe-hold for influence. (The famous experiments by the psychologist Bartlett on nonsense-syllables showed that they could hardly be remembered, unless a meaning or order could be read into them.) To the extent that this strip can have its effect, then, it must have done so by *reminding* its readers that it was horrible.

What about the alternative complaint, that such horror—being horrible—will induce a generalised reaction of disgust at the world—generalised, that is, beyond the medium and its immediate contents? There are two reasons why I do think this is not even logically conceivable.

The first reason relates back to the reader's relations with such strips. In saying that the reader is *dared* to enter a particular relation with them, I am not pointing only to the Crypt-Keeper's invitation into his nest of snakes. It is a relation with the whole narrative form. The more successful the strip, the more it glues us into the relationship which the narrator-guide demands of us. We shall see that, to be damaging in the way this criticism implies, it would require us to 'identify' with the characters in the strips, and thus be affected. But this is not conceivable, because we would not know how to. The form of the stories, governed by the narrator's control of the process, won't let us settle in such a way.

Second, within the logic of these strips, there is not strictly horror, but the idea of horror. Compare them with a horror film. This will typically work on us—perhaps give us nightmares—by using a set of conventions that create atmosphere. For example: the lights are dim; the person (usually a woman) is alone, hearing strange noises. S/he walks into the dark (why do they always do this?), terrified but unable to stop her/himself. Camera angles and lighting tell us that something is looming. Then suddenly . . . The conventions have engrossed us if they are well used, and we feel the shock with the character. These comic-strips don't attempt to create atmosphere. Instead, they work by tying beginnings and endings together in ways that leave us startled. If 'The Way to a Man's Heart' is typical, it shows the dominant convention in comic-horror to be a *logic of shock*. It shocks us by jangling our logical expectations.

Let us call this kind of story-structure a shock-logic formula. I am suggesting that this formula was one of the main motifs of the horror comics. The formula can be used well or badly. The best way to think of it is as a cookbook which describes a recipe without dictating ingredients. It indicates cooking and serving procedures, indicates the *kind* of effect you should aim at, but gives the cook freedom to choose his or her own mixtures. A good cook can do it well, recognising that the instructions will work to good effect if such and such ingredients are used, prepared in the following ways, introduced at the right times and worked on for the right periods. But unlike the cook who seeks to give us pure enjoyment and total immersion in the food, with the horror-strips we have a real paradox: the more they succeed in involving us, and the more we agree to be involved, the less we are certain where we stand in relation to the strip.

What sorts of job can this formula do? I want to show that it is more suited to some forms of use than others. I wouldn't dare claim that I can offer a complete list—I neither know the full catalogue of horror comics past and present well enough, nor would I wish to challenge the artists who still work in the medium to prove me wrong. Nevertheless, I am prepared to argue that the following are among the commonest uses of the formula

I have outlined: (1) appearance-*vs*-reality stories; (2) human relativity stories; (3) objects-come-to-life stories; (4) parody stories and (5) subversion-of-stereotype stories. Let us look at an example of each of these in turn.

APPEARANCE VS REALITY

One of the most basic uses of shock-logic is to play with the distinction between how things may seem, and how they are. This has been done in a variety of ways: using dreams, premonitions, nightmares, madness, or, along another line altogether, using the media as appearance-carriers.

There are very many examples of this use of the formula. I have chosen one which can show one of the truly radical uses to which it can be put, yet against which the critics, in their blindness, would surely have inveighed. Entitled 'Whirlpool', it was introduced by the Vault-Keeper. With an expression of leering glee, VK puns us in extravagantly: 'Hang on to your *normality,* or this one will really have you *hanging* on the ropes!'

A young woman stands helpless as three disembodied faces appear to her. Who are you? What's your name? Tell us your name! They come closer and closer, but she can't remember. A hundred questions, but she can't answer. Still they torment her. She thrashes about in desperation and . . . crashes through a window. Escape! No, they follow her, still demanding answers. Suddenly, there's a building in front of her, with a door but no windows. She runs to the door, pleading for help, and seems to fall right through it. Now she is on the floor. Rough hands of a huge fiend haul her up by the hair and carry her, helpless, to drop her into a bath of scalding water. Then up by the hair again, and into a bath of ice. This is too much for her, and she faints amid howls of laughter. When she opens her eyes, it is still going on. Now she is tied to a board, and an old hag is jabbing her with a needle; again and again jabbing her until . . . at last a tall silent man orders the hag from the room. Gently he unties her and she sobs into his arms. When she is better, he leads her to a chair, to rest . . . no! Suddenly she is being strapped in, and the man, another fiend now, throws a lever and electricity slams through her body . . . When at last she awakes she is in a dark room, no doors, no windows. The walls start to close in on her, making the room tighter and smaller, cramping and crushing, until . . . she breaks right through the walls and falls to the floor. Now another man tenderly lifts her to her feet and helps her down the corridor. It is over. At last someone who will really help her. Here are three men who are kind, and try to explain to her. It was all in her mind. She has been ill. What she thought was an electric chair was only shock treatment. The hag with the hatpin was just a nurse giving her a sedative when she became violent. The hot and cold water were therapies to stimulate her and get her mind in contact with her body again. And the dark room was a padded cell so that she couldn't hurt herself. Doesn't she understand now? This is an insane asylum. But that can't be true; the room seems to go dim around her. They urge her to try hard, now, try to remember. Who are you? What's your name? A hundred questions, she can't remember . . . And there is VK again. 'Heh, heh, heh! Right back where we started, eh? Round and round she goes, and where she stops who the devil cares?'

I would be prepared to go to court to defend this strip. It uses an appearance/reality version of the shock-logic formula to embody something that would be hard to do by any other means. We see the medical process and experience it as many a patient must see it. Helplessly, she suffers what she knows are pointless, merciless, murderous assaults on what is left of her personality. We feel it with her. If we were not distanced a little at beginning and end by VK's blasphemous mockery, it might well be too much. As it is, I am left stunned. No judgement is passed. But, by using the woman's point of view, it leaves me with a mind full of worries and queries. Was she so very mad, or were the treatments making her so? Or is it just hopeless in such cases? And are not some of these methods just as if she had been frozen, boiled and electrocuted? And yet, for a moment she has recovered after them. Without ever passing judgement, the shock-logic forces me to consider my judgements—now having to include patient-experience in reaching them. 'Whirlpool' is a mood piece, and perhaps not the most typical of appearance-*vs*-reality uses of the formula. But in one respect it is typical, in that the formula is a mechanism to be used—in this case for deadly serious intent.

Yet think how a Wertham might have distorted the point of this story by abstracting one frame of, say, the woman tied up to the board with a fiend menacing her.

HUMAN RELATIVITY

This is really a sub-theme of the appearance/reality use of the formula, and is particularly to be found in the science-fiction or science-fantasy comics and strips. A brief example will show how it works.

The story they come from went as follows. People are getting increasingly worried about what appears to be an alien invasion. A leading scientist is convinced that aliens have been landing for a number of years, and infiltrating in disguise. As yet, the investigators can find nothing to distinguish the aliens. The scientist tells his anguish to his beautiful daughter, who also tells it to her lover. But no solution is forthcoming from anywhere. Untouched by this worry, the private life of the daughter and her lover develops happily, and they are eventually married. A passionate night follows, and the daughter, now wife, rises contentedly the next morning—only to stop and look with horror at her husband lying naked asleep on the bed. Seizing the needle-sharp knife we see in the frame, she stabs him to death. He was an alien. But how did she know? We see her sobbing with her father, who now knows the distinguishing mark of the aliens. They have navels—whereas true people are born from eggs hatched outside the body. To have a navel is alien and horrible.

You would never know from Wertham that the point of the story was to throw doubt on the notion of what makes a human, what makes people different.

OBJECTS COME TO LIFE

In his fine book *Fear: a History of Horror in the Mass Media,* Les Daniels makes an interesting case that one of the prerequisites for the emergence of horror as a distinct genre was the secularisation of society. Whilst religion held sway, the supernatural world would seem as natural as, if not more so than, the scientific. This meant that surprise and amazement at the odd and the inexplicable could not be separated out, and treated as exceptional and as a possible subject for bravura and delicious daring. The fears were too central and close to home to be the subject for fantastic reconstruction; but in another sense they were also taken as too normal, however terrifying. But with the decline of religion, especially the decline in its pretensions to 'explain' the natural world and its movements, the mysterious, the macabre and the dangerous could be siphoned-off elsewhere. The bits that science found difficult to explain, or that people found difficult to accept despite science, could be handled in a special way. And all the emotions that surround dark, and death, and bad luck, and the uncontrolled areas of human life could be leaked away, aroused but controlled, in their own special genre: horror.

For no category of horror does this explanation make better sense than for the objects-come-to-life kind. It is still a use of the same formula, still a shock-logic. But now the shock is not necessarily merely an ending that reverses expectations (though it may do that anyway), but more a stepping outside the ordinary, an approach that is maintained *throughout* the narrative. Many strips at this end of the horror spectrum have a lot to do with raising doubts of a Hamlet kind: there are more things in heaven and earth than are dreamed of in our philosophies. Or at the very least, they have to do with the emotions of uncertainty that surround what that statement entails. Of course, it is a darkness in our hearts that needs expunging by horror—something which Bruno Bettelheim wisely notes about fairy-tales, something which Fredric Wertham never admits.

Hence, when Wertham read 'Operation Massacre' in *The Thing,* all he saw fit to tell us about it was that it contained a nasty panel of a man's face being trodden on. The Thing himself, a monster-like character who was, variously in his own comic-history, a danger, a sympathetic alien and other things beside, is our horror-guide on this occasion:

> Ever heard of the maniac who tried to wipe out the human race, so HE could rule the earth? There's a grisly tale that sends chills of horror down *my* own spine! And *I*—hee, hee—don't frighten easily, as *you* probably know. (Signed, The Thing)

The story begins with an old scientist demonstrating a robot which will respond directly to his brainwaves. It works, brilliantly. But one among the audience, Marko, is not happy when the cautious scientist declares he will only tune such robots to other people's thoughts when he is sure of their good intentions. Marko breaks into the scientist's workroom that night to study the plans. Surprised by the humble inventor, he kills him. Then, turning back to the technical specifications, he simply ignores the corpse.

Comes the morning, and he has worked out how to operate the mental control. His first experimental order—it works!—is to one of the robots, to bury the inventor. A look of triumph covers his face. 'I'll control the world with the power in my hands . . . in my brain! Caesar never knew such a might! Alexander the Great will be like an errand boy next to me!' Having tested his control, he flexes his power. Threatening extermination to the City Fathers, he orders them to give him the keys to the treasury. They give the robots a key, but Marko is infuriated to find that it fits only the local asylum. He prepares for war, activating all the robots—but so do the authorities, who surround his place, demanding his surrender. In his rage, he orders his robots to 'crush everyone in your path . . . mutilate . . . massacre!' And they do. Being robots, however, they do the nearest person first, and crush Marko (in the head—hence the panel Wertham showed us). Of course, the moment he dies, the robots cease to function—and so the troops, breaking in, find a frozen tableau. As the narrator says: 'As long as there is evil in men's hearts and minds, they cannot be trusted with such power.' And The Thing adds: 'Sort of a lesson there, is there? But . . . hee, hee . . . I'm sure you *humans* will manage to ignore it!'

Many of the 'mad scientist' stories are of just the same sort. All are premised on the idea that things can and will go out of control; they will not do the expected—and that the vaunting ambitions of humans will be defeated by their very own creations. The world is not subject to simple controls, as some might think. Aside from overt teaching themes as these, the comics in the objects-come-to-life category are the ones which come closest to cinematic ideas of horror. Many strips deal, for example, in supernatural revenge: dead objects coming to life to equalise a crime, and so on.

These, I suspect, are among the ones which can have the greatest *emotional* impact—and not simply because of the presence of the weird and the supernatural. The best examples of this kind of strip are effective because the audience, invited to feel themselves within the story, participate at the cost of being helpless. We are there as victims. It is the sense of helplessness in the face of unpredictable objects and processes that make such narratives work as horror. In this, once again, they come closest to film horror, where the classic motifs—dark nights, unknown threats, and ritual incantations to control the forces of evil—are just what leave us deliciously shuddering when they are well manipulated.

PARODY

With parody, we are right back in the heart of the horror comics. What is parody? It is a way of showing something which accentuates, alters or distorts it so that elements of its nature, formerly concealed, are shown up. It is, in the words of the Oxford English Dictionary, to 'make ridiculous by imitation'. The imitation has to be set off-key so that what had previously seemed normal now appears in a new light.

In the NUT [National Union of Teachers] filmstrip were four pages of a story, (also from *Haunt of Fear* 1) which perfectly typifies this category. Called 'The Grim Fairy Tale', it was just what that title suggests: a spoof version of the original tale, with a twist and hearty tweak in the tail. This one was a version of 'Hansel and Gretel', spicily introduced to us by the Old Witch. In the original tale, Hansel and Gretel were nice, innocent little children. That had to go. Instead, we meet a pair of greedy, loudmouthed, complaining young oafs who are eating their not-much-better parents out of house and home. Even the parents despair, and decide, as in the original, that the children will have to go—and for a time, the *story,* but not the characterisation, proceeds as Grimm's original. When the children reach the old woman's house in the middle of the forest (Hansel having eaten the bread—no nonsense about giving it to the birds for Hansel refuses to waste anything edible), she turns out to be a sweet old thing. She takes them in when, tired and hungry, they arrive at her door. She feeds them tenderly. But Hansel and Gretel can't reward kindness with anything like love. What a stupid old woman to be taken in so! So they play her along and persuade her to bake them a nice big cake. And when she opens the oven to pop it in to bake, they seize the opportunity and pop her in with it. They make off home with the trunk of gold and jewels which they had spotted. There they are reunited with mum and dad, who are agreeably astonished at what the kids have brought home. However did they manage it? they ask. And, as the Old Witch delightedly informs us, that is when Hansel and Gretel made up the story about the wicked witch—just as we now know it! (George Pumphrey summarises it as follows: 'An extraordinarily repulsive version of 'Hansel and Gretel', with one likeable character whom the two children push into an oven and burn to death.' What a way to kill story-telling.)

This is, in one sense, a parody of the content of the original tale; however, I do not think that this is the most important aspect. It is true that the nature of the characters has been subverted, but that is not the heart of it. Bearing in mind the point I have tried to press—that in the horror comics the function of the shock-logic is to unfix our perceptions retrospectively—then we can see that the point of the Old Witch sneaking back in at the end is to question the *authorship* of fairy-tales. Through this, we are put at a distance from fairy-tales, and their magic circle is undermined. What is being parodied in the end is the relation of reader to fairy-tale. It is as if the Old Witch had said to us that we should never be sure we know what is the true story behind a fairy-story. It all depends who made it up! It is the very medium of fairy-tales that is being parodied.

Through this, something else is parodied and thrown into doubt. The more we let the shock-logic work on us, the more it unclothes the character of children in the original fairy-tale. How do we know they were so nice and innocent? Who told us so? The truth is, we took it for granted. We did it because it seems normal to us to take for granted in stories that children are innocent. For a moment, our presumptions are put under an arc light. It is not simply that we are shown two children who go against the standard image: rather, it is that we realise the possibility that they used the idea of innocence as a *mask,* a form of concealment. The strip, and those like it, is a demythologiser—and that has relevance to Lucy.

Because of the way parody is built into such strips, we can see why horror comics can always be close to parody. Parody is not, I want to suggest, *a* version or *a* use of the formula, but its central version and use. For in inviting readers to test themselves to the limits of the customs and conventions, they have to maintain an *almost* joking relationship with us. Whatever effect these strips have is via the shock-logic formula. This works by distancing us and throwing us into uncertainty. Thus there is an inbuilt unease in our relationship with the genre. We might then expect to find within the genre strips that play with the very boundary between horror and parody. Being self-parodying, such strips would make no sense unless we see them as acknowledging where they stand, on a fine line between horror and a parody of horror, and as playing with the fact that they are on that line.

And, indeed, we do find them. Predictably it is in the EC comics—ever the most self-aware, and the most exploratory—that they are to be found. Consider the following, and why it is a sample of the kind I have predicted, from *Haunt of Fear* 17 (US edition, September-October 1950). The Old Witch invites us in to listen to her tale as she lights the fire under her cauldron, brewing a tale 'about the inhabitants of my horrible abode . . . the vampires . . . the werewolves . . . the shapeless ghosts . . . This time, due to the many requests I have received, I am going to tell you a strange tale about two men . . . two men who are the editors of the EC comics magazine publishing company . . . and how they encountered . . . HORROR BENEATH THE STREETS! . . . My story begins on a dank, dismal night. The city is asleep! . . .' And we hear, and then we see, Al (Feldstein) and Bill (Gaines) packing up after a long night's work on their comic *Modern Love.* As they walk the darkened streets home, they think creepy thoughts—and Bill hits on the idea of creepy comics. But Al isn't convinced—readers wouldn't go for them. They argue on until (*sotto voce,* small print) Al mutters that they're being followed. They hurry, but whatever it is keeps pace. Taking a wrong turning, they hit a dead-end—and the only way out is down a manhole. When a hooded figure turns after them, they chance it—only to see the lid close over them and hear a terrible laugh. Silence falls. The manhole is jammed. With mounting terror, they wade through the sewers. Al is beginning to believe all those ghost stories. Now he treads on something; it floats up—a bloated body. Thoroughly panicked, they rush on blindly until Bill is on the point of collapse. He rests for a moment while Al forges on towards a light he has seen. But when he turns back, Bill is gone; the wall had opened and a hand had smothered him into it. Al turns and races for the light, rounds a corner and . . . 'Come in! I've been waiting for you!' Meanwhile, Bill faces *his* captor. 'Who . . . who are you?' 'I? I am the Keeper of the Crypt of Terror!' 'The Crypt of what?' 'TERROR! Don't you know what *Terror* is?' And Al meets his match: 'What . . . do you . . . want with me?' 'Come in and we'll talk it over. I—am the Keeper of the Vault of Horror!' Time passes, and a dazed Bill wanders lost until 'Bill, is that you?' Shaken, they tell their stories to each other—and they turn out to be identical. They wouldn't be released until they each signed a contract, to publish horror-comic stories by the Crypt-Keeper and the Vault-Keeper. 'Well, Al, they got us! I guess we'll *have* to publish their stuff!' And the Old Witch chuckles at us from the last panel. *She* hadn't let them out of the sewer until *she* had a contract, too, for this very comic *Haunt of Fear!*

The strip is apparently about the origins of the EC horror comics. But it embodies this in a story which plays continuously between horror and parody. The very characters, yet to be, come to life to demand their right to be. They use the techniques of horror—dark alleyways, foul sewers, corpses and clutching hands—to persuade their very publishers. There are so many layers here of play with the horror-reality distinction that it necessarily becomes a parody of itself. And because this tendency to self-mockery is built into the very relationship which such horror strips have with their readers, there is a sense in which we are always held off with one hand. All these processes remind us that it is not terror, but the idea of terror, not horror, but the sense of horror, and not fear, but the tasting of fear, that is going on. Working well, horror is a supremely self-conscious medium. Therefore it is no surprise that EC went on from the horror comics to produce *Panic,* and the still-running *MAD*. It is almost as though the very horror medium is unstable, tending to slide either into impoverished weird tales, or into a very parody of itself and thus into satire and self-mockery.

THE TEACHING PARADOX

Let me try to summarise. At the start of this account, I posed the idea of the dare—to test ourselves to the limits. But the limits of what? Once we have been dared, and have accepted the challenge, what is added to or taken away from us? It is at this point that I can hear the renewed chorus of the protestors, pointing to moral confusion, undermining of conscience and pity, and general destruction of innocence and creation of cynicism and degradation. The more sophisticated among them would probably argue that there is no guarantee that children or young people will react to the comics in the way the comics might even intend or propose. Will they not tend to abstract the ghoulish bits—the fear and horror, the deaths, the degradation—and leave the subtleties unmarked?

I cannot deny the possibility. Equally, I wouldn't deny the possibility for almost every sort of reading-matter. As someone who, when younger, managed to find the well-thumbed pages of *Lady Chatterley's Lover* with magnetic precision, I don't dispute that almost any medium allows unorthodox uses. But that was not the critics' case. Their case, crucially, was that the more young readers get involved in such comics, the more they lived in that relation, the greater would be the damage to their souls. My case is a diametrical opposite. The more young people become involved in these comics, the more they cannot help but notice and react according to the conventions, the procedures and the relations which the comics themselves offer. Therefore the further a reader goes into the genre, the more she or he learns the rules and roles and relations of it. They learn to recognise the cues to the types of strip that are included; they can learn to distinguish the successful from the unsuccessful. In learning how to follow the narrative-structure of the horror comics, and learning the nature of shock-logic, they are involved in an end-product which I call the *teaching paradox*.

To understand what this is, consider directly one of the critics' main claims: that children are prone to identify with characters in these comics, and that the harm is done by crossings over the bridge thus created from comics to minds. By getting children to identify, comics put a Trojan horse in their brains, from which spew forth all the things bad for them. This presupposes that we can say *how* a child could identify with a (character in a) horror comic. I want to show that this is in fact impossible unless we so thoroughly revise the standard notion of 'identification' that it could no longer work this way.

Summarising some of what we have seen, then, we can apply its meaning to the idea of identification. Typically, a horror-strip opens by putting us firmly into a situation. This is achieved, very often, by opening with a view of the closing situation, posed as a question or problem. The first frame tells us where we are going to arrive: perhaps not exactly where, but at least we know the *sort* of dénouement it will be. The title may assume this function (recall the pun 'The Way to a Man's Heart'). Or else there could be a narrator telling us how s/he got there. Then the strip unfolds to its conclusion, which is the 'explanation by shock' of the beginning. The narrator often guides us there, speaking to us from outside the frames, occasionally intervening to reveal how far we've got. The arrival at the shock-logic takes the suggestion of climax from the first frame, title or whatever, and transmogrifies it. Now we are in possession of all the facts, we see why the beginning and the end have to be transformed versions of each other. If the strip has worked, we see the logic holding first and last frames together. What sort of a logic is it? It is always a logic of unity, which allows movement by an inexorable process from start to finish. It might be an emotion—jealousy, hate, excessive love, ambition, greed, lust, selfishness—all can be exemplified. It might be a state—innocence, guilt, power—again, the list is a long one. The strips work by making their characters into embodiments of these within relationships, so that these emotions, states or whatever, express their own logic.

So consider an example, from *Shock SuspenStories* 11 (US edition, October-November 1953), called 'The Tryst'. The opening panel shows a wide-eyed young woman (as only Jack Kamen could draw them) walking apparently innocently in the woods; she is watched by a man with a gun who looks upset, or angry—or what? The story's explanation of this first frame sees the world through the eyes of an employer. 'All his life John Hendricks had been searching for someone completely *pure,* someone completely *unsullied* by life—and by MEN!' Here, in front of him, is the perfect example of innocence, in the form of a woman applying to be his secretary. He hires her, keeps her working late at nights to stop her meeting other men, and eventually marries her to make sure her innocence remains perfect. Obsessively, he buys a country estate to install her, and extracts a promise from her that she will not leave it without him. But she gets to be so lonely, and wants something to occupy her—a baby perhaps? No, that would spoil her for him. A colleague comes to dinner, much to John's displeasure, insisting the while on talking about the pleasures of having children. And when John discovers that his wife is taking walks in the woods, he gets jealous and suspicious. Convinced that his colleague is implicated, he murders him. But the walks in the woods continue. One day he follows her, and sees her meet someone, sees her undressing. Mad with jealousy, he tracks and shoots a young man. But as he returns home feeling that he has again secured her innocence, she greets him to tell him how she has been meeting, picnicking and swimming with a boy from a local orphanage. She'd been lonely, so she was sure he wouldn't object. Could the boy come and meet him? 'He's *dying* to meet you,' says the last frame; and we see the body floating face-down in the pool where they swam.

How to identify in this? It would have to be with the man, who is the active centre. The woman is an object, both in the sense that she is only watched—we do not see her thoughts, her motives except as they are refracted through being reactions to John's watching—but also in being characterised first and foremost by passivity. Her innocence is what is being watched, and thus she is essentially object-like. Even to have a baby would make her sufficiently independent and active to destroy the picture-like innocence that is her desirable commodity. So, identification would have to be with the man. And that itself is problem enough for any reader who doesn't easily match. Suppose a woman reader, or a poor reader for whom buying an estate to satisfy a mad whim is forever beyond even dreams. Suppose a child, pre-adolescent, to whom attraction is either innocence or sexuality is not yet an issue. This is an acute problem for the traditional notion of identification assumes *becoming the character, psychologically.* According to that view, we will look at the world through the eyes of the man and, to the extent we identify with him, we will experience our own surrogate versions of his emotions and motives.

But there is another problem. The woman is drawn paradoxically. On the one hand, her face bespeaks innocence. On the other, her body bespeaks sexuality. Kamen, the artist, was famous for what is known in the trade as a 'good girl art'; that is, he was adept at drawing extremely sexy women, with big 'headlights' (as breasts were known, according to Wertham's report from a group of boys). And no doubt, by distancing himself from the story-line, a male adolescent reader could get a thrill from the tautness of her thrusting bust. But, ironically, within the story, it is absolute absence of sexual response in the man who becomes her husband that is focused on. In seeing her as she is in front of him, we see the ambiguity. She *is* innocent, but she has the capacity to be something else. We can understand the growing dilemma of the story-line only by seeing something which John Hendricks refuses to see. Two tensions in the strip do this for us. The story, though told from the angle of John Hendricks, is not told in the first person. We are watching him, his actions and his motives. The pictures also heighten the paradox. The man is crucial, and yet the woman is constantly foregrounded—and the foregrounding is used to emphasise her active sexual potential.

What form, then, could identification take? The most that is possible is *identification with the dilemma* of John Hendricks, for the purposes of seeing where it leads. We are sympathetic in that we are not encouraged to be dismissive of his problem. It is real and immediate to us through the story. When the end comes, the man's world goes to pieces. If we had identified with him, the end would have had to be, for us as well, a meaningless jumble of lost sense. But identification with the dilemma leaves us in an interesting position. We had followed him sympathetically through his glorification of the innocence of Julia's womanhood. Now that very addiction has proved his downfall. By the form of identification allowed by the story, we are now in a teaching paradox. It is a paradox which teaches us, not a set response, but that this kind of 'glorification' of women has problems. The man was caught in a dilemma of his own making, and lived it out. Having followed him, we are caught into seeing the dangers of simplistic notions such as 'innocence'. Julia did, in a sense, remain innocent to the end. Had she not done so, the implicit dilemma would have been different. It remains John's dilemma because the entire strip operates according to the rules of his own motivation. Only he is active, and he destroys himself through the logic of his own obsession.

The concept of identification proves dreadfully inadequate for understanding the processes into which such a strip invites us. I want to use this new approach to the way we are invited to relate to such stories, in looking at a last strip. It is a test case, one that is very significant to me. In the *Daily Worker* in 1954, there appeared one frame from a strip, also published in that nefarious *Haunt of Fear* 1. A single frame from the same strip appeared in the *Daily Dispatch* just a short time earlier. The former treated the strip as a clear case of children being led, through identification (though the word was not directly used), to virulent anti-Communism. The latter saw the strip as just another example of the leering and degraded properties of the horror comics, perhaps best exemplified by one of their banner headlines: 'Horror, Crime, Sex—and the Teenagers Pick It All Up'. (Pumphrey also reproduced the frame which the CP used, in his pamphlet.)

So, what is this strip, and can it be understood in the way the critics are suggesting? Called 'You, Murderer', it originally appeared in the same edition of *Shock SuspenStories* in America as 'The Orphan'. It was in the tradition of a kind of strip about which I shall say something more in a moment, EC's 'social comment' strips. And its point was just exactly the opposite of what both the *Daily Worker* and the *Daily Dispatch* assert.

The story's logic is impeccable. The shock-logic at the end suddenly throws into doubt our certainty that we are always in control of our actions. At the end we realise that, all the way through, the angle of vision has been that of ourselves looking—the angle of vision of the hypnotised, of the chain-wielder, the unknowing murderer. It is very cleverly done, and leaves us with the teaching paradox: just how far are our actions rationally chosen? From that question comes the strong suggestion that, all right, we wouldn't murder someone for no reason. But what sort of reason is this blind unthinking McCarthyite hatred? Isn't that just another form of hypnotism, which makes us gullible, suggestible? The form of the strip makes it very significantly anti-McCarthyite—the exact opposite of what both the *Daily Worker* and the *Daily Dispatch* assert.

I find it fascinating to ask what form of identification would be possible in the case of 'You, Murderer'. We clearly cannot identify with the hypnotist: he is gross, evil, and hostile. Anyway, it is clear that he is in some sense speaking out from the strip to us, or to someone outside. Always his face peers and leers out from the frames. To identify, then, would be to identify ourselves *as* the person addressed. And to do that, would precisely raise as problems the issues I have pointed to. Have *we* been hypnotised? How do we know we haven't? How can we be sure that we aren't capable of this kind of murder, under the influence of a kind of hypnotism—called anti-Communism, or something like it? In so far as we succeed or agree to putting ourselves into the required relation with this strip, it resolves us into a teaching paradox which questions McCarthyism.

The conclusion should be crystal-clear by now. Typically, a horror comic is not an exercise in degradation, but an exercise in doubt. Of course, there are tremendous variations in what they leave us in doubt about, and I am not trying to say that all kinds of doubt are automatically worth while. Many of the simpler horror-strips operate only at the level of leaving us surprised at the workings of the story itself. Others are much more like Hammer horror films—they work on suggestibilities about the supernatural and the like. Ironically, the subtler the strip, the more likely it was to be the object of vilification. Yet these are the very ones of which it would be nonsense to say that they teach anything definite. They are, I would say in summary, exercises in agnosticism and worry—and that is not a bad thing.

John Springhall

SOURCE: "Horror Comics: The Nasties of the 1950's," in *History Today*, Vol. 44, No. 7, July, 1994, pp. 10-13.

[*In the following essay, Springhall delves into Great Britain's 1950s campaign against crime and horror comics.*]

'Moral panic' occurs when the official or press reaction to a deviant social or cultural phenomenon is 'out of all proportion' to the actual threat offered, implying a periodic tendency towards the identification and scapegoating of agencies whose effects are regarded by hegemonic groups as indicative of imminent social breakdown. "Unparalleled evil and barbaric killers" says judge—but did horrific video nasty trigger James's murder?' queried a tabloid headline, rekindling the 'video nasty' debate the day after the conviction of two eleven-year-old boys for the murder in February 1993 of two-year-old James Bulger in Bootle, Merseyside. 'Moral panic' surfaced again in April this year, engendered by the rantings of the tabloid press and by Home Secretary Michael Howard's climbdown in the face of cross-party Commons' support for Liberal Democrat David Alton's illiberal amendment to the Government's Criminal Justice Bill, an attempt to ban films for home viewing on video that could cause 'psychological harm' to children.

Alton's proposal and the surrounding press clamour had a precedent nearly forty years ago with the passage through Parliament of the now-forgotten Children and Young Persons (Harmful Publications) Act. In the early 1950s lurid American 'crime' and 'horror comics' reached Britain as ballast in ships crossing the Atlantic: unsold copies were also imported from Canada and Australia. Few penetrated much further than the environs of the great ports of Liverpool, Manchester, Belfast and London. Seeking out elusive copies from London's East End street markets, one anti-comic-book campaigner confessed that 'I put on an off-white accent and an old coat before I won the vendor's confidence'. Using blocks made from imported American matrices, ensuing British versions of *Tales from the Crypt* and *The Vault of Horror* were printed in London and Leicester to be sold in small back-street newsagents.

On May 17th, 1952, *Picture Post,* the popular Hulton Press photo-magazine, drew widespread public attention to the British 'horror comic' trade in a provocative article ('Should US "Comics" Be Banned?') by Peter Mauger, a Communist teacher anxious to exploit anti-American feeling. 'Who can look at these comics and escape the conclusion that there is a connection between them and the increasing volume of juvenile delinquency?' queried a reader's letter. If Hulton, publishers of the irreproachable *Eagle* range of British comic papers, feared American competition for the juvenile market, parliamentary deputations of teachers and churchmen feared American mass culture invading Britain. All gave voice to an orchestrated groundswell of opinion demanding urgent government action.

'The problem which now faces society in the trade that has sprung up of presenting sadism, crime, lust, physical monstrosity, and horror to the young is an urgent and a grave one', thundered *The Times* on November 12th, 1954. 'There has been no more encouraging sign of the moral health of the country than the way in which public opinion has been roused in condemnation of the evil of "horror comics" and in determination to combat them'. Yet the relatively small sales of American 'horror comics' in comparison to home-grown British comics was openly admitted by eminent paediatrician, Dr Sam Yudkin, an active British Communist Party lobbyist and force behind the Comics Campaign Council (CCC). Yudkin, somewhat disingenuously addressing the Tory Education Committee, estimated that perhaps only 10 per cent of British school children bought 'horror comics' but 'swopping' led to their circulation being rather wider. This small circulation did not prevent such unlikely allies as the CCC, the British Communist Party, the established church, and the National Union of Teachers (NUT) from vigorously campaigning against their diminishing sales. The NUT eventually distanced itself from the CCC, made aware of the political affiliations of many of those active in the anti-comic book campaign.

Ultimately, the Government could not afford to ignore the swelling chorus of 'moral panic' amplified through the press. The new Home Secretary, Major Gwilym Lloyd George, told the Tory Cabinet, meeting in premier Winston Churchill's office at the Commons on December 6th, 1954, that a bill to outlaw 'horror comics' would be difficult to frame. Yet if the Government failed to take the initiative, 'there was a risk that legislation might be brought forward in the form of a Private Member's bill, which would involve the Government in even greater embarrassment'. To forestall such action, Lloyd George was authorised to make an early statement in the House that legislation was being considered, restricted to the type of publication which had 'aroused so much public concern in recent weeks'.

On January 27th, 1955, the Cabinet expressed general support for legislation along the lines of an Alton-like draft bill that banned the sort of comic book which, as a whole, 'would tend to incite or encourage to the commission of crimes or acts of violence or cruelty, or otherwise to corrupt, a child or young person into whose hands it might fall'. It would become an offence to sell or publish 'horror comics', punished by up to four months in prison or a fine not exceeding £100, with the option of trial by jury.

The Children's Department of the Home Office, a liberal bastion, felt that this draft bill was misconceived because it laid too much emphasis upon 'horror comics' as an incitement to juvenile delinquency, statistically declining in mid-1950s Britain. 'First, there is no evidence that the kind of publication aimed at does incite to the commission of crimes by juveniles and, second, crimes of violence, cruelty or horror . . . are definitely infrequent among children and young persons'. Attorney-General Sir Reginald Manningham-Buller felt that the cumulative effect of 'horror comics' on the young was the real evil, leading to 'contempt for the law and an entirely wrong view of adult society'. Furthermore, the Eisenhower administration was concerned, according to the Foreign Office, 'about the extent to which American participation in the production of horror comics is being used to foster ill-feeling between the United States and this country'. The Commander of American Forces in England even attempted to get American PX's to stop bringing 'horror comics' into the country, so desperate was the threat to basic British values.

Fuelled by a 'moral panic' given fresh impetus with the British publication of New York psychiatrist Dr Fredric Wertham's tendentious *Seduction of the Innocent: The Influence of Comic Books on Today's Youth,* the Harmful Publications Bill was piloted through the House of Commons by Major Lloyd George and the Attorney-General in just a few months. The bill's second reading on February 22nd, 1955, was attended by a full house and the debate lasted for over six hours, with strong views being presented both for and against.

The Commons traditionally got excited whenever a question of the liberty of the subject was involved and this debate was no exception. Roy Jenkins and Michael Foot for Labour took up the cudgels in defence of freedom of expression, seeing no apparent contradiction in arguing that a more comprehensive measure should have been introduced to reform the 1857 Obscene Publications Act (eventually modernised by the 1959 'Jenkins Act'). Tory backbenchers who caught the Speaker's eye protested an ardent desire to protect children from being corrupted by the sort of reading matter so graphically exposed in the NUT's highly selective exhibition of 'horror comic' illustrations, conveniently allowed in the Palace of Westminster for two weeks. Several MP's were worried that legislation against 'horror comics' could be given a wider application than intended by the bill's framers. On the other hand, Parliament's interference in liberty of publication was justified by both Government spokesmen and Labour's shadow Home Secretary, Sir Frank Soskice, as necessary to plug gaps in existing obscenity legislation.

'It is true that the public outcry last autumn and the decision to introduce this bill have stopped the publication of "horror comics" in this country', confessed Major Lloyd George, 'but I am convinced that, if the House had not been resolute in its determination to deal with this evil, we would have been faced with a much more serious problem'. The already redundant bill passed its second reading by a unanimous majority and became law on May 6th, 1955. Six months later, only one complaint had reached the Home Secretary and of three other comic books brought to the attention of the Attorney-General none were proceeded against. The sledge-hammer of parliamentary legislation had been wielded in order to crack a very small nut indeed.

The Act was renewed without discussion in 1965 and is still on the statute books. The first, and seemingly only, prosecution under this legislation came on October 22nd, 1970, when W.L. Millers and Co. of Stepney, East London, was charged at Tower Bridge Court with importing from America 25,000 copies of *Tales from the Tomb, Weird, Tales of Voodoo, Horror Tales* and *Witches Tales*. Part early-1950s reprints, part poorly drawn originals, they had already been allowed past customs. Despite being fined only £25 with £20 costs, the firm closed down soon after.

Intellectual rigour and honesty are in short supply on all sides of the current debate about the effects of violent forms of entertainment on a young audience. There can be no easy answers based on inconclusive or contradictory evidence. Scapegoating then censoring the media offers little solution to juvenile delinquency, primarily a complex structural and pathological problem. Equally problematic is the term 'moral panic', popularised in 1972 by sociologist Stanley Cohen to represent a press outcry in the 1960s against those modern 'folk devils': rampaging teenage gangs of Mods and Rockers. One of those deflating phrases used by social scientists to condescend to excitements among the general populace, there is a danger of minimising the contemporary sense of worry and crisis by an account of its repetitious and historically relative character. People may be right to feel 'panic' about rising crime levels, for example, and hence undeserving of academic disdain.

The very fact of a recurring historical cycle might suggest not so much a persistent irrationality or media-induced 'moral panic', argues criminologist Richard Sparks, rather the expression of fundamental contradictions in relations between classes and generations. Assigning each successive 'crisis' to the inclusive category of 'moral panic' risks disregarding particular features of historical context, new technology, or social anxiety. We should, perhaps, give more emphasis to the continuity of the fear and loathing of modern technology which such fears represent and the specificity of the various constituencies, populist, conservative, and fundamentalist, from which they emerge. Violent or sensational forms of popular culture can be offered in any historical age, but the public reaction to them belongs to that age alone.

Brian Siano

SOURCE: "Tales From the Crypt," in *The Humanist*, Vol. 54, No. 2, March-April 1994, pp. 40-2.

[*In the following essay, Siano presents a defense of comic books against a new trend of censorship reminiscent of that practiced during the 1950s.*]

In the early 1950s, a respected psychiatrist and well-meaning reformer named Fredric Wertham published a book entitled *Seduction of the Innocent* and nearly destroyed an indigenous American art form. Wertham alleged that comic books were a major cause of juvenile delinquency, violent crime, social disaffection, and deviant sexuality (sound familiar?). Not only did he wax apocalyptic over the lurid horror comics of the time—EC Comics' *The Haunt of Fear, Tales from the Crypt,* and *The Vault of Horror*—even the superheroes fell under his ever-critical eye. Wertham accused Wonder Woman of promoting lesbianism (under the very scientific theory that dykes wear skimpy flag costumes and fly about in invisible airplanes) and fearlessly sniffed out the homosexual undertones in the relationship between those costumed bachelors, Batman and Robin. The end result of the 1950s comic-book-violence controversy—which ranged from community bonfires to Senate Judiciary Committee hearings—was the creation of the Comics Code, which managed to keep comics from maturing for at least 20 years.

Because the code actually prohibited the use of the words *horror* and *terror* in comics' titles, EC publisher William Gaines was forced to shut down his popular horror comics. As a result, EC editors Harvey Kurtzman and Al Feldstein threw all their efforts into the company's one remaining moneymaker: *Mad* magazine.

For the smarter kids of two generations, *Mad* was a revelation: it was the first to tell us that the toys we were being sold were garbage, our teachers were phonies, our leaders were fools, our religious counselors were hypocrites, and even our parents were *lying* to us about damn near everything. An entire generation had William Gaines for a godfather; this same generation later went on to give us the sexual revolution, the environmental movement, the peace movement, greater freedom in artistic expression, and a host of other goodies. Coincidence? You be the judge.

William Gaines and Harvey Kurtzman both died in 1992 but are fondly remembered by legions of fans. Fredric Wertham is currently on the same infernal chain gang as Anthony Comstock—using his bare hands to lay down hot asphalt along the Good Intentions Expressway. (I hope the Crypt-Keeper's there too, with a shotgun and mirrored sunglasses, shrieking, "What we have here, boys and ghouls, is a *failure to communicate! Eee-hee-hee-hee!*")

Like most predators, censors thrive when the culture can provide lots of weak, disorganized, wiggly little creatures for them to chew up and swallow—and the past 15 years have seen a virtual Cambrian-scale explosion of such organisms. The advent of the printing press helped facilitate the Protestant Reformation; today, for any number of reasons, people have greater access to more forms of expression and entertainment than ever before. I don't think rap music would be half as vital if the Reagan administration hadn't spent years kicking the hell out of the underclass, and it wouldn't be anywhere near as technically complex and sonically challenging as it is without the advent of digital sound technology. Suddenly, kids who would never be able to afford a whole studio could mount assaults of sound with merely a boom box and a Yamaha DX-7 synthesizer. In publishing, desktop systems helped such radical efforts as *On Our Backs* and *Z* to be born, and thanks to advances in software, nearly anyone can design a magazine that looks as cool as *Mondo 2000* or *Spy*. There's a nifty device for Amiga computers called the Video Toaster that lets video freaks create special effects that rival those of Industrial Light and Magic (for example, the new TV series "Babylon 5" does its effects with a bank of Toasters).

Of course, this good stuff isn't *all* due to technology. Inspired by the creative independence of the "underground" comics of the late 1960s, as well as the desire of many comics workers to gain some control over their work, artists and writers have been starting their own companies, taking care of their own distribution, and throwing off the constraints imposed by the code. The result? Draw $200 out of your bank account, go to your local comics store, and check out the following titles: *Cerebus* by David Sim; *Concrete* by Paul Chadwick (a member in good standing, by the way, of the American Humanist Association); a novel called *Watchmen* by Alan Moore and Dave Gibbons; *Omaha the Cat Dancer* by Reid Waller and Kate Worley; *Sin City* and *Hard Boiled* by Frank Miller; *Neat Stuff* and *Hate* by Peter Bagge; *Jim* by Jim Woodring; *The Tick* by Ben Edlund; and *Love and Rockets* by the Hernandez brothers. Pick up anything else that looks interesting; there are hundreds of great comics out there.

Comics are as American as the banjo, jazz, and motion pictures. We don't own them, but we *invented* them, and we should have a parent's protective instincts when they're in danger.

—Brian Siano

Comics are as American as the banjo, jazz, and motion pictures. We don't own them, but we *invented* them, and we should have a parent's protective instincts when they're in danger. Despite the genius evident in the work of Winsor McKay (*Little Nemo*), Walt Kelly (*Pogo*), Al Capp (*Li'l Abner*), George Herrimann (*Krazy Kat*), and many others, comics have generally been treated as worthless trash to keep the kids quiet. This has made them easy targets for the Werthams of the world—no self-respecting adult wants to defend something everybody "knows" is worthless. Few comic-book stores, companies, or artists can afford to protect themselves as effectively as a major media conglomerate can. Comics, in short, are easy prey for the Forces of Darkness.

That is why recent crackdowns on comics—mirroring attacks on other entertainment media—are so disturbing. For example: Timothy Parks, 42, is the owner of Comic Book Heaven, a shop in Sarasota, Florida—the same town where Pee Wee Herman was busted for masturbation, in the same state that gave us 2 Live Crew's obscenity trial and Janet Reno's anti-satanism crusade. On April 1, 1992, a group of kids went into Parks' store and tried to look at the plastic-bagged "adults only" comics. Parks, in accordance with state obscenity statutes, took the comics away from the kids and asked them to leave.

One of the kids' parents filed a complaint with the Sarasota County Sheriff's Department, which in turn went into Parks' store and confiscated several of the "adults only" titles. Parks was arrested and spent a *month* in jail; during the months that followed, the sheriff's office continually revised the original charges (the kids couldn't deliver a coherent deposition), Parks spent his weekends in jail on additional charges, and his business all but collapsed. By late 1993, Parks was convicted.

In El Cajon, California, the local police have never exactly specified just *what* laws governing the sale of comic books applied to the Amazing Comix store they raided in 1992. The police department claims it sent a 17-year-old "undercover decoy" into the store to buy adult comics; store owners deny ever having sold "obscene" comics to minors.

In Chino Hills, California, a new city ordinance requires that "minor-oriented" businesses (arcades, baseballcard shops, comic-book shops) be licensed by the city. It is widely suspected that this ordinance is aimed at forcing Carlos Tortora's City Comics store out of town. Last December, Tortora's stepson pleaded guilty to selling a signed collector's copy of the comic book *Faust* to a 17-year-old. Applying for the new license—essentially a license to sell books—Tortora was photographed and fingerprinted. It should be mentioned that Chino is also the home town of Chick Publications, whose "evangelical" horror comics are notorious for their lurid imagery (mainly of hellfire, drug abuse, and satanic cults) and religious hatemongering.

In what could be the most difficult of comic-book battles, the Board of Equalization in the state of California has ruled that comic-book artwork does not qualify as an "original manuscript." Art Speigelman, who won a Pulitzer prize for *Maus* (a two-volume comic book about the Holocaust), says that the implication here is that "comics are not literature but simply a commodity." Poems, music, novels, even comic-book scripts are not subject to sales taxes, but comic-book *artwork* is considered to be commercial art and is therefore subject to the sales tax.

California is the birthplace of underground comics. It is also a state desperately looking for revenue and not averse to squeezing the thousands of artists in all media who live in the state and would now be forced to cough up the sales tax. For example, the BOE claims that artist Paul Mavrides—collaborator with Gilbert Shelton on *The Fabulous Furry Freak Brothers,* well known for his own political cartoons and paintings and his work for the Church of the SubGenius—owes back taxes for several years' worth of royalties. For Mavrides, like most artists, paying these taxes would require retroactively billing five years' worth of clients for the sales tax. But the BOE means to make an example of Mavrides; it has already placed a lien on his property. Some observers of the situation say that, if the BOE can successfully put the bite on Mavrides and others like him, it will work its way up the media ladder. "The tax collectors need it spelled out sweetly and simply," says *Simpsons* creator Matt Groening. "Comics are free speech, and you don't put a tax on free speech."

In his amazing TV series, "The Day the Universe Changed," James Burke cited the anti-Catholic pamphlets of Martin Luther as examples of the first "propaganda war," an important result of the new printing presses with movable type. Holding up one of these onesheet tracts, Burke pointed to its separate elements: Latin for the churchmen, German for the everyday folk, and woodcut cartoons for the illiterate. The cartoon depicted two men baring their asses at the pope, with thick plumes of fart gas curling like roses in his holiness' direction. Okay, so it's not exactly Noel Coward wit, but it does demonstrate that rudeness and bawdy laughs are pretty universal.

Most comics "zines" have a lot in common with Luther's pamphlets: they are the frequently raw, crude work of someone just trying to communicate with that big herd of folks beyond the walls (the zines are usually photocopied after hours at the day job, hand-stapled, and mailed out to small lists of subscribers). The subject could be anything: masturbation fantasies, frustration at media junk, science-fiction monsters, the local buffoons in city government. They are the print equivalent of hanging in a local bar, nursing 50-cent beers while your friend's band plays Velvet Underground covers on stage. It's not high art, but it's good to get it out of your system.

Mike Diana's zine *Boiled Angel* is just such a project. Its circulation never topped 300 copies or so, and its subject matter—horrifying depictions of rape, child molestation, dismemberment, and the sadomasochism implicit in Christian imagery—wasn't about to get Diana nominated to the Chamber of Commerce. It did earn him some attention from the Federal Bureau of Investigation, which reasoned, through very scientific, criminological techniques, that because Diana drew a comic-book about gross subjects, he might be a *serial killer* they were looking for in Gainesville.

In fact, Diana works at his dad's convenience store, likes comics and zombie movies, and lives in a trailer with his younger brother. Not only does he *not* have the bucks to pay a decent lawyer, but Diana fits a blue-collar profile that some middle-class, "decent" folks look upon with contempt and suspicion. It's cases like Diana's that demonstrate the need to defend free speech for everyone.

Human beings *need* a rich and varied culture to keep their minds vigorous, supple, and informed. When someone demonstrates some new insight to you, or some private way of seeing the world, you can't help but be enriched by it. Sadly, there are thousands of terrified people who can't bear this wonderful anarchy—the same frightened or frustrated people who bitch about the evils of "multiculturalism" and how people should be reading Plato and Goethe instead of Alice Walker and Carlos Fuentes. A single, unified culture is an Alzheimer's of the soul. We *need* craziness, lunatic theories, incoherent rage, and fart jokes every so often, even if it's just to piss off the popes of our time.

SUPERHEROES

Reinhold Reitberger and Wolfgang Fuchs

SOURCE: "Super-heroes," in *Comics: Anatomy of a Mass Medium*, translated by Nadia Fowler, Little, Brown and Company, 1972, pp. 100-29.

[*In the following essay, Reitberger and Fuchs analyze the modern mythology of superheroes, concentrating on the powers, foes, companions, and female counterparts of Superman, Batman, and others.*]

MODERN MYTHS

Superman—the man of steel, helper of all those in distress, defender of the weak and oppressed, strongest of all men, invincible, handsome as a god, noble and gentle—in short, a man far superior to any other human being. He is the ultimate hero, the epitome of his young readers' dreams.

There are so many heroes with superhuman qualities. Jules Feiffer once said that if they joined together with the even more numerous super-villains they would darken the skies like locusts. And all of them experience adventures without a break—mostly adventures of dimensions, countless times the earth, no, whole galaxies are rescued from destruction or enslavement and, on a smaller scale, America is made safe for democracy. Cosmic super-policemen, they patrol the universe, but they do not seek adventure in the same way as the old legendary heroes of mythology and legend did. They do not have to search for evil to combat: evil positively leaps at them and never lets them rest. Without pause they have to prove their super-faculties and powers, for their *raison d'être* is constant battle. They go to battle as the ordinary man goes daily to his office.

The concept of the super-hero was new to comics. It arrived in 1938 in the shape of Superman. Tarzan, The Phantom, Flash Gordon and Buck Rogers, already established in comics at that time, were of course also superior beings; just like The Shadow, Nick Carter, Doc Savage or Sherlock Holmes, who had hunted down villains for decades in millions of cheap pulps.

But Superman and Co. presented a new species of hero to the comic book world—godlike, invincible creatures. Even the way they dressed was quite different. They wore colourful tights, with or without mask or cape, and this intriguing garb was a kind of trade-mark, like Hercules' lion skin.

Superman is as old as the ages. Achilles and Siegfried stood at his cradle—and they are all three invulnerable, except for Achilles' heel, the spot on Siegfried's back and Superman's susceptibility to kryptonite.

Super-heroes, these new 'characters' as they were at first referred to in the comics industry, all bore traces of old myths and legends. Joe Siegel described his 'Man of Steel' as 'the world's greatest adventure strip character', a 'character like Samson, Hercules and all the strong men I ever heard tell of rolled into one'. (In the beginning Superman did not have the exaggerated powers he later assumed.)

But not only Superman, other characters of comics also had mythical ancestors: the first *Flash* is a reincarnation of Mercury (note his costume!); the modern Icarus, *Hawkman,* of the Egyptian prince Knufu (a later version of Hawkman hails from the planet Thanagar); *The Green Arrow,* based on an Edgar Wallace tale, is a descendant of Robin Hood; *Hawkeye* is a modern Philoctet. Bill Finger must have had Aladdin in mind when he created *The Green Lantern* (he wanted to give Green Lantern the name of Alan Ladd to indicate his secret identity!) and Bill Everett, creator of Namor (Roman read backwards) was inspired by some lines in Coleridge's *The Ancient Mariner*.

Most super-heroes draw their special faculties from very ancient sources, but their characters are modified and changed to such an extent that today, with their modern images, they may be regarded as original. They express in today's idiom the ancient longing of mankind for a mighty protector, a helper, guide, or guardian angel who offers miraculous deliverance to mortals.

Marvel Comics have chosen the Nordic gods as their speciality. Olympians, such as Hercules, drop in on occasional visits. The noble Sif now prefers black hair, Thor is blonde, clean-shaven and no longer as uncouth as he used to be. He is super-hero and god rolled into one; with the help of lesser gods, goddesses and heroes he protects 'Midgard' (the Earth) and the whole of the universe. Stan Lee and Jack Kirby, creators of this commercialized heroes' paradise, have dressed up Thor, God of Thunder, and the *Tales of Asgard* so expertly, in such thrilling modern versions, that American readers of Marvel Comics know more about Ragnarök, Yggdrasil or Bifröst than the direct descendants of the Old Teutons.

Is it surprising that the adventures of super-heroes are called modern myths and that Marvel's Stan Lee, the great bard of these modern epics, is hailed as the Aesop and Homer of pop culture?

HISTORY OF THE SUPER-HEROES

The first super-heroes of modern comic epics were unleashed upon mankind at the end of the 1930s, after thousands of years of preparation through myth and legend. A foretaste of things to come was given in 1936, when Lee Falk's *The Phantom,* a mixture of mythological figure and super-hero, appeared on 17 February.

Although he was not endowed with supernatural powers the Phantom seemed immortal, for behind the mask he wore his personality remained forever hidden. True to the first Phantom's oath, his successors kept up the tradition throughout four centuries and created the impression of immortality. The absence of reality is expressed not only in the behaviour and the legendary deeds of the main character, but also in the localities chosen: the Phantom's realm is a large island called Bengali, off the East African coast. He rules in the deep forests, where his skull throne stands in the depths of the skull cave. This cave of memories is a forerunner of the super-heroes' haunts and hiding places where they keep their trophies and souvenirs, like Superman's fortress of solitude, or Batman's bat-cave.

The double identity aspect of super-heroes is also outlined in *The Phantom,* though in reverse and in a particularly complicated way: The Phantom divests itself of its individual personality in order to become a hero and the hero in turn takes on the additional aspect of Mr Walker (the Ghost Who Walks). Superman, in contrast, is first and foremost hero, and he dons his second identity (Clark Kent, the reporter) to hide his true 'super' nature from the ordinary mortals amongst whom he works.

Jerry Siegel and Joe Shuster, spiritual fathers of Superman, hawked their brainchild around for five years before they persuaded *Action Comics* to start publishing Superman in June 1938. The verdict of publishers had always been that it was too fantastic or not commercial, but time was ripe for the superman idea and *Action Comics* reaped a tremendous commercial success. Their editions doubled and in 1939 *Superman* conquered the newspaper strip columns as well. During the Second World War Superman belonged to the American soldier's equipment. He gave them hope and became their symbol of courage and determination, almost a substitute for conventional religion—to the horror of the army chaplains. The Second World War really established the super-heroes, for the Axis Powers provided an enemy against whom they could launch themselves with no holds barred. The fight started in earnest in 1941 and chauvinistic appeal was buttressed by encouragement to buy war bonds.

The enemies were now 'Nazi beasts' and 'Banzai'-yelling 'Nips'. Super-heroes found real adversaries against whom they could pit their strength, for the concept of the super-*villain* had not yet been fully developed. So far, super-heroes had mainly gone into action to combat natural catastrophes; now they found U-boats, battleships and all manner of enemy war potential to fight: 'twisting submarines into pretzels'. Superman really overshadows all other super-heroes for he possesses all the qualities imaginable for a super-hero: he is invulnerable, superstrong, superfast (he is faster than the speed of light and can therefore travel through time); he has X-ray eyes that can penetrate anything and microscopic view to detect the smallest atomic particle. His only weakness is connected with 'kryptonite', a radioactive, rock-like substance that was created through the explosion of Superman's home-planet Krypton. Kryptonite exists in a variety of colours: green kryptonite can weaken, even kill (!) Superman; it has no effect on ordinary human beings. Red kryptonite, invented in the fifties to create a new story potential, has qualities that affect Superman and other creatures of the planet Krypton in the most astounding way: it changes Superman's faculties and alters him physically or mentally; it can give him the ability to read minds, can change his head into that of a lion, can make him invisible or even transfer his faculties to others.

The magic potential of the red rock as well as other magic, can vanquish the noble hero—at least temporarily, but usually he perceives in good time what is afoot. He realizes, for instance, when Mr Mxyzptlk has played a magic trick on him, and induced by a ruse to pronounce his name backwards, the Superman-scorner disappears into the fifth dimension for another ninety instalments.

In *Captain Marvel,* one of the most successful super-heroes in competition with *Superman,* magic also played an important role. The Captain transformed himself with the help of the magic formula Shazam, compounded out of the first letters of the names of ancient gods and demi-gods, to an accompaniment of thunder and lightning provided by a youthful radio-reporter called Billy Batson, into the superstrong hero Captain Marvel. Superman could only ask contemptuously: 'Shazam? What is Shazam?' and out of this contretemps arose one of the few disputes about plagiarism in the history of comics (launched by *Superman*'s publishers, DC National Comics).

Superman's claim to the sole rights in a whole array of superpowers forced Captain Marvel to abandon the super-world. The argument that he was a Superman imitation won and permission to continue drawing his adventures was withdrawn. It was of no avail that Captain Marvel differed from Superman in important details and that he—though inspired by Superman—was more of a take-off of the real thing, drawn in an original and refreshingly new style; nor that a band of anthropomorphic animals were regular members of his crew. Jules Feiffer maintained that he did not even look like Superman, but resembled Fred MacMurray.

Superman's publishers also brought out *Detective Comics* (March 1937), a series which has in the meantime produced over 400 issues. Into this series *Batman* was born in issue No. 27 in May 1939. Batman stands at the other end of the super-hero spectrum. In contrast to the seemingly almighty Superman, he is an ordinary human being, like the Phantom, who trains (under the guidance of his creators Bob Kane and Bill Finger) until he is so well equipped in every way that he can tackle even the most dangerous criminals. Like many of his successors he is of independent means and can attend posh social functions—which always seem to attract crime—in the guise of playboy Bruce Wayne.

Around 1960 *Batman* was slowly dying, but a television series infused new life and vigour into him. True Batman fans were horrified at this pop version of Batman. At the end of the series, however, the enraged fans were mollified by the fact that on his thirtieth birthday Batman returned to his detective role with an added touch of the mysterious. His appearance on television had, needless to say, a most invigorating effect on the sales of *Batman* comic books. Finally, in December 1969, Batman closed his bat-cave temporarily and sent his young assistant Dick Grayson—who had aged only about four years since his first appearance in 1940—to college.

After their successful debut Superman and Batman had their own magazines, bearing their respective names as title; but they still remained faithful to the comic books that had sealed their fame. Superman was so successful that even the adventures of his boyhood were related in special series for *Adventure Comics* and *Superboy.* Some casual critics thought they were the adventures of his kid brother!

In 1950 comic books about Superman's girl friend Lois Lane and his friend Jimmy Olsen started to appear. The latter had been invented specially for a radio series. To top it all Superman and Batman appeared together and shared adventures in *World's Finest Comics,* and here the two heroes took the opportunity of revealing to each other their otherwise strictly secret identities. (This instance apart, nobody, except perhaps President Kennedy, has ever been told!) The two super-heroes also appeared together in *Justice League of America,* a collection of National Comics' most popular heroes.

The success of the super-heroes encouraged many imitations; but they had to have their special gimmicks, choose their own names, apparel, town of origin, etc. Generally speaking National Comics heroes live in imaginary towns, which all belong to the same type of city: Superman lives in Metropolis (a name inspired by Fritz Lang's famous film); Batman in Gotham City; Flash, the super-sprinter, in Central City. Marvel Comics are more realistic in their approach: most of their heroes live and work in New York City.

Many heroes who followed in Superman's wake experienced a short blossoming between 1940 and 1949 before the market became saturated and the readers lost interest. The patriotic flames that had inspired the heroes and had spurred them on to action during wartime had died down. But during the years between 1958 and 1962—and this was still before the comics renaissance—some super-heroes were dug up again and reinstated in a modernized version, or were created anew. The new creations appeared together with some of the old heroes, and the super-heroes' long absence was explained by National Comics, for instance, by the existence of parallel worlds situated in the same space in the universe, but in different dimensions. So as to distinguish them these parallel worlds are called Earth One, Earth Two, etc., up to any number, and their invention opened up many possibilities for new themes and variations of themes.

It is almost impossible to prove that a comics firm has copied super-hero-ideas from another; anyhow, nowadays competition is no longer quite so keen on the hero market. It is practically divided into two groups only: Marvel and DC, and if heroes like sprinters Flash (DC National), Lightning (Tower) and Quicksilver (Marvel) all seem to have the same quality of speed, each one attained it in a different way. Flash received it through a chemical reaction induced by lightning; Lightning through a machine invented by two scientists, and Quicksilver had been born with it through some happy mutation of genes.

Other newly awakened heroes proved to be particularly tough and indestructible as, for instance, Captain America who lay frozen in the Arctic ice for twenty years—as this series had in fact been 'on ice' the idea had a nice, ironic touch. But Captain America had been seen to throw his shield about him in heroic fervour during the days of the Cold War around 1955! A clever reader found an explanation: the interim Captain had not been the real Captain, but only his brother. As a brother had been mentioned in earlier *Captain America* stories, it seemed a reasonable suggestion.

Publishers leave it to their readers to explain apparent incongruities arising out of the difference between real time and comics time. In comics, as in Shakespeare's dramas, a dual time system is used; but whilst in drama years are telescoped into a manageable period of action, in comics the life span of a hero is extended like elastic in order to press as many episodes into it as possible.

Flash, Green Lantern and some of the others were given a new lease of life even before the second comics boom started in the sixties; however, no new ground was broken until 1962, when Marvel Comics' Stan Lee invented *The Fantastic Four* and *Spider-Man* and a fresh wind began to blow through the wilting super-hero epics. The new, modern, more reality-orientated super-heroes were joined in the years that followed by Thor, Daredevil, Iron Man, Hulk, Silver Surfer, the resurrected Captain America, Submariner and others. The new 'Marvel Age of Comics' had broken upon mankind—at least for the next decade. For Shakespeare lover Stan Lee (in private life Stanley Lieber) the super-hero stories have the same function that fairy-tales, myths, legends and romances had for earlier generations.

Marvel Comics, whose heroes have very human failings, produce stories of a humorous, slightly ironic vein, and the same recipe helped many an ailing hero of the great competitive firm National Periodical Publications to new life and vigour.

The enthusiasm for new experiments, which triggered off the boom of the sixties, led also to more socially orientated themes. Some of the heroes such as Green Lantern and Green Arrow even cast off their uniforms—at least for a while—and in their search for truth found themselves face to face at last with reality and the social problems that beset the land.

MARVEL—A NEW ERA

1962 the new 'Marvel Age of Comics'—as Marvel themselves modestly called it—started triumphantly. Nostalgic memories of days when Stan Lee and Jack Kirby produced all that was best in comics almost single-handed!

Marvel continued the work of the Timely Comics Group which had started this 'squinky division of the comics business'—the super-heroes—in November 1939. When, at the end of the forties, the super-heroes lost their hold on the public, romances and modified horror took their place. At this point Timely changed their name to Atlas Comics. In 1962 they decided to start again where thirteen years earlier—as Timely—they had stopped. Stan Lee was at the head of the undertaking and they now changed their name to Marvel, because of the tremendous success of *Marvel Comics* during the Golden Age.

Marvel called itself the 'House of Ideas' right from the start, and many of the themes taken up really were new. Not only were the heroes themselves fresh products of their creators' imagination, the ways in which they were presented had an entirely new and original approach. Serials, in many instalments, made it possible to give the characters a much greater complexity than they had ever had before.

The first of the new super-heroes were The Fantastic Four. On the title page of their booklets the words 'The World's Greatest Comics' were printed in all modesty, starting with the very first issue. Through cosmic radiation the scientist Reed Richards changes into a rubber-like man (reminiscent of Plastic Man and Elongated Man) called Mr. Fantastic; the same cosmic incident turns Benjamin Grimm into an orange-coloured colossus, 'The Thing', with only four fingers on each hand (like Mickey Mouse); Sue Storm becomes the Invisible Girl and her brother Johnny the Human Torch. Thus endowed by fate with superhuman qualities, these chosen ones decide to stay together as a group and they call themselves The Fantastic Four.

In his own way each Marvel hero is also an anti-hero. The Hulk, for instance, described by a reader as the 'true existential man', is the comic's Dr Jekyll (Dr Bruce Banner) and Mr Hyde (Hulk). The Hulk's green-coloured body and square-cut face call Frankenstein to mind. He is a truly tragic character.

Dr Strange, master of the mystic arts, explorer of every dimension of every fantastic realm, whose psychedelic adventures were superbly drawn by Steve Ditko and Gene Colan, attained his powers only after he had experienced and overcome a depression so deep brought him to the very edge of crime.

Daredevil is a blind lawyer who finds new dimensions in his blindness; his 'radar sense', brought about through radioactivity, allows him to 'see' with his ears.

One of the heroes, Marvel's Spider-Man, has to tend his torn spider's costume again and again and experiences in business and in private life one mishap after another. He goes through traumatic crises of identity and suffers from almost paranoiac attacks of self-doubt; but he never gives up, despite all his near misses, disappointments and outrageous accidents. He is the most tenacious and absurdly heroic character of them all.

Spider-Man, in his secret identity of Peter Parker, is handicapped by constant fear for his Aunt May, for whom the slightest excitement could mean death. He is always short of money and earns a precarious living by photographing himself in battle with an automatic camera, and selling the pictures to the *Daily Bugle* for a pittance. J. Jonah Jameson, editor of the paper, has out of envy of the hero denounced him to the press and television as a public menace, so that the police as well as the public are in doubt as to whether Spider-Man is a friend or a foe of society.

Peter Parker could become a brilliant scientist if he were not so preoccupied with his super-hero existence. He is an outsider at college, just as he had been at high school, and as he keeps on missing his lectures his marks are not as good as they should be. His Spider-Man *alter ego* constantly comes between him and the normal joys of a healthy young American; his love life too is just one long misery. His intense suffering and frustration make of Spider-Man the most human of all the super-heroes, and because the reader himself suffers with his hero, Spider-Man is above all other Marvel heroes the most popular on the university campus. Readers' letters from his fans, the 'spidophiles', beg that their 'Spidey' may at last be given just a little bit of good luck; but whatever happens one thing is certain: any good luck coming the way of the 'friendly neighbourhood wallcrawler' will be of short duration only!

The most controversial Marvel hero is *Captain America,* super patriot and spirit incarnate of the USA. Dressed in the Stars and Stripes he incorporates American ideology and the establishment-perpetuating principle expressed by all the super-heroes.

—*Reinhold Reitberger* and *Wolfgang Fuchs*

The most controversial Marvel hero is Captain America, super patriot and spirit incarnate of the USA. Dressed in the Stars and Stripes he incorporates American ideology and the establishment-perpetuating principle expressed by all the super-heroes. Captain America's first action on the title page of his first issue (March 1941) was to crash his fist into Hitler's face. He went on fighting in this vein, his little battle companion Bucky at his side, against Nazis and Japs until 1949. It strikes one as odd that this fervent defender of American democracy, of all people, should personify an idea preached by Nazi ideology: the concept of breeding supermen. Captain America starts as plain Steve Rogers, a weakling who is not accepted by the army despite all his patriotic enthusiasm. Steve, however, is taken in hand by Professor Reinstein (!) who turns him, through a scientific experiment, into a superman. He is the first of a planned series of super-agents. But Professor Reinstein is killed by Nazi agents and takes the secret superman formula with him to the grave, and so Captain America (alias Steve Rogers) remains the only Super-American.

In the McCarthy era 'Cap', as he was affectionately called, awoke to brief life again as a 'Commie-Smasher'; but he only came back permanently in 1964, as a 'Living Legend of World War Two'. Towards the end of the sixties, when America's image began to alter, Captain America became something of an anachronism. His creators are aware of this. Torn by self-doubt, Captain America even searched for a new image as a sort of Easy Rider (1970)—whilst controversy still rages on around him.

The one hero through whom Stan Lee openly moralizes—if we forget about the many short Marvel Westerns through which a strong moral wind blows—is the Silver Surfer, a quasi-messianic figure. 'We try to portray this without satire,' says Stan Lee. The Silver Surfer's former name was Norrin Radd and he used to live on the planet Zenn-La (!). He becomes the messenger of Galactus, a super-super creature who feeds on the energy of whole worlds; but one day, when Galactus' appetite turns earthwards, Norrin refuses to obey his master. In punishment, he loses some of his powers and is banished to earth. Norrin has to accept the cruel exile from his home planet, and gliding through the air on his surfboard, he tries to better mankind. Sometimes he despairs of his self-imposed task and feels like destroying the whole, graceless globe. What puzzles him most of all about human beings is the fact that they are the only inhabitants in the universe who kill in the name of justice.

Marvel also produced the first black super-hero. The Black Panther appeared for the first time in July 1966 on the pages of the *Fantastic Four* comic book. The name, however, was chosen in ignorance of later developments.

The ingredient which above all others contributed to the success of Marvel Comics was a new special type of communication with the readership. Readers' letters pages were nothing new and 'Brand X', or 'Ecch' (Marvel's name for their competitors) ran them as well; but the long, witty replies to readers' comments, written in a personal and friendly tone, extended the 'letter corner' to two pages and it became the most popular feature of the comic book. Marvel invented the 'No-prize', which is not given for the best readers' letter, and the non-existent Irving Forbush. The reader was made one of the Marvel family, a 'keeper of the flame'. Marvel started a comics club, just as the defunct E.C. Comics had done, and called it 'MMMS'. But unfortunately after having fallen into other, purely commercial hands, and lost its connection with the publishers, the club had to be disbanded in 1971. Since 1962 the author's and the artist's credits appear in Marvel publications on the first page of each story. This means that the reader can always see straightaway who wrote and drew the comics; other comics publishers have never done this. In 1965 the 'Bullpen News' page was introduced, which revealed editorial secrets and made of readers true insiders. This personal approach was later successfully copied by other publishers.

The high standard of Marvel publications made them interesting also to older readers, and the average age of the Marvel Comics readership is far higher than that of any other comics publishing concern. In the mid-sixties Marvel was favourite reading matter on the campus for both students and professors.

THE SUPER-HERO BOOM

Anything that is successful is imitated or produced in series. This principle is valid in America for all popular arts. No wonder, then, that Superman and Batman started the first super-hero boom in the forties. But it took twenty years before something similar happened again.

The contents of *Superman* and *Batman* stories were direct continuations of the type of adventure-novel themes around Doc Savage, Black Bat and other characters published by the pulps. The firm Timely (now Marvel) also picked up threads of pulp stories in their comics when the penny dreadfuls themselves were suffering heavy readership losses. Pictured in comics, those stories became even more exciting.

During the first, wild founder years, plagiarism was considered at the worst as ungentlemanly; 'swiping', that is copying other artists, or pinching ideas and producing them slightly modified, was common practice and accepted as a legitimate means of improving output. A firm inventing an original character, a first-born among super-heroes, had to expect a series of imitations to spring up in all the other comics. Great artist like Alex Raymond, Hal Foster or Burne Hogarth would find imitations of their work an everyday occurrence. Timely's *Human Torch* soon had his descendants—such as Firehair, Firefly, Fiery Mask, Firebrand and Pyroman, to name but a few. 'Swiping' was simply part of the business. Bill Everett, creator of Timely's *Submariner,* designed two copies of his own character for other firms and drew for them Hydroman and The Fin.

The number of super-heroes grew and became legion. To name only a few of the most important: The Angel, Atom, Blue Bolt, Comet, Crimson Avenger, Destroyer, Dr Fate, Dr Mid-Nite (!), Guardian, Hangman, Hour-Man, Hurricane, Johnny Quick and his magic formula [3x2(9y)4A], Ka-Zar, Manhunter, Marvel Boy, Plastic Man, Robotman, Sandman, Skyman, Starman, Thunderer, Web and Wildcat.

Captain America began in March 1941 by practically deciding the outcome of the war singlehanded; and on the crest of a tremendous patriotic wave were born no less than forty (!) *Captain America* imitations, among them *The American Avenger, The Super American, The Flag, The Patriot,* and *Major Liberty.* Chauvinism was mirrored in such titles as *The American Comic Book, All Star Comics, Star-Spangled Comics, All-American Comics,* etc. Timely even produced a comic book called *U.S.A.* and a hero of the same name.

The pulps had been only a kind of foundation stone for the super-heroes; what really triggered them off were tensions within the social structure of the country—just as happened again later, in the sixties. Superman and Batman were born just before a great world conflict. They mirrored the spirit of the era and America's attitude towards political problems; they expressed the idea that America was the saviour and preserver of all true social values, guardian of democracy, deliverer of the oppressed from the bondage of Fascism and National Socialism.

After the Korean War interest in super-heroes began to dwindle. Cheap patriotic morale boosters and bloodthirsty horror comics were no longer in demand.

Patriotic enthusiasm could not always find the outlet against someone which Gustave Doré had pointed out but in comics such emotions could be kept alive, compensated, and guided into suitable channels. Publishers of comics kept a finger on the public's pulse and had an instinct for trends among their readership. Comics written and designed on Government contracts for the army were, of course, a different matter. They mirrored the government's political line.

Then came the renewed American comics boom of the early sixties. This boom too was initiated by super-heroes. But the new type had their own particular neuroses and foibles: a reaction to the public's growing boredom with stereotyped black and white presentation of good and evil by all the mass media. To this were added the explosions of social conflict and the Vietnam War. Once again the success of comics was promoted by war; but this was not the only reason for their resurrection. The first boom still glowed across two decades. The old comics awakened nostalgia for lost childhood and the new generation of grown-ups did not forbid their kids to read comics—as their parents had done.

Publishers of comics took note of the trend. The reappraisal of the American consciousness was taken into account. That is why the 'message' of comics is no longer as crystal clear as it used to be. It is still oriented towards law and moral principles, but it has at least become thoughtful and probing. The innocent naïvety of the Golden Age of comics has been lost and the concept of the super-hero is being questioned; comics are drawing ever closer to reality and the great problems of our day.

For these reasons the second boom is also drawing to its end, but the near future has certainly some surprises in store for us. Marvel will have to kindle fresh enthusiasm and will surely come up with ideas of how to modernize the family of super-heroes.

EXTENDED POWERS

Only one hero is mightier even than Superman: The Spectre, a spirit who walks the earth and has practically unlimited powers. He can alter his appearance at will, can make himself invisible, can transform matter, etc., etc. Compared with Superman and Spectre, all other super-heroes have very limited powers. They possess only one, or at best a few specially developed faculties. Their particular 'speciality' or sometimes their origin, is expressed in their name: *Spider*-Man, *Aqua*-Man, or the *Elongated* Man, and often alliteral second names are lovingly added, like The Winged Wonder for Hawkman, The Sultan of Speed, The Viscount of Velocity or The Scarlet Speedster for Flash; Batman is The Caped Crusader.

Any one of us can become a super-hero by mere accident! It is so easy: usually no more is needed than a scientific experiment that slightly misfires; the inhaling of vapours released, the accidental touching of a substance, chemicals combined with the striking of lightning (shades of Frankenstein?) and hey presto! a new super-hero is born!

Batman, however, shows us that we can attain to super-heroship through sheer industry, tenacious endeavour, and a large enough private fortune—running into millions—to acquire all the necessary super-hero equipment. There is no bodily function except sexual prowess (strictly taboo) that could not be suitably extended or adjusted to serve super-hero purposes.

Flash, for instance, can run at such speed that even the surface of water seems to be solid; he can deflect bullets with air compressed by a wave of his hand, or he can agitate his atoms into such high vibrations that bullets pass straight through him without causing any damage. He can also 'vibrate' himself through locked doors and solid walls by the same method. Speed has, in his case, also a most detrimental effect: in his private life he seems to be the slowest, most unpunctual of human beings. No wonder, when he has to tear off on some tricky mission just as he is supposed to keep some ordinary humdrum appointment as plain Mr Barry Allen.

Green Lantern has, at first glance, no special faculties. He achieves his incredible feats with the help of a ring; but the ring functions at the will of its master. Hal Jordan, in his Green Lantern identity, finishes off any adversary with his unlimited fund of clever ideas and his unbreakable willpower; but he must also do the bidding of the guardians on planet Oa, for they supply the energy (which always lasts for 24 hours) from a lantern-shaped source of power. The ring, however, has one weakness: it is powerless against anything of yellow colour. A man who sees (nearly) all his endeavours crowned by success thanks to such a device is always in danger of gradually losing faith in his own personal abilities and so Green Lantern started to hit out with his own fist from time to time, instead of conjuring a giant plasma fist from out of the ring. To restore his self-confidence the guardians of Oa cut down the supply of energy, so that he could no longer rely on a last power reserve to get him out of mortal danger. Now that Green Lantern knows he has to apply his own strength and mind and can no longer rely on completely automatic salvation, he has become much more human and understanding and willing to tackle ordinary problems of everyday life instead of battling endlessly against a host of imaginary enemies.

To augment their various super-powers and use them collectively, super-heroes often band together in super-hero organizations or groups. Among such bands of super-heroes are DC's Justice League of America (a new group modelled on Justice Society of America of Golden Age days), the Legion of Super-heroes and the *T*een Titans. Marvel drew several of its heroes together in *The*

Avengers, so that they could unite in battle against superfoes who had formed themselves into super-villain organizations. For the reader the main attraction probably lies in the opportunity of seeing several super-darlings in action at the same time.

SUPER-SEX

Due to the strictly enforced rules of the Code Authority (1954), it is only in caricatures like those in *MAD* that Superman gives rein to his exhibitionist tendencies whilst changing his clothes in a telephone box (in reality he prefers broom closets or dark alleys), or used his X-ray eyes to glance furtively into the ladies' toilet.

For one super-power is denied all super-heroes: super-sexual powers; and the widespread longing among ordinary mortal men for a penis of super dimensions can never be compensated through the figure of a favourite super-hero. Super-heroes as well as super-villains seem to have absolutely nothing to show underneath their tight-fitting tights; they all appear to be poor androgynous beings—hermaphrodites who lack the primary sexual organs. Jack Kirby's figures, who always stand with their feet at least four feet apart, make this lack pretty obvious.

By simply omitting to mention sex, comics authors achieve the same effect as the loincloth or the fig-leaf does in some paintings or sculptures, and the youthful reader is denied compensation for his most secret and private inferiority complexes.

A sterile, 'clean' world is created in which all the heroes are—at least to look at—androgynes.

The sexual self-denial of the super-heroes may be based on masochism connected with their high battle morale. Their chaste, at best monogamous behaviour stands in glaring contrast to their potential virility. What a paradox, that super-heroes should have to act towards women like ordinary, shy, merely human men! And so the super-hero remains, in one of the most important and vital aspects, a highly unsatisfactory figure of identification for ordinary, frustrated men.

Just imagine Superman's sexual possibilities! He could offer wish fulfilment to every male; he could possess the most beautiful women of the universe, either by subduing them with charm like some super-Casanova, or by taking them by force—and enjoying super-orgasms at any time and for any length of time. But as it is the question must remain: Portnoy Superman still going strong after thirty-two years?

Super-heroines have to behave in an even more absurdly Victorian manner. What possibilities have been missed here! What about Supergirl, Superman's female counterpart? The professionally trained female Circassian slaves of Suleman the Second's harem would appear as naïve beginners compared with Supergirl's super-powers of vaginal muscle contraction.

It is idle to try to imagine the sexual practices of super-heroes. As far as we know, Iris Allen, Flash's wife, has never yet complained; and what would Captain America's girl friends say if they saw that their hero's underpants also bore the Stars and Stripes?

Possibly, but not very likely, further liberalization may loosen the Code in the course of the seventies and allow heroes with hypertrophied sexual powers to appear not only in the pages of underground comics.

THE 'SIDE-KICK'

When comics were accused of having a bad effect on youth, critics pounced on seemingly homosexual traits in super-heroes. Dr Wertham saw a direct link with homosexual fancies in Batman and the Boywonder Robin. His attitude triggered off a controversy, if not to say a libellous propaganda campaign, that is still raging today.

The youthful 'side-kick' is really based on an old tradition of American minor fiction and serialized pulp literature. Tough, resilient, self-reliant, unafraid and honest: this was the image of the typical, one-hundred-per-cent American boy. He was also expected to be clever, humorous and clean. More often than not he was an orphan boy who had had to stand on his own feet from a tender age. Horatio Alger Jr's books had a great part in creating this archetype of the All-American boy. In his many cheap novelettes such boys blossomed in the asphalt jungle of New York—they usually hailed from Brooklyn—and on their way from rags to riches they caught many a grown-up gangster. Such boys, salt of the (American) earth, were of course immediately snapped up by comics and made into boy heroes. Much better identification-figures for young readers than the grown-up heroes! There were also boys who clubbed together in teams and the leader was always the toughest and most American of them all. They fought in countless booklets of the Golden Age during the forties and naturally helped win the war. The Boy Commandos under the leadership of Captain Rip Carter, The Young Allies, The Tough Kids Squad fought behind or in front of the enemy lines. The Newsboy Legion fought at home against crime and the infiltration of enemy agents. When Jack Kirby changed over again from Marvel to DC in 1970 he could take his Newsboy Legion into battle again; but now a little Negro boy had joined their ranks.

It was natural that publishers should try to enhance the success of grown-up heroes by letting boy heroes fight at their side, or by giving the boys a grown-up helper. The Newsboy Legion fought together with the Guardian! Kids were so popular as comics heroes that they quite often pushed a super-hero out of his own comic book; many heroes went into battle with smaller editions of themselves at their side: The Human Torch and Toro, The Sandman and Sandy, The Shield and Rusty, The Green Arrow and Speedy, Captain America and Bucky, and many other teams. All of them, just as Superman and Jimmy Olsen, or as Achilles and Patrocles, Dietrich of

Bern and Hildebrand, King Arthur and the Knights of the Round Table, for that matter, may be suspected for their friendships.

In *Love and Death in the American Novel* Leslie Fiedler explains that there is more between men than just the sacred element of friendship and cites Ishmael and Queequeg, Natty Bumppo and Chingachgook, Huck and Nigger Jim as examples. And so, if we follow the Freudian interpretation, the super-heroes and their young battle companions are but an extension of a truly American tradition. This is neither the time nor the place to contradict Leslie Fiedler, one of the few quotable apologists of the comics culture.

Feiffer adds his comment when he says that American society as a whole takes a misogynist's view of women: 'not only homosexuals, nobody likes them'. This is expressed in all American forms of entertainment from the party joke to comics to films and literature.

Stereotyped clichés of the early comics era naturally fostered the idea of repressed sexual undertones; but for a long time now the tendency has been towards emphasis of the heterosexual, and modern super-heroes have proved their virility by the many marriages that have taken place in their ranks. The Fantastic Four couple has already produced—after the appropriate time lag—splendid progeny. Batman has sent teenage-wonder Robin to college where he seems to show a normal and lively interest in the opposite sex. Young battle companions, however, since they have aroused such unhealthy suspicions, are no longer popular with publishers.

MOTIVATION

Super-heroes have little or nothing in common with Nietzsche's Superman. They live by comparatively conventional morals; they are for good against evil, whereby they adhere strictly to the law's definition of good and evil.

They are always ready to avert catastrophes, help damsels in distress, prevent crimes being committed or injustice being done and to save the earth, or even other, faraway planets from destruction; under the Code Authority rules they undertake never to kill intentionally in their battles against villainy.

Super-heroes mete out their punishment in such well-measured doses that the enemy is either knocked out, can be captured without difficulty, or is able to flee—suitably humiliated, of course—only to return to a revenge attack. This saves the authors from having to invent ever new antagonists, and if they cannot think of anything new they can fall back on a series of hard- boiled, tough villains who, either out of greed or lust for revenge, are always willing to risk another round. The noble super-heroes enjoy their role of helper in distress which allows them to jump into the arena when some worthwhile heroic deed beckons—without being saddled with the responsibility of solving social problems. The criminals they fight are super-criminals and the big gang rings are just super-criminal syndicates; that crime is a symptom of sickness in a society is never stated, because the super-heroes are interested primarily in the *battle* against crime, not in the removal of its causes. They are rarely concerned with the rehabilitation of a criminal, even less with circumstances that led him into crime. Sometimes (as once in an adventure of Spider-Man) a hero can persuade a criminal to change his ways, but on the whole super-heroes accept that a power of evil exists which not even they can break. All they can do is to fight against it. A Sisyphean task that has kept them young for decades.

For a long time super-heroes believed that they were faultless knights in shining armour. They had so many gallant deeds to perform that they never found time to think; or the thought of revenge that had prompted them to take up super-heroism as a career (Batman) closed their minds against the realities that ruled society. They thought, spoke and acted in clichés, were fitted with spiritual blinkers and saw everything in harsh contours of black and white; in-between shades did not exist: democracy was good, Fascism, Nazism, Communism bad. In Senator McCarthy's days they were his allies and staunchly toed the government line and the line of Hoover's FBI; their spiritual heritage was middle-class and petty bourgeois; they were liberal-conservative like their inventors, belonged to the silent majority and believed that tough measures resolved conflicts.

In the course of time and with the birth of a new species of the genre, however, super-heroes have changed. They have undergone (and are still undergoing) a process of reappraisal. Suddenly heroes like Green Lantern are becoming aware of the existence of racial problems, and of the fact that villains sometimes sit behind desks. Nothing is resolved as yet; but this is only natural. Today's problems are too complicated to be treated to rash quick-fire action solutions—and to prove entertaining into the bargain. But it is to be expected that progressive publishers, editors, authors and artists will continue to humanize their heroes; which means, among other things, that they will have to accept a defeat from time to time.

THE SECRET IDENTITY

What is not going to change in the forseeable future is the rigid convention of giving super-heroes a secret identity. It is part of their psychological defence mechanism. Each super-hero chooses in the beginning of his career a disguise and a battle name. Usually he decides to frighten his adversaries, so as to defeat them psychologically as well as physically. He dons a mask and in doing so reaches back to the age-old custom of exorcising demons and evil spirits by frightening them with a terrifying disguise. Today the villains stand in the place of evil spirits. The super-hero's disguise has therefore a mythical element.

Apart from any deeper meaning, costume and mask satisfy a natural urge to have fun, to dress up. The super-hero divides himself into two component parts, each playing its role: the *alter ego* and the secret identity. The dream half (*alter ego*) expresses all that the author or designer—and with him the reader—would like to be; the other half, rooted in reality, is a symbol of the ordinary everyday man following the behaviour pattern ordained by society. It is a division of life into dream and reality typical for the average citizen and serves to strengthen the individual's self-confidence and to justify his personal way of thinking.

There is a serious drawback, though, to the super-hero's dual life: he cannot (and usually does not want to) marry. A family would lay him open to blackmail and all kinds of pressures. 'Darling, I can't marry you, you wouldn't be safe,' are the words the marriage-bent Lois Lane, Superman's girlfriend, has to hear again and again. Celibacy does, of course, aid the popularity of super-heroes; just as it enhances the success of pop stars. To compensate for marriage DC comics have hit upon the idea of imaginary stories; that is, stories are told within the story, in which Superman marries and goes through imaginary experiences. This leads to the paradox that Superman remains single but can, nevertheless, enjoy married bliss in his own personal dreamworld; the reader, of course, gets the best of both worlds.

Lately, however, weddings have not been as taboo in the super-hero world as they used to be. Reed Richards (Mr Fantastic) and Sue Storm (Invisible Girl) of the Fantastic Four have become Mr and Mrs; so have Yellowjacket (alias Goliath, alias Ant-Man, alias Henry Pym) and the Wasp of the Avengers. Barry (Flash) Allen took an ordinary mortal as wife: his girlfriend of long years standing Iris West, the journalist. On the first day of their marriage he confesses that he is Flash—only to be told that she has known this long since, because he talks in his sleep.

Could not each one of us be a disguised super-hero? Our visible appearance only the façade of our much more exciting *alter ego*? The super-hero's secret identity is made in our own image, and it is not a particularly flattering one, as the example of Clark Kent shows. Super-careers force super-heroes to lead particularly drab private lives. They cannot make use of their special faculties in the course of normal, everyday life without betraying their secret; their tragedy is that they have to live one half of their lives as normal, humdrum mortals without being able to find fulfilment in that sphere. (Feiffer calls it the super-heroes' masochism.)

The 'little man' likes to project his wishful thinking into the shape of a big, strong man. Super-heroes are no more than the expression and fixation of narcissistic self-aggrandisement; they show how the adolescent reader, or the infantile grown-up sees himself in his dreams. Super-heroes fulfil the youngster's longing to be like the heroes of legend, fairy-tale and myth, and offer him a perfect identification figure.

It is interesting to note that characters like Superman, Captain America and Batman were invented by their creators when they were still of school age.

As identification figures the super-heroes also express the current ideals of masculine beauty; and it is not always packed muscle, but more often the movement of the figure in action that primarily interests the designer. Jack Kirby supplies his heroes with muscles no anatomy chart would ever show, and yet they appear organically quite sound; not because they enhance the quality of strength portrayed in the figure of Captain America or Thor, but because they introduce an impression of explosive action into a static picture. Bull-necked Superman and Captain America were fashioned according to the taste of their time: modelled on the Charles Atlas body-building-school ideal with Herculean muscles as a narcissistic aim for which to strive. Modern super-heroes mirror a different ideal of male shapeliness and the Silver Surfer, for instance, reminds us of statues by Praxiteles or Lysippos.

SUPER-HEROINES

The relatively small number of beautiful females in comic books of the sixties seems to reflect America's misogyny, but is, in fact, mainly the result of the strict censorship introduced in 1954; also most comics writers and artists are male and they quite naturally express their own dreams and repressed wishes first.

In the glorious days of the forties, the heyday of the comics hero, a great many shapely heroines firmly stood their ground in comics pages and competed with the men. Captain America had a whole range of female imitations: Miss America, Liberty Bell, Miss Victory, Pat Patriot and Yankee Girl, all of them even more patriotic than their male model. Captain Marvel had his female counterpart in Marvel Girl, Hawkman in Hawkgirl, and today, as then, a Batgirl sometimes crosses Batman's path.

In the world of legends and fairy-tales it is always the prince who rescues the maiden, never the other way round. Girls who act like men could only be found among Amazons, and so the first and most famous of all super-heroines was a descendant of the Amazons. *Wonder Woman,* created in 1941 by William Moulton Marston, inventor of the lie-detector, under the pseudonym of Charles Moulton and drawn by H. G. Peters in a strangely flat, two-dimensional style, was the daughter of the Queen of Paradise Island, an Amazon realm no male was allowed to enter. These Amazons were under the protection of Aphrodite; like her companions Wonder Woman was created by breathing life into a statue—the problem of the Amazons' procreation was solved.

Wonder Woman was sent to America to help defend democracy against Fascism. She wore, as befitted her mission, Stars and Stripes on her shorts and her breasts were supported by the wings of the American Eagle. For two and a half decades she fought with her magic lasso, her invisible aeroplane and her bracelets of Amazonium (which deflects all missiles) against all sorts of crimes, which often took the shape of an evil female adversary.

Wonder Woman was no creature of harsh masculinity. In her secret identity of Diana Prince, the bespectacled W.A.C. nurse, she could be of almost helpless femininity. She also had strict moral principles. Helpless girls, gagged and bound, struggled through many a Wonder Woman story and a fat little friend called Etta Candy was for a long time battle companion in most of her adventures. No wonder that the critics not only cried sado-masochism, but also suspected the same goings on between Wonder Woman and Etta which they suspected between Batman and Robin.

Up to 1968 Wonder Woman remained an Amazon. She held Steve Trevor, the pilot who had fallen in love with her, at arm's length, though she had fallen for him at first sight. In October 1968 she took off her uniform—at least for the time being. Her role had become anachronistic. She opened a fashion boutique and plunged headlong into the sorrows of love, because she now fell for the wrong guy.

Feminine softness in the midst of the hard, cruel battle against evil—girls who could put men on the rack—it needed a very delicate touch to make such things acceptable to the mainly male readership. Lee Elias was superbly successful with his black-haired *Black Cat* (appeared 1942 in *Speed Comics*) and so was Syd Shores when he launched *The Blonde Phantom* in 1944.

After 1948 sex was beginning to be strongly emphasized in comics and Gregory Page created *The Phantom Lady,* a very feminine super-heroine indeed, as her generous décolleté proclaimed. But after 1954, when the Code Authority had come into being, all the girls except Wonder Woman, whether they had super-powers or lived in the jungle, disappeared into the comics limbo, and only a few made a comeback in the sixties, notably the Black Canary and The Black Widow. For a while comics denied American matriarchy and sexual behaviour and showed a world ruled exclusively by men. Even the slightest suggestion of sex stimulus was avoided; censorship would have clamped down immediately on any accentuation of the female form. What, girls in tight-fitting tights? Impossible!

Some years after Superman's cousin had landed on earth—'She's been among us for years, and we never suspected! Imagine that!!'—she became Supergirl, the world's greatest heroine. Superman introduced her to the astonished world in February 1966 (*Action Comics* 285). 'She's terrific! Cute, too!' and 'What a Superdoll!!' were some of the delirious comments. In the same story Kruschev remarked laconically: 'It must be a capitalist hoax!'

A new readership draw had been found. Supergirl's second identity is that of Linda Lee Danvers, model of the perfect American college girl; and that is probably the reason why the Code Authority did not object to Supergirl's well-shaped legs being set off to their best advantage by the shortest of miniskirts.

When Marvel introduced the new 'Marvel Age of Comics' in 1962 and censorship was beginning to loosen its iron grip, the firm poured more and more heroines onto its pages: Invisible Girl (now a mother), The Wasp, The Scarlet Witch, Medusa, Crystal and Marvel Girl.

SUPER-VILLAINS

Super-heroes and super-heroines upset the balance between good and evil by their mere existence and to redress this balance super-villains were invented. Normally, each super-hero has his counterpart in the world of villainy. This is a method well tried by many authors of serial novels. We only have to think of Sherlock Holmes and his adversary Dr Moriarty. Comics copied the theme and produced Captain America and the Red Skull, Superman and Lex Luthor, Batman and The Joker, Reed Richards and Dr Doom, and many others.

Each super-hero has an enemy tailored to challenge and match his own particular faculties. The perfect examples are Human Torch and his adversary, The Asbestos Lady; but to match, for instance, The Spider-Man against Galactus would mean the hero's certain death, and to avoid such outrageous catastrophes each hero fights only within his own heroic class.

But in the long run one enemy alone is no challenge for a full-blooded super-hero. The enemy has to disappear behind bars from time to time or even to be presumed dead. If the same villain arrested at the end of one story should reappear at the beginning of the next, the reader might be tempted to conclude that the punishment did not fit the crime. Criminals must always get their just deserts in the end and are often seemingly killed stone dead; a few stories later, however, the reader learns to his surprise that once again, as many times before, a miracle has saved the evil-doer's worthless life. Once more, he can go into action and challenge our hero with his deeds of villainy and deceit.

If the popularity of a hero drops to such a low level that his particular comic book has to be discontinued, it still does not mean that he has to die. In a few years' time readers may like to hear of him again—and up he pops in a modernized version. Hence the saying goes in comics: 'Old super-heroes (like soldiers) never die, they only fade away. . . .' They fade into the comics limbo, that uncertain region where jobless heroes and villains go until recalled.

Since the censorship of 1954 came into force death is only shown as fiction in comics: a kind of unreal state of non-existence which can never figure as a satisfactory solution to any problem. There are only a few exceptions and these made history: Tower Comics let Menthor, hero of *Thunder Agents,* die a true hero's death in issue No. 7 and Marvel allowed Zemo, an old Nazi villain, to be well and truly killed. The latter event did not deter another Nazi fiend from appearing in Zemo disguise and threatening Captain America. No fan would seriously believe that Dr Xavier of *X-Men* was really dead, and sure enough, three years later he re-emerged.

Each super-hero has 'pro bono contra malum' invisibly stamped on his forehead and can, therefore, never be defeated. No wonder that under such a scheme the super-villains are often drawn much more interestingly and hold more fascination for the reader than the hero himself. Just as super-heroes, super-villains too usually acquire their super-gifts through some accident; but when they realize their new potentialities, their warped brains think only of the advantages they can gain for themselves, the power they will be able to wield over their fellow beings, the damage they can inflict on society in revenge for some injustice they suffered in the past.

Lex Luthor, Superman's arch enemy, enjoyed experimenting with chemicals in his youth. Carelessly released vapours robbed him of every hair on his head. It had been Lex's own fault, but he blamed Superboy who had wanted to rescue him—taking the vapour clouds for the smoke of a fire—for the accident and his ensuing baldness. Luthor convinced himself that Superboy was envious of his scientific genius, broke off their friendship and decided henceforth to use his powers in the furtherance of crime.

An important part in the Superman saga is also played by Brainiac, a green-faced computer in human shape, largely immune against Superman's attacks. Brainiac's particular hobby was to scale down whole towns, including inhabitants, to minute size and add them to his growing collection; but when he started on terrestrial towns Superman managed at last to stop this fiendish pastime. He successfully returned towns and inhabitants to their normal size, only one town he could not help: Kandor, a town which his green adversary had popped into one of his bottles, just before the final destruction of the planet Krypton. Brainiac's bottle was filled with an atmosphere which permitted the inhabitants to survive. Since then Kandor—in its bottle—stands in Superman's fortress. Sometimes a group of mini-super-heroes issues from the bottle, to aid Superman in particularly tricky cases. This town is, by the way, the town of Supergirl's parents and they still live there—in reduced circumstances.

Another super-villain who was given a fiend's appearance by a chemical reaction is Batman's adversary, The Joker. His hair turned green, his face white and his lips blood red. At first he was one of those particularly sinister fiends who torture their victims just for the fun of it; but gradually he became the real 'joker' of the world of crime, who commits his villainies for the sole reason of annoying Batman.

The best and most effective villains personify the greatness in evil; they are lonely, tragic figures, demanding our pity. Their crimes are committed out of a desire for revenge, a feeling of bitterness, for they are denied the ordinary human emotions—soulless, despairing creatures. Frankenstein was made of such stuff, and also Marvel's Dr Doom, a super-villain so popular with readers that he became the first evil character to be title-hero of his own series of stories.

Dr Doom, dictator of Latveria, has the greatness as well as the loneliness of Shakespeare's Richard III, and resembles him in more than just an unprepossessing appearance. He is absolute master over his realm. Human beings are no more to him than figures on a chessboard, and he pushes them around as he pleases. He is also a scientific genius—just like his adversary, Mr Fantastic (Reed Richards).

Another highly successful Marvel villain is The Red Skull, the man with the red death's-head mask. He was originally created by Hitler to do his bidding, but gradually became the power behind Hitler's throne, and is now the personification of dictatorship, world-domination and enslavement of mankind. His driving motive is blind hatred against Captain America who for over thirty long years has thwarted his wishes, humiliated him, beaten him in countless battles and repeatedly seemingly killed him; but Red Skull always rises like a phoenix out of the ashes to make another attempt at bringing Hitler's heritage to the USA.

Apart from the great ones there are the smaller evil-doers who have attained some sort of super-faculty through long, painstaking efforts. They are no less inventive in brewing trouble and confront lesser heroes, like Flash; but their super-villainies never succeed in amassing the fortunes for which they pine and the tailors who fashion their costumes never receive payment for their bills.

BRAIN VERSUS BRAWN

Some critics see in the super-heroes' fights a simple brain versus brawn theme which labels the intellectual as negative and inferior.

Super-hero wars are always fought for the highest possible stake: 'Shall earth survive?' It is only logical to give the super-heroes enemies with the most advanced technical know-how and the scientific means to blow earth right out of the universe. Only mad scientists have this particular know-how in comics, and so a simple, straightforward analogy with reality exists. (The comics' atom bomb appeared long before the real one.) The American archetype of the 'tinkerer' of the Edison brand became the Mad Scientist who dabbles in world destruction as a scientific experiment.

In the cruder stories of the Golden Age, when mad scientists and thinkers most often worked for the Nazis (rumours of German 'wonder weapons' abounded), they were usually portrayed as small, misshapen men with large 'egg' heads. Later designs were subtler and much more inventive. Brainiac, Lex Luthor and Marvel's aptly-named Mad Thinker are not displeasing to look at and are rather tragic characters. Super-heroes, however, need enemies they can tackle physically and so mad scientists generally work via robots or other artificially created beings. The Frankenstein theme is endlessly varied and modified.

A repeated show of primitive physical strength and superiority on the part of super-heroes would be boring in the long run, and Superman therefore functions in many a story as super-sleuth. In such cases he becomes a veritable Sherlock Holmes, and Batman too has to make good use of his grey matter when he tries to unravel the mysteries left behind by the Riddler. Batman's super-detective adventures in *Detective Comics* are well worth reading. On the whole it is intelligence rather than crude strength that wins the final super-hero victory.

Jeffrey S. Lang and Patrick Trimble

SOURCE: "Whatever Happened to the Man of Tomorrow? An Examination of the American Monomyth and the Comic Book Superhero," in *Journal of Popular Culture*, Vol. 22, No. 3, Winter, 1988, pp. 157-73.

[*In the following article, Lang and Trimble trace the tendency towards demythologizing comic book superheroes in American popular culture.*]

It happened just a short time ago, the summer of 1986. DC Comics, the publisher of the Superman family of comics, turned 50 years old and, to celebrate, decided to do some housecleaning. They cleared away the dead wood: Green Lantern, the Flash, Hawkman, Hourman, Sandman and many other heroes from what is now called the Golden Age of Comics, the years 1938 to 1946.

Many of these characters were laid to rest without much fuss or bother. They had long ago passed from the public's notice, their gold tarnished. Underneath there was only lead. Or, in the case of Superman, only steel.

Superman is dead.

Of course, he didn't *stay* dead. He was resurrected in a new title. In July 1986, you could have gone down to your local newsstand and bought a copy of *Superman* volume 2, number 1. If you stuck it in a plastic bag and stored it away, maybe it'll be worth something in another 50 years. It sold more than 400,000 copies, which by today's standards is very impressive. Superman just brushed himself off, slicked back that damned forelock and launched himself into the sun. Everybody agreed he looked pretty spry for a 50-year-old.

But it wasn't the same Superman. This one was referred to as the Man of Steel. Of course, they always called him that, but there was another name he used to go by, one you don't hear very often anymore.

Whatever happened to the Man of Tomorrow?

PART I: THE CLASSICAL MONOMYTH AND THE AMERICAN MONOMYTH

The myths of the Greeks and Romans, the legends of King Arthur and the Knights of the Round Table, even the tales of Christ in the Bible—all of these are part of popular culture, mythology. They give the culture form and identity. Richard Slotkin describes mythology as

> . . . a complex of narratives that dramatizes the world vision and historical sense of a people or culture, reducing centuries of experience into a constellation of compelling metaphors . . . Myth provides a scenario or prescription for action, defining and limiting the possibilities for human response to the universe.
>
> [Richard Slotkin, *Regeneration Through Violence: The Mythology of the American Frontier.*]

A monomyth is "a myth occurring cross-culturally." As Billie Wahlstrom and Carol Deming describe it in their article "Chasing the Popular Arts Through The Critical Trees":

> Some patterns of events and figures persist in myths around the world and over time. The similarities in the expression of these myths occur because they represent human behavior and embody human behavioral patterns towards which humans seem to be disposed.

In the classical monomyth,

> A hero ventures forth from the world of common day into a region of supernatural wonder. Fabulous forces are there encountered and a decisive victory is won. The hero comes back from the mysterious adventure with the power to bestow boons on his fellow men.
>
> [Joseph Campbell, *The Hero with a Thousand Faces.*]

Examples would include the Herakles myths of the Greeks, the tales of Lancelot and Tristan, the fairy and folk tales of hundreds of cultures, and, most especially, the Odyssey.

Contrast this with what Robert Jewett and John Shelton Lawrence describe as the American monomyth:

> A community in a harmonious paradise is threatened by evil. Normal institutions fail to contend with this threat. A selfless hero emerges to renounce temptations and carry out the redemptive task, and, aided by fate, his decisive victory restores the community to its paradisal condition. The superhero then recedes into obscurity.
>
> [Robert Jewett and John Shelton Lawrence, *The American Monomyth.*]

The difference between the two is the difference between rites of initiation (the classical monomyth) and tales of redemption (the American monomyth). The American monomyth secularizes Judeo-Christian ideals by combining the selfless individual who sacrifices himself for others and the zealous crusader who destroys evil. This supersavior replaces the Christ figure whose credibility has been eroded by scientific rationalism, but at the same time reflects a hope of divinity and redemption that science has never been able to eradicate. If we take these two concepts, the awareness that a culture needs heroic mythology to provide a scenario or prescription for action and the idea that the American monomyth is an embellishment on the classical monomyth, it is logical to assume the American monomythic hero is different from the heroes of other cultures.

Daniel Walden writes that cultures choose heroes as an indication of their national character. As a relatively new society, America created monomythic heroes that best personified the way Americans wished to see themselves—youthful, physically vigorous, morally upright, a people capable of existing in the melting pot of American technological society without sacrificing an individual sense of value. Conflict was a major part of that figure's life. As a frontier nation, the idea of struggle was inbred into the American monomyth; the hero's struggle was one of vertical mobility, raising himself from humble beginnings until he had forced society to recognize him as a successful individual. The rise from the masses into the light of individual success became the beacon for others to follow.

While the earliest monomythic heroes were usually politicians like Washington or scientist-statesmen like Franklin, the rise of technology and growing corporatism changed the shape of the American hero. Intuition and instinct replaced reason as the physical hands-on experience of the hero became central. Figures like Henry Ford and Thomas Edison were revered not so much as thinkers as individuals struggling with the physical limitations of science and mechanization, their sleeves rolled up, confronting a difficulty that sat immediately before them. Such images emphasize the physical involvement of the monomythic hero in the process of problem solving. We remember Teddy Roosevelt less as a politician than as a larger-than-life figure leading the charge up San Juan Hill.

During the twentieth-century, as America became even more technological, the hero came to represent the needs of the masses. While rich industrialists were lionized, the real monomythic heroes came from the lower classes or the great American mid-west. Charles Lindbergh and Babe Ruth are almost anti-intellectual in their simplicity and appeal. Both relied on instincts, something the average American, grown fearful of rationalism and technology, could identify with. They achieved their greatness through their own physical actions and by depending on an inherent native wit. The message was clear: as Americans, everyone has these innate characteristics and can also achieve social success.

The cultural catastrophe of the 1930s changed the shape one more time. America, in the midst of the Great Depression, became aware of the fragility of monomythic illusion. War threatened Europe, breadlines of middle class businessmen filled the newsreels, and, more important, heroes of the day proved to be all too human. Corporate leaders and politicians became mistrusted; Babe Ruth, heavy and old, left the sport that made him famous. Lindbergh, already victimized by the kidnapping and murder of his son in 1932, fell from grace because of unpopular views about isolationism and Nazi Germany. Real-life heroes proved too fragile to meet the responsibilities of a true American monomythic superhero.

PART II: THE EMERGENCE OF THE AMERICAN MONOMYTHIC SUPERHERO

Jerry Siegel and Joe Shuster were 18 years old in 1933, the year they first conceived of Superman. Growing up in one of the most difficult periods in American history, perhaps, to them, the only means of finding the promised American dream was through the intervention of a superpowered strongman.

Superman is the purest example of the twentieth century American monomythic superhero.

> . . . distinguished by disguised origins, pure motivations, a redemptive task, and extraordinary powers. He originates outside the community he is called to save, and in those exceptional instances when he is a resident therein, the superhero plays the role of the idealistic loner. His identity is secret, either by virtue of his unknown origins or his alter ego, his motivations a selfless zeal for justice.
>
> [Jewett and Lawrence]

Superman is from the distant Krypton, and is motivated by an abstract concern for justice and fair play that transcends nationalistic or religious boundaries. While the most powerful man on Earth, he hides his powers in the guise of Clark Kent to better commune with human beings. He is the benevolent watchdog of the society, and even as Clark Kent, he takes the role of the outside observer, a journalist.

Superman's mission, as every child knows, is to fight for "truth, justice and the American way." Superman was therefore the embodiment of all the values that Americans cherished in the 1930s. For Superman, truth was not an abstract concept but the blueprint for action. Superman never lies. He represents individual dignity and moral integrity while believing in justice for all, rich and poor, strong and weak. The ultimate egalitarian, Superman is fair to everyone in equal measure; he finds the means to give to the poor without taking from the rich. He does not compromise because his moral strength does not require compromise. He upholds the values of the law and the establishment while representing the best of personal freedom and anti-establishment feeling. Superman rises above the law. When he smashes into a criminal's lair, no search warrant is needed.

Superman demonstrates that power and humility can exist in one form. When Superman is not needed, he hides himself away in the weak, mild-mannered form of Clark Kent—a man who, to our eyes, is not only average but is humble about his averageness. Superman's mission is not to punish the wicked but to save the innocent. He does not represent the American legal system, but a secularized version of New Testament justice. He personalizes the values of the Puritan work ethic in its most virtuous form.

Superman's past is the past of all our forefathers: he is an alien, a castaway. Superman comes from Krypton, a planet doomed to destruction because an arthritic, repressive society refused to accept bald-faced reality. He is taken in by a kindly, mid-western couple, the Kents, who teach him all the basic American virtues. As farmers, the Kents are responsible for Superman learning the agrarian values of the American heartland. Through them, he understands the need for humility and the value of hard labor. They teach him the importance of selflessness and that a good deed is its own reward. The Kents shape Superman into the embodiment of the rugged individualist while also teaching him the powers of the individual when acting in concert with the will of the masses. Superman redeems the dreams of the common man where religion and politics have failed. Both figuratively and literally, Superman can fly. Thus, he transcends the petty political illusions of statehood and shows us all how wide the sky can be.

> The thirties were a period of trial, and many of us had lost our old faith in the traditional virtues. War imminent in Europe, Hitler seemed the personification of evil with unlimited power. Superman may have been partly a wish fulfillment: hesitant to accept battle with the evil loose in the world, parents quietly approved the presence of the fictional strongman who would have been a comfort had he existed.
>
> [Jewett and Lawrence]

Superman's first adventure was published in 1938. Hitler had by then begun his march across Europe, and Americans were trying to convince themselves that it was not their fight. Too many had died in the last World War—the Depression had taken too great a toll. The lesson was bitter. Evil, we had learned, was not just an abstract concept. And it did not lurk only across the wide Atlantic: evil could exist wherever there was a desperate need to survive. In 1938, Americans realized that good people could die because other good people had lost the capacity to feel empathy for suffering. Though things were beginning to improve economically, the shadow of the Depression still sat like a malevolent blackbird on everyone's doorstep. Everyone still felt vulnerable, and needed something bright and fearless to chase the blackbird away.

Superman was created to shore up the sagging spirits of a country that had lost its innocence in the Great Depression. Superman did not turn his back on the poor and disenfranchised. In early issues of *Action Comics* and *Superman,* he saved victims in the Tennessee flood valleys, helped families in the Oklahoma dust bowl and, even as late as 1948, he helped city dwellers by rebuilding slums for the poor. He was everywhere at once, a godlike redeemer, but he didn't ask for worship and redemption only cost a dime.

It is impossible to overestimate the impact of the myth of Superman on the American psyche. Les Daniels comments, "Superman, the ultimate expression of human aspiration to pure power and freedom, was an instant triumph, a concept so intense and so instantly identifiable that he became perhaps the most widely known figure ever created in American fiction."

Circulation figures showed the sales of *Action Comics* and *Superman* comics eclipsing those of almost every other comic magazine on the stands. In 1939, the character appeared in syndicated comic strips, in the early 1940s, on radio and in a series of Max Fleisher cartoons. Random House even published a hardback edition of the Superman legend in 1942, so popular was the character's appeal. Other companies imitated the Superman formula, some successfully, others less so. In the words of Jules Feiffer, soon there were so many superheroes that had they all existed together on the same planet, "they would have blackened the skies."

Jewett and Lawrence recognize the decade between 1929 and 1939 as the period when most of the conventions of the American monomythic hero emerged. The presence of Superman dictated a change in the concept, from hero to superhero, offering readers a figure more magnificent than any real-life hero could possibly be. Two conditions were necessary to complete the metamorphosis: the superhero had few personal relationships and no sexual contact with mortals (a convention easily accepted since superhero comics were generally sold to pre-teens). The superhero could have no distractions from the responsibilities of saving the world, and such an emotional distance allowed the superhero to maintain an almost superhuman sense of objectivity. The second condition, serialization, began as a method of merchandising the adventures of a particular superhero. Sexual renunciation and serialization made it possible for the superhero to move from adventure to adventure without the restrictions of normal social relationships. These innovations became the basic plot pattern that comic book writers would exploit for almost 50 years; unfortunately, this foundation also created a formalized structure with which more innovative writers found difficult to dispense.

The list of heroes includes the Lone Ranger, the Shadow, Batman, Doc Savage, the Flash, Green Lantern, Plastic Man and many more. As a culture, we have outgrown some of these figures and no longer find anything in the details of their myths that reassure or instruct us; and yet occasionally, old myths are brushed off and refolded into the needs of modern society. Why some and not others? Why has the Batman continued to exist to this day and not the Shadow? What is there about Superman that remains interesting while Captain Marvel has faded away? And what about Captain America?

PART III: THE POLITICIZED SUPERHERO

Captain America was created in 1941, only three years after Superman made his first appearance. At first glance, we see many superficial similarities between the two characters, but there are many more significant differences. Captain America fits much of the pattern for the monomythic superhero: he has disguised origins and exceptional powers; his identity is secret and he frequently plays the role of the idealistic loner. The single item on the superhero agenda that separates Superman from Captain America is that Superman is motivated by a higher calling—abstract idealism—while Captain America was created specifically to fight one particular threat: the Nazis.

Captain America was a government agent, created during the war years to bash Nazis. Where Superman's alter ego, Clark Kent, served a "philosophical" purpose, Captain America's secret identity, Steve Rogers, was a mere plot device. Superman, in his godlike invulnerability, was difficult to identify with, while Clark Kent was a 90-pound weakling—in other words, Everyman. Captain America wasn't as powerful or as godlike as Superman. His powers were given to him through the intervention of science and American know-how. Steve Rogers happened to be at the right place at the right time when he was chosen to be the first subject of the "Super Soldier" experiment. Private Rogers existed as a method to get Cap to and from the field of battle. Initially one might question the wisdom of having a nation's finest soldier disguise himself as a common infantryman. However, one must realize that Captain America, at bottom, was a propaganda device. The message was that inside every private lay the potential for a Captain America.

The origin of Captain America is a commentary on how the feelings of the American people had changed in a brief time. In 1938, the only possible savior had to come from outside society. In 1941, not only did the savior come from inside society but, because of the nature of the Super Soldier formula, he could have been just about anyone. The American mood had changed from despair to can-do zeal in less than five years. Unfortunately, Captain America's limitations as a hero were built into his origins.

When the war ended, so did Captain America. His publisher, Timely Comics, kept him around for a few years more, trying to fit him into a mystery/horror format, but sales dropped precipitously. The reason Cap failed after the end of the war seems to be that his audience could not accept him in non-political situations. Contrast this with Superman and many of the other National Periodical Publications characters who did not fight in Europe. Superman, less firmly rooted in reality, did not suffer as great a loss in popularity when the temper of the times changed. The Timely comics were more . . . well, timely. Limited by their topicality, sales for the entire line plummeted. Superheroes all but disappeared from the racks.

Other superheroes, Captain America among them, were locked too firmly into a formula of the traditional American monomyth. One of the side effects of the war years was that Americans in general became more sophisticated. Soldiers returned to their homes, many to stay, but they had seen the world. Women had been allowed, however briefly, to leave their traditional roles as housewives and would never again be satisfied with the limitations of the old days. The children of these men and women would not be able to identify with Captain America as a single-minded fighting machine devoted solely to the destruction of a fascist state. There were no more Nazis, only Commies, and though Cap took a lick at them too, somehow it wasn't the same. Nazis wore hobnailed boots and helmets. Communists weren't quite so easy to spot. That was what was so frightening: you couldn't tell them from the good guys. Sending Captain America after the Communists was like using a sledgehammer to cut out a tumor—not only was it ineffective, it also made a mess. Superheroes in general were pretty useless in the 1950s unless they were fighting monsters from outer space, and there were only so many of those to go around.

American comic book companies had no heroes left—at least, no convincing heroes. They began instead to tell stories about the villains, who somehow never changed. The most popular comics genres in the 1950s were horror and crime stories. They dominated the medium with titles like *Crime and Punishment* and *Crime Does Not Pay*. Such comics described the deeds of the lowlifes and misfits of the society, perhaps because, at the time, the standards of what was considered socially acceptable behavior were so strict. In their secret hearts, everyone in the 1950s was an outlaw.

When concerned parents and issue-hungry politicians became aware of the violent and suggestive contents of these comics, the result was a campaign that led to the creation of the Comics Code Authority. This organization's charter proudly proclaimed that it had adopted "the most stringent code in existence for any communications medium." The Comics Code almost proved to be comics' death knell. With the standards the Code enforced, there was very little comics publishers could present that appealed to the prurient interests of what they assumed to be their major audience: 12-year-old boys. In this atmosphere, publishers quickly discovered that superheroes—with their black-and-white depictions of moral values and their antiseptic violence—once again would sell.

Of course, awareness of an opportunity and the ability to do something about it are two different things. National (which later became DC Comics), the publishers of both Superman and Batman, had a corral of superhero characters left over from the '30s and '40s. National began to produce updated versions of the Flash, the Green Lantern, the Hawkman and others. Whereas their predecessors had been rooted in a sort of mysticism (superheroes were called "mystery men" in the 1930s), the new superheroes all were products of advanced super-science. The new Flash gained his powers through a fortunate accident (chemicals combined with a flash of lightning). The new Green Lantern was a member of an interplanetary peace-keeping organization. The new Hawkman actually was an alien sent to Earth to study our police techniques. (Apparently old broadcasts of Superman radio programs from the 1940s had reached his home planet.)

Though different in style from their predecessors, the Silver Age (1959 to 1980) comics characters were not so different in content. Older readers found many fond memories of former heroes in the new superhero titles, but the novelty quickly wore off. The problem was simple: superheroes were locked into the American monomythic formula. All the bells and whistles, new origins and alien monsters couldn't disguise the fact that the basic plot structure of superhero comics hadn't changed in 20 years.

PART IV: HUMANIZING THE SUPERHERO

Superheroes have continued to exist to the present day, mostly because of the intervention in the 1960s of Stan Lee, then editor-in-chief of the Marvel Comics Group, formerly known as Timely Comics.

Lee made superheroes flexible by giving them more human personalities. Where readers had come to expect archetypes with only one dimension, Lee insisted on giving his characters more complex personalities. Spider-Man was neurotically obsessed with status and worldly success. The members of the Fantastic Four, a nontraditional but recognizable family unit, spent almost as much time squabbling among themselves as they did confronting bad guys. The Incredible Hulk was really Bruce Banner, a meek nuclear scientist transformed into a brutal behemoth by a gamma ray bomb. All of these characters were the kind of heroes America seemed to need: readers could admire them but, more importantly, readers could identify with their human frailties.

> We have, in effect, rejected the old, infantile superhero—who represents the strong father who will rescue us (as individuals, who are weak and powerless, and as a society in general) and have accepted responsibility for ourselves and the social order. . . . The comics generally show a new conception of the relationship between individuals and society. The old idea of the self-reliant "individualistic" hero who can do everything on his own, with no help from anyone else—who can save the world because he is a Superman, for example, has been replaced by a view which sees everything as interrelated and everyone's fate being related to the fate of everyone else. it is a much more complex view of man and society than we found in the "caped crusader" comics of the forties and fifties.

Arthur Berger's analysis, while correct in its essence, ignores the fact that the Marvel superheroes generally still resolved a situation in the quaint, old "individualistic" method of beating the living crap out of the bad guys. This much is held over from the American monomyth elements found in Superman. Richard Slotkin calls it the myth of regeneration through violence. It originated in Puritan colonists' tales of Indian wars. Through killing the pagan Indians, the colonists made the frontier safer for virtuous white Christians. Slotkin's myth "depicted violence as the means both of cleansing the wilderness and regenerating true faith in the believing community." Regeneration through violence suggests a world view in which the most powerful or most clever members of the community are also the most moral. The superhero formula thus becomes only a logical extension of this idea brought into the present.

Slotkin's account implies, however, that the hero can originate within the community and may re-enter it after the completion of the violent act. The American monomyth posits a superhero who must remain separate from the community in order to remain pure. The new mythology, the Marvel mythology, suggests a compromise between the two scenarios. In this new myth, the hero is often alienated from the community, fearsome, misshapen, or sometimes only misunderstood, yet still seeks community approval. The superhero seeks to re-enter society through the completion of some violent act that the rest of society is incapable of performing (as in the American monomyth), but also finds abhorrent. In the new myth, the redeemed society does not recognize the redeemer as a hero but instead frequently thinks of him as a menace. He is freakish, different, outside society—and therefore dangerous.

For example, Spider-Man must defeat Doctor Octopus when Doc Ock threatens the order of the society. But Spider-Man does not want to fight, and even tells this to the villain. Frequently Spider-Man wishes that someone else would assume the responsibility of being society's protector, and talks about giving up the superhero role. However, his alter ego, Peter Parker, recognizes his social responsibility. This was driven home to him rather poignantly when an indiscretion on his part as a novice superhero led to his uncle's death. Spider-Man's motto became "With great power comes great responsibility." But as long as he continues to accept his role as a superhero, he will remain outside society. He will always want to be accepted, but knows he cannot unless he renounces his Spider-Man identity, something he feels he cannot do and remain true to his uncle's memory. His dead uncle represents an era gone by in which a hero obeyed a moral code and, even though Spider-Man may not recognize it as such, the code is that of the American monomythic superhero.

This new wrinkle—the superhero's awareness of his place (or lack of it) in society—is one of the few things that has changed about superhero comics in the history of the genre. The new heroes feel ambivalence toward society and their place in it. Not coincidentally, these heroes began to emerge in the early 1960s, an era when many Americans began to entertain serious doubts about the viability of using old methods to solve new, more complex problems. It was an era that promoted self-doubt. Even Captain America—that venerable old war-horse—was brought back and given a healthy dose of angst. He agonized over the death of his young partner, Bucky, who had been killed for a particularly useless reason at the conclusion of World War II. It was a brave statement to make: that young men could be killed for foolish reasons in war. But once again it proved that Captain America is best used as a propaganda tool. This time, however, he was being used *against* the Establishment.

The American monomyth has never, and probably will never, completely disappear from superhero comic books. For any comic book superhero, from 1939 to 1980, the formula works. Superman is still Clark Kent, and Clark Kent is still a wimp, even though he is a television news anchorman instead of a newspaper reporter. The Fantastic Four still live apart from the rest of society in their skyscraper apartment building and regularly fly off to fight Doctor Doom—although sometimes they have to go to a tenants' meeting first. Small alterations have been made to keep the attention of a public that has become more and more sophisticated. As the years have passed, however, and as the education and cynicism of the average reader has become greater, it has become more and more difficult to reach the desired state of suspended disbelief. Details—such as Spider-Man needing to sew himself a new costume, or the Hulk's alter ego, Bruce Banner, pinning traveler's checks inside his pants' waistband so he won't find himself penniless upon waking up from a rampage—make the fantasies more palatable.

PART V: THE DEMYTHIFICATION OF THE SUPERHERO

The process of having superhero characters lose their mythic stature could be described as progressive demythification. The comic book companies' original goal was to make the hero seem fallible so that when he performed an heroic act, the reader would be all the more impressed. This gives the writer greater flexibility in what he may write and the reader more interesting things to read about. Tales of Superman saving the city quickly become boring when there is no sense of peril, no chance he might fail. New elements must be introduced: kryptonite, time travel, Lois Lane—anything that will make the plot more complex. Can Superman save the city *and* find Lois a birthday present? The step from myth to soap opera is a short one, easily made when the comics writer is consistently forced to be interesting in the face of deadline pressure. The more rigid the symbolic character, the more formula it must rely on. Human frailties soften the formula and give it more flexibility. Deviations from the norm start to become more preferable because they are less predictable.

> Captain America, the star-spangled superhero from the hallowed halls of Marveldom, has undergone a metamorphosis that parallels America's movement from the super-patriotic Forties to the disillusioned present. His development is significant not simply for its reflection of emerging American values, but also as an object lesson in the way America's rapid change swallows up its cultural heroes, allowing the out-dated to fall by the wayside, while tolerating only the most flexible in a curious type of Darwinian selection.
>
> [Steve Englehart, *Captain America*]

The demythification process, once begun, is difficult if not impossible to reverse. If Captain American becomes the conscience of the nation rather than its defender, how should he be expected to react when he discovers the heart of the nation has become less than pure? How can a symbol of idealistic patriotism be expected to react when it comes face to face with tawdry reality?

The tale referred to is a Captain American story from the mid-1970s in which Cap uncovers a Watergate-style conspiracy in the upper levels of the American government and is reduced to watching impotently while the conspiracy's leader (Richard Nixon, by implication) shoots himself. Much of the story could be viewed as allegorical, Cap's anguish being representative of the entire nation's. It was a turning point for the character, and for a time he quit his role as Captain America. He took up the identity of Nomad, a man without a country. Eventually, he returned to being Captain America, but only after having gone through an extended period of soul-searching. He decided the value of having a symbolic persona such as Captain America is in its representation of *all* the people—which cannot be thwarted by the small-mindedness of petty individuals.

Steve Rogers, the individual, resubmerged his own personality into the mythic identity of Captain America. Rogers sacrificed himself, and by so doing, gave the myth greater impact by making it clear to the reader that the mythic stature of the hero had grown out of a genuine human conflict.

> Whatever the validity of Marvel's symbol of American patriotism, it is certainly consistent with the larger trends of American intellectual thought. Captain America moves from an almost rural simplicity to an urban complexity; from a simplistic faith in the Melting Pot to nagging doubts that a metaphor can perform its alchemy and become reality; from a morality play naivete in which good battles evil to a questioning of the very terms.

It may not come as a surprise to learn that current issues of *Captain America* feature a storyline in which Cap is forced to quit his role as the nation's defender after refusing to do covert work for the National Security Council that he feels is not morally proper.

Captain America's heroic persona changed as the culture's needs and expectations of a hero changed. The level of complexity of the hero's character, his moral viewpoint, is altered as the society alters. But as the society becomes better educated and more aware of ambiguities, the mythic character must reflect the awareness of those ambiguities in some way. The hero must act, but he must also reflect a complex society's anxiety about direct action. Society's representative must agonize, and through that agony, our collective guilt over our lack of action is purged. We see the results of the action and are seduced into believing that someone else is more capable of effecting social change that we are.

When describing this process, Jewett and Lawrence refer to Ernest Becker's concept of the Demonic. The Demonic, Becker states, ". . . comes into being when men fail to act individually, and willfully, on the basis of their own personal responsible powers." The renunciation of personal responsibility is seen by Jewett and Lawrence as an inevitable consequence of the embracing of the American monomyth. They fear it compels individuals to believe that there will always be someone better, stronger, somehow more capable of handling any given situation.

> Without denying that democracy often fails to live according to its own heritage, one can clearly see that the monomyth betrays deep antagonism towards the creative exercise of reason on the part of the public as well as the individual. In the exercise of redemptive power, purity of intention sufficies. Heroes are either static, innately possessing all the wisdom they need, or they learn all they require from a single incident.
>
> [Jewett and Lawrence]

It is possible that Jewett and Lawrence have overlooked the socializing of superheroes in the 1960s and their consequent humanizing and demythification. They have, in essence, tailored their evidence to ignore characters like Spider-Man who feel great anguish about assuming responsibility for the mass of society.

> From 1962 to 1967, Spider-Man mirrored an era still dominated by Cold War diplomacy and a citizenry more concerned with personal gratification than public service. During the late sixties and seventies, Spider-Man helped to keep alive the liberal tradition among the young, a tradition stressing cooperation among individuals and minorities rather than conflict, moderation in politics rather than conflict, and the right of each American to social recognition and economic opportunity.

By trying to create a formula that would encompass all monomythic superheroes, Jewett and Lawrence have missed understanding the true importance of the American monomyth. And that is: as the culture has grown and changed, the myth has changed. Americans have become more cynical and narcissistic and, perhaps, more mature.

To quote Salvatore Mondello, "Superman came to us in a period of consensus; Spider-Man had to find consensus in an era of conflict." This is the key. Different social pressures on a nation create the need for different types of heroes. The American monomythic character described by Jewett and Lawrence is the prototype for many of our pop-culture heroes, particularly superheroes, but often it is only that: the prototype,

Jewett and Lawrence state:

> . . . Heroes were necessary both as gods and as part of the ritual that kept the external world secure and tolerable. But epic heroes such as these essentially belong to rural worlds, to societies living near the wilderness. And no wonder then that they are dying, particularly in the Western world where nature has become benign.
>
> [Jewett and Lawrence]

It is undeniably true that the concept of the epic hero grew out of the rural world, but to say that the hero is dying—and more, to say that his time has come to die—ignores the fact that evolution is possible and even desirable. Jewett and Lawrence feel that the American monomyth is dangerous and hopelessly beyond repair. They ignore the good the myth may have created and the ideas that it may have inspired. And while it may be true that the American monomythic superhero discourages individual initiative, it is equally true that it creates admirable role models.

All of this aside, Jewett and Lawrence also fail to acknowledge that they may have witnessed an evolution of the comic book superhero. Possibly they just didn't look long enough; the process only became clear relatively recently. They may have missed the chance to see the monomyth rendered less susceptible to conjuring the Demonic. They might not have seen what was happening to the Man of Tomorrow.

Most people, including DC's editors, think poor sales killed him. There has been a noticeable and steady decline in interest in Superman since the mid-1960s. As long ago as 1970, the editors of Superman knew that there was something wrong. "Superman was created in the Depression as an icon," said then-editorial director Carmine Infantino. "At that time, they needed a perfect being. But now they want someone they can relate to. Like kids today, Superman will suffer from an inability to belong." Unfortunately, the few changes made in 1970 couldn't stop the perhaps inevitable loss of readership. It's hard to identify with a man who can do anything. It's even harder to feel any sympathy for his alter ego, the wimp, when we know he doesn't have to suffer. The original idea of Clark Kent was to bring Superman down to a human level. Unfortunately, the 40 years of plot embellishments made him less than human, beneath contempt. In a way, they nearly sank the man who could fly. So, in its 50th anniversary housecleaning, DC changed everything.

First, Superman's home planet, Krypton, is no longer said to have been destroyed because of a shortsighted, repressive government. Instead, it was doomed, as Su-perman's natural father now explains, because of a sterility, a decay that set into a society that had stagnated for too long. Superman's mother boasts of how they can control the rainfall and fears the world to which her husband intends to send their son because the men are hairy and their skins touch the air.

Mostly, though, the editors changed Superman by changing Clark Kent. He's still a reporter, but no longer simply mild-mannered. If anything, he's the epitome of virility: he lifts weights. Women find him attractive—even Lois Lane does, though she would never say so to his face. Clark Kent is no longer an isolated, idealistic loner. He is a member of society, who thinks and feels as a human being does. He does not learn he is an alien until early adulthood (no more Superboy), and when he finds out, he is somewhat perturbed by the idea. Eventually, however, Superman decides that as long as he is accepted as a human being, there is no reason for anyone, including himself, to think of him as anything else.

Furthermore, Superman is no longer portrayed as all-powerful. He can't push planets out of orbit, fly faster than the speed of light and see all the way around the world. To survive in the upper reaches of the atmosphere or dive beneath the waves, he has to hold his breath. He isn't as forgiving or as just either. He grows angry enough at a small Middle Eastern nation that sponsors terrorism to fly into the capital city and destroy any and all munitions he finds there. This isn't a Christ-like redeemer.

The most important change in the new Superman, though, is that his adoptive parents are still alive. In the original myth, the Kents were killed rather quickly and unceremoniously off-panel. The implication was the Superman had learned everything there was to know from them. In *Superman* volume two, the Kents are still Superman's moral center, and they're still preaching small-town American values. But their ideas—and consequently Superman's—aren't chiselled into their gravestones. They still grow and change. They give Clark advice on how to cope with his role as hero, reassuring him that his deeds are worthwhile. There is an incident when Superman is mobbed after saving an airplane. He is stunned by it, and leaves the scene feeling very cynical:

> And it was all demands! Everyone had something they wanted me to do, to say, to sell. They'd taken everything you've taught me and ripped it apart. I know I have to use my powers to help people who really need me, but now they're going to be expecting me. And I just don't know if I can deal with it.
>
> [John Byrne, *The Man of Steel*]

This isn't the American monomythic superhero talking. He is a less self-possessed being. Distinctions between right and wrong aren't so clear-cut. There are ambiguities everywhere, and, as all of us must, Superman now acknowledges them and tries to deal with them. Certainly there's still the requisite amount of mayhem and violence. The bad guy still gets punched out in the end, but that's not the point.

The only conclusion that can be drawn is that, as Am-erica and Americans have learned and matured, their conception of what a hero must be and their choice for a being who reflects their values and ideals have changed. The Man of Tomorrow, the all-purpose hero, is dead.

UNDERGROUND COMIX

Les Daniels

SOURCE: "Underground Comics," in *Comix: A History of Comic Books in America*, Bonanza Books, 1971, pp. 165-80.

[In the following excerpt, Daniels studies the origins and development of underground comic books and surveys the major figures who published in this genre during the late 1960s and early 1970s.]

[Underground] comics, which have existed in one form or another for as long as the medium itself, have come into new prominence through the concentrated efforts of a handful of dedicated practitioners. The underground publications are indisputably the most controversial comics ever to be produced, and what makes them controversial is their totally uninhibited treatment of sex. The newest wave of such comics, which has made the "underground" designation particularly its own, is distinguished as well by a defiance of convention, a defiance which, embracing a variety of social issues as well as warm bodies, has distinctly political overtones.

Underground comics fall into three distinct groups, representing with some overlap three eras in American culture. The first is the small, pocket-sized pamphlet devoted steadfastly to the theme of sexual intercourse, and referred to by various designations including "eight-pagers" (the least colorful but most accurate of the names) and "Tiajuana bibles" (an attempt to identify a point of origin, which identification may actually be completely spurious). While no accurate documentation of this clandestine enterprise will ever be possible, internal evidence suggests that at least a few of these eight-pagers were in print during the twenties, thus giving them a claim to the title of the first comic books. They were definitely in vogue by the thirties, and continued to crop up for several decades before going into a decline which now has given them a current standing as antique items.

The second type which might be considered underground has never been described by a generic term, although they might be called "kinky comics." Again the prevalent topic is sex, but the emphasis has turned away from documentation of copulation. The feature of these comic books—printed without color, half-size, and sold for several dollars apiece—is the depiction of various forms of sadistic or masochistic behavior. Considering the possible range of these deviations, the variations employed are not very extensive, consisting generally of some mild flagellation and bondage, using every possible male and female combination. The material in most instances is presented with a distinct emphasis on comedy and cooperation to lighten the ostensibly grim nature of the subject matter. In contrast to the eight-pagers, bodily exposure in the kinky comics is kept within strictly defined limitations, without depictions of the legally questionable genital areas. Consequently, although the topics under consideration in the kinky comics may represent for some the ultimate in erotic appeal, the breasts and buttocks they traditionally bare are not specifically censorable, and so these comics are available over the counter at retail outlets in most major American cities. The date of their first appearance is fuzzy, but elements of their style and content seem to suggest that they came into their own during the forties, after the standard comic book form had been firmly established.

There is not much to be gained from a study of kinky comics. Distinguished by an extremely narrow range of subject matter, their settings and characters are as abstract and vaguely realized as any ever presented. A few artists who demonstrated a considerable technique emerged from this school; the most widely known are Stanton, Eneg, and Willie. But the monotony of the plotting, and the ludicrous ease with which characters fall into their perverted poses, make them the least impressive of underground comics, worthy of the term only because there is no other way to classify them, and included here primarily for the sake of the record.

The third and most significant group of underground comics are a far more public phenomenon. While the eight-pagers were without any legitimate circulation or recognition, and the kinky comics have remained generally unknown (due perhaps to the very specific and personal nature of their appeal), the new underground comics have had a sizable effect. They have alternately altered or reinforced the opinions of their readers, they have earned supporters and detractors through widespread publicity, and their dogmatic insistence on totally unrestricted self-expression has had a considerable impact not only on the "overground" comic book but on other arts with an ostensibly more serious purpose than comics. Also, they have come as far as they have in a very short time: this type of underground comic was unknown before 1965, and the first important title, *Zap,* did not appear until 1968.

The new underground comics are part of a larger movement which is bent on inducing drastic changes in America's state of mind, not to speak of American society. As such, the artists producing them should be considered not only in terms of their individual achievement but as representatives of a philosophy of which they are both a cause and an effect. On the other hand, controversy over the general underground ethic often obscures the variations in viewpoint which exist among even the most prominent creators in the field. More to the point, it is important to note that a deliberate ambiguity exists in the concepts promoted in certain stories, and that any messages which might be gleaned from one piece may be apparently contradicted by the next, even if both are the work of the same hand. If some underground comics are pure propaganda, the best of them are distinguished by an irony denoting skepticism at the notion of any simplistic solution. Such comics are equally likely to overstate their cases for the purpose of shock, a type of exaggeration that the undergrounders use as a major comedy device, gleefully secure in the belief that it will pass over the heads of the uninitiated.

The original shock value comic books, of course, were the eight-pagers, famed in mail-order advertisements (which were actually for fraudulent, censored imitations) as "the kind men like." The authentic items were created and circulated anonymously, and despite their rumored origin south of the border, they have a distinctly American flavor. Strangely enough, they are not entirely without what the courts refer to as "redeeming social content." Indeed, it is possible that these hot items have been thought to represent the depths of depravity not only because of their concentration on sex but because of their sociological and revolutionary implications. These implications, humanistic and anti-authoritarian, make some of the eight-pagers the obvious but unacknowledged predecessors of today's underground press. Simply by defying the ban on the explicit depiction of sexual activities, forbidden despite the fact that they are personally familiar to most readers and conceptually familiar to all but the youngest child, these comics were an avatar of the current growing insistence on the right to present all human activities in works of the imagination without restriction. Moreover, the concept of introducing the sexual element among familiar personages from the headlines and funnies pages often had a liberating effect exclusive of titillation by demonstrating the vacant and emasculated quality of "approved" entertainment.

There seems to be an important difference between the comics that draw on other comics characters and those that draw on public figures. The most widely known of the eight-pagers are those that used characters from the most familiar of comic strips and comic books as the protagonists of erotic adventure. . . . [This] use of established personalities in activities which their creators would never have sanctioned anticipated by a generation the *Mad* innovation of the fifties. Yet it would be inaccurate to imply that the eight-pagers examined the themes of the legitimate sources in any thoughtful manner. Operating in a twilight mode halfway between parody and plagiarism, the eight-pagers were clearly less concerned with exploration than with exploitation. The real commentary on the material which they treated was implicit in the contrast between the immaculate originals and the inflammatory imitations. Somewhere between the two extremes of purity and pornography lay the truth about human behavior, and the exaggeration of the eight-pagers, as a response to asexual entertainment, impressed many readers as eminently reasonable.

The other (and earlier) type of eight-pager, involving fantasies concerning actual public figures, had a more specific type of comment wrapped up inside it. One of the recent examples of this form presented Alger Hiss in a number of compromising situations, and the new undergrounders have made a lot of mileage out of the possibilities of presenting their prominent political opponents in scandalous situations. However, the original type of character to move from the headlines into these two-by-four inch comic books were notorious criminals. The Depression created a mystique around such infamous figures, based on their willingness to defy a power structure which seemed to be in a state of near collapse, and on their apparent freedom and financial success during a period of crippling poverty. One example features "Pretty Boy" Floyd in a story called "The Fugitive," which brings the fleeing gunman to the exclusive "Madame Dora's School for Girls," an institution which the context endows with most of the qualities of a prison. He seduces an innocent inmate and lures her off into a life of passion and adventure. The hero's armed aggression is presented as a symbolic equivalent of sexual power, success with the former automatically giving way to success with the latter.

More directly anti-establishment is the attitude presented in a John Dillinger eight-pager, "A Hasty Exit," which elaborates the simpler plot of "The Fugitive" by expanding to include two girls and a police detective. Contrasting personal and official attitudes toward underworld behavior, "A Hasty Exit" is also tied in with certain aspects of the cultural changes wrought by industrial development, most specifically the mass-produced automobile. The auto changed the face of crime, and, even before the advent of the drive-in theatre, increased mobility made Henry Ford the father of the sexual revolution. His most impressive public statement was "history is bunk," and this story serves to undermine the official historical view of gangster morality.

Dillinger, like Floyd, is presented as attractive to women, but the two girls in this piece are far from naive, and they are in fact attracted by his infamy, rather than merely tolerant of it. Their rivalry for his affections begins when the outlaw encounters Evelyn and Nellie under their broken-down car, and casually donates his own stolen vehicle in exchange for their company—a small demonstration of the appeal of illegal affluence. A potential three-way love scene is degenerating into an argument when the law arrives in the form of Captain Tracy, who presumably got his name from the comic book detective, although there is no physical resemblance. The law's incompetence is demonstrated when Evelyn disarms its representative, and its corruption is shown in the last panel where Tracy and Dillinger have discarded their social roles as aggressive antagonists and formed a camaraderie born of similar desires. They share the girls, and Tracy gives the police chief a telephoned report that the criminal has escaped to Mexico. The "revolutionary" note here is that Tracy's devotion to duty is undermined not by force but by passion.

Such material indicates that there was often more to the eight-page comic booklets than has usually been considered. If their commentary was a peripheral issue, it was still discernible in numerous cases.

Finally, one can also say that the eight-pagers doubtless had an educational value in introducing some readers into the mysteries of sexual behavior, which was presented in their pages in a reasonably straightforward and comprehensible manner. At their first appearance, they were probably the only place in America where such information was available on a wide scale. Perhaps it was the recent surge of open discussion of sexual matters which cast the form into oblivion.

The new wave of underground comics, which are undoubtedly the most significant despite their comparatively brief lifespan, progressed through their speedy growth in a manner which reduplicated the progress of the standard comics. They began in newspapers, and gradually branched out into the comic book form. But since the new comics were to be totally free of censorship, they could evolve only in a new kind of newspaper.

The first newspaper to afford an opportunity for such uninhibited comics was New York's *East Village Other,* which began in 1965. By the spring of 1966, there were at least four other papers in the nation with similar policies: the Berkeley *Barb,* the Los Angeles *Free Press,* the Detroit *Fifth Estate,* and the Michigan *Paper*. These five became the nucleus of the Underground Press Syndicate, an organization devised to provide free exchange of features among member publications committed to the same radical point-of-view. To fully explore or explain the policies or the politics of the underground press would require a separate book, but certain positions were obvious: opposition to the draft and the war in Vietnam, opposition to drug prohibition, support for oppressed minority groups, demands for sexual freedom including women's liberation, and a general mistrust of government and academic institutions. The newspapers mentioned above were gradually to be joined by dozens of others to become the most readily indentifiable voice of what has been described as the "new left."

The importance of comics to the success of the Underground Press Syndicate was made immediately clear when the announcement of its formation was printed with an illustration by Robert Crumb, who rapidly moved into the spotlight as the underground's most prominent cartoonist. He was probably not the first, however. The earliest continuous comics to appear in the underground press were the work of William Beckman, whose miniscule strip, "Captain High," was a pioneer effort in the pages of the *East Village Other*. Drawn in a style which suggested that the time taken to read the strip equalled the time taken to create it, "Captain High" was a slight effort which constantly abandoned its tentative grip on continuity to involve its characters in bouts of marijuana smoking. The casual attitude taken toward drugs was somehow more effective in defining the editorial position of the underground press than any number of reasoned or impassioned prose arguments, and the door had been opened for the freewheeling treatment of controversial social issues which was to distinguish underground comics.

The comics became the most continually impressive material available for syndication through the various outlets of the U.P.S. (the initials coincidentally duplicated those of the widespread United Press Syndicate)—and the comics succeeded because they were entertaining. Whatever one may think of the underground views of life and society, it is reasonably clear that they have had their best moments when expressed through the arts rather than rhetoric. What shines through the comics medium is the open-mindedness about human and artistic experience that is the movement's spiritual core, a notion too often obscured by the debilitating dogmatism of narrowly focused debate.

To Robert Crumb must go the credit not only for contributing many of the best underground newspaper comics, but also for making the independent underground comic book a viable form.

—Les Daniels

To Robert Crumb must go the credit not only for contributing many of the best underground newspaper comics, but also for making the independent underground comic book a viable form. In addition to his early experience with *Help,* Crumb had solidified his technique through a job drawing for the American Greeting Card Company, where he specialized in the modern snide style of cheer for a line of cards labeled Hi-Brow. He also began developing his first major character, Fritz the Cat, a funky feline who with successive appearances took on more and more the attributes of the bohemian. Serialized adventures of this character appeared in *Cavalier* magazine after they had been drawn in a wallpaper sample book, and they were finally collected in a paperbound volume, *Fritz the Cat.*

What appears to be Fritz's earliest manifestation is a piece dated April 1964 but not published until 1969, in the small pamphlet, *R. Crumb's Comics and Stories,* clearly named in tribute to the famous *Walt Disney's Comics and Stories*. Actually, this pamphlet contained only one story, which saw a vagabond Fritz returning to his home with vague stories of worldly success, and ended with him seducing his younger sister after a midnight swim, an incestuous incident suggested rather than seen. The story ended in a blackout which, in Crumb's future work, would be replaced by unblinking illumination. The more fully realized Fritz pieces in *Fritz the Cat* include a negligible spy spoof, and two others which are keen depictions of the sources and substance of the developing "hippy" life style. At first a glib yet searching college student, the cat soon drops out to become "Fritz the No-Good," a disillusioned disaffiliate who loses his wife and home and becomes a revolutionary political activist more out of boredom than conviction. He runs into enough trouble to drop out of that, too, and eventually becomes the type of bewildered, downtrodden figure who is everywhere in his creator's work.

Fritz is in a sense the source of many of Crumb's characters; he actually traveled the route that brought the protagonists to the state we find them in at the beginning of their stories. As such, it was perhaps inevitable that he be abandoned to leave the way open for personalities who are at home at the point where he seemed to have reached the bottom (even if his optimism is essentially unimpaired by the fall). Discarding Fritz also indicated a significant change for the artist, who has since concentrated primarily on human characters. Strangely enough, they rarely behave in as normal or naturalistic a manner as their animal forebear. It is indicative of Crumb's reversals that he should depict bestiality as an especial attribute of people rather than beasts.

Crumb wrote and drew the first important underground comic book, *Zap,* in 1967. Its appearance was delayed when a misguided acquaintance walked off with the original unprinted artwork, which is rumored to have ended up in England. As a result, it was a second volume that was finally released in 1968 as the first *Zap*. The previous collection of stories was rescued when the artist re-inked Xerox copies of his own missing drawings. The result was an issue numbered *Zap* zero so as to preserve the correct sequence. These two issues are the only *Zap* comic books to contain just Crumb's work, although he continued to appear in later issues and has also issued a number of other solo efforts under different titles, including *Despair, Motor City, Big Ass, Uneeda, Home Grown Funnies* and *Mr. Natural*. In addition, he has contributed to such titles as *Yellow Dog, Bijou, San Francisco Comic Book* and *Slow Death Funnies.*

The Zap comic books, printed in black and white with color covers by Don Donahue's Apex Novelty Company, contain the necessary ingredients for tracing many of the important developments in the underground comics field. To date there have been six irregular issues, the "original" zero plus one through five. The inside cover of zero featured what was to become a frequent occurrence in Crumb's comic books: pages offering the author's message in ludicrous self-portrait-style strips. "Mr. Sketchum is at it again!" proclaims the headline, beneath which a smiling figure with a pencil behind his ear stalks a ramshackle studio littered with old copies of both *Mad* (its last comic book issue) and *Humbug.* He cheerfully promises readers "the latest in humor! Audacious! Irreverent! Provocative! You Bet!" By *Zap* 1 the same chap had become "a raving lunatic" who threatened his audience with strange powers and warned that they were putty in his hands. The title was "Definitely a Case of Derangement!" Two years later, the *Despair* comic book saw the same figure cackling at the desperate plight of others, confessing that from childhood he had been afflicted with a "Morbid Sense of Humor." No longer content to be simply manipulating reactions, he had become a proponent of "psychological sadism . . . with you, the reader, as victim!!" These statements, tongue in cheek though in some respects they are, offer about as complete a sketch of the cartoonist as he is likely to provide; he remains an elusive subject for interviewers, reluctant to discuss his work or its implications.

The same elusiveness infuses his stories, which gain much of their humor from the manner in which they teeter on the brink of a distinct and possibly even profound significance, only to retreat into obscurity or nonsense at the moment when revelation seems at hand. A case in point is "Meatball," the lead story in *Zap* zero, which transformed round hunks of hamburger into a source of spiritual awareness. Dropping out of the sky onto the heads of a chosen few, the inexplicable meatball brings equally inexplicable relief to all it touches, becoming in the story a somehow convincing symbol of transcendence while still retaining the physical properties which make it such an unlikely choice for a source of the sublime. In the last panel the meatball comes alive, winking and waving a greeting to its converts and to those who wait in vain for its approach. (Part of the irony of the piece lies in the contrast between its use of "meatball" and the use that had been crystallized by the article in *Mad* No. 32 of radio personality Jean Shepherd, "Night People versus Creeping Meatballism." In this article, the term was used to describe the kind of materialistic mindlessness which the Crumb meatball cures.)

Crumb's range of targets is indicated by the last story in the same *Zap.* Having explored the possibilities of transforming humanity through miracles of the mind, he moved into "The City of the Future," where scientific development has alleviated all human suffering. Here the cartoonist mocks the pronouncements which assure the public that technology will make life perfect within a decade or two. Such absurd devices as soft plastic buildings and vehicles (to avoid accidents) appear side by side with such dream creations as android slaves and machines that give the individual complete fantasy existences. Yet the pitfalls of the completely controlled society come to the fore at the end of the piece, when the clowns organized "just to keep us on our toes" take on a sinister cast as they deliver a pie in the face of an elderly golfer, the pie poisoned to bring about compulsory euthanasia used as a population-control measure.

The same issue presented some of Crumb's regularly featured characters, including the "snoids," grotesque, snickering little creatures who pop up at the perfect moment to increase embarrassment. Also featured was his most fascinating and enigmatic creation, Mr. Natural, an ancient wiseman who wavers between inspiration and charlatanry. Some brief early appearances featured the sage with a black, shaggy beard, but it soon became the fluffy white one which gives "Natch" some of the physical qualities of Santa Claus, although he is less likely to give gifts than to receive them. His relationship with his followers suggests that he is some sort of confidence man, surviving on contributions for which he offers nothing in return except the opportunity to search fruitlessly for truth in his presence. There is no doubt, however, that he is happier and more competent than those who seek him out. His attitude toward life is based on a wide range of adventures recounted in a prose biography in the *Mr. Natural* comic book. Bootlegger, medicine man, magician, musician, migrant, and taxi driver in Afghanistan, the crusty old philosopher embodies much of the history of the bohemian movement in the United States and abroad. On a few occasions he has proved himself capable of performing something that could pass for a miracle. He does have strange powers, then, but they are "natural," the result of his own personality and experience, and thus impossible to transmit to followers through the sort of simplistic formula they demand. The result is that attempts to uncover his secret finally drive the wiseman to wisecracks and sometimes even to slapstick violence, as on the cover of *Mr. Natural,* where his hobnailed boots are delivering a swift kick in the pants to his disciple, Flakey Foont.

Flakey, Mr. Natural's most consistent foil, is a neurotic young man whose fervent desire for enlightenment leads him into confrontations with the guru which seem to teach him nothing. "Why do I keep thinking you can tell me anything?" he asks. Yet he will not quit, perhaps because his efforts to defy the sage end in complete futility. This was never more apparent than in *Zap* 5, where he determined to spend the rest of his life in a bathtub.

This bizarre bit of behavior might have been more readily accepted from another Crumb creation, Shuman the Human, a bald truth-seeker even more desperate than Flakey. Shuman has had his head reduced to minute proportions for his effrontery in demanding a confrontation with God; he has also suffered a nervous breakdown when Mr. Natural frustrated his attempt to became an eastern mystic. His ability for self-pity and self-deception point up the value of Mr. Natural's attitude.

Other important personalities developed in Crumb's early comic book period include "Whiteman," a business executive obsessed with the need to maintain his inhibitions while striving for success, and mocked by a group of relaxed blacks who then invited him to join in their celebration. The artist's treatment of blacks is based on the stereotype common to an out-dated tradition, but it seems certain that this is less a reflection of prejudice than it is a commentary on the prejudice he sees around him. The point was emphasized by the introduction, in *Zap* 2, of "Angelfood McSpade," a voluptuous native of Africa whose existence is an endless series of exploitations by white lechers.

The pages of *Zap* 2 were opened to three other artists besides Crumb—Rick Griffin, Victor Moscoso, and S. Clay Wilson. Griffin and Moscoso have very similar styles and techniques, almost indistinguishable at first glance. They are the most careful draftsman of the underground cartoonists; the straight lines of their panel borders are one feature which sets them apart from their more casual cohorts. Their "stories" are comics only in a very limited sense. They generally abandon both plot and text to concentrate on conglomerations of abstract shapes and symbols which change from panel to panel in progressions based solely on the visual value of the material. Both have a fondness for Disney characters, mice and ducks who are reduced, especially in Moscoso's work, to their component parts and then rearranged with other objects like light bulbs and empty, shaded speech balloons. The effect of disintegration and reintegration provides the only subject matter, and apparently is intended to suggest the visual effect of psychedelic drugs. While Moscoso's objects seem to be chosen arbitrarily, Griffin's material reflects an interest in the occult, and some of his best pieces are full of arcane symbols like sphinxes, scarabs, and flaming hearts. Originally a poster artist, Griffin is most impressive in single pages which rely less on linear development than on direct relationships between component parts. His most coherent piece, "Bombs Away," reflects the doctrine of Karma in its tale of a duck and a mouse converting a pig into a sausage while a bomb drops from the sky onto their home.

The drawings of Griffin and Moscoso have been a relatively isolated phenomenon; the only other comics with similar concerns are the attractive but unintelligible productions of John Thompson. The debut of S. Clay Wilson, on the other hand, was to have immediate and powerful repercussions. He is, for better or worse, the cartoonist and writer who defies more taboos than any other in the history of comics. He has shocked and amazed every reader who encounters his work not only because of the subject matter but because of the repellent but fascinating drawing style in which it is presented. While Crumb's great popularity is doubtless increased because of a certain roundness and cuteness in even his most reprehensible characters, Wilson's figures are as hideous as his considerable skill can make them. Yet his work has had a direct and acknowledged influence on Crumb and all the other underground cartoonists, by making them aware of how much further they could go in challenging conventions of taste and judgment. Wilson's fantasies of depraved sex and violence made everything that preceded him, even in the underground, seem tame indeed. He makes the eight-pagers look romantic, and the kinky comics look chummy.

Zap 2 featured three of his stories. One saw the contents of an unflushed toilet bowl flung into the faces of three characters, another featured a sailor whose oversized sex organ was amputated and eaten. Each of these pieces was only a page in length, with the ultimate outrage ending the story the way a punch line ends a humorous strip. The indignities which Wilson gleefully inflicts on his protagonists are so incredible that they actually do become jokes; it is because they are intolerable that they are absurd, and thus, in the last analysis, they are funny. The technique of exaggerating and exposing morbid fears is one which Wilson's comics have developed to the point where their crudity becomes cathartic.

Wilson has a number of thematic concerns. The third story in the same issue of *Zap*, "The Hog Ridin' Fools,"—a longer story than the others—explored one of the artist's favorite subjects: the world of contemporary motorcycle gangs. In this comparatively restrained effort, the "Fools" have the misfortune to tangle with the Checkered Demon, one of the rare Wilson characters who survives long enough to appear in more than one story. Various sorts of demons populate Wilson's tales, using their supernatural powers as a sort of moral force to restore order among survivors of his typically bloody battles. In addition to the bikers, Wilson has a fondness for depicting eighteenth century pirates. There are similarities between these groups, which have been emphasized in a series of "time warp" tales in which the two types are mysteriously juxtaposed, resulting in predictable mayhem. More staggering are pieces that depict the battle of the sexes in its most debased form, involving mortal combat between gangs of equally vicious men and women.

While the *Zap* comic books and Wilson's conflicts poured out of the West Coast, a New York cartoonist was creating a different sort of conflict in the pages of the *East Village Other*. This was Manuel Rodrigues, who works under the name "Spain." Wilson's violence has its sources in the domain of abnormal psychology, Spain's comes from the arena of political ideology. His major creation is Trashman, a radical revolutionary struggling against a repressive government in an indistinct period of the future. The Trashman series, which Spain produced and in which he kept a reasonably organized plot line in progress for over a year, constitutes the most sustained effort yet attempted in the field of underground comics. When the best strips were reprinted in a tabloid-size comic book by the Berkeley *Tribe,* the total effect suggested some of the qualities of an epic. In late 1970, years after the character's initial appearance, Spain produced an origin story for the *Subvert* comic book. The story made it clear that the civilization that produced Trashman was the result of an atomic war which had created a new ruling class, only partially in control of the population, and afflicted with a megalomania which found expression in mass slaughter, human sacrifice, and cannibalism. The hero, originally auto mechanic Harry Barnes, became a rebel after his wife was murdered by government agents. He received instruction from mysterious cloaked figures, gaining mastery of obscure skills described as "parasciences." Despite such hints of supernatural guidance, the bearded, black-clad Trashman is clearly a mortal, with magical powers apparently limited to the ability to interpret instructions from such unlikely sources as cracks in the sidewalk. Although the science-fiction elements make it possible to view the series as simply a work of imagination, there is little doubt that it is intended to reflect contemporary reality. Indeed, certain events over the past few years have shown the accuracy of Spain's implied predictions as the new radicals have moved away from a philosophy of peace and love toward the kind of militant confrontation embodied by Trashman and his band of urban guerrillas. Politics aside, Spain is closer to the traditional action comic book style than any of his colleagues. His backgrounds and battle scenes are often reminiscent of the work of Jack Kirby, and his theme is in the tradition of *Blackhawk.*

More recently, Spain has returned to the present with a new protagonist, Manning, a vicious plainclothes police detective who prefers force to reason. Crude, corrupt, and not very bright, Manning represents the radical's concept of the policeman as a "pig." His favorite investigative technique involves administering a brutal beating or a few bullet wounds to whoever happens to be on the scene when he arrives. Probably the rottenest cop ever to be imagined, Manning finally surpasses belief, although his presence in comics is an important indication of the extent to which certain groups, whose attitudes are exposed in the underground press, view "law and order" as a threat to their security. Spain frequently manages to include sordid sex scenes amidst the carnage his characters create (Trashman is one of very few comics heroes to catch a venereal disease), but his real importance is in his portrayal of the violence seething within contemporary society.

Another important contributor to the *East Village Other* is Kim Deitch, who dreamed up a number of weird personalities during a long stint as one of the paper's leading cartoonists. His most memorable creations are Sunshine Girl, whose round body is topped by a daisy-shaped head, and Uncle Ed, the India rubber man and acrobat of love. Deitch was eventually to become editor of the *Other*'s comic supplement, *Gothic Blimp Works,* which was inaugurated in 1969 under the editorship of Vaughn Bode, a cartoonist with a fondness for drawing reptiles.

This tabloid-sized publication, which lasted only a few issues, featured most of the top underground artists, and set itself apart from other productions in the field by including a few pages in color. The color separations were the work of Trina Robbins, who has gained a reputation as the foremost female creator of underground comics. She had some success in *Gothic Blimp Works* with Panthea, a creature half lady and half lion who was transported from Africa with painful results. The somewhat submerged concern for feminist principles which this series suggested was to emerge in 1970, when Trina became the principal contributor to *It Ain't Me Babe,* the first comic book devoted exclusively to Women's Liberation. The cover, which featured renderings of Sheena, Wonder Woman, and Mary Marvel, suggested how much comic book fantasies have done to provide images suitable to a new view of women and her place in the world.

Possibly the most widely syndicated of all underground cartoonists is Gilbert Shelton. After years of producing first the Wonder Warthog series for *Help!* and then *Drag Cartoons,* Shelton moved into high gear in 1968 with the *Feds 'n' Heads* comic book, which established his position as second only to Crumb in the ranks of the radical cartoonists. The Hog was to be gradually abandoned, perhaps because his predilection for crime-fighting made him too much of a "pig" for the new audience. He did exhibit some tolerance when, after accidently knocking a hole in the house of four shocked pot smokers, he remarked, "You folks go back to what you were doing, and I'll be back in a minute to fix your wall."

This sympathy for the drug culture was to take its most impressive form in the adventures of Shelton's new heroes, Those Fabulous Furry Freak Brothers, who have become a regular feature of the Los Angeles *Free Press.* Living by the motto "Grass will carry you through times of no money better than money will carry you through times of no grass," those three long-haired clowns have become the most consistently humorous characters in underground comics. Fat Freddy, Phineas and Freewheelin' Frank demonstrate the pleasures and pains of life on the outskirts of society in a manner reminiscent of the great silent film comedians. Most of these stories are a single page in length, and they appear regularly throughout the Underground Press Syndicate as well as in various comic books. Their longest adventure to date is "The Freak Brothers Pull a Heist," from the second Shelton comic book, *Radical America,* a special issue of a journal ordinarily devoted to revolutionary prose. The ingenuity employed to feed the ravenous pothead Fat Freddy provides an amusing commentary on the gullibility of a public conditioned by television giveaways and similar mass media nonsense.

Shelton has also produced at least two classic pieces that

do not involve the Freak Brothers. One is a poetic tale of a farmer who liberates his chickens in a psychedelic frenzy; the other is "Believe It or Leave It" from *Zap* 5. The latter presents radical complaints concerning policies of the American government, thinly disguised as descriptions of conditions in foreign lands, the argument being presented in vividly contrasting pictures and captions.

Just as the underground comics have their own newspapers, so they have their own presses and, as has been seen, their own comic book titles. An important feature of Shelton's career is his involvement with San Francisco's Rip-Off Press, a cartoonists' cooperative which prints many of the important underground comic books. Until recently, most of the rest came out of Berkeley's Print Mint, operated by Don Schenker. He has distributed the *Zap* comic books, the tabloid *Yellow Dog* (recently converted to standard comic book format) and even the Chicago-originating *Bijou Funnies*.

Next to *Zap, Bijou* is the most consistently impressive title currently being produced. Crumb and Shelton have been regular contributors, but the *Bijou* staff also includes two artists, Jay Lynch and Skip Williamson, with important individual achievements. Lynch, the editor, has a low-key, slightly archaic style which works to good advantage in his tales of "Nard 'n' Pat," which features a dimwitted, straight-laced man with a radical pet cat. Williamson's principal hero is a nattily attired, genial halfwit named Snappy Sammy Smoot. Williamson has also created a series of half-sarcastic views of armed rebellion under the title "Class War Comix."

The underground cartoonists have produced a few comic books with specific themes. Most notorious are the one issue of *Jiz* and the two issues of *Snatch,* titles devoted exclusively to sex, and printed in a smaller size, perhaps in tribute to the old eight-pagers. For some reason, these remarkably graphic entries seem to have had less trouble with the law than *Zap* 4, which has been seized by the authorities in several cities, apparently because of a Crumb piece called "Joe Blow," in which parents seduce their children. Since several of Crumb's stories in *Snatch* and elsewhere show more physical details, it seems that it is the incestuous theme that is intolerable, rather than any specific word or picture.

The untrammeled underground comics may represent the coming trend, or they may be only a temporary aberration. Regardless, there is a sense in which they can be considered part of a larger comic book tradition, a tradition in which realism gives way to exaggeration, and even exaggeration gives way to pure fantasy. The world of comic books is inhabited by supernatural monsters and pseudo-scientific heroes, by animals who act like human beings and human beings who act like animals. Such subjects, because they have a slight relationship to the mundane events of ordinary existence, have caused comic books to be treated condescendingly even by those who can overcome the traditionalist's suspicion of a mixed medium which combines the visual and the verbal.

In the last analysis, however, it must be recognized that the incredible subject matter is not a weakness, but rather the greatest strength of the medium. The surface irrelevance masks a deeper significance. The best comic books probe the subconscious, creating concepts and characters of mythic proportions. Free from the burden of respectability, comic books have provided, for creator and consumer alike, an opportunity to explore the wild dream and desires which seem to have no place in our predominantly rationalistic and materialistic society. In so doing, comic books have won themselves a small but significant place as a key to the American character.

Joseph Witek

SOURCE: "The Underground Roots of Fact-Based Comics," in *Comic Books as History: The Narrative Art of Jack Jackson, Art Spiegelman, and Harvey Pekar*, University Press of Mississippi, 1989, pp. 48-57.

[*In the following essay, Witek discusses the underground comic books of the late 1960s and 1970s as a reaction against the 1954 Comics Code, focusing on the publications* Skull *and* Slow Death Comix.]

E.C.'s *Mad* magazine was able to evade the strictures of the Comics Code only because in 1955 publisher William M. Gaines shifted the format of his biting parodies of American media and social customs from a standard-sized color comic book to a black-and-white magazine. Otherwise the grip of the Code was ironclad; by the late 1950s few comic books were sold in America without the distinctive Comics Code Authority seal of approval. The Comics Code Authority is an independent board established in 1954 by the comic-book industry to review the editorial content of comic books and ensure that they abide by the provisions of the Comics Code, self-proclaimed the "most stringent code in existence for any communications media." The Comics Code established rigid and sweeping rules for the content of comic books: "Guidelines of the authority prohibit displays of corrupt authority, successful crimes, happy criminals, the triumph of evil over good, violence, concealed weapons, the death of a policeman, sensual females, divorce, illicit sexual relations, narcotics or drug addiction, physical afflictions, poor grammar, and the use of the words 'crime,' 'horror,' and 'terror' in the title of a magazine or a story." The nearly universal adoption of the Comics Code is perhaps the single most influential event in the history of the American comic book medium; it efficiently squelched the few postwar comic books that were groping toward a sophisticated audience, and in effect it decreed that all comic books would become the ill-crafted pap toward which most American comics tended anyway. The Comics Code functioned perfectly as an economic instrument of social censorship; magazine distributors, fearful of parental protests, simply refused to handle non-Code-approved books, and dozens of small comic-book publishers folded when they failed to replace their ersatz-E.C. horror and suspense comics with products which were both socially respectable and commercially viable on the newsstands.

Sex, violence, and anarchy in the comics did not disappear after the introduction of the Comics Code, of course; Dr. Wertham, whose inflammatory *Seduction of the Innocent* mobilized the public indignation which spawned the Code, was nonplussed to find in the post-Code comics the same dangerous themes as ever, now, as one writer says, "[disguised] in a hypocritical aura of good taste where the ghastly effects of heartless cruelty were never realistically depicted. Murder looked more like a game than ever under the new self-awarded seal of approval" [Les Daniels, *Comix*].

But despite the chaos peeking through the new bourgeois clothes, comic books were sorely limited in their narrative and thematic possibilities. The Code's ostensible intent was the protection of young and impressionable readers from graphic violence and celebrations of crime, but its provisions work mainly to quell the vitality of the comics and to ratify authoritarian social control. Along with its rules against "violations of good taste or decency," the Code intones: "Policemen, judges, government officials and respected institutions shall not be presented in such a way as to create disrespect for established authority." The Code's insistence that "good" must always triumph over "evil" fossilized the comics' tendency toward oversimplified conflicts and led to thematic and generic stagnation; it stripped away even the vestiges of plot suspense from the crime and adventure comics, and it damned in one phrase the soul of the horror genre, which requires at least the possibility of evil triumphing over good. Not until the introduction of the psychologically torn "hero-villain" in the Marvel superhero comics of the middle 1960s would a semblance of moral ambiguity return to mainstream comic books; the overt conflicts remained as stereotyped as ever, but soap-opera self-doubt eventually replaced melodramatic self-righteousness as the dominant tone of the comic-book hero.

The final effect of the Comics Code was to force comic books to depict a world that was either a denatured view of American social reality (à la Archie and Jughead) or an overtly fantastic never-never land of superpowered Manichean fisticuffs. Historical narratives in comic book form became nearly impossible; the ban on "all scenes of horror, excessive bloodshed, gory or gruesome crimes, depravity, lust, sadism, [and] masochism" can be taken to rule out nearly everything in the history of Western civilization except inspirational biographies and patriotic exemplum. Of course, the rule forbidding "disrespect for established authority" made political satire nearly impossible.

To bash the Comics Code is easy enough: its patent (and successful) attempt to eliminate specific "undesirable" comics publishers is reprehensible; its naive assumption of the unproblematic nature of terms like "good" and "evil" and "excessive violence" would be laughable were its effects not so repressive of free speech; the bland and tedious comic books it mandated are a literary stigma from which the medium has been hard-pressed to recover. But it is important to remember that the Comics Code was not imposed on the industry by the government. In fact, its provisions make hash of the First Amendment and could stand no legal test. But the Code's rules are not laws; they are self-imposed industry guidelines, and as such they simply codified the existing editorial leanings of most American comics. E.C.'s powerfully written war comics failed because of lagging newsstand sales, not because of the meddling of the Comics Code, and while the Code killed off the most sophisticated American comic books, for many other comics the Code simply meant business as usual. The Code officially ruled out overtly mature treatments of adult themes in American comic books, but few such books had existed before the Code anyway, and to blame only the Comics Code Authority for the lack of serious literature in comics form is badly to underestimate the puerility of the comic book publishers and of the mainstream comics audience.

The Code did serve to articulate in an unusually direct and peremptory form the bourgeois artistic (read "moral") standards of postwar America. The bureaucratically enforced wholesomeness of American comic books (parodied unmercifully by their bastard offspring *Mad*) made the medium a specially circumscribed cultural space in which the terms of social rebellion were strictly defined: a comic book which violated the supposedly universal "standards of good taste" was simply not suffered to exist. As a result, when America's rebelling youth of the 1960s set about breaching their culture's established taboos, the comics medium offered a particularly fruitful ground for iconoclasm. Besides the much-heralded innovations in popular music, the most influential and distinctive artistic achievements of the 1960s counterculture were the uninhibited and socially defiant underground comic books, which distinguished themselves from their Code-approved counterparts by adopting the soubriquet "comix." Underground comix were cheaply and independently published black-and-white comics which flourished in the late 1960s and early 1970s as outlets for the graphic fantasies and social protests of the youth counterculture.

To celebrate sex and drugs, as the counterculture did, was offensive to Middle America; to do it in the supposedly simon-pure comic-book form made the violation doubly piquant. The comix often paid homage to their comic-book ancestors by aping the unmistakable cover format and typography of the now-banned E.C. comics and by parodying the ubiquitous Seal of the Comics Code Authority; the interest of the comix in slaughtering sacred cows is clearly seen in the title of the long-running underground anthology *Dr. Wirtham's Comix and Stories,* which lampoons both anti-comic-book crusader

Fredric Wertham and that hoary exemplar of good taste in comics *Walt Disney's Comics and Stories.*

The comix creators cultivated an outlaw image, and their works systematically flung down and danced upon every American standard of good taste, artistic competence, political coherence, and sexual restraint; in so doing they created works in the sequential art medium of unparalleled vigor, virtuosity, and spontaneity—after the underground comix, the Comics Code would never be the same. But comix were a short-lived phenomenon. By the middle 1970s unfavorable court decisions closed most of the drug paraphernalia shops ("head shops") which were the main retail distribution outlets for underground comix, the institution of "community standards" tests for obscenity restricted the areas where comix were allowed, and much of the counterculture's political and artistic energy had dissipated. Major comix artists still work in a format which may be called "underground," but surviving undergrounds retain only a shadow of their former vitality and transgressive force.

The underground comix were too idiosyncratic in approach and too multifarious in subject matter to be adequately summarized here. In fact, their diversity was one of the revolutionary things about them, since they did not have to appeal to the widest possible audience, as did the Comics Code comics. They were a crucial phase in the development of sequential art as a means of artistic expression, and the underground comix movement of the late 1960s and 1970s formed the matrix from which emerged in the 1980s comic books that, unlike the iconoclastic comix, make a new and unprecedented bid for acceptance as literature. Jack Jackson was one of the earliest and most prolific contributors to the comix; Art Spiegelman began his career as a comic-book artist and editor in the undergrounds; Harvey Pekar's earliest work appeared in underground comix, and Pekar's most prominent collaborator on *American Splendor* is Robert Crumb, the greatest talent of the underground movement and one of the major figures in comic-book history.

The underground comix were the first significant group of comic books in America aimed at an entirely adult audience, and the comix proved to a whole generation of readers who had been raised on the vapid Code-approved comics that the sequential art medium is a powerful narrative form capable of enormous range and flexibility. The comix blazed the way for the present-day historical and autobiographical comic books by developing both a group of artists who could write fact-based narratives in comic-book form and an audience prepared to read them.

But while comics such as *American Splendor, Maus,* and *Comanche Moon* would not exist had there been no underground comix, they are not themselves undergrounds, and the difference lies in their attitude toward mainstream America; such writers as Jackson, Spiegelman, and Pekar now actively court a general reading audience. As the words "underground" and "counterculture" suggest, the comix set themselves up in opposition to the dominant culture of the 1960s and 1970s, and much of their energy comes from their persistent efforts to offend the sensibilities of bourgeois America. The comics of the 1950s, with their gory horror and crime extravaganzas, are as nothing, mere innocuous yarns of genteel taste and impeccable morality, compared with such underground classics as S. Clay Wilson's gross and hilarious "Captain Pissgums and His Pervert Pirates," Jim Osborne's tale of drug-induced murder and disembowelment, "Kid Kill!" from *Thrilling Murder Comics,* and Robert Crumb's nightmare/fantasy of castration in "The Adventures of R. Crumb Himself" from *Tales from the Leather Nun.*

Still, the adversarial stance of the undergrounds imposed its own limitations. Works of art which set out to offend most of the public are, if successful, reduced to preaching to the converted, and the unrestrained satire of the undergrounds did at times descend to sophomoric ingroup smugness. Then too the thrill of breaking taboos palls with repetition as iconoclasm itself becomes a rote stylistic gesture. By the late 1970s what had been the underground comix movement was, like the counterculture at large, fragmented and dispersed in its energies. The characteristic psychedelic graphics of the comix had been coopted by American commercial designers; some of the less offensive satirists were absorbed into more respectable outlets for their work such as *Mad's* spiritual heir, the *National Lampoon;* and the end of America's involvement in the Vietnam War found the culture as a whole weary of the political and social confrontation on which the underground comix had thrived.

As a widespread cultural and artistic force the undergrounds lasted barely a decade. But their legacy continues, not only in the work of such established artists as R. Crumb, S. Clay Wilson, and Kim Deitch, who still create vital comic-book work, but also in a growing number of comic-book creators who take from the undergrounds new visions of possibility for comic-book narratives but without that antagonism toward a general audience which so often led to the self-ghettoization of the underground comix.

While all of the undergrounds made an implicit political statement in flaunting the Comics Code, many comix did and still do make overt political critiques of contemporary American society. Naturally enough, given the long tradition of comic books as a humorous form, the primary mode of ideological expression in the comix was satire, Juvenalian with a vengeance, and usually as salacious, scatological, and libelous as possible. For example, the cover of *Yellow Dog* no. 17 features a grinning, cigar-smoking devil, squatting hindquarters-on, defecating a suburban American landscape; in *Uncle Sam Takes LSD,* Uncle Sam similarly relieves himself of the head of Richard Nixon. Faced in their daily lives with the twin terrors of nuclear anxiety and the Vietnam War, the comix creators appropriated the horror genre to political and social satire.

Writers and artists such as Greg Irons, Tom Veitch, Dave Sheridan, William Stout, Rand Holmes, and Richard

Corben used the conventions of horror comic books to satiric effect in comix that included *The Legion of Charlies,* which posits a military coup of the United States by the combined forces of Charlie Manson's murderous "family" and Lt. Calley's Charlie Company from the My Lai massacre. Politics and gore are inseparable in stories such as "You Got a Point There, Pop!" from *Deviant Slice Comix* no. 2, a tale of "the last war between men and women" featuring the black Amazon warrior "Ruth O'Leary of the fighting Fifty-first"; O'Leary informs her male captive that "the roots of the physical struggle between the sexes lies [*sic*] in the SEXISM and IDEOLOGICAL SUPREMISM of the masculine ego" just before she fries and eats his testicles.

Among the longest running of the horror/satire anthologies were *Skull Comix* and *Slow Death Comix. Skull* was not as overtly political as its more didactic and issue-oriented counterpart *Slow Death,* but the two comix shared many of the same contributors, and both took much of their tone and graphic format from the pre-Code E.C. horror comics. For example, advertising blurbs for *Skull* announced it as a comic "in the great old EC horror tradition," the front cover of *Skull* no. 1 sports an E.C. stamp ("An Exorpsychic Comic"), and on its inside cover the underground version of one of E.C.'s trademark "horror hosts," a grinning skull, welcomes his readers:

> Hi kids! Ever wonder what happened to those great old *HORROR* comix that used to scare the shit out of ya way back in the 50's? Well, they all disappeared, an' it wasn't *BLACK MAGIC* what done 'em in, either! Those comix are *GONE*! Until *NOW,* that is! Things bein' as they are these days, a few of us ol' characters decided it was time to revive th' *HORROR* comix . . . in keepin' with th' *times,* y'understand! . . . so here goes—Skull Comix gonna lay it on yer skull. . . . But ya better buy this *FAST* (or better yet, steal it)—cause ya never know when they'll have another great comic book cleanup!

Here the suppression of comic books by the Comics Code is implicitly equated with contemporary political oppression, "things bein' as they are these days," and the paranoia about "another great comic book cleanup" further connects the underground comix project to the unfettered comics of the early 1950s. The salutation "Hi, kids!" is clearly figurative, since the cover reads "ADULTS ONLY, KIDS!" The comix were hardly protective of tender sensibilities (R. Crumb was especially scathing about the American cult of childhood), but like most underground comix, *Skull* and *Slow Death* tried to protect themselves from confiscation and censorship by openly proclaiming their "adult" nature.

Slow Death too was inspired by E.C. comics, but its emphasis on environmental issues made the E.C. science fiction comics rather than the horror comics its natural forebears; *Slow Death* nos. 6 and 7 both mimicked the cover format of E.C.'s *Weird Science-Fantasy,* with its trademark rocket-ship sidebar. For almost a decade *Slow Death* hammered away at the problems of overpopulation, environmental pollution, the extinction of animal species, and nuclear safety by means of stories which wed the conventions of science fiction and horror comics to social satire and didactic essays in sequential art form. For example, Greg Irons's "Our Friend Mr. Atom" in *Slow Death* no. 9 incorporates lists of facts about nuclear bombs and atomic energy in a discussion of geopolitics and cultural attitudes about nuclear arms; the story includes one panel in which a studio audience chuckles and applauds as a Johnny Carson-like talk-show host quips, "There are now enough atomic weapons to destroy the world 600 times over;" in another scene a Donald Duck-like Everyman figure has a huge atomic bomb hammered up his rectum.

In some underground comix which used facts as part of their stories, the simple presentation of the horrifying data of pollution, corruption, and military insanity seemed to make the satiric point without using narrative at all. For example, Greg Irons's "Murder, Inc." from *Slow Death* no. 10 ("Special Cancer and Medical Issue"), includes a two-page spread which both embodies and comments upon the twin poles of sensationalism and didacticism characteristic of the use of facts in the undergrounds (and in historically based comic books in general). Most of the two pages are taken up by large blocks of closely spaced print, one headed "Fun Facts about the Medical Industrial Complex," the other entitled "More Fun Facts . . . The Doctors & the AMA." Across the top of both sections of print runs a comic strip in which a jackass and a baboon dressed as surgeons alternately butcher their comatose patient and attack each other over a botched drug deal. A rakish cigarette-smoking death's-head explains the relation between the two sections: "Now here at Last Gasp we realize that not all of you go for dry, informative, educational-type comic strips. All you sex and violence freaks can just SKIP the following fine print and groove on th' little cartoon here while the rest of you scholarly types read on." Here in "Murder, Inc." the uneasy solution of sober fact and brutal satire in the comix separates out into its component parts.

The educational impulse, with its implicit appeal to empirical authority, works against the visceral impact of the burlesque horror in the comix, which attacks authority by means of ruthless exaggeration and repulsive images. Satiric horror was an effective mode for recreating the anxiety and ugliness of modern industrial culture, but its penchant for shocking overstatement made it less effective in teaching about the particulars of a historical and political situation. Didactic and horror comix still exist, though now in separate venues. The present-day spiritual heirs to *Skull* and *Slow Death* are Kitchen Sink Press's *Death Rattle,* which published the work of horror stalwarts like William Stout and Rand Holmes, and the Educomics series, published by Leonard Rifas, which puts out informational comic books on topics such as nuclear power *(All-Atomic Comics, The Anti-Nuclear Handbook)* and corporate greed *(Corporate Crime Comics, Net Profit).*

Besides their philosophical connections with the E.C. comics, the relevance of the now-defunct *Skull* and *Slow Death Comix* to the present discussion of true stories in the comics is that both comix were the most consistent underground sources for sequential art stories which combined the conventions of horror comics with factual data and history. They were likewise the principal outlets for the work of the artist whom one comics observer has called "the comics' foremost history teacher," the Texas-born Jack Jackson.

Bob Abel

SOURCE: "Up from the Underground: Notes on the New Comix," in *Mass Culture Revisited,* edited by Bernard Rosenberg and David Manning White, Van Nostrand Reinhold Company, 1971, pp. 423-43.

[*In the following essay, Abel interviews underground artists like Art Spiegelman, and notes when underground comic books first came to the attention of Middle America.*]

For the great majority of Americans, probably the first news of underground comics—or comix, to speak a properly underground English—came with the arrival of a late 1970 issue of *Playboy* which signalled the advent of "The International Comix Conspiracy." The blurb for the article, which was by Jacob Brackman, was no less sweeping: "obscene, anarchistic, sophomoric, subversive, apocalyptic, the underground cartoonists and their creations attack all that Middle America holds dear." Moreover, since *Playboy* is a liberal magazine—pubic hair was being liberated from the tyranny of the air brush around this same time—its readers could feel secure from the hostile scrutiny of the underground artists.

Now the *Playboy* audience, large though it may be, is dwarfed by the prime-time evening television audience, and so a great many Americans doubtless first learned of underground comix while watching CBS-TV's *Sixty Minutes* program on the underground press movement in January 1971. Although the program did not dwell on the strips for any length, it did mention them as a regular feature of many of the underground papers.

However, lest future cultural anthropologists be ill-advised on the matter, be it here noted that it was on the 15th of December 1968—roughly two years earlier—that underground comix officially came of age. On that date, *The National Insider,* whose editorial attributes include being "informative," "provocative," and "fearless," not to speak of "entertaining," exposed—the favorite headline verb of this scandal sheet par excellence—the "Latest 'Art' Trend—Hippie Sex Comics." Inside the *Insider,* along with stories on Barbra Streisand ("Color Barbra Sexless") and the civilized world's latest sexual hangup ("Big Breasts Scare Men Stiff!"), the tabloid's puritanical readers were apprised that most of the comic strips found in underground newspapers will "make you sick." A highly indignant article predicting that "If the sick, sick comics continue in Underground newspapers, we will soon see the end of the movement" was surrounded on three sides by specimens of the offending strips, and it is interesting to note that the *Insider* had no compunction about reproducing strips with nasty words in them, nor did it bother about the niceties of running copyright notices or even crediting the material. Oh, well, one editor's sense of legality is another editor's freedom of choice, and the significant thing is that, given this scolding by *The National Insider,* which clearly enough leans toward (and on) a moral imperative, underground comix had surely arrived.

The National Insider notwithstanding, no one has ever accused American culture of being too generously predictable. Thus, while the journey of comix from the easily smudged pages of the *Insider* to the smart walls of the Whitney Museum in Manhattan and other prestigious strongholds of Real Art would seem to be a highly unlikely one—even along those routes so recently charted by the counter-culture—it is nonetheless a fact that by mid-1970 underground comix had already proved intriguing enough to the straight culture for museums to be including them in major shows and for major publishing houses to be readying collections of the work of several artists. Robert Crumb, the best-known artist in the field has had his drawings exhibited, among other places, as part of the Whitney's powerful "Human Concern/Personal Torment" show during the fall of 1969 and both the Viking Press and Ballantine Books have published his work in oversized paperbound editions. (Ballantine now publishes both *R. Crumb's Fritz the Cat* and *R. Crumb's Head Comix,* which Viking originally issued.) In addition, Bantam Books and Dell Books, two of the nation's paperback giants, had by early 1971 committed themselves to underground comix collections, and so the Great American Reading Public was about to be tested on whether it would accept in the home these new subversives out to crease its middle brow. On the other hand, these soft-cover volumes, written by young people with young people in mind, could be sales triumphs simply if enough young people bought them—which if nothing else would keep the whole movement nicely incestuous.

Of course what this may also prove is that whatever American culture does not reject outright, it somehow manages to assimilate. Prior to their modest integration into the straight culture, the creators of underground comix—whatever their degree of professionalism as artists and writers—were characterized chiefly by their unwillingness even to *try* and produce work that might be acceptable either to newspaper syndicates or the publishers of comic books. So, logically enough, underground comix got that way because the first medium in which they appeared for the edification and entertainment—not to speak of titillation—of large numbers of readers was the underground newspaper. Later on, there was a small population explosion of comix magazines, usually sold in paperback galleries—*Zap, Feds 'n Heads,*

Yellow Dog, and *Bijou Funnies* were the important pioneering titles, followed in profusion by (are you ready, Middle America?) *Radical America Komics, Big Ass, Hydrogen Bomb, God Nose, Armadillo, Conspiracy Capers, Captain Guts, Mom's Homemade Comics, The Adventures of Jesus, Slow Death, Despair,* women's lib-uplifting *It Ain't Me, Babe,* and perhaps thirty other titles—but the original impetus to the movement was definitely through the underground papers.

For example, some late 1960s issues of Seattle's *The Helix* were little more than comix and ads, and any one strip originating in an underground paper might appear, via syndication, in scores of other papers. The *East Village Other,* flagship of the underground press movement, was a virtual fountainhead for comix as it attracted a regular group of artists to its pages. These included: of course, Robert Crumb, who is at once the Lenny Bruce and W. C. Fields and Marx Brothers of the field; Spain Rodrigues, whose creation, *Trashman,* features a Che-like, street-fighting "agent" of the 6th Internat'l" who usually won't take leave of his machine gun even to indulge in some nonpartisan sex 'n violence, although some of the other characters in the strip have no such compunctions; Kim Deitch, whose choice of weekly titles for his page in the paper—*Kryptic Kapers, Cul de Sac Comics, Scarey Comix*—do not do justice to a truly uninhibited imagination (Waldo is a super-hip Felix the Cat and Uncle Ed [The India Rubber Man] is a dirty old man worthy of Nabokov); Art Spiegelman, whose *Adventures of Jolly Off, the Masturbating Fiend,* raise the world's least honored but also least expensive sport to new heights; Roger Brand, whose title character, Strawbrick, would have made Candide look like a functioning super-hero and whose collective neuroses ("WHY was I born different . . . ?") would have turned Freud to a different line of work; and Vaughn Bode, a highly gifted, astonishingly prolific artist whose mind turns to fantasy worlds both long ago and long off—machines battle mutants in a world of post-atomic madness, a caveman ponders the wonders of the universe with his best friend (a spear), and talking lizards are warriors in the most bestial human tradition unless confronted with nubile maidens chock full of humanistic sexual responses—and whose draftsmanship already far exceeds most workers in the comics field, whether underground-bound or nationally syndicated.

On the other side of Middle America, another band of drawing renegades were initiating underground comix in their own fashion. (It used to be that San Francisco reflected New York; now there is a cross-cultural, cross-continental transference.) In the Bay City, the peripatetic Robert Crumb—who by virtue of his very large talent, constant output, and widespread syndication throughout the underground press had become the Johnny Appleseed of underground comix—created *Zap Comix* at the same time he was contributing the anti-heroic, pro-hedonistic adventures of Fritz the Cat to *Cavalier* Magazine (then a very lively and provocative magazine of the *Playboy* genre) and also producing deliberately pornographic comix books (*Reader's Digest*-sized at that) which unfortunately were more distinguished for their arrests record than for their contents. Crumb soon became associated with the Print Mint, a Berkeley hostel for underground culture. Its owner, Don Shenker, became at age forty the Instant Grand Old Man of Underground Comix. He not only distributed subsequent *Zaps* but published a tabloid comix paper called *Yellow Dog* (later to switch to comic-book format) that ran not only strips but contributors' sketches and drawings as well, and this latter was some of the more interesting work in the field. [Shenker wrote me at the end of 1968]:

> *Yellow Dog* got started because, partly, interest in posters lagged. We were in the poster business from its inception and when it waned, I turned to comix because the almost violent young public desire which produced the poster boom needed in some way to keep being turned on. For the second part, the artists were present. Here in the Bay Area. Joe Beck (who, I suppose, you might call the father of "underground" comix; he started with the University of California *Pelican* back in the days of the FSM), John Thompson and, finally, the giant of them all, R. Crumb. *Yellow Dog* is a pun and switch of many other things. An American title, out of The Yellow Kid of Pulitzer, out of a nitty gritty dog pissing upon the deepest symbol of the American subconsciousness, Capt. Ahab, who searched and still searches for the White Whale (who, too, pissed on all his black masses and soul-selling.) If Melville was right when he said, about *Moby Dick,* I have written a naughty book, then *Yellow Dog* was designed to be a naughty paper.
>
> Underground comix definitely represent a reaction away from the current comix the same way a loving child leaves home or rots. In the movies the kid sees this chick with her face painted and her tits all trussed up so's they'll look pointy and "sexxy." Well, if you consider this (somewhat like D. H. Lawrence did) with a mind either turned on or fresh in some other way, it's pornographic, and the little books you buy about Popeye and Dick Tracy—"hot books"—are, at least, honest, direct, and done with considerable talent. All of the artists in *Zap, Dog,* etc., pay homage to the old comix you used to buy for 12¢. Harvey Kurtzman is their idol, but they are not tongue-tied before him. They feel his equals. Both Crumb and Gil Shelton (*Feds 'n Heads*) both worked with him before he went to *Playboy.* He himself admires them. But from our correspondence, Kurtzman must, I feel, think of himself now as an old man.

Kurtzman's "prime target in his original *Mad Comics,*" Shenker subsequently pointed out in an article written for *The Daily Californian's Weekly Magazine,* "was the institutionalization of the funnies . . . Where there had been a marvelous, disgruntled quality to the pronouncements of cartoonists, a delightfully anti-usual air, a sourly fantastic and individualistic series of styles and manners before the war, there began to appear a shift. Comics . . . became propagandistic. In short, establishmentarian." Well, it may be argued, I suppose, that the characters of the comic strips had been mobilized in a Great Cause—the defense of democracy and the defeat of fascism—but it is certainly true that after the war the new strips tended toward adventure or soap opera rather than the human comedy. For almost a decade after the war, *Beetle Bailey, Pogo,* and *Peanuts* were the sole distinguished exceptions to the "realistic" turn the postwar strips had taken.

For their part, the contributors to *Yellow Dog* owed no allegiance to comic-strip tradition—except to kid it—and toward American institutions there was scarcely a bugle call except for an occasional cacophonic rendition of *Taps*. Crumb of course was a regular participant—kidding God and man, kidding the State versus man, kidding man versus man, kidding the estate of man, kidding self-knowledge as religion, kidding sex and sexiness, spiritual acne and *angst,* to mention but a few of his comic concerns—as was Gilbert Shelton, who ranks perhaps next to Crumb as the seminal figure of the movement. An émigré from Austin, Texas, Shelton had spent much of the past decade either as student or satirist, or both, and his Wonder Wart-Hog—"the hog of steel"—is unquestionably the ugliest undergrowth super-hero of recent centuries, and properly so. More recently he has concentrated on the Freak Brothers, now appearing under the banner of *The Fabulous Furry Freak Brothers,* not super-heroes but super-"heads" who always keep a huge stash of dope and sometimes get to enjoy it without governmental interdiction. Not necessarily a strip for the "high"-minded only, Shelton's creation may well represent the comic apotheosis of the drug culture in America. Like Crumb, and a few others in the comix field, Shelton can generally be expected to tell a funny story and there exists in his work a sense of broad comedy that is itself a kind of maturity, and evidence that an artist not only is enjoying what he is doing, but is reasonably certain of his achievement.

This is not to say, for a moment, that Crumb and Shelton were the only talents associated with *Yellow Dog* worth a bit of critical howling about, one way or the other. Joel Beck, a former Berkeley student who had already published two books—*The Profit,* a mixed bag of clever and under-realized satire, and *Lenny of Laredo,* good fun, a bit obvious, but, happily, no part of the Lenny Bruce industry that emerged after the comedian's death—continued his acerbic spoofs of American society in the comix paper (first of its kind, it was followed by *Gothic Blimp Works,* originally edited by Vaughn Bode, then by *East Village Other* editors, but now defunct). Ron White, who appears a Beck disciple, did a nice turn on the comic-strip medium itself (and its Pleistocene Era rules) via his B. Bear character whose specialty is getting arrested "for appearing in a comic strip without a morality card." And John Thompson's *The Spiritual Stag Film,* never to be an art director's delight, was nonetheless refreshingly irreverent because of its ofttimes sly and/or cranky lead character, Sam God, who concedes without too much rancor that "all prayers have two parts: one: butter him up [and] two: ask for something." There was also frequently arresting visual material by a variety of artists, including Franz Cilensek and Buckwheat Florida, Jr.—who owns the grandest name in underground comix—which suffered somewhat because of the newsprint on which *Yellow Dog* was then printed (and on which the capricious canine, with undisguised glee, always pisses).

There are also four other artists who contributed to the early issues of *Zap* and *Yellow Dog* whose work—if one is going to apply serious standards to underground comix—requires more extensive analysis. Three of them are demonstrably among the half-dozen or so finest draftsmen in the field. The exception to this is S. Clay Wilson, a transplanted Kansan who is easily the most violent artist in the comix field, and so all enjoy distinction.

Robert Crumb has credited Wilson with inaugurating the "sex revolution" in comix, and this is a little bit like Washington crediting Jefferson for the whole Revolution bit. Still, no one in the comix field has utilized sex and bloodshed to such a degree as has Wilson—and what Crumb refers to is Wilson's apparent refusal from the beginning to accede to any self-censorship. His plots are usually short on narrative and his visual center-piece is frequently an orgiastic clash between various adversaries (pirates, both sides mostly homosexual; motorcycle gangs, both sides in part homosexual; monsters and people, the sexual climate confusing, but predictably violent; pirates and their modern counterparts, Hell's Angels, with a time warp providing the drama) that culminates in a literal or metaphorical ship's hold of sperm and gore. Wilson's work is generally too non-stop violent to be very pornographic, sometimes too pornographic to be entertaining, and depressingly restrictive in terms of the characters he depicts—all are physically repulsive and treacherous if not evil incarnate. Yet there is a raw power and compelling quality to his work—in particular the group clashes—and a legitimate exploitation of the grim strain of violence in American life that make him an artist if not worthy of the associations with Hieronymus Bosch that have cropped up in some writings about him—then at least one well worth a continuing critical attention. If nothing else, it makes for good reading—and can be just as deliciously cultist as the writing about films these days.

For example, in the Summer 1970 (No. 12) issue of *Funnyworld,* an excellent comics fanzine—fan magazine devoted to a certain field, in this instance comic strips and books and animated cartoons—Bob Follett, a veteran observer of the comic art field, responded to the sharp criticism of Wilson made by Mike Barrier, *Funnyworld*'s editor, in a previous issue. "I can't really write a rebuttal to your comments on Wilson," he wrote, doing just that. "Your argument used the premise that there are subjects and styles which should be closed to the cartoonist for reasons of propriety. Wilson fails, in your opinion, because his characters, draped in an abundance of warts and a paucity of clothing, are invariably involved in pastimes that will never make it to the late late show."

Follett goes on to say that this sort of criticism is useless to the underground comix reader "since he generally doesn't share your aversions," and an examination of Wilson's techniques and achievements as a cartoonist—not "the moral suitability of his subjects"—is a more legitimate measure of his work. "Wilson's pluses are as magnificent as his failings," Follett continues his auteuristic style-before-substance argument. "I would imagine that he fails as a cartoonist in the normal sense. There is little if any coherence to a Wilson's 'story line.' Wilson produces images—vivid, vivid images . . . the major fault in Wilson's work and one which may relegate him forever to the group of also-rans—given the absence of a story line and limiting himself to 'meth' freaks, motorcycle bandits, dyke queens, and tide monsters—give or take a wall-eyed professor of two—Wilson can only come up with a certain very finite number of combinations for his drawings. The 'meth' freaks can only meet so many 'Screaming Gypsy Bandits' before the work loses its charm. But Wilson will answer this question for us in the next couple of years."

Writing in that same issue, Barrier, who publishes *Funnyworld*—now a magazine grown from its mimeographed days to one professional in looks as well as contents—as a sidelight to his columnist job at the *Arkansas Gazette,* returned to his criticism of Wilson in an article which deals, among other things, with what he feels is a sex obsession among underground cartoonists. "There can be no valid 'moral' objection to Wilson's work," he wrote, apparently utilizing editor's prerogative in responding to material elsewhere in the magazine, "even though every imaginable sexual practice takes place in his strips. No girl is ever going to be seduced in an underground comic book. My basic complaint about Wilson's work is that it *is* moral, in the narrowest, nastiest sense. I said back in *Funnyworld* No. 10 that S. Clay Wilson impressed me as an uptight little old lady in disguise. By that I mean that he seemed to share an attitude common to many little old ladies, that sex—and, by implication, life itself—is dirty and disgusting. It is in his strips, certainly. His people are all warts, moles, sweat, flab, and body hair (he can make any part of the human anatomy unappealing) and all freaks in one way or another. However there's no indication that 'normal people' would come out looking any better. He looks at humans as a Houyhnhnm might. Wilson refuses to see human beings as a whole; rather, he seizes on physical imperfections and magnifies them. This may be preferable to what happens in syndicate comic strips and traditional comic books, where everyone seems to have been photographed through those Doris Day gauzes, but it's still a distorted and limited way of looking at things."

Now whereas Wilson—and it may be fairly argued, I think, that his distortions of behavior as well as physiognomy are precisely what make his work distinctive (and of course could make it ultimately repetitious and boring)—is among the best known, and easily the most controversial artist in the field, another West Coast artist, Andy Martin, is hardly known, apart from readers of *Yellow Dog,* yet his is a talent that is all the more remarkable for being unique in the field. Martin does not draw comix—he draws political cartoons utilizing the strip form. His line is extremely fine—one is reminded of Lyonel Feininger, the artist who also drew comic strips in the first part of the century, and certain German expressionists—and it is applied to truly savage caricature that builds its effects through distorted bodies with recognizable faces and arresting compositions within the individual panels. His is an inside-out Alice in Wonderlandish trip—picture Alice high on LSD—sounding as though it must be written, though the dialogue is sparse, simultaneously by Thomas Pynchon, Paul Krassner, Timothy Leary, the late Dr. Eric Berne, and Jean Shepherd, with walk-ons by Norman Mailer and Jules Feiffer. Yet it is more the surreal art that makes Martin's work so different. There is nothing like it in comix, comics, or political cartooning in this country.

For example, an early *Yellow Dog* cover depicted Lyndon Johnson defecating on top of a toilet bowl that bore the features of the 1968 Democratic candidate for President—surely a vulgar comic conceit—but the meaning behind the image made this a powerful cartoon and one that many readers might find more telling than, say, a caricature of Johnson by David Levine or one by England's Gerald Scarfe, whose distortions always go for the jugular and thus have become somewhat predictable. Martin's satiric world is one in convoluted progress: His *Hop-Frogian Bible,* "Featuring Dr. Caligari as gynecologist," and dealing with the adventures of Prof. Murayev, Mr. Pueno, Ave, Trippeta, Ahab, and of course Hop-Frog himself (partial cast of characters at that) practically requires a magnifying glass to read because so much is going on. But it is worth the effort because what's there is a visual looney tune deliberately playing against our notions of expectation and order. It is at once chaotic and richly entertaining: Nothing is resolved except our desire to see what happens next. And in that regard, the observations of Don Shenker, who, after all, published Martin, are particularly relevant. Shenker points out that Martin's characters "dwell in a machinistic landscape: they are twisted and crippled by the horror of steel bulkheads which end in vanishing points. Also they are extraordinarily literate. It is not enough that they leer and wring their hands in expectation of imminent catastrophe, but they fly to and fro about it, packing machines like 'fallacy filters' and screaming, 'Dissect the political animal!'" Martin, Shenker adds, agonizes over his work and I doubt if his total published output would consume one issue of *Yellow Dog,* but he is an artist whose promise is not merely looming—it is here with us now, exciting and significant—and whose future work should provide additional reason for our admiration.

The question of what is and what is not estimable in the comix field now logically leads us to consider the cases of Rick Griffin and Victor Moscoso, whose published fantasies are much admired in the field and much emulated. Picture the entire Walt Disney Studios high on something or other and you perhaps may then be able to conjure up a vision of Griffin's and Moscoso's work, which seems at once so private—seemingly drawn while on drugs and probably best enjoyed in the same state—and yet so adroitly drawn that it represents a wing of underground comix that is both fascinating and more or less inaccessible. Here I omit Moscoso's delightful on-going orgy in *Zap* No. 4, in which comic strip and movie cartoon characters as well as a variety of other creatures—most notably Mr. Peanuts of candybar fame—participate for several pages in what must be comix' most densely-populated orgy to date, but it is hardly a generalization to regard these two gentlemen as deliberate (though not necessarily self-conscious) proponents of something avant-garde in the comix field. And, as I say, they have their followers.

For what it is worth, and I do not mean to be snide when I say that I am not at all certain *what* it is worth, I offer Jacob Brackman's explanation in *Playboy* as to what Griffin and Moscoso are up to:

> Much as experimental playwrights pare theater back to basics, Griffin and Moscoso break down comics into their fundamental integers, toy with reassembling them in slow motion, at odd moments freezing transformations midway. Griffin uses words nonsensically. Moscoso hardly uses them at all. Both are fascinated with speech and thought balloons, floating exclamation points, idea bulbs—all of which gain a third dimension, open to reveal their innards, interact with characters and landscapes. The continual flux of their worlds, in which every element is equally animate, achieves the obliviousness of pure play—suggesting true liberation from the old necessity for significance, from any obligation to one's readers.

Anyone familiar with the bulk of Brackman's writing knows him to be a writer of intelligence, but one has to question the true significance of a comic artist's not wishing to communicate. And if "pure play" is a virtue, it should be fun to witness. Saul Steinberg, for instance, makes no concessions to easy comprehension of his work and the greatest accomplishments in comic strips have been creations that manage to communicate on a multitude of levels. It's a silly business to over-intellectualize the funnies, but *Krazy Kat* provided more visual pleasure than just the business of seeing Krazy get hit in the head with a brick thrown by Ignatz (George Herriman's shifting backgrounds, best seen in the Sunday colored pages, and his use of phonetic language were both things of joy), and Walt Kelly's *Pogo* has provided some of the more salient political satire of the past two decades. Being syndicated and being "something else"—both in the usual and hip senses of the term—is what divides the best of popular art from the packaged goods. Brackman rightly observes that Griffin and Moscoso share with other underground artists a fascination with comic strips' past, but theirs is a psychedelic vision, and not a shared vision, and I fail to see—which may be *my* failing, of course—that it affords much pleasure. Neither artist is under any obligation to do other kinds of drawing, but one suspects that they will find their present mode of expression rather constricting and it will surely be interesting to see where their sense of playfulness may lead them. This observer, at least, would welcome a de-Disneyized comic world in which Snow White ravishes the Seven Dwarfs, and Minnie Mouse and Donald Duck are guilty of miscegenation.

Turning away from the San Francisco area, which is unquestionably the hot center of underground comix these days, we head eastward toward the Bijou Publishing Empire, which appears on no map of Chicago. *Bijou Funnies,* one of the best of the underground comix magazines, is the co-conception of a pair of energetic artists, Skip Williamson and Jay Lynch, whose comix capers are the core of *Bijou Funnies*. The magazine itself represents the happy end product of a lifetime interest in comic art. Throughout their teens both Lynch and Williamson had edited and contributed to numerous fanzines and their mimeographed columns of disputation, worship, and scholarship, and it is worth a lengthy examination of the role of fanzines in leading artists to the comix field for the simple reason that so many underground artists *have* followed this route. Moreover, for purposes of authenticity, we may look to Lynch himself, who offers a highly personable and informative story of his (and Williamson's) odyssey into the underground.

Lynch writes (and his letter is reproduced more or less in the free-form style in which it was written):

> In 1960, when normal teens were going to sock hops and doing th' stroll and stuff, Skip Williamson, Artie Spiegelman and I were involved in producing cartoons for what was and still is known as "fandom." I was living with my parents in Miami, Fla., and was going to high school. Skip was living in Canton, Missouri, and going to high school. Artie was living in Rego Park, N.Y., and going to junior high school. Then somehow the three of us started doing cartoons for fanzines. Fanzines are little mimeographed or hectographed magazines that deal with a specific topic. There are science fiction fanzines, classical music fanzines, there are even fanzines that just ramble on for entire issues about how they went about putting out each issue of the previous fanzine. We were into what was called satire fandom. We did cartoons for satire fanzines, which would try to imitate old *Mad* comics. The first satire fanzine we were exposed to was *Smudge,* which was edited by Joe Pilati, who is now a columnist for the *Village Voice*. *Smudge* had a circulation of eighty. Soon other satire fanzines began to appear. *Wild* and *Jack High* were two of the ones to come out immediately after *Smudge*. *Wild* lasted ten issues, more than any satire fanzine of the early sixties. After a while Skip started his own fanzine called *Squire* and Spiegelman started one called *Blasé*. We all contributed to each other's fanzines, and everything went along pretty much the same till 1963. So for three years the three of us were into fandom. Robert Crumb was doing a fanzine called *Foo* around this time, but none of us paid much

> attention to it. Robert was into what was known as funny animal fandom. Walt Bowart of the *East Village Other* (formerly editor and publisher) was doing a science fiction fanzine in the early sixties. Harvey Ovshinsky, who now edits *The Fifth Estate,* which is Detroit's underground newspaper, did a fanzine then called *Transylvanian Newsletter*. Harvey was into monster fandom. Fanzines were not only the original underground press, but many underground cartoonists started out in fandom as well. Trina, a girl cartoonist who does these art nouveau comics for *E.V.O.* was into what is called *femmefandom*. Trina was a femfan. Femfans just put out magazines about how neet it is to be a girl.
>
> Fanzines were good because doing stuff for fanzines taught me to discipline myself. For three years I turned out at least ten pages a month of comic strips.

It wasn't, of course, merely the discipline of fanzine cartooning which profited Lynch and the others, but also the camaraderie of the thing.

Recalls Lynch:

> In 1961, Spiegelman and his parents visited Miami. I got together with Artie and we talked about what the cartoonists we admired were up to and stuff. I used to correspond with Skip and Artie, and it was very good that we did this. We'd share all the knowledge that we were gaining by writing each other and telling the other guy what was happening. Artie would write to tell me of a new comic book that came out. He'd send the address, and I'd mail away for a copy. If it weren't for this correspondence network we had I'd have missed a lot of good stuff. We really dug the work of Jack Davis, Basil Wolverton, Wally Wood, all the old comic book guys.
>
> In 1962 I contributed to *Cracked,* an imitation of *Mad; PREP;* a teen age mag for which I did a regular comic strip about an Archie-type guy called *Hoagie*. Hoagie was hip and neet and sharp. He had a hot rod with twelve cams and he could do the twist. I also did some cartoons for *Zig Zag Libre,* a Cuban exile newspaper in Miami. Everybody must have a cause, so I began to identify with the Cuban exiles. Nobody would print integration cartoons then, especially in Miami.

At some point in the narrative, Lynch has moved to Chicago, a move which augers all kinds of big-time possibilities. [Lynch continues:]

> Canton, Missouri, where Skip lived, is only 250 miles from Chicago, Skip came to visit me, and I went to visit Skip, and soon we were planning stupendous feats of cartooning together. The first thing we did was to visit the cartoon editor at *Playboy,* a fruitless pursuit which we had repeated every six months for several years. *Playboy* doesn't use new cartoonists. The cartoon editor has all these really nice cartoons on the wall of her office—great stuff by dynamic new guys—but, alas, they'll never see print. 1963 was a year when *Playboy* was going through a fantastic rate of growth—not wanting to risk their reputations, they decided to use only the cartoonists which they'd been using before. *Playboy* hasn't had a new cartoonist for six years. [Author's note: This communication from Lynch reached me in early 1969]. Eventually Skip and I got sick of going to *Playboy*—we realized that there was no hope of getting into the magazine at this point.
>
> Skip and I took to sending gag cartoons through the mail to magazines in other cities. I appeared in Harvey Kurtzman's *Help* then, and Skip did, too. Soon we had stuff in *The Realist* and many other mags, but it got to the point where more stuff was lost by the various editors than was printed.
>
> Now the year is 1965. College mags were going out and underground newspapers were starting up. The first underground comic strip that I saw was a thing called 'Captain High' in an early issue of the *East Village Other*. This was about a guy who would take LSD and turn into a super hero. It was really crude. The art was poor. Soon Gilbert Shelton had a thing in *EVO* called 'Clang Honk.' By this time I had started doing surrealist comic strips. I don't know why. I hadn't taken acid yet. I hadn't seen anybody else doing surrealist strips, but everybody started doing them in '65. For me it was a Bob Dylan influence—I was trying to do the same thing in comic strips that Dylan was doing in music. Some early surrealist strips that Skip and I did are in the *Chicago Mirror*. We did them two years before the *Mirror,* came out, though. The early surrealist strips that I did were printed in *Nexus,* a San Francisco literary magazine, and in *Oyez,* the literary magazine at Culver Stockton College which Skip edited. I was working nights as a short order cook in a restaurant. Soon I started doing cartoons for the *Chicago Seed,* the local flower kids' newspaper. In 1966 I took LSD and didn't draw anything but paisleys for the *Seed* for six months.
>
> So now it's 1967 and Skip, who has moved to Chicago, and I are doing things for the *Seed,* but the paper is not printing our stuff well. As soon as we give the *Seed* a cartoon, they photostat it so someone can take home the original art to hang on their wall. Then they make a reduction of the photostat and make an offset negative from that, so by the time it gets printed it's fourth generation instead of second, and it's all blurry and illegible. So Skip and I decide to do our own magazine.
>
> We did the *Chicago Mirror,* which we published quarterly for three-fourths of a year—1967-68—we called it the *Mirror* because we couldn't think of anything better. We decided that if a better title came up, we'd just change it. So I wanted to call it *Bijou* Magazine. Then we realized that we're cartoonists and we really wanted to do a comic book anyway. *Zap Comix,* Crumb's thing, partially inspired *Bijou,* but not totally, since some of the stuff in *Bijou* No. 1 was done before *Zap* came out. It's kind of a spontaneous generation thing—comix are happening all over the place. But without Crumb's breakthrough with the first *Zap,* nobody

> would have done any one hundred percent comix magazine. I can't really say that, though—underground comix have always been around. Jack Jaxon in Austin, Texas, did one called *God Nose* in 1963. It was a great comic book about God and his magical nose. . . .
>
> The other day Skip said to me, 'You know, if there ever *is* a revolution, we'll be big folk heroes after it's over.' But the thing is that there *is* a revolution going on right now! It's a revolution of the mind—of perception and sanity. The sanity of mankind is changing, and a whole new anti-intellectual generation of kids is growing up. Comix books will fill the space that the death of newspapers will leave. Comix will be an integral part of the life of humans in the future. This is why old ladies are down on comic books—they *know* what it's all about. The very old and the very young know. People's opinions were formed by comic books they read in the first seven years of their lives. Now a new wave of adult comix books comes along and changes their opinions. It's the ultimate medium! No question about it.

On this question, Lynch might get some argument from authorities who have busted bookstores selling underground comix in at least two cities—in particular *Zap* #4, with its chronicle of good-natured incest among members of the Joe Blow Family—but among comix artists in general there does exist a carryover of youthful interest in comics that has now matured into white heat enthusiasm for the new strips *they* are now creating.

Vaughn Bode: "I started drawing when I was six, and by the time I was in college I had 1,500 named cartoon characters—recorded in a book. It became a fetish to invent and invent—out-invent everyone on earth . . . I built my own planets—I believe in those planets—and most of the equipment I use in the strips (fighting machines with the worst of human traits), I've designed," he says, adding with a small smile the information that his "Hypocket Infantry Machines, Model 1940" have "developed a disease—empathy—they cry." Bode does elaborate model sheets for his "machines" before putting them into action, and if all this begins to sound a bit compulsive, he'd probably be the last one to deny it. The important thing, of course, is that the work is so well-drawn, genuinely offbeat and often highly perceptive in its analysis of mankind's foibles. "I need to express myself," says Bode. "The work is me. I can't be at ease—all my emotions go into my work. I think Kim Deitch is the same. I know Crumb is the same."

Peter Bramley (who is both underground cartoonist and above-ground commercial artist):

> I've been interested in doing comics, literally, all my life. I think the strongest thing about the cartoon is the vulgarity of the drawing—the whole lack of subtlety is what visually happens . . . when you see a Japanese or Chinese comic book, you realize you don't *need* writing.

Art Spiegelman:

> You're very aware you're working in the comic book form . . . We've all gone through a phase of treating comics as art instead of comics—then after a certain phase, you *know* they're art and treat them like comics again . . . It *is* a groovy form—you do the words *and* the art.

Moreover, as in any other field, there are both the broad general influences and the private jokes, as it were, which really turn on an artist.

Peter Bramley:

> I'm into *Smokey Stover* and *Krazy Kat,* and I'm into mouses a lot—I really love mouses!

Art Spiegelman: "I'm into Winsor McCay (creator of a fabulously drawn comic strip of yesteryear called *Little Nemo in Slumberland*) and Jay Lynch is into funny animal comics and Crumb is into Rube Goldberg." (Apparently there is a subdivision of underground comix entirely given to assigning influences to Robert Crumb. The artist himself told an interviewer that he had been influenced by Jules Feiffer, Chester Gould [*Dick Tracy*], Harold Gray [*Little Orphan Annie*], Elzie Segar [*Popeye*] and Harvey Kurtzman. Roger Brand allows Crumb Elzie Segar, adds Billy DeBeck [*Barney Google*], then insists "it's quite obvious his biggest influence is Basil Wolverton." Mike Barrier observed in *Funnyworld* No. 12 that Crumb's work "looks 'old-fashioned' but no one agrees on which 'old-fashioned' cartoonists had the most to do with shaping his style. Billy DeBeck, Elzie Segar, Carl Barks, Basil Wolverton, John Stanley . . . the list is a long one. Anyone whose style seems to reflect that many influences . . . and yet is clearly in thrall to no one of them . . . has to be a good cartoonist, and a supreme synthesizer.")

Kim Deitch:

> I was a painter—I *came* to New York to be a painter—and Winsor McCay really snapped my mind. Then, during the winter of '66, I started getting interested in *Marvel Comics* and my paintings started to look like comics. I just fell into the *EVO* thing. The first thing I brought there wasn't accepted by Walter Bowart because he wanted something psychedelic, but when I came back with *Sunshine Girl,* Walter thought it was a real underground character. To me, *Sunshine Girl* was about the most organic thing possible, but I guess it was a case of being in the right place at the right time.

Interestingly enough, the emergence of underground comix—it is surely propitious timing, as Deitch infers, that the underground papers were there to provide a forum for artists whose material wouldn't stand much chance of exposure in the professional cartoon field—has happened at the *same* time that professional cartoonists have also been raising fandom to a new level. Some working cartoonists, weary of following the commercial formulas of the marketplace, have been contributing more personal—and frequently more imaginative—efforts to various magazines which exist for just that purpose. *Star-Studded Comics,* published by two Carrollton, Texas, comics buffs named Howard Keltner and Buddy Saunders, is actually pretty conventional comic book stuff with its *Xal-kor, the Human Cat, Doctor Weird,* and *Powerman,* but *Nick Fury, Agent of S.H.I.E.L.D.* is, at the least, graphically impressive. More significant to our examination of the underground comix phenomenon, however, are two publications, *Graphic Story Magazine* and *witzend,* where both underground artists and professionals have been—let the phrase be forever buried after this one, last, dastardly usage—doing their thing.

Graphic Story Magazine, formerly *Fantasy Illustrated,* is edited and published by a Los Angeles gentleman named Bill Spicer, and he does nice work. The magazine, printed on heavy stock, serves as a forum for comic book buffs to indulge in scholarly critiques and launch broadsides at one another, but its more arresting function for the outsider is to publish innovative graphic material. Issue Number Nine, for instance, had an engrossing twenty-one-page rendering of a story by Robert Sheckley, the noted science fiction writer, drawn by Vincent Davis, which found three criminal entrepreneurs searching on a deserted Mars for the ultimate weapon that had destroyed the inhabitants there. It turns out to be a genie-like creature—if that is the term for it—with a voracious appetite for protoplasm. End of Mars, it is explained, and end of the explorers from Earth. *Graphic Story* has also been running the work of George Metzger, whose *Kaleida Smith* and *Master Tyme and Mobius Tripp* represent a level of intricacy and sophistication of story that I strongly doubt is matched anywhere in the commercial comic-book field. Metzger's exciting—an interesting head in action. He's also damn hard to read and could stand an art editor who would make his work even more provocative—science fiction come to startling graphic realization.

Issue Number Ten ran featured two Vaugh Bode sections—*The Man,* an early caveman series, and *The Machines,* another Bode World War III-plus projection—that seemed to split *Graphic Story* readers almost diametrically (it's nice they react). The more recent issues of *Graphic Story* seem to be devoting proportionally more space to long interviews with veteran artists from the comics field, which, while certainly a valuable service, is not likely to have much influence on young cartoonists whose only artistic theory seems to be that radical culture at first borrows freely from the past, then rapidly creates its own cultural antecedents. It would be too bad if Spicer cannot afford both to honor the past and provide a proving ground for the future. But this is observation, not criticism, because without a doubt the work Spicer and the editors of other fanzines are doing will be of more than passing interest to libraries and future historians of comic art.

Witzend is another matter, entirely. True, both magazines, professional as they are, avoid the marketplace entirely and are only available by subscription. Even getting back issues can be a problem. Still, *witzend* started off with a specific future cast—the cultivation of a sophisticated audience and the utilization of the magazine as a sounding board and preview theater for artists.

Wallace Wood, whose parodies of comic strips are delightfully familiar to anyone who read the first decade of *Mad,* founded *witzend* in 1967 as an occasional "public service." Wood wrote in the second issue of *witzend* that he regards the magazine as a "unique publication comprised of *editorless* [emphasis added] artistic creations from the minds and hands of some very talented people. It is a place to experiment, as well as to display some previously unpublished work done by professional artists for their own enjoyment. And to establish copyrights on properties which may have commercial possibilities." He also noted that the magazine "does not and will not seek general distribution by diluting any contribution to suit the preconditioned tastes of a mass audience."

Given these bold words, it's only fair to apply them, as a critical frame of reference, to what *witzend* has published to date. The magazine has featured, among others, Vaughn Bode, Roger Brand, and Art Spiegelman, plus such well-known "pros" as Harvey Kurtzman *Mad*'s Don Martin, Jeff Jones, and Steve Ditko—the latter two comic-book artists—and of course Wood himself. Perhaps the most experimental element, at least in contrast to comics published under the Comics Code, has been a fondness for drawing bare breasts. Since the artists supplying these works of art are good-to-excellent draftsmen, this has not been an unpleasant surprise—there are tons of tits in underground comix, but, taken as a group, the artists are not superior draftsmen and, indeed, would seem to prefer drawing grotesque creatures—and the breasts have helped decorate some interesting science fiction and fantasy material.

However, the best of these strips has been Jones' outer space tale, entitled *Alien,* in *witzend* No. Six, which relied on breastworks not at all, instead utilizing extremely fine graphics to tell a story with almost no reliance on dialogue. *Alien* is an example of the service the magazine can provide its readers, but some of the other professional artists have merely given *witzend* more extreme versions of what they regularly produce for the comic-book racks. The most controversial of these artists has been Ditko, whose *Mr. A.* and *The Avenging World* (this a visual lecture rather than a strip) depict a moral universe strictly divided by an East Berlin Wall of good versus bad. Ditko's work has prompted one reader to cite the artist's "small-minded, arrogant ignorance . . . this piece is a total failure in its blind hatred," and in *witzend* No. Seven, Bill Pearson, now editor of the magazine, and artist Tim Brent parodied Mr. A. with their Mr. E., a "crusading moralist and amateur economist of the quid pro quo" whose "rigid, stony facemask [conceals] the rigid, stony face beneath." By my lights, *Mr. E.* was the most interesting thing in this issue, but the issue was hardly a milestone in *witzend*'s first four years of publishing.

The contributions of underground artists to *witzend* have also been uneven in roughly the same scale that *witzend* has been uneven. I enjoyed Brand's *Homesick,* a time-travel fantasy set in Atlantis and in the here and now, but Bode's brutal salute to war, *The Junkwaffel Invasion of Kruppeny Island* was cruelly crowded on four pages and far too text-heavy. Ironically enough, the most admirable work to date has been Wood's delightful on-going "fairy tale," *Pipsqueak Papers,* but the artist is no longer formally associated with the magazine, having sold it, after four issues, to the Wonderful Publishing Company for the vast sum of one dollar. The only proviso to the purchase, apart from the selling price, was that *witzend* publish at least four more issues in an attempt to achieve artistic, if not financial, solvency.

In 1970 Bill Pearson, who is both editor and publisher, moved his home and the magazine to Arizona, where he hopes to continue publishing it. He recognizes that there must be far more to *witzend* than merely providing a showcase for unpublished commercial material. On the other hand, he doesn't expect to find salvation emanating solely from the underground activity. "It's a great personal artform," he observes, "and you can do things with it. But not enough of the guys have, yet. You have to have a theme."

Thematic direction, of course, usually implies firm editorial direction, and my equally firm suspicion is that underground comix magazines will most prosper when they either are drawn by one person (Crumb has done several entire magazines) or else are run by a strong editor, one kicking the amateurism and self-indulgence out. But this is precisely *not* the way most underground comix are being published—usually they are happening, not being published—and the artists *are* right when they say that the most important aspect to the field is a freedom of expression which would be virtually impossible to attain in the commercial world.

Just as important, this freedom takes many forms. For Jay Lynch, whose *Nard n' Pat* is one of the most "traditional"-looking strips, the fun and charm (rare commodity in the comix field as yet) of his work may simply be the reversal of roles whereby his human character, the chinless, and feckless, Nard has to play foil to Pat th' Cat, a lascivious-minded "kitty-kat" who places ads in the underground press ("Chicks, howdjya' like ta' share my pad? I'm a groovie cat with a way-out mustache.") and who will good-naturedly seduce the "Avon calling" lady at the ring of a doorbell. Lynch's drawing calls up a host of influences (would you believe *Andy Gump*?) but his dialogue and writing are more irreverent and far more playful than will be found in all but a few syndicated comic strips. And, like Crumb, his strips often kid the comic strip medium itself, and in general break all the rules with which above-ground art cartoonists have to live.

Lynch's *Bijou* buddy, Skip Williamson, draws terrific covers and his continuing strip, *Snappy Sammy Smoot,* is one of the more highly stylized in the field—(there is more cross-hatching in some individual panels than there is artwork in some of the cruder comix strips). But what is even more interesting about *Snappy Sammy Smoot* is that it manages to be politically radical at the same time it is satirical and funny and looks like nothing else in the field. Sammy is a well-meaning *nebbish* to whom things happen and this strip and others of Williamson's often take the logic of Establishment dicta to their painfully logical consequences—flower power is no match for police power. However, in a marvelous one-page strip in *Bijou* No. Three entitled *Class War Comics,* a hairy revolutionary echoes the "BRA DAP! FOOM!" of his machine gun with this roar: "EAT LEADEN DEATH IMPERIALISTIC REACTIONARY BUSINESS ADMINISTRATION MAJORS!!" And in the last panel, he reminds us: "An' when yer smashing th' state, kids . . . don't fergit t' keep a smile on yer lips an' a song in yer heart!" Williamson may not be working to overthrow "the System" in some secret revolutionary cell (indeed, now that he is a parent he holds down a day job at *Playboy,* that formerly unhospitable corporation), but his strips slyly, and not so slyly, get a lot of ideas out. "For me," Williamson explains, "it's like an absurd reflection of what happens to me personally. I don't write a script—I work from panel to panel—it's sort of a stream of consciousness comic strip."

Not sex or politics or Mom or any of our hallowed notions but censorship itself may be the only taboo in the comix field, and so for many of the young artists there is a rite of passage equivalent to masturbating in public. Hopefully this is simply a growth point, since most of this work is neither very erotic nor very funny. In any case, S. Clay Wilson and Robert Crumb got there first, although my own feeling about Crumb is that he always tries to be funny and therefore will always manage to produce a kind of smut rather than pornography because there is too much joy and fun in his work to allow prurient interest, his *or* ours, to become dominant in his work. He has already created the largest and most memorable cast of characters in the field: Fritz the Cat, Mr. Natural, Flakey Foont, Whiteman (I'm an AMERICAN! . . . A real hard charger! . . . A Citizen on the go!"), Schuman the Human, Angel Food McSpade, Edgar and Mary Jane Crump, Lenore Goldberg (and her Girl Commandos), plus that epitome of slobdom, Bo Bo Bolinski. His comedy, taken as a body of work, has been the most ebullient force in the comix field. As Don Shenker has written of him, "Nothing is sacred except talent; that is life. Nothing is forbidden except not exercising talent/life," and when I spoke to Crumb some months back and mentioned that *Snatch Comics* ("Are you tired of sex books that promise but never deliver? Tired of looking for the good stuff? Search no further, Bud!") had seemed to zap (yes! an underground pun) all taboos in a single outing, his response was spontaneous: "If taboos were broken by *Snatch Comics*—groovy? Then we can move on to something else. There are millions of other ideas—

I've got so many ideas for comix I wish I had more time to draw!" Similarly, Art Spiegelman, whose work has been both lyrically psychedelic and cheerfully scatological, points out that an artist's kicks derived from violating taboos can be simply another form of conformity. "Professionals think it's a big thing to draw a bare tit," he says. "I'll only transgress them [taboos] when I've something to say. Originally I was going to take a book by Dave Breger called *How to Draw and Sell Cartoons* and violate each taboo he listed. Sex, nudity, religion, motherhood, the whole lot. Hell, then I decided not to bother."

Vaughn Bode is an artist whose industry and commitment to comix represents a slightly astonishing level of dedication. He believes that the freedom allowed him by *Cavalier,* where his *Deadbone Erotica* strips are a regular three-page feature, has helped him to grow not only as an artist, but as a human being as well. "As I have changed, so have the creatures in *Deadbone* (or vice versa!), since I don't know where I end and where the creatures begin," he said recently. "When I first started the series, I was so inhibited that I couldn't draw women, even though I'd taken years of life drawing at school, and now, look at the chicks! Even my lizards were sexless, but now they're all hung. It's been very good therapy for me—very cathartic." Bode's catharsis aside, his work has clearly improved. There is less of the "dis-da" dialogue and text-heavy strips of which Mike Barrier has rightly complained in *Funnyworld,* and his women *do* look delicious. There is more attempt at political and social satire, this reflecting his need to have his work "endure and not become dated." Perhaps reflecting his lack of admiration for most professional comics toilers, he now labels his work "pictography"—picture-writing ("I write and then illustrate what I write"). Whether or not this is more pretentious than portentous, there is simply no doubting his sincerity. "I would like to be a good part of the underground thing and mold it for the future," says Bode, speaking with a strange mixture of boyishness and intensity which somehow *does* come out as a kind of super-sincerity. "What they're all trying to do, I'm *sure,* is express themselves, and this is the only place they can do it. There are so many facets to what they're trying to do—their work is maybe going to have rejuvenated cartooning in this country, loosened it up—they're going to be important people."

Naturally enough, the progress and future importance of comix do rest with its artists, but much also rests with the future of America. There are no nice, benevolent cops in comix, no Presidents en route to sanity, no authority figures who aren't the enemy—representatives of a nation in which reality imitates satire, as witnessed by the front pages of our newspapers, a nation at once in a high state of stasis and frenetic *angst.* The American Dream has become polluted by real life, *has* become a psychedelic nightmare, and at least some of the underground artists recognize, as Don Shenker has pointed out, that the language itself "has been fragmented into a host of rhetorics, most of them authoritarian and totalitarian. Americans are talked at, talked down to, and not with." In his view, the underground comix "undermine by simply being true." Just as the best of the posters have done, he observes, "so are the underground comix providing the place in life and the language which is spoken there, depicting the new country to which so many of us have an earnest desire to be deported. Comix, posters—these are the media of the new poetry, and this is why the police bust them."

If Shenker is right, and unless he is speaking of "dropping out," it is difficult to fault *his* rhetoric, we may reasonably anticipate more suppression of comix as the artists mature and really begin doing that important subversive work of which Shenker and Bode and others speak. But it is still too early to tell if this is going to happen. Thus far the only arrests have been made because the police were afraid someone would get horny by looking at a comix book. The only trend discernible at this writing is a depressing number of "horror comix" that usually just extend what is already admissible in the commercial titles. On the other hand, there are intriguing new artists, for example, Dave Sheridan, Greg Irons, Fred Schrier, "Foolbert Sturgeon" (pseudonym for a college professor who is the creator of *The New Adventures of Jesus* and *Jesus Meets the Armed Forces*), and Jack Jaxon. The last two are making a return debut, as it were, since they each produced one of the earliest comix while living in Texas. The work of these artists is provocative both in terms of graphics and writing. Also, a number of new comix publishing enterprises have been formed (usually in San Francisco) for the dual purpose of maintaining artistic freedom and getting a larger hunk of the cover price, so presumably outlets for comix are expanding into more bookstores, "head shops," and other underground chambers of commerce. This should mean wider distribution for comix and an increased ability to defend themselves should any kind of suppression occur. But whether or not they will become a vital part of America's radical youth subculture and politics strictly remains to be seen. If no girl has ever been seduced by an underground comix book, it may be too much to hope for something along those lines for our political system.

Still, underground comix are exciting because some of them have been clever and funny and have made telling points about America in a new way, and because the times have called them forth. Thus, if it is true, as has been observed, that America without its comic strips would not *be* America, then America with its new comix would be a much more somber America. I think we're witnessing the mere beginnings of a cultural kick with real kick in it.

Imagine. . . .

S. Clay Wilson becoming political, versus the American involvement in Latin America!

Vaughn Bode intercepting our egocentric probes of outer space!!

Gilbert Shelton outwitting the entire Narcotics Bureau by implanting an entire kilo of grass in Bugs Bunny's ears!!!

Jay Lynch's Pat th' Cat practicing whatever Masters and Johnson have preached!!!!

Robert Crumb versus Spiro Agnew!!!!!

Robert Crumb versus Spiro Agnew!!!!!?

I *like*—no, I'm afraid I relish—the match-up. After all, it'll only be satire imitating reality once again.

COMIC BOOKS AND SOCIETY

Clinton R. Sanders

SOURCE: "Icons of the Alternate Culture: The Themes and Functions of Underground Comix," in *Journal of Popular Culture*, Vol. VIII, No. 4, Spring, 1975, pp. 836-52.

[*In the following excerpt, Sanders considers the social, political, and commercial aspects of underground comic books.*]

Much of the popular culture literature is devoted to the discussion of the theoretical constructs and methodological approaches which are most useful in the study of "non-elite" cultural products. I agree with Gillespie that clarity will not be achieved until standardized interpretive concepts are developed. This framework can be built only when the foci and explanatory perspectives employed are clearly and consistently presented.

This paper deals with a relatively new cultural product—underground comix. It is a study of an artistic phenomenon which focuses on the socially constructed definitions of reality which shape both form and content. In that the effect of this medium/message on the perceptions and values of its consumers is emphasized, the discussion relates generally to the sociology of art.

The premise that art is shaped by the interaction of the artist, the public and the distribution network underlies the following discussion. Art is not created in a vacuum. The artist has learned the values and perceptions which are generally accepted within the host society. Similarly, underground comix artists are conscious members of an alienated group which has developed a body of lore and a particular view of reality. Comix clearly reflect the subcultural socialization of their creators.

Is it legitimate to view underground comix as a part of contemporary popular culture? Not if Nye's definition is employed. Comix are not "widely diffused, generally accepted (and) approved by the majority". I prefer, however, to use the broader definition of popular culture offered by Ray Browne.

> (A) viable definition for Popular Culture is all those elements of life which are not narrowly intellectual or creatively elitist and which are generally though not necessarily disseminated through the mass media. . . . "Popular Culture" thus embraces all levels of our society and culture other than the Elite—the "popular," "mass" and "folk."

Comics, as an artistic product, provide an excellent mirror in which the careful observer can see reflected the values, hopes, concerns and perceptions of the society. Further, in that comics function to promote social change by mocking that which is held sacred and provide a medium for bringing socially disapproved topics to the public consciousness, they offer an excellent source of data on how social change mechanisms operate. These aspects of comics will be used to focus a later discussion of the subcultural and societal impact of underground comix.

The following discussion begins with a brief history which touches on the major graphic forms and social forces which are important in the development of underground comix. Next, a description of the thematic patterns to be found in the comix is presented. This description provides the illustrative base for an analysis of the impact which comics, in general, and undergrounds, in particular, have on American culture. Comix exist because they provide *some* people with *something* they need. A meaningful discussion of an artistic product must deal with the function of the product for its audience. As Van Den Haag states:

> In my opinion, emphasis on cultural objects misses the point. A sociologist (and to analyze mass culture is a sociological enterprise) must focus on the functions of such objects in people's lives: he must study how they are used; who produces what for whom; why, and with what effects. To be sure, value judgments cannot be avoided, but the qualities of the product become relevant only when related to its social function.

The paper concludes with an analysis of the cohesive role which comix play in the growing alternative culture with which the majority of the artists identify.

I will admit to some personal discomfort with this discussion at the outset. While potentially leading to a greater understanding of cultural products and social mechanisms, academic analyses of artistic creations tend to hide their real beauty. Unfortunately, a feeling for the *experience* of art rarely survives linear analyses. Comix are fun, thought provoking and aesthetically pleasing. I am hopeful that this discussion does not obliterate the fact that underground comix often provide the reader with an exciting and rewarding experience.

A decade or more before McLuhan presented his analysis of comics, various social observers were noting their rising popularity with considerable alarm. They maintained that the form, values and content of the comics were turning young people into violent, semi-literate animals with bloated egos and an inability to delay gratification. While disagreeing with the dire consequences predicted by anti-comics crusader Fredric Wertham, many writers in the 40's and 50's stressed the importance of comics in molding and reflecting national values. Bakwin, for example, states:

> Comics are recognized as valuable aids in influencing people's understanding and attitudes. They inculcate children with common concepts, doctrines, attitudes, sentiments.

This presentation of the socializing function of comics is directly relevant to the specific focus of this paper.

Underground comix do more than simply reflect the social definitions shared by members of a loosely knit counterculture. Comix also transmit a consistently patterned ideological system to those who feel an "affinity" for a group which maintains an alternate view of reality. In Matza's terms, comix may be an important factor in the "affiliation" process through which individuals come to reconsider their values, perceptions and relationships in light of newly presented possibilities. As Wald and Gussow state:

> Kids who stopped reading comics when they could no longer relate to Uncle Scrooge or Batman found—in Those Fabulous Furry Freak Brothers and Crumb's characters and all the others—images of the new style of life which they were uncertainly grouping after.

Undergrounds have roots which are sunk deep in the American comic tradition. The first American comic books were reprinted collections of newspaper strips. The most famous of these early books was a collection of Mutt and Jeff strips which appeared in 1911. George Delacorte, owner of the Dell Publishing Company, brought out *The Funnies,* a tabloid size comic book which ran for thirteen issues, in 1929. From this modest beginning a popular art form has developed which has considerable impact on the lives of countless American young people.

The work of comic artists is of primary importance in shaping the style and approach of many underground artists. Robert Crumb, one of the best known comix creators, attributes much of his style to the influence of Basil Wolverton, Walt Disney, Chester Gould, Walt Kelly and Harold Gray. Underground artist Roger Brand reports that 30% of his fellow artists are dedicated to the study and collection of "commercial" comics.

Another comic form which has influenced undergrounds is the "eight-pager" or "Tiajuana bible"—pocket-sized pamphlets which first made their clandestine appearance in the twenties and were devoted primarily to the depiction of sexual intercourse.

In the mid-50's an anti-comic crusade was led by Fredric Wertham, a psychiatrist whose book *Seduction of the Innocent* (1954) played a seminal role in the creation of the Comics Code Authority. This organization set up a set of restrictions with which all comics (under threat of boycott) were obliged to comply. This crude censorship mechanism was aimed primarily at William Gaines' horror and violence-ridden E.C. Comics and Harvey Kurtzman's satire comic *Mad* (also published by Gaines). While the Comics Code signaled the death of the E. C. horror line, *Mad* (despite Kurtzman's departure) continued to exist—though in a magazine, rather than comic, format. *Mad* and similar publications such as *Help, Trump, Humbug,* and *Panic* provided a watered-down model for the biting political and cultural satire which abounds in contemporary undergrounds.

In the mid-60's, aided by dope and political activity, a youth culture began to emerge out of the comfortable apathy of the 50's. A growing number of people found themselves increasingly alienated from the racist, cold war, property-over-people mentality of main-stream America. An important aspect of this emergent social movement was the creation of new artistic and propagandistic media experiments. The ballrooms of the Haight-Ashbury, that mid-60's mecca of the counter-culture, were filled with pulsing sounds and flashing projections designed to mimic and enhance the psychedelic drug experience. Young artists began creating posters—some strangely distorted by new chemical experiences, some reminiscent of late 19th century poster art—which advertised these multi-media presentations. A number of these poster artists, especially Rick Griffin and Victor Moscoso, later became highly respected comix creators.

Another development of the "flower-power era" which was important to the emergence of comix was the "underground paper." Daniels points out the interesting parallel between the evolution of commercial comic books and that of undergrounds.

> (U)nderground comics . . . progressed through their speedy growth in a manner which reduplicated the progress of the standard comics. They began in newspapers, and gradually branched out into comic book form. But since the new comics were to be totally free of censorship, they could evolve only in a new kind of newspaper.

Underground papers and "sick humor" magazines which developed in and around university communities (e.g., the *Pelican, The University of California, The Texas Ranger*) provided the necessary arena in which young comic artists could display their artistic skills and anti-mainstream values. In 1965, New York's *East Village Other* began printing William Beckman's "Captain High," the earliest continuous strip to appear in the underground press. The *EVO* went on to print the early works of Kim Deitch, Crumb and Art Speigelman. Philadelphia's

Yarrowstalks was printing R. Crumb's work, while Gilbert Shelton was producing graphic insanity for *The Texas Ranger* and the *Rag* in Austin. In the Midwest Skip Williamson and Jay Lynch, two Chicago artists, were creating the *Mirror,* an underground magazine filled with their own cartoons and satire. Early work by Williamson and Lynch also appeared in The *Realist,* the *Chicago Seed* and *Aardvark.*

By 1968, underground media heads saw the budding popularity of underground cartoon strips and San Francisco's Print-Mint (previously devoted primarily to the printing and distribution of poster art), brought out *Yellow Dog,* the first all comic newspaper. In New York, the *EVO* launched *Gothic Blimp Works Comics* (originally edited by Kim Deitch and Trina Robbins). This monthly comic tabloid featured the works of Crumb, Shelton, "Spain" Rodrigues, S. Clay Wilson and other underground artists, as well as some material produced by aboveground comic artists. At about the same time Shelton put out *Radical Amerika Comix* and *Feds and Heads* and a college professor who signed himself "Foolbert Stugeon" published *The New Adventures of Jesus.*

As is stated in the introduction, it is necessary to focus attention on the distribution system in order to understand the development and social impact of a popular cultural form. The style and content of comix limit their acceptability, distribution and popularity. Bensman and Gerver emphasize that artists must take care that "the thematic treatment should not alienate any interest group of the potential audience" if their artistic product is to be accepted into the corpus of "mass art."

The freedom from censorship which makes comix vigorous, humorous and exciting also creates severe economic and legal problems for their artists and distributors. A limited audience and distribution network necessitates limited press runs which, in turn, decreases profits. Small profits limit the amount of money which can be paid to artists and which can be utilized to expand the distribution network. For example, Denis Kitchen's Krupp Comic Works currently has a catalogue of some 36 books of which there are about 1,000,000 copies in print. Marvel and D. C., the two major commercial comic publishers, sell 1,000,000 copies a month! Kitchen comments on the problems of the comix publisher:

> Straight comic publishers have the distinct advantage of large press runs, which cuts printing costs per book, and commercial advertising, which brings in revenue beyond that which is produced by the sales of books. Underground comic publishers have severe handicaps in economic terms because of small press runs and no advertising.

Hope for the healthy economic growth of the comix industry lies in the ability of the undergrounds to reflect the interests, values and fantasies of a growing number of (mostly young) people. The commercial comics, despite relatively limited attempts to deal with current social issues, are simply getting old. Constrained by a mass audience, the abovegrounds deal cautiously with social issues. Their artistic quality is rapidly declining. Titles, story lines, artistic style and subjects are monotonously similar. Further, new young artists are no longer willing to be hacks for the large comic firms, preferring artistic freedom to economic security.

Any thorough discussion of a popular cultural form must, at some point, focus on the identifiable thematic patterns which are presented in the works being analyzed. This section will deal with the following major underground themes: culture conflict, drugs, sex, politics, ecology, and religion/mysticism.

A common creative premise found in comix is the confrontation between the upstanding, white, middle-class, middle-aged citizen and the cultural or racial deviant. As can be expected, the deviant is usually victorious. The language, values, appearance and activity of the "freak" are usually so foreign or repellant to the "straight" that the latter is rendered defenseless. In many cases, the hip protagonist is simply more intelligent than his straight antagonist. Shelton Freak Brothers (*Fabulous Furry Freak Brothers* #1, *Further Adventures of the Fabulous Furry Freak Brothers*), Crumb's Mr. Natural (*Mr. Natural* #s 1 & 2) and Rand Holmes' Harold Hedd (*The Collected Adventures of Harold Hedd*) are prime examples of the freak characters who commonly win out because of superior wit or simple good luck.

Another assumption upon which a number of culture conflict episodes are based is that the exotic hedonistic pleasures of the hip subculture exert a powerful pull on straights. The middle-class American's hesitant taste of the hip life is usually relatively disastrous.

It is clear where the cultural sympathies of the artists lie. A number of pages present open invitations to join the fun-loving counterculture (see, for example, the back cover of *Zap* #1.

Not all cultural confrontations portrayed are between hips and straights. Conflict between blacks and whites is common (e.g., Crumb's "Whiteman" in *Zap* #1, and "Fritz Bugs Out" in *Fritz the Cat*). Wilson often has deviants meeting other deviants (Dykes vs. Fags, Pirates vs. Dykes, Pirates vs. Demons, Bikers vs. Dykes, etc., etc. See *Bent* or any of Wilson's work in *Zap* #1 through *Zap* #7).

Drugs are commonly encountered in underground comix. Some of the underlying messages transmitted promote the use of illegal drugs (e.g., Shelton *Freak Brothers,* Holmes' *Harold Hedd*). The inside back cover of Crumb's *Zap* #0 proclaims, "Help build a better America! Now you don't need a 'shrink' to flush out Karmic conjestion! GET STONED!" This is followed by instructions on how to smoke marihuana. Similarly, the back cover of *Tales*

From the Ozone is devoted to a plea for the legalization of marihuana. The message reads:

> It's time to end the sham and hypocracy of America's anti-pot laws! Marihuana is a harmless, benevolent herb known to man for thousands of years as a gentle, non-addictive and pleasant high. Pot is less habit-forming than tobacco and has none of the life destroying properties of alcohol. So jump on the band wagon and join the millions of patriotic Americans who say: Make mine pot!

Not all drugs are presented favorably. The use of speed, and opiates and barbiturates is never portrayed as a desirable activity. In fact, a number of artists present a clear anti-drug line (excluding reefer and psychedelics). In "Street Corner Daze" (*Zap* #3) Crumb offers "a public service comic strip on the subject of SPEED for the good of the community." *Junk Comix* and Williams' *Tuff Shit* both deal primarily with heroin use, displaying hard anti-jive attitudes.

Strips which focus on drug themes often present extensive drug use and effective political action as contradictory activities. In his story of three young men who have just been released from prison (*Inner City Romance* #1: *Choices*), Colwell clearly presents these two alternatives. In both *Choices* and its sequel, *Radical Rock,* the artist stresses the value of political activity over chemical escape. Hayes deals similarly with the politics vs. drugs issue in his strip "Dear Crusader" (*Conspiracy Capers*).

Another predominant message found in the comix is that sex is fun. Because of their open depiction of sexual acts all undergrounds carry the caution "adults only" and mail order distributors require that all purchasers sign a statement that they are over 21 years old. Sex is the most common topic used to orient single theme comix. A partial list of sex comix includes, *Bizarre Sex, Young Lust* #s 1-3, *Snatch* #s 1-3, *Jiz, Cunt, Sex and Death, Zap* #4, *Big Ass, Turned on Cities, Clits and Tits,* and *Facts of Life Comix*. It is here that the impact of the old "8 pagers" on the undergrounds is most obvious. In setting down their most juicey fantasies, comix artists go far beyond the stiff sexuality of *Little Annie Fanny, Barbarella, Phoebe Zeitgeist* or any of the other commercial "sexy" comics.

The development of an organized and vocal women's movement has given rise to a serious and valid critique of comix. Women's Liberation does not object to the fact that undergrounds display sexual activity, it is *how* women and sex are presented which is ideologically repugnant. Women are often depicted as objects whose primary functions are to "get laid and/or nag her old man." Those active in the women's movement feel justifiably betrayed—comix are humorous and cohesive journals created primarily by and for members of a culture which should present values, perceptions and activities which are in opposition to those of the dominant society. Yet, the roles, activities and images of both men and women portrayed by underground artists are not radically different from those cherished in the mainstream culture. Why? And what can and is being done?

First, the vast majority of underground artists are men; men who have been socialized in a male-dominated culture. Dominance is difficult and uncomfortable to give up, particularly when there is often little male peer support for the struggle.

In her thought-provoking article, "Guilt Comix," Gretchen states:

> What the comix presently depict is the sickness and hungupness inside most of us. Perhaps getting this out in the open is the first step, but how do you raise the consciousness of both the artist and the reader? How do you change the artist so he depicts women as equals?

The author later suggests that one important step is for women to get more involved in the creation of comix. Further, those concerned with the sexist values displayed in undergrounds must continuously challenge the artists so that they are aware of the consequences of their artistic actions.

Gretchen's suggestion that more women should become involved as underground artists and writers has been heeded in the last three years. In 1970 Trina Robbins and a staff of women artists produced *It Ain't Me, Babe*. In 1972 four other women's comix were published (*Tits and Clits Comix, All Girl Thrills, Wimmen's Comix* and *Girl Fight Comics*). In addition, more of the recent comix created by men are openly (particularly those which present a clear political message) disavowing male-dominance, objectification of women and sex role stereotypes (esp. London's *Merton of the Movement* and *Left Field Funnies,* Colwell's *Inner City Romances* #s 1 & 2, and Sturgeon's *Amazon Comics*).

Perhaps the presentation of a political ideology is the most common way in which comic art has historically been utilized. Artists from Hogarth and Dore through Walt Kelley, Al Capp, Harold Gray and Chester Gould to Fieffer, Steadman and the contemporary multitude of political cartoonists have all used the comic medium to transmit a political message. In his discussion of comics McLuhan maintains that American popular art, in general, represents "an authentic imaginative reaction to official action."

Given this well established comic function and the fact that *all* underground artists have more or less vast disagreements with the political structure and priorities of establishment America, it is hardly surprising that *all* comix present either overt or covert political commentary. These presentations vary considerably. Some artists (e. g., Crumb's *Motor City* #s 1 & 2, and *People's Comix,* Crawford in *High-Flying Funnies Comix and Stories,* and Sutherland in *American Flyer Funnies*) ridicule both the reactionaries and the radicals. Other comix such as *Conspiracy Capers* and *Radical America Komix* were produced to raise money and propagandize for radical groups.

Often the forces of right and justice are aided by a radical super-hero in their fight against the suppressive powers of the state. Manuel "Spain" Rodrigues has created Trashman (*Subvert Comics* #s 1 & 2), a hero who uses his mastery of para-science to combat the tyrannical government which rises to power after the great nuclear war. In order to counter-balance the effect of his rightist super-hero, Captain Guts, Larry Welz has created Wyatt Winghead, a freak with a drug expanded cosmic consciousness, psychic powers and considerable technological know-how (*Captain Guts Comics* #s 1-3, *American Flyer Funnies*).

Greg Irons, an extremely accomplished artist who sees little humor in the current political situation, has produced some of the most striking political commentary to be found in any art form. In *Heavy Tragi-Comics,* for example, Irons tells the story of Fou, a young man raised alone in the ideal Rouseauian wilderness. Fou returns to civilization typified by a Disneyland made up of the ugliest aspects of American society ("GHETTOLAND. Ride the el over seamy side streets. Gloat at death, despair and deprivation at no personal risk.") and run by a junkie Mickey Mouse who commands a redneck park guard and a harem of ex-mouseketeers. Mickey gives the naive young man "a place in the society of man" and in the final panels a newly crew-cut and button-down Fou quietly declares:

> Everything's just wonderful since I started working for Mr. Mouse. After a short rehabilitation program I was assigned to one of the animation departments in Mr. Mouse's studios. It's a relatively unimportant job, really, but it's interesting and there's lots of opportunity for advancement. Besides, the pay's really great and the benefits like paid vacations, hospitalization, insurance, and a retirement fund that allows one to draw a full pension when I'm only sixty-five. Besides all that, I'm working with a great bunch of fellows and we get together a lot after work and on weekends and have lots of fun bowling and drinking and telling jokes and swapping wives. But best of all, I don't have to worry about any of those silly *questions* anymore. . . .

Irons does not use his powerful artistic style to bludgeon home any particular political line. He simply says, "Look at the stupidity of the violence which you wreak on each other and which you justify with short-sighted political ideologies" (see *Legion of Charlies* and Irons' work in *Hydrogen Bomb*).

There is one newer work which deserves mention in this discussion of political comix. Barney Steel's *Armageddon* #s 1 & 2 present an anachronistic, highly individualistic social philosophy which has its roots in Ayn Rand's Objectivism. The hero and heroine are strong, independent and intelligent. Social organization, faith, altruism, all are evils which limit individual freedom and which must be destroyed. On one page of *Armageddon* #1 the hero and heroine, both naked, are battling the forces of social order. The hero wields an ax labelled "9th Amendment" while his partner screams "Laissez-Faire, you statist, socialist, commie, Fascist, Christian Pigs!" Steel takes Irons' distrust of organized ideology and creates an ideological world in which the most extreme individualism is tempered only by the necessity of a monogamous sexual relationship. Steel's political message is clear; politics is evil. Irons suggests avoiding it, Steel is bent on its destruction.

Ecological concerns are often used to focus political statements made in underground comix. The ideological framework employed by those artists most concerned with the condition of our ecology is pop anti-technological elitism—the ecological battle is between people and machines. The primary exponent of this position is George Metzger, an excellent artist whose favorite story setting is the vigorous rural society formed by those people who moved to exurban communes before the great war turned the urban areas into nuclear slag-heaps (see *Moondog* #s 1 & 2, *Truckin',* and Metzger's work in *Slow Death* #4, *Yellow Dog* #s 17 & 21, *Fantagor* #2, *Laugh in the Dark* #1 and *San Francisco Comic Book* #3). The message that our culture's cavalier ecological attitude will bear disastrous fruit is commonly presented through the depiction of a future society struggling for survival in a ravaged and inhospitable world. Irons ("It Grows," *Slow Death* #1) clearly lays out the ethic of ecological responsibility which he and the other artists who deal with the environmental theme wish their readers to adopt.

> Ultimately, the solution comes down to the actions of the individual. We have most of the answers already. What is necessary is the willingness to carry out what we know is the answer. This means changing whole life styles. *Living* the solution. WHAT ARE YOU DOING?

Mockery of established religious institutions is not the only way in which underground artists bring religion into comix. Sturgeon (*The New Adventures of Jesus, Jesus meets the Armed Forces*) and Jaxon (*God Nose*) both evidence deep respect for traditional Christian values and precepts. Sturgeon delights in showing Jesus as he comes up against the absurd, present-day interpretation of the principles which he originated. In his article on the Jesus comix, Greeniones views Sturgeon as attempting to prompt the reader to reevaluate and adopt the "original" Christian perspective.

> He is funny in the right places and is aware of the higher purpose he must fill of making Christ more familiar to us again on our terms so that we may be receptive to his message.

John Thompson (*Eternal Tales* #1, *The Kingdom of Heaven is With You Comix* and *Cyclops Comics* #1) deals solely with mystical/occult/religious themes. His work is a bizarre amalgam of mythical, occult, Christian,

Indian and oriental symbols and characters. Thompson's comix are so personalistic and esoteric that, while it is apparent that his work has some mystical religious significance, the message (if there is a message) is difficult to grasp.

Another comix artist who deals with religious themes is Dan O'Neill. In *Hear the Sound of My Feet Walking . . . Drown the Sound of My Voice Talking,* a collection which was commissioned by Glide Church, O'Neill's religious concerns are most apparent. The introduction of this volume somewhat pompously maintains that O'Neill "captures the nature of existence and struggles with picturization of metaphysics."

The comic form is low in definition and segmented. It requires that the observer fill in the missing detail out of his/her own desires, fantasies and experiences. The personal participation required by comics fosters interest and engagement. The simplicity, availability and familiarity of the comic form often obscure its aesthetic value. Comic art has a central place in our shared cultural heritage; it is experienced less as an art form than as a familiar aspect of day-to-day American reality.

It is not surprising that artists who are concerned with creating relevant "museum art" using objects and forms which are commonly shared, understood and encountered in everyday life have shown an interest in comics. Roy Lichtenstein is the artist primarily responsible for bringing the popular comic form into the elite setting of the fine arts museum. Lichtenstein isolated and enlarged comic panels, emphasized the lines and filled the spaces with screen-patterned color dots to create paintings which were faithful to the form and content of the comics. He carefully chose panels which portrayed "archetypical situations" and climaxes of action.

The efforts of Lichtenstein, Rauschenberg, Jasper Johns and Chicago's Hairy Who group opened the way for the acceptance of comics as serious and significant graphic creations which merited museum exposure. The Phoenix Gallery in Berkeley has had a number of showings of the work of underground artists. In 1971 Chicago's Museum of Contemporary Art devoted an entire floor to a showing of the work of Moscoso, Williams, Griffin, Crumb, Wilson and other of the better known underground artists.

A significant amount of comix material is devoted to an exploration of the artistic potential of the medium. It is here that the importance of the Haight-Ashbury poster art of the mid-60's in the development of contemporary comix is most apparent. The perceptual changes produced by hallucinogenic chemicals is another important factor which has shaped the comix aesthetic.

The comix artists whose work is least constrained by thematic content and who, consequently, emphasize composition, execution and style are Victor Moscoso and Rick Griffin. Both artists have similar styles and employ similar techniques. Both were poster artists prior to their involvement with undergrounds. Apart from the almost perfect graphic work of Corben (*Fantagor, Slow Death* #4, *Wierdom, Tales of the Plague,* etc.), Griffin and Moscoso produce the most careful and technically accomplished underground art.

Moscoso and Griffin are surrealists; their curvilinear characters live on barren plains with stark, flat horizons. They are unencumbered by plot or direction and required to push out only an occasional word balloon. As students of aboveground comics Moscoso and Griffin people their panels with familiar comic and cartoon characters. Moscoso is particularly fond of the Planter's Peanut Man, Maggie and Jiggs, Minnie Mouse, and Donald Duck. Donald Duck and Mickey Mouse are also commonly encountered in Griffin's work. They are, however, accompanied by a nightmare hoard of talking eyeballs with arms and legs, scarabs and pythons. Moscoso's work is somewhat simpler than Griffin's; he uses fewer words and his arrow straight panel borders enclose sizable areas of unused space. The majority of the action in Moscoso's work is due to the disintegration and integration of his characters and the appearance and disappearance of empty thought balloons, stars, pyramids and lightbulbs. Sex plays a more important thematic role in Moscoso's comic art than it does in Griffin's (see *Zap* #s 3 & 4 and *Color*).

Griffin's art is clearly executed and jammed with symbolism, characters and activity. He constantly plays with palindromes—live/evil, god/dog, OXO, AAA. Lightbulbs, cue balls, wings, swords, roses and hearts encircled by thorns commonly appear in Griffin's work. The gravitational field in the fantasy worlds which he creates seems to be weak—his characters are often floating a bit off the "ground." Griffin's characters are also more verbal than those created by Moscoso. They say interesting things like "It's getting better all the time," "Howdy," "I am the vacuum of pure spirit" or "Zounds."

A few other comix artists attempt to achieve the technical and conceptual heights of Moscoso and Griffin. Ron Lipking's work in *Spiffy Stories* is, for the most part, crude, simplistic imitation. Ric Sloane (*Ric Sloane Comics #1*) is a somewhat more accomplished technician than Lipking but his symbols and composition are an embarrassingly blatant rip-off of Griffin.

Greg Irons is as accomplished a comix artist as can be found. In *Light,* Irons' collection of plot-less, essentially non-verbal color drawings, the careful observer finds many of the symbolic objects which abound in Griffin's art (scarab, wings, light bulbs, skulls). The first half of the book presents the progressively terrifying mutation of a young man's head. The last half of the book contains some dozen pages of graphic horror. On each page sit one or more crazed monsters drawn with meticulous attention to each putrefying detail. Irons does not attempt to utilize the flat horizon/barren plain surrealist convention favored by Moscoso and Griffin and all of his work clearly emphasizes anti-establishment values. Nonetheless, his mastery of technique, his rejection of words for graphic symbols and his frequent nonreliance on the crutches of plot and story line, indicate that Irons, along with Griffin and Moscoso, is a master of the visionary, nonlinear, artistic tradition which had its birth a decade ago in the San Francisco poster phenomenon.

It is apparent from the increasing number of publishers, active artists, available titles and distribution sources that underground comix are growing in popularity. This growth indicates that the structure of contemporary American society and the perceived needs of its constituents provide fertile ground for the growth of a cultural product with the form and content of the undergrounds. I will conclude with a specific discussion of the various ways in which structure, needs, form and content interact to sustain comix. The discussion will focus on the impact of undergrounds on dominant American values and the functions of comix for the nebulous alternative culture whose members are primarily responsible for their creation, distribution and consumption.

What is the basis for the increasing popularity of the comic medium in contemporary America? The answer is relatively simple. Comics emphasize action, reflect current values and concerns, and are generally easy to understand. In addition, they are inexpensive, readily available and have become a familiar component of the popular entertainment alternatives from which we choose our leisure-filling activities.

There is a close relationship between the social and technological structure of a society and the artistic and media forms which are appropriate, satisfying, utilized and supported. McLuhan maintains that the existence of instantaneous electronic technology determines the form of the human environment. Members of contemporary Western society are encased in an electronic techno-cultural reality. Consequently, non-linear, low definition ("cool") media forms which demand significant observer participation are most acceptable to those whose perceptions are shaped by the reality of the electronic era.

McLuhan sees comics as a collection of crude images which present the observer with limited, but immediately apprehended, information. The appropriate "coolness" of the comic form, according to McLuhan's theory, accounts for its current popularity.

In his interesting cross-cultural study of the relationship between social structure and the manipulation of pictorial elements in dominant art forms, Fischer (1961) indicates that the artistic products which are accepted in a hierarchical social system will share certain characteristics. In short, the choice and arrangement of pictorial elements, according to Fischer, mirror the structure of the society in which the art is produced.

On the basis of Fischer's analysis, what pictorial choices and arrangements would one expect to find in popular American art? The graphic products accepted in America's hierarchically structured social system would be typified by a) the incorporation of a number of unlike elements, b) asymmetrical design, c) enclosed figures, and d) the utilization of all available space. In that these characteristics are descriptive of the comic form, the popularity of comics in our hierarchically structured society is imminently understandable. The theoretical discussions presented by McLuhan and Fischer indicate that the current popularity of the comic form derives from the fact that it meets the needs and expectations which are shaped by social structure and shared perceptions of reality.

Do underground comix have any impact on the rigid structure of the society's mainstream values, attitudes and social definitions? To restate a major premise of this paper, I maintain that comix *do* play an important role in social change. They present healthy alternative values, perceptions and artistic techniques under the guise of smut, art and entertainment.

Given the anti-comic furor which arose in the mid-50's, and the current wide-spread use of the comic medium to "painlessly" educate young people about the dangers of drug abuse, sex and various other disapproved behavior, it is difficult to maintain that the comic idiom is an ineffective educational medium. Thirty years ago Gruenberg stated:

> For a century we have looked to the *schools* to develop a national unity in our heterogeneous population by inculcating children, as they grow up, with common concepts, doctrines, attitudes, sentiments. But the comics, claiming to be no more than toys, have been doing just that, reaching continuously more than the schools, more than the newspapers.

The educational possibilities of comix are not lost on their creators or those members of the alternative culture who are seriously committed to seeing Americans go through some necessary humanizing changes. As was touched on in the previous section on comix themes, undergrounds have been created which are intended to educate people about such vital issues as sex role oppression (e.g., *It Ain't Me Babe*), pregnancy and venereal disease (*Facts of Life Comics*) and impending ecological disaster (e.g., *Slow Death*). Comix also are created to provide people with useful information on various aspects of daily life from personal hygiene (*National Hair Care Comix and Stories*) to hitch-hiking (*Hit the Road*). Though comix probably have some impact on dominant values, this is severely hampered by the comix limited audience.

While the extent to which undergrounds have a significant and direct effect in promoting alteration in either individual or group value structures is open to question, I maintain that the comix do open ways for change to begin. They do provide the vacillating straight with a new way to look at reality and a repertoire of alternate behavioral models. As comix critic, Paul Buhle, observes:

> Like any potentially subversive cultural mechanism, komix serve at best to destroy an old view of the world and to replace it with a new one. They must provide a means of self-expression for the artist or be false—and in a healthy political movement, the artist's attitudes will correspond to the needs of the larger movement, making his self-expression a new way for masses of people to see their own lives.

It is clear, therefore, that the most important current function of the comix is the cohesion of a group of people who feel alienated from the dominant culture and who are seeking social support for their anger and disgust. In that they reflect shared values and sharpen shared perceptions the comix sustain the alienated group and play an important role in the affiliation process by which new members are socialized and become a part of the counter-cultural community.

Because they clearly present a new world view and portray the stupidity, uptightness and inhumanity of "accepted" values and behaviors, comix may play an important initial role in the conversion process. Yet undergrounds are not widely available and, consequently, the number of potential converts that they reach is severely limited. It is unrealistic to expect that comix will have significant direct effect on the existing social order.

Two other cohesive functions of the underground comix should be mentioned. Comix are important in that they help define boundaries; they separate "us" from "them." The graphics, values and priorities presented in the undergrounds outrage the sensibilities of straight America. They are part of the wall which separates the "friends" from the "enemies." In the eyes of those who are united in their opposition to the changes desired by the alienated "class," comix are cultural artifacts which "serve the function of underscoring class levels" they are "tags or indicators of one's stratum within the American class system.

Finally, underground comix are counter-cultural journals. They are a major component of the material culture which is valued by the alienated subculture. They are a creative art form in which the members can take pride; they are the *icons* of the counter culture—symbolic, value-laden, message-carrying objects. Underground comix entertain us, titillate our senses, raise our consciousness, touch our souls, and stir the anger in our guts. The increasing popularity and availability of comix clearly indicate that these filth-ridden, absurd, beautiful, over-priced books present, for a growing number of people, an acceptable picture of contemporary American reality and appropriate ways of dealing with this reality.

M. Thomas Inge

SOURCE: An introduction to "The Comics as Culture," in *Journal of Popular Culture*, Vol. XII, No. 4, Spring, 1979, pp. 631-39.

[*In the following essay, Inge assesses the comic as an art form.*]

The comic strip has been defined as an open-ended dramatic narrative about a recurring set of characters told in a series of drawings, often including dialogue in balloons and a narrative text, and published serially in newspapers. The daily and Sunday comic strips are part of the reading habit of more than one hundred million people of all educational and social levels. During the first half of this century, surveys have indicated that sixty percent of newspaper readers consider the comic page the priority feature in their reading. Along with jazz, the comic strip as we know it perhaps represents America's major indigenous contribution to world culture.

Comic books, on the other hand, originally an offshoot of the comic strip, are regarded with considerable suspicion by parents, educators, psychiatrists and moral reformers. One critic has called them "crude, unimaginative, banal, vulgar, ultimately corrupting." They have been investigated by governmental committees and subjected to severe censorship. Yet even in today's uncertain market, more than two hundred million copies are sold a year, and the comic book collecting business has become an important area of investment with its own price guides and publications to facilitate exchange and trade.

Any phenomenon which plays so heavily on the sensibility of the American populace deserves study purely for sociological reasons if for no other. The comics serve as revealing reflectors of popular attitudes, tastes, and mores. Because comic strips appear in daily newspapers, a publication designed for family consumption, the syndicates, editors, and publishers submit strips to the severest kind of scrutiny and control to be sure that no parent, political bloc, or advertiser whose support it courts will take offense. In the thirties conservative Harold Gray once had to redraw a *Little Orphan Annie* sequence because of its attack on one of Franklin Delano Roosevelt's New Deal programs, and the liberal slanted *Pogo* strip by Walt Kelly was often banned in the fifties in southern newspapers because of its satirical thrusts at school segregationists.

Examine the comics in any daily newspaper and each will be found to support some commonly accepted notion or standard of society. *Blondie, Archie, Mary Worth, Li'l Abner* and *Gasoline Alley* support the idea that a family is the basic social unit. *Judge Parker, Rex Morgan, Mark Trail,* and *Gil Thorpe* support the concepts of decency and fair play among the professions. While *The Wizard of Id, B. C., Peanuts, Funky Winkerbean, Doonesbury,* and *Shoe* are overtly satirical, they also provide a rational standard against which the aberrations they portray can be measured and found laughable. Why is Andy Capp, who drinks heavily, gambles and commits adultery, permitted to violate these social taboos on the pages of the funny papers? Possibly because he is British and Americans are willing to forgive such behavior on the part of Europeans. It is little wonder that Andy has such a large following—he is a stubbornly unpredictable and incorrigible individualist among many repetitious and mindless Caspar Milquetoasts. In the last few years, I should note, a few strips have daringly dealt with such hitherto forbidden topics as homosexuality, pre-marital sex, unmarried teen-age mothers and mental retardation, but with trepidation and frequent local censorship.

Comic books are submitted for approval prior to publication to the Comics Code Authority, which exercises the most severe censorship applied to any mass medium. Guidelines prohibit displays of sex, adultery, divorce, drugs, corrupt authority or unpunished crimes. Submission to the authority requires a medium mainly irrelevant to reality; thus characters escape into a world of fantasy, dominated by super-heroes, a world in which both might and right are on the side of morality. When needed to support his country in time of war, however, no superhero has ever dared to refuse.

The underground press comic strips and books, which came into being partly to defy the restrictions of the Comics Code Authority, ironically have failed to escape the basically political nature of American comic art. The defiance of American materialism by Robert Crumb, however, approaches anarchy, the rejection of society's sexual taboos by S. Clay Wilson is absolute, and the doomsday vision of Spain Rodriguez predicts the total destruction of civilization. These are radical stances beyond the pale of political ideology, and the underground cartoonists have had the incredible luxury of unrestricted artistic freedom. Perhaps their work thus holds promise of a politically untrammeled comic art of the future.

The comics also derive from popular patterns, themes and symbols of Western culture. Chester Gould has credited Sherlock Holmes as the inspiration for Dick Tracy (compare the shape of their noses), and Superman was based on Philip Wylie's novel *Gladiator. Bringing Up Father,* better known as "Maggie and Jiggs," by George McManus, was inspired by a popular play—*The Rising Generation*—and Philip Nowlan based *Buck Rogers* on his own short story, "Armageddon 2419." Dick Tracy's gallery of grotesque villains draws on the gothic tradition and follows the medieval concept that the outward appearance reflects the inner character. Flash Gordon, Prince Valiant, Captain Marvel and the Fantastic Four draw on the heroic tradition to which Hercules, Samson, King Arthur, Beowulf, Davy Crocket and Paul Bunyan belong.

If the comics have absorbed much of Western tradition, they have also had their influence on popular language and culture. Word coinages deriving from comic strips, and still found in general currency, include *jeep, balony, yardbird, horse feathers, googled-eyed* and *twenty-three skidoo.* There are Rube Goldberg contraptions and Mickey Mouse courses. Certain foods are inextricably associated with certain characters: Popeye's spinach, Wimpy's hamburgers, Jigg's corned beef and cabbage and Dagwood's incredible sandwiches. Buster Brown clothes and shoes can still be bought, and the Prince Valiant haircut has been popular at times. While Charlie Brown did not invent the expletive "Good Grief!" it will be several decades before anyone can use the phrase without automatically associating it with Charles Schultz's diminutive loser in the game of life.

Perhaps a major reason for recognizing and studying the comics is the fact that they are one of the few native American art forms. Literature, drama, music, film and the other forms of popular culture were largely established in Europe and most American practitioners (with perhaps the exception of film) have followed the patterns and standards established by foreign masters—Joyce in the novel, Ibsen in the drama or the Beatles in popular music. In the comic strip and comic book, however, Americans have defined the forms, expanded their aesthetic possibilities, and become the first masters of their unique visual and narrative potential. Winsor McCay, George Herriman, Alex Raymond, Hal Foster, Roy Crane, Milton Caniff, Will Eisner and Harvey Kurtzman are just a few of the internationally recognized geniuses of the comic strip, and all are Americans.

In a great variety of ways, the comics have influenced the general culture of the United States and the world. Pablo Picasso was supplied with American funny papers in France by his friend Gertrude Stein, and he drew inspiration from them for much of his work, such as *The Dream and the Lie of Franco* (1937). When samples of George Herriman's *Krazy Kat* pages circulated in France, they were recognized as early examples of dada art, and a few great modern masters, such as George B. Luks and Lyonel Feininger, produced comic pages early in their careers. The pop art movement of the 1960s witnessed the wholesale appropriation of the forms, symbols and style of comic art for the individual aesthetic intentions of a number of contemporary artists such as Andy Warhol, Roy Lichtenstein, Mel Ramos, Claes Oldenburg and Ray Yoshida, among others. They have appropriated the iconography of comic art as an appropriate idiom for communicating their contemporary visions. Comic imagery is liable to crop up in the most unlikely places. In Crystal City, Texas, the "Spinach Capital of the World," there stands a statue of Popeye, erected by a grateful community. The command module of the crew Apollo 10 answered to "Charlie Brown," while the LEM was named "Snoopy." Blondie helps sell margarine in Norway, and in France Mandrake the Magician promotes Renault automobiles. The Phantom is the subject of a series of highly popular novels published in ten languages throughout Europe.

In addition to their sociological value and their cultural significance, the comics are also of importance unto themselves, as a form of creative expression apart from their relationship to other forms of art. This is the most difficult area to write about because we lack the critical vocabulary and have not even begun to define the structural and stylistic principles behind successful comic art.

Instead, we tend to rely on terms borrowed from other areas of creative expression.

For example, we can talk about the comics as a form of communication and how they can be used for propaganda, in advertising, for the dissemination of information or as instructional aids. Reading teachers have only recently begun to realize the effectiveness of comic books in teaching reluctant or unresponsive children to read—fascinated by the pictures and the story being portrayed, they are led to study the words to figure out what is happening. Contrary to the notion that comic book reading serves as a cop-out and escape from reading "real" books, young readers are often led to novels and plays after reading the comic book adaptations, in the same way adults want to read a book after viewing the movie version of it (a trend so popular that now a book is often not written until after the film version has been released).

We can talk about the comics as graphic art, and clearly the visual attraction is the first thing that captures our attention. The comic artist must confront and solve the same problems of spatial relationships, balance and form that every artist must face, and nearly all modern artistic movements and styles have either been anticipated by or reflected in the comics. In the case of pop art, they inspired a whole school of painting.

Narration or story telling is also a main function of the comics. They are meant to be read, as opposed to traditional narrative art meant to be viewed and interpreted. While they have never competed with the classics, they have seriously altered popular reading habits by attracting readers away from pulp magazines, dime novels and cheap tabloids (only detective and science fiction have withstood the competition and survived). The total work of some cartoonists constitutes something like a novel on the pattern of Balzac's human comedy or Faulkner's Yoknapatawpha County cycle. *Little Orphan Annie* follows the picaresque pattern of *The Adventures of Huckleberry Finn,* and *Gasoline Alley* anatomizes an entire midwestern community much in the tradition of Sherwood Anderson's *Winesburg, Ohio* or Sinclair Lewis's *Main Street* (especially with the recent emphasis by Dick Moores on the provincial grotesque).

It has been suggested that the comics are closest to drama in that both rely on the dramatic conventions of character, dialogue, scene, gesture, compressed time and stage devices, but probably the motion picture is closer. Will Eisner, distinguished for his visual innovations in comic art, has stated that "comics are movies on paper." Eisner's work in *The Spirit* has always demonstrated a brilliant use of angle shots, framing, lighting, mood and detail characteristic of the film medium. When William Friedkin, producer of *The French Connection* and *The Exorcist,* announced his intention to do a film version of *The Spirit* for television, he paid tribute to Eisner's influence on his own work: "Look at the dramatic use of montage, of light and sound. See the dynamic framing that Eisner employs, and the deep vibrant colors. Many film directors have been influenced by *The Spirit,* myself included." Displaying an Eisner cover with a man being chased by an elevated train, Friedkin noted, "This is where I got ideas for the chase in *The French Connection.*" Federico Fellini, Orson Welles, Alain Resnais, and George Lucas are other film makers who have acknowledged their indebtedness to the comics for cinematic concepts and techniques. In fact, many standard techniques were first employed in the comics—montage (before Eisenstein), angle shots, panning, close-ups, cutting, framing, etc.

Yet none of these relationships and functions discussed above elucidate comic art for the distinctive and separate medium it happens to be. Text, artwork and meaning cannot be judged independently of the whole work. Word and picture interact in the best examples without one dominating the other, and quite literally the medium is the message. There has been nothing else quite like comic art on the cultural scene since the invention of the novel for potential in creative challenge and imaginative opportunity.

Historical studies, biographies, appreciations, anthologies, encyclopedias and periodicals on the subject of comic art have begun to proliferate recently (for a detailed survey, see my chapter on comic art in *Handbook of American Popular Culture,* edited by M. Thomas Inge). Partly this has resulted from publishers wishing to tap the lucrative nostalgia market, but in many cases because individuals have begun to recognize the importance of documenting this part of our national heritage. The study of comics has become a part of high school, college and university curricula throughout the country, as well as at the Sorbonne and the University of Brasilia.

Organizations for the advancement of the comic arts have been established abroad, such as Socerlid founded in Paris in 1967 and ICON founded in Brazil in 1970; and special journals are devoted to the reprinting and study of classic American comic strips, such as *Phenix* in France, *Linus* in Italy and *Bang!* in Spain. At least two research centers now exist in the United States and are open to the public—the San Francisco Academy of Comic Art and the Museum of Comic Art in the town of Rye/Port Chester, New York. The latter has instituted a Hall of Fame.

Those who hesitate to accept comic art as a significant form of expression might remember that Shakespeare was once merely a contributor to Elizabethan popular culture who spoke to the pit as well as to the gallery, and it took decades for the elite to grant his work the respectability it deserved. Perhaps the day will come when some of our major comic artists will be granted the place they deserve in the pantheon of American culture.

William W. Savage, Jr.

SOURCE: "Introduction: The Rise and Decline of Escapism, 1929-1945" and "Terminus Ad Quem," in *Comic Books and America, 1945-1954*, University of Oklahoma Press, 1990, pp. 3-13, 111-20.

[*In the following essay, Savage places the comic book hero in a historical context, from World War II to the Vietnam era.*]

During the 1930s, purveyors of popular culture offered escape to the American people. Perhaps they were simply trying to ease Americans through a difficult time by making no offensive reference to the extent of economic calamity wrought by the Depression. If so, the tactic led them conveniently away from the arena of social commentary and thus from the taint of controversy. Concern over Communist activity (the legacy of the Red Scare of the 1920s), distrust of some labor unions, and reaction to even the vaguest of utterances suggestive of socialist sentiment in response to the perceived collapse of capitalism—easy enough to imagine in the 1930s—had all worked toward the kind of consensus that made most social (and necessarily, political and economic) criticism suspect. So, whether the Depression was too dangerous to contemplate or merely too unpleasant, popular culture tended to focus on either the past or the future. Rarely did it examine the present in any relevant manner.

In films—and they are the sole consistently recurring evidence of the era, thanks to the recycling of television and related technologies—the unemployed, if they were revealed at all, were cast as buffoons (the brothers Marx, the Three Stooges, and variations thereon), and their comedic misadventures pointed to the strong prospect of their utter unemployability, even in flush times. Most of the children of Our Gang seemed oblivious to the poverty in which they were mired, relishing instead the striking range of possibilities for innovation it offered to enterprising youngsters. The poor, in short, were usually hilarious; and if poverty could be treated so obliquely, so could a great many other issues. The ramifications of such notions as class distinction were confronted only indirectly, customarily through the genre of romantic comedy, a la Frank Capra. Otherwise, hard-boiled detectives and an array of oriental sleuths, singing cowboys, and gymnastic lords of the jungle, athletic interstellar heroes and high-stepping gold diggers, and a regular posse of man-made monsters, migrating vampires, and enormous apes carried the day. Such fanciful things were matinee fare at everyone's Bijou or Rialto; and they bore little relationship to the real world.

And thus it was with the comics medium. Before 1929, newspaper strips and Sunday comic sections, important cultural transmitters since the turn of the century, were known as "funnies," a term implying humorous intent. Funnies offered slices of life, situation comedies of brief duration and generally domestic in their orientation. After 1929, however, they seemed something less than funny to increasing numbers of readers who failed to find amusing prospects in the framework of daily life. The world was in turmoil, the economy was in serious trouble, and the antics of assorted flappers, high rollers, and down-and-out immigrants could not relieve, even for the moment, the gloomy aspect of the rest of the newspaper. Hard times had blunted the appeal of the so-called funnies.

On January, 7, 1929, the adventures of "Tarzan" and "Buck Rogers" first appeared on newspaper comic pages, heralding the advent of what would become known as the "adventure strip." Following "Tarzan" in the 1930s were "Dick Tracy," "Jungle Jim," "The Phantom," "Terry and the Pirates," and dozens of others. All of them featured continuing stories, exotic locales and/or characters, virtually nonstop action, and little if any humor. They served to transport readers elsewhere—to a jungle, a desert, the Far East, a distant planet or some other atypical environment where heroes struggled against tall odds or fabulous creatures, and where nothing had any real bearing on the problems of the day. As the decade progressed, adventure strips grew in popularity, fueling escapist fantasies for the economically distressed. Because comic books developed from comic strips, they reflected the same shifting emphases.

The comic book emerged as a discrete medium of American cultural expression early in the 1930s. In its initial form, it contained only reprints of newspaper comic strips and was offered by publishers in bulk to companies in search of premiums and giveaways to increase their sales of everything from breakfast cereal to children's shoes. So popular was the comic book in this entrepreneurial venue that some publishers were led to believe it could be marketed directly to youngsters through news dealers, drugstores, and other retail outlets for a dime per copy. Early comic books—*Funnies on Parade* (1933) and *Famous Funnies* (1934) were two of the first-bore titles that belied the newspaper trend toward adventure comics, although they did reprint some of the post-1929 adventure strips. But by the end of the decade, such publications as *Detective Comics* (1937) and *Super Comics* (1938) bespoke a significant thematic change, as comic books began to offer more and more original material prepared specifically for the new medium. These items were among the precursors of the vaunted "golden age" of comic books, which began during the summer of 1938 with the debut of Superman in the first issue of *Action Comics*.

The impact of the Superman character upon the subsequent development of the comic book would be difficult to overestimate. Here was a seemingly human being who possessed a number of superhuman powers, a costumed hero with a secret identity, an alien from a dying planet who embraced American ideals and Judeo-Christian values—a kind of spectacular immigrant, as it were, come from afar to participate in the American dream. He had speed and strength and was invulnerable to manmade weaponry. He could not fly, but he could jump well enough to sustain the illusion. He was the nemesis of criminals, extracting confessions of their misdeeds by displaying his awesome powers; but, withal, he did not kill, or at least not more than was absolutely necessary—and there was an index of his healthy psyche and wholesome persona. As a cultural artifact, Superman gained an enormous audience in fairly short order, passed from comic books into a variety of media including animated cartoons and radio, and endured in his basic format, though further translated by television and motion pictures, for half a century. If imitation is, as Charles Caleb Colton said, the most sincere flattery, then Superman was the most flattered of all comic-book creations, spawning a host of look-alike, act-alike costumed heroes, all owing their existence to the norms and conventions his character established.

The appearance of Batman in the May 1939 issue of *Detective Comics* marked the emergence of another kind of heroic prototype. In this instance, a man of means (he had millions), when summoned by police, donned a bizarre costume (intended both to conceal his real identity and to terrify crooks) and swung into action (literally on the end of a rope, in most cases, even though the other end of it did not appear to be attached to anything). Batman possessed no superhuman powers. The skills he offered in behalf of law and order were merely those of the superior athlete and the brilliant scientist, and that was probably as close to reality as the story line came—which is to say that it missed by quite some distance. Like their adversary, Batman's criminal opponents were peculiar characters, altogether unusual in appearance and demeanor; and they contributed much to the surreal, nearly gothic aura of the Batman comic books.

Batman, too, was widely imitated, especially after the appearance of Robin as his adolescent sidekick in the April 1940 issue of *Detective Comics*. Within a matter of weeks, the duo appeared in the first issue of *Batman Comics*. Batman and Robin established the comic-book precedent for heroic partnerships between grown men and young boys, and their success made such pairings very nearly *de rigueur* in the medium during the 1940s. Here, after all, was a telling point of identification for an eager juvenile readership with dimes to spend.

Superman, Batman, and their numerous cultural clones were wholly fantastic constructs, in keeping with the escapist thrust of Depression-era popular culture. Arguably, they owed much to the renditions of other media. If, for example, radio's Lone Ranger and Tonto (no kid, granted, but clearly possessed of limited talents and abilities and thus kidlike) had been demonstrating since 1933 that a hero and a half were better than one, Batman and Robin merely offered further evidence. And if audiences appreciated the costumed flummery of, say, Buster Crabbe's Flash Gordon movie serials, then perhaps Superman succeeded no less from a growing general interest in science fiction as an entertainment genre than from his exhibition of hybrid qualities revealed onscreen by Flash's friends as well as his enemies—strong men with wings, and all of that. But comic books could carry heroes beyond the limits of possibility imposed by radio (sounds without pictures and thus without depth or significant personification) and film (sounds with pictures, but constrained by technology). Radio, short on data, gave the consumer's imagination too much latitude, while film, rife with data, refused to give it enough. Comic books, however accidentally, managed to split the difference. They could show whatever the artist could draw, their lines and colors directing imagination, their balloon-held texts defining time and space. Comic-book artists and writers could produce that which could be conceived, which was more than the creators of motion pictures and radio programs could claim. Moreover, comic books escaped consideration according to aesthetic criteria established by adults for the evaluation of media offerings intended for the grown-up world. They were for children, and they enjoyed a certain freedom.

As the 1940s began, comic books were being published in larger and larger quantities, and new characters were appearing every month. Heroes proliferated. The Green Lantern, Captain Marvel, and the Atom led the parade in 1940—respectively, an ordinary mortal endowed with alien powers, a boy who could become a man at will, and an extremely small fellow to whom size, or rather his lack of it, was no handicap in a world of frequently malicious larger folk. By 1941, The Justice Society of America had made its appearance as the first consortium of comic-book heroes: Green Lantern, the Atom, the Flash, Hawkman, Hourman, Sandman, the Spectre, and Dr. Fate collaborated against criminals in a continuing alliance, a unique association that would establish yet another trend within the comic-book industry. Captain America, Plastic Man, Daredevil, and Fighting Yank were among the other heroes who first appeared in 1941. Their very names revealed their unreality.

The presence of so many colorfully-clad strongmen in comic books suggested to some observers that young female readers were being ignored. The masked and caped crime fighters seemed ideally structured to serve as role models for boys, so why should there not be a corresponding model for girls? In response, psychologist William Moulton Marston, in collaboration with artist Harry G. Peter, developed a costumed heroine he named Wonder Woman. She first appeared in the November 1941 issue of *All-Star Comics* as yet another prototype, albeit one who lived for years in the shadow of the male protagonists.

All these new heroes had plenty besides crime with which to contend, since, by 1940, war raged in Europe and Japanese militarists were having their way in the Far East. International politics had replaced economics as the major public preoccupation in the United States, and comic-book publishers, seeing fresh opportunities, began paying editorial attention to the real world for the first time. Their heroes, who had been unable to grapple with the complex issues of the Depression, could now set sights on the political arena, at first fighting fascism as a form of international crime in a limited involvement that came several months before America's entry into World War II.

It may have been an appropriate cultural response in the context of the time, given the burgeoning nationalism of the Axis powers; but in any case, impelled by world affairs and the public mood, the comic-book industry fashioned a number of patriotic heroes for popular consumption. These included Fighting Yank, descendent of a Revolutionary War soldier who received his powers from that long-dead ancestor; Captain America, a chemically enhanced human being created by the military as the first member of a proposed army of super-soldiers; and perhaps the most peculiar—and peculiarly American—hero of all, Uncle Sam, who first appeared in the aptly named *National Comics* in July 1940. Once these and other such characters were in place, it was a relatively simple matter to match them against Axis villains, anticipating the day when the United States surely would have to join the conflict in an official capacity.

Many in the comic-book industry seemed to believe that American involvement in the war was inevitable. The attitude led to intense speculation and some rather loud rattling of cultural sabers. In that regard, it was less surprising than it might now seem that the eighteenth issue of *National Comics,* on newsstands early in November 1941, depicted the Japanese attack on Pearl Harbor that would not happen until a month later. Viewed in retrospect, the comic book's striking cover does not suggest the prescience of the medium; rather it indicates that when a single medium explores enough dramatic possibilities proceeding from a given set of circumstances, one or two such explorations are likely to be right on the money. It was simply that a year and a half of guessing on the part of *National Comics* staff had paid expected dividends, since from the perspective of comic books American participation was a foregone conclusion.

If rumors of war hinted at the end of escapism in American comic books, the fact of war presented empirical evidence of it. The questions at hand concerned national survival and the ability of the individual American to cope with the inevitable stress of awaiting an outcome. Comic-book heroes had new roles to play. Whereas crime fighting may have qualified as escapist fare during the 1930s (to the extent that crime was not a thing that touched every life), war was a different matter. Even the Depression had not affected the entire population, which may help to explain why popular culture could have afforded to ignore it. Moreover, crime had been the dilemma of local, state, and federal agencies, and the Depression had been widely viewed as a problem depending upon national political leadership for satisfactory resolution. In contrast, war concerned all Americans, and the cooperation of all would be required to insure a successful conclusion. It was not, as a rule, a time for cultural fun.

Comic books brought much to the American cause. In addition to lending support to such necessary activities as bond drives and paper drives, comic books became an integral part of the Allied propaganda machine, emphasizing the need for a maximum war effort by portraying the enemy as the inhuman offspring of a vast and pernicious evil. Writers coined epithets like "ratzi" and "Japanazi," and artists drew rodentlike Japanese and bloated, sneering Germans. Japanese troops wore thick glasses and displayed prominent teeth, while German officers possessed monocles and dueling scars, much as they did in the wartime renditions of Hollywood filmmakers—although comic-book illustrators took greater liberties than Hollywood could, and to greater effect, given the nature of caricature. Comic books of the war years often bore dramatic covers—the full-color strangling of Hitler by a costumed hero, for example—which suggested an intensity of feeling but nevertheless frequently belied the contents of the issue. While the details of Hitler's agonized death might not (and probably would not) be recounted on the inside, comic-book heroes still could be relied upon to do something grand for the war effort and to wave the flag at regular intervals. Once the cover had stirred the blood, the slightest thing should serve well enough to keep it circulating, such books suggested.

Once America entered the war, the prevalence of heroes with superhuman powers created problems for comic-book publishers. Were the United States to unleash these impervious patriots upon the Axis, the war could reasonably be expected to end in an hour or less. Some explanation of why that would not happen had to be forthcoming if the credibility, and ultimately the utility, of the heroes were to be maintained, even among unsophisticated juvenile audiences. Publishers responded according to the characteristics of their heroes. Some risked having their less-powerful creations travel abroad, where protracted struggle could indicate that the enemy was altogether tougher than anyone had expected and explain why the war would not end quickly. Others allowed their heroes only indirect participation in the war, lest the plausibility of the characters be lost. On the one hand, Superman might indeed have asserted that "our boys" could handle the nasty business of war without his help; but on the other hand, it was also true that Superman's alter ego, Clark Kent, had managed to fail his preinduction physical, which had conveniently kept the "man of steel" from any involvement in a foreign theatre. While Superman did eliminate the occasional spy or saboteur at home, he did not routinely have the chance to strangle Hitler. Nor did Captain Marvel, who also stayed home and fought saboteurs, although in one story his creators did opt for allegory, allowing their hero to encounter a pair of malevolent trolls who closely resembled the leaders of Germany and Italy. They, it seemed, were ruining the lives of the rest of the trolls, who were ordinary, though small and subterranean, folk desiring only a return to peace in their time. And so forth and so on, in as many permutations and variations as there were costumed and powerful characters.

War stimulated the comic-book industry, not only by providing much of the editorial matter but also by expanding the audience for comic books. Hundreds of thousands of comic books were shipped to American service personnel around the world. True, the books were inexpensive and portable and thus logical fare for troops in transit; but, as well, they satisfied the requirement which dictates that popular culture appeal to the lowest common denominator, in this case the individual with limited language skills and the capacity to respond to only a narrow range of cultural symbols. The mobilization of a total of some 16 million Americans by war's end suggested a number of possibilities to comic-book publishers, and they made every effort to capitalize on them. The quality of their product was of no concern in that economic environment.

Sending comic books to military personnel testified to the utility of the medium in raising morale through patriotic fervor, even if it should be achieved through appeals to racism. Laden as they were with unlikely heroic models, comic books could still inform about unity on the home front and indicate the extent to which American soldiers were glorified in a predominantly domestic medium. Even an illiterate could discern from comic books the virtue of the American cause and the sterling qualities of the American fighting man. Comic books served up a four-color version of a war in which the issues were black and white; they questioned nothing; and they dealt almost exclusively in happy—which is to say, victorious—endings. If this were indeed the "last good war," the comic books of the period bear witness to the accuracy of the label.

The war changed the appearance of comic books, probably because so many servicemen read them. By 1945, their art-work had developed a sexual orientation remarkable in a medium ostensibly still intended for juvenile audiences. A typical wartime cover might reveal in the foreground a scantily clad woman, tied with ropes or chains, at the mercy of some leering Axis villain, while in the background an American hero struggled forward, intent upon her rescue. The woman's clothing inevitably was torn to reveal ample cleavage and thigh, her muscular definition enhanced by forced contortion into some anatomically impossible position. Sometimes, her clothing was completely ripped away, leaving her to face her tormentor clad only in her unmentionables—which, presumably, gave added incentive to that struggling hero back there. The stories inside rarely if ever fulfilled the promises of such a cover, but they usually paid sufficient attention to female secondary sex characteristics to warrant a fellow's perusal.

World War II may have ended in 1945, but in comic books it raged on for another year or two, until publishers had exhausted their backlogs of war-related stories. But by then, they had created a serious problem for themselves. By 1946 or 1947 readers, whether they were children or belonged to the older audience built by the war, were jaded by the redundant deeds of redundant heroes. The costumed types, pale copies of Superman and Batman to begin with, had exhausted the dramatic possibilities of the medium as well as of their individual personae by having done, in four action-packed years, everything that anyone could imagine them doing. By the end of the war, comic-book heroes had been pushed to all manner of improbable pastimes, including tearing Axis tanks in half and leaping from one aircraft to another in the middle of a dogfight. Such foolishness continued for awhile, thanks to those backlogs, but it was simply too much for readers to bear, and comic-book sales plummeted.

Once the backlogs were exhausted, heroes had to return to crime fighting to make their contributions to society—and thus to earn their keep, for what good is a hero who does not practice his trade? But in the wake of a world war, that was nothing if not anti-climactic. Any number of heroes fell by the way, unable to pull their weight on an issue-to-issue basis. The survivors retained a loyal following, but a small one by comparison to what once had been. The very survival of comic books may well have been problematical in the minds of some publishers after 1945.

But of course the medium did survive, and it did so by adapting to a new socio-cultural climate with a radically different psychological construct. The war had brought current affairs into the comic pages, and there could scarcely be retreat from that, owing to the circumstances of war's end. Hiroshima and Nagasaki had rather emphatically illustrated the futility of the kind of escapist fantasy prevalent before 1940. Comic books, like other entertainment media, could not ignore what the world had become, nor could they effect a return to simpler times. Who needed a superman when we, with our atomic bombs, had become supermen? Comic-book publishers were willing to change, to adjust their focus, because they supposed that there was plenty of money still to be made. But first, they had to relearn their constituency. Like most other Americans, they had to discover what the nation had become, in consequence of victory.

I have referred throughout to the postwar decade, the period 1945-1954. And yet the chronology is unhandy. Our brackets (the end of the war and the end of a certain kind of comic books) defy convention. Customarily, one may discuss a thing "since 1945," suggesting that the text will bring us to the day before yesterday; or one may deal with "the Fifties," by which is usually meant Dwight Eisenhower's two-term presidency. Either approach will lead to a pause at 1952 to assess what followed: those were culturally sterile years, some historians think, though lately others have argued otherwise. As a child of "the Fifties," I find it all condescending in the extreme. In my family, Ike was a savior of sorts, presiding over the end to the foolishness that made Harry S. Truman try planting (figuratively, but with literal possibilities) my older brother in Korea. That aside, and at work in the liberal academy, I once tried to discover what was the matter with Eisenhower, the old soldier from Kansas whose critics said he spent too much time indulging himself in popular culture, notably paperback westerns. There was Nixon, of course, and John Foster Dulles's nuclear brinkmanship, and other unpleasantries like those. But, undeniably, Ike had more on the ball than most. Indeed, he was our last president to write his own English; and that means more to me with each new administration. But even *that* aside, how could he be linked with the nation's culture and roundly damned because some thought the culture did not come up to snuff? As a boy, I reveled in that culture, or at least the part with which I had anything to do: Saturday matinees, radio drama, television in its infancy (when I could watch it), bubble-gum trading cards, comic books, pulp magazines, and more.

Decades later, I acknowledged that a good bit of it had been sheer drivel; but I noticed also that what had replaced it represented no significant improvement. There were better technologies, better delivery systems for transmitting culture to kids, but content had deteriorated beyond belief. Except perhaps in the realm of popular music, the Sixties and Seventies seemed drab by comparison—and productive of considerably less cultural documentation to assist subsequent students of those periods. *De gustibus* and all of that, but for me the indicators of what we had become all dated from earlier times—from the Thirties, which linked culture with economy to help us cope; from the Forties, when politics resolved economic problems in some deadly ways and offered the misdirection of a "good" war; and from the Fifties, wherein we began learning to adjust to what we had wrought beneath Stagg Field and at Los Alamos, while examining ourselves, our society, and our enemies (who were, as Pogo wisely reminded, sometimes "us") with particular intensity. There were issues aplenty in those three decades. It seemed to me, first through nostalgic recollection and then in consequence of formal research, that comic books had touched them all. The trouble was, few historians had touched comic books, despite the corresponding (however coincidental) chronology of the medium.

The content of comic books from 1945 to 1954 mirrored the concerns, preoccupations, and beliefs of American society during the post-World War II decade. Occasionally, the mirror may have been concave, convex, or convex-concave, in the manner generally associated with reflections in the carnival fun house; but never was the distortion so great as to obscure the proper identification of the object at hand. As a mirror, the medium was sufficient and effective. It was not without flaws, but no mirror is.

Comic books from 1945 to 1954 reflected a society attempting to adjust to profound changes. America had won its war against the Axis in what its allies termed deplorable fashion, and Americans had been made to realize that they had more in common with their enemies than their national myths had led them to believe. Therefore, the postwar comic books took no delight in recounting the horrible fate of the Japanese at Hiroshima and Nagasaki, although they did rejoice in America's great technological achievement. When the Soviet Union developed its own nuclear weaponry, comic books followed the federal government's lead in declaring that such devices, even in enemy hands, threatened only America's enemies, and in demonstrating a strong belief in the survivability of atomic war.

Comic books pertaining to the Korean War were pessimistic exercises, reflecting the difficulty Americans had in working up enthusiasm for the sort of limited conflict that the Bomb had supposedly rendered obsolete. As well, the Korean War was not that at all, but an undeclared conflict, a protracted and deadly police action against minions (North Koreans) of stooges (Chinese) of Russians, who themselves had been America's allies not long before, in the war against Hitler. The comic books mirrored the political confusion of the day, the uncertainty of events, the concern over the pernicious nature of monolithic Communism. They suggested that spies and counterspies were more effective than soldiers in meeting and dealing with the Red Menace; and the notion made sense to the extent that the Korean War was news (and the pessimism was thus inescapable), whereas the doings of spies and counterspies were classified (permitting optimism as a function of literary license).

In times of stress, some sort of positive constant is always helpful to the national psyche; and if Communist insurgency, the Bomb, and Korea all pointed to the irrelevance of costumed superheroes, then more traditional types might be refurbished to respond more believably to new socio-political situations. Thus it was that Roy Rogers could become an anti-Communist cowboy in the early 1950s. Like those costumed superheroes, he was originally a product of the Depression, and he dressed almost as strangely as they did. But, perhaps because he was supposed to be a mere mortal with at least a modicum of contact with historical reality, he was better qualified than creations whose antecedents lay in somebody's recollection of Mount Olympus or the Old Testament to rally America toward resolution of a few geopolitical problems.

Blacks and women were second-class citizens in comic books of the postwar decade—blacks, because they were either seldom seen or servile; women, because they depended so frequently upon the good offices of men. Blacks and women shared defects of intellectual capacity, according to comic books, or perhaps it was simply that they tended to be ruled by their emotions. Comic books revealed a world owned and operated by white men, wherein avenues to power were closed against all who were not white men. The unfortunates dispossessed by gender or ethnicity roamed, for the most part, the side streets and alleys and frequently the cul-de-sacs of that world. Within the structure of the story, they were generally props, those women and blacks (and Indians, Mexicans, and Chinese), supporting the scenery, or serving as handy victims, or providing comic relief. Again, comic books were mirrors, this time for a racist, sexist society which, at the time, took racism and sexism as part of the normal state of affairs.

It was an ageist society, too, although the word means more now than it did then. One might suppose that a medium for youngsters would advocate a degree of juvenile autonomy—or that it might even encourage a bit of playful anarchy. But comic books reinforced popular perceptions of traditional roles within the family: mother in the kitchen or cleaning the house; father at the office or other place of business; and both (but especially father) largely oblivious to their children, who nevertheless developed normally on account of school, peer interaction, or some innate desire for the approbation of adults in positions of authority. Even in comic books of the "teenage" genre, where the normal authority figures (parents, teachers, principals, police) were customarily buffoons, kids still managed to learn in school, obey the law, fulfill the expectations of parents, and otherwise demonstrate traits characteristic of good citizens. In ordinary family or school situations, children were creatures clearly superior to the adults with whom they had to deal; but they were also subordinate to them, in comic-book deference to the social system the medium served. In action-oriented comic books, heroes were the superior characters, and children—even those who were the heroes' sidekicks—had much to learn. Heroes, we note, were role models. Parents and teachers were not. Heroes were adults younger than parents and teachers and thus closer in age to their little companions, and to their audience. Indeed, the older the comic-book character, the more negative his or her image was likely to be. Whether villain or fool, the senior citizen was no object of veneration.

Comic books of the postwar decade reflected something of the moral equivocation associated with a society in crisis—or with a society that imagines itself in crisis. Normality is always a statistical proposition, and awareness of changes in numbers that pertain to something considered important will generally fuel commentary. Why the increase in the divorce rate? Did it foreshadow the end of the family as a basic national institution? Did that have anything to do with perceived growth of the homosexual population? Were we becoming a nation of sissies? How were these things related to the performance of American troops in Korea? Were juvenile delinquents (whose numbers were increasing) the products of broken homes? Did a broken home mean that Mom had too much influence on youngsters, or that Dad did not have enough? In view of the prevalence of such questions in the popular press, might one anticipate the imminent moral collapse of the United States? Comic books belonging to the horror/science-fiction genre regularly responded in the affirmative—but not so much, one gathers, from pessimism about the future of the nation as from a basic philosophical commitment to the proposition that human nature was sufficiently perverse to destroy the most stable of social institutions.

By 1954, of course, comic books were viewed by increasing numbers of critics not as mere symptoms of social malaise but as root causes of it—or at least of that portion affecting the nation's youth. Beset by all who sought convenient solutions to complex problems, the medium barely survived onslaughts by the civic minded. Comic books comprised a four-color scapegoat for ills that even their virtual extermination could not cure. Once the fact that no cure could be easily found became clear, the concerned public lost interest; but by then it was too late for the many publishers already driven from the field by single-minded critics. If nothing else, the mortality rate among comic-book publishing houses, circa 1954, indicated the undercapitalized status of the industry. Corporate giants were abundant in other branches of the entertainment business, but among comic-book publishers they were few and far between. So were the survivors of 1954.

That comic books were the sole components of the comic/cartoon spectrum selected for criticism in the early 1950s owed more to their manner of presentation than to their content. Racism and sexism were not uncommon in the animated cartoons of the day, for example; and animated cartoons were viewed by millions each week in the nation's movie theaters. As well, lurid and unseemly material occasionally made its way into comic strips, staples of the daily newspaper and thus regular visitors in the American home. Comic books enjoyed a smaller audience than either comic strips or animated cartoons, but theirs was a targeted audience—children, teenagers, young adults—and their presentations to it were made largely without restraint. Graphic violence brought most of the complaints; and here, in fact, was the one area in which comic-book producers took greater liberty than cartoon studios or comic-strip syndicates could dare to permit. Evisceration, disfigurement, torture—comic books showed it all, and a great deal more. The argument that some of them were textbooks for aberrant behaviors resulting in extensive tissue trauma may be casually dismissed nowadays, owing to the ubiquity of exploitative "splatter flics" (the various *Halloween* and *Friday the 13th* films) as the prevalent pastime of many youthful consumers of popular culture; but the fact remains that examination of certain pre-1954 comic books can be a stomach-turning experience. Such books, though relatively few in number in comparison to the hundreds of titles produced in the postwar decade, must persuade the skeptic that the concerns of some critics—especially parents and teachers—were sincerely motivated by a desire to remove unpleasant impressions from the purview of the impressionable. Whether comic strips and animated cartoons were psychologically healthier amusements is perhaps problematical, but the strips dealt in a gentler way with human issues, and the cartoons were usually anthropomorphic and always absurd. Their content could not have initiated or sustained a broadly based critical assault.

Would that we had some sort of viable, statistical measure of the effect of comic books upon juvenile readers—not to apply to Fredric Wertham's interpretation, but to evaluate the medium's influence in shaping subsequent attitudes and opinions. What views in adulthood may be attributed to childhood readings of comic books?

We have more testimony about the impact of television proceeding from the postwar decade than we do about any other medium; and that is so, in my judgment, largely because of the pervasiveness of the medium and thus its perceived potential for causing harm to youngsters. But, while one medium did indeed supplant the other, there is nothing empirical to indicate that television's images entirely replaced those of comic books or rendered their recollection any less potent.

When I was eleven years old, I acquired, at a school rummage sale, a coverless copy of what, years later, proved to be the fortieth and penultimate issue of *Two-Fisted Tales* (December 1954—January, 1955). Its opening story was entitled "Dien Bien Phu!" and concerned the failed French defense of that outpost in what was then known only as Indo-China. Told in the first person, the story ended with a panel showing the narrator's own blood spreading over discarded pin up pictures on the floor of the last French bunker, "even as the Red tide is spreading over Indo-China," for goodness' sake. It was a troubling story, and I read it many times.

I cannot say that the politics of "Dien Bien Phu!" disturbed me. By then, the "police action" in Korea had ended, my big brother was safe, and at school we were ducking and covering as per federal instructions—that is, we were diving beneath our wooden desks whenever a teacher flipped the light switch, persuading ourselves and the adults responsible for us that we could handle an atomic blast. Indeed, we would emerge from under our desks unscathed. This was in Chicago; and if we needed further evidence of our own security, we had only to ride the Illinois Central up to the Loop and observe the anti-aircraft implacements and the Nike missile installations on the greensward along the Outer Drive. But there were no Commies overhead, and none in our neighborhood, that we knew of, anyway. And for most of us, the Red tide had ebbed—if, in our cowboy-and-Superman-soaked consciousnesses, it had ever really flowed in the first place.

Somehow, I never managed to forget "Dien Bien Phu!" Long after that ragged copy of *Two-Fisted Tales* and I had parted company, the story would rise to the surface of my memory, drawn there most often by current events. Indo-China became Vietnam, and Kennedy committed us to it, Johnson made a fetish of it, and those of us in college developed a keen interest in the Selective Service classification system. Occasionally, some journalist would reprise the French defeat at Dien Bien Phu, but for the most part it was overshadowed by outrageous political rhetoric, up to and including Lyndon Johnson's promise to "nail the coonskin to the wall" in celebration of an American victory. At such times, I remembered that old comic-book story. I could see the French officers drinking a final toast to flag and country and going out to die, and I could see the blood spreading across the bunker floor. I realized that repeated readings of "Dien Bien Phu!" a decade before had led me to conclude that the United States did not have a ghost of a chance to win a war—any war—in Vietnam.

Some thirty years after my first encounter with the fortieth issue of *Two-Fisted Tales,* I acquired another copy and reread "Dien Bien Phu!" This time around, it seemed to me that the story contained a warning, not about the futility of a land-war in Asia (after the advice of Douglas MacArthur), but about the importance of halting the spread of Communism. In fact, it was as much an early plea for American involvement in Indo-China as it was an antiwar tract. At age eleven, I had ignored that, noting only the massacre of French soldiers who, despite their formidable skill and training, were nevertheless outgunned by determined Commies in pith helmets. Not much of a nationalist in the mid-1950s (despite the best efforts of my teachers, I suppose), I did not assume automatically that American troops would succeed where elite French paratroopers had failed. Nor did I have any real idea why the people in the pith helmets fought with such vigor and determination. From the perusal of hundreds of Korean-era war comics, I was well aware of the shortcomings of the American soldier; but I could not account for the tenacity of the various Communist minions who were our enemies—at least not beyond the standard good-versus-evil dichotomy offered by popular culture in those days. At age eleven, though, I knew that it was difficult to be seriously and consistently bad, unless you happened also to be demented. And yet, comic books did not preach the existence of entire nations of demented people—or, as I discovered much later, they had not done it since the end of World War II.

During the Vietnam years, I often wondered how so many people could be so optimistic about the prospects for American victory. Not the politicians or the Joint Chiefs of Staff or veterans of earlier wars or right-wing clergy, all of whom had different axes to grind, but the people who were, or were to become, the soldiers who would do the fighting—how could they maintain the hope that a bit of trivia like "Dien Bien Phu!" had long since snatched from me? I have never met a veteran of Vietnam who recalled having read the story, or *Two-Fisted Tales,* or very many comic books of any kind, and yet we all belonged to a generation supposedly threatened by the sheer ubiquity of the comic-book medium and its messages.

Since American withdrawal from Vietnam, there have been millions of words written by former soldiers recounting their experiences during the conflict; and not a few of the memoirs proceeding from service in Vietnam have accepted the chore of explaining the preenlistment mentality of American troops. Almost without exception, the accounts stress the influence of motion pictures and television in establishing the norms of patriotic, masculine, American behavior. Middle-aged veterans now confess to early seduction by John Wayne, Audie Murphy, and even Hopalong Cassidy. We must assume that the impact of screens, whether large or small, pushed other images aside, so that, even if these veterans ever contemplated comic books in the first place, the visuals wrought by New York and Hollywood were finally more pervasive and more easily recalled.

We have no similar body of memoirs from the people who opposed the war at home, especially in the late 1960s. If we did, perhaps we would learn who had been reading all those comic books that depicted war as something less than a blessed event. All we know with any degree of certainty is that millions read them—although we can say so only because we know that many millions of copies were printed and sold. Perhaps, as some have said, it was television, not Wertham, that caused the departure of comic books from the cultural marketplace. Perhaps the only children who read them in the early 1950s were, like me, those whose parents foreswore television until the middle of the decade or until they were prepared to accept the inevitability of the medium, whichever came last. But, that aside, there were so many comic books in the postwar decade, they must have meant something, and academics have taken a little too long in finding out what that is. Now that we have some idea of the lessons, perhaps it would be well to know who learned them.

Ariel Dorfman and Armand Mattelart

SOURCE: "Introduction: Instructions on How to Become a General in the Disneyland Club" and "Conclusion: Power to Donald Duck?" in *How to Read Donald Duck: Imperialist Ideology in the Disney Comic*, translated by David Kunzle, International General, 1975, pp. 27-32, 95-9.

[*In the following excerpt, Dorfman and Mattelart attack Disney's Donald Duck comics as purveyors of what they consider a perniciously capitalist ideology.*]

It would be wrong to assume that Walt Disney is merely a business man. We are all familiar with the massive merchandising of his characters in films, watches, umbrellas, records, soaps, rocking chairs, neckties, lamps, etc. There are Disney strips in five thousand newspapers, translated into more than thirty languages, spread over a hundred countries. According to the magazine's own publicity puffs, in Chile alone, Disney comics reach and delight each week over a million readers. The former Zig-Zag Company, now bizarrely converted into Pinsel Publishing Enterprise (Juvenile Publications Company Ltd.), supplies them to a major part of the Latin American continent. From their national base of operations, where there is so much screaming about the trampling underfoot (the suppression, intimidation, restriction, repression, curbing, etc.) of the liberty of the press, this consortium, controlled by financiers and "philanthropists" of the previous Christian Democrat regime (1964-70), has just permitted itself the luxury of converting several of its publications from biweeklies to weekly magazines.

Apart from his stock exchange rating, Disney has been exalted as the inviolable common cultural heritage of contemporary man; his characters have been incorporated into every home, they hang on every wall, they decorate objects of every kind; they constitute a little less than a social environment inviting us all to join the great universal Disney family, which extends beyond all frontiers and ideologies, transcends differences between peoples and nations, and particularities of custom and language. Disney is the great supranational bridge across which all human beings may communicate with each other. And amidst so much sweetness and light, the registered trademark becomes invisible.

Disney is part—an immortal part, it would seem—of our common collective vision. It has been observed that in more than one country Mickey Mouse is more popular than the national hero of the day.

In Central America, AID (the U.S. Agency for International Development)—sponsored films promoting contraception feature the characters from "Magician of Fantasy." In Chile, after the earthquake of July 1971, the children of San Bernardo sent Disneyland comics and sweets to their stricken fellow children of San Antonio. And the year before, a Chilean women's magazine proposed giving Disney the Nobel Peace Prize.

We need not be surprised, then, that any innuendo about the world of Disney should be interpreted as an affront to morality and civilization at large. Even to whisper anything against Walt is to undermine the happy and innocent palace of childhood, for which he is both guardian and guide.

No sooner had the first children's magazine been issued by the Chilean Popular Unity Government publishing house Quimantú, than the reactionary journals sprang to the defense of Disney:

> The voice of a newscaster struck deep into the microphone of a radio station in the capital. To the amazement of his listeners he announced that Walt Disney is to be banned in Chile. The government propaganda experts have come to the conclusion that Chilean children should not think, feel, love or suffer through animals.
>
> So, in place of Scrooge McDuck, Donald and nephews, instead of Goofy and Mickey Mouse, we children and grownups will have to get used to reading about our own society, which, to judge from the way it is painted by the writers and panegyrists of our age, is rough, bitter, cruel and hateful. It was Disney's magic to be able to stress the happy side of life, and there are always, in human society, characters who resemble those of Disney comics.
>
> Scrooge McDuck is the miserly millionaire of any country in the world, hoarding his money and suffering a heart attack every time someone tries to pinch a cent off him, but in spite of it all, capable of revealing human traits which redeem him in his nephews' eyes.
>
> Donald is the eternal enemy of work and lives dependent upon his powerful uncle. Goofy is the

innocent and guileless common man, the eternal victim of his own clumsiness, which hurts no one and is always good for a laugh.

Big Bad Wolf and Little Wolf are masterly means of teaching children pleasantly, not hatefully, the difference between good and evil. For Big Bad Wolf himself, when he gets a chance to gobble up the Three Little Pigs, suffers pangs of conscience and is unable to do his wicked deed.

And finally, Mickey Mouse is Disney in a nutshell. What human being over the last forty years, at the mere presence of Mickey, has not felt his heart swell with emotion? Did we not see him once as the "Sorcerer's Apprentice" in an unforgettable cartoon which was the delight of children and grownups, which preserved every single note of the masterly music of Prokoviev [a reference no doubt to the music of Paul Dukas]. And what of *Fantasia,* that prodigious feat of cinematic art, with musicians, orchestras, decorations, flowers, and every animate being moving to the baton of Leopold Stokowski? And one scene, of the utmost splendor and realism, even showed elephants executing the most elegant performance of "The Dance of the Dragonflies" [a reference no doubt to the "Dance of the hours"].

How can one assert that children do not learn from talking animals? Have they not been observed time and again engaging in tender dialogues with their pet dogs and cats, while the latter adapt to their masters and show with a purr or a twitch of the ears their understanding of the orders they are given? Are not fables full of valuable lessons in the way animals can teach us how to behave under the most difficult circumstances?

There is one, for instance, by Tomas de Iriarte which serves as a warning against the danger of imposing too stringent principles upon those who work for the public. The mass does not always blindly accept what is offered to them.

This pronouncement parrots some of the ideas prevailing in the media about childhood and children's literature. Above all, there is the implication that politics cannot enter into areas of "pure entertainment," especially those designed for children of tender years. Children's games have their own rules and laws, they move, supposedly, in an autonomous and asocial sphere like the Disney characters, with a psychology peculiar to creatures at a "privileged" age. Inasmuch as the sweet and docile child can be sheltered effectively from the evils of existence, from the petty rancors, the hatreds, and the political or ideological contamination of his elders, any attempt to politicize the sacred domaine of childhood threatens to introduce perversity where there once reigned happiness, innocence and fantasy. Since animals are also exempt from the vicissitudes of history and politics, they are convenient symbols of a world beyond socio-economic realities, and the animal characters can represent ordinary human types, common to all classes, countries and epochs. Disney thus establishes a moral background which draws the child down the proper ethical and aesthetic path. It is cruel and unnecessary to tear it away from its magic garden, for it is ruled by the Laws of Mother Nature; children *are* just like that and the makers of comic books, in their infinite wisdom, understand their behavior and their biologically-determined need for harmony. Thus, to attack Disney is to reject the unquestioned stereotype of the child, sanctified as the law in the name of the immutable human condition.

There are *automagic* antibodies in Disney. They tend to neutralize criticism because they are the same values already instilled into people, in the tastes, reflexes and attitudes which inform everyday experience at all levels. Disney manages to subject these values to the extremest degree of commercial exploitation. The potential assailer is thus condemned in advance by what is known as "public opinion," that is, the thinking of people who have already been conditioned by the Disney message and have based their social and family life upon it.

The publication of this book will of course provoke a rash of hostile comment against the authors. To facilitate our adversaries' task, and in order to lend uniformity to their criteria, we offer the following model, which has been drawn up with due consideration for the philosophy of the journals to which the gentlemen of the press are so attached:

INSTRUCTIONS ON HOW TO EXPEL SOMEONE FROM THE DISNEYLAND CLUB

1. The authors of this book are to be defined as follows: indecent and immoral (while Disney's world is pure); hyper-complicated and hyper-sophisticated (while Walt is simple, open and sincere); members of a sinister elite (while Disney is the most popular man in the world); political agitators (while Disney is non-partisan, above politics); calculating and embittered (while Walt D. is spontaneous, emotional, loves to laugh and make laughter); subverters of youth and domestic peace (while W.D. teaches respect for parents, love of one's fellows and protection of the weak); unpatriotic and antagonistic to the national spirit (while Mr. Disney, being international, represents the best and dearest of our native traditions); and finally, cultivators of "Marxism-fiction," a theory imported from abroad by "wicked foreigners" (while Unca Walt is against exploitation and promotes the classless society of the future).

2. Next, the authors of this book are to be accused of the very lowest of crimes: of daring to raise doubts about the child's imagination, that is, O horror!, to question the right of children to have a literature of their own, which interprets them so well, and is created on their behalf.

3. FINALLY, TO EXPEL SOMEONE FROM THE DISNEYLAND CLUB, ACCUSE HIM REPEATEDLY OF TRYING TO BRAINWASH CHILDREN WITH THE DOCTRINE OF COLORLESS SOCIAL REALISM, IMPOSED BY POLITICAL COMMISSARS.

There can be no doubt that children's literature is a genre like any other, monopolized by specialized subsectors within the culture industry. Some dedicate themselves to the adventure story, some to mystery, others to the erotic novel, etc. But at least the latter are directed towards an amorphous public, which buys at random. In the case of the children's genre, however, there is a virtually biologically captive, predetermined audience.

Children's comics are devised by adults, whose work is determined and justified by their idea of what a child is or should be. Often, they even cite "scientific" sources or ancient traditions ("it is popular wisdom, dating from time immemorial") in order to explain the nature of the public's needs. In reality, however, these adults are not about to tell stories which would jeopardize the future they are planning for their children.

So the comics show the child as a miniature adult, enjoying an idealized, gilded infancy which is really nothing but the adult projection of some magic era beyond the reach of the harsh discord of daily life. It is a plan for salvation which presupposes a primal stage within every existence, sheltered from contradictions and permitting imaginative escape. Juvenile literature, embodying purity, spontaneity, and natural virtue, while lacking in sex and violence, represents earthly paradise. It guarantees man's own redemption as an adult: as long as there are children, he will have the pretext and means for self-gratification with the spectacle of his own dreams. In his children's reading, man stages and performs over and over again the supposedly unproblematical scenes of his inner refuge. Regaling himself with his own legend, he falls into tautology; he admires himself in the mirror, thinking it to be a window. But the child playing down there in the garden is the purified adult looking back at himself.

So it is the adult who produces the comics, and the child who consumes them. The role of the apparent child actor, who reigns over this uncontaminated world, is at once that of audience and dummy for his father's ventriloquism. The father denies his progeny a voice of his own, and as in any authoritarian society, he establishes himself as the other's sole interpreter and spokesman. All the little fellow can do is to let his father represent him.

But wait a minute, gentlemen! Perhaps children really *are* like that?

Indeed, the adults set out to prove that this literature is essential to the child, satisfying his eager demands. But this is a closed circuit: children have been conditioned by the magazines and the culture which spawned them. They tend to reflect in their daily lives the characteristics they are supposed to possess, in order to win affection, acceptance, and rewards; in order to grow up properly and integrate into society. The Disney world is sustained by rewards and punishments; it hides an iron hand with the velvet glove. Considered, by definition, unfit to choose from the alternatives available to adults, the youngsters intuit "natural" behavior, happily accepting that their imagination be channelled into incontestable ethical and aesthetic ideals. Juvenile literature is justified by the children it has generated through a vicious circle.

Thus, adults create for themselves a childhood embodying their own angelical aspirations, which offer consolation, hope and a guarantee of a "better," but unchanging, future. This "new reality," this autonomous realm of magic, is artfully isolated from the reality of the everyday. Adult values are projected onto the child, as if childhood was a special domain where these values could be protected uncritically. In Disney, the two strata—adult and child—are not to be considered as antagonistic; they fuse in a single embrace, and history becomes biology. The identity of parent and child inhibits the emergence of true generational conflicts. The pure child will replace the corrupt father, preserving the latter's values. The future (the child) reaffirms the present (the adult), which, in turn, transmits the past. The apparent independence which the father benevolently bestows upon this little territory of his creation, is the very means of assuring his supremacy.

But there is more: this lovely, simple, smooth, translucent, chaste and pacific region, which has been promoted as Salvation, is unconsciously infiltrated by a multiplicity of adult conflicts and contradictions. This transparent world is designed both to conceal and reveal latent traces of real and painful tensions. The parent suffers this split consciousness without being aware of his inner turmoil. Nostalgically, he appropriates the "natural disposition" of the child in order to conceal the guilt arising from his own fall from grace; it is the price of redemption for his own condition. By the standards of his angelic model, he must judge himself guilty; as much as he needs this land of enchantment and salvation, he could never imagine it with the necessary purity. He could never turn into his own child. But this salvation only offers him an imperfect escape; it can never be so pure as to block off all his real life problems.

In juvenile literature, the adult, corroded by the trivia of everyday life blindly defends his image of youth and innocence. Because of this, it is perhaps the best (and least expected) place to study the disguises and truths of contemporary man. For the adult, in protecting his dream-image of youth, hides the fear that to penetrate it would destroy his dreams and reveal the reality it conceals.

Thus, *the imagination of the child is conceived as the past and future utopia of the adult*. But set up as an inner realm of fantasy, this model of his Origin and his Ideal Future Society lends itself to the free assimilation of all his woes. It enables the adult to partake of his own demons, provided they have been coated in the syrup of paradise, and that they travel there with the passport of innocence.

Mass culture has granted to contemporary man, in his constant need to visualize the reality about him, the means of feeding on his own problems without having to encounter all the difficulties of form and content presented by the modern art and literature of the elite. Man is offered knowledge without commitment, a self-colonization of his own imagination. By dominating the child, the father dominates himself. The relationship is a sado-masochistic one, not unlike that established between Donald and his nephews. Similarly, readers find themselves caught between their desire and their reality, and in their attempt to escape to a purer realm, they only travel further back into their own traumas.

Mass culture has opened up a whole range of new issues. While it certainly has had a levelling effect and has exposed a wider audience to a broader range of themes, it has simultaneously generated a cultural elite which has cut itself off more and more from the masses. Contrary to the democratic potential of mass culture, this elite has plunged mass culture into a suffocating complexity of solutions, approaches and techniques, each of which is comprehensible only to a narrow circle of readers. The creation of children's culture is part of this specialization process.

Child fantasy, although created by adults, becomes the exclusive reserve of children. The self-exiled father, once having created this specialized imaginary world, then revels in it through the keyhole. The father must be absent, and without direct jurisdiction, just as the child is without direct obligations. Coercion melts away in the magic palace of sweet harmony and repose—the palace raised and administered at a distance by the father, whose physical absence is designed to avoid direct confrontation with his progeny. This absence is the prerequisite of his omnipresence, his total invasion. Physical presence would be superfluous, even counter-productive, since the whole magazine is already his projection. He shows up instead as a favorite uncle handing out free magazines. Juvenile literature is a father surrogate. The model of paternal authority is at every point immanent, the implicit basis of its structure and very existence. The natural creativity of the child, which no one in his right mind can deny, is channelled through the apparent absence of the father into an adult-authoritarian vision of the real world. Paternalism *in absentia* is the indispensable vehicle for the defense and invisible control of the ostensibly autonomous childhood model. The comics, like television, in all vertically structured societies, rely upon distance as a means of authoritarian reinforcement.

The authoritarian relationship between the real life parent and child is repeated and reinforced within the fantasy world itself, and is the basis for all relations in the entire world of the comics. Later, we shall show how the relationship of child-readers to the magazine they consume is generally based on and echoed in the way the characters experience their own fantasy world within the comic. Children will not only identify with Donald Duck because Donald's situation relates to their own life, but also because the way they read or the way they are exposed to it, imitates and prefigures the way Donald Duck lives out his own problems. Fiction reinforces, in a circular fashion, the manner in which the adult desires the comic be received and read.

. . . . .

Attacking Disney is no novelty; he has often been exposed as the travelling salesman of the imagination, the propagandist of the "American Way of Life," and a spokesman of "unreality." But true as it is, such criticism misses the true impulse behind the manufacture of the Disney characters, and the true danger they represent to dependent countries like Chile. The threat derives not so much from their embodiment of the "American Way of Life," as that of the "American Dream of Life." It is the manner in which the U.S. dreams and redeems itself, and then imposes that dream upon others for its own salvation, which poses the danger for the dependent countries. It forces us Latin Americans to see ourselves as they see us.

Any social reality may be defined as the incessant dialectical interaction between a material base and the superstructure which reflects it and anticipates it in the human mind. Values, ideas, *Weltanschauung,* and the accompanying daily attitudes and conduct down to the slightest gesture, are articulated in a concrete social form which people develop to establish control over nature, and render it productive. It is necessary to have a coherent and fluid mental picture of this material base, and the emotional and intellectual responses it engenders, so that society can survive and develop. From the moment people find themselves involved in a certain social system—that is, from conception and birth—it is impossible for their consciousness to develop without being based on concrete material conditions. In a society where one class controls the means of economic production, that class also controls the means of intellectual production; ideas, feelings, intuitions, in short—the very meaning of life. The bourgeoisie have, in fact, tried to invert the true relationship between the material base and the superstructure. They conceive of ideas as productive of riches by means of the only untainted matter they know—grey matter—and the history of humanity becomes the history of ideas.

To capture the true message of Disney, we must reflect upon these two components in his fantasy world to understand precisely in what way he represents reality, and how his fantasy may relate to concrete social existence, that is, the immediate historical conditions. The way Disney conceives the relationship between base and superstructure is comparable to the way the bourgeoisie conceive this relationship in the real life of the dependent countries (as well as their own). Once we have analysed the structural differences and similarities, we will be better able to judge the effects of Disney-type magazines on the condition of underdevelopment.

It is, by now, amply proven that the Disney world is one in which all materiality has been purged. All forms of production (the material, sexual, historical) have been eliminated, and conflict has never a social base, but is conceived in terms of good versus bad, lucky versus unlucky, and intelligent versus stupid. So Disney characters can dispense with the material base underpinning every action in a concrete everyday world. But they are certainly not ethereal angels flying around in outer space. Continually we have seen how purposefully their lives reflect his view of the everyday world. Since Disney has purged himself of the secondary economic sector (industrial production, which gave rise to contemporary society and power to the bourgeoisie and imperialism), there is only one infrastructure left to give body to his fantasies and supply material for his ideas. It is the one which automatically represents the economic life of his characters: the *tertiary* sector. The service sector, which arose in the service of industry and remains dependent upon it.

As we have observed, all the relationships in the Disney world are compulsively consumerist; commodities in the marketplace of objects and ideas. The magazine is part of this situation. The Disney industrial empire itself arose to service a society demanding entertainment; it is part of an entertainment network whose business it is to feed leisure with more leisure disguised as fantasy. The cultural industry is the sole remaining machine which has purged its contents of society's industrial conflicts, and therefore is the only means of escape into a future which otherwise is implacably blocked by reality. It is a playground to which all children (and adults) can come, and which very few can leave.

So there can be no conflict in Disney between superstructure and infrastructure. The only material base left (the tertiary, service sector) is at once defined as a superstructure. The characters move about in the realm of leisure, where human beings are no longer beset by material concerns. Their first and last thought is to fill up spare time, that is, to seek entertainment. From this entertainment emerges an autonomous world so rigid and confined, it eliminates all traces of a productive, preleisure type of infrastructure. All material activity has been removed, the mere presence of which might expose the falsity of Disney's fusion of entertainment and "real" worlds, and his marriage of fantasy and life. Matter has become mind, history has become pastime, work has become adventure, and everyday life has become a sensational news item.

Disney's ideas are thus truly material PRODUCTIONS of a society which has reached a certain stage of material development. They represent a superstructure of values, ideas and criteria, which make up the self-image of advanced capitalist society, and facilitate innocent consumption of its own traumatic past. The industrial bourgeoisie impose their self-vision upon all the attitudes and aspirations of the other social sectors, at home and abroad. The utopic ideology of the tertiary sector is used as an emotional projection, and is posed as the only possible future. Their historic supremacy as a class is transposed to, and reflected in, the hierarchy established within the Disney universe; be it in the operations of the industrial empire which sells the comics, or in the relations between the characters created in the comics.

The only relation the center (adult-city folk bourgeoisie) manages to establish with the periphery (child-noble savage-worker) is touristic and sensationalist. The primary resources sector (the Third World) becomes a source of playthings; gold, or the picturesque experiences with which one holds boredom at bay. The innocence of this marginal sector is what guarantees the Duckburger his touristic salvation, his imaginative animal-ness, and his childish rejuvenation. The primitive infrastructure offered by the Third World countries (and what they represent biologically and socially) become the nostalgic echo of a lost primitivism, a world of purity (and raw materials) reduced to a picture postcard to be enjoyed by a service-oriented world. Just as a Disney character flees degenerate city life in search of recreation and in order to justify his wealth through an adventure in paradise, so the reader flees his historic conflicts in search of recreation in the innocent Eden of Donald & Co. This seizure of marginal peoples and their transformation into a lost purity, which cannot be understood apart from the historic contradictions arising from an advanced capitalist society, are ideological manifestations of its economic-cultural system. For these peoples exist in reality, both in the dependent countries and as racial minorities ("Nature's" bottomless reservoir) within the U.S. itself.

Advanced capitalist society is realizing in Disney the long cherished dream of the bourgeoisie for a return to nature. It the course of the bourgeoisie's evolution this dream has been expressed in a multitude of historic variations in the fields of philosophy, literature, art and social custom. Recently, from the mid-twentieth century, the mass media have assisted the dominant class in trying to recover Paradise, and attain sin-free production. The tribal (now planetary) village of leisure without the conflicts of work, and of earth without pollution, all rest on the consumer goods derived from industrialization. The imaginative world of children cleanses the entire Disney cosmos in the waters of innocence. Once this innocence is processed by the entertainment media, it fosters the development of a class political utopia. Yet, despite the development of advanced capitalist society, it is the historic experience of the marginal peoples which is identified as the center of innocence within this purified world.

The bourgeois concept of entertainment, and the specific manner in which it is expounded in the world of Disney, is the superstructural manifestation of the dislocations and tensions of an advanced capitalist historical base. In its entertainment, it automatically generates certain myths functional to the system. It is altogether normal for readers experiencing the conflicts of their age from within the perspective of the imperialist system, to see their own daily life, and projected future, reflected in the Disney system.

Just as the Chilean bourgeoisie, in their magazines, photograph the latest hyper-sophisticated models in rustic surroundings, putting mini- and maxi-skirts, hot pants and shiny boots into the "natural environment" of some impoverished rural province (Colchagua, Chiloe) or—this is the limit, why not leave them in peace, exterminators—among the Alacalufe Indians; so the comics born in the United States, reflect their obsession for a return to a form of social organization which has been destroyed by urban civilization. Disney is the conquistador constantly purifying himself by justifying his past and future conquests.

But how can the cultural superstructure of the dominant classes, which represents the interests of the metropolis and is so much the product of contradictions in the development of its productive forces, exert such influence and acquire such popularity in the underdeveloped countries? Just why is Disney such a threat?

The primary reason is that his products, necessitated and facilitated by a huge industrial capitalist empire are imported together with so many other consumer objects into the dependent country, which is dependent precisely because it *depends* on commodities arising economically and intellectually in the power center's totally alien (foreign) conditions. Our countries are exporters of raw materials, and importers of superstructural and cultural goods. To service our "monoproduct" economies and provide urban paraphernalia, we send copper, and they send machines to extract copper, and, of course, Coca Cola. Behind the Coca Cola stands a whole structure of expectations and models of behavior, and with it, a particular kind of present and future society, and an interpretation of the past. As we import the industrial product conceived, packaged and labelled abroad, and sold to the profit of the rich foreign uncle, at the same time we also import the foreign cultural forms of that society, but without their context: the advanced capitalist social conditions upon which they are based. It is historically proven that the dependent countries have been maintained in dependency by the continued international division of labor which restricts any development capable of leading to economic independence.

It is this discrepancy between the social-economic base of the life of the individual reader, and the character of the collective vision concerning this base which poses the problem. It gives Disney effective power of penetration into the dependent countries because he offers individual goals at the expense of the collective needs. This dependency has also meant that our intellectuals, from the beginning, have had to use alien forms to present their vision, in order to express, in a warped but very often revealing and accurate manner, the reality they are submerged in, which consists of the superimposition of various historical phases. It is a bizarre kind of ambiguity (called "barroquismo" in Latin American culture), which manages to reveal reality at the same time as it conceals it. But the great majority of the people have passively to accept this discrepancy in their daily subsistence. The housewife in the slums is incited to buy the latest refrigerator or washing machine; the impoverished industrial worker lives bombarded with images of the Fiat 125; the small landholder, lacking even a tractor, tills the soil near a modern airport; and the homeless are dazzled by the chance of getting a hole in the apartment block where the bourgeoisie has decided to coop them up. Immense economic underdevelopment lies side-by-side with minute mental superdevelopment.

Since the Disney utopia eliminates the secondary (productive) sector, retaining only the primary (raw material) and tertiary (service) sectors, it creates a parody of the underdeveloped peoples. As we have seen, it also segregates spirit and matter, town and countryside, city folk and noble savages, monopolists of mental power and mono-sufferers of physical power, the morally flexible and the morally immobile, father and son, authority and submission, and well-deserved riches and equally well-deserved poverty. Underdeveloped peoples take the comics, at second hand, as instruction in the way they are supposed to live and relate to the foreign power center. There is nothing strange in this. In the same way Disney expels the productive and historical forces from his comics, imperialism thwarts real production and historical evolution in the underdeveloped world. The Disney dream is cast in the same mold which the capitalist system has created for the real world.

Power to Donald Duck means the promotion of underdevelopment. The daily agony of Third World peoples is served up as a spectacle for permanent enjoyment in the utopia of bourgeois liberty. The non-stop buffet of recreation and redemption offers all the wholesome exotica of underdevelopment: a balanced diet of the unbalanced world. The misery of the Third World is packaged and canned to liberate the masters who produce it and consume it. Then, it is thrown-up to the poor as the only food they know. Reading Disney is like having one's own exploited condition rammed with honey down one's throat.

"Man cannot return to his childhood without becoming childish," wrote Marx, noting that the social conditions which gave rise to ancient Greek art in the early days of civilization, could never be revived. Disney thinks exactly the opposite, and what Marx regretfully affirms Walt institutes as a cardinal rule of his fantasy world. He does not rejoice in the innocence of the child, and he does not attempt, from his "higher" level, to truthfully reflect the child's nature. The childish innocence, and the return to a historic infancy which Disney, as monarch of his creation, elevates, is a defiance of evolution. It is like a dirty, puerile, old man clutching his bag of tricks and traps, as he crawls on towards the lost paradise of purity.

And why, readers may ask, do we rail against this deshelved senility, which for worse or worser has peopled the infancy of us all, irrespective of our social class, ideology or country? Let us repeat once more: the Disney cosmos is no mere refuge in the area of occasional entertainment; it is our everyday stuff of social oppression. Putting the Duck on the carpet is to question the various forms of authoritarian and paternalist culture pervading the relationship of the bourgeoisie among themselves, with others, and with nature. It is to challenge the role of individuals and their class in the process of historic development, and the fabrication of a mass culture built on the backs of the masses. More intimately, it is also to scrutinize the social relations which a father establishes with his son; a father wishing to transcend mere biological determinants will better understand and censure the underhanded manipulation and repression he practices with his own reflection. Obviously, this is equally the case for mothers and daughters as well.

This book did not emanate from the crazied mind of ivory tower individuals, but arises from a struggle to defeat the class enemy on his and our common terrain. Our criticism has nothing anarchic about it. These are no cannon shots in the air, as Huey, Dewey and Louie would have it. It is but another means of furthering the whole process of the potential Chilean and Latin American Revolution by recognizing the necessity of deepening the cultural transformation. Let us find out just how much of Donald Duck remains at all levels of Chilean society. As long as he strolls with his smiling countenance so *innocently* about the streets of our country, as long as Donald is power and our collective representative, the bourgeoisie and imperialism can sleep in peace. Someday, that fantastic laugh and its echoes will fade away, leaving a mere grimace in its stead. But only when the formulae of daily life imposed upon us by our enemy ceases, and the culture medium which now shapes our social praxis is reshaped.

To the accusation that this is merely a destructive study which fails to propose an alternative to the defeated Disney, we can only reply that no one is able to "propose" his individual solution to these problems. There can be no elite of experts in the reformation of culture. What happens after Disney will be decided by the social practice of the peoples seeking emancipation. It is for the vanguard organized in political parties to pick up this experience and allow it to find its full human expression.

A. W. Sadler

SOURCE: "The Love Comics and American Popular Culture," in *American Quarterly*, Vol. XVI, No. 3, Fall, 1964, pp. 486-90.

[*In the following essay, Sadler lists the recurring themes, character types, and plot points of romance comics.*]

All across the country, in small town drugstores, at roadside drive-ins, or in big city news-and-tobacco shops, the wall-shelf arrayed with dime comic books is a familiar sight. Here is a form of popular literature, and, like any literature, it must have its *raison d'être*. If you begin to browse, you will soon notice that these little booklets fall into specific categories. There are, for example, the "love comics," which seem to be directed, for the most part, to the interests of teen-aged American girls. Their heroines are usually girls in their late teens. Usually, they are distinctly lower-middle-class girls. Their families have achieved a measure of ease and comfort, but not without impressing upon their daughters the struggle that was required of them. Girls in these stories are ordinarily finishing high school, or else they have just lately graduated and are working at non-career jobs, as stenographers, general office help, or as practical nurses, or in a few cases as waitresses. Their main concern, while ostensibly love, is actually marriage—an early marriage, and one with stability and security.

Where the girl's home life is portrayed, we usually find an aproned mother, looking old before her time, puttering in the kitchen and freely giving advice ("Why do you stay at home, instead of going out with some nice young man?"). The character of the heroine is defined for us in terms of her social background; her job is a temporary affair, and is only incidental to the story. With the men, on the other hand, our impressions are based on occupation and ambitions. The boys who finally win the heroines' affections generally are several years older, and quite well established in their jobs. Some are white-collar workers, and can afford to be free spenders. Others are blue-collar workers (truck drivers, factory foremen, cab drivers), with ambitions of one day becoming a partner in the firm, or having a business of their own. A few are wealthy, and have college degrees. Quite common too (in magazines written predominantly for small-town girls) is the boy who has been promised management of his dad's store.

The names of these magazines, then, may be misleading *(Love Journal, Teen-Age Temptations, True Life Secrets, Romantic Secrets),* unless one understands the special meaning behind these titles. The love comic does not deal simply with the happy anticipation of romance and courtship. But neither does it attempt to deal directly with its readers' specific anxieties regarding an early marriage and security. These separate anxieties are reduced to a single question: How is one to know who is the right man to marry? And the stereotyped answer is this: that for every woman, security and true love are to be found in one and the same man; that she cannot fail to find genuine dollar security with the man who really loves her, and, on the other hand, she will never find security of any kind with a man whose love for her is false. The message of the girls' comics is that there is a mystique that connects (1) a girl's concern for goodness in a man (his honesty, his reliability, his character), (2) her desire for a good provider, and (3) her wish for love and romance. These stories offer their readers two kinds of advice: advice on how to judge character in men, and advice on how a girl can best come to terms with her own ambitions and desires. Above all, they teach the lesson that the girl must know how to recognize and value what is genuine, both in life and in love. Each story is but a dramatization of this lesson.

In each of these magazines there are three or four stories. The stories are endlessly repetitive, all having the same form and roughly the same subject matter. The basic pattern of the narrative is quite simple: the heroine is dissatisfied with her situation in life, and decides to embark on some sort of adventure—either a job in the city, or a more lively circle of friends, or a play for the most handsome boy in the neighborhood—and through this adventure the true nature of love is revealed to her. The little escapade is the heart of the story, and constitutes her "sin."

The locale of most of these stories is the American small town. Occasionally it is given a name, like "Westfield." Boredom with life in her home town is generally what provokes the heroine into her escapade. A few magazines, aimed specifically at city girls, attempt to transplant the frustrations of life in a small town into a city neighborhood setting, but the basic plot remains very much the same. The heroine's boredom may be with her home town, or her parents, or her high school clique, or her "steady" boyfriend—or, most commonly, with all of these put together. The dull boyfriend ("conservative," he is sometimes called) is a recurrent figure, and must present quite a problem to the girls who follow these stories devotedly.

The heroines also feel they aren't being treated royally enough by their boyfriends, that they aren't receiving enough attention, that they aren't the center of excitement for their beaux and their friends. In a word, they would like to be pampered just a bit more. This desire for excitement and for attention accounts always for the heroine's escapade. She may want success and fame (although success may only mean becoming a private secretary in an advertising agency, and fame may only mean going to New York to dance in a chorus line). More important, she wants the luxuries of a glamorous (city) life. She wants the gaiety of night life. She wants fine dresses and furs, and perhaps a yellow convertible. And she wants to be escorted by a Broadway smoothie. In the end, of course, she is taught that all these things are false, and that lasting happiness (and lasting excitement) can be found only in life's simpler things. She is taught to be content with the homey life she grew up with. Yet while she is made to repent her adventure, she generally comes off with a better man than she would otherwise have found; and she is never made to feel that she was wrong in wanting more lavish attention from her beaux than she was getting. She gives up her desire for luxuries; but she is left with at least a promise ("I fell in love with you, not your clothes! After we're married, you'll have all the pretty clothes you want!").

The story may on occasion revolve around some flaw in the heroine's character—jealousy, or deceitfulness, or irresponsibility; but only when the story is to be especially melodramatic. All but a few magazines avoid this sort of material. Ordinarily we are led to believe that there are not good and bad girls; only good girls, who have to learn, through experience, to discriminate between good men and bad men. Some of the better magazines attempt to deal with specific problems of teen-aged girls, in a serious and constructive way, thus avoiding in each case the temptation to moralize. But this too is an exception to the rule.

One does occasionally come upon a story in which the heroine seems to be completely lacking in character, and is tossed back and forth like a football between the good men, who try to help her, and the bad men, who try to use her to their advantage. This type of heroine is a passive agent in a world of men, who contend for her attentions and affections and trust. She makes a very bad sort of heroine, and, happily, she is a rare species.

Most stories conclude with the heroine repentant of her encounter with what is false in life, and joyful over her discovery of the true meaning of love—and of course the prospect of an imminent marriage. In the end, a lesson in morality has been taught—a lesson drawn from a moral code that has vaguely Calvinist undertones. Its emphasis is on loyalty and purity of character, truthfulness, honesty and self-respect. It also endorses a genuine anxiety about success in the workaday world. It teaches self-discipline and self-denial where money is concerned, and often preaches "work hard, and save your money." Surely it is a surprise to find that magazines with titles like *Brides' Romances* and *Real Love* are actually concerned with the religion of frugality; but ostensibly to the writers, and presumably also to the readers of these magazines, frugality and real love can be as closely fitted as the key to the lock. "Love Can't Be Dishonest," reads the title of one of the most revealing of these stories. The heroine, Marge, has been going steady with her classmate, Jimmy. They are rather poor, and cannot afford many of the social functions their school puts on. Jimmy works afternoons at Mr. Robbins' fancy groceries store. One day Jimmy wants so badly to take Marge to the school picnic that he pockets some cash from Mr. Robbins' cash register. Marge persuades him to put it back, and Jimmy tells her: "You're wonderful, Marge, darling . . . I feel clean again!" And she answers: "And that's the way we'll stay, Jimmy—all through life. And after we're grown up and married, you'll be successful, Jimmy. Our good times are coming!"

In some ways this story is not typical. For one thing, it is very unusual for the boy to take the initiative and precipitate the misadventure. For another, this couple is relatively young, and the hero and heroine must wait for financial independence. What is characteristic is that the heroine is *ready* to wait for prosperity. Above all, she has expressly subordinated her desire for affluence to her desire for a clean life and for genuine love. It is this integration of virtue with economic reward that reminds one of the Puritan ethic. If a girl is honest and sincere at all times, if she is truthful with her boyfriend, and if she never pretends to be something that she is not, she will find a good man with these same qualities, and prosperity will come to them, in marriage.

It would be harsh and inaccurate, I think, to say that the morality of the girls' comic is wrong, or that it is unrealistic or harmful. It is over-simplified. It draws the world in black and white—in terms, that is, of the good *versus* the bad; but who can say it is wrong in its fundamentals? We may smile at the overdrawn characters, and the conventions relied upon in telling the story: the older bachelor-villain (probably in his thirties), with his slick black hair and his black moustaches, always lighting his pipe as he schemes (he never actually smokes the pipe), or the younger bachelor-villain, blond and handsome, who is usually a gambler, or a New York promoter. According to the clichés of the love comic, successful career girls always drive yellow convertibles; well-meaning parents always grow anxious when their daughters decide to move to the city and seek their fortunes; and a girl can always rely on just that one decisive kiss to tell her whether or not her boyfriend really trusts and admires her. Yet can we really say, leaving aside these conventions of story-telling, that the girls who read these magazines get a misleading picture of the world they will have to contend with? If we are impatient with the over-simplification of this "world," we should remember that the girl who counts upon love comics to give (or reinforce) a true picture of life cannot wait too long for the values she will act upon; she must marry early. After her marriage, she will have time enough to absorb the ifs, ands and buts of life; for the present her concern is with how to make the best possible marriage. Granting the immediacy of her concern, these comics must serve her wants more than adequately.

Finally, the stranger to these magazines will be struck, I think, by the feeling of stability he receives in reading them. It is a hard thing to explain, but one senses that he is reading of people for whom life is never easy, for whom every common comfort is the reward of hard work, and yet who never find life an unwieldy, incomprehensible thing. Life is ever challenging, continually putting one's virtues to trial; but the good and bad are always clearly discernible; the fundamentals of life are always in plain view. After reading through a sampling of these magazines, one is apt to come away with an inexplicable feeling that everything is right with the world. It is perhaps in conveying this feeling for the stability of society and the world, that popular culture fulfills its most significant function.

Max J. Skidmore and Joey Skidmore

SOURCE: "More Than Mere Fantasy: Political Themes in Contemporary Comic Books," in *Journal of Popular Culture*, Vol. 17, No. 1, Summer, 1983, pp. 83-92.

[*In the following essay, Skidmore and Skidmore identify a new political consciousness instilled in comic books by the Marvel group and other mainstream publishers.*]

To most of us who were in or approaching our teens in the 1940s, comic books were central to our entertainment. Because the pressures of school, parents and economics generally relegated movies to weekends, the only real competition to the comics were radio shows. The contrast with today is striking. Such is the variety of stimulation available now to young persons that many children in this age of television probably never turn to comic books; some in fact may even be unaware of them. As a result, the comics that once were the center of a storm of controversy now occasion relatively little public comment. Now and then there are books or articles describing the phenomenon of the new comic book, but most of them are directed at nostalgia, on the one hand, or at a limited academic audience, on the other.

Those who pay any attention to contemporary comics discover that the quality of the art in nearly all cases has increased immeasurably from that of the Golden Age. A close look indicates also that the plots and story lines are considerably more complex. Most comments upon the comics point out that we are in the age of the "normal" or more human superhero, in the sense that he or she has the same troubles or hang-ups that would exist for any other person. In fact, the possession of superpowers frequently adds to the personal difficulties that face the protagonists.

Only the readers, however, are likely to discern the tendency of many modern comics to shun the older clear-cut simplistic situations, and to adopt a less cut-and-dried approach to values, morality and politics. As the comics have changed, so has the readership. It seems likely that as the audience has become less than universal, it has become more literate; reading anything, even illustrated strips, requires more effort than watching television. The assumption that the reader of comics today is probably older and certainly more sophisticated than his or her counterpart in the Golden Age is consistent with the increasing sophistication of the comics themselves.

Certainly most children of the Golden Age had no notion that their comics were propaganda. The critics centered their attacks upon portrayals of violence and crime, never upon ideology, except insofar as an occasional psychiatrist might complain that the worship of superheroes might induce Fascism. Nevertheless, a substantial portion of comic books have in fact always been intensely political. In the Golden Age, they were chauvinistic, they assumed that in every situation right and wrong were clearly distinct, and they forcefully set forth the United States as the embodiment of all that is right. Moreover, they frequently were overtly racist, sometimes even to the point of including stereotyped "Sambo" characters in attempts at comic relief. The prevailing attitude was well captured during the Second World War by the Golden Age Captain America, who often expressed his opinion that with regard to "Japs," the only task was to "Keep 'em dying!"

The Golden Age reader who turns to today's comics may be impressed or shocked, depending upon his or her orientation. Very likely, however, such a reader would be faintly embarrassed to discover, either through reprints or comic collections, just how blatant are the old works that once afforded so much pleasure.

The world has changed, and comics have changed with it. The simplistic solutions to political situations that had such an appeal throughout much of our existence as a modern nation now seem much less obvious. Contemporary comics often reflect this loss of innocence, and upon occasion have gone considerably beyond the public in their speculation, their inferences, and their predictions. Much of the modern comic effort seems closer in tone to the best of science fiction than to the Golden Age predecessors, and it is common knowledge among comic buffs that such writers as Harlan Ellison and Ray Bradbury have taken the comics seriously. The significance of all this is that, despite the more restricted readership, comics represent very big business, indeed, with enormous sales that dwarf those of most other publishing efforts. Regardless of whether they influence tastes or reflect them, they obviously strike a definitely responsive chord.

The argument that comics deserve to be taken seriously is not new. M. Thomas Inge has discussed the relationship between comics and film, and has pointed out that William Friedkin, Federico Fellini, Orson Welles and Alain Resnais are all film makers who have explicitly acknowledged their indebtedness to comics in one respect or another. Inge concluded that comics from a new and different artistic medium that draws upon the heroic tradition to which Hercules, Beowulf and Paul Bunyan belong, and that they are valuable too as reflectors of popular attitudes. And the comics have had a discernible influence upon contemporary music. Former Beatle Paul McCartney, for example, has used them as a source of inspiration for his lyrics. The *New Republic* has devoted review space to books on comics. Wolfgang Faust has described the graphic techniques unique to comics; speech balloons with sharp edges indicate aggressive speech, for example, and "bubbles" signify thought in a manner linking pictures and words. Although his remark that comic heroes have eternal life and eternal youth is flatly wrong for many contemporary comics, he rightly calls attention to the value of graphics in comic art.

Arthur Berger has written that comics are written for a mass market and they often cater to simple tastes, but that "it is possible to discover important American values showing through." Moreover, they provide a "fusion of art and language which allows ideas to be presented in images that are often emotionally gripping" ["Comics and Culture," *Journal of Popular Culture,* Summer 1971]. Elsewhere he has gone into greater detail regarding the uniqueness of the art form and the "rather unnatural but remarkably intellectual use of language" (which he described as "extremely poetical") ["Marvel Language: The Comic Book and Reality," *ETC: A Review of General Semantics,* June 1972] in the best of the genre, the Marvel group. He pointed out that the vastness of scale upon occasion reaches the level of the epic, and concluded that modern comic books may be considered a kind of "modernized epic." It might be that one should call them "'tertiary' epics," he wrote, "since they make use of other materials and are not 'high literature' as we commonly know it. The interesting thing is that in a literary form that is generally seen as trash and seldom taken seriously we find poetic language, philosophical speculation, and the use of the epic form." He and others have concluded that comic books are a new art form; in his opinion they may best be considered as illustrated plays. Although Geoffrey Gorer's remark that comics are one of the few bonds uniting all Americans in a moment of common experience is more applicable to newspaper strips than comic books, it underscores the importance of the art form, itself.

So whereas there is no longer the concern that once existed that comics might be corruptors of youth, there is as least some recognition that they deserve to be taken seriously, both as an art form and as a socially significant medium. Berger, in fact, has published a study comparing attitudes toward authority in American and Italian comics, and *Psychology Today* has devoted space to them. Strangely, however, there has been almost no attention paid to the striking shift in political themes from the Golden Age to the present. Berger does remark that "frequently biting political comments are made, usually as asides, during the course of the adventures." Although he is correct, he has very much understated the case; many of the stories themselves are explicitly political.

The most notable exception to the statement that there has been no attention to the shift in political themes from the Golden Age to the present is an article by Lindsay and Lawrence Van Geldner, that, while interesting, concludes rather simplistically that because the old chauvinistic attitudes have dwindled and there are now new political themes in the comics, the comics have simply been "radicalized" ["The Radicalization of the Superheroes," *New York,* October 19, 1970]. Berger might agree, since he has said that there is a "radical thrust to many comics now as heroes and superheroes tackle such problems as ecology, racism, the Vietnam war, frigidity and alienation," though his treatment of political themes is minimal. The Van Geldners in colorful language described the contemporary situation in comic books.

They began by remarking that things now are different for Superman and the others in the legion of caped and cowled superheroes. "To turn the pages of comic books today," they said, "is to revisit not the old world of good and evil and of virtue triumphant on a field of yeggs, but to plunge to the nostrils in the bleeped-up world of today." The travelling superhero now finds hunger in Appalachia, corrupt politicians and public officials, cultists working to inflame race-war, victimized American Indians and superpatriotic—and right-wing—actors in Hollywood Westerns. One of Iron Man's antagonists, for example, was Firebrand, a former peace activist who had become bitter and disillusioned, concluding that the only solution was to destroy everything and begin again. Even in these circumstances, however, there was considerable complexity and a great amount of ambiguity. Not only were the issues not cut-and-dried, but Tony Stark (Iron Man) subsequently renounced his previous role as an arms supplier and converted his industrial empire to peaceful research and production.

Certainly the Van Geldners document the change that has taken place since the simplistic days of the Golden Age. Blacks no longer are stereotyped, there are black superheroes and villains, and Stan Lee, the inventive Marvel editor, has had blacks in his stories for so many years that he can say with justification "I don't even think it's worthy of comment". The comics clearly deal with topical issues. Among the illustrations for their article is a reproduction of the cover of *Green Lantern and Green Arrow,* No. 80 (Oct. 1970), consisting of a newspaper's front page with the headline "GUILTY! Conspiracy Trio Sentenced to Die," and a picture of the defendants, including Green Lantern and Green Arrow, bound and gagged before a stern judge bearing a marked resemblance to Judge Julius Hoffman.

The Van Geldners had their facts correct, and their article is one of the few dealing with modern comics that takes full note of politics. Their implication, however, is that the world is being radicalized, and that the comics are reflecting that radicalization. Perhaps it is easier to judge with less passion now than it was in the tumultuous days of 1970, but few today would argue that the world has been radicalized. It seems rather that the world has developed a bit in its attitudes and that the comics anticipated some of that development. It seems that the comics, instead of being radicalized (and of course that would depend upon one's definition of "radical") have merely become more mature and less simpleminded.

A look at some of the comics, themselves, will illustrate how they have developed, how they have become concerned with serious issues, and in fact how upon occasion they have dealt with those issues in a manner that required a willingness to withstand, at the very least, considerable criticism. The most explicit reversal of the chauvinistic atmosphere of the Golden Age may be seen in the most patriotic superhero of them all, Captain America, whose new attitude was revealed in his comment, "I guess I've learned a *lot* since the days I reveled in my enemies' *deaths*. . . ." Moreover, his new partner, The Falcon, is a black man who in his civilian identity is a social worker in the ghettoes. The evolution of the character of Captain America not only reflects his American values but is significant "as an object lesson in the way America's rapid change swallows up its cultural heroes" [Virginia and Andrew MacDonald, "Sold American: The Metamorphosis of Captain America," *Journal of Popular Culture,* Summer 1976].

Plagued with self doubts and shaken in his unquestioning belief in America, Captain America for a time surrendered his identity to take another. Although eventually he returned to his old costume and name, the former assurance was gone forever, especially after he had uncovered corruption at the highest levels of government. His girl friend Peggy at first could not understand his discomfiture. She tried to reassure him by saying that there were many who fought crime, and even provided inspiration, but only he did it "for the United States of America!" His response would have been heresy in the Golden Age:

> There's just *one problem* with that argument, Peggy. . . . America is *not* the *single* entity you're *talking* about. It's *changed* since I took my name. There *was* a time, yes, when the country faced a *clearly hideous aggressor,* and her people stood *united* against it! But now, nothing's that *simple*. Amer-icans have *many* goals—*some* of them quite *con-trary* to others! In the land of the free, each of us is able to do what he wants to do—think what he *wants* to think. That's as it should be—but makes for a great many different *versions* of what *America* is. So when people the world over look at me which American am I supposed to symbolize?
>
> The government created me in 1941—created me to act as their agent in protecting our country . . . and over the years I've done my best! I wasn't perfect—I did things I'm not *proud* of—but I always *tried* to serve my country well—and now I find the government was serving *itself.*
>
> I'm the one who has to be or not be Captain America . . . and I'm the one who's seen everything Captain America fought for become a *cynical sham!*

Some explanation is in order for Captain America's age; if medical science produced of him a super soldier in 1941, how is it that his age is considerably under the 55 or so that should be minimum? The answer is that he had been frozen in a state of suspended animation, as the result of an accident shortly after the Second World War, and had been recovered only twenty years later. This helps to explain the Captain America of the 1950s who returned in one series as a villain. This Captain America began with the same dreams as the original, but "ended as an insane, bigoted, superpatriot." He wanted to help freedom-loving people "to battle the clutching hand of all communism all across the globe." As he explained it, he and his partner "Somehow . . . seemed to outgrow the world. We began finding Reds where others saw nothing, like in Harlem and Watts." "In fact," he said, "we found that most people who weren't pure-blooded Americans were communists."

The source of Iron Man's conversion is significant also. He had returned to the war and to a village that he remembered only to find it wiped out. As he stood near the remains of a home with the bodies of a slain mother and child, he mused " . . . An Thoc, the village I fought to 'save,' winds up in my former 'enemies' control—and *destroyed* by my previous 'allies'! I used to feel *proud* of my support of the war—but things like this—first-hand—

really fog up one's thinking." Such discoveries, first hand or not, likewise "fogged the thinking" of many in a generation of Americans.

Just as themes of the environment and materialism came to be of concern to many Americans, so too did they invade the realm of the comics. In one episode, the Submariner intervened on behalf of demonstrators who were protesting against a company that was severely damaging the environment, finally to reconcile a father, the company president, with his son, one of the demonstrators. Similarly, in one of the Spiderman adventures demonstrators halt a truck carrying nuclear materials. The driver and his partner discuss what to do and they agree to turn back saying, "It ain't our job to fight 'em . . . an' besides, I kinda *agree* with 'em!" A rather lengthy series in another Marvel Comic, *Man Thing,* pitted the Indians of a small village in the middle of a swamp against efforts to drain the region and construct an airport, thereby destroying the Indians' home land. Reflecting the tensions that frequently surface between union members, whose jobs may depend upon a certain activity, and others who for one reason or another protest that activity, the workers are portrayed essentially as persons who simply are trying to make a living, and are infuriated by the Indians and their supporters. "I don't work—my kids don't eat," one says, "simplest ecology there is. Heck, we ain't villains, just hard working' guys tryin' to earn a dollar." On the other hand, the confrontation led to violence, and some of the Indians were shot and killed as they ran after burning a bulldozer. The supervisors and owners are shown as anything but sympathetic. With a very heavy hand, the author chose to name the company the "F. A. Schist Construction Company."

Such themes are not limited to magazines of the Marvel group. The Green Lantern and the Green Arrow, for example, exposed the government officials of a small community who had seized total power for their own ends. The town, Piper's Dell, was severely polluted by its one factory, the only employer in the region. Residents accepted the propaganda that pollution was a "small price to pay for progress," and the Mayor described the community as a "progressive township, growing everyday, the American way." Afterward, one character said that the people of Piper's Dell must have been crazy to give up their freedom of decision so easily, and the Green Lantern responded, "Not crazy, baby, different! A bit more greedy than most . . . a bit less responsible." The Green Arrow, however, said, "I don't know pal," as he saw a sign advertising a special pre-Christmas July sale of plastic Christmas trees, "You really think they were different?"

Another staple of contemporary comic books is attention to civil rights and civil liberties, and attacks upon bigotry. The vocabulary of the villainous Captain America from the 1950s (as he was reincarnated in the 1970s) typically ran to such comments as "We can take a darkie and a Frail," and other racial slurs. Although many comics now clearly decry racial prejudice, they do not attempt to deny various racial and ethnic groups their own identities by submerging them into a "melting pot." Typical is Luke Cage, the first black superhero to have his own magazine, and the Falcon, Captain America's partner and friend who nevertheless often feels more comfortable with the Black Panther (the suave technological wizard and superhero who is equally at home with the African tribe he rules and in the most sophisticated Western gathering) because the Panther, too, is black.

The civil liberties theme causes one once more to remember Judge Julius Hoffman. The authorities have subdued the Hulk, and have brought him to trial sedated and in bonds, whereupon his lawyer, Matt Murdock (in reality, Daredevil), charges that "This trial is the biggest farce in the history of American law." Even more in contrast with the attitudes of the Golden Age, and more indicative of the trend away from the previous over-simplified and often simple-minded situations, was a story that had Superman and Batman break into the home of a suspect and charge him with a crime. After it became clear that the man was innocent, Superman asks how they could have been so wrong, and the Batman responds that the answer is prejudice; prejudice against the "known criminal type."

Also reflecting an abrupt departure from the past is the tendency now to treat the role of the leader or the hero less simplistically, and more ambiguously. Captain America is made to ask, "How can people trust 'heroes' anymore—and how can I blame them? Maybe hero-worship does as much *harm* as good." Mere physical force no longer is able to settle issues and insure that good triumphs over evil. Spiderman (Peter Parker) occasionally is pitted against foes who are considerably more powerful, and he usually, though not always, wins. The god-like villain Galactus asked, "Is this madness so deep-rooted that force is their only answer? And will they never learn there is always a greater force?" Moreover, one of Spiderman's most prominent characteristics is his "willingness to question power and to assume public responsibilities." It is a remarkable development for the superhero comic book to question power, the genre's mainstay. The comics now and then have even raised the question whether pacificism, or at least nonviolence, may be equally as effective as other methods of dealing with malevolence; at times, in fact, the implication has even been that it is the most effective method. The new attitude toward unquestioning obedience is beautifully illustrated by an exchange between Captain America, who is also the leader of the group of superheroes called the Avengers, and another Avenger, The Beast. Upon being admonished for carelessness, The Beast replied, "Aaah, go *pledge allegiance,* will ya?"

One of the most amusing, offbeat, and interesting of the comics is *Howard the Duck.* Although bearing a superficial physical resemblance to Donald (even to the extent that he now must wear pants to lessen the resemblance!) Howard could hardly be more different. He was "trapped in a world he never made" when "the cosmic axis shifted," and he was torn from his planet of civilized ducks and materialized on earth. His ever-present cigar, cynical outlook on the world of "hairless apes," and sophisticated wit and social consciousness are far from the world of Disney.

He has dealt with the brainwashing tactics of a religious cult, the Yuccies, whose leader conducted a "bicentennial prayer meeting and Korean Karate exhibition," and Howard even ran for President. His campaign was forthright, but futile. His victorious opponent, Jimmy Carter, said, "Our fowl may find that even forth-rightness carried to its *extreme* may be deleterious to the long view. Maybe not though." His other opponent, Gerald Ford, "never could figure out what it was that Howard was saying." One might wish for a similar story for the campaign of 1980, or 84.

In another episode, Howard confronts the members of the Soofi movement (Save Our Offspring From Indecency!), who burn immoral books, perverted movies, and depraved records. After he escapes from their clutches and their efforts to treat him with the blanditron, a "patented Soofi device for cerebral ablution," he destroys the organization and exposes its leaders, the Supreme Soofi, who turns out to be a "girl from the Sunshine State," whom the Almighty had instructed to carry the "standards of Dade County to the whole world." Her last words are, "No! Don't go! Please! I need you! A day without imposing my morality on someone else . . . is like a day without . . . well, you know!"

The comics, then, have dealt directly with current political issues, sometimes openly, and sometimes with a view only thinly veiled. Mondello argues that "*The Amazing Spider Man* is a historic document that reflects three periods from our recent past," with the 1962-1967 stories representing Cold War diplomacy and a preference for self gratification as opposed to public service. The second period, he says, began with the issue of July, 1967. Mondello even says that this issue "is an important historical document for it marks a turning point in the development of the superhero and perhaps of the nation," and from then to 1973 "Spiderman addresses himself to every important issue confronting American society" ["Spider Man: Superhero in the Liberal Tradition," *Journal of Popular Culture,* Summer 1976]. One need not go this far to recognize that something of importance was happening. "Spiderman became a subtle persuader fashioning and reflecting public and popular attitudes under the rubric of entertainment."

It is one thing to publish a story concerning broad principles, whether relating to violence, leadership, the environment, political corruption, or whatever. The stories take on a different meaning, reflect a different quality, and probably have considerably different effects when they are tied to specific happenings or specific characters in the real world of politics. Richard M. Nixon, for example, appears in an adventure of the Fantastic Four early in 1972. The earth is threatened with annihilation by the cosmic force of Galactus, and there is an appeal to the President. Nixon says, "Wait! Wait! I'll call a *meeting*—form a *Committee!* Kissinger says—," then, "The fate of the *world* at stake—and all our armed might is useless! Everything depends on one man—Reed Richards! I've no choice but to trust him! And yet, with an *election* coming up—." This unflattering portrayal of Nixon did not, of course, lessen his landslide victory, but it reflected a view of him that deteriorated further with the coming of Watergate.

Just as Watergate jarred American society, so also did it enter the world of the comics. Kamandi, the last human being left alive sometime in the future, came upon a race of apes that worshipped what they thought was the voices of spirits. The voices were tapes that the apes played at great speed, producing a horrifying sound. He could understand certain things, "plumbers," "at this point in time," "Let the culprit twist and turn slowly in the wind." When he captured the tapes and slowed them down he heard, "I want to make this perfectly clear." The tape then snapped. He elected not to fix it, saying, "It doesn't mean much—now—."

One of the harshest political judgments ever published came shortly after the Kamandi story. It is significant that it appeared not in a political journal, not in a scholarly analysis, not even in a journalistic attack, but in a comic book. It was the episode, mentioned above, that so traumatized Captain America, as, indeed Watergate traumatized America itself. It is important to note dates. The story appeared in *Captain America and The Falcon,* no. 175, dated July, 1974, (story by Steve Englehart). Comic books, however, appear on the newstands months before the date indicated; this one began to circulate near the first of the year. At that time, although talk of impeachment was in the air, it was by no means assured that Mr. Nixon would leave the presidency prior to the end of his term. The White House-edited version of the transcribed tapes appeared the last day of April, and the House Judiciary Committee did not begin its impeachment hearings until the 10th of May. It was not until June that it became known that Nixon had been named an unindicted co-conspirator. The Supreme Court ruling requiring him to turn over the tapes came only on the 25th of July, and it was not until the 31st that he actually relinquished the first batch. His resignation came on the 9th of August.

Before all this occurred came the climax of Captain America's battle against the Secret Empire, a mysterious and sinister organization that sought ultimate world domination. The series dealing with the Secret Empire lasted for months. There were many interesting elements, such as a congressional committee that acted as a front for the Secret Empire, but nothing to prepare one for the final shock. As the Empire began to crumble under assault from a variety of sources, its leaders fled to Washington, D.C., relentlessly pursued by Captain America. The final battle occurred on the White House lawn.

With victory clearly in the offing, Captain America saw the commander of the Secret Empire, the shadowy "Number One," robed and hooded as always, break away from the fighting and try to escape by running into the White House. Captain America cornered Number One in the Oval Office and subdued him; he reached down to the fallen ringleader and snatched off his hood. The reader never sees his face, and there is no mention of his name. "Good Lord!" said Captain America, "You!" But you—you're—" Number One responded, "*Exactly!* But high *political* office didn't satisfy me! My power was still too constrained by legalities! I gambled on a coup to gain me the power I craved—and it appears that my gamble has finally *failed!* I'll cash in my chips then!" Whereupon he grabbed a gun and committed suicide.

Captain America was shattered. The narrative said, "A man can change in a flicker of time. This man trusted the country of his birth . . . he saw its flaws. . . . But trusted in its basic framework . . . its stated goals . . . its long-term virtue. This man now is crushed inside. Like millions of other Americans, each in his own way, he has seen his trust mocked!"

It was not until some months later that the Watergate investigators found in the tapes the "smoking gun" that they had sought. That figurative smoking gun ended the reality of a presidential career as completely as the literal smoking gun brought an end to the fictional Secret Empire—and a fictional president. Notwithstanding its exaggeration and the sensationalism of its treatment, a medium of popular culture, the usually scorned comic book, demonstrated a remarkable political prescience.

Comic books vary as do the other media. Certainly not all of them, or even most of them, are political. It is not important whether those that we have discussed are typical or not. What is important is that the comic books of today do deal with political themes, both directly and indirectly. To a considerable extent, they reflect the political conditions around them, just as most media of popular culture reflect the social and cultural conditions.

We do not suggest that the political analyst should turn to the comics for information unavailable elsewhere. On the other hand, one would be hard-pressed to discover anything in the formal literature of political and social science more pertinent to the conditions of the real world than some of the themes and stories in that medium of popular fantasy, the comic book. The significance of the comic, its artistic and graphic techniques, its linguistic usage, and its reflection of the political, social and cultural themes of the age, is clear. The comic book of today is often more than mere fantasy.

David Huxley

SOURCE: "The Real Thing: New Images of Vietnam in American Comic Books," in *Vietnam Images: War and Representation,* edited by Jeffrey Walsh and James Aulich, Macmillan Press, 1989, pp. 160-69.

[*In the following essay, Huxley discusses* Savage Tales, In-Country Nam, *and other examples of post-Vietnam-era war comics.*]

Since 1980 there have been a wide range of texts in the field of American popular culture which have laid the groundwork for a recuperation of the Vietnam War. Many of these texts took the form of television series in which Vietnam was presented as part of the credentials which formed the background of heroes in violent professions—for example, *Magnum, Airwolf, The A-Team.* These were followed by comic books such as *Jon Sable, Freelance,* which used the idea of Vietnam in a very similar way. Gradually the influence of Vietnam moved from the background of some of these texts to the foreground, notably by the use of a recurring formula: the return-to-Vietnam or 'missing in action' story. A variation of this type of story has been used by all the examples mentioned above, and it also forms the basis of the second Rambo film, *Rambo: First Blood II.*

However it is in the field of American comic books that stories set specifically during the Vietnam War began to make a reappearance in 1985. Marvel Comics' *Savage Tales,* no. 1, contained a seven-page story called 'The 5th to the 1st' about a battalion of Air Cavalry in Vietnam in 1967. *Savage Tales* is a comic 'magazine' aimed at an adult audience and is therefore published outside the control of the American comics code. The tradition that led to this kind of large-format adult comic, and the impact of the comics code on American comic, will be discussed later.

A closer inspection of one '5th to the 1st' story—'The Sniper' (*Savage Tales,* no. 4) reveals some of the characteristics of the series. The basic plot of 'The Sniper' is this: the battalion, having failed to find an enemy supply route, goes to help some inexperienced Marines under attack. One of their pilots is shot and the helicopter carrying the story's narrator, Captain Young, crashes. While he is dazed his sergeant tracks down and kills the sniper who has had the Marines pinned down. On returning to base the sergeant tells Young that the whole attack was the work of one young girl.

Although the story is written by Doug Murray, a Vietnam veteran, it still follows some of the formulas which occur in many other American war comics. First, the sergeant in 'The 5th to the 1st' is an archetypal figure in the tradition of *Sgt Rock,* one of DC comics' long-running publications. This sergeant is identified in the first story of the series as 'Rich Heidel . . . hell on wheels in the field—a drunken disaster in garrison'. Apart from the detail about his drinking (the reasons for which will be discussed later), Heidel fits perfectly into the precept that a sergeant must be the most effective member of the group. This apparently invincible sergeant-figure has dominated a large number of long-running American war comics.

Secondly, as an almost necessary comparative adjunct to the sergeant, the captain is less effective. Again, the initial story underlines this. The captain introduces himself as 'Roger Young . . . six months ago I was in college worrying about my grades and my girl'. His surname is perhaps meant to indicate his problem—he is too young to have all the requisite experience for his job. Although he is not necessarily ineffectual, there is no doubt that he is dependent on his sergeant, particularly for important tasks such as tracking down the sniper.

Finally, and perhaps most interestingly, the stories so far have continued the tradition in Vietnam comic books of pushing the enemy virtually out of sight. In 'The Sniper' there is only one appearance of the enemy sniper in six pages—and this is in the final frame, where he is almost hidden in a tree surrounded by foliage. Of course, some of these characteristics can be said to be reflections of the true situation in Vietnam. For example, the difficulty of tracing an elusive enemy was one of the features of the war. In comic-book fiction, however, these three devices: dependable sergeants, inexperienced or inefficient officers and peripheral Vietnamese appear with such regularity that they begin to appear ubiquitous. Furthermore, it is possible to break away successfully from all these formulas, as we shall see later.

On the other hand, 'The 5th to the 1st' does vary radically from standard American war comics in several ways. The most important of these differences stems from the freedom which is permitted when publishing outside the comics code. One of these freedoms is the ability to deal with problems such as the sergeant's drinking. The kind of archetypal sergeant already discussed (Sergeant Rock, for instance) would presumably have been identified as a hard drinker already if this had been permissible within the code. More surprising is the admission of drug-taking: for example, in *Savage Tales,* no. 1, we are introduced to 'Paul Hogan and John Duff . . . these two experiment with consciousness-expanding drugs, but they get the job done'.

Such a semi-favourable comment on drugs of any kind rarely occurs outside the true 'underground' comic. Until 1971 reference of *any* kind to drugs (even in condemnation) was forbidden by the code. At present anti-drug stories are permitted, but the comment that drug-takers 'get the job done' would not be. Similar rules apply with regard to violence. In 'The Sniper' Captain Young is awakened by blood from the dead pilot dripping on his face. Such an explicit demonstration of the result of violence would be banned in a code comic.

'The 5th to the 1st' is drawn by Mike Golden, who uses a strong, clear 'cartooning' style which follows the tradition of American comic-book drawing. This style is unusual in its precision and clarity, which makes it effective for delineating machinery and landscape as well as figures. Golden's landscapes in particular give the *Savage Tales* stories a genuine sense of place that is missing from most other Vietnam stories—of any period. On the second page of 'The Sniper' one panel shows a helicopter flight passing over simply expressed jungle hills that evoke the beauty of the Vietnamese landscape. Perhaps even more remarkable are Golden's jungle 'interiors', in which distant foliage is rendered in a stylised, almost geometric pattern. It is a form of 'graphic equivalent', derived perhaps from a study of photographs of light breaking through dense foliage. It works perfectly.

To English eyes Golden's 'cartooned' figures can look strange in a comic of serious purpose. Facial features and figures are exaggerated enough to imply humorous intent in an English context because of the differing traditions of comic-drawing style in the two countries. Occasionally, however, this fine balance of exaggeration can slip, even in American terms. In the first story in the series we only see the Vietcong in three frames. In the third frame they are taken by surprise in an American ambush. Golden expresses the figures in a beautiful thin line, unlike the solid black which he uses on foreground figures—a device he uses to dramatic effect in this story in order to suggest depth and aerial perspective. But with the face of the central Vietcong figure Golden moves from 'cartooning' into broad caricature. The huge, startled eyes of this figure seemed to have escaped from a humour comic, so that the image jars, particularly at a moment of extreme violence: the figure becomes a racial stereotype.

In fact the visual manifestation of extreme violence is an area where Golden's artwork would be seen to be inadequate, or rather, inappropriate. 'The 5th to the 1st' actually avoids very explicit violence, presumably through a kind of self-censorship. Of course it is true also that demonstrating the result of violence (for example, the incident of blood dripping on Captain Young's face) can sometimes be more effective than showing the violence itself. In 'The Sniper' we do not actually see anyone being shot. The second frame of Vietcong in the first story in the series illustrates the potential problems when Golden represents explicit violence. In this, two Vietcong are caught in a hail of gunfire. Golden expresses the force of the bullets in single broken lines, and the two figures in semi-silhouette have white holes torn through them where the bullets strike. It is the most violent image in a '5th to the 1st' story and, in many ways, tremendously effective. The problem is that it is also beautiful. It aestheticises the moment of violence in a way that is, presumably, unintended. It is difficult for a competent artist to avoid this duality in effect: to some extent there is similar danger inherent in all image-making of this kind. Even documentary war photography, channelled through the eye and compositional ability of a photographer, can sometimes make images of horror more palatable. But again, as we shall see later, it is possible to minimise this effect.

In December 1986 Marvel comics published the first issue of *The Nam.* The editorial explained, '*The Nam* is the real thing—or at least as close to the real thing as we can get in a newstand comic bearing the comics code seal. Every action, every fight is based on fact.' The letter columns of *Savage Tales* reveal that 'The 5th to the 1st' was a popular feature, so the move to a regular full-colour comic presumably made economic sense. But the previous examination of *Savage Tales* indicates that trying to produce a war comic within the code is fraught with problems. The censorship of the code makes the task of depicting the horror of war extremely difficult. Marvel are clearly aware of this and later in the same editorial they admit, 'Yes, we had to make some compromises. The real language used by soldiers in the field can be quite raw.' But sanitised language is only one of its problems. The violence and acknowledgement of the role of drink and drugs which appears in 'The 5th to the 1st' will not appear in *The Nam*. Given that *The Nam* has made strenuous efforts to make every possible detail factually correct, it seems counter-productive to work in a format that imposes so many restrictions. The only justification for it is an economic one.

The Nam and 'The 5th to the 1st' are part of a long tradition of American war comics which have strived for absolute accuracy. The most illustrious of these predecessors were EC comics' *Frontline Combat* and *Two Fisted Tales,* which were edited, and sometimes designed, written and drawn, by Harvey Kurtzman from 1951 to 1954. Kurtzman's meticulous research and broad dynamic drawing made the best of these stories into terse and believable anti-war stories. They were produced before the introduction of the code in 1954, so they were published with the same freedom as *Savage Tales* and produced in a similar format. One strength of this format is that it presents several short stories per issue. This allows stories to be succinct and concentrated whilst avoiding the restrictions which continuing characters can impose. Kurtzman's characters, for example, are quite likely to be killed at the end of the story. One of his most famous and widely reproduced stories is 'The Big If' from *Frontline Combat,* no. 5 (1952). In this an American soldier in Korea is shown, fatally wounded, reflecting on how he came to be separated from the rest of his unit. In the final panel of the story the soldier collapses and dies, the victim of a shell-burst. The various choices which have led him to this tragic end constitute the 'Big If'.

The attack on comics by various critics which subsequently led to censorship did not concentrate in the main on war comics. Geoffrey Wagner, writing in 1954, did include them in his criticism. He wrote of a Battle Brady comic: 'Battle dotes on action. . . . Hooray for the Brooklyn Dodgers! he yells as he plunges his bayonet hilt-deep in yet another red. . . . It is all gorgeous carnage, topped off with a joke or two in dreadful taste.' The comics code ended the 'gorgeous carnage' of which Wagner complained. Ironically, this carnage was replaced in later war comics by scenes in which bullets did not kill and the wounded did not bleed. And yet, in spite of this, the Americans were still the victors.

As part of their striving for factual reality, Marvel have also taken the decision to publish the stories for *The Nam* in 'real time'. Thus, as each new issue is published, one month will have passed for the characters in the comic. Therefore the comic is intended to last for eight years, with an annual change in personnel as they are transported back to America. To understand what a radical departure this plan is from the standard scheme of time in American comics, and what this portends, it is useful to examine in more detail the more usual use of the concept of time in comics. Umberto Eco has analysed the use of narrative and timescale in Superman comics, and many of his conclusions are equally applicable to much popular fiction. The main points of his analysis can be summarised thus.

> 1 The hero has incredible powers which make him almost invincible.
>
> 2 The narrative depends on the surprise value of each new situation or villain.
>
> 3 But each inevitable victory is an achievement locating the hero in a timescale, and thus aging (consuming) him.
>
> 4 The solution to this is to ignore timescale *in between* each adventure.
>
> 5 The hero therefore does not need to plan, and has no responsibility.
>
> 6 His appeal to readers is in a series of idiosyncrasies ('tics' or 'gestures').

In fact the basis of this model can be applied to most standard continuing war-hero characters. Eco concludes that the plot possibilities of this type of story are severely limited and what the reader is actually looking for is a reaffirmation of what he or she already knows about a character. Thus the repeated series of 'gestures' or idiosyncrasies (for example, James Bond's martinis, shaken not stirred, Hercule Poirot's vanity) are actually what makes a character popular, and the main function of the plot is to allow these 'gestures' to be displayed.

Eco argues that Superman will never perform a major act of global significance (or even marry), as this would 'consume' the character and place him in a 'real' timescale. From this it can be seen that, by using 'real time' publishing, *The Nam* represents a serious and unusual attempt to give comic-book characters a sense of reality. The continuing war hero in comics is generally a kind of sub-super-hero, even if he *claims* to be just an ordinary GI just doing his job. The characters of *The Nam* are therefore a great rarity in a continuing series: they are central figures who are merely protagonists.

In *The Nam* Golden's design is as excellent as ever: the cover of the first issue is a *tour de force* incorporating two complicated scenes of action with a map of Vietnam. However there are two problems with the use of colour in *The Nam*. First, the cruder interior colour seems inappropriate to the imagery of war. This is true of the interior colour of most American comic books, which compare badly in this respect with the black-and-white interiors of *Savage Tales*. Indeed the coarseness of this kind of colouring, done by hand separation and using 'benday' dots for tone, was parodied by Roy Lichtenstein's paintings of comic-strip frames in the early 1960s. Because immense skill is required to reproduce naturalistic colour with limited means, colour in American comics is often 'expressionistic'. When this happens in *The Nam,* it demonstrates the second problem: on p. 14 of *The Nam,* no. 1, an ambush is coloured mainly in solid reds to highlight the moments of violence. Unfortunately this has the effect of obscuring the more delicate parts of Golden's linework, and it also lessens the depth and impact of the heavy black shadows which he has used. Similarly, colour can obscure the quality of the artwork when it is used in a more naturalistic manner. At the top of p. 8 in the same issue of *The Nam* a frame showing the infantry base is marred in this way. The tonal range available is insufficient, so that much of the sense of depth in the panel is broken down.

It is interesting to compare *The Nam* with another comic specifically set in the Vietnam War. This comic, *In-Country Nam,* which began publication in 1986, appears at first glance to be of the 'underground' variety: its cover is simply printed in only three colours and its artwork displays a crude naïveté not associated today with professional comics. The interior of *In-Country Nam,* printed in black and white with similar artwork, reinforces the latter impression. Overall it differs in tone from most underground comics of the late 1960s: rather than being obviously anti-war in intent it is, according to its own editorial, 'a gritty account o[f] the war in Vietnam with emphasis on small unit combat actions'.

In fact *In-Country Nam* is the product of a new movement which has radically affected the American comic-book industry in recent years. This is a movement of small unconnected publishers loosely known as the 'independents' who produce a wide range of material normally published outside the comics code. The basic similarity between these publishers is that they aim their product at the evergrowing collectors market. Their comics have quite small print runs and are likely to cost over twice as much as the usual variety. The actual content of these comics varies to a marked degree: some reprint 'classic comics' of earlier periods; several carry on the anti-establishment tradition of 1960s underground comics; while others produce versions of standard newstand comics which are more *risqué* or violent but which are frequently executed with far less competent artwork.

In-Country Nam is published by the Survival Art Press, and its rear cover advertises another of its comics, *The Survivalist Chronicles*. The plot of this is described thus: 'From newly occupied Russian Alaska a paratroop drop by the Russians to survey the damage done by their nuclear bombs to the mainland of America.' Survival Art Press, therefore, appears to be part of a company which produces right-wing comics similar to some titles which were published during the Cold War. This is in line with recent American 'red invasion' cinema films, whose history can be traced back to the status insecurities and isolationist tradition of the postwar Truman administration. A cursory examination of *In-Country Nam* seems to confirm this view. On p. 18, for example, after the North Vietnamese have suffered a defeat, a North Vietnamese colonel says to his major, 'Tell the popular front allies to continue their massed attacks with zeal—that will give us time to withdraw back into the safety of the mountains.'

Despite the fact that the story shows a clichéd, wily oriental officer willing to sacrifice his allies in order to save his own troops, it does at least *show* the North Vietnamese. Furthermore, in an earlier sequence we see the colonel and his major actually discussing tactics for a page and a half. Whatever the shortcomings in the characterisation of the Vietnamese, this kind of acknowledgement of the careful planning of the enemy and its effectiveness is unheard of in any Vietnam War comic book of any period. *In-Country Nam* also avoids the worst excesses of the stereotypical oriental officer, who is generally shown as some sort of sub-human sadist.

In-Country Nam, no. 1, avoids the standard jungle ambush narrative and concentrates on a major North Vietnamese attack aimed at securing a rice crop. Although a US battalion wins the ensuing battle, the final page explains, 'The rice was harvested eventually, under the eyes of the ARVN forces, but still many tons of it made its way into the mountains. . . .' This almost throwaway line undercuts the whole narrative by showing that, for all their effort and apparent victory, the Americans have, in the end, lost the battle.

This is not to say that *In-Country Nam* offers an examination of the war which is novel or enlightened. R. Ledwell's drawing-style reveals that the comic may indeed have right-wing sympathies. At times the anatomy in the drawings and the brushwork used to express it is incredibly crude. Yet the style is reminiscent of one of America's most famous war-strip artists, Milton Caniff. Certain panels, such as the one showing an American colonel on p. 5 of the first issue, reflect Caniff's influence. Caniff's most famous strip, *Steve Canyon,* was 'seen in the Pentagon as a propaganda voice for the Air Force', and one page from an earlier strip, *Terry and the Pirates,* was included in the Congressional Record in 1942 for this reason. The visual references to Caniff's work in *In-Country Nam* mean that it inevitably carries some of the strong progovernment overtones associated with his work. Other incidents in the narrative support this. On p. 14 of the first issue, at the height of the fighting, a North Vietnamese soldier is straddled by two rockets. Murph, an American soldier, comments, 'Holy shit, Jaw, did'ja see the look on that bastard's face?' Although this kind of gloating could be seen as a reflection of real attitudes among many American troops, the decision to publish that particular attitude does denote a specific ideological value judgement.

On the other hand, it could be argued that it is difficult to generalise about *In-Country Nam*. On p. 7 of the first issue there is a frame which parallels 'The 5th to the 1st' panel in which two Vietcong are shot. This frame also features two figures under attack, except that they are American troops. In terms of drawing-technique there are no comparison between Golden in 'The 5th to the 1st' (or *The Nam*) and Ledwell in *In-Country Nam*. Golden's composition, motifs and execution are all totally superior. Yet the frame by Ledwell, which has its foreground figure apparently disintegrating along one side, is somehow potently effective. It is crude rather than beautiful, but the final image appears to be a truer, and therefore more unpalatable, vision of violence than can be found in *The Nam*.

Comics, such as *Savage Tales* and *In-Country Nam,* that have operated outside the code have been able, by contrast, to be more forthright and realistic in many respects.

—David Huxley

In-Country Nam contains very little characterisation of its two main characters. One, Jaw, gets a chance to complain about unfair duties and at one point admits he is 'scared shitless'. The other, Murph, is frightened when trapped by enemy fire and it is he who gloats over the effect of the rockets on the enemy soldier. But these men fade in and out of the narrative and in fact do not appear at all in the last seven pages of the story. As an account of combat in Vietnam this lack of focus reduces the impact of the comic into that of an army manual. Yet as such it contains a truth about Vietnam. *In-Country Nam* expresses one view that is not particularly sympathetic to the Vietnamese, but it does make an attempt to be even-handed.

The styles of the main titles of *The Nam* and *In-Country Nam* are indicative of the difference between them. *The Nam* imitates army-style stencils, suggesting its intentions towards military realism. But the letters are smoothed out and elongated so that their rough edges are flattened—just as the narrative itself is. *In-Country Nam's* main title is much less proficient, but its greater attempt to consider the enemy is indicated by the words 'In-Country', which is in oriental-style lettering.

The Nam, for all its efforts to achieve visual accuracy, particularly in matters involving small detail, has to tell some lies because of the decision to publish within the comics code. To conform to this, characters have to be 'frightened' instead of 'scared shitless'. Comics, such as *Savage Tales* and *In-Country Nam,* that have operated outside the code have been able, by contrast, to be more forthright and realistic in many respects. In particular, the '5th to the 1st' stories in *Savage Tales* had, within their chosen format, the potential for development of all kinds. *The Nam,* in spite of its striving to locate accurately every catch on every gun, is effectively sterilised, and for all its verisimilitude fails to add up to any cohesive truth.

ADULT COMICS AND GRAPHIC NOVELS

George S. McCue and Clive Bloom

SOURCE: "The Moderns," in *Dark Knights: The New Comics in Context*, Pluto Press, 1993, pp. 55-66.

[*In the following essay, McCue and Bloom trace the development of comic books during the 1970s and 1980s, in terms of both their subject matter and marketing strategies.*]

Comic books in the early 1970s looked surprisingly like those of the early 1950s. The medium was dominated by heroic action books and sales were dropping rapidly. Social relevance had failed as a direction for the medium. Other sources of comic book art were beginning to find a market and underground comic books began making real inroads into the readership, further contributing to the mainstream industry's economic woes. DC was hit harder than Marvel during this time because of personnel problems and the lack of the fiercely loyal readership that Marvel's discursive style had earned them. Nonetheless, both companies were in trouble and they scrambled to bring out a cavalcade of new characters: 'vigilantes and barbarians, gods and jungle lords, monsters and pulp heroes, every stripe of hero and anti-hero, both original and adapted, in a mad scramble to find something that would keep comics alive' [Will Jacobs and Gerard Jones, *The Comic Book Heroes*].

Comic book companies knew they had a devoted core audience from the letters, conventions, fanzines and comic-book speciality shops that began springing into existence. The problem was that such a core was too small to support the industry. Companies had to find a format or genre they could use to expand the readership. This 'try anything' approach led to a chaotic atmosphere in which it was difficult to hold on to creative people or standards or, subsequently, a public and a market.

Moreover, the books aimed at the existing market suffered from a similar malaise. As more and more fans-turned-pros entered the medium, they developed a kind of artistic inbreeding. The advantages were obvious: for the first time creators were no longer working under the impression that their craft was throwaway literature, and they approached comic books as legitimate art. [In a 1990 interview, Dennis O'Neil of DC Comics] points out:

> The big difference today with the young guys, say under 30, is they make no apologies about it. They see it as a 'Capital A' art form. In their minds it is very much on a par with cinema or anything else. They regard it as an art form in which they express themselves and reach out and touch their world. We regarded it as a job, hopefully the best job we could do, but it was basically not a lot different than journalism.

The drawback was that these were fans writing for fans and the stories and techniques became repetitive and even absurd caricatures of the best of the Silver Age. Stan Lee's characterization was copied and standardized. Every hero got a stock personality profile to go with his powers and union suit.

> All heroes had to be either hot-headed, alienated, bitter, frivolous, hard as nails (if female), or slow and genial. Between any two given heroes, a conflict had to be contrived where there had formerly been no reason for any to exist.
>
> [Jacobs and Jones]

A typical example was the feud between Green Arrow and his new space-cop foil, the Thangarian Hawkman, to inject 'characterization' into *The Justice League of America*. Marvel had lost the lustre of newness from the ploy but DC had lost the quality scripting that had been its hallmark in its own attempt to ape Marvel.

This is not to say that there were absolutely no worthwhile comic books, but most of the ones worth reading weren't about superheroes. Barry Smith's *Conan* and Mike Grell's *Warlord* were barbarian swordsmen of the first order. Joe Kubert provided DC with some of the finest war comics in its history and the most beautiful Tarzan ever seen. Even when Marvel and DC seemed to copy each other exactly, as in the case of Swamp Thing and Man-Thing, when handled with the care of Berni Wrightson and Steve Gerber, respectively, they were effective and compelling horror books. There was even a brief resurgence of interest in Golden Age characters as several histories of comic books were published, most importantly, Jim Steranko's *History of Comics*. This resurgence was weak and short-lived, fuelled only by hardcore fans who were still few in number.

The problem was one of synthesis. Marvel had introduced characterization to comic books and attracted a slightly older, more sophisticated market. Their work, however, suffered from inconsistent quality and excess. DC had prided itself on well-crafted books and clear story-telling but lost out trying to out-Marvel Marvel. The first signs of this synthesis came in the form of a few superheroes who, characteristically, had been too tough to kill off entirely even in the slump. A new age was coming but it followed the path of ambitions and innovative creative teams rather than entire companies, and it would require almost ten years to gather strength.

One of the few books to show glimmers of hope in this period was *The Legion of Superheroes*. The Legion had been brought back after a guest shot in *Superboy* showed that there was tremendous interest. The key to the strip was a unique recontextualization of traditional minutiae to introduce new themes. Artists became aware that they could use supporting characters and objects from the Legion's past to evoke very particular images since there was a long-standing notion of what they were supposed to involve. An imaginative treatment of an old artefact could be highly effective. The complex and extensive lore of the Legion was excavated by writers Jim Shooter and Cary Bates, both trained in traditional DC writing by Mort Weisinger. Combined with the art of Mike Grell, whose realism rivalled Neil Adams, they were spurred to bring true-to-life issues to the book. Adult themes seemed to creep in beneath the storyline.

> In 'Brainiac 5's Secret Weakness', for example, Brainiac 5 builds a robot of Supergirl in his sleep and later convinces himself that the machine is his real, flesh-and-blood lover; in 'The Trillion Dollar Trophies', the Legion is attacked by Grimbor, the 'greatest master of bondage, restraint, and security in the universe', and his woman Charma, a mutant whose powers evoke abject devotion from men and violent hatred from women.
>
> [Jacobs and Jones]

Grell's art served to highlight the subtexts and create a book that could appeal to several different age groups simultaneously.

Marvel achieved their version of this kind of success with Jim Starlin's cosmic mix of superhero, science fiction and fantasy in *Captain Marvel*. Starlin was originally assigned only as the artist, but he quickly took over both the writing and drawing. He took some of Marvel's unused characters, particularly the galactic level ones, and began to build a separate corner for them in the Marvel Universe. There he crafted *Warlock*. The series' star character was a space messiah who battled the evil Magus. Unfortunately, they were manifestations of the same energy. To kill the other was to be destroyed oneself. They waged glorious, futile battles across space with a wide and varied supporting cast of Starlin's invention.

With themes so far-reaching, Starlin needed to be fairly wordy to explain his plots. Nevertheless, he deftly avoided the over-characterization that plagued Lee's imitators by making sure that each word moved the totality of the art work forward. Starlin also designed his pages so that the numerous word balloons were not oppressive and added to the total artistic composition. He did not allow his philosophizing to become either gratuitous or silly.

> [Starlin] developed a repertoire of personal story-telling gimmicks—symbolism, shifting visual/narrative viewpoints, quick panel progressions suggesting stop-action camera work—that told stories in terms uniquely suited to the comic book medium.
>
> [Jacobs and Jones]

Starlin's work made a lasting impression on the artists who came to dominate the medium in the 1980s—in particular John Byrne and George Perez, whose work on *The X-Men* and *The New Teen Titans,* respectively, would be instrumental in the first books of the Modern Age.

The *X-Men* had vanished through lack of sales in 1970, along with many of their comic-book colleagues. Writer Len Wein and artist Dave Cockrum revived the team for a one-issue shot of nostalgia in *Giant-Size X-Men* in 1975. Nevertheless, the cover proclaimed '68 Big Pages' and 'Senses Shattering First Issue' in the usual Marvel manner. The first page read, 'From the ashes of the past there grow the fires of the future. The grandeur and the glory begin anew with Second Genesis!' Wein could not have known he was speaking for the entire medium.

In this tale, it seems the original X-Men were captured by an evil mutant, and a Professor X had to gather a new team to rescue them. He went to Russian wheat farms, the jungles of Africa, aristocratic Japan, the Bavarian Alps and the American Southwest. The team he assembled was the most diverse ever seen in comic books. Chris Claremont soon took over from Wein and used this mix to create the premier superteam of the late 1970s and early 1980s. Rather than use their ethnicity or special powers to determine a stock character attitude, Claremont worked at developing them into characters as complex as their backgrounds. One of the characters, Kurt Wagner, is Nightcrawler—a blue fuzzy mutant who was endlessly persecuted in his native Germany. Rather than becoming embittered or alienated like the Thing, he is devoutly religious and fancies himself a swashbuckling adventurer, Ororo is the mutant Storm, whose powers control the elements. Originally an orphan pickpocket on the streets of Cairo, she found her way to an African tribe who revered her as a goddess. She is the maternal figure of the team who is simultaneously enthralled and repulsed by her own power. The most famous team member, and arguably the most popular character in comic books for the past decade, is Wolverine. His untold origin and multifaceted persona have contributed to his high sales. He is as comfortable with Zen philosophy as he is in a barroom brawl in a berserker rage.

There is a strong sense of atmosphere in the books and Claremont worked to maintain a feeling of oppression. The theme of racial persecution drew the characters together as a family rather than as a superteam, creating one of the most extended comic book soap-operas ever written.

> a book about racism, bigotry, and prejudice. . . . It's a book about outsiders, which is something that any teenager can identify with. It is a story about downtrodden, oppressed people fighting to change their situation, which I think anybody can empathise with.
>
> [Jacobs and Jones]

Claremont also tried to break through the traditional gender barrier in comic books. Working with Cockrum, he created the character Phoenix from Jean Grey, formerly Marvel Girl. Her immense power, her love affair with Cyclops (based on a relationship between equals), and her personal heroism and intelligence were the first real attempts to appeal to women in a medium dominated by male-power fantasies. Phoenix's death under Claremont and Byrne, as she tried to prevent her power from destroying a planet, is still one of the most famous events in comic-book fandom.

Claremont's consistent efforts with Cockrum and then Byrne showed that all the superhero mainstream needed for success was the consistent ministrations of talented people. This, of course, meant acquiring and retaining creative talent that could hold audience interest. For a mature artist-audience relationship to flourish, newsprint and poor four-colour printing sold on old rusty metal revolving racks just wouldn't do.

The problems of the 1970s were more than merely a content gone thin and stale. Comic books were marketed primarily on what was called 'the news-stands'. There were in fact very few true news-stands that sold comics and these usually appeared in convenience stores, delis and soda fountains. Comics were invariably stacked at the bottom of a rack of every other type of magazine available, which proved both frustrating and disappointing to people such as Dick Giordano.

> A distributor would come in and say, 'I've got a hundred comic books for you, Joe', and he'd say, 'Fine put'em up on the rack.' They were never identified by title or by company. They were just comic books and they were put on the rack. It became impossible then for us to tell which of our books were popular because of accident and which were popular by design. If they got out there, they might have sold, but they didn't all get out there. We were certainly aware that a lot of our books came back with our wrapping on them. In the news-stand outlets, sales have diminished every year for the past 20 or 25. There has been no year that has been better than the previous, no matter what material was put out.
>
> [Interview with Dick Giordano of DC Comics]

The material in comic books, which had been sold for years to children in this offhand manner, had worked its way from those children through adolescents and teens, and now it was attracting adults. Creative pressures and more sophisticated audiences demanded new formats and new sale venues. Comic-book speciality shops were the obvious answer, but there had never been a demand that could support them.

Phil Seuling was the father of the modern comic-book shop. Such a retail network, however *ad hoc,* would put the final piece in place for continuance and renewed success of the medium.

> The existence of the shops is almost an accident in terms of somebody having an idea about supplying comic books to his friends. Literally, the shops came into existence because of Phil Seuling. Phil Seuling was a comic book fan and he and his friends used to go to the same stores every month and couldn't get the same comic books. Phil Seuling lived in Brooklyn and he called up here and said, 'Look, can I buy 10,000 copies from you, wholesale, so that I can sell some to my friends and keep some in the back room?
>
> [Giordano]

Up until that point, comic books had been supplied to the market through magazine distributors. To sell comic books, you had to be willing to sell *Playboy* and *Time* as well. With the work of Seuling in the eastern US and similar moves made by Bud Plant in California, comic books went directly from producers to sales shops. The industry was revolutionized.

The first effect of these stores was that while DC and Marvel were saved, they were no longer the only companies doing business. Newsstand outlets had been dominated by distributors and small grocery stores were hesitant to carry comic books because of the small profit margin available, so the industry had been effectively dominated by the two big houses. Now, anyone who could staple pages together had a place to sell his comic book. Independent companies, with no allegiance to the Code, began to thrive. The first of these included the now famous *Cerebus the Aardvark* by Dave Sim, and Wendi and Richard Pini's *Elfquest*.

DC and Marvel were not slow to realize that this was where the future would be found.

> . . . we realized at that time that the possibility existed that the whole thing could collapse. I mean the direct sales market, but it was the only chance we had. So . . . Paul Levitz and Jeanette Kahn developed a plan that would have us direct our entire line to that audience. If it survived, we survived with it. If it didn't survive, we were gone anyway. I don't think we were quite that negative but each of us knew that there was that possibility . . .
>
> [Giordano]

Marvel's first attempt to target this new market came with the first new comic-book term: the graphic novel. 'Graphic novel' is a term used by some comic-book intellectuals (who may be the same as intellectuals who read comic books!) to denote a new respect for comic products of old. For Marvel it meant a very specific magazine-sized book with high quality glossy paper. The first paper graphic novel was called *The Death of Captain Marvel*. The company recalled their Kree Captain and gave him to Jim Starlin, who wrote a one-episode tale of the heroes of earth gathering to help their friend battle not another villain but cancer. In a classic Starlin style, he managed to have the Captain come to terms with his own mortality and the heroes with their relative impotence.

DC began to see that their market could be tapped to support limited projects that would have strong followings but not support a long-term series. They introduced mini-series and maxi-series. Minis were normally four issues long and maxis twelve. Each issue contained a complete story that could stand on its own and usually delighted fans with a strong character who was not a star in his own right, for instance The Atom, Green Arrow and *The World of Krypton*. DC's first maxi-series demanded more development than an established character needed since there were only twelve issues with which to explore the possibilities. Their first maxi was *Camelot 3000,* enjoyably done by Mike W. Barr and Brian Bolland who used some inventive touches as they reincarnated the Knights of the Round Table to ward off an alien attack. The most memorable character was Sir Tristan reincarnated as a woman. However, with *Camelot 3000,* DC took an even bolder step. All twelve issues were available only in comic book speciality shops, which had come to be known as 'direct-sales outlets'. The natural home for the medium had been found. Then came the deluge.

Once the new path for comic books had been cleared, the two major companies did not allow themselves to be left behind. The key was to synthesize DC's scripting and Marvel's characterization from the Silver Age while utilizing the marketing possibilities of their new audience and the comic shops. Marvel had less ground to regain even though their mainstream product line was as erratic in quality as DC's. Nevertheless, by matching books and creative people properly they were able to achieve some truly wondrous books for their new audience, such as John Byrne's *Fantastic Four* and Walt Simonson's *Thor*.

DC's first real contribution in this arena came packaged in an unremarkable team-up between Superman and Green Lantern in issue 26 of *DC Comics Presents,* where they met and defeated a typically menacing alien. The interesting part was a bonus insertion about the reforming of a team from the Silver Age. The Teen Titans—whose gimmick had been to bring together a team consisting exclusively of sidekicks: Robin, Kid, Flash, Wonder Girl, Aqualad and Speedy—still included most of the above but now added such figures as Cyborg, a scientist's son who was half-man-half-machine; Raven, sorceress and empath, daughter of the demon Trigon; and Starfire, princess of an alien warrior race. This blend of old and new seemed to strike the same chord for DC that the *X-Men* had struck for Marvel. Their differing backgrounds made each character unique while threats from the vastly different pasts of Raven and Starfire forged them into a family.

DC revived *The Legion of Super-Heroes* under Paul Levitz and Keith Giffen. Levitz was a long time Legion fan who was able to excavate arcane details of Legion lore to great effect while Giffen's art was a thoroughly comprehensive and convincing vision of the future. The pinnacle of old entertainment synthesized with new techniques came when Roy Thomas moved to DC and began both *All-Star Squadron* and *Infinity Inc. All-Star* showed Thomas's love for comics history as he retold the wartime adventures of the Justice Society and their innumerable Golden Age counterparts. Thomas rarely radically altered the myths so much as retold and fleshed out the origin stories. *Infinity Inc.*, its modern companion, chronicled the adventures of the Squadron's superheroic children in the present. More significantly it was only for direct sale. While Thomas's painstaking attention to detail attracted older readers and a few younger fans fascinated by the Golden Age, he was never able truly to reach the new fans who had come to expect radical departures for their superheroes and who were now increasingly being influenced by the independent and non-super comics flooding their local shops.

Comic fans nowadays have become a well-educated group, and independent books vie, often successfully, to take sales away from the major houses. Today's more demanding readers have also attracted the attention of artists and writers who want to work unfettered by the rules of Marvel and DC and successful books such as Howard Chaykin's *American Flagg* and Mike Grell's *Jon Sable Freelance* have emphasized the need for reviewing the terms by which major companies employ their creative people.

> . . . We're selling *Blackhawk* because Howie Chaykin did it because nobody has any real interest in Blackhawk. I'm talking about the prestige series. Chaykin likes to work with your characters and likes to work with his own stuff. he likes to fool around with his own stuff for another publisher. He hasn't created anything new for us. He always takes our characters and messes with them. Anything new he has he brings someplace else. Then there's other people who just want to create their own stuff. They really aren't interested terribly in working on your characters. Frank Miller is one of those. He would rather do his own stuff. Dave Gibbons can go either way.
>
> [Giordano]

Thus, the major companies began exploring other formats and genres to entice artists, writers and fans with interests decidedly different from the usual superhero comic. During the 1980s Marvel began to publish expensive, square-bound books such as Barbara Slate's *Yuppies From Hell*—a black-and-white book in comic strip style that mocks money-grabbing, status-seeking yuppiedom. DC has gone so far as to create a separate publishing company called Piranha Press for their own adult titles. Such books are specially designed for older and more sophisticated readers in comic shops. Stories such as 'The Crypt of the Magi' in Piranha's *Beautiful Stories For Ugly Children* shows that they certainly warrant the cover warning, 'For Mature Readers'. In 'Crypt', for instance, a husband moonlights in a factory to earn money to buy coloured contact lenses for his wife who has always hated the drab colour of her eyes. He mutilates his hands in a machine during his last night on the job but returns home on Christmas Eve with the lenses. She, of course, has sold her eyes to a medical school to buy brass knuckles so he will no longer be mugged for his paycheck! These grim and gothically amusing stories are becoming increasingly common as adults are discovering or rediscovering comic books and as the medium becomes more sensitive to the demands of adult entertainment. Independent productions such as Bill Sienkiewicz's *Brought To Light,* which shows the American Eagle defending the Iran-Contra affair with barroom bravado, and *Maus,* a holocaust history with mice as Jews and cats as Nazis, have begun to show the range of potential in the medium, a medium long used for adult entertainment in Europe and Japan.

As comic book fans have become increasingly willing to define themselves in terms of this medium, comic books have tried to speak to them in techniques reminiscent of, albeit far more accomplished than, Lee and Kirby. By playing with the codes and conventions of superhero comics, fans gratify themselves by buying books that show they are 'in the know'. Often this is played for laughs as semi-logical extensions of well-known superhero characteristics are extended. DC has done very well by casting its Justice League International books in this mould. League members regularly make fun of Batman's 'ears', join the group to make money because heroing is usually a non-profit profession, and get lost because they don't know a local language.

These kinds of jokes only work if your audience knows what usually happens in comic books, or more accurately, what is supposed to happen. Everyone knows that while Batman is an incredibly menacing figure, his ears are funny, especially when drawn as impossibly elongated as some artists have done for horrific effect. Satiric magazines using super-heroes are not unusual. One of *Mad*'s earliest successful issues featured 'Super-Dooper Man'. These comics are different because they are aimed at very specific readers with knowledge about the magazine they read and the people that produce it. It's no accident that the most prolific mainstream producer of these meta-comics is Marvel. They pioneered the chatty, humorous atmosphere between artists and readers. Their *Damage Control* series has the interesting premise of a construction firm dedicated to rebuilding property wrecked in super-battles.

Perhaps the steadiest self-parody has come from *The Sensational She-Hulk,* also in the Marvel line. She-Hulk is already a character of dubious seriousness simply because of her name and her green-skinned relative. John Byrne is well known as a star artist of modern comic creations and the magazine sells partly because he is featured as writer and artist. Byrne's affection for the character is long-standing, dating back to his work on her own special graphic novel. The attraction of the book lies in its use of comic conventions. She-Hulk will yell at Byrne for not getting the story right and, if she is truly frustrated, she will say, 'I can't wait until this issue is over' or will have her fight scene censored for the Comics Code.

She-Hulk is with all that a mainstream book and is, in fact, approved by the Comics Code. Marvel's alternative publishing firm, Epic Comics, is not under such restrictions. The idea of twisting unique superhero codes was carried to its extreme in Epic's recent *Crime and Punishment: Marshall Law Takes Manhattan* by Pat Mills and Kevin O'Neil. Marshall Law is a hero hunter garbed in black leather. In a world that mocks and mirrors Marvel's own products, almost every major hero and convention is taken to task. Although their names are not spelled out, their identities are obvious. A true knowledge of the Marvel Universe is necessary to decipher all the coded messages from the clues given. The superheroes of this world were created by government experiments that eventually drove them mad and caused them to murder several innocents. They all end up in a ward for the insane, allowed to 'wear a costume of [their] choosing to assist in recovery'. The magazine is full of psychological case studies for each hero, such as this version of Spiderman.

> *Case 5:* A shy and sexually inhibited young man, who was experiencing difficulties with his marriage and coping with his super-powers, he was diagnosed as suffering from a psycho-sexual neurosis. He tried to overcome his marital problems by a blatant form of exhibitionism. Namely: spending his nights leaping from building to building in a hairy spider suit, 'Web-Shooting'. The sexual significance of this, along with the circumstances under which he was arrested, is discussed below.

The heroes speak in the overblown Lee style of heroic nobility:

> 'Hmm . . . those stairs . . . I suspect they could lead up to the next floor!'
>
> 'Well spotted, my friend! It's there we shall make our Last stand!'
>
> 'And ours shall be victory!'
>
> 'I am with you! Yours shall not be the glory alone!'
>
> 'I, too! For a true hero never abandons his comrades.'

Their version of Daredevil walks about in a costume in which none of the colours match and bumps into walls in the background of panels. When the heroes are thrown from the top of a skyscraper at the climax, each assumes that his own power will save him in the way that superpowers have performed in countless previous comics. Daredevil senses a flagpole coming up and it tears his arms off as he reaches out for it. Captain America grabs a satellite dish antenna, mistaking it for his 'trusty shield'. Dr Strange recites that immortal spell that will open a portal to another dimension; 'Jondag, Jondag, Jiggle, Matmitty, Matmitty'. In the end they all plunge to their deaths in the streets below, and the post-holocaust cannibals that live there roast the Punisher over the Human Torch. In the final panel Marshall Law utters the Marvel slogan, 'Nuff Said'.

An Epic comic of this type is unusual not only for its content but also for its physical form and high price. The characters and events are copyrighted to Pat Mills and Kevin O'Neil, reflecting a growing trend towards creative rather than corporate control over artwork and text. The book is also printed on high-grade paper with no advertisements and is 'square' bound. These kinds of comics are becoming increasingly common for a multitude of reasons. An adult market means a demand for a higher quality product as well as an ability and willingness to pay for such quality. The higher price helps to steer the book into the right hands—a twelve-year-old is less likely to end up with an adult comic when it carries a 5 dollar price tag. Dick Giordano points out:

> The formats and the production values have become more important to us because we don't think of it as throw away literature anymore. We think of it as something you're going to put on your bookshelf and we try to produce material that will at least live as long as you do. With exceptions, almost all of them are printed on good paper with good quality inks and so forth so that they're likely to last as long as the person who purchases them. Not only because it needs to be collected but because it needs to be read 20 years from now by somebody else . . . because it will still be readable 20 years from now without any extraordinary steps being taken to preserve it. Most of the stuff will last longer.

The adult reader and the serious material both seem to demand a comic book that fits well on a bookshelf or coffee table, not merely in a cardboard box. One of the most popular new forms for the medium is the trade paperback. A softbound book with square binding, it is the size of a comic book, only thicker. A series usually consists of four to twelve issues. The limited series of the 1980s, such as *Camelot 3000, WatchMen, Batman: The Dark Knight Returns,* and other mini- and maxi-series, have been the most successful because the books are visualized as complete and homogeneous productions. However, when a particularly popular artist or writer has a successful tenure on a continuing series, these issues are likely to find their way into the trade paperback also. These formats have expanded creative and marketing possibilities as comic book companies such as Marvel and DC are becoming fully fledged publishers. Marvel's graphic novels, featuring such well-liked characters as Dr Strange teamed with Dr Doom or Wolverine and Nick Fury, are now hardcover books and have reached a level of artistic maturity and acceptance previously unknown. DC's long-awaited *Arkham Asylum* is both a hardcover and multimedia production, using experimental methods and avant-garde techniques.

> . . . We started talking about, 'Gee can we paint covers? Why not? Let's try some new covers.' That led to painting a whole book. That's what *Arkham Asylum* is. It's a book that's painted. It's not black and white drawing with good colouring on it. It's painted artwork. It's multimedia painted artwork. It's got things pasted on it. The artwork

> weighs a ton. Some of the things that you see there weren't painted, they were glued to the board. [The artist] decides, 'Oh, this is interesting, this will make a special effect', and he glues that to the painting. You'll see some of those things when you see the book. We've encouraged people to take those kinds of chances and they're doing it.
>
> [Giordano]

Perhaps the best example is *The Complete Frank Miller Batman,* which was leatherbound and sold in bookshops for 25 dollars for the 1989 Christmas season.

Comic books are no longer restrained by any rules other than those generated by the medium. There are only the relationships between words and pictures and artists and audiences. The evolution of comic books from a stunted, retarded medium with only one genre, only one physical form and an audience of perpetual children to one in which a full range of readers from children to adults can enjoy graphic works which are both mature and intellectually satisfying has opened new directions for the comic books of the 1990s and beyond.

Terri Sutton

SOURCE: "Adventures in Adult Comics Land," in *Utne Reader*, No. 59, September-October, 1993, pp. 111-12, 114.

[*In the following essay, Sutton surveys autobiographical comic books for adults.*]

Masturbation, nose picking, stupid jobs, and unsatisfying sex—the subject matter of most autobiographical adult comic books is so pathetically routine that it's past parodying. This strain of alternative comics was born the day Robert Crumb's nebbish alter ego first drooled over a big booty in a tight dress. At their worst, such self-referential stories are the graphic equivalent of getting stuck next to a nonstop talker on a five-hour flight from L.A. to New York. At their best, though, they flash a real-life informality like a lure, and then hook you with the barbed ends of good storytelling.

The past few years have seen a resurgence of autobiographical work by a New Wave of young cartoonists influenced by Crumb, Harvey Pekar (who has solicited Crumb and others to illustrate his own stories in *American Splendor* since 1976), and Gilbert and Jaime Hernandez. While the latter's 10-year-old *Love & Rockets* is for the most part fictional, the Hernandezes' vibrant depictions of day-to-day relationships in marginalized communities—Hispanic punks, white slackers, Central American villagers—undoubtedly encouraged aspiring writers to look to their own backyards for inspiration.

Along with any renaissance comes the backlash, of course, and the Hernandez brothers in particular have hammered on autobiographical comics for their claims to honesty and realism, noting rightfully that a fictionalized narrative is usually more emotionally "true" than a first-person account, which can be hampered by its struggles to "tell the truth."

But that criticism ignores one of the more potent roles of autobiographical writing: witnessing. When female reactions to the misogyny of underground comix came together in the early '70s, the anthologies that resulted—*It Ain't Me Babe, Wimmins Comix, Tits 'n' Clits,* and the like—were generously spiked with personal anecdotes aiming for political impact. The truth of these stories of sexual misadventure, abortion, dyke bashing, and survival was more significant than their form (although these women artists' skill bore its own message). This testimony underscored the reality of events and feelings that were invisible, or demonized, in mainstream media.

It's revealing, then, that contemporary autobiographical work by women weighs in as the most adventurous of the genre. Perhaps because women continue to be underrepresented in popular culture, both as creators and as characters, truth telling likewise remains an effective tool for female cartoonists. But, just as feminism's focus has moved from rights to the often deeply rooted reasons for oppression, women's stories today unfold in the private sphere. Artists such as Fiona Smyth, Julie Doucet, and Renee French play with dreams, memories, what-ifs, acted out primarily on the bodies of their cartoon alter egos.

These comics pointedly explore a more complex femaleness than the cultural left or right has acknowledged. In *Dirty Plotte,* Doucet has repeatedly rummaged through the stock wardrobe of her belly-button-gazing peers, but self-absorption fits differently on her—and registers differently on a reader—if only because the image of a woman stroking her crotch still surprises. More daringly, Doucet has put her big-eyed, goofy cartoon self-image to work unpacking the idea of gender. Doucet flirtatiously fills panels with dicks and cunts in fantasies that don't so much fight sexual oppression as confound it. For Doucet, the language and logic of dreams serve her purpose, which is to peel away the skin of the stories we like to tell ourselves and uncover the jumble of secrets underneath.

Like Doucet, Renee French messes with expectations of female identity—especially expectations about sexuality. Her new comic *Grit Bath* strikes out on the well-worn road of childhood memory, but takes a left before it reaches Norman Rockwell country. This is uncensored girlhood, complete with ritualistic sexual exploration and cruel fascination with geeks and younger sisters (what *else* can we make her do?). French's drawings push normality into the grotesque: braces are mouth wounds and everybody looks like little Wednesday from *The Addams Family.*

Meanwhile, in her aptly named *Nocturnal Emissions,* Fiona Smyth investigates her mind's landscape with a fourth-grade girl's fascination with ornamental detail. Smyth's snakeheaded, multiorganed, and tattooed creatures make Peter Max posters look like minimalism: Nearly every panel is covered with squiggles, flowers, flames, and circles within circles. Explicitly sexual *and* spiritual, the book presents a psychedelia with Frida Kahlo's face—an elaborately sensual, pro-female space where drugs, dreams, and myths meet. Smyth re-envisions the self-loathing porn fantasies of too many boy cartoonists with celebratory zeal.

To read these comics as personal revelations brings the possible into the real: The impudent female qualities portrayed here are not mere potentials, they're alive and kicking.

In a similar way, Joe Sacco's series *Palestine* uses impressions and conversations from his travels around Jerusalem and the West Bank to give character to people many Americans narrowly view as terrorists. Sacco admits his own biases: He remembers the athletes murdered in Munich, but, he writes, "if Palestinians have been sinking for decades, expelled, bombed, and kicked black and blue, even when it's made the evening news I never caught a name or recall a face." That, in effect, is his task: to find those faces, and to figure out why, as an American, he's never seen them before.

Both as an artist and as a reporter, Sacco fiddles with perspective. He draws his slope-shouldered, big-featured figures from either knee level or bird's-eye perspective, juxtaposing points of view. At the same time, he's interspersing stories (of idealistic American Jews in Jerusalem, sadistic rock-throwing Palestinian kids, grieving mothers, angry nurses) into his own rapid-fire commentary (I'm scared; what are they asking of me; cute soldiers—whooee!).

It's a sensitive project that could easily fall into superficial cultural rubbernecking or, worse, dogmatism. Sacco cleverly plays off both. Mostly he emphasizes the loss and pain that register in the faces of those he meets, allowing their words to carry the narrative. The ace he holds is a fine sense of incongruity—something he used to great effect in the Gulf War ruminations from his last book, *Yahoo*. Here, he describes a night in Balata (in the West Bank) with a group of refugees who entertain him by playing a videotape of *Delta Force*. The Chuck Norris film depicts a Beirut hijacking by a group of evil but cowardly Palestinians, who are eventually "blown to bits by Norris from his rocket-firing motorcycle." Sacco's hosts "watch impassively, shaking their heads from time to time." In the morning, he leaves by taxi, gunfire popping behind him.

Palestine works as a comic because Sacco's a skillful, subtle storyteller, but its urgency comes from the very real voices he's made known. Ditto David Greenberger's *Duplex Planet Illustrated*. Greenberger, who works at a nursing home in Boston, first began collecting stories from its aged residents in 1979. Soon after, he put the interviews and anecdotes together in a small fanzine, *The Duplex Planet,* which he's still publishing; he started the picture book version this year.

These are autobiographical bits and pieces told to Greenberger and drawn by a host of cool cartoonists (Dan Clowes, Roberta Gregory, Drew Friedman). Again, the potential for emotional tourism is high, not to mention the risk of relating these fragile stories with condescension or treacly melodrama. Fortunately, Greenberger manages a light touch; the focus is on strikingly told sketches, like one about a National Guardsman's farcical experiences with communist partying in the early '40s. *Duplex Planet* is careful to capture the individual voices of its speakers, and it's a real pleasure to read cadences of the English language not shaped by MTV or *Fast Times at Ridgemont High.*

One side effect of drawing from amateur storytellers is a sort of narrative zigzagging, a dreamlike spiraling off from facts, old movies, and reminiscences that can get as delightfully weird as any *Twin Peaks* episode. Or a story's very simplicity may provide its charm: In its entirety, "What I Learned from Francis McElroy" reads, "If you are an old man, and you go into a bar in pajamas, people will buy you drinks." Sly, poignant, sometimes absurd, *Duplex Planet Illustrated* reminds the smug younger reader that human nature is a wacky, complicated thing, whether you're 9 or 90.

And, yeah, that goes for middle-class, white, thirty-something men as well. Chester Brown's autobiographical stories in *Yummy Fur* have run through almost every hackneyed routine in the autobiographical genre: *Playboy* bunnies, obscenity, bizarre masturbation techniques, '70s pop cult references, first dates, body fluids, troubled relationships with women. So why are they so good? Joe Matt, a pal of Brown's, pulls the same shit in *Peep Show* and you want to force-feed him Michael Douglas movies until he tires of self-centered disaffectedness and learns to prefer Judy Davis over Sharon Stone. So why doesn't *Yummy Fur* make me seethe?

The difference is the absence of the Crumb factor. The reigning wisdom among a lot of attitude-copping male cartoonists seems to be "Yeah, I'm fucked up—how about some sympathy?" But in Brown's best and most startling work, concerning his adolescence, distance allows him to depict his subjects and his characters (including himself) with a tough, discerning, and moral eye.

Not that he's overt about his message; that wouldn't be good storytelling. In fact, Brown's examination of his adolescent obsession with *Playboy* elicited responses across the spectrum, from boys who wanted to know more about his jack-off methods to women upset that he was endorsing objectification of females. Fascinated by the cartoon Chester's ugly desperation, I read it as straightforward testimony: This is the way he learned about sex, about desire; this is the sexual model he's had to carry around, struggle against, strive to change. Reading it, living it myself, I understood better. And that's the magic of witnessing from a life.

Benjamin DeMott

SOURCE: "Darkness at the Mall: The 'New Wave' in Adult Comic Books Features Defeat, Cynicism and Despair," in *Psychology Today*, Vol. 18, No. 2, February, 1984, pp. 48-52.

[*In the following essay, DeMott takes a dim view of the dystopias presented in more recent adult comic books like* American Flagg *and* Edge of Chaos.]

The world of comic books is no match for the violent world of video games, but it does change significantly from generation to generation. And there is a major transformation in full progress right now, with potentially large cultural consequences. The good news is commercial; a hitherto untapped national market is emerging, made up of young males in their late teens and early 20s. They patronize an estimated 3,000 specialty outlets, mostly in shopping malls, spending up to $50 a month to stay abreast of such current adult comic-book favorites as *Edge of Chaos, Camelot 3000, Warp, E-Man, Ronin, The Omega Men, American Flagg,* and *Jon Sable, Freelance,* and dozens more. The bad news is non-commercial; it flows from the darkness of the attitudes and assumptions that dominate the new books.

No single medium shapes the mind of today's youth. But because successful mass-culture productions usually are fine-tuned to the publics they serve, it's conceivable that the themes in the new comics echo the beliefs of the target audiences. And those themes are troubling. Freedom, fairness, integrity, sympathy, individuality and other familiar values surface now and then; in their name heroes and heroines occasionally wage last-ditch holy wars. But defeats far outnumber victories, and victories are often tarnished; the key article of faith seems to be that turning the tides of political corruption, fending off nuclear disaster or breaking the manacles of Big Brother thought control will be, in the long run, impossible. The world of adult comics is full of downers; the tone aimed at, in general, is knowing cynicism, and the feelings evoked are, more often than not, grim, self-taunting and hopeless.

The extent of the negativism can be missed in casual browsing. Fans of *Superman* or *Donald Duck*—or of *Batman* or *Spider-Man* or *Wonder Woman*—might conclude, after a quick glance through the pages of *Warp* or *E-Man,* that the more things change, the more they stay the same. Gory sock-'em-ups, the staple of old comic books for kids, play the same role in comic books for young adults. And the presence of interplanetary wars and other items stolen from ordinary science fiction hardly adds up, in itself, to a radical departure from time-honored tradition. Is there really anything so adult about adult comic books?

Indeed there is, starting with sex. The new magazines don't cross the line into porn, but they commonly show heroes and heroines in bed together before or after galactic adventure. By exploiting time-warp conventions, moreover, they contrive pseudo-historical justification for outfitting females in sexually piquant costumes. For example, the hero of *Edge of Chaos* is time-warped to ancient Greece; in most panels, he appears in the company of Diana, a voluptuously bare-breasted, compliant female assistant to Zeus. And in revising old legends and myths, the story-and-art departments often introduce transformations. DC Comics' *Camelot 3000,* in which King Arthur is reincarnated after a nuclear holocaust, centers much of its action upon a female Tristan caught up in lesbian passion for Isolde; Tristan's price for selling out the Knights of the Round Table is a guarantee, by Morgan le Fay, of a magical sex change.

But it's not just frankness about sex that distinguishes the adult's from the child's comic book; there is also the eagerness to play pedagogue. In adult comic books, war and intrigue are regularly interrupted for mini-lectures on topics ranging from cultural relativism to existential despair, from fluorocarbons to data banks. In the opening issue of one series chronicling a post-holocaust, end-of-the-line struggle against a universal monolith called the Citadel, much is made of the differences among the 22 planetary cultures obliterated by the monolith; a letter to the reader, at the back of the book, stresses that the story's focus is the "vast variety of alien worlds" that existed prior to the Citadel's hegemony, "each [world] with its own unique attitudes and culture."

Moreover, the genre's publishers hype their products as offering news unobtainable elsewhere about the frontiers of contemporary thought. A book called *Mars,* for instance, is advertised as "an extrapolation from current theories about the mind." Eclipse Comics' *DNAgents* instructs readers in genetics jargon. Allusion to contemporary political rows in adult comics can be explicit: *E-Man* takes on evangelical Christian fundamentalism, mocking the current attack on "secular humanists." And recommended reading lists—works in the traditional print media—turn up in both editorial and letters columns. The book called *American Flagg* recommends Huxley's *Brave New World,* Orwell's *1984,* two volumes by Alfred Bester and *Revolt in 2100* by Robert Heinlein.

Ideas also have a place in the traditional comic press, as Ariel Dorfman has demonstrated in a series of witty Marxist analyses of *Donald Duck* and *Superman.* But the new comics stress their teaching mission, even as they are stuffed with cliches, misinformation and errors.

But what's most striking about the new comics is the gloom, the pervasive atmosphere of defeat. They repeat the theme that the future belongs to the Oppressors: Tiny bands of resisters may struggle for independence, but they have terrible difficulty simply staying alive; individual efforts to stand up for oneself or protest some exceptionally outrageous practice by the Oppressors tend to fail. A typical segment of First Comics' *American Flagg* illustrates the pattern. The place is Chicago, the time is 2031, decades after a pivotal year of cataclysm marked by an East Coast meltdown, crop failures, plagues, the collapse of the international banking system and the nuking of London by a reunited Germany. "Every surviving corporate head" and elected leader has been relocated to Mars, where they function as a puppet government jerked about by PLEX, a giant communications conglomerate. The people obliged to go on living in Chicago's rubble and elsewhere are drugged on "entertainments"—chain houses of prostitution (venereal disease from these "Adult Centers" is rife); a sports gambling industry run, in the Windy City, by a black mayor; and, most notably, a weekly, televised, world-syndicated riot called "Firefight All Night Live!" and starring two or more of Chicago's 70-odd "registered paramilitary clubs," murderous gangs armed by PLEX.

Comes a lone resister—decent young Reuben Flagg, a bribe-rejecting college dropout who, after losing an acting job, manages to find work as a uniformed security guard. Depressed by the seedy, PLEX-controlled shysterism surrounding him, Flagg hunts for a way to strike back. But his coworkers set him up. They tape his seduction by the madam of a branch Adult Center so that his claims to integrity are compromised. And his attempts at challenging PLEX come across as pointless. Alerted to the existence of subliminal signals on television that stimulate ever-more intense demands for violence among viewers, Flagg risks his life to rip out the "sublims" signal system, whereupon—the close of the segment—a wilder riot than any hitherto known commences. The last word is a taunt from Flagg's oily, deceitful boss: "Now, thanks to you, we'll see what happens . . . when a horde of murdering sociopaths are deprived of the only thing they love."

American Flagg's portrayal of the media as manipulative providers of "bread and circuses" achieves, at moments, satirical edge. But its pessimism about the engulfing forces of thievery and injustice remains unrelieved from start to finish. And roughly similar views of life appear in countless other adult comic books. *Ronin,* perhaps the most visually impressive publication in the field—at $2.50, it's also among the more expensive—offers images of New York City's future that are staggeringly bleak. A single corporate complex spreads itself over midtown; the rest of the city consists of burning buildings, monster rats and huddled, starved, half-naked bums preying miserably on each other. (New York is "warlike, desperate, hopeless, evil to the root. . . .") The savagery and greed of *Ronin*'s corporate giant, called SAWA, is matched, in *DNAgents,* by that of a chemical combine called Matrix. When futuristic comics are set in post-corporation ages, the survivors are programmed to tear each other apart—see *The Omega Men*—in mindless struggles for the leadership of forlorn groups that haven't a prayer of prevailing against the going universal tyranny. And when comics develop reincarnation themes, a standard plot feature is an act of shameless turpitude committed by a standard-brand politician upon some upright figure out of the past. In *Camelot 3000,* the sitting President in the White House, presented as a conventional American Yahoo, double-crosses King Arthur.

It's fair to acknowledge that a few humorous adult comics continue to be marketed—the best of them is Pacific Comics' *Groo The Wanderer,* a send-up of quest motifs that borrows the idioms of Mel Brooks' 2,000-year-old man. And in contemporary adult mass media, melancholia, self-pity and despair are scarcely unique to adult comics; the lyrics of the Talking Heads or Lou Reed or of many Iggy Pop albums don't exactly overflow with good cheer. And before long, some observers no doubt will announce that it's not the content of the new comics that's significant but, instead, the age of their consumers. Once upon a day, comic books meant kids in their subteens, bike-riding youngsters who dropped by the drugstore or stationery store to check out Bugs Bunny and the rest on innocent Saturday afternoons. Is it not proof of the onset of mass adult illiteracy that the new comic-book audience is composed of people who work for a living and drive to malls, at night, to lay out hard-earned dollars for junk?

Still, the range of allusion and vocabulary in the majority of the adult comics goes beyond that of standard daily newspapers. It's less likely that adult comics are read because they're easy than because they seldom affront the deepest beliefs and intuitions of their audiences. It's hard to be precise about the nature of these audiences: Comic-book publishers don't take complicated readership surveys. Asked what he knows about his adult customers, Mike Flynn, promotion manager at DC Comics, could say confidently only that most are males between the ages of 16 and 24, and that two-thirds had completed some college; he had no information on income levels.

My guess is based partly on the comments I listened to, particularly about *American Flagg,* in the local branch of Moondance, an important Eastern chain of comics stores, and partly on scrutiny of the letters columns of a score of magazines, which seem not to be housewritten. That guess is that dropouts and community-college students, uncertain of their direction, constitute the bulk of the readership. Preached at since childhood about American abundance, the dream of success and upward mobility, these readers find themselves increasingly remote from the success culture, alienated from what Herbert Marcuse once spoke of as "the cosmos of hope." They thus have good reason to value any indirect, non-humiliating explanation of their exclusion from the American Dream.

Sounder explanations than those offered in adult comics are available—versions of the present and future of "opportunity" that take into account shifts in the nature of the economy and the composition of the work force. In theory, public education in a democracy has an obligation to acquaint younger citizens with such historical factors. They also should be informed about the ways in which ideological competition with noncapitalist nations has stimulated extravagant expectations about free enterprise. But that obligation is not met, and one result is that the country's young losers have little choice, when attempting to interpret the more punishing contemporary realities, except to fall back on fantasy, moral oversimplifications and stylized, knowing cynicism about the evil of all who hold power.

A speculative analysis, granted. Equally speculative is the notion that adult comics are a better safety valve for the millions who read them than, say, membership in crypto-Fascist youth groups. What's clear, in any case, is that the new adult-comics press, with its smotheringly enormous corporate giants and hopelessly situated, yet young and decent, American Flaggs, is too disturbing a cultural phenomenon to be pigeonholed under casually dismissive labels. The deep, broad-based cynicism expressed and reflected in adult comics has not been a norm in this country's working-class youth; its advent could have a powerful impact on politics and culture.

Adam Gopnik

SOURCE: "Comics and Catastrophe," in *The New Republic*, Vol. 196, No. 3779, June 22, 1987, pp. 29-34.

[*In the following essay, Gopnik examines Art Spiegelman's* Maus, *a comic book about the Holocaust, in the historical context of traditional cartoon imagery and caricature.*]

If you ask educated people to tell you everything they know about the history and psychology of cartooning, they will probably offer something like this: cartoons (taking caricature, political cartooning, and comic strips all together as a single form) are a relic of the infancy of art, one of the earliest forms of visual communication (and therefore, by implication, especially well suited to children); they are naturally funny and popular; and their gift is above all for the diminutive.

But these beliefs about cartooning are not merely incomplete; they are in almost every respect the direct reverse of the truth. Cartoons are not a primordial form. They are the relatively novel offspring of an extremely sophisticated visual culture. The caricature, from which all other kinds of cartooning descend, first appears around 1600 in Italy, within the circle of Bernini and the Carracci—and then not as a popular form, a visual slang, but as an in-group dialect, an aristocratic code.

Some of the devices that belong to cartoon and caricature might seem to be very ancient. There may appear to be precedents in Egyptian and Assyrian art for the device of combining human and animal elements in one figure; and we find distorted or grotesque human faces on everything from Greek pots to Gothic cathedrals. But these ancient practices have essentially nothing in common with apparently similar devices in modern cartoon and caricature. Before 1600 the tradition of combining human and animal elements in a single figure was a tradition of splicing—usually placing an animal head on a human body in order to symbolize reverence (as in Egyptian art) or contempt (as in certain Roman graffiti). It was only around 1600 that the tradition of splicing human and animal elements was replaced by a tradition of melding those elements together in such a way that the abstract likeness of man and animal was made into an animated visual fusion.

Similarly, grotesques before 1600 were never portraits: Roman and Gothic grotesques are meant to depict sub- or transhuman types. They are not meant to be striking, much less affectionate, likenesses of individuals. Distortion of the human face for the purposes of caricature, rather than the creation of monsters or satyrs, and the device of melding, as against splicing, human and animal features together are unique to the cartoon tradition, and are at most 300 years old (though, inevitably, certain kinds of simple caricature and cartoon are haunted by earlier "grotesque" traditions).

It took more than a century before the caricature was reimagined, in England in the late 18th century, as a form of popular political and social satire. And the "diminutive" cartoon, the kind of cartoon we associate in this country with the work of Walt Disney, is not a simple extension of the cartoon tradition, but a real departure from it, an American invention of the same vintage as contract bridge or the NFL.

Our mistaken beliefs about cartooning testify to the cartoon's near magical ability, whatever its real history, to persuade us of its innocence. Even though cartoons are in fact recent and cosmopolitan, we respond to them as if they were primordial. If we could understand why this happens, we might begin to understand the special cognitive and even biological basis of our response to the form. That educated people don't know very much about cartooning just shows that we don't usually think it worthwhile to educate people about it. But this situation is changing. That, for the first time, educated people are coming to have an opinion about cartoons is largely due to the influence of one remarkable work, Art Spiegelman's book *Maus: A Survivor's Tale.*

By now everyone has heard something about *Maus*. It has been widely and enthusiastically reviewed, has sold a surprisingly large number of copies, has been nominated for a National Book Critics' Circle Award. And by now everyone knows what *Maus* is: the Holocaust Comic Book. This label is one of those oxymorons—like "nonfiction novel" and "rock opera"—that put reviewers into a kind of hypnotic trance. Rising from their baskets and swaying back and forth, they worry ponderously about categories rather than values. *Maus* is a work in progress, a serial that has appeared in installments in Spiegelman's magazine *RAW,* a magazine of what used to be called "underground" cartooning. (*RAW* is to New York painting in the '80s, which often draws heavily on cartoon imagery, what *Minotaure* was to Paris painting in the '30s—a kind of *prêt-à-porter* catalog of avant-garde form.)

On one level, *Maus* is an autobiographical documentary about Vladek Spiegelman, the artist's father, and his experiences in Poland as a Jew during the Second World War. *Maus* begins with Art visiting Vladek today in Rego Park, Queens. "We weren't very close," Art admits. (We learn later that the two men had been torn apart by the suicide of Art's mother, Anja, a few years before.) In part to encourage a warmer relationship with his father, in part because it seems important for its own sake, in part because it offers a new avenue for Art's work, Art decides to write a book about Vladek's experiences during the war, experiences that, we discover early on, took him into Auschwitz. The story then moves freely from Rego Park today to Poland during the horror, as we both follow the track of Art's inquisition of his father and move back into the lost world Vladek's memories evoke.

Vladek, we are informed, came from a family of well-off Polish Jewish merchants. As a young man he married the plain and troubled daughter of a much wealthier family. (It is a measure of Spiegelman's extraordinary intelligence and delicacy as a kind of novelist that he manages to make his father's mixed motives in this marriage perfectly apparent without seeming censorious.) When the war breaks out, Vladek joins the army. (There is a hilarious flashback to the Spiegelman family's distinguished history of draft evasion.) Vladek participates in a single, doomed battle with the Polish army, in which, quite unremorse fully, he kills a wounded German soldier ("I was glad to do something"). He is sent to a prison camp, where, interestingly enough, his Jewishness doesn't seem to single him out for especially sadistic treatment. Then he is released, and returns to his family. Practical and exceptionally enterprising, he begins to build up his business again—and then, in its oddly impersonal way, the Nazi "noose begins to tighten" around the throats of Vladek and his family.

Spiegelman makes the bureaucratic sadism of the Germans uncannily vivid—all the steps and reroutings and sortings and resortings that preceded mass murder. *Maus* is a work of hyperrealist detail. Nobody could have anticipated that a comic book about the Holocaust could have told so much about the way this particular endgame was played out: precisely how the black market worked within the ghettos; exactly what happened, in sequence, when the Germans occupied a town; why in 1943 a Jew would have thought Hungary a haven, and how he would have tried to get his family there. The book version of *Maus,* published by Pantheon in 1986, ends with Vladek and Anja in Auschwitz, and the latest installment in *RAW* picks up their story again in the camp.

At the same time, we see Vladek as he tells his story today. Vladek is not exactly Elie Wiesel. He is a pinched, mean-spirited, and hilariously miserly old man. In the middle of telling Art how Anja's parents were the first among the family to be sent off to Auschwitz and the ovens, he breaks off the conversation to pick something up from the street. Art: "What did you pick up?" Vladek: "Telephone wire. This it's very hard to find. Inside it's *little* wires. It's good for tying things." Art: "You *always* pick up trash! Can't you just *buy* wire?" Vladek: "Pssh. Why always you want to *buy* when you can find!? Anyway, this wire they don't have it in any stores. I'll give to you some wire. You'll see how useful it is." Art: "No thanks! Just tell me what happened with Haskell." And then we are back in Poland.

No summary can do justice to Spiegelman's narrative skill—his feeling for the dramatic juxtaposition of hideous and comic material; his rendering of the exasperated love of a son for his inadequate, persecuted father; above all his ear for voices. No writer in any genre since the young Philip Roth has managed make the Jewish speech of several generations sound so fresh or uncannily convincing, an achievement that's all the more impressive since it has been done within the incredibly tight confines of comic-strip balloons.

But none of this is what has made *Maus* famous in its time. That notoriety due to a simple, hallucinatory device: all the characters in *Maus* are drawn as animals—the Jews as mice, the Poles as pigs, the Germans as cats, and the Americans as dogs. It's extremely important to understand that *Maus* is in no way an animal fable or an allegory like Aesop or *Animal Farm.* The Jews are Jews who just happen to be depicted as mice, in a peculiar, idiosyncratic convention. There isn't any allegorical dimension in *Maus,* just a convention of representation. In fact, at one key moment in the book real mice, animal mice, appear, and the Anja and Vladek characters, though drawn as mice, respond exactly as real people would respond to real rodents.

But the cartoon device in *Maus* has been widely seen not as a way of organizing the horror vividly and effectively, but as a way of denying the horror altogether, of turning remembrance into folktale. It's even been said that *Maus* marks the end of real Holocaust literature, the moment when, in the hands of the survivors' children, the horror settles into folktale and fable. Or else, in the hands of those few reviewers committed to the "underground" cartoon as a form, Spiegelman is seen not as an artist working within the best traditions of the cartoon, but as the Spartacus of the underground comic strip, the hero of a movement that has emancipated the cartoon from mere cuteness—liberated the seven dwarfs from the Disney mines, so to speak, and turned them into underground men of a better and different kind.

Both these views are fundamentally ahistorical. Working not against the grain of the cartoon but within its richest inheritance, and exploring the deepest possibilities unique to the form, Spiegelman has reminded us what the cartoon is capable of: *Maus* is an act not of invention, but of restoration. And in rediscovering the serious and even tragic possibilities of the comic strip and the cartoon, Spiegelman has found another way to do what all artists who have made the Holocaust their subject have tried to do: to stylize horror without aestheticizing it.

Working not against the grain of the cartoon but within its richest inheritance, and exploring the deepest possibilities unique to the form, Art Spiegelman has reminded us what the cartoon is capable of: *Maus* is an act not of invention, but of restoration. And in rediscovering the serious and even tragic possibilities of the comic strip and the cartoon, Spiegelman has found another way to do what all artists who have made the Holocaust their subject have tried to do: to stylize horror without aestheticizing it.

—Adam Gopnik

Mostly we think about the problems of art about the Holocaust in literary terms, and not sufficiently about how the problem has been addressed in the visual arts. It is the visual arts, after all, that memorials to national disasters and martyrdoms have traditionally been made. Some of the terms and concepts evolved in art criticism and art history may help us to understand what is, after all, an iconoclastic dispute, a debate about the legitimacy of images. To borrow a distinction from Meyer Schapiro, we want art about the Holocaust to be both narrative and iconic. We want to be told or shown exactly what happened, but because we know in advance that what we're going to see is more horrible than anything we can imagine, we want the style of the depiction to be elevated and even a little mysterious, like great religious art.

Even the few inarguably great public statements about suffering in our time seem inadequate to the events of the Holocaust. If we were told, for instance, that Picasso's *Guernica* is a memorial to, say, Lublin, I think we would feel a little disgusted. *Guernica,* after all, is an elegy to the losing side in a conflict: the painting takes sides, and has a point. But the uniquely horrible thing about what happened to the Jews in Europe is that the "sides" existed only in the paranoid fantasies of their persecutors. (And in *Guernica,* as in *The Charnel House* of 1945, we can't help but feel that we're being had a little. Picasso's great achievement in art was to ask us to read "distortions" of human form not merely as horrific, but as capable of expressing an enormous range of emotion. In their way these pictures are too beautiful.)

Of course, the notion that modern warfare has brought with it a new kind of evil—not merely cruel, but senseless—does not begin with what happened in Europe in the '40s, and neither does the corresponding notion that the traditional forms of elegiac art are in some sense inadequate. Goya saw clearly that the traditional forms of ennobled suffering were utterly incapable of dealing with a new kind of horror—and he was the first to see, too, that it was the tradition of the cartoon, of all things, that might offer a solution. What may strike us most about Goya's etchings in *The Horrors of War* or *The Third of May* is their documentary realism, but, as E. H. Gombrich has pointed out, it wasn't firsthand experience that gave form to Goya's art; rather, it was the tradition of popular imagery, of caricature and political cartoon, that Goya borrowed and reimagined as the appropriate armature on which to hang his indignation.

One of the most frightening and memorable of Goya's devices in *The Horrors of War* is borrowed from the popular tradition of making men look like animals and animals look like men—the tradition of "physiognomic comparison." What's most striking about the major examples of the tradition, even before Goya, is how fascinatingly ambiguous they are, and how essentially humorless. If we look at, say, Charles Lebrun's *Comparisons* of 1667, the most encyclopedic of all the essays in physiognomy, we seem to be seeing something proto-Darwinian in its vision. Are these images of the bestiality latent in man, or of the humanity latent in beasts? Even those animal types that have become, in our time, stock instances of the diminutive cartoon (rabbits and mice) have in Lebrun's drawings an utter gravity and melancholy. The faces of Lebrun's little humanized rodents not only look uncannily like the faces in *Maus*; they also look like us. They seem, for all their obvious grotesqueness, so much more modern than any of the portraits Lebrun painted precisely because of their ambivalence—not man secure in a social role but man staring into the abyss of his own possible bestiality.

Thus the tradition of the cartoon, far from being essentially diminutive and escapist, has been from its beginnings well suited to expressing certain kinds of high seriousness. Again and again throughout the history of the cartoon, serious artists have drawn not just on the satiric potential of the form, but on its ability to stylize a certain kind of horror as well, the horror that occurs not when human beings behave wickedly but when they lose (or are robbed of) their humanity altogether. This is a tradition Lebrun articulated and Goya ennobled. (It is also the tradition of cartoon that Picasso drew on in his political comic strip of the '30s, *The Dream and Lie of Franco.*)

What needs explaining, then, isn't the emancipation of the cartoon tradition by Spiegelman and the *RAW* stable of artists, but its previous domestication. Stephen Jay Gould has explained the essential psychological device that allowed the artists of the Disney studios, in particular, to transform humanized animals from totemic beasts into pets. Gould demonstrates that Mickey gradually became more and more "neotenic" as time went on; that is, he came to have more and more of the features of human infants: large forehead, floppy joints, head out of proportion to body size, and so on. Mickey, in short, came increasingly to look like a human baby, and, as Gould goes on to suggest, this transformation turned the cartoon mouse into a kind of red flag waved at the most basic of human instincts. We are prewired, it seems, to respond with passionate affection to anything that has a certain set of infantile features; the anonymous artists of the Disney studio had forged a key that fit a primal lock in the human mind.

What Gould didn't point out (and had no need to) was how utterly discontinuous this discovery was with the rest on the history of cartooning. The Disney invention was so astonishingly successful that in some respects it effectively expunged any other kind of cartooning or any other potential for the cartoon, from the memory of educated people. We see here the source of the paradox with which we began: the neotenic cartoon has overwhelmed not just all other kinds of cartoons, but our memory of all other kinds of cartoons.

This was possible, in part, because at a deeper level cartoons and caricature have always had more direct access to basic types of human cognition than almost any other kind of drawing. Some cognitive psychologists theorize that caricatures and cartoons are so memorable because their external forms in some way mirror the internal structure of our mental representations, the idealized and schematized mental imagery that our minds use to presort and structure perception. The mind's eye, they argue, in effect sees caricatures when it looks at the world and sees cartoons when it tries to remember what it has seen. The discovery of caricature, on this view, is as much an episode in the history of psychology—a fundamental discovery about the way the mind works—as it is an episode in the history of art.

I do not invoke Goya and Picasso to provide *Maus* with a tony pedigree. *Maus* is, by comparison, visually timid and even a little crude. In fact, *Maus* is considerably less daring, as drawing and design, than almost anything else in *RAW,* and less daring than much of Spiegelman's own earlier work. (An episode of an earlier Spiegelman strip, "Prisoner of Hell Planet," is inserted into *Maus* to make this plain.) The drawing here is, even by Spiegelman's own standards, deliberately folklike, stiff and unvaried.

If *Maus* depended for its effect only on the cartoon device, it would not be much more than an interesting curiosity. But *Maus* draws its power not from its visual style alone, but rather from the tension between its words and pictures, between the detail of its narration and dialogue and the hallucinatory fantasy of its images. At the heart of our understanding (or our lack of understanding) of the Holocaust is our sense that this is both a human and an inhuman experience. We know that it happened to people like us, but we also know that what happened to them is not what happens to people, that what happened was not just discontinuous with the rest of human history, but also with our notion of what it is to be a person, and of how people behave. In order to show that these events are in some way sacred to us, we have to indicate, in art, that they are at once part of human history and outside it.

This overlay of the human and the inhuman is exactly what *Maus,* with its old form, is extraordinarily able to depict. On the one hand this is entirely history of the motives and desires of particular people, the story of Vladek and Anja's hundred individual decisions, failures, betrayals and disappointments. On the other hand it is a history in which all human intention has been reduced to the hunted animal's instinct for self-preservation, in which all will and motive has been degraded to reflex. The heart-wrenching pathos of *Maus* lies in its retrospective, historical sense: Art, drawing *Maus,* knows that Vladek and Anja are finally as helpless and doomed as mice fleeing cats—but *they* still think that they are people, with the normal human capacity for devising schemes and making bargains.

Maus thus gives form to something essential to our understanding of the Holocaust. It is both loving documentary and brutal fable, a mix of compassion and stoicism. This is the consequence of its strange form, which pays perfect and unerring respect to the fate of particular people caught up in the horror, and at the same time makes it plain that the horror cannot really be understood or explained as a sum of individual actions and desires. Our fear about the depiction of the Holocaust is not only that it will be trivialized, but also that it will be assimilated to the Western tradition of tragedy, that organizing it will allow us in some sense to dismiss it—to leave the theater of history, purged. But with its seemingly bizarre juxtaposition of visual and literary struggles, *Maus* manages to give dignity to the sufferers without suggesting that their suffering had any "meaning" in a sense that in some way ennobled the sufferers, or that their agony has a transcendent element because it provides some catharsis for those of us who are told about, or are shown, their suffering.

Spiegelman's animal metaphor captures something crucial about the psychology of Holocaust survivors. Those few I have met are remarkably articulate about their story, but they are interestingly uncurious about the motives of their persecutors. They do indeed seem to see them as cats, as natural and unthinking predators who simply do what they are born to do. But the Germans weren't cats. They didn't have to do what they did. The cartoon form can supply a perfect mix of literary and visual metaphor, but metaphors aren't explanations.

If *Maus* is a nearly magical description of what happened—if it manages to sum up the experience of the Holocaust, for the survivors and their children, with as much power and as little pretension as any other work I can think of—it still must be said that the book succeeds so well in part because it evades the central *moral* issue of the Holocaust: How could people do such things to other people? The problem with the animal metaphor is not that it is demeaning to the mice, but that it lets the cats off too easily.

There is also a deeper level of image magic at work in *Maus,* which accounts for both its power and its extraordinary fit with its subject. I have mentioned earlier that a tradition of "spliced" animal and human forms precedes the "melded" forms of caricature. The image of a human body with an animal head is one of the very oldest in art, and it occurs frequently for the same reason: not, as in the physiognomic tradition, to compare man and animal, but to symbolize the presence of the sacred. In a way that I am almost certain is completely unconscious, *Maus* is also haunted by the older tradition, and, particularly and strangely, by a peculiar Jewish variant of the older tradition.

Spiegelman's animal heads are, purposefully, much more uniform and mask-like than those of almost any other modern cartoonist. His mice, while they have distinct human expressions, all have essentially the same face. As a consequence, they suggest not just the condition of human beings forced to behave like animals, but also our sense that this story is too horrible to be presented unmasked. The particular animal "masks" Spiegelman has chosen uncannily recall and evoke one of the few masterpieces of Jewish religious art—the Bird's Head Haggadah of 13th-century Ashkenazi art. In this and related manuscripts, the Passover story is depicted using figures with the bodies of humans and heads of animals—small, common animals, usually birds.

Now, in one sense the problems that confronted the medieval Jewish illuminator and the modern Jewish artist of the Holocaust are entirely different. The medieval artist had a subject too holy to be depicted; the modern artist has a subject too horrible to be depicted. For the traditional illuminator, it is the ultimate sacred mystery that must somehow be shown without being shown; for the contemporary artist, it is the ultimate obscenity, the ultimate profanity, that must somehow be shown without being shown. But this obscenity, this profanity, has become our sacred subject, in the sense that our contemplation of it has become nearly liturgical.

Yet still we want a sacred art that isn't a transcendent art. We want an art whose stylizations are as much a declaration of inadequacy to their subject as they are of mystical transcendence. And this is the quality that *Maus* and the Bird's Head Haggadah, for all their differences, share: in both these Jewish works, the homely animal device is able to depict the sacred by a kind of comic indirection. The device is so potent precisely because it seems, at first, so disarming.

So the self-conscious element of primitivism in Spiegelman's drawing has the deepest affinity with the very small body of important Jewish art. It is an affinity that may help lead us to a better understanding of what a modern Jewish art can be, a Jewish art that leads away from Chagall and his levitating Hassidim, away from banal affinities rooted in sentimental imagery, from ersatz connections between ancient form and modern abstraction such as those made by modern Israeli artists who draw on Hebrew calligraphic traditions. The affinity between the medieval Jewish illuminators and Art Spiegelman may be rooted in a much more profound set of solutions—solutions that turn deliberately to the homely and the unpretentious, rather than to the transcendent and mystical, in order to depict the sacred.

One of the platitudes about modern art is that it exists in the face of the failure and dissolution of religious art. In some sense, of course, this is true. And yet the human need to see depicted all those things that used to be the province of religious art—the geography of good and evil, of heaven and hell—remains constant. The deeper preoccupation of modern art, from Matisse's Arcadia to Francis Bacon's infernal interiors, has been to find some secular visual language to fulfill that need. Cartoons reflect this preoccupation too, and have been surprisingly successful in making these images for us: images of Eden in the work of George Herriman and Winsor McCay, and now potent images of extreme horror in *Maus*. If all the old forms of religious art have gone into diaspora, there seem to be moments in heaven, and circles in hell, that have taken shelter in the comic strip.

FURTHER READING

Anthologies

Barrier, Michael and Williams, Martin eds. *A Smithsonian Book of Comic-Book Comics.* Washington, D.C.: Smithsonian Institution Press, 1981, 336 p.

A collection of reprints from the history of comics, from Superman and Little Lulu to the lesser known Scribbly, are presented with short introductions, plus a bibliography.

Estren, Mark James. *A History of Underground Comics.* Berkeley, CA.: Ronin Publishing, 1986, 319 p.

This reissue of a 1974 edition is arranged impressionistically rather than for scholars, with historical and bibliographic information on underground comix.

Gifford, Denis. *The International Book of Comics.* New York: Crescent Books, 1984, 256 p.

A carefully inventoried collection of comic book covers from around the world are presented in color and black and white, with a historical overview and index.

Hirsh, Michael and Loubert, Patrick. *The Great Canadian Comic Books.* Toronto, Ontario, Canada: P. Martin Associates, 1971, 264 p.

Genre comics dating from the days of WWII , from the publishing house of Cyril Vaughan Bell, are introduced and annotated.

Lee, Stan. *Bring on the Bad Guys.* New York: Simon and Schuster, 1976, 253 p.

Stories involving the villains of classic Marvel comics, like the Red Skull, are introduced with some information on their origins.

———. *Origins of Marvel Comics.* New York: Simon and Schuster, 1974, 254 p.

Comic book covers are reprinted, with original stories starring the Hulk, Spiderman and more, introduced by editor Lee.

———. *Son of Origins of Marvel Comics.* New York: Simon and Schuster, 1975, 249 p.

A companion book to *Origins* is devoted to the likes of the X-Men and Silver Surfer.

O'Neil, Dennis ed. *Secret Origins of the Super DC Heroes.* New York: Warner Books, 1976, 239 p.

Debut comic book sequences for ten of the most popular DC Comics characters, including Wonder Woman, Batman and Superman, are introduced by artist Carmine Infantino.

Schodt, Frederik L. *Manga! Manga! The World of Japanese Comics.* Tokyo, Japan: Kodansha International, 1983, 260p.

A bibliography, index and translated sequences illustrate an industry with its own character and history.

Scott, Naomi ed. *Heart Throbs, the Best of DC Romance Comics.* New York: Simon and Schuster, 1979, 256 p.

A series of the publishing house's stories is reprinted, with a separate credits index.

Superman from the Thirties to the Seventies. New York: Crown Publishers, 1971, 386 p.

A sourcebook for original publication information on 28 Superman adventures, reprinted in color and black and white; introduced by a history of mass media representations of this enduring character.

Uslan, Michael ed. *Mysteries in Space, the Best of DC Science-Fiction Comics.* New York: Simon and Schuster, 1980, 251 p.

Science fiction comics dating between 1951 and 1964 are reprinted, with a bibliography of all DC comics in the same genre.

Secondary Sources

Abbot, Lawrence L. "Comic Art: Characteristics and Potentialities of a Narrative Medium." *Journal of Popular Culture* 19, No. 4 (Spring 1986): 155-176.

An analysis of the interaction of text and picture in sequential art in terms of perceptual psychology.

Adams, Kenneth Alan and Lester Hill, Jr. "Protest and Rebellion: Fantasy Themes In Japanese Comics." *Journal of Popular Culture* 25, No. 1 (Summer 1991): 99-127.

Certain recurrent themes in manga are interpreted according to the Freudian psychology of psychosexual developmental stages.

Bailey, Bruce. "An Inquiry into Comic Books." *Journal of Popular Culture* X, No. 1 (Summer 1976): 245-248.

The effects of the Comics Code Authority on romance comics is shown to have resulted in less severe censorship of their most typical storylines.

Barker, Martin. *Comics: Ideology, Power and the Critics.* New York: Manchester University Press, 1989, 320 p.

An inquiry into the trustworthiness of sociological studies, particularly of mass media and their effects on adult and child consumers.

Brent, Ruth S. "Nonverbal Design Language in Comics." *Journal of American Culture* 14, No. 1 (Spring 1991): 57-61.

A study of the use of visual symbols in Calvin and Hobbes and Batman cartoons, that invokes the ethnography of Victor Turner.

Butler Flora, Cornelia. "Roasting Donald Duck: Alternative Comics and Photonovels in Latin America." *Journal of Popular Culture* 18, No. 1 (Summer 1984): 163-183.

Examples of graphic novels published outside the mainstream press coincide with social protest movements in various South American countries like Peru, Chile and Ecuador.

Eisner, Will. *Comics and Sequential Art.* Tamarac, FL: Poorhouse Press, 1990, 158 p.

The author's trademark cinematic approach to writing, laying out and decorating the comic book page is set out step-by-step.

Gifford, Denis. "The Evolution of the British Comic." *History Today* XXI, No. 5, (May 1971): 349-358.

A history of the earliest British cartoons, 1821-1897, from simple broadsides and caricature magazines to the first comic hero Ally Sloper and his popular series.

Havig, Alan. "Richard F. Outcault's 'Poor Lil' Mose': Variations on the Black Stereotype in American Comic Art." *Journal of American Culture* 11, No. 1 (Spring 1988): 33-41.

The author argues that in Outcault's famous Yellow Kid, Buster Brown and Poor Lil' Mose cartoons, a contradictory portrayal of blacks seems to be the norm.

Hinds Jr., Harold E. and Charles M. Tatum. *Not Just For Children: The Mexican Comic Book in the Late 1960s and 1970s.* Westport, Conn.: Greenwood Press, 1992, 264 p.

A detailed study of the most popular Mexican cartoons of the day, including Kaliman, Chanoc and Los supermachos.

Kempkes, Wolfgang. *International Bibliography of Comics Literature,* 2nd. ed., rev. Munich, Germany: Verlag Dokumentation, 1974, 293 p.

Studies of comics which fall under five major chronological categories are listed according to their areas of concern: commerce, psychology, education, and more.

Lanyi, Ronald Levitt. "Comic Books and Authority: An Interview with 'Stainless Steve' Englehart." *Journal of Popular Culture* 18, No. 2 (Fall 1984): 139-148.

The comic book writer talks about his tempestuous career with the publishing houses of Marvel and DC.

Marvel, Bill. "Comics for the Underground." In *The Arts Explosion,* edited by Clifford A. Ridley, pp. 152-161. Princeton, NJ: Dow Jones Books, 1969.

This essay on comix focuses almost exclusively on Robert Crumb.

McConnell, Frank. "Frames in Search of a Genre." In *Intersections of Fantasy and Science Fiction,* edited by George E. Slusser and Eric S. Rabkin, pp. 119-130. Carbondale IL: Southern Illinois University Press, 1987.

This essay breaks down all storytelling into two groups: jokes and shaggy-dog yarns, categories then applied to everything from Homer to Garfield.

McLuhan, Marshall. "Comics: Mad Vestibule to TV." In *Understanding Media: The Extensions of Man,* pp. 164-169. New York: McGraw-Hill Book Company, 1964.

To the author, *Mad* magazine is a mass culture hybrid that shows the effects of the print medium's new rival, television.

Perebinossoff, Philippe. "What Does a Kiss Mean? The Love Comic Formula and the Creation of the Ideal Teenage Girl." *Journal of Popular Culture* VIII, No. 4 (Spring 1975): 825-835.

An outline of the chaste melodramas in romance comics and how they enforce the norm of the nuclear family unit.

Richler, Mordecai. "The Great Comic Book Heroes." *Encounter* XXVIII, No. 5 (May 1967): 46-48, 50-53.

A tongue-in-cheek look back at Fredric Wertham's scare tactics, and an overview of broadly satirical cartoon parodies of the late 1960s.

Scobie, Alex. "Comics and Folkliterature." *Fabula* 21, No. 1 & 2 (1980): 70-81.

The author compares cartoonists to old folklorists who made their living as storytellers, and claims that the group efforts of comic artists result in an anonymity much like that of the unnamed originators of folk tales.

Scott, Randall W. *Comic Books and Strips: An Information Sourcebook.* Phoenix, AZ: Oryx Press, 1988, 152 p.

A list of books, periodicals and library collections which either anthologize cartoons, reprint them or offer critical analysis.

Silbermann, Alphons and H.-D. Dyroff. *Comics and Visual Culture: Research Studies from Ten Countries.* New York: KG Saur, 1986, 264 p.

Comic strips, books and films are discussed within national contexts, with essays devoted to Kenyan mass media, production and consumption in India, kid's comics in the former Soviet Union and elsewhere.

Smoodin, Eric. "Cartoon and Comic Classicism: High-Art Histories of Lowbrow Culture." *American Literary History* 4, No. 1 (Spring 1992): 129-140.

The author lists the innovations and shortcomings of serious analyses of comics as culture, within a review of three books on comic art published between 1989 and 1990.

Thompson, Don and Dick Lupoff. *The Comic-Book Book.* New Rochelle, NY: Arlington House, 1973, 360 p.

An overview in which the editors train a spotlight on lesser known talents in the comics industry.

Tucker, Ken. "Cats, Mice and History—The Avant-Garde of the Comic Strip." *The New York Times Book Review* (May 26, 1985): 3.

To the author, Spiegelman's *Maus* is a post-counterculture example of avant-garde cartoonery, that takes the shape of a popular narrative form and format, but drives home a psychohistorical political commentary.

Multimedia

Mann, Ron. *Comic Book Confidential,* anthology CD-ROM, New York: The Voyager Company, 1994.

Mann's documentary film of the same name is included, along with supplementary artist biographies and bibliographies, and 120 pages of art dating from the 1930s to the 1980s.

Spiegelman, Art. *The Complete Maus,* anthology CD-ROM, New York: The Voyager Company, 1994.

Spiegelman's book *Maus* is reproduced page by page, with multimedia annotations including preliminary sketches, alternate drafts, historical documentation, and interviews with Spiegelman and his father.

Vallejo, Alejandro. *The History of the Comics,* television documentary miniseries, Spain: Euskal Pictures International, S.A., 1990.

Comic art from the days of teacher and cartoonist Rudolphe Topffer (ca. 1850) to European graphic artists of the 1980s is assessed in this four-part series, with an English soundtrack and subtitles.

Zur, Patricia. *Spiegelman,* documentary short, New York: WNYC-TV, 1994.

A thirty-minute interview with Art Spiegelman focuses on his work ethic, thoughts on the critical reception of comic art, and *Maus.*

Zwigoff, Terry. *Crumb,* documentary feature, US: Sony Classics, 1995.

A full-length biography, filmed by a close friend, includes interviews with family members and other intimates of Robert Crumb, as well as the artist himself.

Disease and Literature

INTRODUCTION

The subject of disease—whether as a metaphor for spiritual corruption manifested in the body or as symbol of social ills—is one of the most prevalent in modern literature. While the allegorical presence of sickness was observed by the ancient Greek dramatists and exploited by medieval writers, the topic was elevated to a much greater prominence by the Romantics and their successors. In France, the Symbolist and Decadent movements embraced disease, especially mental illness, as part of the artist's natural state. Arthur Rimbaud, for example, wrote that the visionary poet must undergo a thorough derangement of the senses in order to achieve his ends. In Russia, Fyodor Dostoevsky pioneered the modern conception of the anti-hero, a criminal or otherwise marginal figure, whose malaise of the brain was his defining characteristic. With the Modernists came a new, almost clinical, approach to disease in literature. In 1930, Virginia Woolf wrote, "Considering how common illness is, how tremendous the spiritual change that it brings, how astonishing, when the lights of health go down, the undiscovered countries that are then disclosed . . . it becomes strange indeed that illness has not taken its place with love and battle and jealousy among the prime themes of literature." Thomas Mann explored this theme in relation to the individual in such works as *Doctor Faustus* and *The Magic Mountain*, and also broadened the scope of the disease metaphor, using it to represent the ills of modern European society. This symbolism was later adopted by such writers as Albert Camus, whose novel *The Plague* makes disease emblematic of the wholesale corruption of twentieth-century Europe in the midst of the second World War. Others—notably Alexander Solzhenitsyn, who in his *Cancer Ward* delved into the personal aspects of an illness he himself had suffered and overcome—approached the topic on its most basic, visceral level as well as in its psychological and spiritual contexts. In more recent years the spread of AIDS (acquired immune deficiency syndrome) to epidemic proportions has opened a new chapter in the literature of disease, as writers have begun to confront an illness that daily becomes more of an inescapable part of ordinary life.

REPRESENTATIVE WORKS

Burgess, Anthony
The Doctor Is Sick (novel) 1960
Camus, Albert
La Peste [*The Plague*] (novel) 1947
Céline, Louis-Ferdinand
Voyage au bout de la nuit [*Journey to the End of the Night*] (novel) 1932
Chekhov, Anton
Palata nomer 6 [*Ward Six*] (novella) 1892
Defoe, Daniel
A Journal of the Plague Year (novel) 1722
Dostoevsky, Fyodor
Zapiski iz myortvogo doma [*The House of the Dead*] (novel) 1862
Zapiski iz podpolya [*Notes from Underground*] (novella) 1864
Idiot [*The Idiot*] (novel) 1869
Besy [*The Possessed*] (novel) 1872
Brat'ya Karamazovy [*The Brothers Karamazov*] (novel) 1880
Flaubert, Gustave
Madame Bovary (novel) 1857
Gide, André
L'immoraliste [*The Immoralist*] (novel) 1902
Gilman, Charlotte Perkins
The Yellow Wallpaper (short story) 1899
Hemingway, Ernest
"The Snows of Kilimanjaro" (short story) 1961
Mann, Thomas
Der Tod in Venedig [*Death in Venice*] (short story) 1913
Der Zauberberg [*The Magic Mountain*] (novel) 1924
Doktor Faustus [*Doctor Faustus*] (novel) 1947
Molière
Le medecin malgre lui [*The Doctor in Spite of Himself*] (drama) 1666
Le malade imaginaire [*The Imaginary Invalid*] (drama) 1673
Poe, Edgar Allan
"The Fall of the House of Usher" (short story) 1839
"The Masque of the Red Death" (short story) 1842
Proust, Marcel
A la recherche du temps perdu [*Remembrance of Things Past*] (novel) 1954
Selzer, Richard
The Rituals of Surgery (short stories) 1974
Shaw, Bernard
The Doctor's Dilemma (drama) 1906
Solzhenitsyn, Alexander
Rakovyi korpus [*Cancer Ward*] (novel) 1968
Sophocles
Philoctetes (drama) 409 B.C.
Thomas, Dylan
The Doctor and the Devils (drama) 1953
Tolstoy, Leo
Smert Ivana Ilyicha [*The Death of Ivan Ilych*] (novella) 1886

OVERVIEWS

Virginia Woolf

SOURCE: "On Being Ill," in *Collected Essays*, Vol. 4, The Hogarth Press, 1967, pp. 193-203.

[*In the following essay, Woolf reflects on the ways in which being ill altered her perspective on life as well as her approach to reading works of literature.*]

Considering how common illness is, how tremendous the spiritual change that it brings, how astonishing, when the lights of health go down, the undiscovered countries that are then disclosed, what wastes and deserts of the soul a slight attack of influenza brings to view, what precipices and lawns sprinkled with bright flowers a little rise of temperature reveals, what ancient and obdurate oaks are uprooted in us by the act of sickness, how we go down into the pit of death and feel the waters of annihilation close above our heads and wake thinking to find ourselves in the presence of the angels and the harpers when we have a tooth out and come to the surface in the dentist's armchair and confuse his 'Rinse the mouth—rinse the mouth' with the greeting of the Deity stooping from the floor of Heaven to welcome us—when we think of this, as we are so frequently forced to think of it, it becomes strange indeed that illness has not taken its place with love and battle and jealousy among the prime themes of literature. Novels, one would have thought, would have been devoted to influenza; epic poems to typhoid; odes to pneumonia; lyrics to toothache. But no; with a few exceptions—De Quincey attempted something of the sort in *The Opium Eater;* there must be a volume or two about disease scattered through the pages of Proust—literature does its best to maintain that its concern is with the mind; that the body is a sheet of plain glass through which the soul looks straight and clear, and, save for one of two passions such as desire and greed, is null, and negligible and non-existent. On the contrary, the very opposite is true. All day, all night the body intervenes; blunts or sharpens, colours or discolours, turns to wax in the warmth of June, hardens to tallow in the murk of February. The creature within can only gaze through the pane smudged or rosy; it cannot separate off from the body like the sheath of a knife or the pod of a pea for a single instant; it must go through the whole unending procession of changes, heat and cold, comfort and discomfort, hunger and satisfaction, health and illness, until there comes the inevitable catastrophe; the body smashes itself to smithereens, and the soul (it is said) escapes. But of all this daily drama of the body there is no record. People write always of the doings of the mind; the thoughts that come into it; its noble plans; how the mind has civilized the universe. They show it ignoring the body in the philosopher's turret; or kicking the body, like an old leather football, across leagues of snow and desert in the pursuit of conquest or discovery. Those great wars which the body wages with the mind a slave to it, in the solitude of the bedrooms against the assault of fever or the oncome of melancholia, are neglected. Nor is the reason far to seek. To look these things squarely in the face would need the courage of a lion-tamer; a robust philosophy; a reason rooted in the bowels of the earth. Short of these, this monster, the body, this miracle, its pain, will soon make us taper into mysticism, or rise, with rapid beats of the wings, into the raptures of transcendentalism. The public would say that a novel devoted to influenza lacked plot; they would complain that there was no love in it—wrongly however, for illness often takes on the disguise of love, and plays the same odd tricks. It invests certain faces with divinity, sets us to wait, hour after hour, with pricked ears for the creaking of a stair, and wreathes the faces of the absent (plain enough in health, Heaven knows) with a new significance, while the mind concocts a thousand legends and romances about them for which it has neither time nor taste in health. Finally, to hinder the description of illness in literature, there is the poverty of the language. English, which can express the thoughts of Hamlet and the tragedy of Lear, has no words for the shiver and the headache. It has all grown one way. The merest schoolgirl, when she falls in love, has Shakespeare or Keats to speak her mind for her; but let a sufferer try to describe a pain in his head to a doctor and language at once runs dry. There is nothing ready made for him. He is forced to coin words himself, and, taking his pain in one hand, and a lump of pure sound in the other (as perhaps the people of Babel did in the beginning), so to crush them together that a brand new word in the end drops out. Probably it will be something laughable. For who of English birth can take liberties with the language? To us it is a sacred thing and therefore doomed to die, unless the Americans, whose genius is so much happier in the making of new words than in the disposition of the old, will come to our help and set the springs aflow. Yet it is not only a new language that we need, more primitive, more sensual, more obscene, but a new hierarchy of the passions; love must be deposed in favour of a temperature of 104; jealousy give place to the pangs of sciatica; sleeplessness play the part of villain, and the hero become a white liquid with a sweet taste—that mighty Prince with the moths' eyes and the feathered feet, one of whose names is Chloral.

But to return to the invalid. 'I am in bed with influenza'—but what does that convey of the great experience; how the world has changed its shape; the tools of business grown remote; the sounds of festival become romantic like a merry-go-round heard across far fields; and friends have changed, some putting on a strange beauty, others deformed to the squatness of toads, while the whole landscape of life lies remote and fair, like the shore seen from a ship far out at sea, and he is now exalted on a peak and needs no help from man or God, and now grovels supine on the floor glad of a kick from a housemaid—the experience cannot be imparted and, as is always the way with these dumb things, his own suffering serves but to wake memories in his friends' minds of *their* influenzas, *their* aches and pains which went unwept last February, and now cry aloud, desperately, clamorously, for the divine relief of sympathy.

But sympathy we cannot have. Wisest Fate says no. If her children, weighted as they already are with sorrow, were to take on them that burden too, adding in imagination other pains to their own, buildings would cease to rise; roads would peter out into grassy tracks; there would be an end of music and of painting; one great sigh alone would rise to Heaven, and the only attitudes for men and women would be those of horror and despair. As it is, there is always some little distraction—an organ-grinder at the corner of the hospital, a shop with book or trinket to decoy one past the prison or the workhouse, some absurdity of cat or dog to prevent one from turning the old beggar's hieroglyphic of misery into volumes of sordid suffering; and thus the vast effort of sympathy which those barracks of pain and discipline, those dried symbols of sorrow, ask us to exert on their behalf, is uneasily shuffled off for another time. Sympathy nowadays is dispensed chiefly by the laggards and failures, women for the most part (in whom the obsolete exists so strangely side by side with anarchy and newness), who, having dropped out of the race, have time to spend upon fantastic and unprofitable excursions; C. L., for example, who, sitting by the stale sickroom fire, builds up, with touches at once sober and imaginative, the nursery fender, the loaf, the lamp, barrel organs in the street, and all the simple old wives' tales of pinafores and escapades; A. R., the rash, the magnanimous, who, if you fancied a giant tortoise to solace you or a theorbo to cheer you, would ransack the markets of London and procure them somehow, wrapped in paper, before the end of the day; the frivolous K. T., who, dressed in silks and feathers, powdered and painted (which takes time too) as if for a banquet of Kings and Queens, spends her whole brightness in the gloom of the sick-room, and makes the medicine bottles ring and the flames shoot up with her gossip and her mimicry. But such follies have had their day; civilization points to a different goal; and then what place will there be for the tortoise and the theorbo?

There is, let us confess it (and illness is the great confessional), a childish outspokenness in illness; things are said, truths blurted out, which the cautious respectability of health conceals. About sympathy for example—we can do without it. That illusion of a world so shaped that it echoes every groan, of human beings so tied together by common needs and fears that a twitch at one wrist jerks another, where however strange your experience other people have had it too, where however far you travel in your own mind someone has been there before you is all an illusion. We do not know our own souls, let alone the souls of others. Human beings do not go hand in hand the whole stretch of the way. There is a virgin forest in each; a snowfield where even the print of birds' feet is unknown. Here we go alone, and like it better so. Always to have sympathy, always to be accompanied, always to be understood would be intolerable. But in health the genial pretence must be kept up and the effort renewed to communicate, to civilize, to share, to cultivate the desert, educate the native, to work together by day and by night to sport. In illness this make-believe ceases. Directly the bed is called for, or, sunk deep among pillows in one chair, we raise our feet even an inch above the ground on another, we cease to be soldiers in the army of the upright; we become deserters. They march to battle. We float with the sticks on the stream; helter-skelter with the dead leaves on the lawn, irresponsible and disinterested and able, perhaps for the first time for years, to look round, to look up—to look, for example, at the sky.

The first impression of that extraordinary spectacle is strangely overcoming. Ordinarily to look at the sky for any length of time is impossible. Pedestrians would be impeded and disconcerted by a public sky-gazer. What snatches we get of it are mutilated by chimneys and churches, serve as a background for man, signify wet weather or fine, daub windows gold, and, filling in the branches, complete the pathos of dishevelled autumnal plane trees in autumnal squares. Now, lying recumbent, staring straight up, the sky is discovered to be something so different from this that really it is a little shocking. This then has been going on all the time without our knowing it!—this incessant making up of shapes and casting them down, this buffeting of clouds together, and drawing vast trains of ships and wagons from North to South, this incessant ringing up and down of curtains of light and shade, this interminable experiment with gold shafts and blue shadows, with veiling the sun and unveiling it, with making rock ramparts and wafting them away—this endless activity, with the waste of Heaven knows how many million horse-power of energy, has been left to work its will year in, year out. The fact seems to call for comment and indeed for censure. Ought not someone to write to *The Times*? Use should be made of it. One should not let this gigantic cinema play perpetually to an empty house. But watch a little longer and another emotion drowns the stirrings of civic ardour. Divinely beautiful, it is also divinely heartless. Immeasurable resources are used for some purpose which has nothing to do with pleasure or human profit. If we were all laid prone, stiff, still the sky would be experimenting with its blues and its golds. Perhaps then, if we look down at something very small and close and familiar, we shall find sympathy. Let us examine the rose. We have seen it so often flowering in bowls, connected it so often with beauty in its prime, that we have forgotten how it stands, still and steady, throughout an entire afternoon in the earth. It preserves a demeanour of perfect dignity and self-possession. The suffusion of its petals is of inimitable rightness. Now perhaps one deliberately falls; now all the flowers, the voluptuous purple, the creamy, in whose waxen flesh the spoon has left a swirl of cherry juice; gladioli; dahlias; lilies, sacerdotal, ecclesiastical; flowers with prim cardboard collars tinged apricot and amber, all gently incline their heads to the breeze—all, with the exception of the heavy sunflower, who proudly acknowledges the sun at midday and perhaps at midnight rebuffs the moon. There they stand; and it is of these, the stillest, the most self-sufficient of all things that human beings have made companions; these that symbolize their passions, decorate their festivals, and lie (as if *they* knew sorrow) upon the pillows of the dead. Wonderful to relate, poets have found religion in Nature; people live in the country to learn virtue from plants. It is in their indifference that they are comforting. That snowfield of the mind, where man has not trodden, is visited by the cloud, kissed by the falling petal, as, in another sphere, it is the great artists, the Miltons and the Popes, who console not by their thought of us but by their forgetfulness.

Meanwhile, with the heroism of the ant or the bee, however indifferent the sky or disdainful the flowers, the army of the upright marches to battle. Mrs. Jones catches her train. Mr. Smith mends his motor. The cows are driven home to be milked. Men thatch the roof. The dogs bark. The rooks, rising in a net, fall in a net upon the elm trees. The wave of life flings itself out indefatigably. It is only the recumbent who know what, after all, Nature is at no pains to conceal—that she in the end will conquer; heat will leave the world; stiff with frost we shall cease to drag ourselves about the fields; ice will lie thick upon factory and engine; the sun will go out. Even so, when the whole earth is sheeted and slippery, some undulation, some irregularity of surface will mark the boundary of an ancient garden, and there, thrusting its head up undaunted in the starlight the rose will flower, the crocus will burn. But with the hook of life in us still we must wriggle. We cannot stiffen peaceably into glassy mounds. Even the recumbent spring up at the mere imagination of frost about the toes and stretch out to avail themselves of the universal hope—Heaven, Immortality. Surely, since men have been wishing all these ages, they will have wished something into existence; there will be some green isle for the mind to rest on even if the foot cannot plant itself there. The cooperative imagination of mankind must have drawn some firm outline. But no. One opens the *Morning Post* and reads the Bishop of Lichfield on Heaven. One watches the church-goers file into those gallant temples where, on the bleakest day, in the wettest fields, lamps will be burning, bells will be ringing, and however the autumn leaves may shuffle and the winds sigh outside, hopes and desires will be changed to beliefs and certainties within. Do they look serene? Are their eyes filled with the light of their supreme conviction? Would one of them dare leap straight into Heaven off Beachy Head? None but a simpleton would ask such questions; the little company of believers lags and drags and strays. The mother is worn; the father tired. As for imagining Heaven, they have no time. Heaven-making must be left to the imagination of the poets. Without their help we can but trifle—imagine Pepys in Heaven, adumbrate little interviews with celebrated people on tufts of thyme, soon fall into gossip about such of our friends as have stayed in Hell, or, worse still, revert again to earth and choose, since there is no harm in choosing, to live over and over, now as man, now as woman, as sea-captain, or court lady, as Emperor or farmer's wife, in splendid cities and on remote moors, at the time of Pericles or Arthur, Charlemagne or George the Fourth—to live and live till we have lived out those embryo lives which attend about us in early youth until 'I' suppressed them. But 'I' shall not, if wishing can alter it, usurp Heaven too, and condemn us, who have played our parts here as William or Alice, to remain William or Alice for ever. Left to ourselves we speculate thus carnally. We need the poets to imagine for us. The duty of Heaven-making should be attached to the office of the Poet Laureate.

Indeed it is to the poets that we turn. Illness makes us disinclined for the long campaigns that prose exacts. We cannot command all our faculties and keep our reason and our judgment and our memory at attention while chapter swings on top of chapter, and, as one settles into place, we must be on the watch for the coming of the next, until the whole structure arches, towers, and battlements stands firm on its foundations. *The Decline and Fall of the Roman Empire* is not the book for influenza, nor *The Golden Bowl* nor *Madame Bovary*. On the other hand, with responsibility shelved and reason in the abeyance—for who is going to exact criticism from an invalid or sound sense from the bedridden?—other tastes assert themselves; sudden, fitful, intense. We rifle the poets of their flowers. We break off a line or two and let them open in the depths of the mind:

> and oft at eve
> Visits the herds along the twilight meadows

> wandering in thick flocks along the mountains
> Shepherded by the slow unwilling wind.

Or there is a whole three-volume novel to be mused over in a verse of Hardy's or a sentence of La Bruyère. We dip in Lamb's letters—some prose-writers are to be read as poets—and find 'I am a sanguinary murderer of time, and would kill him inchmeal just now. But the snake is vital', and who shall explain the delight? or open Rimbaud and read

> O saisons o châteaux
> Quelle âme est sans défauts?

and who shall rationalize the charm? In illness words seem to possess a mystic quality. We grasp what is beyond their surface meaning, gather instinctively this, that, and the other—a sound, a colour, here a stress, there a pause—which the poet, knowing words to be meagre in comparison with ideas, has strewn about his page to evoke, when collected, a state of mind which neither words can express nor the reason explain. Incomprehensibility has an enormous power over us in illness, more legitimately perhaps than the upright will allow. In health meaning has encroached upon sound. Our intelligence domineers over our senses. But in illness, with the police off duty, we creep beneath some obscure poem by Mallarmé or Donne, some phrase in Latin or Greek, and the words give out their scent and distil their flavour, and then, if at last we grasp the meaning, it is all the richer for having come to us sensually first, by way of the palate and the nostrils, like some queer odour. Foreigners, to whom the tongue is strange, have us at a disadvantage. The Chinese must know the sound of *Antony and Cleopatra* better than we do.

Rashness is one of the properties of illness—outlaws that we are—and it is rashness that we need in reading Shakespeare. It is not that we should doze in reading him, but that, fully conscious and aware, his fame intimidates and bores, and all the views of all the critics dull in us that thunder-clap of conviction which, if an illusion, is still so helpful an illusion, so prodigious a pleasure, so keen a stimulus in reading the great. Shakespeare is getting flyblown; a paternal government might well forbid writing about him, as they put his monument at Stratford beyond the reach of scribbling fingers. With all this buzz of criticism about, one may hazard one's conjectures privately, make one's notes in the margin; but, knowing that someone has said it before, or said it better, the zest is gone. Illness, in its kingly sublimity, sweeps all that aside and leaves nothing but Shakespeare and oneself. What with his overweening power and our overweening arrogance, the barriers go down, the knots run smooth, the brain rings and resounds with *Lear* or *Macbeth,* and even Coleridge himself squeaks like a distant mouse.

But enough of Shakespeare—let us turn to Augustus Hare. There are people who say that even illness does not warrant these transitions; that the author of *The Story of Two Noble Lives* is not the peer of Boswell; and if we assert that short of the best in literature we like the worst—it is mediocrity that is hateful—will have none of that either. So be it. The law is on the side of the normal. But for those who suffer a slight rise of temperature the names of Hare and Waterford and Canning ray out as beams of benignant lustre. Not, it is true, for the first hundred pages or so. There, as so often in these fat volumes, we flounder and threaten to sink in a plethora of aunts and uncles. We have to remind ourselves that there is such a thing as atmosphere; that the masters themselves often keep us waiting intolerably while they prepare our minds for whatever it may be—the surprise, or the lack of surprise. So Hare, too, takes his time; the charm steals upon us imperceptibly; by degrees we become almost one of the family, yet not quite, for our sense of the oddity of it all remains, and share the family dismay when Lord Stuart leaves the room—there was a ball going forward—and is next heard of in Iceland. Parties, he said, bored him—such were English aristocrats before marriage with intellect had adulterated the fine singularity of their minds. Parties bore them; they are off to Iceland. Then Beckford's mania for castle-building attacked him; he must lift a French *château* across the Channel, and erect pinnacles and towers to use as servants' bedrooms at vast expense, upon the borders of a crumbling cliff, too, so that the housemaids saw their brooms swimming down the Solent, and Lady Stuart was much distressed, but made the best of it and began, like the high-born lady that she was, planting evergreens in the face of ruin. Meanwhile the daughters, Charlotte and Louisa, grew up in their incomparable loveliness, with pencils in their hands, for ever sketching, dancing, flirting, in a cloud of gauze. They are not very distinct it is true. For life then was not the life of Charlotte and Louisa. It was the life of families, of groups. It was a web, a net, spreading wide and enmeshing every sort of cousin, dependant, and old retainer. Aunts—Aunt Caledon, Aunt Mexborough— grandmothers—Granny Stuart, Granny Hardwicke—cluster in chorus, and rejoice and sorrow and eat Christmas dinner together, and grow very old and remain very upright, and sit in hooded chairs cutting flowers it seems out of coloured paper. Charlotte married Canning and went to India; Louisa married Lord Waterford and went to Ireland. Then letters begin to cross vast spaces in slow sailing ships and communication becomes still more protracted and verbose, and there seems no end to the space and the leisure of those early Victorian days, and faiths are lost and the life of Hedley Vicars revives them; aunts catch cold but recover; cousins marry; there are the Irish famine and the Indian Mutiny, and both sisters remain to their great, but silent, grief without children to come after them. Louisa, dumped down in Ireland with Lord Waterford at the hunt all day, was often very lonely; but she stuck to her post, visited the poor, spoke words of comfort ('I am sorry indeed to hear of Anthony Thompson's loss of mind, or rather of memory; if, however, he can understand sufficiently to trust solely in our Saviour, he has enough') and sketched and sketched. Thousands of notebooks were filled with pen-and-ink drawings of an evening, and then the carpenter stretched sheets for her and she designed frescoes for schoolrooms, had live sheep into her bedroom, draped gamekeepers in blankets, painted Holy Families in abundance, until the great Watts exclaimed that here was Titian's peer and Raphael's master! At that Lady Waterford laughed (she had a generous, benignant sense of humour); and said that she was nothing but a sketcher; had scarcely had a lesson in her life—witness her angel's wings scandalously unfinished. Moreover, there was her father's house forever falling into the sea; she must shore it up; must entertain her friends; must fill her days with all sorts of charities, till her Lord came home from hunting, and then, at midnight often, she would sketch him with his knightly face half hidden in a bowl of soup, sitting with her sketch-book under a lamp beside him. Off he would ride again, stately as a crusader, to hunt the fox, and she would wave to him and think each time, what if this should be the last? And so it was, that winter's morning; his horse stumbled; he was killed. She knew it before they told her, and never could Sir John Leslie forget, when he ran downstairs on the day of the burial, the beauty of the great lady standing to see the hearse depart, nor, when he came back, how the curtain, heavy, mid-Victorian, plush perhaps, was all crushed together where she had grasped it in her agony.

Jeffrey Meyers

SOURCE: "Introduction: Disease and Art," in *Disease and the Novel, 1880-1960*, The Macmillan Press Ltd., 1985, pp. 1-18.

[*In the following excerpt, Meyers examines works by nineteenth- and twentieth-century authors that reveal differing attitudes and ideas relating to disease.*]

I

Disease and the Novel explores an important theme in modern fiction. *The Death of Ivan Ilych,* "The Snows of Kilimanjaro," *The Immoralist, The Magic Mountain, Doctor Faustus, The Black Swan, The Rack* and *Cancer Ward* concern the mental and physical changes that take place when a character is attacked by disease—cancer, gangrene, tuberculosis, syphilis—and threatened by death. In all these novels illness isolates, exposes, intensifies and transforms character; structures the work as we follow the progress of the diseased heroes to recovery, remission, invalidism or death. These works portray what Freud calls the "pathology of cultural communities," the sickness of society. For the effect of disease on a victim is both the realistic subject of the book and the symbol of moral, social or political pathology; the illness of the hero, who is both an individual and a representative of his epoch, is analogous to the sickness of the State.

Disease has always been a great mystery: a visitation, a curse, a judgment. The creation of literature is one way of transcending mortality and celebrating human existence, despite the threat of death. We have inherited from the Greeks a view of the artist that explains the phenomenon of creativity and its relation to disease, and that has persisted in our culture, with many variations, until the present time. This Greek concept is revived by Neoplatonic thought in the Renaissance, reappears in the Romantic period, is exalted by Dostoyevsky and Nietzsche, and exerts a powerful influence on twentieth-century literature. *Disease and the Novel* considers how these ideas about the relation of disease and the artist have been challenged and changed by modern novelists.

The Greeks provided two important and quite distinct ideas about creativity, which was closely related to disease and derangement. First, the concept that poets have fallen foul of the gods and are cursed with a physical defect. The idea that the artist is diseased, that his illness gives him psychic knowledge, spiritual power and creative genius, originates with the figures of Tiresias the blind prophet and Homer the blind poet. Edmund Wilson used such a figure to represent a dominant theme in modern literature. In the symbolic myth of the wound and the bow, as interpreted by Wilson, the essential sickness of the artist is represented by the Greek archer Philoctetes, who is degraded by a malodorous disease that renders him abhorrent to society, but "is also the master of a superhuman art which everybody has to respect and which the normal man finds he needs."

The Greek heritage suggests that art, which is synonymous with knowledge, truth and insight, is available only to those who suffer for it like the mythic figures of Oedipus, Orpheus and Prometheus. (In modern times Camus has given a similar interpretation to Sisyphus, whose moment of insight comes when he returns to his rock and renews his suffering.) The belief that suffering is a necessary, even indispensable component of creativity is basic to our culture, and to a large degree our literary history traces the way artists have dealt with this paradox. The power of this idea rests in the meaning it gives to suffering and death; it has continued for centuries despite the intervening Judeo-Christian period, which provides another, redemptive purpose for physical pain and decay.

The second, quite separate Greek idea of the deranged artist found expression in the primitive and archaic cult of Dionysos, whose worshippers sang and danced themselves into a frenzy. This concept is expressed in Plato's *Ion,* which equates poetic power with a state of divinely inspired insanity: "For the authors of those great poems which we admire, do not attain to excellence through the rules of any art, but they utter their beautiful melodies of verse in a state of inspiration, and, as it were, *possessed* by a spirit not their own. Thus the composers of lyrical poetry create those admired songs of theirs in a state of divine insanity, like the Corybantes, who lose all control over their reason in the enthusiasm of the sacred dance. . . . For a poet is indeed a thing ethereally light, winged, and sacred, nor can he compose anything worth calling poetry until he becomes inspired, and, as it were, mad, or whilst any reason remains in him." Nietzsche, whose philosophical thought had the greatest influence on modern literature, combines both these ideas. He uses the concept of the diseased artist to define himself as a creator and the concept of the deranged artist to define the nature of creativity.

The idea that suffering and insanity are necessary to learn the truth and the consequent image of the mad poet were introduced into English literature during the Renaissance and reached their tragic apotheosis in Shakespeare. In *Lear* the heroic truth-seeker pays for his perceptions with madness, degradation and death. Artists have been treated like madmen since the Renaissance, when Neoplatonic doctrine extended the prerogative of the saint and the prophet to the poet and artist, and accounted for the superhuman achievement of the secular genius by a godlike inspiration that produced what Plato had called divine madness. This dangerous gift places the creative mind on a lonely height and threatens to topple him into the abyss of insanity. The artist sees the normal ways of established society as corrupt, while mental illness appears to him as spiritual health.

The idea that poets themselves were likely to be mad was also current in the age of Swift and Johnson. While insisting on the necessity for a sane and rational grasp of life, Dryden acknowledged the poet's proximity to insanity:

> Great wits are sure to madness near allied,
> And thin partitions do their bounds divide.

In the *Life of Savage,* Johnson develops another important aspect of this idea. He draws on his own experience in depicting a life of neglect, exploitation and poverty; and his portrait also emphasizes the idea that the artist is cast out by a society which needs his insight and beauty.

II

During the early part of the nineteenth century, writers associated creativity with one specific disease, tuberculosis. At this time a number of factors combined to revive and reinforce the traditional connection between disease and art: the growth of cities; the advance in medical knowledge; the portrayal of disease in literature and (later on) in immensely popular operas like *La Traviata* (1853) and *La Bohème* (1896); the sudden interest in the aesthetic aspects of consumption; the number of mad poets (Collins, Smart, Cowper, Hölderlin, Kleist); the early death of important literary figures (Chatterton, Keats, Shelley, Byron); the extraordinary appearance of a whole series of tubercular artists. As Rudolf and Margot Wittkower observe in their study of the melancholic artist, the relation of genius and madness was extended to include physical illness: "During the nineteenth century clinical diagnosis confirmed the previous assumption of an alliance between genius and madness. Early in the century Lamartine already talked of '*cette maladie qu'on appelle génie*'; by the end of the century the idea of disease was so firmly established that a popular magazine declared 'evidence is not lacking to warrant the assumption that genius is a special morbid condition.' "

At the turn of the century, when the maximum morbidity for tuberculosis in England occurred among the ill-housed and ill-fed inhabitants of industrial towns, medical evidence began to replace superstitious and religious explanations of disease and epidemics. The major scientific contributions of Jenner, Dalton and Davy coincided with Auenbrugger's discovery of chest percussion (1761) and Laënnec's invention of the stethoscope (1819), which led to important advances in the understanding and diagnosis of tuberculosis.

The horrors of tuberculosis were described as early as Deuteronomy 28:22: "The Lord shall smite thee with a consumption, and with a fever, and with an inflammation, and with an extreme burning . . . and they shall pursue thee until thou perish." But in nineteenth-century literature "the disease was rarely presented as something loathsome. . . . Rather, it was used as a device to enlist the sympathies of the reader. . . . It was believed to affect chiefly sensitive natures, and conferred upon them a refined physical charm before making them succumb to a painless, poetical death." Tom Moore's account of Byron's posturing shows how appealing the consumptive had become by 1810, when physical disease followed fashion: "Standing before a looking-glass one day, Byron said to Sligo: 'I look pale; I should like to die of a consumption.' 'Why?' Sligo asked. 'Because the ladies would all say, "Look at that poor Byron, how interesting he looks in dying." ' "

Writers of the Romantic period continued to interpret the phenomenon of tuberculosis, an infectious and incurable disease of epidemic proportions, in terms of the ancient Greek paradox. The disease was fearful and marked the end of one's life, but it bestowed privileged perceptions upon the poet-victim and was seen as a spur to creativity. Goethe defined the difference between the literature of the eighteenth and nineteenth centuries in terms of disease: "I call the classic *healthy,* the romantic *sickly.* In this sense, the *Nibelungenlied* is as classic as the *Iliad,* for both are vigorous and healthy. Most modern productions are romantic not because they are new; but because they are weak, morbid, and sickly." Schlegel unequivocally declared: "Health alone is loveable." But even Goethe, who described Kleist's stories as "tainted with an incurable disease," expressed the ambivalent attraction-repulsion toward disease that was characteristic of his age. He complained that "The poets all write as though they were sick and the whole world a hospital," but also acknowledged that wisdom could be won only through pain: "Misery too has its virtues. I have learned much in illness that I could have learned nowhere else in my life."

The definition of the consumptive personality in Havelock Ellis' *Study of British Genius* (1904) perfectly matched the literary qualities of the Romantic hero: intense, instinctive, individualistic; intuitive, imaginative, idealistic; tormented, escapist, rebellious. This definition once again brought disease and art into pathological conjunction: "The psychology of the consumptive [is] marked by mental exaltation, hyper-excitability, the tendency to form vast plans and to exert feverish activity in carrying them out, with . . . egoism, indifference, neurasthenia. . . . [Consumptives] with their febrile activities, their restless versatility, their quick sensitiveness to impressions, often appear the very type of genius."

The poet-hero whose life and writings most perfectly embody the Romantic idea of the diseased and doomed artist is John Keats, who contracted consumption while nursing his brother. In sonnets like "After dark vapours" and "When I have fears that I may cease to be" Keats expressed his fear that death would prevent the full realization of his genius but also conveyed his intense desire for dissolution. These morbid feelings reach an apotheosis in "Ode to a Nightingale," which describes the death of a tubercular youth and the longing to escape the limitations of the flesh through the morbid transcendence of the songbird. Keats associates dreams, fantasy and poetry with death, which is transformed into a positive experience and leads to welcome oblivion:

Fade far away, dissolve, and quite forget
What thou among the leaves hast never known,
The weariness, the fever, and the fret
Here, where men sit and hear each other groan;
Where palsy shakes a few, sad, last gray hairs,
Where youth grows pales, and spectre-thin, and dies;
Where but to think is to be full of sorrow
And leaden-eyed despairs,
Where Beauty cannot keep her lustrous eyes,
Or new Love pine at them beyond tomorrow. . . .
Darkling I listen; and for many a time
I have been half in love with easeful Death,
Called him soft names in many a musèd rhyme,
To take into the air my quiet breath;
Now more than ever seems it rich to die,
To cease upon the midnight with no pain.

Keats lived the last year of his life under the constant threat of death. He had been trained in medicine and recognized his fate on the very day of his hemorrhage in February 1820: "I know the colour of that blood," he exclaimed, "—it is arterial blood—I cannot be deceived in that colour; that drop is my death warrant. I must die." After that date he led an intensified "posthumous existence" and was alienated from ordinary life. Keats explained to Fanny Brawne that "A person in health as you are can have no conception of the horrors that nerves and a temper like mine go through." But, like Goethe, he also believed that suffering would lead to spiritual insight: "Do you not see how necessary a World of Pains and troubles is to school an Intelligence and make it a Soul?"

The Romantic attitude toward the suffering Keatsian artist was brilliantly expressed in a poetic apologue by Kierkegaard, who synthesized the idea that pain was intrinsic to art. He compared the torments of the artist to the prisoners roasted by Phalaris within the brazen bull, in whose nostrils reeds were placed so that their agonizing shrieks were transmuted into music: "What is a poet? An unhappy man who in his heart harbors a deep anguish, but whose lips are so fashioned that the moans and cries which pass over them are transformed into ravishing music. His fate is like that of the unfortunate victims whom the tyrant Phalaris imprisoned in a brazen bull, and slowly tortured over a steady fire; their cries could not reach the tyrant's ears so as to strike terror into his heart; when they reached his ears they sounded like sweet music." Kierkegaard also distinguished between the positive pain of the isolated Philoctetes, which he effectively transmuted into military action (the bow), and the negative paralyzing pain of the unheroic man, which can become involuted and self-consuming (the wound). Philoctetes "complains that no one understands his pain. . . . Here is manifested the difference between his pain and the reflective pain which always wants to be alone with its pain, which seeks a new pain in this solitude of pain."

The Romantic theory of disease is constructed out of literary and social history, for as Gottfried Benn remarks: "The early death of so many men of genius [is] something that the bourgeois-romantic ideology likes to connect with the notion of the consuming and devouring character of art." But in *The White Plague,* René and Jean Dubos note that the toxins and low fever produced by the infecting organism actually stimulate intellectual capacity and quicken artistic powers: "Throughout medical history there runs this suggestion that the intellectually gifted are the most likely to contract the disease, and furthermore that the same fire which wastes the body in consumption also makes the mind shine with a brighter light." They explain that art can compensate for disease, and justify the theory on physiological and psychological grounds: "There may be, nevertheless, some basis for the statement that consumption fosters and nourishes genius. Within certain limits fever from any source can heighten emotion, sharpen perception and render intellectual processes more lucid and rapid. . . . Since consumptives often experience mild fever without gross toxemia and without physical prostration, they may crave a full life and exhibit eagerness to seize the fleeting moments for creative efforts. Furthermore, the decreased physical vigor of the tuberculous patient limits his ability to fulfill natural urges and thereby increases his tendency to sublimate them into those forms of mental activity that are most natural to him." Though there is no scientific proof that tuberculosis inspires genius, this idea has been used as a literary theme for one hundred and fifty years.

III

The Romantic attitude toward disease was developed and deepened in the second half of the nineteenth century by two of the greatest writers of the age—neither of whom admitted the possibility of an exotic Keatsian escape: the epileptic Dostoyevsky and the syphilitic Nietzsche. Four characters in Dostoyevsky's novels—Nellie in *The Insulted and Injured,* Myshkin in *The Idiot,* Kirilov in *The Possessed* and Smerdyakov in *The Brothers Karamazov*—are epileptic. The epilepsy of Prince Myshkin, the most striking example, is a metaphor for spiritual insight, for his moments of ecstatic devotion and perfect harmony attempt to transcend the limitations of the disease that is responsible for the disintegration of his personality: "There was a moment or two in his epileptic condition almost before the fit itself (if it occurred during his waking hours) when suddenly amid the sadness, spiritual darkness and depression, his brain seemed to catch fire at brief moments, and with an extraordinary momentum his vital forces were strained to the utmost all at once. His sensation of being alive and his awareness increased tenfold at those moments which flashed by like lightning. His mind and heart were flooded by a dazzling light. . . . But those moments, those flashes of intuition, were merely the presentiment of the last second (never more than a second) which preceded the actual fit. This second was, of course, unendurable. . . . [But] all those gleams and flashes of the highest awareness and, hence, also of 'the highest mode of existence,' were nothing but a disease. As Dostoyevsky insists in *Notes From Underground,* "too great lucidity is a disease, a true, full-fledged disease," because this heightened consciousness forces one to see terrible truths about the nature of human existence. Proust agrees that "An invalid, a Baudelaire, better still a Dostoyevsky, in thirty years, between their crises of epilepsy or whatever, can create a work of which a long line of healthy writers could not have produced a single word."

In a similar fashion, Rimbaud follows the Greek tradition and calls for an artificially-induced, self-destructive, deliberate derangement of all the senses that would enable the tormented, sacrificial, even insane artist to become "the great invalid, the great criminal, the great accursed" and to plunge into unknown, "unheard of, unnameable" spiritual visions. Nietzsche—who confessed that Dostoyevsky was "the only psychologist, incidentally, from whom I had something to learn"—also associates exuberance of the spirit with extreme pain and mental anguish. Like Dostoyevsky and Rimbaud, Nietzsche believes that artistic greatness can be earned only by physical suffering: "To make oneself sick, mad, to provoke the symptoms of derangement and ruin that was [equated with] becoming stronger, more superhuman, more terrible, wiser."

Nietzsche defines man as "*the* sick animal" and believes that disease stimulates the strongest feelings, deepest thoughts and highest energies: "The sick and weak have had fascination on their side: they are more interesting than the healthy. . . . The great 'adventurers and criminals' and all men, especially the most healthy, are sick at certain periods of their lives: the great emotions, the passions of power, love, revenge, are accompanied by profound disturbances." Nietzsche feels that disease can bring new awareness to the artist who is able to survive its grave assaults, for the damage can be valuable when physical pain is transformed into intellectual achievement: "Sickness itself can be a stimulant to life: only one has to be healthy enough for this stimulant." "We seek life raised to a higher power, life lived in danger. . . . What does not destroy us makes us stronger." Nietzsche, who believed the artist's derangement gave him the power to see and tell the truth, exclaims: "One pays dearly for immortality: one has to die several times while still alive." He would have agreed with Keats' insight: "Until we are sick, we understand not." Nikos Kazantzakis, a disciple of Nietzsche, declares that illness both inspired and destroyed the philosopher:

> Disease served as your great enemy and also your greatest friend, the only one that stayed loyal to the death. It never permitted you to relax or remain where you were, never allowed you to declare: I am fine here, I shall go no further. You were a flame; you flared up, you were consumed.

The final phase of the Romantic idea that the artist is necessarily sick and socially outcast, and that this condition alone produces the greatest art, reaches its apotheosis in Thomas Mann, the most important Nietzschean of the twentieth century. Mann believes: "Romanticism bears in its heart the germ of morbidity, as the rose bears the worm; its innermost character is seduction, seduction to death." He gives the ideology of disease its most profound and ironic portrayal in *The Magic Mountain* and *Doctor Faustus,* and employs this theme to diagnose the sickness of German culture.

In his great essay on "Goethe and Tolstoy" and his more cautious "Dostoyevsky in Moderation," Mann places himself firmly in the Romantic tradition by an exaltation of the aesthetic aspects of "genius-bestowing disease." In the first essay he paradoxically claims that disease gives dignity to man because it brings out his spiritual qualities; inspires gravity, reverence and respect: "Disease has two faces and a double relation to man and his human dignity. On the one hand it is hostile: by overstressing the physical, by throwing man back upon his body, it has a dehumanizing effect. On the other hand, it is possible to think and feel about illness as a highly dignified human phenomenon. . . . In disease, resides the dignity of man; and the genius of disease is more human than the genius of health."

In the second essay Mann quotes Nietzsche's dictum: "Exceptional conditions make the artist . . . conditions that are profoundly related and interlaced with morbid phenomena; it seems impossible to be an artist and not to be sick." He then connects Dostoyevsky's and Nietzsche's psychological insight and artistic genius with their diseases. He concludes with the Rimbaudian paradox that the health of humanity can be achieved only by the sacrifice of its artists: "Certain attainments of the soul and intellect are impossible without disease, without insanity, without spiritual crime, and the great invalids are crucified victims, sacrificed to humanity and its advancement, to the broadening of its feeling and knowledge in short, to its more sublime health."

Disease in Mann's fiction is always based on a germ of reality: *Death in Venice* on a cholera epidemic that took place in Italy in August 1910; *The Magic Mountain* on Mann's three-week visit to his wife in a Davos sanatorium in May-June 1912; *Doctor Faustus* on the medical history of Nietzsche; *The Black Swan* on the true story of a middle-aged woman deluded by the return of her monthly periods. In Mann's works, as Erich Kahler observes, the artist is portrayed as an outcast who renounces life in order to create art: "culture and intellect are represented as decadence, love is associated with decline; the artist is seen as a pariah from the start, iridescent with suspect hues, shading into the daemon, the invalid, the social outcast, the adventurer, the criminal; already he is stranded in the ironic situation of expressing a life he himself is unable to live."

The Romantic tradition found its finest expression in Mann, who accepted and dramatized in his fiction Nietzsche's ideas about disease and art, but it also persisted in English literature throughout the twentieth century. Katherine Mansfield, dying of tuberculosis, complains that her husband Middleton Murry (who was infatuated with Keats) was fascinated by the aesthetic connotations of her disease. He believed tuberculosis endowed its victim with spirituality and creative genius, and was more than half in love with Katherine's easeful death: "This illness getting worse and worse. . . . He stood it marvellously. It helped very much because it was a romantic disease (his love of a ' romantic appearance' is *immensely* real)." Yet Katherine Mansfield also makes a direct, Keatsian connection between suffering and insight: "I, being what I am, had to suffer *this* in order to do the work I am here to perform. . . . The more I suffer, the more of fiery energy I feel to bear it. . . . I do not see how we are to come by knowledge and love except through pain." Auden says in "Letter to a Wound": "Knowing you has made me understand." And even the reserved and reticent T. S. Eliot, who wrote *The Waste Land* while recovering from a nervous breakdown, confesses: "I know that some forms of ill-health, debility or anaemia, may (if other circumstances are favourable) produce an efflux of poetry."

IV

In her essay "On Being Ill" (1930), Virginia Woolf—fascinated by morbid psychic states and the extraordinary perspective of the sick notes the importance of disease as a means of moral exploration. She develops Jane Austen's belief that "A sick chamber may often furnish the worth of volumes" and wonders why literature has not seriously concerned itself with this crucial area of human experience: "Considering how common illness is, how tremendous the spiritual change that it brings, how astonishing, when the lights of health go down, the undiscovered countries that are then disclosed . . . it becomes strange indeed that illness has not taken its place with love and battle and jealousy among the prime themes of literature."

Disease and death are traditionally used to reveal the psychological development of the characters and to structure the events of the novel. But in nineteenth-century English fiction the facts of the characters' pain, treatment and death are rarely the focus of interest. Disease is always symbolic (Esther Summerson's smallpox in *Bleak House,* Mr. Rochester's blindness in *Jane Eyre*); characters in deathbed scenes are always etherealized. Even in Flaubert the details of disease are used more for moral than for realistic significance. The operation of Hippolyte's clubfoot reveals the ignorant ambition of Charles Bovary; the death by prussic acid is a cruel punishment for the desperate adulteries of Emma.

But in the twentieth century European writers (including a number of doctors) have increasingly turned to the kind of clinical literature that English authors tended to avoid. Modern European literature often concerns the abnormal and the pathological. It is characterized by a macabre sensibility, an attraction to decay and nothingness, an obsession with physical corruption and death; defined by a mood of dissolution and disintegration, of paralyzing anxiety and metaphysical despair. Disease both expresses and emphasizes the dominant themes of the modern age: hyper-sensitivity, self-doubt, loneliness, alienation, loss of identity. Bernanos emphasizes the traditional connection between sin and disease by observing: "All the wounds of the soul give out pus." But after the loss of faith in the twentieth century, disease replaced hell and became one of the most horrible punishments imaginable.

The modern anti-hero who experiences a physiological dialectic of suffering, a painful life and early death is typified and condemned by disease. He is the archetype of the artist, the martyr and the criminal. He is inwardly infected; tormented in body and mind; tested by the endurance of pain; estranged from himself, from his fellow-sufferers and from healthy men. Disease is a punishment that inspires guilt and shame, fear and self-hatred; as in Kafka's Penal Colony, the "crime" is imprinted on the body of the victim.

Disease puts its mark on a high percentage of writers and sets them apart from society. Illness *seems* to stimulate creative genius, for the constant anxiety, terror and sense of doom intensifies isolation and introspection; heightens the intellectual defiance of the social outcast who questions and challenges conventional ideas about morality; and encourages him to control the potentially dangerous element in his character through the order and form of art. As Nietzsche exclaims: "one must still have chaos in oneself to be able to give birth to a dancing star."

Disease is a grim but fascinating subject that provides insights about how to deal with the ultimate threat of death. Sickness is a shocking experience that exposes the victim's physical and psychological nakedness; plunges him into the anguished aesthetics of despair; jolts him to a recognition of his loneliness and vulnerability; forces him to contemplate the destruction of his body in the silence and solitude of the sickroom. The grand mortuary moment provokes self-probing and internal inquiry, inspires an inward voyage of self-discovery. It often leads to an attempt analogous to aesthetic or religious experience to transcend the limitations of the body and draw on the resource of illness for intellectual illumination and spiritual enlightenment. As Alice James recorded when her fatal cancer was diagnosed: "It is the most supremely interesting moment in life, the only one in fact, when living seems life, and I count it as the greatest good fortune to have these few months so full of interest and instruction in the knowledge of my approaching death."

The horrors of dissolution, not through the natural process of aging but by the hasty and tremendous experience of disease, also resemble the extreme situations that characterize the modern age. The patient lives close to catastrophe; his radical treatment is a form of torture, the hospital like a prison or concentration camp in which the condemned man endures the cruelty of power and the threat of execution. Like the prisoner, his will to live is of crucial importance; if he abandons himself to Arab fatalism, like the *Musselmänner* in the camps, he has no hope of survival.

The freedom to choose life or death, to determine one's destiny, places the sick hero in an existential situation. He discovers that "it is possible to live *without appeal*" and accepts "the certainty of a crushing fate, without the resignation that ought to accompany it." Man knows he is mortal; disease makes mortality visible and forces the victim to realize what it means to be an isolated being irreparably condemned to death. Illness makes the victim aware that his existence can be destroyed, that he can lose himself and his world, that he can become nothing. As Stevenson, a lifelong tubercular invalid, observes: "The changes wrought by death are in themselves so sharp and final, and so terrible and melancholy in their consequences, that the thing stands alone in man's experience, and has no parallel upon earth."

In the modern age a number of complex biographical, religious, social, scientific, medical and moral factors have contributed to the creation of and interest in the literature of disease. Goethe's distinction between healthy and sick writers has disappeared, for disease has become a virtual necessity for creation. Like D. H. Lawrence, modern writers use art for catharsis and insight, and would agree that "One sheds one's sicknesses in books repeats and presents again one's emotions, to be master of them." The moral authority of these writers is based on the paradoxical privilege of sickness and suffering.

The sceptical modern writer no longer assumes that death leads to salvation and a new life, and must attempt to find meaning in suffering and extinction without the consolation of religion. For Keats, easeful death was a release from pain into oblivion; for Tolstoy, a revelation of spiritual truth. But for Ellis and Solzhenitsyn, personal agony has no redemptive quality.

V

Because of the great number of novels about disease it was necessary to be selective. I have therefore chosen [for inclusion in *Disease and the Novel*] both difficult and significant fiction that was written between 1880 and 1960 when this theme achieves its finest literary expression, that treat the complex theme in various ways and that lend themselves to intensive analysis from this point of view. I feel it would be more valuable and interesting to concentrate on a small number of great works than to write a general survey of novels about disease.

These eight works are significantly related to each other. *The Death of Ivan Ilych* was the model for "The Snows of Kilimanjaro." Tolstoy and Mann had a profound influence on Solzhenitsyn and on Ellis. The ideas of Dostoyevsky and Nietzsche strongly influenced Gide and Mann (Gide wrote a book on the Russian, Mann composed several essays on both masters). Mann suggests his thematic similarities to Gide when he describes him as a kind of successful Gustave von Aschenbach "who won out over guilt and neurosis through the discipline of his art, for whom this art had become the saving instrument of self-control, and for whom language and style had turned into the blessed remedies for the anarchy within."

All these novels consider the complex connection between disease and love, and emphasize their emotional and physical similarities: the physiological changes in the body (and orgasm as the "little death"); the painful progress and desperate yearning for a satisfactory resolution; the connection between frustration or consummation in love, crisis or cure in disease. In Tolstoy and Hemingway the heroes, who resent their healthy wives, realize during illness that they have never really loved them. In Gide the revival of the hero is linked to the decline of his wife, who is rejected for young boys and virtually murdered when the husband recovers his health. In *The Magic Mountain* frustrated love causes and consummated love intensifies disease; in *Doctor Faustus* sexual relations lead to venereal disease and to an inhuman renunciation of love; in *The Black Swan* the heroine is cruelly deceived by nature when love causes apparent rejuvenation and actual disease. In Ellis the hope of physical salvation through sexual love is brutally disappointed. In Solzhenitsyn the temporary cure of disease by radiation renders the hero physically incapable of love.

These works also concern the relation between physical, psychological, sexual, emotional, intellectual and moral change. In Tolstoy disease has a positive quality: it emphasizes the spiritual element in man, provides insight and illumination, teaches the Christian acceptance of death. Hemingway substitutes Art for Christianity, but reveals a Tolstoyan pattern of personal redemption. In Gide disease leads not to self-discovery and personal freedom, but to intellectual and ethical derangement.

The Magic Mountain is Mann's critique of the hero's stimulating infatuation with disease, an endemic condition that can neither be cured nor fully understood. *Doctor Faustus* concerns the disease of body and soul, music and love; the relation between artistic sterility, demonic possession and political destruction. *The Black Swan,* a cathartic defense against old age and failing health, is a satire on the Romantic concept of life-enhancing aspects of disease. In Ellis the trapped and tormented hero can never escape the consequences of disease. In *Cancer Ward,* as in *The Rack,* the hero is both released and destroyed at the end of the novel; but Solzhenitsyn's book is a tribute to human dignity and man's power of survival.

Writers like Chekhov, Kafka, Lawrence, Mansfield and Orwell, who died of tuberculosis, rarely wrote fiction about their own disease (though there are hints of it in the heroes of *Lady Chatterley's Lover* and *1984*.) These writers confined their descriptions to personal letters and journals, which I have used to illuminate the novels in [*Disease and the Novel*]. Ellis and Solzhenitsyn—who suffered from tuberculosis and cancer, endured the dreadful stages of dying, pondered the nature of life and death—write directly about their own illness. But they were only able to transmute their disease into art *after* they were cured and had the strength to perceive their sickness more objectively. In their novels, disease is horrible, suffering extreme, cure impossible.

Disease and the Novel concerns the final phase of a Romantic idea that prevailed for a century and a half, reaches its peak in *The Magic Mountain* and *Doctor Faustus,* and is decisively rejected in *The Rack* and *Cancer Ward,* which nevertheless continue through an emphasis on the body the Romantic mode of self-exploration. Unlike Tolstoy, Hemingway and Mann, who observed illness objectively, Solzhenitsyn earned his insight through actual experience. He writes in the tradition of Russian realism, of Tolstoy and Chekhov, and resolutely renounces the Romantic attitude toward disease. He does not believe the artist is sick or that disease inspires creative genius, aesthetic insight, spiritual knowledge or human dignity. And he does not think that the artist must stand outside society.

Cancer Ward rejects the spiritual self-destruction of *Notes From Underground,* in which the masochistic hero proclaims: "I'm a sick man . . . a mean man. There's nothing attractive about me. I think there's something wrong with my liver. . . . I'm fully aware that I can't spite the doctors by refusing their help. I know very well that I'm harming myself and no one else. But still, it's out of spite that I refuse to ask for the doctors' help. So my liver hurts? Good, let it hurt even more!" It also rejects the physical disgust for the human body portrayed in Baudelaire's "Une Charogne" and in Gottfried Benn's horrifying "Man and Woman Go Through the Cancer Ward":

> Here in this row are wombs that have decayed,
> and in this row are breasts that have decayed.
> Bed beside stinking bed. Hourly the sisters
> change.
>
> Come, quietly lift up this coverlet,
> Look, this great mass of fat and ugly humours
> was precious to a man once, and
> meant ecstasy and home.
>
> Come, now look at the scars upon this breast.
> Do you feel the rosary of small soft knots?
> Feel it, no fear. The flesh yields and is numb.
>
> Here's one who bleeds as though from thirty
> bodies.
> No one has so much blood.
> They had to cut
> a child from this one, from her cancerous womb.

The literary precursor of *Cancer Ward* is Chekhov's "Ward Six." In that bitter but compassionate story the sane doctor is locked up in a mental ward by lunatics who symbolize the hopelessness and corruption of Czarist Russia. Solzhenitsyn as well as Tolstoy, Hemingway, Gide, Mann and Ellis share Chekhov's profound sympathy, his transformation of the clinical into the poetical, his concern with the moral aspects of illness, his use of sickness to symbolize social pathology.

The course of European history and thought from 1880 to 1960 can also be traced in this sequence of novels. Tolstoy expresses the crisis of faith in the late nineteenth century; Hemingway's portrayal of Art, rather than God, as the highest good reveals the transition from a religious to a secular age. Gide's hero exchanges Christianity for paganism in a Nietzschean transvaluation of all values. *The Magic Mountain* represents the dissolution of Europe on the eve of the Great War. *Doctor Faustus* allegorizes the rise and fall of Nazism between 1933 and 1945. *The Rack* symbolizes the pathological state of Fascism in the 1940s. *The Black Swan* (which ostensibly takes place in 1924) concerns America's inability to cure sick Europe after the destruction of World War Two. *Cancer Ward* shows the extinction of the principles of the Russian Revolution, the creation of the Arctic concentration camps and the political upheavals that took place after Stalin's death in 1953. Though the novelists offer no easy solutions to the ghastly historical realities of the twentieth century, they reveal how men can confront disease and politics with courage and conviction.

Gian-Paolo Biasin

SOURCE: "From Anatomy to Criticism," in *Literary Diseases: Theme and Metaphor in the Italian Novel*, University of Texas Press, 1975, pp. 3-35.

[*In the following excerpt, Biasin focuses on disease as a theme in modern European literature.*]

> Considering how common illness is, how tremendous the spiritual change that it brings, how astonishing, when the lights of health go down, the undiscovered countries that are then disclosed, what wastes and deserts of the soul a slight attack of influenza brings to view, what precipices and lawns sprinkled with bright flowers a little rise of temperature reveals, what ancient and obdurate oaks are uprooted in us by the act of sickness, how we go down into the pit of death and feel the waters of annihilation close above our heads and wake thinking to find ourselves in the presence of the angels and the harpers when we have a tooth out and come to the surface in the dentist's armchair and confuse his "Rinse the mouth—rinse the mouth" with the greeting of the Deity stooping from the floor of Heaven to welcome us—when we think of this, as we are so frequently forced to think of it, it becomes strange indeed that illness

> has not taken its place with love and battle and jealousy among the prime themes of literature. Novels, one would have thought, would have been devoted to influenza; epic poems to typhoid; odes to pneumonia; lyrics to toothache. But no; with a few exceptions—De Quincey attempted something of the sort in *The Opium Eater;* there must be a volume or two about disease scattered through the pages of Proust—literature does its best to maintain that its concern is with the mind; that the body is a sheet of plain glass through which the soul looks straight and clear, and, save for one or two passions such as desire and greed, is null, and negligible and non-existent. On the contrary, the very opposite is true.

Virginia Woolf's words, elegant as always and seemingly unstudied, are a good introduction to our essay. To her acknowledgment of the importance of the body (an acknowledgment that harkens back to Arthur Schopenhauer and Friedrich Nietzsche), we must immediately add that disease actually is a prime theme of literature, although it has not been sufficiently recognized as such by readers and critics alike; that, therefore, many other names should be added to those of Thomas De Quincey and Marcel Proust; and, finally, that literature, while being concerned with bodily phenomena, will always tend to transform these according to its own procedures and norms.

In the writer's quest for the world, man, and truth (a truth), he neglects no aspect of experience; even the most banal or secondary one acquires its well-defined meaning at a cultural, historical, existential, and structural level. Each of these aspects, to the very degree that it is absorbed into the literary universe, is transformed into images, themes, and *topoi* through which reality is perceived, organized, and ultimately known.

One of these themes, a very ancient one, concerns disease, which is part of life and often an announcement of death, both an individual fact and a social datum: Philoctetes and Prince André, Hercules *furens* and Orlando *furioso,* the *dame aux camélias* and Henry IV, Madame Merteuil and Zeno, and the plagues described by Giovanni Boccaccio, Alessandro Manzoni, and Albert Camus (in differing co-ordinates of time and space) are included in this theme. Outside literature, one remembers Leonardo da Vinci's anatomical drawings or El Greco's figures modeled after Toledo's madmen in the insane asylum (according to Gregorio Marañon); then, following the macabre-scientific combination peculiar to the anatomies of the seventeenth century, one can cite the Dutch physician Friedrich Ruysch and his true-to-life mummies that were to inspire Giacomo Leopardi later on or Francesco Susini's intriguing anatomical waxes in Florence's Specola Museum. It is also interesting to note how, according to Raymond Klibanski, Erwin Panofsky, and Fritz Saxl, the leper became a figurative *topos* in Albrecht Dürer's painting. (But a history of how many leper hospitals were transformed into insane asylums and of the underlying reasons for such a phenomenon has yet to be written, notwithstanding the chapter on "the great imprisonment" in Michel Foucault's *Raison et déraison: Histoire de la folie à l'âge classique.*)

At any rate, today the dichotomy between sane and sick, normal and pathological seems to be predominant in scientific, sociological, and moral thought, as well as in the average man's typical mental attitudes. In a recent interview, Foucault stated: "Every society establishes a whole series of systems of oppositions between good and evil, permitted and prohibited, lawful and illicit, criminal and non-criminal, etc. All of these oppositions, which are constitutive of society, today in Europe are being reduced to the simple opposition between normal and pathological. This opposition not only is simpler than others, but also has the advantage of letting us believe there is a technique to bring the pathological back to normal." On this side of the Atlantic, Susan Sontag wrote in an essay, somewhat peremptorily, "Ours is an age which consciously pursues health, and yet only believes in the reality of sickness."

If we turn to consider the origin of today's disturbing scene, we are likely to find it in the Romantic Movement, especially if we accept Morse Peckham's idea, developed from the views of Arthur Lovejoy and René Welleck, that the major revolutionary discovery of the romantics was the conception of reality as "organicism," as a "dynamic organicism" (rather than as a preordained "mechanism"). Disease is inherent in an organism. So is vitality, and so are evil and death. To give an example, Leopardi's description of a garden as a "hospital" of suffering beings can be taken as emblematic of a whole poetry that fully expresses the dichotomy between the recognition of the negativity of the universe, on one side, and the irreducible vitality and sentiments of the poet, on the other; according to Sergio Solmi's conclusions, "his wound had to remain open." This metaphorical "wound" seems precisely what G. W. F. Hegel diagnosed as "the Romantic malady of his age" according to Erich Heller: "a severance of mind from world, soul from circumstance, human inwardness from external condition." This "Romantic malady" can be considered the very root of today's alienation.

Turning now to the development of medicine as a scientific, social, and historic background of literature, one fact stands out: the scientific attitude toward death as a source of vital knowledge is paralleled in romantic literature by an analogous evaluation of death as a factor of individuality. Often the death of a romantic hero who has been sick with that most spiritual of diseases, tuberculosis, represents an affirmation of his exceptionality, of his spirituality. The *dame aux camélias* and Violetta in *La traviata* are indeed exemplary for the characterization of their epoch. In them the romantic tendency to equate passionate love with disease appears quite clearly. (Of course, I am omitting other characteristic and important attitudes, such as melancholy and sadness, because they are less extreme and less directly related to the theme under examination.)

On the other hand, the romantic period also considered disease and death as punishments with a moral or divine character; one thinks of Madame Merteuil's smallpox in *Les liaisons dangereuses* or of Don Rodrigo's plague in *Fermo e Lucia* (then in *I promessi sposi,* with a less obvious interpretation). In these instances the scientific data were used in an unscientific, almost metaphysical way that did not have much to do with a faithful rendering in literature of actual medical progress, perhaps because the latter remained in the isolated world of clinics for a long time.

However, as Albert Béguin reminds us in *Le Romantisme Allemand,* disease had an importance for certain romantics that can only be fully recognized today, in the light of the literary developments of the late nineteenth century. The most profoundly romantic disease was intimately linked with knowledge and artistic creation in a rich and ambiguous relationship. For instance, in Novalis's *Fragmente* one reads: "Likely, diseases are the stimulus and the most interesting subject for our meditation and activity. . . . Only, we know little the art of using them"; "Medicine must transform itself into the doctrine of the art of living"; "Diseases should be considered as bodily madness and, partially, as fixed ideas"; "Life is a malady of the spirit, since in it one hopes with passion. . . . Death is the principle that makes our life romantic. Death is life. Through death life is reinforced"; "Every disease is a musical problem, healing is a musical solution"; "If a man began to love disease or sorrow, the most exciting pleasure would penetrate him"; "Poetry is the great art of constructing transcendental sanity. Therefore the poet is a transcendental physician"; "Could disease not be a means of higher synthesis?"

Even though such thoughts seem not to have found a large and immediate following, they did have implications and consequences that were fundamental for the nineteenth century. On the one hand, they are a prelude first to Schopenhauer's and Nietzsche's philosophic interest in biological matters, then to naturalism and the emphasis on scientific knowledge of disease. On the other hand, they foreshadow a whole morbid trend that leads through J. C. F. Hölderlin and Gérard de Nerval to symbolism, decadence, and, ultimately, Antonin Artaud's and Raymond Roussel's literature of the irrational.

The scientifically generic and poetically vague way in which the romantics treated the theme of disease was replaced after the second half of the nineteenth century by a cold and precise, clinical and positivist tone. Disease-passion inexorably became physical illness in all its terrible concreteness and painful evidence; disease-punishment disappeared along with what J. Hillis Miller, echoing Nietzsche, has called "the disappearance of God" or at any rate with the fading of the interest in transcendence. No longer a punishment, it remained pure and simple disease, whether physical or (especially later on) psychic, so that from Sigmund Freud's discoveries a wholly new morality was born, one based on the dynamics of the guilt complex. The death of Emma Bovary, described by Gustave Flaubert with relentless clinical attention to the painful and cruel symptoms of poisoning, dramatically marked the end of the romantic hero in France, while in Italy something similar occurred a few years later with the death of Narcisa Valderi in Giovanni Verga's *Una peccatrice.*

From then on, disease was dealt with more and more extensively and frequently in literature. The naturalists, under the impulse of positivism and with the purpose of scientific research, focused their attention not so much on inner, individual aspects of reality as on outer, social ones (in the direction foreshadowed by Novalis), not so much on moods as on this or that atmosphere. As a consequence, their major interest was in the poorest class of the population, its miserable living conditions in urban slums (those of Paris were famous), and certain typical illnesses transmitted from one generation to the next by heredity (like the hereditary madness in Émile Zola's *La bête humaine,* a truly social as well as literary document). The results were works in which the most realistic details of a given sickness were described carefully, technically, and, more often than not, morbidly; it is well known that Zola said he was inspired by a treatise on experimental medicine by Claude Bernard. (I would emphasize "experimental" even more than "medicine.") His statement can enlighten us about the type of interest, substantial and methodological, of literature in medicine from the middle of the last century.

In Italy, the industrial revolution, although somewhat delayed, brought developments analogous with those that had occurred in France and England and bearing similar consequences in the literary field. The *veristi* writers, however, in general abstained from the representation of the most extreme aspects of a pathological nature, yet the lesson of naturalism was deeply felt and left its mark upon the Italian cultural milieu. Verga's restraint whenever he describes the agony and death of one of the characters in his mature novels from La Longa to Mastro-don Gesualdo remains exemplary; so does Luigi Capuana's in his description of pathological cases, from Giacinta to Eugenia.

On the contrary, the Milanese group of *Scapigliati* often indulged in an exasperated and morbid representation of illness. By taking up again melancholy (of the Adolphe type) and Novalis's romantic disease, they in fact anticipated a certain tendency of literature at the end of the nineteenth century—the tendency toward decadence (and even to G. A. Borgese's *Rubè*), which has its roots in this direct relationship between literature and medicine.

Foucault has clearly shown how a whole line of clinical studies in the late 1800's was oriented toward the concept and the status of "degeneration," a concept that some physicians had utilized "to characterize the weakening of the robust human naturalness, condemned by society, civilization, laws, and language to a life of artifices and diseases." Such a negative stance was to be reversed only gradually by medical science, starting with Xavier Bichat: "At the very beginning of life, degeneration is the necessity of death, from which it is indissociable, and the most general possibility of sickness. The structural link between this concept and the anatomo-pathologic method appears now clearly. In the perception of anatomy, death was the high point of view from which disease opened upon its own truth; the trinity life-disease-death was articulated in a triangle whose top was death." It is interesting to note the extraordinary cultural coincidence between degeneration as a negative medical concept and degeneration as a philosophic conception in the works of Schopenhauer, Nietzsche, Paul Bourget, and Max Nordau. An entire area of European culture is usually designated, perhaps a bit too conventionally, by the name of "decadence." In Italy the most important and up-to-date representative of this trend was Gabriele D'Annunzio, whose sensitivity to the theme of physical decadence, disease, and death was not accidental. In France, a similar attitude can be found in Joris-Karl Huysman's *À rebours.*

Examples from D'Annunzio's works are innumerable, but two will suffice. One is taken from the early short story "Il cerusico di mare": "The following day the cuticle of the tumor was swollen by a bloody serum and broke. The whole part took on the appearance of a wasp's nest, from where purulent materials gushed out abundantly. The inflammation and the suppuration were deepening and extending rapidly." The second example is from the late *Il compagno dagli occhi senza cigli* and seems to illustrate clearly the link between D'Annunzio and Novalis: "Disease and death are the two blindfolded Muses that lead us in silence to discover the spirituality of forms." Between these two examples, one could of course add famous pages from *Il piacere, Il fuoco,* or *Il notturno.*

But, concurrently with the pseudoscientific incorporation of medical data in naturalist literature, which sought to master pathology in order to understand the world better, toward the end of the nineteenth century an equally important phenomenon occurred. Medicine evolved radically in a particular field, that of mental illnesses, and these diseases became the focus of predominant interest. Foucault has shown that those who were mad were kept in a status of social and cultural freedom until circa 1650. However, during the seventeenth century they were isolated and burdened with a more or less marked sense of guilt, and this attitude lasted precisely until the end of the nineteenth century. Cesare Lombroso, even with his efforts to liberalize the treatment of madmen, idiots, and criminals, is perhaps the most dramatic and saddest example of a whole social and clinical trend on which Michel David has made pungent remarks and that, unfortunately, persists even today, notwithstanding a few exceptions.

In the field of mental illness there had already been numerous but isolated intuitions, forerunners of psychoanalysis, so many as to lead Carlo Emilio Gadda to suggest that "Freud did not discover anything entirely new, but only ordered, schematized, settled, and reduced into terms a material already known for centuries." Gadda's suggestion was a certainty for Thomas Mann, who in his lecture "Freud and the Future" (1936) showed that the use of disease (especially mental disease) as an indispensable instrument of knowledge was an idea common to great writers and philosophers of the nineteenth century, such as Novalis, Nietzsche, Sören Kierkegaard, and Schopenhauer (not to mention his precise references to Richard Wagner and Feodor Dostoevski).

More recently Lancelot L. Whyte has systematically examined *The Unconscious before Freud,* analyzing how from 1680 to 1880 human thought established the idea of the existence of the unconscious mind and how the structure of the mind has been explored, especially in our century. After noting that in the idea of the unconscious mind at least three groups of elements converge (*a.* German *Naturphilosophie,* romanticism, and scientific individual psychology; *b.* biology, vitality, and organicity; *c.* Oriental mystical ideas), Whyte reminds us that the term *unconscious (Unbewusstsein)* was invented by Ernst Platner and dates back to 1776, while Hegel, Friedrich Schelling, Schopenhauer, Nietzsche, and Eduard von Hartmann (all of them anticlassical, anti-European, anti-Enlightenment) are undoubtedly Freud's major precursors during the nineteenth century. Nine editions of von Hartmann's treatise on *Philosophie des Unbewussten* (1868) had been published in Germany by 1882.

It seems amply demonstrated then that Freud did not come out of a void but was rather the culmination of a whole trend in the culture of the nineteenth century. At any rate, Freud had the great merit of systematizing the theoretical study of the irrational and its practical utilization for therapeutic purposes by instituting psychoanalysis, a new discipline. Certainly, only with Freud can the dialogue between reason and nonreason really begin again. Psychoanalysis is recognized in its scientific autonomy, social function, and cultural status, all of which are inevitably reflected also in literature.

Paradoxically, literature's appropriation of medical discoveries begins the inner erosion of the solid, positivist world; the diseases described acquire an elusive, suggestive character (although the method of description remains partially realistic and documentary). In fact they express the inner breaking down of one whole *vision du monde* that is to be replaced by another. The world of objects is no longer a datum, a certainty; the world of others is no longer meaningful in itself, in its institutions; in an apparently contradictory but intimately rigorous way, reason now implies non-reason within itself. The absolute of objectivity becomes, by varying degrees, the relative of subjectivity. What comes to the fore is the awareness of the self with all the ambiguities and the anguish inherent in the discovery of how unstable, contradictory, and absurd the relationships of the self to the world of others and of objects can be. Henri Bergson's *Essai sur les données immédiates de la conscience* and Freud's first psychoanalytical writings were published toward the end of the last century, almost at the same time.

In Italian literature these dramatic developments are recorded and worked out by two writers in particular: Italo Svevo, who proceeds from a quasi-naturalistic attitude in *Una vita* to the much subtler representation of disease in *Senilità* and then to the complex and articulated view of *La coscienza di Zeno* in which the free use of psychoanalysis acquires an exceptional cognitive and literary value; and Luigi Pirandello, who deliberately uses madness as a means of expressing his theories (especially in *Uno, nessuno e centomila* and in *Enrico IV*), perhaps by adhering to Émile Durkheim's conception of the marginality of disease considered as a mirror of the writer's own marginality.

Svevo is more rigorous and, in my opinion, more effective than Pirandello in his use of disease as a metaphor for inner analysis (of the Freudian type) and as a protest against his society (capitalistic, bourgeois). On the other hand, Pirandello is more openly polemical than Svevo in acknowledging the sharp juxtaposition existing between reason and nonreason and in the paradoxical and ferocious demolition he makes of it, especially through the social "role" (in Peter Berger's and Thomas Luckmann's sense) and the "mask" (in Ludwig Binswanger's sense) with their related problems.

Both of them, Svevo in a polite and subtle way, Pirandello desperately and dramatically, express the dissatisfaction and alienation of modern man. (Perhaps it is not by chance that in Italian a madman is also called *alienato*.) But, whether the protest is expressed through neurosis or madness, it goes back to that moment of inner reflection and self-analysis that marks the beginning of the twentieth century in literature.

It is important to note that the contrast between the self and the world is conveyed not only through the imagery of mental diseases; certain traditional illnesses, like tuberculosis, continue to be thought of and used by some writers as revealing symptoms, as symbols of precisely that contrast. A famous case is that of Franz Kafka, about whom Paolo Milano wrote:

> It is well known that Kafka, from the first moment, in his disease saw the physical manifestation of an inner conflict ("my wound, of which the lung's lesion is only a symbol"). He wrote in one of his notebooks: "The world, of which my fiancée is a representative, and my Self shatter my body in an irreconcilable contrast." At one and the same time, sickness excused him from his duties, in which he believed but to which his strength was unequal. Wagenbach reminds us that this psychogenesis of tuberculosis, sounding like a poetical hypothesis in Kafka's time, today is a diagnosed datum accepted by medicine without difficulty for certain cases.

Actually it has been demonstrated that sickness can be associated with the failure of an individual organism to maintain its integration in the social *telos*: there is a high death rate among motherless children; somatic diseases are frequent among those who have had a traumatic break in their social relationships; and in laboratory experiments some animals brought up in isolation are more subject to cancer than others brought up in groups. In any case it is significant that in his works Kafka did not use physical disease to express his *vision du monde,* but rather preferred to employ the inner world of obsession, guilt, and persecution (from *Das Schloss* to *Der Prozess* and *Die Verwandlung*). He lived his epoch with dramatic awareness and showed it through his characters' sick and morbid introspection.

Another contemporary author can be quoted in this connection: Antonin Artaud, who in his letters to Jacques Rivière and in *Le pèse-nerfs* has brought introspection to bear on the very root of thought, on the phenomenon and process of thinking—the birth, articulation, and manifestation of thought. Here are some examples from his letters to Rivière:

> I suffer from a frightening disease of the spirit. My thought abandons me continuously, from the single fact of thinking to the extreme fact of thought's materialization into words.
>
> This constant breaking down of my thought should be attributed . . . to a central giving way of my soul, a sort of essential and at the same time fleeting erosion of thought. . . . There is then something that destroys my thought, something that prevents me from being what I could be, but that leaves me, if I may say so, suspended. Something stealthy that takes away from me the words *I have found,* . . . and that constantly destroys the mass of my thought in its substance.

Similarly, in *Le pèse-nerfs* he writes:

> A concordance of words with the moments of my states of mind is lacking. . . . At every stage of the mechanics of my thinking there are holes, stops—try to understand me— . . . a strained becoming fixed, the sclerosis of a certain state. . . . I am the one who best felt the awful losing itself of his language in relation to thought. I have detected the very moment of my thought's most intimate, unsuspectable crumbling.
>
> The nervous itinerary of thought, rather than the spirit that remains intact, is hit and derouted by this crumbling. It is in the body and in the blood that this absence and this standing make themselves particularly felt.

As did Artaud, and actually before him, with the same effectiveness, the Italian Federigo Tozzi expressed the same type of penetrating and disquieting intuition, full of anguishing questions on the process of thought, hallucinations, the subtle and fleeting borderline between reason and madness, between normal and pathological, in his letters to Annalena dated February 1903:

> What is this hand that obeys my thought and traces on the paper signs they made me learn? . . . Who am I? What is my thought? And from what does it derive? Will it be able to die like the flesh dies? Or will it merge once again with the infinite force of all the things of the universe, in the form of another phenomenon, which then, in its turn, will transform itself into another, and then into another, in order not to die and to feel forever? And where will the awareness I have of that thought end up? . . .
>
> And now I have something like a dizzy spell. It seems to me that I am being swallowed by the chasm of a precipice, together with the snow that has enshrouded and overwhelmed me completely. I plunge into it without even touching bottom.

It seems almost unnecessary to underline the dramatic quality of this desperate and lucid introspection on the limits of the self, on the limits of the world and society.

This introspection can be seen precisely as a manifestation of the solitude of the individual vis à vis the society and reality in which he happens to live, milieux that at the beginning of the twentieth century are dominated by bourgeois capitalism, with all the cultural and ideological consequences inherent in it, described from opposite viewpoints by such critics as Erich Auerbach and Georg Lukács. According to Auerbach: "In a Europe unsure of itself, overflowing with unsettled ideologies and ways of life, and pregnant with disaster—certain writers distinguished by instinct and insight find a method which dissolves reality into multiple and multivalent reflections of consciousness. . . . But the method is not only a symptom of the confusion and helplessness, not only a mirror of the decline of our world. . . . There is in all these works a certain atmosphere of universal doom, especially in *Ulysses*. . . . There is often something confusing, something hazy about them, something hostile to the reality which they represent." Auerbach's diagnosis is all the more impressive in that it seems to foreshadow what Frank Kermode has recently called "the sense of an ending," a quality that characterizes our Western culture and is to be found in all of our major writers. As for Lukács, in an essay on the aftermath of naturalism in Germany—an essay containing assertions that are valid for the rest of Europe as well—he points out and explains that "the individual personality, juxtaposed to society, finds only in itself a point of reference for its moral life and decidedly rejects any social criterion of behavior." Therefore, in many literary works "there is the accusation against a society in which and because of which man withers and succumbs; there is a feeling that the authentic man can realize his inner capabilities only against and beyond present society." As Lukács notes in another essay, there is above all an escape into the pathological as "a moral protest against capitalism," a protest that, however, often lacks "a sense of direction" and expresses only "nausea, or discomfort, or longing." The extreme, psychopathological cases to be found in William Faulkner's *The Sound and the Fury* and in Samuel Beckett's *Molloy* seem to be very pertinent examples of such a literary and cultural development.

Along with Federigo Tozzi, two more Italian writers fit well into both Auerbach's and Lukács's diagnoses: Svevo, "judging and destructive poet of the bourgeoisie," who continued what Verga had begun, and Pirandello, demystifying "conscience" of European decadence. Their characters take on a significance that transcends their personal cases by far and that, precisely through the common denominator of disease, can be linked to similar contemporary experiences of such writers as Thomas Mann (*Der Zauberberg, Buddenbrooks, Der Tod in Venedig*) and Robert Musil (*Der Mann ohne Eigenschaften*), for whom the pathological plays a similar role; they anticipate typical patterns and attitudes to be found today. One thinks of certain works of Jean-Paul Sartre (*La nausée*), Albert Camus (*La peste*), François Mauriac (*Thérése Desqueyroux*), André Gide (*L'immoraliste, Les faux-monnayeurs*), Jorge Luis Borges (especially "El Sur" in *Ficciones*), Elias Canetti, or Günter Grass (*Die Brechtrommel,* in whose "transcendental dwarfism" there is a deliberate, clearly antinaturalistic attitude toward and use of disease as social protest). One also thinks of similar attitudes to be found in Elio Vittorini (*Conversazione in Sicilia*), Cesare Pavese (especially the diary and *Il diavolo sulle colline*), Alberto Moravia (from *La disubbidienza* to *La noia*), Dino Buzzati (*Sette piani, Un caso clinico*), Giorgio Bassani (*La lunga notte del '43*), Mario Soldati (*Le due città*), P. P. Pasolini (*Una vita violenta*), Italo Calvino (especially *La giornata di uno scrutatore*), and Gianna Manzini (*La Sparviera*). Even at the level of today's popular literature, as in the case of the Anglo-Saxon horror novel, the psychopathological has become common and is often posited as "metaphor of the anormalization of daily experience"; through the device of the diaristic form, "the psychopathic character becomes Everyman—the ironic-tragic sign of a universal condition."

In an example taken from Italian literature, Vittorini used disease in a clearly planned and symbolic way as a necessary stage of the "return to man" and the assertion of his dignity by Silvestro in *Conversazione in Sicilia.* "I knew all this, and more besides. I could understand the misery of a sick member of the human race of toilers, and of his family around him. Does not every man know it? Cannot every man understand it? Every man is ill once, half-way through his life, and knows this stranger that is the sickness inside him, knows his own helplessness against it. Thus every man can understand his fellow."

Or, in another example, involving the most typically literary aspects of bourgeois society, Calvino noted apropos of his novel *Il visconte dimezzato,* "For me the leprous have come to mean the hedonism, irresponsibility, happy decadence, the nexus aestheticism-disease, in a certain way the artistic and literary decadence of today, but of all times as well (e.g., the Arcadia)."

Even in the narrative work of a great critic like Edmund Wilson (one remembers especially his psychoanalytic study *The Wound and the Bow*), the metaphoric value of disease stands out as clear and deliberate. In "The Princess with the Golden Hair," according to the rendering by Paolo Milano of the Italian translation,

> Imogene confesses her secret to her lover; in fact she shows it to him: a metal corset, with which the lady protects herself from a disease of the spinal column, an ailment that the man will soon discover to be wholly imaginary. Imogene's invisible lesion, her erotic caution, slowly crystallize into a symbol, an "objective correlative" of an imaginary invalid, a secretly guilty rich America. But the blennorrhea with which the courageous but unlucky Ann infects her finally loving partner is the mark of the poor and oppressed America, bearer of something so strong and instinctive as to outlive any offense.

But, going back to Italian literature, we see that in Svevo and Pirandello disease is also, perhaps, something more than a metaphor. It becomes an existential condition, a true ontological category (of an ontology always historicized). That is why their influence on contemporary writing is so effective and lasting. It would be impossible to review all of today's novels and short stories dealing with diseases, especially mental diseases, which seem to have been multiplied by the Italian economic boom during the past fifteen years. By applying the notion of "pitiatism" to the contemporary situation, one may note that neuroses appear to be a direct consequence of an affluent society, while such traditional illnesses as malaria and tuberculosis progressively disappear from the literary scene as they diminish, obviously, in social reality. Therefore, the writers who are most attentive to the phenomena of their time continue to use disease as a critical, cognitive instrument by applying it to social and cultural circumstances, first at a representative (or naturalistic) level and also at the levels of metaphor (as a social protest) and ontology.

For instance, one thinks of Giuseppe Berto's *Il male oscuro,* which is so far the most immediate and faithful rendering of a psychoanalytical experience in literary form (although this novel, as such, retains perhaps too much of its autobiographical origin), or of the novel-documentary *Angelo a capofitto* by Franco Fornari, the scholar who is well known for his essays on individual and generalized situations of violence, especially atomic war. Other examples that come to mind are *Le libere donne di Magliano* and *Per le antiche scale,* novels set in insane asylums by the writer-physician Mario Tobino; *Cancer oecumenicus* by Mario Miccinesi, with the emblematic title; and *Il gioco e il massacro* by Ennio Flaiano, with its equally emblematic transformations.

Then there is the long gallery of novels with more or less neurotic protagonists: the "methereopatic" ones *á la* Musil in Giuseppe Cassieri's *Andare a Liverpool* and in Sandro De Feo's *I cattivi pensieri;* or the clearly representative one (in a social sense) of Alcide Paolini's *Lezione di tiro;* or the narrators in Gianni Celati's *Comiche* and in Sebastiano Vassalli's *Tempo di màssacro,* where neurosis is revealed also through stylistic tics; or the lucid mythomaniacs in Luigi Malerba's *Il serpente* and *Salto mortale,* in Enzo Siciliano's *Dietro di me,* and in Aldo Rosselli's *Professione: Mitomane.* In particular, one should remember Mario Spinella's *Sorella H, libera nos,* where all the levels of neurosis can be traced, from the existential to the social, from the literary to the ontological; Torino Guerra's *L'equilibrio* and *L'uomo parallelo,* dealing with the difficult problem of how to maintain a mental equilibrium and how not to succumb to one's double; and, to name the latest specimens of the series, Ottiero Ottieri's *Campo di concentrazione,* with its deliberately ambiguous title, and J. Rodolfo Wilcock's *Lo stereoscopio dei solitari,* with the almost necessary reference to Borges.

The most interesting and meaningful case among those just mentioned seems to be that of Tonino Guerra, who is Michelangelo Antonioni's screenplay writer, because he makes evident the fact that the theme examined so far is not strictly a literary one, but also one that has invaded other forms of art more immediately expressive than literature, like the cinema. Besides *Diario di una schizofrenica* directed by the poet Nelo Risi, we shall mention only the neurotic heroine in Antonioni's *Deserto rosso;* the mad hero of Carel Reisz's *Morgan,* a movie with the appropriate subtitle "A Suitable Case for Treatment"; the psychopathic girl in Roman Polanski's *Repulsion;* the depressed maniac in Liliana Cavani's *L'ospite;* the young epileptic in Marco Bellocchio's *I pugni in tasca;* and the paralytic nephew in Salvatore Samperi's *Grazie, zia.* Referring to the latter two movies, Moravia wrote, "Risking a symbolic interpretation of epilepsy and paralysis, it could be said that they represent the obsession of today's youth with social and cultural integration, conceived of as an infection; that is, the obsession of feeling sick with the same sickness against which one revolts." Moravia's assertion seems to transcend by far the strictly cinematographic context and to apply to the characters of many contemporary novels. Among them the best results at the artistic level seem to have been achieved by Paolo Volponi (*Memoriale, La macchina mondiale*) and Carlo Emilio Gadda (especially *La cognizione del dolore*), whose characters are animated by an attitude of protest revealing itself first and foremost as disease.

Volponi and Gadda, then, appear significant precisely because they view as privileged the condition of illness—the former portrays disease in the context of an industrial setting and of theoretical utopian reflections; the latter portrays it with a geographic and sociological invention that points to a well-defined reality and culminates in a metaphysical climate. Therefore, they exemplify the present-day interest in everything abnormal and confirm the continuing validity of Auerbach's and Lukács's remarks about the beginning of the century. They also confirm the truth of some of Foucault's conclusions:

> There is a lot of talk about contemporary madness, linked with the universe of machines and the waning of direct, affective relationships among men. . . . In fact, when man remains a stranger to the facts of his language, when he cannot recognize any human and living meaning in the products of his activity, when he is limited by economic and social determinations without being allowed to find his homeland in this world—then he lives in a culture that makes a pathologic form like schizophrenia possible; stranger in a real world, he is sent back to a "private world," which no longer can guarantee any objectivity; at the same time, subjected to the limitations of this real world, he feels it as a destiny.

Disease, far from being a simple aspect of reality, is an integral element of a given historical and social structure taken into consideration by literature; therefore, disease often becomes a point of view, an instrument of knowledge and of totalizing judgment for an author.

But, what is disease for a literary critic? Preliminarily, at a superficial but nevertheless meaningful level, it is easy to note that even the language of criticism has been influenced by medical terminology, as if to emphasize the definitive and metaphoric value of the word, which establishes unsuspected relationships between seemingly distant disciplines. Some examples of terms being used currently are *diagnosis, symptom, prognosis,* the already classic *"referto"* introduced by Gianfranco Contini, *anatomy,* as in Ezio Raimondi's *Anatomie secentesche* and Northrop Frye's *Anatomy of Criticism* (although Frye is reviving an older, genre use of the term), and *physiology,* as in Albert Thibaudet's *Physiologie de la critique* or in Mario Untersteiner's *La fisiologia del mito.* In this connection, the following passage by Heller on Nietzsche is a beautiful example of contemporary critical prose: "Thinking and writing to the very edge of insanity, and with some of his last pages even going over it, he read and interpreted the temperatures of his own mind; but by doing so, he has drawn the fever-chart of an epoch. Indeed, much of his work reads like the self-diagnosis of a desperate physician who, suffering the disease on our behalf, comes to prescribe as a cure that we should form a new idea of health, and live by it." Heller's critical language adheres so closely to his subject matter that one does not know which to admire more, his metaphors or his insight.

Another beautiful example is the following passage by Armando Gnisci: "There is a point where the text reveals itself as incomplete and requires an intervention. It is the point when the reader discovers that the work betrays itself as a fiction of an illusion, as writing and *récit,* and then it flees from itself or doubles back on itself and is thematized. At this moment the critical space is opened, where another text is introduced like a surgical instrument into the wound of the primary text to extract its 'meaning.'" The medical metaphor used by Gnisci apropos the critical and literary texts seems to indicate a level that deeply surpasses language in its most common usage and to point out fundamental, hidden possibilities.

At this further level, it is also true that, on the one hand, critics like Foucault and Jean Starobinski have devoted volumes to the cultural status, meaning, and history of medicine, while, on the other hand, physicians like Pedro Laín Entralgo and Juan Rof Carballo have been concerned respectively with the relationships between "disease and biography" and between "medicine and creative activity." A scientist like Ludwig Binswanger has examined "the problem of self-realization in art" and that of the artistic, literary, and clinical status of mannerism (a "form of failed existence"), and Jacques Lacan and Sergio Piro have brought their attention to bear upon the language of the unconscious and schizophrenia. Thus one observes a useful interchange between fields of study, including working methods and critical categories and concepts; the point of convergence is structuralism. A very pertinent example is found in the following remarks by Umberto Eco concerning Lacan's Unconscious-*Autre*: "The Other . . . speaks in the same way as the poetic discourse does according to Jakobson, through a succession of *metaphors* and *metonymies.* A symptom, which substitutes one symbol for another and makes the process of displacement obscure, is precisely a metaphor; while desire, which focuses on a substitutive object and makes the ultimate aim of any expectation undecipherable, is a metonymy. Because of this aim, every desire, though a chain of metonymic shifts, reveals itself as a desire for the Other." With this example we are well inside the most striking phenomenon of contemporary criticism: psychoanalytic terms, patterns, and methods are taken up and applied in the literary field.

Freud's writings on art have remained exemplary of their kind. In them Freud has clearly formulated some fundamental propositions: the language of a work of art (*Gradiva*'s text or Leonardo's paintings) is the sublimation of given impulses that are repressed or not satisfied in life, and it is, therefore, at one and the same time symptom and cure—an ambivalence that gives rise to a significant chain. The psychoanalyst (the critic) must unwind this chain. Furthermore, Freud instituted fundamental parallelisms between the interpretation of dreams and that of poetry and, in another field, between primitive mentality and neurosis.

Perhaps the best assessment of Freud's limits and contributions to date is Lionel Trilling's "Freud and Literature." Trilling arrives at the conclusion that Freud "finds in human pride the ultimate cause of human wretchedness, and he takes pleasure in knowing that his ideas stand with those of Copernicus and Darwin in making pride more difficult to maintain"; but Freud's man has nonetheless a great dignity, which begins with the recognition that he is "an inextricable tangle of culture and biology."

As Mario Lavagetto recently wrote, "Dr. Freud found himself caught between science and literature," with an "invincible nostalgia" for physiology and biology and an equally invincible attraction and innate inclination toward the written word. Equating science with objectivity and literature with subjectivity, he concludes that "the psychoanalytic paradox consists precisely of the systematic utilization of subjective totality."

I am not pretending to fix the landmarks of psychoanalytic criticism, but since Freud's first writings the contributions on and analyses of famous or less well known texts have increased in a crescendo remarkable for the quantity and subtlety of results. These results have been particular and concrete. Sometimes they concern the interpretation or deciphering of single works or authors such as Ernest Jones's perhaps too famous *Hamlet and Oedipus,* Marie Bonaparte's *Edgar Allan Poe,* Walter Benjamin's definition of Proust's style as "asthmatic," Michel Butor's *Baudelaire,* Sartre's *Flaubert,* Michel David's "Manzoni e il fiore del male," Giacomo Debenedetti's "Presagi del Verga," and Dominique Fernandez's *L'échec de Pavese.* On the other hand, there have been methodological results, especially in Charles Mauron's "psychocritique," Gaston Bachelard's phenomenology of the imagination, and Sartre's existential psychoanalysis, and one should not forget the psychoanalytical implications of René Girard's *La violence et le sacré.* These results have established the psychoanalytic instrument alongside the traditional ones of literary criticism, from linguistics to stylistics, from symbology to structuralism. In taking stock of contemporary psychoanalytic criticism, David recently remarked: "The ideal would be that a sound philologist and stylistic critic coexist within the same person together with an experienced psychoanalyst."

Freud's studies on primitive mentality were taken up and developed in a completely different direction by Carl Gustav Jung, who, following a teleologic (not etiologic) conception of disease, often appears, in Debenedetti's words, as "a mystic of illness," "the ally of artists, perhaps their accomplice." Jung in his turn influenced literary criticism with his work on the collective unconscious, the myths and archetypes of mankind. Jung gave impetus to a whole trend of ethnographic and anthropological research (Carl Kerenyi, Mircea Eliade) from which mythologic-symbolic criticism took inspiration. In Italy this type of criticism has only recently been developed successfully, mainly through Ezio Raimondi's teaching and work (and the particular contributions by Furio Jesi on Pavese, Emerico Giachery on Verga and D'Annunzio, and Edoardo Sanguineti on Vittorini).

On the other hand, Freud's studies on the ambiguity of the written word have been explicitly taken up by Jacques Derrida: his "Freud et la scène de l'écriture" is the basis for research that, while being juxtaposed to the ontological structuralism of the other great Freudian, Jacques Lacan, is also perhaps the richest in suggestions and developments for a reexamination of the idea of literature, and particularly for the theme of disease.

There are signs today that Freudian psychoanalysis is felt to be inadequate to deal with the complexities of the contemporary world and does not provide a satisfactory explanation of the nature of art and its relation to society; witness the importance attained by modern biology (Jacques Monod's *Le hasard et la nécessité*) and anthropology (from Claude Lévi-Strauss to Edmund Leach to Victor Turner and to Girard's *La violence et le sacré*). Within psychoanalytic criticism, in particular, Gilles Deleuze's and Félix Guattari's *L' Anti-Oedipe: Capitalisme et schizophrénie* is perhaps the latest and most extreme example of the "beyond Freud" perspective. They acknowledge the insufficiency of the concept of individual personality and propose that this concept be completely destroyed. "Schizo-analysis" should take the place of psychoanalysis and help us fight the evils of capitalistic society; the unconscious should be conceived of as "non-figurative and non-symbolic, . . . abstract, in the way abstract painting might conceive it."

On the other hand, Morse Peckham's *Man's Rage for Chaos: Biology, Behavior, and the Arts* is perhaps the most interesting example of the "aside from Freud" perspective. His biological and behavioristic approach deliberately does away with any psychoanalytic explanation of the artistic phenomenon; art is part of man's biological adaptation to the environment.

It seems clear that our argument so far concerns a field that is at the same time wider and less specialized than medicine and psychoanalysis considered in themselves. This argument starts with the acknowledgment that disease in general has literary autonomy, which manifests itself first as a theme and as such has a status and meanings that are decidedly its own. For instance, the thematic-symbolic analysis of "literary" diseases is justified and functional in that through it, diachronically, one can obtain an exact *aperçu* of a culture, I should say verified in vitro; thus, through a series of what Cesare Segre called *cronòtopi,* it is possible to outline the historic development from romanticism to positivism, or from positivism to decadence, with scientific and at the same time textual precision.

On the other hand, the theme of disease, even if considered with all of its implications, may not be sufficient to provide the framework of an analysis encompassing all the major themes of a given writer synchronically examined. In this case the theme of disease can be privileged above the others and become in a way only a pretext for a total comprehension, without losing anything of its specific and autonomous importance. In other words the critic can perform the same selective operation on the writer that the latter performed on reality in the first place.

This is the point where structural thematic criticism comes closest to symbolic criticism. Disease is indeed considered as a metaphor for our time, and the critic must study the terms, the movement, and the meaning of this metaphor inside any literary structure, defining not only its semantic and stylistic characteristics, but also the historical, sociological, existential, and ontological ones. Here, "metaphor and history" (according to Ezio Raimondi's title, beautiful in its juxtaposition of seemingly unrelated terms) really converge, or constitute the dialectical poles on which the progress of culture is articulated. Metaphor (the text, the author) is linked with history (the event, the reader) through an uninterrupted series of codes—in this connection a certain line of Russian formalism, from Mikhail Bakhtin to Jurij Lotman, should be remembered, not to mention Roman Jakobson's statement that a metaphor is destined, in time, to become a metonymy.

Furthermore, and perhaps above all, disease is a metaphor for literature. At this level, explored by Derrida with disquieting insight, the theme of disease can undergo the most unthought-of and stimulating developments because it becomes grafted onto the ancient dispute about the art-sickness relationship and opens up new, vertiginous perspectives.

In his search for the *trace* and *différance,* in his pursuit of the elusive nature of human language and *écriture,* Derrida made a fruitful visit to "Plato's Pharmacy." In an ancient Egyptian legend analyzed by Plato, Thot, the god of writing, is also the master of numbers, calculus, the calendar, funeral rites, and death: "The god of writing therefore is the god of medicine as well. Of medicine: a science and at the same time a hidden drug. Of remedy and poison. The god of writing is the god of *pharmakon.*" Presented as a gift to Ra-the-Speaking-God, writing can only be considered as contrary to life, a *pharmakon* that does nothing but displace and maybe irritate pain; therefore, writing is a supplement (or displacement) that, as such, contains a "fateful impulse toward redoubling," that is, toward *dissémination.*

Derrida then goes on in his development of the chain of meanings implicit within the ambivalent nature of *écriture,* passing from the word in the Greek *polis* to writing as error, from "pharmakos" as scapegoat to the death of Socrates, from the figure of Socrates the Father to Plato's "parricide" word, from cosmos to cosmetics, from *mimesis* to play. All these concepts and themes seem self-generating in a complex system of semantic, structural, and symbolic associations, and all are to be found in contemporary literature and criticism. We should not forget that in his work Derrida comes back *à rebours* from Plato to Jean-Jacques Rousseau to Ferdinand de Saussure to Lévi-Strauss; thus, he is concerned with structural linguistics and anthropology, today's typical "sciences of man." His purpose, in Alexander Gelley's words, is to define accurately "the boundaries of an epoch, to define the cultural enclosure (*clôture*) in such a way that its limits are both acknowledged and breached. . . . Derrida does seek to reveal as explicit structure what has generally been an unacknowledged or surreptitious devaluation of the textual." In doing so, he makes a further fascinating contribution to what Ernst Curtius called "the symbolism of the book," by proposing an "open" alternative *à la* Borges.

Significantly, Ezio Raimondi refers precisely to Borges, this "fantastic architect of Babel's library," in giving a teleology to the "bibliographic ritual" inherent in his critical method; if "every book one happens to read, whether great or small, puts back into discussion some elements of one's own mental library," then "actually he who accumulates references and lateral observations seconds not only an instinct of information, but also a more secret line of disquiet, of curiosity ever turning upon itself and almost aspiring to its own transcendence. He acts like the collector about whom Benjamin wrote, whose search is dialectically guided by the double calling of order and chaos, of tactics and adventure."

The theme of disease seems particularly fitting for verifying Raimondi's and Derrida's methods of literary analysis and their results, precisely because it goes to the very roots of the literary fact and has an inherent polysemy. But it is important to keep in mind an essential difference between Raimondi and Derrida. The latter is exclusively concerned with literature; society has disappeared almost completely from his critical horizon. The former, on the contrary, begins with literature (rhetorics, style) but is also interested in history (erudition, philology), and from history he is led to a concern for society. For Raimondi, literature and criticism are clearly valid insofar as they strike a rapport with the society and the history around them, insofar as they are able to mirror and to be mirrored by political-cultural events. In this connection it seems significant to note that Raimondi's latest book, dealing with Bolognese humanists and Renaissance and, in particular, Machiavelli's theater, is entitled *Politica e commedia,* confirming the previous *Metafora e storia* in a more "public" context. Unlike Derrida, Raimondi is the latest representative of a tradition that can be considered as beginning with Giambattista Vico (where one finds not only concern for the word as symbol, but also an interest in language as activity) and continuing with Francesco De Sanctis (with his constant relating of literature to society and history) and Benedetto Croce (who was not only the aesthetician of intuition, but also and perhaps above all a liberal historian). Raimondi is fully aware of the problems of literature in contemporary industrial society, and his rigorous work reflects the image of a critic who is at the same time a citizen.

The essays [in *Literary Diseases*] deal with some great Italian writers of the late nineteenth and twentieth centuries who were selected at least in part as specimens. Verga, for instance, can certainly be seen as a figure who epitomizes the transition (not necessarily a chronological one) between romanticism, *Scapigliatura,* and positivism, but it is hoped that he will appear also, or perhaps above all, in his individuality, in his "Verghianity," so to speak. Because it is based on specimens, this book is not intended to be a history of modern and contemporary Italian literature, not even so far as the novel is concerned; but I hope it will demonstrate its validity (of method and results) by giving an explanation (synchronically and diachronically) of the major points of this history.

Some provisional or momentarily definitive conclusions (as Eugenio Montale and Musil would say) should be clear by now. On the intertextual level, an analysis of the theme of disease allows a consideration of Italian literature differing in many respects from the more conventional approaches by periods or "isms," especially because through this theme one can focus on "tradition" as much as on "the individual talent" (to quote T. S. Eliot). Thus the theory of the impersonality of literature can be put to a test in the close reading and analysis of literary texts.

On the contextual level, an analysis of the theme of disease is a valid instrument for tracing the very precise emergence and development of social consciousness in Italian literature, along with the related problem of marginality, from the individualistic death of Narcisa Valderi described by the early Verga to the preindustrial bourgeois society surrounding Gesualdo and witnessing his hopeless struggle with cancer; from Svevo's smiling and pensive irony in dealing with Zeno's neuroses in a well-established and commercial milieu to Pirandello's indictment of that milieu through Moscarda's "mad" rebellion and to Gadda's inquiry into the modes of identity in a technological society, an inquiry coupled with the anguishing memories of a recent Fascist past and a painful uncertainty about the future.

The third conclusion is consonant with the nature of the methodology adopted to interpret the texts and of the texts used to test that methodology: [*Literary Diseases*] has no conclusion, partly because it is designed to be open (a scholar of Mann or James Joyce or Pavese could easily add his chapter to the ones present) and partly because it has to be open if one is to believe in the symbolism of the book and in the unending pursuit of some truth. In this connection, it might be proper to recall also Leo Bersani's "esthetic of incompleteness," which "is equivalent to an ethic of incompleteness for a self too open to be defined and confined by the fixed design of a permanent identity." David Caute's comments about art can be applied to criticism as well: "The struggle against social alienation (*Entfremdung*) and false consciousness requires an alienated (*Verfremdung*), anti-magical art, a dialectical literature which recognizes its own nature and which is self-conscious, anti-mimetic and self-critical. It never aspires to completion. It knits, unravels, knits . . . It is a process as well as a product. This process is both synchronic and diachronic, both genetic and structural."

Through a thematic, symbolic analysis of disease in some texts by Verga, Svevo, Pirandello, and Gadda, it will be possible to reaffirm the cognitive function of criticism and literature, both of which are engaged against death, both of which lean over the abyss of a truth that is no longer (or perhaps has never been) anthropotheological.

Oliver Jelly

SOURCE: "Fiction and Illness," in *A Review of English Literature*, Vol. 3, No. 1, January, 1962, pp. 80-9.

[*In the following essay, Jelly argues that modern fiction has become increasingly concerned with portraying characters who are afflicted with disease.*]

It probably began because Flaubert's father was Resident Surgeon at the Rouen Hospital, which may not constitute all the cause but makes a convenient start for what is now a universal condition: the fiction of the world is full of sickness. This might be thought inevitable amidst the general introspection of our time if we were not bound by the honour due to prophets to think that fictional introspection should precede, not follow, its public appearance. If this is so, then the European attitude to illness will deteriorate further unless these novelist-seers prove wrong; and this is possible because such prophecy is only worked out by hindsight. For example, Stendhal gave his forecast that the released bourgeois energy of his day, fortified with their youth and excellent education, would in no time control the professions, administration, universities, churches and academies, while the appreciation of art would remain in the hands of the elegant relics of the *ancien régime.* This worked out pretty accurately for an important part of the century's French culture and Daumier shows the fact by drawing the patron erect and cavalry and the painter tuberculous. True, the emerging class produced their own Balzacian crust but there was an equally powerful clique which kept aesthetics an acquired taste which only the initiates could share. Such an exclusive attitude was exemplified by the Goncourts, Flaubert himself and, amongst others, Dégas, Proust and Gide; none of them were absolute aristocrats, but all were of independent means, quintessential, representing a type of metropolitan amateur who is almost absent today, that is, extinguished within half a century of his peak.

Just as the fiction of this group had a weakness for the bedside, so *Madame Bovary,* one of their products, is the archetype of the clinical novel and it is necessary to emphasise the following facts in this side of its construction. First, and only to be expected, its clinical detail is extremely accurate; secondly, Flaubert makes full use of the clinical incidents to influence the reader; thus, the clubfoot tragedy makes Charles a fool while the hysteria and ultimate suicide of Emma destroy any sympathy the reader may still feel for her; thirdly, the clinical features are unobtrusive although so important, and Flaubert could have easily raised a defence against these charges. For all that, he undoubtedly set a fashion in the matter and earlier novels had very rarely been clinical; *Werther* is not, in spite of a suicide climax, nor is *Wilhelm Meister,* and although Stendhal is self-clinical in his journal he is much less so in the novels. But after *Madame Bovary* it is hard to find a major novelist who is not also a clinician, some, like Proust, more obviously so than others. Much of this clinical writing is extremely skilful and Svevo's *Confessions of Zeno* is a masterpiece of the genus. Supposedly written to the request of the narrator's psychiatrist Svevo allows himself fair comment on his master's works of reference, from Trieste in the early 'twenties; psychoanalysis is 'not difficult to understand, but very boring'. He is even more cunning than Flaubert in concealing sickness but a masterly description of Basedow's disease (exophthalmic goitre) can be pieced together and how glad this makes the writer that he married the other sister. Lawrence was also a good and careful clinician and with him Ford Madox Ford springs to mind, extending the scale in *Last Post* by laying down the ageing Tietjens after a stroke which has left him with understanding but no speech, an ingenious solution to the problem of providing a critical eye without the active liability of belonging to a partaking character.

II

More modern novelists have transgressed this technical and unobtrusive use of malady and it is the dangers of the present licence which need review. Requiring that all deal with people, novels otherwise whittle down into essays of either thought, word or deed, and on each of these primary elements the influence of sickness can now be seen.

Novels of thought set out to illuminate a human aspect or situation and it is remarkable to realise that what is agreed or accepted in the sphere of invalid morality has arrived in our society through the gates of fiction or drama: for there are simply no other moral rules of sickness available. The Christian faith lays down no law on the matter but blows with the vogue, breezy and muscular fifty years ago, subconscious and psychosomatic today; doctors themselves have always funked the issue and when they get moral they turn to hieratics (Hippocrates), Christianity (Thomas Browne) or animal urge (the modern psycho-social-behaviourists). A code of invalid conduct is springing up from the tall pot of national administration but it is a grasping, material code, strengthening the courage perhaps but not the will to get well. So, rightly or wrongly, fiction has moulded our attitude to illness more than anything else over the last hundred years. Pictorial art began to enter the field as a rival but luckily desisted after realising it could only end in pathos while fiction and drama with their slower evolvement and less instantaneous use of contrast have fattened, or fastened, nicely on the problem.

Fastening is more apt than fattening but not wholly so because novels while getting thinner have not always shown more grip on the invalid situation. To this there are exceptions and, using the world of the T.B. sanatorium as a constant, it is profitable to judge Thomas Mann's *The Magic Mountain* against two modern novels on the same theme, *The Rack* (A. E. Ellis) and *The Vodi* (John Braine).

The Magic Mountain was published in 1924, although it refers to events up to 1914; it has therefore a pointed reference to the sick society of Europe as well as the sick individuals within the cover. As a document of illness it is unsurpassed and it should be compulsory reading for all medical students in the West, all officials, voluntary or paid, in the Health Service, and indeed a film of it should be made for everyone else in 'British Health' who cannot ride its 700 pages. Almost every aspect of the invalid problem is studied, with the appropriate emphasis that each has a different meaning for the hale spectator (reader), the professional attendant, and the patient. For clarity, the tradition of European thought is sharply divided by Mann through the use of two bitter opponents: first, Settenbrini, Italian, freemason, liberal, humanist and classic, with the key words of Renaissance, Risorgimento, reason, enlightenment, democracy (nationalism), and progress; and against him Naphta, Pauline, Jew, Jesuit, proselyte, fanatic, and scholastic, with the key words of Spirit, Faith and Passion.

Invalid morality is only one of the themes this book approaches but it is a recurring motif throughout and can be traced as follows. The first reference comes from the young hero, Hans Castorp, who has found himself in the sanatorium more or less by accident. He expresses amazement that his fellow guests, or patients, can be stupid as well as ill. This is something he cannot understand: surely the process of being ill is a refinement to the individual. Settenbrini explains that there is no logical reason why illness should bring refinement or intelligence, except the relic of old superstition that infirmity carries a pass to heaven and well-being comes from the devil. This point is extraordinarily important and Mann is wise to clarify it at the outset; of course the superstition remains as it was and both the later writers, Ellis and Braine, and Gide before them, fall cellar-steps through the hatch.

To return to *The Magic Mountain;* Settenbrini is allowed full control for the first half of the book while the hero becomes an accepted patient and falls silently in love with another inmate. He listens to an analyst's lecture, disease is love transformed; he wonders if physicians can still be physicians if they are themselves ill, if their spiritual mastery can be retained; and he begins to realise that disease makes men more physical and leaves them with nothing but body: but these are sidelines to the Settenbrini doctrine. Hans is confined to bed when the humanist arrives and characteristically floods the room with electric light. He chides Hans and hints that he has been fooled by the medical management. Hans tackles the progressive; do you believe in science, are there spots on your own x-ray plate, are you really ill yourself? At this Settenbrini stays silent, allowing Hans to air his anxiety on the materialism of Hamburg, his native city, on his own weakness to this materialism, and his own early introduction to death; he is an orphan. Settenbrini is now released again, death must not be divorced from life in any way; severed from life death becomes a spectre, death must have no separate reverence, nor must illness, as he had previously explained to his pupil.

Hans takes his time to accept this and keeps making allowances for his fellow patients, whose behaviour is not gilded in the print. Settenbrini tells him not to listen to them; they have no right to imagine themselves entitled to pity. But they are ill, says Hans. Disease is depravity, he is told, but he tries his best to avoid this conclusion: surely illness may be a consequence of depravity, or an excuse for depravity, but depravity itself, never. Settenbrini tells him again not to defend illness, but Hans parries that the analyst too has told him that disease is a secondary phenomenon. Settenbrini scoffs, how pure is that kind of idealism, and goes on to divide psychoanalysis itself, good as an instrument of enlightenment or destructor of conviction but bad, very bad as it stands in the way of will and action. The Italian is largely having his own way but keeps floundering into this dilemma of modern medicine: what is good and what is bad about it, why has progress to carry its own degeneration? He can only be horrified by his attitude to his own illness, and to its effect on him, that he can be prevented by his physical or animal nature from indulging in services to reason. This is his horrible dichotomy, that he has to honour the body as the vehicle of beauty, freedom, joy and desire, yet despise it as representing the inescapable principle of disease and death. Ultimately Hans accepts most of this and the book's half-way is marked by his first bold conversation with the beloved, a flighty Russian. Her contribution to this true European is the claim that it is her illness which gives her liberty. Unshaken, Hans makes his declaration on the purest Settenbrini principles; body, love and death are one.

Naphta now appears, well heeled and provided by his Order, redolent, his coat of mink lining contrasting with Settenbrini's mangy specimen. They fall on each other, arguing, scratching, biting, and finally fighting a ridiculous duel when Naphta's fanaticism slips the bond of sanity. Legitimately enough he shoots himself once Settenbrini has aimed and fired at the sky. So far as this is a solution, it means presumably that medievalism is dissolved but enlightenment as aerial as ever.

And indeed, the forty odd years since *The Magic Mountain* have shown that the rationalist's victory was pretty thin, and that his scorn for the reverence of illness has not been supported, as he hoped it would, by his admiration of health (though ill himself) nor by his incorporation of death into his conception of life. Nor has he had any more luck with the idea that sympathy for the sick from the fit is an impossible transference, because the sick at once adjust themselves to their state and do not feel a corresponding jealousy for the healthy. Western development on this matter seems to have identified the healthy and sick with a mutual reverence for each other and any idea of death has been excluded from either side; in fact the kindest thing which has appeared about death during these last forty years is the recognition that when it approaches by age or illness it brings its own calm which the victim enjoys but his relations, attendants, and his earlier self are quite incapable of recognising.

And it is on these lines of thought that the second pair of books must be judged because in each case the hero is established solely on the fact of his phthisical crisis. Settenbrini would have gustily condemned this at the outset as being invalid, and the feature does veer to the religiosity of Naphta who was prepared to see a good in illness, a good in torture, and a good in corporal or capital punishment, each and all condemned by Settenbrini. The modern attitude is a flagrant compromise, with all sides trying to patch up with the rest, and it is difficult to find the fallacy, although it is obvious that in conditions of ethical parity between the sick and well it is the latter who will suffer, however much the first may gain. Moreover, this modern compromise is a firm and productive union: Settenbrini welcomed medical progress although professing to despise illness, ultimately hoping to eradicate it, while Naphta called medical progress bourgeois materialism, all very well but opposed to Faith and Spirit; it is the wedding of these two views, the worship of medical progress and the retention of Faith and Spirit, together and in the same breath, that has produced the palpable result before us, that medical progress has created more illness, not less.

In such a balanced atmosphere it is not surprising that Braine and Ellis have produced a very similar hero in the throes of tuberculosis. True to the clinical doctrine that well or ill the patient has this for life, neither book reaches a firm conclusion, each hero being left with his worst disease but deprived of his best girl. Both books are medically accurate but Ellis spends more time on the technical side, to the finick of being documentary, apart from the careless spelling. By inflicting more pain on his hero in this way he sets out to produce more emotion and succeeds in doing so. Braine's hero leaves his bed for long spells to hobnob with some gipsy Vodi (Aunt Nelly and Co.) or to go on nostalgic Sergeants' Mess outings to the next pubs.

Both books survive or die on whether the crisis of illness is a fair plank for a fictional hero, and if this is accepted then the next stage must also be accepted, that of the real-life invalid cashing in on his illness, by writing it up. It is worth while repeating that Settenbrini would have condemned both ventures utterly and to add that Naphta must have accepted them. Does this mean that Naphta should have won the duel? But not by Settenbrini committing suicide?

III

Clinical infiltration into the novel of words is a less universal problem but interesting in the annals of letters. Word-spinners must find metaphor and the number of sources is not infinite. Most are obvious and already overplayed, any of the arts, for example, and most of the activities, preferably stirring and dangerous. Novelists are using technical metaphor more and more, including medical feature and colour. The modern monarch of word and phrase, Joyce, reveals a memory full of medical student talk, particularly the lurid Burke and Hare variety. Two typical examples concern Bishop Arius and judicial hanging. The first is ready-made for Joyce, a fellow heretic of lengthy argument, and any account of Arius gives the manner of his death which occurred in the private part of a public place from fulminating rectal haemorrhage, with 'clotted buttocks', which is Joyce's finis to the heresy. The medical effect of hanging was even more attractive, and Joyce grabbed the priapism, with its hideous symbolism; for biologically the male sex act must be deemed akin to if not accompanied by death, as it is in some forms of life, and here was a man-made parody of the fact.

This comparison between overdrawing a medical event and using a medical event to overdraw provides a natural bridge to the next genus, the novel of deed. Medical incident has long been of the highest use in narrative and it is a pity that rules for its fair employment have never been laid down. Overcharging is again the common crime and as Braine's *Vodi* has been mentioned on a big issue perhaps it is excusable to quote a detail. His hero is on the crest of his easy wallowing days, just engaged to a suitable fast girl; he has to be deflated and his author chooses that night to pronounce the malignant doom of his mother: that seems overcharged. Inaccuracy is also reprehensible; as a rule the masters are careful but here is a blatant blunder of 1960, in a very high place: 'she [the wounded woman] would be drinking blood through the eye of a silver needle. Drop by drop it would be passing into the median vein, heart beat by heart beat.' This is a rich transfusion: 'drinking blood', hardly, but excusable on a poet's licence; 'the eye of a silver needle', the eye of a needle is never lengthwise, nor can a needle be made of silver, but admittedly it may be silver in appearance; the eye of this silver needle then means the lumen (channel) of either a steel needle or a silver cannula. 'Heart beat by heart beat', whose heart? Some pump is clearly envisaged, but even arterial transfusion has a pump of its own, and so did the old direct transfusion. 'Drop by drop it would be passing into the median vein', this much is accurate.

The most virile novel of deed is still criminal and it is obvious how much this type of tale owes to medicine, all the way from its professional prototypes, Doyle, Holmes and Watson, to its advanced propounders of toxicology, traumatology, and forensic problems. Less obvious is the trick perfected by one of its outstanding performers, Simenon, who can be called the modern master of minor illness. In the first place Simenon appears to be personally conditioned to minor malady. On receiving literary 'annunciation' he makes plans for 'accouchement'. The first person summoned is his doctor, to assure the author that he has no illness upon him which might interfere. Not only is the author examined, but his family and servants too; there must be no colds, sick attacks, influenza, and the like. If there is anything lurking through the house, 'labour' is postponed by tranquillisers: once the work is under way no interference is allowed until it is finished. Not content with encouraging minor malady to emphasise his own situation Simenon uses it freely in his constructed circumstances, as punctuation and heightening. The bond of sympathy between reader and character is at once tightened if they are both capable of the same sensation. It is very effective to drop some criminal on a Western air-mac, and describe not the objects around but the blinding headache he has; we know at once that is just how we should feel ourselves. In the same way the judge who is struck with grippe during the hearing of a murder trial at once 'overhears' the evidence and passes on these overtones; moreover the duration of the grippe laces up the length of the procedure and the case clears with the judge's temperature. There is hardly a Simenon novel without this clinical bracing; it is skilful, masterly, and probably subliminal to most readers.

IV

Apart from Conan Doyle and his First Detective, novelists from the medical profession have not been very much responsible for these invalid introductions to modern fiction. When they do write medical novels they tend to write more about their colleagues and other internal professional relations than about the effect of illness or medicine on their patients. Curiously too, Somerset Maugham, who is characteristically footsure at all levels of society and in all parts of the globe, can falter at the bedside. It seems that experience as a patient or spectator is more productive to a novelist than any training as a doctor, and this supports the earlier claim that this infiltration of sickness into European fiction was not medical propaganda but dated from Flaubert and was nourished by the fastidious amateurs who went on appearing until the First War. Those gentlemen were as fussy on their health as they were about their lovely hand-made boots, so that whether they were really crocks, like Proust, or not, like Gide, they were bound to be taken up by the influence of illness on the individual. As well as being obsessional on this matter, these practitioners were also men of independent means, at a time when both illness and health were very easy if you were lucky, and appalling if you were not. Now it is a fact that the society which can see the horror of sickness can best see the advantage of health and unfortunately any depression of the former detracts equally from the latter. It is this visible example of a class which cleverly learnt to disregard the distinction between illness and health which has helped to alter our views. Thomas Mann at least faced the dilemma and went some way to solving its morality, even if he avoided its economy by restricting his remarks to people who could afford to be ill, but Gide gybed the sail, and this is what he said in his Journal: 'I have never met one of those who boast of never having been ill who was not in some way or other a bit stupid; like those who have never travelled; and I remember P. very prettily called illnesses the poor man's travels.'

This depressing opinion does not even level the well with the ill but loads sickness to defeat health. Obviously that is wrong, and society will soon become unworkable if invalids transcend sympathy and score heroics from their sick state.

DISEASE IN NINETEENTH-CENTURY LITERATURE

Audrey G. Peterson

SOURCE: "Brain Fever in Nineteenth-Century Literature: Fact and Fiction," in *Victorian Studies*, Vol. XIX, No. 4, June, 1976, pp. 445-64.

[*In the following essay, Peterson elucidates the medical disorder described in the nineteenth century as "brain fever" and examines its representations in works of fiction during this period.*]

When Heathcliff returned to Wuthering Heights Catherine Linton was subjected to such severe emotional stress that she developed a "brain fever" which ultimately contributed to her death. When Emma Bovary learned that her lover Rodolphe had abandoned her, she fell into "une fièvre cérébrale" and was unable to leave her bed for nearly six weeks. When Lucy Feverel was prohibited from seeing Richard as he lay wounded, her mind gave way and she died five days later of "cerebral fever." These are but three of the many victims of this curious disease, which reached the height of its vogue in the nineteenth century. "Brain fever" is so rarely encountered today in either medical or popular vocabulary that contemporary readers who note the phrase at all are inclined to wonder whether it was a real disease or merely a fictional one created by novelists to suit the exigencies of plot or character. If a physician today is asked what is meant by "brain fever," he is likely to look puzzled for a moment and then say that it must refer to some form of encephalitis or meningitis, but a study of the medical treatises of the period shows that in the nineteenth century the disease was very real indeed in the minds of both doctors and patients and thus in the minds of fiction writers as well.

I

The term brain fever grew out of the classical term "phrensy," usually defined as inflammation of the brain. In the eighteenth century fevers were often classified according to the recurrence of symptoms as intermittent, remittent, and continued, or according to various pathological theories as putrid, malignant, or nervous. The word "fever" itself usually denoted a disease, not merely an elevation of body temperature. Often a particular organ of the body was regarded as the "seat" of a given disease or group of diseases. Thus the medical dictionary of Robert James, the friend of Dr. Johnson, notes under the heading PHRENITIS that "there is no Inflammation, or particular Fever, of so great importance in Medicine, as that which is lodged in the Brain, the noblest of all the Parts." James then separates inflammation of the brain from madness, stating that although, "according to the ancients, a Phrenitis may degenerate into a Mania, there is yet a great difference between them; for in a Phrenitis there is always a Fever, accompanied with a quick, hard, and small Pulse. There is also a delirium. . . . But a Mania is a Chronical Disorder without an acute Fever."

There were many attempts to trace the pathology of inflammation and fever. John Huxham's important treatise on fever in 1750 suggests that "the mere simple accelerated Motion of the Blood" will produce an "Inflammatory Fever." The classification then depends upon the affected organ: "If the Inflammation seizes the Lungs, a Peripneumony; if the Pleura, a Pleurisy; if the Brain, or its Membranes, a Phrensy is generated." Many theorists subdivided Phrensy into cases in which inflammation affected only the membranes of the brain and those which affected the "substance" of the brain. Postmortem evidence sometimes confirmed this distinction, although in other cases both membranes and "substance" were affected. For this reason, William Cullen, the most influential figure of the Edinburgh school, denied the separation. "Nosologists," he wrote, "have thought, that the two cases might be distinguished by different symptoms, and therefore by different appellations; but we do not find this confirmed by observation and dissection; and therefore shall treat of both cases under the title of Phrensy, or Phrenitis."

Whatever the differences in classification, however, a disease known as inflammation of the brain was a recognized medical entity at the close of the eighteenth century, a disease which became more familiarly known as "brain fever." There was no dramatic introduction of the term as a new concept; medical writers simply began using "brain fever" as an informal synonym which gradually replaced the older term "phrensy." For example, in a treatise appearing about 1807, Thomas Beddoes, while tracing the nosology of fevers, refers to brain fever without further definition. A typical classification appears in John Mason Good's widely used textbook of medicine. Under the heading "EMPRESMA CEPHALITIS," defined as Inflammation of the Brain, we find "Meningica. Phrensy. Brain-fever." The terms are intended to be synonymous, but their order indicates degrees of formality, from the formal Latin *meningica* to the familiar or common term "brain fever."

What, then, were the symptoms of brain fever? In 1781 Cullen gave the classic description of "Phrensy, or Phrenitis" as "an acute pyrexia, a violent headache, a redness of the face and eyes, an impatience of light or noise, a constant watching, and a delirium impetuous and furious". This description, with some additions and variations, remained essentially constant throughout the nineteenth century until the disease passed out of official recognition. As late as 1858 James Copland identifies the symptoms of "Brain Fever" as "acute pain in the head, with intolerance of light and sound; watchfulness, delirium; flushed countenance, and redness of the conjunctiva, or a heavy suffused state of the eyes; quick pulse; frequently spasmodic twitchings or convulsions, passing into somnolency, coma, and complete relaxation of the limbs." Sometimes cases of brain fever developed gradually, but more often the attack was described as coming on abruptly, a feature which is especially significant for the writers of fiction. Symptoms often include "restlessness or moaning" and in severe cases the patient rolls the head from side to side and engages in "noisy vociferation or screaming," while in other cases he is quiet or even somnolent. Mental confusion is a universal symptom, accompanied at times by erratic behavior, forgetfulness, and irritability.

Although there is no precise present-day equivalent for brain fever, many of the symptoms and the post-mortem evidence were consistent with some forms of meningitis or encephalitis. However, when we turn from the symptoms to the assigned causes of the disease, we see the marked differences between earlier and current medical theory. Without the knowledge that bacteria could produce disease, earlier physicians were at a disadvantage. However, as the medical historian Lester King points out, doctors in earlier periods often made many keen observations despite the differences in available techniques. It had always been observed that some fevers were epidemic in character, and many theories developed to account for the spread of disease. King cites Cullen's edition of 1786 as representative of the later eighteenth-century belief that fevers arose from matter floating in the atmosphere. "These effluvia were of two sorts, the *contagions* arising from human bodies suffering from a particular disease and capable of exciting the disease in some other person; and *miasmata,* stemming from marshes and moist ground, that is, from sources other than human." Various forms of this theory prevailed into the latter part of the nineteenth century until negated by advances in microbiology.

Apart from contagion, the causes for all fevers presented an interesting mixture of physical and emotional factors. Alexander Tweedie's discussion of the topic in 1833 is characteristic of the period. Among the causes of fever he cites famine, fatigue, and those events which give "a severe shock to the nervous system. The various kinds of mental emotion—fear, anxiety, disappointments, long continued watching on a sick bed, intense study, want of sleep—may individually be ranked among the predisposing causes of fever." Less is known, he says, of the "exciting" (more immediate) causes of fever, but it is certain that "any undue mental fatigue . . . powerfully aids the operation of the exciting causes of fever," and in such cases "the violence of the disease falls on the brain and nervous system, producing what is emphatically termed *brain fever.*"

Similar causes are cited by Bouillaud, the physician who was the prototype for Blazac's Dr. Bianchon. In his treatise on inflammation of the brain, which he calls "l'encéphalite," Bouillaud gives the case histories of many victims of the disease. Some developed symptoms following physical injury or illness, but in others the fever arose from emotional causes. One had experienced "des chagrins violents et prolongés"; another could not speak well, but he was able to say that his illness developed following "une affection morale triste"; yet another (like Emma Bovary) had received a letter bringing bad news. In his summary of "principal causes" Bouillaud includes "les travaux immodérés de l'esprit."

Such information appeared not only in the medical texts and treatises of the period but also in more popular works of wide circulation among the literate classes. Almost every middle-class home would be likely to contain some book of medical reference, such as William Buchan's *Domestic Medicine,* which first appeared in 1769 and went through many editions well into the nineteenth century, not only in Great Britain but in America and on the Continent as well. Among the general causes of disease, the work lists "sedentary occupations," among which the most dangerous is that of study. In fact, says Buchan, "Intense thought is so destructive to health that few instances can be produced of studious persons who are strong and healthy." Later on, speaking specifically of inflammation of the brain, Buchan notes that "the passionate, the studious, and those whose nervous system is weak, are very liable to it."

It is clear enough, then, that brain fever was not a fictional invention, but that both physicians and laymen believed that emotional shock or excessive intellectual activity could produce a severe and prolonged fever. In the examples with which we began, each of the heroines—Catherine Linton, Emma Bovary, and Lucy Feveral—fell ill directly following a severe emotional shock. The modern physician attending these ladies might well anticipate some sort of temporary emotional trauma, but he would not expect his patient to develop, say, a case of typhoid fever. Yet the nineteenth-century physician, following the pathological theories of his day, could confidently diagnose brain fever in such cases.

The disease was particularly attractive to writers of fiction because of its dramatic onset and long duration.

Although most fictional accounts follow the medical descriptions closely, some general differences in the two are evident. For example, the disease is more often fatal in medicine than in fiction. Some literary victims die but most survive and continue to function in the narrative. Also, the method of treating the disease in fictional descriptions does not always follow medical practice but is often suitably vague. The vision of those impeccably dressed ladies who sit by the bedside and allow no one else to assist in nursing the loved one does not correspond with the usual treatment, consisting of copious bleedings, purges, and emetics. Such evasions are understandable, however, given the limitations imposed by public taste upon even the most realistic of nineteenth-century novelists. Tuberculosis was similarly romanticized, until the graceful fading away of all those ladies of the camellias was once and for all demolished by Tolstoy's description of the death of Nikolay in *Anna Karenina.* Even Flaubert, whose description of Emma's death from poisoning at the end of the novel is grim enough, does not give details of her medical treatment during her attack of brain fever.

II

I should like to turn now to a more detailed examination of some ways in which nineteenth-century authors used this interesting disease. By far the most common cases in literature are those which arise as a result of emotional shock. In *Wuthering Heights* (1847) the first Catherine might have developed any sort of disease if Emily Brontë had merely wanted her heroine to fall ill at that point in the novel. But brain fever is particularly appropriate because it reveals the depth of Catherine's passionate attachment for Heathcliff. The attack comes on immediately after Edgar Linton tries to force her to make a choice:

> "Will you give up Heathcliff hereafter, or will you give up me? It is impossible for you to be *my* friend and *his* at the same time; and I absolutely *require* to know which you choose."
>
> "I require to be let alone!" exclaimed Catherine, furiously. "I demand it! Don't you see I can scarcely stand?"

She dashes her head against the arm of the sofa, gnashing her teeth, and then (in Nelly Dean's words) "stretched herself out stiff, and turned up her eyes, while her cheeks, at once blanched and livid, assumed the aspect of death." Even though she has blood on her lips, and Edgar is alarmed, Nelly insists scornfully that Catherine is merely in one of her "senseless, wicked rages." Catherine then locks herself in her room, and it is not until she emerges on the third day, pale and wasted and with wandering mind, that Nelly is forced to recognize that she is seriously ill. The doctor at first spoke "hopefully" but to Nelly "he signified the threatening danger was not so much death, as permanent alienation of intellect" and warned that she must be in an atmosphere of "perfect and constant tranquility." For two months Catherine "encountered and conquered the worst shock of what was denominated a brain fever," precipitated by the violence of her emotions. The precise cause of Catherine's death is not clear. She had made a partial recovery from her illness before the climactic scene of her final meeting with Heathcliff. The circumstances imply that the premature birth of the child is brought on by the violent emotion of that meeting. Evidently her weakness from the attack of brain fever was a contributing rather than a direct cause of her death.

In the case of *Madame Bovary* (1856), Flaubert derives some of his most celebrated ironies from the whole episode of Emma's attack of brain fever. When the letter from Rodolphe breaking off their affair arrives in a basket of apricots, Emma's wild distress is counterpointed against Charles's impervious innocence in the incomparable scene at the dinner table:

> Charles, without noticing his wife's colour, had [the apricots] brought to him, took one, and bit into it.
>
> "Ah, perfect!" said he; "just taste!"
>
> And he handed her the basket, which she put away from her gently.
>
> "Do just smell! What an odour!" he remarked, passing it under her nose several times.
>
> "I am choking," she cried, leaping up. But by an effort of will the spasm passed. . . .

But when she sees Rodolphe's blue tilbury pass through the square, "Emma uttered a cry and fell back rigid to the ground." At her bedside, the theme of the apricots is taken up again by Homais, who embarks upon one of his pompous disquisitions, and now it is Charles who is distressed and Homais who is blithely unobservant. In reply to his question, Charles tells him that she had been taken ill suddenly while eating some apricots, and Homais's first comments reflect the miasmatic theory of disease: "'Extraordinary!' continued the chemist. `But it might be that the apricots had brought on the syncope. Some natures are so sensitive to certain smells; and it would even be a very fine question to study both in its pathological and physiological relations. The priests know the importance of it, they who have introduced aromatics into all their ceremonies.'" The significance of the apricots to Emma is thus ironically underscored by both Charles and Homais.

The severity of her illness is finally apparent when she becomes delirious, and they recognize that a "brain-fever has set in" ("une fièvre cérébrale s'était déclarée"). Although Charles is himself a doctor, he feels that the case is too serious for his own skills and calls in two eminent physicians for consultation. The duration of the illness is specified—"For forty-three days Charles did not leave her." After the first delirium, Emma's symptoms are less violent than those of many sufferers from the disease. In fact, Charles was most alarmed by "Emma's prostration, for she did not speak, did not listen, did not even seem to suffer, as if her body and soul were both resting together after all their troubles." Her condition resembles that described by Bouillaud in his second stage of "l'encéphalite," in which the delirium is followed by a period of "assoupissement." (Bouillaud's treatise appeared in 1825 and would have been a recent text at the time Charles Bovary was studying medicine in the early 1830s.) The final irony which Flaubert derives from Emma's attack of brain fever arises from Charles's slavish devotion during the long course of her illness and his entire ignorance of the real cause of that illness.

Both Catherine Linton and Emma Bovary were married women who were involved either emotionally or physically with another man. In the case of Lucy Feverel, Meredith's purpose is to present a character whose purity of mind and heart are exalted to the highest degree of perfection in order to point up the hypocrisy of Sir Austin's System. The tone of high comedy which informs the novel as a whole is abruptly swept away in the swift and tragic conclusion. Whatever one may think of the appropriateness of the tragic ending, there can be little doubt that brain fever is the appropriate vehicle for Lucy's death, for it is Sir Austin who is most to be punished and who must be made to realize that scientific systems cannot prevail against the human heart. Lady Blandish, whose letter to Austin Wentworth comprises the final chapter of the novel, describes the scene at the French inn where Richard was taken after the duel:

> The doctors had not allowed his poor Lucy to go near him. She sat outside his door, and none of us dared disturb her. That was a sight for Science. His father, and myself, and Mrs. Berry, were the only ones permitted to wait on him, and whenever we came out, there she sat, not speaking a word —for she had been told it would endanger his life—but she looked such awful eagerness. She had the sort of eye I fancy mad persons have. I was sure her reason was going. We did everything we could think of to comfort her. . . . Of course there was no getting her to eat. What do you suppose *his* alarm was fixed on? He absolutely said to me—but I have not patience to repeat his words. He thought her to blame for not *commanding* herself for the sake of her maternal duties. He had absolutely an idea of insisting that she should make an effort to suckle the child. I shall love that Mrs. Berry to the end of my days. I really believe she has *twice* the sense of any of us—Science and all. She asked him plainly if he wished to poison the child, and then he gave way, but with a bad grace.

When "Science" at last relents, it is too late.

> When I told her she might go in with me to see her dear husband, her features did not change. M. Desprès, who held her pulse at the time, told me, in a whisper, it was cerebral fever—brain fever—coming on. We have talked of her since. I noticed that though she did not seem to understand me, her bosom heaved, and she appeared to be trying to repress it. . . . Had she seen her husband a day or two before but no! there was a new *System* to interdict that! Or had she not so violently controlled her nature as she did, I believe she might have been saved.

When the delirium takes over, Lucy is no longer conscious of her actions and exhibits the severest symptoms of brain fever. Lady Blandish reports that "her cries at one time were dreadfully loud. She screamed that she was 'drowning in fire,' and her husband would not come to her to save her." Lucy "died five days after she had been removed. The shock had utterly deranged her." No disease could be more perfectly suited to Meredith's purpose than brain fever, for Sir Austin is made to suffer the knowledge that the cumulative effect of his System has been the cause of Lucy's death. Even worse, he must suffer the knowledge of what his System has done to Richard, for Lady Blandish declares that although "he has saved his son's body, he has given the death-blow to his heart. Richard will never be what he promised."

In *Great Expectations* (1860) Pip suffers from a prolonged illness which is closely related to brain fever, although Dickens does not specifically designate it as such. After the death of Magwitch, Pip's emotional exhaustion overcomes his efforts to stave off the fever. He lies "on the sofa, or on the floor—anywhere," with "a heavy head and aching limbs, and no purpose, and no power." Then follows a long period of delirium in which he often loses his reason and sees phantasmagoric creatures. Dickens uses the device of the illness to reveal the final turning point in Pip's awareness of his own past folly and of the moral goodness of Joe Gargery, who comes to London to nurse him. In a brilliant passage of characteristic rhetoric, Dickens describes Pip's emergence from delirium:

> After I had turned the worst point of my illness, I began to notice that while all its other features changed, this one consistent feature did not change. Whoever came about me, still settled down into Joe. I opened my eyes in the night, and I saw in the great chair at the bedside, Joe. I opened my eyes in the day, and, sitting on the window-seat, smoking his pipe in the shaded open window, I still saw Joe. I asked for cooling drink, and the dear hand that gave it me was Joe's. I sank back on my pillow after drinking, and the face that looked so hopefully and tenderly upon me was the face of Joe.
>
> At last, one day, I took courage, and said, "*Is* it Joe?"
>
> And the dear old home-voice answered, "Which it air, old chap."
>
> "Oh Joe, you break my heart! Look angry at me, Joe. Strike me, Joe. Tell me of my ingratitude. Don't be so good to me!"
>
> For, Joe had actually laid his head down on the

> pillow at my side, and put his arm round my neck, in his joy that I knew him.
>
> "Which, dear old Pip, old chap," said Joe, "you and me was ever friends. And when you're well enough to go out for a ride—what larks!"

Joe's faithful devotion during Pip's illness signals the final stage of the bildungsroman: Pip has achieved maturity.

The foregoing are but a few examples of countless cases in fiction of brain fever brought on by emotional causes. But emotions (or "the passions," in earlier terminology) were not the only recognized cause for the disease. Medical writers, as noted above, consistently warned against excessive study or over-use of the mind as a dangerous prelude to brain fever. Women, as the weaker sex, were considered particularly liable to this malady, a popular notion which could not have been helpful to such later nineteenth-century movements as that of education for women. Sophia De Morgan, for example, who had been active in founding the first Ladies College in the University of London, eventually "became doubtful about the wisdom of higher education for girls—hard work and examinations might bring on attacks of brain fever."

An interesting case of an American young lady who recklessly failed to limit her mental activities is reported by Mary Gove Nichols, a practitioner of the popular Water-Cure treatment:

> Miss———, aged 24 years. I first saw this young lady on the 24th of June, 1848. She was then entirely delirious from brain fever; her whole system seemed on fire, particularly the brain. Her employment was that of musical and mathematical teacher, and she had made great and long continued exertions in both departments, and had acquired a high reputation. . . . She was very energetic and persevering [and] these two excellent qualities had well nigh wrought her death.

The treatment, consisting of wrapping the patient in a wet sheet and of immersions in cold and hot baths, was at least more humane than the rigorous blood-lettings and purges of the traditional school, but we may wonder if its effectiveness could match the claims of the author that she "has treated lung, typhus, scarlet, ship, and brain fever, and has never lost a patient."

Among literary examples of the effects of the overtaxed mind, none is perhaps more tragic than the case which forms the central theme of Conrad Ferdinand Meyer's novella, *Das Leiden eines Knaben* (1883). Julien Boufflers, the son of a marshall in the court of Louis XIV, is a boy of fine and gentle character but of limited mental ability. Placed in a Jesuit school, he is at first treated with great consideration by the fathers; but when the Marshall, through a political incident, becomes their enemy, the boy is no longer favored and suffers from mental cruelty:

> A subtly poisonous atmosphere of creeping revenge filled the rooms of the college. Not only all friendliness but every just consideration for Julien had stopped. The child suffered. Every day and every hour he felt humiliated, not through open censure, least of all through scolding words, which are not used by the fathers, but subtly and impersonally, for they no longer supported the deficiency of the fair-headed boy in a friendly way, but exposed his mental inadequacy to shame after refusing him help. And now the child, goaded by a desperate ambition, began to lengthen his vigils, to shorten his sleep brutally, to torture his brain, to undermine his health.

Ultimately, after an incident of undeserved physical chastisement, Julien developed *"einer Gehirnentzündung"* (literally "inflammation of the brain") which ended in his death. Fagon, who narrates the story, is himself a physician and was present at the boy's deathbed, thus lending credibility to the accuracy of the medical diagnosis. When the boy's father asks if Julien will live, Fagon replies simply: "No. His brain is exhausted ["Sein Gehirn ist erschöpft"]. The boy has overworked himself."

In his introduction to the novella, Harry Steinhauer states that "*The Sufferings of a Boy,* written in 1883, anticipates modern analytical psychology with its profound understanding of the retarded boy who is crushed by his environment and an overdemanding father." In one sense this is true, for Meyer traces with delicate artistry the anguish of the sensitive boy in an unpropitious environment. But I believe that we must not overlook the very real belief of the nineteenth century that excessive strain upon the mind could produce a violent fever of the brain. When Meyer speaks of Julien "undermining his health" by "torturing his brain," and when the physician-narrator declares that the boy cannot live because "his brain is exhausted," these are likely to be more literal statements of "fact" than most post-Freudian readers realize.

Dostoyevsky, most noted of all novelists for anticipating Freudian theory, gives "brain fever" to a number of characters throughout his novels. The wider implications of these cases in relation to psychological theory would constitute a separate topic outside the scope of this essay. For present purposes I should like to cite the case of Ivan in *The Brothers Karamazov* (1880), whose illness arises chiefly from intense mental preoccupation. (Other victims in Dostoyevsky's novels include Raskolnikov's mother in *Crime and Punishment,* whose fatal illness arises from worry over her son, and Nikolay Stavrogin in *The Possessed,* whose eccentric behavior is "explained" by the doctor's declaration that he has brain fever.) The subject of "The Grand Inquisitor" so obsesses Ivan that later in the novel his hallucinations take the form of the renowned visit from the devil with their bitter debate about the nature of morality. The reader is told at the beginning of the chapter that Ivan "was at that moment on the verge of an attack of brain fever." Certainly emotional causes also add their weight, for he has just heard Smerdyakov's confession of guilt and is desperately anxious to save Dmitri. He tries by an effort of will to delay the illness which he feels is coming on, for "he loathed the thought of being ill at that critical time, when he needed to have all his faculties to say what he had to say boldly. . . ." But of course the disease prevails, and he is so incoherent in the courtroom that at last Alyosha leaps up and cries out: "He is ill. Don't believe him: he has brain fever." A recent reference to Ivan's illness stresses the mental causation. Ivan "is led, through a stubborn pride of intellect, into a revolt against God; his final breakdown, due to a medically vague 'brain fever,' is dramatically appropriate." The analysis of Ivan's intellectual trauma is accurate enough, but I believe, as I have shown, that brain fever was less "medically vague" at that period than twentieth-century readers recognize.

In the occurrences of brain fever in fiction so far examined, the disease has been closely integrated in each case with the character who is its victim. Whether the cause was emotional or intellectual, the illness added in some way to the reader's comprehension of the character. In some cases, however, brain fever functions more simply as a device of plot rather than of character. In Elizabeth Gaskell's *Ruth* (1853), for example, Mr. Bellingham develops brain fever at a point in the novel when his illicit affair with Ruth needs to be terminated. It is true that he has been somewhat moody and depressed, but it is Ruth who is deeply disturbed by the irregularity of their situation and who would therefore be a more likely victim of the disease. Mr. Bellingham's illness comes on after nothing more distressing than a game of cards with Ruth at the inn in Wales where the pair are stopping:

> ". . . Do you know, little goose," [says Bellingham,] your blunders have made me laugh myself into one of the worst headaches I have had for years."
>
> He threw himself on the sofa, and in an instant she was by his side.
>
> "Let me put my cool hands on your forehead," she begged; "that used to do mamma good."
>
> He lay still, his face away from the light, and not speaking. Presently he fell asleep.

His symptoms follow a familiar course: he turns his face "away from the light"; his "breathing became quick and oppressed"; he "seemed stupefied and shivery"; he "moaned and tossed, but never spoke sensibly." The doctor arrives, but when Ruth questions him "he only shook his head and looked grave." The verdict has the distinction of being pronounced in Welsh, as the doctor takes the landlady aside out of Ruth's hearing:

> "I am afraid this is a bad case," said Mr. Jones to Mrs. Morgan in Welsh. "A brain-fever has evidently set in."
>
> "Poor young gentleman! poor young man! He looked the very picture of health!"
>
> "That very appearance of robustness will, in all probability, make his disorder more violent. However, we must hope for the best, Mrs. Morgan."

Mr. Bellingham is not only handicapped by his former good health; he may also be in greater danger because of his superior birth. For it was commonly believed that when "brain fever . . . attacks persons in the upper classes of society . . . the delirium and impairment of the mental faculties are more constant, earlier in their development, and more marked."

Ruth insists upon nursing the patient and assures the doctor that she can put on leeches or follow any instructions he wishes to give her. But the arrival of Mrs. Bellingham to nurse her son drives Ruth from the sick room. The plot is then served by Mrs. Bellingham's haughty refusal to see Ruth as anything but a despicable and profligate girl. She "did not understand Ruth. She did not imagine the faithful trustfulness of her heart." As soon as her son is able to travel, Mrs. Bellingham sweeps him away from this baleful influence, and Ruth is left to make her way alone. The character of Bellingham is never developed in the novel; he is merely a weak and selfish creature who is the instrument of Ruth's downfall. His illness from brain fever tells us nothing of interest about Bellingham himself, but it provides a dramatic means of removing him so that Ruth's subsequent history can be developed. The disease that Bellingham contracts at the end of the novel is an epidemic fever, bearing no relation to brain fever. Ruth again nurses him, but this time, because the fever is infectious, she contracts it herself and dies, having fittingly given her life for his.

The use of brain fever purely as a device of plot can also be seen in two examples from the Sherlock Holmes stories. Conan Doyle, himself a physician, accurately depicts current medical theory and practice. In "The Naval Treaty" young Percy Phelps writes to Watson to enlist the aid of Holmes. Phelps, through the influence of his uncle, Lord Holdhurst, had occupied a position of some responsibility in the Foreign Office and had proved himself in every way reliable and trustworthy until an incident occurred which threatened to destroy his promising career. A highly secret naval treaty with which he had been entrusted mysteriously disappeared from his desk. Young Phelps was so shattered by this event that he fell at once into a brain fever and was taken down to Woking to the home of his fiancée, Anne Harrison. Her brother Joseph was abruptly turned out of his bedroom to make way for the invalid, whose illness is described first in his letter to Watson: "I have only just recovered from nine weeks of brain-fever and am still exceedingly weak. . . . Assure [Mr. Holmes] that if I have not asked his advice sooner it was not because I did not appreciate his talents, but because I have been off my head ever since the blow fell. Now I am clear again, though I dare not think of it too much for fear of a relapse." The solution of the mystery hinges upon both the suddenness of the onset of Phelps's illness and its duration. Holmes learns that during those nine weeks either Phelps's fiancée or a nurse had always been in the room with him. On the first night that he was alone, an attempt had been made to enter the room. Holmes then sets a trap by sending Phelps and Watson to London and himself surprising Joseph Harrison, the culprit, as he enters his own bedroom, vacated at last, by lifting the missing document from a floorboard under the carpet. As Holmes later reconstructs the crime to Phelps, Harrison had happened upon the document on Phelps's desk and taken it on the impulse of the moment. Then:

> "He made his way to Woking by the first train, and, having examined his booty and assured himself that it really was of immense value, he had concealed it in what he thought was a very safe place, with the intention of taking it out again in a day or two, and carrying it to the French embassy, or wherever he thought that a long price was to be had. Then came your sudden return. He, without a moment's warning, was bundled out of his room, and from that time onward there were always at least two of you there to prevent him from regaining his treasure."

Phelps might have suffered from any sort of prolonged illness if only the duration of time was needed, but "brain fever" also provided the abrupt onset following emotional shock which was necessary to make the plot effective.

In "The Copper Beeches" Holmes solves the mystery of the young governess who was hired at an inordinately high salary to compensate for the eccentric requirements of her employers—that she cut her hair short and sit at given times at the window wearing an electric blue dress. This obvious attempt to impersonate someone was revealed as the scheme of the villainous Rucastle, who had imprisoned his daughter Alice in order to obtain use of her money. The governess' appearance at the window was designed to allay the suspicions of Alice's fiancé and to assure him that she was well and happy. The plot turns upon the custom of shaving the heads of victims of brain fever in order to facilitate the use of plasters, leeches, and compresses to the "affected organ." For example, in a work intended for household use, the following treatment is recommended: "Application of leeches to the temples. Putting the feet and legs into warm water, and pouring vinegar and water on the head, previously shaved. Blisters to the head, neck, and legs." John Mason Good's textbook recommends that the "head should be shaven as soon as possible, and kept moist with napkins wrapped round it dipped in cold vinegar, or equal parts of water and the neutralized solution of ammonia." The request to sit in the window wearing a particular dress would probably not have disturbed the governess in the story, but for a Victorian lady to cut her hair was another matter, and it was this which caused Miss Hunter to seek advice from Sherlock Holmes. In the end, the woman servant recounts that all had been well while Mr. Rucastle had control of Alice's money, but when she had met Mr. Fowler at a friend's house, Rucastle's control was threatened:

> "When there was a chance of a husband coming forward, who would ask for all that the law would give him, then her father thought it time to put a stop on it. He wanted her to sign a paper, so that whether she married or not, he could use her money. When she wouldn't do it, he kept on worrying her until she got brain-fever, and for six weeks was at death's door. Then she got better at last, all worn to a shadow, and with her beautiful hair cut off; but that didn't make no change in her young man, and he stuck to her as true as man could be."

Happily the loyal fiancé was not deceived and managed to rescue Alice from her captivity, and the mystery of the shorn hair was solved.

Whether the occurrence of brain fever was used by the author to illuminate a character or merely to further the plot, all of the literary cases so far examined were precipitated in some way by emotional or mental causes. Occasionally, however, literary references to the disease appear to deal with purely physical causes or effects. Such conditions as drug addiction or battle wounds may threaten to give rise to the disease. DeQuincey, in an entry in his *Confessions* dated June 1819, speaks of his desperate efforts to break away from the opium habit, for "death by brain-fever or by lunacy seemed too certainly to besiege the alternate course." In "Lancelot and Elaine," from Tennyson's *Idylls of the King,* Lancelot called his wound "a little hurt" but he was "at times brain-feverous in his heat and agony." In Herman Melville's *The Confidence Man* (1857), it is the physical effects of brain fever which are stressed when the "man with the weed in his hat" makes use of the disease to perpetrate a fraud. Accosting the merchant, Mr. Roberts, he claims an acquaintance of six years back which Mr. Roberts, of course, cannot recall. Persuasively he asks: "Tell me, was it your misfortune to receive any concussion upon the brain about the period I speak of? If so, I will with pleasure supply the void in your memory by more minutely rehearsing the circumstances of our acquaintance." After some hesitation the merchant confesses that, though he had never received any injury of the sort named, yet, about the time in question, he had in fact been taken with a brain fever, losing his mind completely for a considerable interval. He was continuing, when the stranger with much animation exclaimed: "There now, you see, I was not wholly mistaken. That brain fever accounts for it all." Relying upon the merchant's belief in the physical effects of his illness, the confidence man proceeds to trade upon the "forgotten" acquaintance to relieve his victim of his money.

Except for this incident from the Melville novel, most fictional uses of brain fever so far examined have occurred in situations that were serious, even tragic. Occasionally, however, references to brain fever occur in a comic context. In *The Old Curiosity Shop* (1840) the absurd machinations of Dick Swiveller appropriately cause him to fall ill. The "spiritual excitement of the last fortnight" proves too much for him; he is stricken with a raging fever, accompanied by a "distempered brain," and has no recollection for three weeks. Again, as in *Great Expectations,* Dickens does not specifically designate brain fever but the resemblance is close. In Samuel Butler's *The Way of All Flesh* (1803), Dr. Skinner, the headmaster of Roughborough, was formidable enough for the most part but had one amusing weakness:

> His hair when he was a young man was red, but after he had taken his degree he had a brain fever which caused him to have his head shaved; when he reappeared he did so wearing a wig, and one which was a good deal further off red than his own hair had been. He not only had never discarded his wig, but year by year it had edged itself a little more and a little more off red, till by the time he was forty, there was not a trace of red remaining, and his wig was brown.

Perhaps the most memorable comic use of brain fever occurs in Mark Twain's *The Adventures of Huckleberry Finn* (1884) when Huck has stolen the butter and hidden it under his hat. It begins to melt and run down his neck and presently ". . . a streak of butter come a-trickling down my forehead, and Aunt Sally she see it, and turns white as a sheet, and says: 'For the land's sake, what *is* the matter with the child? He's got the brain-fever as shore as you're born, and they're oozing out!'"

Humorous uses of brain fever in fiction are uncommon, however. Even in children's literature of the period, when the disease appears it is in a context which was intended, at least by the author, to be serious. For example, in the second of Martha Finley's *Elsie Dinsmore* series, *Elsie's Holidays at Roselands* (1870), the dramatic crisis occurs when Elsie, an excessively pious little girl, is commanded by her worldly father to read a secular book to him on a Sunday. Torn between the unthinkable alternatives of disobeying papa and acting in conflict with her religious convictions, Elsie worries herself into a brain fever, during which her golden curls are cut off. So remorseful is her father at the near loss of his child that he becomes wholly converted to Elsie's particular brand of pietism and remains so throughout the succeeding two dozen or so volumes of the series.

References to brain fever still appeared after the turn of the century, as laymen continued to use terms which the vanguard of science was discarding. A particularly lurid description of the disease occurs in Frances Hodgson Burnett's *A Little Princess* (1905). Little Sara Crewe's father had died in India believing that his friend Carrisford had betrayed him and caused the failure of their diamond-mine venture. Carrisford himself had at the time mistakenly believed that the mines had failed, but his greatest distress arose from the realization that his friend Crewe had "died thinking I had ruined him—I Tom Carrisford, who played cricket at Eton with him." This seeming betrayal of the old school tie was too much for poor Carrisford, but a friend who was with him at the time urged upon him the extenuating circumstances:

> "You ran away because your brain had given way under the strain of mental torture," he said. "You were half delirious already. If you had not been you would have stayed and fought it out. You were in a hospital, strapped down in bed, raving with brain-fever, two days after you left the place. Remember that."
>
> Carrisford dropped his forehead in his hands.
>
> "Good God! Yes," he said. "I was driven mad with dread and horror. I had not slept for weeks. The night I staggered out of my house all the air seemed full of hideous things mocking and mouthing at me."
>
> "That is explanation enough in itself," said Mr. Carmichael. "How could a man on the verge of brain-fever judge sanely!"

The term "brain fever" has not absolutely disappeared even today but current references are meager. For example, *Black's Medical Dictionary* (1971) lists "BRAIN FEVER" as a "popular name" for various forms of encephalitis or meningitis; *Stedman's Medical Dictionary* (1972) calls "brain f[ever]" an "inexact term for encephalitis of unknown etiology." Such references make it clear that the term is no longer medically viable. In popular parlance the term may still linger, particularly in rural areas or among the elderly. One individual, for example, told me that during his childhood in a Yorkshire village in the 1930s his grandfather warned him not to study too much lest it bring on a brain fever. Another recalls that when he was at school in Cornwall during the Second World War, one of the boys was pronounced by the local doctor to be suffering from a brain fever. Such uses of the term may still exist today, particularly when the speaker intends to use a layman's term, but there is no parallel now in medical texts for the long and serious discussions of the disease in the medical treatises of the nineteenth century.

The modern reader who encounters "brain fever" in fiction is likely to attribute the disease to psychological causes. Certainly both real and fictional persons do sometimes become seriously ill as a result of grief, emotional shock, or even excessive study. What makes the nineteenth-century description of brain fever unique is that it assigns emotional causes to a disease which then follows a prescribed physiological course like that of other recognized diseases. Just as the gradual wasting away of tuberculosis made that disease a popular one for fictional purposes, so the combination of emotional cause and physical effect made brain fever attractive to the novelist, according to the needs of the specific work. However, since the tuberculosis of the nineteenth century is essentially the same disease today, whereas brain fever is no longer a recognized medical entity, it would be easy enough for the modern reader to assume that many features of brain fever were fictional inventions. This, as we have seen, is not the case. When the nineteenth-century physician arrived at the bedside of the patient, shook his head gravely, and said that he feared a brain fever was setting in, he was speaking of a disease which was specifically described in the medical textbooks of his day and which was just as real to him and to his lay contemporaries as measles, smallpox, or consumption. The novelists who used brain fever were following medical descriptions, not inventing them.

Miriam Bailin

SOURCE: "'Varieties of Pain': The Victorian Sickroom and Bronte's Shirley," in *Modern Language Quarterly*, Vol. 48, No. 3, September, 1987, pp. 254-78.

[*In the following essay, Bailin views Charlotte Brontë's* Shirley *as exemplary of the way in which Victorian novels portray the events and experiences surrounding a character's illness as reflective of human life in general.*]

There is scarcely a Victorian narrative without its ailing protagonist whose physical suffering is metaphorically, or even causally, related to the larger social and moral disorder of the world outside the sickroom walls. The physician in these works, with his privileged access to the intimate revelations and bodily exposure of the sickroom and his interest in the hidden causalities of disease, often provides an apt analogue for the realist author as diagnostician of social ills and scrutinizer of the minds and hearts of his or her characters. One thinks in this regard of Lydgate in *Middlemarch,* who, "enamoured of that arduous invention which is the very eye of research, . . . wanted to pierce the obscurity of those minute processes which prepare human misery and joy," or of the physician in *Little Dorrit* "who really has an acquaintance with us as we are, who is admitted to some of us every day with our wigs and paint off, who hears the wanderings of our minds, and sees the undisguised expression of our faces."

The presence of illness in such narratives, however, is not always, or even primarily, a sign of social pathology, nor is the sickroom attendant always a semiomniscient healer upon whom such a cure depends. By giving rise to a hallowed space of connection without corrupting entanglement, of repletion without excess, of self-substantiation without self-assertion, illness frequently serves as the cure for the very disorders it signifies. It is this therapeutic aspect of illness that George Eliot celebrates in the following passage from "Janet's Repentance":

> [In the sickroom] you may begin to act without settling one preliminary question. . . . these are offices that demand no self-questionings, no casuistry, no assent to propositions, no weighing of consequences. Within the four walls where the stir and glare of the world are shut out . . . the moral relation of man to man is reduced to its utmost clearness and simplicity: bigotry cannot confuse it, theory cannot pervert it, passion, awed into quiescence, can neither pollute nor perturb it.

As the passage suggests, illness serves as much as a structural principle and declaration of a preferred narrative mode as it does a metaphorical equivalent to a social condition or state of mind. Although the sickroom is located at the domestic center of Victorian life and thus set squarely within the domain of realism, it remains atypical of realistic settings. The "stir and glare of the world are shut out," and "the moral relation of man to man" is disengaged from complication, from "self-questionings," and most notably, given Eliot's characteristic emphases, from the "weighing of consequences." In addition to Eliot's comments on the subject, we have similar testimony from other sickroom devotees. In *Notes from Sickrooms,* Julia (Mrs. Leslie) Stephen mentions with approval that in the sickroom one can "ignore the details which in health make familiar intercourse difficult"; and in *Life in the Sick-Room: Essays by an Invalid,* Harriet Martineau cites among the "gains and sweets of invalidism" the "extinction of concern" about "the ordinary objects of life" and the "abolition of the future—of our own future in this life." Visitors to the sickroom, according to Martineau, "may easily perceive that it is not the appropriate field for demonstration. In its own province Demonstration is supreme. . . . But we sufferers inhabit a separate region of human experience." These exclusions from sickroom life amount to a list of the primary attributes of mimetic realism: the significance of the particular, of causal relations, of ordinary life, of temporal sequence, of "Demonstration."

The narrative mode more appropriate to this view of illness and to the circumstances to which it gives rise is romance, which, in the absence of the realist insistence upon the "hard unaccommodating Actual," can shape experience more fully at the behest of desire. Using as my focus Charlotte Brontë's novel *Shirley,* I will be arguing that scenes of illness and convalescence in Victorian fiction serve as a means of ministering to the disabling oppositions and discontinuities that the realism of the main narrative uncovers and examines, including realism's own opposing commitment to the particularity of experience and to the shaping of that experience into coherent, closed, and meaningful structures. Leo Bersani observes that "the realistic novelist desperately tries to hold together what he recognizes quite well is falling apart." The sickroom "romance," with its private dreamlike intensities, its formal symmetries, its archetypal figures, its suspension of linear development, and, as we shall see, its capacity to grant a fulfillment equal to desire, is a primary means by which such novelists attempt to restore coherence to narratives that are themselves in danger of falling apart. The location of that coherence within a continuing condition of deviation and sequestration from existing social norms and from the dominant narrative mode is, however, an unsettling indication of the disabling terms upon which it could be envisioned.

In *Shirley,* her third novel, Brontë attempted to extend her fictional range beyond the single perspective of the isolated and displaced heroine and to restrain her romantic flights with a cooling dose of realism. As she puts it:

> If you think . . . that anything like a romance is preparing for you, reader, you never were more mistaken. Do you anticipate sentiment, and poetry, and reverie? Do you expect passion, and stimulus, and melodrama? Calm your expectations; reduce them to a lowly standard. Something real, cool, and solid, lies before you. . . .

Shirley, it should be noted, was written during the fearful eleven-month period during which all three of Charlotte's surviving siblings died. Written under these harrowing conditions and with the author straining against her natural bent, the novel presents in its most acute form the disjunction common in her work between subject and object, desire and experience, romance and realism. Although initially she addresses this disjunction in terms of labor unrest and domestic discord, she turns to physical illness when she seeks a cure and not merely a diagnosis. In her fiction, generally, illness both signals dispossession and designates the range of what is possible in the way of accommodation and affective ties to this world. In *Shirley,* somatic disorder becomes the primary form of self-assertion, convalescence the measure of comfort, and physical dependency the enabling condition for intimacy.

Although scenes of illness and convalescence serve a reconciliatory purpose in works by Victorian men as well as women, including the modification of narrowly defined gender roles, the kind of protest and accommodation that I describe above has particular significance for women, as *Shirley* poignantly demonstrates. In the preface to her enormously popular how-to book, *Notes on Nursing,* Florence Nightingale wrote that "every woman is a nurse." She could as easily have stated as her cultural given that every woman is a patient. (Nightingale herself was not only the world's most famous nurse but also an invalid who, for more than fifty years, scarcely left her invalid's couch.) Sandra M. Gilbert and Susan Gubar note that "nineteenth-century culture seems to have actually admonished women to *be* ill. In other words, the 'female diseases' from which Victorian women suffered were not always byproducts of their training in femininity; they were the goals of such training."

In *Shirley* Caroline Helstone discovers that the two modes of self-expression available to women of the middle and upper classes, sickness or the nursing of sickness (in the home or among the neighboring poor) were simply, as Caroline herself characterizes her opportunities, "varieties of pain." "Professional work," as Ann Douglas puts it, "was hardly a socially acceptable escape from a lady's situation, but sickness, that very nervous condition brought on by the frustrations of her life, was." In her discussion of women of the landed gentry in nineteenth-century England, Jessica Gerard takes note of the other possible escape "from the isolation, self-abnegation, and conformity of domestic roles" the "traditional duty of tending to the sick, elderly, and destitute on a personal basis." However different they may have seemed on the face of it, and however much they may have seemed to offer an at least partial escape from frustration and powerlessness, both nurse and patient roles confined women within the same restricted sphere.

The roles of nurse and patient were nonetheless repeatedly pressed into the service of contending against the very limitations they signified. Indeed, it is this paradox that allowed the sickroom to represent a social order more amenable to female desires even as it confirmed women in their isolation. As a realm of freedom fashioned from the materials of restriction, the sickroom mediates what are essentially conflicting desires—the desire to go beyond the restrictive social roles designated for women and the largely internalized imperative to renounce that desire. The sickroom scenes in *Shirley* are the expression of this longing for a less prescriptive assignment of gender attributes and for a less punitive prescription in general of the nature and range of women's desires. Given Brontë's own internal assent to the prevailing constraints, such longing could be represented only as a form of violence against the self.

Set in Yorkshire during the final years of the Napoleonic Wars, against the background of the Luddite riots and the paralysis of trade brought on by the Orders in Council, the novel depicts not only a division between men and women and among women, but a whole society in profound disorder, its various social units radically at odds—workers from employers, the state from the manufacturing classes, clergy from laymen, high church from low. Furthermore, individuals are forced by circumstances to deviate from their own inclinations or to oppose their own prescribed destiny or condition.

What the narrator says of "old maids" is true for all of the major and many of the minor characters as well: to a greater or lesser extent they have "violated nature," thus "their natural likings and antipathies are reversed: they grow altogether morbid." Robert Moore, the presumptive heir to a great Antwerp merchant firm, must, because of reversals in the family fortune, content himself with a cottage and cloth mill "in an out-of-the-way nook of an out-of-the-way district" in Yorkshire. Shirley Keeldar, the titular heroine and heiress of Fieldhead Manor, should have been a man with a man's advantages and perquisites: "They gave me a man's name; I hold a man's position. . . . they ought to make me a magistrate and a captain of yeomanry. . . ." The Reverend Matthewson Helstone "should have been a soldier, and circumstances had made him a priest." Louis Moore should have been master of a household and is instead a servant to one. Mrs. Pryor, despite her maternal longings, abandons her only child. And Caroline Helstone, her daughter, destined to be a lovely and compliant wife, must face the purposeless life of a spinster in the absence of a sufficient dowry to attract the man she loves. One could add to this list of "struggles with . . . the strong native bent of the heart" Brontë herself, the trance writer and romantic, fighting her own aesthetic and temperamental inclinations to write a realistic novel.

Caroline Helstone's relations and position in society make her, in a sense, the vulnerable point of conduction of all the embattled factions and displaced lives in the novel. Linked to foreignness and the Whig manufacturing interest through her kinship to the Moores and her love for Robert, to the established church and high Toryism through her uncle, the Reverend Matthewson Helstone, and to the landed gentry through Shirley, Caroline is both genteel and poor a member of the middle class with access to the wealthy families of the neighborhood and sympathetic to the unemployed laborers, to whom she, as a single, portionless woman without a vocation, is compared throughout the novel. Most important, given the central conflict of the novel, as a woman, Caroline is the reluctant ally of the novel's neglected old maids, abused wives, and resentful, rebellious girls, trapped by their sex in monotonous, restricted, and self-denying roles. If, as Gilbert and Gubar contend, "*Shirley* is about impotence," then Caroline (rather than the more defiant, if no more successful, Shirley) is the impotent center of this deadlocked world, and it is in the workings of her fate in her interaction with others, in her response to seemingly intractable circumstances, and in the fulfillment she is allowed to achieve that we can trace what Brontë views as the limits of accommodation and redress that can be wrested from "the accepted order of things."

Although the plight of the single woman is an important focus of Brontë's social commentary in the novel, marriage is portrayed as unsatisfactory at best, self-destructive and enslaving at worst. As Caroline's Uncle Helstone tells her, "Millions of marriages are unhappy: if everybody confessed the truth, perhaps all are more or less so." In a characterization of marriage that, ironically, describes the terms upon which the "happy" marriage of Robert and Caroline will be transacted, he concludes, "A yokefellow is not a companion; he or she is a fellow-sufferer." Later, Mrs. Pryor warns Caroline against the "false pictures" of marriage given in romances: "They are not like reality: they show you only the green tempting surface of the marsh, and give not one faithful or truthful hint of the slough underneath." The domestic relations depicted in the novel bear out this grim testimony. The Reverend Helstone's marriage to the silent Mary Cave, for instance, "was of no great importance to him in any shape"; he neglected her so utterly that he "scarcely noticed her decline." And Mrs. Pryor, who has escaped from her drunken and abusive husband, James Helstone, is left "galled, crushed, paralyzed, dying."

In addition to these marriages (which were based, at least initially, on sentiment) are those proposed for economic reasons without regard to the inclinations of either party. Robert, in an effort to secure the future of his mill and to release himself and his family from debt, forswears his love for Caroline in order to propose to Shirley, upon whose land his mill is located. Shirley, meanwhile, who loves Robert's brother Louis, has a series of wealthy and aristocratic suitors pressed upon her by her guardian, Mr. Sympson. In the following passage she decries the mercenary god presiding over marriages:

> Behold how hideously he governs! See him busied at the work he likes best—making marriages. He binds the young to the old, the strong to the imbecile. He stretches out the arm of Mezentius, and fetters the dead to the living. In his realm there is hatred secret hatred: there is disgust— unspoken disgust: there is treachery—family treachery: there is vice—deep, deadly, domestic vice.

The primary transgressors in this dismal state of affairs are clearly the men, who are described by Robert Moore as "a sort of scum" ruled almost exclusively by competitive and appetitive forces. Contentious, arrogant, and rapacious, the men of Brontë's Yorkshire seem to embody Shirley's and Caroline's worst fears about them—fears about inconstancy, tyranny, and the possibility that behind a pleasing exterior lurks a dangerous stranger. Mrs. Pryor tells Caroline that "it was my lot to witness a transfiguration on the domestic hearth: to see the white mask lifted, the bright disguise put away, and opposite me sat down—oh God! I *have* suffered!"

Imprisonment and deprivation, then are shown to be the lot of both the married and the unmarried woman. The conflict between a desire for romantic fulfillment and for autonomy, often considered to be the central opposition in Brontë's narratives, is, in *Shirley,* a false dilemma. Rather than equally attractive but incompatible alternatives, both desires are shown to be chimerical—the stuff of romance hiding "the slough underneath."

The intimate conflicts between men and women in the novel parallel the larger social conflicts between the powerful and the powerless. The workers, like the women, are at the mercy of their masters: their needs are ignored, their protests are unheeded, their material well-being is urgently threatened. The parallel between the unemployed workers and the powerless and oppressed women, however, stops short at their common dependency on masters for material and emotional well-being and their privation in a society ruled by unrestrained competition rather than justice and compassion. Parallel becomes contrast when redress and resistance are at issue. Whereas "misery generates hate" among the workers, who seek relief through direct action, the women invert their resentment and, like Mary Cave, Mrs. Pryor, and Caroline, retreat into passivity and illness. The women's rebellion, if it manifests itself at all, does so in a socially acceptable way, registering the inadequacy of the social order without overtly threatening that order or risking the identity, however partial, that is confirmed by it. As Talcott Parsons pointed out in *The Social System,* "From the point of view of the stability of the social system the sick role may be less dangerous than some of the alternatives." The force of Caroline's protest against Robert's treatment of his workers and against male neglect of women's education is diffused by her conflicting need for the love and acceptance of those who determine her deprivation. Direct demand, as Caroline herself implies, risks both a loss of love and permanent abandonment: "Obtrusiveness is a crime; forwardness is a crime; and both disgust: but love! no purest angel need blush to love!"

The internal logic of Brontë's self-imposed realism seems inevitably to lead to narrative stalemate, so incommensurate in her view is the "true narrative of life" with even the most modest expectations of fulfillment, so hopeless is the possibility of effective resistance to the powers that be. Realism is put into sadistic relation to romance rather than serving as a corrective to it. Wish, expectation, and desire are "crush[ed]" by the "inexorable," the "resistless" authority of Experience, with her "frozen" face and her "rod so heavy." "Reason," contends Lucy Snowe in *Villette,* is a "hag" who commands obedience at the price of "savage, ceaseless blows"; and "Truth," the sovereign of "the dread, the swift-footed, the all-overtaking Fact," is a "Power whose errand is to march conquering and to conquer" any "temporary evasion of the actual."

The narrative consequences of this disabling relation between the actual and the desired are exacerbated by Brontë's attempt in *Shirley* to substitute "something unromantic as Monday morning" for "sentiment, and poetry, and reverie." The structure of the novel itself is bifurcated between "reality," the external narrative of social facts and action, which is unresponsive to human wish and agency, and "the life of thought," the interior life of romantic imaginings. The expression of this inner life is almost wholly contained in a kind of textual substratum of the "objective" narrative in diaries, recitations from secondary texts, impassioned reveries, and mythic excursuses—only to regain full narrative status within the sickroom.

Caroline expresses her affection for Robert, for instance, by reading to him "the sweet verses of Chénier" and reveals her view of his character by giving him Shakespeare's *Coriolanus:* "Now, read, and discover by the feelings the reading will give you at once how low and how high you are." She expresses her growing despair, though without acknowledging it as her own, by reciting Cowper's "Castaway," which she murmurs to herself at the "farthest and darkest end of the room" while Shirley listens. We learn of Louis Moore's feelings for Shirley through his private meditations; even the scene of their declaration of love for each other is not dramatized but rather contained in a "reading" of his diary. And there are Shirley's own mystical visions of female equality, of Titanic Eves, heroic struggles, and mythic couplings, which are revealed to Caroline or read aloud from her schoolroom copybooks found hidden away in Louis's drawer.

Only through Caroline's domesticated counterfiction to Shirley's mystical visions—her fantasy of union with her mother—is this suppressed libidinal and romantic material brought to the surface and represented as objective narrative:

> The longing of her childhood filled her soul again. . . . that her mother might come some happy day, and send for her to her presence look upon her fondly with loving eyes, and say to her tenderly, in a sweet voice:
>
> "Caroline, my child. I have a home for you: you shall live with me. All the love you have needed, and not tasted, from infancy, I have saved for you carefully. Come! it shall cherish you now."

Through the mediation of the sickroom, Caroline's wish to be claimed, to assert her being without committing the "crime" of "forwardness," is fulfilled. Unable to imagine a viable identity for her character through political, marital, or occupational means, Brontë secures Caroline within the protective enclave of the sickroom, where exemption from the entanglements and frustrations of the real is a duty a prescription for recovery. Caroline's surrender to the obduracy of the Real ("to wait and endure was her only plan") calls into being its repressed opposite, a sanctuary of perfect harmony and gratified wishes—a kind of intermediary realm of fulfillment between the extremes of Shirley's blasphemous defiance of the existing order (which can be imaged only in mythic terms) and complete subjugation to "the dark, cold side" of "the world and circumstances."

The central scene of Caroline's illness is meant to be a crucial episode in the rite of passage from "Elf-land" to the "shores of Reality," described below as the passage from a romance to a realistic narrative:

> Caroline Helstone was just eighteen years old; and at eighteen the true narrative of life is yet to be commenced. Before that time, we sit listening to a tale, a marvellous fiction; delightful sometimes, and sad sometimes; almost always unreal. Before that time, our world is heroic; its inhabitants half-divine or semidemon; its scenes are dream-scenes. . . .
>
> At that time—at eighteen, drawing near the confines of illusive, void dreams, Elf-land lies behind us, the shores of Reality rise in front.

Instead, her illness marks the transition from the "true narrative of life," which has run aground on the barren and forbidding "shores of Reality," to the surreptitious reemergence of romance (of "sentiment, and poetry, and reverie") as a fundamental structural principle governing the narrative. Just as protrusions on the skull provide telltale evidence in phrenology—the pseudoscience to which Brontë so frequently turned in her assessment of character—illness figures the involuntary emergence into visibility of the self, which, if read aright, makes legible its secret longings. Indeed, the scene of Caroline's illness and convalescence, viewed in the context of a sequence of parallel scenes and images, suggests a realignment and reinterpretation of the novel's overt realist mode and ideology. But the fact that continued debility is the enabling circumstance of this encounter and conciliation between inner and outer testifies to the persistent incompatibility of these two realms of experience. "I shall hardly wish to get well, that I may keep you always," Caroline tells Mrs. Pryor—a statement that proves prophetic of the terms upon which the relationships in this novel, among many others written during the same era, are transacted and sustained. In Elizabeth Barrett Browning's novel-poem *Aurora Leigh* (also an examination of restrictive gender roles that ends with the heroine nursing the shattered hero), Marian Earle expresses a similar sentiment when she wishes she could "be sicker yet, if sickness made / The world so marvellous kind."

The proximate cause of Caroline's collapse into illness is the apparent loss of any hope of Robert's love and, with that loss, the closing off of any means of self-definition: "She returned from an enchanted region to the real world: for Nunnely wood in June, she saw her narrow chamber; . . . for Moore's manly companionship, she had the thin illusion of her own dim shadow on the wall." This illusion of another self is, more generally, a projection of Caroline's fading sense of relationship to the external world in the absence of any fulfilling ties to it. To return to the "real world" is to become unreal, a "pale phantom" of oneself—a familiar enough phenomenon in Brontë's novels, in which the heroines often seem to haunt rather than to inhabit their own lives. In the introduction to *Villette,* Tony Tanner mentions, for instance, the "defamiliarized void . . . which in more muted forms is [Lucy Snowe's] daily experience."

Caroline's illness literally embodies this impasse and through the embodiment "resolves" it. By exchanging her experience of ontological indeterminacy for the determination of the body in distress by making her loss of identity and relation concrete illness not only renders that loss susceptible to redress, attention, and concern, but also allows for a passive form of self-assertion. It makes the self palpably present to itself, a process made manifest by the appearance at her bedside of Mrs. Pryor—Caroline's nurse, mother, and likeness. Formerly suffering from deprivation, solitude, and physical and mental restriction in her "narrow chamber," Caroline now finds in that bedroom turned sickroom identity and ease of mind through an intimate reciprocal connection that is immune to the disruptive aspects of male desire and domination. "My own mamma," Caroline says, "who belongs to me, and to whom I belong! I am a rich girl now: I have something I can love well, and not be afraid of loving." Mrs. Pryor and Caroline's intimacy as nurse and patient, even before they are known to each other as parent and child, creates a wholly loving community of two. Caroline's vision of the ideal marriage, in which "affection is reciprocal and sincere, and minds are harmonious," is realized to a degree that is inconceivable elsewhere. "[L]oneliness and gloom were now banished from her bedside; protection and solace sat there instead. She and her nurse coalesced in wondrous union." Mrs. Pryor lives with Caroline "day and night," touches her gently, encircles her in her arms, yields to her caresses. The privileged "proximity of a nurse to a patient" eulogized in *Villette* allows for an emotional and physical intimacy divested of the disturbing male erotic element that has made such direct interaction dangerous outside the sickroom. Passion, "a mere fire of dry sticks, blazing up and vanishing," according to Shirley, becomes the more enduring "passion of solicitude." Accordingly, Robert is placed in a subordinate position to Mrs. Pryor, a position from which he is only partially redeemed. This supplantation of the marital or sexual union by the female relationship of nurse to patient is suggested earlier in the novel in a mention of Caroline's aunt (and Mrs. Pryor's sister-in-law), Mrs. Matthewson Helstone, and "a female attendant, who had waited upon Mrs. Helstone in her sickness; and who, perhaps, had had opportunities of learning more of the deceased lady's nature, of her capacity for feeling and loving, than her husband knew. . . ."

The nurse-patient relationship preserves the intensity and significance of familial and communal ties while remaining outside the economic, political, and sexual considerations that complicate and distort them. As such it supplants its professional counterpart, the doctor-patient relationship, as well as that between husband and wife. Despite such figures of compassion and romantic interest as Dr. Woodcourt in *Bleak House* and Dr. Crofts in Trollope's *Small House at Allington,* in Victorian novels generally the doctor's interest in his patients is determined chiefly by material issues of profit, reputation, or the assertion of professional authority. Purportedly come to heal illness—that most intimate and emotionally charged area of human experience—the doctor contaminates the sickroom with the very ills that infect society as a whole. The doctor called in to see Caroline "wrote some prescriptions, gave some directions—the whole with an air of crushing authority—pocketed his fee, and went." Even Dr. John in *Villette* is stigmatized with the other members of his profession for his "dry, materialist views" and by his purely scientific interest in pain and disease. The "eye of research" for which Eliot commends Lydgate is at once too penetrating and too remote for the healing process of the sickroom, and perhaps, as I noted earlier, it too accurately mirrors the Victorian novelist's own potentially dehumanizing realistic methods. Finally, however, the "eye of research," or as Brontë puts it in *Jane Eyre,* "the eye of science," is a male eye, and as such indifferent or blind to the real sources of female distress. While Jane is lost in sobs, St. John Rivers is described as looking on "like a physician watching . . . an expected and fully understood crisis in a patient's malady." Brontë's distrust of physicians in this regard was not unwarranted. It is only one of the ironies of the sickroom as sanctuary for women from existing gender roles that medical research during the nineteenth century was engaged in grounding the social and political inequality of women in the "incontrovertible evidence" of the body in the supposedly innate instability and weakness of female structure and physiology.

The relationship between nurse and patient, on the other hand, provides a model of exchange that depends for its efficacy on a quarantine on all the divisive elements marring such exchanges outside the sickroom walls. For this reason, the "hireling" nurse as well as the doctor must be replaced by the "self-elected nurse." The professional nurse is a common butt of humor and contempt in Victorian fiction. Drunken, licentious, and avaricious by reputation, she seems to be reviled in proportion to the value placed on the cherished notion of natural female benevolence and nurturing propensities as antidotes to social ills. The monstrous and brutal Mrs. Horsfall, Robert Moore's nurse at the end of the novel, provides a horrific example. Her bullying of the enfeebled Robert also manifests the implicit aggression that the more idealized feminine authority in the sickroom often disguises.

The relations between the voluntary nurse and patient are presented as reciprocal, each in turn soothing the other in a cycle of dependency. At one point, grieving for the absent Robert, Caroline lies "mute and passive in the trembling arms on the throbbing bosom of the nurse"; shortly thereafter, Caroline bids Mrs. Pryor to come and be comforted, and "she sat down on the edge of her patient's bed, and allowed the wasted arms to encircle her." Still later, when Mrs. Pryor is shaken by her memories of her husband, "the child lulled the parent, as the parent had erst lulled the child." Their union dispels the disruptive "other" in a female bond of reciprocal solace.

Thematically, then, the nurse-patient relationship represents a preferable alternative to marriage and the work place, to the instabilities of passion and competition, domination and subjection, and to the stifling malady of the quotidian. But a much more specific and formally subtle process of substitution and inversion takes place in a series of structurally analogous sickroom scenes. The process represents a romantic replacement for the dominant narrative mode (which threatened to end in stalemate) and is, in a sense, the structural equivalent of the sickroom itself. Unconstrained by the web of probable circumstance and motivation, stable characterization, and linear progression of traditional realism, these scenes effect a symbolic interchange of identity and relation, in the process of which the negative qualities primarily associated with men are, at least temporarily, neutralized or expelled. At the same time, Caroline moves from her peripheral status as abused child and forsaken lover to nurturing wife and daughter, or, in the idiom of the scenes themselves, from patient to nurse. Moreover, this internal narrative of sickroom scenes restores formal consistency to a novel that is floundering in a welter of styles, points of view, and unassimilated plots in its attempt to reconcile competing impulses. In these dream scenes, the determined pulse of desire (the "strong, native bent of the heart") dominates over "the check of Reason." Thus, Brontë's own narrative is given the "contrary turn" that Caroline wishes to give to St. Paul's First Epistle to Timothy on the position of women while still maintaining her claim to orthodoxy, just as illness registers the inadequacy of the accepted order without overtly threatening that order.

We begin with Caroline's "dark recollection" of her father, James Helstone. Although he is only a posthumous presence in the novel, he haunts it as the primal figure of debased appetite and corrupt authority. His disruptive presence as seductive and punishing father, husband, and lover is gradually feminized and transformed during the course of the sickroom scenes. He first appears before Caroline as a figure of romance, "dim, sinister, scarcely earthly," following her uncle's denunciation of marriage. The hallucination images her own fears about such a union: She sees "another figure standing beside her uncle's—a strange shape . . . the half-remembered image of her own father, James Helstone, Matthewson Helstone's brother." Caroline then recalls being left alone and starving, "shut up, day and night, in a high garret-room" to which her father would return each night "like a madman, furious, terrible; or—still more painful—like an idiot, imbecile, senseless":

> She knew she had fallen ill in this place, and that one night when she was very sick, he had come raving into the room, and said he would kill her, for she was a burden to him; her screams had brought aid, and from the moment she was then rescued from him she had never seen him. . . .

The second scene, Caroline's reunion in the sickroom with the mother she had never known, recapitulates the central elements of the earlier scene with her father. It, too, is precipitated by thoughts of marriage—in this instance, the collapse of Caroline's hopes of marriage to Robert, the attenuated version of her demonic father, who, like that father, has "deserted cruelly, trifled wantonly, injured basely." Haunted by Robert's memory, Caroline undergoes solitude, deprivation, confinement to her "narrow chamber," and illness. This time, however, the nurturing mother, herself a victim of male depredation, appears to Caroline in an almost hallucinatory recuperation from the earlier pain, loss, and, perhaps, guilt ("for she was a burden to him"). Just as Mrs. Pryor replaces James Helstone, the father, in this scene, Caroline replaces, or becomes a feminine version of, James Helstone, the husband. (The husband also becomes the child.) Mrs. Pryor calls Caroline his "fairy-like representative," "this living likeness"; "this thing with [his] perfect features . . . has nestled affectionately to my heart, and tenderly called me 'mother'."

In the third of these scenes and, at least ostensibly, their *terminus ad quem,* the elements of apparent abandonment, confinement, deprivation, illness, and sudden reprieve are again present, as is their precipitating occasion, the contemplation of marriage. Following his confession to Mr. Yorke of his mercenary proposal of marriage to Shirley and the betrayal of his true feelings for Caroline, Robert is shot and wounded by a madman, confined in an upstairs room in the Yorke household (where he is almost killed as a result of the incompetence of Mrs. Yorke and Hortense Moore), and later battered and starved by the ferocious Mrs. Horsfall. Just as Caroline was "shut up, day and night," by her father, these women "held the young millowner captive, and hardly let the air breathe or the sun shine on him." In Martin Yorke's exaggerated but narratively definitive account (he is our only access to the events), he describes Moore as "mewed up, kept in solitary confinement. They mean to make either an idiot or a maniac of him. . . ." Later Martin tells Caroline, "It is my belief [Mrs. Horsfall] knocks him about terribly in that chamber. I listen at the wall sometimes when I am in bed, and I think I hear her thumping him. . . . I wish she may not be starving him." His words link Robert's treatment to Caroline's at the hands of her father, while Robert's impending fate as "an idiot or a maniac" associates him with Helstone ("idiot, imbecile").

This scene, like the others, is marked by the archetypal, dreamlike patterns of romance, complete with Caroline's storming of the dungeon where her captive lover lies imprisoned and the defeat of "the dragon who guarded his chamber," Mrs. Horsfall. The besieging of the Yorke household appropriately begins with Martin sitting alone in a wintry wood under the moon, reading "not the Latin grammar, but a contraband volume of Fairy tales," thus underscoring the romantic, fabular nature of this episode as well as its illicit, or at least guarded, presence in a "realistic" novel. "He reads. . . . a green-robed lady, on a snow-white palfrey . . . arrests him with some mysterious question: he is spellbound, and must follow her into Fairy-land." At this point, Caroline appears before him, becoming "like some enchanted lady in a fairy tale," the fate that Rose Yorke had urged upon her earlier in place of her "long, slow death . . . in Briarfield Rectory." With Martin's help Caroline manages to penetrate the fastness of Moore's sickroom and to revive her broken Coriolanus. The only difference between this and the fairy tales Martin reads is the sexual role reversal between the liberator and the liberated.

In this final transposition of identities, Robert takes Caroline's place as the patient, the helpless victim of aggression and neglect, "a poor, pale, grim phantom" of his former self. He also takes over her provisional role in the second scene as a feminized James Helstone. By his experience "unmanned," and thus denuded of his threatening otherness, Robert is kept from becoming "an idiot or a maniac" or, more probably, a faithless tyrant. Furthermore, just as Mrs. Pryor (the good nurse) supplants James Helstone (the bad nurse) in the first two scenes, Caroline supplants Mrs. Horsfall, whose avarice and aggression are displaced and then fully expelled (or, to be more exact, paid off). Through the progressive transposition of structural relation and symbolic identity within and among these scenes, Caroline not only moves from abandoned child and lover to beloved wife and daughter, but also becomes the maternal rather than the "unnatural"—Mrs. Pryor to Robert's pacified and domesticated James Helstone. Within the romantic space of successive sick-rooms, which together seem like so many oneiric images emanating from a single consciousness, Caroline's initial fearful image of her parents' marriage has been exorcised and transformed into a benign equivalent.

The apparent closure afforded by this process is, however, by its very nature unstable. Indeed, even the quarantine provided by the sickroom subnarrative and enclave serves as a somewhat flimsy barricade for the problems they exclude. As an intermediary realm between a total withdrawal into fantasy and the "black trance" of reality, the sickroom enclave neither achieves autonomy from the real nor does it, in ritual fashion, inform or revitalize the world outside its walls. On the contrary, it is necessarily deviant and subordinate to the conditions of ordinary life that it abjures; the unity and solace it offers is forged out of the very untoward conditions that make that solace necessary—isolation, passivity, powerlessness, marginality, alienation, and sexual antagonism. The nurse-patient idyll itself is thus contaminated by the conflicts it seeks to expunge and is, in some cases, underwritten by the same power structure that it formally represses.

With this in mind, I would like to return to the union of Caroline and Robert and the terms by which it is achieved. As we have seen, the frightening potential for unreliability, aggression, neglect, or domination in heterosexual relations is excluded from the sickroom through the "unmanning" of Robert (itself, of course, achieved and sustained through acts of domination and aggression). In the solipsistic manner characteristic of Victorian sick-room scenes in general, Caroline, in a sense, makes everyone over in her own image, becoming father, lover, mother, and child in the progressive transposition of identities in the three major sick-room scenes. Such a conflation of identities is also characteristic of the romance mode which, according to George Levine, embodies "the secret lust of the spirit to impose itself on the world." In Brontë's case, I would stipulate that such a secret lust is, at least in part, a response to the imposition of the world upon the spirit, and of the spirit upon the body.

Robert's "unmanning" in the sickroom has a familiar parallel in Rochester's fate as perpetual patient at the end of *Jane Eyre*. In *Jane Eyre,* however, there is no need for a Mrs. Pryor to guarantee future domestic felicity; Rochester is more permanently secured by his continuing incapacity and sequestration with Jane in Ferndean. Like the Nunnwood of *Shirley* ("the sole remnant of antique British forest" with a "deep, hollow cup" at the center), Ferndean is clearly a female location, "deep buried in a wood." Most critics have viewed Rochester's debility as a chastening or domestication of his power—mythical, sexual, or social. What I wish to stress, however, is not so much the symbolic significance of his disability as its outcome enabling the "perfect concord" of the sickroom relation, which here, as elsewhere, seems predicated on the exorcism of all potential sources of discord in a fusion of identity so complete and so secluded from others that it appears invulnerable to rival affections, breaches of trust, or even differences in perception. "To be together," Jane says of her relation to Rochester, "is for us to be at once as free as in solitude, as gay as in company. We talk, I believe, all day long: to talk to each other is but a more animated and an audible thinking. All my confidence is bestowed on him, all his confidence is devoted to me; we are precisely suited in character—perfect concord is the result." In other words, nurse and patient "coalesced in wondrous union."

This state of identity seems to require either the utter incorporation of the other or, in narrative terms, the invention of a romance in which one can pass for two. Rochester, in effect, *is* Jane, just as Robert, at least temporarily, becomes Caroline. Rochester's physical debility symbolically marks him as feminine or, like Robert, "unmanned"; furthermore, because of his blindness (no more male "eyes," scientific or otherwise), Rochester must submit to Jane's imaginative re-creation of the world and perforce participate in her world. "He saw nature—he saw books through me; and never did I weary of gazing for his behalf, and of putting into words the *effect* of field, tree, town, river, cloud, sunbeam—of the landscape before us; of the weather round us and impressing by sound on his ear what light could no longer stamp on his eye" (my italics). Her imaginative re-creation of the world into words becomes his sole reality.

One evident personal source for this regressive longing for perfect concord only imaginable as total identity in secluded enclaves can be found in the tightly knit, exclusive society and joint imaginative lives of the Brontë siblings, "their oneness as a family in temperament, outlook, and sensibility." As Charlotte described Haworth in a letter written while she was a governess for the Whites,

> My home is humble and unattractive to strangers, but to me it contains what I shall find nowhere else in the world—the profound, the intense affection which brothers and sisters feel for each other when their minds are cast in the same mould, their ideas drawn from the same source—when they have clung to each other from childhood, and when disputes have never sprung up to divide them.

To an extent, all of Charlotte's fictive couples commemorate that harmony before the Brontës' enforced separation, before the harsh intervention of financial need and ambition directed their attention toward what they perceived to be a hostile and unresponsive external world, and before they directed their desires toward the inhabitants of that world—Monsieur Heger, Mrs. Robinson, William Weightman—the loved ones who did not reciprocate their love. The inability of the Brontës to adjust to the world beyond Haworth Parsonage and the fictional worlds they created there condemned them to remain in it as a prison as well as a refuge of privileged intimacy, a place of premature burial ("I feel as if we were all buried here," wrote Charlotte). The parsonage becomes, like the sickroom of Charlotte's fiction, an asylum for their ailing selves. Here, too, the conditions of deprivation doubled as the available terms of fulfillment, just as the final scene of illness in *Shirley* recasts in positive terms the essential attributes of the first or as illness itself registers both the loss or diminution of self and its sole means of preservation.

The sickroom secures for its inhabitants what they started out with, albeit under the guise of protection and solace: it exempts them from an active role in their own affairs; it attains their willing dependency; it sequesters them from society in closed rooms under a carefully observed regimen, obedient to the authority of the figure in charge or, alternatively, in the position of nurse. Ferndean is, after all, "insalubrious" and isolated, and Jane, however willingly, a perpetual nurse to an aging, half-blind invalid. Moreover, if her possession of Rochester suggests domination, it is also a form of subjection. The narrator of George Eliot's *Felix Holt* comments that "strength is often only another name for willing bondage to irremediable weakness." In a sense, the inversion of the intolerable into the desirable occurs not only within the novel, but in the author's re-creation of her own life as well. It is, for example, not difficult to see in the ending of *Jane Eyre,* transmuted into a "happy succeeding life," the shape of Charlotte's life at Haworth itself an insalubrious and isolated setting caring for her half-blind father and obliged to re-create the world in words.

It remains to be seen how the sickroom relation not only bears within itself the imprint of the reality it wishes to transform but also is underwritten or perpetuated by the struggles for money and power that it seeks to exclude. Although Robert remarks to Mr. Yorke that with Caroline's love an "unselfish longing to protect and cherish" would replace "the sordid, cankering calculations of . . . trade," it is the latter that makes the former not only possible, but necessary.

Comparing Caroline's fate to that of the workers reveals the complicitous relation between the sickroom and the ills it seeks to heal. Although their modes of resistance are divergent, the women and workers converge in their return to powerlessness. Submission and defiance alike are shown to lead to debility and defeat. Yet that very debility, for the workers as well as for Caroline, becomes the avenue of redress. The defeated workers have their immediate physical needs tended by the women at Fieldhead Manor after their abortive revolt is put down by soldiers. Once the power of the masters has been demonstrated and consolidated by the disabling of the workers and of their protest, the workers' condition can be recognized and improved through the intermediary agency of nursing women. No longer invisible (either as superfluities in a machine age or as a faceless, mutinous mob), the workers suddenly are visible objects of compassion as patients and victims. Yet their capitulation to dependency effectively secures their subjection. This process of substantiation with a price is given succinct expression in the response of Hiram Yorke to Robert's own disabled condition following the attack on his life:

> This utter dependence of the speechless, bleeding youth . . . on his benevolence, secured that benevolence most effectually. Well did Mr Yorke like to have power, and to use it: he had now between his hands power over a fellow-creature's life: it suited him.

If Robert's experience of powerlessness, when he is shot by a "half-crazed" weaver, put within Mr. Yorke's power, then bullied and starved by a woman, seems to avenge by proxy his earlier actions against the workers and against Caroline, it should be noted that the means by which this is achieved endorse by imitation the inescapability of the disabling process; the relative positions of the participants have been reversed, only to be reversed again. An appropriate finale to this series of power plays between Robert and his workers restores Robert to his position as their master, just as he will be restored as Caroline's. When the newly paternalistic Robert chooses not to pursue his attacker, sickness does his work for him, providing a further opportunity for him to display his benevolence even as he is avenged: "the poor soul died of delirium tremens a year after the attempt on Moore, and Robert gave his wretched widow a guinea to bury him."

For Brontë, there seems to be no available alternative to relations based on the cruel opposition between domination and submission; there are only more or less consolatory variants—"varieties of pain." If *Shirley* registers a protest against such a state of affairs, it also raises it to the level of cosmic principle. As Robert tells Mr. Yorke before he is shot down,

> "I believe—I daily find it proved—that we can get nothing in this world worth keeping, not so much as a principle or a conviction, except out of purifying flame, or through strengthening peril. . . . we are sickened, degraded; . . . our souls rise bitterly indignant against our bodies; there is a period of civil war; if the soul has strength, it *conquers* and *rules* thereafter." (my italics)

The way of the polity and the hearth is the way of the soul as well.

Jane Eyre is permitted a triumph of the soul over the body and the only reprieve from the prevailing power structure that Brontë could envision when the heroine secures her incapacitated lover—a perpetual convalescent from the "crushing, grinding" lessons of experience—under her domination as his nurse and guide in a secluded, primal, and female location. Caroline, on the other hand, in accordance with the dictates of Brontë's professed realism, must be returned to "the shores of Reality" outside the sickroom walls, a reality that belongs to Robert, as the subdivision of Nunnwood and the correspondent subduing of female harmony under male dominance demonstrate. With Robert's restored health, the repeal of the Orders in Council, the advantageous marriage of his brother Louis, and the development of new markets, "the manufacturer's daydreams [were] embodied in substantial stone and brick and ashes—the cinder-black highway, the cottages, and the cottage-gardens; . . . a mighty mill, and a chimney, ambitious as the tower of Babel." Caroline's daydreams, meanwhile, and the Elf-land she has surrendered, have after a brief fulfillment in the sickroom reverted to tales told by women, to women.

> "What was the Hollow like then, Martha?"
>
> "Different to what it is now; but I can tell of it clean different again: when there was neither mill, nor cot, nor hall, except Fieldhead, within two miles of it. I can tell, one summer-evening, fifty years syne, my mother coming running in just at the edge of dark, almost fleyed out of her wits, saying, she had seen a fairish (fairy) in Fieldhead Hollow; and that was the last fairish that ever was seen on this country side. . . . A lonesome spot it was—and a bonnie spot—full of oak trees and nut trees. It is altered now."

TUBERCULOSIS AND LITERATURE

Lewis J. Moorman

SOURCE: An introduction to *Tuberculosis and Genius*, University of Chicago Press, 1940, pp. ix-xxxiii.

[*In the following excerpt, Moorman speculates on the possible connection between tuberculosis and literary genius.*]

Disregarding certain mythological references, including the vague, symptomatic pictures found in the songs of Orpheus and in the Homeric poems, we are convinced that the serious study of history justifies the belief that tuberculosis may have been the first-born of the mother of pestilence and disease. Exhumed skeletons of prehistoric periods bear the marks of tuberculosis. Thus we see that before the time of recorded history tuberculosis left an ineradicable record of its ravages. The code of Hammurabi, written before 2,000 B.C., indicates a knowledge of the disease. In Deuteronomy (seventh century B.C.) we find: "The Lord shall smite thee with a consumption, and with a fever and with an inflammation." In the fifth century B.C. Hippocrates and other Greek writers recognized its essential features and described them well. They observed its wasting proclivities and appropriately called it "phthisis."

Aretaeus, in the second century A.D., gave accurate clinical descriptions of tuberculosis and suggested routine treatment similar to that employed today. Galen, contemporary with Aretaeus, preserved the teachings of Hippocrates and recorded his own observations. He was one of the first to employ climate in the treatment of tuberculosis, recommending the balmy zones immediately surrounding Vesuvius.

In many individuals suffering from tuberculosis there seems to be a strange psychological flair—a phenomenon not fully accounted for, not of established scientific lineage, yet quite evident to the student of clinical tuberculosis. Everyone who deals intelligently with tuberculous individuals knows how patiently they bear their lengthening burdens; how courageous they are, often in the face of insurmountable obstacles; how optimistic they may be even when life is literally being cut down by the inevitable sweep of the Great Reaper. This unusual display of courage and hopefulness has been termed *spes phthisica.*

Charles Dickens must have recognized the subtle power of this intangible influence of the tubercle bacillus when he wrote as follows: "There is a dread disease which so prepares its victim, as it were, for death; which so refines it of its grosser aspect, and throws around familiar looks, unearthly indications of the coming change—a dread disease, in which the struggle between soul and body is so gradual, quiet, and solemn, and the result so sure, that day by day, and grain by grain, the mortal part wastes and withers away, so that the spirit grows light and sanguine with its lightening load, and, feeling immortality at hand, deems it but a new term of mortal life—a disease in which death takes the glow and hue of life, and life the gaunt and grisly form of death."

Many writers of fiction have presented characters, obviously tuberculous, exhibiting exceptional mental qualities, with exuberance of spirit and swift temperamental flights between hope and despair, so characteristic of tuberculosis and genius. Though the list is too long for inclusion in this volume, the numerous examples of the peculiar psychology which often dominates the lives of intellectual victims of the disease should be kept in mind as our theme develops.

It is well known that tuberculosis may give rise to two distinct manifestations: the depletion of physical energy and, directly or indirectly, the stimulation of mental activity. The human organism's response to environment is materially influenced by these two factors. In those who are endowed with exceptional mental qualities, and are at the same time suffering from tuberculosis, there often seems to be a strange psychic stimulus bent on creative accomplishment. Inescapable physical inactivity begets mental activity; giving up the ordinary pursuits of life must be recompensed. In his Introduction to Dr. J. A. Myers' *Fighters of Fate* Dr. Charles H. Mayo says: "The years spent in voluntary obedience to the rules of treatment may have a lasting influence and remove the one great obstacle to success in life." In some individuals only the vision of death brings a consciousness of "the divine reality of life." It has been said that "success dwells in the silences." Certainly, during the silent watches accompanying the course of tuberculosis many a sufferer has discovered the saving presence of a creative instinct. It is appropriate to add that those afflicted with this disease are among the first to appreciate the truth of Hippocrates' famous aphorism: "Life is short and art is long."

In the course of a long illness the essential elements of personality must be ultimately revealed. Often an otherwise imperious individual gradually yields to the inevitable mandates of his disease and exhibits an enviable poise, accompanied by growing tenderness and tolerance.

In *Greek Thinkers* Gompertz refers to the "heightened respect for reason and reflection as the supreme arbiters of human affairs, which may perhaps be termed intellectualism." He goes on to say that "on the soil of Italy and Sicily, the new confidence, which was produced by the reign of criticism and by the revolt from authority, went hand in hand with the growth of refinement of thought." In a sense, the chronic invalid's detachment encourages the Hellenic spirit. He has time for reflection and the quiet exercise of reason. He is no longer wholly subject to the world's conventional authority; consequently, he is in a position to exercise a free, critical spirit.

Erich Ebstein in *Tuberkulose als Schicksal* referred to the fact that biographers and critics have long recognized progressive tuberculosis in geniuses as a possible factor contributing to their individual greatness. He does not admit that the disease causes genius but agrees that it may fan into flame an otherwise dormant spark. On the other hand, he believes that advanced tuberculosis with physical prostration may inhibit creative effort.

Again quoting Dr. Charles H. Mayo's Introduction to *Fighters of Fate*: "We know that victims of chronic tuberculosis have learned the significance of unusual vitality and vigor that often precedes increase in cough, slight fever and another bout with the enemy. Man is not the only creature whom Nature has cunningly equipped for the struggle of life; the little speck of living matter known as the bacillus of tuberculosis paves the way for its destructive action by stimulating its host to overactivity. Like the Roman gods, whom it seeks to destroy, it first makes mad."

Erich Stern is inclined to attribute the manifestations of genius to the toxic action of the tubercle bacilli. The poet Novalis, who died of tuberculosis in early life, said: "The disease consists probably of the most interesting products and stimuli of our thoughts and activities." He also inquired "if disease might not be a means of higher synthesis." The tuberculous poet Klabund believed that a history dealing with the literature of the tuberculous should be written, because "this constitutional malady possesses the peculiarity of altering the mentality of its victims."

In *The Psycho-Pathology of Tuberculosis* D. G. Macleod Munro calls attention to the stimulation of the mental faculties with an unusual desire for accomplishment. "The patient has an insatiable craving for a full and active life. He lives in an atmosphere of feverish eagerness to seize the fleeting moments before they pass. These characteristics are particularly noticeable in those of naturally artistic or literary tastes."

In another chapter Munro discusses the psychoneurosis accompanying pulmonary tuberculosis and makes the following statement, which is significant in that it helps to explain the occasional diversion of genius from its original goal. "The theory of cerebral intoxication by the products of the tubercle bacillus, which has been taught by Cornet and others, appears to be the one most generally held at present, and I am unaware of any more plausible explanation."

In the first chapter of his book on *The Development of Our Knowledge of Tuberculosis* Dr. Lawrence F. Flick said: "In individuals in whom the tubercle bacillus grows meagerly, in whom it has produced but slight toxemia, and in whom it has set up no serious changes in the tissues, it not only may give no discomfort but may stimulate the functional activity of those organs of the body which have to do with the enjoyment of life. In this way the tubercle bacillus may make life more pleasant and make the individual more profitable to society than he otherwise would be."

Dr. J. A. Myers in Fighters of Fate made the following statement: "Havelock Ellis, in *A Study of British Genius,* has pointed out that tuberculosis was present in at least forty British personages, each of them a genius. What is true of British genius is no doubt true for the most part of other nations. Tuberculosis does not produce genius, but the life of physical inactivity which the tuberculous patient is frequently compelled to live may give him an opportunity to discover or to develop his native power. Such is the case of Eugene O'Neill. Tuberculosis is accredited with causing a mental exaltation and increased excitability, during which great visions and plans for their realization come to the patient. Chopin is said to have been motivated in the composition of some of his masterpieces by such a condition. In some measure this may be true, but the greater opportunities for increased mental activity as a result of the decreased physical capacity account for most of the relationship between tuberculosis and genius."

In Dr. Arthur C. Jacobson's *Genius: Some Revaluations* we find the following: "Now it is entirely conceivable that the tuberculous by-products are capable of profoundly affecting the mechanism of creative minds in such a way as to influence markedly their creations. Indeed, they are bound to do so, for the *spes phthisica,* admittedly a result of such by-products, must necessarily affect the whole psychologic switchboard." Dr. Jacobson also said: "Were the present writer to give an almost sure recipe for producing the highest type of creative mind, he would postulate an initial spark of genius plus tuberculosis."

In a recent editorial in *Medical Times* Dr. Jacobson laments the decline in the quality of American writing, and, after discussing the unfavorable influence of political events on our "cultural front," he offers the following rather disturbing suggestion: "We believe that there is another aspect to this matter a medical reason why the candles are snuffed; why the fires smolder; why genius is dead; why the descending curtain signalizes the end of the show. The decline in tuberculosis coincides with the decline in creative writing. . . . In the healthful days to come we may not apprehend the past role of tuberculosis in quickening creative faculties; and by way of compensation for good health we may lack certain cultural joys." In a previous editorial we find the following: "No other disease with equally extensive lesions exalts a victim physically and psychically [*spes phthisica*]. Other diseases, as they devastate tissues, devastate creative powers. Tuberculosis, paradoxically, prods a Shelley or a Keats into finer productivity."

One of the critics of John Millington Synge is quoted as having said: "He was of such an intense super-sensitive temperament that he naturally clutched at extremes with all the hectic greediness of a consumptive."

J. Middleton Murry said of Katherine Mansfield: "When the full tide of inspiration came, she wrote till she dropped with fatigue sometimes all through the night, in defiance of her illness."

In *The Psycho-Pathology of Tuberculosis* Munro quotes Matthew Arnold as having said of Maurice de Guérin: "The temperament, the talent itself is deeply influenced by the mysterious malady; the temperament is devouring; it uses vital power too hard and too fast."

After Thomas Hood had "submitted to a decline" and his health had improved, he again developed active disease, and one of his biographers said that he manifested that "fever for work which has been observed in the consumptive." Munro said of Hood: "As his health declined his poetical fire seemed to burn more brightly, and the 'Song of the Shirt,' as he pathetically put it, came from a man on his death-bed. 'The Bridge of Sighs' soon followed this, and these two poems, written within a few months of his death, set the seal upon his greatness as a poet." Discussing the life of John Addington Symonds, who, at Davos, shared with Robert Louis Stevenson the conscious stimulation of disease, Munro said: "Symonds seems to have been fully aware that he was in a febrile condition while carrying on his mental and physical activities, but confessed that he felt the recklessness of disease, and was possessed of that nervous, fretful, and fitful energy which is so characteristic a feature of the artistic or intellectual phthisical [tuberculous] patient."

Haldane Macfall in his biography of Aubrey Beardsley made this significant statement: "Beardsley knew he was a doomed man even on the threshold of manhood, and he strove with feverish intensity to get a lifetime into each twelvemonth."

Writing about *Sunrise*, Sidney Lanier's "ultimate symphony," Lincoln Lorenz said: "His bodily fever heightened the temperature of his spiritual passion, and indeed permitted him to peer the better over the sea's brink as the first rays diverged." The following reference to Lanier's work at Johns Hopkins, when "life seemed about to vacate the physical tenement," is interesting: "The energy of his thought showed little relation to the weakness of his body; in fact, his lectures now often achieved their best design and farthest reach."

In the *Journal of the American Medical Association*, June, 1932, the London correspondent said: "The number of great writers who have suffered from tuberculosis has long been a subject of remark. Some authorities have held that the disease has an effect in promoting mental development." Continuing to quote from his London letter, we find the following: "At the Congress of the Royal Institute of Public Health, Dr. S. Vere Pearson, physician to Mundesley Sanatorium for Tuberculosis, delivered an address on the psychology of the consumptive. Referring to such authors as Tchekov, Stevenson, Keats, Elizabeth Browning, and D. H. Lawrence, he said that some people ascribed their genius to the stimulating powers of the toxins of tuberculosis. Undoubtedly, a sort of restless agitation was produced in certain phases of pulmonary tuberculosis. There was also a feeling of apprehension lest life should be shortened. Both the apprehension and the restlessness might act as a stimulus to production and particularly to the production of authors, who could pursue their calling without much bodily exertion." The letter closes with the following interesting comment: "It might be said in criticism of Dr. Pearson's interesting address that he somewhat misses the point, which is not the effect which the trouble of tuberculosis has in molding the writings of authors, but that the toxins of the disease act in some way as a stimulus to the brain in the production of the imagination. The list of writers who have suffered from tuberculosis, some, such as Keats, the Brontës and Stevenson, supremely great, is so long as to suggest something more than coincidence."

Discussing John Keats's reaction to his tuberculosis, Dr. Robert L. Pitfield said: "It is more than likely that the tuberculous poisons intoxicated and enriched the imaginations of Stevenson and Chopin and other geniuses. These poisons no doubt added much to the fervid vision of this man. I am sure that they guilded his genius. A peculiar mental hyperesthesia characterizes this disease in even the most commonplace minds. There can be no doubt that Keats was hyper-esthetic, acutely so. He, by this time, had a little fever, yet his disease was to run for years."

Sidney Colvin said of Keats: "It was not often nor for long that the stings either of love or of poetry abated for him the least jot of their bitter sweet intensity, or the anticipation of poverty or the fever of incipient disease relaxed their grip."

With keen perception, perhaps sharpened by the swift discernment of disease, Katherine Mansfield described her doctor as follows: "He has the disease himself. I *recognized* his smile—just the least shade too bright—and his strange joyousness as he came to meet me—the gleam—the faint glitter on the plant that the frost has laid a finger on."

Quoting Jeannette Marks in *Genius and Disaster*: "It has been said that a man is what his microbes make him, and in nothing, it would seem, is this more true than with the man of genius." After referring to James Thomson's pessimism as possibly pathological, she said: "It should be remembered that there are types of optimism equally pathological which are due to the quick burning of disease. For example, the buoyant hopefulness created by tuberculosis." She suggests that "in Shelley's 'Ode to the West Wind' it is doubtful whether the flight of his song and the tumult of wind and leaves would have been so swift without the quickening which Shelley had from tuberculosis. In the case of Emily Brontë, life may have been shortened physically by consumption, but study convinces the reader that psychically in *Wuthering Heights* and in her poems power and passion were made the greater by the *spes phthisica.*"

Again referring to her discussion of James Thomson, she writes: "In any event, the nearer disease and death press on a sensitive mind perhaps all the more passionately does that mind press towards the consolation of art which is immortal."

John B. Huber in his work on *Consumption and Civilization* made the following statement: "It appears to me that the quality of the genius of a great man, if he be consumptive, may be, in some cases at least, affected by his disease."

Dr. John Brown of Edinburgh, author of *Rab and His Friends,* observed a certain mental exuberance as he studied the psychology of his tuberculous patients. In the latter part of the nineteenth century he recorded the results of his observations in a beautiful tribute to his young friend and colleague, Dr. William Henry Scott, who died at the early age of twenty-four. The conclusions of this careful observer are quite obvious, as shown by the following: "He died of consumption and had that sad malady, in which the body and soul, as if knowing their time here was short—burn as in oxygen gas—and have 'hope, the Charmer' with them to the last—putting into these twenty years the energy, the enjoyment, the mental capital and rapture of a long life." Of the same "marvelous boy, whose sun went down in the sweet hour of prime," Mr. George Sim said: "It is difficult to imagine how it was possible in so short a life to acquire so varied an amount of knowledge as Dr. Scott possessed, especially when we consider his delicate constitution and toilsome course of education."

Nevinson has said of Schiller: "It is possible that the disease served in some way to increase his eager activity, and fan his intellect into keener flame."

Aretaeus, the well-known Cappadocian anatomist and physician, who lived in the second century A.D., in describing death from the "pouring out of blood" said: "Really, this is not much to be wondered at; but what is most wonderful is that in a case where the blood comes from the lung, in which the disease [tuberculosis] is most serious of all, patients, even when it is about to come to the end, do not give up hope." We also find the following reference to chronic lung conditions: "Such patients are hoarse; they are short of breath; they speak in a weak voice; their chest walls are dilated yet they do not seem to be broad enough, because a great deal of humor is pent up within them; the black part of the eye flashes; in such cases it is simply wonderful how the strength of the body holds out; the strength of the mind even surpasses that of the body." Aretaeus made additional references to "the confidence and hopefulness of persons expectorating matter from the lungs."

In many cases the mental activity and creative powers seem to vary directly with the progress of the disease. As striking examples of this, we might mention Voltaire, Robert Louis Stevenson, Marie Bashkirtseff, Keats, Shelley, Sidney Lanier, Thomas Hood, and John Addington Symonds. As Dickens has suggested, even after the body becomes a mere mummied crucible, the fires of genius may be observed to burn with a brightness not often seen in the nontuberculous. On this point it would be interesting to let some of the sufferers speak for themselves.

Sidney Lanier, lyric poet and psychic counterpart of Edgar Allan Poe, furnishes a striking example. His creative powers were not in evidence until after his disease was well under way, and his capacity for mental work increased as the disease advanced. He well expressed the peculiar psychology of the tuberculous, when, in 1873, he wrote as follows: "Were it not for some circumstances which make such a proposition seem absurd in the highest degree, I would think that I am shortly to die, and that my spirit hath been singing its swan-song before dissolution. All day my soul hath been cutting swiftly into the great spaces of the subtle, unspeakably deep, driven by wind after wind of heavenly melody. The very inner spirit and essence of all wind-songs, sex-songs, soul-songs, and body-songs, hath blown upon me in quick gusts like the breath of passion and sailed me into a sea of vast dreams, whereof each wave is at once a vision and a melody." Again he wrote: "Know, then, that disappointments are inevitable, and will still come until I have fought the battle which every great artist has had to fight since time began. This—dimly felt while I was doubtful of my own vocation and powers—is clear as the sun to me now that I know, through the fiercest tests of life, that I am in soul, and shall be in life and utterance, a great poet."

Marie Bashkirtseff, whose frail young body was constantly overtaxed by the sheer exhilaration of her exceptional mind, when only twenty-four exclaimed that art alone was the sustaining factor in her life.

Balzac, who died at fifty-one, was a prey to physical frailty and "a horrible spasmodic cough" which recurred from year to year. In 1836 he wrote: "My forces are being exhausted in the struggle; it is lasting too long; it is wearing me out. . . . A nervous sanguineous (!) attack. I was at death's door for a whole day." In 1838: ". . . if there is success, success will come too late. I feel myself decidedly ill. . . . Such fevers . . . crush me." In 1846: "I feel young, full of energy . . . before new difficulties." In 1848: "I have had to get a valet—being unable to lift a package, or to make any movement at all violent. . . . I am as thin as I was in 1819. . . ."

Katherine Mansfield, while resting at 47 Redcliffe Road, lamented the slow delivery of the many stories already written in her mind. "And don't I want to write them? Lord! Lord! it's my only desire—my one *happy issue.* And only yesterday I was thinking—even my present state of health is a great gain. It makes things so rich, so important, so longed for—Changes one's focus."

Dr. Jacobson suggests that Francis Thompson was thinking of his own struggle with tuberculosis when, in *The Hound of Heaven,* he said:

> Ah! Must—
> Designer infinite!—
> Ah! Must Thou char the wood ere Thou
> Canst limn with it?

Ebstein reported the following as coming from the pen of an inquiring patient:

> Many questions trouble me
> Torture also in the stillness,
> Is perhaps my knack of rhyming,
> Caused by the dread bacillus?

Ralph Waldo Emerson, who suffered from a chronic form of tuberculosis, seemed to be quite sure of his dual personality. In his own words, the one "toiled, compared, contrived, added, argued"; the other "never reasoned, never proved; it simply perceived; it was vision; it was the highest faculty." He added: "In writing my thoughts, I seek no order, or harmony, or results." After going south in November, 1826, to escape the "northeast winds," the following May we find him writing: "I am still saddled with the demon stricture [pleurisy], and perhaps he will ride me to death. I have not lost my courage, or the possession of my thoughts. . . ." Approximately a year later he said: "It is a long battle, this of mine betwixt life and death, and it is wholly uncertain to whom the game belongs. . . ."

Keats once said: "I feel more and more every day as my imagination strengthens, that I do not live in this world alone, but in a thousand worlds."

If we accept the teaching that there is a dual personality in every individual, the two personal entities being designated as primary and secondary—the primary personality as that part which conforms to the usual conventions of life, constantly being restricted by established habits and customs, and the secondary personality as that part, which, under ordinary conditions, is kept in leash but occasionally released through the influence of some subtle force to override all conventions and restraints—we can readily see how the world may be blessed or cursed by the unconventional sway of this secondary personality. In those of superior intellect this release of the secondary personality may paralyze restraining inhibitions and cause a flair of genius with power to open the doors leading to the magic fields of creative achievement, doors otherwise closed by the prohibitions of intellectual, moral, and social locksmiths.

How unhappy many pious, prohibiting souls might be if they really knew through what questionable avenues the most beautiful and significant creations of genius have traveled. Fortunately, our archives contain no recorded fingerprints for the detection of psychic derelicts. How surprised these same prohibiting individuals might be if they knew what a frightful price has been paid for many of the literary, artistic, and scientific treasures in which we are permitted to revel without thought of their laborious birth. Certainly, we must admit the intimate relationship of many of these treasures with disease, drugs, and alcohol. As contributing factors we should also consider poverty, persecution, imprisonment, isolation, and often the consciousness of approaching death and, for the scientist, not infrequently, the voluntary risk of life. On the other hand, in those of inferior mental qualities the primary personality may be submerged by the reign of the secondary personality with the danger of irrational behavior. According to Dr. Jacobson, it is in this low-mentality group that we usually find the so-called medium, claiming supernatural communications. There is also a tendency toward vagabondage, while those of exceptional mentality rise on the wings of genius.

As mentioned above, among the factors and forces which seem to destroy inhibition and temporarily set free the secondary personality are alcohol, opium, and possibly the toxins of tuberculosis. While scientific proofs may be wanting, it is easy to build up plausible evidence by the enumeration of many cases which apparently have been influenced by these agents.

Having referred to alcohol and opium as being among the agents which occasionally release the secondary personality and lead to strange and fantastic flairs of genius, we should digress for just a moment in order to call attention to the fact that the alcoholic or the drug addict always pays a frightful price. Among the literary geniuses who have been addicted to alcohol and opium we might mention De Quincey, Coleridge, Edgar Allan Poe, Gabriel Rossetti, James Thomson, Elizabeth Barrett Browning, Swinburne, and Francis Thompson. Two of these, Edgar Allan Poe and James Thomson, "died in the gutter." Another, Francis Thompson, was rescued from the streets in London in an almost dying condition. Jeannette Marks states that two of the remaining five "made ineffectual struggles to get free. And one made no struggle at all but quietly closed the door of his house upon the world. . . . One was made well by a great love, another by a great friendship. But of De Quincey, Coleridge, Poe, Rossetti, James Thomson and Francis Thompson, is recorded both physical and mental shipwreck."

We are now concerned with the alleged influence of the toxins of the tubercle bacillus. After allowing for the increased mental activity which is apt to accompany enforced physical rest and the fear of impending death, many students of tuberculosis have expressed the belief that there is a decided excitation of the mind with increased capacity for creative accomplishment and that this excitation is due to toxic agents manufactured by the tubercle bacillus. Even though we question the intangible conception of a dual personality and the unproved theory of a psychic stimulant among the toxins of tuberculosis, it must be admitted that we have not reduced the number of exceptional minds in conflict with the disease.

During the past few decades the tubercle bacillus has inspired much investigative work, including that of the Research Committee of the National Tuberculosis Association. This Committee has been particularly interested in the chemical composition of the tubercle bacillus. Through the Committee's various assignments to carefully selected workers in well-chosen laboratories, many interesting observations have been made, and some significant facts have been established. If there is a chemical factor possessing the power of mental excitation, the continuation of these investigations may ultimately lead to its discovery and identification.

In the meantime, we must agree that the present evidence of such a stimulus is founded wholly on the clinical observations of those who have witnessed the strange phenomena of mental excitation in many individuals suffering from tuberculosis. While we await the proof of a stimulating toxin, all well-informed physicians who think in terms of tuberculosis will recognize the genuineness of past observations with reference to unusual psychic phenomena in those already endowed with exceptional mental qualities, and the majority of them will continue to attribute such phenomena to compensatory efforts on the part of the patient to meet the insistent demands of a dread disease, to defeat the annulling vision of approaching death, and, in some, to disguise a consciousness of the dismal truth.

In addition to this brief summary of opinions expressed in semiscientific and popular writings, attention is called to the fact that textbooks on tuberculosis recognize the profound influence of tuberculosis on the nervous system. In some of them the surprising euphoria accompanied by a desire for creative accomplishment is frankly discussed.

Dr. Maurice Fishberg in his book on *Pulmonary Tuberculosis* says: "As an exquisitely chronic disease, phthisis is accompanied by many morbid manifestations of the nervous system; in fact, nearly every symptom of the disease is often influenced by the effects of the tuberculous toxins on the nervous system. The neurotic phenomena may make their appearance immediately at the outset, in some they precede the actual onset of phthisis, while most confirmed consumptives have a psychology peculiarly their own, and show symptoms of nervous aberration which cannot escape the vigilance of the observant physician."

Under psychic traits he adds: *"Many tuberculous patients show a remarkable change in their mental traits and character, a disturbance in their emotional life and a striking divergence from their previous customs, habits, affections, and tastes.* In some, this change precedes the evident onset of the disease, in many it appears synchronously with the symptoms of active disease; it may ameliorate with each improvement, and aggravate with each acute exacerbation." He goes on to say: "Engel points out that the original, innate temperament or character of the individual becomes strikingly pronounced in the chronic consumptive: The pessimist suffers from marked despondency; the optimist becomes unreasonably hopeful of the ultimate outcome, etc. These phenomena may be explained by the discordance between the subjective feelings of the patient who is not as disabled as the objective findings of the physician would lead to expect. The mental make-up of the patient depends greatly on his physical condition which, in tuberculosis, is subject to great oscillations; aggravations and improvements coming and going quite unexpectedly. The mental traits *per se* do not change, but such traits as were characteristic during youth but, as a result of education, training, and the vicissitudes of life, have been suppressed, reappear boldly, unhindered by conventionalities."

Discussing euphoria and euthanasia, he says: "Optimism, despite many evidences of progressive disease which saps the body, is frequent; only a copious hemorrhage, or, more rarely, a spontaneous pneumothorax, will terrify the average tuberculous patient. Otherwise, all the symptoms amount to little or nothing. . . . It is often astonishing to behold the sinking man make plans for the future, engage in new enterprises, plan long voyages not for a cure, which he believes he has almost attained, but for pleasure or, as I have seen, arranging for his marriage a few days before his death."

Referring to patients with advanced tuberculosis, Dr. Fishberg says: "His bright eyes with dilated pupils, which are at times contracted unilaterally, the flushing cheeks, the keen intellect which is so often met with among those who before the onset of the disease were rather dull in this respect, coupled with a flickering intelligence which brightens up suddenly for a few hours, but is soon followed by mental depression or fatigue, bear close resemblance to the average person who is under the influence of moderate doses of alcohol, or a narcotic drug.

"In tuberculous patients, particularly young talented individuals, it is noted that for weeks or months, now and then, they display enormous intellectual capacity of the creative kind. Especially is this to be noted in those who are of the artistic temperament, or who have a talent for imaginative writing. They are in a constant state of nervous irritability, but despite the fact that it hurts their physical condition, they keep on working and produce their best work. . . ."

He quotes Létulle as having said: "They astonish everybody with their mental and intellectual activity; their memory, their quick judgment, their delicate reasoning powers are of incomparable amplitude."

Dr. Robert H. Babcock in *Diseases of the Lungs* says: "The one peculiarity of the consumptive which probably strikes the observer most forcibly is his hopefulness, the *spes phthisicorum* of the ancients. This is not usually seen, or at least is not pronounced, in the beginning of the disease, but late in its course, when it is only too apparent to his friends that death is not far off, the consumptive is possessed with a belief in his speedy recovery. He not only talks hopefully of his condition, but actually makes plans for the future which to his friends are absurd and distressing. It is this sanguine expectancy which makes the bedridden consumptive so ready to undertake journeys to some vaunted resort."

Dr. Sherman G. Bonney did not believe that the byproducts of the tubercle bacillus could cause a toxic excitation of the mind, but in his textbook, *Pulmonary Tuberculosis and Its Complications,* he admits that "there is a vast difference in the degree to which pulmonary invalids retain their nervous energy. . . . Some exhibit an astonishing vitality almost to the very end, although their physical strength may be very seriously impaired."

From the above discussion it is obvious that the proper understanding of the psychological phenomena accompanying tuberculosis requires careful reasoning with skilful integration of the known factors and conservative consideration of the unknown.

It is well to remember that every person suffering from tuberculosis presents individual problems. In each case the hereditary factors are distinctive, and the individual's reaction to disease and other external influences is conditioned by these factors—the fundamental traits of character. Though the sum-total of life is to be found in the hereditary and the environmental factors, it is obvious that the range is so wide, the possibilities so varied, that there is no formula which will fully interpret behavior at any period in a person's life. The tubercle bacillus has its own individual characteristics, and the response to its presence in man is to some extent dependent upon the strain or the virulence of the invading bacillus. The behavior of the bacillus and the progress of tuberculosis are greatly influenced by the temperament and constitution of the person infected and the environment in which he lives. Finally, the psychology of the individual suffering from tuberculosis may vary with the acuteness or chronicity of the disease, the stage it has reached, and in some the periods of quiescence and activity. . . .

To mention briefly the work of all the creative minds influenced by tuberculosis would mean the accumulation of sufficient data to fill a series of thick volumes. The following incomplete list, chosen from the field of literature alone, will immediately bring a realization of the close relationship of this disease with creative effort and accomplishment. While the diagnosis cannot be verified in many of the persons listed, the available clinical evidence seems to warrant their inclusion. It is interesting to note that they nearly all lived before the discovery of the tubercle bacillus, before early diagnosis was possible, and before toxemia was limited by modern management.

Milton, Pope, Shelley, Voltaire, Hood, Keats, Walt Whitman, Elizabeth Barrett Browning, Francis Thompson, Goethe, Schiller, Molière, Channing, Mérimée, Thoreau, Descartes, Locke, Kant, Spinoza, Beaumont, Samuel Johnson, Goldsmith, Sterne, De Quincey, Scott, Leigh Hunt, Jane Austen, Charlotte, Emily, and Ann Brontë, Stevenson, Balzac, Rousseau, Washington Irving, Hawthorne, Gibbon, Kingsley, Ruskin, Emerson, Cardinal Manning, Lanier, Marie Bashkirtseff, Robert Southey, Westcott, Georges de Guérin, David Gray, Amiel, John R. Green, Robert Pollok, Hannah More, James Ryder Randall, N. P. Willis, John Addington Symonds, Stephen Crane, Katherine Mansfield, Paul Laurence Dunbar, Eugene O'Neill, Novalis, Klabund, Tchekov, Llewelyn Powys, W. E. Henley, William Cullen Bryant, John Greenleaf Whittier, Maxim Gorky, Feodor Dostoevski, Aubrey Beardsley, Eugene Albrecht, Beranger, Richard Lovelace, George Ripley, Blackmore, Joseph Rodman Drake, Kirke White, Adelaide Ann Proctor, Henry Timrod, H. C. Bunner, John Sterling, Havelock Ellis, and John Millington Synge. Cicero has also been listed among those who may have suffered from tuberculosis.

Even this limited list opens a field for interesting studies in the realm of psychology conditioned by affliction and places before the biographer the intriguing trend of genius through its difficult course in defiance of disease. . . .

Dan Latimer

SOURCE: "Erotic Susceptibility and Tuberculosis: Literary Images of a Pathology," in *MLN*, Vol. 105, No. 5, December, 1990, pp. 1016-31.

[*In the following essay, Latimer observes that in works by such authors as Thomas Mann and Edgar Allan Poe characters afflicted with tuberculosis are associated with erotic and artistic qualities.*]

What is striking about tuberculosis as a disease—in contrast to other important disease representations—syphilis, let's say, or leprosy—is that tuberculosis gets remarkably good press from writers of belles lettres—especially in the first two-thirds of the 19th century. René and Jean Dubos characterize this literary treatment as "perverted sentimentalism," and indeed, considering the nastiness of the disease and its ubiquity, it is hard to imagine at first why permanent diarrhea, ceaseless coughing, spitting up of yellow phlegm then bright red blood, having a grotesquely swollen neck after the lymph nodes have bagged a few of the circulating bacilli, not to mention the night sweats, fever, sleeplessness, opium addiction, emaciation, sunken chest, and clawlike hands—it is hard to imagine how the disease could have been romanticized at all. Nor was it exactly the privilege of the few to have it. In the 19th century, according to Dubos, one-half of the population of England suffered from it with varying degrees of severity. At the beginning of the 20th century, practically all Americans were tuberculin positive, that is, had been exposed at one time or another to the disease. In the first half of the 20th century, it killed 5,000,000 people in the United States, and in 1952, the date of *The White Plague,* Dubos calls it still the greatest killer of those between 15 and 30 years of age. Fifty million were still suffering from it world-wide in 1952, and of those it killed three to five million every year.

The disease, it seems, has always been around. There are Egyptian skeletons from 1000 B.C. with bone lesions, and there are neolithic remains showing signs of spinal curvature, both hallmarks of tubercular infection. But there have been epidemics, periods when the disease was far worse than at other times. In the middle of the 17th century, there was a mini-epidemic in England, though the disease was rare in the country districts. Twenty percent of total deaths were attributed to it. The disease then declined spontaneously to 13 percent of total deaths around 1715, at which point tubercular mortality began again to rise. At the end of the 18th and beginning of the 19th centuries, the mini-epidemic was replaced by a very major one. Then around 1850, the mortality of the disease began to decline gradually of its own accord—before medicine had really figured out what to do about it, whether even it was infectious or not, whether the patient should relax or rough it (as in Mark Cook's wilderness cure), breathe fumes of cow dung or go into the mountains, before Koch had determined that a bacillus caused the disease, and certainly before streptomycin was used against it—not really as a cure, it turns out, since the bacillus lives a long time in dead tissue, through which blood, hence anti-bacterial drugs, cannot circulate.

Mortality declined for several reasons, but the spontaneous decline was probably due to the ubiquitous exposure, the melancholy absence of progeny from those who had been susceptible and had died young, on the one hand, and, on the other, the resistance put up by the bodies of everyone else who did survive it—all rather a Darwinian answer to how epidemics decline on their own. Within this period of gradual decline, there were other periods when mortality shot up aberrantly, even among those groups known previously for considerable resistance. Tuberculosis mortality always rises during times of social upheaval and disruption, during wars and revolutions, when life is unpleasant and stress is high. During the Prussian siege of Paris in 1871, for instance, tuberculosis deaths rose. Eastern European Jews from the ghettos, whose mortality from consumption was low compared to the general population, soon had a worse mortality rate than the general population once the pogrom-like activities of the post-World War I period were under way. Denmark, which was not involved in World War I—neither fighting, nor occupied—but was surrounded by mutually hostile neighbors, had an increased mortality rate. For Dubos, the reason was in part at least that Denmark's own consumption of animal protein was disrupted by heavy sales to England during the war. Mortality declined again once submarine warfare disturbed the meat shipments on the high seas. This relation of animal protein intake to resistance to tuberculosis is supported by the high mortality among vegetarian African tribes (the Akikuyu) as opposed to such meat eaters as the Masai.

Dubos's theory on the causes of the great epidemics of tuberculosis rests mainly on the spreading industrial revolution, in particular the era following Marx's so-called "primitive accumulation," the most rapacious era of early capitalism. Of course Dubos emphasizes the unhealthy living conditions of the workers driven off the land, out of the loveliest villages and into the hellish tenements of new industrial towns, with their night shifts, child labor, and bad nutrition; and, appropriately enough, we find Dubos quoting extensively, and by the way anonymously, from *Capital* here (though the less threatening Engels does get a fleeting mention). A propos of nutrition, one textile manufacturer noticed that the flying fingers of his working girls slowed down after breakfast, so he forbade them breakfast in order to make them, he thought, more alert. Soon sagging surplus value was the least of the problems they and their boss had. In fact, the tuberculosis epidemic was probably the first big price the middle class had to pay, Dubos says, for its capitalist revolution. It was not just the exploited employees who were dropping like flies; the bourgeois gentleman, after a hard day of making others work for him, would come home himself puffing out little toxic clouds of bacilli. This explains why the leisure classes also died from the disease, despite their ample board and enviable idleness.

But it was not just the physical living conditions, the dust, the smoke, the crowded and stuffy rooms of industrialized cities that got the epidemic going. It was also, Dubos says, a matter of the mind—the psychic disruption of the worker as he or she was torn away from a world which, in spite of its poverty, was one where the worker had felt at home and secure to an extent, one where ancestral values were clear, where one was close to the land, and had a comprehensible place in a family and a community. The new urban life offered unusual new cruelties and solitude, and certain hopelessness as well, and consequently vice, including alcoholism and other chemical substitutes for a natural sense of well-being.

This connection between a disrupted psyche and a disrupted soma is something the theoreticians, as well as the poets, of tuberculosis make much of. Dubos mentions without apparent skepticism the statements of physicians who wrote of severe emotional dislocations as preceding the onset of tuberculosis in practically all their patients. Théophile Laënnec, an early student of the disease, inventor of the stethoscope, and therefore of "mediate auscultation" in the examination of tubercular patients, said that unsatisfied desires, nostalgia, and passions of profound melancholy can and do lead to the onset of the disease. Such emotions can and do proceed from financial difficulties, unhappy love affairs, and family tragedies. Thus it was said that Keats's case of miliary consumption was brought on by Fanny Brawne or some bad reviews of *Endymion.* I cite only by way of illustration, and not as evidence, Thomas Mann's fictional treatment of Hans Castorp in *The Magic Mountain* (1924). Castorp's "disease" manifests itself at the same time that some long-buried memories of a boyhood attachment to Pribislav Hippe return during a strenuous walk around *Kurort* Davos. This attachment had only been a matter of a borrowed pencil, an exchange of a few words, and the preservation of some sacred fetishistic pencil shavings. But by the time Castorp gets back to the Berghof, he is in a state of nervous prostration and is spattered with his own blood. He sinks into a chair just in time to hear Dr. Krokowski explain to a roomful of smouldering female patients that the power of repressed desire always returns in the form of disease. This diagnosis also helps explain Castorp's cousin Joachim's difficulty in getting well, since he is desperately enamored of the young Russian woman

Marusja in the Berghof but remains faithful to what he considers his military duty. For Castorp the pencil itself returns, along with Hippe's epicanthic eyes and a new opportunity for love, in Clavdia Chauchat on Walpurgis Night. "Don't forget to bring me my pencil," she says, as she repairs to her bedroom, an exciting if confusing moment for the reader, if only because it emphasizes what really has been clear all along, namely that those who are diseased supposedly because of erotic repression are nevertheless erotomaniacal. One can cite the "unmanierliche" Russian neighbors of Castorp early in the novel who make love noisily and incessantly, as well as the Dionysian entourage of Mynheer Peeperkorn to whom Chauchat (the "hot cat") later becomes attached. The orgies of the Berghof are joined by way of allusion in this text to Faust's orgies on the Brocken with witches as well as the medieval sojourn on the Venusberg by Tannhäuser. Responsibility in Castorp's case is in the flatland, the mercantile world of buying low and selling high, of regular work, of family, and of the unreflecting accumulation of solid property. Eventually responsibility appears as the defense of the fatherland during World War I, a responsibility which Castorp accepts after years of self-indulgence. Irresponsibility is, on the other hand, quite pleasant—a matter not only of erotic experimentation, but of letting go in other ways, in lying around with a low-grade fever reading, thinking, eating massively five times a day (including six-course lunches), having lovely conversations, and cultivating the soul.

Before coming back to Thomas Mann and the suspicious vacillations and waverings of *Tristan* (1902), I would like to take a turn through Dubos again if only to suggest that Mann's vacillations are typical of the contradictory representations of the disease in the years leading up to Mann's *fictional* accounts. We cited Laënnec's position that repressed desire pops up as tuberculosis, a point reiterated by the lecturing lecher of *The Magic Mountain,* Krokowski. What of the other chord, sounded just as often, just as insistently in Mann, that sickness and orgiastic sexuality are two sides of the same self-abandonment? And if this sexual sickness is one that leads to death—think of the terminal relaxation of Aschenbach on the Lido in Venice after he had caught a different, but just as deadly, disease chasing along the canals in pursuit of Tadzio—why is Mann just as likely to make sickness attractive as he is to be censorious about it? When the disease was so common and emerged from an abused proletariat, how did it become in the iconology an aristocratic affliction? When it was so revolting (phlegm and bloody hemorrhages), how did it become the sign of a refined, ethereal nature? Why was Elizabeth Barrett Browning, in Italy for her own consumption, overheard to say, "Is genius, then, only a matter of scrofula?" One might mention that the disease could have been more revolting if the ulceration caused by the extreme toxicity of the bacillus in the moist tissue of the brain, lungs, intestines, even the royal anus in the case of Louis XIV—if this ulceration had been visible, or less disguisable in the case of scrofula by high collars and fashionable neckwear, it would have been less easy to associate tuberculosis with love. As it was, the poets, whose whole gift, Aristotle says, consists in making certain lies plausible, had an all too easy time of it (*Poetics* XXIV).

One curiosity of the taste of the time involved, says Dubos, a change in what was considered attractive in women. Or was this change in taste a matter of necessity thanks to the universality of consumption? In any case, the revolutionary female of 1789, boisterous and lusty, had given way to the vaporous, languishing, delicate, diseased—sometimes even deceased women—of Edgar Allan Poe. Poe's heart leapt up when his wife Virginia would pause during her recitals at the piano while bright red blood ran down the front of her white dress. Nothing was more thrilling to the men of the time. William Cullen Bryant said a dead beautiful girl was the most poetic of themes. Women wore white muslins to look even more consumptive than they already were. They blanched their faces with whitening powders. Pre-Raphaelite painters preferred tubercular women for their models. One such model was the renowned Elizabeth Siddal, a pale redhead with long thin limbs, a cadaverous physique, and a red, sensual mouth. She became Rossetti's wife and a favorite model for everyone from Burne-Jones to Millais. The painters loved to make her lie in a tub of lukewarm water, though at times it was considerably colder than that, while they pretended that she was Ophelia. She died in 1862 at the age of 30 of a laudanum overdose, laudanum being the drug of choice of the time, a mixture of alcohol and opium, just the ticket for diarrhea and a hacking cough. Jane Burden was the woman with whom William Morris afflicted himself (in 1859). She was tubercular, inconstant if not wildly so and sported the same body type as Elizabeth Siddal.

A few years earlier, love and death had already been joined in the feverish example of Marguerite Gauthier, the *dame aux camélias,* and courtesan friend of Dumas, *fils*. After she died at the age of 23, it became fashionable for young lovers to seek the blessing of her spirit by bringing camellias to her grave in Paris. *Camille,* translated into English had a great success in New York, and Verdi's *La Traviata* (1853) it seems, never leaves off drinking, dancing, copulating, and being free. Henri Murger gave his tubercular flower girl-girlfriend eternal life in his *Scenes of Bohemian Life* (1849). When Murger put pen to paper, Mimi was scarcely cold, having died only the year before. Puccini's popular opera, *La Bohème* (1896), is based, of course, on the text of Murger. So compelling was the sexy image of this disease that the Goncourt Brothers, despite their professed realism, were unable to resist a certain romanticization of the sickness in their novels. Dubos mentions the Goncourt novel of *Madame Gervaisais* (1869), whose seraphic seductiveness increases with the progress of her disease. *Germinie Lacerteux* (1864) is an even better example for our purposes here, if we say that our main purpose is to trace the supposed relationship of sex and disease. Germinie is a working-class woman whose frantic erotic excesses—frantic at least for the Goncourts—and her inordinate love of alcohol sentence her to certain pulmonary hemorrhage and death. In this novel, the association of sexual freedom with the grave seems so suspiciously like punishment, in fact, that one thinks of Fontane's *Effi Briest* (1895), another adulteress with lung trouble. For Germinie, though, the need for punishment seems to come less from the central character, as in the Fontane novel, than from the authors, who are clearly appalled by the notion of a woman sleeping around and getting away with it.

Germinie needs to get drunk to let go, needs a *Liebestrank,* or at least a *Liebesgetränk,* much like Castorp, whose desire is also abetted by its translation into a language other than his own. He drinks punch and speaks French to seduce Chauchat. Not that most 19th-century consumptives needed to get drunk to be amorous, since they were almost invariably drunk already. Dubos says that it is safe to assume that every consumptive became an opium addict. Opium generates unnatural brain states. So does fever, also part of the consumptive's lot. Dubos mentions that there is a theory that consumption produces in its victim a microbial toxin, which gives the opium-eating, fever-ridden patient an extra jolt of giddiness. Whatever caused it, it made the consumptive wild, restless, hyperactive, and visionary. Activities suggesting such wildness were widely regarded not only as the result of consumption but also as its cause. One could contract tuberculosis both while sitting in the rat-infested gutter clutching one's gin bottle and while whirling about in a ballroom sipping champagne with Violetta. Indeed, waltzing itself supposedly lubricated the slippery slope to disease, though whether it was as dangerous in this regard as the polka *morbus* is hard to tell. These are the activities of city life, in any case, and consumption was in its inception a disease of the cities. Whatever happened in the cities was perverse and unnatural and likely to upset healthy equilibrium.

If one was sick, then, one was precipitous, hectic, intoxicated. As Stevenson tells us, though, in "Ordered South," strength is soon at an end, even while restlessness remains. The consumptive is therefore necessarily focussed on indoor sports or even sublimations into mental activity of his (or her) natural drives. One can suppose, therefore, a metaphorical leakage between the patient's fever to the idea of a consuming fire, that seemed to burn the patient up from within, and then to the brightness of intellectual achievement. The mental restlessness of the consumptive was a sign of genius. Sidney Lanier, bard of the Chattahoochee, believed his creativity was encouraged by his disease. He was shocked to find Walt Whitman perfectly healthy. The Goncourt brothers were similarly disappointed in Victor Hugo, who would have been a much better poet had he been a physical wreck like Heine or indeed like themselves. The characteristic fire of the consumptive was noted in ancient times by physicians like Aretaeus, who called it *spes phthisica,* "consumptive hope". It manifested itself as a race with death, a hectic drive toward achievement or experience before the disease had burned itself out and the consumptive up. Stevenson's productivity is often mentioned as an example of *spes phthisica*: *A Child's Garden of Verses* (1885), *Dr. Jekyll and Mr. Hyde* (1886), and *Kidnapped* (1886) were all written under these hectic conditions. But it is hard to imagine such works being produced by a consumptive who had only the disease, and no talent, to help him along. Nevertheless intellectual sensitivity and culture were linked with the disease as irresistibly as were unconventionality or hypersexuality. Any one of these linkages would bring us back again to Thomas Mann, but it is surely the first, the alliance between *art* and disease, that opens the path to *Tristan* (1902). Or is it?

Hypersexuality does exist in the story, of course, but it is characteristic of the healthy Klöterjahn, whose name suggests a dialect word for "testicles." It is he who is discovered, compromisingly, with the maid in the hall of the sanatorium Einfried practically the instant he has checked his wife in as a patient there. It is not surprising that he has chosen as his son Anton's nanny a woman of "exuberant figure" and "swelling hip." She is the woman regarded by Spinell with revulsion as she takes the Klöterjahn baby, another relentless man of action and instinct, for an airing in the garden. Klöterjahn *père* is robust of whisker and appetite, devouring an English breakfast every morning with an English family he discovers staying—though they are apparently quite healthy—at Einfried. His overall Anglophilia suggests simplicity and absence of any neurotic tendencies. He is a solid businessman and frankly rapacious. His gaze is open and direct. His eyes are blue with pale lashes; he is short, solid, sociable, and noisy. He is contrasted with Einfried's resident author, Detlev Spinell, who is quiet, solitary, and looks a bit like an undertaker with his lanky, dark form and black coat with tails. When he stands at the piano in the light of the two candles and beckons to Gabriele to play, it is as if he is inviting her to her own coffin. Mann insists on the association of his name with the thorny crystalline mineral "spinel." But the name also suggests *Spinne,* "spider," as well as *Spindel,* the bobbin which gives death to Dornröschen. *Spinner,* "madman," may also be part of the name's resonance. His "deer-like brown eyes," his "gentle" expression and beardless face suggest either feminization or total lack of sexuality. The eyes cannot bear to search out much reality, the defects of which are only too abundant, he says. He prefers his fantasy, his mental impression, to the tangible and actual. Consequently he transforms the image of the young Gabriele in the garden with her six girlfriends into a Pre-Raphaelite *hortus conclusus,* a garden "wild and overgrown," with crumbling, mossy walls, and a fountain bordered by lilies. He has the girls, like fairytale figures, singing instead of crocheting and sharing recipes for potato pancakes, which, according to Klöterjahn, is what they were really doing. Spinell places a little golden crown on Gabriele's head which was not there in reality but which in her increasingly pathological "self-satisfaction" and self-absorption she comes to believe in. When Klöterjahn bursts from the shrubbery to tear her away from the artistic father and girlfriends, Spinell sees the event in Tennysonian terms, and Gabriele as a German lady of Shalott also used, in her weaving, to indirect, reflected contact with the outside world who rises to look directly at her knight, and is crushed by reality. Similarly her tapestry, her web of art, unravels, her mirror shatters, and she dies. We are told several times that Gabriele's eyes have a slight tendency *not* to look directly at things: "sie zeigen eine kleine Neigung zum Verschiessen."

Spinell's decadence, his lack of fitness for life, the impaired nature of his appetites are signalled by his "carious" teeth. His sleeping late would be another sign of decadence, at least for the businessman, for whom the daylight hours are sacred for "getting ahead." It is precisely the day which is rejected for night and love in the piano score of Wagner's *Tristan and Isolde* (1865). Day separates the illicit lovers, who then are reunited at night. No doubt the sacredness of night gives us the principal motivation for Gabriele's opening her forbidden concert with Chopin's *Nocturnes* as well—Chopin, of course, another consumptive.

One positive thing can be said about Spinell's irresponsible behavior in this scene: he does have a sense of the beautiful. He does bring Gabriele (the music-making angel) back to her true artistic nature, tears her away from her reluctant respectability, her healthy child, her priapic husband, indeed from life itself in all its banality, and redevotes her to art and beauty, for which we are told she has an extraordinary talent. To cultivate the beautiful is to be a dreamer, someone who is impractical and self-absorbed. Spinell, who hates the practical, the useful, manages "to rouse in her a quite novel interest in her own personality" (eine seltsame Neugier, ein nie gekanntes Interesse für ihr eigenes Sein). She nourishes "secret thoughts . . . about herself." She finds herself mildly intoxicated during these pensive moods when she is "a little affected, self-satisfied (selbstgefällig), even rather self-righteous (ein wenig beleidigt)." This intoxication is nothing compared to the massive drunkenness of Wagner's piano score, the *Liebestrank* which she and Spinell share. After she has played the second act duet and has paused with a question about the text, Spinell explains to her what it means for the lovers to say "Even then I am the world" (Selbst dann bin ich die Welt). It seems the perfect phrase for what she has become now, self-fulfilling, self-sufficient, the imaginative source of her own reality, all dissonant elements of the real world banished for the secret delights of the night of mystic death and love. The duet in question (from Wagner) begins,

> O sink' hernieder,
> Nacht der Liebe,
> gieb vergessen
> dass ich lebe;
> nimm mich auf
> in deinen Schooss,
> löse von
> der Welt mich los!
>
> (Descend,
> O night of love,
> let me forget,
> that I live;
> take me
> in your lap,
> release me
> from the world!)

This beauty that she produces is her death, of course, because it is precisely her disease which feeds her artistry. She would not be so talented, in the logic of consumption's interpreters, if she were not so ill. Her physique, too, with its ethereal, white, translucent fragility is precisely the otherworldly "muslin beauty" of Virginia Poe or Elizabeth Siddal. The "red, sensual mouth" of Siddal is here "beautiful and wide," with "exceedingly sharp and well-cut contours." Under Spinell's influence, she drops her knitting in her lap, dreams, wastes away, and dies from the massive aural orgasm of the *Liebestod.* This is all so obvious that it is perhaps a pity to have the narrative—actually, Spinell—also make the point that Gabriele dies not of art but of reality, *das Respektabelste,* her husband and child—dies from being torn away from her magic musical garden in Bremen, from her fountain and lilies, and perverted from her true nature by the plebeian gourmand, Mr. Testicles. It can't be that she dies of both, but, of course, she does. Mann as usual is reluctant to take too unequivocal a position.

There may be another reason that she dies, as well. What, besides mutual hatred of reality and love of beauty, is the true relationship between Gabriele and Spinell? What else does the dubious Spinell encourage in his protégée? We mentioned her "self-absorption" and "self-satisfaction," her refusal to consider her own "bodily welfare" when she takes up Wagner's music. There is the mysterious allusion to self-sufficiency in "Even then I am the world," explained by Spinell to Gabriele but not to the reader. The nature of the love between Spinell and Gabriele is an artistically mediated one, a love of distance, indirection, and images. He bows to her from a safe distance of twenty feet; he is speechless, his shoulders are heaving with (one assumes) genuine emotion. His devotion to her "lifts her up on billowy cushions of cloud," away from himself and away from all earthly impurities.

The clearest hint of the nature of their relationship comes in his reasons for being in the sanatorium in the first place. He is having himself *elektrisiert.* His powers have drained away. He needs charging up again. Such was one medical remedy for exhaustion at the time. He explains, paradoxically, that what has brought on this exhaustion is sleeping late. He has a bad conscience. He refuses to be useful. He leads an unhealthy life, troubled by a sense of his own futility. His "whole inner life . . . his way of working is . . . frightfully unhealthy, undermining, irritating (aufreibend)." It is unhygienic, undisciplined. He had gotten to the point of being "wund und krank," sore and sick; the condition has advanced to such an extent that there is not a healthy spot anywhere on his person (kein heiler Fleck an [ihm]). He came to Einfried for a counterirritant, to be forced to get up early, to take cold showers, to take healthy exercise in the garden. The ladies to whom he is speaking give a name to his way of life. Perhaps they are trying to characterize him as an ascetic when they use the term *Selbstüberwindung,* "overcoming" or "controlling" himself. On the whole, they think he is too hard on himself; he frets, torments, abuses himself too much:

> —Sicher grämen Sie sich zu viel.
> —Ja, ich gräme mich viel.

We know by now, or ought to, thanks to the retrieval by Sander Gilman of the medical literature of Europe, and therefore the discursive context of belles lettres heretofore considered self-sufficient and exclusive, how to recognize representations of sexual pathology. In this regard, it is hardly a good sign that Spinell is a *Langschläfer;* always lying in bed late leaves the door open for any number of pathologies to develop, which would then show themselves physically as emaciation, lethargy, fleshy lips, attenuation of powers, and melancholia, which can advance even to the horrors of *Uranismus* or madness. I quote from Richard von Krafft-Ebing, *Psychopathia Sexualis*:

> Die geistige Liebe dieser Menschen [die Urninge] ist vielfach eine schwärmerisch exaltierte. . . . Es bestehen Neurosen (wie Hysterie, Neurasthenie . . .). Geweckt und unterhalten wird sie [die Neurasthenie] durch Masturbation oder durch erzwungene Abstinenz. . . . In der Mehrzahl der Fälle finden sich psychische Anomalien (glänzende Begabung für schöne Künste, besonders Musik bei . . . originärer Verschrobenheit) bis zu ausgesprochenen psychischen Degenerations-zuständen (Schwachsinn, moralisches Irresein).

> The spiritual love of these people [he's speaking of homosexuals] is usually an enthusiastic exalted one. . . . Neuroses (like hysteria, neurasthenia) arise . . . . Neurasthenia is awakened and sustained by masturbation or through forced abstinence. . . . In most of the cases one finds psychic anomalies (a splendid capacity for fine arts, especially music, along with peculiar perversity) to the point of marked psychic conditions of degeneration (imbecility or moral delirium).

To be mad, to be a woman, to be a child, as we can learn from influential physicians like Dr. Paul J. Mobius, is all part of this pathology. (See *Über den physiologischen Schwachisnn des Weibes,* fifth edition, 1909, pp. 17, 21). And Spinell is a child, a degenerate baby (ein verwester Säugling). He has no beard on his round, white, bloated face. He has the soft, doe-eyed gaze of a woman, oblique and indirect. His handwriting is full of gaps and nervous quavers (Zittrigkeiten), according to Herr Klöterjahn. But what of this *Verwesung,* this degeneration, nervousness, and neurasthenia? It is not enough to recognize that Spinell, who characterizes himself as weak and vengeful, the creature of *Geist und Wort,* is most probably a Jew, having been identified by Dr. Leander as coming from Lemberg (Lvov) Galicia, in other words, where " . . . das jüdische Geblüt vorzüglich gedeihen soll," according to that exemplary student of the Jewish guests of the Austrian Monarchy, Joseph Rohrer. One does not have to get too far into George Beard's *Sexual Neurasthenia* (1884) or Max Nordau's *Degeneration* (1892) to see that the cause of Spinell's decay, nervousness, and regressive appearance would have to be the nature and frequency of his sexual emissions. Given all these other pathologies, one would hardly be taken aback to discover that Spinell was also Jewish. How else besides general degeneration to explain the attenuated novel with the deeply confusing cover which can be read in a quarter of an hour? Or the fact of his own self-absorption in always reading it? Or the extraordinary number of letters that leave the sanatorium to find no response at all in the outside world? Perversion is no doubt Dr. Leander's diagnosis as well, for that, and not the normal dislike of the man of science for the artistic *Schwarmer,* would explain Leander's unrelenting contempt for Spinell.

It is as professor of perversion that he infects Gabriele as well, about whom it is probably not enough to say that she becomes a sublimated version of what he is on the physical level. We have mentioned her gaze and her languid, exhausted, translucent form. Her hands are mentioned just as often as Spinell's and are one aspect of their direct kinship. Hers are beautiful and white. His are white and finely shaped. Hers are in her lap more than they are anywhere else. When we first see her, "ihre schönen blassen Hände . . . ruhten in den Schossfalten eines schweren und dunklen Tuchrockes." At the piano after she finishes playing, her hands drop naturally to her lap, *die Hände im Schosse*. It is an image of her self-absorption and self-sufficiency: *Selbst dann, o Wunder der Erfüllung, selbst dann bin ich die Welt.* But the best image of the mediated eroticism she and Spinell share is the repeated foaming up under her laboring hands of the dark musical passion, the *masslose Befriedigung, unersättlich wieder und wieder,* of Wagner's music.

A curious aspect of the story, though, is the way that Mann, the artist allows his diagnosis of Spinell and Gabriele to indict art itself. It is of course true that Wagner, a special favorite of almost all educated homosexuals, according to Dr. Magnus Hirschfeld, is parodied in Mann's style ("Denken und Dünken versank in heiliger Dämmerung"); Einfried, the house of the sick, sounds like Wagner's villa in Bayreuth, Wahnfried. Spinell is not a real artist. The circuit of passion that flows between Spinell and Gabriele is not a strictly physical one. The mediated orgasm of the *Liebestod* is very far removed from the love recommended by Gottfried von Strassburg whose lovers do not play the prude but cure their sickness, *Lameir,* with the remedy of each other, ridding themselves thereby of a host of ills and sorrows. "This death suits me well," says Tristan jauntily,

> ine weiz, wie jener werden sol:
> dirre tot der tuot mir wol.
>
> (12,494-12,498)

Instead of the love that heals, we find in Mann the love that kills. Should we say then that not all art, but only its perverted versions in Wagner and Spinell, are being called into question? Perhaps only life-denying forms of art are included here?

We could say that only if Mann did not show such a favorable inclination toward life-denial himself. It is hard not to see the enthusiasm with which he paraphrases Wagner's musical ideas. Surely it is a measure of his self-hatred that Mann identifies the perverse love between Gabriele and Spinell and its supposed consequences of disease and death with a genuinely breathtaking musical score, with art, beauty, indeed with composition itself, the dubious activity which consumes most of Spinell's average day "so hasst man im anderen nur, was man nimmer sein will, und doch immer zum Teile noch ist," as Otto Weininger puts it so well in *Geschlecht und Charakter* (1903). Mann gestures by implication toward the source of art in disease, a point which he seemingly never tires of making, nor would he exclude his own art from the indictment. Tonio Kröger's background comes quite close, after all, to Mann's own, and the point of that novella, too, is that Tonio is an artist because he is intimately acquainted with abnormality, perhaps even with criminality. It is consequently justifiable to say that the clearly satirical elements of the *Tristan* novella do not exhaust its range. Spinell parodied is still not completely ridiculous. What he loves is beauty, while Klöterjahn only loves beauty's medium. Life defeats Spinell in the person of Klöterjahn and his robust son, and Spinell has to withdraw from the field the battle. But it is not a graceless retreat. Despite some appearances to the contrary, then, it is not impossible to count Thomas Mann among those belles lettrists who—perversely for René Dubos—speak favorably of disease and death as sources of art and beauty. Such words of praise for disease would, after all, only be a measure of Mann's self-love.

WOMEN AND DISEASE IN LITERATURE

Diane Price Herndl

SOURCE: "The Writing Cure: Women Writers and the Art of Illness," in *Invalid Women: Figuring Feminine Illness in American Fiction and Culture, 1840-1940*, The University of North Carolina Press, 1993, pp. 110-40.

[*In the following excerpt, Herndl discusses invalid women in nineteenth-century American life and literature.*]

By the 1870s, the invalid had become such a popular object for both writers and artists that she was one of the most familiar cultural figures. Abba Goold Woolson devoted a whole chapter in *Woman in American Society* (1873) to "Invalidism as a Pursuit," in which she complained that "the familiar heroines of our books, particularly if described by masculine pens, are petite and fragile, with lily fingers and taper waists. . . . A sweet-tempered dyspeptic, a little too spiritual for this world and a little too material for the next, and who, therefore, seems always hovering between the two, is the accepted type of female loveliness." In *Idols of Perversity,* a recent study of turn-of-the-century painting, Bram Dijkstra notes that the same was true of women in art: "Throughout the second half of the nineteenth century, parents, sisters, daughters, and loving friends were kept busy on canvases everywhere, anxiously nursing wan, hollow-eyed beauties who were on the verge of death." Joy Kasson has identified a fascination with the "romantic invalid" in nineteenth-century American sculpture. Wherever women turned in literature, art, medical or religious tracts, or even their own parlors they were confronted with the figure of the invalid woman. Sickly women and, to a lesser extent, sickly men were thought more aesthetically pleasing and interesting than healthy people. As Susan Sontag explains in *Illness as Metaphor,* the "tubercular" look was fashionable and was considered romantic. Abba Goold Woolson claimed that "with us, to be ladylike is to be lifeless, inane and dawdling. . . . Instead . . . of being properly ashamed of physical infirmities, our fine ladies aspire to be called *invalides*" (*Woman in American Society*). Women courted ill health in an attempt to be "beautiful," eating arsenic to achieve pale skin, wearing corsets, avoiding exercise. Whether these habits were destructive to women's health (as nineteenth-century feminists claimed), positive expressions of independence and sexuality (as David Kunzle argues in *Fashion and Fetishism*), or simple signs of continuing human interest in appearance and eroticism (as Valerie Steele contends in *Fashion and Eroticism*) ultimately may be impossible to tell. What we can know for sure is that in the mid- to late nineteenth century, illness became not only the subject of art but itself a kind of cosmetic art.

The invalid was not the only model of womanhood offered in the late nineteenth century, however. By the late 1880s and through the turn of the century, thousands of women were rejecting the cultural stereotype of woman as weak and sickly. Through both feminist and domestic social housekeeping movements women were becoming activists. They were entering both the professional world and the world of social work, thereby forming increasingly important political forces. Educated and intelligent women had more options than ever; as a result, though, it was incredibly difficult to define a proper womanly role. In *Imaging American Women,* Martha Banta claims that "the images by which ideas about the American female were being offered to the public between 1876 and 1918 were . . . varied to the point of potential self-contradiction."

Feminists were more organized than they had been in the middle of the century to respond to claims that female physiology stood in the way of women's political progress, but they were still worried by doctors' claims and uncertain about their own assertions of strength. M. Carey Thomas, who headed Bryn Mawr College, looking back to the 1870s, wrote in 1908, "We did not know when we began whether women's health could stand the strain of education." (quoted in Mary Walsh, "Doctors Wanted: No Women Need Apply,") The medical discourse had grown so powerful in the late nineteenth century that even feminists had begun to doubt their own claims.

One influential physician who was sure that women could not stand the strain of equality was Dr. Edward H. Clarke, who published *Sex in Education; or, A Fair Chance for the Girls* in 1873. He argued that menstruation necessitated regular rest periods that would make it impossible for girls to receive an equal education with boys. Perhaps no other work so solidified the feminist resistance to male medical pronouncements; an almost instant best-seller, *Sex in Education* nonetheless elicited a deluge of counterattacks. Julia Ward Howe edited a volume of replies to Dr. Clarke in 1874, and at least three other collections of feminist responses were published that year. More importantly, Clarke's claims led to the first scientific study of women, menstruation, and education: Mary Putnam Jacobi's *The Question of Rest for Women During Menstruation* (1877), which concluded that normal work was more beneficial to menstruating women than was bed rest. Feminists finally found the means to make their resistance to medical definitions of woman as invalid coherent. Clarke's monograph ultimately had the effect of strengthening the feminist opposition to medical practice.

Given the climate of activism, change, and conflict at the turn of the century, one would expect to find that fictions written by active and productive women who had, themselves, overcome invalidism would represent equally active and productive women who defy the stereotype of the invalid woman. Instead, in fictions like Charlotte Perkins Gilman's "The Yellow Wallpaper" (1891) and Edith Wharton's *The House of Mirth* (1905), we find the same passive and defeated invalid that had figured in the fictions of Southworth, Hawthorne, and Poe fifty years earlier. Despite the fact that Gilman and Wharton themselves worked hard to avoid invalidism, they nonetheless continued to create female figures in their fiction that appear strikingly similar to the earlier ones. The woman in "The Yellow Wallpaper," like Poe's women, goes mad and, apparently, takes her husband with her. Even though, as Annette Kolodny argues in "A Map for Rereading," her story is a "willful and purposeful misprision" of "The Pit and the Pendulum" that emphasizes that Gilman's narrator cannot be "released to both sanity and freedom" as can Poe's, it nonetheless leaves the figure of the invalid woman as drawn by Poe intact—driven insane by her intellectual needs. In the same way, Lily Bart in *The House of Mirth,* like Georgiana in "The Birthmark," Beatrice in "Rappaccini's Daughter," and Zenobia in *The Blithedale Romance,* dies at the end of the story, her body serving as an edifying object for the male gaze.

The apparently stable figure of the invalid woman in turn-of-the-century women's fictions is related specifically to issues of women's power through and over illness. Much recent feminist criticism of "The Yellow Wallpaper" and *The House of Mirth* has evaded the questions about individual power these texts specifically raise, celebrating the power of the author even though the texts work to challenge the possibilities for individual action. While much medical treatment at the turn of the century was still "somatic," that is, treating all ailments (even mental ones) with physical cures, theories stressing the power of mind over body came into prominence during the 1890s and 1900s. Physicians and laypeople alike were fascinated with "mental illnesses"—both insanity and psychosomatic illnesses—and with new cures that sought to directly treat the mind. "Mind cures" ("New Thought" as well as neurology and psychology) developed the idea that the individual has the ability to control his or her mind and therefore his or her body, regardless of environmental factors or social inequities. These medical and social theories emphasized the power of the individual rather than the normative power of society, so that illness became a mark of individual, not social, failure—of individual, not societal, "dis-ease."

Many of these new mind cures were religious in origin, like Mary Baker Eddy's Christian Science, and sought cure through belief. Others were secular or only vaguely religious, celebrating a "life force" or an "All-Supply" of energy. For the purposes of this discussion, I will refer to both the religious and the secular mind cures as "New Thought," as they were called at the time. Perhaps the simplest definition of New Thought was set out in the purpose statement of an early New Thought group, the Metaphysical Club of Boston, in 1895: "To promote interest in and the practice of a true philosophy of life and happiness; to show that through right thinking one's loftiest ideals may be brought into present realization; and to advance intelligent and systematic treatment of disease by spiritual and mental methods." (quoted in Charles Braden, *Spirits in Rebellion*). New Thought eventually became the medical equivalent of the economic individualism urged in the "success" literature at the turn of the century. Elizabeth Towne, who published her own religious New Thought poetry with the New Thought Publishing Company, started a publishing house and printed Bruce MacLelland's *Prosperity through Thought and Force* (1907), a treatise that explained how to use New Thought to achieve wealth as well as health. Just as one could rise on the corporate ladder with hard work and willpower, so, too, could one achieve perfect health. The discourse of self-help, mind over matter, and *willed* health may have provided Gilman and Wharton with the chance to effect for themselves a "writing cure," a personal version of Freud's "talking cure," that was related to New Thought.

Nonetheless, in "The Yellow Wallpaper" and *The House of Mirth,* Gilman and Wharton resist this representation of the individual's capacity for health. Instead, they portray seriously "sick" societies in which social and sexual oppression makes women ill. But these writers' own experiences of "willed" health, as well as their immersion in contemporary culture, make it impossible for them to maintain a consistent stance: the New Thought that had saved the writers indicts their heroines. Illness in these texts becomes, then, a matter of both subversion and collusion. Illness becomes a way to resist the sexist norms of nineteenth-century society, a specifically feminine form of revolt against male control, and a sign of *real* health in a *sick* world. At the same time that Gilman and Wharton celebrate this kind of resistance almost to the point of glorifying victimage they also condemn the women who allow their own victimization. Illness also becomes, then, a sign of acceptance of patriarchal power. As Deirdre David argues of George Eliot in *Intellectual Women and Victorian Patriarchy,* Gilman and Wharton were "collaborateurs" and "saboteurs" whose heroines' ends help reconcile the writers' ambiguous attitudes to past and present, to the male and female traditions in fiction, and to the ideology of "self-advancement" through "disciplined work."

MENTAL HEALING AT THE TURN OF THE CENTURY

By the turn of the century "New Women" and suffragists had begun to challenge Victorian stereotypes of femininity. Of course, most women were not "New Women." Even at the height of the first women's movement, only a very small percentage of women (around 4-5 percent) actually went to college (although by 1910, 40 percent of all college students were women [Glenda Riley, *Inventing the American Woman*]) and only about half of female college graduates went on to actively pursue professional careers. (ibid. and Carroll Smith Rosenberg, *Disorderly Conduct*) Still, 17 percent of all women were in the work force in 1900—four times as many as there had been in 1870. Another of the major changes in the lives of late nineteenth-century women was their involvement in various reform movements. After the Civil War, many were involved in actively feminist causes, but even greater numbers of women led, organized, and staffed social housekeeping campaigns like the temperance movement, care for orphans and veterans, urban planning, aid for the poor, and educational and health reform. Some women undertook these causes as active feminists. Most, however, saw their activism as consistent with the ideology of domesticity: they were expanding their role as moral guides from the nursery and kitchen to the world outside the home. One of the most active of these reform movements was aimed at health; these activists read the dire assessments of women's failing health and, guided both by feminism and by domesticity, determined to do something about it. Following in the footsteps of Mary Gove Nichols, health reformers like Dorothea Dix, Marie Zakrzewska, Elizabeth Blackwell, Jane Addams, Margaret Sanger, and Mary Putnam Jacobi, to mention but a few of the most famous, were instrumental in reforms of health and medicine (see Regina Morantz-Sanchez, *Sympathy and Science,* and Judith Leavitt, *Women and Health in America*). They founded hospitals; advocated dress reform, diet reform, health education, better hygiene, and birth control; and fought for reforms in regular medical practice that became standard policy by the mid-twentieth century. Women's movements of various kinds caused great changes in nineteenth-century culture, but a side effect of those reforms was increased contradiction among differing definitions of "woman's proper sphere." More than ever, women declared themselves fit to hold responsible positions outside the home; more than ever, medical authorities decried the public health dangers created when women devoted themselves to activities other than mothering.

Turn-of-the-century medical authorities by no means presented a unified front, however. The profession was still fragmented by differing theories of disease and treatment. Until the discovery of bacteria and specific etiology for disease at the end of the nineteenth century, allopathy was only one among many competing techniques. "Irregular" practices, like homeopathy, hydropathy, Grahamism, mind cure, and eclecticism, seemed pretty much equal at the time. Self-doctoring, accomplished with the help of the growing patent medicine business, was much in vogue. The medical profession was further fragmented by the entry of a fair number of women into active competition. By 1900, 6 percent of the practicing physicians in the United States were women; in some cities, like Boston and Minneapolis, women accounted for 20 percent of the physicians (Morantz Sanchez, "So Honoured, So Loved?"). These women served as living proof against the accepted "regular" medical position that women were not strong enough to be professionals or to step outside limited roles in the family.

A decades-old (if not centuries-old) belief does not die easily. Despite growing evidence that women could leave the home and not face life-long suffering and despite new theories of disease based on a medical model of specific etiology rather than closed energy, male physicians continued to caution against women taking on roles outside the home. Many of these medical authorities turned their attention from specific physical ailments to interest in "nervous diseases." Late nineteenth-century physicians were fascinated by mental disorders. In Europe, this fascination would lead to Freud's development of psychoanalysis; in the United States, it led to S. Weir Mitchell's development of the "rest cure" and William James's *Psychology,* as well as the proliferation of mind cures.

The second half of the nineteenth century saw an unprecedented increase in the diagnosis of "nervous" illnesses. Medical and cultural observers everywhere noted the staggering and ever-increasing numbers of people (male and female) who suffered from ailments grouped under the general label "nervousness." Edward Wakefield, a physician writing in *McClure's Magazine* in 1893, called nervousness the "national disease of America." Despite studies showing no rise in the actual incidence of insanity between 1885 and 1910, neurologists like George M. Beard and S. Weir Mitchell, among many others, believed that nervousness posed an imminent threat to modern civilization. Not surprisingly, the diagnosis of "nervousness" often represented cultural attitudes toward both disease and its sufferers; similar symptoms in men and women, the rich and the poor, those of American stock and those who had recently immigrated, were attributed to different causes. Therefore, while recent immigrants and the poor went insane, members of the upper middle class most often became "nervous." One study reveals that in 1911 the foreign-born were almost twice as likely as the native-born to be committed to insane asylums in New York State (Nathan Hale, *Freud and the Americans*). Middle-class men, no matter the severity of their symptoms, were most often described as having "neurasthenia," a disease newly discovered (or at least named) by Beard in 1869; middle-class women, too, were often diagnosed as neurasthenic, but if the symptoms were more severe, especially if they included "paroxysms" or "fits," women were described as "hysteric" and the blame for the disease was placed on their sexual organs (as the etymology of the word *hysteria*—from the Greek *hyster,* meaning "womb"—suggests).

Neurasthenia was the disease of the upper middle classes; almost any symptom could be a sign of it (the same was true of hysteria for middle-class and upper middle-class women). Robin and John Haller describe it in *The Physician and Sexuality in Victorian America* as the late nineteenth-century "pathological dumping ground for moralists within and outside the medical world." Almost anything, from tenderness of the scalp, forgetfulness, and ticklishness to dyspepsia, insomnia, and abnormal secretions, could be a sign of neurasthenia; in a few cases, impotence, headaches, yawning, and depression were also symptoms. Nineteenth-century physicians, influenced by Herbert Spencer's Social Darwinism, believed that neurasthenia in a man was the result of a too-speedy evolution from physical to mental work; his illness, though certainly not pleasant, was nonetheless a sign of his "higher" evolution and, therefore, at least tolerable. Many neurologists and psychologists, including Weir Mitchell and William James, were themselves sufferers of neurasthenia.

Nervousness in women, on the other hand, did not have such a specific etiology. Neurasthenia and hysteria, as one encounters them in medical writings of the time, seem to differ only in the severity of symptoms, but that, too, varies from doctor to doctor and among patients. (I will use "nervousness" to refer to mental ailments unless the context calls for a specific designation of either neurasthenia or hysteria.) Nervousness was sometimes understood in the same light as male neurasthenia: troubling but a sign of good breeding and intellectual achievement. More often, though, nervousness was interpreted as female inadequacy to deal with any intellectual endeavor at all and a tendency toward the more severe disease, hysteria. Nineteenth-century physicians believed male neurasthenia was the result of man's ever more demanding role in society, while female neurasthenia was the result of her inadequate brain capacity for dealing with complex thought and roles outside of the home (Haller and Haller, *The Physician and Sexuality in Victorian America*).

Nor was cause the only gender differentiation in neurasthenia. Treatment for male nervousness was increased activity, a return to physical exertion that was seen to counteract too much mental exertion. This treatment signaled the beginnings of a changed attitude about the relation between mind and body. Unlike the mid-nineteenth-century belief in the necessity of shepherding energy, new theories advocated balancing energies and even building energies in the treatment of men. But physicians most often suggested an intensified domesticity as the "cure" to female nervousness, assuming that domestic life was more peaceful than the world outside the home. If the disease were caused by overexertion, rest could be its only cure and a quiet life the only way to prevent it. One could describe the rest cure, which kept women not just at home but in bed in their rooms, as an almost parodic exaggeration of domesticity. Even some women physicians advocated a return to the domestic sphere for nervous women (see Morantz-Sanchez, "So Honoured, So Loved?," and Haller and Haller, *The Physician and Sexuality in Victorian America*). As Tom Lutz observes in *American Nervousness, 1903,* "Both cures [for women and for men] were represented in terms of a return to traditional values of passive femininity and masculine activity." Domesticity, which had begun as a woman-led movement to establish feminine power within the home, became by the turn of the century the means for doctors to confine women there. The suturing of difference between medical and domestic ideologies that we saw at work in Southworth's *Retribution* had, by an intensification of their similarities and a dismissal of their differences, become a tool for doctors to use to extend their own cultural and professional influence. (This occurred despite the extension of one kind of domesticity out of the home into "social housekeeping" reforms.)

Some physicians, however, suggested that female neurasthenia might be the result of boredom and idleness; one such physician, Herbert Hall, argued in 1905 that neurasthenia most often happened to creative women who were generally more clever and artistic than other people (Haller and Haller, *The Physician and Sexuality in Victorian America*). Even those who held this theory of the disease, however, usually suggested not professional or artistic work but charity work. Whatever their theory, though, theorists of nervousness agreed that it was somehow a culturally induced disease. "Their descriptions of the commonest nervous disorders of women and men emphasized conflicts within individuals who could not fulfill social norms, yet, because they had internalized them, could not consciously reject them" (Hale, *Freud and the Americans*).

Regular, allopathic, treatments for neurasthenia between about 1880 and 1910 were usually physically oriented. Nathan Hale, in *Freud and the Americans,* has characterized medical treatment during this period as the "somatic style" because it sought to treat mental ailments by exclusively physical means. Weir Mitchell, a pioneer in the field of neurological treatment, argued against what we would today identify as mental treatment. While he recognized that the causes of patients' ailments "are often to be sought in the remote past" and that patients will tell their physician "more than he may care to hear," Mitchell did not advocate eliciting such "confessions" (Mitchell, *Doctor and Patient*). It will surprise modern skeptics to learn that the somatic style did achieve notable results; rest, diet, exercise, electrical stimulation, hydropathy, and drugs often worked wonders. These means did not, though, work as well as the claims made for them; many patients tried doctor after doctor, treatment after treatment, and still found no real relief. This dissatisfaction led to widespread experimentation with "irregular" treatments, many of which were genuinely mentally oriented; hypnosis and New Thought were extremely popular during this period. According to Hale, "medical and popular interest in hypnosis, suggestion, mental healing and multiple personality peaked in the early 1890s, declined slightly after 1895, then waxed rapidly after 1900" (*Freud and the Americans*).

These new kinds of cures share some characteristics with the earlier somatic cures, especially with Mitchell's "rest cure." This is not particularly surprising since many curists started out as neurologists or as the patients of neurologists. The most significant aspect of all the cures—whether rest cure, hypnosis, hydropathy, dietetic treatment, or New Thought—was a confidence that nervous illness was a matter of an *intent* to be ill, that if the patient decided to be well, she could be. Weir Mitchell rejected almost all of the new psychotherapeutics, but his treatment reveals an attitude towards nervous disease that suggests, at root, an understanding of illness as intentional and of cure, therefore, as a matter of will. His cure's aim was to instill the self-discipline to fight against the "moral failures" of "selfish invalidism." New Thought, while holding that cure could be achieved by "floating in harmony" with the deity, nevertheless encouraged its practitioners to "hit hard and win" against illness (Gail Parker, *Mind Cure in New England*). Freud, at least in his earlier works, shared this attitude and even extended it. In the "Dora" case, he discusses "motives of illness," noting that some diseases are "the result of intention" and even weapons "as a rule leveled at a particular person." He further notes: "The crudest and most commonplace views upon the character of hysterical disorders such as are to be heard from uneducated relatives or nurses are in a certain sense right. It is true that the paralysed and bed-ridden woman would spring to her feet if a fire were to break out in her room and that the spoiled wife would forget all her sufferings if her child were to fall dangerously ill or if some catastrophe were to threaten the family circumstances" (*Complete Psychological Works*). Arguing that the "intention to be ill' is an unconscious rather than conscious process, Freud nevertheless asserts that in many hysterical diseases, a prerequisite to cure is "an attempt . . . to convince the patient herself of the existence in her of an intention to be ill."

The attitude that illness was the result of the will to be ill developed from the rethinking of the relation between mind and body that occurred at the turn of the century. Many late nineteenth- and early twentieth-century physicians and psychologists agreed with the idea described in an early article by William James called "We Are Automata" (1879): "Feeling is a mere collateral product of our nervous processes, unable to react upon them any more than a shadow reacts on the steps of the traveler whom it accompanies. . . . It is allowed to remain on board, but not to touch the helm or handle the rigging" (quoted in Hale, *Freud and the Americans*). But a larger number, including James himself in later works, were fascinated by the possibilities that the mind and body were not as profoundly split as philosophers had suggested since Descartes. The effect of questioning the mind/body split was the burgeoning of a whole new attitude toward the power of the mind to make the body ill and, in turn, to cure it.

In the United States, this attitude reflected a refinement and scientific verification of transcendentalism adapted to an age of pragmatism. Practitioners of New Thought saw Emanuel Swedenborg and Ralph Waldo Emerson as their immediate precursors and would find an ally of sorts in William James. Like transcendentalism, New Thought explicitly rejected the Calvinist religion of sin and death and substituted instead a faith in an "All-Supply" of light and hope. New Thought taught that disease was a man-made entity, because God would never have created something so bad. In complete agreement with the position Emerson propounded in "The Transcendentalist," New Thought maintained that changing one's thinking would change one's reality. Unlike transcendentalism, though, New Thought was both pragmatic and active; practitioners and patients believed in it because they saw its results, and they saw themselves not as passive recipients of the deity (the "transparent eyeball") but as active workers, trying to achieve the diety's will in the world.

The activism of New Thought, its insistence that one must work hard for health, reveals its ties with the reform and self-help movements of the day, reflecting the strong American faith in the individual's ability to determine his or her own fate. One of the most popular mind cure authors, Orison Swett Marden, published the self-help journal *Success* (a publication, incidentally, for which Charlotte Perkins Gilman wrote frequently). Marden's work altered the focus of success literature from instructions in how to achieve professional success to "a call for methodical character-building" (Parker, *Mind Cure in New England*). One of the most important proponents of a kind of New Thought, Mary Baker Eddy, extended the reformism and woman-centeredness of domesticity. She used women's social reforms as patterns for self-reform, their control of the household as a model for self-control. She developed the domestic notion that woman could best direct the moral life of the nation into a belief that women were the chosen of God (see Gail Parker, "Mary Baker Eddy and Sentimental Womanhood"). Mind cure, in most of its forms, united several turn-of-the-century reformist and materialistic movements; it combined women's rights, health, and social reforms with a determination to "succeed" worthy of a Horatio Alger novel.

The popularity of mind cure and various other psychotherapies was supported and extended by the new style of sensational mass journalism. Journalists, many of whom had themselves been "saved" by the revolutionary mental therapies, extolled the virtues of the treatments. This journalistic fervor for mental cures was the strongest in women's magazines (Hale, *Freud and the Americans*). In fact, women were quite involved with the New Thought movement, finding in its teachings an outlet for their ambitions and beliefs. Many feminists discovered that it could prove to be a philosophical basis for their demand to be treated as equals as well as a relief from the prevailing sexism of medical treatment. Elizabeth Cady Stanton was an early proponent of mind cure, urging that a woman should become her "own physician of body and soul" (quoted in Parker, *Mind Cure in New England*).

New Thought helped provide the discourse for a coherent and articulate critique of the medical profession that had been lacking in earlier decades. . . . "Mind cure became one outlet for an articulate feminism that demanded equal access to positions of spiritual leadership, freedom from the pretensions of a male medical elite, and the right to use sexual intercourse (as experienced by women) to depict the relationship between mortals and the All-Supply [the deity]" (Parker, *Mind Cure in New England*). In New Thought, women found a way to take their cure into their own hands, a way to try to avoid the patriarchal dicta of the medical men. Many other women embraced it merely because it offered a cure for their ailments, but once they had been cured, they often joined the crusade for mental healing. Mary Baker Eddy is perhaps the most famous of these women, but she is far from alone; the health reformer Annie Payson Call, the popular poet Ella Wheeler Wilcox, and popular mind cure authors Elizabeth Towne and Mary Ferriter were but a few of the other women who took mind cure as their personal crusade.

Other women, many of them "regular" physicians and feminists, also argued that women should take charge of their own lives, direct their own health, and resist the cultural tendency to seek femininity through illness. Abba Goold Woolson spoke for many when she argued for health education and a reform in the attitudes toward sickness and health: "When women shall learn to desire good health as essential to both beauty and efficiency, and shall look upon their present pernicious indulgences as not only inexpedient but as morally wrong, we may hope to see our people taking a vast stride in all departments of progress" (*Woman in American Society*). As early as the 1840s, Mary Gove Nichols had urged the same; by the turn of the century, women's health reformers following in Nichols's footsteps continually exhorted women to take charge of their lives and health.

THE WRITING CURE

One of the most famous women who took up this call for better health through self-discipline was Charlotte Perkins Gilman. In her autobiography, she claims to have cured herself by working and writing, despite her doctor's orders to stop both activities (*The Living of Charlotte Perkins Gilman*). She claimed that it was writing, especially, that had returned her to health and that had helped other women to follow her example. Gilman had been a victim of "nervousness" throughout her childhood and continued to suffer periodic bouts throughout the rest of her life. But shortly after the birth of her first (and only) child, her symptoms worsened and she feared a complete breakdown. As is well known by now from the numerous studies of "The Yellow Wallpaper" and Weir Mitchell's rest cure, Gilman rejected Mitchell's advice to "never touch pen, brush, or pencil" and to "live as domestic a life as possible" (*The Living of Charlotte Perkins Gilman*), in favor of a life of writing, public speaking, and feminist crusading. Gilman later claimed that "The Yellow Wallpaper" had even convinced Mitchell to change his rest cure to include, for some patients, the chance to write.

One of the beneficiaries of this change was Edith Wharton. Wharton, like Gilman, was a sufferer of "nervousness"; she had suffered a serious breakdown in 1894-95, and when she felt another coming on in early 1898, she went to Weir Mitchell's clinic in Philadelphia for treatment (she was, however, an outpatient and was treated by one of his colleagues, not by Mitchell himself [R. W. B. Lewis, *Edith Wharton: A Biography*]). While there, like most rest cure patients, she was isolated, forced to rest and eat abundantly, given massages, and, unlike Gilman, encouraged to write. R. W. B. Lewis rebuts the "legend" that Wharton began writing during the rest cure as a mode of therapy (a claim mentioned and accorded respect by Suzanne Poirier in "The Weir Mitchell Rest Cure"), pointing out that she had published enough for a small volume before her first breakdown, but he admits that 1898 marks the beginning of her sustained career as a writer. Wharton may not have *learned* to write from her cure, but she did learn that writing could be encompassed in a cure and did not have to be, as Lewis suggests it had been, illness inducing.

Gilman and Wharton found that writing could be curative, whether they had consciously undertaken it as therapy or not. It became for them their own independent form of mind cure because it allowed them to "remake their circumstances," to change their "thoughts and motives" in order to transform their "conditions and economies." It also seemed to work; Gilman was never entirely free of her nervousness, but after becoming an active writer and speaker, she never suffered from it to the same degree as she had earlier. Wharton became healthier in direct relation to her success as an author. But in the texts that mark each woman's emergence as an important writer, the fictions generally accepted as their first "masterpieces," the female characters are not granted the authors' newly won health. The woman in "The Yellow Wallpaper" descends dramatically into a complete breakdown just as Gilman ascends from the threat of a breakdown; in *The House of Mirth,* Lily Bart's physical health deteriorates as a result of her increasing depression. She falls into a cycle of insomnia and drug abuse and finally succumbs to an overdose that may or may not be accidental. The defeat of these female characters may well have been the price of Gilman's and Wharton's own victories over illness and invalidism. In *writing* the story of the invalid, they were able to avoid *living* it.

In *The Madwoman in the Attic,* Sandra Gilbert and Susan Gubar argue that the activity of writing, or producing art, was fraught with anxiety for most nineteenth-century women. They argue that the lively or imaginative girl growing up in the nineteenth century was "likely to experience her education in docility, submissiveness, selflessness as in some sense sickening. To be trained in renunciation is almost necessarily to be trained to ill health, since the human animal's first and strongest urge is to his/her own survival, pleasure, assertion. . . . Learning to become a beautiful object, the girl learns anxiety about perhaps even loathing of her own flesh." This is the reason, they contend, that so many women in the nineteenth century were ill. Gubar, in "'The Blank Page' and the Issues of Female Creativity," argues that "many women experience their own bodies as the only available medium for art"; she associates this art of the body with blood and pain. She argues that women who have not been allowed the education or opportunity to write, paint, or sculpt have learned to make art of their bodies through clothing, makeup, and their shapes: "The woman who cannot become an artist can nevertheless turn herself into an artistic object." For Gilbert and Gubar, making art of the body is itself illness inducing.

In contrast to this view, David Kunzle and Valerie Steele argue that learning to turn herself into an art object was, for the Victorian woman, a way of taking control over her own body. Kunzle goes much further on this point than Steele; he argues that Victorian men were, if anything, against the corsets, cosmetics, and elaborate dresses worn by Victorian women. He sees such body shaping as forms of sexual expression and self-assertion, even of independence from male norms. In his view, it was the corseted lady, not the feminist, who was the real sexual radical in the nineteenth century. Steele's view is more moderate than Kunzle's—in part because her research leads her to believe that reports of corset wearing and tight lacing have been much exaggerated—but she contends that the art of fashion has always been a healthy way to express self and sexuality and accepts the idea that nineteenth-century fashions were, at least in part, a way for women to express self-control rather than male control.

If we allow that illness could be a kind of "cosmetic" for women, as Abba Goold Woolson claimed it was, and if the cosmetic arts were a way to rebel against male control, then illness itself could become both an art and a form of rebellion against patriarchy. The woman who grew up with nineteenth-century standards of moral and social conduct would then have found illness a congenial role in several ways. First, if she, like the women Gilbert and Gubar describe, came to loathe her own flesh, she could punish that flesh with illness. But if she also discovered that the illness with which she punished her body was aesthetically pleasing, then she could turn her self-punishment into art. In this way, the woman who had grown up with fiction and visual arts that exalted the holy and beautiful illnesses of female characters could come to experience suffering and making her body ill as artistic activities. For the woman caught between medical discourses that defined her as ill, aesthetic discourses which asserted that she was better that way, and New Thought arguments that she could take control of her own life and urged her to do so, the self-discipline of willed and artistic illness could offer the simplest resolution to these competing forces.

Making an art of illness, then, represents one extreme kind of self-control. If illness can be understood as a kind of artistic self-discipline, a way of taking control of one's own body, of "working" it to artistic ends, then illness can be *both* a matter of art and of self-punishment, a way of enjoying and loathing the flesh. In *Discipline and Punish,* Michel Foucault argues that punishment, as a part of discipline, "has the function of reducing gaps. It must therefore be essentially *corrective*. . . . Disciplinary systems favour punishments that are exercise intensified, multiplied forms of training." If illness comes to be a *discipline,* then, it can be both punishment and art. It can be either an art intensified into punishment or a punishment meant to "correct" imperfections of the body. It can therefore be both collusion with moral and social standards that oppress women and a subversion of those standards at the same time. The woman who makes an *art* of her illness accedes to her "place" in a patriarchal system, but *she* controls that place.

Alice James may serve as an illuminating case in point. She writes repeatedly in her *Diary* of "achieving" illness and of "getting herself dead" as a feat equal to or surpassing Henry's and William's writing. Jean Strouse, Alice James's biographer, argues that Alice maintained a kind of "negative superiority" about her illness. "All her life Alice had been in conflict over just who she could be. . . . The intelligence and energy Alice might have used in some productive way went into the intricate work of being sick. . . . Her miserable health *was* her career" (*Alice James: A Biography*). And Ruth Bernard Yeazell writes, "Alice retired permanently to her bed and took up the profession of an invalid" (*The Death and Letters of Alice James*). At one point, quoting "un ange philosophe," she explicitly describes suffering as a way to make one's life a work of art: "Sous cette inspiration [souffrance] les existences les plus humbles peuvent devenir des oeuvres d'art bien supérieures aux plus belles symphonies et aux plus beaux poèmes. Est-ce que les oeuvres d'art qu'on réalise en soi-même ne sont pas meilleures? Les autres, qu'on jette en dehors sur la toile ou le papier, ne sont rien que des images, des ombres. L'oeuvre de la vie est un réalité." Alice's "work" was directed destructively at her own body, not exactly as punishment but as self-discipline, as making a work of art of her life. It was this destructive, punishing work that allowed her to construct a sense of self and self-control. The self she defined was ill; the one piece of writing she published in her lifetime, a letter to the editor of *The Nation* (4 July 1890), was signed "Invalid." Alice's writing of her diary was an extension of this work, not a revision of it, because she attempted to write *herself,* as invalid, into it.

Writing could then be an extension of illness-as-art. Gilbert and Gubar claim that it was the stress of making art that caused women writers' illnesses in the nineteenth century, that moving from the "feminine" art of the body to the "masculine" art of the pen was illness inducing. But it seems more likely that illness and writing exist not as opposing options for women but as different points along a continuum of artistic self-discipline. Therefore, as a woman began to make other kinds of art, she no longer needed to experience her sense of art through making herself ill. Ironically, then, the best way to overcome the sense that one's body and illness are the only media for art would be to make art in other ways. Illness would, then, resume its original character as punishment, not self-discipline, not art. Gilman and Wharton both came to believe that writing made them feel better—Wharton had, in fact, used "making up" stories as a kind of a therapy since she had been a child (see Cynthia Wolff, *A Feast of Words*). This was true of other women writers, too. Kate Chopin consciously took up writing as therapy for the depression she experienced after her husband's and mother's deaths, and even Alice James believed that writing her *Diary* helped to relieve her illness.

Writing and making art also were part of the prescription offered by female mind curists to women. Harriott K. Hunt, one of the first female physicians in this country (although she never attended a medical school because none would admit her), was one of Mary Baker Eddy's early proponents and wrote in her autobiography, *Glances and Glimpses,* that her treatment of women consisted of "telling [them] to throw away their medicines, begin a diary, and think of their mothers" (quoted in Ann Douglas Wood, "The Fashionable Diseases,"). Mary Ferriter, a popular mind cure author, wrote in 1923: "Tell the girl that every twenty-eight days she will have a call from nature and that then she will have the sex urge, or the creature instinct, strong upon her; that then is the time for her to express in art, music, poetry" (from *Truth of Life Love Liberty,* quoted in Gail Parker, *Mind Cure in New England*). Gilman and Wharton, who were both extensively exposed to New Thought philosophy, undoubtedly internalized some of this thinking, especially when they found it so successful.

This "writing cure" would, of course, have been coincident with Freud's development of the "talking cure," through which patients were able to speak their anxiety and stop directing it internally. It also parallels much current feminist psychoanalytic theory about the role of language in effecting cures. Psychoanalysts like Luce Irigaray and Michèle Montrelay argue that women growing up in a world dominated by masculine signifying systems often lack the necessary representational structures to articulate sexuality and anxiety: "Women do not manage to articulate their madness: they suffer it directly in their body" (Irigaray, quoted in Diana Adlam and Couze Venn, "Women's Exile"). Language, the "pure cathexis in the word as such," they argue, allows the woman to turn painful experiences into a discourse in which "words are *other*" than herself (Montrelay, "Of Femininity"). Freud wrote that "hysterics suffer mainly from reminiscences" (*Complete Psychological Works*). Irigaray and Montrelay argue that by articulating those reminiscences, women no longer have to live them.

For women writing at the turn of the century, this "writing cure" went further than just articulating painful reminiscences, though. It also fundamentally changed the woman's role. As Jonathan Culler puts it, women have historically been the subject *of* literature, or the inspiration *for* literature, but not the subject who writes literature (*On Deconstruction*). But in becoming a writer, a woman comes to inhabit an altogether different position in society and history. Writing about illness, then, allows the woman writer to separate the experience of it from herself; becoming a writer who creates narratives of illness allows her to control it, to avoid experiencing the sickness herself. Unlike Alice James, who merely wrote her self into her text as invalid, Gilman and Wharton wrote the *illness* into their texts, leaving themselves apart from it, as *authors,* not invalid women.

By writing, Gilman and Wharton produced irrefutable evidence of their changed position from invalid women to writers: a visible, material creation that attests to their activity. In *Discipline and Punish,* Foucault maintains that "disciplinary power . . . is exercised through its invisibility; at the same time it imposes on those whom it subjects a principle of compulsory visibility." This visibility, he argues, allows them to be controlled. In "The Yellow Wallpaper" and *The House of Mirth,* Gilman and Wharton try to make the disciplinary power of patriarchy visible, to reveal the painful effects of women's compulsory visibility (both female characters are "watched"), and to redefine that visibility in the process, in favor of something that can stand for the woman writer herself—the writing.

The "writing cure" is a remedy that provides a way for the woman writer to present her illness so that it is "written and simultaneously erased, metaphorized; designating itself while indicating intraworldly relations; it [is] *represented*" (Jacques Derrida, "Freud and the Scene of Writing"). The writing she produces will *take her place* in two ways, then: first, it can be Other, it can represent the illness she no longer has to embody, and second, it can represent her in her absence. But like the *pharmakon,* writing is a cure that is also a poison because to cure the woman writer, it must kill the invalid woman.

THE ART OF ILLNESS

Both "The Yellow Wallpaper" and *The House of Mirth* center on female characters who are in some sense frustrated artists, trapped in an ugly and uncomfortable world that does not allow them viable alternatives to the traditional world of wifehood and motherhood. These two women, the narrator of "The Yellow Wallpaper" and Lily Bart, therefore turn their artistic urges destructively on themselves. Both Gilman and Wharton refuse the ideal of feminine domesticity in these narratives and, with it, the traditional happy endings of women's fiction. Both narratives reject domestic ideology—marriage and the home do not provide a happy alternative to the heroine's problems—and domestic narrative structure—the heroine does not save herself from an exterior threat but succumbs to an interior one. The emphasis both texts place on art and the rejection of dominant ideology is important to the notion of a "writing cure" and to the place of these narratives in feminist literary history.

"The Yellow Wallpaper" is written in first-person narrative, in the form of the journal of a nameless woman who has been taken to an "ancestral hall," "a hereditary estate," to spend the summer on a modified rest cure while recuperating from some "nervous" condition. Since the narrator remains nameless—she neither mentions her own name nor records anyone calling her by name—she seems not to experience herself as a subject but as a wife, her child's mother, a "sick" woman, or as "a woman" in the "hereditary estate" of all women, which, under patriarchy, makes women sick.

While the woman maintains that she is sick, her husband, a physician, maintains that she is not. This contradiction of her experience leaves her confused; as she puts it, "If a physician of high standing, and one's own husband, assures friends and relatives that there is really nothing the matter with one but temporary nervous depression—a slight hysterical tendency—what is one to do?" She is "absolutely forbidden to 'work' until [she is] well again," even though she is told she is not sick and even though she disagrees with the prescription: "Personally, I believe that congenial work, with excitement and change, would do me good. But what is one to do?"

Throughout the story, her doctor-husband contradicts her representations of reality and imposes his representations on her. She tells him she feels something strange and ghostly in the house, and he says it is a draught and closes the window. Confessing that her "nervous troubles are dreadfully depressing," she states, "John does not know how much I really suffer. He knows there is no *reason* to suffer, and that satisfies him. . . . Nobody would believe what an effort it is to do what little I am able." She does, however, keep trying to tell John how she feels. In every case, he tells her she is wrong, that he knows better than she what is true for her. Still, she tries to maintain her role as speaking and desiring subject, even though John continues to treat her as a child—as *infans,* the one who does not speak, the one who is to be taken care of. She tries to tell him that she "is not gaining" and that she wants to leave the old house; John's response is, as we might expect, "Of course, if you were in any danger, I could and would, but you really are better, dear, whether you can *see* it or not. I am a doctor, dear, and *I know*" (emphasis added).

Despite these repeated instances reinforcing her idea that "nobody would believe" her, she continues trying to tell someone. Her writing of the journal we read is one indication of this attempt to continue representing, even though it is the very work she has been told not to do. She is, at least initially, trying to somehow maintain her subjectivity despite male interdiction. She rebels against John's attempts to control her by instituting her own system of self-discipline: writing. Such a rebellion on her part, however, has marked consequences. She says, "I did write for a while in spite of them; but it *does* exhaust me a good deal having to be so sly about it, or else meet with heavy opposition. I sometimes fancy that in my condition if I had less opposition and more society and stimulus—but John says the very worst thing I can do is to think about my condition, and I confess it always makes me feel bad." When she writes at one point, "I would not say it to a living soul, of course, but this is dead paper and a great relief to my mind," the effects of the continual denial of her representations of reality start to become apparent. In writing only for "dead paper"—writing only *to* death—her language use becomes less governed by existence in the world outside her. She ceases to function as a "speaking-subject" in the world. Continually denied recognition as a subject, treated as a nonspeaker, as one whose representations are invalid (because they are the representations of an invalid?), she comes to reject the effort of maintaining this "invalid" subjectivity: "I don't know why I should write this. I don't want to. I don't feel able. And I know John would think it absurd. But I *must* say what I feel and think in some way—it is such a relief! But the effort is getting to be greater than the relief."

The narrator's attempts to produce her reality, to realize her "representations," are failures and are eventually more frustrating than helpful. Gilman presents not just an image of a woman's "education in docility" but also the defeat of a woman writer, as Annette Kolodny and Paula Treichler have both pointed out. Kolodny describes the story as a woman's giving up writing in favor of reading "the symbolization of her own untenable and unacceptable reality" in the wallpaper ("A Map for Rereading"). Treichler argues that the diagnosis imposed by the physician-husband is not merely a representation of reality that contradicts the narrator's but a mechanism for controlling her ("Escaping the Sentence"). For Treichler, the wallpaper becomes a symbol of the escape from this control: women's writing "becomes possible only after women obtain the right to speak," but women's language remains merely "metaphorical and evocative."

But if we understand that writing here is a form of "control," too, then we see that although her system of self-discipline is radically at odds with that which her physician-husband would impose on her, eventually the distinction between the two becomes unclear. Studying the wallpaper, becoming one with its unknowable artistic principles, is another attempt at self-control but one that eventually becomes indistinguishable from the control of her husband: the wallpaper, like John, watches her.

"The Yellow Wallpaper" is a story about the loss of distinctions—between writing and reading, doctor and patient, medical and self-discipline, art and the body. Early in the story the narrator begins to reexperience her childhood sense that the furnishings of her room have a life of their own. Later, the wallpaper develops "absurd, unblinking eyes," and she eventually sees another woman in the wallpaper. In other words, the furnishings in her room seem to take on a threatening subjectivity of their own; they watch her, attempt to frighten her, and eventually cooperate with her. Throughout, she continues to assert her identity as a speaking subject, but that sense is continually denied by John, who does not listen to her or contradicts her when he does, and becomes more and more difficult to maintain. Coupled with her treatment as an object—something to be watched (by John and the wallpaper) but not listened to—we see that the distinction between subject and object becomes meaningless for her. She does not come to an awareness or rejection of her own "untenable and unacceptable reality"; rather, she becomes part of the world of objects. Her existence as a subject breaks down. Frustrated in her attempt to produce a readable text, she becomes one. Her body—through illness—becomes the outlet for her creativity. Denied the opportunity to make external representations, to write, she is forced to turn these creative impulses on herself. Gilman here illustrates how similar the two activities are.

Walter Benn Michaels, in his introduction to *The Gold Standard and the Logic of Naturalism,* argues that "The Yellow Wallpaper" is not about "a woman being driven crazy by Weir Mitchell's refusal to allow her to produce, [but] is about a woman driven crazy . . . by a commitment to production so complete that it requires her to begin by producing herself." He is right to claim that Gilman accepts the notion that the self must be produced, but he reads past the indications that "The Yellow Wallpaper" is the scene of a battle over who has the *right* to that production. The conflict in this story is between culturally accepted and culturally forbidden modes of self-production. The point of the woman's desire to write is not, as Michaels argues, to "produce evidence that [she is] still the same person"; it is, instead, to produce evidence that she is *different.* Gilman does not write "herself *into* her body" (emphasis added), as Alice James had done. She writes her way *out* of it. While all other distinctions in the story break down, one remains: the distinction between Gilman and her narrator, a distinction Michaels collapses. For even though it is an autobiographical story, Gilman maintains a sharp difference between herself, as writer-producer, and the woman in the story whose writing fails.

The problem in "The Yellow Wallpaper" is not production itself but who has control over production. The story becomes a rewriting of the Poe and Hawthorne stories ["Ligeia," "The Oval Portrait," "The Birthmark," "Rappaccini's Daughter," and *The Blithedale Romance*] at the point when the woman resists the male attempt to produce her as the perfect woman (in this case, the quiet and domestic wife). Unlike the cooperative Georgiana or the painter's wife in "The Oval Portrait," the narrator of "The Yellow Wallpaper" does not submit entirely to her husband's productive efforts. But the woman's resistance is not much more successful than the earlier women's cooperation had been; she does not end up dead, but she does end up mad.

The difficulty of "The Yellow Wallpaper" springs from uncertainty about the woman's writing and its relation to her illness. In the second half of the story, it is not clear who is writing or when. As the woman's position as a subject becomes more tenuous, it becomes impossible to sort out who or what is writing. Tenses shift back and forth between present and past ("I am securely fastened now" and "Now he's crying" to "said I" and "I kept on creeping"), the persona shifts from the woman in the room to the woman in the wallpaper, and the final scene—the tethered woman crawling around the edges of the room, creeping over her unconscious husband—leaves open the question of whether we are reading a madwoman's text, a sane woman's post facto description of madness, or an entirely impossible text, one that could never have been written. As a feminist critic I would like to read this story as that of a woman who has achieved "transcendent sanity" (Treichler, "Escaping the Sentence") because she has been able to imagine "mirages of health and freedom" (Gilbert and Gubar, *The Madwoman in the Attic*), but I must eventually recognize that it is a tale of defeat. As Treichler herself has pointed out, the woman is tied up in the nursery and will undoubtedly be "sent to Weir Mitchell" when John regains consciousness.

A happy ending is not compatible with the tone or context of this story. In fact, "The Yellow Wallpaper" may go out of its way to avoid a happy ending, to emphasize its complete rejection of domesticity and the ideology of domestic fiction. Far from upholding motherhood as a means to power and self-expression, Gilman here represents motherhood and domesticity as the paths to confinement and madness, the death of self-expression. The narrative instability at the end of the story, then, is not the "communal voice" that Treichler finds but the voice of no one, the voice of one with no self. It is the voice of domesticity as Gilman imagines it: confined and mad. Denied the opportunity to make art, or the audience to appreciate it, the woman turns her artistic impulses to her own body, becoming thereby just another of the indecipherable furnishings of the "hereditary estate."

In *The House of Mirth,* the relationship between illness and art is central to an understanding of the character of Lily Bart and to Wharton's writing. Throughout the novel Lily is depicted and admired as an artistic object. Lily's beauty is central to her existence and is represented by Wharton as the result of painstaking production. Our first view of Lily is through Selden's eyes and shares his "confused sense that she must have cost a great deal to make." Lily's value is directly related to her beauty, to her status as a beautiful object. She has no money, no real family connections, and not much of a desirable character; she is a shallow gambler with no interest in high art, literature, or anything practical. Lily's one talent is as an artist of the body; as Dale Bauer argues in *Feminist Dialogics,* she "creates herself as a work of art." She is merely a beautiful commodity on the marriage market; she is in many ways the exemplar of Thorstein Veblen's women who are valuable to a future husband only to the extent of their ability to represent his wealth. . . . Lily's value in the marriage market is doubly dependent on her beauty and her remaining virginal. The novel is, in one sense, a tale about the difficulties of "keeping up appearances"—both Lily's physical appearance and the appearance of innocence. Lily's life is devoted to the "art" of appearances. When that art fails—when she can no longer make art of her body by traditional methods (for example, clothes and makeup), Lily gradually becomes ill, losing sleep and abusing drugs. Her death, which leaves her body artistically arranged on her bed, is a culmination of her art of the body and her illness.

Wharton goes out of her way to emphasize that Lily is an artistic object, turning her at one point into "living art": at the Brys' *tableaux vivants,* Lily appears, unadorned, as a painting. She does not need decoration; she is decoration. It is significant that this moment when she is merely a silent painting is Lily's one moment of unmitigated triumph and the moment when it is *she* who becomes the producer. But, as Bauer points out, she only gains recognition "by inserting [herself] as the representation of another woman in a male-created text."

Susan Gubar argues that Lily's overdose is a logical extension of her objectification into art; once she had become an artistic object, there was little else to do but "kill herself into art" ("'The Blank Page' and the Issues of Female Creativity"). Gubar points to the fact that before taking the overdose, Lily examines her beautiful dresses and thinks about the *tableaux vivants* and then "thinks that there is 'some word she had found' to tell Selden. . . . This word is Lily's dead body; for she is now converted completely into a script for his edification, a text not unlike the letters and checks she has left behind to vindicate her life." Gubar argues further that this equation of body and word "illustrates the terrors not of the word made flesh but of the flesh made word." Like Alice James, Lily had to "get herself dead" in order to speak to Selden. But in contrast to Georgiana in "The Birthmark" and Beatrice Rappaccini, Lily is not made into an object by a man but turns herself into one. (Gubar's use of the passive disguises this.) She therefore takes control and refuses to let society define her; she does not merely leave her body as a text but also leaves those same checks that Gubar mentions and then looks past. She pays off Gus Trenor, making herself completely independent from his demands. Unfortunately, neither her checks nor her body are easily readable. Like the woman in the wallpaper, she finds that women's "language" remains, at least in part, incomprehensible. Lily's death exemplifies how "artistic discipline" can intensify into punishment, how the subversion of society's norms can be interpreted as collusion with them.

Lily fails at every artistic attempt that is not directed at her own body. Even when she is employed at the millinery shop in the "art . . . of [creating] ever varied settings for the face of fortunate womanhood," she is a complete failure, unable to make straight or even stitches. Lily's every attempt at communication is a failure, too. Finally, she even fails at her artistic specialty, herself: her looks begin to fail and she loses her reputation. Lily's only artistic success, the only effort that achieves the effect she desires—the compassion and love of Selden—is her death. She (as Wharton does in creating Lily's character) makes an art of death.

Gubar does not examine the artistry involved in Lily's death scene. Lily does not merely become "a word"; she also becomes, as she had done in the *tableaux vivants,* a painting. In *Idols of Perversity,* Bram Dijkstra shows that one of the most popular genres of turn-of-the-century painting was the "death" or "sleep" painting; Shakespeare's Ophelia and Tennyson's Lady of Shalott and Elaine were among the most popular subjects for the visual arts, as were anonymous dead women. These paintings were an extension of the drowned women paintings and sculptures described by Joy Kasson and Olive Anderson and, as Dijkstra maintains, exhibited "the erotic ambiguity of the Victorian ideal of passive womanhood—the dead woman—indicating how easily a painterly homage to feminine self-sacrifice could shift toward a necrophiliac preoccupation with the erotic potential of woman when in a state of virtually guaranteed passivity."

Many of these paintings, especially those depicting Albine (the heroine who dies at the end of Emile Zola's *The Sin of Father Mouret* [1875]), surround the dead woman with flowers; the dead woman is "nature's flower" who will "die like a flower among the flowers" (Dijkstra, *Idols of Perversity*). Lily, as her name indicates, is also a flower, and like the women in Romaine Brooks's *Le Trajet* or *Dead Woman* (ca. 1911), Hermann Moest's *The Fate of Beauty* (1898), Paul-Albert Besnard's *The Dead Woman* (1880s), John Collier's *The Death of Albine* (ca. 1895), Lucy Hartmann's *Albine* (ca. 1899), Frances MacDonald's *The Sleeping Princess* (1897), Madeline Lemaire's *Sleep* (1890), and Sarah Bernhardt's self-portrait, *Sarah in Her Coffin* (ca. 1870s), Lily, too, becomes a dead but aesthetic object for a male viewer. It is only at her death, when she has literally embodied one of these paintings—her body aesthetically arranged on the bed, in stark contrast with her dingy surroundings—that Selden, like the Victorian male Dijkstra describes, is able to love her.

It seems remarkable that many of these paintings, like *The House of Mirth,* were created by women artists. Even on the stage, the undisputed queen of the theater, Sarah Bernhardt, specialized in death and madness scenes; her *La Dame aux camélias* set the worldwide standard for beauty and grace. Dijkstra argues that these women artists participated in and refined a male-defined genre. But if we examine their works in the context of the stresses involved in being a woman artist, these works appear not so much to conform to the male-defined genre as to turn that genre to their own psychic needs. If these women produced artistic objects to satisfy the demands of patriarchal disciplinary power, then those productions could take their places in that power structure; the women would therefore not have to turn themselves into artistic objects. "Killing the invalid," then, could become an activity quite similar to the one described by Virginia Woolf as "killing the angel in the house": an act of violence necessary to free the female artist from a dangerous and debilitating system of power ("Professions for Women," in *Collected Essays*). That dead invalid would then shield the woman artist from having to embody cultural norms.

Elaine Showalter argues in "The Death of the Lady (Novelist)" that this kind of exorcism of the "Perfect Lady" in *The House of Mirth* allowed Edith Wharton to become a novelist:

> In choosing to have Lily die, Wharton was judging and rejecting the infantile aspects of her own self, the part that lacked confidence as a working writer, that longed for the escapism of the lady's world and feared the sexual consequences of creating rather than becoming art. . . . If Lily Bart, unable to change, gives way to the presence of a new generation of women, Edith Wharton survives the crisis of maturation at the turn of the century and becomes one of our American precursors of a literary history of female mastery and growth.

Lily's death thus serves two purposes: it shows the horror of the body's objectification, the dangers for women of the self-discipline of body-art, and it also provides Wharton with the same kind of surrogate ill woman that Gilman found in "The Yellow Wallpaper." For in creating ill flesh in words, Wharton was able to will herself not to create illness in herself.

Like Wharton, Charlotte Perkins Gilman managed to cure herself through her representation, her "story" of a breakdown. Just as *The House of Mirth* is a narrative of the world Edith Wharton had experienced when she was younger, so, too, is "The Yellow Wallpaper" a representation of much of what Gilman herself experienced. But while the woman in her story does not benefit from her writing, Gilman's writing proved to be restorative. In writing out an alternative narrative, in writing a breakdown rather than continuing to have one, Gilman not only made the patriarchal disciplinary system and woman's place in it visible, but she found that the writing could *take her place*. In creating a narrative of her hysterical condition, she no longer had to embody illness directly but could represent it in her text. Her story and her subsequent writings were published and allowed her a revision of her metaphorical place. She became a social worker, feminist crusader, and *writer*—a visible subject in the outer world, with new concrete possibilities open to her.

The "writing cure" as it can be seen in Gilman's and Wharton's work is not identical to turn-of-the-century mind cure or New Thought. Neither woman could "let go" and "surrender" her individual will to the "All-Supply," as most curists advocated. But in another sense, their writing does conform to the strain of New Thought and mind cure that developed in tandem with economic individualism. Success authors like Orison Swett Marden linked health, wealth, and character; health and wealth were signs of moral strength, sickness and poverty of moral failure (see Gail Parker, *Mind Cure in New England*). Writing became for Gilman and Wharton a self-reliant, active, and determined attempt to defeat the will to illness; they regarded illness as weakness and a moral failure (as Wharton's attitude toward her husband's illness reveals . . .), to which neither writer would succumb.

HAPPY ENDINGS

While *The House of Mirth* and "The Yellow Wallpaper" may have proven curative for their writers, they have nonetheless left an interesting dilemma for the feminist critic. These two fictions surely must be among the unhappiest of the fictions of feminine defeat in American literature. In both, the women's repeated mistakes and bad judgments, or at least their acquiescence in others' bad judgments, becomes, to the modern feminist reader, almost embarrassing. In both, the lack of viable alternatives is frustrating.

As a result of our desire to read past this defeat, contemporary feminist critics often attempt to "recover" a happy version of these unhappy endings. We either rewrite the endings—Lily's suicide becomes a release into freedom from social strictures, or the narrator's madness at the end of "The Yellow Wallpaper" becomes a burst into female creativity—or we turn, as I have done, to biography to deal with these two works. Rewriting the endings, it seems to me, is to argue that women's only option is to be completely outside the system, that our only escape is madness and death. This seems both false to our own experience and to refuse the genuine social criticism in the novel; to rewrite these endings as somehow "happy" is to deny that the society should be changed.

Biography, then, remains the only way to create happy endings for these two fictions. No one discusses "The Yellow Wallpaper" without mentioning Gilman's own triumph over Mitchell's rest cure; very few feminist readers look at *The House of Mirth* without some mention of Wharton's emergence as an important writer. And yet these fictions became central in the "feminist canon" long before others that feature victorious feminine characters. Nineteenth-century novels that feature women who not only avoid the invalid stereotype but become physicians have only come back into print in the last few years; New American Library brought out an edition of Sarah Orne Jewett's *Country Doctor* in 1986, and Elizabeth Stuart Phelps's *Doctor Zay* was reprinted by the Feminist Press in 1987. *Christine*—an openly feminist novel with a triumphant heroine—is not only out of print but still very difficult to find. "The Yellow Wallpaper," on the other hand, was one of the very first volumes published by the Feminist Press in 1973, and Wharton's *The House of Mirth,* of course, has never gone out of print. It is important to our understanding of both the "writing cure" and feminist criticism to evaluate why this has come about.

One important factor in understanding this phenomenon lies in the relation of these texts to women's writing, which, as Helen Papashvily (and others) would have it, is typified by happy endings (the title of her book on the subject is *All the Happy Endings*). "The Yellow Wallpaper" and *The House of Mirth* both belong much more clearly to the mainstream, canonical tradition in American literature in style, form, and substance than they do to domestic (or women's) fiction. In other words, they were read by feminist critics at least in part because they were not seen as "feminine" texts. They could be read in the same way and on the same critical ground as "masculine" fiction; they were texts of which feminist critics could be proud because they resisted the "sentimentality" of the happy ending. Gilman and Wharton did in fact, to an extent, reject or revise the basic tenets of domestic fiction. Gilman explicitly rejected the notion that motherhood and managing a household offered women a path to power; like many twentieth-century feminists, she saw the home as a prison for women (as the imagery in "The Yellow Wallpaper" so clearly suggests). Despite her rejection of much of their ideology, Gilman nevertheless has affinities with the previous generation of women writers. Like them, she centers her fiction on female characters, and like them, her work is deeply distrustful of men while it focuses on a community of women. "The Yellow Wallpaper" is atypical of much of her work because it concentrates so exclusively on one woman, but it does so only to reveal how dangerous the lack of "society and stimulus" can be. In Wharton's case, the situation is reversed: she has affinities with domestic ideology—as Elaine Showalter has argued, the warm kitchen scene at Nettie Struther's is symbolic of the feminine community and warmth that Lily has missed and that might have saved her—but she attempts to break with the previous generation of women writers when it comes to structure, style, and narrative outcome. At every point, *The House of Mirth* seems like a novel determined to rebut nineteenth-century women's fictions in which the heroine ends up happy after long years of suffering. In *The House of Mirth,* mistakes only lead to further mistakes, suffering to more suffering.

In contrast to the traditional plot of women's fiction, neither "The Yellow Wallpaper" nor *The House of Mirth* offers the reader the satisfaction of the heroine's triumph over adverse circumstances. Gilman and Wharton are, in fact, relentless about creating fictional worlds in which their heroines have very few options; the narrator of "The Yellow Wallpaper" could, of course, have rebelled against John, but she would only have been "sent to Weir Mitchell" later. Lily could have saved herself by sacrificing Bertha Dorset, or by blackmailing her, but would then have only become a part of the corrupt society Wharton condemns. Both writers therefore reject domestic ideology precisely at the point of suggesting that a happy ending is possible within the structure of existing society. For Gilman, it is the "happy ending" of domestic fiction—wife- and motherhood—that causes the problem in the first place. Wharton's attitude is more complex. In one sense, marriage is the one possibility for Lily's survival and happiness; in another, it is the degradation of husband hunting that is the problem in the first place. Wharton offers the scene of Nettie

Struther's happy ending as a foil to Lily's unhappy one but assures the reader that such an ending is impossible for Lily within the world of New York high society. Gilman and Wharton use their heroines as proof that women's lives needed to be changed, that it was the social structure that was really sick.

In both fictions, the woman's defeat is closely linked to her social class. Just as the options that are open to Nettie Struther, the working-class woman, are closed to Lily Bart, so, too, are the chances for "congenial work" closed to the narrator of "The Yellow Wallpaper," a woman who has a nurse, a housekeeper, and a wealthy husband. Both fictions subscribe to the Social Darwinist/Spencerian concept of the world outlined by Gilman in *Women and Economics* (1899): "When man began to feed and defend woman, she ceased proportionately to feed and defend herself. When he stood between her and her physical environment, she ceased proportionately to feel the influence of that environment and respond to it." Gilman theorizes that women's social problems and their unequal standing in the culture are a result of generations of selective breeding in which woman's only value is "sex-attraction" and of being shut out of productive labor. "To be surrounded by beautiful things has much influence upon the human creature: to make beautiful things has more. . . . What we do modifies us more than what is done to us. The freedom of expression has been more restricted in women than the freedom of impression, if that be possible."

Gilman argues that the only hope for women and the whole human race lies in women becoming workers, earning their keep, and becoming producers instead of consumers because "to do and to make not only gives deep pleasure, but is indispensable to healthy growth. . . . To carve in wood, to hammer brass, to do 'art dressmaking,' to raise mushrooms in the cellar . . . is a most healthy state." The hope of the race, she argues, lies with the "increasing army of women wage-earners, who are changing the face of the world by their steady advance toward economic independence." The only women who are fit to face motherhood without fear of the "gates of death," she continues, are the "savage woman, the peasant woman, the working-woman everywhere who is not overworked" who is allowed to "mingle in the natural industries of a human creature."

Wharton, too, was influenced by Social Darwinist thought and the new medical theories of inheritance and environmental influence (as the title of one of her story collections—*The Descent of Man and Other Stories*—attests). Like Gilman's *Women and Economics, The House of Mirth* maintains that women who have been bred for leisure are not fit for a life of self-sufficiency. Wharton seems to share Gilman's view that there is little hope for a change in this situation, and both writers idealize the "innate" strength of the working class. Nettie Struther is able to overcome tuberculosis, poverty, and the stigma of single-motherhood to find health, happiness, and a good marriage. Lily suffers much less adversity, yet it proves fatal. Wharton goes to great lengths to show that this failure is not Lily's fault but the fault of her upbringing, the weakness she inherits from both her parents, and the society in which she lives; the result is a Social Darwinist argument of survival of the fittest. Lily (and her entire class) proves as fragile as the flower whose name she bears.

The female protagonists of these fictions do not, however, remain blameless; Social Darwinism is not the only important and popular cultural theory to find its way into Gilman's and Wharton's work. In the age of self-help, mind cure, and New Thought, Lily and the narrator of "The Yellow Wallpaper" must necessarily be examined not just as helpless pawns in a capitalist, patriarchal, evolutionary system but as autonomous creatures in control of their own destinies. Accusation is implicit in Gilman's story of the defeat of the woman writer. When the narrator complains that writing "*does* exhaust me a great deal," one can almost hear Orison Swett Marden condemning the weakness that would give in to a little exhaustion; after all, Gilman herself managed to write despite such adverse circumstances.

Throughout *The House of Mirth* is the dream of a better society, Selden's "republic of the spirit," which sounds remarkably like a New Thought paradise. New Thought philosophy advocated a notion of success in which virtue triumphs over materialism. Selden, in describing his "republic" to Lily, defines it in terms of "success": "'My idea of success,' he said, 'is personal freedom. . . . [Freedom] from everything—from money, from poverty, from ease and anxiety, from all material accidents. . . . That's what I call success. . . . It is a country one has to find one's way to one's self'." Selden's vision is comparable to Orison Swett Marden's: "Happiness today, now, is our duty. . . . How contemptible mere money-wealth looks in comparison with a serene life, with a life which dwells in the ocean of truth, beneath the waves, beyond the reach of the tempests in eternal calm" (*The Young Man Entering Business* [1903], quoted in Gail Parker, *Mind Cure in New England*). While many modern critics dismiss Selden's "republic of the spirit" as hypocritical or faddist and discredit his vision of a better world, it nevertheless seems to be the sort of world Wharton advocates as a remedy to the diseased New York society that destroys Lily, even if Selden proves a poor citizen of it. The kind of methodical character building urged by New Thought writers is the only remedy possible for Lily's degrading attempt to acquire money through marriage. Only in a world that valued people for what they were, rather than what they appeared to be or owned, could Lily have developed less materialistic desires.

"The Yellow Wallpaper" and *The House of Mirth* both illustrate that it is the culture that is more diseased than the woman or, at least, that it is the diseased culture that causes her illness or death. In each novel, nevertheless, the woman is condemned for lacking the strength or fortitude to overcome society's ills. Had the narrator of

"The Yellow Wallpaper" continued to write despite her fatigue, she might have recovered, like Gilman herself; had Lily Bart not given in to the physical ease and pleasure seeking she had been accustomed to, she might have stayed alive or married Selden.

One does not undertake a biographical reading intending to undermine the fiction, of course. Feminist criticism that focuses on the biography of Charlotte Perkins Gilman and Edith Wharton (as I and many others have done) provides a "recovery" of the happy ending by redescribing the context in which to read the fiction. Such criticism sets out what Michel Foucault calls an "author-function," that is, a way to classify the text, define it, compare it with some texts, and contrast it to others. It allows us to "reveal" or "characterize" the text's "mode of being" ("What Is an Author?"). We can then read "The Yellow Wallpaper" in the context of *Herland, Women and Economics,* and Gilman's autobiography to find a feminist parable. And we can read Lily Bart's failure in the context of Wharton's own escape from the strictures of New York's "polite" society and in the context of *Custom of the Country* and *Age of Innocence* to define it as a novel of brilliant social criticism. As Annette Kolodny has pointed out, such criticism allows us to appreciate the individual text because we know "the whole in which it was embedded" ("Reply to Commentaries"). We can therefore reexamine the figure of the invalid woman against a different ground. Such criticism allows us to read the narrative of feminine defeat within the context of the woman writer's victory and to derive our satisfaction from the fact that Gilman and Wharton managed to avoid the fates that they so eloquently described. But before I close on this happy note, I want to examine the impulse the ideology that drives this kind of criticism: why do we continue to read and praise novels of feminine defeat only to reinscribe them in biographical stories with happy endings?

Other feminist critics have tried to answer this question, but so far, none have really resolved the conflict between feminist ideology and masculine aesthetics. One answer to this question is suggested by Myra Jehlen in one of the more interesting feminist works on narrative endings, "Archimedes and the Paradox of Feminist Criticism." Jehlen suggests that the "feminine success story" of domestic fiction may be good ideology but remains bad writing; she suggests that the successful female character makes for neither good fiction nor, she implies, a good subject for feminist criticism. In contrast, she suggests that the novel of feminine defeat (best exemplified by Samuel Richardson's *Clarissa*), while worse ideologically (from a feminist standpoint), is more interesting as fiction.

When the conflict Jehlen foregrounds—that between aesthetics and ideological judgments—is taken up in traditional literary criticism, it becomes an unproblematic denial of feminist ideology's literary value. In *Beneath the American Renaissance,* the only criticism to deal at any length with Bullard's *Christine,* David Reynolds argues that *Christine* manages to be a wonderful novel despite its focus on a mid-nineteenth-century feminist spokeswoman. He claims:

> The real success of *Christine* . . . lies not in its advocacy of women's rights or its portrayal of women's wrongs but in its power as a compelling, taut novel written by a progressive American woman. . . . Here we come upon a central paradox of American women's fiction, indeed of women's literature in general: that is, it most often succeeds artistically when it leaves behind feminist politics. In this sense, it becomes women's *literature* when it refuses to be women's *propaganda* and asserts its power as an expression of universal themes. (emphasis in original)

It is doubtful that Jehlen would agree with Reynolds in his assessment of the "artistic success" of women's literature or in his assertion that great literature discusses "universal themes," thus flattening all questions of gender. But she does conclude that feminist criticism, if it is to find a way to reconcile ideological analysis and artistic analysis, must find a way to deal with this paradox. She suggests that we resolve this paradox through a reevaluation of the epistemology that upholds our aesthetic judgments.

Gilbert and Gubar suggest a different possibility for resolution; in their response to Frank Lentricchia's attack on their work, "The Man on the Dump versus the United Dames of America," they claim that they have "long believed that it is necessary to disentangle political ideology from aesthetic evaluation." Despite a fundamental disagreement on most issues, then, Jehlen and Gilbert and Gubar agree that it is somehow possible to separate ideological and aesthetic judgments. But such a separation is impossible, as the "happy endings" of the critical evaluations of "The Yellow Wallpaper" and *The House of Mirth* show.

Feminist critics who read stories of feminine defeat but embed them in the "whole" that includes the woman writer's dramatic victory over illness and society's structures are, it seems to me, trying to find a way to sidestep the contradiction in their ideological and aesthetic evaluations. This paradox is configured by traditional (male) standards of literary value on one side (what counts as "good fiction") and by New Thought standards of success on the other (what counts as a "happy ending" for the authors). It is an attempt to find a feminist-ideological justification for an aesthetic evaluation based on traditional literary critical standards, without recognizing that it is a capitalist, patriarchal ideology of self-discipline that informs that "feminist" evaluation in the first place. I do not mean to suggest that the "endings" would have been happier for Wharton and Gilman had they, like their heroines, succumbed to the forces of their society, but we should recognize that the move on the part of feminist critics to "recover" happy endings for these fictions does exactly what the fictions themselves argue against: it provides an individual solution to the problem of societal "disease" without fundamentally challenging the structure or ideology of that society. Like most feminist fictions, "The Yellow Wallpaper" and *The House of Mirth* explicitly challenge societal norms and the power of the individual to overcome them. To then celebrate the individual writer's triumph over those norms is to disavow the social criticism in the fiction. The same feminist critics who value fiction like Wharton's and Gilman's because it, like masculine realist fiction, resists the "happy ending" of domestic novels nevertheless reenact that happy ending in their criticism by subscribing to a theory of individual power.

It would be nice if I could offer a "happy ending," an easy resolution to this dilemma, at this point. But I find that whatever solution I offer has a new set of problems, creates a new kind of unhappy ending of its own.

If we continue to read these unhappy fictions and resist the impulse to add on our critical happy endings, we create two new problems. First, we are left with only a negative feminism, an argument about what the world should not be like, not an argument for what changes we might make. But it also leaves that aesthetic of defeated women in place; the sense that only dead or mad women are beautiful remains unquestioned. If we are to find any way to reconcile ideology and aesthetics, we cannot continue to read merely the same texts.

Of course, we could also revise our aesthetic evaluations entirely and recuperate the lost sentimental tradition; we can urge publishers to bring back into print the sentimental texts we have lost. This is, of course, a project already underway with Rutgers University Press's American Women Writers Series, with the Feminist Press, and with New American Library's Plume Women Writers Series, among others. The problem with this—aside from the need to completely reeducate our aesthetic sensibilities—is that what counts as a "happy ending" for many sentimental fictions—the woman's eventual marriage and her coming into wealth is not really what we would advocate today as a happy ending. For better or for worse, New Thought philosophy is deeply embedded in the American success ethic today, perhaps especially among feminist scholars who had to will their way through graduate school and into the profession. If one listens to contemporary conversations with an ear for New Thought phrasing, one hears the same self-reliance, determination, willpower, and "stick-to-itiveness" that Gilman urged in the pages of *Success*. Nineteenth-century sentimental fiction advocates a completely different ethic of "success" and has a different notion of what counts as a happy ending. As professional women, feminist critics may be uncomfortable with the wholesale move into a sentimental canon that holds marriage out as the only "happy ending."

We could therefore turn to "New Woman" fictions, where heroines manage to defy social convention, become successful professionals, and sometimes even couple that professional success with romantic success. These novels—like *Dr. Zay, Country Doctor,* and *Christine*—give us an individual who fundamentally changes society: a woman whose success is predicated on a change in the world and who uses her success to help other women. This "solution," though, continues to uphold individualistic, New Thought, capitalist notions of success, at least to a certain extent, while simultaneously forcing us to reevaluate aesthetic judgments. It would not be an easy or trouble-free solution.

Perhaps the best solution is to try to do some of all of the things suggested here: read unhappy endings as social criticism, and read the different kinds of happy endings with a critical eye. We can also search for texts that resist the dichotomy happy/unhappy at all; texts like Zora Neale Hurston's *Their Eyes Were Watching God* can be categorized as neither happy nor unhappy. But we need to foreground the relation between ideology and aesthetics as well as the questions of the uses of aesthetics and of whether one ever "escapes" ideology. We should, I think, work to keep Jehlen's paradox problematized.

Barbara Fass Leavy

SOURCE: "Plague, Physician, Writer, and the Poison Damsel," in *To Blight with Plague: Studies in a Literary Theme*, New York University Press, 1992, pp. 157-83.

[*In the following excerpt, Leavy analyzes literary works that closely associate women with disease.*]

When Fournier published his book on *Syphilis and Marriage* in 1880, he had several purposes. Like his other treatises on venereal disease, this one provided medical education. The important discoveries concerning the diagnosis and treatment of syphilis were yet to occur, and Fournier's careful look at and classification of symptoms and patterns of transmission—many of his conclusions arrived at deductively—were being communicated to physicians who would encounter and attempt to treat the disease. The book could also educate that segment of the general public that would read it, ironically the same group that he was depicting as more dangerous in the spread of the disease than it as a class wished to admit to itself. For Fournier was also addressing a virtually taboo subject, shifting the site of the disease from the streets and their vices to the bedrooms of respectable households. The doctor's role was no longer restricted to that of healer. Unlike the speaker in Blake's "London," who from an objective distance remarks on the plague that blights the "marriage hearse," the physician that Fournier addresses must be directly concerned that a bridegroom might "give a virtuous young woman the pox as a wedding present." In asking the question, what conditions ought the groom "fulfill, medically, in order that we may be justified in permitting him to marry," or "conversely, in what conditions will it be our duty to defer or even absolutely interdict the marriage"? Fournier implicates the medical profession not only in the course of the marriage and its issue, and in ethical (eventually, in legal) dilemmas, but also in matters of conscience ordinarily dealt with by the clergy. Moreover, the physician's examining room had been extended to the arena of public health; inevitably this involved the doctor in conflicts concerning individual patients, the larger circle of people around them, and society as a whole.

For all of these reasons, Fournier was also attempting to change the public image of the syphilitic, the middle- or upper-class patient he was regularly seeing being one whose need to maintain privacy and avoid scandal was not only acute but also capable of being achieved. But this demand for concealment by respectable people as well as the hypocrisy that governed their sexual lives made them especially insidious spreaders of the disease. Again, these classes were then, as they probably are now, the same ones likely to read books about the diseases that plagued them, to be educated by such reading, and in turn to educate their families. A major source of the problem, they constituted a potentially major source of the solution. Fournier's work is intended as a guide to insure healthy marriages and families, and its immediate translation into English indicates that its public usefulness was quickly recognized outside of France.

This brief survey of Fournier's intentions is based not only on *Syphilis and Marriage* . . . but also on a dramatic work often mentioned in connection with Ibsen's, a play that virtually dramatizes Fournier's profile of the "new" syphilitic: Eugene Brieux's *Damaged Goods,* whose French title, *Les Avariés* is a term that euphemistically identifies a syphilitic patient as well as morally and socially designating him as "damaged." The first and third of its three acts take place in the offices of its main character, a doctor, the second act in the home of a family devastated by his advice having gone unheeded. The doctor had diagnosed the medical condition of one George Dumont to be syphilis, and had dissuaded the young man, who was about to be married, from committing suicide by assuring him that his disease had a 95 percent chance of cure. But when, following upon his relief, George is informed that he must postpone his wedding for three or four years, since it is likely if not definite that he will infect his wife, the young man seizes on the off-chance that this will not happen and proceeds with the marriage. For he has also contracted to buy a notary's practice, for which his prospective bride's dowry is necessary. Moreover, he is overwhelmed with his own sense of not deserving what had happened to him, for, or so he argues, compared to many other men of his generation, he had practised what his age might have considered safe sex. He had restricted himself to the wife of a best friend he knew to be faithful in the marriage, and to a young woman whose family enjoyed the economic privileges of the relationship and hence carefully guarded her on behalf of her sexual partner and benefactor. George claims indignantly, as if he were victim rather than accomplice in his own plight, that it was only a single encounter with a woman whose sexual history should have made him particularly careful that had brought him to his present condition. The doctor wryly responds that one careless instance was sufficient. In any event, George defies medical advice and takes matters into his own hands: drawing, ironically enough, on a more respectable plague, tuberculosis, he finds in vague respiratory symptoms an excuse to postpone his marriage for six months and then pronounces himself cured and ready to wed.

Act 2 finds the married couple a year later, lamenting the absence of their three-month-old daughter, who, in accord with the traditions of their class, is in the charge of a wet nurse. But then disquieting news reaches Dumont. His mother accompanies both nurse and infant to her son's home after learning that the nurse has probably been infected by the baby, who has visible if relatively minor symptoms of congenital syphilis, such as a rash and pimples in her mouth and throat. The same doctor who had diagnosed George is called to the house, and he and the grandmother are embroiled in a verbal battle over the well-being of the nurse (or future nurses) versus that of the child, who—or so its family believes—might not survive if bottle fed according to the doctor's instructions. The father and grandmother are immune to moral issues, although sensitive to the possibility of a lawsuit, several nurses having already been awarded large settlements by the courts for having contracted syphilis from infected infants nursing at their breasts. Moreover, a new law has made doctors who knowingly neglect to warn such nurses if they are in danger also liable to suit, so what is essentially a moral issue is now also a legal one. The Dumonts pay off their nurse, who has now cunningly understood how she can use her situation to get money but has not grasped the full danger to her health. She leaves, but not before the young Mrs. Dumont discovers the truth, act 2 ending with her histrionically "shrieking like a mad woman" at her husband, "Don't touch me! Don't touch me!"

Act 3 returns the audience to the doctor's office, this time in a hospital, where the younger Mrs. Dumont's father, M. Loches, arrives to procure a certificate testifying to his son-in-law's condition prior to marriage so that his daughter can obtain a divorce. The doctor refuses to comply on several grounds. The first has to do with the confidentiality George can expect from his physician. The second involves the doctor's disagreement concerning the divorce being in the best interest of the family in general, the young woman in particular. The third concerns his indictment that the father must accept some of the responsibility for the debacle, since he had made many inquiries about his future son-in-law's character and income, but none about his health. And when all arguments fail, the doctor asks Loches if he is in a position to judge the young man: had he never exposed himself to the danger of contracting syphilis? If uninfected, could he claim more than luck where his son-in-law had been unlucky?

> Come, come, let us have a little plain speaking! I should like to know how many of these rigid moralists, who are so choked with their middle-class prudery that they dare not mention the name syphilis, or when they bring themselves to speak of it do so with expressions of every sort of disgust, and treat its victims as criminals, have never run the risk of contracting it themselves? It is those alone who have the right to talk. How many do you think there are? Four out of a thousand?

Persuading the man that his daughter can construct a good marriage out of the present debacle, that "there is much truth in the saying that reformed rakes make the best husbands," that "we will make sure that when they are reunited their next child shall be healthy and vigorous," the doctor draws the father, a legislator, into his vision of a more enlightened society. This, perhaps, explains the "we" ("nous nous arrangerous") who will insure the well-being of future generations, educating the public about syphilis as a medical disease while addressing the moral issue, which does not rest on any inherent sinfulness attached to sex but rather on hypocritical sexual behavior. To this end, the doctor introduces one of his patients, a prostitute, whose story presents her as a stereotypical fallen woman, victim of her society, thwarted in her striving towards respectability, paying men back for her misery by, at this point, willfully spreading the disease with which she has been afflicted. When Loches excoriates her for being a poisoner, the doctor must remind him that she had herself first been poisoned. In effect, Blake's harlot has finally been allowed to speak for herself.

As a problem play, *Damaged Goods* announces its content to the audience when it is addressed by the theater manager before the curtain goes up: "The object of this play is a study of the disease of syphilis and its bearing on marriage." By substituting the word "object" for the French "sujet," the English version emphasizes the rhetorical *aim* of the drama, the intention both to promote social reform and to educate the audience about the individual's role in the spread of syphilis, as well as to provide advice about how persons might protect themselves and those they are concerned about. When the doctor reproves Loches for failing to investigate the health of his future son-in-law as carefully as he had investigated his character and his finances, Brieux is sending a message directly to every father in the audience concerning his daughter's future.

The playwright is drawing on the traditional advantage of literature in describing a social problem or making an ethical point over other forms of writing because literature alone has pleasure as its means and can give flesh to abstract ideas by way of characters whose actions will affect outcomes. Brieux dedicates his play to Fournier in a brief letter that prefaces his text:

> Monsieur,
>
> I request your permission to dedicate this play to you. Most of the ideas that it attempts to popularize are yours.
>
> I believe, with you, that syphilis will lose much of its gravity when one dares to speak openly of a sickness [mal] that is not a shame nor a punishment and when those who are infected [atteints], knowing what misery [malheurs] they are capable of spreading, are more aware of their responsibilities towards others and towards themselves.
>
> Believe, Monsieur, my respectful sympathy. . . .

Brieux's use of the word "sympathie" indicates more than his agreement with the renowned syphilologist's views on the disease. Rather, he suggests an inherent identification between himself and Fournier, who is represented in the play as an unnamed physician known variously as "le docteur" and "le medicin," which terms emphasize his role as an abstract representative of his profession. Brieux is, in effect, putting Fournier on stage, supplying him with a medium that promises a wider public than his books alone could hope to gain.

In this way Brieux and Fournier, playwright and physician, exchange identities. The writer becomes healer, and conversely the doctor as literary character becomes one who uses *words* rather than dispenses medicines to heal private and public disease. . . . [The] psychological function of the doctor is traditional, and, according to McNeill, was even more so when the medical profession was ineffective against diseases and epidemics. But *Damaged Goods* appeared at a time when the very advances in medicine complicated the physician's role. The play stood at the threshold of crucial scientific discoveries: identifying the spirochete that causes syphilis, devising a reliable test for it (the Wassermann test), and developing effective antibiotics whose side effects did not threaten to be almost as bad as the disease itself. But such progress post-dates *Damaged Goods,* and Brieux's physician can be accused of being too cavalier, too optimistic about the ease with which George might be healed. But, again, Brieux's doctor is not primarily dispensing medical treatment. The prescription that he writes for George Dumont in the first act is a miniature text, a symbol of the play.

For it is language itself, its use and misuse, that supplies *Damaged Goods* with one of its major themes. People who shamelessly entered into the most immoral sexual relations insisted on surrounding the "act that reproduces life by the means of love" with a "gigantic conspiracy of silence." The same persons who took their children to music halls where they were exposed to the most licentious language and acts yet adhered to some ignorant preconception of childhood innocence and would not "let [their offspring] hear a word spoken seriously on the subject of the great act of love," thus denying sex education a role in the schools. It is because he "was afraid to tell" his father that he had syphilis that a young man consulted medical quacks, the disease having progressed very far before he came under the care of Brieux's hero-doctor.

But adults were also shielded from reality, from the language of disease. George's father had owned a small provincial paper and George admits that had they "ever printed that word"—*syphilis*—they would have lost their readers, although that same readership was hungry for "novels about adultery." In a scene reminiscent of the encounter between Dr. Stockmann and Hovstad, George insists that the press must conform to public taste. Thus the word *syphilis* is taboo, and what the doctor insists is that the disease cease to be treated like a mysterious evil the very name of which cannot be pronounced. The "ignorance in which the public is kept of the real nature and of the consequences of this disease helps to aggravate and to spread it." It is the contagiousness of this concept as much as the illness itself that the doctor attacks when he responds to Loches's demand for his complicity in divorce proceedings.

> Few things exasperate me more than that term "shameful disease," which you used just now. This disease is like all other diseases: it is one of our afflictions. There is no shame in being wretched—even if one deserves to be so.

What he calls for is some "plain speaking" concerning those who "dare not mention the name syphilis" or speak of it with "every sort of disgust" and "treat victims as criminals," as if they themselves "have never run the risk of contracting it themselves." It is neither morality nor divine judgment that separate the sick from the well—just luck in the past and possibly education and understanding in the present.

But in the isolated realm of the syphilis patient, the words from outside are as afflicting as the microparasites that destroy from within: the *record* of syphilis proves more incurable than the disease itself. When the doctor tries to talk Loches out of separating his daughter from her husband, he argues that this father has failed to consider that his "daughter has been exposed to the infection," and that a statement to that effect "will be officially registered in the papers of the case." But his daughter's ensuing inability to remarry is nothing compared to the effect of public record on his granddaughter, whose inheritance will be to endure a double infection:

> Indeed! you think that this poor little thing has not been unlucky enough in her start in life? She has been blighted physically: you wish besides to stamp her indelibly with the legal proof of congenital syphilis?

This family's misfortune threatens to dissolve into words, into story, and against Loches's threat to kill his son-in-law and his confidence that he will be acquitted, the doctor counters, "Yes; but [only] after the public narration of all your troubles ['la révélation publique']. The scandal and the misfortune will be so much the greater, that is all."

It is thus in a realm of language rather than science that Brieux's doctor moves. It is what his patients say to him, not their physical symptoms, that allows him to know "better than anyone" what constitutes the morals of his time. And when George begs for assurance that he can look forward to cure and eventually to marriage, the doctor answers, "Je vous le jure," the translation, "I give you my word on it," true to the spirit rather than the letter of the French text. For in *Damaged Goods,* the doctor must counter words with words, and when George repeats some erroneous information he has been told is true, the doctor, part in mockery and part in frustration, can only mimic, "You have been told! You have been told!" "On vous avait dit. . . . On vous avait dit!"

It is as a debater rather than a physician that the doctor confronts Loches, significantly a deputy for his town famous because he is a "regular orator." At first, refusing Loches his request for documentary evidence to use in the divorce, the doctor is reluctant to engage in controversy with his opponent, but he eventually concedes: "Since I have let myself in for it, I may as well explain my position." Once having prevailed with Loches, the doctor must tell the father, at a loss as to how to "persuade" his daughter "to return to her husband," that there are "arguments that you can use." His ability to sway George had been unfortunately undermined by another syphilologist, Ricord, who, if Brieux's presentation is accurate, apparently differed with Fournier about the inevitability of contagion. Although Brieux's doctor responds to his patient, "I will answer you," he cannot muster the irrefutable facts of science to sustain the rhetoric that is almost by default his strongest weapon. When the prospective groom argues that not only his future happiness but also his economic well-being is at issue, his position is thrown back at him with the implications of his words:

> DOCTOR: . . . I can easily show you the way out of the difficulty. Get into touch with some rich man, do everything you can to gain his confidence, and when you have succeeded, rook him of all he has.
>
> GEORGE: I'm not in the mood for joking.
>
> DOCTOR: I'm not joking. To rob that man, or even to murder him, would not be a greater crime than you would commit in marrying a young girl in good health to get hold of her dowry, if to do so you expose her to the terrible consequences of the disease you would give her.

At those times when he is most discouraged about how to halt the spread of syphilis, it is his failure with language that overwhelms the doctor. Coming to examine the infected Dumont infant and recognizing George, he exclaims, "You married and had a child after all I *said* to you" (italics added). But George's predicament is not the doctor's first discouragement, and he had earlier admitted to the prospective bridegroom that he was ineffectual with other patients:

> I am almost afraid of not having been persuasive enough. I feel as though in spite of everything I were in some sort the cause of their misery. I ought to prevent such misery. . . . Give me your word that you will break off your engagement.

But more often than not, the self-interest of the syphilitic patient would prove insurmountable, impervious to the logic of the disease and its epidemiology. What he cannot expect to achieve with George, the doctor may with Loches—outraged father, true, but also legislator entrusted with public welfare. And so he will move Loches to action not with words but, finally, with what the doctor alone can provide, a parade of the hapless and helpless victims of syphilis and their devastated families: the father whose son waited perhaps too long to admit to his family that he was sick; or the poverty-stricken woman who suffers the disease passed on by her now-dead husband and, lacking both money and time off from work for treatment, remains without even the luxury of outrage enjoyed by the bourgeois Mrs. Dumont, who can indulge in screams of horror and fury, and who has her father to fight for and protect her.

But the most important case history for the doctor's argument is the prostitute who is "at once the product and the cause" of so many social ills, her potential for spreading syphilis the result not of her fallen nature but of her own victimization. Her narrative is typical, an account of a maidservant being seduced by her master, whose wife then turns her out on the streets. Ironically, the prostitute has the ambition to be an actress, to make of the stage rather than the streets a livelihood. As a ruse to elicit her life's history, the doctor informs her that Loches can help her realize her goals, when, in fact, it is the doctor himself who supplies the dramatic arena on which she may act out her narrative. More literally, Brieux as playwright transforms the prostitute's dream into actuality: he provides her with a stage, a script, and even—in the person of his doctor—a director.

It is at this point that the doctor and the playwright, whose identities had been merged throughout the play, diverge, the rhetorical aims of the play not entirely consistent with the power of art. Since *Damaged Goods* is the very antithesis of art for art's sake, Brieux must confront the limitations of his medium, which can aim at reform but not assure it. Thus the playwright must constantly gauge his own rhetorical effectiveness. About the prostitute's story, the doctor asks Loches, "Was I not right to keep that confession for the end?" For it is on Loches the legislator rather than on either doctor or playwright that the power to make changes rests. To the prostitute's own words, the doctor has "nothing more to say" ("rien à ajouter"), passing rhetoric back to the person in whose domain it really belongs: "But if you [Loches] give a thought or two to what you have just seen when you are sitting in the [legislative] Chamber, we shall not have wasted our time."

Such a separation between the devices of art and the realities of science and action apparently frustrated Brieux's translator, who seems to have found the playwright's language more suited to lectures on venereal disease than to a play based on them. For despite McNeill's claim that the "learned discussion of syphilis was as florid as the symptoms of the disease itself when new," the French text is matter-of-fact, often more so than the English version, to which is added the metaphor that stands behind the title *Damaged Goods*. That is, to the case histories of syphilitics, which are the last ploy by Brieux's doctor to persuade those capable of action to act, are added the verbally induced images capable of eliciting the sympathies of the audience that was experiencing a play, not listening to Doctor Fournier lecture on syphilis and marriage. When the doctor proposes to Loches that he meet some of his patients, he assures the deputy that their physical condition will not shock him. Brieux's words are straightforward:

> Rassurez-vous, je ménagerai vos nerfs, aucun de ceux et de celles que vous allez voir n'a de tare apparente. Je m'étais dit hier: "Enfin, voilà un député qui va prendre en main la cause qui nous est chère. . . ." Je m'étais trompe. Vous veniez pour un autre sujet. Tant pis.
>
> (Be assured, I will spare your nerves; none of those you are going to see have obvious symptoms. I said to myself yesterday, "Finally, here is a deputy who will take up the cause that is to us so dear." I was mistaken. You came for another reason. Too bad.)

The version of this passage in the translated play not only supplies the strategies of literary language but also draws attention to what it conceives of as its own contribution to Brieux's work:

> To outward appearance [these patients] have nothing the matter with them. They are not bad cases; they are simply the damaged goods of our great human cargo. I merely wished to give you food for reflection, not a lesson in pathology.

The shifting relationship between physician and writer, as well as the comparison between Brieux and his English translator, ultimately rests in *Damaged Goods* on differences in language. The artist's *self* is always at stake in writing about plague rhetoric and art, means and ends frequently in conflict. The way words are used as persuasive devices and the role of persuasion itself in *Damaged Goods* have to do with the playwright's self-definition as social critic and artist, the language of each not always compatible. In the play, this concern is expressed in the doctor's own struggle to define his role. When George Dumont implores him to prescribe a treatment for syphilis that works more rapidly than the ones he presently has at his disposal, the doctor responds that the days of miracles are past.

> DOCTOR: . . . I am a physician, nothing but a physician. . . .
>
> GEORGE: No, no! You are more than a physician: you are a confessor as well. You are not only a man of science. You can't observe me as you would something in your laboratory and then simply say: "You have this, science says that. Now be off with you!" My whole life depends upon you.

George is correct: Brieux's doctor is more than a physician. And he may be a confessor as well. But the "more" that he is is a rhetorician, and his words may be no more immediately consoling to his patients than the limited cures he offers. His predicament has already been seen in Kramer's *The Normal Heart*. Like Brieux's physician, Dr. Emma Brookner has something compelling to say, and in both cases the doctors' words have to do with the sexually transmitted diseases they are diagnosing and to vastly different degrees of success treating. The content of these doctors' argument is likely to be disregarded by the very persons they most want to reach. In both plays, the limitations of medicine, the absence of an easy cure, call into play the powers of language which the writer must direct either towards social reality or towards helping to create, if unwittingly, the illusions out of which humans build their fantasies.

Moreover, doctors themselves may contribute to the dangerous social construction of the diseases that plague their patients. When George Dumont reveals obvious signs of ignoring the doctor's advice, the latter tries yet another persuasive tack to convince the young man of his fiancée's danger:

> . . . Take this book—it is my master's—work here, read for yourself, I have marked the passage. You won't read it? Then I will. (*He reads passionately.*) "I have seen an unfortunate young woman changed by this disease into the likeness of a beast."
>
> "J'ai eu le spectacle d'une malheureuse jeune femme convertie en un véritable monstre par le fait d'une syphilide phagédénique."

Between "beast" and "monstre" as an image of a syphilis-infected woman there is not much to choose from. Outside of the romantic celebration of nature, for example Wordsworth's description of "glad animal movements" in "Tintern Abbey," the likening of people to beasts carries with it a strong condemnation and the assumption that they have lost or surrendered their moral selves. But why should the woman ravaged by syphilis be assumed to be less than human, even, as a monster, outside of nature itself? Especially if she is a victim rather than perpetrator of the disease? There are traditional and dangerous assumptions behind the doctor's image that he seems unwittingly to perpetrate.

Thus his simile for syphilis effectively personifies the disease as a woman:

> . . . I have one thing that I always tell my patients: if I could I would paste it up at every street corner. "Syphilis is like a woman whose temper is roused by the feeling that her power is disdained. It is terrible only to those who think it insignificant, not to those who know its dangers."
>
> "La syphilis est une impérieuse personne qui ne veut pas qu'on méconnaisse sa puissance. Elle est terrible pour qui la croit insignifiante et bénigne pour qui sait combien elle est dangereuse. Elle est comme certaines femmes, elle ne se fâche que si on la néglige."

The feminization of the disease carries with it implications that the play bears out. Just as the disease must be controlled, so must women be—or protected, which is but the other side of the coin.

The female characters in this play are recognizable stereotypes, and it is telling that in the French edition, the cast of characters segregates male and female players, the women listed after the men. The young Mrs. Dumont is a naive woman about whose fate the male characters—her fiancé and eventual husband, her father, and the doctor—are embroiled in arguments. That she has given birth to an infant daughter only extends her role in the play, since the vulnerability of helpless female citizens is supposed to elicit the protectiveness of patriarchal society. Thus the syphilitic widow who appears in act 3 is passive, helpless, and totally dependent on the doctor's skill and direction. On another side, when George's wife does finally learn the truth, her unleashed fury likens her to her angry mother-in-law, whose self-interest, pettiness, and intense emotions surrounding her granddaughter make it impossible to elicit rational thought from her in the matter of dealing prudently with the family predicament. And the wet nurse is merely a cunning, lower-class version of the older woman. Finally, although Brieux obviously meant to arouse sympathy for the infected prostitute, what he also conveys is that men, in whose hands rest the laws of society and the forms of its institutions, would do well to protect themselves of course by enlightened means—against her dangers.

Thus metaphor and gender combine in *Damaged Goods* with sinister results, since social assumptions about women tend to obliterate the distance between Brieux's metaphor for syphilis and its referent. The young and naive Mrs. Dumont and the anything-but-innocent prostitute are morally and socially polar opposites. Yet both are infected with syphilis and are thus both carriers of the disease. Actually, the play hedges this point and it is never definite that George's wife is infected. . . .

French syphilologists were debating the very question of whether an uninfected mother would or could give birth to a diseased child. That George will almost certainly infect his wife is the doctor's primary concern; the danger to their children becomes an important but additional argument.

But if a virtuous woman could carry the disease as readily as a prostitute, a widow infecting a new and healthy husband, for example, then what M. Loches says of the whore is equally applicable to his daughter, that these miserable women are veritable poisoners ("ces misérable femmes [sont] véritables empoisonneuses"). Despite their shared victimization, then, both Mrs. Dumont and the prostitute are dangerous—if to statistically differing degrees. Add to this initial ambiguity that Brieux's virtual personification of the disease as a woman may be—as will soon appear to be the case—conventional, then what *Damaged Goods* constructs is another portrait of the poison damsel, a legendary figure evoked by Loches's contemptuous use of the word "empoisonneuses."

It is the poison damsel who supplies a contextual framework for Nathaniel Hawthorne's renowned and enigmatic story, "Rappaccini's Daughter." Many of its puzzling features have been explained by Carol Marie Bensick, who argues that it is syphilis and not some mysterious disease or generalized evil that is at issue in a tale in which the rivalry between two doctors blights the hopes of one's would-be protégé, Giovanni, and kills the other's daughter, Beatrice. Bensick's argument is a strong one, carefully documented, and the following discussion will follow its assumptions and conclusions, stressing perhaps more than she, however, the image and significance of the polluted and polluting woman epitomized in the poison damsel legend.

In the *Gesta Romanorum,* the Queen of the North, bearing a grudge against Alexander the Great, "nourished her daughter from the cradle upon a certain kind of deadly poison," and when the child grew up, the queen sent her daughter as a gift to Alexander. But his tutor Aristotle at once perceived the danger posed by the young woman and arranged to have her kissed by a condemned prisoner, who immediately died. The deadly girl was summarily returned to her mother. In "Rappaccini's Daughter" a slightly altered variant of the legend is attributed to "an old classic author" who euphemizes the sexual connotations of other variants and tells of

> an Indian prince, who sent a beautiful woman as a present to Alexander the Great. She was as lovely as the dawn, and gorgeous as the sunset; but what especially distinguished her was a certain rich perfume in her breath—richer than a garden of Persian roses. Alexander, as was natural to a youthful conqueror, fell in love at first sight with this magnificent stranger. But a certain sage physician, happening to be present, discovered a terrible secret in regard to her.

In his evocation of the "sage physician," Dr. Baglioni is preparing Giovanni for his own part in protecting the young man from Beatrice's so-called poisonousness. But the substitution of doctor for philosopher also helps point "Rappaccini's Daughter" away from a generalized theme often treated by Hawthorne, the crimes committed by science against the human heart, toward a specific and historically based depiction of physical disease and cure. The connection between the poison damsel and medicinal healing might have come to the author from various sources, one of which has recently been argued to be a Renaissance text, Timothy Bright's *Treatise on Melancholy,* which describes how poisons coexist in nature with "wholesome fruit and soveraigne medicine." Bright's analogue to the poison damsel legend would be the account of how certain persons in Italy (where Hawthorne's story takes place) "did without hurt sucke the poyson of vipers, and without perill did usually hunt them."

Before turning to "Rappaccini's Daughter," it will be useful to pursue some of these associations. First is the account of persons who immunize themselves against vipers by gradually imbibing their poison. The poison damsel's story has been studied in detail by N. M. Penzer, whose search for meanings in widely disseminated folktales and legends is usually attached to his interest in how they traveled from their point of origin, which he believes to be India. Thus Penzer rejects the idea that the poison damsel's meaning can be traced to venereal diseases because of his conviction that syphilis appeared in India only after the story was long established there. But his denial of a specific connection does not preclude Penzer's tracing noteworthy connections among poison damsels, venereal disease, serpents, and traditions of women as polluters. For example, he discusses the *vagina dentata* motif, the belief held by many peoples that some women have teeth in their vaginas and that men who have intercourse with them will be castrated. To extend Penzer's references, Apaches also tell stories of Vulva Women and the ingenuity of men who insert wooden sticks into their genitals, breaking off the threatening teeth and rendering them harmless. Similar stories depict poisonous female characters, for example, Rattlesnake Woman, who first ingests the venom of her natural mate, then metamorphoses into a beautiful woman, attracts men, and kills them by transferring the poison to them. If men resist her, she will die of the venom she has accumulated. Corollary stories, less well known, are told by women, who complain of being invaded by vaginal serpents: "The animals enter the female reproductive system, where they may hatch a whole litter and mutilate or kill the woman, or (in one text) they may merely wriggle around in her vagina and drive her crazy." That gynecological disorders and venereal diseases may contribute to such tales adds a fascinatingly realistic layer of meaning to what is a virtually endlessly provocative symbolism.

Moreover, if Hawthorne did read Bright's treatise on melancholy, it might have reminded him of another, the more renowned seventeenth-century *Anatomy of Melancholy* by Robert Burton, in which the story is told of a lamia (a snake woman) who married a philosophy student, Lycius, his teacher Apollonius Tyanaeus attending their wedding to expose the bride as evil illusion, at which disclosure she vanishes. One of Hawthorne's sources for "Rappaccini's Daughter" is Keats's rendition of this anecdote in his own poem "Lamia." Hawthorne is, however, unlikely to have realized that his own substitution of physicians for philosophers would have touched one of Keats's major concerns. Having decided against being a surgeon after his training at Guy's Hospital, Keats turned to writing poetry and was thereafter torn between medicine and literature—to use the words of one of his letters, between women who had cancers and Petrarchan coronals. In one of his last poems, "The Fall of Hyperion," he asks if poets might not be physicians to all men. For the English poet, sometimes the muse herself might as well have been a poison damsel, substituting the illusion of pleasure for the reality of a world of real diseases, one in which the "fever and the fret" of life causes men to "sit and hear each other groan" a world where

> palsy shakes a few, sad, last gray hairs,
> Where youth grows pale, and spectre-thin, and
> dies.
>
> ("Ode to a Nightingale")

The realistic medical basis for their themes strengthens the connection between Hawthorne and Keats. In "La Belle Dame sans Merci," the narrator perceives that the knight who has loved the mysterious temptress is wasting away:

> I see a lily on thy brow
> With anguish moist and fever dew,
> And on thy cheeks a fading rose
> Fast withereth too.

The White Plague, tuberculosis, the disease from which Keats died, may stand behind this image, which may have been borrowed by Hawthorne for "Rappaccini's Daughter." Often described as feverish, Giovanni perhaps as a result of disordered senses believes he sees the withering of a fresh bouquet of flowers being held by Beatrice Rappaccini.

Strikingly, Hawthorne, too, had contemplated a career in medicine, if only to reject outright the idea that he would derive his living from other people's miseries, in contrast to Keats, who thought being a poet was self-indulgent because people *needed* doctors. Despite this difference, the two writers shared a concern for art's role in a world in which it was losing ground almost in proportion to the growing influence of science and medicine. Keats's poems and Hawthorne's tales are linked not only by common literary sources and images borrowed by Hawthorne from his English romantic predecessor, but also by their shared literary motifs, again, grounded in medicine.

Because of its frequently shifting narrative perspective, events and characters being depicted not necessarily as they are but rather as what one character or another thinks they are, "Rappaccini's Daughter" is difficult to summarize. Its basic plot, however, resembles such stories as that of the lamia or poison damsel. Early in the sixteenth century, one Giovanni Guasconti comes from Naples to Padua in order to attend the university famed for its medical studies. From his lodgings he is able to observe a lush and strange garden with exotic and unusual herbs and flowers, the gardeners who tend the plants proving to be one of the university's most renowned if unorthodox professors of medicine, Giacomo Rappaccini, and his daughter Beatrice, close to her father in learning and the possession of arcane knowledge. Giovanni notices, however, that the father tends the plants from a slight distance as if afraid of their influence on him, whereas Beatrice has no fear of the blooms and moves about and handles them as if attached to them by a special sympathy. He also believes he has witnessed from his window above the garden several strange events: that a bouquet of fresh flowers that he throws down to Beatrice has withered in her arms, and that a lizard and an insect that have come close enough to Beatrice for her to breathe upon them have died. From then on a mingled desire and revulsion intensify Giovanni's attraction to and obsession with Beatrice. His ambivalence is fueled by the mixed signals he receives from another physician, Pietro Baglioni. It is Dr. Baglioni who characterizes Dr. Rappaccini for Giovanni, claiming that his rival cares more for science than human life and would sacrifice anyone—his daughter and Giovanni included—"for the sake of adding so much as a grain of mustard seed to the great heap of his accumulated knowledge." The narrator, whose point of view is distinct from the characters, and should not be taken for granted to be that of Hawthorne, comments,

> The youth might have taken Baglioni's opinions with many grains of allowance, had he known that there was a professional warfare of long continuance between him and Doctor Rappaccini, in which the latter was generally thought to have gained the advantage. If the reader be inclined to judge for himself, we refer him to certain black-letter tracts on both sides, preserved in the medical department of the University of Padua.

The controversy divides Baglioni, a traditional Galenist who adheres to traditionally approved methods of curing disease, from Rappaccini, an empiricist and follower of Paracelsus, who experiments with drugs distilled from the blooms in his garden, concocting toxic brews to fight the systemic poisons that he believes make people ill. Rappaccini is credited with some near-miraculous cures, admits his rival, although he, Baglioni, believes that these are the "work of chance." Here is a noteworthy difference between Brieux's play and Hawthorne's story. Brieux treats the transmission of syphilis as a social problem, arguing that in a large number of cases only chance separates the infected from the uninfected. Treatment of the disease is handled in the play as if it were a simple matter. In Hawthorne's reconstructed Italian

Renaissance, the source of disease (whether or not it is syphilis) recedes into the background, and the cure is a matter of either science or chance, depending upon whether this is seen from the view of Rappaccini or Baglioni.

It is Baglioni who tells Giovanni the story of the poison damsel and of the sage physician who discovered her terrible secret; and playing on Giovanni's suspicions, his growing propensity to believe that the beautiful Beatrice is tainted with moral as well as physical evil, Baglioni suggests that "the poisoner Rappaccini" has created a daughter "poisonous as she is beautiful." But he also claims to possess the antidote to Rappaccini's vile brews, one "little sip" of which "would have rendered the most virulent poisons of the Borgias innocuous." He encourages Giovanni to feed his medicine to Beatrice and await the effects, which turn out to be her swift death: "As poison had been life, so the powerful antidote was death." The young woman dies with an enigmatic reproach to Giovanni: "Oh, was there not, from the first, more poison in thy nature than in mine?" And as she dies before her father and lover,

> Professor Pietro Baglioni looked forth from the window, and called loudly, in a tone of triumph mixed with horror, to the thunder-stricken man of science,
>
> "Rappaccini! Rappaccini! And is *this* the upshot of your experiment!"

The story, again, follows a well-known narrative pattern. A young man finds himself torn between his attraction to a beautiful but strange and perhaps dangerous woman, on one side, and a wise man, often a philosopher or priest, intent on saving him from her, on the other. Hawthorne's story plays a significant variation on this narrative pattern by, again, assigning the role of philosopher or priest to a doctor—indeed, two doctors, who represent radically different approaches to medicine. That one of them is the father of the possibly dangerous young woman is consistent with the world's folklore and legends, where many tales involve a male protagonist who enters into a relationship with an ogre's daughter. Dr. Rappaccini is to Beatrice, for example, as Aeetes is to Medea, another enchantress schooled in poisons. Moreover, whereas Lycius and Alexander find no evil in the lamia or the poison damsel until the philosophers alert them to danger, Giovanni's assessment of Beatrice rests, as Bensick argues in convincing detail, on why Giovanni is predisposed to distrust the beautiful young woman.

Bensick's study, itself an intriguing narrative that moves towards rather than begins with the startling idea that syphilis supplies a major clue to the story's meaning, is not the only work on "Rappaccini's Daughter" to shift interpretation away from the story as an allegory of science versus imagination to a focus on the specific medical controversies that inform Hawthorne's tale. From other Hawthorne critics one learns that the practice of medicine was undergoing significant changes in the nineteenth century and supplied many contentious disputes with which the author was familiar. It has been argued that there were six significant areas in which doctors were severely criticized, only two of which are absent from "Rappaccini's Daughter": the love of gold that characterizes Chaucer's physician, and the lack of respect towards death implicated in vivisection. The four interrelated indictments of the medical profession reflected in "Rappaccini's daughter" are the indifference to life supposedly characteristic of Rappaccini but ultimately of Baglioni as well, since being proven correct is for both of them more important than human health or concerns; the preoccupation with an opportunity to enhance personal reputation even if at the patient's expense . . . ; the seemingly heartless experimenting on people to prove new theories, science counting more than cure; and the internecine squabbles that pitted doctors against each other as Rappaccini and Baglioni were, their disagreements further undermining the public's confidence.

An unwitting pun is employed by M. D. Uroff when he writes that when the public "looked at the profession as a whole, they were apt to say, 'A plague on both your houses.'" Although Uroff does not say so, the many plagues suffered in the United States in the nineteenth century—for example smallpox, typhus, yellow fever, cholera—would have been a spur to, pressure, on, experimentation by, and criticism of the medical profession. Ironically, a legacy of controls instituted because of concerns over what patients might or might not endure is today contended by some to be a worse evil, because treatments that show promise are either withheld or restricted to small control groups until their effectiveness can be solidly demonstrated, while people with little to lose are denied their possible effectiveness and die. Hawthorne's story is an early example of the search for the magic bullet, and, ironically, Rappaccini's garden, the "Eden" to which the story frequently refers, an allusion that has lent itself to a variety of interpretations of Hawthorne's use of the garden motif, is akin to a medical laboratory, making it a unique rendition of the earthly paradise theme in plague literature. This point will be returned to.

Uroff points out that in Hawthorne's time, the medical profession in Massachusetts "was in a state of flux over licensing practices, educational requirements and the large number of charlatans who dispensed cures." One of the strongest debates concerned the confrontation between allopathic and homeopathic practices of medicine, the former based on traditional medical procedures of the sort advocated by Baglioni, the latter represented by Rappaccini:

> Homeopathic doctors regarded disease not as a separate entity affecting a specific organ but as a derangement of the "immaterial vital principle" pervading and animating the body. This vital principle, homeopaths believed, had the capacity to expel morbid disturbances but its

> natural tendency to restoration was temporarily paralyzed by disease. To start the curative process, homeopathic practitioners afflicted the system with a more intense but similar disease whose presence spurred the vital principle to new efforts.

And as Bensick notes as an addition to this way of reading Hawthorne's tale, an instance of the "immemorial conflict between the Galenists and the Paracelsians, the dogmatics and the empiricists" was the enormous controversies over innoculation in the eighteenth century, controversies with which, again, Hawthorne was familiar. Innoculation may make itself felt in his story by way of Rappaccini's theories, innoculation being, as Bensick points out, a "literal application of the principle that like cures like."

This recent critical emphasis on the particulars of medical practice reflected in "Rappaccini's Daughter," when added to the historical specificity of names, locales, and other details in the story, supplies further weight to Bensick's argument that even the disease in question is specific, and is syphilis:

> A naturalistic account of the poison plot of "Rappaccini's Daughter," then, goes something like this. Like his suppressed prototype Paracelsus, who wrote on syphilis, and like Giacomo Berengario da Carpi, who is implied in the tale's allusion to Cellini [who made the artful vial that held the supposed antidote that would cure Beatrice], Rappaccini has a special interest in the treatment of syphilis. He is using the Paracelsian emphasis on experiment as well as the Paracelsian principle that like cures like in his research into poison as a possible cure for syphilis. Rappaccini's interest in syphilis may have begun because he himself is a sufferer [he is always described in the story as ill]; or, just as likely, he may have contracted syphilis while engaged in the study of it. Then also, he may have a special interest in the disease because his daughter has a latent case. Or it may be that Beatrice was born sound but that he has innoculated her with poisons designed to immunize her to syphilis, so that at his death she will be in no danger of ever contracting the disease of the age [the Renaissance].

Bensick's argument is further strengthened by a book she has located but did not use in her study. Two years before Hawthorne's story first appeared (1844), a translation of Philippe Ricord's treatise on syphilis was published in Philadelphia, its very title striking because of the emphasis on experimentation and innoculation: *A Practical Treatise on Venereal Diseases; or, Critical and Experimental Researches on Innoculation, Applied to the Study of These Affections* (1842). Like the works of other nineteenth-century French syphilologists, Ricord's is a storage house of medical and sociological information about venereal disease, much of it validating McNeill's contention, already quoted in the discussion of Brieux, that there was a correlation between the "florid" descriptions of syphilis after it first appeared and the learned discussions that ensued. Early in Ricord's book, among his "General Remarks," is a piece of legendary history about syphilis that is not only perhaps more florid than most, but also brings together a variety of themes: the association of syphilis with women so that the disease is virtually personified as female; the motif of poison; and the connection between sex and contagion that is by implication moral as well as physical:

> Alexander Benedictus, a Veronese physician, was the first to admit, as a contagious principle, *a venereal taint produced in the sexual organs of women by the alteration of humors which they exhale;* this was admitted by Fernel, and received the name of *lues venerea,* poison, venereal virus, &c., and since that time most writers on syphilis have acknowledged the existence of a specific cause, of a peculiar deleterious principle.

The ambiguous placement of "they" makes it unclear whether it is the women or their sexual organs that exhale the poison, but the dual possibility links the two sides of Hawthorne's analogy between the poison damsel with whom, according to tradition, sexual union will prove deadly, and Beatrice Rappaccini, who supposedly need only breathe on a plant or insect in order to kill it.

There are other connections between Ricord and Hawthorne worth noting. Not only is the French physician an advocate of medical experimentation, but he also locates the scientific work on venereal diseases within a problematic context supplied by theology. For example, he refers to the earlier experiments of one Luna Calderon, which were badly received during the scientist's age because "the search for a preservative against diseases sent by Heaven to punish libertinism, was perhaps still regarded as a sacrilege." Ricord congratulates his own time because "the foolish prohibitions of false morality no longer compel [him] to regard venereal disease as a punishment" for immoral living. Ricord thus effectively draws lines to separate sex, sin, and medical studies, differentiating what Giovanni tends to merge, sometimes indiscriminately. For Ricord, "the truly wise, virtuous, and philanthropic moralist will say . . . that he must be considered as the true benefactor and preserver of his race, who should discover the true secret of preserving us from the most terrible contagion which ever threatened mankind."

Giovanni may have been predisposed to view Beatrice as a poison damsel because he too is infected by syphilis and may be inclined to think of himself as already poisoned by some woman—to invoke, that is, any number of the myths of feminine evil available to men seemingly forever. Naples was, according to one prevalent theory, the place from which syphilis spread through Europe, and at one point in the story Giovanni is asked by Baglioni what "disease of body or heart" has him "so inquisitive about physicians?" Such a question might implicitly be extended: one might ask if he had come to Padua, a seat of medical learning and new cures, only for study. Dr. Rappaccini, whose medicines are supposed to have effected near-miraculous cures, is said at one point to have been "heard of as far as Naples." And as already noted, Hawthorne may have drawn from

Keats's poem the image of a feverish knight for his portrayal of Giovanni, whose frequently alluded to feverish state infers a physical problem, a disquieted state of mind, or both. Or, as Bensick points out, there may be a literal meaning to Beatrice's dying words that there was more (physical) poison in Giovanni than the (moral) poison he attributed to her. As with other details in the story, the situation is ambiguous: in Bensick's words, Giovanni

> may have been a healthy youth who became infected by contact with Beatrice or, in his own right, an unwitting carrier of Neapolitan syphilis. In the latter case, he could have been marked as a carrier by the professional eye of Rappaccini, who therefore chooses him to be his daughter's appropriate bridegroom. . . . Giovanni's statement, "She is the only being whom my breath may not slay," may well translate poetically as, "she is the only one whom sexual intercourse with me would not infect."

Once the argument is made for the presence of syphilis as a submerged theme in "Rappaccini's Daughter," what can be done with it to resolve the differing interpretations of "Rappaccini's Daughter"? Bensick herself admits that in her study of how Hawthorne drew on the "famous sixteenth-century pandemic of syphilis" to create an allegory of New England debates over theology, it is not absolutely necessary to her thesis that anyone in the story actually have syphilis, although the pandemic is sufficient to account for one of the most puzzling aspects of Giovanni's behavior, his "automatic conflation of poison with sex and sin." The specific disease rather than a vaguely conceived of poison has further significance, however, and while simplistic arguments for the "relevance" of a past literary work to the concerns of the contemporary world probably involve an insult to both, Hawthorne's story is particularly telling, not only for the past but also for today. For "Rappaccini's Daughter" addresses one of the major, extraphysical afflictions suffered by one who has a contagious disease, especially if it is associated with sexual transmission. Whatever Hawthorne's specific intentions, Beatrice Rappaccini becomes a case study of the crisis experienced by one struggling to free herself of an identity that *equals* her illness, of the assumption by others that her physical condition automatically reveals her character.

In Chaucer's "Physician's Tale," it will be remembered, nature formed a beautiful but still mutable Virginia, whose soul no natural power could supply, and Pygmalion the artificial but soulless Galatea. So do Rappaccini, Baglioni, and Giovanni forever create and recreate Beatrice. The process is best illustrated when Baglioni begins by admitting that he knows "little of the Signora Beatrice" and urging Giovanni to ignore "absurd rumors," and ends not only by planting the idea of the poison damsel in the young man's consciousness but also by supplying the supposed antidote. What Dr. Rappaccini's intentions were with regard to his daughter are never clear because the reader never hears from Rappaccini himself about them; but Beatrice, who would "fain rid [herself] of even that small knowledge" that her father has taught her about his science of plants, believes he has tampered with her very being. Dying, she reproves him with, "I am going, father, where the evil, which thou hast striven to mingle with my being, will pass away like a dream." Her confidence in herself as a secure subject had apparently survived her transformation by others into an object for study; as Bensick argues, "Beatrice evidently has an absolutely assured sense of an essential 'I' independent of the earthly accident of mortal matter, of which poisonousness is finally only a parody."

But Beatrice has nonetheless failed to communicate that about which she has remained secure. Unable to present a coherent self to Giovanni, she asks him first to ignore others and "believe nothing" of her save what he sees with his own eyes, and then realizes that the "outward senses" of her lover cannot grasp her true "essence." Taken alone, her body is as ambiguous as the garden in which she walks, its essence seemingly confused and hence unknowable. But she assures Giovanni that "the *words* of Beatrice Rappaccini's lips are true from the depths of the heart outward [and] those you may believe!" (emphasis added). And when Giovanni's own "terrible words," his accusations of a poisoned *being* as well as a poisoned body, turn into a rejection of her own claims for a language faithful to truth, she herself points out his error by drawing the distinction between her body and whatever beyond the corporeal constitutes her self:

> "I dreamed only to love thee and be with thee a little time, and so to let thee pass away, leaving but thine image in mine heart. For, Giovanni believe it though my body be nourished with poison, my spirit is God's creature, and craves love as its daily food."

In differentiating between Beatrice's body and the essence that is her *self,* Hawthorne raises issues that are not only philosophical and psychological but also sociological. For if syphilis is the poison to which Beatrice refers, then Hawthorne is also effectively writing about the venereal infection of what Fournier called a virtuous woman. It is also worth an ironic note that given the acknowledged influence of Keats on Hawthorne, of "Lamia" on "Rappaccini's Daughter," Keats's reference in a letter to taking mercury as well as his angry words directed at women in general has provoked speculation that the English poet was being treated for syphilis. Keats's life explains his obvious ambivalence towards women: his belief that they would not find him attractive, and his uneasy feelings about a mother who, after his father died, had lovers until she married again, and who died young of tuberculosis; his wish to marry Fanny Brawne, whom, however, he would have to support, perhaps at the cost of abandoning poetry. Keats's biography, that is, can be invoked to interpret the *belles dames sans merci* of his poems. But Keats was also aware that traditionally the muse was a woman, vulnerable to attacks by science, in need of the artist's protection.

The romantic poet asks in "Lamia" whether all charms do not "fly / At the mere touch of cold philosophy?" Science is blamed by Keats for clipping an angel's wings and unweaving the rainbow. In Rappaccini's garden converge the elements of science and art. Within the rivalry between them can be located the problem of Lamia's and Beatrice's identity. Keats asks whether his serpent woman is the demon's self or a penanced lady elf. Giovanni similarly queries himself about Beatrice: "What is this being?—beautiful, shall I call her?—or inexpressibly terrible?" later expressing his ambivalence by deciding, temporarily, that it "mattered not whether she were angel or demon." Is Beatrice, "maiden of a lonely island," Shakespeare's Miranda or Porter's Miranda—the latter another possible poison damsel, perhaps infecting Adam with the influenza from which he died and she recovered? If Hawthorne's Miranda, does Beatrice await her "Ferdinand" only to be betrayed by Giovanni as she already had been by the false Prospero, her father? Or does Beatrice Rappaccini inhabit less a lonely island than a bower of bliss far more complex than any Spenser could have imagined, an Acrasia not necessarily because she *is* a dangerous temptress but because Giovanni reads the signs that he thinks say she is and ignores those that argue that she is not? Or, to put this another way, Giovanni cannot separate Beatrice's identity from that of the garden she inhabits.

Of all the gardens and pseudoparadises in plague literature, Hawthorne's in "Rappaccini's Daughter" is the least susceptible to coherent interpretation. The varying literary sources from which Hawthorne drew depictions of the earthly paradise, and the different meanings he could derive from them, suggest in themselves the expulsion from Eden, from a centrality of vision to a diversity that resists patterning. These other literary gardens exist in Hawthorne's tale almost as separate languages, the scattering of meaning suggesting the Tower of Babel—another story of a fall. Hawthorne himself can be invoked to confirm such a reading of his tale. In a story written about a year earlier, "The New Adam and Eve," he depicts an uninhabited, corrupt world that remains intact and a newly created man and woman who are born into it and who instinctively react positively to the few remaining signs of nature and recoil from the cultural signs they encounter. One of the buildings they chance upon is a library, but the story's narrator reacts against a supposedly new literature in the future that will be merely a reworking of the old: "And his literature, when the progress of centuries shall create it, will be no interminably repeated echo of our own poetry, and reproduction of the images that were moulded by our great fathers of song and fiction, but a melody never yet heard on earth."

"The New Adam and Eve" also creates another context for Rappaccini's garden, beginning with the claim that "Art has become a second and stronger Nature; she is a step-mother, whose crafty tenderness has taught us to despise the bountiful and wholesome ministrations of our true parent." Therefore, it is not to be "adequately know[n] how little in our present state and circumstances is natural, and how much is merely the interpolation of the perverted mind and heart of man." It is this puzzle that informs Dr. Rappaccini's strangely landscaped domain, with its admixture of the natural, the exotic, the beautifully crafted, and the decadently artificial.

By now, the appearance of the false paradise in the midst of pestilence will be an easily recognized theme in plague literature. On one side Rappaccini's domain is likened in the story to Eden, but because it is the place of Rappaccini's experiments, it is also the origin of poison rather than a realm free of it—at least according to Baglioni, who says of his rival that Rappaccini "cultivates" his poisonous plants "with his own hands, and is said even to have produced new varieties of poison, more horribly deleterious than Nature, without the assistance of this learned person, would ever have *plagued* the world withal" (italics added). Giovanni's landlady similarly points out that the "garden is cultivated by the own hands of Giacomo Rappaccini," a doctor whose fame is widespread. By her and Baglioni's description, Rappaccini rules over his garden as a private kingdom. In this he is comparable to Poe's landscape gardener, who seeks to create a new paradise through the art of horticulture, although Rappaccini, who remains aloof from his own blooms, holds an uneasy position between art and science. Beatrice herself refers to the "flowers of Eden" when she dies, and she distinguishes them from her father's "poisonous flowers," seeming to believe she had dwelt in a ruined paradise. And whereas Poe's landscaper looks back to a world before the fall and epidemics, Rappaccini brings pestilence *into* his garden in order to conquer plagues.

Early on, Beatrice had told Giovanni not that Rappaccini cultivated his garden but that he "created" the mysterious shrub from which, or so Giovanni believes, Beatrice derives her poison. But when she says her father created the plant, she uttered her words "with simplicity," as if unaware of the tension between her meaning and the word she employs to convey it. For if Rappaccini creates these blooms rather than cultivates them, then his work is *outside* of nature, which would sustain Giovanni's "instinct" concerning the garden's "appearance of artificialness," indicating an "adultery of various vegetable species," a "production" that is "no longer of God's making," but rather "an evil mockery of beauty." Rappaccini's science is thus akin to artifice, medicine itself reduced to a deceptive artfulness that would seem to bear out Baglioni's contention that the miraculous cures attributed to Rappaccini came about merely by chance.

Thus the shrub that figures as an important image and symbol in the tale would be accurately described in terms of the false and artificial blooms characteristic of Spenser's garden in book 2 of *The Faerie Queene*. The gorgeous plant seems to Giovanni to hang its "gem-like flowers over the fountain." Giovanni is displeased with them; they later seem to him "fierce, passionate, even unnatural." Like Sir Guyon, Giovanni is prepared to destroy the bower of bliss. More to the point, under Baglioni's influence, he is equally ready to destroy Rappaccini's garden-laboratory. But there is a special irony in Giovanni's confusion concerning artifice and science, and he is symbolically, if not literally, employing Rappaccini's method when he carries Baglioni's antidote into the supposedly false garden in order to bring Beatrice, "this miserable child within the limits of ordinary nature." For the antidote itself is contained in the "little silver vase" artfully "wrought" by Cellini.

That artifice and poisonous medicines coexist in the garden is not a view confined to Giovanni, however. The narrator describes the plants and herbs whose "individual virtues" were "known to the scientific mind that fostered them." Some of these were placed in "common garden-pots," others in "urns, rich with old carving." The gorgeous but fatal shrub with which Giovanni identifies Beatrice and with which she identifies herself is "set in a marble vase in the midst of a pool," the flower as much a work of art as its container, but also a product of esoteric knowledge nurtured by pure elements. This commingling of opposites is also reflected when Rappaccini views his daughter and Giovanni together in the garden, apparently satisfied by what he looks at:

> As he drew near, the pale man of science seemed to gaze with a triumphant expression at the beautiful youth and maiden, as might an artist who should spend his life in achieving a picture or a group of statuary, and finally be satisfied with his success.

The use of "as might" reduces the metaphor to a simile, sustaining a distance between "man of science" and "artist," between the garden of medicinal herbs and the palace of art. Moreover, time and mutability have resulted in images that work against any positive identification of doctor with creative artist. In Rappaccini's garden "there was the ruin of a marble fountain, in the centre, sculptured with rare art, but so woefully shattered that it was impossible to trace the original design from the chaos of remaining fragments." But Giovanni has not yet decided that Rappaccini's is a false garden, an inverted Eden of poisonous medicinal plants, and he feels "as if the fountain were an immortal spirit that sung its song unceasingly, and without heeding the vicissitudes around it; while one century embodied it in marble, and another scattered the perishable garniture on the soil." Again, the "as if" reveals that Giovanni has not yet decided how to read the garden.

Giovanni is an allegorizor—if an unreliable one. He had come from Naples to Padua to study medicine, but is "not unstudied in the great poem of his country." In his acquired knowledge, he represents the antithesis of Hawthorne's newly created Adam, and there is in Giovanni's reading of Rappaccini's garden and, ultimately, of Beatrice, the potential cacophony in the "interminably repeated echo" of past masters that Hawthorne alludes to in "The New Adam and Eve." Moreover, as Deborah Jones has argued, the genre of the *Divine Comedy,* allegory, presuppose a "fall," a descent from transcendent unity to chaos. It is such chaos that is figured by the ruin of Rappaccini's garden, where science and art are in conflict. But the allusion to Dante's work also evokes the disadvantage Hawthorne would have to have experienced, for the great Italian poet could adhere to a moral centrality significantly weakened by the nineteenth century. Dante, not Hawthorne, could defend himself against old and traditional accusations that art was a veritable poison damsel. By Hawthorne's time, the artist had experienced another "fall," which is why Jones is probably correct to argue that Hawthorne's story is in part about the "conditions of its own unreadability." To take that argument a step further, Beatrice's death is paradoxically, then, a relatively coherent symbol of that incoherence, of the seeming impossibility of writing meaningfully about plague.

PLAGUE LITERATURE

George Kurman

SOURCE: "A Methodology of Thematics: The Literature of the Plague," in *Comparative Literature Studies*, Vol. 19, No. 1, March, 1982, pp. 39-53.

[*In the following essay, Kurman perceives common elements in six works in which a plague is prominently featured in the narrative.*]

Should an alert and omnivorous modern reader chance to reconsider comparatively the Old Babylonian *Atrahasis Epic* and the first book of Samuel (chapters 4-7); book seven of Ovid's *Metamorphoses* and Pearl Buck's *The Good Earth;* Ingmar Bergman's *The Seventh Seal* and Kurt Vonnegut's *Cat's Cradle,* it would soon occur to her, among other things, that all six texts deal, in substantial part, with plague. But what is she subsequently to make of such a connection, beyond merely noting it?

Fortunately for the essay at hand, upon reflection plague turns out not to be the only common thematic element uniting these six otherwise quite diverse texts: our hypothetical reader may realize, with a flash of insight, that in all of these works separation of the nuclear family unit precedes the advent of plague.

And with increasing excitement the further realization may dawn upon her that each of the six works in question presents an instance of what might be termed "unnatural birth." As a result, the presence of all three thematic elements (viz. family separation, plague, and unnatural birth) in all six works mentioned above, usually in the sequence given, becomes awkward to ascribe to mere chance, and our comparatist faces a familiar set of questions: can the perceived pattern be due, then, to influence or to tradition? To similar and causative psychological or societal or economic circumstances present at the genesis of each work? To biological or medical inevitability? To a heretofore undiscovered regularity tending to govern imaginative literature? Or merely to our sample of six texts being neither random in general nor representative of plague literature in particular, but rather, contrived? And how many more—and which?—texts should one now consult in order to frame an adequate reply to the above questions? Or would we be best advised to abandon our inquiry in view of the depth and breadth of the formidable difficulties confronting us; difficulties augmented by the menacing prospect of arriving at unpublishable results?

Before we pursue such vexing matters, we can note that although many adepts of comparative literature may agree with Robert J. Clements that "the real excitement of our discipline . . . and indeed its challenge, remains in the mythic, generic, and other homogeneities inexplicably occurring over two millennia on our five continents," the apparent contradiction between Clements' use of "discipline" on the one hand and "inexplicably" on the other should not be taken lightly. Yet the problem here is not all that different from a recurrent one in the exact sciences. Albert Einstein, for example,

> considered scientific theories to be "free creations of the human mind." . . . Such theories are the outcome of the mind's activity: its unceasing attempt to make sense of its surroundings. This drive seems to be basically the same in both the sciences and the arts. In both cases the data of experience are continually shuffled, consciously and/or unconsciously, until a meaningful pattern is obtained.

However, Einstein's term "meaningful pattern" begs a key question and it is well to note that even in the quantitative sciences, statisticians have not yet rigorously solved the problem of determining the optimal size of a statistical sample and have of course conceded that determination of "meaningful" levels of statistical significance is essentially arbitrary. Thus it is not only in the humanities that the number or proportion of contrary instances regarded as sufficient to contravene an apparent—albeit limited—"homogeneity" or "meaningful pattern" is flexible; methodology continues to be problematic in statistics as well as in the humanities. As Professor Clements puts it with regard to the comparative study of literature: "It is more exciting to discover that a great number of folk epics include a trip to the afterworld than to observe that a lesser number do not. Little is to be gained by proving that there are exceptions to Otto Rank's comparative observation about the birth and death of the epic hero."

But let us now return to the six works mentioned at the beginning of the present essay. In the fragmentary Babylonian-Assyrian *Atrahasis Epic,* Enlil, the chief of the gods, "became disturbed by their [i.e., mankind's] gatherings," and in retribution sent drought, plague, and a flood. Yet prior to the advent of any actual disaster (save, perhaps, a famine), "the mother does not open her door to the daughter" but rather "prepared the daughter for a meal, / For food they prepared the child." Then drought and plague strike, and "Disease was let loose upon the people. / The womb was closed, so that it could not bring forth a child." Further in tablet V of the *Atrahasis Epic* the theme of disease "let loose upon the people" is repeated, concluding with the recreation or rebirth of humankind from clay kneaded by the gods.

The first book of Samuel not only reiterates the themes of separation of the nuclear family, plague, and unnatural birth, but with the sense of grim justice typical to the Old Testament, sees plague as a punishment inflicted by God. I Samuel 4-7 recounts the struggle of Israel with the Philistines, where it is military service and death that separate Phineas from his wife, who "was with child and near her time." Upon hearing of her husband's and father-in-law's death, "her labor suddenly began and she crouched down and was delivered. As she lay dying, the woman who attended her said, 'Do not be afraid; you have a son'." Shortly thereafter, the Lord afflicts Israel's enemies: "He threw them into distress and plagued them with tumors, and their territory swarmed with rats." Our pattern has been bent here, but not broken: although the plague in I Samuel follows shortly a birth that can be termed "unnatural" on the basis of its precipitateness and the death of the mother, our three essential elements appear, albeit out of sequence.

With one exception, the other references to plague in scripture do not contain both separation of the family and unusual birth. The exception occurring in Genesis is worthy of our attention, however. In order to preserve his own life during their wanderings in Egypt, the aged Abram (Abraham), it will be remembered, instructs his wife Sarai (Sarah) to tell the Egyptians that she is his sister a realignment if not a break in the family unit. Pharaoh, struck by her beauty, subsequently takes her into his household, as a result of which her "brother" (i.e., Abram) also prospers. "But the Lord struck Pharaoh and his household with grave diseases . . ." Many years later, the reunited married couple, now both of exceedingly advanced age, miraculously conceive a son, Isaac:

> God said to Abraham, "As for Sarai your wife, . . . " I will bless her and give you a son by her. . . .Abraham threw himself down on his face; he laughed and said to himself, "Can a son be born to a man who

is a hundred years old? Can Sarah bear a son when
she is ninety?"

As is the case for the two works of near-Eastern literature just discussed, in Greek and Roman texts plagues are also often interpreted as manifestations of God's revenge. In Ovid's *Metamorphoses,* for example, the seventh book contains a story cleverly inset, in the Ovidian fashion of the wrath of Juno upon Aegina:

. . . . A plague struck at us through the heat
Of Juno's anger and she hated us
Because our island had her rival's name.

. . . . .

Then countrymen were struck down to their
doom
And the Great Sickness walked through city
walls:

. . . . .

. . . . all vanished
To the blind wilderness of wind. Nor earth to
hide
Plague-spotted bones and flesh, nor wood for
fire.

Not only is Juno, the goddess of marriage, jealous of her husband's love of Aegina, for whom the land she ravages has been named, but Ovid's plague narrative is preceded by a retelling of the ill-fated marriage of Jason and Medea; what is more, it is immediately followed by the tale of Cephalus' accidental slaying of his wife, Procris. And within the plague narrative itself, the birth of the Myrmidons from a colony of ants in order to repopulate the plague-stricken country is anticipated by reference to Carthaea, whose father saw her "Deliver a mild dove from her heaving body," and to a "sacred spring," where "men grew from rainswept fungus." Thus once more we see an account of plague flanked, as it were, by references to drastic family separation and unnatural birth.

Ovid's sources for his account of plague were, of course, Thucydides, Lucretius, and Virgil (of the *Georgics*). We are interested to note that Pericles' funeral oration, which immediately precedes Thucydides' account of the outbreak of plague in Athens, concludes with commiseration with the parents, sons, brothers, and widows of the Athenian war dead. Likewise, the outbreak of plague in Sophocles' *Oedipus the King* as well as in his *Antigone* is immediately preceded by a violation of the nuclear family unit (via parricide compounded with incest, and reciprocal fratricide, respectively), and accompanied by the presence of Oedipus' "unnatural" children, in the former case, and by Antigone's lamented barrenness in the latter.

To be sure, there are a number of classical texts treating the subject of plague that do not conform with the pattern enumerated above (Livy's *History of Rome,* for example). But we have already called attention to the lack of a generally accepted (however arbitrary) quantitative level of significance in scholarship in the humanities in general, and in comparative literature in particular. Thus the question of the significance of the recurrent pattern so far discovered remains largely a matter of selection and emphasis, and therefore, it seems, of what might be termed rhetoric—an attempt to persuade that such a pattern in fact exists (or is somehow useful to be thought to exist).

Even a cursory survey of the vast medieval plague literature is beyond the competence of the present author. Likewise the fourteenth and fifteenth centuries, while giving us both Boccaccio's and Chaucer's literary responses to the black death that swept Europe, are beyond the purview of the present essay, as is the plague literature of the more than three following centuries. Yet it is precisely a screenplay set in the medieval period, namely Ingmar Bergman's *The Seventh Seal,* that can serve to initiate our discussion of modern plague narratives.

Bergman's film takes place in a land ravaged by a "terrible pestilence." Repentant flagellants course from village to village and a church painter is at work depicting the Dance of Death. Max von Sydow, as the knight and returning crusader Antonius Block, is engaged in a game of chess with Death. More to the present point, however, is the knowledge that ten years earlier Block abandoned his then-recent bride for his quest of faith and of the Holy Land. Block's cynical squire, Jöns (Gunnar Björnstrand), was also wed before departing for the Holy Land, but expresses hopes for his wife's death. But Bergman's account of plague does not only refer to antecedents of drastic familial separation; there is also a disquieting reference to unnatural births. We learn of "terrible omens. . . . Worms, chopped-off hands and other monstrosities began pouring out of an old woman, and down in the village another woman gave birth to a calf's head." The only people to escape the plague and to witness the cinematically memorable Dance of Death are Jof, Mia, and their small, healthy child. Pursued by Death but rescued by the knight Block (who thus continues his solicitude for the Holy Family, now represented by its namesakes), Jof, Mia, and their child huddle in a small wagon, as all of the others (including Plog, the smith, who, interestingly, is still searching for his unfaithful wife) perish.

Indeed Plog's situation restates the plot of the skit or play set within the broader plot of Bergman's film: the playlet is "a tragedia about an unfaithful wife, her jealous husband, and the handsome lover."

The device of a play within a screenplay is strikingly similar to Albert Camus having his pestilence-menaced characters in *La Peste* (1942) attend an opera—Gluck's *Orfeo*—where the theme of family separation is reiterated. That is to say, not only are four of the leading characters of Camus' novel (i.e., Grand, Rieux, Rambert,

Castel) separated from their wives and families before or because of the plague, but, in the inset opera, Orpheus is seeking his lost Euridice. Then, with a dramatic stroke, Camus has the singer playing Orpheus die on stage, but for real. But this is not all. Camus, providing an eerie echo of the dwarf waitress who appears in cameo role in Thomas Mann's *Der Zauberberg* (1924, where tuberculosis patients, separated from family, patiently await their cure or their death), writes in a dwarf barkeep ("Un petit homme . . . le nabot"), thereby prefiguring the title of yet another Nobel prize-winning author's novel.

Per Lagerkvist's *The Dwarf* (*Dvärgen,* 1944) likewise gives the theme of plague a prominent place. A prince, who has a sterile dwarf as an advisor, also has a mistress and is in doubt about the paternity of his daughter. As though he didn't have sufficient problems, after this prince decapitates his poisoned enemy's son upon discovering the latter in bed with his daughter, plague strikes to teach everyone a lesson.

But what can all this mayhem have to do with still a fourth Nobel prize-winning novelist's—Pearl Buck's—*The Good Earth* (1931), the fifth of six titles cited at the beginning of this essay? Little, except that the pattern centered on plague is the very same: following the breakup of the nuclear family as a result of the husband Wang Lung's taking of a second wife, a "plague" of locusts descends; there occur also unnatural birth in the person of a "fool"—Wang Lung's deaf and dumb daughter—and incest of sorts (the second wife traffics with her husband's eldest son); and this second wife remains barren.

An extremely cursory and selective perusal of nineteenth-century literature does not do violence to the pattern we have so painstakingly extrapolated from near-Eastern, classical, and twentieth-century works. Confirmation (whatever that might mean—vide passim) of such a sweeping hypothesis in comparative literary study is, as we have seen, of course quite another matter; and the utility or application of such hypotheses is altogether problematical. Nevertheless, before mentioning four nineteenth-century texts, we can tentatively—taking a cue from Northrop Frye and other theorists of his persuasion—hypothesize that literature is a descendant and extension of myth. Myth serves the purpose of fostering the continuance of the civilization which has created it for just this purpose; violation of the family unit is seen as a threat to the survival of the civilization in question, and is therefore punished in fiction by plague; and subsequent unnatural birth compounds the fictional punishment, confirms the propriety of such punishment, and symbolizes the civilization's projected decay. The function of myth in art (comparable to the function of myth in government, history, etc.) is therefore not merely to reproduce or modify reality but to store potentially useful capacities of the species at a time when they might not be immediately applicable, but with a view toward a future when they might or must be applied for survival. Or to put it in another, Darwinistic manner: for civilizations myth and literature are positively selective traits. Myth and literature can be regarded as the cold storage of things that we cannot for the moment use but are loath to relinquish; the repository of truth, justice, beauty, tears, magic, and the like. Artists can thus be regarded as the guardians, not the counterfeiters, of lasting value. Literary representations of plague, therefore, tend to take place following literary violations (sexual, violent, etc.) of a basic unit which must remain integral if society as we know it is to survive. Further support for this viewpoint can be found in the more frequent occurrence of our pattern in fictional rather than in historical accounts of plague. Thus not only is truth stranger than fiction, but fiction more conservative than truth (cf. " . . . more philosophical than history"). We can, with Frye, see the historical source of a plague narrative as constituting, perhaps, its material and efficient cause, but the governing "myth" furnishing the formal and final cause of the shape of the fictional narrative.

But to continue with our nineteenth-century texts, Heinrich von Kleist's unfinished historical tragedy, "Robert Guiskard" (ca. 1802), is set in an armed camp before the walls of Constantinople. Guiskard, the Duke of Normandy, is father to a widow who is also the beloved of his nephew an aspirant to Guiskard's throne. The camp is ravaged by plague. Some three years earlier, America's first professional novelist, Charles Brockden Brown, preceded his description of the 1793 yellow fever epidemic in Philadelphia (in *Arthur Mervyn*) with an account of the disintegration of the hero's family, including his mother's death, his father's remarriage, the suspicion that Mervyn has been his stepmother's lover (which the hero, however, denies), concluding with young Mervyn's marriage to an older woman, whom he avows to be a replacement for his "lost mamma." Interestingly enough, the epidemic described by Brown in *Arthur Mervyn* may have been the same one (historically) from which Longfellow draws his final scene in *Evangeline* (1847). Many years after the violent eviction of the Acadians in 1755 (an event that led to the massive separation of families), Evangeline, working as a nurse in Pennsylvania during an outbreak of "pestilence," is reunited with her long-lost betrothed—alas upon the latter's deathbed. While these three nineteenth-century texts dealing with plague lack the element of unnatural birth consequent to the advent of the pestilence (although all three stress separation of the family as an antecedent), Manzoni's *I promessi sposi* (1840) is the exception that conforms to our rule. Separated lovers, characters in a "marriage story, the story of the foundation of a household, a home," encounter a variety of adversities, among them plague. Subsequent to the plague we have a still-birth and "when Renzo returns to his village. . . . The first person upon whom his eyes fall is, symbolically, the village idiot."

Like Manzoni's important novel, Kurt Vonnegut's *Cat's Cradle* (1963, the last of the six works mentioned at our essay's start) presents, albeit disjointedly, the pattern we are, by now, not entirely surprised to uncover repeatedly in the plague literature of the world. In Vonnegut's novel, within the context of an account of a disaster that ends all life on earth, we learn that the wife of "the father of the atomic bomb" had been unfaithful: another man is reputed to have fathered her three unusual children, one of whom is a midget! In the meantime, far away on a Caribbean island, an epidemic of bubonic plague in a development hardly central to the main plot decimates the populace.

A final reference to recent novels might well be to Anthony Burgess' *The Wanting Seed* (1962). While there is, strictly speaking, no literal plague in this dystopia, the society Burgess portrays suffers from overpopulation, institutionalized war and homosexuality, a grain blight, cannibalism, and a variety of other collective (and infectious) misfortunes. True to our pattern, Burgess' work begins with the death of the leading characters' child, and continues with the wife's adultery while the state encourages homosexuality and fraternal enmity. Subsequent to the various "plagues" that ravage the society depicted in *The Wanting Seed,* the heroine gives birth to twins, fraternal twins whom she believes to be fathered—one each!—by her husband and his brother, her lover; hardly the most conventional of births, to be sure. Offered still one more confirmation of our pattern by Burgess' novel, we are able to essay a sweeping historical generalization: while texts dealing with plague from the Bible through seventeenth-century British literary accounts tend to emphasize plague resulting from God's wrath, modern texts see mankind plagued by the absence of God, an absence of love. As Gian-Carlo Biasin puts it, "after the second half of the XIXth century. . . . Disease-passion inexorably became physical illness in all of its terrible concreteness and painful evidence; disease-punishment disappeared." In any case, in both traditional and modern views of the essence of literary plague, the pattern of: (1) disintegration of the family; (2) plague; (3) unnatural birth recurs sufficiently enough to warrant our recognition of it as significant.

We have now completed a perfunctory, selective, and somewhat superficial inventory of a three-part pattern (including some permutations) in the vast territory of world literature. Such an inventory could be readily extended to folklore. Consider, for example, the motifs of "Plague as punishment," "Unborn child affected by mother's broken Tabu," "Misshapen child from brother-sister incest," and the like. A more contemporary sociological inventory would soon encounter the "plague" of drug abuse an affliction that is conventionally often preceded or accompanied by family separation and, as various medical authorities claim, endangers the drug abuser's ability to bring forth normal offspring. Likewise the recent epidemic of venereal disease in the West had similar antecedents and consequents, further reinforcing the significance of our pattern. But even if we confine our inquiry to imaginative literature, two things are certain: a number of texts dealing with plague can be found that contravene the pattern I have been so determinedly pursuing, and a number of plague narratives will display the pattern with what will be perceived by me as sufficient rigor. Or as William H. McNeill phrases this methodological quandary in his introduction to his monumental revisionist volume on the history of world plagues:

> Study of simultaneity among multiple processes is presumably a better way to approach an understanding. But the conceptual and practical difficulties here are enormous. Recognition of patterns, and observation of their endurance or dissolution is, at most levels of organization, about as much as people are capable of; and at some levels, including the social, there is profound uncertainly and dispute about which patterns are worth attending to, or can, in fact, be reliably detected. Divergent terminologies direct attention to different patternings; and finding a logically convincing test, acceptable all around, that can determine whether one such system of terms is superior to its rivals, is often impossible.

Thus we are inevitably brought back to the question of the proper methodology of comparative literary study, including its congruences with, and departures from, procedures in other disciplines—most of them presumably more precise ways of knowing. It might first of all be pointed out that the notion of absolute regularity in literary history (indeed in all history, and by extension in any branch of the humanities) is demonstrably absurd. One can, for example, hypothetically contravene any regularity postulated in literature through writing (or commissioning) and publishing a sufficiently large number of suitably contrived texts. Furthermore, all plague texts written subsequent to the appearance and diffusion of, say, the present essay may theoretically be "contaminated" by their author's awareness of my hypothesis. Fortunately, the works discussed in the present essay almost all have literary stature; knowledge of literary history will help us identify "contaminated" works in any future sample; and there remains a large number of literary texts dealing with plague of which I am unaware, or have not read, or cannot read. Thus the continued verification (or refinement, or rejection) of the pattern discerned in the present essay is not an unreasonable hope. Of far greater import, however, would be the development of a theory of sampling and level of significance, cast in terms appropriate to humane studies in general (and comparative literature in particular), in order to enable us to choose among patterns contending for general validity, in the meantime of course avoiding both triviality and outright falsehood.

The continued status in comparative literature of methodology as *Schmerzenskind* (far more so than problems of self-justification, organization, and definition) can be seen, for example, in critical responses to papers presented at the Budapest Congress of the International Comparative Literature Association in 1976. "The disasters" among the papers read there were deemed by Frederic Garber to be "due, once again, primarily to problems of methodology." Yet two pages later Garber continues: "If the text is at all meaningful and complex, it will resist every kind of categorization, proving itself bigger than our scholarly straitjackets, richer than any facts we can learn about it." Garber's sentiments illustrate nicely how western comparatists have traditionally been torn in opposite directions: on the one hand, it is desirable on a number of counts to have and be part of a "discipline," hence practice a more or less rigorous methodology; on the other hand, likewise on a number of solid grounds, it is desirable to resist all irrelevant reductionism, positivism, and the like in favor of the meaningfullness, complexity, bigness, and richness (all four Garber's words) of literature attributes that have drawn men to imaginative literature and its study for millennia. In practice, of course, we do our best with an ad hoc combination of, on the first hand, more or less flexible "scholarly straitjackets," reinforced by as many historical facts as seem convenient, and, on the other hand, we devise fictions of our own with which we embellish the avowedly fictitious (but decidedly useful—see above) texts that inspire or amuse us.

An illustration of this point with reference to the pattern recurrent in plague narratives described earlier in the present essay should prove helpful. Rene Girard, in a recent article, argues that "there is a strange uniformity to the various treatments of the plague, not only literary and mythical but also scientific and nonscientific, of both past and present. . . . the differences, at close range, turn out to be minor." Girard goes on to isolate a

> thematic cluster that includes, besides the plague or, more generally, the theme of epidemic contamination, the dissolving of differences and the mimetic *doubles*. . . . [and, finally, the "sacrificial element"—Girard's italics;] this same thematic cluster *almost never fails* [emphasis added] to gather around the plague in a great many texts that may appear to have very little in common. Some of the elements may be more emphasized than others; they may appear only in an embryonic form, but it is *very rare* [emphasis added] when even one of them is completely missing.

Now Girard, in an effort to support his analysis, has had to go out on some extremely shaky limbs. For example, speaking of Sophocles' *Oedipus,* Girard has Oedipus, Creon, and Tiresias "all turn into each other's doubles." And once he is beholden to his "thematic cluster," Girard apparently must unearth it everywhere. Thus we are told that in Bergman's *Seventh Seal,* "The mimetic *doubles* are there, and Death is one of them"—surely a forced interpretation to no apparent purpose other than to shore up the original analysis. Yet the purpose of the present remarks is not necessarily to argue for the advantages of my proposed "thematic cluster" over Girard's (or Sontag's, or anyone else's) but to pose once more the venerable question of method: on what grounds is one "thematic cluster" or interpretation or explanation or explication to be preferred to another? Possible answers include: parsimony, predictive power, explanatory power, and conformity with the larger number of texts (ignoring for a moment the obvious *petitio principi* difficulties of, especially, the lattermost). Perhaps the phrase "at close range," used rather glibly by Girard and cited above, introduces still another complication. Compare, for example, the delightful interplay of notions of closeness-of-range and triviality in the case of the hypothetical physical scientist who observes, first, the motion of atoms of a gas at the molecular level and concludes they are random, chaotic, and hence trivial; then at the molar level, eventually hitting upon the gas laws; and finally at some extremely remote remove, over an enormous span of time. . . . leading to his formulating God knows what kind of analytically ingenious proposition that best explains what the gas molecules seemed to be doing. (We are of course not trying to be frivolous or obscurantist here by citing such rough and ready parallels with the philosophy of science, but rather seeking a broad and stable base for the framing of method in literary study.)

In the meantime, I am convinced that—when met by difficulties such as those rehearsed above—we should not abandon our search for patterns in literature in favor of concentrating only on the specific, aesthetic use made by an author of a theme such as plague in a specific work or works. That would be tantamount to abandoning a vision of regularity (i.e., the pattern we think we see) for the "reality" of a work that implicitly avows its fictionality in the first place. In comparative literature we must continue to exercise the choice between embellishing single fictions with fictions of our own or drawing rather weak, necessarily "ill defined generalizations" about a larger number of fictions, or retreating to a time-honored—but still as stodgy and sterile as ever—applied positivism in literary study.

Perhaps temporary relief from this vexing selection of the lesser-most methodological evil lies in the emphasis of the suitability of rhetorical models for literary study. Rhetoric has been defined, of course, in a variety of ways; one is as the art of persuasion: "Rhetoric as distinct from the learnings which it uses is . . . concerned with movement. It *does* rather than *is*. It is method rather than matter. It is chiefly involved with bringing about a condition rather than discovering or testing a condition." Or as Walter J. Ong puts it when recapitulating Aquinas: "Rhetoric . . . and poetics both differ from the logic of the sciences in that neither requires certitude for its arguments." Now statistics is like rhetoric in that the former too "is an art, a science, and a technique. . . . concerned with the making of wise decisions in the face of uncertainty." Therefore, to take a sanely cynical view, the *inventio* for authors of literary essays, if they are to be successful, must usually be fraught with gross and intentional sampling errors (i.e., with rhetorical technique), in order to favor convincingly the hypothesis proferred. What is more, the purpose of the entire rhetorical performance can be regarded as being directed towards persuading editorial boards to publish the essay in question, thereby advancing the career of the author, who as a result succeeds to the extent that her "sampling errors" are forgiven. Thus in the article referred to above, Rene Girard is well advised to be selective in the texts he analyzes at greater length (as opposed to those he cites in passing); it is understandable that contrary evidence is gently suppressed and there is resort to such locutions as: "The sacrificial element is sometimes an invisible dimension, something like an atmosphere that pervades every theme but cannot be pinpointed as a theme. . . ."; ". . . the plague . . . must be viewed, I believe, as a mask for the crisis leading to the scapegoat process. . . ."; ". . . our entire cluster is strikingly intact"; and the like. There is no other way. Almost all of us system-mongerers do it. That is to say, we remain rhetoricians rather than discoverers of absolute truth; our truth remains impacted in our rhetoric. Thus the presentation of general discoveries in the humanities is a "rhetorical situation."

It remains for us to dwell with this recognition, as well as with the possibility that if the comparison offered above (between rhetoric and methodology in literary study) is forced, it becomes false; and if not, it remains trivial—a situation not unlike the one confronting the "alert and omnivorous modern reader" whose apercu concerning plague texts launched the present essay.

Sharon Achinstein

SOURCE: "Plagues and Publication: Ballads and the Representation of Disease in the English Renaissance," in *Criticism*, Vol. XXXIV, No. 1, Winter, 1992, pp. 27-49.

[*In the following essay, Achinstein observes that the publication of ballads in sixteenth and seventeenth-century England was closely associated in the public mind with the dissemination of plague.*]

The scope of devastation by bubonic plague in early modern Europe is hard for us to imagine today, even as some call AIDS a modern plague. The Black Death haunted Western Europe from its first great appearance in 1348 for over four hundred years. The initial catastrophe of plague in England in 1348-9 swept away one third of the population, at a minimum. Though this first outbreak was the most severe, the epidemic continued to threaten English society over the next four hundred years. Plague deaths were part of daily life in early modern England, with repeated outbreaks of the disease in almost every year between 1348 and 1665 not just in the landmark years of plague—1603, 1625 and 1665. It is no wonder that the plague was a subject of much thought and writing, and that it even became a trope in English literature.

It may seem incongruous to write about the plague and ballads together, but the unlikely fact is that these two subjects were linked in the moral discourse of the period. Renaissance notions of contagion and transmission linked plagues and ballads; the evil in plagues and ballads was thought to disseminate in similar ways. Ballads, like the plague, were perceived to exert evil effects both morally and physically. William Prynne's now-famous criticism of the theatre inveighs against ballads, his language consistent with plague discourse: "Such songs, such poems as these [are] abundantly condemned, as filthy and unchristian defilements, which contaminate the souls, effeminate the minds, deprave the manners, of those that hear or sing them, exciting, enticing them to lust; to whoredom, adultery, prophaneness, wantonness, scurrility, luxury, drunkenness, excess; alienating their minds from God." Like the plague, the ballads were "filthy" and had their effects through "contamination"; their corruption worked on the spirit as well as on the body.

Ballad-sellers, and not just the corrupting ballads themselves, were frequently attacked as conveyors of plague. The 1636 Plague Orders, issued by the Royal College of Physicians in London, required not only that London citizens take specific health precautions and that those who were infected be submitted to quarantine and surveillance within their homes—the usual responses to plague epidemic—but also that "loose persons and idle assemblies" be regulated, that no "wandering beggar be suffered in the streets of this City." Along with restrictions on plays, bear-baitings and other games, the order specifically prohibited the singing of ballads. The offenders were to be severely punished. Since the ballad trade in the seventeenth century depended upon chapmen and wandering peddlers, who were often considered beggars, such orders effectively eliminated the sale of ballads during times of plague.

The case of the restrictions on ballads in the first half of the seventeenth century opens up new possibilities for understanding responses to plague and to the printing economy in early modern England. The association of plagues with ballads is an example of how disease was beginning to be perceived as a material phenomenon, and not solely as a providential one. The discourse on ballads presents this dual explanation of disease inhabiting the minds of seventeenth-century medical practitioners, lay and clerical.

Furthermore, the material explanation of disease by London health authorities was accompanied by a social commentary that articulated anxieties about urban disorder, poverty and vagrancy. As medical explanations offered a substantially modified view of the natural order of things in the late sixteenth and early seventeenth centuries, English society was also coping with the social upheavals of an urbanizing society. The analogy between disease and popular literature was used by civic authorities, in London especially, to control and suppress certain social groups that threatened civic order, and the association of plagues with ballads illustrates how rhetoric functioned by the use of this powerful analogy to control the popular force of printing. This essay is a chiastic attempt to consider the play between moral and material explanations in the medical discourse of Renaissance England, on the one hand, and, on the other, the articulation of fears about urban disorder as a function of a literary genre, ballads. Put simply, why were ballads blamed for England's literal and figurative ills?

1

Social and cultural norms always shape the ways disease is represented, interpreted, and treated, since ways of perceiving disease are historically constructed. This is as true for the AIDS epidemic today as it was for the plague of the early seventeenth century. Writing about AIDS in the 1980s, Douglas Crimp pursues the idea that disease does not exist apart from the "practices that conceptualize it, represent it, and respond to it. . . . We know AIDS only in and through those practices." Crimp is quick to add: "This notion does not contest the existence of viruses, antibodies, infections, or transmission routes. Least of all does it contest the reality of illness, suffering and death. What it *does* contest is the notion that there is an underlying reality of AIDS, upon which are constructed the representations, or the nature, or the politics of AIDS." There is of course a political interest in deconstructing myths of AIDS today at a time when AIDS is still treated not just as any health issue, but one charged with anxiety about alternate sexualities. Awareness of the politics of medical perception only sharpens the call for a cultural analysis of this, and other, diseases.

The aim here is not to dismiss studies in the history of medicine which concern the history of the plague, but to encourage a dialogical and discursive approach to that history, one which seeks to enliven the study of historical representations by invoking the contemporary cultural meanings against which those representations were posited. Historians of medicine might gain by looking into the associations between the plague and certain forms of literature, so as to see the ideas about transmission as a moral and as a physical matter, and those concerned with early printed literature might better understand how medical and philosophical discourses give us guides for interpreting the position of that literature in society. We need to expand the kinds of contexts and preconditions we might use to inform our studies of literary representations, as well as to encourage historians of ideas and of society to look to literature as a way to understand the diversity of cultural response that is offered by the archive.

What was the language of the plague in early modern England? Dating from its first appearances, the plague was coded by Christian theology, and instances of plague were likened to Biblical examples of divine punishment. As early as the sixteenth century, houses where infected people were found were marked with a red cross on the door as part of civic programs for monitoring and containing the illness. This red cross and its accompanying slogan, "Lord have mercy upon us," drew symbolic power from the Bible, and the use of the Biblical trope of marked doors coded the plague as divinely sent. City health officials used the Biblical story of the Passover, where the Angel of Death passed over the marked houses of the Israelites in Egypt (Exodus 12:13), with an inversion: they marked doors of those infected with the plague, as if to say the Angel of Death *would* visit there. These marks were, like the Passover tokens of blood, red. The sign and slogan reinforced theories that the infection had a divine source, that God had sent the plague to punish sin. By alluding to the Bible in this way, the English added their own history to a long series of divine punishments for sin.

Yet the health officials' placement of these marks upon the doors of contaminated households also promoted materialist explanations of the disease. The doors were marked so that other citizens would stay away; and in these acts of quarantine and segregation, city officials practiced a theory of disease closer to our modern treatments of infection and contagion. Their use of the Biblical trope accompanied reforms in sanitation and hygiene which promoted a radically different explanation of disease, one that was rooted in physiology, not in theology. If God sent the plague to punish those sinners who were spiritually unclean, then only spiritual reform would work; or could human physical hygiene contribute to disease conditions? This conflict in explanatory models was a source of debate between English civil and ecclesiastical authorities between 1590 and 1640. As Renaissance theorists of contagion, such as Fracastero (*De Contagione* [1546]), turned to physical causes to explain the transmission of disease, so civic authorities sought to control the spread of plague by material measures—quarantine, isolation of the sick, and hygienic reform. The very idea of a program for public health required that diseases be considered to be within the realm of human prevention.

This essay concerns ideas about the plague roughly between the years 1597 and 1630 in England, during which time there were significant outbreaks which destroyed between ten and thirty percent of the population of communities in a single year. The clash between Renaissance health authorities and the Church in their analyses of disease, and thus the ideological clash between providential and material understandings of the world, is evident in the representation of the plague and in its link to the attack on ballads.

2

Renaissance notions of contagion blurred the distinction between moral and physiological causes of disease. Thomas Lodge, a self-proclaimed "Doctor in Physicke," explained what contagion was in his *A Treatise of the Plague* (1603). A contagion was: "An evil quality in a body, communicated unto another by touch, engendering one and the same disposition in him to whom it is communicated. So as he that is first of all attainted or ravished with such a quality, is called contagious and infected". In Lodge's account, contagion was a process of "communication," but one with both physical and moral properties: it was an "evil quality" which performed an action from outside, a "ravishment" upon its victims. The plague made both men and women passive victims of a pollution. Yet the moral factor, the "evil quality," was transmissible via physical contact, touch. It had some material properties, which careful civic regulation might inhibit. Lodge's dedication of his tract to the Lord Mayor, Aldermen and Sheriffs of London, the city's chief public health authorities, offered a "scientific" approach to the pestilence, calling for practical responses to the disease, including street cleaning and fumigation.

Mary Douglas's analysis of the idea of pollution is helpful here. In her account, ideas of uncleanness and pollution reveal a society's concerns with the "relation of order to disorder." She writes: "Dirt . . . is never a unique, isolated event. Where there is dirt there is system. Dirt is the by-product of a systematic ordering and classification of matter, in so far as ordering involves rejecting inappropriate elements." The Renaissance conception of plague as a kind of pollution, an "evil quality," required that the stricken society do moral penance. That moral penance took diverse and ritualized forms: municipal cleanliness; the exclusion of unruly elements of society, beggers, the poor and vagrants; as well as suppression of some forms of popular literature. These measures reveal the multivalent understanding of pollution. For the municipal authorities, the evils of the city ranged from the physical aspects of dirt to the spiritual ideas of uncleanness, idleness, or unruliness.

For early seventeenth-century medical practitioners, purging was to be accomplished on the social, not only on the individual, level. One author presented this theory by speaking in the voice of a disconsolate London: "I hope it [the plague] will purge my body from bad humours, as vicious persons. Nay, I know it hath already of abundance." In a cruel conclusion, London concedes, "God hath swept my house, so desire to garnish it with virtue, and furnish it with graces." London in particular, and cities in general, were made to shoulder both the moral and physical burden of especially high mortality rates in times of plague.

Cities were seen as the particular targets of God's wrath. The plague was associated with cities—it was an urban phenomenon; and it fed the idea of the metropolis as an eater of people. The city itself was portrayed as the cause of the infection. The plague was seen as a punishment for urban vice, and this anti-city perception may be interpreted as a sign of concern about urbanization in early modern England. The poet John Taylor summed up this theory in his 1636 plague pamphlet, *The Fearefull Summer:*

> Fair *London* that did late abound in bliss,
> And wast our Kingdom's great *Metropolis,*
> 'Tis *thou* that are dejected, low in state,
> Disconsolate, and almost desolate,
> The hand of Heaven (that only did protect thee)
> Thou hast provoked most justly to correct thee,
> And for thy pride of heart and deeds unjust,
> He lays thy pomp and glory in the dust.

The idea that "citizens [were] plagued for the city's sins" was a common one. Those sins could be physical or spiritual ones: "what ignorance and blindness, what infidelity and prophaneness, what pride and idleness, what gluttony and drunkenness, what whoredom and uncleanness, what deceit and lying, what blasphemies and all cursed speaking, what riot and all manner of excess, do reign in most places," railed one Bible-thumper, who saw moral failings as the cause of plague. All of these civic corruptions deserved punishment, and the plague was just that punishment sent by God.

Metaphoric civic "purges" were chief among the many social responses during times of plague, and the logic of purgation led to restrictions on travel, fairs, crowd-gatherings, warnings about immoderate eating and sexual activity, and the regulation of human movement by state surveillance. The city, the body social, must imitate the body personal on a large scale, as prescribed in the frequent reports of the Royal College of Physicians of London. Orders included streetcleanings, civic fumigation, and establishing examiners to determine the exact causes and numbers of deaths. And knowing that their own measures would meet resistance from the divines, members of the Privy Council warned ecclesiastics in particular to buckle under to the regime of public health. Some divines followed Royal command, like Thomas Thayre, who first stressed civic repentance before God. But he also hedged his bets by reminding the Lord Mayor, Aldermen and Sheriffs to uphold their public duties of keeping the streets clean, cleaning sewers and ponds, burying all the dead and fumigating and burning infected property.

The policy for enforcing surveillance of individuals and of households by the Privy Council in 1625 and again in 1629 used the two conflicting models for understanding communication of the plague, the moral and the material. Unlike the leprosarium, which instituted a space for the ill *apart* from the social space, according to Michel Foucault's tracings in *Madness and Civilization,* the plague, by contrast, was represented as *inside* the body social. The quarantines and orders for segregation required that infected persons be shut up inside their own houses, the healthy with the sick, and a lock put on the outside door. The plague fractured community, closing community institutions. Parliament recessed; courts closed; trade, theatres, fairs were ordered to cease functioning. The precautions ordered that citizens become prisoners in their own houses. The plague was domestic; it attacked the house, the house on the street and the house of the flesh. The plague was inside—inside the body, inside the house—not outside, like leprosy.

The plague atomized the community. Humans were locked inside their homes, left to live or to die alone. Images of a desolate city recur throughout the plague literature of the period: "Our houses are left desolate . . . we are afraid of one another, men hardly trust themselves, yea, scarcely the clothes of their back. Where are our solemn meetings, and frequent assemblies; men stand afar off; the streets and highways mourn: traffic ceaseth: merchandise decayeth; the craftsman and cunning artificer is ashamed of his poverty" [William Muggins, *Londons Mourning Garment,* 1603]. The description ascribes no human agency to the half in city operations: "traffic" simply "ceaseth." Flight, the most common response to the plague, was based on material fear of contagion: doctors warned citizens to "depart from contagious places, unto a purer air," as if the locus of the city exerted some evil equality. Many who stayed behind lamented the desolation of their communities, and they criticized their fellow citizens for failing to take care of each other in times of need.

Civic regulators sought to contain the plague, but their measures also effectively controlled unruliness in a society that was increasingly filled with anxieties about urban disorder, not only about disease. The city of London itself at this time did provoke many worries, since it was rapidly becoming fixed as the center of a new kind of cosmopolitan economy, as the nation's administrative and commercial hub, and as the nexus of leisure and culture. But at the same time, the plague worked to break down the emerging patterns of metropolitan community and civic consciousness. During the time of plague, the city lost its urban character, "streets bare, Temples empty, shops shut up." Those who could fled from the city into the country; those who could not afford to do so holed themselves up in their houses and huts, hoarded supplies and refused to go out into the streets. The plague was associated with cities, and yet it un-citified cities.

Theories about transmission of the plague relied upon particular facts about city life that provoked anxiety. Thomas White complained that "the city is full" of sinning people: "adulterers and harlots, theives and vagabonds do swarm in most places of the same, and no marvel, for Dicing houses, Dancing Schools, bowling alleys, Alehouses, are almost lawless in every place." These places of disorderly and unauthorized society were likened to places infected by plague: "me thinks the policy were good to note on those places (LORD HAVE MERCY UPON US) as on infected houses," White concludes. The equation between social outcasts inhabiting the city and the victims of plague is explicit.

These fears about unruliness were epitomized in the ballad-trade, an unauthorized economy which transmitted morally suspect materials to a non-elite audience. Later in this essay, we shall see how these several aspects of the trade in ballads contributed to the discourse of the plague.

3

Lodge's language concerning contagion, "an evil quality in a body, communicated unto another by touch, engendering one and the same disposition in him to whom it is communicated," applies also to the communication through the media. Despite the idea that God had sent the plague to punish the city for its sins, the contrary interpretation was that the plague was communicable from one human to another through physical means—by paper, for example.

Plague was carried along transport routes, often arriving in London by ship and moving along predictable trade circuits. The growth of London and the increase in road traffic made the rest of the country more susceptible to plague influence. Certain goods were particularly suspect, especially cloth and paper goods, even books. Heretical ballads and other forbidden published matter were sometimes smuggled into England, but in addition to the dangerous content of published material, the very physical object itself was a potential carrier of disease, since the rags from which paper was made were thought to be able to carry plague. Archbishop William Laud angrily blamed trade and the consumer culture for the rapid spread of disease in 1637: "And it is now clear as the sun, that the last increase [of plague] came by the carelessness of the people, and greediness to receive into their houses infected goods. To this add great defect in inferior governors, and great want among the poor, by reason of so many base tenements . . . and you have all the causes under God himself of the present infection."

It was thought that the plague could reside in many material substances, and this was the reason that the household goods of a plague victim, especially his clothes and linens, were burned upon his death. In *The Fearful Summer* (1625), John Taylor recounted how even private correspondence through letters was suspended out of fear that the plague would be carried along with the paper:

> Nor *London* letters little better sped,
> They would not be receiv'd (much lesse be read)
> But cast into the fire and burnt with speed
> As if they had been *Hereticks* indeed.

Taylor's analogy between letters and heretics is not a casual one; heresy and treason were often planned by letters, the exposure of which formed magnificent scandals in the early seventeenth century. Thus both the content and the material of the letters could transmit disease.

Thomas Dekker played upon the fear that paper could carry disease in *The Wonderful Year* (1603): "If you read, you may happily laugh; tis my desire you should, because mirth is both *physical* and wholesome against the *plague,* with which sickness (to tell truth) this book is, (though not sorely), yet somewhat infected." His own book was "somewhat infected": Dekker here correlates political or moral corruption with the dissemination of ideas in print. The reader was not to worry, though; the reader's resistence to the plague would improve with his pamphlet, since mirth itself would be a corrective.

Dekker here applied the Galenic model of disease, where disease was cured by righting an imbalance in the humours.

The physician Thomas Lodge recommended preventing contagion by restricted modes of social intercourse: "it behoveth every man to have special care that he frequent not any places or persons infected, neither that he suffer such to breathe upon him." To stem the spread of plague, circuits of physical communication were to be regulated—touching, breathing, traveling. In this common view of contagion, even human conversation was suspect. The preacher Roger Fenton explained that the scriptural word commonly used for the pestilence was "derived from a verb that signifieth to speak, as some think, because where it is, everyone speaketh of it, enquireth after it, how it encreaseth, what remedies there be for it, what preservatives against it, what be the symptoms and qualities of it." Fenton's etymology of plague blurred the distinction between the thing spoken of and the act of speaking.

Defining the plague was itself a kind of plague. Thomas Dekker traded on this equation between discourse about the plague and the plague itself in the epistle dedicatory to his plague-poem, "News from Grave's End." Dekker employs the common belief that the plague could reside in the paper of books, that the distribution of books through trade could spread the plague. "Shall I creep (like a drowned rat)," he asks, "into thy warm bosom, (my benefique Patron!) with a piece of some old musty Sentence in my mouth . . . and so accost thee? Out upon't!" Dekker's own writing works like a plague upon his reader, "creeping" like dead vermin into the reader's warm, living flesh. The equation works the other way round as well; writing about the plague gives the writer symptoms of the plague: "A stiff and freezing horror sucks up the rivers of my blood: my hair stands on end with the panting of my brains: mine eye-balls are ready to start out, being beaten with the billows of my tears: out of my weeping pen does the ink mournfully and more bitterly than gall drop on the pale-face'd paper, even when I think how the bowels of my sick country have been torn." Dekker is infected with plague merely by writing about it. Thinking of the plague is enough to disfigure him: his very organs are expelled from his body in so doing. This passage plays on the associations of the plague with civic sins, which need to be purged from the "bowels of my sick country." Like Lodge's "evil quality," the disease is inside the body, or the state, and it struggles to escape through any orifice.

As a metaphor for verbal communication, the plague could also signify the spread of subversive ideas, religious dissent, or even treason. In the Bible, plague in Egypt was punishment for an entire nation's political mistake, and political ramifications were never far from the surface of fears about plague. When plague struck Barnstaple in 1646, for example, some inhabitants blamed the local congregation of Independents, and had them chased out of town. Bottles of plague-infected air were said to have been brought by the French to poison the English in 1665, and Catholics were sometimes suspected of spreading the disease as an act of warfare. The Laudian innovations in the church were seen by some Puritans as a cause of plague: "The plague of God is in the land for the new mixture of religion that is commanded in the Church," said John Dod in 1635. Plague was also seen as punishment for civic corruption, and the coincidence of plague with the deaths of Elizabeth in 1603 and James in 1625 was seen by some as a warning of God. Anti-monopolists took the metaphor of plague in their attacks on crown policy in 1641.

The idea of plague purging the evil within the state is found in many critiques of state policy. George Wither associated plague with the difficulties of Parliament in 1628:

> Some did so counsel, and so urge
> The Body politic to take a purge
> To purify the parts that seemed foul.

And the anonymous author of *The Plague at Westminster* (1647) makes the connection between plague and political evil outright, imitating plague orders for a "sick Parliament, grievously troubled with a new Disease." The sorrows, brought about by the House of Lords, are like the plagues of Egypt on the Israelites: "besides your continual taxes, collections, assessments, and the like (a burden that breaks our backs and very hearts); which continually follow one on the neck of another, with every particular belonging to our trade and livelihoods; our wives, our daughters, our sons, our houses, our beds, our apparel, our horses, our hay, our beeves, our muttons, our lambs, our pigs, our geese, our capons, and the rest of our goods are forced from us. . . ." The author here imitates Pharaoh's piling up of burdens on the Hebrews, and he evokes the punishment of God upon the rulers who are too hard. The author ends with a burst of irony: "O almighty and everlasting Lords, we acknowledge and confess from the bottom of our hearts, that you have most justly plagued us these full seven years for our manifold sins and iniquities. . . . For we know too well (O Lords) understand we have grievously sinned.

Plague as a physical entity and as a circumstance of political subversion collided in the physical matter of paper. Sir Simonds D'Ewes wrote in his journal of a letter sent to Mr. Pym in the House of Commons in 1641 which contained "an abominable rag full of filthy bloody atter," that is, pus from a sore. The letter turned out to be a "scandalous libel" in which Mr. Pym was called a "Bribe-taker, Traitor and other opprobrious names," and that the sender of the letter "had sent him a cloute [cloth] drawn through a plague sore which he had running upon him hoping that the same should kill him by infection." This paper, just as it might communicate slander and political opposition figuratively, could also communicate disease and death literally.

This political dimension of plague discourse depended upon a model of disease that made a cosmic analogy between the state of the individual and the political state. Galenic medical theory combined the moral and the material explanations of disease in this analogy, which connected political ills and physical ills. Galenism gave an account of the origin of disease—humoural imbalance, which might be caused by the stars, by lapses in personal discipline (errors in eating, sleeping, or sexual activity), by communal sins or by God's punishment. Those who ascribed to this Galenic model of disease sought to restore the nation's health by typical Galenic means: purging and bloodletting. Clean people and clean states resisted infection. One doctor recommended internal purgation, "it should be good to evacuate and expel those superfluities of humours," including hemorrhoids, ulcers, menstrual blood, itches and boils. This returns us to Douglas's idea of pollution and uncleanness.

Though the plague was often imagined as arriving from foreign shores, the plague was treated as if the dangers were *inside* the body social. The "purge" was to take place on a social level, and regulations specified particular control of those "superfluities" in human terms—beggers, the poor, wandering chapmen, and players. All these seemed to be outsiders, to pose a threat to society. Plague was often accompanied by riots by the poor, who were hit hardest. The fact that more poor folk suffered from the ravages of the plague seemed proof that they were morally degenerate. Suffering sometimes led to protest: "the unruliness of infected persons and want of government" were the occasion of riots in Manchester in 1605. The wanderers, too, were morally suspect because they were "masterless men," but they were also dangerous as potential carriers of infection because of their itinerant behaviors and their spreading potentially subversive mores.

4

In the ample body of literature concerning the plague and the playhouses, the notion of the plague's moral foundation in sin lent authority to the public health officials' attacks on idleness, leisure, and playgoing. According to the dictates of the Royal College of Physicians during plague-time, plays and other crowd-gathering events were to be prohibited, including "Bear-baitings, games, singing of Ballads, Buckler-play, or such like assembly of people." Opponents of the theatre made use of the threat of the plague to quell popular entertainments since such activities were already morally and spiritually suspect. Francis Herring wrote that popular entertainments left the body "disposed to infection, and the contagion dangerously scattered both in city and country." The moral became material, as the body was weakened by its moral failings.

A body could predispose itself toward infection by certain behaviors, both physical and spiritual, according to theories about plague. Idleness was seen as particularly risky. The reasons for this were part physiological and part moral. According to Thomas Thayre, idleness "dulleth the body, filling and repleting it with superfluous and evil humours, which breed many sicknesses." Thayre was not bashful in explaining the social costs of idleness: "As exercise and labour is a preserver of health, so idleness is the shortener of life, enemy unto the soul and body, and very unprofitable in a Commonwealth."

The state would go far in prosecuting idleness, as an example from Manchester in 1605 shows. One Philip Fitton, a vagrant, "of evil demeanor and behaving himself lewdly and dangerously in going to the places and persons infected with the plague," was punished for so doing, first by being locked in a cabin by the constables. But he escaped, and continued in his disorderliness without fear of the plague. He ignored the plague orders, traveled freely within the town, sleeping in out-houses, and wherever else he would. This was too much, and the constables sent him to the Manchester dungeon, not explicitly for carrying infection, but for his "disordered behavior." In the case of Philip Fitton, fears about the plague and about social disorder were one and the same.

The moral explanation for the plague was often confused with the material one in the voices of the Royal College of Physicians. Their orders concerning "loose persons and idle assemblies" during times of plague did not clarify how the infection worked, but rather elided the material explanation with the moral one: "Nothing is more complained on, than the multitude of Rogues and wandering Beggars, that swarm in every place about the City, being a great cause of the spreading of the infection." These 1636 plague orders connected ballad-selling with another set of worries: fears about spreading the plague by "Rogues and wandering Beggars," morally suspicious persons who spread not only disease, but possibly other kinds of dangers as well. Vagrants were impounded during times of virulent infection.

Ballads were unlike plays and other types of crowd gatherings, since not only did they spread "infection" by drawing a crowd, but they also spread "infection" around the countryside. Ballad-hawkers were restricted in 1581 and again in 1608. The cultural construction of contagion hit at a specific economy, that of disseminators of popular culture. The laws punishing rogues and vagabonds were carried to their fullest extent during times of plague, and chapmen, peddlers and pot-men especially were to be apprehended, searched, sometimes sent home, whipped or even incarcerated.

Philip Stubbes opposed the ballad-sellers, those "bawdy Parasites as range the Counties, rhyming and singing of unclean corrupted and filthy songs in Tavernes, alehouses, Inns, and other public assemblies" because the threat of such "filthy Ballades and scurvy Rhyme" was a public one, and more specifically, one on the move. The ballad-sellers were travellers who might spread contagion through physical contact. Those singing and selling ballads were morally debased and debasing; the material itself was evil: as "corrupt meats do annoy the stomachs, and infect the body, so the reading of wicked and ungodly books" (*Anatomie*). The evil, moreover, was contagious, as the "infection" of these men spread through social contacts found in low places, taverns, inns, alehouses. Some writers themselves condemned the extent of ballad circulation, and their criticism told a story of movement from the city into the country. In 1631, William Brathwaite described how ballads travelled from the city into the country, "till at last they grow so common there too, as every poor milk-maid can chant and chirp it under her cow." Likewise, John Earle scorned the popularity of the ballader's product, particularly in the country: "chanted from market to market, to a vile tune, and a worse throat, whilst the poor Country wench melts like her butter to hear them." The complaint was about their widespread influence.

In a society that mistrusted forms of idleness, the ballad-singers appeared to transmit the worst forms of this vice. Philip Stubbes turned against the *distributive* nature of the bawdiness; he worried about the public dissemination of such material. Ballads and other literary wares hawked by travelling salesmen carried stigmas, moral and material: "These Basilisks [the ballad-sellers], these bad minded monsters, brought forth like vipers by their mothers' bane, with such lascivious lewdness have first infected London the eye of England, the head of other Cities, as what is so lewd that hath not these contrary to order been printed, and in every street abusively chanted." Most important in this writer's attack, the ballad-sellers' wandering permits the spread of evil; like a disease, the "infection" of these men was spreading by contact with many. The thorough dissemination of the ballads, their pervasiveness, their being changed in "every street," all terrified the critic. The ballads posed a public threat, not confined geographically to London (already regarded as morally corrupt), but sweeping into every location in the land.

According to this writer, ballad sellers were "able to spread more pamphlets by the State forbidden than all the Booksellers in London" because of their uncontrollable means of dissemination. The chapmen could evade more easily the censures of the civic authorities than the booksellers, whose stock stayed in one place. Part of their threat was that they were dispersed without proper authority, and dispersed through routes that were uncheckable, like the plague's progress.

The repeated printing orders concerning ballads issued by the Stationers' Company attempted to restrict ballad production because of piracy, but also because of their moral and morally-transmissible danger. The Orders of 1612 restricted the number of ballad printers to five, because of "great abuses" daily practised in the ballad industry, but also because of the ballads' lewdness, "offensive both to God, the Church and the state," leading to "the corrupting of youth and evil disposed people." Like other forms of idleness, listening to ballads corrupted those already predisposed to sin. This explanation of the route of corruption into already corrupt matter follows the Galenic interpretation of the plague: like attracts like, both in moral and in material arenas. A soul's morality could be "evil infected" like a body.

There were many reasons the Stationers' Company sought to keep ballads under control, and it did its utmost to restrict ballad production. As the regulatory body charged with the mission of administering all printing and publishing in England, the Stationers' Company maintained records of ballad production. Though only 3081 of the estimated 15,000 broadside ballads published between 1557 and 1709 were listed in the records of the Stationers' Company after formal licensing, there is evidence of a considerable structure of regulation for the market in ballads in the Court records of the Stationers' Company. Unlawful publication of ballads fell largely under two categories: publication of indecent and lewd ballads and literary piracy; fines could be a mere five shillings for printing without license, to forty shillings for piracy and indecent printing. The presses of a ballad printer were on occasion seized and his stock burned. Ballads were persistently an object of worry about unruly economic and moral behavior within the printing industry.

Such concerns about dissemination of this material reveal a real pressure point in early modern English society. The attacks which focused on the public setting of ballads, on their distribution, specifically their route of travel from London into the outlying countryside, were also attacks on their audience. The ballads were being communicated to an audience specifically vulnerable to the plague: the poor, the outcasts. The printing trade brought urban vice—moral and physical vice—to the countryside. Yet the country was supposed to be a place of refuge, a place to fly to. This was the kind of communication circuit that was under regulation because of the plague, yet regulation with respect to the wandering chapmen in the printing industry was especially fraught with worries, since social outcasts were involved.

5

The plague was a disease with mortal consequences, spots, buboes and fever, but it also provided a rhetoric for dealing with anxieties about the body social. Along with the outbreaks of the malevolent, mysterious and invisible disease came forms of communication concerned with plague matters. We still need further inquiry into the ways in which certain social and economic groups were stigmatized through their association with the plague, and especially the theories of contagion and communication the plague provided. This is no more pressing than today, when a second generation of people with AIDS lives with what is still a stigmatized condition.

The trade in ballads is one example of an unauthorized economy in early modern England which was intwined in the rhetoric of the plague. The concern about dissemination of ballads also tells us something about early modern notions of transmission, both of ideas and of disease. The use of the plague metaphor with respect to this commercial literature reveals Renaissance ideas of communication in the media: the plague gave a ready rhetoric for expressing worries about social and cultural changes experienced and felt in the society of early modern England: urbanization, masterless men, and also institutional threats like those of the theatre and the printing industry. Not just any metaphor would do, since the plague was understood both as a moral and a physical accomplishment, and it seemed to work invisibly.

By the early seventeenth century, public health officials were increasingly adopting a material understanding of disease, and their regulations stressed the kinds of actions that followed from that understanding: quarantines, civic sanitation, and the like. But common notions about the moral worth of certain social groups, and fears about social and political subversion colored public policy. Citizens had to explain why the plague struck one person and not another, and the observation that there was selective punishment gave rise to the many explanations of the disease. Physicians stressed that infection could be communicated from one human to another, and this was why their main efforts to regulate public health imposed quarantine and segregation on infected persons. One should abstain from social intercourse of all sorts.

A moral code also determined reactions to the plague, and that moral code was concerned with wanderers like ballad-sellers. The ballads threatened public order, not only in London, but especially as they carried vice into the countryside. The printed nature of the material was a problem, since many balladeers also transgressed against the regulations of the printing authorities, and they engaged an audience that was unacceptable. Hawkers of ballads were one example of the kinds of carriers thought to be dangerous because theirs was an unauthorized economy, and also because the literature they purveyed brought morally controversial material to a morally controversial audience. It is true that as a public and specifically urban problem, the vagrant and idle poor were becoming increasingly visible. Contemporaries saw this however as a decay in morals. As idlers, vagrants, and as distributors of alternative social practices, the hawkers of popular literature were the real foci of worries their early modern English contemporaries had about the social changes they were experiencing.

Raymond Stephanson

SOURCE: "The Plague Narratives of Defoe and Camus: Illness as Metaphor," in *Modern Language Quarterly*, Vol. 48, No. 3, September, 1987, pp. 223-41.

[*In the following essay, Stephanson elucidates the differing symbolic functions served by the plague in two novels: Daniel Defoe's* A Journal of the Plague Year *and Albert Camus's* The Plague.]

In her essay *Illness as Metaphor,* Susan Sontag writes:

> Any important disease whose causality is murky, and for which treatment is ineffectual, tends to be awash in significance. First, the subjects of deepest dread (corruption, decay, pollution, anomie, weakness) are identified with the disease. The disease itself becomes a metaphor. Then, in the name of the disease (that is, using it as a metaphor), that horror is imposed on other things. The disease becomes adjectival.

Sontag's essay explores the ways in which tuberculosis in the nineteenth century and cancer in the twentieth have had "the widest possibilities as metaphors for what is felt to be socially or morally wrong." The same can be said about the plague, which, though eradicated in the West after its last spectacular appearance in Marseilles in 1720, has continued to kill millions in the Third World into this century. The plague—whether bubonic, septicemic, or pulmonary—has always been (like tuberculosis and cancer) a horridly mysterious and impenetrable essence whose pathological might is made even more unsettling by its invisibility. Given the enigmatic and unpredictable nature of plague, it is hardly surprising that symbols have been projected onto the face of this unseen predator in order to explain or justify its catastrophic biological, social, economic, and political consequences. The scores of plagues from the Plague of Justinian (542) through the Great Plague of London (1665) accounted for more than one hundred million deaths. The bubonic plague of 1346-49, known as the Black Death, swept away between one-quarter and one-half of Europe's population; the 1664-65 plague that Defoe describes in *A Journal of the Plague Year* claimed roughly seventy thousand lives in one year; about forty thousand deaths (nearly half the city's population) occurred in Marseilles in 1720. In the face of chaos and trauma of this magnitude, it is natural for humans to ask: what does the plague mean?

Literature has reflected the tendency to make plague a vehicle for allegory, and the interpretive bent is usually religious: plague is the punishment of a sinful people by an angry god. Such is the meaning of plague in Book 1 of *The Iliad* and in the opening scenes of Sophocles' *Oedipus*. Boccaccio situates the privileged storytellers of his *Decameron* near a plague-stricken Florence that suffers "because of God's just wrath as a punishment to mortals for our wicked deeds." The plague in *A Journal of the Plague Year* is meant to be similarly didactic; few readers have disagreed with Louis Landa's view that plague symbolizes "man under the wrath of God," although the astute reader Max Byrd adds that the "allegory a modern reader may search for in the plague might be political or economic or sociological" and cites "the potential for estrangement" as one symbol inherent in Defoe's plague.

The signposts of plague as a symbolic vehicle are relatively obtrusive in Defoe's narrative; Camus's *Plague* is more indirect about what plague "means," preferring ambiguity and multiple possibility to the narrow symbolism of a single doctrine. This is not to say that Camus's narrative has lacked literary commentators eager to transform his tale into allegory. Readings of his plague have included "cosmic alienation," "human indifference," "the abstract logic of the Marxist-Hegelian theory of history," "Nazi occupation of France," and "the human tendency to abstraction per se." Confronted with plague's devastation and murky causality, the modern literary critic reacts in the same way as the authors he reads and the characters he reads about: to pestilence he gives symbolic significance. Antonin Artaud understands the value of plague as a symbol, and in his essay "The Theater and the Plague," he uses plague to epitomize his notion of how theater is both catalyst and mirror of life:

> The plague takes images that are dormant, a latent disorder, and suddenly extends them into the most extreme gestures; the theater also takes gestures and pushes them as far as they will go: like the plague it reforges the chain between what is and what is not, between the virtuality of the possible and what already exists in materialized nature. It recovers the notion of symbols and archetypes which act like silent blows, rests leaps of the heart, summons of the lymph, inflammatory images thrust into our abruptly wakened heads. The theater restores us all our dormant conflicts and all their powers, and gives these powers names we hail as symbols. . . .

Plague has never failed to elicit a symbolic cast—philosophical, religious, or political—from the mind that contemplates it.

It is precisely the capacity of plague to generate symbol making that interests me. Beneath the array of symbols engendered by pestilence can be seen a common human activity—imaginative projection in the face of the unknown and the unseen. The agonies of painful swellings in the groin and armpits, coughing, swollen tongue, thirst, fever, impaired vision, aching limbs, and delirium are in one sense bearable because we can imagine them. What we cannot bear is confronting an invisible presence that has no immediate identity and hence no imaginative coordinates. This is the imaginative threat of plague. For how does one grasp the reality of tens of thousands of deaths in one place at one time? How does one engage an ominous, lurking presence that secretly infects thousands of human bodies and poisons the very air we breathe? Through an act of the imagination. Because it is unknown and unseen, and because its presence can be inferred only by its effects, the plague in a sense compels an imaginative response, just as the darkness of night, outer space, and infinitude have never failed to engage the symbol-making energies of the mind. The unknown unleashes the imagination from the restrictions of ordinary experience. But plague is an unknown that also focuses the other end of imaginative life—the confinement and emptying of the imagination as it confronts the intimate yet impersonal ravages of the body, the devouring of the self's terrain by an invading, mysterious other. Responses to the plague form the spectrum of imaginative life itself: at one end is the initial release of the imagination excited by the novel or unknown and at the other end a return to the demands of a more prosaic material reality. Plague initially is a symbol of imaginative potential, a symbol whose unformed significance we create ourselves; but plague also becomes an unsymbolic fact that confronts us with our imaginative emptiness in the face of the permanence of time, matter, and the contingencies of human existence.

A Journal of the Plague Year (1722) and *The Plague* (1947) are the most profound plague narratives in Western literature. They do not relegate pestilence to a peripheral or background role. Both writers imagine themselves at the center of human contact with plague and try to create some sense of what it means. Their sustained imaginative encounter with the experience and significance of plague makes both narratives an ideal testing ground for my argument that the deepest meaning of plague concerns typical energies and limits inherent in imaginative activity. Neither Defoe nor Camus wrote about plague for the sole purpose of dramatizing vital features of the human imagination; the authors' immediate intentions are located in moral, social, and political issues. But from plague as subject matter necessarily emerge fundamental issues concerning the imagination that both writers pursue. And what Defoe's narrative suggests is as true in 1722 as it is for Camus in 1947 and for readers in the late twentieth century: the imagination is unrestrained in its potential for creativity at the same time it is confined by experience.

When, in the *Spectator* of 30 June 1712 (No. 418), Addison commented that "the Imagination can fancy to it self Things more Great, Strange, or Beautiful, than the Eye ever saw," he was reflecting the increased self-consciousness in eighteenth-century queries about the imagination, especially in regard to contact with the infinitely vast or infinitesimally small worlds thrown open by the new science. Newtonian physics and the anatomical discoveries of the new physiology provided vistas of enormous imaginative possibility, vistas whose theoretical and mathematical models awaited a corresponding set of imaginative touchstones and a concrete imagery. New insights into the shadowy realms of astronomy and microbiology, made possible by improved telescopes and microscopes, inspired an intense imaginative reaction, as the creative responses of eighteenth-century poets and the metaphors and analogies of the scientists themselves have testified. And so it is with plague: the blank face of a ghastly pestilence provokes the imagination to create images to fill the void. But there are no visual hints to prefigure the alien identity of plague; the imagination is radically free to invent its own shape for the unseen.

Thus the frequency with which Defoe refers to the imagination of the people, particularly in the first quarter of the text, should come as no surprise. "The poor People were terrify'd, by the Force of their own Imagination" is a typical observation by H. F., the tenacious narrator of the *Journal*. Defoe senses that plague, lacking imaginative anchor for the mind, allows for a creative projection of extravagant and fabulous imagery onto the unseen protagonist. And he uses considerable space to dramatize imaginative response to the plague, including substantial accounts of the people's attraction to magic and addiction "to Prophesies, and Astrological Conjurations, Dreams, and old Wives Tales," of hallucinations, of reported ghosts, and of "Charms, Philtres, Exorcisms, Amulets":

> Some heard Voices. . . . Others saw Apparitions in the Air. . . . but the Imagination of the People was really turn'd wayward and possess'd: And no Wonder, if they, who were poreing continually at the Clouds, saw Shapes and Figures, Representations and Appearances, which had nothing in them, but Air and Vapour. Here they told us, they saw a Flaming-Sword held in a Hand, coming out of a Cloud. . . . There they saw Herses, and Coffins in the Air. . . . Heaps of dead Bodies lying unburied, and the like; just as the Imagination of the poor terrify'd People furnish'd them with Matter to work upon.

Unconstrained by conventional modes of identification, the imagination is free—painfully and fearfully free—to create its own picture of the unseen foe. For the people as well as for the reader, the thing without becomes the thing within: plague is internalized and the mind is set free to create and then confront its own scenario, however bizarre or grotesque.

Camus's Dr. Rieux, calm and scientific, reacts to the first halting, tentative use of the word "plague" in the same way as Defoe's Londoners do. After a moment of astonished recoil, his imagination rushes forward to meet this covert foe for the first time, carrying with it a creative adrenalin so intense that even the lifeless statistics of history are charged with colors, smells, and sounds:

> . . . a word was echoing still, the word "plague." A word that conjured up in the doctor's mind not only what science chose to put into it, but a whole series of fantastic possibilities utterly out of keeping with that gray and yellow town under his eyes. . . . Athens, a charnel-house reeking to heaven and deserted even by the birds; Chinese towns cluttered up with victims silent in their agony; the convicts at Marseille piling rotting corpses into pits; the building of the Great Wall in Provence to fend off the furious plague-wind; the damp, putrefying pallets stuck to the mud floor at the Constantinople lazar-house, where the patients were hauled up from their beds with hooks; the carnival of masked doctors at the Black Death; men and women copulating in the cemeteries of Milan; cartloads of dead bodies rumbling through London's ghoul-haunted darkness. . . . Dr. Rieux called to mind the plague-fires of which Lucretius tells, which the Athenians kindled on the seashore. The dead were brought there after nightfall, but there was not room enough, and the living fought one another with torches for a space where to lay those who had been dear to them. . . . A picture rose before him of the red glow of the pyres mirrored on a wine-dark, slumbrous sea, battling torches whirling sparks across the darkness, and thick, fetid smoke rising toward the watchful sky.

To such "fantastic possibilities" the doctor reacts with stern objectivity: "He was letting his imagination play pranks—the last thing wanted just now." But as Camus realized, the doctor's response is not some eccentric prank; his imaginative energy is archetypal. Plague excites the innermost recesses of imaginative flight, and out of plague's mysterious presence the mind creates a drama of intense life.

During a time of plague, when human attention is thrust onto the threshold of the unknown, there are always dream merchants, the grasping fakes who sell imaginative fodder to a public eager for images that will satisfy their hunger for shape, vision, and meaning. The "Apprehensions of the People" in the *Journal* prompt a "running about to Fortune-tellers, Cunning-men, and Astrologers . . . to have their Fortunes told them, their Nativities calculated." Dr. Rieux takes note of "the remarkable interest shown in prophecies of all descriptions" and points to the "printing firms," "journalists," and "popular prophets" who were "quick to realize the profit to be made by pandering to this new craze" for "predictions," "apocalyptic jargon," "Nostradamus and St. Odilia," "superstition." The purveyors of imaginative wares—charlatans who shamelessly sell dreams, fortunes, and predictions—are a symptom of the people's need for an imaginative act that is equal to the stifling power of the invisible plague. H. F. writes of finding (even "before the Plague was begun," when Londoners were only dreading its recurrence) "a Crowd of People in the Street"

> all staring up into the Air, to see what a Woman told them appeared plain to her, which was an Angel cloth'd in white, with a fiery Sword in his Hand, waving it, or brandishing it over his Head. She described every Part of the Figure to the Life; shew'd them the Motion, and the Form; and the poor People came into it so eagerly, and with so much Readiness; YES, *I see it all plainly,* says one. *There's the Sword as plain as can be.* Another saw the Angel. One saw his very Face, and cry'd out, What a glorious Creature he was! One saw one thing, and one another.

Camus's Jesuit priest, Father Paneloux, though sincere, fills the same need and offers the same release as do the conjurers. First, he challenges his anxious congregation with the ominously vacant symbolism of plague, and then he fills his sermon with Old Testament imagery calculated to harrow the hearts of his listeners. More important, the concrete imagery provides an outlet for the pent-up imaginative energy of the people:

> "For plague is the flail of God and the world His threshing-floor. . . . See him there, that angel of the pestilence, comely as Lucifer, shining like Evil's very self! He is hovering above your roofs with his great spear in his right hand, poised to strike, while his left hand is stretched toward one or other of your houses. Maybe at this very moment his finger is pointing to your door, the red spear crashing on its panels. . . ."
>
> At this point the Father reverted with heightened eloquence to the symbol of the flail. He bade his hearers picture a huge wooden bar whirling above the town, striking at random, swinging up again in a shower of drops of blood. . . .

These passages (and others like them) provide evidence of the mind's need to "picture" the unknown entity. Plague becomes a mirror of the imagination, calling forth heightened creative energy by liberating the imagination from the quotidian. And the direction this imaginative projection takes will vary from person to person and from one historical moment to another: the response of the common people in 1664-65 is characterized by superstition; Defoe's response is dominated by the notion of divine retribution; for Camus, the plague suggests the dangers of moral and social ennui. The content of these various responses is not particularly relevant; what is significant is their shared genesis—the encounter of the creative fire and flight of the imagination (sometimes exhilarating and satisfying, sometimes frenetic and fearful) with the unknown. In the process of grappling with the enigmatic plague, the imagination itself becomes the subject as well as the object of its own surging energy, signaling its vast potential for the creation of life, form, and meaning.

While plague may at first liberate the imagination, it soon represses that inherent freedom. Camus's narrator, Dr. Rieux, appreciates this other side of plague as symbol for imaginative life:

> The truth is that nothing is less sensational than pestilence. . . . In the memories of those who lived through them, the grim days of plague do not stand out like vivid flames, ravenous and inextinguishable, beaconing a troubled sky, but rather like the slow, deliberate progress of some monstrous thing crushing out all upon its path.
>
> No, the real plague had nothing in common with the grandiose imaginings that had haunted Rieux's mind at its outbreak.

Camus is not suggesting that Rieux's earlier imaginative response was not "real," but rather that the brutal, inescapable statistics of plague accumulate and oppose the creative activities of the imagination, finally forcing a confrontation with the possibility of imaginative closure and death. H. F.'s use of the weekly "Bills of Mortality" and his citation of various social, economic, and political statistics function in this way. As the biological and social effects of pestilence begin to touch men and women directly, as the metaphorical thing without threatens to become the physical thing within, the initial energy of the imagination begins to fade.

Rieux observes, for instance, the initially carefree attitude of the people of Oran: "They went on doing business. . . . How should they have given a thought to anything like plague, which rules out any future, cancels journeys, silences the exchange of views. They fancied themselves free, and no one will ever be free so long as there are pestilences." What the people in both narratives come to experience is the social alienation, physical imprisonment, and threat of other that plague entails. Plague means physical separation from lovers and family, quarantines and the shutting up of houses by city officials, paralysis of business and trade, death of a husband or daughter, and invasion by a mysterious, invisible other (far more potent than the footprint in *Robinson Crusoe*) that can consume the self and its imaginative horizons: "unperceiv'd by others, or by themselves," plague "prey'd secretly on the Vitals," "the penetrating Poison insinuating itself into their Blood in a Manner, which it is impossible to describe, or indeed conceive" (*Journal*). Pestilence also brings the overwhelming fear of contagion. To the imagination, such realities are forms of confinement and dispossession that ultimately deplete and exhaust our creative potential. Imaginative life in a world of plague quickly veers from the energetic and endless possibility in the unknown toward stasis, toward an oppressive inertia in which physical, social, economic, and intellectual possibilities threaten to cease altogether. For Camus's narrator, pestilence eventually causes "that sensation of a void within":

> Sometimes we toyed with our imagination, composing ourselves to wait for . . . a traveler coming by the evening train . . . and though we might contrive to forget for the moment that no trains were running, that game of make-believe, for obvious reasons, could not last. Always a moment came when we had to face the fact that no trains were coming in. . . . In short, we returned to our prison-house. . . .

Although one might "set the trains running again in one's imagination" and "[fill] the silence with the fancied tinkle of a doorbell," there is always the inevitable return to a world of plague in which real doorbells are "obstinately mute."

Camus describes a similar imaginative impotence that claims those who dwell on their separation from lovers and spouses:

> At the beginning of the plague they had a vivid recollection of the absent ones and bitterly felt their loss. But though they could clearly recall the face, the smile and voice of the beloved, . . . they had trouble in picturing what he or she might be doing at the moment when they conjured up

> these memories, in a setting so hopelessly remote. In short, at these moments memory played its part, but their imagination failed them. During the second phase of the plague their memory failed them, too. Not that they had forgotten the face itself, but . . . it had lost fleshly substance and they no longer saw it in memory's mirror. Thus, while during the first weeks they were apt to complain that only shadows remained to them . . . by the end of their long sundering they had also lost the power of imagining the intimacy that once was theirs. . . .

Pestilence finally defeats man's power to imagine. While the imagination gazes at it in fascination, plague moves inexorably, crushing dreams and life itself. Before long, the miserable fate of the city and its people becomes a metaphor for what awaits the imagination: "The silent city was no more than an assemblage of huge, inert cubes" suggesting the "final aspect, that of a defunct city in which plague, stone, and darkness had effectively silenced every voice." Defoe's narrative also images the ultimate confinement of the collective imagination as physical emptiness and cessation of human activity: "whole Streets seem'd to be desolated, and not to be shut up only, but to be emptied of their Inhabitants; Doors were left open, Windows stood shattering with the Wind in empty Houses, for want of People to shut them." Even the dream makers and false purveyors of imaginative expansion are gone: "all the Predictors, Astrologers, Fortune-tellers, and what they call'd cunning-Men, Conjurers, and the like; calculators of Nativities, and dreamers of Dreams, and such People, were gone and vanish'd, not one of them was to be found." Camus's Father Paneloux also is gone, victim of plague.

If initially a liberator of the imagination, plague finally leaves the imagination no escape. In the *Spectator* of 23 June 1712 (No. 412), Addison writes,

> Our imagination loves to be filled with an Object, or to graspe at any thing that is too big for its Capacity. . . . The Mind of Man naturally hates every thing that looks like a Restraint upon it, and is apt to fancy it self under a sort of Confinement, when the Sight is pent up in a narrow Compass, and shortened on every side by the Neighbourhood of Walls or Mountains.

Where Camus deals literally with imaginative confinement, Defoe expertly dramatizes imaginative restriction and paralysis through physical confinement—a "Neighbourhood of Walls." The words "confin'd" and "Confinement" are everywhere in the *Journal,* and the sense of imprisonment both in anecdotes and in diction and imagery is overwhelming. The reason is not hard to find: the threat of plague means the shutting up of houses, and in a world besieged by plague, "here were just so many Prisons in the Town, as there were Houses shut up. . . ." Many people have "lock'd themselves up" to avoid contagion, and those unfortunate victims in the agonies of swellings and fever are occasionally "ty'd in their Beds and Chairs, to prevent their doing themselves Hurt." Being "restrain'd" and "ty'd" by force is "counted a very cruel and Unchristian Method, and the poor People so confin'd made bitter Lamentations," but these domestic confinements are only part of a much larger, more appalling picture of stasis and constriction. When H. F. reports that "it was said, there was at one Time, ten thousand Houses shut up, and every House had two Watchmen to guard it," Defoe is suggesting a kind of physical confinement whose claustrophobic implications are staggering. Defoe describes a people who, at the height of the plague's mastery, are paralyzed and imprisoned in a city whose activities have been negated and confined by the plague's menacing void: trade and navigation are "at a full Stop"; "Employment ceased"; "The Inns-of-Court were all shut up"; "All the Plays and Interludes . . . were forbid to Act; the gaming Tables, publick dancing Rooms, and Music Houses . . . were shut up and suppress'd; and the Jack-puddings, Merry-andrews, Puppet-shows, Rope-dancers, and such like doings . . . shut up their Shops. . . ." What the imagination confronts is the specter of a city that has been captured, confined, and emptied by plague: "London was as it were entirely shut up." In response to this oppressive landscape, the imagination adopts a defensive posture, and its creative energies are quickly replaced by a fear of contagion.

Confinement is not limited to the intercourse of trade, commerce, and exchange. It also afflicts social relationships: "a vast Number of People lock'd themselves up, so as not to . . . suffer any . . . Company, to come into their Houses, or near them." Plague severs the normal bonds between people, who now confine themselves to their tiny window frames and maintain only a distant contact with a dying world: "I look'd thro' my Chamber Windows (for I seldom opened the Casements) while I confin'd my self within Doors . . ."; "They had no way to converse with any of their Friends but out at their Windows, where they wou'd make such piteous Lamentations."

Physical features and tableaux such as these offer an objective correlative for the centripetal movement of the imagination as it is hemmed in and threatened by the "acute penetrating Nature of the Disease." The sick are confined with the healthy, people fleeing London are confined in the spaces between towns, people are "imprisoned," houses are shut up, many have *"lock'd themselves up, and live on board"* ships, neighbors are confined to their homes, the sick are tied down to beds and chairs, and there is, finally, the ultimate confinement in the Aldgate pit or in a pine box. While such diction and imagery refer literally to forms of social, economic, and physical imprisonment caused by the pestilence, they also provide an effective emblem of imaginative stasis and retreat: every imaginative avenue normally allowed by ordinary experience is either nonexistent or locked up. One cannot move; one cannot touch neighbors with the loving stuff of small talk; one cannot do business. One can only be shut up with the dying and the dead; the earlier flights of the imagination are now in thrall to plague.

These various kinds of restriction and imprisonment are the metaphorical vehicles in the *Journal* for imaginative immobility in the face of a threatening and incomprehensible void, and such structures of confinement are a feature in most of Defoe's anecdotes. One narrative sequence, for example, concerns "Another infected Person" who visits the family of a close friend to announce that he has "got the Sickness, and shall die to morrow":

> The Women and the Man's Daughters which were but little Girls, were frighted almost to Death, and got up, one running out at one Door, and one at another, some down-Stairs and some up-Stairs, and getting together as well as they could, lock'd themselves into their Chambers, and screamed out at the Window for Help. . . . The Master . . . was going to lay Hands on him . . . but then considering a little the Condition of the Man and the Danger of touching him, Horror seiz'd his Mind, and he stood still like one astonished. . . . And so he [the infected friend] goes immediately down Stairs: The Servant that had let him in goes down after him with a Candle, but was afraid to go past him and open the Door . . . the Man went and open'd the Door, and went out and flung the Door after him.

What is noteworthy here and elsewhere in the *Journal* is the claustrophobic, almost pathological quality of the scene: the oppressive sense of futile flight, confinement, physical and social paralysis, fear of touch or movement, and the final sense of being shut up in one's own domain. This powerful sense of physical confinement is an effective way to illustrate how the plague shackles both physical and imaginative movement.

But Defoe ultimately is interested in re-creating in us a tangible experience of what this confinement is like. The ubiquitous presence of paralysis and confinement in diction, imagery, anecdotes, and subject matter profoundly influences our realization of the text. Like the Londoners faced with a diminishing physical and social world, we recoil from repeated accounts of inertia and decreasing possibility. The story of the soldier, sailor, and carpenter (the longest anecdote in the *Journal*) is paradigmatic in precisely this way. The preparations of the men as they ready themselves to escape London are the stuff of romance or adventure; what the narrative stresses is their excited voyaging forth into a realm of possibility that will test and reward their individual talents. This narrative formula, with its predictable resolutions and adventure plots, also presages a setting forth of the reader's imagination. The sudden possibility of imaginative excursion into the world of adventure and romance stands in sharp contrast to the typically claustrophobic events in the *Journal*. Having encouraged the imaginative flight that attends any adventure formula, Defoe then stifles and neuters that energy by concluding with confinement and stasis. What might have been escape and expansion for the three men becomes an entrapped, glum survival in an area between communities; what might have been imaginative flight for the reader becomes yet another exercise in imaginative entropy and narrative inertia.

This vicarious experience of imaginative confinement is evident even in the apparently unstructured shape of the plot itself. The traditional claims that the *Journal* is "an incoherent jumble" lacking a plan and that the structure of the narrative is "repetitive" and "undisciplined" fail to account for the way in which Defoe's organization of incident and anecdote contributes to the powerful feeling of confinement that the *Journal* evokes in its readers. The forward progress of the "journal" and its chronological advance in particular are frequently suspended; the ponderous movement of the daily and monthly account very often seems to give way to a more static representation of the plague year in which temporal and spatial features tend to recede altogether. This is true of many of Defoe's more striking anecdotes, which, although specific in detail, are characterized as without clear temporal or physical location. This paratactic or disjunctive narrative process can be attributed in part to H. F.'s use of the unique "case" to substantiate some general historical point. But the narrative structure can be accounted for in a different fashion as well.

As much as Defoe dramatizes temporal flux (however haltingly) in H. F.'s journalistic account of the events of 1664-65, he also restricts the reader's experience of the passage of time by developing a chronology of events in London only so far and then returning to issues that he already has handled. Numerous transitional sentences take the reader backward in time: "But I must go back again to the Beginning of this Surprizing Time, while the Fears of the People were young . . ."; "But I come back to the Case of Families infected, and shut up. . . ."; "But I return to the shutting up of Houses"; "But I must go back here . . . to the Time of their shutting up Houses . . . "; "But to return to the Markets"; "But I return to the Coals as a Trade." This retrogressive, da capo movement creates an illusion of time stopping, of the normal experience of narrative duration being held in abeyance, and this structural feature effects another form of imaginative inertia for the reader a sense that even the ordinary progress of time has been paralyzed. And the focus of the majority of these circular moves involves the reader's repeated confrontation with both the imaginative and spatial confinement that accompanies the shutting up of houses. Such movement is not "incoherent" or "undisciplined"; it is rather an effective rhythm of closure, a re-creation of the imaginative paralysis brought by the plague.

The narratives of both Camus and Defoe dramatize the symbolic import of pestilence in ways that go beyond religious, social, or political allegory. At its deepest and most threatening level, plague means the erasure of imaginative potential through a negation of those social and physical categories whose presence we need to maintain even a modicum of sanity. As plague devours those imaginative avenues we take for granted, our initial thrust of imaginative energy against the unknown is quickly confined by our fear of bodily disintegration, death, and nothingness.

If the threat of plague in part follows from its invisibility and lack of imaginative coordinates, then an equally unsettling implication is that once an image or symbol has been supplied, the imaginative structure finally fails to "contain" plague. Pestilence ultimately refuses to yield to the very act of imaginative appropriation it has precipitated and threatens to obliterate the self. We are left with our dwindling imaginative energy and with the realization that our apprehension of the world of others is like our experience of plague: the attempt to possess or neutralize through imaginative projection always will be met with that unknowable, irreducible essence that makes its own claims on us and that refuses to become a malleable figure in our psychological tableau.

Indeed, plague and the threat of infection force the drama of self and other to be played out at its most intimate and terrifying level. The site of confrontation is not some accidental place of contact, but within. The other has been literally internalized as a physiological presence, telling us that *we* are other. To be a victim of plague dramatizes an essential truth about our imaginative transactions with the other, namely, that our attempts to "know" or to translate the significance of the foreign entity are really about how we create a fictional second self, an alter ego, and locate it at arm's length, often forgetting that such an act is as much a measure of self as it is an understanding of other. Plague does not permit us to forget; its simultaneous invitation and impenetrability to the imagination, as well as its concurrent embodiment as abstract statistic and intimate physical presence, paradoxically suggest that to grapple with the unknowable other compels a better knowledge of self, however disquieting such insights may prove.

Both texts constantly imply the drama of self/other and the fundamental fear of the dissolution of the ego, although Defoe and Camus seem more interested in the temporal dynamics of the imagination than in the ontological status of the imagination and its objects. Their plague narratives offer a structure and focus for the nature of imaginative life itself, revealing both the corporeal tenterhooks against which the charging imagination strains and the typical sequence of imaginative passage through time. What both texts pose is a fundamental paradox: the transcendental quality of the imagination creates significance beyond its immediate location in space and time, but this generative quality is finally never free of its physical and temporal definitions. The plague intensifies these two ends of the imaginative spectrum by representing first an unknown that draws the imagination into heightened activity and then a hostile other that threatens a confiscation of the ego and its imaginative potential.

Defoe presents an apposite image of these complementary yet opposed aspects of the imagination when he speaks of a plague world in which "confining the Sound in the same House with the Sick" becomes a pressing physical threat, and Camus speaks of the gruesome possibility of "the dying embrac[ing] the living" in public squares. Such a union of the dying and dead, sick and well offers a compelling image of what imaginative life entails: plague confronts the mind's eye with its creative power at the same time it extinguishes that power through the certainty of closure and death, and the generative force of imagination finds its own death in the very act of giving imaginative life to the unseen void. The spirit is indeed trapped in clay.

But the *Journal* and *The Plague* also reflect the typical sequence of the imagination as it moves through time—first, a moment of imbalance or uncertainty as the imagination is seized and then released by metaphorical potential, then a headlong flight into the dark mysteries of the cavern or excited ascent into empyrean light as the mind's eye is carried by the energy of its own creativity, and finally, the inevitable return, that sobering decrescendo into thoughtful repose when we attempt to reconcile the imagined and the "real," editing and discarding so that the shape of our visions will fit the limits of a mundane, material world. The structure of both narratives reflects this sequence: anecdotes and episodes that dramatize the initial release and flight of the imagination are followed in both texts by an exploration of the inevitable deflating and closing of the imagination as it collides with an intractable physical reality.

The presence of these underlying truths and deep structures makes the *Journal* and *The Plague* such moving (and, one might add, disquieting) reading experiences. The narratives of Defoe and Camus explore the experience of plague as a mirror of the imagination, thereby witnessing one of the great dramas of mental life. "I know positively," says one of Camus's characters, "that each of us has the plague within him; no one, no one on earth, is free from it."

Barbara Fass Leavy

SOURCE: "Microparasites, Macroparasites, and the Spanish Influenza," in *To Blight with Plague: Studies in a Literary Theme*, New York University Press, 1992, pp. 127-55.

[*In the following excerpt, Leavy discusses works by Wallace Stegner and Katherine Anne Porter in which the influenza epidemic of 1918 figures prominently.*]

The influenza pandemic of 1918 has been called by one of its historians "the most appalling epidemic since the Middle Ages," but, according to another who has studied it, the "average college graduate born since 1918 literally knows more about the Black Death of the fourteenth century" than about the epidemic. The disease came to be called the Spanish influenza and sometimes, more colorfully and perhaps more insidiously, the Spanish Lady, the feminization of influenza perhaps not as dangerous as the portrayal of syphilis as a woman, but nonetheless contributing to the stereotype of woman as polluter. In any event, there is indeed a glaring disparity between the dramatic possibilities of describing the pandemic and the relatively slight impact it has made on the consciousness of the world and of the United States, where it coincided with America's entry into World War I. And this disparity has caused puzzlement:

> The important and almost incomprehensible fact about Spanish influenza is that it killed millions upon millions of people in a year or less. Nothing else—no infection, no war, no famine—has ever killed so many in as short a period. And yet it has never inspired awe, not in 1918 and not since.

If it does exist for some as a "folk memory," it has nonetheless failed to produce any enduring folklore, for it has been claimed that the "Spanish Lady inspired no songs, no legends, no work of art." In American literature, however, the influenza pandemic has provided at least two authors, Wallace Stegner and Katherine Anne Porter, with major subject matter and themes for fiction. The former has used the outbreak of influenza as a motif in several works, one of which, his "Chip off the Old Block," is on its way to becoming a classic short story. The latter's novella, *Pale Horse, Pale Rider,* is acknowledged to be "one of the twentieth century's masterpieces of short fiction," a work that also provides the historian with a "most accurate depiction of American society in the fall of 1918," synthesizing what otherwise could be gleaned only from the popular press.

Both Stegner and Porter make use of the coincidence of two of what each author would call plagues, the war and the flu, a conjunction that supplies a blatant instance of McNeill's depiction of human life as caught between macro- and microparasites, it being an additional point of interest that the influenza epidemic would strike hardest at the same segment of the American population as would the war. As Alfred Crosby has described it,

> The interweaving of the war and the pandemic make what from a distance of a half-century seems to be a pattern of complete insanity. On September 11 Washington officials disclosed to reporters their fear that Spanish influenza had arrived, and on the next day thirteen million men of precisely the ages most liable to die of Spanish influenza and its complications lined up all over the United States and crammed into city halls, post offices, and school houses to register for the draft.

In Stegner's work, war and flu spell the end of the American dream, whose demise renders futile the attempt to achieve a personal identity that presupposes its existence. For Porter, who depicts the ironic death of a soldier, not from wounds suffered in battle but from influenza, the disease has a broader and more existential symbolism where it comes to her heroine's quest for self-definition. For despite the existence in *Pale Horse, Pale Rider* of religious themes in which some readers find Porter's belief in personal redemption, the American scene depicted in her novella comes very close to resembling the absurd world of Camus's *The Plague*.

Wallace Stegner tells the story of twelve-year-old Chet Mason, who becomes the man of the house when his father, mother, and brother—all ill of influenza—are taken to their town's makeshift hospital. His father's condition is complicated by frostbite incurred during a journey to purchase the whisky believed to be an effective medicine for flu. While his family is recovering, Chet remains in contact with the infirmary, supplies it with the excess milk piling up at his house, hunts for meat as food, wards off with a gun the half-breed Louis Treat and an unnamed companion intent on stealing the brew, sells the liquor for more money than his father would have charged, and, when the end of World War I is announced, holds a party to which he invites neighbors who were spared during the epidemic or were already released from the infirmary. At this celebration the whisky is imbibed freely, and in the midst of the merrymaking, Chet's father returns home and angrily confronts his son, accusing him of mishandling affairs while the family was away.

There are two ways for a reader to experience Chet's encounter with the pandemic believed to have killed over twenty million people throughout the world and to have infected about five times that number, the infection rather than its threatening fatality being central to Stegner's themes, since in this story no important character dies of the flu. The episode appears in Stegner's saga of the Mason family, *The Big Rock Candy Mountain,* and is alluded to again in its sequel *Recapitulation*. It also exists as a separately published short story. The context supplied by the novels reveals Chet to be a relatively minor character compared to his father and brother, but only in the novels is it clear how pervasive are Stegner's metaphors of disease. *The Big Rock Candy Mountain* begins with the early life of Chet's mother and the death of his grandmother from what appears to be tuberculosis and thematically concludes with the death of Chet's mother from cancer and with the impact of her illness and death on her husband and surviving son, Bruce. For by this time, Chet too is dead, his earlier triumph during the epidemic rendered ironically futile not only because he escaped the flu only prematurely to die of pneumonia while still a young man, but also because of the bleakness of his young manhood and the hopelessness of his future. As Stegner critics suggest, the Mason family deaths parallel the demise of the myths upon which America was supposedly built. There is a bitter irony that Chet's end comes about through the transformation of nature into a commercial venture by the society that trapped his father in the perpetual quest for the quick buck:

> If Chet had not been generous and good-natured, he would not have worked up a sweat on a cold and windy day, helping dig somebody's car out of the snow at the Ecker ski-jumping hill outside of Park City. If he had been born luckier, he would have waited to catch pneumonia until after antibiotics had tamed it. Being generous, unlucky, and ill-timed, he dug and pushed, he got overheated, he fell sick and he died within

> six days. . . . Then he escaped from his future, which was drab, and his marriage, which was in trouble, and abandoned to others the daughter he had conceived before he was legally a man. . . . Like his catch-up reading, his instruction in real life had much ground to cover in only a little time.

In effect, the brevity of Chet's final illness mirrors his life, and, significantly, the short tale Stegner carved out of his long novel commences with a passage about time:

> Sitting alone looking at the red eyes of the parlor heater, Chet thought how fast things happened. One day the flu hit. Two days after that his father left for Montana to get a load of whisky to sell for medicine. The next night he got back in the midst of a blizzard with his hands and feet frozen, bringing a sick homesteader he had picked up on the road; and now this morning all of them, the homesteader, his father, his mother, his brother Bruce were loaded in a sled and hauled to the schoolhouse-hospital.

The requirements of short fiction necessitate such condensation of events, and in "Chip off the Old Block," genre actually duplicates the quick course of the disease, and, symbolically, the brief span of a human life. Such a connection between form and content is implied in Stegner's 1989 foreword to his *Collected Stories*. He describes how "increasingly, in [his] own writing the novel has tended to swallow and absorb potential stories," how he "found fairly early that even stories begun without the intention of being anything but independent tended to cluster, wanting to be part of something longer."

In life as well, incidents become part of what will hopefully constitute the extended biography of the individual self. As the celebrity queried about his feelings about having reached a quite advanced age replied, he felt very well considering the alternative. One wants to survive, to make each event part of something longer. Mortality in general and plague in particular threaten this hopefulness. The rapidity of Chet's sudden passage from youth to young adulthood in the short story, and the successive failures of the generations of Masons are as in all family sagas—actually condensed in Stegner's long novels. Time bears an uneasy relationship to narrative, and, again, genre itself mirrors history, the relation of incident to the larger picture. The promise and collapse in rapid succession of the American dream parallel Chet's story, which is but part of the family chronicle treated in the novels. Similarly, in Europe, where World War I had crushed hopes that the Congress of Vienna marked the end of such global battles, the apparent progress of a century was suddenly rendered a mere illusion. The appearance and disappearance of the influenza pandemic that came to be known as the Spanish Lady, virtually personified the grim reality of the era, joining with the war to mock the human hope to achieve that which endures.

To read "Chip off the Old Block" outside *The Big Rock Candy Mountain* is, however, to view Stegner's metaphors of disease through a more optimistic lens, to avoid learning that Chet was untouched by the influenza epidemic and its often-fatal respiratory complications only to succumb in early adulthood to pneumonia at that very time when the early hopefulness of his life was past and the discovery of antibiotics was not far off. Time creates in Stegner's work the gap between promise and reality, but in this story, despite its explicit introduction, time can be ignored. There are, in addition, formal benefits to reading the story in isolation, for by itself it obviates the criticism that has been leveled at *The Big Rock Candy Mountain,* that whatever its power, it is structurally flawed, lacking a consistent focus of interest (is it primarily about the patriarch Bo Mason or about his son Bruce, and in either case, why does the novel begin and end with the lives and deaths of Bruce's grandmother and mother, with so much of the narrative being about his mother's life?); without a consistent point of view; and deficient in the literary use of "myth, symbol, current psychology, or neo-theology" that are among the elements of a great novel. Joseph Warren Beach has asked of this novel, "what of the distinctive pleasure which one takes in a work of art?" and he continues with gentle reproach that Stegner, committed to realism, "refrains from using the 'distortions' of art, and . . . does not greatly command the finer tools of irony, suggestion, pathos, fancy, or intellectual abstraction, which variously serve in the masters to give esthetic point to a neutral subject."

By itself, "Chip off the Old Block" meets these objections and is a satisfying work. It has a consistent focus of both interest and point of view, Chet himself, and it employs the art of fiction to write about the impact of a plague on the developing identity of the young boy. There is no doubt that for the youth the influenza epidemic has accelerated the inexorable movement towards adult responsibility and adult consciousness. One of Chet's activities during his lonely hours is to write a story in which a young explorer encounters many dangers, among which are menacing snakes he significantly mislabels "boy constructors." From the real perils he faces, and from the narrative he invents, Chet creates his own rite of passage.

Stegner's depiction of influenza and its impact on a small western American town is accurate. For example, Chet wonders at his father's contracting flu, he being a man "who seldom got anything and was tougher than boiled owl." In fact, Chet's father is particularly ill, and it is reported to his anxious son that at one point his survival had been in doubt. That influenza hit hardest such a man, in the age group of twenty to forty, who, because he lived in a rural area isolated from the illnesses prevalent in the cities and thus had not built up many antibodies to disease, is part of the history of the 1918 pandemic. McNeill contends that when a population is depleted of persons in such an age group, its leaders and most productive workers, the community is likely to suffer a greater demoralization than when the very young or the very old suffer the highest mortality rate. Again, the age group described by McNeill corresponds to that of the soldiers likely to be lost in the war that was at that time still raging. But it is Katherine Anne Porter, not Stegner, who makes use of that coincidence.

Moreover, Stegner's story combines naturalistic detail with popular belief, such as the relationship of plague to sin (more about that shortly). Finally, "Chip off the Old Block" is almost a perfect rendering of McNeill's description of human life participating in a universal food chain in which one creature feeds off another and normal existence is capable of being expressed in images of hunting, warfare, and disease. At one point Chet affirms his ability to take care of himself while alone by reporting, "I shot rabbits all last fall for Mrs. Rieger. . . . She's 'nemic and has to eat rabbits and prairie chickens and stuff. She lent me the shotgun and bought the shells." And at the conclusion to the story, when the struggle between father and son reaches a boiling point, the angry but also proud parent invokes a cannibalistic figure of speech to proclaim of his son, "He'd eat me if I made a pass at him." If the generation gap is, as Stegner's critics argue, a primary theme in his fiction, then fathers themselves are macroparasites against which sons must defend themselves, and Bo Mason's imagery could extend from the universal but naturalistic food chain to the myth of Cronos, who literally swallowed his own children in order not to be symbolically swallowed by them.

Indeed, the structure of "Chip off the Old Block" persistently involves the interaction of micro- and macroparasites. Stegner draws heavily on the coincidence of World War I and the influenza epidemic: it is the war rather than the pandemic that one of his characters labels a "plague." Thus the "emancipation" of Chet's father from the "dread sickness" is writ symbolically large in the "emancipation of the entire world." Chet himself had been entrusted to "hold the fort" of the familial house, and had warded off the invasion of Louis Treat. And, of course, the father-son relationship is depicted as it often is in literature, as an archetypal battle. When Bo Mason berates Chet for wasting the whisky he had almost died to procure—"Will you please tell me why in the name of Christ you invited that God-damned windbag and all the rest of those sponges over here to drink up my whiskey?"—Chet declines to "defend himself." "The war was over," he says, taking the offensive. "I asked them over to celebrate."

Stegner employs a biting irony when the elder Mason invokes Christ and God in proclaiming his patriarchal right of property, for this family can be read as a figure for American society, oscillating as it does between nurturing generosity (feeding) and exploitation (eating). Chet selflessly hunts animals for the woman whose anemia requires meat; he unquestioningly acts as part of the community in donating bedding to the hastily constructed infirmary; he takes the initiative in donating milk that collects and that will go sour if not used. But he also luxuriates in the increased self-esteem he enjoys after selling the supposedly medicinal whisky for even more profit than his father expected to make. What the pestilence has done is to bring into sharp relief the contradictory elements intrinsic to American life. And as Chet crosses the line from youth to adulthood, he carries with him these conflicting reactions to the plague-created crisis:

> "People wanted [the whisky] for medicine," Chet said. "Should I've let them die with the flu? They came here wanting to buy it and I sold it. I thought that was what it was for."

His father articulates an older, but no less contradictory ethic that eschews price gouging: "'You didn't have any business selling anything,' he said. 'And then you overcharge people.'"

Stegner's ironic perspective on the relation of business to crisis appears reflected in one of the townspeople, Vickers, who comes to collect the bedding for the infirmary and stays to buy some whisky. As he and Chet negotiate the price of four dollars or four-fifty for a bottle, "Vickers's face was expressionless. 'Sure it isn't five? I wouldn't want to cheat you'." When Chet sets the price at four-fifty, Vickers buys twenty-seven dollars worth and asks with what is presumably both an approving and knowing laugh, "What are you going to do with that extra three dollars?" On a larger plane, the cost of things threatens to spill over into a major social problem, and one of the characters in the story recognizes that the community will be put to a test both as individuals and as a group concerning how far it is willing to go to help those left helpless by the death of the persons who were their support.

> He wouldn't be surprised if the destitute and friendless were found in every home in town, adopted and cared for by friends. They might have to build an institution to house the derelict and the bereaved.

Stegner is considered a regional writer, a describer of the American West compounded of raw nature and legend, the writer invoking and at the same time debunking traditional myths. The town in which the Masons reside is no Eden, but the image of an earlier paradise is implied when the same character worries that after the epidemic, "the town would never be the same." "Chip off the Old Block" employs images of a fall and of an expulsion, both of which inform the themes involved in Chet's maturity and his defense of his own disobedience when confronting a threateningly punitive patriarch, his father. Much later, in *Recapitulation,* Bruce Mason contemplates the search for a new Eden:

> But Paradise. . . . He feels that quiet back lawn of the city of his youth as a green sanctuary full of a remote peace. "Paradise is an Arab idea," he says. "Semitic, anyway. It's a garden, always a garden. They put a wall around it because that's

> how their minds work, they're inward-turning, not outward-turning."

"Paradise," he concludes, is, however, "safe, not exciting," like the "lawns of his youth." This nostalgia for security illuminates "Chip off the Old Block." It is out of the relative security of childhood that Chet is about to be thrust as he confronts the epidemic.

Chet, who "resolved to be a son his parents could be proud of," stands at a boundary not only between the world of children and that of adults, but also between a safety perhaps as illusory as paradise itself and adventure, symbolic of the promise that will be extinguished with his life. The boundaries that separate the ideal and the real are also those that separate nature from culture, and it is here that the story of the "boy constructor," the tale Chet writes for himself, picks up significance, for it is about the quest for a "lost city" of gold. Even Chet's title, "The Curse of the Tapajós," contains echoes of the punishment motif attached to the fall. First the young author "*hunts* up a promising locale" (emphasis added), which he finds in an uncivilized tributary of the Amazon. He then "created a tall, handsome young explorer and a halfbreed guide very like Louis Treat," the predator whom Chet runs out of the Mason family home with a gun. Later, when his fictional counterpart must not only dodge the snakes too "thick" (undoubtedly in both size and number) to handle, but also evade the half-breed guide "who was constantly trying to poison the flour or stab his employer in his tent at midnight," Chet begins to wonder at his own story and to ask himself "why the explorer didn't shoot the guide." Now Chet is stymied by his own tale, whose ending he cannot yet glimpse, and intuitively he collapses predators and infectious disease into a collective vision: "And then suddenly the explorer reeled and fell, mysteriously stricken, and the halfbreed guide, smiling with sinister satisfaction, disappeared quietly into the jungle."

The explorer, Chet's persona, probably refrains from killing the half-breed because of Chet's natural identification with the menacing guide (who may also be a figure of his father). Like Caliban, Louis Treat is an image of the wild man, neither pure nature nor assimilated to culture. Chet remembers what his father had told him, that "you could trust an Indian, if he was your friend, and you could trust a white man sometimes, if money wasn't involved, and you could trust a Chink more than either, but you couldn't trust a halfbreed." In this ethnic and ethical scale is laid out the history and the paradoxes of the American scene, a scale that, in a time of plague, picks up particularly disturbing reverberations. Nature, like Indians, could be trusted if its benign face was turned toward one (as it never is in a time of pestilence); and culture, in some high form, such as that represented by China, held out at least the possibility of a social ideal. Neither nature nor culture in their pure forms match the reality of America. In another Stegner short story, "The Chink," an inhabitant of the town in which the Mason boys live, Mah Li, is from the point of view of its inhabitants as much an "other" as if he were not human, "as much outside human society as an animal would have been." The narrator, this time Bruce Mason, tells how "I loved Mah Li as I loved [a] colt, but neither was part of the life that seemed meaningful at the time."

In a disquieting fashion, Stegner reveals the parallels between the supposedly civilized white man, who *sells* medicine, and the half-breed who tries to steal it. Like Caliban, who uses the language Prospero has taught him only to curse his master and wish a visitation of the Red Plague upon him, Chet's half-breed guide is associated with the "curse" of the Tapajós, slinking away as the explorer-hero is mysteriously stricken with illness. Chet has difficulty fathoming his own tale and its meaning:

> It was going to be hard to figure out how his hero escaped. Maybe he was just stunned, not killed. Maybe a girl could find him there, and nurse him back to health. . . .

Just as the expulsion from Eden is sometimes joined to the promise of a female redemptress with her heel on the neck of the deceitful serpent, so is the curse of the Tapajós and the jungle full of snakes mitigated by the healing presence of a young girl. This female function is exemplified, significantly, during the party to celebrate the end of the war, during which one of the guests makes two toasts, the first being to "those heroic laddies in khaki who looked undaunted into the eyes of death and saved this galorious empire from the rapacious Huns." It is only through aggression that men can achieve selfhood in the terms established by patriarchal culture, and at one point Chet revises his story and imagines that in the jungle there is a "beautiful and ragged girl, kept in durance vile by some tribe of pigmies or spider men or something," so that he would need to "rescue" her and "confound [her] captors." Consistent with such an image of female helplessness is the other toast, made to "those gems of purest ray serene, those unfailing companions on life's bitter pilgrimage, the ladies." The possible blurring of "laddies" and "ladies" paradoxically only serves to intensify the distinction made in the toasts.

In "Chip off the Old Block," the nurturing woman is Chet's mother, mediator between the boy and the fearsome patriarch, Bo Mason. Her role is echoed by another female character, Mrs. Chance, who in the face of Bo Mason's anger pulls her husband away from the party with a "quick pleading smile" that virtually epitomizes woman's function in the aggressively interactive world of men. But the importance of Chet's mother extends beyond the traditional parallels between the good mother archetype and the gentler side of human culture. In Stegner's story, the maternal figure also suggests an artistic ideal, although one more likely thwarted than fulfilled in time of plague. The relation of gender to the redeeming potentialities of language can only be apprehended, however, after recognizing communication itself to be one of Stegner's themes in "Chip off the Old Block."

By writing so much of what he only partially comprehends in his own story, Chet, as youthful author, represents the uncertainties of an authorial voice. In this way, Stegner may join Boccaccio and Poe in confronting the marginality of literature, Stegner perhaps formulating a new metaphor: the author as half-breed, inherently "other" in the practical world yet necessary because it is the coherence of language that bestows structure on the incoherence of events. The difficulties surrounding language become motifs woven through "Chip off the Old Block." For example, when Louis Treat faces Chet in his attempt to take the whisky away from the young boy by pretending he had been sent to fetch medicine for the community, he tries to reduce the struggle between them to one of mere language: "'We 'ave been sent,' Louis said; 'You do not understan' w'at I mean'"—to which Chet replies, "'I understand all right'." But Chet's composition, the story within Stegner's story, suggests that narrative can only struggle to comprehend and be comprehended. Chet will never develop sufficient self to grasp the possibilities of his own symbolic autobiography, which is probably why—to invoke Stegner's metaphors of disease—he will eventually succumb to infection. For he *is* a chip off the old block, and his life will end, as the passage from *Recapitulation* suggests, as an unfinished story.

"Chip off the Old Block" parodies the literary endeavor itself in the person of a character nicknamed Dictionary Chance because "he strung off such jaw-breaking words." He is described at one point as "voluble to the last," and it is he who takes upon himself the role of bombastic party speechmaker and who makes a defense of Chet's celebratory party when Bo Mason's son stands silent before his angry parent. A survivor of the flu himself, Chance had also brought Chet the frightening news that his father almost died as well as the reassuring news that Bo Mason did recover. Chance's connection with language points to how plague strikes at verbal communication itself, a theme that Camus insistently and profoundly explores in *The Plague*. Stegner, like the French author, creates a world in which surviving the influenza epidemic is as arbitrary as dying from it. That is why Dictionary Chance, whose name signifies not only a capricious universe but also the tenuous relationship of language to events, does not tell Chet his father is all right before he tells Chet that Bo Mason almost died: words can be as confused and confusing as events.

It is therefore only an added irony that Chance does not see matters this way and that there is a darker side to eloquence, for he depicts a world in which epidemics are part of some horrific moral order. Like a pompous preacher he instructs Chet to "mark [his] words" and heed his prophesy that the epidemic signals the decline of the town. Chet listens to Chance "tell [stories] about the Death Ward," but these prove to be moral exempla. On one side Chance tries to be kind to the young boy who is alone, tries to substitute as father, playing the part of good father in contrast to Bo Mason's wielding of power over his son. But all Chance really does is manipulate words for authority where the elder Mason is more likely to exploit the paternal role and the privilege he assumes with it.

Like some kind of hell-and-damnation preacher—he is described as dominating the Mason kitchen like an "evangelist"—Chance associates the pestilence with sin and punishment. Describing the horrors of the makeshift infirmary, he refers with disgust to a "hard to kill" townsman whose incontinence, the result of his illness, necessitated that his bed be cleaned six times a day.

> "I hesitate to say before the young what went on in that ward. Shameful, even though the man was sick." His tongue ticked against his teeth, and his eyebrows raised at Chet. "They cleaned his bed six times a day," he said, and pressed his lips together. "It makes a man wonder about God's wisdom," he said. "A man like that, his morals are as loose as his bowels."

Stegner's imagery involves not only language but also the mechanics of articulation as well as the gap between the mouth that moves and the silence that is always, in this story, ominous. Chet writes his story with "his lips together in connection"; he "gnawed his pencil" as a sign of his struggling over his tale of the Tapajós. Chance's tongue ticks against his teeth and he presses his lips together in a sign of moral disapproval when he describes the incontinent influenza patient. There is a distinction drawn between the party guests who imbibed Bo Mason's whisky and "smacked their lips" in noisy pleasure, and the "moment of complete silence" that follows Bo's return home and his obvious displeasure.

Although Chance's wife, elsewhere described as "incoherent" and portrayed at one point as crying "every time she spoke," protests against her husband's harsh view of the ill man, Chance wagers "that a man as loose and discombobulated as that doesn't live through this epidemic." It is telling that Chance's so-called eloquence should always hover on the verge of becoming a kind of verbal diarrhea: Bo Mason contemptuously dismisses him as a "windbag." At the same time, it is Chance whose dissonant volubility expresses the ambivalence of his community. He links the influenza epidemic, the "terrors of the plague," with the "dread plague of war," but it is only the former that he views in terms of a moral and social decline. As influenza attacks his microcosmic world, he envisions his town as irrevocably changed by the epidemic, a fallen place. His choice of words suggests equivocality: he "wouldn't be surprised" if the destitute were found in every home; the town "might" have to build institutions to house them. Bo Mason may be correct in repudiating Chance's verbiage, but his dismissal picks up disturbing intimations if it can be read as applicable to the narrative voice itself.

Having created a youthful persona whose use of language falls short of what in any event he can only imperfectly comprehend, a patriarch who almost deliberately surrounds himself with his family's silence, and a parody of the writer who distorts language because his own vision is sometimes clear and sometimes twisted, Stegner is hard pressed to create a model character who can uphold language, and—by extension—literature. In the end, he may have taken recourse to a device used by many male writers who wish to create a fictional perspective that is both within and outside the dominant society: he creates a symbol for literature out of the female voice.

At the beginning of "Chip off the Old Block," Chet has received his father's instructions, expressed negatively in terms of what his son should *not* do, as well as his mother's "words," a "solemn burden on his mind." Mrs. Mason is more than mother: she stands as a verbal intermediary between father and son, concerned to explain the husband who "didn't understand" his son and who in any event will not "admit he was wrong." As mediator, she hopes to close the gap that separates father from son. But the mother who can use language to break through silence must remain subordinate to the husband she must interpret and in effect give shape to. In contrast to Mrs. Chance's wordless tears, language is available to Chet's mother but the only time when she is named in the story she is called "Sis," a diminutive that reduces the matriarch to the role of another child. Ultimately, the only real metaphors available to the redemptive female are those of a man's world. It is his mother who metaphorically draws on a world of aggressors when she tells Chet to "hold the fort" while the family struggles with influenza.

"Chip off the Old Block," like its miniature analogue "The Curse of the Tapajós," ends inconclusively. Chet's parents are proud of him, but the tensions within the family are as unresolved as the fate of Chet's imagined hero-explorer; no one can see the direction of his or her personal narrative. In the end, Chet's experience with plague is that of an author for whom plot and language remain uncertain in a world embroiled in a persistent struggle to ward off micro- and macroparasites.

According to Crosby, *Pale Horse, Pale Rider* lacks attention outside of literature courses because "it is about a person undergoing a traumatic experience as the result of something most people do not recognize as having been of much importance: the 1918 pandemic of Spanish influenza." When the novella begins, Miranda experiences the first symptoms of flu; at the end, she emerges transformed as a person from a long bout with the illness. In between, as her headaches increase and she becomes convinced that something terrible and perhaps fatal is about to befall her, her increasingly tenuous connection to external reality brings into sharp relief her struggle for other kinds of survival. But even those likely to teach Porter's novella do not appear to view Miranda's illness as critical to a reading of it. Usually the disease is treated as but a metaphor: the "influenza epidemic is also, of course, the physical counterpart of the illness of society at war." As is true of Stegner's story, however, it is the coexistence of micro- and macroparsites that lends *Pale Horse, Pale Rider* its thematic intricacy and depth.

The structure of *Pale Horse, Pale Rider* can be described in two ways, one of them having to do with the external events surrounding Miranda's fight with influenza, the other with a series of dreams and visions, among them what Porter later described as the "Beatific Vision, the strange rapture that occurs, and maybe more often than we can ever know, just before death," a religious concept that has strong psychological significance for Miranda's attempt to achieve personal identity in the face of threats to her body and to her striving to maintain individuality. Miranda's delirium during the flu allows the reader the sense of experiencing a character's struggle for self-hood from within that place where the struggle is actually taking place, the unconscious. The perspectives of "Chip off the Old Block" and *Pale Horse, Pale Rider,* that is, are quite different. Stegner's young Chet projects his developing self onto the narrative he invents of the young explorer who falls stricken with a mysterious disease in a jungle he cannot imagine his way out of. Miranda's self remains internalized, persistently subjective. She too has visions of a jungle, a "writhing terribly alive and secret place of death," and part of the ambiguity surrounding her recovery from influenza, her sense that in being alive she had been "condemned" to the "dull world" whose efforts "to set her once more safely in the road . . . would [only] lead her again to death," has to do with whether she too is trapped in her symbolic jungle.

Miranda is a young journalist who with a female coworker named Towney (she writes the town gossip column) had once suppressed a story about a scandalous elopement in order to protect the reputation of a young woman and her family. When another paper was therefore able to scoop the story, Miranda was demoted from reporter to theater reviewer. Even her profession, that is, can be conceived of in terms of hostile invasions of people against others: the young woman who had attempted a flight to freedom is described as "recaptured." Miranda's unwillingness to participate in this mutual aggression makes her susceptible to attack: her illness is both real and historically based in the 1918 pandemic but also a sign of her alienation in her world. The very place in which she lives, an impersonal rooming house, can hardly be called home, nor can it promise another home to be shared with Adam, the young soldier who takes up a brief occupancy there until he is sent overseas to serve with the ground troops, his coming back a "returned hero" unlikely. Despite this unfriendly place in which they meet, however, Miranda and Adam try to escape the real world for the brief few days in which she pretends to hope. But it is difficult to maintain her illusions: "'I don't want to love,' she would think in spite of herself, 'not Adam, there is no time and we are not ready for it and yet this is all we have'." Their situation is glossed by Camus's *The Plague,* in which the narrator relates how "plague had gradually killed off in all of us the faculty" of love, "since love asks something of the future, and nothing was left us but a series of present moments." But even such precious moments are cut short when Miranda collapses with flu. It is Adam who nurses her through the night before she enters the hospital, perhaps contracting the illness in that time, for it is he who dies—not of war, but influenza. Miranda must face a life without her Ferdinand, not in the brave new world of Shakespeare's heroine, but in what she perceives to be a "world" in which there is "too much of everything" threatening and hostile. Wanting only to sit down and die, she can be contrasted with Miranda of *The Tempest,* and perhaps for this reason it is significant that she also wants to lose her memory and "forget [her] own name."

An important feature of *Pale Horse, Pale Rider* that sets it apart from other works of plague literature is that it is written by a woman about a woman. Miranda must not only establish her individual self in a world resistant to its development but also affirm a female identity. Gender plays an obviously important thematic part in the story, war particularly differentiating male and female roles. One of the characters, Miranda's coworker Chuck, is particularly important in this sense. His own lung disease disqualifies him for battle, a matter about which he is particularly defensive. It is he who vehemently protests against what he views as the feminization of war:

> "It was Florence Nightingale ruined wars. . . . What's the idea of petting soldiers and binding up their wounds and soothing their fevered brows? That's not war. Let 'em perish where they fall. That's what they're there for."

At the same time, from the male-dominated view of his own culture, Chuck exhibits sex role confusion. Miranda is demoted from reporter to a "routine female" job when she is made theater critic, the very position Chuck wants. And although he maintains a hard attitude toward a war he cannot fight in, in his own personal war with an alcoholic father, Chuck evidences the same kind of softness that had led Miranda to suppress the story of the elopement.

Meanwhile, Miranda's reluctant contribution to the war effort involves participation in areas filled with woman's work, such as rolling bandages, knitting socks and sweaters for the troops, visiting the wounded in hospitals, or attending social events in which, for example, women dance with lonely soldiers and generally provide companionship for them. When Towney is found knitting a rose-colored garment, Miranda asks her what soldier would be the recipient of this gift with such a sprightly (and, implicitly, decidedly feminine) color, to which Towney replies, "Like hell. . . . I'm making this for myself." In general, however, Towney does not allow this minor rebellion to interfere with her doing what was expected of a woman during the war. In contrast, Miranda's resistance presages a conflict with Adam had they ever had the time for their relationship to develop. Several examples could be cited, but one telling one should make the point clear. Adam knows very well that Miranda does not easily wear woman's role:

> "I can see you knitting socks," he said. "That would be just your speed. You know perfectly well you can't knit."
>
> "I do worse," she said, soberly; "I write pieces advising other young women to knit and roll bandages and do without sugar and help win the war."
>
> "Oh, well," said Adam, with the easy *masculine* morals in such questions, "that's merely your job, that doesn't count." (italics added)

The final ambiguity is hardly accidental. What does not count? That Miranda urges other women to knit rather than knitting herself, or her job, her source of her meager income but, nonetheless, her independence?

Miranda has been held to be typical of Porter's female protagonists in illustrating

> a basic psychological conflict . . . [between] a desire, on the one hand, for the independence and freedom to pursue art or principle regardless of social convention, and, on the other, a desire for the love and security inherent in the traditional roles of wife and mother.

Adam's death from influenza not only deprives Miranda of his love and the possibility of fulfilling such traditional roles, but it also, and perhaps more significantly, thwarts Miranda's ability to work through her ambivalence.

In an important letter, Porter responded to an essay about her work she professes to have loved but whose basic tenet she attacks thoroughly, rejecting both Freud himself and any Freudian theory (such as female penis envy) that would result in the idea that what Miranda wants in *Pale Horse, Pale Rider* is to be a man. It is, writes Porter,

> almost impossible for any woman to convince any man that this is false. . . . What [women] really want, I think, is not a change of sex, but a change of the limited conditions of their lives which have been imposed because of their sexual function. . . . A woman who knows how to be a woman not only needs and must have an active force of character and mind, but she has invariably, I have never known it to fail, an intense self-respect, precisely for *herself,* her attributes and functions as a female. . . . What she wants is the right *really* to be a woman, and not a kind of image doing and saying what she is expected to say by a man who is only afraid of one thing from her—that one day she will forget and tell him the truth!

Porter continues with a point quite significant for a reading of *Pale Horse, Pale Rider,* because it suggests that Adam's nursing of Miranda through their last night together may be the only ministering to her needs that he could ever really be capable of, his concern for her body's health, however tender, being another manifestation of the sexual desire that draws him to her. To provide in addition any essential support for her attempts to establish an autonomous female identity would require a transcendence of gender conflicts he could never achieve. Porter writes in the same letter,

> I know that when a woman loves a man, she builds him up and supports him and helps him in every possible way to live. . . . I never knew a man who loved a woman enough for this. He cannot help it, it is his deepest instinct to destroy, quite often subtly, insidiously, but constantly and endlessly, her very center of being, her confidence in herself as woman.

One of the poignant aspects of *Pale Horse, Pale Rider* is that Adam and Miranda seek to *know each other* during their brief time together. Again, a tender and caring person, Adam is nonetheless stereotypically masculine. He wants to be an engineer and does not read much beyond engineering textbooks. He loves driving his roadster very fast and sailing a boat. He would have preferred to be a pilot than part of the ground troops, but he had given in to his mother's hysterical fear, she, implicitly typical of a woman, not realizing that flying is safer than what he is fated to do.

During his talking about himself, "Miranda knew he was trying to tell her what kind of person he was when he had his machinery with him. She felt she knew pretty well what kind of person he was." But when he says he wants to know about her, her answer is significantly vague: "There's nothing to tell, after all, if it ends now, for all this time I was getting ready for something that was going to happen later, when the time came. So now it's nothing much." They are "two persons named Adam and Miranda," but he knows far better than she who he is. Her identity is less clear to her precisely because she is a woman. And when, during an "instant that was a lifetime," she is struck by "the certain, the overwhelming and awful knowledge that there was nothing at all ahead for Adam and for her," the insight may go beyond the war and the plague of influenza. In a work of fiction whose essential theme is *survival,* what is at risk for Miranda is that in any permanent union with Adam, she could not preserve a hard-won female identity.

It is survival itself that creates a thematic conjunction out of the historical coincidence of World War I and the influenza pandemic, both of which were conflated in the popular imagination. Plagues are often blamed by some people on others, who become scapegoats, as the Black Death was attributed to Jews who poisoned drinking water, or AIDS to female poisoners or white scientists committing genocide against black people. In *Pale Horse, Pale Rider,* influenza is discussed as an instance of germ warfare by the Germans against the Americans, the conversations betraying an insularity that ignores the prevalence of the illness throughout the world. The reportage is evocative of Defoe's account in his *Journal* of the kind of ignorant superstition the poor in particular were prone to. In Porter's work, a more sophisticated class becomes the carrier of rumors:

> "They *say,*" said Towney, "that it is really caused by germs brought by a German ship to Boston, a camouflaged ship, naturally, it didn't come in under its own colors." (italics added)

At first she pretends to think the report "ridiculous," but as she continues, the space between herself and the "they" whose beliefs she is reporting narrows:

> "They think the germs were sprayed over the city—it started in Boston, you know—and somebody reported seeing a strange, thick, greasy-looking cloud float up out of Boston Harbor and spread slowly all over that end of town. I think it was an old woman who saw it."

Miranda also absorbs the local folklore, for she too has merged in her conscious mind the plagues of war and influenza, tracing the start of her bad headache to the beginning of the war. Her doctor has a German-sounding name, Hildesheim, and while she is delirious in the hospital, the physician becomes transformed in her vision into a killer, "his face a skull beneath his German helmet, carrying a naked infant writhing on the point of his bayonet, and a huge stone pot marked Poison in Gothic letters." But for Miranda, the confrontation with an enemy other is also an extension of a widespread indifference shown by people to each other, fear of contagion during plague thus being merely a literalization of a prevalent human alienation. When Adam returns Miranda to her room after an evening together, she is surprised that he watches her up the stairs:

> Miranda hardly ever saw anyone look back after he had said good-by. She could not help turning sometimes for one glimpse more of the person she had been talking with, as if that would save too rude and too sudden a snapping of even the lightest bond. But people hurried away, their faces already changed, fixed, in their straining towards their next stopping place, already absorbed in planning their next act or encounter.

It is only an additional irony that Miranda's focal point for a generalized social paranoia, Dr. Hildesheim, should be the one to preserve the life about which she is so ambivalent but which she cannot give up. Miranda's drive for physical survival is portrayed at the beginning of the story in the first of her visionary experiences—this one in a dream. It is here that she appears as the rider on a pale horse engaged in a race against another rider—death—that she is determined to win: "I'm not going with you this time—ride on!" When she thinks of the miracle of meeting Adam, it is in terms of their being "alive and on the earth at the same moment." The two of them engage in conversation about their health, for example the dangers of smoking, and Miranda is filled with wonder that despite the perils of war he faces in just a few days, he "looked so clear and fresh, and he had never had a pain in his life," not knowing, of course, that this is precisely the profile of the person attacked most violently by the influenza. In contrast, she, whose way of life involved "unnatural hours, eating casually at dirty little restaurants, drinking bad coffee all night, and smoking too much," strives successfully during her illness "to keep her small hold on the life of human beings . . . no matter what," to the point that she cannot submit to her beatific vision of pure being, instead living to join the "dead and withered things that believed themselves alive."

But the struggle merely to exist goes beyond Miranda's health, for her entire life is engaged

> in a continual effort to bring together and unite firmly the disturbing oppositions in her day-to-day existence, where survival, she could see clearly, had become a series of feats of sleight of hand.

At one point she asks Adam, "Don't you love being alive?" But there is something hysterical in the question, because for Miranda, being alive is to engage in the unremitting effort to remain fit enough to live, the "disturbing oppositions" in her life being not only the conflict between herself and her environment but also the conflict between her instinct for survival and a very pronounced death wish. Part of Miranda's struggle has to do with her resistance to the forms of society, supposedly constructed to insure individual survival but inevitably antithetical to the self's endeavor to preserve itself.

That is, the social contract is as thematically important to *Pale Horse, Pale Rider* as it is to Defoe's *Journal of a Plague Year*. In theory, the contract is an antithesis to chaos and a reference point for civic duty, which is itself a possible antidote to a person's alienating fear of others in the world. In times of plague—as has already been argued—the tensions in the social contract emerge to disclose the separateness of human beings, fear of contagion—again—literalizing an essential antipathy toward others, or, at best, a drive toward self-preservation that under stress alienates even well-meaning individuals. But whereas works such as Defoe's *Journal* affirm the viability of the social contract, *Pale Horse, Pale Rider* looks at it from the opposite point of view. The collective itself becomes a macroparasite against which the individual needs protection. It is interesting in this regard to note David Richter's suggestion that the name of Miranda's "respectable and suspicious" landlady is Miss Hobbe, for in this work in which names are so important, the landlady's name

> recalls that of the seventeenth-century English philosopher, Thomas Hobbes, who postulated that man originally inhabited no peaceful Eden, but a land of perpetual warfare, where every man's hand was against every man, and where life was "solitary, poor, nasty, brutish, and short."

Richter's suggestion reinforces the parallels between Miss Hobbe's rooming house and the state whose preservation was the point of the Hobbesian conception of the social contract. For although the good of the individual is inferred by the agreement people enter into for mutual protection, individual needs rarely prevail. When, for example, Miranda asks for better curtains than the thin ones that do not adequately keep the light out of her room in the morning, she is promised new ones that do not, however, appear. And when Miss Hobbe learns that Miranda has influenza, she orders the ill woman back to bed immediately, not for Miranda's good but for the protection of herself and her other tenants. She is determined that Miranda be sent to the hospital without delay, and protests,

> I tell you, they must come for her *now*, or I'll put her on the sidewalk. . . . I tell you, this is a plague, a plague, my God, and I've got a houseful of people to think about!

That Miss Hobbe's house cannot support itself, that is, "was not paying," may symbolize the precariousness of the state based on the social contract, whose initial premise is the war of all against all. Only the force of punishment (a symbolic as well as real eviction) can guarantee the conformity of a person to the requirements of the group and preserve the abstract whole.

In Miranda's delirious vision, the hospital becomes a place to which criminals are sent, the plague a crime rather than the traditional punishment for one, and the health care workers "executioners" in league with death itself. The old man in the next bed who dies of influenza appears to her a pitiable criminal being dragged away protesting that the "crime of which he was accused did not merit the punishment he was about to receive." In her delirium, Miranda conflates original sin, the fruits of which are plague and death, with the unknown sin of the individual against an order from which the person is essentially alienated. As the "executioners" advance, the

> soiled cracked bowls of the old man's hands were held before him beseechingly as a beggar's as he said, "Before God I am not guilty," but they held his arms and drew him onward, passed, and were gone.

Miranda and Towney are very conscious of punishments meted out in a world in which individual initiative is discouraged. When they had suppressed the news story of the elopement (a symbol of personal choice whose punishment was to be public scandal), they had been virtually court-martialed, their ranks broken. Having "taken their punishment together, [they] had been degraded publicly to routine female jobs." This juxtaposition of punishment and gender creates an added level to the conflict between individual and society, here disclosed as a confrontation between the female condemned and the patriarchal sentencer. Miranda, as already noted, comes out of her bout with influenza to think of herself as "condemned" to live.

The male representatives of the persecuting and prosecuting state are both insignificant and powerfully insidious—

the Liberty Bond salesmen. Miranda's fear is that she will be punished for her failure to buy one. Richter has pointed out that "the name of the bond is an irony Porter did not have to invent." In terms of a social contract, there is additional irony attached to the word *bond* (which Porter later uses to describe the weak relationship Miranda has to the men who return her after a date to her rooming house). The war against Germany presumably represents a solely external threat, the war bond drive the intended mutual cooperation of American citizens to win that war. Instead, those in charge of selling bonds engage in internal warfare, become the aggressors, another group of invading macroparasites against which Miranda feels as helpless as against war and influenza. The man who issues unspecified threats if she does not purchase a bond is an apt candidate for Hobbes's nasty and brutish human being, an enemy attacker or criminal in the war against his own kind: he had a stony stare, "really viciously cold, the kind of thing you might expect to meet behind a pistol in a deserted corner." Miranda and he face each other as enemies, one of them trying in self-protection to avoid the inevitable confrontation. "Usually she did not notice [him and his partner] at all until their determination to be seen was greater than her determination not to see them." It is only a sardonic feature of this symbolic military engagement that her antagonists invoke the common struggle in which supposedly they are all embattled as part of their attack: "We're having a war, and some people are buying Liberty Bonds and others just don't seem to get around to it." Miranda remains "desperately silent," trying to decide on some tactical defense, her words to herself creating an ambiguity about just which battle she is contemplating:

> [Miranda] thought, "Suppose I were not a coward, but said what I really thought? Suppose I said to hell with this filthy war?"

The entire world of *Pale Horse, Pale Rider* seems made up of macroparasites. Miranda thinks about the invasion of her private territory at work: "reminded of the way all sorts of persons sat upon her desk at the newspaper office," she wonders "*why* won't they sit in the chair?" Her job as theater reviewer breaks out as another kind of war, one in which she is both aggressor and attacked. Her reviews of performers are, she realizes, an assault not only on their performances but also on their selves, and she wishes they did not care what she thought. It is when she understands how badly she has hurt someone with a review that she decides, in a weary gesture of identification, that she wishes to die. The object of her review, in turn, says he is "going to take the goof who wrote that piece up the alley and bop him in the nose." When he actually threatens physical violence, he is driven off by Miranda's friends as if repulsed in battle, but not until his own bellicosity is revealed. A seeming antithesis to this pitiable figure turns out to be as pathetic but also insidiously macroparasitic. This is Chuck's alcoholic father, who "beamed upon [his son] with the bleared eye of paternal affection while he took his last nickel." Porter's story shares with Stegner's the image of the universal food chain, as Miranda describes another bond salesman: "Just another nasty old man who would like to see the young ones killed; . . . the tom-cats try to eat the little tom-kittens, you know." In such a world only survival counts. It is because Chuck cannot fight the war and therefore need not live through it (although, ironically, he has to worry about his lung disease) that it ceases to mean anything to him: "I don't care how [the war] started or when it ends. . . . I'm not going to be there."

But among the different kinds of survival dealt with in *Pale Horse, Pale Rider,* survival of the individual self prevails as that under which all other survivals are subsumed. That Porter is portraying Miranda's striving toward selfhood is a point about which most Porter critics agree. Robert Penn Warren contends that there is in the story a "paradoxical problem of definition," a "delicate balancing of rival considerations." Philip Yannella has given Miranda's conflicts an historical context, noting that 1918 was a "crucial year in the history of modern selfhood" and that Porter's novella makes some "acute observations about the attrition of nineteenth-century definitions of selfhood, the development of the twentieth-century self, and the failure of the twentieth-century self to establish suitable patterns of behavior." Thus, according to Thomas Walsh, influenza does not so much cause Miranda's despair as bring "to the surface" what already "lay submerged in her character." The specific rooting of Miranda's problem in her southern origins is added by James Johnson, who says that in Porter's fiction is found the theme of the "individual within [her] heritage." Related themes are cultural displacement and, finally, a slavery to nature and "subjugation to a human fate" that dooms a Porter character to "suffering and disappointment."

But the quest for self in *Pale Horse, Pale Rider* exists as a theme very much as Miranda herself exists, on "multiple planes" of being. But "planes" is perhaps inadequate to Porter's own purposes as Miranda experiences "tough filaments of memory and hope pulling taut backwards and forwards holding her upright between them." Her predicament is more complex than such an image suggests, involving paradoxes whose elements are difficult to separate. As Richter points out, for Miranda "to summon the will to live that will enable her to survive her illness, she must detach herself from all the values that have given her life meaning and, though she ultimately survives, she pays a price that may not be worth the empty life she regains." Miranda is transformed from a potentially loving young woman to one who subsists on her own indifference. What can be inferred from Richter's argument is that *Pale Horse, Pale Rider* addresses the difficult philosophical issue of just what survives in survival. The novella, that is, raises the body-mind problem. Porter is not, of course, a systematic philosopher, and the problem is depicted not through logical analysis but through the images and visions that make up Miranda's conscious and unconscious responses to both body and mind.

One result of Miranda's illness is that it allows her out-of-body experiences. While she lies ill in the rooming house, she has one of her visions, imagining herself sailing into a jungle that—it has already been noted—represents death. The jungle probably also represents her unconscious, in which unformulated terrors and her persistently resisted death wish are revealed. The language of her vision includes words and phrases such as "screaming," "bellow of voices all crying together," "a writhing terribly alive and secret place of death," "danger, danger, danger," and "war, war, war." Miranda's reaction is not to recoil, however, but eagerly to meet these dangers, and in a moment of dissociation one part of her observes the other:

> Without surprise, watching from her pillow, she saw herself run swiftly down this gangplank to the slanting deck, and standing there, she leaned on the rail and waved gaily to herself in bed, and the slender ship spread its wings and sailed away into the jungle.

Later, in the hospital, Miranda experiences a more intense form of dissociation, the struggle between a death instinct and the will to survive described in an image of fission:

> Her mind, split in two, acknowledged and denied what she saw in the one instant, for across an abyss of complaining darkness her reasoning coherent self watched the strange frenzy of the other coldly, reluctant to admit the truth of its visions, its tenacious remorses and despairs.

It is at this point that she approaches what Porter was to call her beatific vision, which Miranda responds to "with serene rapture as if some promise made to her had been kept long after she had ceased to hope for it." What she envisions are "pure identities," without material bodies (although, of course, Porter must use the language of bodies to describe them) and without the conflicts that can result in a mind that "split in two."

> Their faces were transfigured, each in its own beauty, beyond what she remembered of them, their eyes were clear and untroubled as good weather, and they cast no shadows. They were pure identities and she knew them every one without calling their names or remembering what relation she bore to them.

The Miranda thinks she knows them is susceptible to several explanations, but clearly they correspond to very deep wishes on her part to be free of the "disturbing oppositions" that engage her in her unremitting struggle merely to exist. That her visions are "pure identities" means of course that they are free of personal identity, for it is the survival of her individual self that causes Miranda the most difficulty. What Georges Rey says in his essay "Survival" supplies an interesting commentary on *Pale Horse, Pale Rider,* supplying it with the philosophical context it evokes. Rey writes that the "possibility of an *entirely* disembodied, yet still somehow *personal, existence* seems simply capricious: idle 'image mongery.'"

> We are led, then, both by the presuppositions and by the failure of a purely psychological criterion, to our bodies. We were really led there already by considerations of the causal basis of our survival at a given time. . . . We might have been led there independently by even a casual inspection of the notion of a person: whatever the details, such creatures consist at least of a complex of capacities, abilities, dispositions; and, as such, as many writers have rightly insisted, they cannot float about somehow unanchored in space and time.

And, indeed, through the ministering of doctors and nurses as well as through the tenacity of her own will, Miranda comes out of her ecstasy and, as John Donne's famous poem describes the ecstatic out-of-body experience, *descends* to her body.

The body supplies *Pale Horse, Pale Rider* with much of its imagery, for Porter is always specific about the concrete details of her characters' physical existence in their environment. Miranda's conflict is as immaterial as the mind itself, but her emotional withdrawal from a hopeful commitment to her world is described in specifically physical terms: "her hardened, indifferent heart shuddered in despair at itself, because before it had been tender and capable of love." Earlier her body had been foreign to her. She had even asked herself, "Do I even walk about in my own skin or is it something I have borrowed to spare my modesty?" Adam's very health causes her to think of his body as a monster, an image she also evokes for herself, but from a different emotional perspective, Miranda being estranged from her body whereas Adam is comfortable in his. In the hospital, Miranda experiences not relief but entrapment when she recovers from influenza, thinking how

> The body is a curious monster, no place to live in, how could anyone feel at home there? Is it possible I can ever accustom myself to this place? . . . Miranda looked about her with the covertly hostile eyes of an alien who does not like the country in which he finds himself.

For Adam, it is the body that is tantamount to personal identity. When Miranda, who is profoundly depressed by the war, tells him that it is what war "does to the mind and the heart" that is so awful, adding, "you can't separate these two—what it does to them is worse than what it can do to the body," Adam pragmatically replies, "The mind and the heart sometimes get another chance, but if anything happens to the poor old human frame, why, it's just out of luck, that's all." Richter points out that the tragic ending to *Pale Horse, Pale Rider* rests on the irony that "contrary to what Adam thinks, the body may well 'get another chance,' but the heart and mind, once altered, are changed forever." This is perhaps another way to say that for Adam philosophical issues of personal identity are not important, whereas for Miranda they had been critical. She has, in short, resolved the problem of survival by, in the end, adopting Adam's view and abandoning the quest for self-definition. The body that was once alien to her because she sought an identity that was more than it alone could supply is now all she has—or wants.

Richter's argument that Miranda summons the will to survive at the expense of the values she had lived by—that is, in effect, by abandoning that self that is more than just body—touches on another plane of meaning in *Pale Horse, Pale Rider*. The story is illuminated by a concept of selfhood that comes from self psychologist Douglas Detrick, who parallels the tension between the individual and the group with the historical evolution of the unconscious:

> I believe that until the modern era, the archetypal collective unconscious organization was more or less adequate for humans both in the cultural and personal domain. However, this organization was slowly undermined over the last two millennia by the expansion of the personal unconscious.

Among the forces that Miranda must ward off to preserve her personal identity are the archetypes that make up her heritage. According to Robert Penn Warren, Miranda's final insights become her personal myth, and she "must live by her own myth. But she must earn her myth in the process of living." Such a reading may, however, be too optimistic, for the dual plagues of war and influenza may indicate that in her culture, Miranda must learn to live without myths.

If, as Thomas Loe contends, Miranda's visionary experiences involve a symbolic "journey of initiation, necessarily internal," then Miranda is on an archetypal quest to free herself of archetypes. The very opening of the story reveals the tension between the constraints of a heritage and the striving of the individual. In Miranda's first dream, a sign of the onset of influenza, she "knew she was in her bed, but not the bed she had lain down in" earlier. She was in a "room she had known somewhere," and she feels the need to get up, to leave while some unknown *they* "are all quiet." But she cannot at first find her (again, vaguely described) "things," that which is hers alone: "Things have a will of their own in this place and hide where they like." An ambivalent fondness for and rejection of those who crowd upon her, her past and still too much a part of her present, become mixed up with images of death and survival, illustrating Detrick's concept of a struggle between the archetypal and personal unconscious:

> Faces will beam, asking, Where are you going, What are you doing, What are you thinking, How do you feel, Why do you say such things, What do you mean? . . . How I have loved this house in the morning before we are all awake and tangled together like badly cast fishing lines. Too many people have been born here, and have wept too much here, and have laughed too much, and have been too angry and outrageous with each other here. Too many have died in this bed already, there are far too many ancestral bones propped up on the mantelpieces, there have been too damned many antimacassars in this house, she said loudly, and oh, what accumulation of storied dust never allowed to settle in peace for one moment.

The passage seems almost an extension of sections in *Old Mortality* in which Miranda, who had when too young entered into an unfortunate marriage (this is not mentioned in *Pale Horse, Pale Rider*), visits her southern home:

> "Ah, the family," [her cousin Eva] said, releasing her breath and sitting back quietly, "the whole hideous institution should be wiped from the face of the earth. It is the root of all human wrongs." . . . [Miranda] felt a vague distaste for seeing cousins. She did not want any more ties with this house, she was going to leave it, and she was not going back to her husband's family either. . . . She knew now why she had run away to marriage, and she knew that she was going to run away from marriage, and she was not going to stay in any place with anyone that threatened to forbid her making her own discoveries, that said "No" to her.

And yet Miranda asks in *Pale Horse, Pale Rider* about that which anchors her in a concrete world of familiar realities her grandfather, great-aunt, cousins, a decrepit hound, and silver kitten "What else besides them did I have in the world?" When she thinks she is going to die, she wonders if she should go home: "It's a respectable old custom to inflict your death on the family if you can manage it."

One way to define the conflict in Miranda's relationship with Adam is to realize that he represents a series of archetypes, whereas she struggles to free herself of the archaic organization of her world. They are, as earlier noted, two persons *named* Adam and Miranda. As Adam's name suggests, he is the first man, an original (Richter points out the significance of his surname, *bar*-clay). Like Adam in Genesis, Adam Barclay is doomed to fall, "not for any woman, being beyond experience already, committed without any knowledge or act to his own death." He is also archetypally American, a Protestant (Miranda is Catholic), as well as a model for the American soldier. "He was wearing his new uniform [which is custom made to fit him exactly], and he was all olive and tan and tawny, hay colored and sand colored from hair to boots." Stereotypically masculine, he is one of those concerned that wearing a wristwatch (as soldiers had to) would make him a sissy. But he is also a figure of the saintly martyr, and in one of Miranda's visions, they are both shot through with arrows of death, he perishing while she is cheated of this release. Perceived by Miranda to be pure, "all the way through, flawless, complete, as the sacrificial lamb must be," he represents all the soldiers that were to die at the front. And only a few words later, she hopes they "don't come to a mud puddle," for he will carry her over it like the archetypical courtier.

Not that Adam wears his archetypes comfortably. He is described as "infinitely buttoned, strapped, harnessed into a uniform as tough and unyielding in cut as a strait jacket." But then, that is the point about past heritages: in their repressiveness they are never easy to bear. But only Miranda seems to know this. Her very name—borrowed from Shakespeare—promises her release from the burden of her past, represented in part by cousins named Eva and Maria. In these names, of course, are the most basic Western archetypes of woman, the temptress and the redemptress, the one causing the fall, the other the archetype of the good mother who redeems the world after the sin of her counterpart. But Shakespeare had created in *The Tempest* not only the possibility of a brave new world but also a woman free of the archetypal dichotomies implied by Eve and Mary: Miranda, innocent and uncorrupted to the end. To repeat a passage already quoted, it is when Porter's Miranda can no longer bear the world she lives in and wants only to sit down and die that she despairingly says, "I wish I could lose my memory and forget my own name." Shakespeare's Miranda will remain free of Caliban and the Red Plague with which he curses her father; Porter's Miranda will succumb to pestilence. When she emerges from her physical crisis, there will be no "more war, no more plague" but also, in the most profound sense, no more Miranda.

It is therefore quite significant that it is Towney who comes to the hospital when Miranda is ready to be released, and that at this point Porter's reader is reminded of Towney's real name, Mary Townsend. And it is as Mary that Miranda addresses her, longing for some spiritual anchor in the world that she can no longer provide for herself: "Do you suppose, Mary . . . I could have my old room back again?" Mary reassures her that her possessions had been stored with Miss Hobbe, a symbolic confirmation that Miranda has given up striving for individuation. And when the nurse informs her that the taxi that will take her away from the hospital is waiting, "there was Mary. Ready to go."

Interpretations of the conclusion to *Pale Horse, Pale Rider* vary from the extremely pessimistic, to the neutral or mildly hopeful, to the affirmation of Miranda's spiritual rebirth. The story does end with a validation of Eudora Welty's conviction that time is the critical theme in Porter's fiction: the last sentence reads, "Now there would be time for everything"—even, supposedly, time for Miranda to begin again to recreate her self, although Porter critics frequently point out that *Pale Horse, Pale Rider* is the last of the author's Miranda stories. But, in fact, time did play an important part in this piece of fiction that has its roots in Porter's own struggle to survive influenza during the pandemic of 1918. For after almost twenty years, Porter turned her bout with an almost fatal illness into the work considered her masterpiece. Interestingly enough, she writes in a letter to Robert Penn Warren that she is searching for another title; but the title she retained after obvious contemplation may supply *Pale Horse, Pale Rider* with its most obvious hopefulness.

On the night before she enters the hospital, Miranda tells Adam she knows "an old spiritual," which she begins to recite: "Pale horse, pale rider, done taken my lover away." He responds that he had heard it sung by the black workers in Texas oil fields, and reminds her that there are "about forty verses, the rider done taken away mammy, pappy, brother, sister, the whole family besides the lover." Miranda corrects him:

> "But not the singer, not yet," said Miranda. "Death always leaves one singer to mourn. 'Death,'" she sang, "'oh, leave one singer to mourn—.'"

This image of an enduring art that in its own way recreates the world can be found in *Old Mortality,* in which Miranda and her cousin Maria attend concerts and theaters to discover that there

> was then a life beyond a life in this world, as well as in the next; such episodes confirmed for the little girls the nobility of human feeling, the divinity of man's vision of the unseen, the importance of life and death, the depths of the human heart, the romantic value of tragedy.

There are correspondence between this passage and Porter's description of a transcendent beatific vision. And while there is nothing romantic about influenza in *Pale Horse, Pale Rider,* there is in it an expression of the romantic value of tragedy, the word *tragedy* itself inferring not only a catastrophic event but also its rendering through an artistic genre. Like the monument to the surviving singer in "Pale Horse, Pale Rider," that is, the spiritual itself, Porter's novella is a testament to that which can survive even plague, that for which there might always be time, perhaps even enduring through time—the literature of plague.

AIDS IN LITERATURE

Michael Denneny

SOURCE: "AIDS Writing and the Creation of a Gay Culture," in *Confronting AIDS Through Literature: The Responsibilities of Representation*, edited by Judith Laurence Pastore, University of Illinois Press, 1993, pp. 36-54.

[*In the following essay, Denneny views AIDS as a catastrophic event of central importance to both gay literature and social history.*]

In the Preface to *The Birth Of The Clinic* Michel Foucault writes: "It may well be that we belong to an age of criticism whose lack of a primary philosophy reminds us at every moment of its reign and its fatality: an age of intelligence that keeps us irremediably at a distance from an original language. . . . We are doomed historically to history, to the patient construction of discourses about discourses and to the task of hearing what has already been said."

It is perhaps unfair to continue an argument with a man after he is dead, but it is increasingly necessary and I doubt Foucault would have minded, especially considering the gusto he displayed in late night discussions about this issue of primary discourse in our time, specifically the emergence of the possibility of such a thing as gay culture and its corollary, gay literature. I would not presume to try to reproduce Foucault's subtle—and, to my mind, shifting—position on this topic; for my part, this despair about primary discourse seemed to me a result of the commanding position the academic mind has achieved in our culture, reigning over the recording and evaluation of the activity of intelligence in general. The academic mind, I argued, looks out and sees reflections of itself and its interior processes, not the world as it is happening around us. We are doomed not historically but academically to the patient construction of discourses about discourses, to the task of hearing what has already been said. History dooms us to something else altogether.

Acknowledging the enormous loss to this discussion caused by Foucault's death from AIDS, I would like to try to extend this argument to the extraordinary surge of writing that has been occasioned by the advent of the AIDS epidemic, acts of primary discourse whose nature, depth, and value seem to me in danger of being obscured by the natural bent of the academic mind. It is noticeable that secondary discourses about AIDS—how the media speaks when it speaks about AIDS, studies of the metaphors used in AIDS discussions—naturally float to the surface of academic journals or serve as the occasion for thematic issues, while the primary acts of speech uttered in confrontation with the thing itself are neglected or misunderstood.

What history dooms us to is the shock of events, happenings that break over us and challenge the human spirit to give back an answer—"answering back the hammer-blows of Fortune," in the words of the final chorus of the *Antigone.* This urge to answer back, to declare one's presence even at the cost of acknowledging the original blow to the spirit, lies at the very heart of what we mean by culture, that shared collection of individual acts of the spirit that articulate who we are and how we find ourselves in this life.

History dooms us to the shock of events, and an epidemic is a historical event, the unleashing of an infectious—in this case, lethal—disease in a population. AIDS is not a condition to be managed, like high blood pressure or poverty. AIDS is not just a disease, like cancer or sickle-cell anemia. AIDS is not a chronic medical state, like diabetes—though it may become one. AIDS in our time is an *event,* a calamity, like a forest fire, like the blitz of London. AIDS is an epidemic and an epidemic is an event.

More precisely, an epidemic is the occurrence of death as a social event. Usually death is one of the most individualizing and private experiences a person can undergo. But death is sometimes a social event, a shared reality; it was so in the trenches of World War I, in the gas chambers of Auschwitz, in the killing fields of Cambodia. When death becomes a social event, the individual death is both robbed of its utter privacy and uniquely individual meaning and simultaneously amplified with the resonance of social significance and historical consequence. When death is a social event, both the individual *and the community* are threatened with irreparable loss.

An epidemic is a shared social disaster played out on the bodies of the afflicted. AIDS, of course, is not a gay disease. But, given the means of transmission, AIDS managed to gain momentum and achieve epidemic force first in the gay community. As John Preston has said, "AIDS is not a gay disease. . . . It is, however, a catastrophe for gay men." Although it has ravaged other individuals (hemophiliacs, transfusion recipients) and diverse social groups (Haitians, Africans, IV drug users and, through them, the mostly black and Hispanic inner-city underclass, and—soon—American teenagers), it was the happenstance of history that the disease should first achieve epidemic proportions in the gay community. This was to have severe consequences both for the world and for the gay community. The world, motivated by a disastrous combination of prejudice, vicious self-righteousness, murderous indifference to the fate of a group mistakenly thought to be "other," and massive, panicked denial, ignored the problem and blindly allowed the epidemic to get out of control, with grim consequences that have not even begun to be perceived, much less tallied. For the gay community, it meant that the AIDS epidemic was to become the central fact of its history at this moment, as elemental an event for this fledgling community as the Holocaust was for Jews all over the world.

I

It is clear now that the history of the liberated gay community in America is divided into two phases. First was the original act of constitution as a self-acknowledged community, initiated by the Stonewall Riots in June 1969 and unfolded in the seventies when a vast act of social transformation reshaped the lives and attitudes of millions of Americans—a social event of such magnitude that it can only be compared to the half-century-old civil rights movement—but which has characteristically received virtually no attention from our so-called social scientists. The second phase commenced with the advent of the AIDS epidemic at the beginning of the eighties, an event that threatened to destroy this community both physically and spiritually.

The initial shock at this dawning social disaster was compounded by the peculiar relations of the gay community to the surrounding society, which has always favored resounding silence as the most effective means of gay repression. Thus, when gay men found themselves in the middle of a social catastrophe, found themselves and their friends wasting away from an unknown but clearly rapidly spreading disease, their panic was compounded by the hostility of the Reagan political regime, the indifference of the national medical establishment, and the virtual silence of the media. The shameful silence of the *New York Times,* the nation's self-proclaimed "newspaper of record" as well as the hometown paper for the city that was the epicenter of this catastrophe, left gay New Yorkers in a near schizophrenic situation: on the one hand, friends were falling ill left and right, life became a surrealistic series of medical disasters, hospital vigils, and memorial services; on the other hand, everyday life went on as if nothing were happening, the media were nearly silent, and straight friends and co-workers, going about their normal lives, seemed to be living on some other planet. "It was as if a war was going on in our city," said William M. Hoffman, "and half the city was in rubble, but people weren't mentioning it."

Piling the insult of silence on top of the grotesque injuries wreaked by AIDS left the gay community in a state of political confusion and spiritual despair, for the impact of any social disaster is mute until it is articulated in words, reflected in the imagination. Only then do we realize what is happening to us; only when we can relive in the imagination what has happened to us in life does it become real for us. As Hannah Arendt observed, "The impact of factual reality, like all other human experiences, needs speech if it is to survive the moment of experience, needs talk and communication with others to remain sure of itself." It is for precisely this reason that gay writers became pivotal players in the second act of gay history.

During the first decade of gay liberation, the community itself seemed to undergo a process of spontaneous transubstantiation: when the drag queens and the boys in the bars initiated it all by fighting back, it was as if a signal went out, heard by all, calling everyone to the colors. The process of transformation ignited everywhere, and the enormously complex act of redefinition—sexually, politically, morally, psychologically, interpersonally, spiritually—was spontaneous, decentralized, and multiple. Something akin to Nietzsche's "transvaluation of all values" was happening all over the place. This enormous ferment unleashed in 1969 gained velocity during the seventies, creating new social spaces, new relationships, new institutions, even new sexual acts, and igniting the imaginations of the first generation of gay writers, who emerged in the late seventies avid to reflect in their writing these fundamental changes that were already clearly sweeping through our lives.

With the advent of AIDS in the early eighties a new and heavier task fell to the writers: the job of sounding the alarm, mobilizing the community both politically and spiritually, delineating the shape of this disaster breaking over us, and initiating the discourse of AIDS in the face of the silence of the national media and institutionalized medicine. It is notable that it was a gay newspaper, *The New York Native,* that first announced the existence of this disease—before the Centers for Disease Control did—by insisting that a handful of cases of a rare cancer must be connected to the unheard-of pneumonia that was striking people down. It was Larry Kramer's famous 1983 essay in the *Native,* "1,112 and Counting" which swept away the confusion and mobilized gay people from one end of the American continent to the other.

Taken completely by surprise, enraged and demoralized by what seemed like a malevolent symbolism in a disease that not only appeared to target gay men but that seemed to zero in on sexual activity, the locus of most of the hard-won liberation of the previous decade, the gay community reeled. One of the first to confront the panic, conflict, and grief that the sudden appearance of this new and almost unbelievable disease engendered was William Hoffman in his play *As Is.* "Personally, I was trying to cope with the death of friends—four in particular at the time—and the illness around me," he said. At almost the same time, Larry Kramer, furious at the inaction of the gay community, the medical establishment, and political "leaders" from city hall to the White House, took to the stage with *The Normal Heart,* an intensely political play that rang out with a stinging indictment of official indifference and a near-maddened call to arms.

As the epidemic expanded, as more people fell ill and died, as visits to the hospital and the funeral home became regular, if bizarre, social occasions for gay men, the community moved into life in the war zone. Like other gay men in major urban areas, gay writers spent an increasing amount of time caring for the ill; confronted by the epidemic every which way they turned, it began to seem the only serious thing to write about. Robert Ferro's novel *Second Son* was written while the author, ill himself, was caring for his dying lover, and published only months before his own death from AIDS. In his novel *Valley of the Shadow,* Christopher David sought to present the human reality behind the impersonal—and increasingly frequent—obituaries of young gay men appearing in the newspapers. This first-person fiction was a courageous act of imagination and sustained with remarkable beauty a clear-eyed depiction of the grief, loss, and love that would soon become common throughout the gay world.

Randy Shilts, determined to set down the objective record so long ignored by the media, produced *And the Band Played On,* a massive, relentless, hypnotic, and epic narrative of the first five years of the AIDS epidemic that laid bare the unfolding politics and history of this disaster with such persuasive force and detailed accumulation of fact that the book itself became a political event. Paul Monette, seeking to make personal sense of the holocaust that had swept over his life, wrote

Borrowed Time, in which he etched with passion and anger the impact of AIDS on two lovers, while his great poem cycle, *Love Alone,* raised a shattering paean to the death of a whole generation of gay men, "the story that endlessly eludes the decorum of the press."

George Whitmore learned of his own illness while writing *Someone Was Here,* a book of personal reportage in which he managed, before his death, to show people with AIDS (PWAs) as the concrete individuals they were, not just statistics and categories, and not just gay men. At the same time, his friend Victor Bumbalo was working on *Adam and the Experts*, a play about their friendship during the crisis. "Writing the play was a painful experience," Bumbalo told an interviewer, "but also very, very cathartic."

"Did you have to wait a long time after your friend died to be able to write it?" he was asked.

"No, he was alive when I finished it. He read the play. This was George Whitmore. We talked about it, and he loved the idea of the play. And then he said an interesting thing to me. He asked me, 'Is Eddie going to die during the play?' And I said, 'No, I don't think so,' because I was nervous and trying to avoid it. He said, 'Then, as a PWA, I would be very uncomfortable watching your play; it would be denying what may happen to me.'"

"And what did he say when he read the play?" asked the interviewer.

"He really liked the play a lot. But then, George is George; he's also a writer. So first, of course, he had his emotional experience with it, and then he looked at it as a writer. I mean, I was writing this play and he was writing *Someone Was Here*. We were two of the most depressed people in New York!"

Around this time, according to Andrew Holleran, "there came a strange point—this was years into the epidemic—when I realized that all the writing that was not about AIDS that I myself was reading seemed so irrelevant and pointless, that it really was like playing bridge while the Titanic was sinking. It just was impossible to talk about anything else." Holleran's monthly essays in *Christopher Street Magazine,* collected in *Ground Zero,* became like new paths of thought through the wilderness that life with AIDS had become, probing, exploring, grieving the past, mapping the way we live now.

Robert Patrick's searing one-act comedy *Pouf Positive,* printed in *Untold Decade: Seven Comedies of Gay Romance,* was a final gift to an ex-lover whose last request the author found on his answering machine when he returned to the city after the man's death: "You ask if you can do anything for me, Robert? Yes, write a comedy about this absurd mess." And Harvey Fierstein, in his comic trilogy *Safe Sex,* explored the new social conundrums AIDS has established with a rare blend of wit and anger.

Larry Kramer weighed in yet again with his *Reports from the Holocaust,* a collection of passionate essays and thunderous calls to action that proved just how mighty the pen can be—not since Émile Zola's *J'Accuse* has the sheer power inherent in the written word been used with such polemical skill and political impact.

In *Personal Dispatches,* John Preston, who had stopped writing for over a year after he was diagnosed, found a way out of his own panic and despair by collecting essays from some twenty writers who had to put their personal and professional agendas on hold and turn to the written word to confront the plague that increasingly threatened their circle of friends, their lovers, their own bodies. "The drive of each author was to bear witness," said Preston in an interview, "and in rereading the book, I was struck by how often that word was used. . . . and the word 'witness' is not a passive word, it's a very active verb. To 'witness' is not simply to make note, not simply to record, although there is a power in that. It is to go out and see what is going on."

Two of the contributors to Preston's anthology died before the book could be printed. And well over half of all these writers mentioned are seropositive, ill, or already dead.

These writers—and many others I have not mentioned—registered the initial shock of AIDS as a historical event, that moment when a deep shudder seized the soul of the gay community. Because of criminal neglect and indifference, this eminently preventable epidemic, which should have been treated as an emergency but was not, spread throughout the land and became a medical fact and an omnipresent threat. By the late eighties the emergency had become a condition of life, particularly for gay men. "We seem to have reached a plateau of some sort," commented Holleran in 1988, "in which people have adapted to it in a strange way. . . . It's a way of life now."

A way of life that Paul Monette, who continued to be able to write against all odds, explored in two further novels:

> "It's never going to be over, is it?" asked Mark, not really expecting an answer.
>
> "Someday. Not for us."
>
> "Will anyone understand what it was like?" It was curiously easy, perched on the mountain of death, to speak about the future when all of them would be gone.
>
> "Maybe the gay ones will."
>
> "Yeah, but they'll have to see through all the lies. 'Cause history's just white fo!ks covering their ass."

Beyond even anger and grief, gay writers realized they now stood in the full noon of disaster, unrelenting, unending, inevitable; and, like Michael Lassell in his great poem "How to Watch Your Brother Die," they set down a record to stand against the lies. Peter McGeehee, in his two extraordinary novels *Boys Like Us* and *Sweetheart,* describes what life is like when you live amidst a circle of friends, an elective family, that you know is soon going to disappear, when imminent absence is a palpable, felt pressure affecting every present moment. It was his great achievement to wrest comedy from material saturated with such intense mortality.

Edmund White too described the new situation with a precise clarity:

"Mark thought this summer everything was just as it had been the twelve preceding summers. The only thing different was that this summer would end the series.

"He wanted to know how to enjoy these days without clasping them so tightly he'd stifle the pleasure. But he didn't want to drug himself on the moment either and miss out on what was happening to him. He was losing his best friend, the witness to his life. The skill for enjoying a familiar pleasure about to disappear was hard to acquire . . . Knowing how to appreciate the rhythms of these last casual moments—to cherish them while letting them stay casual—demanded a new way of navigating time."

This growing body of work defining the face of AIDS, limning it in our public and collective imagination, seems to me more than a literary accomplishment. These are individual acts of language performed in the full light of the community's crisis. They are, I would argue, the primary discourse of AIDS, a public dialogue that articulates the experience of the community and constitutes, beyond the shadow of a doubt, the creation of a culture. This new writing is not "discourses about discourses"; indeed, it was impelled into being by the urgent necessity to put speech where there had been cultural silence, for in our present circumstances, as the motto of ACT UP succinctly puts it, "Silence = Death." The task was not to "hear what has already been said" but to utter the new word, the word that would reveal what was happening to us and, at the same time, would constitute our answer, our response, our resistance.

This writing lays before us an example of a living culture, culture as a spontaneous act, for culture is a complex social event that creates the public space in which a community comes into being through participation. Generally, we tend to think of culture either objectively, from the outside, as an anthropologist might look at Samoa, or passively, as a tradition that's there, that is somehow fundamental and undergirds our intellectual life today. But we are not outside this culture that is ours, we have no disinterested Archimedian point of view from which to study it; we *are* the Samoans. Nor is culture any longer a tradition handed down to us, shoved at us by the previous generation; indeed, a great portion of the cultural activity of the last century has centered on the collapse of this tradition and its consequences. Insofar as it exists today, culture is an event that requires activity at both ends, on the part of the initiator who raises a voice to speak, and on the part of the hearer who actively attends to the word. Culture *is* the relationship between these two, and that relationship is an activity, of speaking and of attending, and that activity creates the bond that is what we mean by the word *community.*

II

The writing that is emerging from the AIDS crisis is, to my mind, startlingly different from our normal understanding of writing and books in this society—that is, writing as a literary career or profession, on the one hand, and books as a commercial commodity and the object of aesthetic appreciation, on the other. Virtually all the writers I know of who have grappled with AIDS in their work have experienced this as an interruption in their career. They speak of putting aside their personal agendas to care for friends, to do political or volunteer work, to manage their own illness, and finally to confront this disaster with the tools of their trade, to use the imagination and the capacities of language and its forms to comprehend what is happening.

"Many of the contributors to [*Personal Dispatches*] are activists," said Preston. "They are doing things that must be done. There's a quote at the beginning of the book, 'For some of us must storm the castles. Some define the happening,' that I hesitated before using because it seemed to imply a separation of roles. Writing on the one hand, action on the other. I kept it in because I came to understand that it was a corporate statement; that both must be done and that much of it is done by the same people."

"Write as if you were dying," admonished Annie Dillard in the 28 May 1989 *New York Times Book Review,* evidently not imagining that a whole generation of gay writers might be. "At the same time," she added, "assume you write for an audience consisting solely of terminal patients." When this is actually the case, profession and career do not begin to define or situate the activity of writing.

"The purpose of AIDS writing," declared Preston, "has to be found outside of any conventions that contemporary criticism and publishing might try to impose on us. The canons are proven to be ineffective, inappropriate. What is 'literature' becomes a meaningless academic question when what is defined can't accommodate what is happening in our lives. . . . Those of us who are writing about AIDS can't worry about these definitions any more. We can't be concerned with careerism, with academic acceptance, or with having the fashions of the day dictate how we write. We can now only deal with being witnesses" ("AIDS Writing").

The poems in *Love Alone* that coursed out of Paul Monette in the months immediately following his lover's death were not conceived as a literary strategy. "Writing them quite literally kept me alive," said the author, "for the only time I wasn't wailing and trembling was when I was hammering at these poems." When Randy Shilts took a leave of absence from his job as an investigative reporter to write *And the Band Played On,* he intended to change the world, to shock the country into taking action that would end the epidemic. That all he achieved was another book, albeit a best-seller, does not alter the original intention; indeed, the sardonic, even bitter, tone with which he recounted in *Esquire* magazine the story of the book's success and his own utter failure starkly reveals his original intention.

If it is an inescapable irony for the artist that acts of the spirit, when put into the world, immediately become transformed into exchange commodities—for instance, books to be sold and bought—still, this does not change either the author's original intention or the work's essence. In fact, it only creates more paradoxes. "Who wants to read this fiction?" asked Allen Barnett, whose harrowing stories remind us that reading is sometimes a courageous act; "It hurts me to re-read them" (personal communication). "My fear is these works are going to die in the studio," said Kenneth Lithgow, who has produced some of the most powerful depictions of AIDS on canvas I know of: "People see them and cry. Who would want to live with these paintings?" And Holleran writes of books about AIDS, "I really don't know who reads them for pleasure."

Aesthetic appreciation is neither the intention nor the relevant response to such works. "I don't consider myself an artist," writes Larry Kramer. "I consider myself a very opinionated man who uses words as fighting tools. I perceive certain wrongs that make me very angry, and somehow I hope that if I string my words together with enough skill, people will hear them and respond. I am under no delusion that this will necessarily be the case, but I seem to have no choice but to try." And Paul Monette says of *Love Alone,* "I would rather have this volume filed under AIDS than under Poetry, because if these words speak to anyone they are for those who are mad with loss, to let them know they are not alone." Whatever it is, this writing is not about the making of well-wrought urns.

What distinguishes this AIDS writing from other literary production in our time is not only the writers' intention but the unique situation in which the act of writing occurs. This is not strong emotion recollected in tranquility; these are reports from the combat zone. AIDS writing is urgent; it is engaged and activist writing; it is writing in response to a present threat; it is in it, of it, and aims to affect it. I can think of no good parallel for this in literary history. As far as I know, most of the writing done about the Holocaust was published after 1945, when the nightmare was over in reality and began to haunt the imagination. And while the closest parallel might be the poetry that came out of the trenches of the first World War, the bulk of that writing was published, reviewed and read after the war; whereas this AIDS writing is not only being produced in the trenches, as it were, but is being published, read by its public and evaluated by the critics in the midst of the crisis. It is as if Sassoon's poetry were being mimeographed in the trenches and distributed to be read by men under fire—the immediacy of these circumstances precludes the possibility of this being a merely aesthetic enterprise. The aesthetic requires distance and the distance is not available, not to the writer, not to the reader.

Because of this peculiarity, the truth or beauty—that is, the inherent excellence—of this writing will not wait upon posterity—for judgment. In this onrush of death, posterity even posterity as an imagined frame for the activity of writing—is a luxury. The time is not available. Writers who are facing death are writing for an audience that is dying. Never could I have imagined ten years ago hearing regular discussions from writers about whether they would live long enough to finish a project. Never could I have imagined feeling, on a normal basis, this terrible urgency to get the book out while the author is still alive.

"During the year after Roger died," Paul Monette told an interviewer, "I wrote my book of poems and I spent the next eight or nine months writing the book *Borrowed Time,* assuming I would be dead in a year. I felt that I should get up in the morning and write the best I could that day and put it to bed that night, for who knew what would happen the next day. It was a sense of urgency, a calamitous urgency throughout the writing of those two books."

Many artists and art movements in the twentieth century have tried to shake themselves loose from the deadening context of posterity-as-judge, to avoid the spectre of the eternal museum outside time to which art is consigned, in order to free the creative act and its inherent energy. It is a terrible irony that for gay writers AIDS has knocked to smithereens all such constraining cultural frameworks.

A comparison may make clearer the unparalleled circumstances in which this work is being written. Anne Frank's diary, which might at first be thought a good literary parallel, had its own special beauty; but, on the one hand, it was written without her really knowing what would happen, and, on the other hand, we read it knowing there is nothing we can do about the course of events. But AIDS writing is about something we know *is* happening, *now,* and about which we must in fact *do* something. Of necessity this writing arises from the moment and intends to have its impact in the present. As Sarah Pettit has pointed out, what is "wholly different about the present sort of bearing witness is that it's witnessing *in the midst* of the nightmare. Speaking out in the midst of an event has to hold with it the notion that witnessing can effect change."

John Preston agrees: "The purpose of AIDS writing now is *to get it all down.* The purpose of the writer in the time of AIDS is *to bear witness. . . .* To live in a time of AIDS and to understand what is going on, *writing must be action. Writing must be accompanied by action. Writing is not what our teachers told us, something that stands alone.*

"To be a writer in the time of AIDS is to be a truth-teller. The truth is more horrible than anything people want to hear. . . . The truth is devastating. The truth can't be contained in a pleasantly structured short story that will satisfy the readers of a literary magazine" ("AIDS Writing").

III

"This writing about AIDS reports from the thing itself. It unsettles all the assumptions culture codified about how art is supposed to work and how long it is supposed to take for it to work and who decides whether what is working is really art," writes Robert Dawidoff in *Personal Dispatches*. "The reader and writer community of AIDS has rediscovered the roots of any kind of writing, the roots in human survival, expression, ritual and need. We need to have these things written. The information, the truth, the anger, the philosophy, the history, the fiction, the poetry, the spirituality do a job now. Their place in history will be judged by their success in helping to keep the community the writing serves alive, safer, together, comforted in sickness and in loss." Holleran agrees: this writing will be judged "as writing published in wartime is, by its effect on the people fighting."

This idea that the appropriate measure of writing is its impact on the continued existence and well-being of the community is the valuating principle of any ethnic or national literature; it is why Isaac Bashevis Singer is important to Yiddish culture, why the slave narratives undergird all African-American writing in this country, why the underground Russian writers of the last fifty years will be treasured by generations of Russian readers. All such writing has as its innermost principle the act of bearing witness. To bear witness is to declare oneself, to declare oneself present, to declare oneself in the presence of what has come to be. This is the original discourse, the primary word, the logos that opens a space in which we can be present to one another. It is this space that allows a community to come into being, for this is the site of the action of culture and the possibility of memory. Those who bear witness carry the soul of the community, the stories of what it has done and what it has suffered, and open the possibility of its existence in memory through time and beyond death.

This understanding of writing and its inherent nature and excellence stands in opposition to all ideas of universal literary standards, the presence of which is always an outstanding characteristic of the hegemonic urge of any dominant and dominating class, group, or nation. In literary culture the assertion of universal standards of judgment is always the tip-off to the urge to dominate, to subdue the different, to draw all into a uniform order. You reach for the universal when you don't want to tolerate diversity, politically speaking, when you want to abolish the existential fact of human plurality.

This is, of course, an outstanding fact about the literary culture in America today, as anyone who has the misfortune of being in a profession that requires the reading of a large cross-section of book reviews can testify to, or as a brief glance at the furious defenses of the canon coming from our reactionary, but still dominant, cultural commentators attests to. In spite of the fact that this country is composed of a loose assortment of variegated and astonishingly numerous communities all superimposed upon one another, that virtually every individual American participates in a number of overlapping communities, each with its own culture—as a woman, say, who is also Jewish, a lesbian, and an academic—the organs of cultural definition in this country seem hell-bent on asserting a uniform and shared culture, which is in fact a myth, an obfuscation, a curtain drawn over the real mechanics of cultural creation today. The purpose, of course, is to assert control—to absorb those creations which can be assimilated to the cultural amalgam of the dominant class without upsetting the applecart, and, at the same time, to peripheralize the rest into a marginal, regional, special interest, minority reservation—colorful perhaps, worth a visit as a tourist, but in some basic way not the real thing.

This has been the root problem with the reception of works of gay writers by the mainstream press in the last decade. And it is only heightened when the writing concerns AIDS, for as long as the mainstream press does not participate in the community of crisis, which may be defined as those who choose to be affected by AIDS, as long as the mainstream press sees AIDS as something that happens to "other people," it will continue to judge this writing and these writers in terms of conventional aesthetic categories: is this aesthetically pleasing? Does it constitute an advance in the career of the writer? In short, the media will continue to miss the point.

A revealing instance can be found in the long, joint review that *Time* magazine printed in 1988 of three books provoked by the AIDS crisis: Paul Monette's *Borrowed Time,* Andrew Holleran's *Ground Zero,* and Alice Hoffman's *At Risk,* a novel by a heterosexual woman about an eleven-year-old white girl—a gymnast, no less—who got AIDS from a blood transfusion—what they call "an innocent victim." It was utterly predictable that the book that had the strongest impact on the gay community and on those affected by AIDS, Monette's *Borrowed Time,* was the book *Time* found most disagreeable. "*Borrowed Time* demands a sympathetic response instead of inviting one," complained the magazine, as if this constituted an unwonted imposition on the reader by the author. Would they have made the same complaint about Nedezda Mandelstam's memoirs or the tale of any Holocaust survivor, one wonders. Oddly enough, the reviewer didn't notice that the reason

Holleran neither invites nor demands sympathy from straight readers is that he assumes that all his readers are gay, for this is clearly whom he is speaking to when he sits at his typewriter. Of course, the best book of the lot, according to *Time,* was Hoffman's account of an "innocent victim": "Hoffman gets the blend of hope and despair just right," approved *Time,* as if the author were whipping up a cake. What can this possibly mean? Is there a mixture of hope and despair that is just right? Is it right in all cases, or just in this instance? What precisely constitutes hope when your eleven-year-old daughter is dying of AIDS? What the reviewer really meant is that his sensibilities were not unduly disturbed, that his spirit was agitated but still soothed in a pleasing manner. If you want to see the essential vulgarity of this purely aesthetic response, just imagine someone saying, "Anne Frank got the blend of hope and despair just right."

In the gay literary community there was much heated debate about *At Risk* and a good deal of bitterness about the fact that this work of fiction far outsold any other novel on AIDS. While I believe that no author can be told what he or she can or cannot write about, this anger did not seem a surprising response. One could imagine a novel about an eleven-year-old Christian girl in Hannover who, through some mix-up one day on the street, is caught in one of the round-ups of Jews and "mistakenly" sent to Auschwitz—the "mistake" here is equivalent to "accidentally" getting AIDS. This is a perfectly legitimate subject for a novel, but if the book detailed the suffering of this child and her family while virtually ignoring the fate of the Jews at Auschwitz, one would not be surprised to get a chilly reception in the Jewish press. And if that book far outsold any other novel about the Holocaust, one would not be surprised to find bitterness in the hearts of many Jews. This is a hypothetical example, but there was in reality a similar debate over *The Confessions of Nat Turner*. All arguments aside, the point of the matter is that there *was* a heated and public debate—as there should have been—but I did not see one reviewer outside the gay press raise the issue with *At Risk,* and, in fact, few reviewers inside the gay press did either. And surely the matter was worth discussing.

In fact, it raises a serious and troubling question about the judgment of contemporary works of fiction. When I read Allen Barnett's extraordinary story "The *Times* as It Knows Us"—the title signals the sheer contempt this gay New Yorker has for our "newspaper of record"—the author's unblinking vision of the harrowing events that take place during one weekend in a not untypical gay summer house in The Pines both exhausted and impressed me. The story's power derives from its understatement, its lack of hysteria, and its unbending courage to imagine things as they are right now for many of us. It is not an unfamiliar story to me or my friends; it's one I recognize only too well, yet I found it almost unbearable to read. The fact that Barnett's imagination did not buckle under the weight of this horror steadied me and convinced me of the magnitude of his achievement. But what, I wondered, would a straight reader make of it? Would such a reader feel the unstated pressure that made it difficult for me to breathe? And, if not, was I saying that a straight friend of mine would be in no position, would have no right, to judge this story because she did not have first-hand experience of what the story was about?—a position that made me very uncomfortable. When I raised the issue with Barnett himself, he thought a moment and said, "You know, I saw a teenager, a black girl, on the subway today reading Toni Morrison's *The Bluest Eye,* a book that had an incredible impact on me. And I realized that the book could never have the meaning for me that it would have for her. And I was very glad she was reading it, for she is the audience."

For me this little story neatly raises the question of the plurality of cultures in which we live. In one of the last great works of the imperial spirit, T. E. Lawrence wrote in *The Seven Pillars of Wisdom* that to try to view reality simultaneously through the veils of two different cultures would drive a man mad. Though this sounds convincing when you come upon it in that remarkable book, one remembers that Kierkegaard and Nietzsche, the first two thinkers for whom modernity as such was a problematic issue—indeed a crisis—both characterized modernity, or perhaps the crisis hidden within it, as the ability or the necessity of holding contradictory ideas in the mind simultaneously. "Contradictory" was perhaps inexact, but the collapse of a unifying tradition that could take disparate elements and order them into a more or less uniform, or at least noncontradictory, whole, this collapse of tradition is indisputable and glaringly the fundamental datum of twentieth-century culture, articulated over and over again in the works of our thinkers, poets, and artists. By now it should be quite clear to everyone: the center did not hold. And with the collapse of the authority of tradition, all cultures, not only all present but all past cultures, regained a certain viability as a veil that one might borrow to see certain aspects of reality more clearly, as when Picasso raided African art for forms and principles that could rejuvenate his own.

The resulting situation, it seems to me—with all due respect to Lawrence of Arabia—is that today we see reality precisely through a multitude of veils simultaneously. And while this may require some fancy footwork and a greater mental and spiritual dexterity, by no means will it necessarily drive us mad.

All the questions, objections, and arguments about the existence of a separate and distinct gay culture—and the deep-seated hostility with which the spokespeople for the dominant culture in this country react to this possibility—rest on a mistaken notion of the relationship between the two. It is not, as they think, a question of the Greeks versus the barbarians, which in essence boils down to those who have culture versus those who don't, *hoi barbaroi,* the barbarians who babble, who have no language (don't speak Greek) and thus no culture. This paradigm of how a plurality of cultures coexists always comes down to a power relation, a hostile power relation: us versus them. But we *are* a them, each one of us. I am a white American gay man. I participate in gay culture, but I also participate quite actively in mainstream American culture. And, in fact, through my reading of the remarkable burst of superb writing by African-American women in the last decade and a half, not to speak of black music in general, I get to participate in black culture. And when I read Maxine Hong Kingston and Amy Tan, I get to see life in this country through the veil of Chinese-American culture.

These cultures all exist simultaneously, inexactly superimposed upon each other, a great palimpsest, creating a moiré effect in the soul that is the basic texture of cultural life today. And when groups of us—urban male Jews or African Americans or Chinese Americans or gay people—spin our veils, we are creating garments for the spirit which we can share.

Allen Barnett can share *The Bluest Eye,* though perhaps it will never have the resonance and depth for him that it will for an African-American girl. Then again, none of us can participate in Greek tragedy with the transparent clarity it must have had for contemporary Athenians. But still we read it. Which is precisely why we have Greek scholars, specialists who not only tend and preserve the work and its meaning but try to clear away the obscurity that an ever-lengthening distance between us and the work creates.

Time, of course, is not the only type of distance; there are psychic distances, between, for instance, the souls of black folk in America and the dominant American culture, between an emerging gay sensibility and straight America, between those who are living through the maelstrom of AIDS and the rest of the country. But we can bridge these distances by the active power of the imagination, that power, as Hannah Arendt used to say, that makes present that which is absent, that makes near that which is far, that power which is the root and source of all human understanding.

Those who are living through AIDS are spinning an astonishing garment for the spirit, one that offers its gift not only to those stricken but to all who care to reach, to participate in the great life of the imagination and spirit that is human culture. Gay culture is a necessity for us and an offering to the rest. At the moment, the dominant culture mainly rejects the gift and spurns the giver, which is a great foolishness. The gift asks only to be taken, and in that sharing we begin to participate in the communities of all peoples. In that sharing we begin to learn how to live among a plurality of peoples and to move among a multiplicity of cultures, with whom we share the Earth even as they share with us the riches of their experiences and the wealth of their spirit.

James W. Jones

SOURCE: "The Plague and Its Texts: AIDS and Recent American Fiction," in *Journal of American Culture,* Vol. 16, No. 1, Spring, 1993, pp. 73-80.

[*In the following essay, Jones discusses three novels by gay writers to illustrate how the use of plague as a metaphor for AIDS stigmatizes the victims of the disease.*]

It need hardly be pointed out that AIDS has become a major theme in literature. It could scarcely be otherwise, for this syndrome has profoundly affected American culture over the past decade. As writers have translated their experiences and their culture's values and reactions into fiction, they have employed a variety of techniques by which to represent the effects of the health crisis in their works. Early examples of what Shaun O'Connell calls "the AIDS literature" came largely from theater and television. Employing rather one-dimensional characters, some sought to evoke sympathy for the "victims" of this "disease" while others aimed at provoking the audience to action (e.g. demanding safer sex education and governmental funding for drug research). In the relatively short period of time since those works first appeared around 1985, the topic has found a much wider and more varied expression in American literature. By now the list of such works would extend over several pages and encompass all genres.

The American reaction to AIDS has changed enormously—for the better—over the past five years. It is no longer socially acceptable to discriminate against people with AIDS (PWA) or HIV—more importantly, it is no longer legally permissible. Of course, that statement must be qualified with adjectives of class, race and gender. A poor black woman with AIDS is undeniably treated differently than a middle-class white (gay) male. Nonetheless, we are no longer at that point where people burn the home in which someone with AIDS lives or talk about becoming infected by a mosquito. Such reactions, although they may still occur, are generally viewed as arising from a lack of proper education about the topic.

The American reaction to AIDS has been directed by a belief that education and (medical) science can provide answers to the dilemma which the virus poses. The forces of Enlightenment can, we seem to believe, conquer the darkness of that "disease." But the beacon of reason cannot illuminate all the dim recesses created by the crisis, and one of the most potent metaphors for AIDS remains "*plague,*" that Black Death which neither reason nor science could subdue until the discovery of the Pasturellus pestis bacillus in the late nineteenth century. *That* plague may have been conquered, but it lived on in folk memory as an extremely powerful cultural narrative. The appearance of "AIDS" breathed new life into the plague as a cultural metaphor and stirred the folk memory to action.

The question arises: why is it the "plague" that becomes an often used metaphor for AIDS? Susan Sontag's *AIDS and Its Metaphors* (1989) supplies some answers. She points out that the name "AIDS" is itself a metaphor, for it means only some symptoms and diseases from among an extensive list which comprise the syndrome. And that metaphor which has taken on its own quite literal meaning has in turn supplied other metaphors to embody its multiplicity of meanings. Among them, "[P]lague is the principal metaphor by which the AIDS epidemic is understood." While her statement is more true of 1987 and 1988, the plague metaphor, although no longer predominant, retains a central and quite potent position within the syntax of the language of AIDS. The crucial point of Sontag's argument is that by using the metaphor of plague to define AIDS within American culture, we eliminate many possible ways of dealing with the epidemic and revert to methods which are not only inappropriate but also undemocratic and, ultimately, inhumane. Within this cultural construct called "AIDS," the important distinction between "infected but healthy" and "infected but ill" is being lost. Since the discovery of microbes and viruses, the concept of "infected but healthy" has been elaborated in medical science; yet, the discourse on AIDS discards that in favor of older concepts which create an inexorable step by step progression of infection to illness to death. Thus, "AIDS reinstates something like a premodern experience of illness."

Such a "premodern experience" understands the particular illness' plague as a punishment upon the infected/inflicted. Those plague(d)-infected become categorized as Other, for, according to the "usual script for plague," it "invariably comes from somewhere else." That geography of the foreign is charted upon the bodies of individuals who become classified as members of a threatening group due to their deviance from the proscriptions of the majority. Thus, "a person judged to be wrong is regarded as, at least potentially, a source of pollution." These Others lose their humanity through their election to step beyond the norm despite knowledge of those limits and the possible punishments: "people with little reason to expect exemption from misfortune have a lessened capacity to *feel* misfortune." A major reason why the plague metaphor has proved so fitting for AIDS, as opposed to many other diseases which have killed more people, lies in the need for our society to blame: in the twentieth century, a disease which is *sexually* transmitted is necessary in order to fix blame.

While it revokes a "modern" scientific discourse on infection, the plague metaphor also invokes both a powerful cultural narrative of plague as the destroyer of civilization and a mighty Judeo-Christian cultural myth of the plague as retribution for sins. Within both, plague serves the purposes which Sontag outlines: it punishes the transgressors, it marks the foreign within the body politic, it identifies the possible agents of death, it "transforms the body itself into something alienating," not just through the physical disfigurement caused by the diseases but also through estranging the body itself through talk of "body fluids," the interposition of physical barriers between bodies in sexual intercourse, or the distinction between the "vulnerable rectum" and the "rugged vagina," to cite but a few examples.

One of the most potent American cultural narratives about AIDS—and the one with the most dangerous implications for affecting attitudes towards those with AIDS —is that AIDS is a "plague." Of particular interest here is an even more limited metaphor: AIDS is a "gay plague." The continuing need to make such statements as "AIDS. It's not just a gay disease any more" or "AIDS affects all of us" provides ample evidence of the continued wide-spread belief that AIDS is "just" a disease of gay men. [Or of some group which is not "us"; maybe Afro-Americans or Hispanic Americans, but that is a topic for a different paper.] Sontag's analysis demonstrates how the plague metaphor operates to ostracize, categorize, assign blame, and, ultimately, mete out punishment. Quarantine and internment ("concentration") camps become ever more possible and thus ever more real.

Over the past several years, the plague has become an accepted metaphor within the American public discourse on AIDS. It would be impossible to cite all the references to AIDS as a plague, so I shall limit myself to what I believe to be a representative sampling of those which metaphorize AIDS as a specifically gay male plague. One must begin of course with the medical researchers at the Center for Disease Control who in 1981 proposed the name "Gay-Related Immune Deficiency" for the variety of immune-deficiency related diseases which were affecting gay men in urban centers. In 1985, Robert Boucheron published a book of poems about this health crisis, entitled *Epitaphs for the Plague Dead.* David Black published a very superficial book, written with little understanding of gay culture, *The Plague Years: A Chronicle of AIDS, the Epidemic of Our Times* (1986). That subtitle sums up the fear and distress which characterized the reaction of the majority society to AIDS at this time. In the same year, Frances Fitzgerald's article "The Castro," which had appeared in *The New Yorker* in 1985 was published in her collection *Cities on a Hill: A Journey through Contemporary American Cultures* (1986). Although better written, this essay shares with Black's book a view of gay culture from the outside and an unquestioning acceptance of the metaphor of plague for AIDS among gay men. Gay men are "they," not "we." "Their" health crisis receives a history, namely that of the medieval plague. Black describes a gay and lesbian health conference in Boston as "like a medieval fair." Both authors use the health crisis to pass judgement upon the ways gay men have lived. Fitzgerald and Black portray gay culture as based solely upon sexual encounters, with quantity being more important than quality. "[The whole bar and sex culture of the Castro] clearly was unhealthy in many respects," so these people should not really be too surprised at their fate. Thanks to AIDS, the Castro and gay men in general are today "stable and domesticated." The plague seems to have taught its lesson. Both authors see themselves as liberals and identify themselves in their texts as heterosexual. By so doing they reinforce the cultural narrative of the plague with its focus upon dividing them from us and defining disease as punishment. The plague continues as a metaphor in reporting about gay people and AIDS in James Kinsella's recent study on the way the media have treated the topic, *Covering the Plague: AIDS and the American Media* (1990).

But not every reference to AIDS as plague so blatantly evokes the images Sontag describes. The gay poet James Broughton writes: "How will this penetrating plague / deflower our erotic life?" and Karen Finley, a performance artist, speaks of AIDS as the "modern plague." Padraig O'Malley, editor of *The AIDS Epidemic* (1989), refers to AIDS as "a slow plague," and Shaun O'Connell writes in his article on fiction about AIDS: "[We should] understand illness—particularly the collective illness that is called plague—as a distinguished, incomparable thing."

One of the most prolific gay authors on the subject of gay men and AIDS is Andrew Holleran. He continually refers to AIDS as "the plague," as in this recent example from his column "New York Notebook" in the magazine *Christopher Street:* "If, before the plague, a writer had been trying to compose a novel about a group of gay men in New York—based, of course, on the lives of his friends over the years: how they met, changed, grew closer or farther apart—he may well have been stopped by the sheer lack of dramatic content." He unrepentantly defends the past which has led to this our present—which is to say he refuses to capitulate to the desire of the heterosexual majority to desexualize gay men. In this particular essay on "Friends," he describes his early fear about gay friendships: "That our emotional commitment was not so much to the other particular friends, as to other homosexuals, in general: the sea of men that could toss up, at any moment, for whatever length of time, a sexual antidote to loneliness." But that fear was allayed by discovering "If friends are what root us, in lieu of family—if friends are the only family we have, so that in middle age, we do not abandon one another—there was always something complex and communal about the band of men who wandered the city forming erotic attachments with one another."

"The plague" has tested friendships, those bonds that create the gay community. Holleran, an insider intimately affected by the AIDS epidemic, uses the metaphor in a quite different way than authors such as Black and Fitzgerald. For him, the plague has affected gays in particular, but it is in no way a punishment. The plague has decimated the gay community, and it is that community which has had to shoulder most of the load of caring for the sick, fighting for drugs and grieving for the dead. Because of this, he, too, uses the plague metaphor to describe a division between us and them. Here too the division arises out of fear of infection, but it is "their" fear of "us" which strengthens the very bonds of that gay community whose disappearance Black, et al. believe they are describing.

That paradox, that duality within which the metaphor of plague operates, can be found within much of the fiction which portrays gay men with AIDS and which employs that metaphor. That paradox I am referring to evokes a cultural narrative of ostracism, fear, alienation, even quarantine and death with the equation of AIDS and plague. Yet, at the same time, these gay authors want to demystify AIDS and thus remove the beliefs that AIDS is a just punishment, that people with AIDS are essentially Other, etc. If these authors want to achieve that goal, why indeed do they evoke the metaphor of plague? To answer that question, I want to examine some novels in which the metaphor appears.

In *Eighty-Sixed* (1989) by David Feinberg, B. J. Rosenthal tells of his search for love and the friendships he forms along the way. The book is written in two parts: the first takes place in 1980, the second in 1986; thus, AIDS demarcates the life of the novel's narrator just as it has divided the lives of all gay men over a certain age into pre- and post-AIDS eras. Part Two ("Learning How to Cry") comprises just over one half of the book's length (326 pages). The plague metaphor does not appear until the last sixty pages; then, it is used seven times in rapid succession. B. J. himself is not infected, but several of his friends and acquaintances are. The health crisis overwhelms these gay men: "'Most people don't even know seventy people, let alone seventy who have or have had the plague. A.I.D.S.,' he spells out." "'I don't see the end.' 'For Bob?' 'No, the plague'." New York City has become "Plague Central." The deaths mount, more and more acquaintances fall ill. By the end, the plague of AIDS has become a rain which does not cleanse but only floods and destroys: "It begins as a gentle rain. Just a drop, for each illness, each death. And with each passing day it gets worse. Now a downpour. Now a torrent. And there is no likelihood of its ever ending."

The novel well illustrates the points I am trying to make. Once AIDS enters the novel, it becomes slowly a plague, transforming all it touches. By marking gay characters in the novel with HIV-illnesses, AIDS radically alters the life of the narrator. For him, AIDS becomes not "a" plague, but "the" plague. As the plague affects more people he knows, thus coming nearer and nearer to him, his own life begins to lose its multiplicity of meanings. Interspersed between the chapters are fragments of the narrator's thoughts on topics which relate to events that occurred in the previous chapter. In one called "Everything," he lists "everything I am afraid of." The extensive list includes AIDS six times in the first 50 items. The last item is "AIDS," repeated 28 times. AIDS obliterates all else in his life. It is at this point (two pages earlier, actually) when the plague metaphor is employed for the first time. Once "AIDS" becomes "plague" then plague eventually obliterates all other possible meanings for AIDS. Indeed, it infiltrates every conversation between or about gay men. Thus, when B. J. describes his ex-lover, who has AIDS, as having "come back to haunt me, to plague me," we read that final verb not in its metaphorical sense (of harassing someone) but in the AIDS-metaphorical (which here becomes literal) meaning that B. J. is worried that Richard has infected him. Feinberg makes this point himself four sentences later: "Years ago Richard and I exchanged bodily fluids—you know, your typical high-risk sexual activities most conducive to spreading viruses. Fucking. Anal intercourse. *Taking it up the ass.* Didn't some part of me hate Richard for possibly infecting me?"

The last sexual encounter described in a book filled with sexual encounters begins with an image borrowed from Poe's "The Masque of the Red Death": "The specter of death cannot be ignored, forgotten." Caution rules the sex between B. J. and Mario, a man he picks up in a bar. Behind the bolted door of his apartment, with the bedroom door closed, the windows locked, and the phone machine on, B. J. believes he has found respite, if not security. But the plague intrudes, not as in Poe's nineteenth century text in the form of a gruesome specter, but instead it invades that private space by means of the phone line. A friend calls to report the death of their friend Bob.

In Joseph Hansen's mystery novel *Early Graves* (1987), someone is murdering young gay men who have AIDS. Halfway through the novel, the murderer would appear to have been found. A young gay man with AIDS, Leonard Church, has methodically killed six of the 'many men with whom he had had sex because one of them infected him with HIV. All of the men he murdered were dying of AIDS, as he himself is, but his death comes not from disease but a policeman's bullet when he attempts to escape from the Tiberius Baths where he had gone to find his next victim. Church leaves a diary in which he confesses to all the murders except that of Drew Dodge, the man whose murder David Brandstetter, Hansen's detective in this series, is investigating. He, too, had AIDS, although very few knew or even suspected it, since he was married and had a child.

As it turns out, there are two avenging angels at work here. The second, the one who killed Dodge, is his illegitimate son, Cary. The son, reared in a deeply conservative, fundamentalist background in Arkansas, tracks down the well-known and seemingly well-to-do Dodge at his home in California in order to confront him with what he believes to be his father's treachery toward his mother and himself. He also tries to blackmail his father by threatening to expose the latter's prior convictions for fraud. When Dodge refuses to talk with him, they quarrel. After Dodge fires a gun at him, the son fires his own gun and kills his father. Even though Dodge's death is not a direct result of AIDS, his death nonetheless becomes an AIDS-caused death, just as much as those of the gay men murdered by Leonard Church, for his community and family react to it as such. No one comes to his funeral, despite his having been a leader in the community. His wife and mother-in-law castigate him for having infected his wife with HIV.

The common link between all the murders of these gay men with AIDS, however, is a view of AIDS as a plague spread by silent agents of death. Leonard believes the men he kills all knew of their illness when they had sex with him; Dodge hid his homosexuality and his illness from his family and friends. The avenging angels act out the theme of retribution which, as Sontag points out, is one of the major aspects of the AIDS as plague discourse. Leonard and Cary become the agents of a society which needs to fix blame and to eliminate the blamed. Hansen shows the source of homophobia by linking the two characters with religious fundamentalism: Cary's upbringing and Leonard's last name make that link. What Hansen makes most evident is that, if we think of AIDS as a plague, we see people with AIDS as deserving to be done away with. Their murders gain meaning as justified acts of retribution. Only the gay detective, the hero of the novel, can unravel that meaning and by unraveling it begin to remove its discursive power.

Peter, the main character in Joel Redon's novel *Bloodstream* (1988), has returned to Oregon to live with his family of blood while he tries to chart ways in which he can live with AIDS. But haunting every attempt to do so is the certain knowledge that AIDS means death; like the plague bacillus, once it enters the bloodstream, it will not leave until it has destroyed its host. The novel tells the story of Peter and his blood kin, how they have failed him and he them, as well as how they do or do not help him live until the end. Peter is compared to his aunt who never married and who died of tuberculosis at a young age. Tuberculosis serves as another metaphor for plague, a sign from an earlier period of the twentieth century when TB acquired enormous metaphorical meaning, just as AIDS is doing in the present. AIDS as a plague enters the novel most obviously through a quote from the gay poet James Broughton: "AIDS is very much connected to the larger plague on all levels . . . the poisoning of the whole of human life and of the planet. And here it is the homosexual society which is being sacrificed to make people aware of it." That social sacrifice to expiate the moral sins of the general society takes place upon a select minority. But the plague also marks the foreign(ers) within the body of society—that is, gay people—in order to manage the threat they pose, the threat unbridled infection and death.

But AIDS as plague also performs this function on an individual level. Peter lives in a small house on his parents' estate, physically separated from his family. He lives outside the city where his gay friends and members of his support group live, which is to say he lives largely in isolation. AIDS, the plague, has chased him out of New York City (Feinberg's "Plague Central") to the opposite coast in order to find a way of living with the disease. But the disease/plague draws a line around him which only serves to isolate him further. All the advice he receives tells him to love himself, to forgive himself, in other words it directs all his acts inward, not outward, so that not only does the plague/disease concept work upon others to separate themselves from him, it also works within him to separate himself from others.

Taking these three novels as examples, then, we see how the metaphor of AIDS as plague exhibits the signs which Sontag warned us to look for. The plague transforms the body into something alienating. This is as true for the gay man with AIDS as it is for the gay man who is HIV-negative, but who must always be conscious of the possibility of infection that accompanies every erotic exchange. The plague serves as retribution for transgressing a moral code. The plague marks the foreign within the body of society and within the family. These characteristics of the discourse on AIDS are for many gay men, fictional and real, but signposts along the way toward a new kind of "final solution." This kind of discourse on AIDS, based as it is on metaphorizing AIDS as plague which in turn evokes a cultural myth in order to construct a new cultural narrative, proves to be more deadly for gay men than the virus itself.

Three recent novels share a common theme of the virus creating a fear of gays which leads to quarantine and even to death camps. They detail a world in which homophobia has largely or completely triumphed. *Plague* (1987) by Toby Johnson, subtitled "A Novel about Healing," draws the most direct connection between AIDS and plague. The identity of the two is a direct equivalence for one group of people in particular: political conservatives. In a lecture to a Georgetown University audience, one such leader "mentioned Moses and the plagues on ancient Egypt as an example of a well-applied weapon." Another refers to "the homosexual plague." Indeed, it is representatives of that group who literally engineered this plague of AIDS upon America's homosexuals. Johnson builds his novel on the often-heard rumor of the mid-1980s that the CIA manufactured the virus as a biological weapon and it somehow got out of their control while testing it upon selected populations. Using the virus to turn gay men into mobile sites of infection for each other and at the same time invisible threats to the majority, these men seek to eradicate gays from American society not only by killing them off through AIDS but also by invoking quarantine measures and possibly erecting concentration camps.

Gay activists, along with supportive heterosexual friends, reveal the truth, but the "cure" which the virus' inventor had prepared is never mass-produced and its secret formula dies with him. However, "thanks to safe sex and nation-wide education about sex" and to medical research, the plague has become by the end of the novel a controllable disease which has lost its ability to inspire terror. The novel drives its thesis home with the statement of one of the main characters, who is also gay, that "the real plague" is homophobia and fear. Indeed, the gay characters see through that myth of metaphor. Early on, one gay man with AIDS asks another, "Then how come God gave me the plague?" His friend answers him: "God didn't give you the plague. You got sick on account of a virus that mutated over in Africa." Although "the plague" destroys lives, it does not eradicate [the] gay community. That community is maintained by direct, political action, and it is in large part sustained by a kind of EST-philosophy which the novel preaches. Only through a combination of the science fiction and detective genres (good gays hunt down the bad guys—gay and straight—who "caused" AIDS) and a metaphysical, holistic approach to healing the body from disease can the author disarm the power of the myth in his novel's title.

Genocide (1988), Tim Barrus's collection of short stories and poems, centers on the theme of a universe in which gays are being quarantined, interned and ultimately murdered because they are infected with the HIV. In one of the episodes, a kind of gay *2001,* the computer on board a spaceship inhabited by a pair of gay lovers sets the vehicle on a course to flee "the virus universe." That virus has killed or infected (meaning it will kill) all humans except for these two men. Virus means certain death which under these conditions becomes genocide. Here genocide is but a politically motivated and directed plague; thus, genocide, plague, and AIDS are really the same thing. Plague images are present: "earth had baptized its creatures with . . . virus and starvation and plague." The original meaning within idiomatic expressions is revived because of this context: a line in one of the poems which concludes each story speaks of how "we avoid trouble / like the plague because trouble is always the policia." That statement makes the connection between the medical danger of the plague and the political threat in which the plague places its sufferers. The plague here is not medieval but horribly modern. Auschwitz images dominate these stories: gay men disappear inside collective hells of train cars and death camps, or they struggle between escape and enslavement. This dark novel holds out very little hope for survival, much less for change. Barrus does locate one possibility of resistance to that political discourse which separates gays from the majority, figuratively and literally, in order to eliminate them. Gay sadomasochistic sex becomes an avenue by which to rescue some shard of gay identity and gay community, for through it active, armed resistance to quarantine and camps becomes possible.

Gentle Warriors (1989) by Geoff Mains combines elements from both of these novels. Set in a not too distant future, the novel describes how civil rights for gays in the United States have largely disappeared. Most cities have passed "quarantine laws." San Francisco remains the sole metropolitan area which has refused to do so. While internment camps have not yet been devised, gays have become the victims of governmentally planned murder. The CIA and the Pentagon devised the HI virus. The government then intentionally had the virus spread through the gay male community. This secret is revealed by a CIA agent who is proud of the effects this plot has had; his religious beliefs as to the immorality of homosexuality found here an approved method of expression. Images of death and plague predominate. Society has been rendered asunder by the plague. For gay men, it has drawn a sharp black line between the past and the present: "Those times would never come back. And even if time would permit it, reality had placed its shadow across the way." "He knew there was no escape, that a similar death was inevitable." "[N]ow the sidewalks seem to smell of blood." "[M]emories, like a signature for these dark times."

But gay men respond to this medical and political crisis in a variety of ways, personified by three major characters. Allan Bennett runs for district attorney of San Francisco in order to keep the city free of the repressive measures that have choked the lives of gay men across the country. Gregg, a Vietnam veteran who is dying of AIDS, joins with other gay men who have AIDS in a plot to infect the President of the United States with HIV when he visits San Francisco. This is not an act of retribution, but one of blackmail. They believe that they will thus force the government to reveal an "antidote" to the virus. Marc espouses a philosophy of self-forgiveness and of maintaining, even strengthening, the erotic bonds between gay men as one way (but not the only way) to deal with the health crisis. Through his somewhat "New Age" spirituality and his intense ties to a gay male community that is bonded by a shared past of sexual liberation and a love expressed through "leather sexuality," Marc moves between the past and the present. He works at a leather bar which exists only for a select few. To all others, it ceased to exist when AIDS appeared. Yet this space becomes a haven for gay men whenever it is most needed. Someone who is being chased by the police finds the door and runs in, but the police find only a solid wall of brick.

In the end, though, the election has not yet taken place. Allan does seem assured of victory after the city rallies behind its minorities. Gregg dies while waiting to shoot the President; so does another man with AIDS, Jim, who had organized the plot. The phantom bar seems about to disappear forever, irrevocably. Marc concludes the novel with a eulogy for the past. But the future remains decidedly uncertain. It seems the choices must be made whether society will take the path of tolerance and inclusion represented by San Francisco and the majority of its citizens or the path of repression and genocide represented by the neo-fascism of the American president and the religious right.

Several common threads to the gay discourse on AIDS as plague become evident in these three science fiction/fantasy novels. The plague has been created by the American government in order to carry out a program of elimination ("genocide") directed by the religious right. Gay men fight back against this, but stop short (except for some of Barrus short stories) of killing heterosexuals. The military metaphor which Sontag and others have described as a chief attribute of the discourse on AIDS here is applied in a new way. Not physicians nor medical researchers nor even care-givers are the soldiers in the battle against the disease; instead, people with AIDS, that is to say gay men themselves, are the "warriors" in a struggle against homophobia in general and particularly against a government bent on killing every one of them. Centers of gay culture and gay rights (e.g. San Francisco) are threatened by the non-gay majority.

That it is nonetheless gays who die becomes the most interesting point of this discourse which wants to oppose that majority discourse on AIDS and to defuse its power. One aspect of the philosophy of gay liberation, namely using non-violent methods to achieve its goals, prevents the gay characters from murdering their murderers or even from using violence to force the government to release the cure they believe it possesses. But what keeps these authors from concluding their novels with Life?

The most obvious answer is that such an ending is impossible because there simply is no such antidote, as much as they might like to fix the blame for AIDS/plague on a governmental plot. Only education, "Truth," can help now. Such measures may protect, but they cannot cure.

Ultimately, however, it is the very metaphor of plague itself which makes it impossible for these authors to write optimistic endings. Here I refer not only to the three science fiction novels, but also to the three novels discussed earlier. The plague metaphor has entrenched itself within the public discourse on AIDS in America so thoroughly (although I do *not* want to say "overwhelmingly") that literary discourses on AIDS cannot avoid confronting this metaphor. An author may indeed choose to reject the plague metaphor—as many have—but such a choice is a conscious decision, intentionally aimed at diffusing, if not refusing, the power of that particular metaphor to define conceptions of AIDS and of people with AIDS. But if an author does employ that metaphor, an extensive mythology and history accompany that figure of speech into the text. Indeed, they may be said to "infect" the body of the text in analogy to the way in which the HIV virus infects the human body.

Thus, the metaphor of the plague keeps these authors from flights of fantasy that might soar too high. It makes it impossible to imagine a world free of AIDS. The mourning that concludes *Eighty-Sixed* and *Gentle Warriors* is but the beginning, for gays will continue to die. Peter in *Bloodstream* will surely die. David Brandstetter may have solved the murders of gay men with AIDS in this novel, but in the next one we discover that his lover has become infected. Even the most "optimistic" of these, *Plague,* cannot create a completely happy ending, for no cure is to be found. It is impossible then to imagine a world free of AIDS. Plague has become pervasive. All we can do is live with it until we eventually die of it.

When "plague" becomes a metaphor for AIDS, it evokes a cultural myth which can provoke a dangerous reality. *That* is the problem with using this metaphor. It does not eliminate or devour all other meanings of "AIDS" in every text. It does reduce the multiplicity of possible meanings to a small range in which that of "plague" predominates.

Linda Singer has described the plague, in its modern, metaphorical meaning, as marking a "radically anxious point of rupture." It destabilizes significations. It is, as Camus writes in his novel *The Plague,* forever "unusual, out of place." The discourse, in fiction and in society, seeks to restore order and to eliminate the unusual. The discourse of AIDS is, of course, a discourse of the body. The metaphor of plague marks the body so as to identify those who are a deadly threat. But exactly whose body is it?

It is "the body of the male homosexual," as Paula Treichler writes in her insightful essay, "AIDS, Homophobia, and Biomedical Discourse: An Epidemic of Signification." That "'promiscuous' gay male body" is a body that is historically determined, created for this particular historical moment, so as to suture together that rupture which AIDS as plague represents for the non-gay majority. That body exists only as an extension of erotic desire, never as an actual person who might be someone *like* everyone else (i.e. "us"). That body is a reservoir of possible infection, a silent, hidden threat of death since there are no external signs of homosexuality. Plague provides the text by which that body can be read. That this is all a social (which is to say: political) construction need hardly be stressed. This plague text which is constructed upon the mythic gay male body *must* define that body as "not-self" in order to remove the fear of AIDS from the Self. Thus, the discourse of immunology, a "story" in its own right, determines how we speak about and deal with gay men with AIDS. The metaphor of plague creates a story that culminates in Armageddon (or, as several gay authors have termed it, genocide). This scenario makes it possible to inscribe homophobia at a very high level within the discourse on AIDS. The deaths of *all* gays are desired by a homophobic culture, but that culture cannot express that desire openly (due to constraints of a competing discourse of "liberalism" about civil rights, diversity, and tolerance) and so instead it speaks of the "virus" as a plague which in turn becomes a kind of *Götterdämmerung* for the gods of our society: heterosexuals. Thus, by means of these metaphors, that society can achieve its goal of eradication of the non-self.

But here we have discussed novels by gay men about gay men with AIDS. How can they support these homophobic aims? Certainly, they intend to do just the opposite. They want to remove the power of precisely that script which uses AIDS as plague to write the deaths of all gays. But some of these works use the metaphor unquestioningly; thus, they only serve to support that power. While others include passages explicitly denying that AIDS is a plague, they cannot avoid the ability of exactly that cultural narrative to inscribe itself within these texts. Thus, although they seek to defend against it, they become "infected" by that homophobic discourse. In an excellent analysis of this problem, exposing the problematics of the slogan "Silence=Death," Lee Edelman shows how "defensive strategies deployed—in the realm of discourse or disease—to combat agencies of virulence may themselves be informed by the virulence they are seeking to efface, informed by it in ways that do not produce the immunizing effect of a vaccine, but that serve, instead, to reinforce and even multiply the dangerous sites of infection." Because these novels are produced in a culture which wants to define gays as plague-carriers, each evocation of the plague metaphor becomes a possible strengthening of that discourse it would like to subvert: "[A]ny discourse on AIDS must inscribe itself in a volatile and uncontrollable field of metaphoric contention in which its language will necessarily find itself at once appropriating AIDS for its own tendentious purposes and becoming subject to appropriation by the contradictory logic of homophobic ideology."

Edelman concludes: "[T]here is no available discourse on AIDS that is not itself diseased," because we are caught in a system bent on reification, on creating absolute identities, and on thinking in polar opposites. Since, as Edelman summarizes, "homosexuality [in the West] was conceived as a contagion, and the homosexual as parasitic upon the heterosexual community," the plague metaphor is a natural consequence of AIDS within American culture. Further, "Turner's postulates" apply: "(1) disease is a language; (2) the body is a representation; and (3) medicine is a political practice." As Treichler states, "AIDS demonstrates how language can give the illusion of control" ("AIDS, Gender, and Biomedical Discourse").

Are we left then in the pessimism of Edelman's conclusion? Must we capitulate to the power of discourse because we have been taught, as up-to-date cultural critics, that there is no recourse to a meta-discourse nor escape from discourses of power? Must we be content to seek gaps in power in order to find power's source? And can we then only usurp power for new ends?

I am not so pessimistic. There is obviously no simple way out, for this cultural narrative of plague is only one aspect of a complicated discourse of AIDS in America. (I have of course omitted discussion of those on Afro-Americans and Hispanics, drug addicts, and female prostitutes.) We cannot simply refuse its power, for some cultural narrative is going to replace it. We can, however, move the discourse out of the parameters of a discourse on disease, from which the plague metaphor and the definition of the homosexual as inherently sick arise. Gay fiction, including the texts described here, already offers some other possibilities. As in Andrew Holleran's essays, gay community is strengthened, not destroyed, by the AIDS crisis. Gay men reassert their sexuality, thus refusing to become the non-threatening creatures that the majority would like them to become. There are, then, ways to talk about gay men and about gay men with AIDS that can escape the discourse on disease. Cultural critics can play an important role in finding others. They must, if society is to learn to individualize—and thus humanize—not just people with

AIDS, but all people defined as members of a minority. Lofty goals, perhaps. But what choice do we have?

Gregory D. Gross

SOURCE: "Coming Up for Air: Three AIDS Plays," in *Journal of American Culture*, Vol. 15, No. 2, Summer, 1992, pp. 63-7.

[*In the following essay, Gross analyzes three plays that emphasize the political implications of AIDS.*]

Jews, homosexuals, infidels and other devils took more than their fair share of the blame for the Black Death which plagued medieval Europe. No historical drama exists to depict that piece of the gay collective past. Until recently, writers of gay historical drama chose a plague of a different color—the non-biological warfare of persecution, oppression and brutality which crouches at the center of the "three key symbolic events in . . . gay history: Oscar Wilde's trial, the Nazi purge, and Stonewall" [J. M. Clom, "'A Culture That Just Isn't Sexual': Dramatizing Gay Male History," *Theatre Journal* 41, 1989]. *As Is, The Normal Heart,* and *Safe Sex* each allude to the latter two events (indeed, the Holocaust acts as a major symbol in two of the plays); nevertheless, the main point of each of these plays is to sound the alarm over a contemporary event, both real and symbolic, that mirrors the past and also threatens to redefine or undo liberation across the board. These plays, by William Hoffman, Larry Kramer and Harvey Fierstein, respectively, remind audiences that history is political, art is political and even sex is political. These are history plays that are performed in the midst of their own history. The players, the spectators and those walking around outside the theater stand engaged in the same situation. Playwrights have sensed this. Gay writers know that both drama-time and real-time break down into pre-AIDS and post-AIDS. Martin Sherman cancelled the 1983 full-scale production of his *Passing By,* a play about two gay men quarantined with hepatitis, for fear that "the tragic AIDS epidemic . . . would throw the story . . . into a completely misleading light and fan some of the misconceived and prejudicial linkage of homosexuality and physical illness that was then popular in the American press."

Hoffman, Kramer and Fierstein also felt this pressure. The introductions to each of their plays speak to the squeeze of AIDS. Each author wrote under a great sense of urgency. Each felt the press of time. Each had a deadline, not imposed by some editor or producer but, it seems, by civilization itself. These were hurried playwrights: Hoffman—"but one day I realized the depth of my fear and asked God to protect me as I wrote the play"; Kramer—"'This is not a play about measles.' It is about something the Africans call the Horror"; Fierstein—"Never have I felt so of the moment, so 'time-capsulized'." Each wrote his own kind of play about gay men confronting AIDS and each draped his play with an overlay of urgency. None of the major characters die; yet they all come to feel closed in, trapped, out of time. For these characters, AIDS holds the slow horror of suffocation.

Each of the plays gives us characters who struggle with the suffocation of alienation and loneliness. *As Is* tells the story of Rich and Saul who meet to split-up the community property left over from their divorce, a divorce Saul had never wanted. By play's end, Rich and Saul are re-united as a couple facing Rich's rapid AIDS-related physical deterioration. Saul plays the caretaker and serves throughout as a font of love. That scares Rich. During one of the several scenes of Chekhovian overlapping dialogue, Rich flirts with two lines from one of his poems—"The final waning moon / And the coming of the light," while another character describes the play for which she has just auditioned wherein "Everybody in the play is dead [and] The main characters are ghosts." Rich, afraid to truly love or to give, acts as something of a ghost.

Ned, in *The Normal Heart,* is no ghost. He yells and screams too much to be ghostly. Ned, too, is a writer; he, too, closes the play in an AIDS ward; he, too, defends against closeness at every turn. He forms a political action group to fight the disease on the medical/political front. Uncomfortable with his own sexuality, Ned wants to wage war on the sexual front, as well. His political flyer that reads "I am sick of guys moaning that giving up careless sex until this blows over is worse than death" represents just one of the many understandable outbursts that came to be known as the "Ned Weeks School of Outrage." Before working with a string of therapists, Ned approached relationships as a runner; now he approaches them as a fighter. Like Rich in *As Is,* Ned offers a glimpse of alienation in his writing: "[His] novel was all about a man desperate for love and a relationship, in a world filled with nothing but casual sex," and "it sounds to me like [this AIDS crusade is] another excuse to keep from writing." Both of these accusations speak to Ned's need to keep distance from self and other. Ned's harsh activism contains a great deal of heart-felt passion that wins the audience's respect with its rightness. Ultimately, however, the style of Ned's activism eventually alienates the group and they expel him. Like other gay domestic dramas, these two plays end with closeness pressed upon men in desperation, whose time for love and life is rapidly ending.

Fierstein's *Safe Sex,* produced in 1987, two years after *As Is* and *The Normal Heart,* offers a trilogy of plays, each with two major characters. In two of the pieces the author presents a view of the feared AIDS aftermath. *Manny and Jake* open the trilogy with a world in which sex has been banished—at least by Manny. "But I can't kiss," he tells Jake, a would-be seducer. Manny openly mourns the loss of his own humanity and of his relationships with other people. "Another body in a hospital waiting room. Not a patient. Not a survivor. A fact. A statistic. No will. No dream. No choice." Manny can only pray and remember.

The third piece opens much the same way as *As Is,* with two people meeting to claim their belongings. However, Marion and Arthur were never married to each other, though consecutively, each had been married to Collin, who has died from an AIDS illness. The polite veneer of friendly but awkward graciousness while conducting their business soon lifts to reveal jealousy and hostility over who truly mourns and who really loved Collin. Ironically, Marion, absent from his bed for five years, has tested HIV positive, while Arthur has not. She also is remarried and has Collin's son, who serves as a hopeful promise that all their lives will turn out alright.

The center piece of the trilogy bears the play's title, *Safe Sex.* Ghee and Mead are on their second honeymoon, having been a couple for five years before their recent two year separation. The honeymoon is over. Ghee insists upon interrupting lovemaking to check his list of safe sex practices. Mead, who uses calm and cool intellectualization to defend against closeness, rightly proposes that Ghee is misusing safe sex to avoid intimacy. They fight. Mead accuses Ghee of lifelong frigidity; Ghee reminds Mead of his unenticing, non-stimulating personal hygiene. Like Ned and Rich, they are both right and are both wrong. They have made their self-righteous beds and they lie alone. Still, the push for a relationship presses in on these frightened men. Ghee: "Now we enjoy politics and argue sex." Manny, Rich, Ned and Mead could each have said that; each have had that lonely awareness.

Even the stage set underscores the alienation of the characters in *Safe Sex.* Each part of this play contains a small cast surrounded by a large, nearly empty space. Jake strolls around Manny, who sits on a white sofa, center stage. Mead and Ghee each sit on their respective ends of an overly large seesaw, crawling back and forth upon this stage-on-a-stage to punctuate spatially the elastic nature of their closeness-distance continuum. Marion and Arthur occupy a living room stripped of all but a few boxes, ready to be moved out. Perhaps the space and air press down upon all these characters. They occupy the bottom of an oppressive universe—mere specks—and seldom look up, except at the end of each piece when they transcend disease and their own need to control that universe. The less stylized, more representational sets of the other plays also emphasize this existential anxiety.

Ned's personal library serves a similar function. In a mad rush to meet the deadline, he buys books before they go out of print. Felix: "I think you're going to have to face the fact that you won't be able to read them all before you die." In similar fashion, *As Is* utilizes a Greek chorus on stage to comment upon the stifled and stifling nature of Rich's life. For example, Rich asks five doctors from the chorus, "Doctor, tell me the truth. What are my chances?" Each in rhythmic, staccato fashion replies in his turn, "I don't know; I just don't know." Simultaneously, a pre-recorded T.V. announcer concludes an AIDS news summary with a cascade of we-don't-know's.

Larry Kramer weds dialogue, set and theme in a rather complex manner. He recommends that the set walls be painted white as a chilling background for black lettering. Upon these walls, AIDS statistics and press releases such as "TWO MILLION AMERICANS ARE INFECTED—ALMOST TEN TIMES THE OFFICIAL ESTIMATES" are displayed. These Brechtian announcements flash numbers all over the stage and audience—numbers about AIDS cases, numbers about AIDS deaths, numbers of news articles printed in major papers, numbers of dollars spent, numbers of various dates and some corresponding and contrasting numbers related to the 1982 Tylenol scare. Along with the numbers, people's names appear—the fashion of the Vietnam Veterans Memorial in Washington, D.C. Names and numbers are all over the place. Kramer floods the dialogue in a similar way. His Ned Weeks (first name an anagram for "end," last name a time measure) speaks in numbers and lists continuously. Most of his numbers ascend. He first raises $124, then $50,000, then $500,000 before Emma complains that a $5,000,000 grant for AIDS pales along side the $20,000,000 spent on the Tylenol hysteria. Moreover, quite predictably, Ned's statistics on AIDS cases and deaths rise while the number of his own friends, dead or dying, spirals.

Kramer adds a sharp contrast to Ned's numbers and lists with the similarly long but less significant lists of other characters. For example, much is made of Ben's million dollar house that he is about to build even when the cost doubles. When Ned first encounters *Times* writer Felix, whom he will eventually marry, he must listen to Felix's lists. Felix must write about 23 parties, 14 openings, 37 restaurants, 12 discos, 105 spring collections, because "I just write about gay designers, and gay discos, and gay chefs, and gay rock stars, and gay photographers, and gay. . . ." Later when he becomes fully consumed with the disease, Felix's lists take on a far less trivialized nature as he catalogues the names and numbers of treatments he has undergone and paid for. When he settles his will, that final resting place of lists and figures, Felix speaks of numbers hardly at all.

This pattern of descending numbers serves a function that differs from those which ascend. The descending numbers do not serve to flood the audience's consciousness over the size of the plague. Instead, the declining size of the numbers, moving from the big to the small, draws a funnel-like bead on the individual character. Emma starts this pattern when she tells Ned: "That's something over a thousand cases by next year. Half of them will be dead. Your two friends I just diagnosed? One of them will be dead." She moved from the big to the small, from the abstract to the concrete and from the general to the highly personal. Later, Ned expresses his own horror about forty friends now dead of AIDS: "That's too many for one person to know." When the disease eventually hits home and Felix refuses to follow doctor's orders, Ned succumbs: "Felix, I am so sick of statistics, and numbers, and body counts, and how-manys . . . and everyday, Felix, there are only more numbers, and fights . . . You want to die, Felix? Die!" Lists and numbers had suffocated Ned.

Kramer did not use numbers the way Thornton Wilder did in *Our Town* to place a people in their comfortable, right place from the Crofut Farm to the Mind of God. Ned's lists and numbers granted no Epiphany, except in the last paragraph of the play. There, Ned tells of his youth when he had wanted to kill himself "because I thought I was the only gay man in the world . . . they had a dance. Felix, there were six hundred men and women there." Felix had died only a moment before and Ned's soaring, remembered vision proved a proper send-off for Felix's newly released soul.

Fierstein's Manny also plays the numbers, although his final, solitary reverie casts some doubt about whether or not he achieves Epiphany. "I will kiss having learned nothing." Manny often interrupts his dialogue with Jake in order to recite. These recitations carry the quality of a joke-poem that begins with "Two grown men stand in a bar. . ." He starts one of these with two grown men and continues with four, then eight, then twelve grown men. After each grown man speculates about the health of the others, the recitation continues but the number of men standing at the bar decreases incrementally to "One grown man [standing] in a bar looking for someone to look at." Manny finds no safety in numbers; numbers contain danger. Yet squeezed out of the group, he finds little safety, only the press of aloneness in a vast space. Like Ned before him, Manny faces his own need for a group (a lover, family, subculture, culture) and his own lonely distance from that group. Even after his long lists of types of lovers and encounters, he concludes, "And I loved them all. And I missed them when they were gone!"

Fierstein reintroduces, then does away with, numbers in the last piece of his trilogy. Appropriately titled *On Tidy Endings,* this segment not only concludes the play, it also contains two endings within itself. The first half engages Marion with her lawyer, June, who represents the business side of grief. June swamps her client with legal papers—copies and copies of legal papers (wills, insurance policies, real estate documents). June cares about Marion and wants the best deal for her. But there's a time and a place for everything. "This is about tidying up loose ends, not holding hands," advises June. That settled, June exits and Arthur, co-beneficiary, enters for the second half. After some small-talk over who gets this or that from the deceased Collin, they begin to "get messy" with some of the emotional, unfinished business. Marion and Arthur tidy up these accounts, too, and ironically they decide to postpone signing those legal papers. Those numbers will have to wait.

Another set of numbers plagues these plays—6,000,000 Jews. The Holocaust took many casualties from Jews and gays alike. Both claim the Holocaust as a major event in their respective and intertwined histories and all three playwrights here lace their dramas with Nazi images. *The Normal Heart* took its name from *The Informed Heart,* Bruno Bettleheim's seminal treatise on life in the death camps. Kramer's set contains a paragraph on Jewish political strategy during World War II and his characters draw overt parallels between the Holocaust and AIDS and to the Jewish and gay response to both. Ned delivers near soliloquies on the subject. These speeches turn up the heat; they sap the air out of those who wish to hide from the issues. When they finally get to City Hall, Tommy reflects that the government has put them in a "tomb" (basement), thus arousing the twin images of catacombs and Nazi mass graves. Freud is called just another old Jew who couldn't get laid; David, dying, looks "like someone out of Auschwitz"; and Dr. Emma earns the name Dr. Death.

Kramer's men are not only victims; they are victimizers: "So we're just walking time bombs—waiting for whatever it is that sets us off." Again, these men feel the life squeezed out of them, caught in a vice of passivity on one hand and sexual/political action on the other. Both appear futile. The Holocaust smothers the play with the undertones of brutality and oppression. At the same time, as John Clum claimed of *Bent,* a gay-issues play set more directly within the Nazi regime, "the real issue of the play is self-oppression manifested in behavior that would be considered typical for an urban gay man in 1979." *As Is,* too, punctuates AIDS with allusion to Naziism. Saul refers to Rich's agent as Dr. Mengale, and Hospice Worker admires a Lodz Ghetto survivor who accepted death passively but nobly. And then PWA 4 tells the complete joke: "Have you heard about the disease attacking Jewish American Princesses? It's called MAIDS. You die if you don't get it." Jewish humor, sick humor, the Holocaust and 1980s gay experience collide in that one joke. Here the audience may die if *they* don't "get" it. Saul had set this joke up much earlier when he said to Rich, "Why didn't you warn me we were going to play Christians and Jews today? I would have worn my yellow star." Much later Saul quips that if he commits suicide he will "go to hell with all us Jews." Rich replies, "I bet they have a separate AIDS section in the cemetery."

It was no joke in *The Normal Heart* when Bruce described Albert's "cemetery." An orderly "stuffs Albert in a heavy-duty Glad bag . . . and he puts him in the back alley with the garbage . . . and we finally found a black undertaker who cremated him for a thousand dollars, no questions asked." Kramer wrote this scene with such craft that one might even smell the death-smoke and choke on its suffocating odor. This atmosphere of growing persecutory paranoia stemming from both homophobia and societal indifference threatens to explode into oppressive action. Mickey: "Do you think the CIA really has unleased germ warfare to kill off all us queers . . . ?" Ned: "Did you ever consider it could get so bad they'll quarantine us in camps?" Ghee's sexual paranoia in *Safe Sex,* reality based as it is, pales beside Kramer's view of a society gone mad.

Fierstein alludes less directly to the Holocaust, but its spectre squats just beneath the surface. Manny's sober, chant-like prayers place him in a death house. He states he is not a "survivor." Perhaps his soul has gone. In the final play of the trilogy, Arthur calls himself a "prisoner of love" and adds, "Who says I survived?" He and his lover had played the Wandering Jew, together shopping the world over for the newest cure promised—in Reno, Philly, France, New Orleans, Mexico. "We traveled everywhere they offered hope for sale and came home with souvenirs." Collin died and part of Arthur failed to survive the new Holocaust.

With their lists, and their deaths, and their Dachaus, and their dead air, do these plays depress? No. If these plays do not end happily, they at least end hopefully. Fierstein's "Author's Note" advises, "Never lose your sense of humor." *As Is* begins and ends with a laugh, albeit a nervous laugh. These plays are chock full of in-jokes, out-jokes, ethnic jokes, "faggot jokes," affectionate teasing and downright funniness. Much of the humor represents the gallows variety described in previous decades by two Jewish men who wrote non-fiction. Freud said such sick humor "perches on the edge of personal destruction." Victor Frankl, a psychiatrist and a survivor of Auschwitz, called these jokes "one of the 'soul's weapons' in the struggle for self-preservation." Both writers were speaking of a psychic liberation from the proverbial abyss. Each of the three dramas laments the loss of a better time before the AIDS abyss. Whether an audience laughs at this humor out of depravity, therapy or liberation seems beside the point. The point is AIDS has forced a re-examination of liberated spirit as well as liberated behavior. Ghee laments, "We can never touch as before. We can never be as before. 'Now' will always define us. Different times. Too late. . . . Safe sex." "The more open and liberated the movement, . . . the more sexuality is freed to wreak havoc." If Ned articulates a desire for gay men to identify with more than their sexuality, then sexuality today may have to find a way to identify with more than AIDS. Balancing the demands of desire and dread, these three plays pose all the old questions of love and will, freedom and responsibility. Mead: "This is dangerous. You're supposed to be [scared]. These are different times with different rules, but some things never change."

Joseph Dewey

SOURCE: "The Music for a Closing: Responses to AIDS in Three American Novels," in *AIDS: The Literary Response*, edited by Emmanuel S. Nelson, Twayne Publishers, 1992, pp. 23-38.

[*In the following essay, Dewey examines three novels that he considers exemplary literary representations of the realities surrounding AIDS.*]

The American experience has produced remarkably few journals of plague years. After all, our most direct confrontations with the realities of epidemic infection occurred early in our nation's history, long before a tradition in fiction had begun; encouraged by loosely monitored sanitary conditions, chronic food shortages, impure water supplies, and hordes of insects, "epidemic disorders [regular outbreaks of malaria, smallpox, typhoid, and scarlet fever] visited death and destruction upon the American colonies with relentless regularity." Yet with the exception of Charles Brockden Brown's *Arthur Mervyn* (1799) with its dark vision of a Philadelphia ravaged by the yellow fever epidemic of 1793 the early colonial experience with pestilence found little voice in our national literature. Plagues in our literature have been neither bacterial nor viral but rather moral and, hence, metaphoric: our plagues have been rapacity, complacency, racism, political fanaticism, sexual excesses, drug and alcohol abuse. These have been our sicknesses, simpler to diagnose than to treat; and writers as diverse as Jack London and Thomas Pynchon, William Dean Howells and James Baldwin, Henry James and Kurt Vonnegut have created our journals of these plagues. Indeed, despite *Arthur Mervyn*'s unblinking record of the horrific realities of Philadelphia's crowded hospitals and stinking streets, Brown uses the epidemic metaphorically to suggest the moral malignancy his young hero must ultimately come to glimpse as a necessary moment in his maturation.

In America, the record of our confrontations with epidemics has been recorded not in our fiction but in medical treatises. There, in its largely inaccessible language, the medical community has first defined, then isolated, and (with reassuring regularity) vanquished one after another of a score of once terrifying diseases: encephalitis, influenza, smallpox, yellow fever, cholera, tuberculosis, and, most recently, polio. Never in America's history has plague commanded the terror or immediacy that has been recorded in other national literatures. Indeed, from Cotton Mather's courageous campaign to inoculate a decidedly hostile Boston against smallpox to Noah Webster's encyclopedic *A Brief History of Epidemic and Pestilential Diseases* (1799) to the heroics of Walter Reed and Jonas Salk, the American experience with pestilence has been a defiant record of success. A scant decade ago the notion that we might confront a plague—more, a strain of virus never tracked—would have seemed the alarmist premise of bargain-bin science fiction. Yet the devastating potency of the HIV virus, with its dubious distinction as the first plague of the Television Age, has created within a half-decade after its outbreak not only a global awareness of a radically new sort of infection but also for the first time in the American literary experience a substantial body of what must be defined as plague literature.

An artistic response was, perhaps, inevitable given that the HIV virus has struck with particular virulence within the arts community, generating responses in virtually every media. The literary response, largely ignored by the reading public and the established critics in the popular press, chronicles our attempt to come to terms with difficult conditions that have carried us back to a decidedly medieval sort of mind-set. After all, at the decade's start, we sat securely within the smooth walls of our biomedical wonderland only to turn, like Poe's haughty Prince Prospero, to confront an untreatable retrovirus, with a terrifying sort of memory, that slumbers until, after stretches of years, it begins the steady work of destroying the body's fragile defenses against illness, and is so potent that divine wrath becomes a possible explanation for those struggling to answer why.

As a genre, this body of plague literature, of course, has little promise—there is no aesthetic beauty in the caved-in, yellowed faces and skeletal figures in AIDS hospices; a viral infection of this scale creates not the elegant individuality of heroes but rather an overwhelming anonymity of victims, interred within statistics; the plot must operate without the drive of suspense, propelled only by the grind of inevitability; there can be no moral—save that a virus blindly, stupidly destroys what gives it life. And because the epidemic stays immediate and vivid in the oppressive tonnage of newspaper articles, magazine photostories, and television documentaries, it resists the graceful transmutation into metaphor that has long been the aesthetic privilege of those writers who dare to work within the dark sphere of illnesses that destroy the young.

More distressing, plague literature is a body of fiction that must recognize as its first premise its own helplessness. For those who are afflicted, the written word cannot heal, cannot answer why, cannot even concoct an afterlife sufficiently believable to overcome the agony of losing this life. Where, then, can an AIDS fiction begin? Given the alarming novelty of the virus itself, traditional models of plague literature—namely, Boccaccio's *Decameron,* Defoe's *The Journal of the Plague Year,* and Camus's *The Plague*—offer few relevant strategies. The bawdy insouciance of Boccaccio's storytelling with its strategic withdrawal from the plague city to refuge deep within the Italian countryside would seem glaringly insensitive—AIDS is too much with us to permit our indulging in, even with yearning innocence, the casual comedy of whiling away the darkest hours in such pleasant nullity. We cannot *not* write about it. And Defoe's unshakeable conviction that Providence alone could withstand the plague's cold illogic seems at best shopworn in the Secular City where God casts a thin shadow and at worst bald hypocrisy in the face of a disease many can accept as an instrument of divine punishment. And Camus's use of contagion as an undeniable occasion of mortality that tests whether those quarantined in the Algerian port can find significance in life within an infected geography seems too metaphoric, a luxury when compared to what AIDS victims must confront: the indignities of a slow and grinding premature death.

If the genre of plague literature seems inappropriate, so also does the genre of doomed youth. Predominantly war fiction, the literature of doomed youth is a genre of extremes. In its more elegant expression, the genre articulates a heady sort of idealism that defines the sacrifice of young life using a community vocabulary of heightened patriotism. It is a fiction that sustains a community at war and endows the war dead with significance. In this century, however, the fiction more often deals head-on with war's horrific experience to devastate inflated notions of heroism. In either case, war fiction searches for ways to teach the community, to awaken it to awareness. Although the parallel between the at-risk group confronting the HIV virus and doomed, frontline troops has been elaborated by writers (most prominently by Emmanel Dreuilhe in *Mortal Embrace*), the fiction of the AIDS epidemic cannot find its way to either extreme of the genre, to exaggerated idealism or to unsettling anger. The sick die for no ideal; anger here cannot teach. AIDS fiction, like war fiction, is left only the cold business of measuring the attrition, counting the dead.

There are few other genres into which the literature of AIDS could fall. There is the slender group of works that treats the death of the young, characters confronting mortality precisely at the moment of their fullest potential, confronting, as it were, the lie of youth's own assumptions. Such fiction—James's *The Wings of a Dove,* for example—often converts the illness into a dramatic metaphor, making the physical trauma of the disease vague, allowing the young sufferer to leap effortlessly into infinity, leaving behind the weightless advice to live fully. It is a literature that counsels with passionate seriousness to love the fragment of time we are given; in such literature the illness is awkwardly irrelevant—the fact of death is central, not the circumstances of dying. Such characters often die of plot necessity. But AIDS is far too immediate, far too available; from the thick rhetoric of government reports to the shrill white noise of supermarket tabloids, the devastation of AIDS is far too immediate to permit such elegant transmutations.

The magnitude of the illness, the steadily escalating statistical projection of the number of infected people, threatens to turn fiction finally into irrelevancy—leaving AIDS fiction to spin with linguistic opulence the elegies or flowery saintly-buddy pieces; with hope impossible to locate, the only available strategy for AIDS fiction, then, would be adjusting to the illogical intervention of the AIDS virus. Or perhaps, as Andrew Holleran argues, the only writing sufficient to the surreal horrors of the epidemic would be a simple list of the names of those who have died, a list that stretches to disheartening lengths as each month 3,000 new cases of AIDS are diagnosed in the United States alone. Ironically, that necessary realism has moved the literature away from death, or more particularly away from recounting the raw experience of preparing for death's interrupting stroke. The fictional response to the fact of AIDS has turned toward the very face of the epidemic and there it has found a strategy, an approach. Although it is surely possible, given the medical community's unprecedented interest in the AIDS virus, that within a generation the infection may go the way of other pestilent horrors, the irruption of the virus has nevertheless generated a substantial body of human and humane fiction, journals of our plague years, the first generation of such novels in the American experience.

I

> Doesn't it seem as if autumn were the real
> creator, more creative
> than spring, which all at once is; more creative,
> when it comes
> with its will to change and destroys the much-
> too-finished,
> much-too-satisfied picture of summer?
>
> —*Rainer Maria Rilke*

Because of its radical failure of nerve, Alice Hoffman's *At Risk* (1988) is a most instructive starting point in assessing the novel's response to the AIDS epidemic. In Hoffman's novel the settled calm of an affluent family in a small New England town is upended when the 11-year-old daughter, Amanda, is diagnosed with AIDS five years after she has been contaminated by a blood transfusion during an emergency appendectomy. As the family struggles to understand the implications of the diagnosis, Amanda herself adjusts both on a public level (to the casual cruelties of friends and neighbors who, in their ignorance, initially recoil from her) and on a private level (to the reality of her denied future). As she moves uncertainly between planning for a gymnastics competition scheduled for an all-too-distant springtime and imagining what sound her death will make and what color it will be, she strikes poignant responses within the reader. With Dickensian sensibility, Hoffman stage-manages Amanda's narrative. Unlike the mainstream victims of the disease, Amanda, by virtue of her age and the method by which she contracted the virus, can be accepted unambiguously by the reader as a victim. Thus Hoffman manages to elicit sentiment while neatly avoiding the tangling complexity of questions AIDS raises about love, sexuality, and death.

With Hoffman's book, however, we can enter easily into an emotional melodrama in which AIDS serves as well as any contagious, terminal infection. We are free to feel the anger and the sorrow of such an illogical stroke—Amanda is innocence intolerably violated. As such the book succeeds in recording the raw and immediate moments of Amanda's adjustment: weeks after her diagnosis, for example, Amanda, her braces newly removed, peeks into the dentist's mirror and concedes with tears that, indeed, she "would have been beautiful." She is a victim, "murdered," according to her father's passionate anger. The domestic security of Amanda's family is breached much like when the wasp (pregnant, full of eggs) invades the kitchen in the opening scene or when the destructive voles rummage beneath the neat perimeter of the family vegetable garden. AIDS here is an invasion. Instead of confronting AIDS, Hoffman manipulates its impact as a hot buzzword. Forsaking the tensions caused by AIDS on the margins of society to register the impact within the settled middle, Hoffman sanitizes the epidemic, makes its reader-friendly. Not surprisingly, her book received enormous critical attention and significant sales, including movie rights.

But without exploring the effects the virus registers in those whose very identities—sexual, social, political—have been threatened, the book reads as an uncomplicated exercise in the literature of doomed youth. As in such fiction, Hoffman's characters define a natural world irredeemably infected, moving irresistibly toward exhaustion or extinction. At every turn, virtually with every character, we find a death-soaked natural world. Amanda is herself a school champion gymnast, whose stunning routines are the very embodiment of the physical world elevated to grace and near perfection. Amanda's father, an astronomer, specializes in tracking exploding stars, in "looking at dead stars." Her brother is enthralled by dinosaurs. Once his sister is diagnosed, he is trapped within terrifying nightmares in which he imagines extinction creeping over a newborn dinosaur caught in the inexorable slide toward the Ice Age. Amanda's mother, a free-lance photographer, has just completed work on a book about coping with dying and is now covering the séances of a local medium. That medium, who comes to befriend Amanda, is herself haunted by dreams of death because many of her clients are mourning the loss of a loved one and hunger to touch a realm beyond the reach of death.

Yet, Hoffman concedes that the attempt to make contact with the dead is little more than a brave gesture, much like Amanda's brother's naïve campaign to capture on film a prehistoric giant turtle he is certain he has glimpsed in a neighborhood pond. Confirming the prehistoric turtle's existence would, of course, counter the physical world's apparent rush toward extinction. However, since the novel is locked within the iron logic of the literature of doomed youth, death claims Amanda, in this instance, melodramatically: before leaving for the hospital, she dictates her "will," consigning her few possessions to her family, struggling to give even as the illness takes everything; then her father carries her to the hospital amid a swirl of dead leaves on Halloween night. It is an uneasy moment of unearned sentimentality, as emotionally draining as it is effortlessly cinematic. When the novel closes with Amanda's brother patiently waiting pondside for the emergence of the prehistoric turtle, after he has received news that his sister is dead, the reader recognizes it as a bravura gesture and, in its own way, an act of denial. Hoffman's novel is, then, an exercise in relearning the terrifying brevity of life, whether it is measured in the handful of summers Amanda has had or in the unnerving stretches of astral years her father measures in his planetarium.

At Risk is, finally, not about Amanda or about AIDS at all. The virus seems less the subject than an occasion to test a family's resilience. Amanda's family first splinters (after the diagnosis, each family member retreats into separate rooms on different levels in the house) and then slowly, gradually repairs. The mother overcomes her awkward relationship with Amanda by watching the friendship that develops between her daughter and the local medium; the father struggles to forgive the random virulence of the natural world through the calming voice of Brian, an AIDS patient who answers questions at an emergency hotline; and the brother overcomes his all too normal sibling grudges against his older sister and affirms in the closing pages that he will never not have a sister. Stricken, the family struggles to heal in the limited time it has before Amanda's generous presence becomes sheerest absence. Hoffman's chosen vehicle for recovery—the family—is, oddly, the very unit of social support that often is inaccessible to the homosexual community. For gays creating a family, of course, is barred by biology; establishing a family is severely restricted by social webbing; and even retaining the family into which they were born is often jeopardized by the revelation of their sexual orientation and then by the devastating revelation of the infection. Hoffman's resolution of the crisis caused by AIDS that is dramatized in her novel does not ring altogether false—Amanda's hesitant movement toward death is all too immediate—but Hoffman cannot find her way to a satisfying examination of AIDS because she deliberately does not focus on the isolation and anxieties the disease has prompted within the gay community. Amanda's death is unbearably poignant but finally reductive. And because Hoffman steers clear of exploring the contrapuntal urges of love and death that a complete literary treatment of AIDS demands, her narrative can offer not hope but only adjustment. Hoffman's narrative is, finally, unpleasantly exploitative as it summons the images of the epidemic without grappling with its essential definition. As such, Hoffman's work remains at best a powerful reassertion of that leaden feeling (typical in the literature of doomed youth) that a young character has been robbed of the opportunity to experience what life has to offer.

II

Unlike Hoffman's elaborate dodge, Robert Ferro's *Second Son* (1988) directly confronts mortality as well as the more complicated questions of love and sexuality raised by the AIDS epidemic. And, offering characters compelled by such urgencies, Ferro is able to create a very dramatic journal of this plague, offering in his work what Hoffman cannot—a model for those who seek in literature not a cure but rather a strategy for coexisting with a virus of compelling potency.

Ferro centers his argument on the striking comparisons between the traditional family and the gay relationship, or more exactly between the social unit applicable to measuring the stability of presumably healthy heterosexual arrangements and the less conventional partnerships struck when sexual orientation excludes expression within such conventional lines. Against the fashionable stereotype of the homosexual life-style of the 1970s when the gay community found in limitless promiscuity a defiant assertion of identity, Ferro here traces a nurturing relationship that develops between Mark Valerian and Bill Mackey, both stricken with the virus. That construction, so apparently defined by the AIDS epidemic as infected, offers within Ferro's book the possibility of healing against the family, which here is so completely dysfunctional, so totally bankrupt of reassuring support and compassion that it, rather than the relationship defined as diseased, is ailing and terminally infected.

The novel opens with Ferro's devastating portrait of Mark Valerian's family. Although Mark often jokingly refers to the "Filial Wars" that have long wrenched his family, such posturing conceals what is indeed a family deeply divided, a busy family involved in exacting professions (one sister is named Vita). Given the fury of their upscale life-styles, they express familial affection in frictionless holiday gestures and in quick long-distance telephone calls. Mark cannot find his place within this family. Unlike two of his siblings, one a psychologist, the other a lawyer, Mark follows an aesthetic impulse—his eye for "form, decoration"—and has become an interior decorator. His other sister expounds on the wisdom of abandoning the fast track to raise a family, a life-style even further removed from Mark. Mark's diagnosis only reinforces his sense of estrangement, his feeling of being (as the title underscores) one son too many. The family initially recoils from Mark's illness, finding the diagnosis distasteful, dangerous. His father, trying to define the illness within a fundamentalist Christian vocabulary, waffles between repugnance over the "sin" of homosexuality and the lamest clichés of his faith in miracles. But he cannot conceal that he finds the illness and, by extension, his second son, offensive.

Isolated, Mark takes up residence for the summer in the cavernous run-down summer cottage that the family has maintained for nearly 30 years by Cape May, New Jersey. When the family, encouraged by the reptilian older brother, moves to sell the summer cottage to help cover enormous losses incurred by the father's failing business, it is a practical decision uncomplicated by compassion. The inevitable showdown between father and second son over the sale of the house is an ugly recitation not merely of deep-seated homophobia but the far more distressing feelings in the son that his father is waiting for him to die, to be rid of the cumbersome problem of the second son. It is an "annihilating moment" that leaves nothing but "ash." The family with its occasional gestures toward connection (in a tender moment, Mark is allowed to hold his niece) is a decaying construction, like the summer cottage itself. Itself more dead than alive, it cannot minister to the dying second son.

The radical failure of the Valerian family to accommodate the life of the second son defines what has emerged as the dominant theme of the literary response to AIDS—the terrifyingly simple sundering of hearts, the ease with which distance is created. In many ways, the virus and its attendant paranoias have legitimized disconnection. In the government's sobering pronouncements for safe sex, in the hysterical calls for quarantining or tattooing the sick, in the necessities of barrier nursing, in the designation of the sick as pariah, we are shaped by a logic of withdrawal. Apart from the pragmatics of health care, disconnection is part of a larger conspiracy of apathy, a determination by the largest share of the population currently enjoying the illusion of being not at risk to turn away from the flat, dead eyes of the already stricken. It is "their" disease—and unlike other diseases that emerged into prominence during the decade (Alzheimer's, for example) AIDS is perceived to be an affliction that will not cross the threshold if it is not given access. Far more terrifying than the grinding physical erosion of the disease on its victims, Ferro argues, is the fear of being abandoned. Twice marginalized, once by their sexual identity and then again by their infection, surrounded in their community by those who have learned hard lessons of repugnance, estranged from family, even from lovers, and left often with only the cold touch of sympathetic strangers in hospices, AIDS patients too often are left to play at desperate illusions of self-sufficiency. When Mark visits Bill in the hospital, he visits an AIDS patient very much alone, a boy of 23 whose only company, he groans, is death: "I feel it come into the room." Left so finally alone, he confesses to Mark that death would be better than the insufferable days of isolation. His only consolation, his heart so thoroughly destroyed, is that death will finally claim everyone. He lashes out at Mark, "Your lover will die, then you will; then all of them, one after another."

Second Son cites just this irrevocable error of withdrawing into the self and counsels rather a courageous commitment to emotion—the fragile, private, man-made constructions of passion and compassion, that can serve as a heroic counterforce to the sort of poisonous webbing suggested by the insidious spread of the disease. Against the very public campaigns encouraging discipline, celibacy, and abstinence, against the withering away of the urgent, creative combustion of sexual spontaneity, against the acceptance in the gay community to live like Shakers—against, in short, a decade-long drift away from each other, Ferro asserts a most unconventional response—the relationship. Against the collapse of Mark's family, we witness the emergence in graceful counterpoint of his relationship with Bill Mackey, a set designer and theatrical lighting specialist whom he meets while on a working vacation in Rome. Like Mark, Bill has tested positive and begins even as the relationship develops to feel the first symptoms. Yet this relationship defies the grinding inevitability of the virus. When they first make love in Rome under the fabulous vermilion sunsets spoked into color by the poisonous radiation cloud from Chernobyl as it passes over southern Europe, Mark and Bill construct a marvelously fragile bond that revives for both of them emotional responses denied in the two years since their diagnoses, two years of living on the rich details of their memories.

As Mark and Bill make love—the "collected, considerate reserve of elderly lovers who worry for each other's hearts or brittle bones"—it is a potent sort of magic. During the slow, late summer days when Mark and Bill return from Rome to the Berkshires to disperse the ashes of Bill's longtime companion, Mark rows to the middle of a lake one evening on Bill's instructions. He turns toward the distant haze of the shore and in the fading twilight sees flickering against the descending dusk on shore a fabulous "necklace of lights" "bleeding into the darkness," complemented by 60-foot jet streams of water arching into the simple grace of a rainbow. It is a gift from Bill. Mark is enthralled by such a lambent moment of magic that speaks a "language of brightness," all produced by Bill's creative impulse, aided by a noiseless generator, a pump, and miles of extension cords. Like the fragile connection forged between Bill and Mark, the display is not permanent; rather it can be maintained for only a gorgeous moment. But Bill's gesture suggests the magic of the artificial, the man-made, that is powerful precisely because it must flicker, because it must certainly give way to the darkness. Their emotional bond is an assertion against the natural world—that world is represented by the Roman sunsets infected by radiation or by the shoreline hushing into night or by the AIDS infection. The natural, here as in other fictional responses to AIDS, is decidedly limited; the retrovirus strikes, as Susan Sontag has observed, through the blood and semen, the most sacramental networks of biological life. Against the autumn shoreline that moves with its natural determination toward the silences of winter, the fragile string of lights enchants Mark; indeed, it glows stronger, brighter as night descends. And under the tonic of their commitment to each other, Mark and Bill register defiant remission in their illness—lesions fade, headaches dim, appetites return. Theirs becomes a marvelous parable of restoration and reclamation, as Mark's profession might suggest.

But AIDS cannot permit magic. Despite Mark's emotional description of Bill as some fantastic being "lowered from the sky on piano wire" and his heady pronouncements that he simply will not concede to the disease, he cannot shake dreams of boarding a train bound for a "cathedrallike, cavernous nineteenth-century railway station of steel and glass," a haunting suggestion of approaching death. The fiction of AIDS cannot depend on recovery—the disease demands closure. Ferro will not abrogate the imperative of realism. Against a subplot that involves an exchange of letters in which a friend of Mark's (who is likewise infected as the reader gathers from remarks in the letters) writes about the money he is investing in a ludicrous plan to launch a rocketful of homosexuals to a distant planet there to recover and live in peace, Mark shoulders his way toward what must be. Toward the end of the book, the relapse for both Mark and Bill signals that indeed they are poised to acknowledge the end of any new possibilities even as Mark returns to close up Cape May for the winter. There is no cure—simply the steady assurances they offer each other that neither will go it alone.

Ferro argues that such an assurance is the sole gesture against the plague. In a poignant moment, Mark, in the hospital for tests, must deliver a sperm sample and finds himself unable to achieve sufficient erection. He begins to cry, and only in tears does he find himself aroused. That is the lesson of *Second Son*—only the steady pressure of absolute absence engenders absolute emotion. Much as Mark watches a handsome man walk slowly along the beach weaving tight circles above the wastes of the sand with a metal detector to find something of value, Ferro finds within the claustrophobic binding of the disease something of value—the overwhelming magnitude of a disease that defies connection demands connection, not in the heady excesses of cruising but in the gentler gesture of finding another heart. As Mark watches the man on the beach find something, the metal scoop he carries proves "inadequate. Only the human hand will do." Unlike Hoffman's sentimental drama, resolution cannot be found within the constricting webbing of the family. As Mark and Bill prepare, as AIDS patients must, for inevitable closure, they wait with each other. That commitment offers them a healing of a sort, a summer that is in its brevity the very mother of beauty. The disease itself creates the occasion of their passion, for only the knowledge of their mutual infection creates the courage to love. Unable to place sufficient faith in the interminable experiments with blood tests and new drugs, unable to believe as an Italian clairvoyant assures them that the passing radiation cloud will cure them, Mark and Bill define a fragile community, an achievement of manmade magic as artificial, as momentary, as incandescent as the string of lights along an autumnal shoreline.

III

The Sunrise—Sir—compelleth Me—
Because He's Sunrise—and I see

—*Emily Dickinson,* "Poem 480"

George Whitmore's *Nebraska* (1987) would seem to be an odd choice as the most significant journal of our plague years. Whitmore's narrative does not directly treat the virus. Moving from the Eisenhower fifties to the summer of 1969, the very threshold of the sexual liberation of the 1970s, Whitmore's novel traces the difficult maturation of Craig McMullen, a fatherless, one-legged boy who must come to terms with his homosexuality even as his family is devastated by similar revelations about his Uncle Wayne, whom Craig fiercely admires as a surrogate father. Well within the conventions of gay literature, Whitmore centers his coming-of-age story on the difficulty of the double life, or more accurately, the fractured life necessitated by a social network unable to accept sexuality that cannot be contained within the simplest perception of "normal."

One such fractured life is surely Uncle Wayne's. Following his discharge from the navy, he returns to Nebraska to await word from Vernon, a friend from the navy, about opening a garage in California. Wayne is a man of the world, too big, too full of life to be trapped within the iron frame of Nebraska. The engagement ring he wears on his pinkie, he brags, is a token of affection from any one of a number of women who waited for him at any number of ports. Yet, he stays in Nebraska. Each letter he receives from Vernon delays his plans, he says, because of financial inconveniences. Reluctantly, Wayne accepts work, temporarily, he insists.

But Wayne is leading a fiercely destructive secret life. Because Whitmore relates events through the limited perception of a young Craig, we do not learn until much later the actual contents of the letters from Vernon to Wayne. In them, Vernon must tell Wayne that their love cannot be realized and that separation is the only response. Driven by the oppressive confines of a Nebraska home he suddenly cannot leave and by the realization that the simplest expression of his love would not be tolerated, Wayne makes uncertain gestures toward his impressionable nephew; for example, one evening he strokes Craig's penis, checking, he says, for hair. Wayne conceals his sexual identity from his family until he is arrested in a vice sweep of a men's room in a bus depot in nearby Omaha. Then, in quick succession, he loses his job, his family, his home. Without explanation to the young Craig, his Uncle Wayne is simply "gone."

What triggers the sequence of devastating events, not surprisingly, is a lie. Craig concocts an innocent lie about his Uncle Wayne during a sleepover. That night, a sultry Indian summer night, Craig feels good, close to Wesley in ways he does not possess sufficient vocabulary to explain. As they lie together in an improvised tent, a blanket pitched above Craig's bed, Wesley nervously asks to touch the stump of Craig's leg. Finding himself aroused, Craig intrigues to convince his friend to masturbate him by telling him that his Uncle Wayne had bragged that such practices were routine in the navy and that Uncle Wayne had even shown him how to do it "lots and lots of times." It is a devastatingly obvious lie, told without thought during the onset of a hurricane of emotions that the boy at 13 cannot begin to understand. All he wants, he thinks, is to feel his friend's hand warm on his penis, a gesture of the simplest connection that echoes, ironically, the imperative wailed out to him when he watches a television evangelist, who wheezes enthusiastically, "SEIZE LIFE! TAKE LIFE IN THY HANDS! SMELL OF ITS FRAGRANCE." Here, the opportunity is frustrated Wesley, a practicing Baptist, fears such acts are too sinful.

The chain reaction caused by this lie, however, culminates in Craig's testifying after his uncle's arrest. When Wesley's father informs local authorities after Wayne's arrest of what Craig revealed to Wesley, Craig must answer delicately phrased questions about whether his uncle "interfered" with him. When asked if his uncle ever touched him, Craig must admit, of course, that he had—even in the caring gesture of sponge bathing him after the accident that claims his leg. Whitmore offers pages of court testimony that deliver with cold objectivity the devastating judgment against Uncle Wayne. Cornered into testifying against his uncle, the boy, however, only completes the destruction of his uncle begun long before by the systematic refusal of the social webbing to allow him the expression of a normal life, lived as he wanted, as he had to. Destroyed by his trial, ostracized by his family, driven through a series of dead-end jobs, long separated from the companionship of his lover in California, Wayne ends up in a state medical facility where, we find out years later, he is surgically altered against his will, neutralizing what most distresses him but what most defines him—his sexual identity.

When Craig, 10 years later, finally reunites with his uncle in California, he finds a most disturbing creature. Craig first sees Wayne sprawled in four inches of water in a child's wading pool. His uncle does not seem to recognize him. Indeed, now surgically separated from his own sexuality, Wayne lives with Vernon like a child in undisturbed prepuberty. He lives in the room of a "normal" American boy—model airplanes suspended from the ceiling, sports equipment scattered about, pictures of dinosaurs, spaceman wallpaper, sheets and pillow cases with planets. But the normal assumes surreal shadings as Whitmore delivers in a spare and unemotional line of prose the horror of Craig's growing sexual realization. Lost now within the pleasant routines of going to the zoo or to the mall, now giddy in a shrill prepubescent way about sex (he giggles hysterically as he rummages through Vernon's hidden collection of male muscle magazines), Wayne is a shadow of his earlier, tormented self (indeed, in the navy his nickname had been Shadow). Distanced now from the difficult, destructive confrontation with growing up, he lives in a haunting parody of normality, in an eerie sort of suspended animation; he has become a disturbing cross between Peter Pan and Sleeping Beauty. But peace has come at a high cost. Craig observes as Wayne and Vernon watch television each night, Wayne cuddled in asexual security in the crook of Vernon's arm. They are unable now to break through to the genuine expression of passion they had shared in the navy. Vernon, feeling enormously responsible for Wayne's condition because of his hasty letters releasing Wayne from their commitment, understands that now they are each other's life sentences . . . the authentic expression of their passion has been replaced by the colder routine of careful watching. Wayne has vanished into a secret and safe world, like his miniature railroad town in the basement that he shows his nephew, with its miles of tracks, its detailed landscaping, its houses and farms, precise down to stray sheep, streetlights, and picket fences—so compellingly normal, so unnervingly surreal.

Whitmore's narrative, then, would seem a most disturbing variation on the doomed-queen genre, a revelation of the agonies experienced within the closet and the perilous experiences outside its protective darkness. But it is the destructive splintering within the boy that more concerns Whitmore. Uncertain of his sexuality, uncertain of its potency, its acceptability, even its implications, Craig moves through a difficult adolescence unloved. There are no happy couples within Craig's immediate experience. Craig's father, a reformed alcoholic, returns to his son's life quite abruptly after school one afternoon, years after abandoning his family. Despite his fervent declamations about being a born-again Christian, he is, nevertheless, capable of kidnapping his son during the height of a Nebraska snowstorm. When it is apparent the boy is more fearful than forgiving, the father douses the child with gasoline and contemplates sacrificing him to God, Isaac-style, to make up for his past mistakes. And Craig's long-suffering mother is bloated by a life of servility, first to the raging abuses of her husband and then to the petty slavery of her 15 years waiting tables at a Montgomery Ward's coffee shop. She recalls with imperfect emotions the unanticipated pregnancy that led her, years earlier, to begin the elaborate charade as mother. Other marriages in Craig's family are drawn by financial considerations or are brokered after similar unexpected pregnancies; they are sustained by the merest gestures of interest; siblings are horribly distant and casually cruel, grandparents inexplicably hostile and obscure.

It is struggling, finally, against that dead weight of oppression, corroded passion, and deception that marks the emergence of Craig McMullen. Crippled at 12 (on the very threshold of puberty) by a vicious truck accident that forces the amputation of his leg, Craig is forever isolated, marked, denied access to the normal expression of boyhood—Red Cross swimming lessons and scouting, for example. Indeed, normality seems a condition far removed from Craig's experience. He is marked by an aberrant father, an infamous uncle, a missing leg. He hungers to be happy, a condition he defines early on as being normal; yet he struggles against the distance, the sheer inaccessibility of such a condition. He dreams of the heartbreakingly simple, of having "his own blue notebook back with the three-hole paper with the ship flags on it and inside the right number of pencils, a little sharpener for the one you lost, your three-color ballpoint and the pink eraser that works on ink too." He cannot, however, seem to make it all work. He admits to an intolerable, inexplicable weight of unhappiness, comparing himself to a young girl in the hospital who had lived her entire, short life in terrible pain assuming all the time, "This is just life." She dies, Craig overhears, from a tumor no doctor had even suspected she had.

Marked by his accident, confused by the uncertain expression of urges he cannot dismiss, Craig cannot find his niche within his corroded family in Nebraska. After his uncle's trial, his mother remarries (to a lugubrious lawyer with colorless eyes who maneuvers an out-of-court settlement after Craig's accident). No offer is extended to Craig to live with them. He goes, rather, to live with his grandparents in their run-down home. There he feels like another piece of the family junk furniture that crowds the house. When, finally, he heads to California to reestablish ties with Wayne, he goes as much in search of himself as his uncle. As his accident suggests, a piece of him is missing—he is incomplete, splintered. Departing Nebraska marks Craig's first significant gesture toward restoring his splintered interior, toward authentic feeling. Indeed, in the months after the accident, Craig's mother had been accused by concerned doctors of overdosing the boy with painkillers, which leave him like jelly, rather than working him through the first rehabilitation exercises.

The reunion with the shattered remnant of his Uncle Wayne signals Craig's movement toward wholeness, toward emotion, toward his significant split with the charade of being "normal." The undeniable evidence of his uncle's condition at first drives him to run away wildly (like a "poor cartoon creature with his tail on fire"). He ends up in the night world of a Tijuana topless bar where he loses his virginity in an unspectacular tussle with a badly scarred whore (named, ironically, Candy), whom he imagines likes him. To his astonishment in the morning he is asked to pay for her services. His traumatic introduction into the world of heterosexuality is on par with his experiences of the world of his childhood—love defined by the carnal, compelled by the mercenary. Yet against such exploitation and corruption of passion, Craig offers a loving gentler expression—he kisses Candy's heavy network of white scars, the mole she fears is cancerous, the lacerations on her feet from stepping on a nail, the lines on her forehead from a car accident, the jagged line from her appendectomy. Such gentleness, of course, is lost on the prostitute, who scolds him harshly, contemptuously dismisses his efforts at making love, and punches him fiercely.

Finding that expression comes only in the closing sequence when Craig accepts finally that he must love whom he must. Returning to Wayne's house, he stretches out next to his uncle, who is sleeping on the living room couch. At first, Craig wonders if masturbating Uncle Wayne might break the spell his uncle seems to wander in, much as the kiss returned Sleeping Beauty. But, even as Craig places Uncle Wayne's open hand on his stomach, the reader realizes that what may be a gesture too late for the uncle promises awakening for the young Craig. For Craig is the Sleeping Beauty who must be awakened. And as Craig cradles Wayne's hand, he wonders, "God what if this makes me one too? . . . but what if I am after all." It is a moment of interior confrontation, of measuring the schism within. He pulls closer to the slumbering Wayne, and "for long moments, there is no line between [them]." Craig moves gently to place Wayne's hand "down there," on his penis that begins to harden even as the morning sun spokes through the blinds. The action completes the struggle toward identity that had begun long ago with his attempt at a similar gesture with his friend Wesley during the sleep over. That gesture had proven as destructive as this gesture promises to be constructive. Craig, finally, takes life into his own hands. The sky lightens, and Craig affirms that "it is going to be a beautiful day." And in the same breath, he further notes, it is "the day they are going to try landing on the moon"—a day, Whitmore asserts, for Craig himself to begin the successful exploration of a radically new terrain, a terribly beautiful interior geography. It is a haunting moment of closing, finally, the schism within Craig, of restoring what had so long been missing, of rejecting the limiting definition of "normal." The puzzle, at last, is solved, and the reader recalls that as a boy Craig, so socially awkward, had earned his sole moment of local fame (a picture story in the local newspaper) for his amazing agility at assembling puzzles.

What, then, makes *Nebraska* the affirming testament for the AIDS decade although its action concludes in the summer of 1969? After the energetic rush from the closet in the 1970s introduced homosexuals as a rambunctious ethnic group hungry for expression, the AIDS realities introduced an entirely new rationale for suppression and denial. It is to that threat that Whitmore addresses his appeal. Denial would extinguish what Ferro had defined as the magic of the fragile constructions of emotional commitment. Denial puts all gays at risk. Like the child who dies from an unsuspected tumor, only the secret kills. Whitmore leaves Craig, restored and healed, at the very brink of the explosive energy of the 1970s when so much of the damage later defined by the AIDS virus would be accomplished. Without regret, without apology, without anger, without pity, Whitmore launches Craig, his sexual identity now powerfully asserted, into the breaking dawn of a day that would within a scant decade unleash a most absolute night. Even as he completed work on *Nebraska,* Whitmore revealed that he had been diagnosed with AIDS.

IV

Our journals of these plague years, then, are compelled not by Boccacio's supreme escapism, Defoe's religious conviction, or Camus's stern existentialism. They are not compelled simply by the awareness of death or by pity but rather (much as the disease itself) by the contrapuntal pressures of love, sex, and death. Without that countermovement of eros, the literature, as with Hoffman's work, bottoms out in graceful pathos and struggles merely to engage death humanely. Refusing the posturings of anger or frustration against the endgame of the infection, the literature accepts a poisoned universe and offers the slenderest premise of synchronicity. Forsaking the conventional coming-out-of-the-closet novel, these novels (as well as Paul Monette's *After Life,* Edmund White's "Palace Days," Andrew Harvey's *Burning Houses,* David Leavitt's "Gravity") find virtue not merely in identity but in confluence.

It is inevitable, long before the virus is decoded by the medical community, that the intensity of interest generated in the latter half of the 1980s will diminish even as the infection grows exponentially. Inevitably the rhetoric over the AIDS crisis will be lost among other threats perceived significant enough to be cased within the apocalyptic rhetoric that will only increase as the century as well as the millennium close—crises over the steady depletion of the environment, the periodic shaking of significant geopolitical entities in strategic spots, the tectonic shifts in global economic conditions, the silent oppression of nuclear weaponry. And yet AIDS has generated a significant response— novels that are finally not journals of the plague years but rather defiantly journals against the plague years, novels that argue against a disease that escalates with a surreal insistency, against the emerging definition of ourselves as biohazards, against the emerging ideology of protection, against the difficult struggle to understand that sex can kill. These novels remind us, despite the simplest impulse to withdraw from each other, how bound we are each to the other. And they argue, finally, that we are to seize not the day, but rather each other.

Sharon Oard Warner

SOURCE: "The Way We Write Now: The Reality of AIDS in Contemporary Short Fiction," in *Studies in Short Fiction*, Vol. 30, No. 4, Fall, 1993, pp. 491-500.

[*In the following essay, Warner examines several short stories by American writers as effective vehicles for communicating the social, psychological, and medical realities associated with AIDS.*]

> She knew as much about this disease as she could know.

The line comes from "Philostorgy, Now Obscure," a short story first published in *The New Yorker*. Its author, Allen Barnett, died of AIDS in 1992. The "disease" the line refers to is, in fact, AIDS, and the "she" is a woman named Roxy, who asks her friend Preston whether he intends to go on DHPG. Roxy knows DHPG is a drug used to treat CMV (cytomegalovirus), and that it requires "a catheter inserted into a vein that fed directly into an atrium of his heart." Roxy has done her homework. In her room, Preston finds "a photocopy of an article from the *New England Journal of Medicine,*" as well as "a book on the immune system and one on the crisis published by the National Academy of Sciences, and a list of gay doctors." She has read extensively, and she cares deeply, but there is still much she cannot know. I identify with Roxy: I have read extensively (though not as much as she has), written some, and care deeply, but like her, there is much I cannot know. What I do know, however, I have learned not so much from television documentaries, though I have watched them, and not from articles and reports, though I have read them. What I know about AIDS—about living with it and dying from it—I have learned from literature, from novels and poems and essays, and, most of all, from short stories.

Most of us knew little about AIDS when Susan Sontag's story "The Way We Live Now" was published in 1986 in *The New Yorker*. "The Way We Live Now" was one of the first stories on AIDS to appear in a mainstream periodical, and it is still—by far—the best known story on the subject. To illustrate, not only was Sontag's story included in *Best American Short Stories 1987;* it was also chosen for the volume *Best American Short Stories of the Eighties*. Last spring, to raise funds for AIDS charities, the story was released once again, this time as a small and expensive volume, complete with illustrations by British artist Howard Hodgkin. In *The New York Times Book Review* (1 March 1992), Gardner McFall proclaimed this newest incarnation of the story "an allegory for our times."

Presumably, the allegorical elements of the story are in what is left out: the name of the main character—the man who is ill—and the name of the disease. These two subjects, person and illness, we learn about through hearsay, second and third hand in a variety of voices:

> I've never spent so many hours at a time on the phone, Stephen said to Kate, and when I'm exhausted after the two or three calls made to me, giving me the latest, instead of switching off the phone to give myself a respite I tap out the number of another friend or acquaintance, to pass on the news.

Surely, one of Ms. Sontag's intentions was "to pass on the news" to the reader. However, the message may not be getting across, at least not to everyone, and perhaps not to those most in need of hearing it. Last fall, I taught "The Way We Live Now" in a fiction writing class at Drake University. Five years had passed since the story's first appearance in *The New Yorker,* a period in which approximately 120,000 Americans died of AIDS. Even so, several students in my class insisted that the disease in question might not be AIDS at all. One young man was adamant; no amount of argument would serve to convince him. Enlightened members of the class pointed to lines such as this one: "Ellen replied, . . . my gynecologist says that everyone is at risk, everyone who has a sexual life, because sexuality is a chain that links each of us to so many others, unknown others, and now the great chain of being has become a chain of death as well." But the student would not be persuaded; he simply preferred to believe that Sontag intended some other disease—any other disease. The meaning of the allegory, if indeed "The Way We Live Now" is an allegory, was certainly lost on this student.

While Sontag's story may well have been the first to avoid the name of the illness, it certainly was not the last. The first volume of stories on AIDS, *A Darker Proof,* by Edmund White and Adam Mars-Jones, mentions the acronym only once in 233 pages. In the foreword to his newest collection of stories, *Monopolies of Loss,* Mars-Jones comments that the "suppression" of the term in the earlier book was intentional. My own experience with writing about AIDS is similar. In writing a story about a foster mother to a baby with AIDS, I deliberately sidestepped the term until page 6, and thereafter used it only twice. My concern was that editors and readers would be turned off by the subject, so I made sure my audience was well into the story before I divulged the truth. Even in fiction, it seems, we are invested in keeping AIDS a secret.

But more problematic than avoiding the name of the illness is the practice of evading the person with AIDS. In Sontag's story, we never learn the man's name—or much else about him, for that matter—except that he has a large number of devoted and talkative friends. In a very real sense, Sontag's story has no main character. What it has, instead, is, at best, a subject of conversation, at worst, grist for the gossip mill. As several of my students pointed out, "The Way We Live Now" is reminiscent of the children's game, "Telephone," in which players sit in a circle and whisper a message in turn:

> At first he was just losing weight, he felt only a little ill, Max said to Ellen, and he didn't call for an appointment with his doctor, according to Greg, because he was managing to keep on working at more or less the same rhythm, but he did stop smoking, Tanya pointed out, which suggests he was frightened, but also that he wanted, even more than he knew, to be healthy, or healthier, or maybe just to gain back a few pounds, said Orson. . . .

This technique is catchy, but it may well cast suspicion on the veracity of what is at hand. After all, the charm of the children's game comes from the inevitable distortion of the message. (If everyone reported correctly, what fun would it be?) Were it only one of many stories on AIDS, the issues of technique and omitted names might be simply matters to be hashed out among literary critics; but, in fact, "The Way We Live Now" continues to be the best-known story on the topic and one of the few to have been published in a commercial periodical.

By and large, the stories about AIDS that have followed Sontag's have also kept their distance from the subject. (Here, I am speaking of stories that have been published in mainstream literary and commercial publications.) As good as these stories are—and some are excellent—most of them are not stories about people with AIDS—instead, they are stories about people who know other people with AIDS. Once again, the disease and those who suffer from it are kept at a distance.

The main characters in these stories tend to be siblings or friends of people living with AIDS. Three good examples are "Close" by Lucia Nevai, which appeared in *The New Yorker* in 1988; "A Sister's Story," by Virginia DeLuca, which appeared in *The Iowa Review* in 1991; and "Nothing to Ask For," by Dennis McFarland, which appeared in *The New Yorker* in 1989 and was later included in *Best American Short Stories 1990*. Guilt plays a major role in all three. While a friend or a sibling struggles with AIDS, the main characters of these stories struggle with feelings.

In Nevai's story, a social worker named Jorie is flying home for the funeral of her brother Jan, "who had contracted AIDS seven months earlier and had not let anyone in the family know." Jan's lover Hank cared for him, "made sure he never lacked for visitors," "made sure he had painkillers," "helped him write a will." The pain of knowing that she was intentionally excluded from the last months of Jan's life is hard for Jorie to bear, but by the end of the story she realizes that "pain was stronger, pain was hungrier. Pain would win this one."

DeLuca's story also concerns a sister whose brother dies. Much of "A Sister's Story" is told through journal entries, and the effect of this technique is the same sort of distance one feels in Sontag's story. As in Nevai's story, the sister is burdened with guilt, partly because her husband is afraid of AIDS, and therefore afraid of her brother, Mike. At one point, the sister confesses her husband's fears to Mike. His response is rage: "Mike turns to me. 'You shouldn't be married to him. Leave him. How can you stay married to him when he does this to me? LEAVE HIM'." A few days later, the sister writes in her journal that her brother will die faster as a result of the pain she has caused him. Near the end of the story, she writes of her own pain: "So these memories, coming at unexpected times, . . . are like cramps, sudden, fierce, doubling me over—forcing me to clench my jaw."

Of the stories about people who know people with AIDS, "Nothing to Ask For" gets closest to both the illness and those who suffer from it. In the Contributor's Notes of *Best American Short Stories 1990,* Dennis McFarland explains that "Nothing to Ask For" is based on a visit he paid to a close friend just weeks before the friend died of AIDS. He admits that he had trouble with the narrator: "It was hard to let the story be his, while never allowing his concerns to upstage those of the characters who were dying." Perhaps because upstaging was a concern, McFarland's story succeeds in allowing "the horror of the disease to speak for itself." The result is a story full of reverence for life and for those in the midst of leaving it.

The main character of "Nothing to Ask For" is a man named Dan who is spending the day with his friend Mack, who is close to death, and with Mack's lover, Lester, also sick with AIDS. Guilt is an issue in this story as well. At one point, Lester finds Dan in the bathroom sprinkling Ajax around the rim of the toilet bowl:

> "Oh, Dan, really," he [Lester] says. "You go too far. Down on your knees now, scrubbing our toilet."
>
> "Lester, leave me alone," I say.
>
> "Well, it's true," he says. "You really do."
>
> "Maybe I'm working on my survivor's guilt," I say, "if you don't mind."
>
> "You mean because your best buddy's dying and you're not?"
>
> "Yes," I say. "It's very common."
>
> He parks one hip on the sink, and after a moment he says this: "Danny boy, if you feel guilty about surviving . . . that's not irreversible, you know. I could fix that."

> We are both stunned. He looks at me. In another moment, there are tears in his eyes.

McFarland takes pains to develop both Lester and Mack as characters in their own right. To do so, he pulls us directly into their lives, bypassing gossip, memories, and journal entries.

In order to prepare Dan for the sight of him naked in the bath, Mack calls out, "Are you ready for my Auschwitz look?" As Dan bathes him, Mack muses on his fate: "You know, Dan, it's only logical that they've all given up on me. And I've accepted it mostly. But I still have days when I think I should at least be given a chance." A chance is what McFarland gives this character—the chance to express himself, to enter our psyches, to change us in a way hearsay can never do.

As one might predict, most of the writing about AIDS is being done by gay writers, but readers may not realize that most of this writing is published in collections marketed primarily to gay readers. Not until I began searching out stories dealing with AIDS did I begin to realize just how segregated that market is. A number of the stories I wanted to read were unavailable in local bookstores—even in the bigger and better ones—and the books had to be special-ordered. Others were available in a special section set aside for gay readers. So I was not surprised to find that of the 20 entries under the subject heading "AIDS" in the *Short Story Index* for 1990, eight were published in an anthology called *Men on Men 3*. Four were published in a collection by Allen Barnett called *The Body and Its Dangers,* which I could not locate in libraries or bookstores, despite the fact that the book won a PEN/Hemingway award. The eight remaining were either reprints—McFarland's and Sontag's or stories appearing in individual collections. Not one of the stories in the 1990 listing appeared in a periodical of any kind. Because few people outside the gay community are exposed to these stories, few are reading them. And we all need to be reading them. These are the stories that go to the heart of the matter, stories by writers who are either HIV-positive themselves or who know enough to risk writing from the point of view of someone with AIDS.

The Darker Proof: Stories From a Crisis was the first collection of fiction dealing with AIDS. It includes four stories by the British writer Adam Mars-Jones and three long stories by American novelist Edmund White. These stories plunge right in, no intermediaries or secondhand information. For instance, Mars-Jones's story, "Slim," begins this way:

> I don't use that word. I've heard it enough. So I've taken it out of circulation, just here, just at home. I say Slim instead, and Buddy understands. I have got Slim. When Buddy pays a visit, I have to remind myself not to offer him a cushion. Most people don't need cushions; they're just naturally covered. So I keep all the cushions to myself, now that I've lost my upholstery.
>
> Slim is what they call it in Uganda, and it's a perfectly sensible name. You lose more weight than you thought was possible. You lose more weight than you could carry. Not that you feel like carrying anything.

Of the 20 stories in *Men on Men 3,* eight are concerned with AIDS. All are well worth reading, but by far the best is Part One of *Halfway Home* by Paul Monette. Though actually an excerpt from a novel, Monette's piece works remarkably well as a piece of short fiction. Monette is a versatile man—a poet, essayist, screenwriter, and novelist—and one of the finest writers I have read in years. His book, *Borrowed Time: An AIDS Memoir,* was nominated for the National Book Critics Circle Award in 1988. It is the intensely moving account of the life and death of Roger Horwitz. In *Borrowed Time,* Monette remarks that "families do not always come together neatly in a tragedy" and Part One of *Halfway Home* is a poignant illustration of this sad truth.

Tom Shaheen is in his early thirties and has not seen his brother Brian in nine years, not since their father's funeral. He fully expects to die without seeing his brother again, and he fully expects to die soon. Until then, he lives in a bungalow by the sea, rent-free courtesy of a gentle and unassuming man named Gray Baldwin. Every day Tom makes his way slowly down the 80 rickety steps—"my daily encounter with what I've lost in stamina"—to the entrance to a cave by the surf. There, he broods over "missed chances" and "failures of nerve." He does not, however, probe the painful tooth of his childhood—his "scumbag drunk" of a father, his "whimpering" mother. In particular, he avoids thinking about his older brother Brian—beautiful as a Greek god, ruthless as a terrorist. Monette prepares the reader carefully for an unexpected visit, but he is such a skillful writer that Brian's abrupt entrance still takes us by surprise. The encounter is brutal. Monette does not spare Tommy or Brian or the reader. Guilt is an issue here, too, but now we see it from the other side of the gun. When Brian tries to say he is sorry, Tommy feels not forgiveness but the added burden of his brother's regret:

> Suddenly I feel drained, almost weepy, but not for Brian's sake. . . . The whole drama of coming out—the wrongheaded yammer, the hard acceptance—seems quaint and irrelevant now. Perhaps I'd prefer my brother to stay a pig, because it's simpler. And even though he's not the Greek god he used to be, fleshier now and slightly ruined, I feel *more* sick and frail in his presence. Not just because of AIDS, but like I'm the nerd from before too. "You can't understand," I say, almost a whisper. "All my friends have died."

Part One of *Halfway Home* cannot be neatly summed up. It is not simply a story about a confrontation between two brothers, a story about AIDS, or self-pity, or a growing acceptance of death. It is about all these things plus so many others. As George Stambolian explains in the Introduction to *Men on Men 3,* "The epidemic . . . challenges and tests our beliefs, makes time directly perceptible to our hearts and minds." He goes on to quote Robert Gluck: "Now death is where gay men . . . learn about love. . . ." And love is a subject Monette knows more about than any other contemporary writer I can think of. Near the end of the story, Tommy steals into the bedroom where his brother is sleeping. Looking down at Brian, Tommy feels intense hate—"I'm like a bad witch, rotten with curses, casting a spell even I can't see the end of"—and bitter love:

> I take a last long look at Brian, and on impulse I lean above him, hover over his face and brush my lips against his cheek. . . . I've never kissed my brother before. He doesn't flinch, he doesn't notice. Then I turn and stumble back to my room, pleading the gods to be rid of him.

While I was working on my own story about AIDS, a writer friend advised me to change the disease. "I really like this story," she told me, "but why does the baby have to have AIDS?" I had no answer for that question, really. Why does anyone have to have AIDS? The impetus for my story was something I overheard about a single woman in Chicago who nurses babies with AIDS. When one child dies, she simply turns to caring for another. After hearing about that brave woman, I wanted to get to know her, and because I am a fiction writer, that meant writing a story. While I could change many things about "A Simple Matter of Hunger," I could not change the disease. That much, at least, I am sure of.

The tragedy is that babies do have AIDS, that an estimated one million people in the US are infected with the HIV virus. According to the Centres for Disease Control, by the end of 1995, the USA will have at least 415,000 AIDS cases and at least 330,000 AIDS deaths. It is not something we can avoid as writers, as readers, or as human beings. "But I was taught not to write about social issues," my friend explained to me. "They just don't last. In a hundred years, it's possible that AIDS may be completely forgotten." We can hope for that, I suppose, but it does not change the present. Right now, we all need to know as much about this disease as we can know.

Ms. Sontag ends "The Way We Live Now" this way: "I was thinking, Ursala said to Quentin, that the difference between a story and a painting or a photograph is that in a story you can write, He's still alive. But in a painting or a photo you can't show 'still.' You can just show him being alive. He's still alive, Stephen said." Ironically, in this most famous story about AIDS, "he" whoever he might be, isn't *shown* still alive. For that, we have to take Stephen's word. And while his word might have been enough to begin with, now and in the future we will need something more. We will need stories like Monette's, stories whose main characters speak to us directly: "I've been at this thing for a year and a half, three if you count all the fevers and rashes. I operate on the casual assumption that I've still got a couple of years, give or take a galloping lymphoma. Day to day, I'm not a dying man, honestly." See there, Tom Shaheen is still alive. Take it from Monette, someone who knows.

FURTHER READING

Anthologies

Klein, Michael, ed. *Poets for Life: Seventy-Six Poets Respond to AIDS.* New York: Crown Publishers, Inc., 1989, 256 p.

Collection of poetry dealing with the emotional component of the AIDS epidemic.

Bibliographies

Trautmann, Joanne and Pollard, Carol, eds. *Literature and Medicine: Topics, Titles & Notes.* Philadelphia: Society for Health and Human Values, 209 p.

Bibliography of literary representations of medicine, doctors, diseases, death, and dying.

Secondary Sources

Biggs, Penelope. "The Disease Theme in Sophocles' *Ajax, Philoctetes* and *Trachiniae.*" *Classical Philology* LXI, No. 4 (October 1966): 223-35.

Explores Sophocles' use of the disease metaphor to represent heroic suffering.

Brody, Saul Nathaniel. *The Disease of the Soul: Leprosy in Medieval Literature.* Ithaca, N. Y.: Cornell University Press, 1974, 223 p.

Investigates "the association of leprosy with moral defilement" in medieval European literature.

Gallacher, Patrick J. "The *Summoner's Tale* and Medieval Attitudes Towards Sickness." *The Chaucer Review* 21, No. 2 (1986): 200-12.

Examines "the dialectic of self and otherness as it is affected by the conflict between body and soul" in Chaucer's *Summoner's Tale* and *Friar's Tale.*

Gerrard, Charlotte Frankel. "Pestilence in Contemporary French Drama: Camus and Ionesco." *Symposium* XXXI, No. 4 (Winter 1977): 302-22.

Comparative analysis of Camus' *L'Etat de siège* and Ionesco's *Jeux de massacre,* in light of Antonin Artaud's vision of the theatricality of plague.

Gilman, Sander L. *Disease and Representation: Images of Illness from Madness to AIDS.* Ithaca, N. Y.: Cornell University Press, 1988, 320 p.

Discusses how disease and its manifestations are represented in literature from the classical era to the present.

Graham, Peter W. and Sewell, Elizabeth, eds. *Literature and Medicine Volume Nine, Fictive Ills: Literary Perspectives on Wounds and Diseases*. Baltimore, Md.: The Johns Hopkins University Press, 1990, 196 p.

Essays on disease in ten works of literature by writers ranging from Sophocles to Charlotte Perkins Gilman.

Merrill, Reed B. "Brain Fever in the Novels of Dostoevsky." *Texas Quarterly* XIX, No. 3 (Autumn 1976): 29-50.

Traces the biographical and thematic significance of Dostoevsky's representation of brain fever in his major novels, *Crime and Punishment, The Idiot, The Possessed,* and *The Brothers Karamazov*.

Murphy, Timothy F. and Poirier, Suzanne, eds. *Writing AIDS: Gay Literature, Language, and Analysis*. New York: Columbia University Press, 1993, 352 p.

Essays on the effects AIDS has had on writing, especially by and about gay men.

Nelson, Emmanuel S. "AIDS and the American Novel." *Journal of American Culture* 13, No. 1 (Spring 1990): 47-53.

Surveys several responses to the problem of AIDS found in the novels of gay American men, ranging from subtle allusion to open and frank discussions of the disease.

Norden, Edward. "From Schnitzler to Kushner." *Commentary* 99, No. 1 (January 1995): 51-8.

Discusses a variety of plays by Jewish homosexuals, especially in relation to issues surrounding AIDS.

Ober, William B., M. D. *Boswell's Clap and Other Essays: Medical Analyses of Literary Men's Afflictions*. Carbondale and Edwardsville, Ill.: Southern Illinois University Press, 1979, 291 p.

Offers a biographical and medical/biological approach to literary questions of disease and creativity.

Paccaud, Josiane. "Mr. Razumov's 'Disease of Perversity': Of Artistic Lies in Conrad's *Under Western Eyes*." *Forum for Modern Language Studies* XXIV, No. 2 (April 1988): 111-25.

Investigates themes of lying and self-betrayal, typified as a "disease of perversity" in Conrad's novel.

Peschel, Enid Rhodes, ed. *Medicine and Literature*. New York: Neale Watson Academic Publications, Inc., 1980, 204 p.

Collection of essays on the affinities between literature and medicine. Includes selections on the portrayal of doctors in literature, physicians as writers, and disease as a heightened state of consciousness.

"The Politics of AIDS." *The Minnesota Review*, No. 40 (Spring/Summer 1993): 5-159.

Special issue dedicated to AIDS-related literature, including poetry, fiction, and essays on the subject.

Preston, John, ed. *Personal Dispatches: Writers Confront AIDS*. New York: St. Martin's Press, 1988, 183 p.

Collection of outstanding essays on the topic of AIDS.

Rey, W. H. "Return to Health? 'Disease' in Mann's *Doctor Faustus*." *PMLA* 65, No. 2 (March 1950): 21-6.

Comments on the spiritual and spiritualizing dimensions of disease as dramatized in Thomas Mann's novel *Doctor Faustus*.

Román, David. "'It's My Party and I'll Die If I Want To!': Gay Men, AIDS, and the Circulation of Camp in U. S. Theatre." *Theatre Journal* 44, No. 3 (October 1992): 305-27.

Observes the strategies of irony, wit, and humor of what is known collectively as "camp literature" that contemporary gay playwrights have used to position themselves and their works in relation to AIDS.

Rubinstein, Frankie. "They Were Not Such Good Years." *Shakespeare Quarterly* 40, No. 1 (Spring 1989): 70-4.

Describes humorous approaches to the topic of venereal disease used by Shakespeare and other sixteenth-century writers, and its use by these authors as a metaphor for corruption.

Sontag, Susan. *Illness as Metaphor*. New York: Farrar, Straus and Giroux, 1977, 88 p.

Seeks an "elucidation of" and consequent "liberation from" the cultural metaphors of illness.

———. *AIDS and Its Metaphors*. New York: Farrar, Straus and Giroux, 1988, 95 p.

Sequel to *Illness as Metaphor* aimed at confronting the myths associated with AIDS.

Modern Japanese Literature

INTRODUCTION

The modern period in Japanese literature dates from the Meiji Restoration of 1868 and encompasses the Meiji (1868-1912), Taisho (1912-1926), and Showa (1926-present) periods in Japanese political history.

During the Meiji era, such novelists as Futabatei Shimei and Shimazaki Toson sought to devise a new literature that rejected the traditional native forms and subjects in favor of ideas borrowed from contemporary Western literature. Among the most significant Western concepts to gain currency with Japanese writers of the period was the notion of individualism, which found uniquely Japanese expression in the confessional narratives of the *shishosetsu,* or I-novel. The loneliness of the self-aware individual became a sustained theme in novels of the period, notably in the works of Natsume Soseki. In addition, developments in fiction during the late nineteenth and early twentieth centuries included colloquial reform of highly-stylized literary language and the rise of Naturalism, bringing with it a focus on ordinary protagonists and situations drawn from everyday life. Together these changes served to elevate the position of fiction within Japanese literature from mere entertainment into an art form of critical merit and social relevance. Writers of the Taisho and Showa periods continued formal experimentation, and individual authors embraced a variety of currents in world literature, including Marxism, Modernism, and—following the nuclear devastation of World War II—nihilism.

Throughout the phenomenal prosperity that has brought Japan to the forefront of the world economy since the 1970s, the condition of the individual in contemporary society has remained a prominent literary theme, as evidenced by the works of Abe Kobo, Nakagami Kenji, and others. While the period since 1868 has been dominated by innovations in prose, Japanese drama and lyric poetry have seen parallel developments. In drama, the stylized traditional forms of *no, kabuki,* and *bunraku* were maintained by classicists, although translations of Western theatrical productions and the development of *shingeki*, or "new drama," have gained prominence since World War II. In poetry, the introduction of Western concepts of free verse and the transformation, by Kawahigashi Hekigodo and others, of the traditional *haiku* form into a mode of self-expression represent significant innovations of the period.

*REPRESENTATIVE WORKS

Abe Kobo
Suna no onna [*The Woman in the Dunes*] (novel) 1962
Hako otoko [*The Box Man*] (novel) 1973
Agawa Hiroyuki
Ma no isan [*Devil's Heritage*] (novel) 1952
Akutagawa Ryunosuke
Rashomon, and Other Stories (short stories) 1952
Exotic Japanese Stories (short stories) 1964
Arishima Takeo
Aru onna [*A Certain Woman*] (novel) 1919
Dazai Osamu
Shayo [*Setting Sun*] (novel) 1947
Ningen shikkaku [*No Longer Human*] (novel) 1948
Enchi Fumiko
Onnazaka [*The Waiting Years*] (novel) 1957
Endo Shusaku
Umi to dokuyaku [*The Sea and Poison*] (novel) 1958
Chimmoku [*Silence*] (novel) 1966
Kuchibue o fuku toki [*When I Whistle*] (novel) 1975
Sukyandaru [*Scandal*] (novel) 1986
Futabatei Shimei
Ukigumo [*Drifting Clouds*] (novel) 1887
Hagiwara Sakutaro
Tsuki ni hoeru [*Howling at the Moon*] (poetry) 1917
Hayashi Fumiko
Ukigumo [*The Floating Cloud*] (novel) 1953
Hayashi Kyoko
Matsuri no ba [*Ritual of Death*] (novella) 1975
Higuchi Ichiyo
Takekurabe [*Growing Up*] (novella) 1895
Ibuse Masuji
Kuroi ame [*Black Rain*] (novel) 1966
Inoue Yashushi
Ryoju [*The Hunting Gun*] (novel) 1949
Tempy no iraka [*The Roof Tile of Tempy*] (novel) 1957
Tonko [*Tun-huang*] (novel) 1959
Ishikawa Takuboku
Romaji nikki [*Romaji Diary*] (diary) 1909
Ichiaku no suna [*Sad Toys*] (poetry) 1912
Kawabata Yasunari
Yukiguni [*Snow Country*] (novel) 1935-48
Senbazuru [*Thousand Cranes*] (novel) 1952
Koda Rohan
Pagoda, Skull, and Samurai (short stories) 1985

Kurahashi Yumiko
Parutai [*Partei*] (novel) 1960
Masoaka Shiki
Bokuju itteki [*A Drop of Ink*] (poetry and diary) 1901
Mishima Yukio
Kamen no kokuhaku [*Confessions of a Mask*] (novel) 1949
Shiosai [*The Sound of Waves*] (novel) 1954
Kinkakuji [*The Temple of the Golden Pavilion*] (novel) 1956
Hojo no umi. 4 vols. [*The Sea of Fertility: A Cycle of Four Novels*] (novels) 1969-1971
Miyazawa Kenji
Spring and Azura (poetry) 1973
Mori Ogai
"Maihime" ["The Dancing Girl"] (short story) 1890
Wita sekusuarisu [*Vita Sexualis*] (novel) 1909
Gan [*The Wild Geese*] (novel) 1911-13
"Abe ichizoku" ["The Abe Family"] (short story) 1913
Murakami Ryu
Kagirinaku tomei ni chikai buru [*Almost Transparent Blue*] (novel) 1976
Nagai Kafu
Udekurabe [*Geisha in Rivalry*] (novel) 1918
Kafu the Scribbler: The Life and Writings of Nagai Kafu, 1879-1959 (biography and short stories) 1965
Nakagami Kenji
Misaki (novel) 1976
Nakano Shigeharu
Muragimo (novel) 1954
Natsume Soseki
Wagahai wa neko de aru. 3 vols. [*I Am a Cat*] (novel) 1905-07
Kusamakura [*Three-Cornered World*] (novel) 1906
Mon (novel) 1910
Kojin [*The Wayfarer*] (novel) 1912-13
Kokoro (novel) 1914
Nogami Yaeko
Hideyoshi to Rikyu (novel) 1963
Noma Hiroshi
Shinku chitai [*Zone of Emptiness*] (novel) 1952
Oe Kenzaburo
Kojinteki na taiken [*A Personal Matter*] (novel) 1964
Man'en gannen no futtoburo [*A Silent Cry*] (novel) 1967
Ooka Makoto
A String around Autumn (poetry) 1982
Shiga Naoya
An'ya koro. 2 vols. [*A Dark Night's Passing*] (novel) 1938
Shimazaki Toson
Wakanashu (poetry) 1897
Hakai [*The Broken Commandment*] (novel) 1906
Ie [*The Family*] (novel)
Takahashi Shinkichi
Afterimages: Zen Poems (poetry) 1972
Triumph of the Sparrow (poetry) 1986
Takamura Kotaro
Chieko-sho [*Chieko, and Other Poems*] (poetry) 1941
Tanaka Yasuo
Nantonaku kurisutaru (novel) 1981
Taneda Santoka
Mountain Tasting (poetry) 1980
Tanikawa Shuntaro
With Silence My Companion (poetry) 1975
At Midnight in the Kitchen I Just Wanted to Talk With You (poetry) 1975
Tanizaki Jun'ichiro
Tade kuu mushi [*Some Prefer Nettles*] (novel) 1928-29
Sasameyuki [*The Makioka Sisters*] (novel) 1943-48
Kagi [*The Key*] (novel) 1956
Futen rojin nikki [*Diary of a Mad Old Man*] (novel) 1961
Tayama Katai
Futon [*The Quilt*] 1907
Uno Chiyo
Irozange [*Confessions of Love*] (novel) 1935
Yamazaki Masakazu
Zeami (drama) 1969
Sanetomo shuppan [*Sanetomo*] (drama) 1973
Yashiro Seiichi
Hokusai manga [*Hokusai Sketchbooks*] (drama) 1973
Yokomitsu Riichi
"Love," and Other Stories (short stories) 1974
Yosano Akiko
Midaregami [*Tangled Hair*] (poetry) 1901
Yoshioka Minoru
Lilac Garden (poetry) 1976

*The publication date of a work with only an English title signifies the date that the translation was first published, not the original Japanese date of publication.

POETRY

Donald Keene

SOURCE: "The Creation of Modern Japanese Poetry," in *Landscapes and Portraits: Appreciations of Japanese Culture,* Kodansha International Ltd., 1971, pp. 131-56.

[*In the following essay, Keene charts the transition of Japanese poetry during the Meiji era from traditional* tanka *and* haiku *forms to* shintaishi, *or "new-style poems," and also surveys later innovations in Japanese poetic techniques and themes.*]

Modern Japanese poetry, like everything else modern in Japan, is generally traced back to the accession to undisputed authority of the Emperor Meiji in 1868. This political event did not immediately inspire floods of poetic composition; in fact, as far as I can determine, not a single poet sang the glories of the new reign, and no book of poetry of consequence was published for some years afterwards. But the new Emperor was to show himself conspicuously unlike many generations of his ancestors, rulers whose arrivals, activities and departures had been of little concern to poets. Though the Emperor's direct role in the movement of modernization was minor, he set the spirit of the new age in his oath taken in 1868, when he promised, among other things, to end old ignorance and to seek learning throughout the world. Poets were soon to call themselves proudly "Meiji men," meaning that they belonged to the new, enlightened generation.

Eighteen sixty-eight is of interest in the history of Japanese poetry for another reason. In that year two poets died whose works, though in the classical *tanka* form, suggest that they might ultimately have found a way out of the impasse in which Japanese poetry was trapped. The first, Okuma Kotomichi, sounded a new note in his book of poetic criticism *Hitorigochi* (1857): "The poets of the past are my teachers, but they are not myself. I am a son of my time and not of the past. Were I to follow blindly the poets of former times, I should forget my own humble identity. The poems I wrote might seem impressive, but their excellence would be entirely on the surface; they would be merchants in princes' raiment. My art would be pure deceit, like a performance of Kabuki." Despite his insistence that poetry reflect its time, however, Kotomichi's works are scarcely revolutionary: in diction and structure they are sometimes barely distinguishable from the poems in the *Kokinshu* written nine hundred years earlier. It would be hard to conceive of an English poet writing in 1850, with no intention of fraud, verses which might have antedated Chaucer, but in the Japan of the nineteenth century the language of the *tanka* was with few exceptions a thousand years old. Words of other than pure Japanese origin were not tolerated; it was as if the English poets of the eighteenth and nineteenth centuries had been obliged to confine themselves to words of Anglo-Saxon derivation, and Coleridge had therefore written "The Hoary Seafarer" instead of "The Ancient Mariner."

The subjects of poetry were also prescribed with minute exactness. There were, for example, twenty-five varieties of flowers which might properly be mentioned in a *tanka:* cherry blossoms, plum blossoms, wisteria, azalea, etc. Other flowers could be mentioned only at the risk of the poet being denounced as an eccentric or a revolutionary. The standard collections of poetry were known by heart, and the critical works of poetic dicta, most of them dating back to the thirteenth century, were not so much helpful guides as absolute prescriptions. The poet was encouraged to demonstrate originality of conception, while restricting himself to the language of the tenth-century collections, but what this meant in practice was merely minor variation. Perfection of classical diction, successful evocation of the poetry of the past, were the aims of centuries of poets. Of course an expert can trace currents even within this seemingly static poetic: the proportion of nouns might show a tendency to increase in certain periods, or there might be a greater use of metaphor in the love poems. But no self-respecting poet in 1850 would have said, "I enjoyed a quiet smoke," though people had been smoking for two hundred years. That is why Kotomichi's declaration seems so important for its day. Poets of the time reconciled their seemingly contradictory beliefs in the necessity for contemporary expression, and in the desirability of preserving the language and mood of the *Kokinshu* poetry, by writing chiefly about subjects which had not changed much in nine hundred years. "Fragrance alone, I thought, was in the wind, but since this morning the plum garden sends me blossoms too" is a poem which might have been written at any time over the centuries, and could still be composed today; indeed, such relatively static elements in Japanese life as the quiet appreciation of nature within one's own garden contributed to the preservation of the old poetic traditions.

The second of the poets who died in 1868, Tachibana Akemi, is a more striking figure. He was involved in the patriotic movements which resulted in the restoration of power to the Imperial Family, and his poetry reflects his activities far more vividly than Kotomichi's. He wrote, for example, a series of fifty *tanka* on the theme "Solitary Pleasures" including: "It is a pleasure when, a most infrequent treat, we've fish for dinner, and my children cry with joy, 'Yum-yum!' and gobble it down"; or, "It is a pleasure when, in a book which by chance I am perusing, I come on a character who is exactly like me"; or, "It is a pleasure when, in these days of delight in all things foreign, I come across a man who does not forget our Empire." These *tanka* have almost none of the traditional virtues of the form: they lack elegance, tone, depth, melody and so on. But in their different ways they point to possibilities of poetic expression which had largely been ignored: the pleasures (or sorrows) of ordinary life, the pleasures of the intellect, and the involvement of the poet in political activity. Tachibana Akemi's *tanka,* however, barely touched on these larger issues. It remained the task of the specifically modern poets to explore them.

Before 1868 Japanese poets who did not wish to write *tanka* had two other recognized possibilities open to them. The first was the *haiku,* a form which had originally allowed much greater freedom, especially in the vocabulary, than the hidebound *tanka,* but which by this time was even more saddled with hackneyed phraseology. Not one *haiku* poet of distinction was writing in 1868. The most important poetry was probably not that in Japanese but in Chinese. There was a thousand-year-old tradition of Japanese poets writing in Chinese, and probably the finest of this poetry was composed in the early nineteenth century. Poets who felt their thoughts too large to stuff into the thirty-one syllables of the *tanka* or into the even more cramped seventeen syllables of the *haiku* enjoyed the greater amplitude of the Chinese poem, which could run to thirty or more lines. This meant, however, writing in a language as unlike Japanese as Latin is unlike English. But just as English poets at times in the past chose Latin, not only for commemorative addresses but for their most personal poetry, so many Japanese found that certain things could be said easier in Chinese. For them Chinese was not the language of China, a foreign country, so much as a heritage from the Japanese past. Chinese influence was present in almost every variety of Japanese literature prior to 1868. It was only gradually superseded by influences from the West.

Modern Japanese literature was indeed to be distinguished most particularly by the presence of the West. Whether accepted or rejected, the West could not be ignored. The first stage in adapting Western influence was, inevitably, that of imitation. The Japanese have often been taxed with an excessive proclivity towards imitation, but it is difficult to see how they could have achieved the revolution in their literature without translation and imitation. It is surprising in fact how much the poets managed to salvage of the old traditions even when translating. The Japanese preference for alternating lines in five and seven syllables, going back at least to the seventh century, continued to be observed by almost all poets for decades. Even when translating English poetry they adhered to this rhythm, as in the version of "Elegy in a Country Churchyard" done by Yatabe Ryokichi (1852-99):

yamayama kasumi
iriai no
kane wa naritsutsu
no no ushi wa
shizuka ni ayumi
kaeri yuku
tagaesu hito mo
uchitsukare
y oaku sarite
ware hitori
tasogaredoki ni
nokorikeri

The mountains are misty
And, as the evening
Bell sounds,
The oxen on the lea
Slowly walk
Returning home.
The ploughman too
Is weary and
At last departs;
I alone
In the twilight hour
Remain behind.

Sometimes the adaptations were even freer, using Japanese equivalents in the imagery or construction, as in this version of "The Last Rose of Summer":

niwa no chigusa
mushi no ne mo
karete sabishiku
narinikeri
aa shiragiku
aa shiragiku
hitori okurete
sakinikeri

The thousand grasses in the garden
And the cries of insects too
Have dried up.
And turned forlorn.
Ah, the white chrysanthemum
Ah, the white chrysanthemum
Alone, after the others,
Has blossomed.

The rose, a flower without poetic significance for the Japanese, was here transformed into a chrysanthemum, and in place of Moore's "All her lovely companions/are faded and gone," a use of personification unfamiliar to the Japanese, we are told of the "thousand grasses" and "cries of insects" in the garden.

The first collection of modern poetry, *Selection of Poems in the New Style* (*Shintaishi-sho*), was published in 1882. It included fourteen translations of English and American poems, one French poem translated from an English version, and five original poems by the compilers. Among the English poems were "The Charge of the Light Brigade," "Elegy in a Country Churchyard," the "To be or not to be" soliloquy, and two translations of Longfellow's "A Psalm of Life." The translators were scholars of English who happened to have become interested in poetry, and their versions, like the translations of professors elsewhere, had little poetic grace. The original poems are modelled on Western examples, sometimes with ludicrous results, as in Yatabe Ryokichi's attempt at rhymed Japanese verse:

haru wa monogoto
  yorokobashi
fuku kaze totemo atatakashi
niwa no sakura ya mono no hana
yo ni utsukushiku miyuru
  kana
nobe no hibari wa ito
  takaku
kumoi haruka ni maite naku

In spring everything is full of
  charm,
The blowing wind is really warm.
Cherry and peach, blossoming
  bright,
Make an unusually pretty sight.
The lark of the moors, very high,
Sings as it soars far in the sky.

One compiler wrote disarmingly in the preface, "We are rather pleased with this selection of poems, but for all we know, the public may contemptuously dismiss it as an exceedingly strange and uncouth performance. Good and evil, however, are not eternal. Values change with the age and with what different generations believe. Even if our poems win no favor among people today, it may be that future generations of modern Japanese poets will attain the heights of Homer or Shakespeare. Some great poet, impressed by the new style of this collection, may contribute more talent and write poetry which will move men's hearts and make the very gods and demons weep."

As predicted, the collection was subjected to considerable abuse, part of it justified. We can only question the grasp of the principles of Western poetry revealed by Toyama Chuzan (1848-1900), the author of the poem entitled "On the Principles of Sociology," which begins with the lines, "The sun and moon in the heavens and even the barely visible stars all move because of a force called gravity." This was hardly an imitation of any English poem, but rather a combination of the new learning (especially the writings of Herbert Spencer) with the new poetic forms. One man wrote a full-length geography of the world entirely in the new verse! But *Selection of Poems in the New Style* was ridiculed less because of its poetical ineptitude than because the authors had deliberately mingled elegant and unrefined words including, for example, Chinese-derived expressions in Japanese contexts. Despite such criticisms, the collection exerted enormous influence, and the words "poems in the new style" (*shintaishi*) of the title came to be employed as the normal designation of the new poetry. Collections of this verse appeared in rapid succession during the following years.

The instant popularity of the new poetry was obviously not due to its exceptional beauty. It came rather as an explosive reaction to the overly familiar stereotypes of Japanese poetics. Tachibana Akemi in a satirical essay had derided the old poetry: "In early spring one writes of the morning sun gently shining and of the spreading mists; at the end of the year one speaks of the 'waves of years crawling shorewards' and of waiting for the spring. For flowers there is 'the blessing of rain' and for snow 'regret over leaving footprints.' Poetic language has come to mean such phrases and nothing else. A hundred out of a hundred poets, the year before last, last year, and this year too have merely strung together the same old phrases. How depressing!" Tachibana Akemi, not knowing about Western poetry, could offer no way out of the impasse except his homely little verses on daily life. With the new translations, however, it became apparent that poetry could have a much wider range than anyone had previously suspected.

First of all, poetry could be much longer and in many forms. Long poems had been popular in eighth-century Japan, and some new poets justified their long compositions in terms of Japanese tradition, but the inspiration for long poems, particularly on contemporary subjects, came directly from the West. Secondly, the subject matter was entirely new. The variety of topics treated by Western poets made some Japanese novices suppose, not surprisingly, that *any* subject, even the principles of sociology, might be celebrated in verse. The liberation from the old themes was sometimes excessive, and poets were eventually to discover that some hackneyed old topics still had validity, but it would never again be possible to limit Japanese poetry to the obviously "poetic." Finally, the language of Japanese poetry was enormously expanded, though not as much as the pioneers expected. Komuro Kyokuzan, the editor of one of the early collections, wrote, "Persons with unenlightened views, not realizing how the processes of civilization operate, assert that it is wrong to use in poetry any words except the old ones. This attitude in practice often leads to unfortunate results. For example, where once one spoke of a soldier carrying a bow and arrows, today he carries a Snyder, and there should therefore be no objection to writing of a soldier's Snyder. But when the critics insist that the poet must continue to refer to bows and arrows, does this not lead to an unfortunate result? They are mistaken because they do not realize that Snyder has already become a Japanese word." The argument is cogent, but unfortunately for Komuro Kyokuzan, the Snyder gun was not long afterwards replaced by a Japanese-made rifle, and the word Snyder, despite his predictions, never replaced bow and arrows.

Komuro Kyokuzan exemplified his theories of poetry with his "Ode to Liberty," translated in part by Sansom:

> O Liberty, Ah Liberty, Liberty O
> Liberty, we two are plighted until the world
> ends.
> And who shall part us? Yet in this world there
> are
> clouds that hide the moon and winds that destroy
> The blossoms. Man is not master of his fate.
>
> It is a long tale to tell
> But once upon a time
> There were men who wished
> To give the people Liberty
> And set up a republican government.
> To that end. . .

The first volume of new verse by a single poet was the collection *The Twelve Stone Tablets* (*Juni no ishizuka*) by Yuasa Hangetsu, published in 1885. It consists of a series of poems based on the Old Testament, cast into the traditional rhythms in five and seven syllables of the ancient Japanese poetry. The language is replete with the stylistic devices of the past, and the vocabulary rich in old-fashioned elegance, but the presence of the Land of Canaan and the Walls of Jericho remind us that the enlightenment has occurred. The strongest cultural influence of the early Meiji period was indeed the translation of the New Testament, completed in 1879. This period marked the high point of Christianity in Japan, as many people were converted to the religion of the West, the source of the new culture. Believers and non-believers read the Bible and sang hymns. The hymns especially proved important in the development of the new poetry.

The first critical study of the new poetry, published in 1893, began with the remarks, "People constantly tell me, 'I am living in Meiji Japan, and I use the language of Meiji Japan. Why should I study the dead writings of the past and waste my time over the old circumlocutions?'" Owada Tateki, the author of this study, though sympathetic with the point of view expressed, felt that much was still to be learned from the past. He favored the use of modern Japanese, but noted how difficult it was to set standards for the ordinary, contemporary language of the Meiji era. In 1893 there was no standard spoken Japanese. The tradition of writing the spoken language was so recent that people were not even sure how to record common colloquial expressions, nor which words were standard speech and which were dialect. Owada felt that a certain artificiality was therefore inevitable. Above all, he counselled, there should be "moderation" in expression—avoidance of bizarre phraseology merely to achieve novelty of effect. He declared, for example, that "direct imitations of such Western expressions as 'the moon dances' or 'the mountains clap their hands' are likely to surprise, but they are not pleasing."

On the whole, however, Owada was optimistic about the future of Japanese poetry. "A new atmosphere is about to flood into our literary world. Already it is seeking cracks through which to gain admittance. Breathe in! Breathe in! Japanese poetry has its strange, unique beauty, but we must not forget that foreign poetry has extraordinary virtues. It would be a mistake to abandon our own traditions and adopt theirs in entirety, but if we add theirs to our own we shall widen our literary horizons. The long poem is unquestionably the special glory of their literatures; we should therefore transplant it in our garden, tender it, water it, and make Eastern flowers blossom on this Western plant. The Japanese Po Chü-i has long since completed his labors and sleeps in the ground. When will the day come that a Japanese Milton will write *Paradise Lost* at the Ishiyama Temple?"

Japanese Miltons, even of the mute, inglorious kind, were never to abound, but the lyricism of the past, assuming the freer and more varied forms inspired by the West, was to produce before long a fair number of Japanese Wordsworths, Shelleys, and eventually Verlaines. The lyric in the strict sense was to remain the dominant form for thirty or more years; many of the best lyrics are widely known even to school children in the musical settings later given them. Because the Japanese language was unable, like English, to rely on rhyme or a pronounced rhythm to differentiate poetry from prose, a sustained poem was difficult to manage, and the greatest successes continued to be in shorter works even after the *tanka* had been rejected for its excessive brevity.

The first collection of modern poetry still widely read today appeared in 1897. The fifty-one poems in *Seedlings* (*Wakana-shu*) by Shimazaki Toson (1872-1943) described the poet's youthful loves with an overt romanticism which captivated his readers. A few years later Toson related what his feelings had been when he published this collection: "A new era in poetry had at last arrived. It was like the coming of a beautiful dawn. Some poets shouted their words like the prophets of old, others cried their thoughts like the poets of the West; all seemed intoxicated with the light, their new voices, and a sense of fantasy. Youthful imagination awoke from an age-old sleep and clad itself in the language of the common people. Traditions took on fresh colors again. A brilliant light shone on the life and death ahead of them, and illuminated the grandeur and decline of the past. Most of that crowd of young poets were merely simple youths. Their art was immature and incomplete. But it was free of falsity or artifice. Their youthful lives flowed from their lips, and their tears of passion streaked their cheeks. Try to remember that their fresh, overflowing emotions made many young men all but forget food and sleep. And remember too that the pathos and anguish of recent times drove many young men mad. I too, forgetting my incompetence, joined my voice with those of the new poets."

Toson published two more collections of poetry, in 1899 and 1901, before turning to the novel. His most famous poem, "By the Old Castle of Komoro," appeared in 1900. Its opening lines are known to most Japanese:

By the old castle of Komoro
In white clouds, a wanderer laments.
The green chickweed has not sprouted,
The grass has yet to lay its carpet;
The silver coverlet on the hills around
Melting in the sun, the light snow flows.

Toson's indebtedness to the West included imitations of Shakespeare and of the "Ode to the West Wind." Other Japanese poets turned to Keats or to Browning. Susukida Kyukin (1877-1945) wrote one poem beginning, "Oh to be in Yamato, now that October's there." After this comically obvious imitation, he continues quite respectably:

I would follow a lane through the wood of
Kaminabi, with its sparse-
leaved trees,
To Ikaruga, at dawn, the dew on my hair—when
the tall grass
Ripples across the wide field of Heguri like a
golden sea,
And the colour fades from the dusty paper-
window, and the sun is faint—
Between the wooden columns, insatiably, I peer
at the golden letters of
the precious age-old scriptures,
At the ancient Korean lyre, the grey unglazed
pottery and the gold and
silver paintings on the wall.

Without Browning the poet would probably not have conceived of this sentimental journey to Yamato, but once on his way he chooses images that are real and Japanese. In this respect the influence of English poetry on Japanese differed categorically from the centuries-old influence of Chinese poetry. Imitation of Browning enabled Susukida Kyukin to evoke effectively a Japanese scene, but imitation of Chinese poetry had generally imposed the obligation of describing China as well, even on poets who had never seen China. In a real sense, then, imitation of European poetry led to a liberation of Japanese poetry, giving direction to thoughts which poets had long entertained but never known how to express. Fortunately for the Japanese, the European languages were so remote in idiom that no possibility of closely imitating them existed; imitations were thus usually of conception rather than of imagery. The poem on Yamato in October is otherwise indebted to Browning in the use of enjambement, not unknown in traditional Japanese poetry, but generally avoided, in keeping with the dictates of Chinese poetics.

The most powerful Western influence on Japanese poetry came in 1905 with the translations by Ueda Bin (1874-1916) of the French Parnassian and Symbolist poets. Ueda's explanations of the functions of Symbolist poetry, based on the theories of Vigié-Lecoq, were to exert an enormous influence on subsequent Japanese poetry. His translations introduced to Japanese the works of Baudelaire, Mallarmé and Verlaine, all of whom at once became favorite poets of the intellectuals. The popularity achieved by the French Symbolists in Japan is not entirely surprising, in view of the worldwide success of the movement, but that this poetry should have blotted out almost all other Western influences surely indicates some special affinity with the Japanese. In the introduction to his 1905 collection entitled *Sound of the Tide* (*Kaicho-on*), Ueda wrote, "The function of symbols consists in borrowing their help to create in the reader an emotional state similar to that in the poet's mind; they do not necessarily attempt to communicate the same conception to everyone. The reader who quietly savors the symbolist poetry may thus, in accordance with his own taste, sense an indescribable beauty which the poet himself has not explicitly stated. The explanation of a given poem may vary from person to person; the essential thing is that it arouse a similar emotional state."

Such views, as I have indicated, were borrowed from the West, but at the same time they represent quite accurately the special qualities of the traditional Japanese *tanka.* Since the ambiguities of the Japanese language are so extreme—in the *tanka,* for example, personal pronouns are rarely used, there is no distinction between singular and plural, often no distinction in tense, and the subject is usually unexpressed—it is natural for a given poem to produce different effects on different readers. The important thing, as in symbolist poetry, was the communication of the poet's mood, and here the shadings were extremely fine. The relatively straightforward poetic statements of Shimazaki Toson, reflecting the nineteenth-century English traditions, were welcomed by the general public, but the poets responded more enthusiastically to the indirection shared alike by the symbolists and their own country's classical poetry. If they had been urged to look to the past, to avoid contamination by foreign ideas, these poets would have been outraged. They would have declared that such obscurantism was contrary to the spirit of the enlightened Meiji age. But when told that eminent foreign poets had preferred ambiguity to informative clarity, the Japanese responded with double enthusiasm. Foreign appreciation of other Japanese traditional arts was to provide the impetus for Japanese rediscovery. When the German architect Bruno Taut proclaimed the uniquely Japanese beauty of the Katsura Palace, the Japanese rapidly and instinctively echoed his excitement. A Japanese love of ambiguity and suggestion, going back a thousand years, underlay the triumph of the Symbolist school.

Ueda Bin's translations were acclaimed not only because they introduced celebrated European poets to Japan, but because they were exceptionally beautiful as Japanese. He maintained in general the traditional fives and sevens of Japanese poetry, sometimes combining them in novel ways, as in the lines of five, five, five and seven syllables he used in translating Mallarmé's "Soupir." The vocabulary was entirely traditional, even slightly archaic, using the most natural Japanese words (rather than exotic, literally translated phrases) to communicate with remarkable fidelity the mood of the original. Ueda was a polyglot, and his collection *Sound of the Tide* includes a section from d'Annunzio's "Francesca da Rimini," a sonnet by Rossetti, some German lyrics, and even poems from the Provençal, but it was his translations from the French which affected most markedly the dominant stream in modern Japanese poetry.

English and American poetry on the whole has not been of great influence in Japan, at least since the time of Ueda Bin. For many years Japanese poetry remained under the spell of the French Symbolists, and they were succeeded by the Dadaists, Surrealists and so on. English poetry belonging to the same schools was welcomed, and T. S. Eliot in particular worked his gloomy magic on the younger poets, even before the war created bombed-out wastelands for them to celebrate, but his absorption with tradition and religion escaped them. For the most part, English and American poetry excited relatively little interest, perhaps because translations from the French were literarily superior, perhaps because of the allure of Paris, which captivated the Japanese in the twenties and thirties no less than the Americans. By the 1880's English had become the second language of Japan, and every schoolboy, however unlikely ever to leave his farm or fishing village, was required to study English until he could plod through one of Lamb's *Tales from Shakespeare* or an O. Henry story. But English tended to be thought of as a practical language, the language of commerce and information, not of poetry. Translation from the English was therefore generally left to teachers of English grammar, and most Japanese poets, as if to distinguish themselves from schoolmasters, studied French, though a few preferred German or Russian. Ueda Bin's translations influenced a whole generation of Japanese poets.

The volume of translated poetry, *Corals* (*Sangoshu*), published by the great novelist and poet Nagai Kafu in 1913, was also from the French, and consisted chiefly of Baudelaire, Verlaine, Henri de Régnier, and the Contesse de Noailles. Kafu's translations are close to the original, sometimes in the classical tongue and sometimes, a great rarity in those days, in the colloquial. His translation of Verlaine's "Colloque Sentimental" was particularly successful.

> Dans le vieux parc solitaire et glacé,
> Deux formes a tout à l'heure passé.
>
> Samui samushii furuniwa ni
> Ima shi totta futatsu no katachi.

By choosing for "solitaire et glacé" two Japanese words, both beginning with the sound *samu,* Kafu intensified the weariness of the atmosphere. Later in the poem we find

> —Te souvient-il de notre extase ancienne?
> —Pourquoi voulez-vous donc qu'il m'en
> souvienne?
>
> —Omae wa tanoshii mukashi no koto wo oboete
> iru ka?
> —Naze oboete iro to ossharu no desu?

Here the distinction between the *tu* employed by the man to the woman and the *vous* used by her in reply is preserved in the Japanese, though not possible in English. The tone is colloquial yet poetic, and completely natural, replacing such un-Japanese conceptions as *extase ancienne* with the familiar *tanoshii mukashi no koto,* "happy bygone things."

It is striking that although Kafu spent four years in the United States as a young man, including one year at Kalamazoo College, he never felt impelled to translate English poetry. His subsequent residence in France was only one year, including a bare two months in Paris, but his passion for French poetry and all things French remained with him for the rest of his long life, and influenced many younger men.

The next important collection of translated poetry was again from the French. The translator, Horiguchi Daigaku (b. 1892), was to gain fame in his own right as a poet, but his translations of Samain, Jammes, Apollinaire, and Cocteau, published after his return to Japan from France in 1924, exerted an extraordinary influence on modern Japanese writing. Most leading critics of Japanese literature today wrote on French poetry before turning to the works of their compatriots, and many developments in the Japanese novel may also be traced in terms of the effects of translations of novels by Cocteau and his generation. France itself was the dream of most young poets, painters and intellectuals, a sentiment commemorated by Hagiwara Sakutaro, the finest modern poet, in verses beginning:

> I wish I could go to France,
> But France is too far away . . .

The Japanese painters who studied in Paris (most leading contemporaries spent a few years there) all depicted the Riviera, Montmartre, and the other frequently represented scenes. The poets, on the other hand, were much freer in their borrowings. Horiguchi Daigaku, for example, rewrote a fable of La Fontaine in the style of Apollinaire, but managed to remain Japanese:

> *The Cicada*
>
> There was a cicada.
> He spent the whole summer singing.
> The winter came.
> What a fix, what a fix!
> (Moral)
> It was worth it.

Much earlier, the poet Kitahara Hakushu (1885-1942) had exploited the possibilities of exoticism, but his exoticism was drawn from the Japanese past, and not a recent importation:

> I believe in the heretical teachings of a
> degenerate age, the witchcraft of
> the Christian God,
> The captains of the black ships, the marvellous
> land of the Red Hairs,
> The scarlet glass, the sharp-scented carnation,
> The calico, arrack, and *vinho tinto* of the
> Southern Barbarians,
> The blue-eyed Dominicans chanting the liturgy
> who tell me even in
> dreams
> Of the God of the forbidden faith, or of the
> blood-stained Cross,
> The cunning device that makes a mustard seed
> big as an apple,
> The strange collapsible spyglass that looks even
> at Paradise.

Hakushu attempted in this poem to intoxicate the reader with bizarre words derived from the Portuguese or Dutch dating back to the sixteenth and seventeenth centuries, when Japan was first in contact with the West. Often the sound of the words, rather than their meanings, was uppermost; Hakushu delighted in the cadences of *deus, kapitan, araki, bateren, birodo,* and his poetry was heavy with absinthe, the odor of chloroform, the sobbing of violins, the putrefying of marble, and the moans of sick children. His exoticism easily turned into a fin-de-siècle overripeness, but his symbolism was sometimes simple and effective:

> The acacia blossoms gold and red are falling,
> In the dusky autumn light they fall.

My sorrow wears the thin flannel garb of one-
sided love.
When I walk the towpath along the water
Your gentle sighs are falling,
The acacia blossoms gold and red are falling.

In this poem, a lingering trace of his partiality for exoticism, Hakushu deliberately wrote of the acacia, a foreign tree, rather than the normal Japanese cherry blossoms, which to modern poets would be anathema. Hakushu's early fondness for the sound of foreign words, however, eventually led him to appreciate the peculiar capabilities of Japanese sounds. As so often in Japan, the young man's passion for the exotic developed later in life into a rediscovery of the traditionally Japanese. Hakushu published in 1923 one of his most celebrated poems, "Chinese Pines" (*Rakuyosho*), in which sound is at least as important as meaning:

karamatsu no hayashi wo
sugite
karamatsu wo shimijimi to
miki
karamatsu wa sabishikarikeri
tabi yuku wa sabishikarikeri.
karamatsu no hayashi wo
idete
karamatsu no hayashi ni
irinu
karamatsu no hayashi ni irite
mata oku michi wa
tsuzukeri

Passing the forest of Chinese
pines,
I stared profoundly at the
Chinese pines.
How lonely were the Chinese pines.
How lonely it was to travel.
Coming out of the forest of
Chinese pines
I entered the forest of Chinese
pines.
Entering the forest of Chinese
pines,
Again the road within
continued.

The last of the eight stanzas runs:

yo no naka yo, aware
narikeri
tsune nakedo ureshikarikeri
yama kawa ni yamagawa no
oto
karamatsu ni karamatsu no
kaze

Oh world, how sad you are,
Inconstant, and yet joyous.
In the hills and rivers, the sound
of the mountain streams
In the Chinese pines the wind of
the Chinese pines.

In the final stanza Hakushu not only demonstrates the special musical qualities of the Japanese language, but deliberately employs the most hackneyed of the old Buddhist images, the transience of worldly things. The slightly novel twist, the discovery of joy even in this impermanence, suggests the aged philosopher who, after his solitary walk in the forest of pines carpeted with fallen needles, finds a quiet happiness in his solitude. We may think this typically and pleasingly Oriental. Indeed, it is normal for Western critics to observe with satisfaction that the Japanese poet, after years of aping Western ways, has at last returned to the ancient traditions of his own country. We should not, however, forget that these sentiments were expressed by a man whose earlier poetry was chiefly influenced by French symbolism. Moreover, although the emotions are sincerely stated, the fact that Hakushu, writing in 1923, should have chosen the language of a thousand years before to describe the truth taught him by his walk through the forest, suggests how acutely aware he was of performing a Japanese action, doing what Japanese poets traditionally did. In his walk along the towpath amidst the falling acacia blossoms, Hakushu was the poet, the lover, not necessarily Japanese, but not un-Japanese. As he walked through the pine forest he saw himself as a Japanese, almost with the eyes of an outsider, and he relished the beauties of the Japanese language, almost with the ears of an outsider, as once he himself had delighted in the strange music of arrack, *vinho tinto* and velvet. Though he states, using the ancient classical language, that the world is *aware* (sad) and *tsune nakedo* (inconstant), he has not returned miraculously to the outlook of the ancient Japanese; he has discovered that their manner of expression suits him at this stage of his life, as French symbolism had suited him earlier. He himself remains that enigma, the Japanese in the twentieth century.

Hakushu's poem on the pine forest is cast in the traditional alternating lines of five and seven syllables, and is in classical language. This was a deliberate case of archaism, one might suppose, but the retention of these features of traditional Japanese poetry was general until the 1920's, and did not entirely disappear afterwards. The classical language had certain advantages over the modern tongue. Its greater variety of inflections enabled the poet, if he chose, to be more concise than modern language permits, or, on the other hand, to draw out a single word the full length of a line for special effect. For example, in Hakushu's poem "Chinese Pines" *sabishikarikeri,* meaning "it was lonely," is grammatically a single word in seven syllables; the modern word *sabishikatta* is not only two syllables shorter, but its double consonant destroys the prolonged, mournful tone desired.

Japanese poets found it hard to sense overtones in words without poetic ancestry. Writing modern Japanese was for them what writing poetry in Basic English or even in Esperanto would be for us. Even revolutionary poetry was cast in the classical grammar:

We know what we are seeking,
We know what the people want,
And we know what we must do.
We know more than the young men of Russia
fifty years ago—
Yet no one with clenched fist bangs on the table
To proclaim V NAROD.

The modern language was used most effectively when the poet's intent was to disillusion or to be unpoetic. A pioneer effort, published in 1909, was entitled "The Rubbish Heap," and graphically described the odors, maggots, rotting objects and so forth found in the garbage. The poem was a step in the right direction, but not one that all poets wished to take.

The first truly successful poet of the modern language was Hagiwara Sakutaro (1886-1942). He used it not to startle with unpleasant images or vulgar colloquialisms, but for its own music, unlike that of the classical language but no less capable of moving the reader. The dissatisfaction of earlier poets with the modern language had stemmed from their attempts to make it respond in the same manner as the classical language; Hagiwara abandoned that attempt and wrote a free, colloquial verse which, as he himself recognized, altered the course of Japanese poetry. His themes often skirt the neurotic, and his sensitivity is akin to morbidity, but a haunting beauty remains.

The Corpse of a Cat

The spongelike scenery
Is gently swollen with moisture.
No sign of man or beast in sight.
A water wheel is weeping.
From the blurred shadows of a willow
I see the gentle form of a woman waiting.
Wrapping her thin shawl around her,
Dragging her lovely, vaporous garments,
She wanders calmly, like a spirit.
Ah, Ura, lonely woman!
"You're always late, aren't you?"
We have no past, no future,
And have faded away from the things of reality.
Ura!
Here in this weird landscape.
Bury the corpse of the drowned cat!

With Hagiwara modern Japanese poetry attained its maturity. The subject of his poems was the Japanese artist in the twentieth century, attracted by the West, savoring its civilization, but living in the ghost-ridden landscape of Japan. His poetry is in the Symbolist tradition, the fruit of other men's long years of translation. He rejected neo-classicism and the classical language, but equally the coarse realism which many poets assumed was the alternative to formalism. In the twenties, when the proletarian movement in literature was in full swing, Hagiwara insisted on the absolute values of poetry, and scorned what he termed third-rate versifying. His arbitrary judgments won him enemies, but also devoted followers who created the main stream of poetry in the 1930's. Miyoshi Tatsuji (1900-63), after Hagiwara the foremost Japanese poet, wrote a poem entitled "Hagiwara Sakutaro—Teacher!" that begins:

Dark mass of melancholy—
That character I loved,
Doubter and pessimist, philosopher and
wanderer,
Crystallized, unchanged and incorruptible,
Like still-warm lava, of strange music.

Miyoshi was the guiding spirit of the magazine *Shiki* (*Four Seasons*), the leading poetry journal of the thirties, which published most of the poets of the period still esteemed today. They included the eccentric, short-lived Nakahara Chuya (1907-37), whose poetry has gained full recognition only in recent years. Nakahara, after a most erratic scholastic career, graduated at the age of twenty-six from the French Department of the Tokyo School of Foreign Languages, and later translated Rimbaud. In his own day he was famed as the arch example of a Bohemian, a dissolute incorrigible who consciously posed as a Japanese Rimbaud, but his best poems speak unaffectedly of the weariness and despair which occasioned his riotous living.

To a Dragonfly

In an autumn sky too perfectly clear
A red dragonfly is winging.
In the empty field I stand,
Bathed in pale sunset.

The smokestack of a distant factory
Meets my eye, blurred in evening light.
Breathing a great sigh,
I kneel and pick up a stone.

When I feel the pebble's coldness
Warm at last within my hand,
I let it go, and now over grass
Bathed in sunset glow it skims.

The skimmed-over grass
Droops earthwards, just perceptibly.
The smokestack of the factory in the distance
Meets my eye, dim in evening light.

Another poet of the Four Seasons school, even shorter lived than Nakahara, was Tachihara Michizo (1914-39). His poetry is exceptionally lyrical, and some critics believe that it raised the modern Japanese language to its highest peak of expressive possibilities.

For Future Remembrance

The dream always returns to that lonely village
at the foot of the mountain
—Winds stir in the nettle leaves
And crickets endlessly pipe—
Along a road through a wood silent with early
afternoon.

A brilliant sun shines in the blue sky, the
volcano sleeps
—And I,

Though I know no one listens, go on talking
Of things I have seen: islands, waves, headlands,
sunlight and the moon.

The dream never goes beyond that point.
I will try to forget everything, utterly.
When I have forgotten even that I have
completely forgotten,

The dream will freeze amid recollections of
midwinter,
Then open a door and leave in solitude
On that road lighted by scraps of stars.

One unusual writer who stood apart both from the poets of the Four Seasons school and their opposite numbers, the poets of social consciousness, was Kusano Shimpei (born 1902), the master of onomatopoeia. Of all languages of highly civilized peoples, Japanese probably has the richest variety of sound effects to represent every conceivable noise, as well as some phenomena (like the twinkling of a star) which only suggest sound. Kusano exploited this feature of the Japanese language and even invented a language of frogs, delighting readers with the curious, meaningless music. His fondness for frogs, he said, stemmed from his belief that they were the true proletarians—a harking back apparently to his early anarchist days. His use of onomatopoeia (to depict the sound of waves) is evident in this poem:

The Sea at Night

From the distant, deep, heavy bottom,
From the dark, invisible, limitless past
zuzuzuzu zuwaaru
zuzuzuzu zuwaaru
gun un uwaaru

The black sea continues its roar,
In the black the lead-colored waves are born.
Splashing their lead-colored manes, the waves
break,
And crawl on their bellies up the sopping strand.

Leaden waves are born out there,
And out that way too,
Then swallowed in the black of India ink,
But once again appear and press to shore.
zuzuzuzu zuwaaru
zuzuzuzu zuwaaru
gun un uwaaru . . .

Poetry, like all forms of literary activity, fell increasingly under governmental supervision in the thirties with the start of the wars in China. Not surprisingly, the same period saw a marked development in surrealist or dadaist poetry. The escape from reality into fantasy or a pure poetry, which created meanings of itself instead of expressing existing ideas, characterized such avant-garde poets as Kitasono Katsue (born 1902) and his VOU group, celebrated by Ezra Pound. It is tempting to discover in the great vogue which surrealist poetry has enjoyed in Japan since the thirties something of the long tradition of extremely complicated poetry, often filled with irrational verbal associations, encountered in the Japanese drama. Overtones and associations, rather than ideas, absorbed the surrealists, and thereby saved them from possible ideological sins. The Four Seasons poets too, being uninterested in political matters, escaped trouble from the authorities, and by the time of the outbreak of the Pacific War in 1941 had come to be recognized as the most serious group of modern poets. During the war the poets behaved much like the rest of the population, rejoicing over victories and lamenting the deaths of soldiers, on occasion falling into hysterical outbursts of bellicosity.

The immediate postwar generation grew up in a bleak atmosphere. Hunger, the black market, and the collapse of the old moral values induced despair or a blank craving for pleasure. The most important group of new poets gathered around a journal aptly called *The Wasteland* (*Arechi*). The Wasteland poets wrote of their sense of hollowness and futility, taking comfort (if at all) in a desperate search for human values. Tamura Ryuichi (born 1923), a leader of the Wasteland poets, wrote in a typical vein:

"Why do little birds sing?"
At the Press Club bar
My friend Hoshino introduced me to an
American's poem.
"Why do people walk? That's the next line."
We drank our beer
And ate our cheeseburgers.
At a corner table
A middle-aged Englishman lit his pipe;
His wife was lost in a novel about God and the
devil.
After the twentieth of September
The nights in this age without faith become
autumnal.
We walked slowly along the narrow asphalt
streets
And separated at Tokyo Station.
"Why do little birds sing?"
I woke from my dream in profound darkness
Moved
By something falling from extremely high,
Then once again I plunged
Into the dream, towards "the next line."

The wasteland mood appears frequently in the postwar poetry, though sometimes altered by surrealist or even traditional *haiku* techniques, as in this poem by Ando Tsuguo (born 1919) entitled "Tubers" and found in a collection divided in *haiku* fashion by the seasons of year.

Worms, mole-crickets, slugs

When eyeless things
Go searching for the eyes
Of dead things which
Address them amiably

The smell of their breath
From a whole year back
Crowds before them

The corpses of small birds,
Like forgotten tubers,
Lie fallen this month.

Wakeful children
Wander a sky
Which could not be inhumed

Tomorrow,
Peaches. Grasshoppers. Cumulus clouds.

The tubers of this poem suggest *The Wasteland,* though the season is June here, and the roots are not being stirred into activity by the rain so much as rotted away. Only the sky escapes the seasonal decay and offers a promise of the summer of childhood.

A still later generation of Japanese poets, raised in more cheerful times, seems to have escaped from the wasteland and to be intent on creating poetry explosive in its intensity but curiously unconcerned with the moral and political issues that torment older Japanese. Poetic production since the war has remained largely under the domination of the older generation, notably Miyoshi Tatsuji and Nishiwaki Junzaburo, a professor of English literature whose translations of T. S. Eliot have been seminal. Nishiwaki has favored surrealism in his own poetry, and influenced younger poets with his intuitive, flashing style. Contemporary Japanese poetry is generally difficult, both in syntax and imagery, and even when not written under any direct influence from the West is likely to reveal kinship with the works of Eliot, Yeats, Rilke, or the French modernists.

My discussion has thus far been restricted to poems written in the new form—irregular in length and composed directly or indirectly under Western influence. This does not mean that the more traditional Japanese verse forms, the *tanka* and the *haiku,* were abandoned. Far from it. After an initial period of about twenty years of relative inactivity following the Meiji Restoration, a time when the existing schools of *tanka* and *haiku* failed to reflect the changes in the new society, a revolution occurred in the *haiku* with Masaoka Shiki (1867-1902), and then in the *tanka* with Yosano Tekkan (1873-1935). It would be tedious and repetitious to chronicle the successive shifts of taste within these two types of poetry. In both cases revolution meant first of all a rejection of prevailing modes of composition. In the *haiku,* Shiki attacked Basho, long venerated as a god, and advocated instead the pictorial techniques of the eighteenth-century master Buson. Shiki also concerned himself with the *tanka,* rejecting the *Kokinshu,* the ideal of nineteenth-century *tanka* poets, in favor of the ancient collection, the *Manyoshu.* Yosano Tekkan and his wife Yosano Akiko began in 1900 the publication of the magazine *Myojo,* which served as the organ of the new *tanka.* The pages of *Myojo* were soon splattered with such untraditional words as "passion," "blood," "purple," "flesh" and so on, suggesting the wildly romantic strain characteristic of the new poetry. Yosano Akiko's collection *Tangled Hair* (*Midaregami*), published in 1901, stirred women readers in particular, not only because of the lyrical beauty, but because her poetry seemed to proclaim a new age of romantic love. Using the familiar classical language of the old poets, Yosano Akiko moved readers with her self-proclaimed emancipation:

kazu shiranu
ware no kokoro no
kizahashi wo
hata futatsu mitsu
kare ya noborishi

Of the numberless steps
Up to my heart,
He climbed perhaps
Only two or three.

Myojo served as a focal point for activities by *tanka* poets in the early 1900's. One frequenter of the Yosano salon was Ishikawa Takuboku (1885-1912), who emerged in the course of his short life as probably the most popular *tanka* poet in all Japanese history. Takuboku also wrote poems in the modern style (one is quoted in part above), but he owed his fame to his *tanka,* and remains today a literary idol thanks to the dozen or more verses that everyone knows and to the romances spun around his tragic life. The interest he showed in anarchism and socialism has especially endeared him today with "progressive" critics. His most famous *tanka* runs:

Tokai no
kojima no iso no
shirasuna ni
ware nakinurete
kani to tawamuru

On the white sand
Of the beach of a small isle
In the Eastern Sea,
I, my face streaked with tears,
Am playing with a crab.

Many of Takuboku's poems might be dismissed as sentimental, but Japanese find their melancholy charm peculiarly attractive. The lonely boy, weeping as he plays with a crab on the empty shore, certainly struck a warmer chord of sympathy than the poetry of the new style, expressing loneliness in terms of dark and confusing symbols. The simple lyrical impulse of the *tanka* enabled it to survive even after the successes of the new poetry movement had opened to Japanese poets channels of expression far more varied and flexible than the rigid thirty-one syllables of the classical form. The form itself sustained what in a freer verse might be little more than an inarticulate cry of emotion. The poet needed not devise an elaborate structure for his *tanka;* the structure was already there, waiting for its delicate burden. For a poet like Hagiwara Sakutaro the limits of the *tanka* would have constituted an intolerable impediment to his poetic expression, but for innumerable other Japanese, the poetic impulse consisted of a single perception or reflection which could only be vitiated if expanded to greater lengths.

Both the *tanka* and *haiku* were inevitably influenced by developments in the modern poetry. European influence, the adoption of words of foreign origin, the use of the colloquial in place of the classical language, the acceptance of irregular lines in place of the traditional fives and sevens—all aroused the passions and bitterly divided the *tanka* and *haiku* poets, to an even more pronounced degree than the modern poets, if only because it was possible to invoke tradition more effectively. Unlike the case of modern poetry, moreover, the conservative forces proved victorious in the end. Most *tanka* and *haiku* are written today in the classical language, and despite English or French words that may be introduced to lend an exotic note, the themes are often reminiscent of the past. Modern themes, even when employed by good poets, tend to seem contrived or precious when presented in the traditional form and language.

teiden no
yoru no roka ni
inu nemuri
inu no shizukeki
ibiki kikoyuru

Tonight a breakdown
Of electric current: my dog
Snoozes in the hall;
I can hear the murmur of
His tranquil canine snoring.
Miya Shuji (born 1912)

icho ochiba
yogoreshi minato no
machi no tsuji
niguro no hei ni
michi wo kikarenu

Fallen gingko leaves
Have dirtied the harbor streets;
At the road crossing
A negro soldier stopped me
And politely asked the way.
Kimata Osamu (born 1906)

dokubu ni
aku e no shiko wo
wasurekoshi
tomo wa nukegara to
shika omowarezu

I can only think
My friend who has forgotten
His taste for evil
In solitary confinement
Is but the husk of himself.
Kasugai Ken (born 1940)

The *tanka* and *haiku* of today are distinct from modern poetry in one important respect: they are not considered to be exclusively the business of trained poets. Literally hundreds, perhaps thousands of *tanka* and *haiku* groups publish journals devoted to works by members, who are drawn from all levels of society. The daily newspapers carry *tanka* and *haiku* columns in which verses by readers are appraised by leading professionals. Labor union magazines and businessmen's journals alike feature *tanka* and *haiku* columns; the *haiku,* being shorter, is generally more popular.

It is easy for a Japanese, even of modest education, to write a poem in seventeen or thirty-one syllables. An ability to dash off a *haiku* at a drinking party is prized as a social asset. Naturally enough, the quality of most amateur *haiku* is deplorable. However, the most influential article written about the *haiku* since the war (in 1946), "On Second Class Art" ("*Daini Geijutsu-ron*") by Kuwabara Takeo, a professor of French literature at Kyoto University, asserted that the difference between a *haiku* composed by an acknowledged master and one by a bank clerk or a railway engineer was hardly perceptible. Taking a hint from the method used by I. A. Richards in *Practical Criticism,* he asked a group of colleagues to evaluate various *haiku,* some by masters and some by dubs, first removing the names of the poets. The results were so chaotic that Kuwabara felt justified in his claim that most people judge *haiku* by the poet's reputation and not by the works themselves. He asked if it were likely that a short story or a long poem by a master would be confused with one by an amateur, and concluded that the *haiku* must be a second class art, not objectionable as a mildly artistic diversion for amateurs, but certainly not to be considered a serious vehicle of literature.

Kuwabara's article aroused enormous controversy, as was to be expected, and diverted many budding young *haiku* poets to other fields. It is difficult to say that an art with the enormous following of *haiku* is not flourishing, but Kuwabara's article certainly shook the foundations of the art in a manner from which it has not recovered. The *tanka,* though not specifically a target of Kuwabara's, was susceptible to much the same criticism. It moreover has suffered from its intimate association, as the oldest and therefore "purest" Japanese verse form, with the ultranationalistic activities during the war. The *tanka* poets were vociferous in the adulation they offered to the mystique of the Imperial Family and the Japanese civilizing mission. The student who today writes *tanka* is therefore regarded with suspicion as a possible embryonic fascist, no matter what subjects he may choose. The seventeen-year-old boy who assassinated the leader of the Socialist Party wrote a *tanka* in his prison cell before committing suicide.

On the whole, the future of the *tanka* and *haiku* does not seem promising, despite the many magazines and newspaper columns. The two poetic forms will undoubtedly survive, as almost every traditional art has survived in Japan, practiced by retired old gentlemen and smaller numbers of active young men. The future of poetry in Japan would seem to lie, as in other countries, with the professional poets of the modern school. We may regret the diminishing of purely Japanese poetic arts, and fear that the new poetry will be little more than a reflection of Western writing. But modern Japanese poetry has by now achieved its identity. Though part of the larger stream of world poetry and no longer an entirely distinct flow, it is as Japanese as Japan in the middle twentieth century can be. Here is what Takamura Kotaro (1883-1956) wrote about his poetry, and in a sense of all modern Japanese poetry:

> *My Poetry*
>
> My poetry is not part of Western poetry;
> The two touch, circumference against circumference,
> But never quite coincide . . .
> I have a passion for the world of Western poetry,
> But I do not deny that my poetry is formed differently.
> The air of Athens and the subterranean fountain of Christianity
> Have fostered the pattern of thought and diction of Western poetry;
> It strikes through to my heart with its infinite beauty and strength—
> But its physiology, of wheat-meal and cheese and entrecôtes,
> Runs counter to the necessities of my language.
> My poetry derives from my bowels—
> Born at the farthest limits of the far east,
> Bred on rice and malt and soya-beans and the flesh of fish . . .
> Western poetry is my dear neighbour,
> But the traffic of my poetry moves on a different path.
>
> (translation by Ninomiya and Enright)

Kijima Hajime

SOURCE: "On Postwar Japanese Poetry," in *The Poetry of Postwar Japan,* edited by Kijima Hajime, University of Iowa Press, 1975, pp. xi-xxvi.

[*In the following excerpt, Kijima presents an overview of trends in Japanese poetry written after World War II.*]

Postwar Japanese poetry emerged from the ashes. During the wartime, the poets who were not influenced by the ultra-nationalistic military activities were rare, and almost all poets were mobilized to write war-encouraging poems. Spontaneously, rather than by being forced, they participated in this kind of literary effort. And of course, no literary works of endurance could come of such activities. As a result, when Japan was defeated by the Allied Forces in 1945, there was no base upon which the new poets could stand—only the so-called "Given Democracy."

Ashes, vacuum, and "Given Democracy." But nothing creative can be expected from these.

The writers who had been ardent militarists yesterday suddenly became "democrats." Their guilty consciences caused them to accuse the then famous poets of their fascistic literary activities during the wartime. Thus began the long controversy about the responsibility of the poets during the war. Critics pointed out the relation between the ultra-nationalistic totalitarianism and the traditional psyche which was represented frantically in the war poems. Could such a relation be found and analyzed well enough? Hot debates continued.

In 1946 a serious article was published by Professor Kuwabara about the traditional short poem, *haiku.* I want to quote the concise summary of this article and its result as presented by Professor Keene:

> It is easy for a Japanese, even of modest education, to write a poem in seventeen or thirty-one syllables. An ability to dash off a *haiku* at a drinking party is prized as a social asset. Naturally enough, the quality of most amateur *haiku* is deplorable. However, the most influential article written abut the *haiku* since the war (in 1946), "On Second Class Art" ("Daini Geijutsu-ron") by Kuwabara Takeo, a professor of French literature at Kyoto University, asserted that the difference between a *haiku* composed by an acknowledged master and one by a bank clerk or a railway engineer was hardly perceptible. Taking a hint from the method used by I. A. Richards in *Practical Criticism,* he asked a group of colleagues to evaluate various *haiku,* some by masters and some by dubs, first removing the names of the poets. The results were so chaotic that Kuwabara felt justified in his claim that most people judge *haiku* by the poet's reputation and not by the works themselves. He asked if it were likely that a short story or a long poem by a master would be confused with one by an amateur, and concluded that the *haiku* must be a second class art, not objectionable as a mildly artistic diversion for amateurs, but certainly not to be considered a serious vehicle of literature.
>
> Kuwabara's article aroused enormous controversy, as was to be expected, and diverted many budding young *haiku* poets to other fields. It is difficult to say that an art with the enormous following of *haiku* is not flourishing, but Kuwabara's article certainly shook the foundations of the art in a manner from which it has not recovered. The *tanka,* though not specifically a target of Kuwabara's, was susceptible to much the same criticism. It moreover has suffered from its intimate association, as the oldest and therefore "purest" Japanese verse form, with the ultra-nationalistic activities during the war. The *tanka* poets were vociferous in the adulation they offered to the mystique of the Imperial Family and the Japanese civilizing mission. The student who today writes *tanka* is therefore regarded with suspicion as a possible embryonic fascist, no matter what subject he may choose. The seventeen-year-old boy who assassinated the leader of the Socialist Party wrote a *tanka* in his prison cell before committing suicide. (Donald Keene, *Modern Japanese Poetry* [University of Michigan, 1964].)

One thing I wish to add is the fact that *tanka* became the form of death poema by soldiers and generals who were executed as war criminals after World War II. Almost all made death poems as an accompaniment of their rigid rituals. But they never composed *haiku* when they were about to die. Thus, for the relation of the war to traditional poetry, *tanka* was actually more deeply involved than *haiku,* as Professor Keene has pointed out. And after the devastating war, many poets were forced to become keenly aware of the sentimental lyricism in *tanka*. What elements in the Japanese psyche could mold themselves into ultra-nationalistic militarism? Poets could not avoid this question. Modernity in Japan itself did mean the imitation of Western expansionistic civilization, which was the stepfather of militaristic provocative activities by Japan—or was it not? Reflections like these kept coming.

Fundamentally, in modern Japanese lyricism there must have been something fragile that tended to be sentimentally totalitarian, and poets should have criticized this element, but actually they promoted this tendency without being aware of it.

The ultra-nationalistic power oppressed all literary activities: modern, avant-garde, and proletarian. But after the surrender of resistants to this oppression, people who were educated militaristically became rather more and more enthusiastic about the governing class's ultranationalism. So, oppressed by power, and surrounded by the warmongering people, many poets could not write their own personal feelings even clandestinely, or even inside their own hearts.

But the unknown poets or the poets-to-be were mumbling, and chewing over the whole experience, and not a few genuine poets died during the war. Kusuda Ichiro was one of them. He wrote the following lines before he was killed on some battlefield.

> Where this wind blows itself out
> The hollows of valleys
> Without air or clouds
> The cries of beasts nibbling
> At the thistle's stinging leaves,
> All rush up into a blank sky
> Like violent soldiers.
> Humans are being killed,
> Being killed.
> Look at this tree,
> Listen to this stone.
> Inside the cracks of the earth
> Many lives continue.
>
> Various blood billows up
> And gleams in daylight
> Like the coolies' greased foreheads.
>
> . . . . .
>
> Evening was stained and looted
> This eye witnessed the devastation
>
> . . . . .
>
> They were excluded from sleep
> They slept standing, like trees

(from "Dark Songs," translated by Kijima Hajime)

In these lines the young poet was keenly aware of what the war was bringing about.

He can be called a forerunner of the postwar poets. And this poem was published after the war by his friend Ayukawa Nobuo, who became one of the most influential poets and critics, founding the poetry group Arechi (The Waste Land) in 1947. As is clearly shown by its name, this poetry group Arechi started its literary activities under the influence of T. S. Eliot, considering this age of ours as that of devastation, futility, and despair.

It must be added that this forming of the poetry group Arechi was made during wartime, not officially, but with some of the same feeling, coming spontaneously in separate places, that "hope is abominable for us, and despair is more suitable for us in 1941 and 1942" (Ayukawa Nobuo, *The Wartime Diary*). There was no vacuum for them. They were breathing the new poetic air through destruction.

What should not be forgotten is that already in the nineteen twenties and thirties all the trends of modern or post-modern poetry had been introduced into Japan. After 1868 when feudalism ended, within the next forty to sixty years, Japanese poetry changed its dress several times—romanticism, naturalism, symbolism, dadaism, futurism, surrealism, intellectualism, proletarianism—and stood as a contemporary with Western poetry having the same kind of consciousness in common. However, it did not find any tie with Oriental poetry at all, even in the field of folklore or popular lyrics. It faced toward the West always, this tendency still continues, and nobody can foresee the prospect of change. Perhaps this comes from the linguistic and political isolation of Japan, and also from her unprecedented modernization in Asia. But Japanese poets have tended to feel a strong affinity with the West, and in the last stage before World War II they felt the same artistic consciousness as the Western avant-gardists. For example, Takiguchi Shuzo, who was once put into prison and became one of the most respected art critics after the war, was a colleague of those international surrealists like André Breton and Paul Eluard. The reason why the police had arrested surrealists was simple. The men in power thought surrealism not understandable, and therefore dangerous for them. Even though Takiguchi stopped writing poetry very early, his would be considered as one of the forerunners of postwar poetry, and under his influence not a few young poets began to concentrate their energy upon the imaginative. Here is an example of his poetry.

Virgin decorations
Ashes of innumerable inverted candles
Branches and flowers of transparent trees
Roars of infinite mirrors and
Spasms of windows of houses

My whole body
In the water fossil increasing its brightness day
by day

My desire swims none the less
I am the noble bastard of the huge chandelier
called azure

No one calls me the sphinx of love

My dream, in the fable of jasper,
Glitters all the more blue

("The Desire of the Fish," translated by
Sato Hiroaki)

The poet who criticized the rising ultra-nationalistic tendencies most severely before the war was Oguma Hideo. He died in 1940, and was the last major proletarian poet who resisted very strongly the inclination toward fascism until his death. He expressed himself openly, and criticized his fellow poets and novelists bitterly but humorously after the regime forced the proletarian writers union to disband. He tried to write more colloquially than others.

Even if darkness
Blinds the earth forever
Our rights will always
Awaken.
Roses appear
Black in the darkness,
But if sunlight strikes them
Their color burns.

Grief and sorrow are our share,
Not theirs,
But they can have
Neither joy nor laughter.
I know all about darkness.
Therefore I believe light is coming.
Comprehend the hard meaning,
Comrades,
Of our search for fire:
We even strike our fists on stones.

Millions of voices
Cry in the dark.
The air is trembling and it illuminates
The windows.
It feels its way as a key does
And it brings light,
And it brings victory.

Never be useless and silent
When you are near roses.
Surely action
Is the synonym of hope.
Surely your emotion is a brilliant bridegroom.

So get ready.
Your carriage is coming.
You are going to welcome your bride.
You'd better get started.
Blow your horn's thunder,
Whip the horses along,
And make the clear sound
Of your loud wheel-track song.

("Starting Song of Our Carriage," translated by
Kijima Hajime)

When the poetry group Retto (Archipelago) was formed in 1958, it intended to follow and develop this line of Oguma's with much more imaginative experimentation, like that of Takiguchi's.

Between these two main poetry groups, Arechi and Retto, there was one common awareness—the rumination over war experience. Of course, among those poets who did not belong to these two groups, the same feeling existed. How to reorganize the images, sounds, and deep feelings of wartime was the main concern of many poets. In the totalitarian war where almost all Japanese people were involved, nobody could avoid the disastrous results, mental and physical. So the naming of "Postwar Poetry" was irresistible and quite usable, until the generation with no experience and memory of war began to appear.

Every nation has its own memorable dates. Every person, too. Independence, confusion, and revolution. Love, crisis, and self-discovery. For postwar Japanese poetry the special date was 1945, because a new poetry began to emerge. But the date does not mean simply the defeat of militarism and the birth of a new nation. It also indicates a tremendously unfathomable image-burden for us. August 6th. Who can cope with the first event in the whole history of mankind with his imagination?

Together with the helplessness of soldiers, this unprecedented image of actual genocide haunted the postwar poets. *The Inferno* of the present age should have been written in Japanese. Perhaps no overwhelming poem has been written yet about the whole human experience of World War II. Let us read a memorable poem written by Ando Tsuguo who was born in 1919.

"On August 6th, 1945 at 8:15 a.m.
the first atomic bomb in human
history, dropped on Hiroshima,
branded on the granite a human
shadow sitting eternally at rest."

Rosy crystallized sunlight creeps around.
Now over the earth
The damp mold covering the lower world
Widens.
It increases a billion times faster
Than human activity.
It has been a long time
Since we wished to exterminate
That castrated shadow;
Since that day we stopped
Walking on two legs.

But we refuse to walk
On four legs forever—
Since our legs and arms have grown
To unmatching sizes.
With our hands placed forward obsequiously
On the earth,
We crawl around gladly
On our knees.

Since we saw the immense mushroom cloud
A dark purple that day
In the rosy crystallized sky,
Our bellies swelled up
Like those of pregnant women,
And from our navels an oil
Trickles continually.

How fussy we are about its amount—
Increasing? No.
We quarrel with each other about soiling
What was just cleaned.
How we laugh at these pointless arguments
With groans
As if our lungs were translucent.
We have no need now
To hide our genitals,
Nor enough time to bother with them.
All this pain is caused
By one problem: how to get rid
Of this dark red, swollen,
Unmanageable navel.
On the navel eyes grow
And a nose,
And on the bald head
We check for downy hair quivering
Like dry rice in a field;
Turning the navel
Over again and again for a close inspection
Is the most solemn duty
In our daily schedule.
And therefore we crawl out gladly
Into the rosy crystallized sunlight
On our knees.

A long time has passed
Since we began
To extinguish our widening shadows
Over the earth.

A long time has passed
Since we began to forget
The dark home country
From which we'd started.

("The Book of the Dead," translated by Kijima Hajime)

Thus the abnormal mental condition resulting from the war continued. The wounded, the mutilated, and the ghosts were rampant in postwar Japanese society, even though people were taught about democratic reconstruction. How can they disappear in the imagery of sensitive poets?

During this time, curiously enough, or rather naturally enough, the healthy appeared singular and prominent. When Tanikawa Shuntaro began to publish his poems which had no war shadows, his works were thought to be fresh and clear, and attracted attention. But, although he was considered to be totally free from the influence of the war, it was not true. Such an interpretation is superficial.

About Tanikawa's formative years, let us hear the opinion of Iwata Hiroshi who belongs to the same generation:

> Then [during the war—Kijima] the junior high school students, who were too young to be desperately intoxicated with the war cause, but too mature to overlook the war reality, were opening their keen adolescent eyes in the vague freedom that was allowed only for noncombatants. In an over-strained period, to be wise one must always be on the alert, and also be abnormally sensitive. Day and night the junior high school students at that time used much sharper and purer imaginations than those who spent their adolescence in the other periods.

This remark of Iwata's about their adolescence can be applied to Tanikawa Shuntaro and other poets of the same age. And when the new poetic generation gathered together, forming a group named Kai (Oars) in 1953, it was thought that a third group besides Arechi and Retto was appearing. But actually the members of this group, too, were very concerned about the war and its results. The works of the poetess Ibaragi Noriko, one of the founders of this group, show that quite clearly.

So it can be said that paradoxically enough all the intense experiences of the war absurdly nurtured and prepared the important and distinctive voices in postwar poetry. In a sense, its intensity guaranteed the artistic quality of the poetry as long as it lasted in the poets' minds and among the public.

Thus the critical moment for postwar poetry came when the symptoms of the disintegration of this intensity began to appear. What the postwar poets began to suffer then was a lack of intense experience, an oppression of mass production, and the diffusion of poetic themes. Poets suddenly found themselves in the labyrinth of economic over-production and commercialism after violence, starvation, and suicidal devotion. This was a tremendously drastic change. People are becoming paralyzed and apathetic in the mass society, and although poets feel crazed with bitterness they cannot yet discern whether this change is structural or not, and rather feel completely dismayed in the new situation—a rare one in modern Japan. For in the process of Japanese modernization there has never been such a long peaceful term as the one since 1945. Always modern Japan was involved in wars, or rather I must say Japan kept on invading Asian countries, anachronistically imitating Western imperialism. Although modern Japanese intellectuals resisted this tendency, their proposals were all defeated. Not a few committed suicide. If not, they converted—converted not into another belief, but rather into aestheticism.

But if we look back to the premodern age, Japan had more than 250 years of peaceful isolation under the Tokugawa shogunate. And poets, like the anonymous Senryu poets, who belonged to the common people and contributed 17 syllabled satirical verses to the compiler Karai Senryu (1718-90), had to and could endure the staleness of society, yet produce a kind of creative writing. So if we see the Japanese cultural situation from afar, it is the history of long isolation and sudden interference, the sad repetition of the colonial mind and chauvinism, and the peculiarly incomprehensible uniqueness. Can poetry be unrelated to this? I don't think it is possible.

Japanese language itself is considered to be very isolated, and yet inside the country it is an integral part of life and can be understood well anywhere, although there have been numerous dialects. As for the way of inscribing, it absorbed and digested foreign words through its peculiar way of adaptation, especially from the Chinese. For example, poems were written in Chinese from ancient times in Japan, but these poems in Chinese were recited completely differently from the way they were in China.

In the present Japanese language, Chinese characters are used together with two kinds of Japanese phonograms (Hiragana and Katakana) mixed, and Chinese characters (Kanji), which have more than one pronunciation usually but have not yet lost some essential charm to the poets as ideas or as things visualized. This mixed use of ideograms and phonograms at the same time is undoubtedly peculiar in itself. I think this may be very dogmatic, but I want to say from my poetic preoccupation that this mixed use through adaptation has some curious coincidence with religious syncretism in Japan, which appears unbelievable for Westerners, but very natural for Japanese. People believe at the same time in Shintoist Gods, Buddhism, and Confucianism. In everyday life these are combined and embodied in numerous rituals. From the Western theological point of view the Japanese attitude cannot be called religious, but rather too worldly. However, from the Japanese point of view, Western Monotheism is after all connected with that other world—the absolute one—which is a little bit too absurd for contemporary living. So in the contemporary age this syncretism can be the way to be worldly-wise about everything crucial, for good or for evil. And this mixed use, or peaceful coexistence of the various opposing elements, can be seen in every sphere of Japanese cultural life.

Mixture, but not thorough permeation. Transformation after transformation, and yet hard-core preservation. Noh, Kabuki, and the modern theatre. Japanese and Western paintings. Music of traditional, Western classical, and Jazz. They are existing altogether without mutual thorough inter-penetration. About poetry, traditional or modern *tanka* and *haiku* poets are seemingly very indifferent to contemporary free verse, and vice versa. These forms do not dominate each other, and one cannot extinguish the others. Of course, historically *tanka* originated first and was long preserved as a court poetry, and *haiku* came second and spread most widely. The fact that these three kinds of poetic forms can exist, and generally do not interfere with each other, also shows the symptoms of the Japanese cultural situation. I could not find an adequate word, so I am calling this a peaceful coexistence. It is well known that the two short traditional forms have definite regulating devices, but modern Japanese poetry does not have any such lasting regular form. It is free. In the prewar age at the time (1882) of the so-called Shin Tai Shi (the new-styled poetry) some forms of longer repetitive use of 5-7 or 7-5 syllables were about to become standard, but they could not because of their monotonousness. These two fundamental syllabic lines, which derived from classical *tanka* and *haiku,* can be seen now in popular lyrics—full of clichés. Modern poets, who want to put the importance upon the sounds and rhythms of their poetry, make use of some regular phonetic forms, and sometimes invent their own with much experimentation. But as a whole modern Japanese poetry has no regular forms at all—it is completely free—poets must find their own form each time they begin to write: "organic form."

Of postwar poetry, I mentioned only three groups, simply not to confuse readers, but actually there were innumerable groups, many of them publishing their own magazines. In one of the three monthly poetry magazines, *Gendaishi Techo* (*Notebook of Contemporary Poetry*), in its annual December issue a list of some 1,700 poets' addresses is made public. Among this number no *tanka* and *haiku* poets are included. But it should be noted here that on the other hand no major Japanese publisher takes the trouble to produce books of poems from among these numerous poets. The reading of modern poetry has not yet become popular, even though some trials or experimentations are occasionally made. (But annually in January in the emperor's court *tanka* recitation is held. Amateur *tanka* poets whose works have been accepted gather and hear their own *tankas* recited like an ancient ritual: an example of *hard-core preservation.*)

Two reasons, I think, may be mentioned why poetry reading cannot be popular in Japan. Modern poetry reading is actually surrounded not only by those who like *tanka* and *haiku,* but also by those who are pleased with Shigin (peculiar recitation of Chinese poems in Japanese), Rokyoku (sentimental epic recitation about gamblers and outlaws), and Kabuki declamations. Of course, these latter are not called poetry in the modern sense, but rather fall into the general category of entertainment: music with words. In any case, it should be noted that the way of recitation is well-preserved and does not show any signs of disappearing. Even though all these forms differ widely, in their concept of poetry, from the work of contemporary poets, they do have an impact on the auditory sense of the general public.

One more important thing is that contemporary poets use the ideogram Kanji (Chinese characters) very frequently to make their images precise and rich. And these ideograms are understood at once when seen like hieroglyphics, but sometimes misunderstood when pronounced. So it can be said that many contemporary poems are much more understandable when they are seen than when they are read aloud.

Consequently, modern Japanese poetry as a whole is cut off from vital colloquial expressions, but in exchange for this it can seek clear and subtle images full of sensitive feelings and the association of ideas—not with logic, but with seemingly arbitrary imagery. And this association of ideas and images, if it can have some consistency or enduring power, is the keynote of Japanese poetry.

Makoto Ooka

SOURCE: "Contemporary Japanese Poetry," translated by James O'Brien, in *World Literature Today,* Vol. 62, No. 3, Summer, 1988, pp. 414-17.

[*In the following essay, Ooka examines various characteristics that have emerged in Japanese poetry since 1970.*]

About three years ago the Japan Foundation organized an exhibition of photographs. More than two hundred representative works were selected from photographs of nature and society which had been taken in our country over the course of almost fifteen years. Based on the theme "Japan, Its Life and Ways: 1971-1984," this exhibition traveled to various parts of the world. The selection of works was done in two stages. Representatives of the Japan Professional Photographers Society, after much debate, chose three hundred prints from a group of more than six thousand amateur and professional works which had appeared in newspapers, magazines, and other publications. In order to reduce the number to almost two hundred, a group of people without expertise in photography joined the jury of photography specialists for the final round of competition. I was a member of this final group.

Among the three hundred prints there was a considerable variety of subject matter. Needless to say, there were beautiful photos of nature illustrative of seasonal change, as well as views of life in fishing villages, in farm hamlets, and in the large cities. Both children and oldsters appeared in the photographs; people were working in some cases, enjoying themselves at a picnic or some similar function in others. Current fashion was on display, and ritualistic occasions—the coming-of-age ceremony, weddings, funerals, ancestral services—were also included. Indeed, the prints gave a composite picture of modern Japanese society.

As I examined the photographs, I became aware of something peculiar. Hardly a single one was focused on the image of Japanese society most representative of the seventies and thereafter. Our "high-tech" culture, with its computers and information-processing capabilities, was totally absent. Why was this? I asked the photographers on the jury if they had, in the course of culling these three hundred photos from the six thousand, deliberately excluded those which showed the most advanced sector of our country. Not at all, they replied. In fact, they had located such prints but found them uninteresting as photographs. Most had been taken for promotional purposes by various companies and did not fit into the exhibit. Furthermore, the photographers added, in the most advanced sectors of the economy the principal work was now being performed by robots rather than by people. Even if you took a photo, it looked like something out of a catalogue. Finally, the things a photographer would be most eager to show were precisely those a company was most secretive about. Photographing them was forbidden, and this was entirely understandable. That was why, the professional photographers concluded, I did not see any such examples in the exhibit.

Adept at managing vast quantities of information and systematized to a high degree, our high-tech "electronic society" is based on delicate machines which do not lend themselves to interesting photography. Needless to say, the machines themselves are operated by specialized engineers of high intelligence. One might take appealing photos of these engineers enjoying their leisure away from the job.

The group which thoroughly understands the complex structure of these delicate machines constitutes a small elite, the great majority being mere workers who are totally ignorant of such things. These workers only operate some appendage of the electronic device. One imagines the everyday lives of this group, lives rendered quite pleasant by those trivial comforts which all of us are gradually acquiring in exchange for handing over our independence and personal dignity to a bureaucratized and standardized society more and more controlled by computers. I might add that, as a consequence of this development, our inner anxieties, instead of getting resolved, become steadily more acute.

Is it not our teams of robots, with their transcendent and highly precise intelligence, which now have the authority once held by humans to make decisions on important questions? Furthermore, the amplification of these robots sometimes gives them access to destructive power beyond the imagination, as can typically be seen in accidents involving nuclear power plants. Against such eventualities the individual person is virtually helpless. Human intelligence can make these delicate machines; but once the machine gets beyond the control of that intelligence and careens toward violence and destruction, the ability to foresee the final issue of the process and to prevent it is almost nil. In using these teams of robots whose destructive power can grow out of control, mankind has achieved a level of prosperity unprecedented in history. Like children frolicking innocently upon the roof of a powder magazine which might explode at any time—that, one might say, describes the people in the so-called advanced countries.

Assuredly this describes the situation in Japan since the seventies. The younger generation in particular has suppressed the anxiety that ought to accompany this condition, opting instead for a hedonistic attitude of living cheerfully in the present. The rise of the new religions and the flourishing of astrology and other forms of divination probably have some necessary connection to the situation.

To my surprise, photos of large political demonstrations were absent from the aforementioned exhibit. The student riots which had kept Japanese society in turmoil until the end of the sixties quickly subsided in the seventies. In their place an indifference, if not animosity, toward declarations of political intent spread among the young people. The hedonistic attitude mentioned above accompanied this development.

The location of commercial and amusement districts in Tokyo popular among the younger generation has shifted. In place of the Ginza, the fashionable quarter of yesteryear, and Shinjuku, the place where the commoners gathered of old, such centers as Shibuya, Roppongi, Aoyama, Kichijoji, and Harajuku have suddenly taken over. Young people throng into these places and remake them in accord with their own tastes. Such districts play a leading role in fashion, in the computer games which the most advanced technology brings into being, and in sports too. The consumer culture which targets the young grows fat as it serves up change with dizzying speed. One fact concerning the rapidly expanding Japanese economy seems undeniable: it has produced a large class of younger people who are hedonistic and affirm the present while avoiding any social and political responsibilities.

Reflecting on the present situation, one cannot avoid the sense of a profound problem for Japan in what has already been said. I can cite here a characteristic phenomenon. Formerly the younger poets—the more enthusiastic ones at least—recognized themselves as an "avant-garde" and prided themselves on composing work that was experimental both in form and in content. It was only natural that few readers understood their poems. For these poets, however, the notion that poetry in particular ought to be in the forefront of literature and the arts was utterly natural.

Since to be of the avant-garde meant necessarily to go beyond the existing framework of poetry and to seek new methods in unknown territory, poets formerly sought ties with other artists, in fields such as music, the plastic arts, film, drama, and radio. The collaboration thus achieved resulted in the creation of works across the old boundaries. For certain individuals like myself at least, born around 1930 and first active in the fifties, one can definitely state that such collaboration was a clear raison d'être for the poet. My friend Shuntaro Tanikawa and I worked out a proposal for collaboration among poets alone. We would sit down at the same table with other poets, even foreign ones, and together compose dozens of pieces in a kind of chain. This practice of "linked poetry" constitutes a protest against existing ways of writing, reading, and criticizing poems. In carrying on this activity, we unquestionably seek something new in an uncharted land, something we Japanese poets have been looking for since the fifties.

Needless to say, we do not accept inferior and unsightly work under the guise of experimentation. We can only shake our heads at this common practice of the avant-garde. To what extent can we change the existing framework of composing? And can we produce superior and persuasive works by these means? Such are the questions that concern us. Poetry must be new in some sense to be worthy of its name.

From this perspective, the year 1970 seems a kind of symbolic watershed. The term *avant-garde* virtually disappeared from discussions of contemporary Japanese poetry, and young poets quit seeking the cooperation of artists from other fields. Those who still aimed toward original work along collaborative lines generally came onstage in the fifties and sixties. I am talking, in this regard, of my own generation and of poets just a decade younger. This is probably closely related to the fact that, among poets presently in their twenties and thirties, criticism which sums up the poetry of the period with compelling persuasion has ceased to exist. During the seventies the poets themselves were acutely aware of how futile their own words were within the great wave that was rapidly transforming Japan into an electronics and information society, and so they restricted their attention to what might be discovered in their immediate surroundings. The poets might write of their private joys and sorrows with sincerity or irony; but the systematized society, with its vast power and its robots, seemed something merely to be endured.

This focus of interest is reflected in the photographs from the exhibit which I introduced at the beginning of my essay, most of them either recording the quiet and pleasant lives of people seeking domestic happiness or else showing the scenic beauty of the four seasons. Perhaps the average citizen of contemporary Japan merely clings all the more to his middle-class pleasures for hearing at his back the roar of a revolutionary storm which begins to rage in each country as our century comes to an end. A proverb rooted in Buddhist thought speaks of "the candle in the wind." Our young poets should not be insensitive to the fate of our world, so like this very candle. Indeed, when they express in their subtle way the small joys and pains which they discover within middle-class life, the acute reader can sense in the background a nihilism that wears the mask of cheerfulness. One might even call this feature the key to gauging the honesty and talent of the particular poet.

Just now, then, the term *avant-garde* has become nothing other than an anachronism.

There is another phenomenon closely connected to this state of affairs. For approximately the last ten years there has been a marked revival—some might call it a "boom"—in the traditional forms of verse, the haiku and the tanka. For close to twenty years following Japan's defeat in World War II, our traditional values underwent a rapid decline and lost their credibility. However, along with the miraculous revival of the Japanese economy, the opportunity arose to reassess these same values. With this trend there came a general interest in the traditional forms of poetry. This interest reflected a straightforward desire by people to understand the roots of their country's culture.

An interesting phenomenon occurred after the initial phase of this reevaluation of tradition had passed: for the first time women came forward in large numbers to write in classical verse forms. Because of our economic development and prosperity, many household tasks could now be performed by machines. With more time to spend as they saw fit, women looked to creative activity—in literature or the arts—as a means of self-expression that had been suppressed hitherto. They became very active poets.

In cities throughout Japan and in farm and fishing villages too, schools run by businesses or by local governments, as well as cultural centers similar to colleges, have sprung up in great numbers. What we call the "cultural center" is the best-known example of this development. Such centers offer numerous courses of instruction, sustained to a large extent by the number of women who enroll in them. The courses cover such areas as religion, history, language, literature, art, dance, gymnastics, cosmetics, cooking, gardening, flower arrangement, and the tea ceremony. Included too are courses in the writing of modern verse, tanka, haiku, fiction, and essays. For these letter courses professional critics often serve as instructors, and so do poets who write in various forms. Among the women who take these courses, talented writers and haiku poets emerge in significant numbers.

The classes in tanka and haiku composition are quite popular. The need to write in a brief, set form disciplines the student in the use of language and leads to considerable satisfaction and pleasure. However, it must be said that there is a marked difference in the level of language discipline, depending on the quality of the instruction. It is not only that the teacher who is a haiku or tanka poet can give finer instruction and revise the work of the students. It is the students themselves who positively expect and even demand this of such a teacher. From the distant days of the Heian period (794 to 1185), the orthodox method of teaching the composition of traditional forms of Japanese poetry has been along these same lines. The clearest proof of this lies in the nature of the best critical writings in these areas. These are not expositions about substance or principles, but manuals of composition and guidebooks which illustrate how to write and appreciate poetry with reference to specific examples. The tanka writings of Shunzei Fujiwara and Teika Fujiwara, the haikai writings of Matsuo Basho, and the writings on No by Zeami—these last composed under the influence of tanka—are all examples of this.

In other words the most widely read and influential works in the area of poetics and art are not those of pure theory; rather, they are precisely the records and accounts of how the best poets instructed their pupils day by day. Women, it might be generally said, readily accept this type of training; and now, in both the tanka and the haiku, the emergence of women poets is very striking.

Speaking of tanka, mention must be made of a volume of poems published early last summer called *Sarada kinenbi* (Salad Days Remembered). Composed by a woman in her midtwenties named Machi Tawara, the book sold two million copies by the end of the year and continues to sell well this year. Such a record is unprecedented in the publishing world generally. Tawara is a recent college graduate and now teaches high school. Closely observing the traditional verse form, her tanka sing lightly of love, of travel, of music, of books—while regularly using the conversational tone of young men and women. These works are modern popular songs in a classical verse form, and they are highly successful.

This poet has caught the public's eye as a cheerful, outgoing, sociable artist, thus reversing the prevailing image of the artist as dark and introverted. Moreover, as her poems are not flippant in the least, mature men who are not in the habit of the reading tanka end up greatly admiring them. Perhaps these men believe Tawara's poems provide insight into the opinions and lives of the so-called "new talents," a group such men normally regard as a strange new species. In short, this young woman poet has been accepted by all levels of Japanese society and has become a star of the mass media overnight. People are well disposed toward her because she is young and charming.

A hundred years ago, when Akiko Yosano's tanka appeared on the scene, many older people were scandalized by this woman's contempt for their moral sentiment and sexual respectability. As the author of a volume that has sold over two million copies, Machi Tawara is much talked about. There is a certain panache to her reception, but not even a hint of scandal. The Platonic notion of the poet as more or less a danger to society would appear to be outmoded in Japan, where mass culture has, in some sense, developed further than in any other country.

Still, even the popularity of Machi Tawara has already begun to abate; but the stage for women of superior poetic talent will be enlarged hereafter. However, we must be aware of the fact that the subject which women poets have commanded until now has, for the most part, been daily life in the home. One might say that this coincides with the point I made in my earlier comment on the photography exhibit.

Tanka and haiku are written and read by many people because their set forms are very approachable. In contrast, modern free verse will always be distant and forbidding. It can never be said that this kind of poetry, lacking a set form and so various in both its themes and techniques of expression, is really accessible. However, inasmuch as poetry is never something merely approachable and easily understood, this alienation of modern verse and reader could be a passing phenomenon.

As for myself, I began writing linked verse together with fellow poets around 1970. (Even some novelists joined in.) During the eighties we carried on the joint creation of linked verse with poets from such Western countries as America, the Netherlands, West Germany, and France. The poets who worked with me included Thomas Fitzsimmons of the United States; J. Bernlef, Willem Van Toorn, and Robert Anker of the Netherlands; Adrian Henri of Great Britain; Antonio Cisneros of Peru; Oskar Pastior, Guntram Vesper, and Karin Kivus of West Germany; H. C. Artmann of Austria; Jean-Pierre Faye and Alain Jouffroy of France; and Hiroshi Kawasaki and Shuntaro Tanikawa of Japan. In a house by a small lake in Michigan, in a garden on the outskirts of Rotterdam, in the Petite Salle of the Centre Pompidou in Paris, beside the Wannsee in West Berlin, or in the Literaturhaus in the center of the same city, we poets sat around a table and jointly composed linked verse.

A gathering of foreign poets essentially unknown to each other until our sessions together, we soon became close friends as we sat for several hours or a few days around a table and composed poetry as a group. We learned that, at some subterranean level, a burst of laughter or silent pause had meaning. On this breeding ground, where language bubbled up from within the participating poets, we shared in a rare experience: confronting one another as collaborative authors of verses that came from each of us.

One thing stood out as most important. We might have had differing notions of reality and diverging techniques of expression; but we could observe these differences in the very process of their formation and respond to them time after time. Ascertaining how heterogeneous we were, we paid due respect to our differences; and there is probably no path to mutual understanding other than transcending our heterogeneity and carrying on the dialogue. At present the world is full of misunderstanding. The struggles are becoming more fierce among the different peoples, religions, cultures, and societies in different stages of development. So long as there is no method for readily resolving these divisions, we must at least cultivate mutual respect by acknowledging our heterogeneity and striving to reach a point where we love one another. This we might call a duty for all people alive today.

From this perspective, the experiment described above does not, in my opinion, amount merely to making linked poetry. This is a challenge: we head toward a realm rich in productive incitements.

DRAMA

J. Thomas Rimer

SOURCE: "Japanese Theatre: Languages and Pilgrimage," in *Pilgrimages: Aspects of Japanese Literature and Culture,* University of Hawaii Press, 1988, pp. 71-90.

[*In the following essay, Rimer provides a historical overview of Japanese theater, focusing on three representative works of classical and modern Japanese drama.*]

When I first began to attend performances by Japanese contemporary theatre companies in the 1950s, I was puzzled by what I took to be a disparity between the power of the texts chosen for performance and the quality of the acting available to make those texts come alive on the stage. To see Pirandello, Molière, and Kinoshita on the stage in Japan was a rare opportunity, and yet the performances, for all their polish, seemed to lack any real natural elegance. The thoughts that follow here, in fact, have grown from that initial sense of surprise and, perhaps, of disappointment.

The first help I received came in the form of a few paragraphs in Peter Arnott's *The Theatres of Japan.* Arnott, an expert on the Greek classic theatre who visited Japan in 1966, revealed his conception of an important distinction he found between Japanese and Western performing technique.

> The gulf between the Japanese theatre and its Western counterpart embraces more than different social standards and unfamiliar subjectmatter. They are two forms built on different aesthetic foundations, and divided by the actor's concept of his relation to his role. The extrovert and presentational style cultivated for centuries in Japan cannot be easily reconciled with plays written for actors trained in a different mode and expected to identify themselves psychologically with their roles. This is the most serious difficulty that the Japanese actor has to face. He is forced, in effect, to relearn the fundamentals of his trade. Japanese actors, on the whole, are more secure in Western plays to which the traditional methods can be applied. They are conspicuously successful

> in the "epic" style cultivated by Brecht and others, which comes close to, and indeed borrowed from, their own traditions. The "alienation effect" demanded by Brecht from his characters is founded on the premises of presentational acting. But the wholly naturalistic style continues to elude them, with results sometimes disastrous to the play. In Brecht, the [Japanese] actor is moving in a world he knows.

Arnott's suggestion of a profound difference in craft and style seemed to go a long way in answering my question; as it turned out, however, his explanations opened up further questions still. When I translated for an American production a drama by the contemporary playwright Yamazaki Masakazu, one of the most thoughtful and intellectually imaginative writers of his generation, the director, musing over the English script, told me that he was struck by the form in which the drama was cast. "Why," he asked me, "should a contemporary playwright choose to write a metaphysical melodrama? The play is extremely effective, but it is cast in a form difficult for American actors and based on assumptions difficult for us to seek out."

The director's remarks seemed most perceptive; and even though I could not answer his question properly, I realized that perhaps he was struck not so much by a need to search out different acting styles but by the fact that an altogether different view of reality was suggested by this and the other Japanese plays he had read, a genuine reality certainly, but one not based on the concept of mimesis so familiar in Western drama since its very beginnings. Reality in the Japanese theatre was to be found not in imitation but in stylization, the kind of intense simplification and suggestiveness that had so attracted certain important Western poets, composers, and writers to the Japanese traditional theatre. How, then, was the stylization that had so appealed to artists such as Claudel, Britten, Brecht, and Yeats to be understood?

Various angles of analysis seemed possible. One obvious point, and one well understood by Yeats, for example, was that this stylization seemed allied to ritual and could thus provide a means to allow an audience an experience quite outside their everyday comprehension of themselves. The medieval *no* drama shows this ability consistently. An examination of ritual, in turn, can help show the purposes of stylization. In seeking out the psychological basis of ritual, I was led to the work of Victor Turner, mentioned earlier in this book; his discussion of pilgrims leaving their orthodox social environments in order to undergo a special experience, their assumption of voluntary status as pilgrims, and their movements through symbolic time, all in order to seek the state of *communitas,* a universal sense of nonduality, which releases the pilgrim from his everyday "role playing and all its guilts," struck me as highly suggestive of the process through which an audience, albeit an ideal audience, might go.

But to what extent can the theatre be considered a place of pilgrimage? After all, the audience does not participate but rather watches and observes. Still, I thought, a case might be made out that the audience is always on a pilgrimage of sorts. I was reminded of a scene in Paul Claudel's play *L'Échange,* in which some of the qualities Turner points out as typical of a pilgrimage—a strange sense of time, of place, and the possibility of transcendental understanding—are placed in the province of the theatre. Lechy Elbernon is an actress, and at one point in the drama she is attempting to explain the craft of the theatre to a friend.

> LECHY. The theatre. Don't you know what it is?
>
> MARTHE. No.
>
> LECHY. There is a stage, there is an audience. In the evening, everything's closed. They all come, and they sit in rows, one behind the other, and they look.
>
> MARTHE. What do they look at, if everything is shut?
>
> LECHY. They look at the curtain. And what is behind it when it rises. And something happens on the stage just as though it were real.
>
> MARTHE. But it isn't real! It's like a dream you have when you're asleep.
>
> LECHY. Yes, that is why they come to the theatre at night . . . I look at them, the audience; and they are living, clothed flesh. And they cluster on the walls like flies, right up to the ceiling; I see those hundreds of white faces. Man lives his life in boredom, and ignorance that has clung to him from his birth. And because he does not know how anything begins or ends he goes to the theatre. And he looks at himself, his hands on his knees. And he laughs and he cries and cannot bear to leave . . . They look and listen as though they were asleep.
>
> MARTHE. The eye is made to see, and the ear to hear the truth.
>
> LECHY. What is truth? Is it not like an onion, wrapped in seventeen skins? Who can see things as they are? The eye sees, the ear hears, But only the mind can know. And that is why man Longs to take out what he carries in his mind and spirit To see it with his eyes and know it with his ears. And so it is that I show myself on the stage.

Audiences, Claudel suggests, exist in a special state of heightened, detached awareness that is altogether reminiscent of Turner's psychological pilgrim state: dream as reality, time at a stop, the world of the spirit dominating the rule of the senses. In Claudel's vision, an audience comes to the theatre in the hope that its members can make manifest, to actually see before them, what may otherwise exist only inside their own souls, as potential. The spectators, desiring an understanding of themselves, seek that vision in the images they find in their own minds and souls, which are thrown up on the stage for them to examine, to look at and observe. In Turner's terms the spectators participate vicariously in the movement of the images on the stage that parade before them; they *see* the pilgrimage spread out before them.

If such a vicarious pilgrimage can be posited in terms of the theatre, then an examination of the nature of the relationship of an audience to the drama of its time can suggest as well what images a given audience may most desire to see, what kind of mirror it most wishes to have thrown up before it: in short, what kind of reflected pilgrimage it may find itself most wanting to seek out. Individuals, audiences, and societies change, and so will the nature of the pilgrimages on which they embark. By way of example I would like to indicate Japanese dramas from three historical periods that can suggest the dynamics of this process. All reveal a congruence with Turner's scheme: the pilgrimages seem to involve a voluntary act on the part of the pilgrim, the trip to a special place, and a segment of symbolic time. Finally, Turner's idea of a crucial liminal experience, a sense of *communitas,* seems present as well. To anticipate my conclusions, I would like in particular to suggest that a play written as a surrogate pilgrimage surely requires a style of composition and performance at variance with the kind of realism so basic to the modern Western theatre.

My first example is taken from the medieval *no;* closest to European medieval ritual as these dramas are, they provide almost a paradigm for a dramatic version of Turner's conception of pilgrimage. The play I have chosen is one I have translated and the text of which I have studied closely, *Taema,* a play attributed to the greatest figure in the history of *no,* Zeami Motokiyo (1363-1443). The audiences for *no* in Zeami's time were largely popular, with a sprinkling of aristocrats, not unlike the medieval popular audiences in Europe. Whatever the differences in class outlook, the audiences were held together by their common cultural consciousness, which centered on Buddhist belief and psychology. The texts of this and most other plays contain "high" sections of metaphysical poetry, presumably for the highly literate aristocrats, and "low" sections of easier prose for the commoners.

The play is a perfect model of a spiritual journey. The *waki,* or subsidiary character, consists of a priest, plus his two companions; the *shite,* or main character, appears first as a nun, then in the second part of the play as the Princess Chujo. At the beginning of the play, the priests visit Taema temple to see the famous woven mandala there (which, incidentally, modern tourists can do as well, since the original temple, with its beautiful grounds, is about one hour from Osaka by train). They meet an old woman, a Buddhist nun, who is accompanied by a young girl. The pair tell the priest and his companions how Princess Chujo prayed at the temple for the coming of Amida Buddha, and how eventually an aged nun had come to the princess, revealed herself as a manifestation of Amida, and heralded the princess' ascent to paradise. The nun and the girl next reveal themselves to the priest as dream-visions of the princess and Amida, then disappear. During the interlude, a farmer in the vicinity retells the story in simple language, adding the fact that Amida Buddha had presented a mandala woven of lotus threads to the princess. In the final and highly poetic section of the play, the priest and his companions pray for enlightenment; the princess now reappears in dazzling attire and reveals a poetic image of paradise. She praises Amida, presents the priest with a sutra, and bids him pray. As he kneels to do so, the vision fades.

The play follows Turner's schemata closely. The very opening lines of the play show the priests anxious to make a trip toward enlightenment.

> PRIESTS. [*Together.*] Wonderful the Gate
> Of the Wonderful Law: Let us follow the road it discloses.

The priest and his companions have consciously sought out a holy place, a sacred spot, far out of the way; their piety in turn makes it possible for them to identify the two others, the nun and the young girl, who also worship Amida Buddha. Their encounter together suggests the possibility of a shared *communitas,* a oneness that surpasses the individual.

> GIRL. Amida with a single mind
> Shows the way . . .
> BOTH. Let us never neglect
> To say with all our hearts,
> "I put my faith in Amida."
> NUN. And as we praise him,
> All distinction between the Buddha and
> ourselves
> Will disappear . . .

They identify their own pilgrimage as a transcendental one.

> NUN. In that road which leads towards
> Cool purity
> We place our trust.

As the priest and his companions observe these two women, the visitors come to realize that they are beginning to become involved in an experience that may lead them to still greater faith. The nun and the girl describe the various holy relics to be seen at Taema temple, then remind the priests of the proper attitude needed to participate in a real pilgrimage.

> TOGETHER. Many are the well-known places,
> Many the occasions to contemplate
> the Buddha
> And to hear the Wonderful Law,
> But too profound for our
> comprehension.

As a single strand of pure lotus,
Our cry rises from our united
hearts
Amida save us!

Mere observation, cognition, must be abandoned for the deep cry of faith. The nun now explains to the rapt priest how Princess Chujo herself made a pilgrimage to the deep mountains, giving herself up to contemplation and prayers to Amida. As they finish the story, the two reveal themselves.

TOGETHER. We are transformed beings from
the past,
A nun and a girl,
Who appeared in your dream,
And even as we speak these words
CHORUS. Light thrusts,
Flowers fall,
Miraculous odors everywhere,
Voices of music.

Now the priest and his companions fulfill the third of Turner's conditions leading to *communitas:* they will come to move in symbolic time. In the final section of the play, as they begin their prayers to Amida, they are rewarded by a vision that might be classed as a form of extended reality, which will move them toward a transcendent experience.

PRIESTS. Even before we can speak of it,
How surprising!
Wondrous music sounds,
Light floods down,
Boddhisattvas,
Singing, dancing,
Before our eyes,
Sacred manifestations—
Wonderful, oh wonderful.

The princess now appears and tells the priests of the joys of paradise.

CHORUS. Wondrous Paradise!
Magnificence, a vast unending world
of sky
Dazzles the sight, lost in paths of
clouds.
PRINCESS. The sound of the voice
Of the turning wheel of the
Wonderful Law
Fills the air to the vast edges
if Paradise.
CHORUS. The heart, calm and quiet as the
dawn
PRINCESS. Is guided on its cool path to
Paradise
By the light of Amida.

She then presents the priest with a sutra, which he worships. All join together in the unity and oneness of prayer.

CHORUS. Keep your heart without
confusion
PRINCESS. Do not go astray
CHORUS. Do not go astray
PRINCESS. The strength of ten voices
CHORUS. Will rise from your one voice in
prayer.
Gracious Amida!

The vision reaches its climax, then fades as the priests awaken from their dream of bliss just as, with another image of travel, the play ends.

PRIESTS. In the waning night the bell
sounds
And the bell sounds echo
With the voices crying,
"Praise to Amida!"
As we venerate the Buddha
And hear his miraculous word,
His holy truthful teaching
Shines down to light the world:
In all ten directions
Mankind finds welcome from him
As they travel
In the boat of the True Law.
The oars are used in moving
water,
And yet
In the time it takes to push away
an oar
The dream of this short night fades
And dawn comes,
Faintly.

Now the priests are becoming reabsorbed into the real world; their spiritual pilgrimage is ending, and their physical one will now begin again; they will return to their familiar existence enlightened. *Taema* seems a perfect artistic representation of Turner's scheme, in which each layer reinforces the others. All participants, the princess, the nun and the girl, the priests, and, presumably, the audience as well, are seeking an authentic pilgrimage experience; all search out paradise, and the play seems a poetic representation of a vast prayer into which the audience seeks to be drawn. The style of the play is perfectly suited to the theme, rising as it does to the first poetic climax, dropping back for the interlude, then moving up to the final poetic heights. All aspects of the presentational *no* performance—dancing, poetry, masks, and music—help involve the audience in this symbolic act.

My second example is from the world of *joruri,* specifically a play by Chikamatsu Monzaemon (1653-1724) that has been widely performed both by puppets and by *kabuki* actors. By this time in Japanese history, the theatre, as in Europe, was responding to the rapid development of a bourgeois society; the playwright thus provides a secular view of the pilgrimage progress. The audience now moves toward the role of observer rather than that of participant.

By the time of Chikamatsu, the medieval unities had broken down. The audience for the puppet theatre now constituted a class audience, made up largely of urban merchants who wished for their entertainment a chance to see their own values reflected on the stage, particularly in the so-called *sewamono,* or "domestic dramas," based on contemporary events, where the moral tensions of their own society could be portrayed.

Some insights recorded in Arnold Hauser's *Social History of Art,* although dealing with the European situation during the eighteenth century, suggest both a parallel development with the Japanese cultural situation and an occasional striking similarity. His remarks thus provide some useful insight into the interactions between Chikamatsu and his audiences. Hauser remarks that a self-consciousness of social class helps define and limit the work of the playwright at the time. "The assumption is that the spectator is able to escape from the influence of the play much less easily when he sees his own class portrayed on the stage, which he must acknowledge to be his own class if he is logical, than when he merely sees his own personal character portrayed, which he is free to disown if he wants to."

Hauser goes on to say that the characters in European plays of this period often become functions of their environment. Men are posited as social beings, and, "deprived of all autonomy, lose to some extent the responsibility for their actions." His observations on the effect of a growing consciousness of a class structure would seem a useful means to examine a Japanese example, Chikamatsu's *Shinj ten no Amijima* (The Love Suicides at Amijima), written in 1721 and often regarded as Chikamatsu's masterpiece. The play was originally composed for the puppet theatre but its evocative settings and realistic dialogue, and a plot presumably based on a real love suicide, have made it a favorite with *kabuki* actors as well.

The plot of the play is simple and like many of the other familiar "domestic dramas" of Chikamatsu. Jihei, a paper merchant, is in love with a courtesan, Koharu, despite the real affection felt for him by his long-suffering wife, Osan. Osan's love for Jihei is such that, suspecting that the pair may attempt to commit suicide together, she attempts to avoid the worst by helping her husband ransom Koharu from the teahouse where she has been forced to serve as an entertainer. The story as it evolves is crafted with a number of effective confrontations between the characters concerning the nature of love, duty, honor, and so forth. In this, Magoemon, Jihei's brother, plays a particularly effective part, serving to some extent the role of the *honnête homme* of Molière as he seeks to bring his brother to the path of reason and the consolations of social duty. Eventually these tensions push Koharu and Jihei to suicide. The last two scenes of the play form a lyrical pilgrimage not to an immediate transcendence, as in *Taema,* but to a *communitas* through death. The change in tonality is immediately obvious; the realistic and often spirited exchanges of the early scenes that make up the bulk of the play vanish and the language of the text becomes lyrical, indeed highly poetic. This change of tonality is so striking in the last sequence, and the values the playwright propounds there are so different from those expressed in the rest of the play, that the interpretation of the drama as a pilgrimage seems virtually the only means to link the two sections of the text together, at least in terms of the language involved.

In this regard, Turner's conditions again seem to be fulfilled in this final scene. The lovers, Koharu and Jihei, choose to die together. Their decision is voluntary. In fact, they have made the decision to die together early in the play; their real problem, then, concerns how to carry out their vow. During their pilgrimage to death, they also choose a special place, out of the way of normal human traffic. They leave their familiar surroundings and take a fanciful journey, the stage *michiyuki* so familiar in all forms of the traditional Japanese theatre. Their destination is Amijima (which might be rendered into English as "Island of Nets"), and on the way they pass by various islands and bridges that are assigned poetic, often transcendental meanings as they approach the final spot chosen for their death.

> JIHEI. Look, there is Oe Bridge. We follow the river from Little Naniwa Bridge to Funairi Bridge. The farther we journey, the closer we approach the road to death.

When they approach the site where they will kill themselves, the imagery of the play becomes more and more religious.

> JIHEI. Listen—the voices of the temple bells begin to boom. How much farther can we go on this way? We are not fated to live any longer—let us make an end quickly.
>
> NARRATOR. Tears are strung with the 108 beads of the rosaries in their hands. They have come now to Amijima, to the Daicho temple; the overflowing sluice gate of a little stream beside a bamboo thicket will be their place of death.

Finally, time expands as the couple travels their "long last night," as they call it. As in *Taema,* the drama ends as the dawn breaks, but the circumstances are very different. The *communitas* achieved is one of death. Koharu herself sees her voyage, her pilgrimage, as a means to salvation.

> KOHARU. What have we to grieve about? Though in this world we could not stay together, in the next and through each successive world to come until the end of time we shall be husband and wife. Every summer for my devotions I have copied the All Compassionate and All Merciful chapter of the Lotus Sutra, in the hope that we may be born on one lotus.

Here at the moment of their deaths, Koharu and Jihei abandon their normal secular social roles and consciously take on the persona of pilgrims.

> NARRATOR. Jihei whips out his dirk and slashes off his black locks at the base of the top knot.

> JIHEI. Look, Koharu. As long as I had this hair, I was Kamiya Jihei, Osan's husband, but cutting it has made me a monk. I have fled the burning house of the three worlds of delusion; I am a priest unencumbered by wife, children, or worldly possessions. Now that I no longer have a wife named Osan, you owe her no obligations either.
>
> NARRATOR. In tears he flings away the hair.
>
> KOHARU. I am happy.
>
> NARRATOR. Koharu takes up the dirk and ruthlessly, unhesitatingly, slices through her flowing Shimada coiffure. She casts aside the tresses she has so often washed and combed and stroked. How heartbreaking to see their locks tangled with the weeds and midnight frost of this desolate field!
>
> JIHEI. We have escaped the inconstant world, a nun and a priest. Our duties as husband and wife belong to our profane past.

As in *Taema* the pilgrims pray to Amida.

> JIHEI. You musn't let worries over trifles disturb the prayers of your last moments. Keep your eyes on the westward-moving moon, and worship it as Amida himself. Concentrate your thoughts on the Western Paradise.

In her ecstasy Koharu now leads Jihei to the final act.

> NARRATOR. She smiles. His hands, numbed by the frost, tremble before the pale vision of her face, and his eyes are first to cloud. He is weeping so profusely that he cannot control the blade.
>
> KOHARU. Compose yourself, but quick!
>
> NARRATOR. Her encouragement lends him strength; the invocations to Amida carried by the wind urge a final prayer. Namu Amida Butsu. He thrusts in the saving sword.

The combination of images employed by Chikamatsu provides a striking example of how one set of images, those borrowed from the kind of religious terminology so highly developed in the medieval *no,* can now be employed in a self-consciously artistic way in order to create a secular, exteriorized version of a similar religious vision. Artistically, at least, Chikamatsu does believe in his lovers and wants the audience to do so as well. As Jihei kills himself, he calls out, "May we be born on one lotus: Hail Amida Buddha!" And indeed, the last lines in the play suggest that the lovers did earn in death the transcendence they sought.

> NARRATOR. The tale was spread from mouth to mouth. People say that they who were caught in the net of Buddha's vow immediately gained salvation and deliverance, and all who hear the tale of the Love Suicides at Amijima are moved to tears.

There is here an effective pun on the word *ami,* which serves both as the name of the place where the lovers died (Amijima, "Island of *ami,* or Nets"), and as a reference to a traditional saying that the nets of the Buddha are woven meshes able to catch and take up to heaven the most recalcitrant sinner. Chikamatsu's title thus carries the suggestion of a transcendental message.

In the case of Chikamatsu's drama, then, a play that is realistic in most of its details ends with a poetic and religious conclusion which, if not altogether out of keeping with the opening scenes, is certainly scarcely anticipated in them. The audience is taken by the playwright on a journey, but, unlike the voyage of the priests in *Taema,* this trip is really an interior one, moving from exterior action to interior motivation, which is expressed poetically. Chikamatsu's technique in creating this movement is accomplished through his skillful use of the narrator. The characters themselves are never required to speak in a fashion out of keeping with their social milieu, or in a fashion so poetic that the verisimilitude that Chikamatsu sought, that famous "slender margin between the real and the unreal" for which he was famous, is never destroyed; rather, the narrator takes over the task of providing a philosophic and poetic gloss on the actions witnessed on the stage. As his role grows larger, the language of the play expands. In this regard Chikamatsu's use of the narrator provides an ingenious solution to the difficulty of how to put poetic dignity in the mouth of everyman, a stylistic problem that has troubled many modern playwrights. Arthur Miller, for example, in *A View from the Bridge,* was driven to adopt, rather awkwardly, the same sort of device in order to lift his text up to the level of eloquence he sought.

Chikamatsu's lovers may commit suicide together in a kind of triumphant search for *communitas,* but they are themselves no larger than life, no Tristan and Isolde. A case might be made that Wagner's orchestra is his narrator, glossing the words of his characters with a high pitch of emotion, but a reading of the text alone of Isolde's love-death shows that the words themselves are conflated far beyond anything that Chikamatsu would have considered appropriate to a human scale. After all, he was writing in his *sewamono* about contemporary figures, not medieval knights, and for many modern readers of the plays, the figures he creates are more passive than active, more acted upon than acted. They are, perhaps, barely heroic enough.

The same phenomenon has been observed in Western drama of the eighteenth and nineteenth centuries, when plays began to be written for middle-class audiences, whose beliefs and assumptions began to show marked differences with those of other levels of society. Here is Georg Lukàcs' description of the hero of such Western bourgeois drama.

> The heroes of the new drama—in comparison to the old—are more passive than active; they are

> acted upon more than they act for themselves; they defend rather than attack; their heroism is mostly a heroism of anguish, of despair, not bold aggressiveness. Since so much of the inner man has fallen prey to destiny, the last battle is to be enacted within. The greater the determining force of external factors, the more the center of the tragic conflict is drawn inwards; it becomes internalized, more exclusively a conflict of the spirit.

In the case of Chikamatsu, that anguish is transcended through death, which gives Jihei and Koharu their final dignity. In the composition of this play, as in most of his domestic dramas, Chikamatsu was working with a series of givens, the actual accounts of the lives and deaths of the characters he wished to show on the stage. The remarks of Lukàcs suggest that one means to observe the dramatic movement of the characters in Chikamatsu is to follow the progress of their pilgrimage, their voyage out of their class, out of their problems, and, of course, out of the world altogether, where no final solutions are possible. Again, Lukàcs provides striking insights. "The heroes of the new drama always partake of the ecstatic; they seem to have become conscious of a sense that death can vouchsafe them the transcendence, greatness, and illumination which life withheld, and together with this, a sense that death will fulfill and perfect their personalities."

The townspeople for whom Chikamatsu chose to write could certainly appreciate the poetry of this pilgrimage, framed as it was in terms of the conceptions that made up their own consciousness; they might not carry out such an adventure themselves, but there was a satisfaction for them in watching those whose lives served as witness to the fact that heroism was possible. *The Love Suicides at Amijima* was a large, distorting mirror held up to amplify and dignify the lives of those who came to the theatre. The very movement in the language of the play from prose to poetry confirmed the possibility of that beauty.

If Chikamatsu's play can be seen as a secularizing vision of pilgrimage in a changing Japanese society, then in the contemporary secular world, the modern Japanese theatre can offer up as few sacramental occasions as can its Western counterparts. The audience for contemporary theatre in Japan is young, urban, highly educated, and wholly secular, an audience of intelligentsia that constitutes another kind of "class" altogether. Their interest in religion ranges from indifference to skepticism. In that climate, what forms will drama take, particularly when there has been so much influence from Western theatrical forms and ideals admired and absorbed into the assumptions of the postwar dramatists? Is pilgrimage still possible? Some examples, in fact, would suggest that it is, and that, further, the continuation of such themes argues for some fundamental qualities in the art of the Japanese theatre.

The theme of pilgrimage, in its modern guise, is particularly apparent in a work by the contemporary dramatist Yamazaki Masakazu (born 1934). *Sanetomo shuppan,* written in 1974, was successfully performed in Tokyo, and the author chose it for translation and production in the United States. When preparing the translation, I became aware of just how the mental constructs of the pilgrimage mentality were present, almost as unspoken assumptions, in the text. The conception of the drama itself is quite sophisticated and in a sense repeats the structures of Chikamatsu and of *Taema,* where actual locations, events, and characters are placed on the stage. In this case, Yamazaki chose the figure of Minamoto Sanetomo (1182-1219), the young shogun of Japan who was installed after the Heike wars that ended in 1185; a gifted poet and a remarkable statesman, his assassination marked a tragic turning point in the fortunes of the Kamakura shogunate. Sanetomo's character has long fascinated writers, scholars, and thinkers, and Yamazaki has made this fascination part of the construct of his play by superimposing the figure of Hamlet onto that of Sanetomo, in which the same search for truth and the same questions of the significance of existence come to the fore as the protagonist questions all the assumptions of the life he finds around him. Yamazaki has constructed the text as a kind of psychodrama assembled by those who knew him—his mother, uncle, relatives, allies, enemies; they are presented as ghosts who reconstruct and examine various incidents in Sanetomo's life. Much of the central section of the play concerns the young shogun's desire to build a ship to sail to China. As the incidents concerning this event are reconstructed, discussed, relived on the stage, Yamazaki makes use of an expanded poetic time that puts his drama into the expanded psychological atmosphere redolent of the atmosphere of pilgrimage that Turner described. In this regard, Yamazaki's use of the dichotomies of the stage versus reality, acting versus living, memory versus action, effectively combine to reveal his central concerns. As with Chikamatsu, the central events presented by Yamazaki are well known to his audience; both dramatists play on what the audience already understands so as to move them to a higher and different level of understanding and empathy.

The full title of the play, translated into English, is *Sanetomo Sets Sail,* and the events of the play suggest on one level a wholly secular end to the theme of pilgrimage, for the ship never leaves Japan. Sanetomo's sole desire is to go to China, his own idea of a cultural paradise, but his vessel is built without sufficient knowledge of seagoing sail craft and never leaves the beach. Each character in the play has formed a different idea of why Sanetomo wants to go to China, and each of these convictions in turn is based on the differing motives, obsessions, and blindnesses of the particular character who devises them. Does Sanetomo know himself? Early in the play he attempts to articulate to the ghost of his dead father some of his feelings in a scene that comes closest to Yamazaki's chosen model of *Hamlet.*

> SANETOMO. Show me your face . . . I want to tell you something. I want you to do something

for me. Speak. I have the force. And the strength of will. And too much curiosity. I'll do anything, try anything. Risk some adventure? Where should I go? Speak. Tell me. Am I to live? To die?

Despite the mistrust of all those who surround him, Sanetomo makes a decision to build the ship, to prepare his men. His powerful uncle Yoshitoki, who admires and loves his nephew, now becomes convinced that Sanetomo has some sort of transcendental purpose in mind, some purpose which he, Yoshitoki, because of his own view of the world and its scheming politics, cannot understand. Convinced of this, Yoshitoki now sets out to try to grasp in his own terms the seemingly ambiguous purposes of Sanetomo's effort. The huge ship is finally completed, but Sanetomo's Chinese shipwright adviser remains concerned about the impracticality of the voyage.

CHEN. I do not know. I do not. Do you really intend to go on board? Do you plan to board her and sail across the sea?

SANETOMO. What a nuisance you are. Of course.

CHEN. But you must not. It is not a ship. It is an apparition. A ship of two thousand stone. What is more, you had three cabins built. The prow of the ship is too heavy. Too dangerous. And the weights in the bottom have increased three times over. That is bad. So unreasonable. Sailing a ship like that you will sink, even on a fair day. Please. Sanetomo. Listen to what I tell you.

SANETOMO. To sink . . . or not to sink . . . sink . . . not to sink . . .

Is Sanetomo's scheme dream or reality? Yoshitoki thinks in the end that he has come to understand his nephew's motivations. He recites to his sister Masako, the young shogun's mother, a poem by Sanetomo.

YOSHITOKI. "The world itself
Is but a reflection in a mirror:
If it seems to be there, it is;
If not, then there is nothing."

I'm not quite sure I understand the part about being there and not being there. But if the whole world is just a reflection, then where does that leave us, my dear sister? If Kamakura, the Emperor himself, everything is an illusion, then all my strength evaporates. And more awesome is the man who can go on existing, serene, knowing that everything is an illusion. A man who conducts his life with good sense, and without despair, even though nothing, nothing at all makes any difference. With such a strong man nearby, I am overwhelmed. I lose the strength to go on living.

MASAKO. Calm yourself, Yoshitoki. You are over anxious. You are tired.

YOSHITOKI. Now I have only one hope. It is Sanetomo's ship. Because this is the only time he has positively opposed me. The one time he has stepped off the path I have prepared for him. And with such passion. Masako. We will allow him to do it. I want to see it. I want to see him once, firm in the belief that this world is not merely an illusion.

Sanetomo prepares his ship, but the vessel is too large and is destroyed at the launching on the beach. Sanetomo now gives up his transcendental voyage and makes plans instead for a this-worldly political voyage, to become a courtier and a poet. Even those who are shortly to murder him cannot understand his change in motivation.

The play concludes with a scene in which his wife asks all those who knew him to enact an incident that never occurred in life, the moment when Sanetomo would actually set sail. It is his murderer, his nephew Kugyo, who, now watching the sails unfurl at last, comes closest to grasping the meaning of Sanetomo's gesture.

KUGYO. I'm overwhelmed. He's really putting all he's got into it. In the middle of a senseless dream, when he knows nothing will come of it, why does he never become discouraged? Why?

Sanetomo, it seems, has made his interior and transcendental voyage after all.

Yamazaki's play was written in the kind of climate that exists in the postwar theatre movement around the world. His dialogue is realistic and psychologically attuned to the changing inner self-perceptions of the characters. Yet the play's purposes do not stop there; indeed they are intended to lead contemporary spectators from a sterile emphasis on individual motive and obsession to a larger vision of the universe, a world where personal predilections dissolve in a movement toward a larger gathering together. The whole structure of the play is calculated to permit the spectators to transcend the world of those who surround Sanetomo, with their plots and schemes, and rise up with him onto the platform of the ship. In the pattern of the medieval *no,* the person seeking enlightenment went on a pilgrimage himself; now Yamazaki combines the idea of physical pilgrimage, appropriate to the historical Sanetomo, with the image of an internal search for transcendence, so much a part of the way in which contemporary human beings conceptualize the possibilities of understanding life today. If this represents a bonding between Freud and the Buddha, then it must be said that, in theatrical terms at least, they have more in common than might have been supposed.

All three of these plays, then, and the traditions they represent show a poetic style, a thrust away from mimesis, an invitation for the audiences to lose themselves in an experience that can draw them out of their normal mental structures of reality. Metaphysical melodrama turns out to have a logic all of its own. In that regard, the three examples provided here were not chosen with an eye to validating Turner's pilgrimage model; rather, Turner's insights can help illustrate this powerful pattern of a poetic desire for oneness which began with the *no* and continues to exist in the secular theatre of today. The movement beyond the abstract logic of words and social data toward a vision of a shared communal world that lies beyond is as strong an impetus behind, say, the avant-garde theatre of Suzuki Tadashi and his *Trojan Women* as it remains behind *Taema.* It is perhaps for such reasons that the so-called post-modern theatre of Suzuki and his contemporaries has gone back to the roots of the Japanese dramatic experience to come forth and reassert the genius of the Japanese theatre, not in the realm of a Chekhov, an Ibsen, or a Molière, however much has been learned from them, but from a transcendental thrust that, in our culture, has perhaps only been fully visible in the best of modern dance. What Zeami and Chikamatsu knew, and what Claudel, Yeats, and Britten recognized, is finally coming to be appreciated again in contemporary Japan. It is to such new theatre, rather than to the Brecht and Molière that I saw in the 1950s, that spectators around the world are beginning to look with excitement and enormous admiration. The pilgrimage, happily, would seem to continue.

Yasunari Takahashi

SOURCE: "Visionary Gleams," in *Encounter,* Vol. LXXII, No. 5, May, 1989, pp. 25-8.

[*In the following essay, Takahashi provides a survey of Japanese theater from the 1960s to the late 1980s.*]

Statistically, there is little doubt that Tokyo is the world's largest theatre town, even surpassing New York. Probably there are many Japanese, especially outside Tokyo, who would be surprised to know that there are in their megalo-capital about 250 theatre companies, about 120 plays put on every month, and about 60 acting spaces. This includes large companies which produce a play per month, and tiny ones which may disappear after a single show; productions ranging from new plays to *Noh, Kabuki, Bunraku,* and foreign plays in translation; and small studios or other spaces turned into *ad hoc* theatres as well as regular playhouses.

Statistics, however, is a dreary and deceptive business—revealing more about economics than about culture. One can go for that sort of information to the Japan Foundation or the Japanese Embassy. What matters is the significance of theatre in the context of contemporary Japanese culture, and here quantity must give way to quality, for only the best in quality, though few and small in scale, would offer an insight into the problem. And since, in my view, much of the best in the Japanese theatre in the late 1980s derives from the "revolution of the theatre" which took place twenty years ago, any serious attempt to understand the issue cannot but begin there.

There are a number of scenes, if I may start on a personal note, which spring up to my memory as I cast my mind back to the late 1960s. A couple still retain special vividness: one is centred on the figure of Yukio Mishima, the other on that of Arnold Wesker.

In May 1969, a year before his all-too-famous suicide, Mishima accepted a challenge by a group of radical students of Tokyo University (where I happened to be a young assistant professor) to hold an open debate with them on their campus. I managed to sneak into the packed auditorium and, in a tense yet strangely exhilarating atmosphere, watched and listened to the fascinating harangue in which the "ultra-nationalist" novelist manifested his sympathies with and differences from the radically Leftist students. The students had, earlier in the year, achieved a spectacular *succès de scandale* in their rebellion when they were expelled by the police force from the clock tower—the symbol of the University and of intellectual authoritarianism—which they had been occupying for some weeks. (It was a really "spectacular" event, watched avidly nation-wide on the TV screen.)

Mishima told the students that he was all for their attacks on the system of modern values authorised by universities and characterised by the false "affluence" of contemporary Japan; he would, he said, gladly have joined them in their occupied "citadel" if only they had cried "*Viva* Emperor!"—which got a great laugh.

A few months prior to the fall of the "citadel", in September 1968, the project called "Wesker '68" had invited the British playwright to Tokyo to discuss, in a symposium involving half-a-dozen theatre directors and critics of Japan, the situation of theatre in contemporary society and what could be done to change it. I was on the platform, sitting beside Wesker, whispering into his ear as simultaneous interpreter, and interpreting him aloud to the other panelists and the audience. There were misunderstandings on the part of the Japanese about British political and theatrical conditions, and vice versa—which entailed some futile though vehement exchanges of attacks on each other; but there were moments when the sheer force of the critique of the status quo, if not an outline of the possible strategies for "revolution", was movingly communicated. (Quite a few faces on the floor on this occasion could be recognised among the audience at the encounter with Mishima).

These episodes go some way, I believe, towards evoking the kind of milieu in which a new theatre movement was getting into full swing. In a sense, it was part of the global phenomenon of the revolt of the youth in the 1960s. The students' strike in 1968 at the Medical Department of Tokyo University preceded the "May Revolution" in Paris by four months, although without, in all probability, any consciousness of prophecy or synchronicity. By the end of the year, however, no less than 116 universities and colleges in Japan were undergoing "campus turmoils", and the students were fully aware of global solidarity in their revolt against academic authority as well as in their denunciation of the Viet Nam War and their admiration for the Beatles.

At the back of it all lay a profound disagreement with the system of modern Western or Westernised values. In theatre, the younger generation in Japan were reacting no less keenly than their Western counterparts to the contestations of modern realism by Artaud, Brecht, Beckett, Genet, Arrabal, Grotowski and Julian Beck, as well as Wesker.

Nevertheless, it would be wrong to ignore those factors which were specifically Japanese. For instance, no account of the new movement in Japanese theatre in the 1960s would be complete without stressing the importance of one political event: the parliamentary ratification of renewal of the Japan-United States Mutual Security Treaty (ANPO) in 1960. The failure to prevent renewal meant not only a débâcle for the whole of socialist power in the political scene; it also compelled intellectuals to rethink their political standpoint. On those young people in the theatre, barely twenty years of age, who had been actively committed to the anti-ANPO campaign, the effect was double: the traumatic experience irrevocably cured them of the Old Left dream and, by the same token, brought them into a violent clash with the orthodoxy in modern Japanese theatre. The orthodox modern Japanese theatre known as *Shin-geki* (literally, "new theatre") had allied itself politically with socialism since pre-War days, and had adopted socialist realism for its artistic method, though another stream alongside it held a less political and more Chekhovian stance of psychological realism. The defeat suffered in 1960 determined the young people's search during the following decade for an alternative theatre with a radically different ideology and methods.

It was in the 1960s that the so-called "High Growth Period" started. A comparatively higher standard of living had considerably dampened the ideal of "post-War democracy", to the chagrin of the Socialists and Communists, and had consolidated the political supremacy of the Liberal Democratic Party. On the other hand, it did not strengthen the sense of national identity. People just seemed to have started drifting, borne along by a new dream of affluence, but at bottom uneasy and uncertain in the aftermath of the disillusionment of 1960.

This is what lay behind Mishima's apparently only half-serious, but deeply-felt, appeal to the students. But the sociological fact had an ironically rich significance for the emerging new theatre. Japan in the 1960s was on the one hand becoming affluent enough—or just about—to allow the aspiring youth to indulge in their own small-scale theatre activities. At the same time, what would now be called "the postmodern era of playfulness' had not yet set in. The moral and intellectual atmosphere, combined with psychological uncertainty, was earnest enough to encourage questionings of everyday reality and deep probings into Japan's cultural identity; there was an urge to talk of eschatology and utopia (Wesker's title, *Their Very Own and Golden City,* had a special ring to it); of Beckettian futility and yet of a need for transcendence; of madness and carnival. Nowhere did all this bear more stimulating and substantial fruits than in the new theatrical movement of the young.

A cursory look over a chronological table of the late 1960s makes one realise the phenomenal importance of the period. One encounters there all the charismatic names that were to revolutionise the theatre scene in the succeeding decades.

In 1966 Tadashi Suzuki, leader of Waseda Sho-gekijo (Waseda Little Theatre, later re-named SCOT), makes his directorial début with a play by his friend Minoru Betsuyaku.

In 1966 Juro Kara, leading Jokyo Gekijo (Situation Theatre), directs his own play, achieving the first in a long series of semi-outdoor productions in a famous "red tent theatre".

In 1966 Makoto Satoh declares the foundation of Jiyu Gekijo (Free Theatre) with the production of his own play. The company, later renamed Theatre Centre 68/71, is commonly known as "Black Tent".

In 1967 Shuji Terayama, founder of Tenjo Sajiki, directs his own play.

In 1969 Yukio Ninagawa, founding Gendaijin Gekijo (Modern Man's Theatre), produces a play by his friend Kunio Shimizu.

In 1970 Shogo Ohta, leader of Tenkei Gekijo (Transformation Theatre), directs his own plays for the first time.

These young leaders did not rally round common political slogans, whose lies they had come to know only too well. The most explicit in political awareness was Makoto Satoh, whose plays—such as *My Beatles* (1966) and *Cinema and Phantom* (1976)—are probably the best embodiment in Japan of the ideas of the New Left, in a brilliantly Brechtian style. His most recent directorial work (1988) was Brecht's *Threepenny Opera,* which he completely transformed into a story about Japan at the time of the Meiji Revolution; the great success of the production confirmed that he was still a most devoted Brechtian in spirit and style. What marks the passage of time is the fact that, besides remaining the energetic leader of the "Black Tent Theatre", he is now also among the most sought-after directors of Western opera (most recently Berg's *Lulu*) in the large commercial theatres of Tokyo.

Though far from being unanimous in espousing "the theatre of revolution", the young theatrical avant-gardists shared a passionate belief in a "revolution of theatre", a revolution which should be total and far-reaching, aiming at no less than a transformation of the consciousness of the audience. No one was more tirelessly experimental than Terayama in challenging the accepted relationship between performance and audience. His transgression was so bold—e.g. *Blindman's Letter* (1973), performed in total darkness; or *Knock* (1975), which literally took the streets for an indeterminate stage where actors roamed about according to a rough "time-schedule"—as to cause scandalised citizens to sue him. But it would be wrong to see only a theatrical *enfant terrible* and scandalmonger in an artist who was a true avant-gardist if ever there was one, and a fascinating "hunter of theatrical images" (in the phrase of the reviewer in *The Times* of the performance of his *Directions to Servants* at the Riverside Studios in 1978). Teryama's death in 1983 might be interpreted as symbolic, in that he was the only one among the young visionaries of the 1960s who refused until the last to acclimatise to the all-powerful commercial milieu of the 1980s.

Perhaps it was Tadashi Suzuki who did more than any other to bring about a radical re-examination of concepts involving acting and text, actor's body and mind, theatre and culture. And he did this not by critical theorising alone but also, and more powerfully, by directing. The work which established his reputation in the "little theatre movement" was *On Dramatic Passions, Part 2* (1970), a collage of scenes from *Kabuki* and other Japanese drama as performed by a Japanese variant of "mad woman in the attic".

Suzuki won a wider recognition with *The Trojan Women* (1974), in which he used for the main roles a *Noh* actor, an actress trained in the tradition of *Shin-geki,* and a leading actress of his own company—thus creating a clash of acting styles which forced as it were deconstructive rethinking upon both actors and audience. The work also successfully employed a "framing" device whereby the Euripidean play was performed as a fantasised vision of an old Japanese beggar, a woman loitering in the streets of burnt-down Tokyo immediately after World War II. After Terayama's ultra-avant-garde plays, this was the first contemporary Japanese production to tour Europe (including performances at the Riverside Studios in 1985) and America, to great critical acclaim. Suzuki leads the increasingly "internationalising" trend in Japanese theatre today, with his activities such as founding the annual Toga Festival (which has so far invited Robert Wilson, Tadeus Kantor, Lee Breuer, Welfare State International, etc.), lecturing at Juilliard in New York, and producing his boldly reduced all-male version of *King Lear* with a mixed international cast.

Another influential director is Yukio Ninagawa, a name quite familiar by now to British theatre-goers. His fame in Japan has long been associated with the playwright Kunio Shimizu—their early collaboration in productions like *Such a Serious Frivolity* (1969) has now become legend as a most moving portrayal of the revolutionary generation. After a period of separation, they again started working together, and *Tango, at the End of Winter* (1984), for instance, bore eloquent witness to Shimizu's unfailing dramaturgical skill in mixing memory and reality, yearning and despair, as well as to Ninagawa's staggering manipulation of the dynamics of the stage.

Ninagawa is also a witness to the devouring power of time in the sense that, alone among his rebellious colleagues, he has proved himself capable of success in big commercial theatres—something totally unthinkable before his advent. His first venture in this new direction was *Romeo and Juliet* (1974), followed by *King Lear* (1975), *Oedipus Rex* (1976), a new version of Chikamatsu's *Kabuki* plays (1979), the famous *Macbeth* (1980), *Medea* (1985), and *The Tempest* (1987).

The only other name in Japanese theatre today that can claim international recognition is that of Shogo Ohta, whose completely silent piece, *Water Station* (1981), has more than once toured Europe and America. Another major work, *Komachi Fuden* (1979), which is intended for performance on the *Noh* stage, consists mainly of an old woman's silent reenactment of her memories. These apparent *tours-de-force* make a significant contribution to theatre in general because of the amount of participation which has to be extracted from the audience in order to make it possible for the theatrical experience to exist at all. But they are of particular interest to the Japanese because they seem to tap the deep root of the nation's aesthetic sensibility: the aesthetics of silence and void, the refusal to articulate, or the body's resistance to *logos.*

Ohta may resemble in this those Butoh dancers whose grand master, Tatsumi Hijikta, seeking the basis of his art in the decrepit body discarded by the mind in the process of modern civilisation, learnt a great deal from the primitive forms of *Noh* and *Kabuki.* It should be stressed here that Japanese theatrical modernisation started in the Meiji era with a conscious denial of the indigenous tradition of performance. Be that as it may, it is a sad pointer to the state of culture that Ohta, unable to maintain his ascetic activity any longer, was last year forced to disband his troupe.

Juro Kara's revolt against modern intellectualism was arguably fiercer than that of any other Japanese playwright. Though European surrealism was one of the great influences on him, his instinctive sympathies were blatantly committed to the eroticism, freedom, and yearning of popular imagination. His dramatic text, incredibly sophisticated and breathtakingly spontaneous, matched well with the magical power of his actors' "privileged body", which he famously eulogised. His works, ranging from the series of "John Silver" plays (1965-68), *The Mask of the Maiden* (1969), to *The Black Tulip* (1983) and so on, continue to be a stubborn thorn in the affluent theatrical flesh of contemporary Japan.

Last but not least, Minoru Betsuyaku is exceptional in the list of experimentors of the late 1960s in that he alone was and remains a pure playwright, an ascetic in his own right, never involved in any kind of "movement". He started his dramatic career under the decisive shadow of the absurdist theatre, especially Beckett. But he was quick to realise the dangers of the cul-de-sac that it might lead him into, and has developed a unique style of his own whereby he can treat serious subjects such as the sufferings of Hiroshima (*The Elephant,* 1962) or a family crisis involving the killing of an old woman by her grandson (*The Cherry in Bloom,* 1980) with the same perfect expertise that he shows in dealing with abstract problematics such as the nature of social institutions (*Conference,* 1982). What this style might possibly remind one of would be, if anything, that of Pinter. Betsuyaku's quietly methodical mind seems to set his work apart from the vociferous and often amateurish stagecraft of the younger generation.

So those are the "big names", or the so-called "first generation of the little theatre movement", all of them born between 1935 and 1943. They are the ones who, having brought about the "golden age" of experimental theatre twenty years ago, now constitute the solid core of theatrical creativity.

A few words about a solitary figure from the same generation: Hisashi Inoue. He did not belong to any of the "radical" groups, nor did he come from the modern Westernised *Shingeki* tradition. His roots were in popular vaudeville entertainment, which he refined with something of a Brechtian verve. But it would certainly be quite unfair to disregard the sheer joy he has given to theatre-goers in the past two decades, with his fantastically complex chinese-box dramaturgy (*The Navel of the Japanese,* 1969) or his savagely entertaining portrayal of evil (*Yabuhara the Priest,* 1973). And he is still prolific.

Another playwright who resists classification is Rio Kishida. Having long worked for Terayama in many of his important productions, she triumphantly established her own fame with the performance of her play *Itojigoku* (*The Hell of Threads*) in 1984—a hauntingly realised story of Japanese women working in a weaving factory, and one which only the female imagination could have produced. Other female playwright-directors to be mentioned, even though in passing, are Koharu Kisaragi (*Doll,* 1983) and Eriko Watanabe (*Ge-ge-ge-no-ge,* 1982), though they are to be grouped with the "third generation".

The "second generation", comprising playwright-directors now in their early forties, tried to establish their difference by shedding the tragic gestures and revolutionary visions of their immediate predecessors and concentrating on the scaled-down ordinary realities of life. The most prominently talented among them was Kohei Tsuka, whose special importance, however, lies in the fact that he was at the same time responsible for tipping the balance in favour of the following generations. It was his play *The Atami Murder Case* (1973) which turned the tide by pushing the interchangeability of fiction and reality on the stage to the furthest extreme. His characters were intent on playing roles with a dizzying and desperate devotion which somehow both madly intoxicated the audience and left them excruciatingly blasé. That was his way of provoking what he considered to be the growing complacency of Japanese society; and when he thought his "malice" no longer worked, he left the theatre to become a novelist and work in films. Last March, after seven years' absence, he came back to the theatre, with a new play about a film actress. It remains to be seen whether he has found the times sufficiently changed to stimulate him into continued exercise of theatrical "malice".

It would be too scholastic to dwell on the distinction between the "third" generation and the "fourth". Suffice it to say that, despite the differences in individual talents, they do share certain characteristics: a lack of serious concern with social reality, or rather a precocious awareness in advance of the futility of all efforts; an abundant energy of playfulness which might be labelled "post-modern" in contradistinction to the "anti-modern" or "pre-modern" concerns of the "first generation"; a science-fiction-oriented fascination with eschatology or imagery of androids, and so on. The forerunner among them is Hideki Noda, whose company, Yumeno-yuminsha (Idle Dreamers), performed his play *Descent of the Beast* in Edinburgh in 1987. Following him closely in both vitality and popularity are Shoshi Kokami's troupe, Daisan Butai (Third Stage), and Takeshi Kawamura's troupe, Daisan Erotica (Third Erotica).

The present prosperity of theatre in Tokyo, unprecedented in Japanese history and probably unrivalled in the world, owes much to these young playwright-directors. One would, however, be rash to state categorically how much of their work is ephemeral, and how much of enduring substance.

Robert T. Rolf

SOURCE: "Japanese Theatre from the 1980s: The Ludic Conspiracy," in *Modern Drama,* Vol. 35, No. 1, March, 1992, pp. 127-36.

[*In the following essay, Rolf analyzes major characteristics of Japanese theater in the 1980s.*]

Twentieth-century Japanese theatre grew out of attempts to create a new Japanese theatre befitting the new Japan. As was the case with the immense socio-economic reform Japan undertook in the late nineteenth century, the model for the new theatre was the West, specifically the works of Shakespeare, Chekhov, Gorki, and Ibsen. By the late 1920s, what came to be known as *shingeki* (literally, new theatre) had produced a significant body of artists and works. The new theatre was intellectual in tone and lacked a popular audience. Much of it was characterized by a socialist realism that used the stage for the exploration of socio-political issues. Another strain of the new Western-inspired realistic theatre sought a psychological and lyrical complexity in the vein of the works of Chekhov. Even with the upheavals brought about by World War II, this state of affairs lasted into the 1960s.

The generation of artists who began their careers in the 1960s brought about a theatre renaissance that has received increasing scholarly and critical attention. Much has appeared (or is about to) concerning the tent theatres of Kara Juro (b. 1941) and Satoh Makoto (b. 1943), the drama of playwrights Betsuyaku Minoru (b. 1937) and Shimizu Kunio (b. 1936), the avant-gardism of Terayama Shuji (1935-1983), and the theatre aesthetic of Suzuki Tadashi (b. 1939) and Ota Shogo (b. 1939). The new direction taken by these artists is becoming well-documented. Facing a theatre scene dominated by realism and rationality, they worked to restore the primacy of the actor, reduce theatre's dependence on the written word, and re-establish links with an autochthonous premodern Japanese imagination. This involved new configurations of performance and audience space, new relationships between actor and text, actor and spectator. Although most of these figures are still active, their work already constitutes a considerable legacy. Their dramaturgical innovations have taken hold, influencing younger Japanese theatre artists.

A recognizable style has held sway over the past decade, one that seems to some a continuation of the tradition of the 1960s and to others something different. As will be seen, it may be both. Although not encompassing all of today's nontraditional theatre, this approach predominates among younger artists. A description of its characteristics will be followed by a close look at two compelling works as examples. Listing creates the risk of oversimplification or excessive schematization, but should provide a preliminary agenda, a starting point for discussion of this remarkable trend in contemporary Japanese theatre.

I GENERAL TRAITS

1. *Socio-political relativism.* Japanese theatre today seems to have little interest in making statements. Direct concern with social or political morality is often seen as old-fashioned and inappropriate to contemporary theatre. Supporting this apolitical stance is the notion that one point of view is ultimately as valid as the next. Works by many of Japan's more creative younger artists are marked by the absence of any easily identifiable ideology, although the lack of an apparent ideological position could be interpreted as constituting one of sorts.

Many of the more successful works are *tours de force* of the creative imagination, the reality presented in the performance meant to bear little relation to conventional, easily recognizable paradigms of everyday life. At any rate, no attack upon such a reality is intended. Items and figures from history and the social milieu are freely dragged in, but lacking any attempt to valorize them. They are more or less equated, morally neutral, so to speak, being merely different pieces of bric-a-brac from different shelves of the contemporary consciousness.

2. *Preoccupation with childhood and fantasy.* A defining trait of the new Japanese theatre is its frequent use of childhood. Works abound in adolescent and, especially, prepubescent characters. There is a deep fascination with the solipsistic perception that characterizes early childhood, a time of pure experience free from the demands of logic and the need to assess and judge. Setting plays in childhood provides a natural link to the world of fantasy. One source of the new theatre's many elements of fantasy is science fiction, but the result is more akin and indebted to *manga,* Japanese cartoons, than "science."

Manga is the constant link with the sensibility of childhood. One source of this fascination with *manga* is surely its visual nature, which frees it from the domination of language. The drawings of a cartoon possess a reality that precedes that of its captions (even taking into account the pictorial possibilities of the many ideographs in the Japanese writing system). Secondly, Japanese cartoons treat all manner of subjects—from the most naive adolescent romance to the atomic bomb—but the medium involves an inherent simplification. Its essentially unintellectual character makes it a key element in the packaging of contemporary Japanese drama. Not only is a cartoon world created on stage, but programs and promotional materials are similarly marked by cartoons, cutely posed photos, bright colors, and an absence of the critical and biographical commentary found in material for older artists. The artists of the 1980s cultivate an unintellectual image that belies their obvious intelligence.

The typical Japanese cartoon is decidedly emotive. Its onomatopoeia and exclamatory language would shame Batman; in a sense, this finds a counterpart in the unusual, fast-paced acting style of such troupes as that of Noda Hideki (b. 1955; described below). Emotive, rather than cognitive, the cartoon provides the antithesis of the rationality that was common in Japanese drama from the 1920s to the early 1960s. Finally, there is an obvious and satirical unreality about cartoons. Performances suggesting a similar air of unreality call attention to the physical reality of the actors. Distance is created between not only actor and role, but words and their meaning, as well. Although only a child would "believe" the reality of a cartoon (or a stage performance, for that matter), it can communicate an ironic perspective.

Japanese theatre artists and audiences seem drawn to the sensibility of the cartoon by its inherently visual, simple, emotive, ironic character. The fairy tale is another common, more literary source of fantastic, childish, emotive imagery. It remains popular, but its importance (although considerable) seems matched by that of the contemporary cartoon.

3. *Ludic spirit.* Today's Japanese theatre, well rehearsed and skilfully staged, is performed in a spirit of play: the more laughter, the more successful the performance. The reduced distance between actor and audience, like that between actor and text, has become correspondingly more fluid. This has resulted in closer identification by audiences with actors and their predicament as they do battle with the text. The audience and the performers become co-conspirators against the text, working together to undermine and subvert its literal meaning and surface logic. Occasionally, actors even resort to what is essentially a technique of popular comedy—laughing at one's own jokes. This further increases the distance between themselves and their acting, while reducing that with the audience.

Audiences are generally young, mostly in their early twenties, younger than most of the performers. But age alone cannot account for the conspiracy of humor, laughter not being a monopoly of youth. Still, the ludic spirit of today's theatre (like its apoliticalization and absorption in childhood and fantasy) points to a certain mentality: indifferent, self-absorbed, comfortable.

4. *Self-conscious awareness of the drama form.* Much of the experimentation in Japanese theatre of the 1960s and early 1970s involved abandoning the traditions and assumptions of the well-made play. There was a keen awareness of the pliability of dramatic structure. Today's new Japanese playwrights and directors love to engage in metatheatre exercises, an almost mischievous playing with and exploring of theatre's malleable parameters. This is not only to rediscover or reconfirm what is now already well known, but also to make use of a dramaturgical device that is now quite familiar, if not second nature.

Beckett's *Waiting for Godot* was a major impetus for many of the generation of the 1960s. It was performed in May 1960 by the Literary Theatre (Bungakuza), an old and influential *shingeki* troupe, which had done Pirandello's *Six Characters in Search of an Author* in March 1955. Artists of the 1960s often explored the nature of playing and the play in original works, making such exploration an integral part of their approach. Plays today constantly call attention to the fact that they are plays, and the exposure or underscoring of theatre's unreality is often a work's apparent purpose. The effect within the apolitical, ludic cartoon world of today's theatre is to further stress the impossibility and laughableness of constructing a conventionally ordered stage reality mirroring a similarly ordered one beyond.

II ARTISTS AND WORKS

A complete listing of the artists and troupes whose works fit the above description is unnecessary and nearly impossible, but some of the more prominent names should be mentioned (even at the risk of unfortunate omissions). Noda Hideki and his troupe Dream Idlers (Yume no yuminsha), begun in 1976, are early, major practitioners of this theatre, as are playwright/director/actress Watanabe Eriko (b. 1955) and her group Theatre Troupe 300 (Gekidan sanjumaru), founded in 1979. Also relevant is Tin Spontaneity Troupe (Buriki no jihatsudan), founded in 1981 in a reorganization of an earlier outfit. Led by playwright/director/actor Ikuta Yorozu (b. 1949), it features actress/singer Ginpun Cho (b. 1952), an icon of the theatre of the 1980s. A polished organization that shares much of the sensibility that came to typify the 1980s is playwright/director Kokami Shoji's (b. 1958) The Third Stage (Daisan butai), formed in 1981. A grittier outfit is Third Erotica (Daisan erochika), begun in 1982 by playwright/director/actor Kawamura Takeshi (b. 1959). Its works have a socio-political dimension but otherwise belong to this theatre. Play*Machine/Fully Automatic Theatre (Yu *kikai/zenjido shiata), discussed below, appeared in 1983. Project Navi (Purojekuto nabi), led by playwright/director Kitamura So (b. 1952), seems more literary in its approach but shares points of confluence with the dramaturgy of the above artists. Acquiring its current name in 1986, Project Navi grew out of earlier outfits that trace their roots to 1977.

1. *Half a God* (*Hanshin,* 1986). Noda Hideki and the Dream Idlers are at the center of the theatre style that characterizes the 1980s. Noda is playwright, director, and principal actor of his troupe but prefers the designation director or actor. Although he crafts complex dramatic texts, his direction—the unique acting style of Yume no Yuminsha—is meant to force his text into an unwinnable battle with its performance. In his more successful efforts, such as *Half a God,* the contest between text and performance is fought to a stalemate (rather than the text being overwhelmed, which sometimes happens). The success of a performance results from the involved interaction between the two.

As to the acting style, in one brief speech in *Half a God* Noda runs, jumps, rolls on the floor, employs odd hand motions and gestures, and delivers his lines in all manner of pitches, accents, and inflections, many with no apparent semantic relationship to the words themselves. This subversion of normal speech segues into and out of realistic or emotional patches. Such performances can be jarring for one seeking a conventional style, but Yume no Yuminsha audiences appreciate them. Noda and his prominent co-actors, specifically Uesugi Shozo (b. 1955), are masters of the ironic smile that unmasks them as "actors"—people estranged from the text, as is the audience—performing an improbable role in a self-conscious, often silly style. The audience is thus included in the conspiracy to prevent the hegemony of the text by attacking and calling into question its "inherent" semantic logic.

Half a God was directed and adapted by Noda from a cartoon story by Hagio Moto. A clever fantasy involving a grab bag of mythological characters and pseudo-scientific elements, it is set in an isolated lighthouse, where live a couple and their nine-year-old daughters, Maria and Asura—Siamese twins. Maria is a simpleton, endlessly smiling, gurgling, and thrashing about; Asura is a frustrated prodigy, saddled with watching out for her twin, from whom she longs to be free. Into this situation comes the girls' new tutor; other characters include two old mathematicians and a surgeon (all played by Noda), two aunts, and a host of characters from a world of spirits and myths—a mermaid, a unicorn, a Harpy, the angel Gabriel, and, above all, a sphinx. The last group seeks to lure the twins away to the farthest reaches of their spirit world. Asura and Maria are mysterious, given the rarity and strangeness of their condition, and so belong with the sphinx and other myths. The "great doctor," played farcically by Noda, determines that an operation to separate them can save one; otherwise both will die, since they cannot go on sharing the same heart. The operation takes a year and twenty-four hours, during the first year of which Maria is apparently the one saved. But, in the end, the "dead" Asura emerges as the one to live, while Maria joins the world of myth.

The story of *Half a God* is intriguing in itself and bolstered by multilayered imagery. Two contrasting structures (both imagistic and philosophical) are set in binary opposition: the dichotomy and the spiral. The former involves sets of opposites—North/South, left/right, high and low blood pressure, medicine/mathematics, and, of course, the twins. An almost incantatory equation plays a key role in the linguistic and imagistic structure of the play: 1/2 + 1/2 = 2/4. The answer to a sphinx's riddle is always "man," one head over two legs, i.e., 1/2. But in the case of the Siamese twins, mathematical logic is subverted, and 1/2 + 1/2 equals not a whole person, but two heads over four legs, 2/4. In contradistinction to the dichotomy is the spiral, represented by the helix, the lighthouse staircase, whirlpools made by the water draining from bathtubs, cosmic maelstroms, the earth's rotation, a revolving stage (in motion for several minutes during one scene), funnels, and windmills. Uniting everything is the romantic, melancholy Argentinian tango, a whirling dance in 2/4 or 4/4 time, which is used frequently.

Although the above description is not exhaustive, it should suggest *Half a God*'s fantasy and complexity. The story is, of course, not merely played straight. The performance begins with Noda and his actors (referred to by their real names) rehearsing the final scene. When acted in its entirely at the close, it is still in the form of a rehearsal. At two other points, when the audience has become engrossed in the story, director Noda suddenly interrupts and has everything gone through again with a different approach. He chides the actors for their lack of critical detachment, jokingly defined as the actor's feeling of watching himself from a distance. The opening is a wild parody of Yume no Yuminsha's well-known, energetic acting style, which is preceded by a wry description of the superfluous people, needed neither at home nor the office, who would attend such a play.

Along with *The Third Richard* (*Sandaime Richado*, 1990), *Half a God* is Noda's masterpiece and exhibits all the traits of this new theatre.

2. *A Deep Breath of My Time, Vol. 3* (*Boku no jikan no shinkokyu, vol. 3;* 1990). Performances by Play*Machine/Fully Automatic Theatre often provide consummate examples of the childhood fantasy prevalent on Japanese stages. *A Deep Breath of My Time* is a group composition, such as Play*Machine is known for. It is credited, however, as composed and directed by Yoshizawa Koichi (b. 1960), codirected by Shirai Akira (b. 1957), with dialogue by Takaizumi Atsuko (b. 1958); the latter two are the work's featured actors. Volumes One and Two appeared in 1986 and 1987, respectively. A brief look should help reveal the nature of the attraction to the perception of childhood, the sensibility of the cult of prepubescence.

The opening is a monologue by a grade school boy, Yamada Noboru, played by actress Takaizumi Atsuko. Takaizumi is known for her male impersonations, especially the little boy Yamada (who also appears in other works) and a nondescript "salaryman" in late middle age. Home alone, Yamada wants to eat, not just anything but a rice omelette prepared just so. This frustrated desire leads to a favorite Play*Machine technique—using strong desires or thoughts as springboards to fantasy. A French chef appears from inside the refrigerator but is not what the little boy needs. The stage then darkens and bright light pours from the refrigerator, out of which dance many chefs carrying ingredients and cooking utensils. Other settings include school, the swimming school Yamada is forced to attend, a movie theatre, and a bar where he drinks when he imagines how alcohol might give him the strength to face school.

His fantasies never lead to fulfillment. He ends up without his rice omelette, having "killed" it when he throws it on the floor in a tantrum (he and the cooks do hold a proper funeral for it, however). He carries his insecurities and anxieties everywhere. Likewise, he cannot escape the passing of time. That it is his constant companion is clear from the huge round alarm clock he carries everywhere. It being his only friend, he talks to it and even dries its eyes as he and, presumably, his clock cry in the movie theatre at Judy Garland's "Somewhere Over the Rainbow." Garland he sees only on the screen, but he meets many other characters from his fantasies—Superman, Frankenstein, Olive looking for Popeye, Japanese cartoon figures, his favorite baseball player, a sumo wrestler, an Arab, women.

The close of the long day of childhood fantasies segues into the twilight of Yamada's long life. Takaizumi, suddenly dressed as the old salaryman, gives Yamada's retirement speech from the department store where he has quietly worked for thirty-five years. Never married, he has nothing to look forward to in retirement; he regrets nothing except a marketing opinion he once gave that led to an off year in sales. After thirty-three years there had been talk of promotion to a position of responsibility, but he asked for a transfer to the toy department instead.

A Deep Breath of My Time, like many of these works of childhood fantasy, is a psychological drama. Placing insecurity and anxiety in childhood keeps them at a safe distance for adult audiences. There is a longing, a nostalgia, for the simplicity and naivety with which a child conceives of and expresses psychological dilemmas. This feeling is fostered by the cuteness of the child characters on stage, their exaggeratedly childish clothes, walk and, above all, talk. Wanting a rice omelette is probably a simpler, more elemental frustration than those of an audience ranging from many in their twenties to a sprinkling of people in middle age. The frightening nature of Yamada's deep-seated sense of foreboding and personal inadequacies is defused when encountered within the context of childhood fantasy. The ending is moving but somewhat sentimentally so. What saves the performance from being mere escapist entertainment is its imagistic complexity and the troupe's ensemble (and, in many cases, individual) acting skills.

A Deep Breath of My Time implies a critique of society, but the dominant philosophical note is resignation. There is a sad inevitability about Yamada's life, but through nearly all the performance he is a lovable little boy. His sudden appearance as old employee Yamada is too brief to alter the charming image of him already created. The obnoxiousness that a "real" boy such as this would likely convey is obviated by the great distance between character and role occasioned by the use of an adult female. Similarly, two adult actresses play two little girl classmates of Yamada's as obnoxious, but the result is humor. *A Deep Breath* achieves some psychological depth but, as with most such contemporary Japanese drama, the actors' and audience's shared fun in the performance is its real *raison d'être.* As Takaizumi disappears behind the curtain, smiling and waving at the audience a few yards away on virtually the same level, the bond between performer and spectator is deepened; there is the reassurance that the humorous, moving story and expert performance were just that and nothing more. Nothing happening in the theatre is intended as a specific challenge to anything beyond it.

III CONCLUSION

Set in childhood, seeking a cartoon fantasy world, the well-rehearsed, imaginatively staged theatre from the 1980s provides an ironic perspective on all realities—social, political, or theatrical. Revealing no familiar ideology of its own, however, it mounts no concentrated attack upon or challenge to any one specific reality. The theatre event itself becomes the point. Self-referential and playful, it assumes the audience's sympathy as it undermines the text, demonstrating that there can be no single agreed upon meaning or reality. Lessening the distance and deepening the bond between performer and spectator, there is a diminution of the audience's critical attitude toward the performance.

Whether indulging in a pseudo-science-fiction fantasy or exploring the psychology of a lost soul hiding in the shadows of the work ethic, the sensibility of childhood (as it exists in the adult imagination) wraps everything in a soft, protective cocoon. Performers and audience delight in this image of childhood simplicity. The gap between the gray, hard, adult world and what they see as a brighter, more innocent time is mined for considerable humor. In the guise of childhood fantasy, all aspects of human experience can be drawn upon freely for imagery without any thought of logicality. The mind of the child is thus seen as resembling the world of the dream.

Final assessments of the new theatre of the 1980s are problematic; it is impossible to gauge its significance at this early date. There is also the question of its relation to the theatre renaissance of the 1960s. Critic Senda Akihiko sees a direct line of descent from Kara and the others he terms the First Generation down to today's newest generation. His divisions are strictly chronological. Using the metaphor of a romantic voyage, he sees each generation sailing forth on paradoxical voyages of discovery in a world where the ocean has been reduced to an inland sea. Senda's views are opposed by Saeki Ryuko and Tsuno Kaitaro, both with the New Left Black Tent in the 1960s. Saeki sees some continuity, but holds it to be deterioration. Among other things, he objects to Senda's implication that today's theatre achieves more psychological depth through its interiority, free now of the ideological paradigms that characterized the theatre of the 1960s. Tsuno sees artists of the 1980s just repeating the 1960s, the metatheatre Senda regards as a defining trait of the new theatre having also been common in the 1960s. For Tsuno, the earlier theatre was an avant-garde movement that petered out after about five years (1972), as all such movements must, what it stood for probably expressed afterward in other artistic or political forms.

Theatre today, like that in the 1960s, emphasizes the actor's physicality, maintaining the link established by Kara and his contemporaries with such actor-centered older theatre forms as *kabuki* and *taishu engeki* (literally, popular theatre). However, a difference between young theatre artists today and those of the 1960s is the way they see themselves in relation to what was once known as the establishment (*taisei*). Prompted by sympathy with student and labor activism, the theatre of the 1960s was often confrontational in spirit. Its form and style may have survived, but from the start artists today are more career-oriented. As typified by the well-known public persona of Noda Hideki, youth's rebellious pose has been replaced by nonchalance. Noda and his troupe have achieved success and recognition—awards, corporate sponsorship, and a niche in the cultural establishment. In 1985, a Noda play could pun at the expense of the Actors Theatre (Haiyuza), a venerable *shingeki* troupe dating from the 1940s; in 1990, Play*Machine/ Fully Automatic Theatre makes joking (perhaps envious) references to Noda's Dream Idlers.

Many of the traits of Japanese theatre today are in line with international trends, as was also generally true in the 1960s. Much as the earlier theatre could be discussed in terms of the international avant-garde, the vocabulary of postmodernism could be applied to today's theatre. To refer to one persuasive study, it obviously possesses the tendencies of postmodern theatre described by Patrice Pavis: "depoliticization"; much of a performance's "coherence and totality" coming from the "process of its making and its reception"; and, a "plurality of readings." Yet it is equally obvious that, as was true with theatre in the 1960s, a specifically Japanese sensibility and theatrical assumptions are also at work.

Robert T. Rolf

SOURCE: "Tokyo Theatre 1990," in *Asian Theatre Journal,* Vol. 9, No. 21, Spring, 1992, pp. 85-111.

[*In the following essay, Rolf offers a retrospective of trends in Japanese theater and discusses works by six contemporary Japanese playwrights.*]

Tokyo is the scene of extensive theatre activity. Besides the well-known older forms, the world of nontraditional Japanese theatre has expanded. Indeed, a recent directory lists one hundred and seventy-five such troupes based in Tokyo. This theatre, of twentieth-century origin, will be the sole focus here. Of the great number of theatre productions in 1990, six will be described to convey the nature of theatre in Tokyo today. Criteria for selection take into account both the play's intrinsic interest and the manner and significance of its performance. The six performances provide an introduction to many of the theatre artists who are best responding to the circumstances of theatre today. Performances were chosen from fifty seen in 1990; four of the selections happen to coincide with those of Japanese critics. All represent provocative plays and performances of great interest.

A BRIEF LOOK BACK

Early moves to create a modern Japanese theatre, one responding to the new reality of a modern Japan, involved late-nineteenth-century attempts both to reform *kabuki* and to create a new, "up-to-date" *kabuki.* The latter effort resulted in such things as *shimpa,* a hybrid form that survives today—the traditional (female impersonation, for example) side by side with the modern (actresses). The origins of modern Japanese theatre would seem, however, to lie more in two early-twentieth-century phenomena: the staging of Western drama (Shakespeare, Ibsen, Chekhov) and the writing of Japanese plays in that new vein. By the 1920s a nucleus of modern theatre artists had evolved; novelists, too, were fascinated by the drama form, even if not always as interested in having their dramas staged.

From the outset, the new theatre (*shingeki,* literally new drama) was highly intellectual; there was little opportunity or need to acquire a popular following. Consequently, it tended to branch off ideologically into either aestheticism or socialism. The former championed psychological realism or lyricism and aspired to a Chekhovian complexity; the latter was marked by socialist realism and sought to lay bare the essence of socioeconomic and sociopolitical dilemmas—in short, to educate. Such a state of affairs obtained into the 1960s, even with the disruption of theatre activities occasioned by World War II.

By the 1960s *shingeki* had perhaps grown stale. Its realism and rationality were challenged with great success by a generation of young artists. They were inspired by a combination of factors: the example of the absurdism of Ionesco and, especially, Beckett; participation in the nationwide demonstrations against the ratification in 1960 of the U.S.-Japan Mutual Security Treaty *(Ampo),* which removed protest and anti-establishment stance-taking from the exclusive province of the old Left; and the general exhilaration of the youthful international counterculture of the middle and late 1960s.

Shingeki's contributions to Japanese theatre were many and important: the broadening of subject matter to encompass nearly all facets of life; the addition of an intellectual dimension to theatre; the placing of Japanese theatre in a more international context. The new theatre emerging in the 1960s, on the other hand, was usually referred to as underground *(angura)* or the Little Theatre movement *(shogekijo undo)*. Experimentation was active on all fronts. Both from necessity and the desire to free theatre from the tyranny of the proscenium arch, various unconventional performance spaces were used—tents, coffee houses, streets, parks, rooftops. New concepts of theatre space allowed a reconceptualization of the audience, and efforts were made to dislodge it from its customarily passive, nonparticipatory role. Both the role of the director and, even more so, that of the actor received new attention. There was a corresponding reduction in the traditionally central concept of authorship, and much was tried to reduce the role of the text in a performance, which heightened the awareness and importance of the actor's physicality. The new dramaturgy often meant texts structured nonlinearly to create a sense of cyclic or mythic, rather than historical, time. The political spectrum ran from the New Left to the anarchical.

The heyday of the new, post-*shingeki* theatre was from about 1966 (although one might argue that it actually began a few years earlier) to 1973. The golden age ended, but in a sense the post-*shingeki* era continues. Stylistic assumptions that motivated the experimentation of what Japanese critics like to call the "first generation" have for the most part now become the norm. One has trouble ascribing such continuity to Japanese theatre of the past twenty-five or thirty years, however, owing to the ideological differences between the anti-establishment, New Left, or avant-garde pioneers and the more career-minded, typically apolitical artists of today.

The initial group of pioneers—playwrights Betsuyaku Minoru and Shimizu Kunio, playwright-directors Satoh Makoto and Terayama Shuji, playwright/director/actor Kara Juro, directors Suzuki Tadashi and Ninagawa Yukio—and others of about that time (Ota Shogo, Inoue Hisashi) are mostly in their fifties now (Terayama died in 1983); all remain of great interest. Betsuyaku and Shimizu have established themselves as two of the most important living Japanese playwrights, as they have gone on exploring their theatre worlds, mining claims staked out early in their careers. In the 1980s Satoh became a highly respected director, often of musical productions. Kara remains unchanged, pitching his trademark Red Tent theatre in the same old spot—the grounds of Hanazono Shrine near the sleaziest section of Tokyo's Shinjuku Ward. His broad dramaturgy and irreverent bohemianism still serve him well. Unlike others of his time, he has remained popular with young audiences. Director Suzuki has developed an international reputation for his interpretations of the Western classics and a unique approach to actor training based on traditional Japanese aesthetic assumptions. While Suzuki has thus pursued the *shibui* (the quiet or understated), director Ninagawa has appropriated the *hade* (the brilliant and spectacular) for his highly theatrical interpretations of the Western classics. Ota Shogo is well known outside Japan, as well, for his development of a distinctive minimalist dramaturgy. Although without the foreign reputation of Suzuki, Ninagawa, and Ota, Inoue Hisashi is quite famous in Japan and popularly appreciated for his clever, accessible dramas and prose.

Following the seminal developments of the 1960s and early 1970s came a loss of interest in sociopolitical and philosophical issues. Theatre moved toward entertainment. This change sometimes took disappointing turns—for example, an aspiring to the slick theatricality of Broadway musicals. An immensely popular young artist in the middle and late 1970s was the talented playwright Tsuka Kohei, who used considerable irony and lively theatricality to achieve psychological depth. His works, such as *The Atami Murder Case (Atami Satsujin Jiken;* 1973), shifted the emphasis somewhat from the questioning and experimentation of the 1960s and placed it more upon having fun. Rock music, common in the 1960s, was used by Tsuka and others in the 1970s. But the fascination with singing, dancing, and exuberant showmanship grew, reaching a crescendo in the early 1980s, when nearly every Japanese playwright, director, and actor seemed compelled to demonstrate the ability to be musical.

Throughout this period of emphasis on showmanship, artists of a different stripe—Betsuyaku, Shimizu, Suzuki, Ota—continued their more reflective work. Novelist Abe Kobo had by now left the scene. Abe's involvement with theatre dated from the 1950s, including the acclaimed play *Friends* (*Tomodachi;* 1967). From 1973 to 1979, however, he headed the Abe Kobo Studio, which increasingly pursued a theatre of images, emphasizing the physicality of the actor and seeking theatre's emancipation from the word—in short, continuing (like Suzuki) much of the thrust of 1960s experimentation.

In the mid-1980s music returned to the background, though remaining important. Among the younger artists, a phase that continues today had begun. With significant exceptions like Kawamura Takeshi and his troupe Third Erotica (Daisan Erochika), these artists are uninterested in making statements; their "message" seems to be that there is (or should be) no message. There is a preoccupation with the world of childhood—its psychology, iconography, and, above all, school. Their dramas seem to exist in a cartoon world; paradoxically, both thematic superficiality and psychological depth seem to result. (To the 1980s what Tsuka was to the 1970s, Noda Hideki—discussed below—remains an "older" exemplar of such theatre.) Much interesting work was done in 1990 by Third Erotica and other young troupes: Play*Machine/Fully Automatic Theatre (Yu*Kikai/Zenjido Shiato), Libre Ship (Riburesen), and Health (Kenko), Such work will be the subject of a future discussion.

Little Brother!—A Message to Sakamoto Ryoma from Otome, His Older Sister (Ototo yo—ane, Otome kara Sakamoto Ryoma e no dengon)

THE PLAYWRIGHT/DIRECTOR

Shimizu Kunio is one of the most accomplished playwrights writing in Japanese today. First, his plays are marked by skillful attention to language and imagery, his dialogue a compound of the realistic and occasional lyrical patches. His focus is psychological—not meticulous revelation of individual psychology in the manner of a Eugene O'Neill, but thoughts and feelings delineated in broader strokes. His more mature works show an affinity with both Chekhov and Tennessee Williams. There is a fascination with poetry, usually (though not exclusively) Western. Swatches of the poetry of Pushkin, Rilke, and Aragon appear in many of his dramas; their function is crucial—to enfold his characters' mental crises in poetic images, raising them to some higher plane. In such an approach are inherent risks, of which Shimizu is well aware. The trick is to maintain the necessary balance between the two levels of language; with too much elevation, the focus drifts away from the essential and off into the blue. Shimizu's technique for keeping his works firmly grounded is the use of humor, a second characteristic of his dramaturgy, to puncture the seriousness. It runs from repartee to comical characters fainting.

Pervading many of Shimizu's more stimulating plays is a sense of loss, a thematic element that also contributes to a certain stage atmosphere. This may be achieved through language or, as in *Little Brother,* such directorial techniques as *tableaux vivants*. Establishing this mood naturally involves a looking back, but it is much more likely to take the form of wistfulness than hard reexamination of the past. Change, the passing of an indispensable someone or something, the fading of youth—these are frequent occasions for loss in Shimizu's plays. He is an admirer of the aesthetic stance of Tanizaki Jun'ichiro as described in that author's *In Praise of Shadows* (*In'ei Raisan;* 1933)—for example, praise of the shadowy beauty of the traditional Japanese house. Shimizu's persistent awareness of life's evanescence seems another point of affinity with Tanizaki.

A final comment about Shimizu's plays: they frequently contain strong female characters, as often as not to be played by his wife, Matsumoto Noriko. Shimizu describes his attitude toward these characters in terms of the psychology of "older sisters." *Little Brother* is archetypical in this regard, a kind of summing up of Shimizu's insights into the older sister type, a woman more rational than the male characters (or forced to be so in order to look after them). Men in Shimizu's plays are, conversely, romantic to the point of foolishness or even insanity; women who fall under their sway are foolish, perhaps doomed.

Shimizu was a key participant in the theatre renaissance of the 1960s, as well as in the *Ampo* and other earlier political demonstrations. As for the latter, however, describing himself as the dutiful son of a Niigata policeman, he claims to have been decidedly a follower swept along by the crowd. Still, by the late 1960s (past the age of thirty), he was an enthusiastic leader of sorts in the Tokyo youth culture.

Playwright Shimizu has directed all but one of the performances of his theatre group, Winter Tree Troupe (Mokutosha), formed in 1976. Including small-scale atelier pieces, *Little Brother* was Winter Tree's twenty-sixth production; nearly all have been of his works. Shimizu is modest about his directorial skills, but his pieces fare well under his hand. He has an association dating back to the 1960s with director Ninagawa Yukio, who still often directs his works. Shimizu's directorial approach is more or less grounded in realism; primacy is put upon the word. His troupe contains many young actors, but neither his scripts nor his direction normally call for athleticism. Despite his directorial competence, Shimizu's importance is as a playwright.

THE PERFORMANCE

Performed December 8-18, 1990, at Kinokuniya Hall, Tokyo, *Little Brother* opens at night upon a passing vendor of wind chimes; their relentless, hypnotic tinkling is like the spirit of the dead charismatic Ryoma, whose memory will not leave those who knew, loved, and depended upon him. Sakamoto Ryoma (1835-1867) was a samurai from Tosa *han* who worked for imperial restoration until assassinated by Tokugawa Bakufu loyalists. Known both for his swordfighting skills and for his role as an intermediary in consolidating an anti-Tokugawa alliance among traditionally hostile *han,* the young imperial martyr is revered even today.

Sakamoto Ryoma does not appear as a character in *Little Brother*. Rather, he is the obsession of a group of relatives and cohorts a few years after his death, the first years of Meiji (1868-1912); at their center is Otome, an elder sister, who struggles to keep his memory in proportion among the others, although scarcely able to do so herself. Her soliloquies—the first introduces a flashback to the fall of 1866 (more than a year before Ryoma's death) and the last closes the play—establish her role as a kind of narrator, the audience's closest link to the indefinable presence of Ryoma. Her soliloquies are spoken with a wistful solemnity.

Of even greater intensity and impact are the *tableaux vivants,* in particular the one that immediately precedes Otome's final speech. These take the form of all the Ryoma-obsessed characters posing for commemorative photos. They must hold their poses for at least twenty seconds to accommodate the ancient camera. To accomplish this they must look "natural," as Otome (Matsumoto Noriko) says, " . . . With a soft gaze . . . as if you are thinking of something glimmering. . . . Yes, something glimmering; your joys; your sorrows; your dreams; and, your love." Then Otome, alone now, relates how the people in the photo afterward went their separate ways. Photos are, she says, silent things that seem to try to communicate something, no one knows what. Shimizu presents the enigmatic nature of photos as a metaphor for history and legend. Ryoma is now revered unequivocally as a hero, but the truth cannot possibly have been so simple. Still, Shimizu seems to say, what more can be known or said at this juncture? Like the old photos, the history of a time like the early Meiji period just gazes back at us gazing at it, sending a silent message we can never hear.

As usual, Shimizu is dealing on a metaphoric or poetic level with the difficult questions his plays provoke. In that light, *Little Brother* shows great similarities to another masterful Shimizu play, *Dreams Departed, Orpheus* (*Yume sarite, Orufe;* 1986), which also deals with the process of myth-making, the psychological need to reject the death of one's, so to speak, messiah.

Like *Little Brother,* Shimizu's *Dreams* treats a crucial period and a charismatic figure in Japan's history: the 1930s and Kita Ikki (1883-1937), another imperialist (though perhaps of a different sort) put to death by a reactionary government. Sakamoto Ryoma was from Tosa, where he was held in awe. Kita Ikki was another provincial deified at home, Shimizu's Niigata. In *Dreams,* Shimizu relies on the lyric force of a long Pushkin poem; in *Little Brother,* he harnesses the power of the nostalgic image of old photographs created in the audience's mind as it gazes at the *tableau vivant* of the actors.

The set of *Little Brother* is dominated by a raised, wall-less, two-story house stage center. Basically it is conventional period realism such as one sees in standard *shingeki* fare, although designed by Asakura Setsu, a frequent Shimizu collaborator, known for her elaborate sets. Asakura, perhaps the most noted set designer in Japan and also active abroad, has worked often with Ninagawa Yukio, as well as with Tsuka Kohei, Inoue Hisashi, Kara Juro, and countless others. Kara says that Asakura "doesn't concern herself with the abstract core of the play, but instead tries to materialize all of its physical details." Shimizu's directions call merely for a dilapidated old house, and that is all that Asakura materializes.

Costumes in *Little Brother* were also in keeping with period realism; changes in costumes and props were used to illustrate and underscore Japan's rapid westernization between 1866 and 1871. Acting was, likewise, generally realistic, except for lyrical scenes or, naturally, the exaggerated humor of the comic relief. Many scenes were darkly lighted, but seldom beyond the exigencies of Shimizu's generally realistic directorial concept. Music was used sparingly as a quiet undercurrent to scenes of heightened intensity, in particular the *tableaux vivants.*

In conclusion, *Little Brother* reveals Shimizu's preoccupation with a crucial period in Japanese history, one of transition to the modern age, necessitating the beginnings of Japan's ongoing process of westernization. Shimizu hints that even after the Meiji Restoration the often sanguinary struggles that typified pre-Meiji Japan would be continued and, quite possibly, intensified, albeit in other guises; but he goes no further into specific historical assessments, preferring to adopt a relativist stance. Clearly, it is the eternal fact of inevitable change upon which Shimizu wishes to train his considerable writing and directing skills.

Letters from the Wildcat—The Legend of Ihatobo (Yamaneko kara no tegami—Ihatobo densetsu)

THE PLAYWRIGHT

Betsuyaku Minoru was a key figure in the development of the new theatre of the 1960s, the first major pure playwright to emerge from the movement. He has remained a respected writer and has built up an important body of dramatic literature. Into the mid-1970s, Betsuyaku had a deep infatuation with the dramaturgy of Samuel Beckett; critics (and Betsuyaku himself) quite rightly cite that influence regularly. From Beckett he derived an understanding of minimalism, the conviction that the simplest language, sparest sets, and most basic human relationships could be the stuff of powerful theatre experiences and deep psychological insights. A more enduring infatuation is that for the world of the fairy tale, the universal link with the psychology of childhood. Betsuyaku's works incorporate many elements from Japanese children's games and songs, the tales of Miyazawa Kenji (1896-1933), Lewis Carroll, Hans Christian Andersen, the Brothers Grimm, *manga* (cartoons). Betsuyaku sees the absurdist techniques of Beckett and Ionesco, and the psychology of the fairy tale, as similarly useful approaches for liberating theatre from a linear conception of time. Both free us from fear of the illogical and the forbidden, rendering more approachable hidden areas of the human psyche.

A performance of a Betsuyaku play is usually a quiet affair. A certain convention in directing his works has developed, no doubt influenced by the quiet intensity of his two important early works, *The Elephant* (*Zo;* 1962) and *The Little Match-Girl* (*Matchi-uri no shojo;* 1966). Actors speak the typically commonplace lines without relying on the fast, loud delivery traditionally associated with Japanese avant-garde theatre of the 1960s—Kara Juro, for instance. Likewise, actors move slowly, not in the silent, glacial manner of Ota Shogo or with the intellectual stylization of Suzuki Tadashi, but more like preoccupied or weary people from the everyday world. A character who strides purposefully on stage in a play's beginning may be found at the end sad, hesitant, or, more likely, dead.

Many Betsuyaku plays portray a process of victimization in a context of moral relativism. There are few heroes or villains, virtually no concept of character or personality, only situations and circumstances. Notions such as an individual overcoming adversity through force of will are alien to Betsuyaku's world. Victim or victimizer, winner or loser—the inner core of one is indistinguishable from that of the other. A person can be the one just as easily as the other. Some Betsuyaku plays do employ a specific social and historical context, allowing the Betsuyaku who was a passionate participant in the *Ampo* and later political struggles to emerge; but such works seem increasingly in the minority compared to his more abstract efforts.

THE PERFORMANCE

House lights dim to begin *Letters from the Wildcat,* revealing Betsuyaku's most often used set—a telephone pole on an otherwise bare stage. Performed by Bungakuza (Literary Troupe) on November 2-13, 1990, at Kinokuniya Hall, it is a catalog of Betsuyaku's most familiar props, settings, situations, characters: a hand-pulled cart; a baby buggy; a tea party alfresco; a woman with a parasol; men with black umbrellas; an unsuspecting traveling salesman as protagonist/victim; wandering symbiotic couples (including one person leading the other on a rope, like Beckett's Lucky and Pozzo); a Christian "minister" in the incongruous garb of a padre; wind sounds; a voice from a raspy speaker mounted high on the pole; women singing children's lullabies. Over all is a quiet, languid air of absentmindedness and fatigue.

The title derives from tho works of Miyazawa Kenji, in particular his fairy tales "The Restaurant with Many Orders" (*Chumon no oi ryoriten;* 1924) and "The Life of Gusuk Budori" (*Gusuko Budori no denki;* 1932). The Western-style restaurant in the former Miyazawa tale stands alone in the forest, a lure for unwary hunters who enter thinking "many orders" implies good food and many customers, only to find that it means customers are ordered to prepare themselves step by step to be eaten by its proprietor, the Wildcat. "The Life of Gusuk Budori," on the other hand, is a story of ultimate self-sacrifice, whose elements include famine and child abandonment, set in a land called Ihatobo. Other Miyazawa works are drawn upon also—for example, verse from his *Spring and Asura* (*Haru to shura;* 1924-1925) poetry collections is recited by the salesman to close the play. Betsuyaku has based his works upon Miyazawa's before, most notably *Journey to Giovanni's Father* (*Jobanni no chichi e no tabi;* 1987), also directed by Fujiwara for Bungakuza. The fascination with Miyazawa is widespread among contemporary theatre artists; other examples include Inoue Hisashi's *The Ihatobo Drama Train* (*Ihatobo no geki ressha;* 1980) and Kitamura So's *So's Draft of Milky Way Railroad Nights—A Revision* (*Soko: ginga tetsudo no yoru—rivijon;* 1990).

In Betsuyaku's *Letters from the Wildcat* seven characters (of the play's ten) are journeying to Ihatobo, summoned there by letters from the Wildcat. Ihatobo seems to be a kind of endpoint, a terminal station, though not a "heaven" (the presence of the padre/minister notwithstanding). As is usually the case, Betsuyaku's salesman seems drawn into things by the other characters, by the situations and relationships they create. Incest (brother and sister), child abandonment, refusal to take responsibility for these crimes—all are prominent in the play. There is repeated reference to the famines of twenty-three and forty-two years earlier, when the two abandonments took place. The seven reach Ihatobo, where they are welcomed with fireworks and the tea party, then called away by ones and twos by the welcoming voice from the loudspeaker. The salesman, confused that the others seem to know when they are to be called, goes quietly, soliloquizing the poetry of Miyazawa Kenji. Over the whole finish—snow has begun to fall—is an attempt at lyricism and a note of spiritual transcendence.

Interpreting Betsuyaku's suggestive, enigmatic text, director Fujiwara Shimpei saw the characters as fettered by what Betsuyaku terms a "chain of unhappiness." Keeping an anthology of Greek tragedies beside his *Letters from the Wildcat* script, Fujiwara conceived of the dilemma of Betsuyaku's characters as similar in kind to that of an Oedipus destroyed by a chain of events he never understands until too late. He also sees in this and other Betsuyaku works affinities with Buddhist notions of karma—in the sense that even the smallest actions of insignificant people have great cosmic implications. Whereas Miyazawa's works may focus on the great good coming from individual acts of self-sacrifice, Betsuyaku's characters seek, in Fujiwara's words, to expiate their sins. Fujiwara's aim is to somehow direct such weighty matters in a "light" fashion. Betsuyaku's association with Fujiwara and Bungakuza goes back to the 1960s; he has written a new play for them almost annually since 1974.

The Silence of the Sheep (Hitsujitachi no chinmoku)

THE PLAYWRIGHT AND THE TROUPE

Yamazaki Tetsu began his theatre career with a brief but formative stint of less than a year in Kara Juro's Situation Theatre (Jokyo Gekijo), handling lighting and assistant directing chores in 1970. He had begun seeing the theatre of Kara, Terayama Shuji, and other new artists as early as 1967, while a university student. Through most of the 1970s he headed a troupe that approached performing in the Kara manner, trucking their plays about Japan, in the spirit of "riverbed beggars" (*kawara kojiki*), the outcast forebears of *kabuki*. Yamazaki considers actors to be theatre's main element, given their overwhelming physical reality; they are not merely people who memorize. He is uncomfortable with the label of playwright (as well as that of artist) and prefers to be called a director. He places great emphasis on the shared nature of theatre's creative process; indeed, he describes the writing of his plays as a verbal manifestation of his relationship with a group of actors. In 1980, Yamazaki and others formed the troupe Transposition 21 (Ten'i 21), for which he regularly writes new plays that he directs himself.

The Seventh Sick Ward (Dainana Byoto) is a somewhat rare commodity: a successful theatre troupe without an influential playwright or powerful director. Its head *(zacho)* is primarily an actor, Ishibashi Renji, who appeared in some of the early successes of Shimizu and Ninagawa. They perform infrequently, compared to other troupes, with one or even several years between productions. Yamazaki has written for them before, but they are best known for their interpretations of plays written for them by Kara, especially his *Two Women* (*Futari no onna;* 1979). Seventh Sick Ward would seem a good combination with Yamazaki, given his strong feelings about the primacy of the actor. Whereas he views the creation of a performance as a joint effort, a pulling together, Ishibashi describes the rehearsal period as a breaking apart, a process sharpening the actors' awareness of their essentially separate natures. An important member of the Seventh Sick Ward is actress Midori Mako, a key reason for its success and cult status. Post-*shingeki* theatre has produced its famous actresses. Ri Reisen, until recently Kara's wife, matched the gritty, boisterous world of his Red Tent theatre with her hoarse, unpretentious, energetic style. Midori Mako, on the other hand, projects an aura of fragility and mystery.

THE PERFORMANCE

The time is now; the place, a basement coffee shop in a part of Tokyo not far from Disneyland, an area under tremendous pressure from developers and real estate speculators. Across the back wall of the set are a row of windows, at leg level of pedestrians outside, and a glass door entrance at the audience's right. Stairs lead down along the wall from the glass door to the middle of the shop. Construction scaffolding for the adjacent lots is visible through the windows and door; there is the sound of a wrecker's ball battering away. The props follow natural laws—phones ring, the jukebox works. The acting is, likewise, realistic. Many customers come in, all to various degrees desperate.

What comes through clearly is the characters' utter boredom and frustrated communication, the desperation with which they pursue their respective ends—becoming a prostitute to escape the frustrations of a housewife's life; the taking by a young man of any part-time job that pays well and is a little "interesting," even if it means committing acts of violence; being a gangster and forcing people to sell their homes; running a coffee shop as a means of escape from the complications of a career; coming from the country to see Disneyland and deal somehow with the family suicide of one's children and grandchildren. Resembling a compendium of recent social issues, *Silence* is in danger of overdosing on topicality. What sparks it to life is the mad Midori Mako character, a failed actress who claims to have thought up a screenplay that will be used for a Hollywood movie. Actually, it is Arthur Penn's *Bonnie and Clyde,* which she tells (with great skill) in detail on stage to the other characters. They become engrossed in the telling, even though some know it is a famous film, not her creation.

As the vibrations from the wrecker's ball punctuate her story and send dirt down the walls, it becomes apparent that these contemporary Japanese are as desperate as Bonnie and Clyde in the America of the Great Depression—both societies in both times putting corporate finances and economic development first and the individual last. In the end, the greedy, frustrated gangster runs amok in the coffee shop, accidentally shooting Midori, whose script (like Bonnie's poem) is now complete. The last scene uses the light from a filmless movie projector to frame the tableau of the dying actress, her former husband (the proprietor), and his second wife. *Silence* was performed by Seventh Sick Ward, June 9-25, 1990, at the Sangenjaya Chuo Gekijo, an old movie house in a rather outdated shopping district, which further intertwined the worlds of film, theatre, and storytelling.

The Legend of the Mermaid (Ningyo densetsu)

THE TROUPE

The stylistic innovation that characterized the new theatre of the 1960s has largely become second nature to younger artists. One such troupe is Shinjuku Ryozampaku (Ryozampaku alludes to the Chinese classic *The Water Margin*), formed in 1987, primarily by artists from the Red Tent world of Kara's Situation Theatre and Satoh Makoto's Black Tent Theatre 68/71 (Kokushoku tento 68/71). Led by actor/director Kim Sujin (the *zacho*) and playwright Chon Wishin, SR has pursued the same total theatre that typified both the two tents and Terayama Shuji's determinedly avant-garde Tenjo Sajiki (The Gallery). In particular, SR has tried to expand the performance space beyond the confines of their tent theatre, a space no longer so unconventional. Most performances incorporate the special characteristics of the site to achieve spectacular entrances, exits, and backdrops. A link is forged between the sealed, "artificial" world inside the theatre and the open, "real" one beyond. In Chon's *Carmen Nocturne* (*Karumen yaso kyoku;* 1987), the tent was pitched in an abandoned railway station, which allowed actors and stage to enter spectacularly from out of the dark on a flatcar. Another production Kim directed saw SR perform with the back tent flap open: passing commuter trains created a strange backdrop to Yamakawa Santa's *Quest for Ammonites—Night of Distant Thunder* (*Ammonaito kuesto—toku kaminari no kikoeru yoru;* 1988). Street theatre pieces often accompany SR's tent performances; Watanabe Eriko's *Star Cavalry Gathering in the Night—Dark Sunday at the End of Showa* (*Yoru ni muragaru hoshi no kibatai—Showa no owari no kurai nichiyobi;* 1988) had a huge lighted dragon and actors on lighted bicycles rolling through the streets. Shinjuku Ryozampaku's artistic rationale for such glitter and scale is to create a spectacle, more in the nature of *kabuki* than experimentation with some theoretical basis, as with Terayama, Satoh, and Kara. SR seeks to surprise and delight—to inspire wonder, not provoke thought.

THE PERFORMANCE

The Legend of the Mermaid was performed by Shinjuku Ryozampaku on the shore at Enoshima, May 25-27; on the Yokohama waterfront, June 29-July 1 (after touring several regional cities); and by Shinobazu Pond in Tokyo, July 18-August 6. The Yokohama performance of June 29 is described here.

The tent theatre was set up beside a river, which was used for the initial entrance and final exit by boat of much of the cast, during which the back and side tent flaps were raised. A water pit at the front center of the stage was also used with energy and effect. In the tent/little theatre tradition, seating was on the ground; the front two rows of spectators huddled under a large sheet of plastic provided to protect them from the splashing. The cast was active before the performance, mostly doing practical chores such as lining up the audience to enter, but also performing quietly among them. This had some effect in reducing audience/actor distance and audience/performing space distinctions, even among the generally inhibited, unresponsive theatregoers. Sets and props were proletarian—noodle carts, small factories, slum streets, a boxing ring. Also in the tent/little theatre tradition, there was great dependence on lighting and music—abrupt, drastic changes in both, a link as well to the melodramatic world of *taisho engeki* (popular drama), found in such places as the Asakusa area of Tokyo. There was much live singing by the cast, reminiscent of the Black Tent, as was a brief teaching scene, the structure and humor of which called to mind Satoh Makoto's works.

Many things happen in Chon's play. As in Mishima's modern *no* play *Sotoba Komachi* (1956), a poet and an old woman sit on a bench; the poet tells the story of a family with many brothers, which the other actors perform, while the old woman comments on its significance. Trapped in the slum, the family vents its bitter frustrations in crimes of passion. A constant motif is that all life originates and somehow belongs in the sea. The forgotten slum is intended to be like the unseen, unknown depths of the sea. There are ethereal, supernatural characters who forge that link, preparing for the final scene when the earth opens and the sea reclaims the poet, the family of his story having returned to the sea.

Chon was nominated for the Kishida Kunio Drama Prize for *Legend* but failed to gain it—mostly because judges felt his borrowing from Visconti's 1960 film *Rocco and His Brothers* was too liberal. Still, the world of film (to which SR has often referred) is obviously a congenial source for a troupe seeking a theatre world that both embraces and is somehow larger than life.

The Third Richard (Sandaime, Richado)

THE PLAYWRIGHT

Noda Hideki, actor, director, playwright, and leader of the Dream Idlers Company (Yume no Yuminsha), may be the consummate example of the theatre artist of the 1980s. While an underclassman, Noda formed his troupe out of the college drama club in 1976. Often appearing on television, he has become something of a celebrity; his blend of ironic nonchalance and puckish naivety appeals to younger Japanese.

Noda thinks of himself as, first of all, an actor; his awareness of himself as such greatly influences both his directing and writing. Dream Idlers' performances are marked by action. A high school hurdler, Noda leads the charge as the cast scurries and bounds about the stage—not in a display of acrobatics per se, but movement in double time, matching the rapid delivery of the actors' lines. With typical self-effacing irony, Noda claims that Dream Idlers' rapid speech was born of necessity—to cover up deficiencies in student actors—but it has the effect of undercutting the hold of language over the performance. Extremely well rehearsed actors advance Noda's typically involved plots with a delivery that seems disinterested in, distant from, ironic toward, the words' meaning. The story is just a way of holding the audience's attention; its meaning seems of little significance, one story (any beginning, middle, or end) as good as another. The cardinal sin is to be slow or boring. Rather than patiently building toward something (although the plots do run on), each section, every minute, must be interesting, in the sense of fun, in and of itself. There are many pranks and puns. Plays typically present important scenes from childhood; promotional materials and programs are always studiously childish, done in bright colors, with cartoons, cutely posed photos, and a total absence of the critical, biographical, and historical information one finds in programs for works by older artists, such as Betsuyaku and Shimizu. Much like Noda's dramaturgy, this style and the anti-intellectualism it implies seem an attempt to thwart interpretation. One is left with only the experience of the performance itself.

THE PERFORMANCE

The Third Richard was performed at the Tokyo Globe Theatre, October 26 to December 2, 1990 (and in Osaka, December 5-16). Ostensibly an interpretation of *Richard III* (given the title), it becomes, almost from the start, a different play—one about the "historical" Shakespeare and how he manufactured from his imagination a hunchbacked, villainous Richard III, although in fact the king had been neither. Richard is put on trial for war crimes. Shylock (played by Noda) is also a major character, another aggrieved figure made unsavory by Shakespeare, another victim of the Bard's imagination. Underlying this is the notion that the truth of the past exists only in the past and cannot be conveyed to the future. Shakespeare's characters, such as Richard III and Shylock, are the product of—and as such exist only in—Shakespeare's fantasies. By extension a question is posed to the audience: Whose fantasy do you exist in? Noda uses scenes from Shakespeare's childhood—and a troublesome younger brother, Richard Shakespeare—to have the Shakespeare of Noda's fantasies creating such villains as Richard III to work out his own psychological compulsions. The effect of all this is to convey the view that truth is illusory and relative, that value (or judicial) judgments are based on subjective, rather than objective, criteria. The twelve jurors—all members of the audience—are evenly divided (six for conviction; six for acquittal); the thirteenth juror, an actor, who decides the matter, is vindictive.

The description to this point might imply that Noda's work is more "serious" than it is. Whatever its implications and the questions it raises, it was performed in a spirit of play. This approach aided the success of the actors' intrusions into the audience, some of whom (possibly "plants") were made to say a word or two in answer to very simple questions and, in one case, to stand up, turn around, and face the audience. At one point handbills relating to the play were passed out among the audience by actors from the stage. The acting was the customary Yume no Yuminsha style—much running and jumping, lines delivered at odd paces and in a variety of voices and accents unrelated to meaning. The set was somewhat elaborate with arches and several entrances; the costumes were a mix of period, contemporary, and the fantastic. Lighting effects and recorded music were used liberally, but the considerable success of the performance resulted essentially from the interplay of the content of Noda's play and the acting style of his troupe.

People on the Roof (Okujo no hito)

THE PLAYWRIGHT AND PROJECT NAVI

Playwright/director Kitamura So heads the Nagoya-based Project Navi (Purojekuto Nabi), a prominent theatre troupe in the 1980s. Although not a famous actor, Kitamura and his troupe seem cast in a somewhat similar mold to Noda and his Dream Idlers Company. That is, Kitamura's productions are packaged in the same juvenile style implying a similar anti-intellectual stance. But the similarities may be superficial. Kitamura is a skilled playwright; although far from realistic in their approach, Project Navi's performances rely little on fast pacing and athleticism and give attention to the literal meaning of words.

Kitamura has also explored the nature of stage space and questions of authorship. And, like so many other contemporary Japanese theatre artists, he is greatly preoccupied with childhood and its possibilities for revealing basic human obsessions and motivations, which leads naturally to the world of fairy tales and the writings of Miyazawa Kenji, as noted in my discussion of Betsuyaku.

Project Navi's more successful productions combine Kitamura's artfully crafted scripts with the troupe's well-rehearsed acting and highly professional stagecraft. As several of its actors have comedic and musical proficiency, Project Navi is almost always worth watching. Will Kitamura, born in 1952, continue to grow as a playwright/director following a trajectory like that of a Shimizu Kunio? Or will he become trapped in the youthful style with which his troupe has been so successful? The question is of great interest.

THE PERFORMANCE

A cutout city skyline low across the back, the bare stage is covered by a platform a few inches high, which represents the rooftop on which all the action of *People on the Roof* takes place. This comic portrayal of sexual frustration begins quietly and deliberately on a well-lighted stage. The acting proves to be a mixture of the realistic, wistful, and broad; the comedy sometimes borders on slapstick. Tokyo performances were at the Honda Theatre, May 29 to June 3, after earlier presentations in Nagoya and Itami (near Osaka).

Many people come in ones, twos, and threes to the roof, where they encounter one another and reveal their various stories. Pervading all is the theme of sex. A young woman with a baby on her back enters with a young man. She describes a scene of al Fresco sex acts in an explicit way that sets the tone for the play. He tries to convince her he is faithful to her. She claims he has taken a lewd photo of her; when he denies it, she suggests he take one of her next time they come to the roof. They leave with the entrance of three schoolgirls who have lively discussions about sex. A stolid workman enters, as well, followed later by a man in a trenchcoat, a flasher who is aroused to action overhearing the girls' talk of sex. Two more couples round out the eleven rooftop denizens: a blind professor in a wheelchair and his female companion, who reads him the Confucian *Analects* and lewd stories; a young man and a working girl he is trying to dump (although she has aborted two of his children) so that he can marry his boss's daughter.

Going through the humorous warmup rituals of a sumo wrestler, the silent exhibitionist finally speaks toward the end, revealing his dual identity: salaryman/pervert. Adding to the humor, the blind man at one point puts on a demonstration of wheelchair basketball. Toward the close, his companion dramatically steps off the edge of the roof/platform—but nothing happens, destroying the fiction of the stage as a separate reality. After a musical number, "Whatever Will Be Will Be," the close sees the woman with baby flashing the workman, who chooses to go on cleaning the roof rather than take her up on her proposition. She takes it well and goes off, leaving him working, working.

In Kitamura's inventive piece, all actions seem morally equated. It is a humorous treatment of contemporary sexuality, a subject seldom encountered on the recent Japanese stage. Kitamura and Project Navi, in spite of the carefree style they assiduously cultivate, present a performance that is both comfortably entertaining and disturbingly thought-provoking.

FUTURE PROSPECTS

The experimental approaches of twenty-five years ago have become, if not a new orthodoxy, at least well established. Realism, the onetime bugbear, may remain stigmatized but still can produce viable theatre. Among younger and older artists alike, there is a preoccupation with legend and myth rather than history. The prevailing relativism precludes probing and assessment of the past and, not surprisingly, aids the retreat into the nonjudgmental world of childhood and the fairy tale. Human psychology is seen as more compelling than the sociopolitical or philosophical realm. And, especially among younger artists, there is an unabashed embracing of the purely entertainment values of theatre.

There is much theatre in Tokyo to be seen, assessed, and (if worthy) reported on. And the scene may be expanding, for the Tokyo area is in the midst of a building boom. This wealth of new theatres is the welcome fulfillment of a long-standing need and may create equally welcome opportunities for Japanese theatre people. There is a stimulating increase in imported foreign productions, but how will Japanese artists respond to the changing circumstances? Much of the major work of the past thirty years has come from small theatres and avant-garde experimentation. Approaches, assumptions, and techniques that are the product of decades of performances in small or unconventional spaces are not always easily transported to large conventional theatres. Such considerations and the lure of money make the future hard to predict.

FICTION

Noriko Mizuta Lippit

SOURCE: "Ironic Perspective and Self-Dramatization in the Confessional I-Novel of Japan," in *Reality and Fiction in Modern Japanese Literature,* M. E. Sharpe, Inc., 1980, pp. 13-38.

[*In the following essay, Lippit examines the types and major characteristics of the Japanese "I-novel."*]

The most peculiarly characteristic form of the modern Japanese novel is the I-novel, in which the author appears as the protagonist and describes his private affairs and experiences. Avoiding the use of fictional devices, the author presents his state of mind, ideas and realization almost directly. Not only is the subject matter narrowly confined to the author's personal life and experience, but the perspective is almost entirely limited to that of the author-protagonist, and the novel typically lacks such structural and fictional mediation as plot, story-development, dramatic tension and characterization. The author's inward-turning eye observes his inner self in minute detail, leading to a profound insight, a distilled and crystallized sensibility, and a heightened awareness of life which make this type of novel close to poetry, while the lack of fictional devices brings it close to the impressionistic essay and diary.

At the same time, writing about oneself is an act of exposing the hidden self and desire, and often constitutes a challenge to the norms of social morality. It involves a confrontation between the individual and society, resulting in the sacrifice of the individual's (author's) social respectability. The author engages in this confrontation for the sake of art and the pursuit of truth. The self-exposure that characterizes the confessional I-novel is thus at once exhibitionistic and self-destructive.

Two distinct types of I-novel can be discerned in modern Japanese literature. The poetry-like, essay-like I-novel, usually called the "state-of-mind novel" (*shinkyo shosetsu*), reached its peak in the works of Shiga Naoya. It expresses the writer's understanding of life—his realization. It is not necessarily confessional and in most cases is not rebellious toward society, however unconventional and individualistic the author may be. It most characteristically expresses the author's sincere and stoic determination to search for the self, for a higher knowledge of life. Rather than being destructive both to society and to the self, the *shinkyo shosetsu* is a purified form of autobiographical novel in which the author meditates upon himself or herself with a profound, if egocentric, inward-turning eye and with the accurate eye of a realistic painter. It becomes a presentation of the heightened moments of the author's life and thus a philosophic novel as well as a realistic one. In the author's endeavor, the "I" is purified and even approaches selflessness. The optimistic, idealistically humanistic belief that the expansion of one's ego means the expansion of all human consciousness supports this process.

The other form of I-novel, the confessional novel, was established at the same time, in the late Meiji (1868-1912) and Taisho (1912-1926) periods, by the works of Tayama Katai, Shimazaki Toson, Iwano Homei and Chikamatsu Shuko, and was further developed in the Showa period (1926-present) by the works of Dazai Osamu. All of these writers depict their sinfulness, perversity, shamefulness and irrational contradictions without presenting any explicit aspiration for a solution or salvation. The act of exposure becomes the purpose in itself, yet with their persistent, unsentimental presentation of themselves, their novels gain an existential dimension and become expressions of the sinfulness of human nature itself. Underlying this destructive type of I-novel is a view of human beings and of literary expression that is essentially naturalistic. Thus it is not surprising that the first confessional I-novels were produced by such naturalist writers as Katai, Toson and Iwano Homei.

The confessional novel is usually considered to have been initiated by Tayama Katai's *Futon* (The Quilt, 1907), a work strongly influenced by naturalism. Although the unveiling of the self is not an essential element of the original French naturalism and the confessional I-novel is not a simple extension of European naturalism, the basic concepts of the Japanese confessional novel were fundamentally influenced by the tenets of naturalism, and the form or genre of the I-novel emerged from the short-lived movement of naturalism in Japan. Indeed we can even say that the mature era of naturalism in Japan started when the writers became engaged in writing about themselves.

According to the naturalistic view, people are controlled basically by their instinctive drives and conditioned by their social and biological environment. People either struggle unsuccessfully to control their drives through reason and moral will or achieve success only superficially. To understand people's lives as they are, the writer unveils the false social masks they wear and describes the naked human self in all its contradictions as baldly and as truthfully as possible. The reality of human life and nature is understood as determined by objective forces, and thus it can be described precisely through "flat description" (*heimen byosha*) and "one-dimensional description" (*ichigenteki byosha*). Not only is the unfictionalized exposure of one's ugly and secret side thus justified, but also the self and the author's life become the most suitable materials for his art serving as the basis for both intellectual scrutiny and the detailed, realistic description which exists as the core of the naturalists' theory of description.

Both types of I-novel (the *shinkyo shosetsu* and the confessional novel) are also based on the author's sense of crisis, a sense which is not abstract, metaphysical anxiety or despair but the result of a specific crisis in life (such as his wife's love affair or his infatuation with a young girl). While the *shinkyo shosetsu* is an expression of the writer's victory over the sense of crisis or of his effort to overcome it, however, the confessional novel is an expression of the sense of crisis as it is. The sense of crisis in the destructive I-novel stems from the sinfulness and shamefulness inherent in human existence which, unless overcome, leads people to self-destruction. The *shinkyo shosetsu,* on the other hand, is based on a belief in struggle to transcend the sense of crisis and attain enlightenment. The *shinkyo shosetsu* reflects a belief in life according to which art is used as a means for arriving at a higher consciousness of life, while the destructive I-novel reflects an effort to find salvation in art, that is, in the act of writing the novel itself.

In both cases, the question of the relation between art and life is central. For the writers of the I-novel, art was a path of mental and spiritual training, and their ethical passion to live honestly made the artists expose their thoughts and desires openly and frankly, thus converting life to art and making art serve life.

Both types of I-novel dominated the development of the modern Japanese novel. Although there were such writers as Natsume Soseki and Tanizaki Junichiro who strongly opposed both the I-novel and naturalism, it continued to be the dominant form of Japanese novel until the emergence of proletarian literature in the Showa period. For new writers, the I-novel was a heavy burden of tradition to struggle with and to surpass, and in the period following World War II, a major critical effort was devoted to criticism of the I-novel.

The limitations of both types of I-novel are quite obvious. The I-novel excludes almost completely the elements of the outer world, of others and of social problems. It tends to be narcissistic, self-satisfying dialogue with oneself or an exhibitionistic exposure of oneself. The most fundamental problem of the I-novel, a problem which has been pointed out by such critics as Kobayashi Hideo, Nakamura Mitsuo and Hirano Ken, is the writers' lack of a concept of the modern self. The reader can readily discern the easy assumption of the I-novelists that the self could be grasped by themselves and that to know the self was to know human beings in general. While the I-novelists justified their egocentric interest in writing about themselves accordingly, their works in fact present merely impressionistic and often sentimental and self-righteous, if realistically accurate, observations of themselves.

The I-novelists also assumed too easily that to expose oneself was to rebel against society. Their effort, although understood by themselves as an essential part of their struggle to establish the modern ego, became too often merely a personal reaction to their narrow and immediate circumstances, reflecting a fundamental lack of insight into the relationship between the individual and society in the modern age.

The I-novel was originally the product of writers who were influenced by such French writers as Rousseau, Flaubert, Maupassant and Gide, all of whom were concerned with the question of the "I" in society and in the novel. In criticizing the Japanese novelists' superficial understanding of the French writers, Kobayashi Hideo points out that when Rousseau declared in his famous *Confessions* that he would undertake the unprecedented act of exposing himself to society, he was not really concerned with knowing himself or with how he would describe himself, but was concerned with the question of the individual in society. Above all, the Japanese writers never experienced the desperation of Flaubert, Maupassant or Gide over their lack of faith in the possibility of understanding the self and reality with the methods of positivistic science—the French writers were concerned with the question of how to restore the "I" which is killed by positivistic science. For Gide, to believe in the "I" meant to believe in the "I" in his experimental studio. Although the French writers esteemed daily life in art, they did not seek salvation in life itself, unlike the basically ethical Japanese I-novelists, whose primary concern was salvation in life. Kobayashi states that the I-novelists were sentimental and romantic, and that they were fundamentally feudalists with a naturalistic outlook.

The other principal criticism directed toward the I-novel concerned its form and method of expression. The I-novel rejects fictionalization and the mediation of materials through fictional devices. Although the author's limited perspective and firm grasp of the materials convince the reader of the truthfulness and accuracy of the description, the essay-like novel, with its crude, bare facts, hardly entertains the reader; nor does it evoke understanding of people's complex relation to society. It tends, rather, to be boring and irrelevant. Thus it leads to such violent reactions as that of Tanizaki Junichiro, who stated that he loses interest in the work immediately if he senses that the author is going to talk about himself, and who declared that he loves made-up stories with complicated, shocking plots.

In fact, the question of form and the necessity of structural and fictional mediation in the novel became one of the central points of the critical controversy among the young writers of the Taisho period who, dissatisfied with the I-novel and naturalistic writing, began writing neo-romantic literature. The debate carried out between Akutagawa and Tanizaki—which is usually referred to as "the plot controversy"—is typical of the critical disputes which arose during this period.

Dissatisfaction with the I-novel spurred as well the arguments for the *honkaku shosetsu* (the orthodox novel), whose model was the works of European, English and Russian realism. Such dissatisfaction also aroused a critical dispute concerning the difference between the I-novel and the German *Ich Roman,* in which the process of the protagonist's mental growth is traced. Since the critics who favored the *honkaku shosetsu* were usually enthusiastic about the German *Ich Roman,* they could base their arguments against the I-novel only on the grounds that it lacks social scope and fictional devices, both of which the I-novelists deliberately excluded as irrelevant to their endeavor.

The pursuit of the question of the self is a major concern of most modern novelists and a characteristic of the modern novel which distinguishes it from the early nineteenth century and Victorian novels. Although the Meiji I-novel narrowed novel writing to the pursuit of the self, excluding the possibility of social novels, its modernity exists exactly in this fact, that is, in the writers' search for the self in art and indeed in the very act of writing novels during the overly utilitarian Meiji period, when writers were excluded systematically from the mainstream of society's efforts to modernize itself. Although the protected, hothouse situation of the writers' in-group literary circle, the *bundan,* isolated them from the reality of social life and forced them to coil into themselves, it did create a fertile environment for radical and abstract literary and philosophic experimentation. The modernity as well as the fundamental weakness of the I-novel stems, therefore, from the basic isolation of the writer from the reality of society in the process of industrial development, the very situation which characterizes modern Western writers as well.

Underlying the emergence of the genre of the novel, there existed the diaries, confessions and letters in which the private experiences and feelings of individuals are expressed with varying degrees of fictitiousness. The novel as a form and as a literary perspective absorbed these underlying forms of expression. The novel is often a concealed form of autobiography and in particular in modern literature, the modern literary technique of stream of consciousness facilitates this concealment, enabling the author to expose the inner self of the protagonist without necessarily making the work overtly autobiographical, and often resulting in the fusion of dramatic confession with autobiographical confession. Writing about oneself using the device of confession, thus, is an inherent part of the novel as a form. In modern confessional novels, the confession was deliberately isolated by the author and made into the sole basis of the novel. Restoring the self in the novel through confession was a new, if desperate, literary venture for the modern author at a time when writers had become isolated from social reality, and thus the spontaneous relation between the individual and society, life and art, a relation which the novel had taken for granted, had ceased to exist. The I-novel must be viewed then not only in the context of the unique development of the Japanese novel, but also in the context of this overall history of the development of the modern novel in which the self became a major theme—indeed the sole theme—and the artist and art turned increasingly and exclusively to themselves.

In Japanese literature in particular, the I-novel emerged from the naturalistic investigation of the self, but it was modified by and integrated into the romantic tradition of the pursuit of the self, a tradition which was first introduced to Japan through Emersonian romanticism and to which many of the naturalist writers subscribed even before turning to novel-writing. In particular, the confessional I-novel integrates the naturalistic unveiling of the self with the destructive exposé of the inner self inherent in the tradition of Western dark romanticism. Iwano Homei, for example, defined his confessional works as neo-naturalistic and was a proponent of the naturalistic theory of expression which he called "one-dimensional description," yet he was also deeply indebted to the romantic literature both of the West and of Japan in the mid-Meiji period. An ardent admirer of Poe and Baudelaire, he was a proponent of the "diabolism" in the literature of dark romanticism. Thus he embodies the link between the naturalistic unmasking of the self and the diabolical self-exposure inherent in the literature of dark romanticism, a link which is of particular significance in the development of modern Japanese literature. This link between naturalism and dark romanticism in the confessional novel's investigation of the self is responsible for rendering the Japanese confessional novel uniquely modern and is one of the major factors which enabled the I-novel to continue as a dominant form even after naturalism died as a literary movement and when anti-naturalistic—in fact anti-I-novel—aesthetic literature, strongly influenced by the Western decadent literature of Poe, Baudelaire and Oscar Wilde especially, came to be a major literary force in the Taisho period.

Indeed, many of the overly hasty denunciations of the I-novel are due to critics' uncritical identification of the novel with the author's life and their inability to assess the works as part of the emerging modern genre of the confessional novel. Japanese literary criticism ironically has been dominated by a view and method which form a counterpart to the I-novel; it is characterized by the critics' heavy emphasis on the study of the authors' lives rather than their works. Instead of appreciating the works as autonomous works of art, critics have used them as documents which illustrate the writers' minds and lives, reducing too readily every element in the works to the authors' ideas, attitudes toward life and actual experiences. Most of the severest critics of the I-novels failed to analyze the works as separate from the authors' actual life experiences and attacked the authors rather than the works, basing their attacks on their uncritical identification of the authors with the protagonists.

Even if the concern with the author's life is recognized as legitimate in some cases—since the subject matter of the I-novel is usually the author himself or is derived from his life—evaluation and reading of the works solely in the light of the author's life becomes absurd in most cases. Hirano Ken, for example, argues in his essay on Shimazaki Toson's *Shinsei* (New Life, 1920), a confessional I-novel in which the protagonist confesses his illicit love affair with his niece, that the author had no literary or artistic purpose in confessing the love affair in the book but did so in order to end the relationship with her when it became a burden to him. He argues that *Shinsei* thus cannot be understood fully without understanding Toson's real motivation for writing the novel, that is, to rid himself of his niece. Hirano believes that it was only Toson's consistent egotism which caused him to sacrifice others' social life by exposing them in his novels, pretending that he did so for the sake of his art while in fact using art to solve his personal problems.

It is striking that Hirano's criticism lacks completely any analysis of the work itself. *Shinsei* in particular uses the confession of the protagonist as the basic plot, and the confession provides the climactic point toward which the novel develops. Although the story is based on the author's life, the novel assumes the form of an art novel in which the protagonist struggles to bring himself to write a confessional novel (*Shinsei* is the product), and the theme of the novel becomes the process of a man being born anew as an artist. Although Hirano's essay reveals unintentionally the basic structure of the Japanese I-novel (true in particular of the works of T son)—the interweaving of actual life and art in the works, with actual life frequently receiving priority over art and art serving life—his complete failure to analyze the work itself renders the relations between his essay and literary criticism tenuous at best.

One of the central questions of the I-novel is indeed the extent to which it can be appreciated meaningfully without reducing it to the author's actual experiences, and it is to this question that I now turn with an analysis of Tayama Katai's *Futon* (The Quilt), which is considered to be the starting point of the I-novel. I try to show that Katai uses an ironic perspective in portraying the protagonist, creating a critical distance between the author and the protagonist, and that consequently the protagonist emerges as an ironic dramatization of the author, not as a faithful portrayal or subjective self-dramatization. Thus, the protagonist can be viewed as a fictional representation of the Meiji high-collar intellectual or as an ironic representation of the author's self, comical as well as tragic, who is made to typify the Meiji intellectual. According to this reading, the demarcation which is usually made between *Futon* and Shimazaki Toson's *Hakai* (The Broken Commandment, 1906)—treating *Hakai* as a genuine modern novel of realism and *Futon* as a distorted, pseudo-modern I-novel—is not acceptable. Instead, *Futon* is a work close to *Ukigumo* (Floating Cloud, 1888, the "first" modern Japanese novel and a work which Katai himself admired), a work in which the Meiji intellectual, infatuated with the new Western ideas, is portrayed as a quixotic hero with a touch of self-parody on the part of the author. This point will be illustrated in the following analysis of the ironic dual perspective which Katai carefully implants in *Futon* but which is also inherent in the confessional novel in general.

To grasp the dual perspective, it will be necessary to clarify some of the confusions which led critics to read *Futon* exclusively as a document of the author's life. These confusions stem from the very basic fact that the I-novel exists in the "slender margin" between art and life (or fiction and reality) and exploits this fact artistically and intellectually, although sometimes without clear self-consciousness on the part of the author. The fascination of the confessional I-novel, of the masochistic self-exposé of Iwano Homei and Chikamatsu Shuko or of Henry Miller, for example, exists precisely in this artistic exploitation of the "slender margin" between reality and fiction as the sole basis of the genre. Although it is one type of autobiographical novel, the confessional I-novel forms a distinct genre of its own on the basis of its manipulation of the confession and of its ironic perspective in particular, which facilitates both self-search and self-exposé, and both self-glorification and self-parody.

The "evils" of the I-novel are usually traced back to *Futon*. The publication of *Futon* in the fortieth year of Meiji (1907) was received as a shocking event by Katai's contemporaries. *Futon* and Toson's *Hakai*, which appeared a year earlier, mark the beginning of the late naturalism period, a period in which major naturalistic works integrating crude, imported theories into Japanese milieus and themes were produced. *Futon* alone, it has been argued, also determined the direction of the mainstream of Japanese literature in the post-Russo-Japanese-War period by establishing the genre of the confessional I-novel. Thus, Nakamura Mitsuo argues that the I-novel warped and distorted the Japanese literature of realism and that *Futon* played a decisive role in making the autobiographical I-novel the mainstream of modern Japanese literature.

He argues, moreover, that the success of Katai's *Futon* overshadowed *Hakai,* relegating *Hakai* to a state of complete neglect and thus foreclosing the possibility of developing Japanese realism along the lines of the social novel *Hakai.* Even Toson himself followed the path of Katai and after *Hakai* began to write autobiographical I-novels (*Haru* [Spring, 1909], *Ie* [The Family, 1912], and *Shinsei* [New Life, 1920]), until in the end he left the form to write *Yoake mae* (Before the Dawn, 1935), an historical novel describing his father's life and the struggle of the intellectual caught up in the process of cultural dissolution. Thus, according to Nakamura, although *Hakai* and *Futon* are usually recognized as the first modern Japanese novels, the two are almost diametrically opposed in nature; while *Hakai* is a genuine modern novel of realism, *Futon* is representative of the typically Japanese brand of pseudo-modern novel, the I-novel, a confessional, exhibitionistic, egocentric, narcissistic, autobiographical novel.

Toson's *Hakai* is the story of a young man who, belonging to the Eta caste, receives a command from his father not to reveal his Eta identity. Obeying this command faithfully, the protagonist, Ushimatsu, successfully progresses through the educational hierarchy and becomes a teacher in a local town in Nagano prefecture. His colleagues and pupils never suspect his Eta identity. Ushimatsu's self-contempt at his own life's deception increases, however, as he witnesses the merciless ostracism of other members of the Eta caste. His admiration for the Eta intellectual Inoko Rentaro, a humanistic ideologue who openly admitted his Eta identity, increases his desire to lead a life of self-respect and moral and intellectual integrity, and he finally overcomes his fear of social ostracism. At the climax of the novel, Ushimatsu confesses his Eta identity and leaves the school and, in fact, Japanese society altogether.

The central question of *Hakai* is the dilemma of the new Meiji intellectuals who were torn between the desire for an ideal life with moral and intellectual integrity and the feudalistic social values and system which hindered the development of the modern individual ego. The essential tension of the novel, Ushimatsu's fear of social ostracism and his contempt for his own moral and intellectual deception, is that of the modern intellectual of the Meiji period.

Tayama Katai's *Futon* also deals with the inner conflict or dilemma of the new intellectual writer. Takenaka Tokio, a middle-aged writer, feels weary frustration over his lack of success as a writer and his drab marital life. The novel is a bald exposure of his inner struggle over his sexual attraction to his young female pupil, Yoshiko, an attraction which turns into an obsession when he comes to conceive of their relationship as the sole and absolute solution for his life of frustration. Yoshiko is a "high-collar" girl, the new breed of modern Meiji girl. Infatuated with the new Western ideas, she had come to Tokio to be his apprentice, to have him teach her to be a writer.

Takenaka Tokio finds consolation in teaching Yoshiko foreign literature and what the modern woman should be. When he discovers that she is in love with a young man who has given up his religious studies and followed her to Tokyo to become a writer himself, he is tormented by jealousy. Yet he also supports their love, for love is what a new individual must celebrate, and he even defends the young couple before Yoshiko's parents.

His infatuation with Yoshiko is not solely sexual; in fact, his infatuation is with ideas—the new ideas of man, of life and of literature. Katai writes: "Into Japanese literature, which had only Chikamatsu and Saikaku, the great European thought came with the full violence of a typhoon. . . . Every young man aspired to it." Feminine liberation, that is, the creation of the new woman, was one of the imported ideas which inspired Meiji writers. Reading Ibsen to Yoshiko, Tokio urges her to grow out of feudal submissiveness and to develop her modern personality. Free love was central in this female liberation, the establishment of the modern self. Tokio argues the importance of love, yet love of the flesh, sexual love, he rejects as morally wrong.

Tokio's inner conflict is thus dual in nature. On the one hand, he aspires to be a liberated modern individual, and finding life with his old-fashioned, unintellectual wife deplorable, dreams of having an intellectually vital life with the modern Yoshiko. He cannot force himself, however, to act according to his desire and dream, for his moral sense as a teacher, husband and father prevents him from doing so. His romantic ideals meet defeat before his moralistic concern for social integrity, and he emerges as a compromising realist to his own great sorrow.

On the other hand, the novel presents the protagonist as a middle-aged man who, though driven by the dark force of sexual desire, is basically a conventional, feudal moralist. Although he desires Yoshiko himself, he finds her sexual relations with her lover morally unacceptable. He can approve only of spiritual love as necessary for the attainment of the modern self. Thus the inner conflict he experiences is not only between his romantic ideal vision of life and the drab reality of his daily life, and between his uncontrollable sexual longing for a young pupil and his moral social integrity, but also between his Western, radically modern ideals and the old feudal values to which he himself still subscribes. His moral outrage (and subsequent rejection of Yoshiko), which is based on the young lovers' physical relations, exposes his inner feudal self. The most devastating revelation is indeed the fact that the Western ideology of the modern man and the romantic, humanistic idealism to which he enthusiastically subscribed proves to be superficial attire for him. He emerges as a conventional moralist as well as a sentimental dreamer who is unable to accept the burdens and responsibilities of man's daily life.

The novel was accepted as a shocking yet brilliant achievement by Katai's contemporary writers. The main reason for the shock is the bold exposure and description of the protagonist's inner secret, his sexual longing for a young girl. A year before the publication of *Futon,* Katai had written an essay entitled "Rokotsunaru byosha" (Bald Description) in which, rejecting what he called "gilded literature," he advocated the presentation of reality as it is by the one-dimensional, bald description of facts. *Futon* is the implementation of this naturalistic theory of description. Following its appearance, heated debates took place with regard to the legitimacy of sexual description as literary and artistic expression. Erotic realism as a part of the naturalistic theory of literary creation came into focus.

At the same time, the work was considered to be a bold confession of the writer, who was regarded as willing to sacrifice his social respectability, family life and even his relation with his model for the sake of artistic creation. It was considered a confrontation with and even a revolt against the social values confining individuals within the framework of feudal morality. In this way, the novel was accepted as a radically modern novel, a confessional novel through which the writer challenged society fundamentally at the risk of his own social destruction. Katai himself later wrote, using Maupassant's expression in a somewhat different way, that he experienced the pain of peeling off his skin, of exposing himself. It is exactly on these grounds that Nakamura Mitsuo defines *Futon* as the prototype of the confessional I-novel.

It is not incorrect to call *Futon* a naturalistic novel, for we can discern the strong influence of the naturalistic concept of man in Katai's portrayal of the protagonist. Katai presents man as basically controlled by his instinctive drives and conditioned by his social environment. He struggles to control his desire by reason and moral will. In order to understand man as he is, the author unveils the false social mask he wears and describes him as baldly and as truthfully as possible. Before this task of unveiling the truth of human nature, fictionalization or rhetorical devices seem superficial and unnecessary. Indeed, with the publication of *Futon,* the mature era of Japanese naturalism began. The naturalistic concept of man found a congenial genre, the I-novel, the subject of investigation being the author himself. The I-novel supplied a form in which Japanese writers could dramatize their investigation of man in a milieu where a tradition of literary realism was lacking.

What is problematic, therefore, is not the question of the naturalistic elements in *Futon,* but the question of the confession in this I-novel, that is, the relation between the author and the protagonist, and the author's treatment of the protagonist. Nakamura Mitsuo argues that Katai, moved by the protagonist Johannes in G. Hauptmann's *Lonely People,* tried to recreate his own image accordingly without understanding Hauptmann's treatment of his hero. He criticizes Katai for what Tokio is: a sentimental intellectual, fundamentally alienated from the reality of his life, who is infatuated with Western ideas of humanism and the modern self—a romantic dreamer who laments over the drab reality of mundane life yet is himself a conventional, feudal man.

Hirano Ken, on the other hand, disagrees with Nakamura's contention that the protagonist's drama is the direct portrayal of the author's. He states that the author himself behaved perfectly as a teacher and a family man, and that the publication caused no problem to those who were directly related to him or to the events in the novel, for it was evident to them that the story was indeed fiction. He says that Katai's intention was ethical, that the central theme of the novel is the author's struggle for moral growth, for self-reform even at the risk of social respectability. Hirano says that Katai, unlike Toson in *Shinsei,* had no need to reveal or confess his secret infatuation with his pupil. The deliberate confession of his secret desire served only his literary and ethical ambition, his desire to break through the deadlock he felt both as an artist and as a modern man. While Nakamura argues that the hero-author genuinely suffers from the loneliness of modern man in the mold of Hauptmann's Johannes and thus is a self-dramatization as a tragic figure, Hirano argues that the protagonist is the old self which the author outgrew by writing the novel.

While on the surface the point of divergence between Nakamura and Hirano appears to exist in their assessment of the critical and aesthetic distance between the hero and the author, an essential and crucial point in the assessment of the I-novel, in actuality both accept the protagonist as a direct and faithful portrayal of the author, or assume that it was the author's intention to make him so, whether the protagonist is the author in the present or the past. The novel, according to them, is a direct autobiographical confession, and their critical efforts are directed at evaluating the author, present or past, as a person and his motivation for writing the novel.

Here again a simplistic identification of the protagonist with the author exists behind their critical assessment. It is a truism that Katai had both the ethical intention of reforming himself—enabling himself to be reborn as a writer and to break the artistic deadlock from which he felt he suffered—and an urge for self-dramatization, an emotional urge to reveal his inner feelings through his protagonist as a projection of the self. To argue these points can only reveal the motivations of all writers in creating works of art. The central issue is to evaluate the author's artistic treatment of the self, his relation to his art, in terms of the literary or even philosophic perspective of the novel. This is particularly to the point in the confessional novel, in which the treatment of the inner self and the artistic exposé of the self provide the sole structural and thematic basis of the novel.

It is exactly in the ambiguity and complexity of the author's treatment of the protagonist that the main point of *Futon* lies. Indeed, Tokio is portrayed as a hopelessly sentimental intellectual who can see himself only by comparing himself to characters in Western literary works. Western novels are always open on his desk, and when he lectures on them to Yoshiko he is in a heightened or drunken state of consciousness, having identified himself with the heroes of the novels. In his mind he is Johannes, and he believes that his sorrow is that of a high-minded intellectual who has confronted premodern social norms and human relations and met defeat. Tokio believes that he is a tragic hero and is not aware of the fact that his pathetic despair may appear comical to others. He is not himself aware that he has exposed the superficiality of his belief in Western ideas and that his tragic posture reveals only the puerile sentimentality of the intellectual who cannot see himself in the light of reality.

This is exactly how Nakamura sees Katai himself. Basing his opposition on this book, he defines not Tokio but Katai as a product of *bummei kaika* ("the flowering of civilization," a phrase in vogue in the Meiji period), a man who believed joining international society as a modern military power meant the modernization of the Japanese mind. Nakamura states that the comical nature of Tokio's drama, the drama of one who is drunk with ideas, escapes from the author's eye and that to appreciate this novel, it is necessary for the reader to be as drunk with the same ideas as is the author. Thus, according to Nakamura, for the sober reader the book cannot bear critical evaluation.

Actually, however, Tokio cannot simply be Katai, for the author presents a dual perspective for observing his protagonist: Tokio's subjective view of himself and the perspective of ordinary people absorbed in everyday life. Although Tokio himself does not understand fully the complexity of his inner conflicts and above all is not aware of the comical nature of his tragic posture, Katai is aware of it and presents Tokio both from Tokio's own point of view and from this antithetical point of view. Tokio's lack of self-knowledge as well as his genuine suffering becomes the main point of the novel, and according to the dual perspective which Katai presents, Tokio is a comical hero as well as a tragic one.

Tokio's change of mood and obvious high spirits caused by Yoshiko's presence in his house is viewed from the perspective of daily life simply as a nuisance, as an obvious brightening of the spirit any ordinary middle-aged man would experience. Nakamura states that Tokio's infatuation with the young girl is too ordinary for a man of the world to take seriously, and that his inner suffering is not at all intellectual or tragic as Tokio believes it to be. He points out the comical nature of the self-dramatization of an ordinary, mediocre man who thinks his drama is unique and tragic. Yet this is exactly what Katai wishes the reader to think about his protagonist. This is exactly how he is viewed by his wife and his sister in the novel, although they, being old-fashioned women, never articulate their views. His wife and sister, both of whom he ignores or constantly compares to the modern Yoshiko as old-fashioned, ignorant women, consistently present the "healthy," although conventional, realistic viewpoint of daily life and regard him as a big child.

Moreover, Yoshiko is portrayed as she turns out to be—a superficial modern girl who was only attracted to Western ideas as if to fashionable clothes; she was actually interested in men, and her intellectual pretension was an unconscious device to attract them. Katai reveals this true nature of the Meiji "high-collar" girl mercilessly. In fact, Tokio's wife and sister see this from the beginning, and the reader too is led to see Yoshiko from their perspective. Only Tokio is blind to it and continues to defend her free behavior with men (until he finds out that her object of interest is not him but a young man), telling his wife that she does not understand the new woman or the ideas in which she believes.

Yoshiko's lover also turns out to be a vulgar, superficial fellow, and this time even Tokio recognizes it. Although he is critical of the lover, however, he never blames Yoshiko for choosing him. It is his wife who takes the lover's superficiality almost for granted since Yoshiko is herself superficial. Tokio's wife, as if watching the play of children, observes a drama whose ordinariness is hidden from its participants by high language, and it is she who comes to fetch and mother Tokio when, overwhelmed by his misery and frustration, he drinks himself into a stupor. Katai views this drunken, middle-aged man, lying on the floor of the bathroom, through the eyes of his wife, a woman rooted in the business of her daily life and domestic cares. His self-pity and pathetic drunkenness lack dignity and are viewed as such by people in daily life. A stranger passing by Tokio, who is lying drunk in the park and brooding over his loneliness, regards him simply as an ordinary drunkard, a good-for-nothing, while Tokio compares himself to an intellectual hero in Russian literature who is insulted by a crude common citizen.

Tokio's lack of understanding and self-knowledge are also clearly portrayed. Even when he finds out about Yoshiko's sexual involvement with her lover, he does not realize the fundamental shallowness of this "high-collar" girl. On the contrary, he tries to believe that her love is still platonic, while her own father simply laughs at such an idea, taking their sexual relation for granted. When Tokio learns the truth, he believes that they have betrayed the high ideals of love which he advocated, and acting like a severe, moralistic guardian with uncompromising standards, he decides to send her back home. Yet after Yoshiko leaves, he breaks into tears, still dreaming that someday she may become his wife.

Even Yoshiko and her lover Tanaka are somewhat at a loss over Tokio's high language and persistence in advocating ideal, spiritual love. Yoshiko knows too that what Tokio sees in her is not herself as a person but the idea of love, the egotistical projection of his aspiration. Yoshiko knows well, however, that in order to stay in Tokyo, she must please Tokio by pretending to go along with his high ideals. Even when her sexual involvement is revealed, she tries to justify herself to Tokio in terms of the high ideals of the modern woman, while Tokio, torn between his desire to accept her high language and his moralistic indignation over her corrupt love, merely indulges himself in his own misery and loneliness. At this point it is clearly Tokio alone who believes he is the Johannes of *Lonely People*.

The scene in which Tokio sees Yoshiko off describes Tokio's blindness and lack of self-knowledge mercilessly. Tokio, wrapped up in his feeling of sadness, speculates that Yoshiko's mistake, the fact that she is no longer a virgin, might enable her to marry him who is much older and has many children. He then compares his fate to that of the protagonists in Turgenev's novels. He firmly believes that Yoshiko is in the same state of sorrow over their imminent separation; Katai informs his readers that only Tokio did not see that another man was at the station secretly bidding farewell to Yoshiko.

The last scene of the novel depicts Tokio after Yoshiko's departure, indulging himself in inhaling the body odor retained in the *futon* (quilt) which Yoshiko had left in her upstairs room in his house. It is this last scene of the novel which was considered the most shocking.

> When he opened one shutter of the eastern window as he did on the day of separation, the sun's rays streamed into the room. The desk, bookcase, bottles and cosmetic dish were left there as they had been before, and he was caught by the illusion that his beloved was at school, as it had been in the past. Tokio opened the drawer of the desk. An oil-stained ribbon had been left there. Tokio took it in his hand and inhaled the odor. After awhile, he stood up and opened the closet door. Three large chests were packed there, ready to be sent off, and behind these chests was the bedding which Yoshiko used to use—the bottom quilt in pale yellow with an arabesque plant design and a top night-cover with the same design and thickly stuffed with cotton were folded on top of each other. Tokio took them out. The nostalgic odor of oil and the perspiration of the woman made his heart swell. Putting his face to the velvet collar of the night-cover where it was particularly soiled by use, he inhaled to his heart's content the odor of his beloved woman.
>
> Sexual desire, sadness and despair struck his heart immediately. Tokio spread the quilt, covered himself with the night-cover and burying his face in its soiled velvet collar, he cried.
>
> Outside the dark room, the wind blew fiercely.

Nakamura Mitsuo expresses his disgust over Katai and over his sentimental treatment of this folly of a middle-aged intellectual who, after everything is over, still remains without self-knowledge and indulges himself in this pathetic outburst. On the other hand, Hirano Ken argues that the scene is obviously a fiction, that this is not what Katai himself actually did. He says that Katai could not have done this because of what would have happened if his wife had come upstairs and seen him. He also argues that it is highly improbable that a young girl whose father came from far away to take her home would leave her personal belongings behind.

As I have shown, however, *Futon* is not meant to be the author's truthful exposé of his inner self; nor is it simply a moralistic novel in which the author criticizes away his past self by deliberately exposing his inner secret. As Yoshida Seiichi points out, Katai had previously dealt with basically the same theme as that of *Lonely People* in *Onna Kyoshi* (Woman Teacher, 1901), a novel which is not based on his real experience. He had also written a novel called *Shojyobyo* (Young Girl Fanatic) in which a middle-aged, frustrated and sentimental writer who has a "bad habit" of falling in love with young girls is mercilessly parodied. The protagonist, Kojyo, is a sentimental dreamer who, completely lacking self-knowledge, comically becomes isolated from the reality of his life. He is almost the same as Takenaka Tokio, yet is presented clearly as a comical anti-hero. Thus it is not possible to regard *Futon* as a direct dramatization of the author's inner self.

What we see in *Futon* is a dramatization of the sentimentality as well as of the despair and loneliness of the Meiji intellectual who was infatuated with Western ideas and thus was alienated from society; it is a dramatization of the artist's alienation in its tragicomical duality. Viewed from the perspective of daily life, Tokio appears to be a comical, quixotic hero, yet the reader also feels the frustration of a middle-aged writer living in an environment hostile to art and modern ideas, and the despair of a man who fails to find a sense of life. The man who cries in the quilt of the young girl whose very superficiality is the cause of his misery is indeed comical as well as pathetic, and Katai portrays this well. The point of the novel lies in the fact that it is neither a clear self-parody nor an empathetic self-portrayal, but a representation of the Meiji writer in his tragicomical duality. The ironic perspective and use of confession facilitate the presentation of this duality: the novel is indeed an ironic self-dramatization.

The basic structure of such novels as *Futon* is the exposé of the protagonist's inner self—an exposé which destroys his social respectability before the reader. Whether the confession is autobiographical or dramatic is not important, for the reader, forced to hear the confession, is taken into an alliance with the protagonist. The confessor masochistically abandons himself before the reader, who is fully exposed to his embarrassing contradictions or disgusting criminality. The reader's complex reaction to the confession, his disgust and empathy, is caused by the complex psychological relation between the confessor and his audience. Confession, whether it is that of the extrovert or that of the introvert, to use Northrop Frye's terminology, is a masochistic exhibition of the self and thus an aggressive challenge to the consciousness of the other. By deliberately exposing himself, the protagonist becomes a clown, challenging the reader's consciousness but also glorifying his own subjectivity, a subjectivity which is established by the reader's disgust over or moral rejection of his clowning self-dramatization. In most cases it is the reader more than the protagonist himself who is embarrassed by the self-exposé.

The confession of the secret self of the protagonist has been used by various authors, including Edgar Allan Poe, who was influential in Japan, to establish a complex relationship between the protagonist and the reader. Poe's "mad" heroes confess their gratuitous crimes, exposing the perversity of their criminal selves which desire to do wrong for its own sake. Not only do they challenge the reader's moral and social sensibility by fascinating the reader, they also establish their singularity by evoking the reader's sense of disgust at being forced to see something which he does not desire to see. Thus the reader is caught between feelings of disgust over the hero's persistent self-dramatization without self-knowledge and the fascination of glimpsing some forbidden truth about human nature. Poe skillfully draws the reader into the inner world of the protagonist, but at the same time does not forget to remind us that the heroes are mad. Through the use of the confessional technique, therefore, the author introduces dual perspectives for regarding the hero, one involved and the other detached.

Iwano Homei, a writer of confessional I-novels who was greatly influenced by the "diabolism" of Poe and Baudelaire, exploits this existential-psychological challenge of the confession to its extremity in his novels. His persistent exposure of the protagonists' shamefulness, lack of integrity, and self-destructive indulgence in sex is as masochistic and intimidatingly obnoxious as that of Henry Miller's protagonist in *Tropic of Cancer* or Erica Jong's in *Fear of Flying,* yet because of his persistence and extremity, the self-exposure becomes almost an act of conscious self-parody. In the confession, therefore, self-glorification and self-parody, the expression of the singularity of the self and of the universality of human nature, are presented simultaneously. Iwano Homei's novels clarify the integration in Japanese confessional novels of naturalistic self-investigation with the self-destructive self-search inherent in the tradition of dark romanticism. Tanizaki's early works also demonstrate this unique mixture clearly. Dazai Osamu, whose deliberate use of the confession as a fictional device comes very close to that of Poe, also integrates these elements skillfully.

The tragicomedy of the Meiji intellectual, whose radical ideas and Western influence isolated him or her from the reality of contemporary life, is indeed the main theme of *Futon.* This has been one of the major themes of modern Japanese literature. Such major writers as Futabatei Shimei, Mori Ogai, Natsume Soseki, Shimazaki Toson, Akutagawa Ryunosuke and Yokomitsu Riichi pursued it with obsessive concern, revealing both the superficiality and the tragic despair of the Japanese intellectuals in their struggle to modernize themselves. The confessional novel proved to be an effective vehicle for the expression of the theme, enabling the author to present his ironic understanding of the self both as a clown and as a tragic hero. Above all, the dual perspective which the confession itself contains enables the author to present an ironic self-dramatization, a uniquely modern treatment of the self.

Despite its egocentric narrowness and narcissistic obsession with the self, and despite its lack of articulate artistic devices, the confessional I-novel emerged as an extension of the Meiji writers' awareness of realism, as advocated by Tsubouchi Shoyo, and it realizes one extreme possibility of the modern novel. For Meiji writers, isolated from society in the closed world of the *bundan,* the question of one's self and one's relation to art was the sole matter of import. There is no doubt that Meiji writers did not and could not fully understand the struggle of French writers against bourgeois society and against science. Yet the Japanese writers, living in an overly utilitarian yet feudal society that was hostile to art and the artist, shared with them the same isolation and the same concern with the question of the restoration of the self in art. It was only natural that Tsubouchi Shoyo's *hito no nasake* (human feelings) made sense to these isolated artists only as his own *nasake.*

The conflict between art and life is central in their confessional novels. Toson's *Shinsei,* although seriously colored by Toson's desire for purification and self-punishment (bringing the novel closer to *shinkyo shosetsu*), exploits fully the psychological, social and above all literary challenge the confession itself contains. The reader's disgust over the protagonist's egotism stems from the deliberate self-exposure, contrary to Hirano Ken's contention, and the self-righteous insistence that the protagonist's rebirth as an artist will be achieved by it.

Almost all modern confessional novels are in fact art novels, with the protagonist trying to write or to be reborn as an artist. Whether an artist will be reborn, as in the case of Stephen Daedalus, or whether the protagonist continues to be unable to create is irrelevant with regard to the fact that in confessional novels, art and life are curiously interwoven. The confessional novel becomes a form of art novel in which the artist's self-search, the process of making an artist, is the structural basis and major theme. Although the life of the artist is the subject, it is a life justified in terms of art. The art or the seriousness of the protagonist in his attempt to become an artist supplies the fundamental justification for writing about oneself. Thus confessional novels are curiously philosophic and intellectual despite their narcissistic, egocentric perspective.

Yoshida Seiichi dismisses the confession in *Futon* as a pointless display of inner experience, for the protagonist does not suffer from any sense of guilt and his secret infatuation with his young pupil does not merit being called a crime. He argues that in the absence of an absolute God or established religious and social orthodoxy in Meiji Japan, there could not be any serious, uncontrollable urge for confession, except the vague fear of social criticism. Yet in modern confessional becomes not that of a moral sinner seeking religious salvation or spiritual resurrection, but that of an artistic failure trying to be born or reborn as an artist. The loss of imagination or creative sterility is the crime (sin) for which the protagonist seeks salvation. Artistic sterility rather than religious sinfulness drives the artist-hero to confess, and the artistic sincerity or commitment to art justifies the exposure of the inner self as material suitable for art. The Japanese confessional novelists, because they were exempt from religious struggle, were able to attain radical modernity in this sense, presenting the wasteland of art in modern society and the struggle of modern man, for whom art has replaced God as the sole means of salvation.

The interweaving of art and life, one typical characteristic of the Japanese I-novel, is thus a characteristic of the modern confessional novel in general. The protagonist of confessional novels, who is neither an aloof artist nor a realistic social existence, appears tragicomical. He appears to be a comical, quixotic hero without self-knowledge when regarded from the perspective of everyday life, but a tragic hero who suffers enormously in a hostile society and from the artistic sterility caused by it when regarded from the perspective of art. This tragicomical quality itself expresses the isolation of the artist in a utilitarian, industrial society in which art and life are incompatible with each other. Unlike Tanizaki Junichiro, who abandoned life without reluctance for the sake of art, or Shiga Naoya, who assumed responsibility for life by placing it above art, the authors of the confessional I-novels based their artistic creation on this very duality. The confessional novel is a form which enables the author to convert life into art and art into a means of serving the artist. Its raison d'être is its exploitation of the "slender margin" between the real and the unreal, between truth and fiction, and between the author's self-glorification and self-parodization, integrating the artist's egotistical insistence on his artistic self and his awareness of life's retaliation against it.

Irmela Hijiya-Kirschnereit

SOURCE: "Post-World War II Literature: The Intellectual Climate in Japan, 1945-1985," in *Legacies and Ambiguities: Postwar Fiction and Culture in West Germany and Japan,* edited by Ernestine Schlant and J. Thomas Rimer, The Woodrow Wilson Center Press, 1991, pp. 99-119.

[*In the following essay, Hijiya-Kirschnereit considers the intellectual and artistic currents that form the background to Japanese fiction during the forty years since the end of World War II.*]

A common and not necessarily critical understanding of literature presupposes a relationship to general history as well as to the so-called intellectual climate. According to this view, both are "mirrored" in the literary creations of the time, and on the other hand they are, in some way or another, also influenced by history and virulent ideas. So far, so true—but how to establish these relationships in more concrete terms? This [essay] first sketches aspects of the intellectual climate which appear to be of special relevance to our focus of concern, namely the corpus of literature dealing with the war experience. It then proceeds to propose a set of paradigms for screening and classifying the works and closes with observations on some widespread patterns of perception and attitudes in the Japanese literature dealing with the war experience.

THE GENERAL INTELLECTUAL CLIMATE IN JAPAN AFTER THE WAR

First, what does "intellectual climate" mean? Let us assume that this climate can be grasped through the observation of a succession of topics in public discussions on matters concerning society, the focus of media interest in certain issues, or the controversies of intellectuals and other public figures.

Despite the war damage and the shortage of food, housing, and all the materials necessary for printing, the publication industry revived almost immediately after the termination of the war in Japan. Since the early 1930s, rigid censorship and an extensive system of "advisorship" and control had marked Japanese literary creations, allowing nothing but the most conformist texts to appear. Even works as apolitical as Tanizaki Jun'ichiro's *Sasameyuki* (*The Makioka Sisters*) were held back after the first episodes had appeared in *Chuo ko ron* in January and March 1943, on the ground that they ran counter to the national interest in time of emergency; Tanizaki's translation of the classic *Genji monogatari* into modern Japanese also was censored "because of the irregular ties it described in the succession to the throne." Left-wing writers of the so-called Proletarian School had been forced to "convert" (*tenko*) as early as 1933, and with the authorities' grip tightening on all spheres of public life, including literature, writers readily succumbed to the pressure in one way or another. The majority seemed to have regarded it as their duty to cooperate with the war effort in their field. They voiced no opposition to the system, emigration was out of the question for Japanese writers, and only rarely did they consider taking up jobs other than writing in order to avoid compromising. Only a few of the leftists, such as Kurahara Korehito, preferred going to prison rather than "converting."

Writers eagerly volunteered to be sent abroad as war correspondents, and except for perhaps the established figures of Nagai Kafu, who lapsed into silence, and Tanizaki Jun'ichiro, who kept his cooperation to a minimum, Japanese writers and poets seemed to have felt obliged to support what they, too, regarded as the national cause. The streamlining of the press and the "voluntary dissolution" of important general magazines such as *Chuo ko ron* and *Kaizo* serve as further landmarks to indicate what Donald Keene has termed the "barren years," or, in the terminology of Marxist writers, the "dark valley" (*kurai tanima*) in the literary and intellectual history of modern Japan.

The emperor's broadcast on 15 August 1945, declaring Japan's acceptance of the terms of the Potsdam Declaration, caused different reactions in the population, but, while mourning and harboring deep feelings of shame at their nation's first defeat in history—even in the writings of intellectuals such as the author Dazai Osamu, "shame" (*haji*) is the central expression when describing his reaction at the end of the war—the overwhelming majority of Japanese felt relief that the war had come to an end.

Within a few weeks, the Japanese people underwent a transformation of attitude, the rapidity and extent of which surprised members of the occupation so much that they found it hard to trust and feared a possible resurgence of militarism later. But these fears proved groundless. Busy with the task of sheer survival, people had turned away from matters of public concern, and the breakdown of the oppressive system of control inspired the press to write in an increasingly bold tone. The first new literary magazine, *Shinsei* (*Vita Nova*), appeared, along with others temporarily suspended during the war such as *Shincho* and *Bungei shunjo*. The following year saw a boom of already established or new magazines, beginning with *Chuo ko ron* and *Kaizo* and the newly founded *Sekai, Ningen, Tenbo, Kindai bungaku,* all starting in January 1946, as well as *Shin Nihon bungaku* and *Sekai bungaku* following in March and April, respectively.

It may come as a surprise that in view of the radical changes in the political system and in the daily life of the people—and the abolition of the system of pressure and political-ideological claims on literature—literary historians insist on the power of continuity rather than postulating a new beginning. Much evidence supports this view. Those authors who had been established before the war resumed their writing and publishing activities seemingly undisturbed by any sense of obligation to "explain" to themselves and others what had happened in the meantime. Continuity is also obvious in the ease with which the *bundan,* the literary establishment, revived, and in the "surprising tolerance" granted to writers who had closely cooperated with the militarists. A beginning can be claimed only for that generation of younger writers who started their careers in the years after the war, the so-called *sengo ha* (Postwar School), but this fact sets the "beginning" off from any mere reorientation.

The writers generally appreciated the new air of freedom. Kawakami Hajime is reported to have observed that "the Americans and British had bestowed in the course of a few months freedoms that the Japanese could not have won unaided in ten or even twenty years." Others such as Takami Jun expressed shame that this new liberty should have been given to his country by an occupying power, and even the critical Nakamura Mitsuo, who in his history of contemporary Japanese literature chooses to speak of freedom after the war only in quotation marks and who insists in other places in calling postwar literature the "literature under the occupation" (*senryu ka no bungaku*), admits that a new freedom in political and daily life formed the basis of a new and enlarged role of literature in society.

THE DEBATE OVER WRITERS' WAR RESPONSIBILITY

The question of war responsibility and guilt of writers was first put on the agenda in the inaugural edition of another literary magazine, *Bungaku jihyo,* in January 1946, by Odagiri Hideo, who attacked the poet Takamura Kotaro as one of the foremost figures in the world of poetry to carry "responsibility for the war" (*senso sekininsha no iwaba dai ikkyu*). The June 1946 issue of *Shin Nihon bungaku,* organ of the writers of the former proletarian literature movement, featured, again on Odagiri's proposal, a blacklist of twenty-five names of colleagues accused of intensive propaganda for militarist goals. *Kindai bungaku,* founded by Marxist members but less orthodox than *Shin Nihon bungaku,* also brought up the question, this time voiced by Hirano Ken, Ara Masato, and others, but on the whole it seems to have been inseparably connected with Marxist writers who praised their liberation by the Allies, condemned their nonleftist colleagues who had willingly cooperated with the militarists from a moral standpoint, and sought to justify their second "conversion" immediately after the war.

The discussion seems never to have reached a substantial level, touching political or moral issues, but mainly ran to global accusations and reproaches, these being overshadowed by constant hostilities between the two Marxist groups, culminating in Nakano Shigeharu's verdict on the *Kindai bungaku* critics Ara Masato and Hirano Ken as "inhuman and anti-human." Other writers tackled the question by attacking what they saw as the self-deception of the so-called democratic literary movement (leftist literature). Such criticism was voiced by Yoshimoto Takaaki and by Fukuda Tsuneari, who, in an article on "Literature and War Responsibility" ("Bungaku to senso sekinin") in the February 1947 issue of *Asahi hyo ron,* declared that he did not believe in anything like war responsibility for writers, adding that "the attitude of those who pursue the issue of war responsibility has nothing to do with literature."

Needless to say, this dissociation of politics and history

from literature, which as an implicit idea was widespread among intellectuals of the time even if it was not voiced in such a clear-cut manner, was also prevalent during the war, when a writer such as Nakajima Atsushi, while being sent to Micronesia by the government in 1941, could maintain that war and literature were completely separate and unrelated. Other intellectuals and writers, such as Kobayashi Hideo or Dazai Osamu, self-indulgently declared themselves simple citizens without political interests or education, who could not have been expected to see through the machinations of the militarists.

The debate over war responsibility soon ebbed away in literary circles, but the question was approached from a more fundamental angle in the works of the political scientist Maruyama Masao. He related the problem to Japanese political mentality in general as it was formed by centuries of social and intellectual history, and his contributions had exerted wide influence on critically minded Japanese intellectuals since the late 1940s. Maruyama made important statements about the nature of Japanese political mentality.

On the whole, the early postwar years were tinged by a strong progressive current, which also reflected the fact that Japanese intellectuals had regained contacts with the international scene. The "almost completely uncritical acceptance of Marxist ideology" during these years, however, drove Donald Keene to suspect that the writers might have been motivated by the vague anticipation that sooner or later a socialist or Communist government might take over in Japan.

Political developments, however, did not move in the expected directions. Although leftist groups obtained prestige and influence in the immediate postwar period, and the GHQ actively supported a coalition government of Socialists and leftist Liberals, the coalition suffered a severe defeat in the January 1949 elections. Under the strong influence of American policies, priorities shifted from democratization to reconstruction, paving the way for what the political scientist take Hideo recently described as an "anti-communist coalition between militant liberalism and traditional authoritarianism."

From all that we know about it today, censorship under the occupation cannot have represented an important factor in the development of intellectual life. To describe its effects in Jay Rubin's phrasing,

> [It] may have come close to destroying the Kabuki theater and briefly inconvenienced a few determined believers in the imperial myth; it certainly did delay some of the more intense expressions of outrage at the use of the atomic bomb, and it reduced the number of mixed couples holding hands in the literary landscape. None of this qualifies as a general or systematic distortion of postwar literature.

That this view differs markedly from the opinion of many Japanese literary historians is a point to which I must return later.

Under the liberal reactionism (*Otake*) of 1948-49, more often termed reverse course, and a government that increasingly represented traditional authoritarianism under the Yoshida cabinet, the economy made substantial progress toward recovery, further stimulated by the Korean War (1950-53). The prevailing mood in the early 1950s was one of optimism and privatism. People enjoyed consumption, and while one faction of intellectuals, the progressive liberals, were discussing the merits and demerits of Stalinism and while others were still attempting to understand what was by this time termed Japanese fascism (Maruyama Masao contrasted it with German fascism to explain its specific character), the wider public had long accepted the return to office of wartime leaders. The selection of Kishi Nobusuke, former member of the Tojo cabinet, as prime minister in February 1957 was only the most conspicuous case.

The question of writers' wartime responsibility was raised once more in 1956 in a study by Takei Teruo and Yoshimoto Takaaki, *Bungakusha no senso sekinin* (*The War Guilt of Literary Writers*), but, again, their research dealt not with writers in general but only with those left-wing representatives who had been the focus of the discussion in 1946 and 1947. Yoshimoto took them to task for not facing the problem of collaboration among themselves. Leading figures of the democratic literature movement whose task would have been to explain themselves evaded the issue, while the rest of the members of the group merely closed their eyes during the decade after the war. Thus, according to Takei and Yoshimoto, they failed to face up to their wartime responsibility as well as their postwar responsibility; moreover, their avant-garde stance caused the failure of the "democratic revolution" (*minshu kakumei*). This seems to be the last contribution of some consequence to the issue under the heading of war guilt and the responsibility of writers.

The Intellectual Climate of the 1960s and 1970s

The general public meanwhile enjoyed a period of high economic growth and increasing international attention with popular highlights such as the Tokyo Olympics in 1964, which the Japanese public viewed as the most conspicuous sign of international recognition. The nation also appears to have regained national confidence. At the same time, the 1960s and early 1970s represented a phase of sociopolitical activism in the form of mass demonstrations and citizen movements. The mass protest against the signing of the U.S.-Japanese Security Treaty in May and June 1960 was supported by a majority of intellectuals, as were the protests against the U.S. involvement in the Vietnam War and the support of that involvement by the Japanese government between 1965 and 1973. Student riots in the late 1960s, the fierce resistance of Sanrizuka farmers to the construction of

Tokyo International Airport at Narita since 1966, the antimodern movement, and antipollution movements of which the Minamata case in the late 1960s and early 1970s is the most widely known, dominate the picture of Japan during these years.

Most of these citizens' movements appear to have parallels in other countries and thus to have international aspects as well as having concrete economic and ecological motives. Japanese cultural historians such as Tsurumi Shunsuke, however, tend to emphasize the indigenous, premodern roots of these citizen movements. According to Tsurumi, these movements were issue oriented and thus disappeared with the issue. This characteristic seems to set them off, despite surface parallels, from phenomena like the "'68 generation" in Western Europe, which tackled more fundamental issues from an idealistic and socialist perspective. Issue orientation in the Japanese case also implies a spontaneous reaction to concrete problems. It does not grow out of a heightened political awareness as Tsurumi writes:

> Only when he [the ordinary citizen] feels his life affected by the political situation, or his life style hampered by it, does he rouse himself from political apathy and voice his political view in public. The citizen's political interest is in contrast to the political interest of the professional activists whose livelihood depends on being politically well informed.

Writers took an active part in all these movements, and their activities were reflected in their literary works or essays, which often became bestsellers and gained the status of authentic condensations of the *Zeitgeist,* as did Oda Makoto's *Nandemo mite yaro* (*We will look at everything,* 1961) or Shibata Sho's *Saredo warera ga hibi* (*Those were the days, my friend . . . ,* 1963). As the historical distance from the war years lengthens and the interest of the public turns to more immediate contemporary issues, this phase of Japanese history is hardly addressed. Those who do speak about the issue treat it in a clearly affirmative, noncritical manner.

One focus is the reevaluation of the Tokyo war crimes trials, which, according to the leftist liberal Tsurumi, were never accepted by the Japanese people but did serious harm to their notion of justice, although at the time of the occupation, they had to suppress their protests. Now, according to Tsurumi's slightly curious phrasing, "in the wake of the prosperity since 1960 there has been a surge of compassion for the victims of the War Crimes Trials." As a matter of fact, documentary novels on wartime officials such as *Yamamoto Isoroku* (*The Reluctant Admiral: Yamamoto and the Imperial Navy,* 1965) by Agawa Hiroyuki, or Shiroyama Saburo's *Rakujitsu moyu* (*War Criminal: The Life and Death of Hirota Koki,* 1974) were widely acclaimed and won coveted prizes. Kinoshita Junji's play *Kami to hito to no aida* (*Between God and Man,* 1972), first staged in 1970, links Japanese doubts about the legitimacy of the Tokyo war crimes trials with the issues of the dropping of the A-bomb over Hiroshima and Nagasaki and the U.S. involvement in the Vietnam War. Thus, the roles of the accuser and the accused were reversed. Writers who argued for a relationship between the contemporary Vietnam experience and the Japanese role in World War II usually reasoned in this way, using Vietnam as a means of Japan's exculpation.

Another, more extreme example for such a positive reevaluation of the war experience is Hayashi Fusao's *Dai Toa senso kotei-ron* (*In Support of the Greater East Asian War,* 1964, with a sequel published in 1965), which revived the wartime argument that Japan simply functioned as a liberating force against Western imperialism in Asia. According to Tsurumi, these views were widely acclaimed in the Japan of the 1960s. Hayashi, by the way, is also notable as an example of a writer of originally Marxist inclinations who, after the war, never revoked his *tenko.*

THE SWING TOWARD CONSERVATISM AND NIHONJINRON

Whether because the issues of the citizens' protests were settled, as Tsurumi maintains, or because people generally swung toward conservatism after a phase of political idealism and failed aspirations for direct democracy, the late 1970s and early 1980s saw a turning away from humanitarian idealism and solidarity toward more introspective activities. This development occurred not only in Japan but in other advanced nations as well. On the politico-economic plane there was an "almost simultaneous restoration of economic liberalism and traditional conservatism." Around the mid-1970s, popular theories about the so-called national character, which are now known as *Nihonjinron,* appeared in such great numbers that they began to be regarded as a genre per se. This new interest in explanations and definitions of "Japaneseness" was prompted in part by Japan's opening to the world and the need the Japanese suddenly felt to understand themselves and to make themselves understood to the outside world, especially because international criticism tended to satirize the nation as "Japan, Inc." and to characterize its citizens as "economic animals."

Self-explanation as self-defense is, however, only one part of the reason for the new interest in Japaneseness. Growing pride in the nation's economic successes and international standing also provided a new perspective. One important motif in many *Nihonjinron* texts is the refutation of the unconscious or conscious Amero-Eurocentrism in Japanese thinking—or what the authors of popular studies on the origins of the Japanese people, their language, their cultural history, and the "Japanese" brain *held* to be the ethnocentric values of Western nations, which the Japanese had long mistaken for universal ones. Although some of these Japanese criticisms hit the mark, the effect in many cases merely represented a simple exchange of ethnocentric values. If the possibility of universals is denied from the beginning, the task remains only to substitute "genuinely Japanese" attitudes and values for real or supposedly Western ones.

An example of how this attitude has developed since the mid-1970s is the publications of the linguist Suzuki Takao, from his best-selling *Tozasareta gengo: Nihongo no sekai* (*A Closed Language: The World of Japanese,* 1975), down to his most recent *Buki toshite no kotoba* (*Language as a Weapon,* 1985). Suzuki starts with a critique of the history of his discipline and the unconscious Eurocentrism in subject matter and methodology, and then widens his scope to include statements about how to improve the Japanese standing on the international stage. His public influence has grown considerably over the years, as his tone has grown more and more militaristic.

Suzuki is, however, only one prominent spokesman in the chorus of authors dealing with the Japanese language in the form of a *Nihonjinron.* The language is commonly regarded as the core of Japanese culture, symbolizing and representing the essence of Japanese history and race (note the contamination of all these different entities!). Therefore the degree to which the language issue, including the recent discussion about Japanese as a foreign language, dominates public discourse should not surprise us. Roy A. Miller has rightly identified this preoccupation with language as embodying the Japanese essence as a central "modern myth."

As for the issue of World War II, since the mid-1970s a series of publications that document the war experience from the perspective of average citizens have appeared. Tsurumi Shunsuke lists sixteen of them between 1974 and 1983. To this list should be added the series of fifty-six volumes compiled by the youth division of the Buddhist lay organization *Soka gakkai,* which appeared between 1974 and 1979 under the title *Senso o shiranai sedai e* (*To the Generation Which Does Not Know War*). The aim of the latter and many other documentary collections is not to deal with the question of how the war could have happened, but to record the sufferings of the ordinary Japanese in order to show the "inhuman nature of war, with honest appeals that the folly must not be repeated."

Wartime sufferings of ordinary people are also a popular subject for TV dramas. Thus, the serialized TV version of the novel *Oshin* centering on the life of a woman called Oshin and a deserter from the Japanese army in the supporting role for the portion of the story that takes place in the "Fifteen-Year War" (between 1930 and 1945), achieved an unprecedented popularity rating of more than 58 percent in 1983. Although these and other popular dramas of the period intended no critical investigation or enlightenment but were aimed at a sentimental identification, Tsurumi points out that there have been consistent (although unsuccessful) efforts on the side of the ruling party and the government to keep the Fifteen-Year War from being treated as the subject of TV plays.

THE GENERATIONAL MODEL FOR POSTWAR LITERATURE

Japanese literary histories resort to the generational model when classifying postwar literature. They also maintain this division into "generations" when discussing the literary approach to the World War II issue, and the model is extended to include the intellectual scene as a whole. For example, Hashikawa Bunzo identifies four patterns of approach to the issue alongside these generational borders:

> 1. One group, which would correspond to the generation of already established older writers in presentations of literary history, is the generation that has continued to symbolize authority during and after the war, a group supposedly unaffected by war.
>
> 2. The second generation is the one that, according to Hashikawa, had finished its higher education during the war, was critical of the "meaningless" and "pathological" war, eagerly awaited its end, and regarded Japan's defeat as a liberation.
>
> 3. A slightly younger age group, called the *war generation* (*senchu ha sedai*) by Hashikawa, regarded war as a given "natural" fact and as an "everyday myth" (*nichijo no shinwa*). Innocent and young as they were, almost all of them became "unconscious nationalists." Defeat at the end of the war deprived them of all their ideals.
>
> 4. The next generation in Hashikawa's model had no direct relationship with the war experience whatsoever. No reorientation was necessary for this group, which espoused a "healthy materialism and a contractual pragmatism" (*kenzenna materiarizumu, keiyakuteki go rishugi*) and took the initiative in the students' movement.

Hashikawa's model reflects the popularity of generational explanation patterns in modern Japanese history while containing the same blind spots that I have noted elsewhere. (Note, for example, that his model has no room for a "generation" of convinced supporters of the war.)

Despite the obvious biases of the generational model in literary and intellectual history, and despite the fact that it is not an age group model in the strict sense, I suggest a modified version for classifying the literary response to the World War II experience, because it appears useful—and the frequency with which this model is employed seems to back me up. The fact that within modern Japanese culture the war issue is approached predominantly on an individual level, with personal experience being the most important factor, speaks for itself. I propose the following "generations":

> 1. The older generation of established writers, who are, according to popular opinion, aloof,

untouched, and unaffected by the war. Among them, however, we can distinguish between the ones who refused to cooperate (Nagai Kafu and possibly Tanizaki Jun'ichiro) and the rest, who engaged in cooperation to different degrees, such as Kawabata Yasunari, Takamura Kotaro, and Masamune Hakucho. A strategy of this generation in coping with postwar reality was, as it had been with many of them during the war years, an escape into aestheticism and an idealized picture of a "purer" or premodern Japan. To give only one example: Kawabata reports himself to have been completely absorbed by his reading of the *Genji monogatari* when the war ended and, not without an element of self-stylization, he writes, "I might well be surprised at the disharmony between me and the train, loaded with the baggage of refugees and victims of the bombings, making its way irregularly through the charred ruins, in terror of another bombing; but I was even more surprised at the harmony between me and a work a thousand years old."

2. The generation of the activists, an age group old enough to be recruited for "patriotic services." We could distinguish several subgroups, such as straightforward supporters, like the "Romantic School" (*Nihon Roman-ha*); former Marxists who underwent conversion (*tenko*); and a group of writers who started their literary career after the war but were old enough to have taken an active part in the war (whether "voluntarily" or forcibly). This third subgroup makes up the bulk of what is usually subsumed under the heading of the *Postwar Group* (*sengoha*), and for them, the war experience forms the central concern in their literature. The best-known names in this group are Noma Hiroshi, Takeda Taijun, Haniya Yukata, Ooka Shohei, Umezaki Haruo, Nakamura Shin'ichiro, and Shimao Toshio.

3. What is—slightly misleadingly—termed the *War Generation* (*senchuha*) is the next younger age group of writers who grew up during the war and were indoctrinated by the militarist thought and value system but were not yet in position to play an active adult part in the war. This group includes writers such as Mishima Yukio, Abe Ko bo, or the so-called *third generation* of new writers, to whom, as Matsubara Shin'ichi contends, war was not of such a big concern, as they showed that "even during war, daily life continued without being directly affected by the idea of war" and as they "got through war as a simple individual."

4. The generation of writers who at the end of the war were still children includes those who are occasionally called "engagés" such as Oe Kenzaburo or Kaiko Ken. Some of this generation began to publish at the end of the 1950s, but as a whole, the times when they started their literary careers and their motifs and approach in dealing with World War II vary to an even greater degree than in the case of the older generations. Writers such as Kono Taeko, Kaga Otohiko, or Morimura Sei'ichi fall into this category.

5. The generation born after the war does not figure at all in Japanese generational models dealing with writers' attitudes toward World War II. It is presupposed that, for this generation, the war is of no immediate concern and interest. In fact, Japanese literature appears to contain no works of this generation in which they question their fathers about what they did during the war or about "how it all could happen," as is common in the German context. Writers of this generation, such as Murakami Ryu, treat the topic of war abstractly, as in his *Umi no muko de senso ga hajimaru* (*Across the Sea, a War Begins*, 1977).

The generations demonstrate different motivations for dealing with war. The highest degree of relative uniformity, notwithstanding individual differences in ideological outlook, appears to be in the second generation group, where the prevailing motif is the immediately felt necessity to explain, to oneself and to others, and self-justification. At the same time, the period in which these authors have written about their war experiences is relatively short, limited mainly to the immediately postwar years.

The third group deals with the subject over a longer time and across a wider spectrum of accents, their contributions on the topic concentrating on the 1950s and 1960s. The fourth generation shows an even wider variety in time of writing—from the late 1950s to the 1980s—motivation, and topicality.

THREE MORE PARADIGMS

The second paradigm I propose is a topical one, differentiating the writings according to subject matter, such as:

1. War, especially battlefield experience overseas and in Japan;

2. Civilian life during the same period overseas and at home;

3. The end of the war and the capitulation with the large subgroup of so-called A-bomb literature (*genbaku bungaku*);

4. The aftermath of war in postwar everyday life as experienced in physical hardship and value reorientation, generational conflicts because of the war, and the war crimes trials, among other things. Needless to say, this paradigm can be further differentiated.

The third paradigm distinguishes the degree to which the writing focused on the war experience. There are three main categories:

1. War as the central topic;

2. War as a secondary or side aspect; and

3. War as omission or ellipsis (*Ausblendung*).

The second group of works is a large one, containing, for example, many works of the first generation of writers. Kawabata could serve as a convenient example again. In many of his works wartime memories enter into the stories of the characters, frequently and significantly enough to make the reader realize that they constitute a secondary topic. (Again, a certain discrepancy can be noted between a writer's statements about his personal attitude and his literary creation.) This pattern also appears frequently in the works of a writer like Mishima. In the novel *Kinkakuji* (*The Temple of the Golden Pavilion,* 1956), the author's systematic and deeply meaningful allusions to the war in the story, which deals with a young acolyte who burned down the temple in Kyoto in 1950, are so convincing that a Japanese critic classifies the novel as one dealing with the war experience. Nevertheless, *Kinkakuji* belongs to the second category according to our paradigm.

The third group should not escape our attention, especially because although this group is probably substantial in number, the Japanese usually do not take it into consideration when dealing with this topic. Many works that deal with the time of war without referring to war, shutting out this reality, can be found in the narrowly personal genre of *shisosetsu.* Kato Shuichi, in commenting on two famous examples, finds a relationship to the time: "They are of course solely concerned with the author's personal life, not with the fate of the Japanese Empire. However, Dazai did write *Setting Sun* at the time that the sun of the empire was setting and 'unfit to be human' when Japan was found to be unfit to be an independent nation."

The last paradigm I propose differentiates the (prose) genre. Whereas the interest in literary studies clearly lies in the realm of so-called pure literature, in the case of literature dealing with the World War II experience, Japanese critics tend to be more flexible than usual and to include other genres. Therefore it is important to take into account the following groups:

1. *"Junbungaku"* (pure literature, or literature proper). This group is by far the largest one.

2. *"Taisho bungako"* (mass literature). Famous examples are the popular novels *Ningen no joken* (*Human Conditions*), a work in six volumes by Gomikawa Junpei, and *Senkan Yamato no saigo* (*The End of the Battleship Yamato,* 1952) by Yoshida Mitsuru.

3. Personal records (collections of letters, diaries), which, by their publication, gain a status similar to that of literature. Thus the famous collection of letters by student-soldiers who died in the war, *Kike, wadatsumi no koe* (*Listen, Voice of the Sea,* 1949) is treated as a piece of "antiwar literature" in Odagiri's article on "Senso bungaku."

4. Documentary accounts, occasionally fictionalized, also have to be taken into account such as Morimura Seiichi's three-volume novel *Akuma no hoshoku* (*A Devil's Feast,* 1982), dealing with Japanese war crimes of a secret special unit using prisoners of war and civilians in Manchuria as guinea pigs for cruel medical experiments, crimes that have not been brought to court. The book clearly was intended to enlighten and was well researched, but according to Kato Shuichi, many may have read it out of a cruel voyeurism comparable to the "outlet" function ascribed to SM comics in Japan.

The last example reminds us that it is important to note carefully the possible gaps between an author's intention and the work's intention, the critic's interpretation of the work (which may be a projection of the declared author's intention) and the critic's own bias, or countless other factors besides it, and the actual impact the work leaves with the typical reader or several representative groups of readers. Or, to give another example: Oe Kenzaburo's early short stories dealing with war and occupation experiences from the perspective of a boy are usually regarded in Japanese scholarship as fine examples of a decidedly critical stance, the author being known as a representative of a consciously political and anti—A-bomb group of intellectuals. A closer look at the works in question, however, reveals that a far stronger element is his veneration of vitality and power—in fact, the story could well be set in a time other than in the war or occupation.

PATTERNS OF CONTINUITY

The literary work and its reception form the two focuses of the most meaningful approach to the subject of "World War II and Its Legacy in Literature"—at the micro level of one or a group of works, analyzed according to their textual strategies, their "philosophy" and value system, and their effects. Of course, it is vital not to lose sight of the macro level, for even an intratextual analysis necessitates relating elements of a work to inter- or extratextual contexts. Only careful microanalysis will prevent us from producing the stereotypical views that are prevalent in much of the research on the subject so far. There are, however, promising new approaches that dig below surface opinions. In a recent contribution on A-bomb literature, John Whittier Treat shows that Hara Tamiki, a writer famous for his story "Natsu no hana" ("Summer Flowers," 1947), had already developed certain topics, above all, the theme of death, in his writing at an earlier stage, so that he was able to adapt his patterns of description and interpretive schemes to the subject of the atomic holocaust.

It is beyond the scope of this chapter to present practical analyses, but I want to draw attention to some patterns of description and interpretation that can be found in so many examples—regardless of their possible classification within the paradigms presented earlier—that they appear typical for the large corpus of pertinent literature as a whole. I sketch them under the following headings:

Sentimentalization;

Strategies of fatalism: depersonalization and derealization (*Entwirklichung*);

Aestheticizing; and

Transforming history into nature.

Anyone familiar with modern Japanese literature will also know its sentimental traits, which are particularly characteristic of its central genre: the autobiographical *shishosetsu,* which concentrates on a phase in the private life of a person, a "focus figure" that the reader identifies with the author. An autobiographical approach, and a basically sentimental mood, is also typical for most Japanese fiction dealing with the war experience. This mood is also evident in the personal accounts of ordinary citizens collected as documentaries on the war. Reliving one's sufferings by telling them, savoring one's past pains, and expressing quiet resignation add up to a basically affective, emotional attitude that leaves no room for reflection. The result is therefore a purely individual description of an instant of personal suffering, from which the historical dimension is shut out. The strictly apolitical stance of even those texts written to document war as history is symbolized by an example from the two-volume *Waga ko ni nokosu—Senchu, sengo boshi no kiroku* (*To Leave Behind to My Child—Records of the Lives of Mothers and Children in War and Postwar Times*, Tokyo, 1978). The reports of the forty mothers include photographs of the author, in one of which the author is shown posing in front of the Imperial Palace, an obviously inadvertent irony, considering the suffering reported in the story.

The prevailing personal approach to war being emotive and sentimental, the reaction to disaster is one of accepting it as fate. This reaction is not only implied in the attitude but sometimes put into words directly. In the story "Sayonara," by Tanaka Hidemitsu, for example, the author displays a clear consciousness—and thus a degree of detachment and self-criticism—toward this fatalism: Originally published in November 1949, "Sayonara" features an autobiographical account of events when the author was a soldier fighting against the Chinese. The title is explained right in the beginning as being symbolic of the Japanese attitude, for, whereas in most European and other languages, salutations at parting imply a positive attitude, as in "au revoir" and "auf Wiedersehen," the Japanese "sayonara—if things are like this, (we will have to part)" has a resigned, "defeatist" coloring.

The protagonist himself demonstrates this attitude in an incident involving an attractive young Chinese soldier, the only one not killed by the Japanese, who usually did not make prisoners of the Chinese. They used the fourteen- or fifteen-year-old boy as a porter. One day when the soldiers marched on a cliff, the boy, as the only act of revenge possible to him, threw his load into the depth and jumped after it, thus committing suicide. The protagonist witnessing this scene likens the dark spot disappearing to a young eagle and shouts, "Sayonara," behind him, "I only shouted 'sayonara.' (This is fate. Young man, it cannot be helped. If this is so, I am sorry.)"

Having become a "fatalist by necessity" (*yamu o enu unmeironja ni natte ita*), the protagonist reacts to the sudden death of thirty young girls hit by a bomb in a factory with the same, "extremely simple" (*kiwamete assari*) "sayonara" ("I only felt this was their fate").

The narrator is a double fatalist, so to speak, for he attributes this fatalism to a mental attitude deeply ingrained in the Japanese, which becomes clear as he further reflects on the deaths of four young Chinese whom he has just killed by himself: "It was not my hands who have killed these young men, it was fate called war that felled these youngsters." And he continues with a comparison of nations:

> The French, who can say "au revoir" or "bon voyage" at parting and who do not believe in war as an inescapable natural calamity, could continue their resistance unbroken under the Nazi occupation, but the miserable people of Japan, who even when parting from a lover, can only say "sayonara," could not put up any resistance against the takeover of power of the military clique.

This remarkable statement shows that even the slightly ironical reference to his own fatalism is combined with self-justification.

Instead of depersonalization, as in the foregoing example ("It was not my hands . . . "), we may encounter "translation" into the sphere of unreality to cope with reality. Tamiya Torahiko's story "Ashizuri misaki" ("Cape Ashizuri"), first published in October 1949, ends with a scene in which the narrator witnesses a drunken man, a former member of a suicide squad called *Ryu kichi,* stumble through the streets at night shouting his rage against his superiors, the emperor, and all those who told him to die. On hearing the voice gradually fade again as the man disappears in the darkness, the narrator muses, "I suddenly thought that in this voice, I heard the voice of the old pilgrim. It was a dream—everything was a dream. Where is truth which is not a dream? I tried once more to follow the voice of Ryukichi which could not be heard any more but then the street lights which had flickered weakly, suddenly went out."

Aestheticizing is another widespread strategy, for which numerous examples offer themselves. As a conscious attitude it is practiced by Kawabata Yasunari, of whom Nakamura Mitsuo writes that the more Japan "is made to take the position of a loser" (*makeinu no tachiba ni tatasarereba sareru hodo*), the more he feels driven to stress the beauty of "Japan's soul," and this beauty, according to Nakamura, is embodied in the figure of Kikuko in Kawabata's first postwar novel *Yama no oto.*

In literary practice, there are many examples of the

"beauty in destruction" pattern of description—with Mishima Yukio, in a series of novels down to *Akatsuki no tera* (*The Temple of Dawn,* 1970), and in the A-bomb literature. Ota Yoko, in her *Kaitei no yo na hikari* (*A Light as if at the Bottom of the Sea*), the first literary text to be published about the A-bomb, which appeared on 30 August 1945, writes of the "beauty" of the sacrifice with which Hiroshima was decorated at the end of the war. The "horrible beauty" of an air-raid scene is evoked by Kaga Otohiko in his *Kaerazaru natsu:* in consonance with Japanese conventions, he contrasts the sight with cherry trees in full blossom.

Transformation into aesthetic and erotic categories can go to extremes, as in the case of Mishima Yukio, who imagines the relationship between a Kamikaze plane and the ship to be destroyed as penis and vagina. But other writers show this fascination with destruction as well. Sakaguchi Ango, for instance, has repeatedly written of the "beauty of people submitting to fate."

The fourth pattern of description—transforming history into nature—amounts to an extension of the others: The attitude of regarding war as a category of nature is also characteristic of many descriptions of war. For example, Tanaka Hidemitsu's protagonist called war an "inescapable fate resembling calamity" (*tensai ni nita fukahi no unmei*). A resigned aestheticism has marked the Japanese attitude toward natural catastrophes. Shimizu Ikutar recalls the sight of those inhabitants of Tokyo who, after the Great Earthquake of 1923, sat within the ruins. Even those who had lost their houses and families felt an indescribable inner calm as they watched how the setting sun colored the sky over the horizon of destruction.

It is interesting to note that similar photographs, showing families sitting in the ruins regarding a newly discovered nature with a wide horizon after the bombings of the capital can be found in documentaries of Sh wa history, suggesting that the attitude was very similar. The attitude is often likened to the aesthetic resignation, informed by the escapist and pessimistic medieval Buddhist outlook of Kamo no Chomei, who, in his *Hojoki* (*An Account of My Hut,* 1212), enumerates natural calamities like fire, earthquakes, typhoons, and famines, wonders about the ephemerality of the world, and finds peace in the heart of nature in his lonely hut.

It must be more than mere coincidence that I recently came across a comment on Ibuse Masuji's famous A-bomb novel *Kuroi ame* (*Black Rain,* 1966), which states:

> The ancient Greek notion of Fate pervades the atmosphere of the novel. At the same time, we feel that the reason why Ibuse was able to draw this hellish picture of sufferings of people after the atomic explosion without losing his composure, was partly because he viewed it with the same passive resignation he has shown towards unusual calamities beyond human control in *Aogashima Taigaiki* (*Aogashima Tragedy,* 1934) and *Gojinka* (*The Sacred Fire,* 1944). Therefore, it is possible that his attitude towards the atomic bomb calamity, expressed in *Kuroi ame* (*Black Rain*), *is not fundamentally different from his attitude towards natural calamities.* The novel may be an angry one: the inhumanity of using an atomic bomb seems to be amply revealed through the sheer weight of the facts recorded; however, these facts may have been produced with the *resignation to fate characteristic of Japanese sensibility.* If so, what Ibuse Masuji has presented in this novel . . . is the view of a nihilist observer who reacts with the traditional Japanese resignation to fate. In this sense Ibuse in *a spiritual descendant of Kamo no Chomei* . . . , who had a traditional penetrating understanding of the transience of the world.

> Certainly, there are other attitudes and literary approaches to the subject of war and its aftermath in contemporary Japanese literature, but the cluster of attitudes just sketched is undoubtedly a widespread pattern to be found over the whole four decades. I believe that it corresponds to a number of basic patterns in Japanese intellectual life, which can only be hinted at here.

Van C. Gessel

SOURCE: "Postoccupation Literary Movements and Developments in Japan," in *Legacies and Ambiguities: Postwar Fiction and Culture in Germany and Japan,* edited by Ernestine Schlant and J. Thomas Rimer, The Woodrow Wilson Center Press, 1991, pp. 207-23.

[*In the following essay, Gessel discusses major fiction writers and literary movements that emerged in Japan after World War II.*]

Japanese fiction after the occupation is in many ways an extension as well as a rethinking of the two major types of writing that dominated prewar composition—specifically, the works by the socially and ideologically committed proletarian authors (*Puroretaria bungaku sakka*) and the predominantly asocial, semiautobiographical personal narratives (the infamous *shi-shosetsu*). There was little cross-pollenization between these two rival factions; the proletarian writers considered the *shi-shosetsu* writers to be needlessly parochial, overweeningly narcissistic, and dangerously removed from the political and social concerns that were already tearing apart the fabric of experimental democracy in the Taisho period (1911-26). For their part, the creators of autobiographical fiction, with some justification, looked upon the leftist writers as novice artists who were sincere enough in their convictions but inadequately trained in literary technique to be able to present their social messages in anything other than an embarrassing framework.

The polarization between committed social activism and equally sincere artistic purism carries over into the postwar era. The past forty years or so of Japanese literary developments can be described in terms of the constant interplay between the reconstituted versions of these two camps. The postwar Marxist writers represent what might be styled the "social trend" in postwar literature. These are authors who initially highlighted the moral horrors of the war that had just ended and then went on to define a positive path of involvement for the writer in the creation of a new Japanese society. They came to the task of writing with a vision of the potential for social change through imaginative art. These writers, known in Japanese literary jargon as the *Sengoha* (après-guerre faction) were displaced for a time—significantly just as the occupation ends, around 1952—by young writers who were clearly cut off from social and intellectual activism, and who represent what might be called the "private" trend in Japanese fiction. These writers, the first wave of whom are labeled the *Daisan no shinjin* (the third generation of new writers), produced a literature of anxious tension: a placid, well-constructed, modernized surface undercut by a negative vision of internal collapse and despair. As writers, they functioned outside the borders of society, restoring Japanese artists to their traditional relationship with the majority; in their withdrawal, they also returned to—although later I suggest ways in which they simultaneously made significant modifications in—the autobiographical mode of writing.

Even though the third generation of new writers is loosely fashioned here as a group, it is important to observe that literary groupism in Japan—which, in one form or another, was one of its most consistent features in the classical and medieval periods and a mainstay in the development of modern literature from the 1880s through the occupation years—had largely collapsed as a governing influence in the creation and discussion of literature by the early 1950s. The *Sengoha,* the Marxist writers who made their debut shortly after the defeat in 1945 with their own literary journal, *Kindai bungaku* (*Modern Literature*), established and maintained a mutually consistent set of literary goals for themselves, however they may have interpreted and modified those goals individually.

In the third generation, however—the writers who were brought together essentially at random less than a year after the end of the Allied occupation—the sense of unity, shared purpose, and even shared intellectual experience that had characterized the *Sengoha* was gone. Just as their writings began to call into question the spiritual and emotional foundations of the resurgent Japanese social system, their lack of cohesion as a literary group echoed the anxiety they felt just at the time their nation began the march toward economic domination in Asia.

The question of how the war and the defeat were reflected and interpreted in Japanese fiction of the postwar period becomes a complex one, then, because the initial response to those devastating incidents came almost immediately (*Kindai bungaku* published its first issue in January 1946) from the *Sengoha* writers, primarily men in their thirties who had a tantalizing brush with leftist philosophy and existentialism before they were eradicated from Japan by ideological censorship of the 1930s. The war had come between the *Sengoha* and their moral idealism, but the interruption had been temporary, and once the shackles on free speech were removed with the coming of the occupation, they swiftly and easily turned back to their intellectual roots and wrote literary critiques of the war in an attempt to point out the error of militarism and the hope that awaited Japan through a socialist revolution. The first interpretation of the war that was offered to the postwar Japanese reading public was one filled with revulsion for the immediate past, but one necessarily dripping with mea culpa toward the question of war responsibility: although the Japanese readily embraced the belief that they had been too easily duped by militarist propaganda, they resisted grappling with the larger questions of national guilt. But that initial interpretation was also filled with anticipation for the political phoenix that could be resurrected from the ashes of defeat.

THE EARLY POSTWAR SETTING

It is important to recall, however, that this message of optimism was being broadcast to a nation that was largely in ruins. By the time the war ended, more than 3 million Japanese had been killed, almost a third of the population had lost their homes, and industry was operating at one-quarter its previous level of productivity. There were 5.5 million soldiers to be demobilized and another 3.25 million civilians to be repatriated from abroad. And it was no simple matter for Japan to cope psychologically with the first defeat and foreign occupation that their nation had experienced in recorded history. It is understandable that the Japanese populace did not immediately rise to its feet to respond to the call to Marxist revolution: there were so many people too weary and underfed to have the energy to get to their feet, either figuratively or literally.

It is similarly necessary to factor in the style with which General MacArthur administered the occupation: the imperial manner in which he forced democratic reforms on the Japanese government had a certain appeal for the Japanese. MacArthur easily fit into the mold of surrogate rulers who governed in the name of the emperor (the occupation planners wisely decided to keep Hirohito in place to provide legitimacy for their reforms), and the general's popularity in Japan reached such a peak that there was widespread shock and mourning when he was dismissed by Truman. Finally, by 1950 the policies of the occupation had considerably improved the overall quality of life in Japan; hence the extra economic punch provided by the outbreak of war in Korea that summer proved to be mere icing on the cake. It must have seemed to many in the early 1950s that the goals of the Marxist writers were being reached, not through proletarian revolution but through the firm but benign administrative orders that emerged from MacArthur's GHQ.

Because the Japanese occupation was carried out under American direction and thus avoided the carving out of zones of influence that divided Germany, a mood of quiet optimism was evident among the people. When the occupation formally ended in 1952, many in Japan could easily have felt that they had emerged the better for what had transpired over the past seven years. The financial shot-in-the-arm provided by the Korean War, along with the occupational institutions put into place, set the stage for what would be the beginnings of the Japanese "economic miracle" by the late 1960s.

THE EARLY POSTOCCUPATION LITERATURE

It would be natural, then, to expect that the literature that appeared in the wake of the occupation would capture this mood of exhilaration, or at least of hope. But we are accustomed to finding that literature betrays such facile expectations, and the Japanese case is no exception. Most of the writers who began their literary careers at just about the time the occupation troops were withdrawing and the economy was starting to build up steam were young men who had been born a few years on either side of 1920. Few of them had been old enough to absorb Marxist or any alternative philosophical response to the growing militarism of their country, and many had been plucked out of college to serve in the war effort before they had developed any solid concepts of selfhood. In essence, they gave their youth to the war. Almost without exception, those who returned from the battlefield to become the writers known in the 1950s as the third generation of new writers went through utterly bizarre experiences in the war.

Kojima Nobuo (born in 1917), for instance, received his teaching credentials to become an instructor of the English language just six months before Pearl Harbor. When the bombs fell on Honolulu, English became a proscribed subject in Japan, and Kojima fell victim to the draft. He was shipped off to northern China, where his commanding officer ordered him to forget every word of English he had ever learned. In the spring of 1944, however, he was transferred to Beijing to decode transmissions intercepted from American units in the Pacific; when it became evident that Japan would be defeated, Kojima's new commanding officer ordered him to remember all his English, so he could teach his superiors useful English phrases such as "I am not a war criminal." Meanwhile, Kojima's original unit was shipped off to the Philippines, where every single man was killed in the fighting at Leyte.

Kojima's experience was by no means extreme for his age; Shimao Toshio (1917-86), another writer who is sometimes linked with the third generation, was made commander of a suicide torpedo boat squadron stationed on an island north of Okinawa. He spent almost a year there, training under cover of darkness for his mission of death. But that entire year consisted of nothing more taxing than the simple act of waiting. Orders to prepare for launch finally came—on 14 August 1945. The men donned their battle gear, armed their torpedoes, and waited for the final order to launch. That order, of course, never came and Shimao was charged with the duty of reporting to his men that the imperial broadcast, which none of them heard, had ordered unconditional surrender rather than a fight to the death. It comes as no surprise that the engines of war continue to race beneath the surface of Shimao's fiction, whether he is writing about his kamikaze experience or about his wife's going insane after the war.

Armed (or disarmed) with such experiences of war, the new writers of the 1950s could only feel bewildered about the meaning of the war, uncertain about the import of the occupation, and decidedly unconvinced about the desirability of bowing down to the newfound gods of capitalism, democracy, or communism. One writer from this generation, Yoshiyuki Junnosuke, has written about the hesitance that he and his contemporaries felt toward all the new ideas that were being bandied about in Japan:

> The [*Sengoha*] writers spent their youth in league with communism, but mine was spent very differently. As a result, my concerns are unlike theirs. During the war, I couldn't bring myself to sacrifice my life for the sake of any single philosophy, even if its ideals might be realized at some point in the future. Many willingly made that sacrifice, but the very thought repelled me. The idea of becoming a sacrifice gave me no pleasure. I considered myself an "individualist"—not an egotist, certainly, but something more refined. In those days, the word "individualist" was considered equivalent to "traitor," but I bravely used it to describe myself anyway. . . .
>
> Communism enjoyed a great wave of popularity shortly after the war. . . . But the innate resistance I felt toward that philosophy was the same resistance I had felt toward the militarism of the war years. I could not bear the thought of putting on another uniform when I had just taken off the previous one and thereby liberated my individuality. Neither did I care for the thought of martyring myself for the sake of some ideal that might possibly be realized in some distant future.

Because of the ambivalence born of their experience and the mistrust they felt toward any new direction Japan might take, a gulf opened between these writers and their society. The nation embarked on an aggressive, single-minded pursuit of economic expansion; but the authors whose careers commenced contemporaneously with the period of growth were "plagued by an inability to act purposively. . . . For them, the postwar period—which should have been an age of liberation—was instead a time to which they were ill-suited. . . . They could not believe in the outer world, in lofty, absolute philosophies, or even in the pull of their own emotions."

THE IRONIC SHI-SHOSETSU

The literary form that was appropriated by this third generation of postwar writers was, understandably enough, the comfortable, experientially centered *shi-shosetsu* (the autobiographical "I"-novel). But there is a significant difference in the perspective that they bring to a recounting of their private lives. Partly because of the absurdity of their wartime experiences, partly because of their philosophical naïveté, and thanks also to their perception of the gap of incongruity that was opening up between themselves and their society, the third-generation writers brought to the *shi-shosetsu* a vital element that it had been lacking in the prewar period: irony. So while the popular media journals began extolling Japan as a nation efficiently rebuilding in the wake of war, the fiction in the literary magazines turned to describing the process of destruction that was perceived to be taking place within the genteel walls of middle-class civilization. The immediate benefit for literature is that the narrating persona of fiction has become schizophrenic: he or she can relate personal experience with the same degree of sincerity and rhetorical flourish as the prewar writers, but a narrational doppelgänger lurks somewhere in the text, functioning as a second set of eyes to view events from a separate perspective, or as a mocking voice uttering contradictory opinions from between the lines of the discourse. It is no coincidence that *Sukyandaru* (*Scandal,* 1986; translated 1988), the most recent novel by Endo Shusaku (born 1923), a leading member of the third generation, has as its central subject the question of split personality, of evil doppelgängers who mockingly challenge the sincerity of people who are striving to live a moral life.

This ironic, split narrational perspective is most obvious in the novella *Kaihen no kokei* (*A View by the Sea,* 1959; translated 1984), by Yasuoka Shotaro (born 1920). The narrator is a young man whose father has returned from the war with no skills and apparently no desire to provide a livelihood for his fractured family. This pathetic man's wife is finally driven to insanity and death by the bleak circumstances of postwar Japan (and, more specifically, by her son's willful destruction of the bond that links him to her). Through the eyes of the accusing son who blames his father for all this collapse, we see a portrait of a failed patriarch who can no longer guide and sustain his family. But even as we are given that view, Yasuoka subtly provides us with another perspective on this family, and we are able to discern the faint outlines of a father who has struggled desperately to find means to feed an unappreciative wife and son, and who nurses his wife with the utmost solicitude and tenderness once she has passed beyond the boundaries of sanity. The voice of the son in the text condemns the emotionally crippled father, but a second voice beneath the surface of the narrative implicates every member of the family for the severing of the ties that once held them together.

Another novel that makes use of an architectural metaphor to bring the internal collapse of postoccupation Japan into ironic focus is Kojima Nobuo's *Hoyo kazoku* (*Embracing Family,* 1966). The work centers on a physical structure—a house that belongs to the Miwa family. The husband, Shunsuke, is a scholar steeped in the ways of Western civilization, and on the surface he appears to have all the enlightened knowledge he needs to govern his life. But as a human being, he is very much like his trouble-plagued house. That structure is the dominant image throughout the novel; in fact, although one prominent Japanese critic has described *Embracing Family* as the most "anthropocentric" Japanese novel of the modern period, I am inclined to argue that the house is the true protagonist of the work, and that it has taken over as the central "consciousness" because Shunsuke has, in his "enlightened" way, abrogated his responsibilities as master.

The main action of the novel involves several attempts by Shunsuke to rebuild the family house, always at the instigation of his wife, Tokiko. Equal weight is given to the act of "housecleaning." But, tellingly, all the energies of this family are focused on the external concerns of building and cleaning, while inside their whited sepulchre there is an extraordinary amount of moral decay. Shunsuke, caught up in lecturing on contemporary Western family mores and building a house that is described as resembling "a country villa in the highlands of California" (even though it ends up a creaking nightmare of leaking roofs and malfunctioning "foreign" appliances), is not even aware of the fact that his wife has been having an affair with an American marine who remained in Japan after the occupation. Even after the housekeeper tells him of the affair, he does not know how to respond. "What should he say? What should he do? The answers to these questions had not appeared in any book he had read, and no one had ever taught them to him."

The ironic chasm that Kojima gouges into this text suggests an extreme reticence on the part of the narrator. Shunsuke, as in the quotation, is perpetually asking the crucial questions; but Kojima's narrator stubbornly refuses to provide any answers. This third-person narrator essentially mocks Shunsuke's inability to make moral judgments; as a result readers find him ridiculous, frustrating, and pathetic. At the same time, Kojima forces us to fill in ourselves the answers to the questions that Shunsuke poses, or to declare the novel morally vacuous. And observing our struggles alongside Shunsuke's stands the house, solid on the outside but crumbling within.

THE THIRD GENERATION'S INTERPRETATIONS OF THE WAR

The interpretations of the war afforded by the authors of the third generation are naturally far more cynical and personalized than those of the *Sengoha.* If the prototypical *Sengoha* treatment of the war—say, Noma Hiroshi's *Shinku chitai* (*Zone of Emptiness,* 1951)—had as its aim "to analyze the responsibility of the intellectual and the revolutionary . . . to depict the Japanese people as a whole during the war," the standard third-generation novel about the same war made no claims to universalization of experience. The soldiers of their war novels are confused, isolated individuals whose response to the call to arms is neither political nor intellectual; it is, in fact, difficult even to call it "emotional." The reaction is essentially physiological, with chronic diarrhea appearing as a recurrent motif.

The ambivalence of these unwilling warriors can be seen in Kojima's writings, especially in the short story "Hoshi" ("Stars," 1954; translated 1984) and the novel *Bohimei* (*Epitaph,* 1960). The protagonist in both these works is a Japanese-American who has the misfortune of being in Japan when the war breaks out and ends up being drafted to serve in the Japanese army. Perhaps the most effective literary moment in the two works comes at the very end of *Epitaph*: the soldier Tomio (Tom), who looks very much like an American, is sent with his battalion to fight in the Philippines. There, his commander dresses him up in an American uniform and sends him out as a decoy to lure enemy soldiers into ambushes. Tom naturally has mixed feelings about engaging in this bizarre activity and being exploited in this way (much the same way, in fact, that Kojima's English-language talents were exploited by his military superiors). After it becomes evident that the Japanese resistance has failed, the battalion is dispersed and Tom wanders alone through the jungle. He strips off the American uniform, then removes his Japanese uniform. He stops short when he sees a rifle pointed at him from the undergrowth. He cannot see whether the hands holding the weapon belong to an American or a Japanese, and at this stage he is not sure which to consider as enemy and which as ally. He shouts, "Don't shoot! I'm not Japanese! And I'm not American, either!" Then he reaches up to rip off his uniform, but finds himself naked, left with only the noncommittal skin he was born with. That scene epitomizes much of the confusion and anxiety that beset a generation of Japanese during the war, and represents the postwar response to that experience.

OTHER RESPONSES TO THE WAR EXPERIENCE

Let us turn now from the private, visceral reactions to the war experience evident in the writings of the third generation to two other categories of response: (1) the eulogistic and chroniclelike attempts to capture certain key moments of the war and (2) the abstract Marxist-influenced philosophical fiction of the *Sengoha* group mentioned earlier. The categories are less distinct than this breakdown implies, however, because even when works in the first category deal with major battle incidents, such as the sinking of the great warship *Yamato,* they tend to be either very personal records of loss, as in Yoshida Mitsuru's *Senkan Yamato no saigo* (*Requiem for Battleship Yamato,* 1952; translated 1985), or detailed, sensitive portraits of military figures as important for their private doubts about the war as for their heroism. The prime examples of this latter category are the three lengthy, moving biographies of admirals written by Agawa Hiroyuki (who is sometimes classed with the third generation), *Yamamoto Isoroku* (1969; translated as *The Reluctant Admiral* in 1979), *Yonai Mitsumasa* (1978), and the highly acclaimed *Inoue Seibi* (1986).

The most important pieces of war literature in the second category include Noma Hiroshi's *Zone of Emptiness* and many works by Ooka Shohei (1909-87), a student of French poetry and fiction who was drafted to fight in the Philippines and spent nearly a year in an American prisoner-of-war camp. His literary recreation of that experience, *Furyoki* (*A Prisoner's Story,* 1948), is a work of remarkable philosophical detachment. But his most harrowing portrait of the war is in the novel *Nobi* (*Fires on the Plain,* 1952; translated 1969), an unsparing portrait of the manner in which war destroys the last vestiges of individual humanity. Like Kojima's *Epitaph,* this novel deals with a solitary soldier who wanders the jungles of the Philippines at the end of the conflict, but his withdrawal from the human race as a result of his experience is so extreme that he decides he can only unite himself with his fellowmen once again participating in an act of cannibalism, which is described in imagery that links it to the Catholic communion. Ooka suggests, in a literary transformation of his war experience that makes considerable demands on the Japanese reader, that it would require some extraordinary spiritual transmutation to reintegrate a soldier into peacetime society, but the horrifying form that this metamorphosis assumes drives his protagonist mad, and he writes his war reminiscences from an insane asylum.

THE QUESTION OF WAR GUILT

Few of the works in any of the three categories of war writings from the postwar perspective treat Japanese war atrocities, either to deny or defend them or to reflect on their meaning. In fact, the bulk of the war literature with which I am familiar has precious little to do with the confrontation between Japanese and non-Japanese within the framework of war. The great majority of writings deal with the internal conflicts, whether they be among members of the same battalion or within an individual. That tendency, of course, can to some extent be attributed to the long-standing tradition in Japanese prose to focus tightly on the narrow, introspective moment and the individual confessions, but in isolation from their social contexts.

I do not wish to suggest here that Japanese writers have avoided the question of war guilt. Rather, I do not see much consideration of national culpability; instead, there is considerable retrospection about individual responsibility. In fact, I believe that the intellectual responses to war that emerged from the Marxist *Sengoha* writings are something of a cultural aberration, whereas the gut-level, personalized, and even trivialized reactions from the third generation are more in keeping with the traditions of Japanese literature—and, more important, in keeping with the rhetorical potentialities and limitations of the language—in the twentieth century.

THE RETREAT FROM MARXISM IN POSTOCCUPATION JAPANESE LITERATURE

It is, then, somewhat ironic that Marxist criticism has dominated the postwar discussions of the war while the literature itself has focused primarily on private responses to that event. Some of the chief tensions within the Japanese literary establishment have arisen from the disproportionate influence that Marxist critics have exercised in the literary journals. As Donald Keene notes,

> Postwar literary critics were largely Marxists, and they tended to exaggerate the importance of writers of their own persuasion. One is likely therefore to obtain the impression that left-wing writers were much more significant at this time than any of the older generation. . . . In general the literary world of the immediate postwar period, and even much later, was sympathetic to left-wing causes. This was partly because of the opprobrium attached to the right wing, partly by way of reaction to the popularity of the American way of life among ordinary, nonintellectual Japanese. The *Asahi shimbun* (the newspaper most widely read by intellectuals), the government-owned radio and television stations, the leading intellectual magazines—all, to a greater or lesser degree, espoused left-wing causes.

It is a simple matter to identify writers and intellectuals of the past forty years who have been sincerely sympathetic for left-wing causes. It is far more difficult, however, to isolate those who have not become disillusioned with the extraordinary factionalism of the progressive political parties in Japan, or who have sought some philosophy other than dialectical materialism to guide their thinking after an initial flirtation with Marxism. As I noted earlier, virtually all the writers of the *Sengoha* generation were proclaimed Marxists when they began their literary careers. A number, including Noma Hiroshi and Abe Kobo, became members of the Communist Party. One must struggle, however, to find a writer who has not been expelled at least once from the party, while many others withdrew either formally or informally. Most were also closely in sympathy with the wave of existential philosophy that was sweeping the postwar world. Yet within a decade or so, many of these young activists had cooled toward leftist philosophy, and some of the more important of them began looking for some way to reintegrate themselves into their Japanese spiritual heritage through a study of Buddhism, or into the revitalized Western tradition through conversion to Christianity.

Initially, the jarring and tearing and soul-crunching of their war experience had put them on the offensive, turning them against native tradition in all its forms and placing into their hands convenient, foreign weapons of intellectual battle at a time when it seemed likely that the Japanese past had been obliterated. Once the occupation had run its course, however, and Japan appeared to have put its pieces back together again, many of these writers searched for some means to plug themselves back into a tradition that had proved strong enough to survive all the blasts of war. Noma Hiroshi, whose earliest postwar stories, including "Kao no naka no akai tsuki" (Red Moon in Her Face, 1947; translated 1962), argue that the war and defeat had made it impossible to form satisfying relationships with any other human being, by 1960 was absorbed in the writing of a novel, *Waga to wa soko ni tatsu* (*There My Pagoda Will Stand*), which he described as an attempt to "accurately analyze the Buddhism which even now lives and throbs deep within the hearts of Japanese." Without that study, he maintained, "I would be unable to understand most Japanese or to obtain a clear insight into what controls their actions." And Shiina Rinzo (1911-73), a Communist as well as the most Sartre-like writer in Japan in the late 1940s, converted to Christianity at the end of 1950.

The same process can be seen in the second generation of leftist writers, most prominently represented by Oe Kenzaburo (born 1935). Oe's political and social commitment is evident in works such as "Sebuntiin" ("Seventeen," 1961) and the documentary essay collection *Hiroshima noto* (*Hiroshima Notes,* 1964; translated 1981). Disappointed by petty factional conflicts both in the leftist political movement and the Hiroshima peace movement, Oe in 1964 abandoned the overt political methodology of his earlier writings after his first child was born with significant brain damage. In his novel *Kojin-teki na taiken* (*A Personal Matter,* 1964; translated 1969), Oe adopted the autobiographical mode of fiction and transformed it into a medium of social and moral drama. In virtually all Oe's fiction since that time, he presents the very private image of a deformed baby, born with a brain tumor that makes him look as though he has two heads. But Oe's staunch social commitment will not allow him to let the image remain a personal, autobiographical one. It is as though he sees an image of the Hiroshima mushroom cloud superimposed over the grotesque tumor on his baby's head, and his child is transformed into an innocent victim, whose torment Oe has described in the following words: "Could any conscious state be so full of fright and hurt as perceiving pain and not its cause, and perceiving pain only, because an idiot infant's murky brain was apparently to go unsoothed?" The child, unaware of the sources of its own agony, can only open its mouth and form the shapes of a silent cry (one of the images in Oe's 1967 novel, *Man'en gannen no futtoboru,* translated in 1974 as *The Silent Cry*).

In the cavern of that wordless moan echo the tormented voices of those who suffered and perished at Hiroshima, and in his own original way Oe is presenting his readers with a moral choice. We have the memory of Hiroshima placed before us, in the same way that the baby's father has to confront his deformed infant. Do we embrace that memory and accept responsibility for our guilt, as the father does in Oe's *A Personal Matter,* or do we attempt to obliterate the memory altogether, as the father does in "Sora no kaibutsu Aguii" ("Aghwee the Sky Monster," 1964; translated 1977) by conspiring with the doctors to kill his baby?

By equating the personal and the social and making our choice one of global life or death, Oe breathes a new and profound significance into the I-novel. In his best writing, Oe can be movingly intimate and personal in the stories that derive from his own experience, and at the same time publicly and politically forceful in delineating the implications that his private experience has for all of us in the wake of the A-bomb. Here again, for the Japanese writer at least, Marxism appears to have limited value as a literary tool until it is transmuted through personal experience that renders it palpable in the Japanese context.

THE VIETNAM WAR

I can only briefly treat the manner in which the Vietnam War makes its appearance in Japanese literature, and that view will be oblique. The most important artistic treatments of that war, which certainly aroused important debate and controversy in Japanese intellectual circles, may come not from the mainland but from the writings of Okinawan novelists who debuted in the late 1960s. The Akutagawa Prize, the most important new-author award in Japan, was first given to an Okinawan author in 1967: the recipient was Oshiro Tatsuhiro, whose short story "Kakuteru pati" ("Cocktail Party," translated 1989) examines the frustrating relations between Okinawans and the American troops stationed there. A second Okinawan author, Higashi Mineo, received the prize in 1971 for "Okinawa no shonen" ("A Boy from Okinawa," translated 1989), which concerns a young boy who decides to steal a boat and leave Okinawa for the open sea when he can no longer stand being evicted from his bedroom so that the neighborhood prostitutes (for whom his parents pimp) can service American soldiers. Neither story overtly protests the Vietnam War, but both are sensitive depictions of the way in which the American military presence in Japan, of mounting strategic importance to the U.S. effort in Southeast Asia, erodes the moral fabric of the community and renders life on Okinawa unbearable for some.

REVIVAL OF THE CLASSICAL LITERARY TRADITION

Another key feature of postwar literature in Japan is the manner in which the classical heritage has been resuscitated and perpetuated through the efforts of some of the finest writers of the century. Here again, there was some initial speculation after the war that perhaps the defeat and occupation had been sufficiently traumatic to sever all ties with classical culture. One prominent critic of the 1950s, Kuwabara Takeo, wrote, "I do not think much effort should be spent maintaining traditions that have been transmitted without any relation to modernization. The beauties of old Japan that early foreign residents admired will gradually disappear." Although it may be foolhardy to try to give full credit to one person for turning the tide and reestablishing a link with traditional literature, it is tempting to single out Tanizaki Jun'ichiro (1886-1965) for that distinction, and to select his long novel, *Sasameyuki* (*The Makioka Sisters,* 1942-48; translated 1957), as the crucial work in that process of revitalization.

What Tanizaki achieves in *The Makioka Sisters* is a denunciation of the very concept of history by forging a link between postwar literature and the aesthetic heritage that stretches back a thousand years to *The Tale of Genji.* The points of convergence between Tanizaki's novel and the *Genji* have almost nothing to do with plot; it is rather in the sense of time, the perception of the seasons, the centrality of aesthetic values, and the importance of annual observances as a measure of who the family is and how they get along that these two works are joined. And it should be borne in mind that Tanizaki began work on *The Makioka Sisters* shortly after he completed his own translation of *Genji* into modern Japanese, a labor of love in which he engaged three times in his career (twice after the war).

The subsumption of literary tradition in the postwar period can be divided into three large categories. First are the modern translations of classical works by prominent authors. Included here are Tanizaki's *Genji* and another significant version of that tale by the leading woman writer of the postwar age, Enchi Fumiko (1905-86). A score of other major novelists have produced their own modern translations of the classical text that reverberates most persuasively for them; some examples are Yoshiyuki Junnosuke's renditions of Ihara Saikaku's seventeenth-century erotic masterpieces, *Koshoku ichidai otoko* (*The Life of an Amorous Man*) and *Ko shoku ichidai onna* (*The Life of an Amorous Woman*).

A second category includes modern, often cynical, adaptations of traditional works, including Mishima Yukio's modern No plays, Dazai Osamu's retelling of Saikaku's stories about the merchant class, and the reshaping of traditional myths by Oe Kenzaburo, Nakagami Kenji, and others.

Third are the independent creative works that clearly owe a measure of their inspiration to specific classical works, but go far beyond the bounds of simple retelling or adaptation. Tanizaki's *Makioka Sisters* belongs to this category, as does the informal trilogy of novels by Enchi Fumiko, which demonstrates a clear indebtedness to *Genji.* Her *Onnazaka* (*The Waiting Years,* 1957; translated 1971) adopts the male-centered power structure that lies at the heart of *Genji* and examines the ways in which the perpetuation of such a structure in the modern period affects her female protagonist. *Onnamen* (*Masks,* 1958; translated 1983) explores the vengeful spirits of wronged women and the ways in which they have their revenge. And *Namamiko monogatari* (*Tale of a False Shamaness,* 1965) is itself set in the tenth-century court of Heian, recreating an idyllic love relationship between the emperor and his chief consort, but surrounding that pure association with so many layers of falsehood, betrayal, and political manipulation that it becomes clear that Enchi believes such tales can no longer exist in our contemporary, cynical age.

The "new subjectivism" that became the hallmark of Western fiction in the late 1970s actually developed somewhat earlier in Japan, when a second-phase reaction against the sociopolitical concerns of such writers as Oe and Kaiko Takeshi produced what has been labeled a "generation of introverts" (Naiko no sedai), writers who once again, in the manner of the third generation, strip politics and ideology from literature and restore focus to the home, the workplace, and the individual leading a life of "quiet desperation" in various complex social institutions. These authors, virtually none of whose work has been translated into English at this point, include Furui Yoshikichi, Abe Akira, Kuroi Senji, and Sakagami Hiroshi. Like their direct predecessor from the third generation, Shono Junzo, the "introverts" focus on the apparently placid surface of everyday life, while hinting at a gnawing pit widening its circumference beneath. Thus, in their reaction against the overt social consciousness of Oe's generation, these writers calmly depict the solidity of society's structures, while simultaneously, and with great subtlety, probing the hollowness that lies at the core. Abe Akira's "Hibi no tomo" ("Friends," 1970; translated 1985) is a prime example of this: "friendships" among co-workers at a television station are described as healthy, normal, and perhaps a bit distant, but the best one can expect with the hectic pace of contemporary life. Yet as the story unfolds, it becomes evident that these relationships are worse than fragile; they cannot keep several from the brink of madness or even suicide. Even though I emphasize the return to the elements of everyday life in the "introvert" generation, however, it is important to note that these writers demonstrate a more mature sense of outrage, a more indignant belief that alternatives are possible, than can be discerned from the fiction of the third generation.

I want to mention also the existence of an intriguing new subgenre in Japanese fiction that may well be a reaction against the ineffectual activism of the late 1970s. Several prominent writers in recent years have composed novels of "secession," of small communities on the fringes of Japan that quite literally declare their independence from the mother country and launch out on their own. The implicit social criticism is obvious, but the humor and linguistic playfulness introduced into these works suggest that something of a new direction is being carved out here. I have in mind such works as Oe's *Dojidai gemu* (*Contemporary Games,* 1980), Inoue Hisashi's *Kirikirijin* (*The People of Kirikiri,* 1981), and Abe Kobo's bleak *Hakobune Sakuramaru* (*The Ark Sakura,* 1984; translated 1988). One might even expand the collection with Kurahashi Yumiko's *Amanonkoku kanki* (*A Record of Intercourse with the State of Amanon,* 1986), which creates fantasy kingdoms of men and women after the nuclear holocaust.

CONCLUSION

Most of the writers who clung to classical tradition as their means to endure the postwar trauma are now dead, whereas most of the writers associated with the *Sengoha* and the third generation now jostle with one another for positions of leadership in the closed literary establishment of Japan. And yet a moralistic Catholic writer such as Endo Shusaku is now studying Buddhism and Jung and writing about sadomasochism (as a metaphor for unredeemable evil) in an attempt to cope with war atrocities, while some of those who seemed to be the most staunchly humanistic, even materialistic, critics and writers are, in their later years, being baptized as Christians. The legacy of ideological conversion from the prewar years survives. It is this unpredictability within the confines of convention that makes the Japanese literary scene fascinating to observe.

Emiko Sakurai

SOURCE: "Japan's New Generation of Writers," in *World Literature Today,* Vol. 62, No. 3, Summer, 1988, pp. 403-7.

[*In the following essay, Sakurai profiles four recent Japanese fiction writers.*]

In 1976 several young writers in their twenties won the coveted Akutagawa Prize for their starkly original novellas and astonished the literary community by ringing up phenomenal sales. *Almost Transparent Blue* by the art student Ryu Murakami reportedly sold a million copies within sixty days of its publication as a hardcover, setting a postwar record. By year's end some 1,400,000 copies of the slim, almost-transparent-blue volume had changed hands. Publications by other newcomers that year and the next also enjoyed near-record sales. The emergence of these young writers was a major event of 1976. Fiction in the preceding decade had been dominated by authors born in the 1920s and 1930s—among them Junnosuke Yoshiyuki (b. 1924), Kunio Tsuji (b. 1925), Saichi Maruya (b. 1925), and Kenzaburo Oe (b. 1935)—with very few writers in their twenties attracting attention. During the ten years prior to 1976, no writer in his twenties had been awarded the Ak-utagawa Prize.

It was only natural then that the reading public welcomed the emergence of these young writers. They were of a new generation born after World War II under what was a largely American occupation and nurtured with a culture that may be called "hybrid" because of the strong American influence. They had been educated under a system meticulously planned for their democratic well-being by General MacArthur's GHQ, their conduct ruled by a new constitution modeled after the American prototype instead of the previous strongly Confucian *bushido* (the way of the warrior). They had grown up watching American Westerns, science-fiction films, sitcoms on television, listening to American jazz and rock, reading American comic books and best sellers in translation, speaking a language littered with English words. Some also had had direct contact with Americans and American culture through their work or through residence in the United States. The critics called them the "rock and fuck generation." The following brief study focuses on the literary efforts of four writers who emerged between 1976 and 1978—Kenji Nakagami, Ryu Murakami, Masuo Ikeda, and Michitsuna Takahashi—with emphasis on their prizewinning novellas to evaluate their literary worth.

Kenji Nakagami. Nakagami was born on 2 August 1946 in Shingu, an old castle town at the mouth of the Kumano River in southern Kishu, on the Pacific coast. He had originally wanted to become a wrestler and singer, he says, but he started writing fiction shortly before his graduation from high school. He moved to Tokyo after graduation, joined a literary coterie, and submitted his first manuscript, entitled "I, Eighteen Years Old." The story appeared in the March issue of the coterie's magazine, *Bungei Shuto* (Metropolitan Literature), the following year. During the next decade Nakagami supported himself by performing physical labor and contributed more stories to *Bungei Shuto,* then to regular, established literary magazines. Some of the latter were collected in 1974 in a volume entitled *The Map of the Nineteenth Year,* the rest in *The House of Pigeons* in 1975. The earliest works that appeared in *Bungei Shuto* were brought together in 1977 under the awkward title *Eighteen Years Old, to the Sea.*

These early efforts reveal not only Nakagami's contact with jazz, left-wing politics, and small theater groups after his arrival in Tokyo but also his indebtedness to the novelist Kenzaburo Oe. Oe had likewise come to Tokyo straight out of a high school in the hinterlands, ashamed of his provincial accent and stuttering as a result. He regarded the city as a barren desert and portrayed in his early fiction lonely young men bewildered in a hostile metropolis. Influenced by Mark Twain, Oe also wrote a number of teen-age adventure stories and what he called "pastorals"—boys' tales suffused with poetry and set in a faraway village.

Nakagami's story "About the Japanese Language" (1968) depicts the relationship of a black American soldier just returned from Vietnam and a member of the New Left who plots the soldier's desertion, a plot which recalls Oe's "Our Times." *The Map of the Nineteenth Year* features the fantasies of a student in a preparatory school who makes indistinctly articulated threats by telephone when he is off duty as a newspaper carrier, a story line reminiscent of Oe's "Seventeen." Similarly, Nakagami's tale "The First Incident" (1969), which describes a boys' community in a village, brings to mind a pastoral by Oe. Oe's influence on Nakagami, however, waned after 1975 as Nakagami consciously strove to rid himself of the older author's influence.

Among Nakagami's early works, *The Map of the Nineteenth Year* was selected for consideration for the Akutagawa Prize in 1973. "A Burning House" (1974) and "A Tour of the Jyotoku Temple" (1975), the story of a visit to a temple by a group of tourists guided by the young protagonist, followed. *The Promontory* (1975), therefore, was Nakagami's fourth try. Its selection as one of the two winners of the seventy-fourth prize (for the latter half of 1975) was announced in January 1976 and catapulted Nakagami—then a twenty-year-old unemployed laborer—to fame.

The characters of "The Promontory" and their complex family relationships were already delineated in "The First Incident," wherein the protagonist was still a boy. They reappeared in "A Burning House," and after "The Promotory" they are featured again in "The Sea of Kareki" (1977) and "Hosenka" (Touch-Me-Not; 1980). Together these tales form a saga about a family at the mouth of the Kumano River in southern Kishu.

"Arson and murder are specialties of this place," the protagonist Akiyuki says to his mother in "The Promontory." The blame lies in the land surrounded by mountains, river, and sea and baked by the sun; the inhabitants easily go mad. The family saga slowly unfolds in choppy, unadorned, yet vigorous prose. The protagonist Akiyuki is a robust construction worker who at age twenty is still a virgin and afraid to be initiated for fear that he may become dissolute like his natural father. The latter is a "big man" from somewhere whom his mother took as her lover when she was a young widow. When she was pregnant with Akiyuki, she discovered that he had impregnated two other women while living with her. She severed her ties with him and refused to give the boy to him, eventually remarrying and taking the twelve-year-old Akiyuki with her, leaving behind her grown son and three daughters by her first husband. The son came to her drunk, threatening to kill her and Akiyuki for abandoning him and his sisters; but then at age twenty he hanged himself.

Like the protagonist of "A Burning House," Akiyuki is haunted by the memory of his brother and obsessed by loathing for his father, whom he considers a profligate and a scoundrel. The narrative makes clear, however, that despite loathing, Akiyuki has a subconscious wish to be with his father and his half-brother and sisters as family. At book's end Akiyuki takes out his frustration on his half-sister, a prostitute sired by his father. By "raping" this woman, he thinks he is "raping" his father and the rest of his family members; yet even in the act of bought love, the affection Akiyuki feels for his half-sister is palpable. These are the touches that give depth to this tragedy.

The narrative also hints at an incestuous relationship between the brother and his younger sister Mie and an incestuous feeling between Mie and Akiyuki, who resembles his brother. On another level, the story is one of Akiyuki's sexual repression and initiation. The promontory, shaped like an arrowhead sticking into the sea, is intended as Akiyuki's phallic symbol. While picnicking there with his family, Akiyuki would like to hide the promontory from his brother-in-law's view; and when he finally beds down with his half-sister, he applies the metaphor of the promontory to his genitalia.

These two passages are obviously absurd and should have been left out. A mood of repressed sex and incest pervades the story and sets the right atmosphere for the final scene without such additions.

The best and worst part of the novella is its dialogue, which is in the Kishu dialect. It requires time and effort to become accustomed to this dialect, but the dialogue is so real that the reader is amply rewarded. Despite the scarcity of character description in Nakagami's writing, the characters, particularly the women, come alive through their speech. The passages describing the pleasure of doing construction work flow with confidence and eloquence, but overall, Nakagami's rugged, uniformly laconic style is unimpressive.

The Sea of Kareki, Nakagami's first novel, was serialized in *Bungei* from October 1976 to March 1977. The cast, locale, and situation remain the same. Akiyuki, now twenty-six, still haunted by the memories of his brother and obsessed by loathing for his father, has become a prosperous landowner. The obsession leads Akiyuki to kill his half-brother, begotten by the father he cannot forgive or forget. The novel received the Mainichi Publication Culture Prize in 1977 and the Art Sensh Newcomers Prize in 1978.

The Sea of Kareki is a compelling story but contains the usual flaws associated with serialization. The original monthly presentation made artful construction with effective progression impossible and repetition of ideas necessary. Since most of the numerous characters that fill the work are related, kinship is explained fully and repeated with painful frequency to elucidate readers who missed the previous installment.

Viewed from a historical perspective, these works are important because of their departure from the existing literary trends. Before Nakagami many of the leading authors such as Maruya, Furui, Tsuji, and Oe were intellectuals who studied literature—either English, French, or German—at prestigious Tokyo University and therefore came under the influence of such Western superintellectuals as Jean-Paul Sartre. Some lectured on geniuses of Western literature at universities in Tokyo: Maruya, for example, lectured on James Joyce at Tokyo University. Their writing, naturally, was intellectual and also perennially introspective, with the result that intellectualism and introspection became the dominant qualities of the literature of 1965-75.

Nevertheless, Nakagami eventually dropped his allegiance to the superintellectual Kenzaburo Oe, the famous disciple of Sartre, and switched to proletarian literature (popular in the 1920s) and to naturalism and the bucolic southern Kishu. His novella "Woman of Water" (1978) reads like the "I-fiction" of Shusei Tokuda (1871-1943), a leader of the Japanese naturalist school. Nakagami reportedly studied this author meticulously for "Ho-senka," which depicts the life of Akiyuki's mother, but he was already writing like Tokuda in mid-1978. It should also be noted that Nakagami entitled a 1976-77 story "Arakure" (Rough), which is the title of a 1915 novel by Tokuda as well. Nakagami's indebtedness to the naturalist writer seems to predate "Hosenka" by two years.

What is more interesting, however, was the reading public's willingness to go along with Nakagami in his descent to the proletariat in 1976-77. Clearly the public had had enough of intellectualism and introspection.

Ryu Murakami. Born in Sasebo on 19 February 1952 as the son of a music teacher, Murakami formed a rock band and composed songs while he was still in high school. He experienced the hippie culture while on suspension from school for barricading the rooftop of his school building. In 1970 he went to Tokyo and lived in Fussa, near an American air base, and two years later enrolled in Musashino Fine Arts College. In 1975 he entered a new writers' contest with a novella based on his experience in Fussa. Entitled *Almost Transparent Blue,* the story brought Murakami the Gunzo New Writers Prize in May 1976 and the seventy-fifth Akutagawa Prize (for the first half of 1976) in July 1976. He was then twenty-four and a senior at Musashino.

The locale of this work is a town by the Yokota Air Base partly populated by American airmen and their dependents, Amerasians, bar girls, prostitutes, and pimps. Ryu, nineteen, earns money and drugs by supplying women to black soldiers for "parties" featuring rock music, drugs, and group sex. A passive participant at those orgies, Ryu dons makeup as a woman, dances, and lets the racially mixed partners abuse him sexually. Heroin, hashish, marijuana, mescaline, and other narcotics are forever being injected, inhaled, swallowed, and crunched. Violence accompanies each scene: kicking, stabbing, burning, and wrist-slashing. Blood oozes in profusion. The characters are always nauseated or vomiting, especially Ryu, who keeps and eats rotten pineapple. "Ryu eats rotten food," a girl remarks. Ryu also likes insects and at one point puts the wings of a dead moth in his mouth. He goes insane at book's end, babbling about the coming of a big black bird that will destroy the city of his fantasy.

The novel is extraordinary for the sensuousness of its imagery: an assortment of rotten food from pineapple to roast chicken, various types of dirty grease, human vomit, decayed bodies, cancers, the mashed viscera of various insects. The insects clearly symbolize the human race, and the images of decay represent this world. The city with a palace that Ryu fantasizes is the sacred world he seeks, whereas the black bird, of course, stands for death and destruction. Murakami is more a decadent poet, like Rimbaud or Baudelaire, than he is a writer of fiction.

The unprecedented popularity of *Almost Transparent Blue* in 1976 was clearly due to its pornographic subject matter, yet Murakami's description of orgies is not titillating or even erotic. Although some isolated images—such as an insect wet with Ryu's saliva—affect the reader's senses, the writing lacks immediacy, as if the action were taking place behind gauze. The reader fails to become emotionally involved in the story and remains unmoved by the fate of its characters. Many readers, however, find Ryu's gentle, vulnerable, and sensitive character appealing. Overall, the book is boring, with astonishingly long monologues, particularly about dreams and fantasies.

Murakami's full-length novel *War Begins beyond the Sea* (1977) is an expansion of a dream mentioned by Ruy's friend Lily in the previous work. Here Murakami continues his theme of the decomposition of the world and suggests cleansing it by war and annihilation. Despite its sensuous imagery, the book is interesting only to fanciers of other people's dreams.

Masuo Ikeda. The seventy-seventh Akutagawa Prize (for the first half of 1977) was awarded to two newcomers, Masahiro Mita (b. 1948) and Masuo Ikeda (b. 1934) for "What Am I?" and "To the Aegean Sea" respectively. The former is the story of a foolish but likable college freshman caught up in a political fight on campus and swept in all directions at once. The portrayal was so vivid and the underlying humor so engaging that the work was very well received. The Akutagawa made it a great commercial success as well, turning Mita into a darling of the press overnight. The most talked-about book of the year, however, was "To the Aegean Sea."

Ikeda is a world-renowned printmaker and has received many international awards for his modernistic prints and drawings. When he was thirty years old, twenty-four of his prints were purchased by the Museum of Modern Art in New York. He was born in Manchuria, repatriated to Japan at age eleven, and educated in Nagano prefecture until graduation from high school. Unable to pass the entrance exam to Tokyo Art University, he devoted himself to art and the study of literature in Tokyo. His interest in literature had started at age twelve, and by fifteen he was reading Camus and Sartre and had become absorbed in existentialism. He also discovered Jean cocteau that year. At twenty-four, he says, he came under the strong influence of Henry Miller's writing and watercolors. His first work of fiction, "Milk-Colored Oranges," appeared in February 1976 in the prestigious journal *Chuokoron*. "To the Aegean Sea," first published in *Yaseijidai* in April 1976, was his second effort in fiction. The novella won the Yaseijidai New Writers Prize in January 1977 and the Akutagawa Prize six months later.

"To the Aegean Sea" resembles a one-act drama with four characters. It opens with an artist listening to his wife's trans-Pacific reproaches on the phone and watching a fly on his model-mistress Anita's foot. Anita is completely nude and has her legs apart because her friend Gloria has been shooting a pornographic movie. The two women are apparently lovers. The artist, watching the women, thinks of Anita's groin as the Mediterranean Sea and Gloria's as the Aegean; hence the phrase "To the Aegean Sea," which comes to his mind. At the end nothing has changed except that Gloria is holding a hairpin with a needle-sharp end.

The foregoing recalls Jean Cocteau's popular one-act play *La voix humaine* (1930), in which a jilted woman tries to win back her lover during a one-sided telephone conversation. Ikeda must have seen the play performed in Paris during one of his trips to Europe. He had received a lasting impression from Cocteau's *Orphée* while still in high school, and in his 1977-78 essay "I Story: My Wonderings in Literature," Ikeda paid the French author extravagant tribute as his hero. One wonders then if the idea of having the model open her legs came from the Japanese translation of Cocteau's title for his 1923 prose work *Le grand écart*. Translated into Japanese as "Opening Legs Wide," it is mentioned in the essay as one of Cocteau's books that Ikeda read in high school.

In the same essay he also expressed his admiration for Camus's *Étranger* and recalled the impact Camus's opening sentence had made on him. The first sentence-paragraph he wrote in the present work to emulate Camus goes: "There is a fly on the sole of Anita's foot." One would then ask if the use of flies as a dominant image in this work was inspired by Sartre's symbolism in his play *Les mouches* (1947; Eng. *The Flies*). Sartre was another of his heroes.

Ikeda admired Cocteau for his frivolity, his style, and his moral courage. All these qualities are on exhibit here, but he also seems to have inherited Cocteau's superficial method of characterization. Anita and Gloria are mere shadows, and the scolding wife and philandering husband are one-dimensional portrayals. The inebriated wife's relentless denunciation of her dense, errant husband is hilarious, however, and the writing here is brilliant. A feeling of youthful mischief and clean fun rather than offensive obscenity or prurience permeates the novella. The work, moreover, is significant in its emphasis on the visual as a medium of communication in fiction.

Michitsuna Takahashi. In 1974 the seventeenth Gunzo New Writers Prize was awarded to a twenty-six-year-old sportswriter, Michitsuna Takahashi, for "Killing Time." The son of a writer, Takahashi studied creative writing at San Francisco State University for three years while doing odd jobs. Back in Japan, he studied English literature for a time at Waseda University in Tokyo. In July 1978 Takahashi's novella "Sky of September" was selected as one of two winners of the seventy-ninth Akutagawa Prize (for the first half of 1978). Helped by the popularity of Mita, and of Murakami before Mita, he became a favorite of the press as another young writer of the new generation.

"Killing Time" is the story of a Japanese student and his neighbors living in a dilapidated apartment house in a poor district of San Francisco. The array of vivid characters includes Bob, who keeps constant watch on his divorced wife as she practices prostitution in the next building. The latter's death by a bullet intended for her lover, and the bereaved Bob's jump from the Golden Gate Bridge would have been moving if the misanthropic—and misogynistic—personality of the protagonist Junichi did not obtrude. Discovering his neighbor's suicide attempt at the final scene, Junichi laughs aloud in bemusement. Once when Junichi's best friend and occasional lover is sound asleep in his bed, Junichi suddenly kicks her in the abdomen without any provocation or cause. The reader inevitably feels overjoyed when Junichi is later kicked by campus activitists. The story suffers also from excessive attention to Junichi—who is but a Greek chorus of sorts—and insufficient focus on the tragic incident itself.

"The Sky of September" is the kind of story Takahashi likes to write: about boys' ideals and friendships and budding sexuality. "My protagonists value friendship more [than women's love]," Takahashi once said in a conversation with an actress in "Sometimes Sentimental" (1980). The protagonist of "The Sky" is a member of a high-school kendo (Japanese fencing) team who is offended when a girl joins the all-male outfit—apparently out of her interest in him. After he has won a match against a powerful opponent, however, the youth is willing to be more tolerant. The work suffers because the protagonist is so unlovable, and it lacks the energy of the author's "Angry but Powerless Dogs" (1977), probably the most forceful of his stories.

The 1977 piece is a first-person narrative about several dogs kept by the narrator's family since he was three. The first was Kuro, his protector in childhood; the last was Bell, the family's first bitch, who represented the female sex to the narrator during his adolescence. The boy is disappointed when he sees that the stray dog which lingers at his house is female. He soon starts inflicting pain on Bell, even shoving a stick into her vagina and stealthily discarding the food his mother gives her. Once he is sexually aroused by Bell and attempts to have coitus with her, only to be rejected.

The narrative is brilliant and compelling in parts, but the material has not been properly sculpted as a work of fiction, only presented loosely like a memoir. It reveals that by mid-1977 Takahashi still had not learned the techniques of fiction. Despite his engaging prose style, Takahashi is a conventional writer, and his contribution to literature is the slightest among our four authors. Of the four, Nakagami is generally rated the most outstanding and original on the basis of "The Promontory" and *The Sea of Kareki.* Most outstanding he certainly is as a regional novelist—a Thomas Hardy in the making—but his family saga is traditional, reminiscent of the literature of the twenties and thirties, even though his telescoping of time, merging characters and events from the past with those of the present, gives novelty to his writing. Still, one recalls that in "Football in the First Year of Mannen" (1967), also set in a village, Oe had used this same technique, effectively fusing the post-Meiji Restoration era with the post-student-riot days of the early sixties.

If Ikeda's indebtedness to French masters can be forgotten, his "To the Aegean Sea" is fresher and more original than Nakagami's work, and Ikeda certainly writes better prose. As regards the form of fiction, Murakami is the most original of the four. Disliking literary conventions, Murakami wrote *Almost Transparent Blue* like a television script: copious dialogue interspersed with imagistic descriptions in present-progressive form. Only it failed to produce realism. Naoya Shiga's simple recollection of an incident in childhood—told in the past tense—in *A Dark Night's Passing* (1937) far surpasses Murakami's novel in vividness. Despite Murakami's recognized talent with sensuous and decadent imagery, *Almost Transparent Blue* is more interesting from a historical point of view as a natural product of the new age, the kind of writing one would expect from a young generation untainted by the emperor cult, free from the shame of defeat and the guilt of survival, nurtured by television, rock, and jazz, and innocent of prewar morality and taboos.

Yotaro Konaka

SOURCE: "Japanese Atomic Bomb Literature," in *World Literature Today,* Vol. 62, No. 3, Summer, 1988, pp. 420-24.

[*In the following essay, Konaka surveys several works exemplary of a Japanese literary genre known as "atomic-bomb literature."*]

In *On Photography,* Susan Sontag tells of seeing, at the age of twelve, the victims of the Jewish concentration camp at Birkenau, and of how it changed her. For my part, I cannot forget seeing as a youth for the first time in the illustrated weekly *Asahigurafu* photographs depicting the suffering caused by the atomic bomb. In that year, 1952, the U.S. Occupation of Japan ended, and information about victims of the nuclear explosions became generally available. Also, just this year the film *Genbaku no ko* (Children of the Atomic Bomb), directed by Shindo Kanendo and based on a collection of essays by young people from Hiroshima, was released. The hellish conflagration depicted on the screen is branded on my eyelids. These accounts of the atomic-bomb blasts and the Jewish Holocaust, like those describing the burning of Rome under Nero in ancient times, did not simply appear spontaneously in the historical record; they have been passed down to posterity through the determination and the recording activities of witnesses and chroniclers, modern-day Japanese counterparts of the early Christians and of such Jewish authors as Anne Frank and Erich Weil, who wanted to document and tell of their experiences.

In 1982, thirty-seven years after the atomic bomb was dropped, I was privileged to participate in the compilation and publication of a fifteen-volume collection titled *Nihon no genbaku bungaku* (Japanese Atomic–Bomb Literature), the first collection of its kind in Japan. The concept for this collection was formulated as a result of a gathering that same year of some five hundred Japanese writers, who issued a "Writers' Declaration on the Danger of Nuclear War." (The declaration aroused opposition among some who felt it was an inappropriate activity for writers.) The pictures on the covers of each volume in the collection are based on the series "Atomic-Bomb Drawings" by the artists Iri and Toshi Maruki.

In working on this compilation, I decided to read many works of Japanese atomic-bomb literature in order to gain an idea of its flow. I noticed that it proceeded from reports of direct experiences to imaginative accounts, from focusing on the victim to considering the perpetrator, and that, taken as a whole, it has progressed toward the formulation of a view of the world as a global village. Among many other small revelations, I learned from Naruhiko Ito, one of the editors, that Yoko Ota, the author of *Shikabane no machi* (City of Corpses), did not have writing paper but instead wrote on the back of paper used to cover sliding screens (*fusuma*). Having been caught in the Tokyo air raids, Ota was returning to Hiroshima, her birthplace, at the time the bomb was dropped. At the age of forty-three, Ota was already active as a writer. In November, three months after the bomb was dropped on 6 August, she completed a documentary about it, a journalistic record based on her own experiences as well as on the testimony of scientists.

> And corpses were lying all over, left and right, and in the middle of the road. Some were lying face upward and others face down, all of them had been headed toward the hospital. With their bulging eyes, swollen and battered lips, and bloated limbs, they were like hideous big rubber dolls. Weeping copiously, I recorded the image of those people on my heart.
>
> "Big Sister, you've become quite accustomed to seeing them, haven't you? I can't stop and look at the corpses."
>
> "Little Sister, you seem to be reproaching me," I answered. "I am looking at them with the eyes of a human being and the eyes of a writer."
>
> "How can you write about such things?"
>
> "Having seen these things, I must write about them at some time. It is a writer's responsibility."

In Ota's work there is both hatred for the American army and an abiding devotion to the Japanese emperor; with "City of Corpses" she recorded in detail the suffering of the victims, and she has subsequently continued to raise her voice in protest against the bomb.

Tamiki Hara was born in 1905. Introspective since childhood, he was sensitive but temperamental, the kind of poet who could not put Rilke's *Notebooks of Malte Laurids Brigge* aside. A resident of Hiroshima at the time of the bombing, he wrote about his experience in the verse collection *Natsu no hana* (Flower of Summer; 1947) and elsewhere. One of his poems is simply a transcription of the cries of a victim of the bombing.

> "Water, please.
> Ah, water, please.
> Something to drink, please.
> It would have been better had I died.
> Aah.
> Help me, help me.
> Water.
> Anything.
> Anyone, please.
> Ohh. . . .
> Ohh. . . . "

In 1951, at the height of the Korean War, Hara committed suicide by hurling himself under a train. He had been angry about the war and was himself suffering from, among other things, radiation sickness. A deep attachment to his late wife, who had died of tuberculosis, is also a very strong motif in his works.

In 1982, at the time of the New York peace march in which one million people demonstrated, an antinuclear conference was convened by writers opposing nuclear weapons, with the participation of Erica Jong and William Safire. Elementary and high-school students also participated. A poem by Goichi Matsunaga based on Hara's "Water, Please" was read. Through Hara's tragic poem the cries of the bomb victims are heard throughout the world even today.

At the same time, in "Flower of Summer" and in the short story "Shingan no kuni" (Country of One's Desire) one person's feelings of loneliness are extended to encompass images of the destruction of the earth itself. Today, in the 1980s, the prophetic images contained in Hara's personal catastrophe continue to be reflected in the works of such Japanese writers as Shusaku Endo and Kenzaburo Oe. Not only to record, but also to prophesy—these are the twin tasks of those who would write about the atomic bomb.

Masuji Ibuse (b. 1898) continues to be much loved by his readers as a writer who observes human nature and describes it with humor. However, in 1965, twenty years after Hiroshima, he shocked his readers by writing about the extremely painful realities of Japan in the aftermath of the war, basing his work on the records of bomb victims. The title of his novel *Kuroi ame* (Eng. *Black Rain*) refers to the radioactive rain that fell immediately after the bomb was dropped. The work tells the story of a young woman on whom that rain fell, and that of her uncle. The uncle's diary which makes up a portion of the novel is that of an actual person; the niece's diary, however, is Ibuse's creation. Because of the rumor that she is "a victim," the young woman is unable to marry. Later, it is understood that she has leukemia. With this work and its description of daily life, Ibuse shows that the atomic bomb not only brought instant death for many, but also generated problems of chronic illness and subsequently discrimination and contempt within Japanese society for many survivors of the August 1945 attacks. Since then, the atomic bomb has become an ever-present dilemma.

In 1963 Yoshie Hotta (b. 1916) attempted to introduce the bomb into world literature by counterposing the Japanese experience of the bomb—which until then had been discussed only in terms of its victims—against Japan's military invasion of China. In *Shinpan* (Eng. *The Judgment*) one of the two main characters is the American pilot of the *Enola Gay,* the airplane that dropped the bomb, and the other is a Japanese officer who witnessed the actions ordered by his superior officer. Both men are suffering from violent pangs of conscience. Hotta raises questions that we must ask ourselves today, questions concerning the nation and the individual. In particular, the relationship between the emperor and the Japanese people is considered. Nobuko Tsukui of George Mason University, who has prepared the forthcoming English translation of *The Judgment,* summarizes this problem as follows:

> Moreover, although Kyosuke [a Japanese soldier] wonders how the Emperor who sent him into battle can sleep peacefully at night, both he and Paul [an American pilot] reject the plea that they were "only obeying orders." In accepting guilt, both men take the side of meaning. They accept responsibility for what they have done. After accepting responsibility, the problem is how to bear it. The word *kutsu* (pain), repeated by Paul, poignantly reveals the intensity of pain in his effort. Without human help, without love, there is no survival.
>
> The anguish of the *Enola Gay*'s American pilot has been a powerful stimulus to other Japanese writers as well. Iidamomo's *Amerika no eiyu* (American Hero; 1965) is strongly critical of America, and Miyamoto Ken's drama *Za pairotto* (The Pilot; 1964) is a story about that particular American's visit to Nagasaki. It is a spiritual tale about how his personal anguish is engulfed and assuaged at a popular festival. The expression of forgiveness at community folk festivals for the dropping of the atomic bomb is a Japanese characteristic seen in many other works as well.

In *Hiroshima noto* (Hiroshima Notes; 1963) Kenzaburo Oe provides a documentary report about an important time in the history of the Japanese postwar peace movement, when the crusade to ban nuclear and thermonuclear weapons was disintegrating. In describing the medical efforts of Fumi Shigeto, director of the Atomic-Bomb Hospital, and others to save lives in the aftermath of the bombing, Oe tried to focus on the hopes of mankind.

Turning to the field of drama, Hotta Yoshimi, in *Shima* (The Island; 1955), describes a fierce passion for life. As is appropriate to this genre of literature, the Nagasaki and Hiroshima dialects are frequently used, and regional flavors and natural features play a prominent role in this and similar dramatic works. Among them, Chikao Tanaka's *Maria no kubi* (The Head of Mary; 1959) is based on the traditions of the Christian faith, particularly Catholicism, which was prohibited during the Tokugawa period. Adherents of the Catholic faith were relatively numerous in Nagasaki, where there existed a Catholic church in Urakami, and so the fact that an atomic bomb was dropped there was particularly bitter for those who believed in the Christian God. Tanaka based this drama on an actual incident. Describing how someone broke off and cherished a piece of the stone statue of Mary at that church, the author tried to convey the devotion and love of Mary, who herself had become a sacrifice. (In reality, it seems the person who broke the statue sold the stone as a souvenir, but Tanaka treated the incident as an act of devotion.)

In 1965, when Minoru Betchaku wrote *Zo*—the title means "The Elephant," which is also what a keloid scar is called—the Japanese antinuclear movement was bitterly divided along political lines. Moreover, the excitement of the protests against the 1960 Japan-U.S. Security Treaty had dissipated. Betchaku, himself a student during the 1960s, despaired over the Japanese people's lack of independence and depicted the atomic-bomb victims in the style of Beckett's theater of the absurd. In discussing the works of this generation of dramatists, David Goodman, a professor at the University in Illinois in Urbana, saw in this play the source of unease which nuclear weapons create in mankind and wrote:

> *The Elephant* is a play about the survivors of Hiroshima and cannot be understood correctly except as such, and yet it is also more than that. Inasmuch as we are all survivors of Hiroshima, living daily with the knowledge that we possess the means to destroy our planet, we also face the choice posed by the invalid and his nephew, whether to accept the absurd reality of our situation and thus accept death and madness, or whether to reject that reality and embrace the absurd hope for life in the nuclear age.

Women authors, according to their respective generations, have continued to write about the bomb throughout their careers. In her story "Kangen matsuri" (Music Festival; 1978) Hiroko Takenishi focuses on the blossoming of a girl student at the time of the war in juxtaposition to a rite for the purification of the dead at Itsukushima Shrine. Ineko Sata, a writer from Nagasaki, repeats and develops similar themes in, for example, *Iro no nai e* (Picture without Color; 1961), describing the political activities and loves of a woman she knew who was of Chinese origin, and in *Juei* (Shadows of Trees; 1972). Since *Matsuri no ba* (Festival Scene; 1975), published thirty years after the bomb, Kyoko Hayashi has continued to write about the present in her short stories, novellas, and novels. The following comments by Koji Nakano (one of those who joined the "Writers' Declaration on the Danger of Nuclear War") about Hayashi apply just as well to the other two writers mentioned above: "What Kyoko Hayashi did here was the only thing a person can do with regard to such a historical event: namely, even though it was from the vantage point of someone who had lived through the past thirty years, she established a distance from that period and looked at it without prejudice, as one rooted in the present." Shusaku Endo as well, in his "Onna no issho" (A Woman's Life; 1985), followed the life of a woman who lived in Nagasaki.

Turning to the 1980s, Minoru Oda published *Hiroshima* (1981), a wide-ranging work covering a series of events extending in time from Pearl Harbor to Hiroshima and whose characters include an American Indian soldier and a uranium-mine worker who develops cancer. The novel focuses on problems occurring in the American army associated with the atomic bomb and uranium, problems which have recently gained attention. Also, even prior to the accidents at Three Mile Island and Chernobyl, Akiyoshi Nosaka examined several matters relating to nuclear energy in *Jicho no kane* (The Bell of Mourning for Ourselves; 1953), a novel about atomic waste set in the near future. In Japan, which has few natural sources of energy, nuclear power is differentiated from nuclear weapons, and expressions of popular concern are not yet as prevalent there as in Europe and America.

In the category of prophetic works, I would note especially Mitsuaki Inoue's *Asu* (Tomorrow; 1982). In his earlier novel *Chi no mure* (Clod of Dirt; 1963), set in Sasebo, Inoue had already examined the social discrimination brought about by the bomb. "Tomorrow" describes in detail the daily lives that average people led even in Nagasaki the day before the bomb was dropped. A young woman who works in a factory is thinking of the man who made her pregnant and subsequently abandoned her. Another woman is anticipating her wedding ceremony. A streetcar driver also appears. Although the action takes place during the war, the novel describes a modern city where people are leading everyday lives. There are elementary-school pupils and there are teachers. The citizens have no weapons. No one knows that the bomb will be dropped the next day, that a nuclear device will detonate over them "tomorrow." Is this not precisely the fate of modern mankind as a whole?

In 1983, the year after the "Writers' Declaration" was published, I started teaching Japanese literature at a university in the United States. The television film *The Day After* was causing a great sensation at the time. In interpreting these Japanese works on the Hiroshima and Nagasaki bombings I explained that what Inoue was showing in "Tomorrow" is that we are living "the day before." Now, incidentally, in June of 1988, "Tomorrow" has been released as a film under the direction of Kazuo Kuroki. Moreover, *Sakura tai chiru* (The Cherry Blossom Corps Is Scattered), a film about a theater company whose members died in Hiroshima while on tour there, has recently been completed under the direction of Shind Kanendo. Prior to this, in 1983, two animated films by the *manga* (cartoon) author Keiji Nakazawa, who lost his mother in the atomic bombing, were released: *Hadashi no Ken* (Barefoot Ken) and *Ningen o kaese* (Return Our Humanity), which was based on American documentary films.

Compared with the time when there were only such films as Akira Kurosawa's *Ikimono no kiroku* (1955; Eng. *I Live in Fear*) and *Ikiru* (1952; Eng. *To Live*) and later Tadashi Imai's *Jun'ai monogatari* (A Story of Pure Love; 1957), the situation had changed greatly by 1984, when Cynthia Contreras of Brooklyn College concluded her survey of the atomic-bomb experience and its aftermath in cinema as follows: "The audience tastes the terror of the obsessive imaginary presence that was slowly permeating his experience of everyday reality." Even on television, ever since *Yumechiyo nikki* (Dream Diary of a Thousand Ages; 1981) was first shown, numerous quiet masterpieces have been created. Moreover, when I went to America in 1982, I saw Steve Okazaki's *Hibakusha* (Survivors of the Atomic Bomb), a documentary depicting the anguish of survivors in the United States, based on their own accounts.

The 1984 Tokyo conference of the International PEN Club chose as its theme "Literature in the Nuclear Age: Why Do We Write?" The question was discussed by writers from around the world. Kenzaburo Oe subsequently edited an anthology of short stories abut the atomic bomb, *Nan to mo shirenai mirai ni* (Toward an Unknowable Future), which was later published in English as *Atomic Aftermath.*

Whereas the Holocaust was entirely a matter of the Jewish people's victimization, the atomic bombing of Japan may be regarded as a way of ending a war that had been started by the Japanese people. Still, the two bombs that were dropped in August of 1945 not only ended the world war but also sounded a tragic alarm for mankind, ringing in the nuclear age. Therefore, documenting and collecting information on the tragedy of the bomb and probing its historical significance for humanity are not the tasks of the bomb victims and the Japanese alone. I believe these efforts should be of concern to all people throughout the world. Now, as the movement surrounding Japanese atomic-bomb literature seeks a new vision for humanity, we are trying to collect once again those records of the past and reevaluate them.

An editor of one of the poetry volumes in the 1982 anthology "Japanese Atomic-Bomb Literature" has indicated his disappointment over the dearth of verse on the bomb: the Japanese experience is still sleeping within the hearts of the survivors of the atomic bomb. Nevertheless, in the world of poetry the works of such writers as Tamiki Hara as well as Sankichi Toge, who opposed the Occupation authorities, and Sadako Kurihara, who illuminated the point of view of women, leave a strong impression. Among the poems which I read in 1982, those that moved me most profoundly were written in that uniquely Japanese form, the haiku. I have chosen several by the Nagasaki survivor Atsuki Matsuo as a fitting conclusion to this survey.

> On the eleventh of August she piles up the wood
> and burns our children's remains:
> The dragonfly alights on them,
> Three small bodies—
> Siblings.
>
> At daybreak on the twelfth, she gathers up their
> bones:
> Next to the pillow—
> The bones that were her children.
> but still her breasts are full.
>
> On the fifteenth, I burn my wife's remains as
> the Emperor announces the war's end:
> Imperial words of surrender.
> The fires that consume my wife
> Are just now at their height.
>
> Keeping vigil over my firstborn daughter,
> Gravely injured,
> Summer turns to winter.
>
> A single garment—
> My child wears it, I wear it,
> The morning chill.
>
> The couple are bound for Sasa
> With their cups for relief rations
> Wrapped in a cloth.
>
> Helping each other,
> The two of them make their way
> With their two dishes.

WESTERN INFLUENCES

Robert E. Morrell

SOURCE: "A Selection of New Style Verse (*Shintaishisho,* 1882)," in *Literature East and West,* Vol. XIX, Nos. 1-4, January-December, 1975, pp. 9-33.

[*In the following essay, Morrell elucidates the influence on Japanese poetry of* Shintaishio, *an anthology of western poetry published in Japanese translation in 1882.*]

In August, 1882, Maruzen Bookstore in Tokyo—still a favorite haunt for the foreign traveler in Japan—published a small booklet of nineteen poems, fourteen translations from English and five original pieces. The collection's three authors were all professors at Tokyo University; they were not professional poets. The youngest was Inoue Tetsujiro (1855-1944), 27 years old and just that year appointed as Assistant Professor. Two years later, in 1884, he would go to Germany for six years of study, returning to Japan in 1890 to become one of the most distinguished and influential philosophers of the age. Inoue died in 1944.

The other two authors, who contributed most of the poems to the anthology (9 each), had come to the United States together in 1870 for extended periods of study. Toyama Shoichi (1848-1900), after working for a short time at the Japanese legation in Washington, attended high school in Ann Arbor, Michigan, and went on for three years at the University of Michigan, where he became acquainted with the works of Herbert Spencer. (One of the notorious items in the collection was a lengthy poem "On the Topic, 'The Principles of Sociology,'" to which I will return later.)

The third member of the group was Yatabe Ryokichi (1851-1899), who studied botany at Cornell, and who returned to Japan to teach and publish in that field. Although Yatabe had the least literary pretensions, his translation of Gray's "Elegy Written in a Country Churchyard" proved to be the most influential item in the book.

The three amateurs called their production "A Selection of New Style Verse" (*Shintaishisho*). Their purpose was to introduce the Japanese public to the possibility of a new style of poetry writing, a style capable of expressing a broad range of thought and feeling not possible through the traditional forms. These traditional forms were the 31-syllable *tanka* (or *waka*) which had dominated Japanese literature since the days of the first great anthology of poetry, the eighth-century *Manyoshu* (Collection for Ten Thousand Generations); the even shorter 17-syllable haiku, which developed around the beginning of the Tokugawa period; and *kanshi,* poetry written in Chinese following Chinese rules of prosody.

Each of the compilers contributed a preface to the *Shintaishisho* in which they attacked the limitations of the older forms. The proposed solutions are mainly to be seen in the poems which followed. The major points of criticism were these:

> 1. Both *waka* and *haiku* are too short to express any sustained and complex mood or argument;
>
> 2. *Waka* and *haiku* are bound by a traditional vocabulary and grammar which are not readily understood by ordinary people; colloquial expressions should be used instead;

> 3. Traditional poetry has a limited range of permissible subject matter. The New Style poetry should not only be longer, but it should broaden its content;
>
> 4. Poetry in Chinese, although more sustained than the *tanka* or *haiku,* is really an impossibility for the Japanese because it depends on the use of tones. When the Japanese read the Chinese characters in the Japanese manner—as they almost always do—the tones simply disappear.

It is difficult for us to comprehend the sense of constraint which the old traditional forms of Japanese poetry continued to exert on the literary consciousness of the Japanese at the time of the *Shintaishisho.* And we may wonder what is so revolutionary about an awkward collection of twenty-one translations and original verse by three men who did not seriously consider themselves to be poets. The very fact that they had other interests, however, perhaps gave them the brashness to rush in where the professional literary angels feared to tread. Prose writing of the time had similar inhibitions. A major problem, which also bothered the poets, was the unification of literary and colloquial styles (*gembunitchi*). For centuries the Japanese writing styles, with a grammar virtually unchanged since the *Tale of Genji* (ca. 1000), had remained fairly constant while the spoken styles of the living language had inevitably gone their own way. As a result, the divergence between spoken and written styles became something of a crisis for the Meiji writers who were attempting to express contemporary concerns through a readily-comprehensible vehicle. The written and spoken styles of English are generally so close that the Japanese problem may hardly seem real to us. But perhaps we can improve our perspective by recalling the reluctance of many English and American poets to abandon rhyme, or the furor over the new translations of the Bible.

To demonstrate what an alternative style of poetry might be like, our three compilers then provided nineteen translations and original poems of their own. They all employed the traditional 7-5 syllable pattern with stanzas of varying lengths; two of them attempted rhyme. The *Shintaishisho* was intended as a break with the past. The compilers could just as easily have argued that they were merely reviving the glorious tradition of the *choka,* the relatively long poem in alternating lines of five and seven syllables which was brought to perfection by Hitomaro in the eighth-century *Manyoshu.* This line of argument seems to have been suggested in the epilogue to the collection written by the proofreader, Kume Motobumi:

> It has been handed down that since antiquity ours has been a country in which the power of words (*kotodama*) has flourished; generation after generation, men excelling in long and short poetry and prose have not been few. In today's great civilized age we hear of people who have a reputation for *tanka;* but it is very strange that we do not hear much about those who compose long poems (*choka*) or prose. They say that in countries across the sea, in both ancient and modern times, there are men excelling in the way of poetry who, generation after generation, continually compose poems—mostly long—in battle, at celebrations, and during grief and pleasure. This is really what people, all born into the same world, ought to do! Recently when I entered the university and saw that these great men had translated Western poetry into our own language, I could not help admiring them. Would that we could somehow revive what has been cast aside (the long poem in Japanese?) to celebrate the manners of such a new age as our own. By virtue of men accomplished in the skill to do this, the ways of our country in which the power of the word (*kotodama*) flourishes will truly become known. And when men from across the sea hear of it, how could they but translate these words into their own tongue? So is this not an undertaking which is to be a light for the country? The person writing this is the Master of the Tea Cupboard, Motobumi.

But the Meiji period looked to the future, not the past; and so the poetry had to be "new," not "revived." Although the compilers make reference to the earlier *choka,* they see themselves as doing something essentially new. The New Style poetry, as conceived by the compilers of the *Shintaishisho,* did resemble superficially the form of the *choka,* at least as far as the syllable pattern was concerned. The content was another matter.

Our compilers thought of themselves as pioneering a new poetic movement, one that would cast off the pall of tradition and flourish in the climate of colloquial, easily-understood language. And so it is not surprising, given the paradoxical nature of human behavior, that they would introduce their collection with a preface in Chinese!

After the prefaces and a short introductory remark by "The Editors," actually Inoue, we come to the poetry itself. Which poems were selected for translation (paraphrase is perhaps a better word in most cases)? What topics were considered important? And does the collection have any overall organization?

All of the translations are of English or American poems. The editors do not tell us anything about the criteria of selection, but it is reasonable to suppose that some were poems to which Toyama and Yatabe were exposed during their studies at the University of Michigan and Cornell in the 1870's. We also know that in 1875-76 Toyama and Yatabe were lecturers, and Inoue a student, at Kaisei Gakko (later to be known at Tokyo University). An English instructor at the school, James Summers, used as examination topics three of the poems which were later translated in the *Shintaishisho:* Gray's "Elegy," Longfellow's "Psalm of Life," and Wolsey's address. We can also assume that the selection reflects to some extent the predilections of the translators.

With the advantage of hindsight a century later, we would not consider the *Shintaishisho*'s fourteen translations an inspired selection. But it is easy to see them as the kind of poetry likely to have been popular in the United States in the 1870's—the decade of the scandals in the Grant administration (1873), of the massacre of General Custer at the Little Big Horn (1876), of the invention of the telephone (1876) and the electric light (1879), and of the presidency of Rutherford B. Hays (1877-81). Our collection made its appearance in the same year (1882) as Mark Twain's *The Prince and the Pauper*. It was a long time ago. The selection . . . includes Longfellow's "Psalm of Life," Tennyson's "Charge of the Light Brigade" and several other military pieces, Gray's "Elegy," and, inevitably, a few scraps from Shakespeare, including two versions of Hamlet's Soliloquy.

Related to the question of selection is that of organization. The eighth-century *Manyoshu* reflects the separate collections from which it was concocted; the 21 Imperial Anthologies of *waka* beginning with the *Kokinshu* in 905 borrow the form of Chinese collections—poems grouped first according to season and then under several special topics. In the *Shinkokinshu* (ca. 1206) and later we find the materials further organized according to principles of association and progression, as Professors Konishi, Brower and Miner have shown us. The linked verse (*renga*) of the Ashikaga and later periods had its own internal organization by virtue of each segment's necessary relation to that which preceded and followed it.

Are the poems in the *Shintaishisho,* then, organized according to any unifying pattern? Not really. Since most are translations of poems which have little if any relationship to each other in the English original, we should not be surprised that the poems of the *Shintaishisho,* which only number nineteen, should be compiled as a random anthology rather than as an integrated collection. The only obvious pattern seems to be for editorial rather than for literary reasons: Toyama and Yatabe alternate their contributions. After the fifth entry, Toyama's translation of the "Psalm of Life," Inoue inserts his rhymed version. Then Toyama and Yatabe continue taking turns. . . .

When the collection appeared in 1882, it was widely criticized as clumsy and uncouth, as their editors had expected. Professor James Morita in his study, "Yamada Bimyo as Novelist" cites a portion of Bimyo's preface to a collection of new style poems which appeared four years later (1886) called the *Shintaishisen:*

> There are only a few places in our collection which are truly fine poems, but we can be sure that, in comparison with other works which have appeared in the last five or six years, ours are more than just a little superior. The others are so lacking in elegance and faulty in grammar as to make one wonder whether they are not simply direct translations of the original stanzas or just some rural songs.

The poems of the *Shintaishisho* may indeed have been "lacking in elegance and faulty in grammar," but they made up for these defects by being extremely popular and influential. The prominent short story writer and poet, Kunikida Doppo (1871-1908), had this to say in 1897:

> Then appeared the *Shintaishisho,* compiled and promoted by Professors Inoue, Toyama and others. Ridicule arose from the four directions. But in no time at all it had been disseminated as far as the school houses in mountain villages. Even that insipid war song, "We are the government forces, and our enemies are foes of the court . . ." (from Toyama's *Batto tai,* item 8) moved every elementary school student and had them singing all in step. Moreover, works like the translation of Gray's "Elegy" (literally, "chiyaruchi yado") inspired countless young people in Japan with a strange and pure fervor. Unless one were a youth at that time, as I was, it is difficult to understand that this little booklet had an influence on the youth of the entire country which was not anticipated by the leaders of the literary world.

The contribution of the *Shintaishisho* to modern Japanese literature is somewhat comparable to that of Tsubouchi Shoyo's influential *Essence of the Novel* (Shosetsu shinzui, 1885). Both Tsubouchi and our three compilers were far better at rousing the literary world to the need for change than at creating works of merit to reflect this change.

Let us now examine the contents of this early experiment at New Style poetry. In separate sections I wish to emphasize the contributions made by each of the compilers, and, for the most part, to let them speak to us in their own words.

A. INOUE TETSUJIRO (1855-1944)

(Sonken Koji)

> INOUE's Chinese Preface opens the *Shintaishisho:*
>
> Master Ch'eng (?Ch'eng Yi, 1033-1108) says: "The poems of the ancients were like the popular songs of today in that even the village children understood what they meant when they heard them. As a result, they aroused much interest. Today, however, even an old master or an aged scholar cannot easily elucidate the meaning of a poem. How much more difficult it is for an ordinary student! Consequently, people are not aroused by poetry." (Cf., *Analects* VIII: 8, 1-3)
>
> Reading this statement I exclaim regretfully: "The popular songs of today are like the poems of old (in that they express the contemporary mood in the language of the time). But people today do not appreciate this fact. They despise current popular ballads and venerate the poems of the ancients. Ah, what delusion! Why do we not accept the songs of today?"

> Later, while reading his biography, I came upon this remark by Kaibara Ekken (1630-1714): "In our country we should express our aspirations and relate our feeling only through *waka*, There is no need to provoke ridicule by composing clumsy poems in Chinese and making a fool of oneself." So I said to myself: "It is just as Master Ekken states. The people of our country should study *waka*, not Chinese poetry (*shi*). Compared with *waka*, Chinese poetry, even by a contemporary, is difficult to explicate. So why not cultivate *waka?*"
>
> Then I entered college and studied the poetry of the West. Their short poems are comparable to our short poems, but their long poems extend to several tens of volumes; our long poems cannot equal them. Moreover, these Western poems change with the times, so that current poems employ current idioms and their comprehensiveness and elaborateness insure that their readers will not become bored. Perhaps it was in response to this that I again remarked: "It is not enough to stick with the old *waka*. Why should we not cultivate a new-style poetry (*shintaishi*)?"
>
> And then I considered again: "This is an important undertaking. If one does not study the traditional forms of poetry in Chinese and Japanese, both ancient and modern, then he will certainly not succeed in bringing it off." Accordingly, we have re-examined the traditional forms of poetry in Chinese and Japanese, and, having assimilated their excellent qualities, we are about to create a new style of poetry. But we do not yet know what can and what cannot be done.
>
> Recently Chuzan (i.e., Toyama) and Shokon (i.e., Yatable) took turns composing new style poems and showed them to me. I found that although they had mixed together literary and colloquial expressions, the result was plain and straightforward, easy to read and easy to understand, With a sigh of relief I remarked: "This must be it! What difficulty will even a village child have when he hears this? Is it not better to express our aspirations and feelings by composing this kind of poetry than to invite ridicule by making a fool of oneself writing Chinese verse?" I frequently met with these two gentlemen. We did a considerable amount of work modifying the syntax, polishing the style, and finally we collected the better pieces under the title, "Selection of Poems in the New Style." This is Part One. Will those whose business it is to compose poetry criticize it as something uncouth? Perhaps they will. But from antiquity new styles of poetry fortuitously came forth without waiting for the labor a million refinements. Uncouth though this book may be, in the end how can we be sure that we have not created a beginning for a new style of poetry?
>
> May 7, Meiji 15 (1882)
> Sonken Koji, Inoue Tetsujiro

Inoue's Preface is followed by prefaces by each of the other compilers. There are then several paragraphs of "Introductory Remarks" ascribed to "The Editors." From later accounts we know that they were written by Inoue.

> —These verses (no less than those in traditional form) likewise tell of our aspirations. (Cf., Classic of Documents, *Shu Ching*) In China they refer to poetry as *Shi*; in Japan we call it *uta*. But we do not yet have a common word for both *uta* and *shi*. The compositions in this book are not *shi* (i.e., in the sense of Chinese poems), nor are they *uta*. Our use of the word *shi* simply assigns a name which inlcudes both *uta* and *shi*, like the Western word, "poetry" (*Poetorii*). Ours are not the *shi* which have been so called since antiquity.
>
> —The form of long Japanese poems is the 5-7 or 7-5 syllable pattern. The compositions in this book also employ the 7-5 syllable pattern, but they are not bound by the old poetic rules. Moreover, our desire has been to seek out various new styles (*shintai*); and this is why we call our compositions New Style Poems (*shintaishi*).
>
> —In dividing the poetry in this work into "verses" and "stanzas" we follow the example of Western collections of poetry.
>
> —Occasionally there is an introductory note preceding the poem for those items which we previously published in a newspaper or magazine. We have reproduced them here since they are extremely important for a study of the poem. We certainly hope that this does not bore our readers, and that happily they will excuse these intrusions.
>
> April, Meiji 15 (1882)
> The Editors

Inoue's only poetic contribution to the collection is a translation of Longfellow's "Psalm of Life." Toyama also provided a translation. . . . Inoue's version of the "Psalm" and Yatabe's "Spring-Summer-Autumn Winter" (item 19) are the only two poems which experiment with rhyme. The translation is preceded by prefatory remarks.

> For some time now I have had the desire to compose new style poems, but I feared that it would be no easy task. So first of all I studied the various styles of poetry, new and old, Chinese and Japanese; and then gradually tried ways of making new style poetry. One day Shokon Koji showed me the translation of a verse from *Hamlet*. Although this composition incorporated colloquial words, it was more difficult to unravel than the old poetry in Japanese and Chinese. I admired the piece and included it in the sixth issue of the Literary Arts Magazine. Subsequently, Chuzan Senshi also produced a version of Hamlet's soliloquy, as well as Cardinal Wolsey's (speech). Disregarding the issues of old and new, East and West, it is my opinion that the popularity of the new style poetry for the most part came about by chance, and its composition certainly does not require the labor of much training. Thus I cannot know for sure that the works of Shokon Koji and Chuzan Senshi are the first examples of the new

style poetry. So I have translated Longfellow's "Song of the Jewel String" (i.e., the "Psalm of Life"). I prefer not to let these two gentlemen monopolize the credit for having invented the New Style Poetry. My composition is roughly the same as theirs. But whereas they have not used rhyme, I have attempted to; this is the difference. Certain people, seeing my translation, will laugh heartily. But perhaps such people as this do not know the reasons why literature has its rising and declining, its ups and downs; and so they are not in a position to criticize very seriously. Meiji poetry should be Meiji poetry, not ancient poetry. Japanese poetry should be Japanese poetry, not Chinese. This is why we are creating a new style poetry. Now if only we can improve the methods of rhyming and the techniques of rhythm—but it cannot be done all at once. I hope that my readers will view this work with understanding.

6. Song of the Jewel String (or, A Poem on Human Life)

Nemuru kokoro wa shinuru nari
Miyuru katachi wa oboro nari
Asu wo mo shiranu waga inochi
Aware hakanaki yume zo kashi
Nado to aware ni iu wa ashi

That the slumbering soul is a thing that dies
And seen forms but dim before our eyes:
It is wrong to say sadly such things,
And that life unsure of the morrow
Is but a pathetic dream of sorrow.

The poem continues in this way through the remaining eight stanzas.

B. YATABLE RYOKICHI (1852-1899)

(Shokon Koji)

The botanist Yatabe writes the second preface for the *Shintaishisho*. Although, unlike Inoue's, it is written in Japanese, the preface is not without its paradoxical element: when he breaks into verse, the form used is the traditional *waka*. Cultural relativism is one of his prominent themes.

PREFACE TO THE SELECTION OF POEMS IN THE NEW STYLE

People are forever making distinctions between good and bad, and right and wrong, but it is not as though there were any fixed and unchanging criteria for determining these things. We act, saying that this is good and that bad, because, by virtue of the disposition which we have inherited from our forebears and the education we have received from the society in which we live, we feel in our hearts that there is something to be taken as a standard of judgment. To the extent that people make distinctions in this way in countries where the Confucian way is dominant, they take the words of Confucius as the criterion of judgment; in places where the Mormon teaching prevails, the words of Joseph Smith are taken as the truth. Christianity, in which today the peoples of Europe place their faith, was formerly a Judean heresy (*Judaya kuni no jakyo*). And Buddhism, in which the people of our country believe, was formerly expelled from India. Likewise, the explanation of light as wave motion and the theory of evolution (*bambutsu kajun*), which are now employed throughout the world, were unknown to the ancients.

When we come to the Meiji period, we find that for a certain gentleman the fidelity of Lord Kusunoki or Uchikuranosuke is now seen to be comparable to that of Gonsuke, and ordinary menial. Others have come to know for the first time that despotism is a source of liberty. We cannot say that there is no country among the various cultures of the world where it is considered proper to practice cannibalism or to bury the aged alive. Considering, then, differences in country, times, education, and "association of ideas," we cannot speak of good and bad, right and wrong, as something given. And so we sing that:

Yo no naka wa
Ono ga kokoro no
Sugata nari
Yoki mo waruki mo
Hoka ni naku shite

All the world
Takes the form of one's
Own thought,
And neither good nor evil
Exist apart from it

Though I speak in this way, I am none the less greatly disturbed by the decadence in social affairs. Rather than mounting some great project to try to reverse these trends, I have simply taken counsel with one or two like-minded individuals. It is regrettable that our countrymen seldom compose poems using the language of the common people. We have worked out a kind of new-style poetry (*Shintai no shi*) on the European pattern. What we have done here for the most part paraphrases Western poems; and we have collected together a number of verses into a single volume to present to the public. We are rather pleased with the result, but it may be that people will reject it as something strange and uncouth. As I have said above, there are no fixed criteria for right and wrong, good and bad. Since these values differ according to what individuals believe among the new and old in this age, and according to the stage of their cultural development, our poems may win no favor with people today. But perhaps a poet of some future generation might aspire to the heights of a Homer or a Shakespeare. And might not a great poet appear who will champion the principles of this new movement, and, implementing them with increased skill, again compose poetry to move men's hearts and cause the demons and gods to weep. Those who read this compilation should appreciate this fact and under-stand what we have done by not overlooking our objectives.

Thus I venture to record my humble opinion among these introductory remarks.

April, Meiji 15 (1882)
Shokon Koji, Yatabe Ryokichi

Yatabe's first poem (item 2) is a translation of a nationalistic poem by Thomas Campbell (1777-1844), "Ye Mariners of England: A Naval Ode," in four stanzas of ten 7-5 syllable lines. . . . It is of no particular interest, and one can only suppose that it appears here to form a group with Toyama's military pieces that precede and follow it.

His next selection, however, became the most famous poem in the entire collection, "Gray's Elegy in a Country Churchyard." Yatabe translated all thirty-two stanzas in the standard 7-5 syllable pattern, and introduced it with the following comments:

> Very few people in our country translate Western poetry. This is probably because its content *(shuko)* is not the same as that of their own personal poetry. And even such translators as there are model their translations on Chinese-style poetry, so that the kids *(tomogara)* in elementary school cannot comprehend them. This is distressing. For a long time it has seemed to me that Westerners are very skillful in this art, and they always achieve a balance of qualities. In their pieces they are often able equally well to describe a natural scene and to penetrate sympathetically into human emotions. Furthermore, there are many kinds of diction, and poems may be rhymed or unrhymed, measured or brisk. Their variations in stress can almost never be reproduced. The vocabulary all being words in common use, they would not think of borrowing words from other countries as we do. Since they do not utilize the ancient vocabulary of a thousand years ago, even a child three feet tall understands the language of the country down to the last detail and is able to comprehend its poetry. Although Westerners do not dislike short poems, they also think highly of the longer compositions. Not a few of these compositions have come out as a single work more than ten times the size of the thin Japanese-style booklet with which we are familiar. Recently I have consulted with my colleague, Chuzan Senshi, and, as an experiment, we have selected a few Western poems and translated them in the common, everyday vocabu-lary. I am by nature deficient in rhetorical ability, but we have managed to translate several booklets of poems, of which we now present the first to the public for your perusal. May it please you not to laugh at the coarseness of our rhetoric.
>
> Shokon Koji

4. Gray's Poem of Ruminations in a Graveyard (Gure Shi Funjo Kankai no Shi)

yamayama kasumi
iriai no
kane wa naritsutsu
no no ushi wa
shizuka ni ayumi
kaeri yuku
tagaesu hito mo
uchitsukare
yoyaku sarite
ware hitori
tsogaredoki ni
nokorikeri

The mountains are misty
And, as the evening
Bell sounds,
The oxen on the lea
Slowly walk
Returning home.
The ploughman too
Is weary and
At last departs;
I alone
In the twilight hour
Remain behind.

Item 7 is a translation of Tennyson's "The Captain." This is a narrative poem, possibly based on an historical incident, of an ambitious but oppressive ship's captain who so alienated his crew that they refused to fight when the enemy was upon them. The ship and all aboard were blown into the sea and the crew was revenged. One can only wonder what appealed to Yatabe in this poem. Had he been an anarchist he might have seen the captain as the Emperor Meiji, with the crew ready to blow Japan into the Pacific Ocean. But this is just a fantasy . . . Translation in the standard 7-5 syllable pattern with no unusual features.

Item 9 is an original poem, "A Song of Encouragement to Study" *(Kangaku no uta)* in standard format.

Long ago when Chu Hsi of China
Was a great scholar in the world,
Wishing to promulgate his learning
He wrote a poem on youth soon growing old:
An entire lifetime, he lamented,
Is like a spring night's dream.

Without respect to ancient or modern,
Their area of the country, or social status,
For those who follow the way of learning,
Whatever their abilities may be,
Will they not experience
The same feelings in this matter?

The first blossoms of spring, the autumn moon,
Summer's green leaves and the snow of winter—
If we take time to reflect on
All the things that are in this world,
We will review our literary attainments
And ponder the passing days and months.

Even while the short dreams of the spring
Grasses by the pond are unawakened,
The paulownia leaves growing over the eaves
Are lured by the blowing autumn wind.

This year, too, is half over—
Do those who write and read not know this?

Though the days and months of the year are long,
They seem as a single night, a reed stem
In a village by Naniwa Bay.
Shame overwhelms my being, for though
By the light of firefly and snow I read
My books, my work is not accomplished.

The learning of men of antiquity
Was but a single straight road,
And still the wise men lamented.
Today the arts and sciences are many-sided:
To their branches, the last leaves on their twigs
How can the ability of ordinary man reach?

Among the adages which express this idea:
The beginning of a mountain is a single clod of dirt,
The origin of the sea is a single drop of water.
However we may hurry, it is to no avail.
But it is indeed well that we be diligent,
Centering our interests as long as we live!

Even if you do not accomplish much,
If you master just one skill,
For you as a person it will be considerable.
The spider has skill to spin a web;
The bee has ability to make honey.
Whatever you say, are you not as good as an insect?

Strive on, strive on without flagging;
Advance, go forward without stagnating.
Do not tire of a subject for being difficult.
In the sea of learning are ship lanes;
On the mountain of instruction there are guides.
How is the strong man to be intimidated?

Item 11, "Impressions on Visiting the Great Buddha at Kamakura" is another original poem by Yatabe. Standard format with introductory note.

In Western lands people usually compose poetry using the ordinary vocabulary of the people, and everyone directly expresses what is on his mind. In ancient times we did the same thing in Japan, but when today's scholars compose poetry *(shi)* they use Chinese words; and when they write Japanese verse *(uta)* they choose an archaic vocabulary. Ordinary language, treated as inferior and vulgar, is not employed. This cannot but be an error in judgment.

The Chinese studies pursued by our countrymen are almost entirely in the so-called "irregular" *(hensoku)* style—those people being very few who use the actual Chinese sounds to read its literature. Thus, although they know from dictionaries and examples whether a word to be utilized is level or deflected, when they use them to make a poem, they do not in the final analysis utter the actual sounds of a Chinese. They are bound to be frustrated in their endeavors, as though they were to attempt to swim without water. The reason is that although their basic intention is for the poetic content to be elegant and skillful, the fact remains that getting the tones right is extremely important for this kind of composition. But since the tones differ from one country to another, the poet cannot speak with a proper voice, and so he is unable to appreciate the true meaning of the words. He may say that they are clear, but he is like those students of Western learning who compose poems after studying the strong and weak accents from examples in a dictionary. Who does not laugh at such foolishness?

Likewise, it is difficult to compose the traditional long and short Japanese poems to give full play to our feelings and thoughts with precision by using an ancient and elegant vocabulary which, since it is not in everyday use, is like a kind of rare foreign tongue.

This being so, I think that we should frequently mix in a few ordinary words to make a new style of poetry in order to adequately give vent to what we feel in our hearts. However, if I do not put into practice that about which I speak, then people will take me for an irresponsible and talkative fellow. So, without heed to my lack of talent, I have recently as an experiment translated a number of Western poems and published one or two in magazines and newspapers. Now once again I borrow the white margins of this new publication, submitting two feeble compositions, and offering them to you fine people in society. The first is my own work, although the first verse is adapted from the preface to the "Daily Subscription for Material and Spiritual Benefits of the Great Buddha." The other is a translation of a Western poem. I am basically ignorant of literary matters and not well informed about composition. I beg to have the good fortune that the fine people of society may sympathize with my humble intentions.

Shokon Koji (i.e., Yatabe)

11. Impressions on Visiting the Great Buddha at Kamakura

When from today we reckon things past,
In that long ago of six hundred years
During the Encho era in Kamakura
There was built by Lady Itano
A Great Buddha completely of bronze,
The height of whose body was fifty feet
With ever so perfect countenance,
August features which never tire the viewer—
There was nothing like it any where.
But in 1495, they say, the calamity
Of a tidal wave from Yui Beach destroyed
Its great enclosure, and afterwards
Even the gilt Sage was soaked by the rain,
And ravaged by the winds
Now for almost four hundred years—
This is what I have heard people say.
Recently, wandering here and there,
I visited the old remains at Kamakura;
Drawing along my walking stick, heart at ease,
I paid my respects to the Great Buddha.
As I looked directly up at the holy face,
The pure heart of the Tathagata

(To which even the lotus flower cannot attain)
Appeared through that outward form, and
somehow
The word "nirvana" came to me.
Ordinary, unlightened being though I am,
For a moment the clouds in my breast dispersed,
And I woke from the dream of illusion:
I felt that I had seen the perfect light
Of the moon of the Tathagata
(Though in fact I had not).

The coming into being of this phenomenon
Was not, indeed, a matter suddenly arranged!
So with the Roman Empire in antiquity,
It did not flourish by Caesar alone
Brandishing his skill; and as for
The prosperity of the Tokugawa family,
Do not think that it came about
Merely by virtue of Ieyasu.
The conditions of the times and human sentiment
Advance gradually to attain their object.
So with the Great Buddha on Kamakura
Mountain:
The teaching of Gautama came over to Japan
And after eleven hundred years passed,
People's faith having become strong,
A skill in casting also in their possession,
For the first time, perhaps, could they create the
image.

At the time of Lady Itano, people
Prostrated themselves before this Great Buddha
With devout concentration and clasped hands,
Praying for peace upon the earth
And benefits in the life to come.
But those living in the glorious reign of Meiji
Today do not act in this way.
Gazing upon the face of the Buddha,
I think of things long ago
And I merely have admiration
For a skillful job of casting.
When times change, they do indeed change—
No less than the skies of autumn!

That which the people of long ago
Said was right, we now say is wrong:
Today's truth is tomorrow's falsehood,
And tomorrow's teaching will become
Irrational heresy the day after tomorrow.
"Everything in heaven and earth
Evolves according to fixed laws,"
Say the scholars; but no one will ever
Realize them in his heart
As certain specific regulations.

Ah, wondrous Great Buddha!
Six hundred years have passed,
And just as people, year after year,
Praise the flowing water and crimson
Maple leaves of the Tatsuta River,
So, as long as your honored presence is here,
However conditions of the time may change,
People, year after year, will
Come to visit and admire you.

The thirteenth item is a translation of Longfellow's "Spring," from an original ballad by Charles d'Orleans (1391-1465) referred to as "Sur le Printemps," or, from its opening line, as "Bien moustrez, printemps gracieux." Yatabe's version is in three stanzas of four double 7-5 syllable lines, with no rhyme. . . .

Poem fifteen is another translation from Longfellow, "Children" (not to be confused with the better-known poem, "The Children's Hour"), a quite ordinary example of Victorian sentimentality. The translation is in standard 7-5 format with no conspicuous features.

Then there is the inevitable translation of Hamlet's soliloquy (item 17, cf., Toyama's translation, item 18). Here the restrictions of the 7-5 syllable pattern become especially apparent. When Yatabe's and Toyama's versions are compared with a revised translation done in 1928 by Tsubouchi Shoyo (1859-1935) the quality of the latter is apparent even to the foreign student of Japanese. Still, the pioneer translations may be of some interest.

17. A Scene from Shakespeare's Hamlet

Should I go on living? But also,
Should I not go on living?
These are matters to be pondered.
However wretched our fate may be,
Is it only manly to endure it?
Or, on the contrary, does the warrior
Raise his hand against enmity
Deeper than the sea, and dispel it?
We are quite unable to put our minds at rest.
Well then, should we die? Dying
Is like sleep, and while we sleep
We cast off even the heartache
And every kind of bodily misery: this should be
The very consummation of one's hopes!
Ah, to die! To sleep! But when we sleep
If perchance we were to dream,
This seems to be the hitch!
For in that sleep of death who can say
(Though we have left this vile world where we
Are swept up by the winds of impermanence)
If some kind of dream might come—
Well, this does not clear up our doubts.
Though we long bear with calamities,
For whose benefit is it? The reason we ask
Is that we can easily settle our affairs
With a single cut from the tip
Of a mere foot-long dagger.
But this we do not do, we are cautious.
As for the strong man's cruelty, the world's
envy,
The proud man's contumely, the unkindness
Of the beautiful lady whom we love,
The laws of the country which have become lax,
The insolence of dignitaries, and,
(However good one may be)
The ridicule of inferior people—
Why should we put up with all of this?
Living a life unbearable to live,
While enduring misery and hardship
Bearing heavy burdens, wiping off the sweat—
Again, why is this? It is because everyone
Has a fear of what comes after death.

Up the strange road of the Mountain of Death
None have climbed who have returned.
What kind of things might be there?
We feel that they are truly horrible!
Though one abides in this world,
Enduring grief and calamities,
The things of the other world are fearsome.
And because he feels this in his heart,
Even the brave heart becomes weak.
However deep one's resolution may be,
Without opening its blossoms it withers away,
Never to become something real.
Be that as it may—Ophelia!
(Ah, that elegant grace)
Should you pray to the gods,
Please beg forgiveness for my sins.

The final poem in the *Shintaishisho* is Yatabe's attempt at rhyme. One of the collections five original poems, it is in four stanzas of six verses in the 7-5 syllable pattern. Donald Keene, who translated the first stanza, calls the rhyming "ludicrous." Yatabe prefaces the poem with the statement:

In this poem I have rhymed the last two syllables of two consecutive lines *(ku),* e.g., *yorokobashi, atatakashi.*

19. Spring-Summer-Autumn-Winter

In spring everything is full of charm,
The wind blowing is really warm.
Cherry and peach, blossoming bright,
Make an unusually pretty sight.
The lark of the moors, very high,
Sings as it soars far in the sky.

In summer grass and trees grow dense
And the crape myrtle blooms intense.
Evening falls and the bugs that fly
Collect on the edge of the eaves on high.
Now that friends from my house have departed
I will cool myself, for night has started.

In autumn's pampas grass will tendermaids
With season's bellflower open their blades.
Without a cloud in the sky clear blue
The shining moon now shows a brilliant hue!
Yet everywhere the same will be,
The melancholy which outside the house we see.
In winter deep is the frost and snowy storm,
And then our frigid hands and feet to warm,
When, by the fire in the hearth we try,
Sitting in a circle all nearby,
Through the door slit where winds blow cold
When we look outside, a silver world.

Among our three poets, Yatabe shows the broadest range of concern and the greatest sensitivity. He composed three of the five original poems, including one experiment with rhyme. Only our botanist reveals an appreciation of the natural world, that perennial theme for traditional Japanese poetry. (Toyama, as we shall see, is more intrigued by the social dimensions of the human experience.) As a child of the Meiji period, Yatabe has his poems on patriotism and on the need to be energetic, but he also responds to the mood of the seasons and to natural imagery, a trait that may have led him to Gray's country churchyard.

C. TOYAMA SHOICHI (1848-1900)

(Chuzan Senshi)

Toyama Shoichi (or Masakazu), influential reformer and educational leader during the Meiji era, eventually became president of Tokyo University, and Minister of Education. He contributed the third preface to the *Shintaishisho.*

PREFACE TO THE SELECTION OF POEMS IN THE NEW STYLE

A foreigner from the side streets of the T'ang once said: "When things cannot attain equilibrium, they make a noise. Grass and trees are without voice; but when the wind disturbs them, they rustle. Water is mute; but when it is moved by the wind, it murmurs . . . The same applies to the utterances of man. When one is unable to control himself, then he speaks. When he composes a poem, it is because he has something on his mind. When he weeps, it is because something is bothering him. Is it not generally true that those who emit sounds from their mouths are all somehow lacking in equanimity?"

So in our land, whether it be the long verse *(choka),* the thirty-one syllables (i.e., *waka*), satirical lines *(senryu),* or poems in the Chinese style—all are various ways of crying out. We cry our when we seen the moon, snow, flowers, a pretty girl. But however wildly we may sound off, we can never express ourselves adequately and thoroughly. Why is this so? The reason is that although from antiquity we have been able to express ourselves through the long poem *(choka),* it has become extremely rare. Especially when we come to modern times, it is as though the form had been swept off the face of the earth. The methods of expression which we use when we have been moved by something are the thirty-one syllables, *senryu,* and simple T'ang-style poetry. We use them simply because they are not demanding modes of expression. But in the long run, when we view things through such simple modes of expression as this, without a doubt the ideas they encompass will also be simple. This may be a very rude objection to raise, but it seems to me that the ideas which we can exhaustive convey through such modes of expression as the thirty-one syllables, or satirical verse, are those of a duration no longer than fireworks or shooting stars. When we get ideas in our head with the slightest continuity and try to enunciate them, such modes of expression are basically inadequate.

Not a few people in the world these days express themselves at somewhat greater length by composing T'ang-style poetry. Now in Chinese poetry meaning is a basic consideration. But the quality of the tones is also very important. And is it possible that this T'ang poetry is composed by our scholars of Chinese, who read Chinese in the Japanese fashion (where the tones are not indicated)? It is a wellknown fact that a general feature of this poetry is the distinction between level and deflected tones, and that these have a bearing on the meter. But if we were to have a Poppy Seed Head (Chinese) groan out (these T'ang poems composed by Japanese), would the tones be pleasant, or would they sound like a broken pot struck by a pestle? We can never tell. In the end, Chinese-style poetry for Japanese is like the pantomime of a deaf-mute or the hand-posturing of puppets. Should we not pity those who imitate mutes, though they were not born with this affliction; or who imitate dolls, although they were born as men?

We cannot use the one form to incorporate a continuous train of ideas, and we are unable to express ourselves very well in the other with appropriate tones. So we fold our arms together, as it were, in frustration at not being able to employ the thirty-one syllables or the painfully difficult T'ang verse, and we fix our attention on these poems which are like the *choka* of long ago to which we have given the name, "New Style" (*shintai*). With our noses complacently high with self-satisfaction, we have freely brought together a number of translations of Western poems (whose meaning we have not fathomed), as well as our own poorly-written long verse. Taking a hard look at them I exclaim:

> The label
> "New Style" sounds
> New enough;
> But it's just an old style
> Pompous boast.

Knowing it to be a pompous boast,
Our aim the old phrase, "beginning with us,"
You surely ought to ridicule, saying:
"As for the boast, 'beginning with us,'
It were better that it come to nothing."
But when it comes to what people do not do,
This also takes place without the boast.
It is only when someone would express
Something different from the experience of others
That he employs elegant, classy language,
Or the four-sided characters of Cathay
To express the possibilities of Chinese verse.
But we have formed a group, saying:
"Without distinguishing new and old, elegant and vulgar,
And mixing together Japanese, Chinese and Western things,
We concentrate on being understood by others."
Carrying comprehensibility to its limits,
One advantage is ease of composition.
If those of elevated discernment laugh at this
As something ridiculous, then let them laugh.
As the proverb says: "It is a matter of taste
For the bugs that eat smartweed."
So for the great majority of people,
Who knows but that they will say
That it is no foolishness to approve
Of our objectives as commendable,
Even though, regarding what we write
As so much nonsensical gibberish,
In the end (like today's T'ang-style poems)
Others do not much emulate us. Respectfully,

May, Meiji 15 (1882)
Chuzan Senshi, Toyama Shoichi

Toyama's first poem is a translation of forty-six of the seventy-eight lines of "The Soldier's Home." By Robert Bloomfield (1766-1823). An old soldier returns home after being away at the wars for twenty years. He muses on the peacefulness of the old homestead, the futility of war, and his happiness at meeting his aged father and his niece, "a little blue-eyed maid." The translation is in the usual pattern of alternating lines of seven and five syllables.

His next contribution is a Japanese rendition of Tennyson's "Charge of the Light Brigade," with a preface.

> The following poem concerns the events of 1854 when England and France, going to the aid of Turkey, opened hostilities with Russia. This eventually became the famous Crimean War. Among many battles which took place here and there, the most famous was the Battle of Balaclava on June (actually October) 25th of that year. Six hundred riders of the English light cavalry rode into an incredibly strong enemy force. Although they performed an exploit unmatched in past or present, it was a great pity! From the outset the odds were overwhelming and the majority of the riders were shot to death. Some were taken prisoner, and a few made it back safely to their units. The famous poet of the time, Tennyson, put the events of the charge into verse. They say that, regardless of nationality, among those who understand English at all, there is no one who has not memorized this poem.
>
> Chuzan Senshi

Ichiri han nari ichiri han
Narabite susumu ichiri han . . .

Item 5 is a translation of Longfellow's "Psalm of Life." (Cf., Inoue's preface and translation, item 6, pp. 14-15. Like Yatabe's "Song of Encouragement to Study" (item 9) it is an exhortation likely to have appealed to the energetic reformers of the Meiji period. Standard format of 7-5 syllable lines.

5. Longfellow's Poem on Human Life

Surely the soul's slumbering
Is to be called death;
So do not sing the sad lament
That the life of man is a dream:
Unless one is sleeping, he sees no dreams!
You may consider everything in the world
To be a dream—but it is not so.

Indeed, the life of man

Is too concrete to be but a dream.
The end of man is not the grave,
Nor can he be buried in the grave:
To speak of coming from the earth
And returning to earth refers to the body;
It is not a thing of the soul.
In this world neither enjoyment
Nor sorrow are basically the charm
Of man's existence here:
To live is to serve a purpose.
Being mindful day by day,
We must distinguish ourselves today
To the extent that the day allows.

Truly, time is like an arrow,
And Art is not easily mastered.
However brave our hearts may be,
They continue vainly beating in our breasts
The funeral drum of the interment rites,
The sound of a drum which is incessant,
Resounding with great sadness.

This life is a battle; do not act
As a sheep or cow walking about,
Used and driven by others,
Vainly having been born as a man.
In the midst of this battle,
Not being overcome by others, we should
Exert ourselves to perform meritorious feats.

However pleasant we think it may be,
We should not place our hopes in the future.
And however enjoyable it may have been,
The past has gone on to long ago.
The work to be done is in the present!
Those who see that this is their work have
Their hearts in their breasts and God in heaven.

If we attentively turn over in our minds
The lives of great heroes, we find that
Their having lived is not without value to us.
If one does meritorious deeds which surpass
others;
Thereby attaining rare honors,
His name is fair, and to later generations
Will forever be handed down and remembered.

Hearing this fair name,
One who, sailing the seas of society,
Having been buffetted by the wind and waves
Of suffering and hardship and then capsized
Without even a lifeboat—such a one
May take heart and exert himself
To attain an illustrious reputation.

So let us all be not negligent in what we do;
Nor let us delay for even a moment!
However bad our fortunes may be,
Let us not be downhearted;
But let us with composure exert ourselves
And work without faltering or stopping,
Even as we perform meritorious feats.

Toyama appears to have been a rather bellicose individual. We know that during the Sino-Japanese War of 1894-95, he composed a number of war songs: "Walk On, Sons of Japan!" (*Yuke yuke Nihon Danjin*), and "Heroic Captain Kaji of Port Arthur" (*Ryojun no eiyu Kaji taii*). Nothing in the standard biographical sketches suggests that Toyama was ever involved in any military action, either during the struggles attending the Restoration or later. But in every country it is the non-participant who can best afford heroically to urge others to die for the fatherland. Item 8 is an original poem by Toyama in standard format, with a short preface.

In the West in time of war, songs full of vehement indignation are sung to bolster the martial spirit. At the time of the French Revolution, for example, the people attacked singing a most vehement song, the Marseillaise. During the Franco-Prussian War the Prussians sang a song called "Watchmen on the Rhine" (*Uocchimen on ze rain!*) Songs to inspire love of country are all like this. The "Band with Bare Swords" which follows would emulate their example.

8. A Band with Bare Swords

We are the government forces, and our enemies
Are foes of the court not to be tolerated!
Though our enemy's general be a hero
Incomparable in past or present;
Though the warriors who follow him
Be fierce soldiers prepared for death,
Brave men, with less shame than demons,
Yet from antiquity there has been no instance
Of success by those who have raised rebellion
Unsanctioned by heaven.
(*Refrain*)
Until we have destroyed the enemy,
Go forward, go forward, all together;
Our jewel-strewn swords unsheathed,
Let us advance prepared for death!

O that pride of the Japanese sword
That protects the wind of empire
And the bodies of its warriors,
Set aside since the Restoration,
Now again it comes forth into the world.
One and all, our enemies and ourselves
Will die beneath the sword!
For those who have the Japanese spirit,
The time to die is now:
Be not left behind and put to shame!
(*Refrain*)
Until we have destroyed the enemy, . . .

When we look ahead there are swords,
And all have swords to the right and left:
To scale a mountain of swords
Is said to be our future.
Though the prospect before us
Is to scale a mountain of swords,
This is not done to erase the crimes
We ourselves have committed.
In order to subjugate the rebels
What matters a mountain of swords!
(*Refrain*)
Until we have destroyed the enemy, . . .

The glint of rays upon the swords:
Is it not lightning between the clouds?

And the bombardment from all directions:
Is it not thunder in the sky?
Laid low by the blades of the enemy,
Shot down by his shells, the jewel-thread
Of life severed, ephemerally lost,
Their corpses pile up to form a mountain,
And their blood flows to form a river;
They enter the land of death for their lord.
(*Refrain*)
Until we have destroyed the enemy, . . .

Advancing into a hail of shells,
My one-and-only body, ungrudgingly,
Blown by the tempest on the plain,
Reaches its untimely end
Like white dew that vanishes away.
But if I who die for the sake of loyalty
Die with some result attained,
Then I would not at all regret dying.
Ye, who might be tempted to think of self,
Do not pull back even one step.
(*Refrain*)
Until we have destroyed the enemy, . . .

We who now may die here
For our lord, for our country,
To lay down our lives is our destiny.
Though their corpses may have rotted,
The names of those who perished for loyalty
Will favorably and eternally be handed down
To future generations, and will remain.
Let it not be said that it is vain to have been born
A warrior, or that you are a dog without honor.
And do not be reviled as a coward!
(*Refrain*)
Until we have destroyed the enemy, . . .

Poem 10 is a translation of "The Three Fishers" by Charles Kingley (1819-1875). It is a melancholy lyric about three fisherman who put out to sea, their wives who waited for them, and their returning home drowned. An unusual feature of the poem is the refrain in each of the three stanzas, a device which Toyama employed in his "Band with Bare Swords" (Item 8).

Poem 12 is Cardinal Wolsey's farewell speech from Shakespeare's *Henry the Eighth,* in which the Cardinal bemoans the fact that the mighty are at last brought low—a familiar theme in Japanese literature—and ends with the statement:

O! how wretched
Is that poor man that hangs on princes' favours!
There is, betwixt that smile we would aspire to,
That sweet aspect of princes, and their ruin,
More pangs and fears than wars or women have;
And when he falls, he falls like Lucifer,
Never to hope again.

Did Toyama include this fragment merely because it was known to him as a school exercise, or was he addressing the Meiji bureaucrat?

Item 14 is the famous composition on "The Principles of Sociology." Toyama wrote it as the preface to a translation of Herbert Spencer's *Principles of Sociology* (1876-1896), of which the first of three parts had appeared. This was translated into Japanese and published by the economist Noritake Kotaro (1860-1909) in 1882, the year of the *Shintaishisho.* Although the composition was ridiculed for its unpoetic content, the fact that it was conceived as a versified preface makes the undertaking plausible. Heightened prose passages using the 7-5 syllable pattern had been employed by Japanese writers for centuries, and there is nothing to distinguish such a prose composition from new style "poetry" except for the way it appears on the printed page. As we saw earlier, Toyama read Spencer at the University of Michigan.

14. On the Topic: The Principles of Sociology

The things in the universe
All, without exception,
Do indeed follow regulations.
The movements of the sun and moon
In the sky, or the barely-visible stars,
Are all because of a force
Which we call gravity.
The workings of this gravity
Are according to fixed laws:
Things cannot attract arbitrarily.
And the paths traversed by
The heavenly bodies likewise
Are necessarily determined.
That which outwardly appears
Unruly, like the rain and wind,
Thunder and earthquakes, operates
Under a unified system of laws.
The vegetation on mountains and plains,
The insects and quadrupeds which crawl
Upon the earth, and the various birds
Which soar in the sky—all are regulated,
From physical form to behavior.
And nothing exists in all the world
But has evolved interdependently
From the deep past.
Among birds, beasts, and plants,
The traits which are passed on from
Parent to child are all transmitted,
Without exception, by the laws of heredity.
Those who do not adapt, decline.
For all beings in the world today—
Broad bells, pampas grass, valerian flowers,
Plum and cherry, bush clover and peonies
(And the Chinese lion attracted to the peonies),
Butterflies lighting on leaves of rape,
Nightingales singing among the trees,
The robin redbreast foraging near the gate,
Cuckoos in the sky making themselves heard,
And the Child-calling Bird of the same species,
Deer, yearning and belling for their mates,
Treading mountain recess maple leaves,
Cattle and sheep which plod along, driven
Uncomprehendingly by the conch sound;
The monkey, closely akin to the sheep,
But still without understanding—for all,
As also for man, the lord of creation,
If we investigate the origins
Of their present bodies and brain power,
We find that they are the cumulative result

Of small changes age after age.
This is the discovery of Darwin, who saw
The matter through with perspicacity
Unequalled in ancient or modern times,
And whose intelligence is no whit inferior
To that of Aristotle or Newton.
Spencer, who was the equal of these men,
Enlarged upon this same train of reasoning.
His contribution to the law of evolution was
That in respect to all things which exist
(Not just the plants and animals
Which we see before our very eyes),
He did not make the least distinction
Between animate and inanimate things,
Or between the material and spiritual; thus,
This understanding cannot be too highly admired
Which carried truth to its limits.
So inasmuch as the workings of the mind,
The development of thought and understanding,
The ameliorization of language and belief
And social phenomena are all part of the same
(Evolutionary) processes, then indeed the
Fundamental principles of already-developed
Philosophies proceed from this basis
Taking this to be the fundamental principle
Of biology and psychology,
It goes without saying that the core
Of what is written here is (evolution)
As the fundamental basis of sociology.
This book contains and explains the following:
First of all, what do we mean by "society"?
How does its development come about?
What are the societal differences
With respect to organization and operation?
The merits of differing social relationships
Between clan, parents, and children?
Whether it be the relations between men and
women,
Or differences in conditions and treatment
Of children by women; whether it be
Dissimilarities among various governments,
And the reasons for these dissimilarities;
Or why monastic organizations exist,
And the reasons for their changing;
Or the varieties of custom, industry, language,
Theoretical knowledge, art and ethics,
With respect to time and place—
All this will be explained in detail
In a long work in three volumes,
Showing the condition of things
As they move, change, and evolve.
Ah, what a commendable accomplishment!
Among those who have read the first volume
Of this book which has already come out,
There are none who do not praise it;
Truly it is an uncommonly good work.
If those officials with serious duties
Who take in hand the affairs of society
And busy themselves with this and that,
Or those newspapermen and public speakers
Who brag and pretend to be clever,
Claiming to solve all problems at one stroke,
Scribbling away and talking nonsense,
Unable even to express themselves clearly—
If these people would read and ponder this book,
Then might there be some slight decrease
In the crimes and faults which lead people astray.
Setting aside the consideration of such things
As the operations of the sun, moon, and stars,
Or the nature of plants and animals, or metals,
There is the matter of worldly industry,
Take, for example, the making of a floor mat,
Or the sewing of a single foot-covering—
Without a wakeful apprenticeship
Through long years and months,
That which could be done is not accomplished.
Weighing by themselves the problems of society,
But having submitted to no apprenticeship
And having attained no learning about society,
People become newspapermen and officials—
A matter which we take very lightly.
However, when there are many such individuals,
Then suddenly, as seeing it in a mirror,
We find socialists arising in the country,
As well as frightful nihilists.
The upshot of all the hot debate
Is total collapse with nothing accomplished:
Order is not established, there is no liberty,
And society becomes like a muddy sea!
Until the wind and waves again subside
And the sea of society becomes peaceful,
A hundred years may not suffice.
This we can know by observing the condition
Of France after the Revolution.
Bearing all this in mind, let us not
Put our hands recklessly to these affairs,
Nor babble on without restraint.
In this wide world are many things
Which we ought to fear,
But none surpasses the warfare
Between blind comrades: it is dangerous
To join a stick-fencing association
Which has no fixed objectives.
The world today is in a time when
The whirlwinds of thought blow violently.
And if we are whirled, even for a moment,
Into its violent center, we are lost.
Our legs become unstable, our eyes dizzy,
And our heads gradually become unsettled.
We are made to turn round and round,
Turning with no opening through which to
escape.
And the upshot of it all is that we are whirled
Into the air and hurled down again.
When we first come to realize this,
The season for late-sown peppers is already past,
'Repentance never precedes the act.'
When the typhoon blows violently,
We would say it is skillful
Of the helmsman not to erringly
Lead his boat into the gusts.
That those who take the helm of government,
And those who lead public opinion
Make a study of sociology in order to
Carry on with prudence, nor take their work
Lightly—such is my fervent wish.

Toyama's final two contributions are translations from Shakespeare. Item 16 is the monologue by King Henry at the beginning of *Henry IV, Part II,* in which he laments that the mighty, unlike the humble, have a hard time getting to sleep; he ends with the line, "Uneasy lies the head that wears a crown." Item 18 is a translation of Hamlet's soliloquy (cf., Yatabe's translation of the same selection, item 17. . . .).

Unlike Yatabe, Toyama had no interest in nature. His themes are about human interactions: patriotism, war, the need to be energetic, social Darwinism, and the maladjustments of the mighty. His views on what had to be done to revive Japanese poetry are much the same as those of his colleagues.

The *Shintaishisho* is not a graceful work. But I hope that the reader (if I still have his attention) has found something of literary historical interest in the groping, repetitious remarks and in the experiments of our three pioneers.

Noriko Mizuta Lippit

SOURCE: "Western Dark Romanticism and Japan's Aesthetic Literature," in *Reality and Fiction in Modern Japanese Literature,* M. E. Sharpe, Inc., 1980, pp. 70-81.

[*In the following essay, Lippit assesses the influence of such western writers as Edgar Allan Poe and Charles Baudelaire on Japanese writers.*]

The strong response of such major writers of modern Japanese literature as Tanizaki Junichiro, Akutagawa Ryunosuke, Hagiwara Sakutaro and Mishima Yukio to Western writers of dark romanticism (such writers as Poe, Baudelaire and Oscar Wilde) can be readily understood in the light of their shared artistic concerns. Like their Western counterparts, the Japanese writers were concerned with the question of evil, the role of the grotesque and the ugly in art, and the relation of art to life, and they pursued these questions even after they moved away from the obvious influence of the Western writers. This is most evident in the Japanese writers of decadence and aestheticism, whose writing formed a major literary current from the late Meiji period (1868-1912) onward.

The writers of Western dark romanticism, particularly Poe and Baudelaire, explored the realm of the grotesque—psychic fear, the ugly, the irrational, and so forth—in their search for a means of transcending the romantic dichotomy they perceived in reality between body and mind, being and consciousness, and the outer world and inner world. Unlike the earlier romantic writers (Wordsworth and Emerson, for example), who envisioned a return to the original state of harmony or recovery from alienation through a return to nature and a rational scheme of education, such later romantic writers as Poe and Baudelaire, believing that nature and reality were unredeemably corrupt, sought to attain the original unity through destructive transcendence, through delving into the heart of their alienation in an exploration which could culminate only in self-destruction. Paradoxically, therefore, their exploration of the dark psychic realm was an endeavor for transcendence, an attempt to return to the original unity envisioned as original nothingness.

The grotesque for these later romantic writers was at once a symbol of the decadence of reality and consciousness and a symbol of the imagination which could reveal this decadence in its extremity. Yet at the same time, the grotesque was a form of imagination which pointed toward the transcendence of the decadence, a dark imagination which envisioned the original harmony through self-destructive exploration of the realm of the ugly, the fantastic (including the primitive and symbolic) and the subconscious. For Poe in particular, the grotesque was a part of his romantic ideology which understood, through a mythopoeic vision of man, nature and the universe, man's alienation and his aspiration for unity.

The Japanese writers of aestheticism who were influenced by the writers of Western dark romanticism did not necessarily start as romantic writers. The "diabolism" of both Iwano Homei and the early Tanizaki was initially a part of their naturalistic endeavor to unveil the irrational, instinctive side of existence, while the early Hagiwara Sakutaro was concerned mainly with exploring the depths of the wounded psyche. In the process of their literary investigation of the alienated psyche—the realm of the grotesque—however, they turned increasingly to the search for a myth (a vision of a self-sufficient world of dream) which would justify their exploration. Their ultimate "return" to the Japanese cultural heritage and the archetypal creative consciousness which underlies it can best be understood as the result of their aspiration for a larger metaphysical and aesthetic framework which would explain their endeavors as a drama of alienation and recovery. It is with regard to the romantic quest for a vision of destructive transcendence to which this aspiration led that their exposure to and learning from Western dark romanticism bears deepest significance.

From the turn of the century to the 1920s, the consciousness in Japan of European literary and artistic activities grew markedly, and such anti-naturalistic movements as art nouveau and symbolism were accorded an especially favorable reception. Yet during this time, Japanese artists and writers were developing their own world of aesthetic sensibility, producing a unique world of fantasy and imagination which can properly be called indigenous. This period, occurring roughly ten to fifteen years later than its European counterpart, can be called Japan's fin de siècle.

The emergence of Japanese aestheticism in the late Meiji to Taisho periods (1912-1926) was vitally influenced by the activé introduction to Japan of the works of William Blake, Emerson, the pre-Raphaelites, Water Pater, Aubrey Beardsley and art nouveau, Gustave Moreau, and Oscar Wilde. The works of Baudelaire and Poe had already been introduced to Japan in the nineteenth century and had been admired greatly, but with the introduction of this "new" European art and literature, Japanese aesthetic writers became especially impressed with their significance. In this context, such writers as Kitahara Hakushu, Hagiwara Sakutaro, Sato Haruo, Nagai Kafu, Tanizaki Junichiro, Kinoshita Mokutaro and Hinatsu Konosuke, and such painters as Takehisa Yumeji, Aoki Shigeru, Tanaka Kyokichi and Fujimori Shizuo, produced the aesthetic movement, which they regarded as marking the arrival of the "real" modern period in Japan. As in Europe, this was the period during which the aesthetic concerns of art and literature were most closely related.

In the forty-first year of Meiji (1908), two groups of writers and artists, Subaru (Pleiades) and Pan-no-Kai (The Pan Society) were formed, groups which were to be the core of the aesthetic movement. Subaru included such established writers as Mori Ogai, Ueda Bin, Yosano Kan and Yosano Akiko who had been leading members of Myojo, a group at the center of the romantic movement in the Meiji period. The most active members, however, were the poets Kitahara Hakushu, Kinoshita Mokutaro and Yoshi Isamu, all of whom had been dissatisfied with Myojo's optimistic romanticism. Reflecting the sharp impact of European decadent literature, these poets moved toward the exploration of the grotesque, sensualism and exoticism, all of which are evident features of dark romanticism. In addition to these writers, Nagai Kafu and Takamura Kotaro, both of whom had just returned from abroad, and the painters Ishi Hakutei and Yamamoto Tei, among others, joined the new organization. Subaru was clearly an extension of the romantic movement fostered by Myojo, but in determining the direction of the new journal which the group published (under the name *Subaru*), Ueda Bin's introduction of the French fin-de-siècle literature, later collected in *Kaicho-on,* and of Walter Pater's aesthetic theories played a vital role.

Pan-no-Kai was composed of such young members of Subaru as Kinoshita Mokutaro, Kitahara Hakush , Yoshi Isamu, Tanizaki Junichiro and Ishi Hakutei. It was an art salon which, after the fashion of Le Chat Noir, aimed at the integration of art and literature. The members met at a restaurant on the banks of the Sumida River in Tokyo and, talking about the literature and art of Edo Japan (1600-1868) and of France, immersed themselves in an atmosphere of decadence. Nagai Kafu at that time established the journal *Mita Bungaku* (The Literature of Mita), in which he published translations of Western symbolist poems which were later collected in *Sangosho* (The Coral Collection, 1913), a work which proved as influential as Ueda Bin's *Kaicho-on.* In the forty-third year of Meiji (1910), Tanizaki published the sensational "The Tattoo" in *Shinshicho,* a work which was praised by Kafu as the harbinger of the new literature, and a year later Hakushu started his own journal, *Zamuboa* (Shaddock), in which he published works strongly colored by exoticism and dandyism.

In considering the characteristic features of Japan's fin-de-siècle art and literature, we might note first that it is an extension of the romantic movement in the Meiji period and started as an anti-naturalistic movement, yet it was naturalist writers themselves who turned to aesthetic literature and introduced European writers of aestheticism. We can see in the Japanese art and literature of aestheticism a fundamental merging of naturalism and romanticism, particularly dark romanticism. Second, Japanese aestheticism was, culturally speaking, a reaction to the Meiji goal of Westernization and modernization; it reflected a fundamental skepticism toward and criticism of progress, Western civilization and capitalist economic development. Third, after an initial period of enthusiastic learning from European art and literature, most of the artists and writers of aestheticism returned to Japanese and Oriental culture and philosophy, moving in some cases toward a reactionary nationalism in their rejection of Western culture and in their exaltation of the Japanese tradition. Most typically, they developed a nostalgic aspiration for the characteristically erotic and grotesque art and literature of the Edo culture which had developed in the two-and-a-half centuries of Japan's cultural "isolation" prior to the beginning of the Meiji period in 1868.

Yet their "Edo taste" was only a way station in their search for a cultural archetype and spiritual roots; such major writers of the aesthetic school as Tanizaki and Hagiwara Sakutaro, and the painter Aoki Shigeru, even tried to return to the primordial origins of Japanese and oriental culture and aesthetic sensibility, attempting to create their own myth that would integrate life and death, the self, nature and art. After elaborating briefly these three characteristic features of Japanese aestheticism, I would like to turn to a discussion of Hagiwara Sakutaro . . . to illustrate the way in which the ideas inherent in dark romanticism played a significant role in Japanese aesthetic literature.

Soon after the Russo-Japanese War of 1904, Japan reached its peak of naturalism in literature with the works of such writers as Shimazaki Toson, Tayama Katai, Tokuda Shusei, Iwano Homei, Shimamura Ho getsu and Chikamatsu Shuko. These writers, deeply influenced by de Maupassant and even more by Zola, established the genre of the I-novel, which is basically autobiographical and confessional. The confessional novelists' attempt at the naturalistic unveiling of the self often approached the destructive, masochistic exposé of the inner self inherent in the tradition of Western dark romanticism. Here was the basis for the affinity that Japanese writers of naturalism felt toward the "diabolism" of Poe, Baudelaire and Wilde. . . .

Iwano Homei, a most articulate proponent of Japanese naturalism, although he called himself a neonaturalist and thereby distinguished himself from the first generation of Japanese writers of naturalism, was one of the most committed translators and introducers of Baudelaire and Poe; calling Baudelaire Poe's masterpiece, he explained European aesthetic literature as emerging from a core formed by the writings of Poe and Baudelaire. Homei considered the self as the absolute goal of his literary, religious and philosophic pursuit. Regarding Satan as representing the worst self, he pursued evil and the ugly (artificial beauty or the rejection of natural beauty), and delved into the realm of psychic fear and dread opened by his self-destructive pursuit of pleasure. Although he was concerned with the masochistic exposé of his own perverse, evil nature, and with the ruthless pursuit of desire and pleasure, a pursuit which often resulted in the unethical and sadistic exploitation of others, his persistent, unsentimental presentation of himself gains an existential dimension and becomes an expression of the sinfulness of human nature itself. His underlying aspiration for transcendence through evil brings his "mysterious semi-animalism" close to the idea of destructive transcendence in such writers as Poe and Baudelaire.

The link between naturalism and aestheticism is evident in the works of other writers as well. Nagai Kafu had, under the strong influence of Zola, already established himself as a naturalistic writer when he turned to writing the so-called "Sumida-gawa [Sumida River] Stories" after his return from the United States and France, stories which showed his "Edo taste." Although such later writers of aestheticism as Tanizaki and Sato Haruo started their literary careers by attacking naturalism, they too were baptized in the "diabolism" of Japanese naturalism and in essence developed it further. In this respect, Japanese aesthetic literature, although it was an extension of the earlier romantic movement and began with an attack on the then-dominant naturalistic literature, became the major link between naturalism and dark romanticism.

As a part of the national modernization enterprise in the Meiji era, Japanese writers were deeply concerned with modernizing the self by actively learning from Western art and literature. The self-conscious effort to produce modern literature in Japan initiated by Tsubouchi Shoyo and Futabatei Shimei reached its first stage of achievement in the early years of the twentieth century with the appearance of the confessional naturalistic I-novel, including works by such writers as Tayama Katai and Shimazaki Toson. Toson and Katai were the product of learning from the West, and at the same time they typically represented those who came from the rural areas of Japan to Tokyo with the ambition to be "successful" in the new Meiji society. The writers of aestheticism and Natsume Soseki, by contrast, were typically from Tokyo and, with their urbane sophistication, sneered at Toson and Katai's aspiration for success, uncritical worship of the West, and ethical pursuit of life. In essence, aestheticism was a reaction to Meiji utilitarianism and the thrust of modernization. The atmosphere of fin de siècle itself—the artists' separation of art from morality, their extreme sensuality and their pursuit of the grotesque—reflects the artists' basic reaction to Meiji utilitarianism. Although in Meiji Japan, unlike European society at that time, there was neither a firmly established bourgeois class nor a religious orthodoxy to form the core of middle-class morality, the thrust for modernization, backed by utilitarianism, created a similar isolation of artists, evoking in Japan as well as in Europe a strong sense of crisis. It was only natural that the artists' attempt to restore art in a hostile industrial age, their exploration of the senses and of beauty, led them back to the classical culture which existed prior to the Meiji period.

The Edo period in particular was the period when Japanese culture, cut off from the outside world, reached a state of ripeness and produced its own decadence; violence, cruelty and eroticism characterize late Edo literature especially. At the same time, the aesthetic writers were already far removed from Edo, and Edo culture was as exotic to them as Western culture. Their Edo taste was synonymous with their exoticism. Edo presented to them an exotic world of the senses, removed in time and space, yet linked with a strange affinity to the European world of the end of the century in which beauty and the senses were also explored, and in which Orientalism, reflected for example in the influence of Edo art—*ukiyoe* especially—on the French impressionists, was apparent. Although theirs was an escapist attempt to retreat into a world of taste and for some writers this atmosphere was no more than one in which they could be drunk and left no serious impact, for such writers as Tanizaki, Hakushu and Sakutaro, the rejection of Meiji culture and the discovery of Gothic themes in both Western dark romanticism and Edo culture forced them to pursue further their search for the origins of their aesthetic sensibilities and their cultural home. Kafu's return to Edo, Natsume Soseki's return to Zen Buddhism and the Chinese philosophy of Taoism, Tanizaki's return to Heian culture, Sakutaro's return of the wanderer to a mystical home called Japan, Kawabata's return to the *Kojiki* and the aesthetic tradition, and Mishima's metempsychosis all represent the writer's attempt to return to the source and to establish a myth that would recreate a self-sufficient world of the senses. All of these writers tried to restore the original unity by exploring the psychic realm of fear, the world of sensuous beauty and eroticism, and the world of the grotesque. It is in relation to their effort at the creation of myth and the restoration of original unity through destructive transcendence that we can see the most fundamental impact of Western romanticism. A comparison of the works of Sakutaro with those of Poe can help to show this with particular clarity.

Hagiwara Sakutaro (1886-1942), Japan's leading modern poet and one of the first to establish free verse, started his poetic career under the strong influence of Kitahara Hakushu, Kambara Ariake (a symbolist poet), Poe, Baudelaire, Nietzsche and Dostoevski. He admired Poe in particular, and his world of poetry is highly reminiscent of Poe's. Sakutaro began by defining himself as a diseased man, and his world was perceived through nerves sharpened to abnormality by his sickness. It was a world in decay, and at its center a great void opened its mouth, evoking a sense of fear of life. In confronting this nothingness, the poet confronted his own diseased face, his own double.

At the bottom of the earth a face appears
A lonely, diseased man's face appears

In the darkness at the bottom of the earth
Stems of grass begin to emerge waving
Rats' nests begin to appear
Numerous hairs entangled in the nests
Begin to tremble
From the lonely, diseased earth of winter
Around the winter solstice
The roots of thin blue bamboo begin to grow
Begin to grow
That looks truly pitiful
Looks smoky
Truly, truly looks pitiful

In the darkness at the bottom of the earth
A lonely, diseased man's face appears

("A Diseased Face at the Bottom of the Earth"; collected in *Tsuki ni Hoeru* [Howling at the Moon], 1918; my translation.)

The lonely, diseased poet wanders in the universe of "flowing time, darkness and the silent moment," driven by a fear of the unknown and led by the light and shadows that flicker in his subconscious, following the footsteps of fate toward a final vision that awaits him beyond reality.

To the poet who confronts the loneliness that turned into a "faceless woman" clad in a red dress, to the poet who confronts his own soul in the depths of despair and nothingness, there appears gradually a recovery of something spiritual, something transcendental, a recovery which could be achieved only through the destruction of his own body. To recover the spiritual by delving deeply with sharpened sensibilities into inner darkness—a world of fear, loneliness and sterility—to attain transcendence through extreme commitment to the abnormal, grotesque and destructive, is a central idea of dark romanticism. During Sakutaro's later period, his sense of fear, loneliness and the sterility of life became systematized as his sense of the loss of the original home, and recovery through the destruction of his body became his journey of return to his original home. This process of systematization into the loss of the original home and its recovery is the process of his return to his Japanese cultural origins and is indeed the process of his myth-making. Finally, he reached the idea of eternal return through spiral descent into the depths of the poet's soul. Poe's poet in *Eureka,* whose grotesque and arabesque imagination brings the entire universe to its primordial unity through his suicidal and centripetal concentration on himself, is fundamentally akin to the poet of Sakutaro.

Sakutaro, like Poe, tried to express his vision of transcendence and the process of attaining it through the music of words. Words, by destroying their own meanings, grasp and express what exists beyond words, thus creating an inner landscape. The evocative power of words' musicality, the inner landscape where darkness and dawn, dream and reality, mingle is the world of purgatory for the poet. "The Rooster," a poem which Sakutaro wrote inspired specifically by Poe's "The Raven," illustrates the depths of his empathy with Poe's world.

Before the dawn
A rooster cries outside the houses
Its voice long vibrating.
It is the voice of mother
   Calling from faraway nature in the lonely
   countryside
To te ro   Toru mo   Toru mo

In the cold bed in the morning
My soul flutters.
Surveyed from the space between the shutters
The scenery outside looks shining bright
Yet before the dawn
A melancholy creeps into my bed
Crossing over the misty tips of tree branches
It is the voice of a rooster
   Calling from faraway nature in the lonely
   countryside
To te ro   Toru mo   Toru mo

Beloved, beloved,
Behind the cold screen in the dawn
I sense a vague fragrance of chrysanthemums
Like the scent of diseased spirits

The fragrance of white chrysanthemums rotting
   unnoticed
Beloved, beloved,

Before the dawn
My heart wanders in the shadows of the
   cemetery
I cannot bear this pale pink air
Beloved,
Mother.

Come in haste and extinguish the candle
I hear the sound of the storm
   That blows across the far horizon
Toru-mo   to-te-ka

("The Rooster"; collected in *Aoneko* [The Blue Cat] 1924; my translation.)

Sakutaro himself explained that in writing this poem he was inspired by "The Raven" and that he tried to practice the principles of poetry-writing Poe described in "The Philosophy of Composition." The use of a mysterious animal, the use of the refrain, the use of melancholy as a theme, and the evocation of mental scenery by the use of sound and its repetition are all reminiscent of "The Raven."

Dawn, the time of the poem, is appropriate for presenting a special condition of consciousness in which reason is suppressed and the memory of the dream haunts the psyche. The faraway scenery which the poet glimpses through the shutters is his own psychic scenery, evoked most vividly when reason is suppressed. In Poe's poem, the time is midnight, the polar opposite of daytime, yet the dawn reminds us of Poe's state of dreaming consciousness, the condition of the mind just prior to sinking into sleep. The decline of rational thinking is expressed through the sense of decay that pervades the poem, and a strongly sensuous state of consciousness emerges with the sense of decay. Yet most fundamental in making the poem close to "The Raven" is the evocation of something which is lost, something which is buried deep in the psychic realm. In Sakutaro's poem, the beloved and mother are put together, making "faraway nature in the lonely countryside" the primordial origin of life, the original home of the poet. Both in Sakutaro's poem and in Poe's poem, the longing for a deceased lover is turned into a longing for metaphysical existence. What Sakutaro saw in "The Raven" was "transcendental memory," which is what his own poetry always seeks to recapture. Although in Sakutaro's later works an extreme "Japanism" which rejects Western elements can be found, his return to Japanese culture was his attempt to return to the spiritual archetype, an attempt which exists as an essential core of dark romanticism.

In the post-World War II period, we can see further evidence of the significance of dark romanticism and the profundity of its influence on Japanese literature in the writings of Mishima Yukio. The Japanese writers of aestheticism, who form the mainstream of modern Japanese literature, reveal the links between traditional Japanese literature and the ideas and aesthetics of dark romanticism by their conscious effort to associate their literary endeavors with traditional Japanese literature. In each case their introduction to and learning from Western dark romanticism played an important role in their rediscovery of the Japanese literary tradition.

Ko Won

SOURCE: Introduction to *Buddhist Elements in Dada: A Comparison of Tristan Tzara, Takahashi Shinkichi, and Their Fellow Poets,* New York University Press, 1977, pp. 1-30.

[*In the following excerpt, Ko traces the influence of the Dada movement on Japanese literature.*]

The life of Dada as a poetical and artistic movement was by no means lengthy. Historically speaking, the onset of its group activities, whether they were those of "Pre-Dada" in New York, led by Marcel Duchamp, Francis Picabia, and Man Ray; or of Zurich Dada, whose group including Hugo Ball, Emmy Hennings, Jean (Hans) Arp, Marcel Janco, Tristan Tzara, Richard Huelsenbeck, Walter Serner, and Sophie Täuber, all of whom were to frequent the Cabaret Voltaire as their headquarters, had much to do with these expatriates' or deserters' desperate objections to World War I, which broke out in 1914. As the Dada movement took place roughly between 1914 and 1923, spreading over a large number of European and American countries, its major centers including New York, Zurich, Berlin, Cologne, Hanover, and Paris, some aspects of the movement—especially in Germany—were politically oriented. Strangely enough, however, despite the fact that Zurich was the place of exile for Lenin (who lived close to the Cabaret Voltaire) and other would-be revolutionaries during the war, the Zurich Dadaists, who are said to have sympathized with the Russian Revolution, seem to have hardly been inclined to things like Bolshevism in art.

From a literary-artistic point of view, Dada was, in any case, not necessarily the by-product of war experiences. Well before the structured movement began to develop, the way to Dada was already paved in the realms of poetry, art, and drama as well as philosophy. The Symbolist search for the absolute and belief in universal correspondence, the Impressionist discard of the conventional modes of seeing, breaking up the solidity of objects into a multiplicity of fragments, the Expressionist effort to objectify inner experience, the Futurist objection to nature and glorification of the noise and speed, and the Cubist fragmentation of the elements of an experience and synthetic rearrangement of them, for instance, are all related to Dada in one way or the other.

More specifically, as Professor Grossman examines in detail, Alfred Jarry, Arthur Cravan, and Jacques Vaché may well have been "three of Dada's most radical and most immediate predecessors." Far and near forerunners taken together, common to all is a decisive breakdown of the old conception of external reality, coupled with a revolt against present-day conditions and against the traditional manner of expression, and, in many cases, with the rejection of discursive intelligence. With this background and under the moral impact of World War I, there followed a general disgust and despair and a particular distrust of all existing values, including those of beauty, form, logic and words, order and system, among the young artists and poets of the mid-1920s. These were also true pacifists, becoming the core of an international movement which happened to be called Dada.

In the history of Western literature and art, Dada, therefore, stands between the trends of Cubism and Futurism and the following movement of Surrealism, which assimilated many aspects of Dada, with André Breton now assuming its leadership. By way of defining the difference between Dada and the former two movements (Cubism and Futurism) from which Dada broke away, let us simply have the then Dada poets, Tzara and Breton, speak for themselves. Tzara said in 1918 that

> Cubism was born from the simple way of looking at the object: Cézanne painted a cup twenty centimeters

> lower than his eyes, the cubists look at it from above, others complicate its appearance by making one part perpendicular and in putting it nicely on one side. . . . The futurist sees the same cup in movement, a succession of objects one alongside the other embellished maliciously by some lines of force. . . . The new artist protests: he no longer paints (symbolic and illusionistic reproduction) but rather creates directly in stone, wood, iron, tin, rocks, and locomotive organisms that can be turned about on any side by the limpid wind of momentary sensation.

Breton categorized the three trends in the early 1920s as follows: "Cubism was a school of painting, futurism a political movement: DADA is a state of mind. . . . DADA is artistic free-thinking." While admitting that each of these currents differed both regionally and individually within its own scope and according to the period of its development, Dada in general rejected virtually all the Cubist and Futurist "constructive" and modernistic principles. Although Dada shared quite a few methodological aspects of Cubism and Futurism, Dada was definitely against anything decorative and artificial; it was anti*art* and anti*literature;* it never allowed itself to accept the Futurist apotheosis of mechanical and technological civilization. After all, Dada "abolished" everything. At the same time, because of its negative and "destructive" nature, Dada was serious enough to be positive and creative as well. Its accomplishments included the threat to photographic representation, conventional perspective, and syntax in a thoroughgoing manner, replacing all sorts of bourgeois aesthetics with typographical representation, disjointed images, sounds rather than pretentious and limited (inaccurate) words; and the decentralization of logical mind into "nonsensical" humor, paving the way to the movement of the absurd and automatism.

The early phase of Dada became known to the Japanese in 1920, and it served in the following years to change the current mode of Japanese poetry, which now came to see an era of Dada. This new development was far more than accidental. During the 1910s, "modern" Japanese poetry—whose history had started in 1882 with the publication of *Shintaishi-sho* (New style poetry), an anthology of translations of various Western poetry in which the translators introduced the term "new style" as opposed to the traditions of *tanka* and *haiku*—marked an important period of symbolism. Owing a great deal to such anthologies of French and German poetry in Japanese translation as Ueda Bin's *Kaicho-on* (Sound of the tide, 1905); Nagai Kafu's *Sango-shu* (Corals, 1913); Horiguchi Daigaku's *Kino no hana* (Flowers of yesterday, 1918); and to Arthur Symons's *The Symbolist Movement in Literature,* the Japanese translation of which appeared in 1913, most of the Japanese symbolists exhibited at times a fusion of the aspects of European Symbolism and their own Buddhist background. In this Symbolist period, new conventions in Japanese poetry were established: the long-traditional Japanese rhythm pattern of seven-five (also five-seven) syllables was broken to a great extent; the language shifted from a Classic or a Neoclassic literary style (*bungotai*) to a more familiar colloquial style (*kogotai*); poetic vocabularies and metaphorical images were enriched more than ever.

In sharp contrast with this, another aspect of the Japanese poetry of the same period was noted by a tendency toward the popularization of the ideas of democratic and socialistic enlightenments as shown in the so-called *minshushi,* or poetry for the mass. It must be remembered that the end of World War I did not wholly bring about a peaceful and prosperous reign in Japan. Along with the Korean independence movement of 1919, the Siberian intervention of 1918-1922 (which had earlier created the "rice dispute" of 1918 in a Japanese locale) continued, reaching its peak when Japanese troops and civilians were attacked by Siberian partisans at Nikolayevsk, a port of Khabarovsk Territory, in 1920. In the course of "Taisho democracy," a term denoting not so much the democratic accomplishment as the ephemeral experiment of the Taisho era (1912-26), Japan's military activities in Siberia as a whole became the target of criticism in the Diet and the public responded to the expedition with either growing speculation, which caused the rise in the price of rice, or indifference, which was meant to show their disagreement. In a poem by Fukuda Masao, one of the major figures of the "people's poetry school" (*minshushi ha*) of this period, called "A Train and Handkerchiefs," we can visualize the scene:

> Where there passes a train,
> crying out a roar of *banzai,*
> loaded with soldiers on the way to Siberia—
> A mass of handkerchiefs flapping at the windows,
> crowds by the roadside watching them vacantly;
> only an old cartman
> shouted *banzai,* waving his hat.
>
> Soldiers are chosen for death, going off to die.
> What a national tragedy.
>
> I know everything too well to give cheers for
> you.
> Sorry, but I send you off with my tears instead.

Antimilitarism was also exemplified in such poems as "For Country" by Negishi Masayoshi, a man of the working class; "A Night Chat" by Fukushi Kojiro, a free-verse lyricist; and "War Is Bad" by Mushakoji Saneatsu, the individualistic novelist and the founder of the utopian socialist-like New Village movement. Following are some of Mushakoji's least poetic yet exemplary lines: "Since I hate/ to be killed/ I oppose murder,/ and therefore I oppose war./ Only those who/ like to be killed,/ those who like to see/ one whom they love killed,/ only such people/ can praise war."

At this time, Japan's reinforcements in Siberia led to her discord with the United States; and the naval expansion of great powers, including Japan, was so competitive that it was eventually limited at the Washington

Conference of 1921-22. This limitation, however, did not mean the weakening of the military influence on Japanese politics and society. Edwin O. Reischauer, in his *The United States and Japan,* describes the power structure of the new Japan of the 1920s as consisting of "the highly centralized economic empires of the *zaibatsu* [plutocracy, plutocrats], the huge and omnipresent civil bureaucracy, the all-seeing, all-knowing police, and, worst of all, the closely knit and fanatical corps of army officers." As the trends of democracy and individual liberties kept pace with militarism, so did capitalistic development with postwar financial panic. Thus, the better-organized labor movement began to launch political and legal issues, activities of great impact in 1920 including the Yahata iron-steel workers' strike and May Day rallies in Tokyo and Osaka, which demanded, among other things, the abolition of the oppressive "peace maintenance police" law, an article of which suppressed both labor and tenant disputes. While the nation was still struggling for the adoption of universal manhood suffrage, with demonstrations of the masses and the disturbance in the Diet marking political confusion in 1920, the government retaliated with dictatorial measures. According to Ike Nobutake, branches of the Reservists Association were established in the 1920s even "in factories and mines for the purpose of combatting the growth of labor unions."

In academic and intellectual circles, there was also great controversy. The government's anxiety over radicalism was first evidenced by the suppression of the study of anarchism, the movement of which in Japan had already been confronted with difficulties, such as the execution of Kotoku Shusui and eleven other anarchists in 1911 (i.e., toward the end of the Meiji era, 1868-1912). In January 1920, Morito Tatsuo, an assistant professor at Tokyo Imperial University, was indicted for his article, "Kuropotokin no shakai shiso no kenkyu" (A study of Kropotkin's social thought), published in the same month's issue of *Keizaigaku kenky* (Economic studies). His indictment, along with that of Ouchi Hyoe, the editor of the journal, was immediately reported in the daily, *Tokyo asahi shinbun,* which explained the cause as "a result of the government's determination of the assistant professor as a popularizer of anarchism, whose article served to prompt an action of the Society for National Development (Kokoku Doshikai), a student organization." Accompanied by Morito's suspension from teaching, the charge of his "repugnance to the Japanese constitutional order" became a serious public concern, for, Arima Tatsuo observed, "Morito and Ouchi had on their side the sympathy of interested college students, intellectuals and the major newspapers."

This controversy was followed in the same year by the publication of Peter Kropotkin's *Memoirs of a Revolutionist,* translated by Osugi Sakae, the leading anarchist (murdered immediately following the great Kanto earthquake of 1923), and Volume I of Karl Marx's *Das Kapital,* translated by Takabatake Motoyuki, in a Marxism series. Also established in 1920 were a leftist magazine, *Shakaishugi* (Socialism), and the Japan Socialist Union, followed by the founding of the Japan Communist party in 1922. Anarchism and Marxism were, in fact, the two main streams of thought to which Japanese radicals were allied around this time, although one was in conflict with the other. Except for some political activists, however, the ideological basis of the intellectuals was generally characterized by a sort of radical, liberalistic idealism, which was prevailing among the writers too.

Under these circumstances the works of such "democratic" poets as Walt Whitman, Horace Traubel, and Edward Carpenter were published in translation in the beginning of the 1920s. Their ideas attracted some members of Shiwakai, a poets' association, which came to be dominated around 1921 by the "people's poetry" school. Of the two major literary magazines established in 1921, *Nihon shijin* (Japanese poets) and *Tane maku hito* (The sower), the latter, which was founded by Komaki Chikae who had witnessed World War I in France and was under the influence of Henri Barbusse's *Clarté* movement (a kind of ideological International) on his return from Paris, lured laborers, intellectuals, writers, and thinkers with its motto of cosmopolitanism. In its first issue, a manifesto was published, which reads in part: "Man created God in the past. Man has now killed God. . . . We fight for the truth of modern age . . . . We defend the truth of revolution for the sake of our living. Those who sow the seeds rise here—together with the comrades of the world." At a time when a serious dispute between the anarcho-syndicalists and the Bolsheviks of Japan was going on, *The Sower* devoted its pages to writers inclined to the idea of social revolution and paved the way to an era of proletarian literature.

To sum up the climate of the years from 1920 to 1922, the people did not suffer (unlike those in Europe) directly from the havoc of World War I in which Japan also joined, but they wanted a secure peace after the war. There was a fear of war, and people were against militaristic expansion. Postwar prosperity soon evolved into severe financial panic, which created social problems. The Japanese people began to doubt the established order and the values of the past. They were disenchanted with the aristocracy and disgusted with the growing bureaucracy. Intellectuals were aware of what was wrong and concerned with what should be done. In the realm of poetry, while the *minshushi,* which also employed the colloquial style, reached its height in the beginning of the 1920s, it could not escape the looseness of expression, because it was little concerned with aesthetics. Naturally, the poets who belonged to this school were confronted with an attack by those who emphasized poetry as a work of art.

Thus, at the turn of the decade, many younger poets became disgusted with the kind of lyricism which was too personal to express the dramatically changing phases of the age, on the one hand, and the prosaic descriptive style which was too plain for the intensity of modern man's thought and feelings, on the other. They wanted a further modernization of Japanese poetry as much as they were eager to revolutionize the political and social systems of Japan. They wanted an aesthetic revolution in style and expression in order to deal with new subject matter and new sentiment in the modern world. Although their war experiences were not as intimate as those of European writers, they were equally interested in reexamining life and society.

At this point, in the beginning of the twenties, a decade which saw an epoch-making development of avant-garde and of proletarian literature in Japanese literary history, the Dada current made its impact felt. Thus the seeds were sown for some of the sophisticated and revolutionary poets to find immediate kinship with Dada. It was Takahashi Shinkichi who became the pioneering poet of the Dada movement in Japan, which flourished during the first half of the 1920s, a movement which exerted influence in a new development of Korean poetry too.

In general, there is a big difference between the West and Japan in the scale and nature of the Dada movements. Western Dada (in both its inception and development) was a truly organized movement in the sense that those poets who shared similar ideas—often in collaboration with artists, and sometimes with musicians—participated together, although places and times varied, in the publication of their manifestative, theoretical, and creative works in journals, many of which were founded for this particular purpose. In addition, their group activities included demonstrations, theatrical events, and the reading of "simultaneous poetry." On the other hand, Dada in Japan was, strictly speaking, seldom organized as a movement. As far as poetic works are concerned, Takahashi was the sole Dada at the outset, aside from Tsuji Jun's moral support. It was only after some of Takahashi's Dada poems had been published in 1921 and 1922 that there appeared other followers of Dada. Personal contact among those who claimed themselves to be Dadaist was very much limited: Takahashi met Tsuji in 1921 for the first time; and as Kikuchi Yasuo points out, Dada in Japan was "permeated" through the friendship between the two writers. It was in 1922 that Takahashi became acquainted with Hirato Renkichi, the Futurist who was also interested in Dada and whose Futurist works attracted the former. The younger Dada poet, Nakahara Chuya, met Takahashi only in 1927, shortly before Nakahara wrote an essay on Takahashi. Although there were some short-lived little magazines devoted to Dada in the early part of the twenties, they seem to have been least influential. A group of anarchists launched a radical poetry magazine called *Aka to kuro* (Red and black) in 1923, which some of the contemporary Japanese historians tend to associate with the Dada movement, but its member poets were, in a strict sense, anarchists who felt certain affinity with Dada rather than Dada adherents. In this respect, Tsuboi Shigeji seems right in observing the following:

> The impact of Dadaism appears to have been felt to a degree where it produced [a special] atmosphere rather than as a theoretical influence. However, even if it was limited to that extent, Dada as a poetic spirit had the power as strong as to set what was moving within each poet's inner world on fire. A characteristic element common to those poets of that time [the early 1920s] who were more or less Dadaistic was the awareness of self-decomposition, and the explosion of energy accompanying this decomposition served as the basis of their poetic spirit.

While the Japanese Dada and semi-Dada poets brought about a revolution in both subject matter and expression, they soon encountered the communists' criticism that Dada was nothing more than intellectual escapism and that it interfered with the social revolution. As the proletarian literary activity grew vigorous in the latter half of 1925, there followed an uncompromising conflict between the leftist- ideology-oriented writers and the other faction. Meanwhile, the year 1925 marked a point of departure for the Surrealist movement in Japan. Aside from Horiguchi Daigaku's new and influential translation of contemporary French poetry, *Gekka no ichigun* (A group under the moon), which included the poems of Philippe Soupault and Ivan Goll, the professor-poet Nishiwaki Junzaburo attracted young Japanese poets of the time with the French Surrealist publications which he had brought with him on his return from Europe in 1925. In the same year, the writings of Louis Aragon, André Breton, and Paul Eluard were published in Japanese translation in a little magazine, *Bungei tambi* (Literary aestheticism), in which also appeared somewhat Surrealistic poems by Japanese. In due course, the Surrealist movement—perhaps the best organized in the history of Japanese literary movements—surfaced in 1927, when a journal called *Bara, majutsu, gakusetsu* (Rose, magic, theory) was published for the Surrealists, alongside an anthology of their writings, *Fukuiku taru kafu yo* (Fragrant stroker!). This trend lasted for a decade or so thereafter.

It is true that none of the Japanese Dada poets has ever been officially associated with the Surrealist movement in Japan. This was unlike the situation in France, where Dada was "taken over" by Surrealism. Although Dada was preceded by Symbolism and followed by Surrealism in the history of Japanese poetry, it seems proper to say that the Symbolist fashion was still going on, Hagiwara Sakutar having been an important Symbolist poet, along with Futurism in the Dada period.

Despite the fact that the Dada movement in Japan was short-lived and small-scaled, the Dada works of Takahashi Shinkichi, the author of seventeen books of poetry in addition to ten volumes of essays on art and three collections of literary essays, are significant and important not only because they exerted a remarkable influence on other Japanese poets, both Dadaists and non-Dadaists, an influence which served to mature the modernity of Japanese poetry, but also because they reveal a fascinating blend of Dada and Buddhism, especially Zen. Takahashi, as he has repeatedly emphasized, found in Dada a perfect affinity with Zen.

I. THE RECEPTION OF DADA IN JAPAN

Unlike the manner in which Symbolist poetry and Surrealism were introduced into Japan by translator-poets or translator-scholars, Dada became known to the Japanese public through its journalists. It seems reasonable to assume that Kurt Schwitters was the first among Western Dadaists to appear in a Tokyo daily newspaper; it was in 1920 that the *Manchoho* published an anonymous article, "A Strange Phenomenon in the Art Circle of Germany: Schwitter's Merz Pictures," in which the word "Dadaist" was used for the first time in Japanese writing. More than just a report, this short article contained the columnist's comments on the paintings and sculpture exhibited in Germany around 1920: "Externally, it [the tendency] is nothing other than an extension of Futurism, Cubism, and *Berliner Sezession;* internally, however, it may be interpreted as that which has, in a confusion of the cruelty of war and the misery of defeat, fallen into a formless chaotic state." In explaining Schwitter's use of materials, the article defined his *Merzbild* as "not a *Gemälde* but a *Gebilde,* the word *Merz* having no particular meaning." These comments thus seem to have alluded, though at a superficial level, to some aspects of a new artistic movement in Europe, with a slight hint of Dada, namely, an undertone of despair and chaos, the use of unorthodox nonart materials, and the use of chance.

This was followed in the same year by two longer articles more specifically on Dada itself, published together as "The Latest Art of Epicureanism: Dadaism Becoming Popular in the Postwar Era," by Shiran, and "A View of Dadaism," by Yotosei. In an attempt to define the difference between Dada and Futurism, the former, filled with fragmentary information on the Dada movement, and generally more critical than sympathetic toward it, refers to Tristan Tzara's word on "the abolition of everything—home, morality, common sense, memory, archeology, prophets, and the future." Shiran further quotes as one of the Dada principles from Tzara, with no source specified, that "Dada is not madness, nor wisdom, nor irony, look at me, there's a good man. Art was a hazelnut game." Criticizing Dada's "lunatic and playful" manner of expression, the columnist, in attempting to account for the uselessness of man's action and word, argues that many explanations of it can be found in Buddhism and Nietzsche. His overall interpretation of Dada is summed up as follows: "Dadaism is, after all, a kind of Bolshevism and nihilism in literature and art; Dadaists are extreme epicureans, thoroughgoing individualists, nihilists, and realists. . . . They aim at the destruction of love, philosophy, psychology, and everything; they are sort of mad destroyers who will recognize certain senses only."

The other article by Yotosei provides more specific information on the Dada movement, with a list of European, American, and Brazilian Dadas and their publications, including *SIC, Litterature, 391,* and *The Blind Man.* Yotosei also supplies more relevant quotations, such as those from Tzara's "Dada Manifesto 1918," published in *Dada* No. 3, in the following: "I am against systems, the most acceptable system is the one of not having any system, on principle"; "I proclaim the opposition of all cosmic faculties to this gonorrhea of a putrid sun . . . Dada; abolition of the future." Also, referring to Walter Serner's "Manifesto, 'The Last Loosening,' published in *Dada* No. 4," Yotosei cites a quotation, in Japanese, which he equates with "an idler's somniloquy." His translation of Serner's words reads:

> Everybody knows that a dog is not a hammock. Few know, however, that a fist hits the artist's head without this tender hypothesis. And nobody knows that exclamations are the best. The world view is a confusion of words. . . . A rhetorician is not an ass. . . . One can hold women's silk stockings, but he can hardly grasp a genius.

Despite his sarcasm, Yotosei goes on to consider the reason why an outlook of this kind had drawn the public attention as a new literary-artistic principle in a direct relation to the downfall of Futurism. He points out the fact that the major Futurists, including Filippo Marinetti, had turned out in the midst of war to proclaim nationalism, an idea which profoundly disturbed the European writers who had witnessed the misery of war, preferring instead internationalism. Thus the Dada ideas of antiwar and antinationalism were made pointedly clear.

It was in this article that the first excerpts from Western Dada poems in Japanese translation appeared: seven lines from "Attraction" by Walter Serner, and five lines from "Phantastische Gebete" by Richard Huelsenbeck. Yotosei, however, chose to present these poems, not because of a belief in their value, but, in his words, to exemplify the "extreme strangeness of contents" and the "outrageousness of expression" of Dada poetry. His criticism culminates in the observation that "Dadaism is nothing but hedonism, a product of the mentally effeminate writers' unsteadiness."

In the meantime, it is worth pointing out that in October 1920, painter-poet Kambara Tai published *Dai-ikkai Kambara Tai sengensho* (The first Kambara Tai manifesto), which shows some aspects of Dada. Although he has always been regarded in Japan as a Futurist, his manifesto of 1920 seems to be a peculiar modification of Futurism. The opening statement of this sixty-four-page manifesto is eloquent enough to sum up his basic ideas:

> Painters, be gone! Art critics, be gone! Art is absolutely free. There is no poetry, no painting, no music. What exists is creation only. Art is absolutely free. The freedom of its form is also absolute. Say, nerve, reason, sense, sound, smell, color, light, desire, movement, pressure—and furthermore, true life itself which stands at the end

of all—there is nothing that does not fit the content of art; any material and any form cannot be useless in the course of creation.

This statement is reminiscent of what Kurt Schwitters said of *Merz,* the kin of Dada: "*Merz* stands for freedom from all fetters, for the sake of artistic creation." Kambara further rejects "any kind of academism" and "idolatry in the arts." It is true that he emphasizes in his manifesto the beauty of the noise, speed, color, and light of mechanical and industrious urban society, but he did not agree with Marinetti on such points as the praise of "a roaring car. . . is more beautiful than the *Victory of Samothrace*." Referring to this passage, Kambara comments: "It must be noted that he [Marinetti] is confused with the great beauty of the car and the depth and breadth of modern man's nerve, keen to beauty." Despite the widely known fact that he was deeply inspired by the theoretical and creative works of Marinetti, with whom he had a large correspondence, Kambara's quest for new art was heading toward something beyond both Cubism and Futurism, if not a clear acceptance of Dada. His position was, as he declared in his manifesto, not only against "the shallow realism and naturalism . . . and the pretended intellectual tendency," but also against "the Futurists who show off modern art by depicting modernized objects."

About the same time, a new Futurist movement surfaced in Tokyo in December 1921, when poet Hirato Renkichi distributed a leaflet, *Nihon miraiha segen undo* (Japanese Futurist manifestation movement) with a French subtitle, *Mouvement futuriste japonais*. Largely based on the Italian Futurist manifesto which had been introduced into Japan as early as 1909, Hirato added several concrete suggestions for a new manner of writing:

We want to participate in a true creation by employing onomatopoeia, mathematical signs, and all kinds of organic methods. By destroying, as much as possible, syntax and the conventions of expression, especially by sweeping away the dead bodies of adjectives and adverbs, and by using infinitives of verbs, we shall advance toward a realm which will not allow any invasion.

Although much of the rest consisted of a partly plagiarized version of Marinetti's Milan text and was, as his friend, Takahashi Shikichi, later pointed out, quite anachronistic, Hirato's advocacy of a revolution in composition shows, whether intended or not, a certain affinity with Dada. In fact, Hirato's principle evolved into what he called *"doitsu hyogen-shugi,"* the resulting analogism literally translating into something corresponding to a synchronous Expression-ism. It would seem that he meant to synthesize four elements, converted here from his special nomenclature into "time Futurist poetry," "spatial Cubist poetry," "the fourth-side poetry (*Futurisme + Cubisme = Dadaisme = Expressionisme*)" and "post- Futurism or the poetry of *analogisme* (*Imagisme + Expressionisme = Analogisme* = a perfect synchronism of imagery and inner image.)" Whatever expressions he used, it is obvious that his theory shows the impact of Dada, and his "Japanese Futurism" must have been meant to be a Japanese-like modification of the many Western avant-garde currents of the time.

Apart from Hirato's manifesto, more serious discussions on Dada by Japanese critics, scholars, and poets arose in 1921 and 1922, most of them appearing in magazines. Following Kawaji Ryuko's introductory article, "What is Dadaism?" Katayama Koson, in his "A Study in Dadaism," discussed the history of the Dada movement, largely based on Richard Huelsenbeck's *En avant Dada: Die Gechichte des Dadaismus.* With many quotations from the booklet, Katayama most strongly emphasized the difference between Huelsenbeck's activist ideas and the characteristics of the works of other Dadas, including Tristan Tzara, Hugo Ball, Jean (Hans) Arp, and Francis Picabia—"a heretic Dada group," in Katayama's words, "whose activities were more successful than the former's." Katayama's view, on the whole, favored the ideas of Huelsenbeck. One of the relevant points made in Katayama's study is the discussion of three artistic principles, namely, bruitism, simultaneity, and the use of new materials in painting. However, Katayama himself seemed torn between Dada and Expressionism.

A few months later, two articles on Dada by Tsuji Jun, the translator of Cesare Lombroso, Thomas De Quincey, Oscar Wilde, and Max (Schmidt) Stirner, were published. In "Misunderstood Dada," Tsuji points out that although some Japanese thought of Dada merely as a by-product of the tragedy of war in Europe and therefore not serious enough to dwell on, and others were even proud of knowing nothing about Dada, they would eventually ally themselves with its ideas and ramifications. Tsuji then defines this universality from a psychological point of view: "Dada bites at the misery of creatures from its bottom, aiming inwardly at liberating them from their falsehood, their own traps, megalomania, and silly vanity," emphasizing, at the same time, absolute freedom of the individual.

In another article, "A Talk on Dada," published in the same year, Tsuji expounded an interesting view on Laurence Sterne in association with the Dada attitude, quoting his own English sentence from "Tada-Dada" (*"tada,"* meaning "only, alone"), which was included in his book, *Fur mango* (A wanderer's miscellanies), published in 1922. The English part reads: "My dear grand Laurence Sterne (who is the Greatest *Dadaist* ever born in the world, born too early, and lived and died miserably for the sake of his great Dada)." Tsuji's view considers the following:

The pioneer of Dada is, in my opinion, neither Tristan Tzara, Richard Huelsenbeck, nor Marcel Janco, but Laurence Sterne, born in England in the 18th century. Tzara, perhaps, took his name

> Tristan from *Tristram Shandy*. . . . which I think can be claimed to be the Dada bible.

In the same essay, Tsuji again reveals himself as a Stirnerian: "Dada is a fine reality-lover in a Stirnerian sense. When the philosophy of [Max} Stirner transforms itself into the arts, that makes precisely Dada art." He also cites a poem by Takahashi Shinkichi which he mentions he had altered, confirming the fact that Japanese Dada poetry was indeed known, certainly to him, prior to the publication of Takahashi's first Dada poems in 1922.

A little earlier than this, a technical comparison of "Eccentric Schools of Poetry: The Poetry of Futurism, Cubism, Dadaism and Imagism" by Kawaji Ryuko appeared in a university journal. After a discussion of Apollinaire's *Calligrammes,* with an accompanying reprint of "Il Pleut," he points out that "Dada poetry may well be most similar to Cubism, because it applies decomposition even to word; in its manner of writing, in some cases, a Cubistic typographical method is used." At a time when some of the Japanese avant-garde poets were still confused with Futurism, Cubism, and Dada—or perhaps were trying to combine them all—Kawaji's observation does not seem to have offered a clear distinction among them.

In a manner more detailed and favorable to Dada, Moriguchi Tari presented some relevant points in his article, "The Poetry and Painting of Dadaism, published in the same issue of the influential Waseda University literary review. Introducing the program of the Dada demonstration of February 5, 1920, in Paris (in Japanese translation), the originals of "Portrait de Tristan Tzara" and "The Mind of Christ" by Picabia; "Suicide" by Louis Aragon; and "Paroxysme" by Pierre Chapka-Bonnière, Moriguchi discussed Marcel Duchamp's (re-)painting of the *Mona Lisa,* entitled *LHOOQ,* and Tzara's manifestoes, in terms of the negative and rebellious attitude of the Dada spirit. Finally, paying attention to the pronouncement of "the awakening of antihuman action" and of the antagonism against slavish flattery, his comment concludes with a criticism of contemporary Japanese writers who, he thinks, should feel ashamed of their idleness coupled at the same time with their cry for revolution. This criticism had much to do with the new political, social, and intellectual developments in the beginning of the 1920s, an outline of which is given in the Introduction to the present work.

II. TAKAHASHI SHINKICHI, THE PIONEER

Takahashi Shinkichi, who is now regarded as the only living Japanese Zen poet, proved himself in the early 1920s to be the pioneer of Dada poetry in Japan.

Born in 1901 in a small town in Ehime Prefecture as the seventh of eight children of a schoolmaster, Shinkichi led a somewhat unusual life in his teens. Although his mother died when he was eleven years old, she, who had been "an ardent Buddhist," must have exerted some influence on his young years. Awazu Norio sketches Takahashi's boyhood as follows:

> This boy grows watching the noisy village people . . . in the celebration of the victory in the Russo-Japanese War, and listening to the grown-ups talking about the assassination of It Hirobumi and the execution of Kotoku Shusui. At the same time, his independent temperament, which seems to have been inherited from his parents, becomes more and more apparent. One of the most charac-teristic attitudes of this young boy may well be that he is totally and terribly moved by his own emotions and thoughts, and is lacking, unlike many other boys, the capability of relating him to the already existing order of this world.

In this observation, which is based on Takahashi's autobiography, *Dagabaji Jingiji monogatari* (Tale of Dagabaji Jingiji), one can visualize the youthful, rebellious thinker. Takahashi himself speaks of "a metaphysical experience" he had while he was a boy of grade-school age:

> As I was walking along a narrow path on the riverside one day, a thought like this happened to flash in my brain—. . . . If I drew a long thread from this point where I am standing and extended one end several hundred million years into the past, and the other to an infinitely far point in the future, the length of the two threads would be the same. I am always in the center of the past and future. . . . Even if I, grown old 50 or 60 years later, would have extended the thread in two directions, the length would be the same as one I would have now. I am, then, always in the same place and nowhere else. The time I experience becomes extinct all the while and turns out to be nothing. Whether the time is of the past or of the future, all collapses, and the only existence is myself, which stands in the center.

In the same article, he also recalls an incident where, as a young boy, he had witnessed a healthy-looking carpenter who had hanged himself, leaving beside him an uneaten piece of bun. He says that this experience may have influenced him thereafter in forming his nihilistic thoughts.

Evidence of Takahashi's maturing intellect surfaced toward the end of his secondary education. He learned of the Russian Revolution of 1917 while he was attending a school of commerce, and he "grew restless and impatient because of the feeling of world unrest." According to the "Chronology" in his *Complete Poetic Works,* he withdrew from school shortly before his graduation early in 1918 and, without his father's knowledge, went to Tokyo. He had left school feeling that to graduate was to verify his school record, and since his friends had been expelled from the same school because of a strike, he felt his own graduation would stain his career by labeling him a conformist. Takahashi says, "I was rebelling against something invisible. . . . I did not want to be bound to anything." Takahashi's further explanation of this decision reads: "I took up my position to cut, in advance, all possible chains that would disturb my intent to oppose home life and to defy society." Immediately after his furtive departure for Tokyo, he could find little to do there and moved around Kobe and Osaka, doing some least decent work until he returned home late 1918. In the following spring, however, he went to Tokyo again, doing odd jobs for a transportation company, a restaurant, and a bakery until he contracted typhoid fever. Found in the street after having been felled by the disease, he was then admitted to a hospital for infectious diseases. Interestingly, Takahashi considers this serious illness one of the factors which "brought him into contact with the Dada spirit."

Aside from the rebellious milieu of the time in general and Takahashi's personal experience, it seems relevant for understanding his strong inclination to Dada to examine his early literary background, which appears to be more Western than Eastern up to this point. According to the poet's own memoirs, as early as 1914, when he was only thirteen years old, he read, "with enthusiasm," Feodor Dostoevsky's *Crime and Punishment* in Japanese translation; thereafter he did not miss any translated works of the Russian writer and found *The Brothers Karamazov* (translated in 1916) the best of all. (Incidentally, a Japanese collection of the complete works of Dostoevsky appeared in 1920.) In listing his readings in translation before 1920, Takahashi mentions *War and Peace* and *Anna Karenina* by Leo Tolstoy, four volumes of the complete works of Plato, and Plutarch's *Lives* (which the young Takahashi found more interesting than Plato's writings). In addition, as the poet recollects, he read all the newly translated works of Anton Chekhov, August Strindberg, and Gustave Flaubert. It is important to note that he became profoundly interested in Max (Schmidt) Stirner, alongside Dostoevsky, when he read *Yuiitsusha to sono shoy* (The sole man and his possessions), Tsuji Jun's translation (published in May 1920) of a part of Stirner's *Der Einzige und sein Eigentum.* As Takahashi suggests on another occasion, by this time he was also familiar with the works of Friedrich Nietzsche; this familiarity seems to have been equally significant in forming the young poet's philosophical maturity. Although he does not specify what he read, it is worth pointing out that Nietzsche's *Thus Spake Zarathustra* and *Beyond Good and Evil* were translated in 1911 and 1915, respectively, followed by the ten-volume translations of complete works, published in 1919.

In his early years—it is not clear how early, but certainly before 1927—Takahashi also read Karl Marx's *Das Kapital,* the poetry of Omar Khayyám, some of the Greek tragedies, and the poetry of Theocritus (both of which he felt were "exciting"). When he read during this time Edward Gibbon's Roman history, he "came to dislike Christianity." Among the Japanese poets whose poetry he read in his teens, such as Shimazaki Toson, Yamamura Bocho, Hagiwara Sakutaro, and Fukushi Ko- jiro, he says that he was attracted to Shimazaki and Fukushi; all this indicates nothing more than a variety of his interest, ranging over Romanticism, Symbolism, and idealism. Apart from Japanese poets, Takahashi admired the mystical poetry of the ancient Chinese poet, Ch'ü Yüan (c. 340-278 B.C.), the author of a large portion of *Ch'u Tz'u* (The songs of the south, Ch'u), along with the Persian work, *Rubáiyát* of Omar Khayyám. It would seem that the young man was interested more than anything else in various expressions of negative views of life and reality.

Takahashi's literary career began to bud on his return home in 1920: his first fiction piece, "Honoo o kakagu" (Raising a flame), won first place in the *Manchoho* short-story contest. This was followed by a poem called "Taigai shi" (An approximate poem) and an essay, "Dada butsu mondo" (Dada-Buddha question and answer), published in the *Yahata shinbun,* a local newspaper for which Takahashi worked for two months. Unfortunately, these two works are not available for consideration here; however, it is interesting to note that Takahashi, in the title of the latter, combined Dada and the Buddha. Obviously, then, he must have written it after he had become acquainted with the Dada movement in August of the same year.

The year 1920 marked a turning point for Takahashi in that he found in Dada a fresh principle which would be a guide in nurturing his negative attitude toward many kinds of literary and cultural conventions. "When the end of World War I gave impetus to the collapse of Europe," Takahashi recalls, "a wooden horse called Dada started running with its teeth of rebellion pulled out. I was the first Asian to hold its reins." He also recollects how he responded to the two *Manchoho* articles on Dada as follows:

> I came to know Dada when I was 19 years old by reading Tzara's words, "I proclaim the opposition of all cosmic faculties to this gonorrhea of a putrid sun. . . . Dada; abolition of the future." I felt refreshed as if my brain was struck and broken by Serner's manifesto in which he said, "The world view is a confusion of words." All the knowledge I had acquired by that time through reading books now scattered and disappeared all at once. With Dada's poetic methods whereby letters of different sizes are arranged in reverse or obliquely, I felt something like membranes peeling off from my eyes.

Despite the fact that "neither Shiran nor Yotosei, when they wrote about Dadaism, were ever in agreement about it," Takahashi says, " . . . these articles gave me an extraordinary shock." In fact, Takahashi "reacted against the ideas" of the journalists and "was fascinated with Dada itself." While he regarded Shiran as having some Buddhist background and considered certain of Shiran's observations quite valid, Takahashi, refuting Yotosei's comment on the feeble nature of Dada, later defended his own standpoint: "It is an unmistakable fact that not simply men of spiritual weakness alone came under the spell of Dada." The young poet thus readily accepted the Dada spirit: "The driving force of the birth of Dadaism was the spirit implanted in Tzara's brain, and the one who caught it at once in Japan was Takahashi Shinkichi." The Dada method was, as we have seen, an eye-opener to him. Unfortunately, however, he had no friends with whom he could share his excitement and exchange ideas. His imagination, as he said, simply took flight far up into the sky over Paris, a place unknown to him.

Early in 1921, he left home again—not for large cities this time, but for a mountain—to become a janitor-novice in residence at the Kinzan Shussekiji, a Shingon sect temple in Kita-gun. (He thought at that time that he would rather choose to renounce the world and stay celibate all his life.) During his eight-month stay at the monastery, he had many opportunities to read (in Japanese) the *Yuimakyo* (the *Vimalakirti* sutra), which consists of the explanations of Vimalakirti, who was known as a wealthy lay disciple of convincing eloquence, and the *Gezinmikkyo* (the *Sandhinirmocana* sutra). "I tasted satisfaction with my touching a part of the profound doctrines pronounced in these Mahayana sutras," Takahashi recalls, "but I was incapable of understanding them precisely." With these Buddhist ideas, he states that he "came to feel, though vaguely, something different in nature from those of Nietzsche, Stirner, Dostoevsky, and Dada that I had read before." Aside from the difference, one notes a significant combination of interests—significant because the diversity of Mahayana Buddhism, nihilism, individualistic liberalism, and Dada was to serve him in helping to adjust and develop his philosophy in the years to come.

It is also interesting that Takahashi, in a temple where esoteric Buddhist practices were still kept, "objected to the sacred rule and soon the fire of distrust and doubt was burning in his mind, leading him deliberately to act out the transgression of commandments." Accordingly, Takahashi was expelled from the temple involuntarily, and was already on the way to Tokyo for his third visit; he thereafter settled down in its vicinity.

In December 1921, Takahashi made about 100 mimeographed copies of *Makuwauri shishu: DA 1* (Melon poems: DA 1)—"Makuwauri" being his nickname at this time—which the poet claims to be his first book of poetry. The "DA" in the title is, of course, directly suggestive of Dada. Takahashi, in fact, often puns on the Japanese word-ending "da" or the letter "D" in his poems in association with "DADA." The mimeographed edition contained 28 poems, and 25 of them were included in his first printed volume, *Dadaisuto Shinkichi no shi* (Poems of Dadaist Shinkichi), published in 1923. Apparently, then, Takahashi had written many Dada poems as early as 1921 and even earlier.

In 1921, carrying the book of *Melon Poems* with him, Takahashi visited Tsuji Jun, who was to write several articles on Dada beginning in 1922 and subsequently edited Takahashi's 1923 volume. Tsuji may well have been the first Dada associate of Takahashi. According to Tsuji, Takahashi wanted a copy of his entire translation of Stirner's book, published under the title of *Jigaky* (the self sutra) in 1921. Tsuji thus discovered that the visitor understood Stirner "very well indeed" and that Takahashi's "Taigai shi" ("a kind of essay," as Tsuji called it) was largely influenced by Stirner. It should be noted that Stirner's extreme individualism emphasized that the only reality is self or ego, before which home, society, state, and all else are empty and meaningless. Takahashi's continuing interest in Stirner would then seem to indicate that the young poet, having learned something about Dada and Buddhism, was still seeking a personal philosophy of his own. Tsuji says of Takahashi's *Melon Poems* that

> Dada is not limited to a certain, one art. Shinkichi's poetry is his life, religion, and, at the same time, his philosophy. He read through the Buddhist literature, . . . mastered the Dada spirit, translated it [or them] into Stirner, and produced the *Melon* poetry.

Takahashi, however, did not always agree with Tsuji, as will be seen.

The publication in mimeographed form was followed by a long prose poem called "Dangen wa dadaisuto" (Assertion is Dadaist), one of the most—perhaps *the* most—important of Dada poems by Takahashi, written on August 14, 1922, and published in *Shukan nihon* (The weekly Japan) in the following month. As far as the public was concerned, it was through this poem that Takahashi became known as "Dadaist." Furthermore, his was the first voice of Japanese Dada. In 1922 four more poems followed: "Kentai" (Ennui)—later called "Sara" (Dish)—published in *Shimun,* (April); and "Dada no shi mittsu" (Three Dada poems)—"Tsumbo" (A deaf man), "Mekura" (A blind man), and "Oshi" (A mute)—all in *Kaizo* (October). At the time the latter three poems were published, Japanese articles on Dada by Katayama, Kawaji, Moriguchi, and Tsuji had also appeared. All in all, then, it seems that the spirit of Dada in Japan had advanced in 1922 through both theoretical and poetic works.

The year 1923 was another memorable date in the development of modern Japanese poetry. In January of that year a group of young anarchists (Hagiwara Kyojiro, Okamoto Jun, Kawazaki Chotaro, and Tsuboi Shigeji) launched a radical poetry magazine, *Aka to kuro* (Red and black), and a striking "Manifesto" was published on the cover of its first issue: "What is poetry? What is poet? We abandon all the ideas of the past and boldly proclaim that 'Poetry is a bomb! The poet is a black criminal who throws his bombs against the prison's hard walls and doors.'" Tsuboi Shigeji, then editor of this journal, later elaborated upon the manifesto: "Since the poets regarded society as a prison, that same negative spirit pervaded the existing conventions of the poetry of the time, those conventions also being seen as a prison." In the magazine's third issue of the same year, "*Aka to kuro* undo dai-ikkai sengen" (The *Red and Black* movement manifesto 1) was published, which reads in part: "Our existence is negation itself. Negation is creation. Creation is nothingness. . . . Let us devote ourselves entirely to negation! Only by doing so can we exist." Anarchistic, indeed; the *Red and Black* is regarded by some Japanese literary historians as having made an initial contribution to the Dada movement in Japan, a theory with which Tak-ahashi does not agree. What we are concerned with at this point is that these poets' ideas represented the social concerns and avant-garde spirit that had grown in and intruded upon the times.

In the following month, *Poems of Dadaist Shinkichi,* the first book of Dada poetry in Japan, was published. Sato Haruo, in his Introduction to the book, observed the world of Takahashi as follows:

> Takahashi's life and art represent complete opposition and challenge to the pretentious art of the academy as well as the carefree life. His passive—nay, going beyond both passive and aggressive—attitude is, in the sense stated above, powerful. Takahashi always lives by this spirit.

Tsuji Jun, who edited Takahashi's volume, said in his postscript (following the comment on Takahashi's *Melon Poems* cited previously): "He [Takahashi] is the pioneer of Dada [in Japan], who first seized the Dada spirit most strongly and profoundly." To the work of this "Dadaist," the anarchic poet-critic Tsuboi Shigeji responded immediately in his review, "Saijo Yaso and Takahashi Shinkichi":

> The poetry of Takahashi Shinkichi may indeed look like a monster to those who still adhere to the concept of poetry that has been dominant up to now. It is a sharp dagger, a pistol, a bomb. Comparing his poetry with that of Mr. Saijo, in fact, I find there a difference which is greater than that between a bomb and candy.

Listing four important books of poetry published in 1923, Tsuboi later recollects how Takahashi's work was received at that time:

> Of these publications, *Poems of Dadaist Shinkichi* especially caused a great sensation in the realm of poetry since Dadaism . . . had been attracting the young Japanese poets of the time as well. The reason was that not only did the poet, who appeared in public suddenly, interest his audience because of his unusual experience (it was said that he had become psychotic more than once), but also his poetry exhibited before us a poetic world which was entirely different from the already existing one.

Fresh, different, and revolutionary, Takahashi's Dada poetry was thus to influence at once such poets (among others) as Onchi Terutake, who acknowledged the impact of both Takahashi and Murayama Tomoyoshi, and Nakahara Chuya, who wrote, in addition to his own Dada poems, a short essay "On Takahashi" in 1926.

It is important to note here the contribution of Murayama Tomoyoshi, "the Kandinsky of Japan," who exerted an immediate influence after he had returned from Germany in January 1923 with a new idea which he called "Conscious Constructivism." According to Ooka Makoto, while Murayama was staying in Berlin in 1921, he was overwhelmed by such new artistic trends as Dada and Constructivism, and he himself started experimenting with "construction," using hair, shoes, woolen yarn, knitted goods, string, nails, tins, printed materials, photographs, slippers, silk thread, hemp, lace, cloth, artificial flowers, and so on. His one–man show, held in 1923 in Tokyo, "stirred up," as Ooka says, "an unexpected sensation," and he (now with many followers) led a group of avant-garde artists and writers who called themselves MAVO. Murayama, the translator of Kan-dinsky's book of poetry, *Echo,* and the author of *Gendai no geijutsu to mirai no geijutsu* (The art of today and of the future, 1924), also astonished people with his Constructivist stage setting for Georg Kai-ser's *From Morning till Midnight (Von Morgens bis Mitternachts),* performed by the Tsukiji Little Theatre in December 1924. Murayama's influence was not limited to art, it seems, but was felt in poetry as well: Onchi Terutake placed Murayama among the major Dada poets of Japan.

The year 1923 also saw in Japan one of the worst natural disasters in Japanese history, the great Kant earthquake, which turned the entire Tokyo area and its surrounding vicinity into ashes on September 1. What followed was the massacre of civilians who were against the ruling class, most of them being Korean residents; this eventually led to a social revolution.

Some literary historians, such as Onchi Terutake, consider the period from the time immediately following the earthquake up to 1926 the era of Dadaism, the young generation's revolutionary ideas as well as their nihilism having been ignited by the particular social and political conditions of the time. It should be remembered, however, that since Takahashi Shinkichi's poetry preceded the earthquake of 1923, it is he alone who deserves full credit for the inception of Japanese Dada poetry.

FURTHER READING

Anthologies

Hibbett, Howard, ed. *Contemporary Japanese Literature: An Anthology of Fiction, Film, and Other Writing since 1945.* New York: Alfred A. Knopf, 1993, 468 p.

Includes works not previously translated into English by such writers as Kurahashi Yumiko, Abe Kobo, Mishima Yukio, Nagai Tatsuo, and Tanizaki Jun'ichiro.

Bibliographies

Anderson, G. L. "Japan: Modern Literature." In *Asian Literature in English: A Guide to Information Sources,* pp. 139-69. Detroit: Gale Research, 1981.

Annotated guide to primary and secondary sources.

Marks, Alfred H. and Bort, Barry D. *Guide to Japanese Prose.* Boston: G. K. Hall & Company, 1984, 186 p.

Descriptive bibliography of poetry, drama, and fiction anthologies and secondary sources divided into two sections: "Pre-Meiji Literature (Beginnings to 1867)" and "Meiji Literature and After (1868 to Present)."

Modern Japanese Literature in Translation: A Bibliography. Tokyo, New York, and San Francisco: Kodansha International, 1979, 311 p.

Lists translations into English and European languages of Japanese literature published since 1868.

Rimer, J. Thomas, and Morrell, Robert, E. *Guide to Japanese Poetry.* Rev. Ed. Boston: G. K. Hall & Co., 1984, 189 p.

Provides introductory essays and annotations to 225 works of Japanese literature in English translation.

Secondary Sources

Arima, Tatsuo. *The Failure of Freedom: A Portrait of Modern Japanese Intellectuals.* Cambridge, Mass.: Harvard University Press, 1969, 296 p.

Considers "the dominant modes of thought in prewar Japan, primarily in the Taisho era (1912-1926)."

Boscaro, Adriana; Gatti, Franco; and Raveri, Massimo, eds. *Rethinking Japan, Vol. I: Literature, Visual Arts & Linguistics.* Sandgate, Folkstone, Kent: Japan Library Ltd., 1991, 291 p.

Reprints papers delivered during a symposium hosted in October 1987 by the Institute of Japanese Studies in Venice, Italy.

Fowler, Edward. *The Rhetoric of Confession: "Shisho setsu" in Early Twentieth-Century Japanese Fiction.* Berkeley and Los Angeles: University of California Press, 1988, 333 p.

Traces the roots of *shishosetsu* to "Chinese and native literary and intellectual traditions as well as to the structure of the Japanese language itself" and "explores the impact that literary tradition, the naturalist movement and contemporary journalistic realities had on the writing of autobiographical fiction."

Gessel, Van C. *The Sting of Life: Four Contemporary Japanese Novelists.* New York: Columbia University Press, 1989, 326 p.

Focuses on the works of Yasuoka Shotaro, Shimao Toshio, Kojima Nobuo, and Endo Shosaku.

Keene, Donald. *Dawn to the West: Japanese Literature of the Modern Era—Poetry, Drama, Criticism.* New York: Holt, Rinehart and Winston, 1984, 685 p.

Literary history covering such topics as modern tanka, modern haiku, poetry of the Meiji, Taisho, and Showa periods, modern Kabuki, Shimpa and Shingeki, and literary criticism since 1868.

Kimball, Arthur G. *Crisis in Identity and Contemporary Japanese Novels.* Rutland, Vt.: Charles E. Tuttle Co., 1973, 190 p.

Explores identity as a theme in Japanese literature since World War II.

Kokusai Bunka Shinkokai. *Introduction to Contemporary Japanese Literature, Vol. III: Synopses of Major Works, 1956-1970.* Tokyo: University of Tokyo Press, 1972, 313 p.

Includes biographical sketches and synopses of works by seventy-two authors.

Miyoshi, Masao. *Accomplices of Silence: The Modern Japanese Novel.* Berkeley and Los Angeles: University of California Press, 1974, 194 p.

Examines narrative situation, character, plot, and language in the works of Futabatei Shimei, Mori Ogai, Natsume Soseki, Kawabata Yasunari, Dazai Osamu, and Mishima Yukio.

Petersen, Gwenn Boardman. *The Moon in the Water: Understanding Tanizaki, Kawabata, and Mishima.* Honolulu: University Press of Hawaii, 1979, 366 p.

Comprises critical essays, bibliographies, and chronologies on Tanizaki Jun'ichiro, Kawabata Yasunari, and Mishima Yukio.

Powell, Irena. *Writers and Society in Modern Japan.* Tokyo: Kodansha International, 1983, 149 p.

Attempts "to seek some social explanations for the phenomenon of modern Japanese literature, to examine its environment and the forces which formed it."

Rubin, Jay. *Injurious to Public Morals: Writers and the Meiji State.* Seattle: University of Washington Press, 1984, 331 p.

Covers developments in Japanese literature during

the Meiji period (1868-1912), focusing particularly on the rise of Naturalism and the program of government censorship.

Ueda, Makoto. *Modern Japanese Poets and the Nature of Literature.* Stanford: Stanford University Press, 1983, 451 p.

Encompasses the works of Masaoka Shiki, Yosano Akiko, Ishikawa Takuboku, Hagiwara Sakutaro, Miyazawa Kenji, Takamura Kotaro, Ogiwara Seisensui, and Takahashi Shinkichi.

Walker, Janet A. *The Japanese Novel of the Meiji Period and the Ideal of Individualism.* Princeton: Princeton University Press, 1979, 315 p.

Discusses the interpretation of the Western ideal of individualism by major Japanese novelists of the late nineteenth and early twentieth centuries.

Yamanouchi, Hisaaki. *The Search for Authenticity in Modern Japanese Literature.* Cambridge: Cambridge University Press, 1978, 214 p.

Examines the works of Tsubouchi Shoyo, Futabatei Shimei, Kitamura Tokoku, Shimazaki Toson, Natsume Soseki, Shiga Naoya, Akutagawa Ryuno-suke, Tanizaki Jun'ichiro, Kawabata Yasunari, Mishima Yukio, Abe Kobo, and Oe Kenzaburo, focusing on "the ways in which these writers tackled difficult questions—personal, social, and intellectual, including the confrontation with the West, and the ways in which they tried, with or without success, to represent their experiences in an authentic form of literary art."

Twentieth-Century Literary Criticism

Cumulative Indexes
Volumes 1-66

How to Use This Index

The main references

Calvino, Italo
1923-1985.....CLC 5, 8, 11, 22, 33, 39, 73; SSC 3

list all author entries in the following Gale Literary Criticism series:

BLC = *Black Literature Criticism*
CLC = *Contemporary Literary Criticism*
CLR = *Children's Literature Review*
CMLC = *Classical and Medieval Literature Criticism*
DA = *DISCovering Authors*
DC = *Drama Criticism*
HLC = *Hispanic Literature Criticism*
LC = *Literature Criticism from 1400 to 1800*
NCLC = *Nineteenth-Century Literature Criticism*
PC = *Poetry Criticism*
SSC = *Short Story Criticism*
TCLC = *Twentieth-Century Literary Criticism*
WLC = *World Literature Criticism, 1500 to the Present*

The cross-references

See also CANR 23; CA 85-88; obituary CA 116

list all author entries in the following Gale biographical and literary sources:

AAYA = *Authors & Artists for Young Adults*
AITN = *Authors in the News*
BEST = *Bestsellers*
BW = *Black Writers*
CA = *Contemporary Authors*
CAAS = *Contemporary Authors Autobiography Series*
CABS = *Contemporary Authors Bibliographical Series*
CANR = *Contemporary Authors New Revision Series*
CAP = *Contemporary Authors Permanent Series*
CDALB = *Concise Dictionary of American Literary Biography*
CDBLB = *Concise Dictionary of British Literary Biography*
DLB = *Dictionary of Literary Biography*
DLBD = *Dictionary of Literary Biography Documentary Series*
DLBY = *Dictionary of Literary Biography Yearbook*
HW = *Hispanic Writers*
JRDA = *Junior DISCovering Authors*
MAICYA = *Major Authors and Illustrators for Children and Young Adults*
MTCW = *Major 20th-Century Writers*
NNAL = *Native North American Literature*
SAAS = *Something about the Author Autobiography Series*
SATA = *Something about the Author*
YABC = *Yesterday's Authors of Books for Children*

Literary Criticism Series Cumulative Author Index

Andouard
See Giraudoux, (Hippolyte) Jean

Andrade, Carlos Drummond de ...... **CLC 18**
See also Drummond de Andrade, Carlos

Andrade, Mario de 1893-1945..... **TCLC 43**

Andreae, Johann V(alentin)
1586-1654 .... **LC 32**
See also DLB 164

Andreas-Salome, Lou 1861-1937... **TCLC 56**
See also DLB 66

Andrewes, Lancelot 1555-1626 .... **LC 5**
See also DLB 151

Andrews, Cicily Fairfield
See West, Rebecca

Andrews, Elton V.
See Pohl, Frederik

Andreyev, Leonid (Nikolaevich)
1871-1919 .... **TCLC 3**
See also CA 104

Andric, Ivo 1892-1975 .... **CLC 8**
See also CA 81-84; 57-60; CANR 43; DLB 147; MTCW

Angelique, Pierre
See Bataille, Georges

Angell, Roger 1920-.............. **CLC 26**
See also CA 57-60; CANR 13, 44

Angelou, Maya
1928- .... **CLC 12, 35, 64, 77; BLC; DA; DAB; DAC; DAM MST, MULT, POET, POP**
See also AAYA 7; BW 2; CA 65-68; CANR 19, 42; DLB 38; MTCW; SATA 49

Annensky, Innokenty Fyodorovich
1856-1909 .... **TCLC 14**
See also CA 110

Anon, Charles Robert
See Pessoa, Fernando (Antonio Nogueira)

Anouilh, Jean (Marie Lucien Pierre)
1910-1987 ...... **CLC 1, 3, 8, 13, 40, 50; DAM DRAM**
See also CA 17-20R; 123; CANR 32; MTCW

Anthony, Florence
See Ai

Anthony, John
See Ciardi, John (Anthony)

Anthony, Peter
See Shaffer, Anthony (Joshua); Shaffer, Peter (Levin)

Anthony, Piers 1934- .. **CLC 35; DAM POP**
See also AAYA 11; CA 21-24R; CANR 28; DLB 8; MTCW; SAAS 22; SATA 84

Antoine, Marc
See Proust, (Valentin-Louis-George-Eugene-) Marcel

Antoninus, Brother
See Everson, William (Oliver)

Antonioni, Michelangelo 1912-..... **CLC 20**
See also CA 73-76; CANR 45

Antschel, Paul 1920-1970
See Celan, Paul
See also CA 85-88; CANR 33; MTCW

Anwar, Chairil 1922-1949 .... **TCLC 22**
See also CA 121

Apollinaire, Guillaume
1880-1918 .... **TCLC 3, 8, 51; DAM POET; PC 7**
See also Kostrowitzki, Wilhelm Apollinaris de
See also CA 152

Appelfeld, Aharon 1932- .... **CLC 23, 47**
See also CA 112; 133

Apple, Max (Isaac) 1941-........ **CLC 9, 33**
See also CA 81-84; CANR 19; DLB 130

Appleman, Philip (Dean) 1926-..... **CLC 51**
See also CA 13-16R; CAAS 18; CANR 6, 29

Appleton, Lawrence
See Lovecraft, H(oward) P(hillips)

Apteryx
See Eliot, T(homas) S(tearns)

Apuleius, (Lucius Madaurensis)
125(?)-175(?) .... **CMLC 1**

Aquin, Hubert 1929-1977.......... **CLC 15**
See also CA 105; DLB 53

Aragon, Louis
1897-1982 ..... **CLC 3, 22; DAM NOV, POET**
See also CA 69-72; 108; CANR 28; DLB 72; MTCW

Arany, Janos 1817-1882......... **NCLC 34**

Arbuthnot, John 1667-1735.......... **LC 1**
See also DLB 101

Archer, Herbert Winslow
See Mencken, H(enry) L(ouis)

Archer, Jeffrey (Howard)
1940- .... **CLC 28; DAM POP**
See also AAYA 16; BEST 89:3; CA 77-80; CANR 22, 52; INT CANR-22

Archer, Jules 1915- .... **CLC 12**
See also CA 9-12R; CANR 6; SAAS 5; SATA 4, 85

Archer, Lee
See Ellison, Harlan (Jay)

Arden, John
1930- ..... **CLC 6, 13, 15; DAM DRAM**
See also CA 13-16R; CAAS 4; CANR 31; DLB 13; MTCW

Arenas, Reinaldo
1943-1990 ...... **CLC 41; DAM MULT; HLC**
See also CA 124; 128; 133; DLB 145; HW

Arendt, Hannah 1906-1975 .... **CLC 66**
See also CA 17-20R; 61-64; CANR 26; MTCW

Aretino, Pietro 1492-1556 .... **LC 12**

Arghezi, Tudor.................... **CLC 80**
See also Theodorescu, Ion N.

Arguedas, Jose Maria
1911-1969 .... **CLC 10, 18**
See also CA 89-92; DLB 113; HW

Argueta, Manlio 1936-............ **CLC 31**
See also CA 131; DLB 145; HW

Ariosto, Ludovico 1474-1533......... **LC 6**

Aristides
See Epstein, Joseph

Aristophanes
450B.C.-385B.C......... **CMLC 4; DA; DAB; DAC; DAM DRAM, MST; DC 2**

Arlt, Roberto (Godofredo Christophersen)
1900-1942 ..... **TCLC 29; DAM MULT; HLC**
See also CA 123; 131; HW

Armah, Ayi Kwei
1939- .... **CLC 5, 33; BLC; DAM MULT, POET**
See also BW 1; CA 61-64; CANR 21; DLB 117; MTCW

Armatrading, Joan 1950-.......... **CLC 17**
See also CA 114

Arnette, Robert
See Silverberg, Robert

Arnim, Achim von (Ludwig Joachim von Arnim) 1781-1831 .... **NCLC 5**
See also DLB 90

Arnim, Bettina von 1785-1859.... **NCLC 38**
See also DLB 90

Arnold, Matthew
1822-1888 ..... **NCLC 6, 29; DA; DAB; DAC; DAM MST, POET; PC 5; WLC**
See also CDBLB 1832-1890; DLB 32, 57

Arnold, Thomas 1795-1842 ...... **NCLC 18**
See also DLB 55

Arnow, Harriette (Louisa) Simpson
1908-1986 .... **CLC 2, 7, 18**
See also CA 9-12R; 118; CANR 14; DLB 6; MTCW; SATA 42; SATA-Obit 47

Arp, Hans
See Arp, Jean

Arp, Jean 1887-1966............... **CLC 5**
See also CA 81-84; 25-28R; CANR 42

Arrabal
See Arrabal, Fernando

Arrabal, Fernando 1932- ... **CLC 2, 9, 18, 58**
See also CA 9-12R; CANR 15

Arrick, Fran...................... **CLC 30**
See also Gaberman, Judie Angell

Artaud, Antonin (Marie Joseph)
1896-1948 ... **TCLC 3, 36; DAM DRAM**
See also CA 104; 149

Arthur, Ruth M(abel) 1905-1979.... **CLC 12**
See also CA 9-12R; 85-88; CANR 4; SATA 7, 26

Artsybashev, Mikhail (Petrovich)
1878-1927 .... **TCLC 31**

Arundel, Honor (Morfydd)
1919-1973 .... **CLC 17**
See also CA 21-22; 41-44R; CAP 2; CLR 35; SATA 4; SATA-Obit 24

Asch, Sholem 1880-1957 .... **TCLC 3**
See also CA 105

Ash, Shalom
See Asch, Sholem

Ashbery, John (Lawrence)
1927- ...... **CLC 2, 3, 4, 6, 9, 13, 15, 25, 41, 77; DAM POET**
See also CA 5-8R; CANR 9, 37; DLB 5, 165; DLBY 81; INT CANR-9; MTCW

Ashdown, Clifford
See Freeman, R(ichard) Austin

Ashe, Gordon
See Creasey, John

Ashton-Warner, Sylvia (Constance) 1908-1984 .... **CLC 19**
See also CA 69-72; 112; CANR 29; MTCW

Asimov, Isaac 1920-1992 ...... **CLC 1, 3, 9, 19, 26, 76, 92; DAM POP**
See also AAYA 13; BEST 90:2; CA 1-4R; 137; CANR 2, 19, 36; CLR 12; DLB 8; DLBY 92; INT CANR-19; JRDA; MAICYA; MTCW; SATA 1, 26, 74

Astley, Thea (Beatrice May) 1925- .... **CLC 41**
See also CA 65-68; CANR 11, 43

Aston, James
See White, T(erence) H(anbury)

Asturias, Miguel Angel 1899-1974 .... **CLC 3, 8, 13; DAM MULT, NOV; HLC**
See also CA 25-28; 49-52; CANR 32; CAP 2; DLB 113; HW; MTCW

Atares, Carlos Saura
See Saura (Atares), Carlos

Atheling, William
See Pound, Ezra (Weston Loomis)

Atheling, William, Jr.
See Blish, James (Benjamin)

Atherton, Gertrude (Franklin Horn) 1857-1948 .... **TCLC 2**
See also CA 104; DLB 9, 78

Atherton, Lucius
See Masters, Edgar Lee

Atkins, Jack
See Harris, Mark

Attaway, William (Alexander) 1911-1986 .... **CLC 92; BLC; DAM MULT**
See also BW 2; CA 143; DLB 76

Atticus
See Fleming, Ian (Lancaster)

Atwood, Margaret (Eleanor) 1939- ..... **CLC 2, 3, 4, 8, 13, 15, 25, 44, 84; DA; DAB; DAC; DAM MST, NOV, POET; PC 8; SSC 2; WLC**
See also AAYA 12; BEST 89:2; CA 49-52; CANR 3, 24, 33; DLB 53; INT CANR-24; MTCW; SATA 50

Aubigny, Pierre d'
See Mencken, H(enry) L(ouis)

Aubin, Penelope 1685-1731(?)........ **LC 9**
See also DLB 39

Auchincloss, Louis (Stanton) 1917- .... **CLC 4, 6, 9, 18, 45; DAM NOV; SSC 22**
See also CA 1-4R; CANR 6, 29; DLB 2; DLBY 80; INT CANR-29; MTCW

Auden, W(ystan) H(ugh) 1907-1973 ...... **CLC 1, 2, 3, 4, 6, 9, 11, 14, 43; DA; DAB; DAC; DAM DRAM, MST, POET; PC 1; WLC**
See also AAYA 18; CA 9-12R; 45-48; CANR 5; CDBLB 1914-1945; DLB 10, 20; MTCW

Audiberti, Jacques 1900-1965 ...... **CLC 38; DAM DRAM**
See also CA 25-28R

Audubon, John James 1785-1851 .... **NCLC 47**

Auel, Jean M(arie) 1936- .... **CLC 31; DAM POP**
See also AAYA 7; BEST 90:4; CA 103; CANR 21; INT CANR-21

Auerbach, Erich 1892-1957 .... **TCLC 43**
See also CA 118

Augier, Emile 1820-1889 .... **NCLC 31**

August, John
See De Voto, Bernard (Augustine)

Augustine, St. 354-430...... **CMLC 6; DAB**

Aurelius
See Bourne, Randolph S(illiman)

Aurobindo, Sri 1872-1950 .... **TCLC 63**

Austen, Jane 1775-1817 ..... **NCLC 1, 13, 19, 33, 51; DA; DAB; DAC; DAM MST, NOV; WLC**
See also CDBLB 1789-1832; DLB 116

Auster, Paul 1947- .... **CLC 47**
See also CA 69-72; CANR 23, 52

Austin, Frank
See Faust, Frederick (Schiller)

Austin, Mary (Hunter) 1868-1934 .... **TCLC 25**
See also CA 109; DLB 9, 78

Autran Dourado, Waldomiro
See Dourado, (Waldomiro Freitas) Autran

Averroes 1126-1198 .... **CMLC 7**
See also DLB 115

Avicenna 980-1037 .... **CMLC 16**
See also DLB 115

Avison, Margaret 1918- .... **CLC 2, 4; DAC; DAM POET**
See also CA 17-20R; DLB 53; MTCW

Axton, David
See Koontz, Dean R(ay)

Ayckbourn, Alan 1939- ...... **CLC 5, 8, 18, 33, 74; DAB; DAM DRAM**
See also CA 21-24R; CANR 31; DLB 13; MTCW

Aydy, Catherine
See Tennant, Emma (Christina)

Ayme, Marcel (Andre) 1902-1967... **CLC 11**
See also CA 89-92; CLR 25; DLB 72

Ayrton, Michael 1921-1975 .... **CLC 7**
See also CA 5-8R; 61-64; CANR 9, 21

Azorin.......................... **CLC 11**
See also Martinez Ruiz, Jose

Azuela, Mariano 1873-1952 ..... **TCLC 3; DAM MULT; HLC**
See also CA 104; 131; HW; MTCW

Baastad, Babbis Friis
See Friis-Baastad, Babbis Ellinor

Bab
See Gilbert, W(illiam) S(chwenck)

Babbis, Eleanor
See Friis-Baastad, Babbis Ellinor

Babel, Isaak (Emmanuilovich) 1894-1941(?) ...... **TCLC 2, 13; SSC 16**
See also CA 104

Babits, Mihaly 1883-1941 .... **TCLC 14**
See also CA 114

Babur 1483-1530................. **LC 18**

Bacchelli, Riccardo 1891-1985 ..... **CLC 19**
See also CA 29-32R; 117

Bach, Richard (David) 1936- ...... **CLC 14; DAM NOV, POP**
See also AITN 1; BEST 89:2; CA 9-12R; CANR 18; MTCW; SATA 13

Bachman, Richard
See King, Stephen (Edwin)

Bachmann, Ingeborg 1926-1973..... **CLC 69**
See also CA 93-96; 45-48; DLB 85

Bacon, Francis 1561-1626 .... **LC 18, 32**
See also CDBLB Before 1660; DLB 151

Bacon, Roger 1214(?)-1292 ...... **CMLC 14**
See also DLB 115

Bacovia, George.................. **TCLC 24**
See also Vasiliu, Gheorghe

Badanes, Jerome 1937-............ **CLC 59**

Bagehot, Walter 1826-1877 ...... **NCLC 10**
See also DLB 55

Bagnold, Enid 1889-1981 ...... **CLC 25; DAM DRAM**
See also CA 5-8R; 103; CANR 5, 40; DLB 13, 160; MAICYA; SATA 1, 25

Bagritsky, Eduard 1895-1934 ..... **TCLC 60**

Bagrjana, Elisaveta
See Belcheva, Elisaveta

Bagryana, Elisaveta................ **CLC 10**
See also Belcheva, Elisaveta
See also DLB 147

Bailey, Paul 1937- .... **CLC 45**
See also CA 21-24R; CANR 16; DLB 14

Baillie, Joanna 1762-1851 .... **NCLC 2**
See also DLB 93

Bainbridge, Beryl (Margaret) 1933- .... **CLC 4, 5, 8, 10, 14, 18, 22, 62; DAM NOV**
See also CA 21-24R; CANR 24; DLB 14; MTCW

Baker, Elliott 1922- .... **CLC 8**
See also CA 45-48; CANR 2

Baker, Nicholson 1957- .... **CLC 61; DAM POP**
See also CA 135

Baker, Ray Stannard 1870-1946... **TCLC 47**
See also CA 118

Baker, Russell (Wayne) 1925-...... **CLC 31**
See also BEST 89:4; CA 57-60; CANR 11, 41; MTCW

Bakhtin, M.
See Bakhtin, Mikhail Mikhailovich

Bakhtin, M. M.
See Bakhtin, Mikhail Mikhailovich

Bakhtin, Mikhail
See Bakhtin, Mikhail Mikhailovich

Bakhtin, Mikhail Mikhailovich 1895-1975 .... **CLC 83**
See also CA 128; 113

Bakshi, Ralph 1938(?)- .... **CLC 26**
See also CA 112; 138

Bakunin, Mikhail (Alexandrovich)
1814-1876 .... **NCLC 25**

Baldwin, James (Arthur)
1924-1987 ...... **CLC 1, 2, 3, 4, 5, 8, 13, 15, 17, 42, 50, 67, 90; BLC; DA; DAB; DAC; DAM MST, MULT, NOV, POP; DC 1; SSC 10; WLC**
See also AAYA 4; BW 1; CA 1-4R; 124; CABS 1; CANR 3, 24; CDALB 1941-1968; DLB 2, 7, 33; DLBY 87; MTCW; SATA 9; SATA-Obit 54

Ballard, J(ames) G(raham)
1930- .... **CLC 3, 6, 14, 36; DAM NOV, POP; SSC 1**
See also AAYA 3; CA 5-8R; CANR 15, 39; DLB 14; MTCW

Balmont, Konstantin (Dmitriyevich)
1867-1943 .... **TCLC 11**
See also CA 109

Balzac, Honore de
1799-1850 .... **NCLC 5, 35, 53; DA; DAB; DAC; DAM MST, NOV; SSC 5; WLC**
See also DLB 119

Bambara, Toni Cade
1939-1995 ...... **CLC 19, 88; BLC; DA; DAC; DAM MST, MULT**
See also AAYA 5; BW 2; CA 29-32R; 150; CANR 24, 49; DLB 38; MTCW

Bamdad, A.
See Shamlu, Ahmad

Banat, D. R.
See Bradbury, Ray (Douglas)

Bancroft, Laura
See Baum, L(yman) Frank

Banim, John 1798-1842 .... **NCLC 13**
See also DLB 116, 158, 159

Banim, Michael 1796-1874 ...... **NCLC 13**
See also DLB 158, 159

Banks, Iain
See Banks, Iain M(enzies)

Banks, Iain M(enzies) 1954- .... **CLC 34**
See also CA 123; 128; INT 128

Banks, Lynne Reid .... **CLC 23**
See also Reid Banks, Lynne
See also AAYA 6

Banks, Russell 1940- .... **CLC 37, 72**
See also CA 65-68; CAAS 15; CANR 19, 52; DLB 130

Banville, John 1945-.............. **CLC 46**
See also CA 117; 128; DLB 14; INT 128

Banville, Theodore (Faullain) de
1832-1891 .... **NCLC 9**

Baraka, Amiri
1934- .... **CLC 1, 2, 3, 5, 10, 14, 33; BLC; DA; DAC; DAM MST, MULT, POET, POP; DC 6; PC 4**
See also Jones, LeRoi
See also BW 2; CA 21-24R; CABS 3; CANR 27, 38; CDALB 1941-1968; DLB 5, 7, 16, 38; DLBD 8; MTCW

Barbauld, Anna Laetitia
1743-1825 .... **NCLC 50**
See also DLB 107, 109, 142, 158

Barbellion, W. N. P. .... **TCLC 24**
See also Cummings, Bruce F(rederick)

Barbera, Jack (Vincent) 1945-...... **CLC 44**
See also CA 110; CANR 45

Barbey d'Aurevilly, Jules Amedee
1808-1889 .... **NCLC 1; SSC 17**
See also DLB 119

Barbusse, Henri 1873-1935 .... **TCLC 5**
See also CA 105; DLB 65

Barclay, Bill
See Moorcock, Michael (John)

Barclay, William Ewert
See Moorcock, Michael (John)

Barea, Arturo 1897-1957 .... **TCLC 14**
See also CA 111

Barfoot, Joan 1946- .... **CLC 18**
See also CA 105

Baring, Maurice 1874-1945 .... **TCLC 8**
See also CA 105; DLB 34

Barker, Clive 1952- ... **CLC 52; DAM POP**
See also AAYA 10; BEST 90:3; CA 121; 129; INT 129; MTCW

Barker, George Granville
1913-1991 ..... **CLC 8, 48; DAM POET**
See also CA 9-12R; 135; CANR 7, 38; DLB 20; MTCW

Barker, Harley Granville
See Granville-Barker, Harley
See also DLB 10

Barker, Howard 1946-............ **CLC 37**
See also CA 102; DLB 13

Barker, Pat(ricia) 1943-........ **CLC 32, 94**
See also CA 117; 122; CANR 50; INT 122

Barlow, Joel 1754-1812 .... **NCLC 23**
See also DLB 37

Barnard, Mary (Ethel) 1909-....... **CLC 48**
See also CA 21-22; CAP 2

Barnes, Djuna
1892-1982 ... **CLC 3, 4, 8, 11, 29; SSC 3**
See also CA 9-12R; 107; CANR 16; DLB 4, 9, 45; MTCW

Barnes, Julian 1946-......... **CLC 42; DAB**
See also CA 102; CANR 19; DLBY 93

Barnes, Peter 1931- .... **CLC 5, 56**
See also CA 65-68; CAAS 12; CANR 33, 34; DLB 13; MTCW

Baroja (y Nessi), Pio
1872-1956 .... **TCLC 8; HLC**
See also CA 104

Baron, David
See Pinter, Harold

Baron Corvo
See Rolfe, Frederick (William Serafino Austin Lewis Mary)

Barondess, Sue K(aufman)
1926-1977 .... **CLC 8**
See also Kaufman, Sue
See also CA 1-4R; 69-72; CANR 1

Baron de Teive
See Pessoa, Fernando (Antonio Nogueira)

Barres, Maurice 1862-1923 .... **TCLC 47**
See also DLB 123

Barreto, Afonso Henrique de Lima
See Lima Barreto, Afonso Henrique de

Barrett, (Roger) Syd 1946- .... **CLC 35**

Barrett, William (Christopher)
1913-1992 .... **CLC 27**
See also CA 13-16R; 139; CANR 11; INT CANR-11

Barrie, J(ames) M(atthew)
1860-1937 .... **TCLC 2; DAB; DAM DRAM**
See also CA 104; 136; CDBLB 1890-1914; CLR 16; DLB 10, 141, 156; MAICYA; YABC 1

Barrington, Michael
See Moorcock, Michael (John)

Barrol, Grady
See Bograd, Larry

Barry, Mike
See Malzberg, Barry N(athaniel)

Barry, Philip 1896-1949.......... **TCLC 11**
See also CA 109; DLB 7

Bart, Andre Schwarz
See Schwarz-Bart, Andre

Barth, John (Simmons)
1930- ...... **CLC 1, 2, 3, 5, 7, 9, 10, 14, 27, 51, 89; DAM NOV; SSC 10**
See also AITN 1, 2; CA 1-4R; CABS 1; CANR 5, 23, 49; DLB 2; MTCW

Barthelme, Donald
1931-1989 ...... **CLC 1, 2, 3, 5, 6, 8, 13, 23, 46, 59; DAM NOV; SSC 2**
See also CA 21-24R; 129; CANR 20; DLB 2; DLBY 80, 89; MTCW; SATA 7; SATA-Obit 62

Barthelme, Frederick 1943-........ **CLC 36**
See also CA 114; 122; DLBY 85; INT 122

Barthes, Roland (Gerard)
1915-1980 .... **CLC 24, 83**
See also CA 130; 97-100; MTCW

Barzun, Jacques (Martin) 1907- .... **CLC 51**
See also CA 61-64; CANR 22

Bashevis, Isaac
See Singer, Isaac Bashevis

Bashkirtseff, Marie 1859-1884 ... **NCLC 27**

Basho
See Matsuo Basho

Bass, Kingsley B., Jr.
See Bullins, Ed

Bass, Rick 1958-................. **CLC 79**
See also CA 126; CANR 53

Bassani, Giorgio 1916-............. **CLC 9**
See also CA 65-68; CANR 33; DLB 128; MTCW

Bastos, Augusto (Antonio) Roa
See Roa Bastos, Augusto (Antonio)

Bataille, Georges 1897-1962 .... **CLC 29**
See also CA 101; 89-92

Bates, H(erbert) E(rnest)
1905-1974 .... **CLC 46; DAB; DAM POP; SSC 10**
See also CA 93-96; 45-48; CANR 34; DLB 162; MTCW

Benedikt, Michael 1935- . . . . **CLC 4, 14**
See also CA 13-16R; CANR 7; DLB 5

Benet, Juan 1927- . . . . **CLC 28**
See also CA 143

Benet, Stephen Vincent 1898-1943 . . . . . . **TCLC 7; DAM POET; SSC 10**
See also CA 104; 152; DLB 4, 48, 102; YABC 1

Benet, William Rose 1886-1950 . . . . . . **TCLC 28; DAM POET**
See also CA 118; 152; DLB 45

Benford, Gregory (Albert) 1941- . . . . **CLC 52**
See also CA 69-72; CANR 12, 24, 49; DLBY 82

Bengtsson, Frans (Gunnar) 1894-1954 . . . . **TCLC 48**

Benjamin, David
See Slavitt, David R(ytman)

Benjamin, Lois
See Gould, Lois

Benjamin, Walter 1892-1940 . . . . . . **TCLC 39**

Benn, Gottfried 1886-1956 . . . . **TCLC 3**
See also CA 106; DLB 56

Bennett, Alan 1934- . . . **CLC 45, 77; DAB; DAM MST**
See also CA 103; CANR 35; MTCW

Bennett, (Enoch) Arnold 1867-1931 . . . . **TCLC 5, 20**
See also CA 106; CDBLB 1890-1914; DLB 10, 34, 98, 135

Bennett, Elizabeth
See Mitchell, Margaret (Munnerlyn)

Bennett, George Harold 1930-
See Bennett, Hal
See also BW 1; CA 97-100

Bennett, Hal . . . . **CLC 5**
See also Bennett, George Harold
See also DLB 33

Bennett, Jay 1912- . . . . **CLC 35**
See also AAYA 10; CA 69-72; CANR 11, 42; JRDA; SAAS 4; SATA 41, 87; SATA-Brief 27

Bennett, Louise (Simone) 1919- . . . . . **CLC 28; BLC; DAM MULT**
See also BW 2; CA 151; DLB 117

Benson, E(dward) F(rederic) 1867-1940 . . . . **TCLC 27**
See also CA 114; DLB 135, 153

Benson, Jackson J. 1930- . . . . **CLC 34**
See also CA 25-28R; DLB 111

Benson, Sally 1900-1972 . . . . **CLC 17**
See also CA 19-20; 37-40R; CAP 1; SATA 1, 35; SATA-Obit 27

Benson, Stella 1892-1933 . . . . **TCLC 17**
See also CA 117; DLB 36, 162

Bentham, Jeremy 1748-1832 . . . . . **NCLC 38**
See also DLB 107, 158

Bentley, E(dmund) C(lerihew) 1875-1956 . . . . **TCLC 12**
See also CA 108; DLB 70

Bentley, Eric (Russell) 1916- . . . . **CLC 24**
See also CA 5-8R; CANR 6; INT CANR-6

Beranger, Pierre Jean de 1780-1857 . . . . **NCLC 34**

Berendt, John (Lawrence) 1939- . . . . **CLC 86**
See also CA 146

Berger, Colonel
See Malraux, (Georges-)Andre

Berger, John (Peter) 1926- . . . . . . **CLC 2, 19**
See also CA 81-84; CANR 51; DLB 14

Berger, Melvin H. 1927- . . . . **CLC 12**
See also CA 5-8R; CANR 4; CLR 32; SAAS 2; SATA 5, 88

Berger, Thomas (Louis) 1924- . . . . **CLC 3, 5, 8, 11, 18, 38; DAM NOV**
See also CA 1-4R; CANR 5, 28, 51; DLB 2; DLBY 80; INT CANR-28; MTCW

Bergman, (Ernst) Ingmar 1918- . . . . **CLC 16, 72**
See also CA 81-84; CANR 33

Bergson, Henri 1859-1941 . . . . **TCLC 32**

Bergstein, Eleanor 1938- . . . . **CLC 4**
See also CA 53-56; CANR 5

Berkoff, Steven 1937- . . . . **CLC 56**
See also CA 104

Bermant, Chaim (Icyk) 1929- . . . . . . **CLC 40**
See also CA 57-60; CANR 6, 31

Bern, Victoria
See Fisher, M(ary) F(rances) K(ennedy)

Bernanos, (Paul Louis) Georges 1888-1948 . . . . **TCLC 3**
See also CA 104; 130; DLB 72

Bernard, April 1956- . . . . **CLC 59**
See also CA 131

Berne, Victoria
See Fisher, M(ary) F(rances) K(ennedy)

Bernhard, Thomas 1931-1989 . . . . **CLC 3, 32, 61**
See also CA 85-88; 127; CANR 32; DLB 85, 124; MTCW

Berriault, Gina 1926- . . . . **CLC 54**
See also CA 116; 129; DLB 130

Berrigan, Daniel 1921- . . . . **CLC 4**
See also CA 33-36R; CAAS 1; CANR 11, 43; DLB 5

Berrigan, Edmund Joseph Michael, Jr. 1934-1983
See Berrigan, Ted
See also CA 61-64; 110; CANR 14

Berrigan, Ted . . . . **CLC 37**
See also Berrigan, Edmund Joseph Michael, Jr.
See also DLB 5

Berry, Charles Edward Anderson 1931-
See Berry, Chuck
See also CA 115

Berry, Chuck . . . . **CLC 17**
See also Berry, Charles Edward Anderson

Berry, Jonas
See Ashbery, John (Lawrence)

Berry, Wendell (Erdman) 1934- . . . . **CLC 4, 6, 8, 27, 46; DAM POET**
See also AITN 1; CA 73-76; CANR 50; DLB 5, 6

Berryman, John 1914-1972 . . . . . . **CLC 1, 2, 3, 4, 6, 8, 10, 13, 25, 62; DAM POET**
See also CA 13-16; 33-36R; CABS 2; CANR 35; CAP 1; CDALB 1941-1968; DLB 48; MTCW

Bertolucci, Bernardo 1940- . . . . **CLC 16**
See also CA 106

Bertrand, Aloysius 1807-1841 . . . . **NCLC 31**

Bertran de Born c. 1140-1215 . . . . . **CMLC 5**

Besant, Annie (Wood) 1847-1933 . . . **TCLC 9**
See also CA 105

Bessie, Alvah 1904-1985 . . . . **CLC 23**
See also CA 5-8R; 116; CANR 2; DLB 26

Bethlen, T. D.
See Silverberg, Robert

Beti, Mongo . . . . **CLC 27; BLC; DAM MULT**
See also Biyidi, Alexandre

Betjeman, John 1906-1984 . . . . **CLC 2, 6, 10, 34, 43; DAB; DAM MST, POET**
See also CA 9-12R; 112; CANR 33; CDBLB 1945-1960; DLB 20; DLBY 84; MTCW

Bettelheim, Bruno 1903-1990 . . . . . . **CLC 79**
See also CA 81-84; 131; CANR 23; MTCW

Betti, Ugo 1892-1953 . . . . **TCLC 5**
See also CA 104

Betts, Doris (Waugh) 1932- . . . . **CLC 3, 6, 28**
See also CA 13-16R; CANR 9; DLBY 82; INT CANR-9

Bevan, Alistair
See Roberts, Keith (John Kingston)

Bialik, Chaim Nachman 1873-1934 . . . . **TCLC 25**

Bickerstaff, Isaac
See Swift, Jonathan

Bidart, Frank 1939- . . . . **CLC 33**
See also CA 140

Bienek, Horst 1930- . . . . **CLC 7, 11**
See also CA 73-76; DLB 75

Bierce, Ambrose (Gwinett) 1842-1914(?) . . . . **TCLC 1, 7, 44; DA; DAC; DAM MST; SSC 9; WLC**
See also CA 104; 139; CDALB 1865-1917; DLB 11, 12, 23, 71, 74

Biggers, Earl Derr 1884-1933 . . . . . **TCLC 65**
See also CA 108

Billings, Josh
See Shaw, Henry Wheeler

Billington, (Lady) Rachel (Mary) 1942- . . . . **CLC 43**
See also AITN 2; CA 33-36R; CANR 44

Binyon, T(imothy) J(ohn) 1936- . . . . **CLC 34**
See also CA 111; CANR 28

Bioy Casares, Adolfo 1914- . . . . **CLC 4, 8, 13, 88; DAM MULT; HLC; SSC 17**
See also CA 29-32R; CANR 19, 43; DLB 113; HW; MTCW

Bird, Cordwainer
See Ellison, Harlan (Jay)

Bird, Robert Montgomery 1806-1854 . . . . **NCLC 1**

Birney, (Alfred) Earle 1904- . . . . **CLC 1, 4, 6, 11; DAC; DAM MST, POET**
See also CA 1-4R; CANR 5, 20; DLB 88; MTCW

Bishop, Elizabeth 1911-1979 . . . . . . **CLC 1, 4, 9, 13, 15, 32; DA; DAC; DAM MST, POET; PC 3**
See also CA 5-8R; 89-92; CABS 2; CANR 26; CDALB 1968-1988; DLB 5; MTCW; SATA-Obit 24

Bishop, John 1935- . . . . **CLC 10**
See also CA 105

Bissett, Bill 1939- . . . . **CLC 18; PC 14**
See also CA 69-72; CAAS 19; CANR 15; DLB 53; MTCW

Bitov, Andrei (Georgievich) 1937- . . . **CLC 57**
See also CA 142

Biyidi, Alexandre 1932-
See Beti, Mongo
See also BW 1; CA 114; 124; MTCW

Bjarme, Brynjolf
See Ibsen, Henrik (Johan)

Bjornson, Bjornstjerne (Martinius) 1832-1910 . . . . **TCLC 7, 37**
See also CA 104

Black, Robert
See Holdstock, Robert P.

Blackburn, Paul 1926-1971 . . . . . . **CLC 9, 43**
See also CA 81-84; 33-36R; CANR 34; DLB 16; DLBY 81

Black Elk 1863-1950 . . . . . **TCLC 33; DAM MULT**
See also CA 144; NNAL

Black Hobart
See Sanders, (James) Ed(ward)

Blacklin, Malcolm
See Chambers, Aidan

Blackmore, R(ichard) D(oddridge) 1825-1900 . . . . **TCLC 27**
See also CA 120; DLB 18

Blackmur, R(ichard) P(almer) 1904-1965 . . . . **CLC 2, 24**
See also CA 11-12; 25-28R; CAP 1; DLB 63

Black Tarantula, The
See Acker, Kathy

Blackwood, Algernon (Henry) 1869-1951 . . . . **TCLC 5**
See also CA 105; 150; DLB 153, 156

Blackwood, Caroline 1931-1996 . . . **CLC 6, 9**
See also CA 85-88; 151; CANR 32; DLB 14; MTCW

Blade, Alexander
See Hamilton, Edmond; Silverberg, Robert

Blaga, Lucian 1895-1961 . . . . **CLC 75**

Blair, Eric (Arthur) 1903-1950
See Orwell, George
See also CA 104; 132; DA; DAB; DAC; DAM MST, NOV; MTCW; SATA 29

Blais, Marie-Claire 1939- . . . . **CLC 2, 4, 6, 13, 22; DAC; DAM MST**
See also CA 21-24R; CAAS 4; CANR 38; DLB 53; MTCW

Blaise, Clark 1940- . . . . **CLC 29**
See also AITN 2; CA 53-56; CAAS 3; CANR 5; DLB 53

Blake, Nicholas
See Day Lewis, C(ecil)
See also DLB 77

Blake, William 1757-1827 . . . . **NCLC 13, 37, 57; DA; DAB; DAC; DAM MST, POET; PC 12; WLC**
See also CDBLB 1789-1832; DLB 93, 163; MAICYA; SATA 30

Blake, William J(ames) 1894-1969 . . . **PC 12**
See also CA 5-8R; 25-28R

Blasco Ibanez, Vicente 1867-1928 . . . . **TCLC 12; DAM NOV**
See also CA 110; 131; HW; MTCW

Blatty, William Peter 1928- . . . . **CLC 2; DAM POP**
See also CA 5-8R; CANR 9

Bleeck, Oliver
See Thomas, Ross (Elmore)

Blessing, Lee 1949- . . . . **CLC 54**

Blish, James (Benjamin) 1921-1975 . . . . **CLC 14**
See also CA 1-4R; 57-60; CANR 3; DLB 8; MTCW; SATA 66

Bliss, Reginald
See Wells, H(erbert) G(eorge)

Blixen, Karen (Christentze Dinesen) 1885-1962
See Dinesen, Isak
See also CA 25-28; CANR 22, 50; CAP 2; MTCW; SATA 44

Bloch, Robert (Albert) 1917-1994 . . . **CLC 33**
See also CA 5-8R; 146; CAAS 20; CANR 5; DLB 44; INT CANR-5; SATA 12; SATA-Obit 82

Blok, Alexander (Alexandrovich) 1880-1921 . . . . **TCLC 5**
See also CA 104

Blom, Jan
See Breytenbach, Breyten

Bloom, Harold 1930- . . . . **CLC 24**
See also CA 13-16R; CANR 39; DLB 67

Bloomfield, Aurelius
See Bourne, Randolph S(illiman)

Blount, Roy (Alton), Jr. 1941- . . . . . **CLC 38**
See also CA 53-56; CANR 10, 28; INT CANR-28; MTCW

Bloy, Leon 1846-1917 . . . . **TCLC 22**
See also CA 121; DLB 123

Blume, Judy (Sussman) 1938- . . . **CLC 12, 30; DAM NOV, POP**
See also AAYA 3; CA 29-32R; CANR 13, 37; CLR 2, 15; DLB 52; JRDA; MAICYA; MTCW; SATA 2, 31, 79

Blunden, Edmund (Charles) 1896-1974 . . . . **CLC 2, 56**
See also CA 17-18; 45-48; CAP 2; DLB 20, 100, 155; MTCW

Bly, Robert (Elwood) 1926- . . . . **CLC 1, 2, 5, 10, 15, 38; DAM POET**
See also CA 5-8R; CANR 41; DLB 5; MTCW

Boas, Franz 1858-1942 . . . . **TCLC 56**
See also CA 115

Bobette
See Simenon, Georges (Jacques Christian)

Boccaccio, Giovanni 1313-1375 . . . . **CMLC 13; SSC 10**

Bochco, Steven 1943- . . . . **CLC 35**
See also AAYA 11; CA 124; 138

Bodenheim, Maxwell 1892-1954 . . . **TCLC 44**
See also CA 110; DLB 9, 45

Bodker, Cecil 1927- . . . . **CLC 21**
See also CA 73-76; CANR 13, 44; CLR 23; MAICYA; SATA 14

Boell, Heinrich (Theodor) 1917-1985 . . . . **CLC 2, 3, 6, 9, 11, 15, 27, 32, 72; DA; DAB; DAC; DAM MST, NOV; SSC 23; WLC**
See also CA 21-24R; 116; CANR 24; DLB 69; DLBY 85; MTCW

Boerne, Alfred
See Doeblin, Alfred

Boethius 480(?)-524(?) . . . . **CMLC 15**
See also DLB 115

Bogan, Louise 1897-1970 . . . . **CLC 4, 39, 46, 93; DAM POET; PC 12**
See also CA 73-76; 25-28R; CANR 33; DLB 45; MTCW

Bogarde, Dirk . . . . **CLC 19**
See also Van Den Bogarde, Derek Jules Gaspard Ulric Niven
See also DLB 14

Bogosian, Eric 1953- . . . . **CLC 45**
See also CA 138

Bograd, Larry 1953- . . . . **CLC 35**
See also CA 93-96; SAAS 21; SATA 33, 89

Boiardo, Matteo Maria 1441-1494 . . . . **LC 6**

Boileau-Despreaux, Nicolas 1636-1711 . . . . **LC 3**

Bojer, Johan 1872-1959 . . . . **TCLC 64**

Boland, Eavan (Aisling) 1944- . . . . **CLC 40, 67; DAM POET**
See also CA 143; DLB 40

Bolt, Lee
See Faust, Frederick (Schiller)

Bolt, Robert (Oxton) 1924-1995 . . . . . . **CLC 14; DAM DRAM**
See also CA 17-20R; 147; CANR 35; DLB 13; MTCW

Bombet, Louis-Alexandre-Cesar
See Stendhal

Bomkauf
See Kaufman, Bob (Garnell)

Bonaventura . . . . **NCLC 35**
See also DLB 90

Bond, Edward 1934- . . . **CLC 4, 6, 13, 23; DAM DRAM**
See also CA 25-28R; CANR 38; DLB 13; MTCW

Bonham, Frank 1914-1989 . . . . **CLC 12**
See also AAYA 1; CA 9-12R; CANR 4, 36; JRDA; MAICYA; SAAS 3; SATA 1, 49; SATA-Obit 62

Bonnefoy, Yves 1923- . . . . . . **CLC 9, 15, 58; DAM MST, POET**
See also CA 85-88; CANR 33; MTCW

Bontemps, Arna(ud Wendell) 1902-1973 . . . . **CLC 1, 18; BLC; DAM MULT, NOV, POET**
See also BW 1; CA 1-4R; 41-44R; CANR 4, 35; CLR 6; DLB 48, 51; JRDA; MAICYA; MTCW; SATA 2, 44; SATA-Obit 24

Booth, Martin 1944- . . . . **CLC 13**
See also CA 93-96; CAAS 2

Booth, Philip 1925- . . . . **CLC 23**
See also CA 5-8R; CANR 5; DLBY 82

Booth, Wayne C(layson) 1921- . . . . . **CLC 24**
See also CA 1-4R; CAAS 5; CANR 3, 43; DLB 67

Borchert, Wolfgang 1921-1947 . . . . . **TCLC 5**
See also CA 104; DLB 69, 124

Borel, Petrus 1809-1859 . . . . **NCLC 41**

Borges, Jorge Luis 1899-1986 . . . **CLC 1, 2, 3, 4, 6, 8, 9, 10, 13, 19, 44, 48, 83; DA; DAB; DAC; DAM MST, MULT; HLC; SSC 4; WLC**
See also CA 21-24R; CANR 19, 33; DLB 113; DLBY 86; HW; MTCW

Borowski, Tadeusz 1922-1951 . . . . . . **TCLC 9**
See also CA 106

Borrow, George (Henry) 1803-1881 . . . . **NCLC 9**
See also DLB 21, 55, 166

Bosman, Herman Charles 1905-1951 . . . . **TCLC 49**

Bosschere, Jean de 1878(?)-1953 . . . **TCLC 19**
See also CA 115

Boswell, James 1740-1795 . . . . . . **LC 4; DA; DAB; DAC; DAM MST; WLC**
See also CDBLB 1660-1789; DLB 104, 142

Bottoms, David 1949- . . . . **CLC 53**
See also CA 105; CANR 22; DLB 120; DLBY 83

Boucicault, Dion 1820-1890 . . . . . . **NCLC 41**

Boucolon, Maryse 1937(?)-
See Conde, Maryse
See also CA 110; CANR 30, 53

Bourget, Paul (Charles Joseph) 1852-1935 . . . . **TCLC 12**
See also CA 107; DLB 123

Bourjaily, Vance (Nye) 1922- . . . . **CLC 8, 62**
See also CA 1-4R; CAAS 1; CANR 2; DLB 2, 143

Bourne, Randolph S(illiman) 1886-1918 . . . . **TCLC 16**
See also CA 117; DLB 63

Bova, Ben(jamin William) 1932- . . . . **CLC 45**
See also AAYA 16; CA 5-8R; CAAS 18; CANR 11; CLR 3; DLBY 81; INT CANR-11; MAICYA; MTCW; SATA 6, 68

Bowen, Elizabeth (Dorothea Cole) 1899-1973 . . . . . . **CLC 1, 3, 6, 11, 15, 22; DAM NOV; SSC 3**
See also CA 17-18; 41-44R; CANR 35; CAP 2; CDBLB 1945-1960; DLB 15, 162; MTCW

Bowering, George 1935- . . . . **CLC 15, 47**
See also CA 21-24R; CAAS 16; CANR 10; DLB 53

Bowering, Marilyn R(uthe) 1949- . . . **CLC 32**
See also CA 101; CANR 49

Bowers, Edgar 1924- . . . . **CLC 9**
See also CA 5-8R; CANR 24; DLB 5

Bowie, David . . . . **CLC 17**
See also Jones, David Robert

Bowles, Jane (Sydney) 1917-1973 . . . . **CLC 3, 68**
See also CA 19-20; 41-44R; CAP 2

Bowles, Paul (Frederick) 1910- . . . . **CLC 1, 2, 19, 53; SSC 3**
See also CA 1-4R; CAAS 1; CANR 1, 19, 50; DLB 5, 6; MTCW

Box, Edgar
See Vidal, Gore

Boyd, Nancy
See Millay, Edna St. Vincent

Boyd, William 1952- . . . . **CLC 28, 53, 70**
See also CA 114; 120; CANR 51

Boyle, Kay 1902-1992 . . . . . **CLC 1, 5, 19, 58; SSC 5**
See also CA 13-16R; 140; CAAS 1; CANR 29; DLB 4, 9, 48, 86; DLBY 93; MTCW

Boyle, Mark
See Kienzle, William X(avier)

Boyle, Patrick 1905-1982 . . . . **CLC 19**
See also CA 127

Boyle, T. C. 1948-
See Boyle, T(homas) Coraghessan

Boyle, T(homas) Coraghessan 1948- . . . . . **CLC 36, 55, 90; DAM POP; SSC 16**
See also BEST 90:4; CA 120; CANR 44; DLBY 86

Boz
See Dickens, Charles (John Huffam)

Brackenridge, Hugh Henry 1748-1816 . . . . **NCLC 7**
See also DLB 11, 37

Bradbury, Edward P.
See Moorcock, Michael (John)

Bradbury, Malcolm (Stanley) 1932- . . . . **CLC 32, 61; DAM NOV**
See also CA 1-4R; CANR 1, 33; DLB 14; MTCW

Bradbury, Ray (Douglas) 1920- . . . . **CLC 1, 3, 10, 15, 42; DA; DAB; DAC; DAM MST, NOV, POP; WLC**
See also AAYA 15; AITN 1, 2; CA 1-4R; CANR 2, 30; CDALB 1968-1988; DLB 2, 8; INT CANR-30; MTCW; SATA 11, 64

Bradford, Gamaliel 1863-1932 . . . . . **TCLC 36**
See also DLB 17

Bradley, David (Henry, Jr.) 1950- . . . . . **CLC 23; BLC; DAM MULT**
See also BW 1; CA 104; CANR 26; DLB 33

Bradley, John Ed(mund, Jr.) 1958- . . . . **CLC 55**
See also CA 139

Bradley, Marion Zimmer 1930- . . . . **CLC 30; DAM POP**
See also AAYA 9; CA 57-60; CAAS 10; CANR 7, 31, 51; DLB 8; MTCW

Bradstreet, Anne 1612(?)-1672 . . . . . . **LC 4, 30; DA; DAC; DAM MST, POET; PC 10**
See also CDALB 1640-1865; DLB 24

Brady, Joan 1939- . . . . **CLC 86**
See also CA 141

Bragg, Melvyn 1939- . . . . **CLC 10**
See also BEST 89:3; CA 57-60; CANR 10, 48; DLB 14

Braine, John (Gerard) 1922-1986 . . . . **CLC 1, 3, 41**
See also CA 1-4R; 120; CANR 1, 33; CDBLB 1945-1960; DLB 15; DLBY 86; MTCW

Brammer, William 1930(?)-1978 . . . . **CLC 31**
See also CA 77-80

Brancati, Vitaliano 1907-1954 . . . . . **TCLC 12**
See also CA 109

Brancato, Robin F(idler) 1936- . . . . . **CLC 35**
See also AAYA 9; CA 69-72; CANR 11, 45; CLR 32; JRDA; SAAS 9; SATA 23

Brand, Max
See Faust, Frederick (Schiller)

Brand, Millen 1906-1980 . . . . **CLC 7**
See also CA 21-24R; 97-100

Branden, Barbara . . . . **CLC 44**
See also CA 148

Brandes, Georg (Morris Cohen) 1842-1927 . . . . **TCLC 10**
See also CA 105

Brandys, Kazimierz 1916- . . . . **CLC 62**

Branley, Franklyn M(ansfield) 1915- . . . . **CLC 21**
See also CA 33-36R; CANR 14, 39; CLR 13; MAICYA; SAAS 16; SATA 4, 68

Brathwaite, Edward Kamau 1930- . . . . **CLC 11; DAM POET**
See also BW 2; CA 25-28R; CANR 11, 26, 47; DLB 125

Brautigan, Richard (Gary) 1935-1984 . . . . **CLC 1, 3, 5, 9, 12, 34, 42; DAM NOV**
See also CA 53-56; 113; CANR 34; DLB 2, 5; DLBY 80, 84; MTCW; SATA 56

Brave Bird, Mary 1953-
See Crow Dog, Mary
See also NNAL

Braverman, Kate 1950- . . . . **CLC 67**
See also CA 89-92

Brecht, Bertolt 1898-1956 . . . . . . **TCLC 1, 6, 13, 35; DA; DAB; DAC; DAM DRAM, MST; DC 3; WLC**
See also CA 104; 133; DLB 56, 124; MTCW

Brecht, Eugen Berthold Friedrich
See Brecht, Bertolt

Bremer, Fredrika 1801-1865 ..... **NCLC 11**

Brennan, Christopher John 1870-1932 .... **TCLC 17**
See also CA 117

Brennan, Maeve 1917- .... **CLC 5**
See also CA 81-84

Brentano, Clemens (Maria) 1778-1842 .... **NCLC 1**
See also DLB 90

Brent of Bin Bin
See Franklin, (Stella Maraia Sarah) Miles

Brenton, Howard 1942- .... **CLC 31**
See also CA 69-72; CANR 33; DLB 13; MTCW

Breslin, James 1930-
See Breslin, Jimmy
See also CA 73-76; CANR 31; DAM NOV; MTCW

Breslin, Jimmy .... **CLC 4, 43**
See also Breslin, James
See also AITN 1

Bresson, Robert 1901- .... **CLC 16**
See also CA 110; CANR 49

Breton, Andre 1896-1966 ..... **CLC 2, 9, 15, 54; PC 15**
See also CA 19-20; 25-28R; CANR 40; CAP 2; DLB 65; MTCW

Breytenbach, Breyten 1939(?)- ...... **CLC 23, 37; DAM POET**
See also CA 113; 129

Bridgers, Sue Ellen 1942- .... **CLC 26**
See also AAYA 8; CA 65-68; CANR 11, 36; CLR 18; DLB 52; JRDA; MAICYA; SAAS 1; SATA 22

Bridges, Robert (Seymour) 1844-1930 .... **TCLC 1; DAM POET**
See also CA 104; 152; CDBLB 1890-1914; DLB 19, 98

Bridie, James .... **TCLC 3**
See also Mavor, Osborne Henry
See also DLB 10

Brin, David 1950- .... **CLC 34**
See also CA 102; CANR 24; INT CANR-24; SATA 65

Brink, Andre (Philippus) 1935- .... **CLC 18, 36**
See also CA 104; CANR 39; INT 103; MTCW

Brinsmead, H(esba) F(ay) 1922- .... **CLC 21**
See also CA 21-24R; CANR 10; MAICYA; SAAS 5; SATA 18, 78

Brittain, Vera (Mary) 1893(?)-1970 .... **CLC 23**
See also CA 13-16; 25-28R; CAP 1; MTCW

Broch, Hermann 1886-1951 .... **TCLC 20**
See also CA 117; DLB 85, 124

Brock, Rose
See Hansen, Joseph

Brodkey, Harold (Roy) 1930-1996 .. **CLC 56**
See also CA 111; 151; DLB 130

Brodsky, Iosif Alexandrovich 1940-1996
See Brodsky, Joseph
See also AITN 1; CA 41-44R; 151; CANR 37; DAM POET; MTCW

Brodsky, Joseph .. **CLC 4, 6, 13, 36, 50; PC 9**
See also Brodsky, Iosif Alexandrovich

Brodsky, Michael Mark 1948- ..... **CLC 19**
See also CA 102; CANR 18, 41

Bromell, Henry 1947- .... **CLC 5**
See also CA 53-56; CANR 9

Bromfield, Louis (Brucker) 1896-1956 .... **TCLC 11**
See also CA 107; DLB 4, 9, 86

Broner, E(sther) M(asserman) 1930- .... **CLC 19**
See also CA 17-20R; CANR 8, 25; DLB 28

Bronk, William 1918- .... **CLC 10**
See also CA 89-92; CANR 23; DLB 165

Bronstein, Lev Davidovich
See Trotsky, Leon

Bronte, Anne 1820-1849 .... **NCLC 4**
See also DLB 21

Bronte, Charlotte 1816-1855 .... **NCLC 3, 8, 33; DA; DAB; DAC; DAM MST, NOV; WLC**
See also AAYA 17; CDBLB 1832-1890; DLB 21, 159

Bronte, Emily (Jane) 1818-1848 .... **NCLC 16, 35; DA; DAB; DAC; DAM MST, NOV, POET; PC 8; WLC**
See also AAYA 17; CDBLB 1832-1890; DLB 21, 32

Brooke, Frances 1724-1789 .... **LC 6**
See also DLB 39, 99

Brooke, Henry 1703(?)-1783 .... **LC 1**
See also DLB 39

Brooke, Rupert (Chawner) 1887-1915 .... **TCLC 2, 7; DA; DAB; DAC; DAM MST, POET; WLC**
See also CA 104; 132; CDBLB 1914-1945; DLB 19; MTCW

Brooke-Haven, P.
See Wodehouse, P(elham) G(renville)

Brooke-Rose, Christine 1926- ...... **CLC 40**
See also CA 13-16R; DLB 14

Brookner, Anita 1928- .... **CLC 32, 34, 51; DAB; DAM POP**
See also CA 114; 120; CANR 37; DLBY 87; MTCW

Brooks, Cleanth 1906-1994 ..... **CLC 24, 86**
See also CA 17-20R; 145; CANR 33, 35; DLB 63; DLBY 94; INT CANR-35; MTCW

Brooks, George
See Baum, L(yman) Frank

Brooks, Gwendolyn 1917- ...... **CLC 1, 2, 4, 5, 15, 49; BLC; DA; DAC; DAM MST, MULT, POET; PC 7; WLC**
See also AITN 1; BW 2; CA 1-4R; CANR 1, 27, 52; CDALB 1941-1968; CLR 27; DLB 5, 76, 165; MTCW; SATA 6

Brooks, Mel .... **CLC 12**
See also Kaminsky, Melvin
See also AAYA 13; DLB 26

Brooks, Peter 1938- .... **CLC 34**
See also CA 45-48; CANR 1

Brooks, Van Wyck 1886-1963 ...... **CLC 29**
See also CA 1-4R; CANR 6; DLB 45, 63, 103

Brophy, Brigid (Antonia) 1929-1995 .... **CLC 6, 11, 29**
See also CA 5-8R; 149; CAAS 4; CANR 25, 53; DLB 14; MTCW

Brosman, Catharine Savage 1934- .... **CLC 9**
See also CA 61-64; CANR 21, 46

Brother Antoninus
See Everson, William (Oliver)

Broughton, T(homas) Alan 1936- ... **CLC 19**
See also CA 45-48; CANR 2, 23, 48

Broumas, Olga 1949- .... **CLC 10, 73**
See also CA 85-88; CANR 20

Brown, Charles Brockden 1771-1810 .... **NCLC 22**
See also CDALB 1640-1865; DLB 37, 59, 73

Brown, Christy 1932-1981 .... **CLC 63**
See also CA 105; 104; DLB 14

Brown, Claude 1937- ..... **CLC 30; BLC; DAM MULT**
See also AAYA 7; BW 1; CA 73-76

Brown, Dee (Alexander) 1908- .... **CLC 18, 47; DAM POP**
See also CA 13-16R; CAAS 6; CANR 11, 45; DLBY 80; MTCW; SATA 5

Brown, George
See Wertmueller, Lina

Brown, George Douglas 1869-1902 .... **TCLC 28**

Brown, George Mackay 1921-1996 .... **CLC 5, 48**
See also CA 21-24R; 151; CAAS 6; CANR 12, 37; DLB 14, 27, 139; MTCW; SATA 35

Brown, (William) Larry 1951- ...... **CLC 73**
See also CA 130; 134; INT 133

Brown, Moses
See Barrett, William (Christopher)

Brown, Rita Mae 1944- ..... **CLC 18, 43, 79; DAM NOV, POP**
See also CA 45-48; CANR 2, 11, 35; INT CANR-11; MTCW

Brown, Roderick (Langmere) Haig-
See Haig-Brown, Roderick (Langmere)

Brown, Rosellen 1939- .... **CLC 32**
See also CA 77-80; CAAS 10; CANR 14, 44

Brown, Sterling Allen 1901-1989 .... **CLC 1, 23, 59; BLC; DAM MULT, POET**
See also BW 1; CA 85-88; 127; CANR 26; DLB 48, 51, 63; MTCW

Brown, Will
See Ainsworth, William Harrison

Brown, William Wells
1813-1884 . . . . **NCLC 2; BLC; DAM MULT; DC 1**
See also DLB 3, 50

Browne, (Clyde) Jackson 1948(?)- . . . **CLC 21**
See also CA 120

Browning, Elizabeth Barrett
1806-1861 . . . . . **NCLC 1, 16; DA; DAB; DAC; DAM MST, POET; PC 6; WLC**
See also CDBLB 1832-1890; DLB 32

Browning, Robert
1812-1889 . . . . **NCLC 19; DA; DAB; DAC; DAM MST, POET; PC 2**
See also CDBLB 1832-1890; DLB 32, 163; YABC 1

Browning, Tod 1882-1962 . . . . **CLC 16**
See also CA 141; 117

Brownson, Orestes (Augustus)
1803-1876 . . . . **NCLC 50**

Bruccoli, Matthew J(oseph) 1931- . . **CLC 34**
See also CA 9-12R; CANR 7; DLB 103

Bruce, Lenny . . . . **CLC 21**
See also Schneider, Leonard Alfred

Bruin, John
See Brutus, Dennis

Brulard, Henri
See Stendhal

Brulls, Christian
See Simenon, Georges (Jacques Christian)

Brunner, John (Kilian Houston)
1934-1995 . . . . . . **CLC 8, 10; DAM POP**
See also CA 1-4R; 149; CAAS 8; CANR 2, 37; MTCW

Bruno, Giordano 1548-1600 . . . . **LC 27**

Brutus, Dennis
1924- . . . . . **CLC 43; BLC; DAM MULT, POET**
See also BW 2; CA 49-52; CAAS 14; CANR 2, 27, 42; DLB 117

Bryan, C(ourtlandt) D(ixon) B(arnes)
1936- . . . . **CLC 29**
See also CA 73-76; CANR 13; INT CANR-13

Bryan, Michael
See Moore, Brian

Bryant, William Cullen
1794-1878 . . . . . **NCLC 6, 46; DA; DAB; DAC; DAM MST, POET**
See also CDALB 1640-1865; DLB 3, 43, 59

Bryusov, Valery Yakovlevich
1873-1924 . . . . **TCLC 10**
See also CA 107

Buchan, John
1875-1940 . . . . **TCLC 41; DAB; DAM POP**
See also CA 108; 145; DLB 34, 70, 156; YABC 2

Buchanan, George 1506-1582 . . . . **LC 4**

Buchheim, Lothar-Guenther 1918- . . . **CLC 6**
See also CA 85-88

Buchner, (Karl) Georg
1813-1837 . . . . **NCLC 26**

Buchwald, Art(hur) 1925-. . . . . **CLC 33**
See also AITN 1; CA 5-8R; CANR 21; MTCW; SATA 10

Buck, Pearl S(ydenstricker)
1892-1973 . . . . **CLC 7, 11, 18; DA; DAB; DAC; DAM MST, NOV**
See also AITN 1; CA 1-4R; 41-44R; CANR 1, 34; DLB 9, 102; MTCW; SATA 1, 25

Buckler, Ernest
1908-1984 . . **CLC 13; DAC; DAM MST**
See also CA 11-12; 114; CAP 1; DLB 68; SATA 47

Buckley, Vincent (Thomas)
1925-1988 . . . . **CLC 57**
See also CA 101

Buckley, William F(rank), Jr.
1925- . . . . **CLC 7, 18, 37; DAM POP**
See also AITN 1; CA 1-4R; CANR 1, 24, 53; DLB 137; DLBY 80; INT CANR-24; MTCW

Buechner, (Carl) Frederick
1926- . . . . . . **CLC 2, 4, 6, 9; DAM NOV**
See also CA 13-16R; CANR 11, 39; DLBY 80; INT CANR-11; MTCW

Buell, John (Edward) 1927-. . . . . **CLC 10**
See also CA 1-4R; DLB 53

Buero Vallejo, Antonio 1916- . . . **CLC 15, 46**
See also CA 106; CANR 24, 49; HW; MTCW

Bufalino, Gesualdo 1920(?)-. . . . . **CLC 74**

Bugayev, Boris Nikolayevich 1880-1934
See Bely, Andrey
See also CA 104

Bukowski, Charles
1920-1994 . . . . **CLC 2, 5, 9, 41, 82; DAM NOV, POET**
See also CA 17-20R; 144; CANR 40; DLB 5, 130; MTCW

Bulgakov, Mikhail (Afanas'evich)
1891-1940 . . . . **TCLC 2, 16; DAM DRAM, NOV; SSC 18**
See also CA 105; 152

Bulgya, Alexander Alexandrovich
1901-1956 . . . . **TCLC 53**
See also Fadeyev, Alexander
See also CA 117

Bullins, Ed
1935- . . . . **CLC 1, 5, 7; BLC; DAM DRAM, MULT; DC 6**
See also BW 2; CA 49-52; CAAS 16; CANR 24, 46; DLB 7, 38; MTCW

Bulwer-Lytton, Edward (George Earle Lytton)
1803-1873 . . . . **NCLC 1, 45**
See also DLB 21

Bunin, Ivan Alexeyevich
1870-1953 . . . . **TCLC 6; SSC 5**
See also CA 104

Bunting, Basil
1900-1985 . . . . **CLC 10, 39, 47; DAM POET**
See also CA 53-56; 115; CANR 7; DLB 20

Bunuel, Luis
1900-1983 . . . . **CLC 16, 80; DAM MULT; HLC**
See also CA 101; 110; CANR 32; HW

Bunyan, John
1628-1688 . . . . . . **LC 4; DA; DAB; DAC; DAM MST; WLC**
See also CDBLB 1660-1789; DLB 39

Burckhardt, Jacob (Christoph)
1818-1897 . . . . **NCLC 49**

Burford, Eleanor
See Hibbert, Eleanor Alice Burford

Burgess, Anthony
. **CLC 1, 2, 4, 5, 8, 10, 13, 15, 22, 40, 62, 81, 94; DAB**
See also Wilson, John (Anthony) Burgess
See also AITN 1; CDBLB 1960 to Present; DLB 14

Burke, Edmund
1729(?)-1797 . . . . **LC 7; DA; DAB; DAC; DAM MST; WLC**
See also DLB 104

Burke, Kenneth (Duva)
1897-1993 . . . . **CLC 2, 24**
See also CA 5-8R; 143; CANR 39; DLB 45, 63; MTCW

Burke, Leda
See Garnett, David

Burke, Ralph
See Silverberg, Robert

Burke, Thomas 1886-1945 . . . . **TCLC 63**
See also CA 113

Burney, Fanny 1752-1840 . . . . **NCLC 12, 54**
See also DLB 39

Burns, Robert 1759-1796 . . . . **PC 6**
See also CDBLB 1789-1832; DA; DAB; DAC; DAM MST, POET; DLB 109; WLC

Burns, Tex
See L'Amour, Louis (Dearborn)

Burnshaw, Stanley 1906- . . . . . **CLC 3, 13, 44**
See also CA 9-12R; DLB 48

Burr, Anne 1937- . . . . **CLC 6**
See also CA 25-28R

Burroughs, Edgar Rice
1875-1950 . . . . **TCLC 2, 32; DAM NOV**
See also AAYA 11; CA 104; 132; DLB 8; MTCW; SATA 41

Burroughs, William S(eward)
1914- . . . . **CLC 1, 2, 5, 15, 22, 42, 75; DA; DAB; DAC; DAM MST, NOV, POP; WLC**
See also AITN 2; CA 9-12R; CANR 20, 52; DLB 2, 8, 16, 152; DLBY 81; MTCW

Burton, Richard F. 1821-1890. . . . **NCLC 42**
See also DLB 55

Busch, Frederick 1941- . . . **CLC 7, 10, 18, 47**
See also CA 33-36R; CAAS 1; CANR 45; DLB 6

Bush, Ronald 1946- . . . . **CLC 34**
See also CA 136

Bustos, F(rancisco)
See Borges, Jorge Luis

Bustos Domecq, H(onorio)
See Bioy Casares, Adolfo; Borges, Jorge Luis

Butler, Octavia E(stelle)
1947- . . . . . **CLC 38; DAM MULT, POP**
See also AAYA 18; BW 2; CA 73-76; CANR 12, 24, 38; DLB 33; MTCW; SATA 84

Carey, Ernestine Gilbreth 1908- . . . . **CLC 17**
See also CA 5-8R; SATA 2

Carey, Peter 1943- . . . . **CLC 40, 55, 96**
See also CA 123; 127; CANR 53; INT 127; MTCW

Carleton, William 1794-1869 . . . . . . **NCLC 3**
See also DLB 159

Carlisle, Henry (Coffin) 1926- . . . . . . **CLC 33**
See also CA 13-16R; CANR 15

Carlsen, Chris
See Holdstock, Robert P.

Carlson, Ron(ald F.) 1947- . . . . **CLC 54**
See also CA 105; CANR 27

Carlyle, Thomas
1795-1881 . . . . **NCLC 22; DA; DAB; DAC; DAM MST**
See also CDBLB 1789-1832; DLB 55; 144

Carman, (William) Bliss
1861-1929 . . . . **TCLC 7; DAC**
See also CA 104; 152; DLB 92

Carnegie, Dale 1888-1955 . . . . **TCLC 53**

Carossa, Hans 1878-1956 . . . . **TCLC 48**
See also DLB 66

Carpenter, Don(ald Richard)
1931-1995 . . . . **CLC 41**
See also CA 45-48; 149; CANR 1

Carpentier (y Valmont), Alejo
1904-1980 . . . . **CLC 8, 11, 38; DAM MULT; HLC**
See also CA 65-68; 97-100; CANR 11; DLB 113; HW

Carr, Caleb 1955(?)- . . . . **CLC 86**
See also CA 147

Carr, Emily 1871-1945 . . . . **TCLC 32**
See also DLB 68

Carr, John Dickson 1906-1977 . . . . . . **CLC 3**
See also CA 49-52; 69-72; CANR 3, 33; MTCW

Carr, Philippa
See Hibbert, Eleanor Alice Burford

Carr, Virginia Spencer 1929- . . . . **CLC 34**
See also CA 61-64; DLB 111

Carrere, Emmanuel 1957- . . . . **CLC 89**

Carrier, Roch
1937- . . . **CLC 13, 78; DAC; DAM MST**
See also CA 130; DLB 53

Carroll, James P. 1943(?)- . . . . **CLC 38**
See also CA 81-84

Carroll, Jim 1951- . . . . **CLC 35**
See also AAYA 17; CA 45-48; CANR 42

Carroll, Lewis . . . . **NCLC 2, 53; WLC**
See also Dodgson, Charles Lutwidge
See also CDBLB 1832-1890; CLR 2, 18; DLB 18, 163; JRDA

Carroll, Paul Vincent 1900-1968 . . . . **CLC 10**
See also CA 9-12R; 25-28R; DLB 10

Carruth, Hayden
1921- . . . . . . **CLC 4, 7, 10, 18, 84; PC 10**
See also CA 9-12R; CANR 4, 38; DLB 5, 165; INT CANR-4; MTCW; SATA 47

Carson, Rachel Louise
1907-1964 . . . . **CLC 71; DAM POP**
See also CA 77-80; CANR 35; MTCW; SATA 23

Carter, Angela (Olive)
1940-1992 . . . . . . **CLC 5, 41, 76; SSC 13**
See also CA 53-56; 136; CANR 12, 36; DLB 14; MTCW; SATA 66; SATA-Obit 70

Carter, Nick
See Smith, Martin Cruz

Carver, Raymond
1938-1988 . . . . **CLC 22, 36, 53, 55; DAM NOV; SSC 8**
See also CA 33-36R; 126; CANR 17, 34; DLB 130; DLBY 84, 88; MTCW

Cary, Elizabeth, Lady Falkland
1585-1639 . . . . **LC 30**

Cary, (Arthur) Joyce (Lunel)
1888-1957 . . . . **TCLC 1, 29**
See also CA 104; CDBLB 1914-1945; DLB 15, 100

Casanova de Seingalt, Giovanni Jacopo
1725-1798 . . . . **LC 13**

Casares, Adolfo Bioy
See Bioy Casares, Adolfo

Casely-Hayford, J(oseph) E(phraim)
1866-1930 . . . . **TCLC 24; BLC; DAM MULT**
See also BW 2; CA 123; 152

Casey, John (Dudley) 1939- . . . . **CLC 59**
See also BEST 90:2; CA 69-72; CANR 23

Casey, Michael 1947- . . . . **CLC 2**
See also CA 65-68; DLB 5

Casey, Patrick
See Thurman, Wallace (Henry)

Casey, Warren (Peter) 1935-1988 . . . **CLC 12**
See also CA 101; 127; INT 101

Casona, Alejandro . . . . **CLC 49**
See also Alvarez, Alejandro Rodriguez

Cassavetes, John 1929-1989 . . . . **CLC 20**
See also CA 85-88; 127

Cassill, R(onald) V(erlin) 1919- . . . **CLC 4, 23**
See also CA 9-12R; CAAS 1; CANR 7, 45; DLB 6

Cassirer, Ernst 1874-1945 . . . . **TCLC 61**

Cassity, (Allen) Turner 1929- . . . . **CLC 6, 42**
See also CA 17-20R; CAAS 8; CANR 11; DLB 105

Castaneda, Carlos 1931(?)- . . . . **CLC 12**
See also CA 25-28R; CANR 32; HW; MTCW

Castedo, Elena 1937- . . . . **CLC 65**
See also CA 132

Castedo-Ellerman, Elena
See Castedo, Elena

Castellanos, Rosario
1925-1974 . . . . . . **CLC 66; DAM MULT; HLC**
See also CA 131; 53-56; DLB 113; HW

Castelvetro, Lodovico 1505-1571 . . . . . **LC 12**

Castiglione, Baldassare 1478-1529 . . . **LC 12**

Castle, Robert
See Hamilton, Edmond

Castro, Guillen de 1569-1631 . . . . **LC 19**

Castro, Rosalia de
1837-1885 . . . . . . **NCLC 3; DAM MULT**

Cather, Willa
See Cather, Willa Sibert

Cather, Willa Sibert
1873-1947 . . . . **TCLC 1, 11, 31; DA; DAB; DAC; DAM MST, NOV; SSC 2; WLC**
See also CA 104; 128; CDALB 1865-1917; DLB 9, 54, 78; DLBD 1; MTCW; SATA 30

Catton, (Charles) Bruce
1899-1978 . . . . **CLC 35**
See also AITN 1; CA 5-8R; 81-84; CANR 7; DLB 17; SATA 2; SATA-Obit 24

Catullus c. 84B.C.-c. 54B.C. . . . . . . **CMLC 18**

Cauldwell, Frank
See King, Francis (Henry)

Caunitz, William J. 1933-1996 . . . . . **CLC 34**
See also BEST 89:3; CA 125; 130; 152; INT 130

Causley, Charles (Stanley) 1917- . . . . . **CLC 7**
See also CA 9-12R; CANR 5, 35; CLR 30; DLB 27; MTCW; SATA 3, 66

Caute, David 1936- . . . . **CLC 29; DAM NOV**
See also CA 1-4R; CAAS 4; CANR 1, 33; DLB 14

Cavafy, C(onstantine) P(eter)
1863-1933 . . . . **TCLC 2, 7; DAM POET**
See also Kavafis, Konstantinos Petrou
See also CA 148

Cavallo, Evelyn
See Spark, Muriel (Sarah)

Cavanna, Betty . . . . **CLC 12**
See also Harrison, Elizabeth Cavanna
See also JRDA; MAICYA; SAAS 4; SATA 1, 30

Cavendish, Margaret Lucas
1623-1673 . . . . **LC 30**
See also DLB 131

Caxton, William 1421(?)-1491(?) . . . . . **LC 17**

Cayrol, Jean 1911- . . . . **CLC 11**
See also CA 89-92; DLB 83

Cela, Camilo Jose
1916- . . . . . **CLC 4, 13, 59; DAM MULT; HLC**
See also BEST 90:2; CA 21-24R; CAAS 10; CANR 21, 32; DLBY 89; HW; MTCW

Celan, Paul . . . . . . **CLC 10, 19, 53, 82; PC 10**
See also Antschel, Paul
See also DLB 69

Celine, Louis-Ferdinand
. . . . **CLC 1, 3, 4, 7, 9, 15, 47**
See also Destouches, Louis-Ferdinand
See also DLB 72

Cellini, Benvenuto 1500-1571 . . . . **LC 7**

Cendrars, Blaise . . . . **CLC 18**
See also Sauser-Hall, Frederic

Cernuda (y Bidon), Luis
1902-1963 . . . . **CLC 54; DAM POET**
See also CA 131; 89-92; DLB 134; HW

Cervantes (Saavedra), Miguel de
1547-1616 . . . . **LC 6, 23; DA; DAB; DAC; DAM MST, NOV; SSC 12; WLC**

Christie
See Ichikawa, Kon

Christie, Agatha (Mary Clarissa) 1890-1976 . . . . . . **CLC 1, 6, 8, 12, 39, 48; DAB; DAC; DAM NOV**
See also AAYA 9; AITN 1, 2; CA 17-20R; 61-64; CANR 10, 37; CDBLB 1914-1945; DLB 13, 77; MTCW; SATA 36

Christie, (Ann) Philippa
See Pearce, Philippa
See also CA 5-8R; CANR 4

Christine de Pizan 1365(?)-1431(?) . . . . **LC 9**

Chubb, Elmer
See Masters, Edgar Lee

Chulkov, Mikhail Dmitrievich 1743-1792 . . . . **LC 2**
See also DLB 150

Churchill, Caryl 1938- . . . **CLC 31, 55; DC 5**
See also CA 102; CANR 22, 46; DLB 13; MTCW

Churchill, Charles 1731-1764. . . . . **LC 3**
See also DLB 109

Chute, Carolyn 1947- . . . . **CLC 39**
See also CA 123

Ciardi, John (Anthony) 1916-1986 . . . . **CLC 10, 40, 44; DAM POET**
See also CA 5-8R; 118; CAAS 2; CANR 5, 33; CLR 19; DLB 5; DLBY 86; INT CANR-5; MAICYA; MTCW; SATA 1, 65; SATA-Obit 46

Cicero, Marcus Tullius 106B.C.-43B.C. . . . . **CMLC 3**

Cimino, Michael 1943- . . . . **CLC 16**
See also CA 105

Cioran, E(mil) M. 1911-1995. . . . . . . **CLC 64**
See also CA 25-28R; 149

Cisneros, Sandra 1954- . . . . . **CLC 69; DAM MULT; HLC**
See also AAYA 9; CA 131; DLB 122, 152; HW

Cixous, Helene 1937- . . . . **CLC 92**
See also CA 126; DLB 83; MTCW

Clair, Rene. . . . . **CLC 20**
See also Chomette, Rene Lucien

Clampitt, Amy 1920-1994 . . . . **CLC 32**
See also CA 110; 146; CANR 29; DLB 105

Clancy, Thomas L., Jr. 1947-
See Clancy, Tom
See also CA 125; 131; INT 131; MTCW

Clancy, Tom. . . . . **CLC 45; DAM NOV, POP**
See also Clancy, Thomas L., Jr.
See also AAYA 9; BEST 89:1, 90:1

Clare, John 1793-1864 . . . . **NCLC 9; DAB; DAM POET**
See also DLB 55, 96

Clarin
See Alas (y Urena), Leopoldo (Enrique Garcia)

Clark, Al C.
See Goines, Donald

Clark, (Robert) Brian 1932- . . . . **CLC 29**
See also CA 41-44R

Clark, Curt
See Westlake, Donald E(dwin)

Clark, Eleanor 1913-1996 . . . . **CLC 5, 19**
See also CA 9-12R; 151; CANR 41; DLB 6

Clark, J. P.
See Clark, John Pepper
See also DLB 117

Clark, John Pepper 1935- . . . . **CLC 38; BLC; DAM DRAM, MULT; DC 5**
See also Clark, J. P.
See also BW 1; CA 65-68; CANR 16

Clark, M. R.
See Clark, Mavis Thorpe

Clark, Mavis Thorpe 1909- . . . . **CLC 12**
See also CA 57-60; CANR 8, 37; CLR 30; MAICYA; SAAS 5; SATA 8, 74

Clark, Walter Van Tilburg 1909-1971 . . . . **CLC 28**
See also CA 9-12R; 33-36R; DLB 9; SATA 8

Clarke, Arthur C(harles) 1917- . . . . **CLC 1, 4, 13, 18, 35; DAM POP; SSC 3**
See also AAYA 4; CA 1-4R; CANR 2, 28; JRDA; MAICYA; MTCW; SATA 13, 70

Clarke, Austin 1896-1974 . . . . . . **CLC 6, 9; DAM POET**
See also CA 29-32; 49-52; CAP 2; DLB 10, 20

Clarke, Austin C(hesterfield) 1934- . . . . **CLC 8, 53; BLC; DAC; DAM MULT**
See also BW 1; CA 25-28R; CAAS 16; CANR 14, 32; DLB 53, 125

Clarke, Gillian 1937- . . . . **CLC 61**
See also CA 106; DLB 40

Clarke, Marcus (Andrew Hislop) 1846-1881 . . . . **NCLC 19**

Clarke, Shirley 1925- . . . . **CLC 16**

Clash, The
See Headon, (Nicky) Topper; Jones, Mick; Simonon, Paul; Strummer, Joe

Claudel, Paul (Louis Charles Marie) 1868-1955 . . . . **TCLC 2, 10**
See also CA 104

Clavell, James (duMaresq) 1925-1994 . . . . **CLC 6, 25, 87; DAM NOV, POP**
See also CA 25-28R; 146; CANR 26, 48; MTCW

Cleaver, (Leroy) Eldridge 1935- . . . . . **CLC 30; BLC; DAM MULT**
See also BW 1; CA 21-24R; CANR 16

Cleese, John (Marwood) 1939- . . . . . **CLC 21**
See also Monty Python
See also CA 112; 116; CANR 35; MTCW

Cleishbotham, Jebediah
See Scott, Walter

Cleland, John 1710-1789 . . . . **LC 2**
See also DLB 39

Clemens, Samuel Langhorne 1835-1910
See Twain, Mark
See also CA 104; 135; CDALB 1865-1917; DA; DAB; DAC; DAM MST, NOV; DLB 11, 12, 23, 64, 74; JRDA; MAICYA; YABC 2

Cleophil
See Congreve, William

Clerihew, E.
See Bentley, E(dmund) C(lerihew)

Clerk, N. W.
See Lewis, C(live) S(taples)

Cliff, Jimmy. . . . . **CLC 21**
See also Chambers, James

Clifton, (Thelma) Lucille 1936- . . . . **CLC 19, 66; BLC; DAM MULT, POET**
See also BW 2; CA 49-52; CANR 2, 24, 42; CLR 5; DLB 5, 41; MAICYA; MTCW; SATA 20, 69

Clinton, Dirk
See Silverberg, Robert

Clough, Arthur Hugh 1819-1861. . **NCLC 27**
See also DLB 32

Clutha, Janet Paterson Frame 1924-
See Frame, Janet
See also CA 1-4R; CANR 2, 36; MTCW

Clyne, Terence
See Blatty, William Peter

Cobalt, Martin
See Mayne, William (James Carter)

Cobbett, William 1763-1835 . . . . . **NCLC 49**
See also DLB 43, 107, 158

Coburn, D(onald) L(ee) 1938- . . . . . . **CLC 10**
See also CA 89-92

Cocteau, Jean (Maurice Eugene Clement) 1889-1963 . . . . **CLC 1, 8, 15, 16, 43; DA; DAB; DAC; DAM DRAM, MST, NOV; WLC**
See also CA 25-28; CANR 40; CAP 2; DLB 65; MTCW

Codrescu, Andrei 1946- . . . . **CLC 46; DAM POET**
See also CA 33-36R; CAAS 19; CANR 13, 34, 53

Coe, Max
See Bourne, Randolph S(illiman)

Coe, Tucker
See Westlake, Donald E(dwin)

Coetzee, J(ohn) M(ichael) 1940- . . . . . . **CLC 23, 33, 66; DAM NOV**
See also CA 77-80; CANR 41; MTCW

Coffey, Brian
See Koontz, Dean R(ay)

Cohan, George M. 1878-1942 . . . . . **TCLC 60**

Cohen, Arthur A(llen) 1928-1986 . . . . **CLC 7, 31**
See also CA 1-4R; 120; CANR 1, 17, 42; DLB 28

Cohen, Leonard (Norman) 1934- . . . . **CLC 3, 38; DAC; DAM MST**
See also CA 21-24R; CANR 14; DLB 53; MTCW

Cohen, Matt 1942- .... **CLC 19; DAC**
See also CA 61-64; CAAS 18; CANR 40; DLB 53

Cohen-Solal, Annie 19(?)- .... **CLC 50**

Colegate, Isabel 1931- .... **CLC 36**
See also CA 17-20R; CANR 8, 22; DLB 14; INT CANR-22; MTCW

Coleman, Emmett
See Reed, Ishmael

Coleridge, Samuel Taylor
1772-1834 ..... **NCLC 9, 54; DA; DAB; DAC; DAM MST, POET; PC 11; WLC**
See also CDBLB 1789-1832; DLB 93, 107

Coleridge, Sara 1802-1852....... **NCLC 31**

Coles, Don 1928- .... **CLC 46**
See also CA 115; CANR 38

Colette, (Sidonie-Gabrielle)
1873-1954 .... **TCLC 1, 5, 16; DAM NOV; SSC 10**
See also CA 104; 131; DLB 65; MTCW

Collett, (Jacobine) Camilla (Wergeland)
1813-1895 .... **NCLC 22**

Collier, Christopher 1930- .... **CLC 30**
See also AAYA 13; CA 33-36R; CANR 13, 33; JRDA; MAICYA; SATA 16, 70

Collier, James L(incoln)
1928- .... **CLC 30; DAM POP**
See also AAYA 13; CA 9-12R; CANR 4, 33; CLR 3; JRDA; MAICYA; SAAS 21; SATA 8, 70

Collier, Jeremy 1650-1726........... **LC 6**

Collier, John 1901-1980........... **SSC 19**
See also CA 65-68; 97-100; CANR 10; DLB 77

Collins, Hunt
See Hunter, Evan

Collins, Linda 1931-.............. **CLC 44**
See also CA 125

Collins, (William) Wilkie
1824-1889 .... **NCLC 1, 18**
See also CDBLB 1832-1890; DLB 18, 70, 159

Collins, William
1721-1759 .... **LC 4; DAM POET**
See also DLB 109

Collodi, Carlo 1826-1890........ **NCLC 54**
See also Lorenzini, Carlo
See also CLR 5

Colman, George
See Glassco, John

Colt, Winchester Remington
See Hubbard, L(afayette) Ron(ald)

Colter, Cyrus 1910- .... **CLC 58**
See also BW 1; CA 65-68; CANR 10; DLB 33

Colton, James
See Hansen, Joseph

Colum, Padraic 1881-1972......... **CLC 28**
See also CA 73-76; 33-36R; CANR 35; CLR 36; MAICYA; MTCW; SATA 15

Colvin, James
See Moorcock, Michael (John)

Colwin, Laurie (E.)
1944-1992 .... **CLC 5, 13, 23, 84**
See also CA 89-92; 139; CANR 20, 46; DLBY 80; MTCW

Comfort, Alex(ander)
1920- .... **CLC 7; DAM POP**
See also CA 1-4R; CANR 1, 45

Comfort, Montgomery
See Campbell, (John) Ramsey

Compton-Burnett, I(vy)
1884(?)-1969 ...... **CLC 1, 3, 10, 15, 34; DAM NOV**
See also CA 1-4R; 25-28R; CANR 4; DLB 36; MTCW

Comstock, Anthony 1844-1915 .... **TCLC 13**
See also CA 110

Comte, Auguste 1798-1857....... **NCLC 54**

Conan Doyle, Arthur
See Doyle, Arthur Conan

Conde, Maryse
1937- .... **CLC 52, 92; DAM MULT**
See also Boucolon, Maryse
See also BW 2

Condillac, Etienne Bonnot de
1714-1780 .... **LC 26**

Condon, Richard (Thomas)
1915-1996 .... **CLC 4, 6, 8, 10, 45; DAM NOV**
See also BEST 90:3; CA 1-4R; 151; CAAS 1; CANR 2, 23; INT CANR-23; MTCW

Congreve, William
1670-1729 .... **LC 5, 21; DA; DAB; DAC; DAM DRAM, MST, POET; DC 2; WLC**
See also CDBLB 1660-1789; DLB 39, 84

Connell, Evan S(helby), Jr.
1924- .... **CLC 4, 6, 45; DAM NOV**
See also AAYA 7; CA 1-4R; CAAS 2; CANR 2, 39; DLB 2; DLBY 81; MTCW

Connelly, Marc(us Cook)
1890-1980 .... **CLC 7**
See also CA 85-88; 102; CANR 30; DLB 7; DLBY 80; SATA-Obit 25

Connor, Ralph .... **TCLC 31**
See also Gordon, Charles William
See also DLB 92

Conrad, Joseph
1857-1924 .... **TCLC 1, 6, 13, 25, 43, 57; DA; DAB; DAC; DAM MST, NOV; SSC 9; WLC**
See also CA 104; 131; CDBLB 1890-1914; DLB 10, 34, 98, 156; MTCW; SATA 27

Conrad, Robert Arnold
See Hart, Moss

Conroy, Pat
1945- ... **CLC 30, 74; DAM NOV, POP**
See also AAYA 8; AITN 1; CA 85-88; CANR 24, 53; DLB 6; MTCW

Constant (de Rebecque), (Henri) Benjamin
1767-1830 .... **NCLC 6**
See also DLB 119

Conybeare, Charles Augustus
See Eliot, T(homas) S(tearns)

Cook, Michael 1933- .... **CLC 58**
See also CA 93-96; DLB 53

Cook, Robin 1940- .... **CLC 14; DAM POP**
See also BEST 90:2; CA 108; 111; CANR 41; INT 111

Cook, Roy
See Silverberg, Robert

Cooke, Elizabeth 1948- .... **CLC 55**
See also CA 129

Cooke, John Esten 1830-1886..... **NCLC 5**
See also DLB 3

Cooke, John Estes
See Baum, L(yman) Frank

Cooke, M. E.
See Creasey, John

Cooke, Margaret
See Creasey, John

Cook-Lynn, Elizabeth
1930- .... **CLC 93; DAM MULT**
See also CA 133; NNAL

Cooney, Ray .... **CLC 62**

Cooper, Douglas 1960-............ **CLC 86**

Cooper, Henry St. John
See Creasey, John

Cooper, J. California
.... **CLC 56; DAM MULT**
See also AAYA 12; BW 1; CA 125

Cooper, James Fenimore
1789-1851 .... **NCLC 1, 27, 54**
See also CDALB 1640-1865; DLB 3; SATA 19

Coover, Robert (Lowell)
1932- .... **CLC 3, 7, 15, 32, 46, 87; DAM NOV; SSC 15**
See also CA 45-48; CANR 3, 37; DLB 2; DLBY 81; MTCW

Copeland, Stewart (Armstrong)
1952- .... **CLC 26**

Coppard, A(lfred) E(dgar)
1878-1957 .... **TCLC 5; SSC 21**
See also CA 114; DLB 162; YABC 1

Coppee, Francois 1842-1908 ...... **TCLC 25**

Coppola, Francis Ford 1939-....... **CLC 16**
See also CA 77-80; CANR 40; DLB 44

Corbiere, Tristan 1845-1875 ..... **NCLC 43**

Corcoran, Barbara 1911- .... **CLC 17**
See also AAYA 14; CA 21-24R; CAAS 2; CANR 11, 28, 48; DLB 52; JRDA; SAAS 20; SATA 3, 77

Cordelier, Maurice
See Giraudoux, (Hippolyte) Jean

Corelli, Marie 1855-1924......... **TCLC 51**
See also Mackay, Mary
See also DLB 34, 156

Corman, Cid....................... **CLC 9**
See also Corman, Sidney
See also CAAS 2; DLB 5

Corman, Sidney 1924-
See Corman, Cid
See also CA 85-88; CANR 44; DAM POET

Cormier, Robert (Edmund) 1925- .... **CLC 12, 30; DA; DAB; DAC; DAM MST, NOV**
See also AAYA 3; CA 1-4R; CANR 5, 23; CDALB 1968-1988; CLR 12; DLB 52; INT CANR-23; JRDA; MAICYA; MTCW; SATA 10, 45, 83

Corn, Alfred (DeWitt III) 1943- .... **CLC 33**
See also CA 104; CANR 44; DLB 120; DLBY 80

Corneille, Pierre 1606-1684 .... **LC 28; DAB; DAM MST**

Cornwell, David (John Moore) 1931- .... **CLC 9, 15; DAM POP**
See also le Carre, John
See also CA 5-8R; CANR 13, 33; MTCW

Corso, (Nunzio) Gregory 1930- ... **CLC 1, 11**
See also CA 5-8R; CANR 41; DLB 5, 16; MTCW

Cortazar, Julio 1914-1984 ...... **CLC 2, 3, 5, 10, 13, 15, 33, 34, 92; DAM MULT, NOV; HLC; SSC 7**
See also CA 21-24R; CANR 12, 32; DLB 113; HW; MTCW

CORTES, HERNAN 1484-1547 ..... **LC 31**

Corwin, Cecil
See Kornbluth, C(yril) M.

Cosic, Dobrica 1921- .... **CLC 14**
See also CA 122; 138

Costain, Thomas B(ertram) 1885-1965 .... **CLC 30**
See also CA 5-8R; 25-28R; DLB 9

Costantini, Humberto 1924(?)-1987 .... **CLC 49**
See also CA 131; 122; HW

Costello, Elvis 1955- .... **CLC 21**

Cotter, Joseph Seamon Sr. 1861-1949 .... **TCLC 28; BLC; DAM MULT**
See also BW 1; CA 124; DLB 50

Couch, Arthur Thomas Quiller
See Quiller-Couch, Arthur Thomas

Coulton, James
See Hansen, Joseph

Couperus, Louis (Marie Anne) 1863-1923 .... **TCLC 15**
See also CA 115

Coupland, Douglas 1961- .... **CLC 85; DAC; DAM POP**
See also CA 142

Court, Wesli
See Turco, Lewis (Putnam)

Courtenay, Bryce 1933- .... **CLC 59**
See also CA 138

Courtney, Robert
See Ellison, Harlan (Jay)

Cousteau, Jacques-Yves 1910- ...... **CLC 30**
See also CA 65-68; CANR 15; MTCW; SATA 38

Coward, Noel (Peirce) 1899-1973 .... **CLC 1, 9, 29, 51; DAM DRAM**
See also AITN 1; CA 17-18; 41-44R; CANR 35; CAP 2; CDBLB 1914-1945; DLB 10; MTCW

Cowley, Malcolm 1898-1989 .... **CLC 39**
See also CA 5-8R; 128; CANR 3; DLB 4, 48; DLBY 81, 89; MTCW

Cowper, William 1731-1800 ...... **NCLC 8; DAM POET**
See also DLB 104, 109

Cox, William Trevor 1928- .... **CLC 9, 14, 71; DAM NOV**
See also Trevor, William
See also CA 9-12R; CANR 4, 37; DLB 14; INT CANR-37; MTCW

Coyne, P. J.
See Masters, Hilary

Cozzens, James Gould 1903-1978 .... **CLC 1, 4, 11, 92**
See also CA 9-12R; 81-84; CANR 19; CDALB 1941-1968; DLB 9; DLBD 2; DLBY 84; MTCW

Crabbe, George 1754-1832 .... **NCLC 26**
See also DLB 93

Craddock, Charles Egbert
See Murfree, Mary Noailles

Craig, A. A.
See Anderson, Poul (William)

Craik, Dinah Maria (Mulock) 1826-1887 .... **NCLC 38**
See also DLB 35, 163; MAICYA; SATA 34

Cram, Ralph Adams 1863-1942 .... **TCLC 45**

Crane, (Harold) Hart 1899-1932 .... **TCLC 2, 5; DA; DAB; DAC; DAM MST, POET; PC 3; WLC**
See also CA 104; 127; CDALB 1917-1929; DLB 4, 48; MTCW

Crane, R(onald) S(almon) 1886-1967 .... **CLC 27**
See also CA 85-88; DLB 63

Crane, Stephen (Townley) 1871-1900 .... **TCLC 11, 17, 32; DA; DAB; DAC; DAM MST, NOV, POET; SSC 7; WLC**
See also CA 109; 140; CDALB 1865-1917; DLB 12, 54, 78; YABC 2

Crase, Douglas 1944- .... **CLC 58**
See also CA 106

Crashaw, Richard 1612(?)-1649 ...... **LC 24**
See also DLB 126

Craven, Margaret 1901-1980 .... **CLC 17; DAC**
See also CA 103

Crawford, F(rancis) Marion 1854-1909 .... **TCLC 10**
See also CA 107; DLB 71

Crawford, Isabella Valancy 1850-1887 .... **NCLC 12**
See also DLB 92

Crayon, Geoffrey
See Irving, Washington

Creasey, John 1908-1973 .... **CLC 11**
See also CA 5-8R; 41-44R; CANR 8; DLB 77; MTCW

Crebillon, Claude Prosper Jolyot de (fils) 1707-1777 .... **LC 28**

Credo
See Creasey, John

Creeley, Robert (White) 1926- ..... **CLC 1, 2, 4, 8, 11, 15, 36, 78; DAM POET**
See also CA 1-4R; CAAS 10; CANR 23, 43; DLB 5, 16; MTCW

Crews, Harry (Eugene) 1935- .... **CLC 6, 23, 49**
See also AITN 1; CA 25-28R; CANR 20; DLB 6, 143; MTCW

Crichton, (John) Michael 1942- .... **CLC 2, 6, 54, 90; DAM NOV, POP**
See also AAYA 10; AITN 2; CA 25-28R; CANR 13, 40; DLBY 81; INT CANR-13; JRDA; MTCW; SATA 9, 88

Crispin, Edmund .... **CLC 22**
See also Montgomery, (Robert) Bruce
See also DLB 87

Cristofer, Michael 1945(?)- .... **CLC 28; DAM DRAM**
See also CA 110; 152; DLB 7

Croce, Benedetto 1866-1952 ...... **TCLC 37**
See also CA 120

Crockett, David 1786-1836 .... **NCLC 8**
See also DLB 3, 11

Crockett, Davy
See Crockett, David

Crofts, Freeman Wills 1879-1957 .... **TCLC 55**
See also CA 115; DLB 77

Croker, John Wilson 1780-1857 .. **NCLC 10**
See also DLB 110

Crommelynck, Fernand 1885-1970 .. **CLC 75**
See also CA 89-92

Cronin, A(rchibald) J(oseph) 1896-1981 .... **CLC 32**
See also CA 1-4R; 102; CANR 5; SATA 47; SATA-Obit 25

Cross, Amanda
See Heilbrun, Carolyn G(old)

Crothers, Rachel 1878(?)-1958 ..... **TCLC 19**
See also CA 113; DLB 7

Croves, Hal
See Traven, B.

Crow Dog, Mary .... **CLC 93**
See also Brave Bird, Mary

Crowfield, Christopher
See Stowe, Harriet (Elizabeth) Beecher

Crowley, Aleister .... **TCLC 7**
See also Crowley, Edward Alexander

Crowley, Edward Alexander 1875-1947
See Crowley, Aleister
See also CA 104

Crowley, John 1942- .... **CLC 57**
See also CA 61-64; CANR 43; DLBY 82; SATA 65

Crud
See Crumb, R(obert)

Crumarums
See Crumb, R(obert)

Crumb, R(obert) 1943- . . . . **CLC 17**
See also CA 106

Crumbum
See Crumb, R(obert)

Crumski
See Crumb, R(obert)

Crum the Bum
See Crumb, R(obert)

Crunk
See Crumb, R(obert)

Crustt
See Crumb, R(obert)

Cryer, Gretchen (Kiger) 1935- . . . . . . **CLC 21**
See also CA 114; 123

Csath, Geza 1887-1919 . . . . **TCLC 13**
See also CA 111

Cudlip, David 1933- . . . . **CLC 34**

Cullen, Countee
1903-1946 . . . . . . **TCLC 4, 37; BLC; DA; DAC; DAM MST, MULT, POET**
See also BW 1; CA 108; 124; CDALB 1917-1929; DLB 4, 48, 51; MTCW; SATA 18

Cum, R.
See Crumb, R(obert)

Cummings, Bruce F(rederick) 1889-1919
See Barbellion, W. N. P.
See also CA 123

Cummings, E(dward) E(stlin)
1894-1962 . . . . . . **CLC 1, 3, 8, 12, 15, 68; DA; DAB; DAC; DAM MST, POET; PC 5; WLC 2**
See also CA 73-76; CANR 31; CDALB 1929-1941; DLB 4, 48; MTCW

Cunha, Euclides (Rodrigues Pimenta) da
1866-1909 . . . . **TCLC 24**
See also CA 123

Cunningham, E. V.
See Fast, Howard (Melvin)

Cunningham, J(ames) V(incent)
1911-1985 . . . . **CLC 3, 31**
See also CA 1-4R; 115; CANR 1; DLB 5

Cunningham, Julia (Woolfolk)
1916- . . . . **CLC 12**
See also CA 9-12R; CANR 4, 19, 36; JRDA; MAICYA; SAAS 2; SATA 1, 26

Cunningham, Michael 1952- . . . . **CLC 34**
See also CA 136

Cunninghame Graham, R(obert) B(ontine)
1852-1936 . . . . **TCLC 19**
See also Graham, R(obert) B(ontine) Cunninghame
See also CA 119; DLB 98

Currie, Ellen 19(?)- . . . . **CLC 44**

Curtin, Philip
See Lowndes, Marie Adelaide (Belloc)

Curtis, Price
See Ellison, Harlan (Jay)

Cutrate, Joe
See Spiegelman, Art

Czaczkes, Shmuel Yosef
See Agnon, S(hmuel) Y(osef Halevi)

Dabrowska, Maria (Szumska)
1889-1965 . . . . **CLC 15**
See also CA 106

Dabydeen, David 1955- . . . . **CLC 34**
See also BW 1; CA 125

Dacey, Philip 1939- . . . . **CLC 51**
See also CA 37-40R; CAAS 17; CANR 14, 32; DLB 105

Dagerman, Stig (Halvard)
1923-1954 . . . . **TCLC 17**
See also CA 117

Dahl, Roald
1916-1990 . . . . . . **CLC 1, 6, 18, 79; DAB; DAC; DAM MST, NOV, POP**
See also AAYA 15; CA 1-4R; 133; CANR 6, 32, 37; CLR 1, 7, 41; DLB 139; JRDA; MAICYA; MTCW; SATA 1, 26, 73; SATA-Obit 65

Dahlberg, Edward 1900-1977 . . . **CLC 1, 7, 14**
See also CA 9-12R; 69-72; CANR 31; DLB 48; MTCW

Dale, Colin . . . . **TCLC 18**
See also Lawrence, T(homas) E(dward)

Dale, George E.
See Asimov, Isaac

Daly, Elizabeth 1878-1967 . . . . **CLC 52**
See also CA 23-24; 25-28R; CAP 2

Daly, Maureen 1921- . . . . **CLC 17**
See also AAYA 5; CANR 37; JRDA; MAICYA; SAAS 1; SATA 2

Damas, Leon-Gontran 1912-1978 . . . **CLC 84**
See also BW 1; CA 125; 73-76

Dana, Richard Henry Sr.
1787-1879 . . . . **NCLC 53**

Daniel, Samuel 1562(?)-1619 . . . . **LC 24**
See also DLB 62

Daniels, Brett
See Adler, Renata

Dannay, Frederic
1905-1982 . . . . **CLC 11; DAM POP**
See also Queen, Ellery
See also CA 1-4R; 107; CANR 1, 39; DLB 137; MTCW

D'Annunzio, Gabriele
1863-1938 . . . . **TCLC 6, 40**
See also CA 104

Danois, N. le
See Gourmont, Remy (-Marie-Charles) de

d'Antibes, Germain
See Simenon, Georges (Jacques Christian)

Danticat, Edwidge 1969- . . . . **CLC 94**
See also CA 152

Danvers, Dennis 1947- . . . . **CLC 70**

Danziger, Paula 1944- . . . . **CLC 21**
See also AAYA 4; CA 112; 115; CANR 37; CLR 20; JRDA; MAICYA; SATA 36, 63; SATA-Brief 30

Da Ponte, Lorenzo 1749-1838 . . . . **NCLC 50**

Dario, Ruben
1867-1916 . . . . . **TCLC 4; DAM MULT; HLC; PC 15**
See also CA 131; HW; MTCW

Darley, George 1795-1846 . . . . **NCLC 2**
See also DLB 96

Darwin, Charles 1809-1882 . . . . . . **NCLC 57**
See also DLB 57, 166

Daryush, Elizabeth 1887-1977 . . . . **CLC 6, 19**
See also CA 49-52; CANR 3; DLB 20

Dashwood, Edmee Elizabeth Monica de la Pasture 1890-1943
See Delafield, E. M.
See also CA 119

Daudet, (Louis Marie) Alphonse
1840-1897 . . . . **NCLC 1**
See also DLB 123

Daumal, Rene 1908-1944 . . . . **TCLC 14**
See also CA 114

Davenport, Guy (Mattison, Jr.)
1927- . . . . **CLC 6, 14, 38; SSC 16**
See also CA 33-36R; CANR 23; DLB 130

Davidson, Avram 1923-
See Queen, Ellery
See also CA 101; CANR 26; DLB 8

Davidson, Donald (Grady)
1893-1968 . . . . **CLC 2, 13, 19**
See also CA 5-8R; 25-28R; CANR 4; DLB 45

Davidson, Hugh
See Hamilton, Edmond

Davidson, John 1857-1909 . . . . **TCLC 24**
See also CA 118; DLB 19

Davidson, Sara 1943- . . . . **CLC 9**
See also CA 81-84; CANR 44

Davie, Donald (Alfred)
1922-1995 . . . . **CLC 5, 8, 10, 31**
See also CA 1-4R; 149; CAAS 3; CANR 1, 44; DLB 27; MTCW

Davies, Ray(mond Douglas) 1944- . . **CLC 21**
See also CA 116; 146

Davies, Rhys 1903-1978 . . . . **CLC 23**
See also CA 9-12R; 81-84; CANR 4; DLB 139

Davies, (William) Robertson
1913-1995 . . . . . **CLC 2, 7, 13, 25, 42, 75, 91; DA; DAB; DAC; DAM MST, NOV, POP; WLC**
See also BEST 89:2; CA 33-36R; 150; CANR 17, 42; DLB 68; INT CANR-17; MTCW

Davies, W(illiam) H(enry)
1871-1940 . . . . **TCLC 5**
See also CA 104; DLB 19

Davies, Walter C.
See Kornbluth, C(yril) M.

Davis, Angela (Yvonne)
1944- . . . . **CLC 77; DAM MULT**
See also BW 2; CA 57-60; CANR 10

Davis, B. Lynch
See Bioy Casares, Adolfo; Borges, Jorge Luis

Davis, Gordon
See Hunt, E(verette) Howard, (Jr.)

Davis, Harold Lenoir 1896-1960 . . . . **CLC 49**
See also CA 89-92; DLB 9

Davis, Rebecca (Blaine) Harding
1831-1910 . . . . **TCLC 6**
See also CA 104; DLB 74

de Saint Roman, Arnaud
See Aragon, Louis

Descartes, Rene 1596-1650 . . . . . . **LC 20, 35**

De Sica, Vittorio 1901(?)-1974 . . . . . **CLC 20**
See also CA 117

Desnos, Robert 1900-1945 . . . . **TCLC 22**
See also CA 121; 151

Destouches, Louis-Ferdinand
1894-1961 . . . . **CLC 9, 15**
See also Celine, Louis-Ferdinand
See also CA 85-88; CANR 28; MTCW

Deutsch, Babette 1895-1982 . . . . **CLC 18**
See also CA 1-4R; 108; CANR 4; DLB 45; SATA 1; SATA-Obit 33

Devenant, William 1606-1649 . . . . **LC 13**

Devkota, Laxmiprasad
1909-1959 . . . . **TCLC 23**
See also CA 123

De Voto, Bernard (Augustine)
1897-1955 . . . . **TCLC 29**
See also CA 113; DLB 9

De Vries, Peter
1910-1993 . . . . **CLC 1, 2, 3, 7, 10, 28, 46; DAM NOV**
See also CA 17-20R; 142; CANR 41; DLB 6; DLBY 82; MTCW

Dexter, John
See Bradley, Marion Zimmer

Dexter, Martin
See Faust, Frederick (Schiller)

Dexter, Pete
1943- . . . . **CLC 34, 55; DAM POP**
See also BEST 89:2; CA 127; 131; INT 131; MTCW

Diamano, Silmang
See Senghor, Leopold Sedar

Diamond, Neil 1941- . . . . **CLC 30**
See also CA 108

Diaz del Castillo, Bernal 1496-1584 . . **LC 31**

di Bassetto, Corno
See Shaw, George Bernard

Dick, Philip K(indred)
1928-1982 . . . . **CLC 10, 30, 72; DAM NOV, POP**
See also CA 49-52; 106; CANR 2, 16; DLB 8; MTCW

Dickens, Charles (John Huffam)
1812-1870 . . . . . . **NCLC 3, 8, 18, 26, 37, 50; DA; DAB; DAC; DAM MST, NOV; SSC 17; WLC**
See also CDBLB 1832-1890; DLB 21, 55, 70, 159, 166; JRDA; MAICYA; SATA 15

Dickey, James (Lafayette)
1923- . . . . **CLC 1, 2, 4, 7, 10, 15, 47; DAM NOV, POET, POP**
See also AITN 1, 2; CA 9-12R; CABS 2; CANR 10, 48; CDALB 1968-1988; DLB 5; DLBD 7; DLBY 82, 93; INT CANR-10; MTCW

Dickey, William 1928-1994 . . . . . . **CLC 3, 28**
See also CA 9-12R; 145; CANR 24; DLB 5

Dickinson, Charles 1951- . . . . **CLC 49**
See also CA 128

Dickinson, Emily (Elizabeth)
1830-1886 . . . . **NCLC 21; DA; DAB; DAC; DAM MST, POET; PC 1; WLC**
See also CDALB 1865-1917; DLB 1; SATA 29

Dickinson, Peter (Malcolm)
1927- . . . . **CLC 12, 35**
See also AAYA 9; CA 41-44R; CANR 31; CLR 29; DLB 87, 161; JRDA; MAICYA; SATA 5, 62

Dickson, Carr
See Carr, John Dickson

Dickson, Carter
See Carr, John Dickson

Diderot, Denis 1713-1784 . . . . **LC 26**

Didion, Joan
1934- . . **CLC 1, 3, 8, 14, 32; DAM NOV**
See also AITN 1; CA 5-8R; CANR 14, 52; CDALB 1968-1988; DLB 2; DLBY 81, 86; MTCW

Dietrich, Robert
See Hunt, E(verette) Howard, (Jr.)

Dillard, Annie
1945- . . . . **CLC 9, 60; DAM NOV**
See also AAYA 6; CA 49-52; CANR 3, 43; DLBY 80; MTCW; SATA 10

Dillard, R(ichard) H(enry) W(ilde)
1937- . . . . **CLC 5**
See also CA 21-24R; CAAS 7; CANR 10; DLB 5

Dillon, Eilis 1920-1994 . . . . **CLC 17**
See also CA 9-12R; 147; CAAS 3; CANR 4, 38; CLR 26; MAICYA; SATA 2, 74; SATA-Obit 83

Dimont, Penelope
See Mortimer, Penelope (Ruth)

Dinesen, Isak . . . . **CLC 10, 29, 95; SSC 7**
See also Blixen, Karen (Christentze Dinesen)

Ding Ling . . . . **CLC 68**
See also Chiang Pin-chin

Disch, Thomas M(ichael) 1940- . . . **CLC 7, 36**
See also AAYA 17; CA 21-24R; CAAS 4; CANR 17, 36; CLR 18; DLB 8; MAICYA; MTCW; SAAS 15; SATA 54

Disch, Tom
See Disch, Thomas M(ichael)

d'Isly, Georges
See Simenon, Georges (Jacques Christian)

Disraeli, Benjamin 1804-1881 . . **NCLC 2, 39**
See also DLB 21, 55

Ditcum, Steve
See Crumb, R(obert)

Dixon, Paige
See Corcoran, Barbara

Dixon, Stephen 1936- . . . . . **CLC 52; SSC 16**
See also CA 89-92; CANR 17, 40; DLB 130

Dobell, Sydney Thompson
1824-1874 . . . . **NCLC 43**
See also DLB 32

Doblin, Alfred . . . . **TCLC 13**
See also Doeblin, Alfred

Dobrolyubov, Nikolai Alexandrovich
1836-1861 . . . . **NCLC 5**

Dobyns, Stephen 1941- . . . . **CLC 37**
See also CA 45-48; CANR 2, 18

Doctorow, E(dgar) L(aurence)
1931- . . . . . **CLC 6, 11, 15, 18, 37, 44, 65; DAM NOV, POP**
See also AITN 2; BEST 89:3; CA 45-48; CANR 2, 33, 51; CDALB 1968-1988; DLB 2, 28; DLBY 80; MTCW

Dodgson, Charles Lutwidge 1832-1898
See Carroll, Lewis
See also CLR 2; DA; DAB; DAC; DAM MST, NOV, POET; MAICYA; YABC 2

Dodson, Owen (Vincent)
1914-1983 . . . . **CLC 79; BLC; DAM MULT**
See also BW 1; CA 65-68; 110; CANR 24; DLB 76

Doeblin, Alfred 1878-1957 . . . . **TCLC 13**
See also Doblin, Alfred
See also CA 110; 141; DLB 66

Doerr, Harriet 1910- . . . . **CLC 34**
See also CA 117; 122; CANR 47; INT 122

Domecq, H(onorio) Bustos
See Bioy Casares, Adolfo; Borges, Jorge Luis

Domini, Rey
See Lorde, Audre (Geraldine)

Dominique
See Proust, (Valentin-Louis-George-Eugene-) Marcel

Don, A
See Stephen, Leslie

Donaldson, Stephen R.
1947- . . . . **CLC 46; DAM POP**
See also CA 89-92; CANR 13; INT CANR-13

Donleavy, J(ames) P(atrick)
1926- . . . . **CLC 1, 4, 6, 10, 45**
See also AITN 2; CA 9-12R; CANR 24, 49; DLB 6; INT CANR-24; MTCW

Donne, John
1572-1631 . . . . **LC 10, 24; DA; DAB; DAC; DAM MST, POET; PC 1**
See also CDBLB Before 1660; DLB 121, 151

Donnell, David 1939(?)- . . . . **CLC 34**

Donoghue, P. S.
See Hunt, E(verette) Howard, (Jr.)

Donoso (Yanez), Jose
1924- . . . . **CLC 4, 8, 11, 32; DAM MULT; HLC**
See also CA 81-84; CANR 32; DLB 113; HW; MTCW

Donovan, John 1928-1992 . . . . **CLC 35**
See also CA 97-100; 137; CLR 3; MAICYA; SATA 72; SATA-Brief 29

Don Roberto
See Cunninghame Graham, R(obert) B(ontine)

Doolittle, Hilda
1886-1961 ..... **CLC 3, 8, 14, 31, 34, 73; DA; DAC; DAM MST, POET; PC 5; WLC**
See also H. D.
See also CA 97-100; CANR 35; DLB 4, 45; MTCW

Dorfman, Ariel
1942- .... **CLC 48, 77; DAM MULT; HLC**
See also CA 124; 130; HW; INT 130

Dorn, Edward (Merton) 1929-... **CLC 10, 18**
See also CA 93-96; CANR 42; DLB 5; INT 93-96

Dorsan, Luc
See Simenon, Georges (Jacques Christian)

Dorsange, Jean
See Simenon, Georges (Jacques Christian)

Dos Passos, John (Roderigo)
1896-1970 ...... **CLC 1, 4, 8, 11, 15, 25, 34, 82; DA; DAB; DAC; DAM MST, NOV; WLC**
See also CA 1-4R; 29-32R; CANR 3; CDALB 1929-1941; DLB 4, 9; DLBD 1; MTCW

Dossage, Jean
See Simenon, Georges (Jacques Christian)

Dostoevsky, Fedor Mikhailovich
1821-1881 ...... **NCLC 2, 7, 21, 33, 43; DA; DAB; DAC; DAM MST, NOV; SSC 2; WLC**

Doughty, Charles M(ontagu)
1843-1926 .... **TCLC 27**
See also CA 115; DLB 19, 57

Douglas, Ellen .... **CLC 73**
See also Haxton, Josephine Ayres; Williamson, Ellen Douglas

Douglas, Gavin 1475(?)-1522........ **LC 20**

Douglas, Keith 1920-1944 .... **TCLC 40**
See also DLB 27

Douglas, Leonard
See Bradbury, Ray (Douglas)

Douglas, Michael
See Crichton, (John) Michael

Douglass, Frederick
1817(?)-1895 .... **NCLC 7, 55; BLC; DA; DAC; DAM MST, MULT; WLC**
See also CDALB 1640-1865; DLB 1, 43, 50, 79; SATA 29

Dourado, (Waldomiro Freitas) Autran
1926- .... **CLC 23, 60**
See also CA 25-28R; CANR 34

Dourado, Waldomiro Autran
See Dourado, (Waldomiro Freitas) Autran

Dove, Rita (Frances)
1952- .... **CLC 50, 81; DAM MULT, POET; PC 6**
See also BW 2; CA 109; CAAS 19; CANR 27, 42; DLB 120

Dowell, Coleman 1925-1985........ **CLC 60**
See also CA 25-28R; 117; CANR 10; DLB 130

Dowson, Ernest (Christopher)
1867-1900 .... **TCLC 4**
See also CA 105; 150; DLB 19, 135

Doyle, A. Conan
See Doyle, Arthur Conan

Doyle, Arthur Conan
1859-1930 .... **TCLC 7; DA; DAB; DAC; DAM MST, NOV; SSC 12; WLC**
See also AAYA 14; CA 104; 122; CDBLB 1890-1914; DLB 18, 70, 156; MTCW; SATA 24

Doyle, Conan
See Doyle, Arthur Conan

Doyle, John
See Graves, Robert (von Ranke)

Doyle, Roddy 1958(?)- .... **CLC 81**
See also AAYA 14; CA 143

Doyle, Sir A. Conan
See Doyle, Arthur Conan

Doyle, Sir Arthur Conan
See Doyle, Arthur Conan

Dr. A
See Asimov, Isaac; Silverstein, Alvin

Drabble, Margaret
1939- .... **CLC 2, 3, 5, 8, 10, 22, 53; DAB; DAC; DAM MST, NOV, POP**
See also CA 13-16R; CANR 18, 35; CDBLB 1960 to Present; DLB 14, 155; MTCW; SATA 48

Drapier, M. B.
See Swift, Jonathan

Drayham, James
See Mencken, H(enry) L(ouis)

Drayton, Michael 1563-1631......... **LC 8**

Dreadstone, Carl
See Campbell, (John) Ramsey

Dreiser, Theodore (Herman Albert)
1871-1945 .... **TCLC 10, 18, 35; DA; DAC; DAM MST, NOV; WLC**
See also CA 106; 132; CDALB 1865-1917; DLB 9, 12, 102, 137; DLBD 1; MTCW

Drexler, Rosalyn 1926- .... **CLC 2, 6**
See also CA 81-84

Dreyer, Carl Theodor 1889-1968.... **CLC 16**
See also CA 116

Drieu la Rochelle, Pierre(-Eugene)
1893-1945 .... **TCLC 21**
See also CA 117; DLB 72

Drinkwater, John 1882-1937...... **TCLC 57**
See also CA 109; 149; DLB 10, 19, 149

Drop Shot
See Cable, George Washington

Droste-Hulshoff, Annette Freiin von
1797-1848 .... **NCLC 3**
See also DLB 133

Drummond, Walter
See Silverberg, Robert

Drummond, William Henry
1854-1907 .... **TCLC 25**
See also DLB 92

Drummond de Andrade, Carlos
1902-1987 .... **CLC 18**
See also Andrade, Carlos Drummond de
See also CA 132; 123

Drury, Allen (Stuart) 1918-........ **CLC 37**
See also CA 57-60; CANR 18, 52; INT CANR-18

Dryden, John
1631-1700 .... **LC 3, 21; DA; DAB; DAC; DAM DRAM, MST, POET; DC 3; WLC**
See also CDBLB 1660-1789; DLB 80, 101, 131

Duberman, Martin 1930- .... **CLC 8**
See also CA 1-4R; CANR 2

Dubie, Norman (Evans) 1945-...... **CLC 36**
See also CA 69-72; CANR 12; DLB 120

Du Bois, W(illiam) E(dward) B(urghardt)
1868-1963 .... **CLC 1, 2, 13, 64, 96; BLC; DA; DAC; DAM MST, MULT, NOV; WLC**
See also BW 1; CA 85-88; CANR 34; CDALB 1865-1917; DLB 47, 50, 91; MTCW; SATA 42

Dubus, Andre 1936-... **CLC 13, 36; SSC 15**
See also CA 21-24R; CANR 17; DLB 130; INT CANR-17

Duca Minimo
See D'Annunzio, Gabriele

Ducharme, Rejean 1941- .... **CLC 74**
See also DLB 60

Duclos, Charles Pinot 1704-1772 ..... **LC 1**

Dudek, Louis 1918- .... **CLC 11, 19**
See also CA 45-48; CAAS 14; CANR 1; DLB 88

Duerrenmatt, Friedrich
1921-1990 ...... **CLC 1, 4, 8, 11, 15, 43; DAM DRAM**
See also CA 17-20R; CANR 33; DLB 69, 124; MTCW

Duffy, Bruce (?)-................ **CLC 50**

Duffy, Maureen 1933- .... **CLC 37**
See also CA 25-28R; CANR 33; DLB 14; MTCW

Dugan, Alan 1923- .... **CLC 2, 6**
See also CA 81-84; DLB 5

du Gard, Roger Martin
See Martin du Gard, Roger

Duhamel, Georges 1884-1966 .... **CLC 8**
See also CA 81-84; 25-28R; CANR 35; DLB 65; MTCW

Dujardin, Edouard (Emile Louis)
1861-1949 .... **TCLC 13**
See also CA 109; DLB 123

Dumas, Alexandre (Davy de la Pailleterie)
1802-1870 .... **NCLC 11; DA; DAB; DAC; DAM MST, NOV; WLC**
See also DLB 119; SATA 18

Dumas, Alexandre
1824-1895 .... **NCLC 9; DC 1**

Dumas, Claudine
See Malzberg, Barry N(athaniel)

Dumas, Henry L. 1934-1968 ..... **CLC 6, 62**
See also BW 1; CA 85-88; DLB 41

du Maurier, Daphne
1907-1989 .... **CLC 6, 11, 59; DAB; DAC; DAM MST, POP; SSC 18**
See also CA 5-8R; 128; CANR 6; MTCW; SATA 27; SATA-Obit 60

Dunbar, Paul Laurence
1872-1906 . . . . . . **TCLC 2, 12; BLC; DA; DAC; DAM MST, MULT, POET; PC 5; SSC 8; WLC**
See also BW 1; CA 104; 124; CDALB 1865-1917; DLB 50, 54, 78; SATA 34

Dunbar, William 1460(?)-1530(?) . . . . **LC 20**
See also DLB 132, 146

Duncan, Lois 1934- . . . . **CLC 26**
See also AAYA 4; CA 1-4R; CANR 2, 23, 36; CLR 29; JRDA; MAICYA; SAAS 2; SATA 1, 36, 75

Duncan, Robert (Edward)
1919-1988 . . . . **CLC 1, 2, 4, 7, 15, 41, 55; DAM POET; PC 2**
See also CA 9-12R; 124; CANR 28; DLB 5, 16; MTCW

Duncan, Sara Jeannette
1861-1922 . . . . **TCLC 60**
See also DLB 92

Dunlap, William 1766-1839 . . . . **NCLC 2**
See also DLB 30, 37, 59

Dunn, Douglas (Eaglesham)
1942- . . . . **CLC 6, 40**
See also CA 45-48; CANR 2, 33; DLB 40; MTCW

Dunn, Katherine (Karen) 1945- . . . . . **CLC 71**
See also CA 33-36R

Dunn, Stephen 1939- . . . . **CLC 36**
See also CA 33-36R; CANR 12, 48, 53; DLB 105

Dunne, Finley Peter 1867-1936 . . . . **TCLC 28**
See also CA 108; DLB 11, 23

Dunne, John Gregory 1932- . . . . **CLC 28**
See also CA 25-28R; CANR 14, 50; DLBY 80

Dunsany, Edward John Moreton Drax Plunkett 1878-1957
See Dunsany, Lord
See also CA 104; 148; DLB 10

Dunsany, Lord . . . . **TCLC 2, 59**
See also Dunsany, Edward John Moreton Drax Plunkett
See also DLB 77, 153, 156

du Perry, Jean
See Simenon, Georges (Jacques Christian)

Durang, Christopher (Ferdinand)
1949- . . . . **CLC 27, 38**
See also CA 105; CANR 50

Duras, Marguerite
1914-1996 . . **CLC 3, 6, 11, 20, 34, 40, 68**
See also CA 25-28R; 151; CANR 50; DLB 83; MTCW

Durban, (Rosa) Pam 1947- . . . . **CLC 39**
See also CA 123

Durcan, Paul
1944- . . . . **CLC 43, 70; DAM POET**
See also CA 134

Durkheim, Emile 1858-1917 . . . . . . **TCLC 55**

Durrell, Lawrence (George)
1912-1990 . . . . **CLC 1, 4, 6, 8, 13, 27, 41; DAM NOV**
See also CA 9-12R; 132; CANR 40; CDBLB 1945-1960; DLB 15, 27; DLBY 90; MTCW

Durrenmatt, Friedrich
See Duerrenmatt, Friedrich

Dutt, Toru 1856-1877 . . . . **NCLC 29**

Dwight, Timothy 1752-1817 . . . . . . **NCLC 13**
See also DLB 37

Dworkin, Andrea 1946- . . . . **CLC 43**
See also CA 77-80; CAAS 21; CANR 16, 39; INT CANR-16; MTCW

Dwyer, Deanna
See Koontz, Dean R(ay)

Dwyer, K. R.
See Koontz, Dean R(ay)

Dylan, Bob 1941- . . . . . . **CLC 3, 4, 6, 12, 77**
See also CA 41-44R; DLB 16

Eagleton, Terence (Francis) 1943-
See Eagleton, Terry
See also CA 57-60; CANR 7, 23; MTCW

Eagleton, Terry . . . . **CLC 63**
See also Eagleton, Terence (Francis)

Early, Jack
See Scoppettone, Sandra

East, Michael
See West, Morris L(anglo)

Eastaway, Edward
See Thomas, (Philip) Edward

Eastlake, William (Derry) 1917- . . . . . **CLC 8**
See also CA 5-8R; CAAS 1; CANR 5; DLB 6; INT CANR-5

Eastman, Charles A(lexander)
1858-1939 . . . . . **TCLC 55; DAM MULT**
See also NNAL; YABC 1

Eberhart, Richard (Ghormley)
1904- . . **CLC 3, 11, 19, 56; DAM POET**
See also CA 1-4R; CANR 2; CDALB 1941-1968; DLB 48; MTCW

Eberstadt, Fernanda 1960- . . . . **CLC 39**
See also CA 136

Echegaray (y Eizaguirre), Jose (Maria Waldo)
1832-1916 . . . . **TCLC 4**
See also CA 104; CANR 32; HW; MTCW

Echeverria, (Jose) Esteban (Antonino)
1805-1851 . . . . **NCLC 18**

Echo
See Proust, (Valentin-Louis-George-Eugene-) Marcel

Eckert, Allan W. 1931- . . . . **CLC 17**
See also AAYA 18; CA 13-16R; CANR 14, 45; INT CANR-14; SAAS 21; SATA 29; SATA-Brief 27

Eckhart, Meister 1260(?)-1328(?) . . **CMLC 9**
See also DLB 115

Eckmar, F. R.
See de Hartog, Jan

Eco, Umberto
1932- . . . **CLC 28, 60; DAM NOV, POP**
See also BEST 90:1; CA 77-80; CANR 12, 33; MTCW

Eddison, E(ric) R(ucker)
1882-1945 . . . . **TCLC 15**
See also CA 109

Edel, (Joseph) Leon 1907- . . . . . . **CLC 29, 34**
See also CA 1-4R; CANR 1, 22; DLB 103; INT CANR-22

Eden, Emily 1797-1869 . . . . **NCLC 10**

Edgar, David
1948- . . . . **CLC 42; DAM DRAM**
See also CA 57-60; CANR 12; DLB 13; MTCW

Edgerton, Clyde (Carlyle) 1944- . . . . **CLC 39**
See also AAYA 17; CA 118; 134; INT 134

Edgeworth, Maria 1768-1849 . . . **NCLC 1, 51**
See also DLB 116, 159, 163; SATA 21

Edmonds, Paul
See Kuttner, Henry

Edmonds, Walter D(umaux) 1903- . . **CLC 35**
See also CA 5-8R; CANR 2; DLB 9; MAICYA; SAAS 4; SATA 1, 27

Edmondson, Wallace
See Ellison, Harlan (Jay)

Edson, Russell . . . . **CLC 13**
See also CA 33-36R

Edwards, Bronwen Elizabeth
See Rose, Wendy

Edwards, G(erald) B(asil)
1899-1976 . . . . **CLC 25**
See also CA 110

Edwards, Gus 1939- . . . . **CLC 43**
See also CA 108; INT 108

Edwards, Jonathan
1703-1758 . . . . **LC 7; DA; DAC; DAM MST**
See also DLB 24

Efron, Marina Ivanovna Tsvetaeva
See Tsvetaeva (Efron), Marina (Ivanovna)

Ehle, John (Marsden, Jr.) 1925- . . . . **CLC 27**
See also CA 9-12R

Ehrenbourg, Ilya (Grigoryevich)
See Ehrenburg, Ilya (Grigoryevich)

Ehrenburg, Ilya (Grigoryevich)
1891-1967 . . . . **CLC 18, 34, 62**
See also CA 102; 25-28R

Ehrenburg, Ilyo (Grigoryevich)
See Ehrenburg, Ilya (Grigoryevich)

Eich, Guenter 1907-1972 . . . . **CLC 15**
See also CA 111; 93-96; DLB 69, 124

Eichendorff, Joseph Freiherr von
1788-1857 . . . . **NCLC 8**
See also DLB 90

Eigner, Larry . . . . **CLC 9**
See also Eigner, Laurence (Joel)
See also CAAS 23; DLB 5

Eigner, Laurence (Joel) 1927-1996
See Eigner, Larry
See also CA 9-12R; 151; CANR 6

Einstein, Albert 1879-1955 . . . . **TCLC 65**
See also CA 121; 133; MTCW

Eiseley, Loren Corey 1907-1977 . . . . . **CLC 7**
See also AAYA 5; CA 1-4R; 73-76; CANR 6

Eisenstadt, Jill 1963- . . . . **CLC 50**
See also CA 140

Eisenstein, Sergei (Mikhailovich)
1898-1948 . . . . **TCLC 57**
See also CA 114; 149

Eisner, Simon
See Kornbluth, C(yril) M.

Ekeloef, (Bengt) Gunnar 1907-1968 .... **CLC 27; DAM POET**
See also CA 123; 25-28R

Ekelof, (Bengt) Gunnar
See Ekeloef, (Bengt) Gunnar

Ekwensi, C. O. D.
See Ekwensi, Cyprian (Odiatu Duaka)

Ekwensi, Cyprian (Odiatu Duaka) 1921- ...... **CLC 4; BLC; DAM MULT**
See also BW 2; CA 29-32R; CANR 18, 42; DLB 117; MTCW; SATA 66

Elaine .... **TCLC 18**
See also Leverson, Ada

El Crummo
See Crumb, R(obert)

Elia
See Lamb, Charles

Eliade, Mircea 1907-1986 .... **CLC 19**
See also CA 65-68; 119; CANR 30; MTCW

Eliot, A. D.
See Jewett, (Theodora) Sarah Orne

Eliot, Alice
See Jewett, (Theodora) Sarah Orne

Eliot, Dan
See Silverberg, Robert

Eliot, George 1819-1880 ..... **NCLC 4, 13, 23, 41, 49; DA; DAB; DAC; DAM MST, NOV; WLC**
See also CDBLB 1832-1890; DLB 21, 35, 55

Eliot, John 1604-1690 .... **LC 5**
See also DLB 24

Eliot, T(homas) S(tearns) 1888-1965 ..... **CLC 1, 2, 3, 6, 9, 10, 13, 15, 24, 34, 41, 55, 57; DA; DAB; DAC; DAM DRAM, MST, POET; PC 5; WLC 2**
See also CA 5-8R; 25-28R; CANR 41; CDALB 1929-1941; DLB 7, 10, 45, 63; DLBY 88; MTCW

Elizabeth 1866-1941 .... **TCLC 41**

Elkin, Stanley L(awrence) 1930-1995 ...... **CLC 4, 6, 9, 14, 27, 51, 91; DAM NOV, POP; SSC 12**
See also CA 9-12R; 148; CANR 8, 46; DLB 2, 28; DLBY 80; INT CANR-8; MTCW

Elledge, Scott .... **CLC 34**

Elliott, Don
See Silverberg, Robert

Elliott, George P(aul) 1918-1980 ..... **CLC 2**
See also CA 1-4R; 97-100; CANR 2

Elliott, Janice 1931- .... **CLC 47**
See also CA 13-16R; CANR 8, 29; DLB 14

Elliott, Sumner Locke 1917-1991 ... **CLC 38**
See also CA 5-8R; 134; CANR 2, 21

Elliott, William
See Bradbury, Ray (Douglas)

Ellis, A. E. .... **CLC 7**

Ellis, Alice Thomas .... **CLC 40**
See also Haycraft, Anna

Ellis, Bret Easton 1964- .... **CLC 39, 71; DAM POP**
See also AAYA 2; CA 118; 123; CANR 51; INT 123

Ellis, (Henry) Havelock 1859-1939 .... **TCLC 14**
See also CA 109

Ellis, Landon
See Ellison, Harlan (Jay)

Ellis, Trey 1962- .... **CLC 55**
See also CA 146

Ellison, Harlan (Jay) 1934- ...... **CLC 1, 13, 42; DAM POP; SSC 14**
See also CA 5-8R; CANR 5, 46; DLB 8; INT CANR-5; MTCW

Ellison, Ralph (Waldo) 1914-1994 .... **CLC 1, 3, 11, 54, 86; BLC; DA; DAB; DAC; DAM MST, MULT, NOV; WLC**
See also BW 1; CA 9-12R; 145; CANR 24, 53; CDALB 1941-1968; DLB 2, 76; DLBY 94; MTCW

Ellmann, Lucy (Elizabeth) 1956- .... **CLC 61**
See also CA 128

Ellmann, Richard (David) 1918-1987 .... **CLC 50**
See also BEST 89:2; CA 1-4R; 122; CANR 2, 28; DLB 103; DLBY 87; MTCW

Elman, Richard 1934- .... **CLC 19**
See also CA 17-20R; CAAS 3; CANR 47

Elron
See Hubbard, L(afayette) Ron(ald)

Eluard, Paul .... **TCLC 7, 41**
See also Grindel, Eugene

Elyot, Sir Thomas 1490(?)-1546 ..... **LC 11**

Elytis, Odysseus 1911-1996 .... **CLC 15, 49; DAM POET**
See also CA 102; 151; MTCW

Emecheta, (Florence Onye) Buchi 1944- .. **CLC 14, 48; BLC; DAM MULT**
See also BW 2; CA 81-84; CANR 27; DLB 117; MTCW; SATA 66

Emerson, Ralph Waldo 1803-1882 ..... **NCLC 1, 38; DA; DAB; DAC; DAM MST, POET; WLC**
See also CDALB 1640-1865; DLB 1, 59, 73

Eminescu, Mihail 1850-1889 ..... **NCLC 33**

Empson, William 1906-1984 .... **CLC 3, 8, 19, 33, 34**
See also CA 17-20R; 112; CANR 31; DLB 20; MTCW

Enchi Fumiko (Ueda) 1905-1986.... **CLC 31**
See also CA 129; 121

Ende, Michael (Andreas Helmuth) 1929-1995 .... **CLC 31**
See also CA 118; 124; 149; CANR 36; CLR 14; DLB 75; MAICYA; SATA 61; SATA-Brief 42; SATA-Obit 86

Endo, Shusaku 1923- ... **CLC 7, 14, 19, 54; DAM NOV**
See also CA 29-32R; CANR 21; MTCW

Engel, Marian 1933-1985 .... **CLC 36**
See also CA 25-28R; CANR 12; DLB 53; INT CANR-12

Engelhardt, Frederick
See Hubbard, L(afayette) Ron(ald)

Enright, D(ennis) J(oseph) 1920- .... **CLC 4, 8, 31**
See also CA 1-4R; CANR 1, 42; DLB 27; SATA 25

Enzensberger, Hans Magnus 1929- .... **CLC 43**
See also CA 116; 119

Ephron, Nora 1941- .... **CLC 17, 31**
See also AITN 2; CA 65-68; CANR 12, 39

Epsilon
See Betjeman, John

Epstein, Daniel Mark 1948- .... **CLC 7**
See also CA 49-52; CANR 2, 53

Epstein, Jacob 1956- .... **CLC 19**
See also CA 114

Epstein, Joseph 1937- .... **CLC 39**
See also CA 112; 119; CANR 50

Epstein, Leslie 1938- .... **CLC 27**
See also CA 73-76; CAAS 12; CANR 23

Equiano, Olaudah 1745(?)-1797 .... **LC 16; BLC; DAM MULT**
See also DLB 37, 50

Erasmus, Desiderius 1469(?)-1536.... **LC 16**

Erdman, Paul E(mil) 1932- .... **CLC 25**
See also AITN 1; CA 61-64; CANR 13, 43

Erdrich, Louise 1954- .... **CLC 39, 54; DAM MULT, NOV, POP**
See also AAYA 10; BEST 89:1; CA 114; CANR 41; DLB 152; MTCW; NNAL

Erenburg, Ilya (Grigoryevich)
See Ehrenburg, Ilya (Grigoryevich)

Erickson, Stephen Michael 1950-
See Erickson, Steve
See also CA 129

Erickson, Steve .... **CLC 64**
See also Erickson, Stephen Michael

Ericson, Walter
See Fast, Howard (Melvin)

Eriksson, Buntel
See Bergman, (Ernst) Ingmar

Ernaux, Annie 1940- .... **CLC 88**
See also CA 147

Eschenbach, Wolfram von
See Wolfram von Eschenbach

Eseki, Bruno
See Mphahlele, Ezekiel

Esenin, Sergei (Alexandrovich) 1895-1925 .... **TCLC 4**
See also CA 104

Eshleman, Clayton 1935- .... **CLC 7**
See also CA 33-36R; CAAS 6; DLB 5

Espriella, Don Manuel Alvarez
See Southey, Robert

Espriu, Salvador 1913-1985 .... **CLC 9**
See also CA 115; DLB 134

Espronceda, Jose de 1808-1842... **NCLC 39**

Esse, James
See Stephens, James

Esterbrook, Tom
See Hubbard, L(afayette) Ron(ald)

Estleman, Loren D. 1952- . . . . . . **CLC 48; DAM NOV, POP**
See also CA 85-88; CANR 27; INT CANR-27; MTCW

Eugenides, Jeffrey 1960(?)- . . . . **CLC 81**
See also CA 144

Euripides c. 485B.C.-406B.C. . . . . **DC 4**
See also DA; DAB; DAC; DAM DRAM, MST

Evan, Evin
See Faust, Frederick (Schiller)

Evans, Evan
See Faust, Frederick (Schiller)

Evans, Marian
See Eliot, George

Evans, Mary Ann
See Eliot, George

Evarts, Esther
See Benson, Sally

Everett, Percival L. 1956- . . . . **CLC 57**
See also BW 2; CA 129

Everson, R(onald) G(ilmour) 1903- . . . . **CLC 27**
See also CA 17-20R; DLB 88

Everson, William (Oliver) 1912-1994 . . . . **CLC 1, 5, 14**
See also CA 9-12R; 145; CANR 20; DLB 5, 16; MTCW

Evtushenko, Evgenii Aleksandrovich
See Yevtushenko, Yevgeny (Alexandrovich)

Ewart, Gavin (Buchanan) 1916-1995 . . . . **CLC 13, 46**
See also CA 89-92; 150; CANR 17, 46; DLB 40; MTCW

Ewers, Hanns Heinz 1871-1943 . . . **TCLC 12**
See also CA 109; 149

Ewing, Frederick R.
See Sturgeon, Theodore (Hamilton)

Exley, Frederick (Earl) 1929-1992 . . . . **CLC 6, 11**
See also AITN 2; CA 81-84; 138; DLB 143; DLBY 81

Eynhardt, Guillermo
See Quiroga, Horacio (Sylvestre)

Ezekiel, Nissim 1924- . . . . **CLC 61**
See also CA 61-64

Ezekiel, Tish O'Dowd 1943- . . . . **CLC 34**
See also CA 129

Fadeyev, A.
See Bulgya, Alexander Alexandrovich

Fadeyev, Alexander . . . . **TCLC 53**
See also Bulgya, Alexander Alexandrovich

Fagen, Donald 1948- . . . . **CLC 26**

Fainzilberg, Ilya Arnoldovich 1897-1937
See Ilf, Ilya
See also CA 120

Fair, Ronald L. 1932- . . . . **CLC 18**
See also BW 1; CA 69-72; CANR 25; DLB 33

Fairbairns, Zoe (Ann) 1948- . . . . **CLC 32**
See also CA 103; CANR 21

Falco, Gian
See Papini, Giovanni

Falconer, James
See Kirkup, James

Falconer, Kenneth
See Kornbluth, C(yril) M.

Falkland, Samuel
See Heijermans, Herman

Fallaci, Oriana 1930- . . . . **CLC 11**
See also CA 77-80; CANR 15; MTCW

Faludy, George 1913- . . . . **CLC 42**
See also CA 21-24R

Faludy, Gyoergy
See Faludy, George

Fanon, Frantz 1925-1961 . . . . **CLC 74; BLC; DAM MULT**
See also BW 1; CA 116; 89-92

Fanshawe, Ann 1625-1680 . . . . **LC 11**

Fante, John (Thomas) 1911-1983 . . . **CLC 60**
See also CA 69-72; 109; CANR 23; DLB 130; DLBY 83

Farah, Nuruddin 1945- . . . . . **CLC 53; BLC; DAM MULT**
See also BW 2; CA 106; DLB 125

Fargue, Leon-Paul 1876(?)-1947 . . . **TCLC 11**
See also CA 109

Farigoule, Louis
See Romains, Jules

Farina, Richard 1936(?)-1966 . . . . **CLC 9**
See also CA 81-84; 25-28R

Farley, Walter (Lorimer) 1915-1989 . . . . **CLC 17**
See also CA 17-20R; CANR 8, 29; DLB 22; JRDA; MAICYA; SATA 2, 43

Farmer, Philip Jose 1918- . . . . **CLC 1, 19**
See also CA 1-4R; CANR 4, 35; DLB 8; MTCW

Farquhar, George 1677-1707 . . . . **LC 21; DAM DRAM**
See also DLB 84

Farrell, J(ames) G(ordon) 1935-1979 . . . . **CLC 6**
See also CA 73-76; 89-92; CANR 36; DLB 14; MTCW

Farrell, James T(homas) 1904-1979 . . . . **CLC 1, 4, 8, 11, 66**
See also CA 5-8R; 89-92; CANR 9; DLB 4, 9, 86; DLBD 2; MTCW

Farren, Richard J.
See Betjeman, John

Farren, Richard M.
See Betjeman, John

Fassbinder, Rainer Werner 1946-1982 . . . . **CLC 20**
See also CA 93-96; 106; CANR 31

Fast, Howard (Melvin) 1914- . . . . **CLC 23; DAM NOV**
See also AAYA 16; CA 1-4R; CAAS 18; CANR 1, 33; DLB 9; INT CANR-33; SATA 7

Faulcon, Robert
See Holdstock, Robert P.

Faulkner, William (Cuthbert) 1897-1962 . . . . . **CLC 1, 3, 6, 8, 9, 11, 14, 18, 28, 52, 68; DA; DAB; DAC; DAM MST, NOV; SSC 1; WLC**
See also AAYA 7; CA 81-84; CANR 33; CDALB 1929-1941; DLB 9, 11, 44, 102; DLBD 2; DLBY 86; MTCW

Fauset, Jessie Redmon 1884(?)-1961 . . . . **CLC 19, 54; BLC; DAM MULT**
See also BW 1; CA 109; DLB 51

Faust, Frederick (Schiller) 1892-1944(?) . . . . . **TCLC 49; DAM POP**
See also CA 108; 152

Faust, Irvin 1924- . . . . **CLC 8**
See also CA 33-36R; CANR 28; DLB 2, 28; DLBY 80

Fawkes, Guy
See Benchley, Robert (Charles)

Fearing, Kenneth (Flexner) 1902-1961 . . . . **CLC 51**
See also CA 93-96; DLB 9

Fecamps, Elise
See Creasey, John

Federman, Raymond 1928- . . . . . . **CLC 6, 47**
See also CA 17-20R; CAAS 8; CANR 10, 43; DLBY 80

Federspiel, J(uerg) F. 1931- . . . . **CLC 42**
See also CA 146

Feiffer, Jules (Ralph) 1929- . . . . . . **CLC 2, 8, 64; DAM DRAM**
See also AAYA 3; CA 17-20R; CANR 30; DLB 7, 44; INT CANR-30; MTCW; SATA 8, 61

Feige, Hermann Albert Otto Maximilian
See Traven, B.

Feinberg, David B. 1956-1994 . . . . . . **CLC 59**
See also CA 135; 147

Feinstein, Elaine 1930- . . . . **CLC 36**
See also CA 69-72; CAAS 1; CANR 31; DLB 14, 40; MTCW

Feldman, Irving (Mordecai) 1928- . . . . **CLC 7**
See also CA 1-4R; CANR 1

Fellini, Federico 1920-1993 . . . . . **CLC 16, 85**
See also CA 65-68; 143; CANR 33

Felsen, Henry Gregor 1916- . . . . **CLC 17**
See also CA 1-4R; CANR 1; SAAS 2; SATA 1

Fenton, James Martin 1949- . . . . **CLC 32**
See also CA 102; DLB 40

Ferber, Edna 1887-1968 . . . . **CLC 18, 93**
See also AITN 1; CA 5-8R; 25-28R; DLB 9, 28, 86; MTCW; SATA 7

Ferguson, Helen
See Kavan, Anna

Ferguson, Samuel 1810-1886 . . . . . **NCLC 33**
See also DLB 32

Fergusson, Robert 1750-1774 . . . . **LC 29**
See also DLB 109

Ferling, Lawrence
See Ferlinghetti, Lawrence (Monsanto)

Ferlinghetti, Lawrence (Monsanto) 1919(?)- . . . . **CLC 2, 6, 10, 27; DAM POET; PC 1**
See also CA 5-8R; CANR 3, 41; CDALB 1941-1968; DLB 5, 16; MTCW

Fernandez, Vicente Garcia Huidobro
See Huidobro Fernandez, Vicente Garcia

Ferrer, Gabriel (Francisco Victor) Miro
See Miro (Ferrer), Gabriel (Francisco Victor)

Ferrier, Susan (Edmonstone) 1782-1854 . . . . **NCLC 8**
See also DLB 116

Ferrigno, Robert 1948(?)- . . . . **CLC 65**
See also CA 140

Ferron, Jacques 1921-1985 . . . **CLC 94; DAC**
See also CA 117; 129; DLB 60

Feuchtwanger, Lion 1884-1958 . . . . . **TCLC 3**
See also CA 104; DLB 66

Feuillet, Octave 1821-1890 . . . . . . **NCLC 45**

Feydeau, Georges (Leon Jules Marie) 1862-1921 . . . . . **TCLC 22; DAM DRAM**
See also CA 113; 152

Ficino, Marsilio 1433-1499 . . . . **LC 12**

Fiedeler, Hans
See Doeblin, Alfred

Fiedler, Leslie A(aron) 1917- . . . . **CLC 4, 13, 24**
See also CA 9-12R; CANR 7; DLB 28, 67; MTCW

Field, Andrew 1938- . . . . **CLC 44**
See also CA 97-100; CANR 25

Field, Eugene 1850-1895 . . . . **NCLC 3**
See also DLB 23, 42, 140; DLBD 13; MAICYA; SATA 16

Field, Gans T.
See Wellman, Manly Wade

Field, Michael . . . . **TCLC 43**

Field, Peter
See Hobson, Laura Z(ametkin)

Fielding, Henry 1707-1754 . . . . . . **LC 1; DA; DAB; DAC; DAM DRAM, MST, NOV; WLC**
See also CDBLB 1660-1789; DLB 39, 84, 101

Fielding, Sarah 1710-1768 . . . . **LC 1**
See also DLB 39

Fierstein, Harvey (Forbes) 1954- . . . . . **CLC 33; DAM DRAM, POP**
See also CA 123; 129

Figes, Eva 1932- . . . . **CLC 31**
See also CA 53-56; CANR 4, 44; DLB 14

Finch, Robert (Duer Claydon) 1900- . . . . **CLC 18**
See also CA 57-60; CANR 9, 24, 49; DLB 88

Findley, Timothy 1930- . . . . . . **CLC 27; DAC; DAM MST**
See also CA 25-28R; CANR 12, 42; DLB 53

Fink, William
See Mencken, H(enry) L(ouis)

Firbank, Louis 1942-
See Reed, Lou
See also CA 117

Firbank, (Arthur Annesley) Ronald 1886-1926 . . . . **TCLC 1**
See also CA 104; DLB 36

Fisher, M(ary) F(rances) K(ennedy) 1908-1992 . . . . **CLC 76, 87**
See also CA 77-80; 138; CANR 44

Fisher, Roy 1930- . . . . **CLC 25**
See also CA 81-84; CAAS 10; CANR 16; DLB 40

Fisher, Rudolph 1897-1934 . . . . **TCLC 11; BLC; DAM MULT**
See also BW 1; CA 107; 124; DLB 51, 102

Fisher, Vardis (Alvero) 1895-1968. . . . **CLC 7**
See also CA 5-8R; 25-28R; DLB 9

Fiske, Tarleton
See Bloch, Robert (Albert)

Fitch, Clarke
See Sinclair, Upton (Beall)

Fitch, John IV
See Cormier, Robert (Edmund)

Fitzgerald, Captain Hugh
See Baum, L(yman) Frank

FitzGerald, Edward 1809-1883 . . . . **NCLC 9**
See also DLB 32

Fitzgerald, F(rancis) Scott (Key) 1896-1940 . . . . **TCLC 1, 6, 14, 28, 55; DA; DAB; DAC; DAM MST, NOV; SSC 6; WLC**
See also AITN 1; CA 110; 123; CDALB 1917-1929; DLB 4, 9, 86; DLBD 1; DLBY 81; MTCW

Fitzgerald, Penelope 1916-. . . **CLC 19, 51, 61**
See also CA 85-88; CAAS 10; DLB 14

Fitzgerald, Robert (Stuart) 1910-1985 . . . . **CLC 39**
See also CA 1-4R; 114; CANR 1; DLBY 80

FitzGerald, Robert D(avid) 1902-1987 . . . . **CLC 19**
See also CA 17-20R

Fitzgerald, Zelda (Sayre) 1900-1948 . . . . **TCLC 52**
See also CA 117; 126; DLBY 84

Flanagan, Thomas (James Bonner) 1923- . . . . **CLC 25, 52**
See also CA 108; DLBY 80; INT 108; MTCW

Flaubert, Gustave 1821-1880 . . . . **NCLC 2, 10, 19; DA; DAB; DAC; DAM MST, NOV; SSC 11; WLC**
See also DLB 119

Flecker, Herman Elroy
See Flecker, (Herman) James Elroy

Flecker, (Herman) James Elroy 1884-1915 . . . . **TCLC 43**
See also CA 109; 150; DLB 10, 19

Fleming, Ian (Lancaster) 1908-1964 . . . . . . **CLC 3, 30; DAM POP**
See also CA 5-8R; CDBLB 1945-1960; DLB 87; MTCW; SATA 9

Fleming, Thomas (James) 1927- . . . . **CLC 37**
See also CA 5-8R; CANR 10; INT CANR-10; SATA 8

Fletcher, John 1579-1625. . . . . . **LC 33; DC 6**
See also CDBLB Before 1660; DLB 58

Fletcher, John Gould 1886-1950 . . . **TCLC 35**
See also CA 107; DLB 4, 45

Fleur, Paul
See Pohl, Frederik

Flooglebuckle, Al
See Spiegelman, Art

Flying Officer X
See Bates, H(erbert) E(rnest)

Fo, Dario 1926-. . . . . **CLC 32; DAM DRAM**
See also CA 116; 128; MTCW

Fogarty, Jonathan Titulescu Esq.
See Farrell, James T(homas)

Folke, Will
See Bloch, Robert (Albert)

Follett, Ken(neth Martin) 1949- . . . . . . **CLC 18; DAM NOV, POP**
See also AAYA 6; BEST 89:4; CA 81-84; CANR 13, 33; DLB 87; DLBY 81; INT CANR-33; MTCW

Fontane, Theodor 1819-1898 . . . . . **NCLC 26**
See also DLB 129

Foote, Horton 1916- . . . . **CLC 51, 91; DAM DRAM**
See also CA 73-76; CANR 34, 51; DLB 26; INT CANR-34

Foote, Shelby 1916- . . . . . . **CLC 75; DAM NOV, POP**
See also CA 5-8R; CANR 3, 45; DLB 2, 17

Forbes, Esther 1891-1967. . . . . **CLC 12**
See also AAYA 17; CA 13-14; 25-28R; CAP 1; CLR 27; DLB 22; JRDA; MAICYA; SATA 2

Forche, Carolyn (Louise) 1950- . . . . **CLC 25, 83, 86; DAM POET; PC 10**
See also CA 109; 117; CANR 50; DLB 5; INT 117

Ford, Elbur
See Hibbert, Eleanor Alice Burford

Ford, Ford Madox 1873-1939 . . . . **TCLC 1, 15, 39, 57; DAM NOV**
See also CA 104; 132; CDBLB 1914-1945; DLB 162; MTCW

Ford, John 1895-1973. . . . . **CLC 16**
See also CA 45-48

Ford, Richard 1944- . . . . **CLC 46**
See also CA 69-72; CANR 11, 47

Ford, Webster
See Masters, Edgar Lee

Foreman, Richard 1937-. . . . . **CLC 50**
See also CA 65-68; CANR 32

Forester, C(ecil) S(cott) 1899-1966 . . . . **CLC 35**
See also CA 73-76; 25-28R; SATA 13

Forez
See Mauriac, Francois (Charles)

Forman, James Douglas 1932-. . . . . . **CLC 21**
See also AAYA 17; CA 9-12R; CANR 4, 19, 42; JRDA; MAICYA; SATA 8, 70

Fornes, Maria Irene 1930- . . . . . . **CLC 39, 61**
See also CA 25-28R; CANR 28; DLB 7; HW; INT CANR-28; MTCW

Forrest, Leon 1937- . . . . **CLC 4**
See also BW 2; CA 89-92; CAAS 7; CANR 25, 52; DLB 33

Forster, E(dward) M(organ) 1879-1970 . . . . . **CLC 1, 2, 3, 4, 9, 10, 13, 15, 22, 45, 77; DA; DAB; DAC; DAM MST, NOV; WLC**
See also AAYA 2; CA 13-14; 25-28R; CANR 45; CAP 1; CDBLB 1914-1945; DLB 34, 98, 162; DLBD 10; MTCW; SATA 57

Forster, John 1812-1876 . . . . **NCLC 11**
See also DLB 144

Forsyth, Frederick 1938- . . **CLC 2, 5, 36; DAM NOV, POP**
See also BEST 89:4; CA 85-88; CANR 38; DLB 87; MTCW

Forten, Charlotte L. . . . . **TCLC 16; BLC**
See also Grimke, Charlotte L(ottie) Forten
See also DLB 50

Foscolo, Ugo 1778-1827 . . . . **NCLC 8**

Fosse, Bob . . . . **CLC 20**
See also Fosse, Robert Louis

Fosse, Robert Louis 1927-1987
See Fosse, Bob
See also CA 110; 123

Foster, Stephen Collins 1826-1864 . . . . **NCLC 26**

Foucault, Michel 1926-1984 . . . . **CLC 31, 34, 69**
See also CA 105; 113; CANR 34; MTCW

Fouque, Friedrich (Heinrich Karl) de la Motte 1777-1843 . . . . **NCLC 2**
See also DLB 90

Fourier, Charles 1772-1837 . . . . . . **NCLC 51**

Fournier, Henri Alban 1886-1914
See Alain-Fournier
See also CA 104

Fournier, Pierre 1916- . . . . **CLC 11**
See also Gascar, Pierre
See also CA 89-92; CANR 16, 40

Fowles, John 1926- . . . . . . **CLC 1, 2, 3, 4, 6, 9, 10, 15, 33, 87; DAB; DAC; DAM MST**
See also CA 5-8R; CANR 25; CDBLB 1960 to Present; DLB 14, 139; MTCW; SATA 22

Fox, Paula 1923- . . . . **CLC 2, 8**
See also AAYA 3; CA 73-76; CANR 20, 36; CLR 1; DLB 52; JRDA; MAICYA; MTCW; SATA 17, 60

Fox, William Price (Jr.) 1926- . . . . . **CLC 22**
See also CA 17-20R; CAAS 19; CANR 11; DLB 2; DLBY 81

Foxe, John 1516(?)-1587 . . . . **LC 14**

Frame, Janet 1924- . . . . **CLC 2, 3, 6, 22, 66, 96**
See also Clutha, Janet Paterson Frame

France, Anatole . . . . **TCLC 9**
See also Thibault, Jacques Anatole Francois
See also DLB 123

Francis, Claude 19(?)- . . . . **CLC 50**

Francis, Dick 1920- . . . . **CLC 2, 22, 42; DAM POP**
See also AAYA 5; BEST 89:3; CA 5-8R; CANR 9, 42; CDBLB 1960 to Present; DLB 87; INT CANR-9; MTCW

Francis, Robert (Churchill) 1901-1987 . . . . **CLC 15**
See also CA 1-4R; 123; CANR 1

Frank, Anne(lies Marie) 1929-1945 . . . . **TCLC 17; DA; DAB; DAC; DAM MST; WLC**
See also AAYA 12; CA 113; 133; MTCW; SATA 87; SATA-Brief 42

Frank, Elizabeth 1945- . . . . **CLC 39**
See also CA 121; 126; INT 126

Frankl, Viktor E(mil) 1905- . . . . **CLC 93**
See also CA 65-68

Franklin, Benjamin
See Hasek, Jaroslav (Matej Frantisek)

Franklin, Benjamin 1706-1790 . . . . . **LC 25; DA; DAB; DAC; DAM MST**
See also CDALB 1640-1865; DLB 24, 43, 73

Franklin, (Stella Maraia Sarah) Miles 1879-1954 . . . . **TCLC 7**
See also CA 104

Fraser, (Lady) Antonia (Pakenham) 1932- . . . . **CLC 32**
See also CA 85-88; CANR 44; MTCW; SATA-Brief 32

Fraser, George MacDonald 1925- . . . . **CLC 7**
See also CA 45-48; CANR 2, 48

Fraser, Sylvia 1935- . . . . **CLC 64**
See also CA 45-48; CANR 1, 16

Frayn, Michael 1933- . . . . **CLC 3, 7, 31, 47; DAM DRAM, NOV**
See also CA 5-8R; CANR 30; DLB 13, 14; MTCW

Fraze, Candida (Merrill) 1945- . . . . . **CLC 50**
See also CA 126

Frazer, J(ames) G(eorge) 1854-1941 . . . . **TCLC 32**
See also CA 118

Frazer, Robert Caine
See Creasey, John

Frazer, Sir James George
See Frazer, J(ames) G(eorge)

Frazier, Ian 1951- . . . . **CLC 46**
See also CA 130

Frederic, Harold 1856-1898 . . . . . . **NCLC 10**
See also DLB 12, 23; DLBD 13

Frederick, John
See Faust, Frederick (Schiller)

Frederick the Great 1712-1786 . . . . . . **LC 14**

Fredro, Aleksander 1793-1876 . . . . . **NCLC 8**

Freeling, Nicolas 1927- . . . . **CLC 38**
See also CA 49-52; CAAS 12; CANR 1, 17, 50; DLB 87

Freeman, Douglas Southall 1886-1953 . . . . **TCLC 11**
See also CA 109; DLB 17

Freeman, Judith 1946- . . . . **CLC 55**
See also CA 148

Freeman, Mary Eleanor Wilkins 1852-1930 . . . . **TCLC 9; SSC 1**
See also CA 106; DLB 12, 78

Freeman, R(ichard) Austin 1862-1943 . . . . **TCLC 21**
See also CA 113; DLB 70

French, Albert 1943- . . . . **CLC 86**

French, Marilyn 1929- . . . . **CLC 10, 18, 60; DAM DRAM, NOV, POP**
See also CA 69-72; CANR 3, 31; INT CANR-31; MTCW

French, Paul
See Asimov, Isaac

Freneau, Philip Morin 1752-1832 . . **NCLC 1**
See also DLB 37, 43

Freud, Sigmund 1856-1939 . . . . **TCLC 52**
See also CA 115; 133; MTCW

Friedan, Betty (Naomi) 1921- . . . . . . **CLC 74**
See also CA 65-68; CANR 18, 45; MTCW

Friedlander, Saul 1932- . . . . **CLC 90**
See also CA 117; 130

Friedman, B(ernard) H(arper) 1926- . . . . **CLC 7**
See also CA 1-4R; CANR 3, 48

Friedman, Bruce Jay 1930- . . . . **CLC 3, 5, 56**
See also CA 9-12R; CANR 25, 52; DLB 2, 28; INT CANR-25

Friel, Brian 1929- . . . . **CLC 5, 42, 59**
See also CA 21-24R; CANR 33; DLB 13; MTCW

Friis-Baastad, Babbis Ellinor 1921-1970 . . . . **CLC 12**
See also CA 17-20R; 134; SATA 7

Frisch, Max (Rudolf) 1911-1991 . . . . . **CLC 3, 9, 14, 18, 32, 44; DAM DRAM, NOV**
See also CA 85-88; 134; CANR 32; DLB 69, 124; MTCW

Fromentin, Eugene (Samuel Auguste) 1820-1876 . . . . **NCLC 10**
See also DLB 123

Frost, Frederick
See Faust, Frederick (Schiller)

Frost, Robert (Lee) 1874-1963 . . . . **CLC 1, 3, 4, 9, 10, 13, 15, 26, 34, 44; DA; DAB; DAC; DAM MST, POET; PC 1; WLC**
See also CA 89-92; CANR 33; CDALB 1917-1929; DLB 54; DLBD 7; MTCW; SATA 14

Froude, James Anthony 1818-1894 . . . . **NCLC 43**
See also DLB 18, 57, 144

Froy, Herald
See Waterhouse, Keith (Spencer)

Fry, Christopher 1907- . . . . . **CLC 2, 10, 14; DAM DRAM**
See also CA 17-20R; CAAS 23; CANR 9, 30; DLB 13; MTCW; SATA 66

Frye, (Herman) Northrop 1912-1991 . . . . **CLC 24, 70**
See also CA 5-8R; 133; CANR 8, 37; DLB 67, 68; MTCW

Fuchs, Daniel 1909-1993 . . . . **CLC 8, 22**
See also CA 81-84; 142; CAAS 5; CANR 40; DLB 9, 26, 28; DLBY 93

Fuchs, Daniel 1934- . . . . **CLC 34**
See also CA 37-40R; CANR 14, 48

Fuentes, Carlos 1928- . . . . . . **CLC 3, 8, 10, 13, 22, 41, 60; DA; DAB; DAC; DAM MST, MULT, NOV; HLC; WLC**
See also AAYA 4; AITN 2; CA 69-72; CANR 10, 32; DLB 113; HW; MTCW

Fuentes, Gregorio Lopez y
See Lopez y Fuentes, Gregorio

Fugard, (Harold) Athol 1932- . . . . **CLC 5, 9, 14, 25, 40, 80; DAM DRAM; DC 3**
See also AAYA 17; CA 85-88; CANR 32; MTCW

Fugard, Sheila 1932- . . . . **CLC 48**
See also CA 125

Fuller, Charles (H., Jr.) 1939- . . . . **CLC 25; BLC; DAM DRAM, MULT; DC 1**
See also BW 2; CA 108; 112; DLB 38; INT 112; MTCW

Fuller, John (Leopold) 1937- . . . . **CLC 62**
See also CA 21-24R; CANR 9, 44; DLB 40

Fuller, Margaret . . . . **NCLC 5, 50**
See also Ossoli, Sarah Margaret (Fuller marchesa d')

Fuller, Roy (Broadbent) 1912-1991 . . . . **CLC 4, 28**
See also CA 5-8R; 135; CAAS 10; CANR 53; DLB 15, 20; SATA 87

Fulton, Alice 1952- . . . . **CLC 52**
See also CA 116

Furphy, Joseph 1843-1912 . . . . **TCLC 25**

Fussell, Paul 1924- . . . . **CLC 74**
See also BEST 90:1; CA 17-20R; CANR 8, 21, 35; INT CANR-21; MTCW

Futabatei, Shimei 1864-1909 . . . . . . **TCLC 44**

Futrelle, Jacques 1875-1912 . . . . . . **TCLC 19**
See also CA 113

Gaboriau, Emile 1835-1873 . . . . . . **NCLC 14**

Gadda, Carlo Emilio 1893-1973 . . . . **CLC 11**
See also CA 89-92

Gaddis, William 1922- . . . . . **CLC 1, 3, 6, 8, 10, 19, 43, 86**
See also CA 17-20R; CANR 21, 48; DLB 2; MTCW

Gaines, Ernest J(ames) 1933- . . . . **CLC 3, 11, 18, 86; BLC; DAM MULT**
See also AAYA 18; AITN 1; BW 2; CA 9-12R; CANR 6, 24, 42; CDALB 1968-1988; DLB 2, 33, 152; DLBY 80; MTCW; SATA 86

Gaitskill, Mary 1954- . . . . **CLC 69**
See also CA 128

Galdos, Benito Perez
See Perez Galdos, Benito

Gale, Zona 1874-1938 . . . . . . **TCLC 7; DAM DRAM**
See also CA 105; DLB 9, 78

Galeano, Eduardo (Hughes) 1940- . . . **CLC 72**
See also CA 29-32R; CANR 13, 32; HW

Galiano, Juan Valera y Alcala
See Valera y Alcala-Galiano, Juan

Gallagher, Tess 1943- . . **CLC 18, 63; DAM POET; PC 9**
See also CA 106; DLB 120

Gallant, Mavis 1922- . . . . **CLC 7, 18, 38; DAC; DAM MST; SSC 5**
See also CA 69-72; CANR 29; DLB 53; MTCW

Gallant, Roy A(rthur) 1924- . . . . **CLC 17**
See also CA 5-8R; CANR 4, 29; CLR 30; MAICYA; SATA 4, 68

Gallico, Paul (William) 1897-1976 . . . **CLC 2**
See also AITN 1; CA 5-8R; 69-72; CANR 23; DLB 9; MAICYA; SATA 13

Gallo, Max Louis 1932- . . . . **CLC 95**
See also CA 85-88

Gallois, Lucien
See Desnos, Robert

Gallup, Ralph
See Whitemore, Hugh (John)

Galsworthy, John 1867-1933 . . . . . . **TCLC 1, 45; DA; DAB; DAC; DAM DRAM, MST, NOV; SSC 22; WLC 2**
See also CA 104; 141; CDBLB 1890-1914; DLB 10, 34, 98, 162

Galt, John 1779-1839 . . . . **NCLC 1**
See also DLB 99, 116, 159

Galvin, James 1951- . . . . **CLC 38**
See also CA 108; CANR 26

Gamboa, Federico 1864-1939 . . . . . . **TCLC 36**

Gandhi, M. K.
See Gandhi, Mohandas Karamchand

Gandhi, Mahatma
See Gandhi, Mohandas Karamchand

Gandhi, Mohandas Karamchand 1869-1948 . . . . . **TCLC 59; DAM MULT**
See also CA 121; 132; MTCW

Gann, Ernest Kellogg 1910-1991 . . . . **CLC 23**
See also AITN 1; CA 1-4R; 136; CANR 1

Garcia, Cristina 1958- . . . . **CLC 76**
See also CA 141

Garcia Lorca, Federico 1898-1936 . . . **TCLC 1, 7, 49; DA; DAB; DAC; DAM DRAM, MST, MULT, POET; DC 2; HLC; PC 3; WLC**
See also CA 104; 131; DLB 108; HW; MTCW

Garcia Marquez, Gabriel (Jose) 1928- . . . . **CLC 2, 3, 8, 10, 15, 27, 47, 55, 68; DA; DAB; DAC; DAM MST, MULT, NOV, POP; HLC; SSC 8; WLC**
See also AAYA 3; BEST 89:1, 90:4; CA 33-36R; CANR 10, 28, 50; DLB 113; HW; MTCW

Gard, Janice
See Latham, Jean Lee

Gard, Roger Martin du
See Martin du Gard, Roger

Gardam, Jane 1928- . . . . **CLC 43**
See also CA 49-52; CANR 2, 18, 33; CLR 12; DLB 14, 161; MAICYA; MTCW; SAAS 9; SATA 39, 76; SATA-Brief 28

Gardner, Herb(ert) 1934- . . . . **CLC 44**
See also CA 149

Gardner, John (Champlin), Jr. 1933-1982 . . . . . **CLC 2, 3, 5, 7, 8, 10, 18, 28, 34; DAM NOV, POP; SSC 7**
See also AITN 1; CA 65-68; 107; CANR 33; DLB 2; DLBY 82; MTCW; SATA 40; SATA-Obit 31

Gardner, John (Edmund) 1926- . . . . **CLC 30; DAM POP**
See also CA 103; CANR 15; MTCW

Gardner, Miriam
See Bradley, Marion Zimmer

Gardner, Noel
See Kuttner, Henry

Gardons, S. S.
See Snodgrass, W(illiam) D(e Witt)

Garfield, Leon 1921-1996 . . . . **CLC 12**
See also AAYA 8; CA 17-20R; 152; CANR 38, 41; CLR 21; DLB 161; JRDA; MAICYA; SATA 1, 32, 76

Garland, (Hannibal) Hamlin 1860-1940 . . . . **TCLC 3; SSC 18**
See also CA 104; DLB 12, 71, 78

Garneau, (Hector de) Saint-Denys 1912-1943 . . . . **TCLC 13**
See also CA 111; DLB 88

Garner, Alan 1934- . . . . **CLC 17; DAB; DAM POP**
See also AAYA 18; CA 73-76; CANR 15; CLR 20; DLB 161; MAICYA; MTCW; SATA 18, 69

Garner, Hugh 1913-1979 . . . . **CLC 13**
See also CA 69-72; CANR 31; DLB 68

Garnett, David 1892-1981 . . . . **CLC 3**
See also CA 5-8R; 103; CANR 17; DLB 34

Garos, Stephanie
See Katz, Steve

Garrett, George (Palmer) 1929- . . . . **CLC 3, 11, 51**
See also CA 1-4R; CAAS 5; CANR 1, 42; DLB 2, 5, 130, 152; DLBY 83

Garrick, David 1717-1779 . . . . **LC 15; DAM DRAM**
See also DLB 84

Garrigue, Jean 1914-1972 . . . . **CLC 2, 8**
See also CA 5-8R; 37-40R; CANR 20

Garrison, Frederick
See Sinclair, Upton (Beall)

Garth, Will
See Hamilton, Edmond; Kuttner, Henry

Garvey, Marcus (Moziah, Jr.) 1887-1940 . . . . **TCLC 41; BLC; DAM MULT**
See also BW 1; CA 120; 124

Gary, Romain . . . . **CLC 25**
See also Kacew, Romain
See also DLB 83

Gascar, Pierre . . . . **CLC 11**
See also Fournier, Pierre

Gascoyne, David (Emery) 1916- .... **CLC 45**
See also CA 65-68; CANR 10, 28; DLB 20; MTCW

Gaskell, Elizabeth Cleghorn 1810-1865 .. **NCLC 5; DAB; DAM MST**
See also CDBLB 1832-1890; DLB 21, 144, 159

Gass, William H(oward) 1924- ... **CLC 1, 2, 8, 11, 15, 39; SSC 12**
See also CA 17-20R; CANR 30; DLB 2; MTCW

Gasset, Jose Ortega y
See Ortega y Gasset, Jose

Gates, Henry Louis, Jr. 1950- .... **CLC 65; DAM MULT**
See also BW 2; CA 109; CANR 25, 53; DLB 67

Gautier, Theophile 1811-1872 ...... **NCLC 1; DAM POET; SSC 20**
See also DLB 119

Gawsworth, John
See Bates, H(erbert) E(rnest)

Gay, Oliver
See Gogarty, Oliver St. John

Gaye, Marvin (Penze) 1939-1984 ... **CLC 26**
See also CA 112

Gebler, Carlo (Ernest) 1954- .... **CLC 39**
See also CA 119; 133

Gee, Maggie (Mary) 1948-......... **CLC 57**
See also CA 130

Gee, Maurice (Gough) 1931- .... **CLC 29**
See also CA 97-100; SATA 46

Gelbart, Larry (Simon) 1923- ... **CLC 21, 61**
See also CA 73-76; CANR 45

Gelber, Jack 1932- .... **CLC 1, 6, 14, 79**
See also CA 1-4R; CANR 2; DLB 7

Gellhorn, Martha (Ellis) 1908- .. **CLC 14, 60**
See also CA 77-80; CANR 44; DLBY 82

Genet, Jean 1910-1986 ...... **CLC 1, 2, 5, 10, 14, 44, 46; DAM DRAM**
See also CA 13-16R; CANR 18; DLB 72; DLBY 86; MTCW

Gent, Peter 1942- .... **CLC 29**
See also AITN 1; CA 89-92; DLBY 82

Gentlewoman in New England, A
See Bradstreet, Anne

Gentlewoman in Those Parts, A
See Bradstreet, Anne

George, Jean Craighead 1919- ...... **CLC 35**
See also AAYA 8; CA 5-8R; CANR 25; CLR 1; DLB 52; JRDA; MAICYA; SATA 2, 68

George, Stefan (Anton) 1868-1933 .... **TCLC 2, 14**
See also CA 104

Georges, Georges Martin
See Simenon, Georges (Jacques Christian)

Gerhardi, William Alexander
See Gerhardie, William Alexander

Gerhardie, William Alexander 1895-1977 .... **CLC 5**
See also CA 25-28R; 73-76; CANR 18; DLB 36

Gerstler, Amy 1956- .... **CLC 70**
See also CA 146

Gertler, T. .... **CLC 34**
See also CA 116; 121; INT 121

gfgg .... **CLC XvXzc**

Ghalib .... **NCLC 39**
See also Ghalib, Hsadullah Khan

Ghalib, Hsadullah Khan 1797-1869
See Ghalib
See also DAM POET

Ghelderode, Michel de 1898-1962 .... **CLC 6, 11; DAM DRAM**
See also CA 85-88; CANR 40

Ghiselin, Brewster 1903- .... **CLC 23**
See also CA 13-16R; CAAS 10; CANR 13

Ghose, Zulfikar 1935-............. **CLC 42**
See also CA 65-68

Ghosh, Amitav 1956- .... **CLC 44**
See also CA 147

Giacosa, Giuseppe 1847-1906 ...... **TCLC 7**
See also CA 104

Gibb, Lee
See Waterhouse, Keith (Spencer)

Gibbon, Lewis Grassic .... **TCLC 4**
See also Mitchell, James Leslie

Gibbons, Kaye 1960- .... **CLC 50, 88; DAM POP**
See also CA 151

Gibran, Kahlil 1883-1931 .... **TCLC 1, 9; DAM POET, POP; PC 9**
See also CA 104; 150

Gibran, Khalil
See Gibran, Kahlil

Gibson, William 1914- .... **CLC 23; DA; DAB; DAC; DAM DRAM, MST**
See also CA 9-12R; CANR 9, 42; DLB 7; SATA 66

Gibson, William (Ford) 1948- .... **CLC 39, 63; DAM POP**
See also AAYA 12; CA 126; 133; CANR 52

Gide, Andre (Paul Guillaume) 1869-1951 .... **TCLC 5, 12, 36; DA; DAB; DAC; DAM MST, NOV; SSC 13; WLC**
See also CA 104; 124; DLB 65; MTCW

Gifford, Barry (Colby) 1946- .... **CLC 34**
See also CA 65-68; CANR 9, 30, 40

Gilbert, W(illiam) S(chwenck) 1836-1911 ..... **TCLC 3; DAM DRAM, POET**
See also CA 104; SATA 36

Gilbreth, Frank B., Jr. 1911-....... **CLC 17**
See also CA 9-12R; SATA 2

Gilchrist, Ellen 1935- .... **CLC 34, 48; DAM POP; SSC 14**
See also CA 113; 116; CANR 41; DLB 130; MTCW

Giles, Molly 1942- .... **CLC 39**
See also CA 126

Gill, Patrick
See Creasey, John

Gilliam, Terry (Vance) 1940- .... **CLC 21**
See also Monty Python
See also CA 108; 113; CANR 35; INT 113

Gillian, Jerry
See Gilliam, Terry (Vance)

Gilliatt, Penelope (Ann Douglass) 1932-1993 .... **CLC 2, 10, 13, 53**
See also AITN 2; CA 13-16R; 141; CANR 49; DLB 14

Gilman, Charlotte (Anna) Perkins (Stetson) 1860-1935 .... **TCLC 9, 37; SSC 13**
See also CA 106; 150

Gilmour, David 1949-............. **CLC 35**
See also CA 138, 147

Gilpin, William 1724-1804....... **NCLC 30**

Gilray, J. D.
See Mencken, H(enry) L(ouis)

Gilroy, Frank D(aniel) 1925-........ **CLC 2**
See also CA 81-84; CANR 32; DLB 7

Ginsberg, Allen 1926- ...... **CLC 1, 2, 3, 4, 6, 13, 36, 69; DA; DAB; DAC; DAM MST, POET; PC 4; WLC 3**
See also AITN 1; CA 1-4R; CANR 2, 41; CDALB 1941-1968; DLB 5, 16; MTCW

Ginzburg, Natalia 1916-1991 .... **CLC 5, 11, 54, 70**
See also CA 85-88; 135; CANR 33; MTCW

Giono, Jean 1895-1970.......... **CLC 4, 11**
See also CA 45-48; 29-32R; CANR 2, 35; DLB 72; MTCW

Giovanni, Nikki 1943- ...... **CLC 2, 4, 19, 64; BLC; DA; DAB; DAC; DAM MST, MULT, POET**
See also AITN 1; BW 2; CA 29-32R; CAAS 6; CANR 18, 41; CLR 6; DLB 5, 41; INT CANR-18; MAICYA; MTCW; SATA 24

Giovene, Andrea 1904-............. **CLC 7**
See also CA 85-88

Gippius, Zinaida (Nikolayevna) 1869-1945
See Hippius, Zinaida
See also CA 106

Giraudoux, (Hippolyte) Jean 1882-1944 .... **TCLC 2, 7; DAM DRAM**
See also CA 104; DLB 65

Gironella, Jose Maria 1917- .... **CLC 11**
See also CA 101

Gissing, George (Robert) 1857-1903 .... **TCLC 3, 24, 47**
See also CA 105; DLB 18, 135

Giurlani, Aldo
See Palazzeschi, Aldo

Gladkov, Fyodor (Vasilyevich) 1883-1958 .... **TCLC 27**

Glanville, Brian (Lester) 1931- ...... **CLC 6**
See also CA 5-8R; CAAS 9; CANR 3; DLB 15, 139; SATA 42

Glasgow, Ellen (Anderson Gholson) 1873(?)-1945 .... **TCLC 2, 7**
See also CA 104; DLB 9, 12

Glaspell, Susan (Keating) 1882(?)-1948 .... **TCLC 55**
See also CA 110; DLB 7, 9, 78; YABC 2

Glassco, John 1909-1981 . . . . **CLC 9**
See also CA 13-16R; 102; CANR 15; DLB 68

Glasscock, Amnesia
See Steinbeck, John (Ernst)

Glasser, Ronald J. 1940(?)- . . . . **CLC 37**

Glassman, Joyce
See Johnson, Joyce

Glendinning, Victoria 1937- . . . . **CLC 50**
See also CA 120; 127; DLB 155

Glissant, Edouard
1928- . . . . **CLC 10, 68; DAM MULT**

Gloag, Julian 1930- . . . . **CLC 40**
See also AITN 1; CA 65-68; CANR 10

Glowacki, Aleksander
See Prus, Boleslaw

Gluck, Louise (Elisabeth)
1943- . . . . **CLC 7, 22, 44, 81; DAM POET; PC 16**
See also CA 33-36R; CANR 40; DLB 5

Gobineau, Joseph Arthur (Comte) de
1816-1882 . . . . **NCLC 17**
See also DLB 123

Godard, Jean-Luc 1930- . . . . **CLC 20**
See also CA 93-96

Godden, (Margaret) Rumer 1907- . . . **CLC 53**
See also AAYA 6; CA 5-8R; CANR 4, 27, 36; CLR 20; DLB 161; MAICYA; SAAS 12; SATA 3, 36

Godoy Alcayaga, Lucila 1889-1957
See Mistral, Gabriela
See also BW 2; CA 104; 131; DAM MULT; HW; MTCW

Godwin, Gail (Kathleen)
1937- . . . . **CLC 5, 8, 22, 31, 69; DAM POP**
See also CA 29-32R; CANR 15, 43; DLB 6; INT CANR-15; MTCW

Godwin, William 1756-1836 . . . . . . **NCLC 14**
See also CDBLB 1789-1832; DLB 39, 104, 142, 158, 163

Goethe, Johann Wolfgang von
1749-1832 . . . . **NCLC 4, 22, 34; DA; DAB; DAC; DAM DRAM, MST, POET; PC 5; WLC 3**
See also DLB 94

Gogarty, Oliver St. John
1878-1957 . . . . **TCLC 15**
See also CA 109; 150; DLB 15, 19

Gogol, Nikolai (Vasilyevich)
1809-1852 . . . . **NCLC 5, 15, 31; DA; DAB; DAC; DAM DRAM, MST; DC 1; SSC 4; WLC**

Goines, Donald
1937(?)-1974 . . . . **CLC 80; BLC; DAM MULT, POP**
See also AITN 1; BW 1; CA 124; 114; DLB 33

Gold, Herbert 1924- . . . . **CLC 4, 7, 14, 42**
See also CA 9-12R; CANR 17, 45; DLB 2; DLBY 81

Goldbarth, Albert 1948- . . . . **CLC 5, 38**
See also CA 53-56; CANR 6, 40; DLB 120

Goldberg, Anatol 1910-1982 . . . . **CLC 34**
See also CA 131; 117

Goldemberg, Isaac 1945- . . . . **CLC 52**
See also CA 69-72; CAAS 12; CANR 11, 32; HW

Golding, William (Gerald)
1911-1993 . . . . **CLC 1, 2, 3, 8, 10, 17, 27, 58, 81; DA; DAB; DAC; DAM MST, NOV; WLC**
See also AAYA 5; CA 5-8R; 141; CANR 13, 33; CDBLB 1945-1960; DLB 15, 100; MTCW

Goldman, Emma 1869-1940 . . . . **TCLC 13**
See also CA 110; 150

Goldman, Francisco 1955- . . . . **CLC 76**

Goldman, William (W.) 1931- . . . . **CLC 1, 48**
See also CA 9-12R; CANR 29; DLB 44

Goldmann, Lucien 1913-1970 . . . . . . **CLC 24**
See also CA 25-28; CAP 2

Goldoni, Carlo
1707-1793 . . . . **LC 4; DAM DRAM**

Goldsberry, Steven 1949- . . . . **CLC 34**
See also CA 131

Goldsmith, Oliver
1728-1774 . . . . . . **LC 2; DA; DAB; DAC; DAM DRAM, MST, NOV, POET; WLC**
See also CDBLB 1660-1789; DLB 39, 89, 104, 109, 142; SATA 26

Goldsmith, Peter
See Priestley, J(ohn) B(oynton)

Gombrowicz, Witold
1904-1969 . . . . **CLC 4, 7, 11, 49; DAM DRAM**
See also CA 19-20; 25-28R; CAP 2

Gomez de la Serna, Ramon
1888-1963 . . . . **CLC 9**
See also CA 116; HW

Goncharov, Ivan Alexandrovich
1812-1891 . . . . **NCLC 1**

Goncourt, Edmond (Louis Antoine Huot) de
1822-1896 . . . . **NCLC 7**
See also DLB 123

Goncourt, Jules (Alfred Huot) de
1830-1870 . . . . **NCLC 7**
See also DLB 123

Gontier, Fernande 19(?)- . . . . **CLC 50**

Goodman, Paul 1911-1972 . . . . **CLC 1, 2, 4, 7**
See also CA 19-20; 37-40R; CANR 34; CAP 2; DLB 130; MTCW

Gordimer, Nadine
1923- . . . . **CLC 3, 5, 7, 10, 18, 33, 51, 70; DA; DAB; DAC; DAM MST, NOV; SSC 17**
See also CA 5-8R; CANR 3, 28; INT CANR-28; MTCW

Gordon, Adam Lindsay
1833-1870 . . . . **NCLC 21**

Gordon, Caroline
1895-1981 . . . **CLC 6, 13, 29, 83; SSC 15**
See also CA 11-12; 103; CANR 36; CAP 1; DLB 4, 9, 102; DLBY 81; MTCW

Gordon, Charles William 1860-1937
See Connor, Ralph
See also CA 109

Gordon, Mary (Catherine)
1949- . . . . **CLC 13, 22**
See also CA 102; CANR 44; DLB 6; DLBY 81; INT 102; MTCW

Gordon, Sol 1923- . . . . **CLC 26**
See also CA 53-56; CANR 4; SATA 11

Gordone, Charles
1925-1995 . . . . . **CLC 1, 4; DAM DRAM**
See also BW 1; CA 93-96; 150; DLB 7; INT 93-96; MTCW

Gorenko, Anna Andreevna
See Akhmatova, Anna

Gorky, Maxim . . . . **TCLC 8; DAB; WLC**
See also Peshkov, Alexei Maximovich

Goryan, Sirak
See Saroyan, William

Gosse, Edmund (William)
1849-1928 . . . . **TCLC 28**
See also CA 117; DLB 57, 144

Gotlieb, Phyllis Fay (Bloom)
1926- . . . . **CLC 18**
See also CA 13-16R; CANR 7; DLB 88

Gottesman, S. D.
See Kornbluth, C(yril) M.; Pohl, Frederik

Gottfried von Strassburg
fl. c. 1210- . . . . **CMLC 10**
See also DLB 138

Gould, Lois . . . . **CLC 4, 10**
See also CA 77-80; CANR 29; MTCW

Gourmont, Remy (-Marie-Charles) de
1858-1915 . . . . **TCLC 17**
See also CA 109; 150

Govier, Katherine 1948- . . . . **CLC 51**
See also CA 101; CANR 18, 40

Goyen, (Charles) William
1915-1983 . . . . **CLC 5, 8, 14, 40**
See also AITN 2; CA 5-8R; 110; CANR 6; DLB 2; DLBY 83; INT CANR-6

Goytisolo, Juan
1931- . . . . . **CLC 5, 10, 23; DAM MULT; HLC**
See also CA 85-88; CANR 32; HW; MTCW

Gozzano, Guido 1883-1916 . . . . **PC 10**
See also DLB 114

Gozzi, (Conte) Carlo 1720-1806 . . **NCLC 23**

Grabbe, Christian Dietrich
1801-1836 . . . . **NCLC 2**
See also DLB 133

Grace, Patricia 1937- . . . . **CLC 56**

Gracian y Morales, Baltasar
1601-1658 . . . . **LC 15**

Gracq, Julien . . . . **CLC 11, 48**
See also Poirier, Louis
See also DLB 83

Grade, Chaim 1910-1982 . . . . **CLC 10**
See also CA 93-96; 107

Graduate of Oxford, A
See Ruskin, John

Graham, John
See Phillips, David Graham

Graham, Jorie 1951- . . . . **CLC 48**
See also CA 111; DLB 120

Graham, R(obert) B(ontine) Cunninghame
See Cunninghame Graham, R(obert) B(ontine)
See also DLB 98, 135

Graham, Robert
See Haldeman, Joe (William)

Graham, Tom
See Lewis, (Harry) Sinclair

Graham, W(illiam) S(ydney) 1918-1986 .... **CLC 29**
See also CA 73-76; 118; DLB 20

Graham, Winston (Mawdsley) 1910- .... **CLC 23**
See also CA 49-52; CANR 2, 22, 45; DLB 77

Grahame, Kenneth 1859-1932 .... **TCLC 64; DAB**
See also CA 108; 136; CLR 5; DLB 34, 141; MAICYA; YABC 1

Grant, Skeeter
See Spiegelman, Art

Granville-Barker, Harley 1877-1946 ...... **TCLC 2; DAM DRAM**
See also Barker, Harley Granville
See also CA 104

Grass, Guenter (Wilhelm) 1927- ..... **CLC 1, 2, 4, 6, 11, 15, 22, 32, 49, 88; DA; DAB; DAC; DAM MST, NOV; WLC**
See also CA 13-16R; CANR 20; DLB 75, 124; MTCW

Gratton, Thomas
See Hulme, T(homas) E(rnest)

Grau, Shirley Ann 1929- .... **CLC 4, 9; SSC 15**
See also CA 89-92; CANR 22; DLB 2; INT CANR-22; MTCW

Gravel, Fern
See Hall, James Norman

Graver, Elizabeth 1964- .... **CLC 70**
See also CA 135

Graves, Richard Perceval 1945- .... **CLC 44**
See also CA 65-68; CANR 9, 26, 51

Graves, Robert (von Ranke) 1895-1985 ...... **CLC 1, 2, 6, 11, 39, 44, 45; DAB; DAC; DAM MST, POET; PC 6**
See also CA 5-8R; 117; CANR 5, 36; CDBLB 1914-1945; DLB 20, 100; DLBY 85; MTCW; SATA 45

Graves, Valerie
See Bradley, Marion Zimmer

Gray, Alasdair (James) 1934- ...... **CLC 41**
See also CA 126; CANR 47; INT 126; MTCW

Gray, Amlin 1946- .... **CLC 29**
See also CA 138

Gray, Francine du Plessix 1930- .... **CLC 22; DAM NOV**
See also BEST 90:3; CA 61-64; CAAS 2; CANR 11, 33; INT CANR-11; MTCW

Gray, John (Henry) 1866-1934 .... **TCLC 19**
See also CA 119

Gray, Simon (James Holliday) 1936- .... **CLC 9, 14, 36**
See also AITN 1; CA 21-24R; CAAS 3; CANR 32; DLB 13; MTCW

Gray, Spalding 1941- .. **CLC 49; DAM POP**
See also CA 128

Gray, Thomas 1716-1771 ...... **LC 4; DA; DAB; DAC; DAM MST; PC 2; WLC**
See also CDBLB 1660-1789; DLB 109

Grayson, David
See Baker, Ray Stannard

Grayson, Richard (A.) 1951- .... **CLC 38**
See also CA 85-88; CANR 14, 31

Greeley, Andrew M(oran) 1928- .... **CLC 28; DAM POP**
See also CA 5-8R; CAAS 7; CANR 7, 43; MTCW

Green, Anna Katharine 1846-1935 .... **TCLC 63**
See also CA 112

Green, Brian
See Card, Orson Scott

Green, Hannah
See Greenberg, Joanne (Goldenberg)

Green, Hannah .... **CLC 3**
See also CA 73-76

Green, Henry .... **CLC 2, 13**
See also Yorke, Henry Vincent
See also DLB 15

Green, Julian (Hartridge) 1900-
See Green, Julien
See also CA 21-24R; CANR 33; DLB 4, 72; MTCW

Green, Julien .... **CLC 3, 11, 77**
See also Green, Julian (Hartridge)

Green, Paul (Eliot) 1894-1981 ...... **CLC 25; DAM DRAM**
See also AITN 1; CA 5-8R; 103; CANR 3; DLB 7, 9; DLBY 81

Greenberg, Ivan 1908-1973
See Rahv, Philip
See also CA 85-88

Greenberg, Joanne (Goldenberg) 1932- .... **CLC 7, 30**
See also AAYA 12; CA 5-8R; CANR 14, 32; SATA 25

Greenberg, Richard 1959(?)- .... **CLC 57**
See also CA 138

Greene, Bette 1934- .... **CLC 30**
See also AAYA 7; CA 53-56; CANR 4; CLR 2; JRDA; MAICYA; SAAS 16; SATA 8

Greene, Gael .... **CLC 8**
See also CA 13-16R; CANR 10

Greene, Graham 1904-1991 .... **CLC 1, 3, 6, 9, 14, 18, 27, 37, 70, 72; DA; DAB; DAC; DAM MST, NOV; WLC**
See also AITN 2; CA 13-16R; 133; CANR 35; CDBLB 1945-1960; DLB 13, 15, 77, 100, 162; DLBY 91; MTCW; SATA 20

Greer, Richard
See Silverberg, Robert

Gregor, Arthur 1923- .... **CLC 9**
See also CA 25-28R; CAAS 10; CANR 11; SATA 36

Gregor, Lee
See Pohl, Frederik

Gregory, Isabella Augusta (Persse) 1852-1932 .... **TCLC 1**
See also CA 104; DLB 10

Gregory, J. Dennis
See Williams, John A(lfred)

Grendon, Stephen
See Derleth, August (William)

Grenville, Kate 1950- .... **CLC 61**
See also CA 118; CANR 53

Grenville, Pelham
See Wodehouse, P(elham) G(renville)

Greve, Felix Paul (Berthold Friedrich) 1879-1948
See Grove, Frederick Philip
See also CA 104; 141; DAC; DAM MST

Grey, Zane 1872-1939 .... **TCLC 6; DAM POP**
See also CA 104; 132; DLB 9; MTCW

Grieg, (Johan) Nordahl (Brun) 1902-1943 .... **TCLC 10**
See also CA 107

Grieve, C(hristopher) M(urray) 1892-1978 .... **CLC 11, 19; DAM POET**
See also MacDiarmid, Hugh; Pteleon
See also CA 5-8R; 85-88; CANR 33; MTCW

Griffin, Gerald 1803-1840 .... **NCLC 7**
See also DLB 159

Griffin, John Howard 1920-1980.... **CLC 68**
See also AITN 1; CA 1-4R; 101; CANR 2

Griffin, Peter 1942- .... **CLC 39**
See also CA 136

Griffiths, Trevor 1935- .... **CLC 13, 52**
See also CA 97-100; CANR 45; DLB 13

Grigson, Geoffrey (Edward Harvey) 1905-1985 .... **CLC 7, 39**
See also CA 25-28R; 118; CANR 20, 33; DLB 27; MTCW

Grillparzer, Franz 1791-1872...... **NCLC 1**
See also DLB 133

Grimble, Reverend Charles James
See Eliot, T(homas) S(tearns)

Grimke, Charlotte L(ottie) Forten 1837(?)-1914
See Forten, Charlotte L.
See also BW 1; CA 117; 124; DAM MULT, POET

Grimm, Jacob Ludwig Karl 1785-1863 .... **NCLC 3**
See also DLB 90; MAICYA; SATA 22

Grimm, Wilhelm Karl 1786-1859 .. **NCLC 3**
See also DLB 90; MAICYA; SATA 22

Grimmelshausen, Johann Jakob Christoffel von 1621-1676 .... **LC 6**
See also DLB 168

Grindel, Eugene 1895-1952
See Eluard, Paul
See also CA 104

Grisham, John 1955- .. **CLC 84; DAM POP**
See also AAYA 14; CA 138; CANR 47

Grossman, David 1954- . . . . **CLC 67**
See also CA 138

Grossman, Vasily (Semenovich)
1905-1964 . . . . **CLC 41**
See also CA 124; 130; MTCW

Grove, Frederick Philip . . . . **TCLC 4**
See also Greve, Felix Paul (Berthold Friedrich)
See also DLB 92

Grubb
See Crumb, R(obert)

Grumbach, Doris (Isaac)
1918- . . . . **CLC 13, 22, 64**
See also CA 5-8R; CAAS 2; CANR 9, 42; INT CANR-9

Grundtvig, Nicolai Frederik Severin
1783-1872 . . . . **NCLC 1**

Grunge
See Crumb, R(obert)

Grunwald, Lisa 1959- . . . . **CLC 44**
See also CA 120

Guare, John
1938- . . . . **CLC 8, 14, 29, 67; DAM DRAM**
See also CA 73-76; CANR 21; DLB 7; MTCW

Gudjonsson, Halldor Kiljan 1902-
See Laxness, Halldor
See also CA 103

Guenter, Erich
See Eich, Guenter

Guest, Barbara 1920- . . . . **CLC 34**
See also CA 25-28R; CANR 11, 44; DLB 5

Guest, Judith (Ann)
1936- . . . . **CLC 8, 30; DAM NOV, POP**
See also AAYA 7; CA 77-80; CANR 15; INT CANR-15; MTCW

Guevara, Che . . . . **CLC 87; HLC**
See also Guevara (Serna), Ernesto

Guevara (Serna), Ernesto 1928-1967
See Guevara, Che
See also CA 127; 111; DAM MULT; HW

Guild, Nicholas M. 1944- . . . . **CLC 33**
See also CA 93-96

Guillemin, Jacques
See Sartre, Jean-Paul

Guillen, Jorge
1893-1984 . . . . . . **CLC 11; DAM MULT, POET**
See also CA 89-92; 112; DLB 108; HW

Guillen, Nicolas (Cristobal)
1902-1989 . . . . **CLC 48, 79; BLC; DAM MST, MULT, POET; HLC**
See also BW 2; CA 116; 125; 129; HW

Guillevic, (Eugene) 1907- . . . . **CLC 33**
See also CA 93-96

Guillois
See Desnos, Robert

Guillois, Valentin
See Desnos, Robert

Guiney, Louise Imogen
1861-1920 . . . . **TCLC 41**
See also DLB 54

Guiraldes, Ricardo (Guillermo)
1886-1927 . . . . **TCLC 39**
See also CA 131; HW; MTCW

Gumilev, Nikolai Stephanovich
1886-1921 . . . . **TCLC 60**

Gunesekera, Romesh . . . . **CLC 91**

Gunn, Bill . . . . **CLC 5**
See also Gunn, William Harrison
See also DLB 38

Gunn, Thom(son William)
1929- . . . . **CLC 3, 6, 18, 32, 81; DAM POET**
See also CA 17-20R; CANR 9, 33; CDBLB 1960 to Present; DLB 27; INT CANR-33; MTCW

Gunn, William Harrison 1934(?)-1989
See Gunn, Bill
See also AITN 1; BW 1; CA 13-16R; 128; CANR 12, 25

Gunnars, Kristjana 1948- . . . . **CLC 69**
See also CA 113; DLB 60

Gurganus, Allan
1947- . . . . **CLC 70; DAM POP**
See also BEST 90:1; CA 135

Gurney, A(lbert) R(amsdell), Jr.
1930- . . . . **CLC 32, 50, 54; DAM DRAM**
See also CA 77-80; CANR 32

Gurney, Ivor (Bertie) 1890-1937 . . . **TCLC 33**

Gurney, Peter
See Gurney, A(lbert) R(amsdell), Jr.

Guro, Elena 1877-1913 . . . . **TCLC 56**

Gustafson, Ralph (Barker) 1909- . . . . **CLC 36**
See also CA 21-24R; CANR 8, 45; DLB 88

Gut, Gom
See Simenon, Georges (Jacques Christian)

Guterson, David 1956- . . . . **CLC 91**
See also CA 132

Guthrie, A(lfred) B(ertram), Jr.
1901-1991 . . . . **CLC 23**
See also CA 57-60; 134; CANR 24; DLB 6; SATA 62; SATA-Obit 67

Guthrie, Isobel
See Grieve, C(hristopher) M(urray)

Guthrie, Woodrow Wilson 1912-1967
See Guthrie, Woody
See also CA 113; 93-96

Guthrie, Woody . . . . **CLC 35**
See also Guthrie, Woodrow Wilson

Guy, Rosa (Cuthbert) 1928- . . . . **CLC 26**
See also AAYA 4; BW 2; CA 17-20R; CANR 14, 34; CLR 13; DLB 33; JRDA; MAICYA; SATA 14, 62

Gwendolyn
See Bennett, (Enoch) Arnold

H. D. . . . . **CLC 3, 8, 14, 31, 34, 73; PC 5**
See also Doolittle, Hilda

H. de V.
See Buchan, John

Haavikko, Paavo Juhani
1931- . . . . **CLC 18, 34**
See also CA 106

Habbema, Koos
See Heijermans, Herman

Hacker, Marilyn
1942- . . . . **CLC 5, 9, 23, 72, 91; DAM POET**
See also CA 77-80; DLB 120

Haggard, H(enry) Rider
1856-1925 . . . . **TCLC 11**
See also CA 108; 148; DLB 70, 156; SATA 16

Hagiosy, L.
See Larbaud, Valery (Nicolas)

Hagiwara Sakutaro 1886-1942 . . . . **TCLC 60**

Haig, Fenil
See Ford, Ford Madox

Haig-Brown, Roderick (Langmere)
1908-1976 . . . . **CLC 21**
See also CA 5-8R; 69-72; CANR 4, 38; CLR 31; DLB 88; MAICYA; SATA 12

Hailey, Arthur
1920- . . . . **CLC 5; DAM NOV, POP**
See also AITN 2; BEST 90:3; CA 1-4R; CANR 2, 36; DLB 88; DLBY 82; MTCW

Hailey, Elizabeth Forsythe 1938- . . . **CLC 40**
See also CA 93-96; CAAS 1; CANR 15, 48; INT CANR-15

Haines, John (Meade) 1924- . . . . **CLC 58**
See also CA 17-20R; CANR 13, 34; DLB 5

Hakluyt, Richard 1552-1616 . . . . **LC 31**

Haldeman, Joe (William) 1943- . . . . . **CLC 61**
See also CA 53-56; CANR 6; DLB 8; INT CANR-6

Haley, Alex(ander Murray Palmer)
1921-1992 . . . . **CLC 8, 12, 76; BLC; DA; DAB; DAC; DAM MST, MULT, POP**
See also BW 2; CA 77-80; 136; DLB 38; MTCW

Haliburton, Thomas Chandler
1796-1865 . . . . **NCLC 15**
See also DLB 11, 99

Hall, Donald (Andrew, Jr.)
1928- . . **CLC 1, 13, 37, 59; DAM POET**
See also CA 5-8R; CAAS 7; CANR 2, 44; DLB 5; SATA 23

Hall, Frederic Sauser
See Sauser-Hall, Frederic

Hall, James
See Kuttner, Henry

Hall, James Norman 1887-1951 . . . **TCLC 23**
See also CA 123; SATA 21

Hall, (Marguerite) Radclyffe
1886-1943 . . . . **TCLC 12**
See also CA 110; 150

Hall, Rodney 1935- . . . . **CLC 51**
See also CA 109

Halleck, Fitz-Greene 1790-1867 . . **NCLC 47**
See also DLB 3

Halliday, Michael
See Creasey, John

Halpern, Daniel 1945- . . . . **CLC 14**
See also CA 33-36R

Hamburger, Michael (Peter Leopold)
1924- . . . . **CLC 5, 14**
See also CA 5-8R; CAAS 4; CANR 2, 47; DLB 27

Hamill, Pete 1935- . . . . **CLC 10**
See also CA 25-28R; CANR 18

Henryson, Robert 1430(?)-1506(?).... **LC 20**
See also DLB 146

Henry VIII 1491-1547............. **LC 10**

Henschke, Alfred
See Klabund

Hentoff, Nat(han Irving) 1925-..... **CLC 26**
See also AAYA 4; CA 1-4R; CAAS 6; CANR 5, 25; CLR 1; INT CANR-25; JRDA; MAICYA; SATA 42, 69; SATA-Brief 27

Heppenstall, (John) Rayner
1911-1981 .... **CLC 10**
See also CA 1-4R; 103; CANR 29

Herbert, Frank (Patrick)
1920-1986 ...... **CLC 12, 23, 35, 44, 85; DAM POP**
See also CA 53-56; 118; CANR 5, 43; DLB 8; INT CANR-5; MTCW; SATA 9, 37; SATA-Obit 47

Herbert, George
1593-1633 .... **LC 24; DAB; DAM POET; PC 4**
See also CDBLB Before 1660; DLB 126

Herbert, Zbigniew
1924-......... **CLC 9, 43; DAM POET**
See also CA 89-92; CANR 36; MTCW

Herbst, Josephine (Frey)
1897-1969 .... **CLC 34**
See also CA 5-8R; 25-28R; DLB 9

Hergesheimer, Joseph
1880-1954 .... **TCLC 11**
See also CA 109; DLB 102, 9

Herlihy, James Leo 1927-1993 ...... **CLC 6**
See also CA 1-4R; 143; CANR 2

Hermogenes fl. c. 175-........... **CMLC 6**

Hernandez, Jose 1834-1886...... **NCLC 17**

Herodotus c. 484B.C.-429B.C..... **CMLC 17**

Herrick, Robert
1591-1674 ..... **LC 13; DA; DAB; DAC; DAM MST, POP; PC 9**
See also DLB 126

Herring, Guilles
See Somerville, Edith

Herriot, James
1916-1995 .... **CLC 12; DAM POP**
See also Wight, James Alfred
See also AAYA 1; CA 148; CANR 40; SATA 86

Herrmann, Dorothy 1941-......... **CLC 44**
See also CA 107

Herrmann, Taffy
See Herrmann, Dorothy

Hersey, John (Richard)
1914-1993 .... **CLC 1, 2, 7, 9, 40, 81; DAM POP**
See also CA 17-20R; 140; CANR 33; DLB 6; MTCW; SATA 25; SATA-Obit 76

Herzen, Aleksandr Ivanovich
1812-1870 .... **NCLC 10**

Herzl, Theodor 1860-1904........ **TCLC 36**

Herzog, Werner 1942-............. **CLC 16**
See also CA 89-92

Hesiod c. 8th cent. B.C.-......... **CMLC 5**

Hesse, Hermann
1877-1962 .... **CLC 1, 2, 3, 6, 11, 17, 25, 69; DA; DAB; DAC; DAM MST, NOV; SSC 9; WLC**
See also CA 17-18; CAP 2; DLB 66; MTCW; SATA 50

Hewes, Cady
See De Voto, Bernard (Augustine)

Heyen, William 1940- .... **CLC 13, 18**
See also CA 33-36R; CAAS 9; DLB 5

Heyerdahl, Thor 1914-............ **CLC 26**
See also CA 5-8R; CANR 5, 22; MTCW; SATA 2, 52

Heym, Georg (Theodor Franz Arthur)
1887-1912 .... **TCLC 9**
See also CA 106

Heym, Stefan 1913-.............. **CLC 41**
See also CA 9-12R; CANR 4; DLB 69

Heyse, Paul (Johann Ludwig von)
1830-1914 .... **TCLC 8**
See also CA 104; DLB 129

Heyward, (Edwin) DuBose
1885-1940 .... **TCLC 59**
See also CA 108; DLB 7, 9, 45; SATA 21

Hibbert, Eleanor Alice Burford
1906-1993 .... **CLC 7; DAM POP**
See also BEST 90:4; CA 17-20R; 140; CANR 9, 28; SATA 2; SATA-Obit 74

Hichens, Robert S. 1864-1950..... **TCLC 64**
See also DLB 153

Higgins, George V(incent)
1939- .... **CLC 4, 7, 10, 18**
See also CA 77-80; CAAS 5; CANR 17, 51; DLB 2; DLBY 81; INT CANR-17; MTCW

Higginson, Thomas Wentworth
1823-1911 .... **TCLC 36**
See also DLB 1, 64

Highet, Helen
See MacInnes, Helen (Clark)

Highsmith, (Mary) Patricia
1921-1995 .... **CLC 2, 4, 14, 42; DAM NOV, POP**
See also CA 1-4R; 147; CANR 1, 20, 48; MTCW

Highwater, Jamake (Mamake)
1942(?)- .... **CLC 12**
See also AAYA 7; CA 65-68; CAAS 7; CANR 10, 34; CLR 17; DLB 52; DLBY 85; JRDA; MAICYA; SATA 32, 69; SATA-Brief 30

Highway, Tomson
1951- ..... **CLC 92; DAC; DAM MULT**
See also CA 151; NNAL

Higuchi, Ichiyo 1872-1896....... **NCLC 49**

Hijuelos, Oscar
1951- .... **CLC 65; DAM MULT, POP; HLC**
See also BEST 90:1; CA 123; CANR 50; DLB 145; HW

Hikmet, Nazim 1902(?)-1963....... **CLC 40**
See also CA 141; 93-96

Hildesheimer, Wolfgang
1916-1991 .... **CLC 49**
See also CA 101; 135; DLB 69, 124

Hill, Geoffrey (William)
1932- ... **CLC 5, 8, 18, 45; DAM POET**
See also CA 81-84; CANR 21; CDBLB 1960 to Present; DLB 40; MTCW

Hill, George Roy 1921-........... **CLC 26**
See also CA 110; 122

Hill, John
See Koontz, Dean R(ay)

Hill, Susan (Elizabeth)
1942- .. **CLC 4; DAB; DAM MST, NOV**
See also CA 33-36R; CANR 29; DLB 14, 139; MTCW

Hillerman, Tony
1925- .... **CLC 62; DAM POP**
See also AAYA 6; BEST 89:1; CA 29-32R; CANR 21, 42; SATA 6

Hillesum, Etty 1914-1943 .... **TCLC 49**
See also CA 137

Hilliard, Noel (Harvey) 1929-...... **CLC 15**
See also CA 9-12R; CANR 7

Hillis, Rick 1956-................ **CLC 66**
See also CA 134

Hilton, James 1900-1954......... **TCLC 21**
See also CA 108; DLB 34, 77; SATA 34

Himes, Chester (Bomar)
1909-1984 .... **CLC 2, 4, 7, 18, 58; BLC; DAM MULT**
See also BW 2; CA 25-28R; 114; CANR 22; DLB 2, 76, 143; MTCW

Hinde, Thomas .... **CLC 6, 11**
See also Chitty, Thomas Willes

Hindin, Nathan
See Bloch, Robert (Albert)

Hine, (William) Daryl 1936-....... **CLC 15**
See also CA 1-4R; CAAS 15; CANR 1, 20; DLB 60

Hinkson, Katharine Tynan
See Tynan, Katharine

Hinton, S(usan) E(loise)
1950- .... **CLC 30; DA; DAB; DAC; DAM MST, NOV**
See also AAYA 2; CA 81-84; CANR 32; CLR 3, 23; JRDA; MAICYA; MTCW; SATA 19, 58

Hippius, Zinaida .... **TCLC 9**
See also Gippius, Zinaida (Nikolayevna)

Hiraoka, Kimitake 1925-1970
See Mishima, Yukio
See also CA 97-100; 29-32R; DAM DRAM; MTCW

Hirsch, E(ric) D(onald), Jr. 1928-... **CLC 79**
See also CA 25-28R; CANR 27, 51; DLB 67; INT CANR-27; MTCW

Hirsch, Edward 1950- .... **CLC 31, 50**
See also CA 104; CANR 20, 42; DLB 120

Hitchcock, Alfred (Joseph)
1899-1980 .... **CLC 16**
See also CA 97-100; SATA 27; SATA-Obit 24

Hitler, Adolf 1889-1945.......... **TCLC 53**
See also CA 117; 147

Hoagland, Edward 1932-.......... **CLC 28**
See also CA 1-4R; CANR 2, 31; DLB 6; SATA 51

Hoban, Russell (Conwell) 1925- .... **CLC 7, 25; DAM NOV**
See also CA 5-8R; CANR 23, 37; CLR 3; DLB 52; MAICYA; MTCW; SATA 1, 40, 78

Hobbs, Perry
See Blackmur, R(ichard) P(almer)

Hobson, Laura Z(ametkin) 1900-1986 .... **CLC 7, 25**
See also CA 17-20R; 118; DLB 28; SATA 52

Hochhuth, Rolf 1931- ..... **CLC 4, 11, 18; DAM DRAM**
See also CA 5-8R; CANR 33; DLB 124; MTCW

Hochman, Sandra 1936- .... **CLC 3, 8**
See also CA 5-8R; DLB 5

Hochwaelder, Fritz 1911-1986 ...... **CLC 36; DAM DRAM**
See also CA 29-32R; 120; CANR 42; MTCW

Hochwalder, Fritz
See Hochwaelder, Fritz

Hocking, Mary (Eunice) 1921- ..... **CLC 13**
See also CA 101; CANR 18, 40

Hodgins, Jack 1938- .... **CLC 23**
See also CA 93-96; DLB 60

Hodgson, William Hope 1877(?)-1918 .... **TCLC 13**
See also CA 111; DLB 70, 153, 156

Hoeg, Peter 1957- .... **CLC 95**
See also CA 151

Hoffman, Alice 1952- .... **CLC 51; DAM NOV**
See also CA 77-80; CANR 34; MTCW

Hoffman, Daniel (Gerard) 1923- .... **CLC 6, 13, 23**
See also CA 1-4R; CANR 4; DLB 5

Hoffman, Stanley 1944- .... **CLC 5**
See also CA 77-80

Hoffman, William M(oses) 1939- ... **CLC 40**
See also CA 57-60; CANR 11

Hoffmann, E(rnst) T(heodor) A(madeus) 1776-1822 .... **NCLC 2; SSC 13**
See also DLB 90; SATA 27

Hofmann, Gert 1931- .... **CLC 54**
See also CA 128

Hofmannsthal, Hugo von 1874-1929 .... **TCLC 11; DAM DRAM; DC 4**
See also CA 106; DLB 81, 118

Hogan, Linda 1947- .... **CLC 73; DAM MULT**
See also CA 120; CANR 45; NNAL

Hogarth, Charles
See Creasey, John

Hogarth, Emmett
See Polonsky, Abraham (Lincoln)

Hogg, James 1770-1835 .... **NCLC 4**
See also DLB 93, 116, 159

Holbach, Paul Henri Thiry Baron 1723-1789 .... **LC 14**

Holberg, Ludvig 1684-1754 .... **LC 6**

Holden, Ursula 1921- .... **CLC 18**
See also CA 101; CAAS 8; CANR 22

Holderlin, (Johann Christian) Friedrich 1770-1843 .... **NCLC 16; PC 4**

Holdstock, Robert
See Holdstock, Robert P.

Holdstock, Robert P. 1948- .... **CLC 39**
See also CA 131

Holland, Isabelle 1920- .... **CLC 21**
See also AAYA 11; CA 21-24R; CANR 10, 25, 47; JRDA; MAICYA; SATA 8, 70

Holland, Marcus
See Caldwell, (Janet Miriam) Taylor (Holland)

Hollander, John 1929- ...... **CLC 2, 5, 8, 14**
See also CA 1-4R; CANR 1, 52; DLB 5; SATA 13

Hollander, Paul
See Silverberg, Robert

Holleran, Andrew 1943(?)- .... **CLC 38**
See also CA 144

Hollinghurst, Alan 1954- .... **CLC 55, 91**
See also CA 114

Hollis, Jim
See Summers, Hollis (Spurgeon, Jr.)

Holly, Buddy 1936-1959 .... **TCLC 65**

Holmes, John
See Souster, (Holmes) Raymond

Holmes, John Clellon 1926-1988 .... **CLC 56**
See also CA 9-12R; 125; CANR 4; DLB 16

Holmes, Oliver Wendell 1809-1894 .... **NCLC 14**
See also CDALB 1640-1865; DLB 1; SATA 34

Holmes, Raymond
See Souster, (Holmes) Raymond

Holt, Victoria
See Hibbert, Eleanor Alice Burford

Holub, Miroslav 1923- .... **CLC 4**
See also CA 21-24R; CANR 10

Homer c. 8th cent. B.C.- ..... **CMLC 1, 16; DA; DAB; DAC; DAM MST, POET**

Honig, Edwin 1919- .... **CLC 33**
See also CA 5-8R; CAAS 8; CANR 4, 45; DLB 5

Hood, Hugh (John Blagdon) 1928- .... **CLC 15, 28**
See also CA 49-52; CAAS 17; CANR 1, 33; DLB 53

Hood, Thomas 1799-1845 .... **NCLC 16**
See also DLB 96

Hooker, (Peter) Jeremy 1941- ...... **CLC 43**
See also CA 77-80; CANR 22; DLB 40

hooks, bell .... **CLC 94**
See also Watkins, Gloria

Hope, A(lec) D(erwent) 1907- .... **CLC 3, 51**
See also CA 21-24R; CANR 33; MTCW

Hope, Brian
See Creasey, John

Hope, Christopher (David Tully) 1944- .... **CLC 52**
See also CA 106; CANR 47; SATA 62

Hopkins, Gerard Manley 1844-1889 .... **NCLC 17; DA; DAB; DAC; DAM MST, POET; PC 15; WLC**
See also CDBLB 1890-1914; DLB 35, 57

Hopkins, John (Richard) 1931- ...... **CLC 4**
See also CA 85-88

Hopkins, Pauline Elizabeth 1859-1930 .... **TCLC 28; BLC; DAM MULT**
See also BW 2; CA 141; DLB 50

Hopkinson, Francis 1737-1791 ...... **LC 25**
See also DLB 31

Hopley-Woolrich, Cornell George 1903-1968
See Woolrich, Cornell
See also CA 13-14; CAP 1

Horatio
See Proust, (Valentin-Louis-George-Eugene-) Marcel

Horgan, Paul (George Vincent O'Shaughnessy) 1903-1995 ...... **CLC 9, 53; DAM NOV**
See also CA 13-16R; 147; CANR 9, 35; DLB 102; DLBY 85; INT CANR-9; MTCW; SATA 13; SATA-Obit 84

Horn, Peter
See Kuttner, Henry

Hornem, Horace Esq.
See Byron, George Gordon (Noel)

Hornung, E(rnest) W(illiam) 1866-1921 .... **TCLC 59**
See also CA 108; DLB 70

Horovitz, Israel (Arthur) 1939- .... **CLC 56; DAM DRAM**
See also CA 33-36R; CANR 46; DLB 7

Horvath, Odon von
See Horvath, Oedoen von
See also DLB 85, 124

Horvath, Oedoen von 1901-1938 ... **TCLC 45**
See also Horvath, Odon von
See also CA 118

Horwitz, Julius 1920-1986 .... **CLC 14**
See also CA 9-12R; 119; CANR 12

Hospital, Janette Turner 1942- ..... **CLC 42**
See also CA 108; CANR 48

Hostos, E. M. de
See Hostos (y Bonilla), Eugenio Maria de

Hostos, Eugenio M. de
See Hostos (y Bonilla), Eugenio Maria de

Hostos, Eugenio Maria
See Hostos (y Bonilla), Eugenio Maria de

Hostos (y Bonilla), Eugenio Maria de 1839-1903 .... **TCLC 24**
See also CA 123; 131; HW

Houdini
See Lovecraft, H(oward) P(hillips)

Hougan, Carolyn 1943- .... **CLC 34**
See also CA 139

Household, Geoffrey (Edward West) 1900-1988 .... **CLC 11**
See also CA 77-80; 126; DLB 87; SATA 14; SATA-Obit 59

Housman, A(lfred) E(dward) 1859-1936 ...... **TCLC 1, 10; DA; DAB; DAC; DAM MST, POET; PC 2**
See also CA 104; 125; DLB 19; MTCW

Ibuse Masuji 1898-1993 . . . . **CLC 22**
See also CA 127; 141

Ichikawa, Kon 1915- . . . . **CLC 20**
See also CA 121

Idle, Eric 1943- . . . . **CLC 21**
See also Monty Python
See also CA 116; CANR 35

Ignatow, David 1914- . . . . . . **CLC 4, 7, 14, 40**
See also CA 9-12R; CAAS 3; CANR 31; DLB 5

Ihimaera, Witi 1944- . . . . **CLC 46**
See also CA 77-80

Ilf, Ilya . . . . **TCLC 21**
See also Fainzilberg, Ilya Arnoldovich

Illyes, Gyula 1902-1983 . . . . **PC 16**
See also CA 114; 109

Immermann, Karl (Lebrecht)
1796-1840 . . . . **NCLC 4, 49**
See also DLB 133

Inclan, Ramon (Maria) del Valle
See Valle-Inclan, Ramon (Maria) del

Infante, G(uillermo) Cabrera
See Cabrera Infante, G(uillermo)

Ingalls, Rachel (Holmes) 1940- . . . . . **CLC 42**
See also CA 123; 127

Ingamells, Rex 1913-1955 . . . . **TCLC 35**

Inge, William Motter
1913-1973 . . **CLC 1, 8, 19; DAM DRAM**
See also CA 9-12R; CDALB 1941-1968; DLB 7; MTCW

Ingelow, Jean 1820-1897 . . . . **NCLC 39**
See also DLB 35, 163; SATA 33

Ingram, Willis J.
See Harris, Mark

Innaurato, Albert (F.) 1948(?)- . . **CLC 21, 60**
See also CA 115; 122; INT 122

Innes, Michael
See Stewart, J(ohn) I(nnes) M(ackintosh)

Ionesco, Eugene
1909-1994 . . . . **CLC 1, 4, 6, 9, 11, 15, 41, 86; DA; DAB; DAC; DAM DRAM, MST; WLC**
See also CA 9-12R; 144; MTCW; SATA 7; SATA-Obit 79

Iqbal, Muhammad 1873-1938 . . . . . **TCLC 28**

Ireland, Patrick
See O'Doherty, Brian

Iron, Ralph
See Schreiner, Olive (Emilie Albertina)

Irving, John (Winslow)
1942- . . . . . **CLC 13, 23, 38; DAM NOV, POP**
See also AAYA 8; BEST 89:3; CA 25-28R; CANR 28; DLB 6; DLBY 82; MTCW

Irving, Washington
1783-1859 . . . . . **NCLC 2, 19; DA; DAB; DAM MST; SSC 2; WLC**
See also CDALB 1640-1865; DLB 3, 11, 30, 59, 73, 74; YABC 2

Irwin, P. K.
See Page, P(atricia) K(athleen)

Isaacs, Susan 1943- . . . **CLC 32; DAM POP**
See also BEST 89:1; CA 89-92; CANR 20, 41; INT CANR-20; MTCW

Isherwood, Christopher (William Bradshaw)
1904-1986 . . . . **CLC 1, 9, 11, 14, 44; DAM DRAM, NOV**
See also CA 13-16R; 117; CANR 35; DLB 15; DLBY 86; MTCW

Ishiguro, Kazuo
1954- . . . . . . **CLC 27, 56, 59; DAM NOV**
See also BEST 90:2; CA 120; CANR 49; MTCW

Ishikawa, Takuboku
1886(?)-1912 . . . . **TCLC 15; DAM POET; PC 10**
See also CA 113

Iskander, Fazil 1929- . . . . **CLC 47**
See also CA 102

Isler, Alan . . . . **CLC 91**

Ivan IV 1530-1584 . . . . **LC 17**

Ivanov, Vyacheslav Ivanovich
1866-1949 . . . . **TCLC 33**
See also CA 122

Ivask, Ivar Vidrik 1927-1992 . . . . **CLC 14**
See also CA 37-40R; 139; CANR 24

Ives, Morgan
See Bradley, Marion Zimmer

J. R. S.
See Gogarty, Oliver St. John

Jabran, Kahlil
See Gibran, Kahlil

Jabran, Khalil
See Gibran, Kahlil

Jackson, Daniel
See Wingrove, David (John)

Jackson, Jesse 1908-1983 . . . . **CLC 12**
See also BW 1; CA 25-28R; 109; CANR 27; CLR 28; MAICYA; SATA 2, 29; SATA-Obit 48

Jackson, Laura (Riding) 1901-1991
See Riding, Laura
See also CA 65-68; 135; CANR 28; DLB 48

Jackson, Sam
See Trumbo, Dalton

Jackson, Sara
See Wingrove, David (John)

Jackson, Shirley
1919-1965 . . . . **CLC 11, 60, 87; DA; DAC; DAM MST; SSC 9; WLC**
See also AAYA 9; CA 1-4R; 25-28R; CANR 4, 52; CDALB 1941-1968; DLB 6; SATA 2

Jacob, (Cyprien-)Max 1876-1944 . . . **TCLC 6**
See also CA 104

Jacobs, Jim 1942- . . . . **CLC 12**
See also CA 97-100; INT 97-100

Jacobs, W(illiam) W(ymark)
1863-1943 . . . . **TCLC 22**
See also CA 121; DLB 135

Jacobsen, Jens Peter 1847-1885 . . **NCLC 34**

Jacobsen, Josephine 1908- . . . . **CLC 48**
See also CA 33-36R; CAAS 18; CANR 23, 48

Jacobson, Dan 1929- . . . . **CLC 4, 14**
See also CA 1-4R; CANR 2, 25; DLB 14; MTCW

Jacqueline
See Carpentier (y Valmont), Alejo

Jagger, Mick 1944- . . . . **CLC 17**

Jakes, John (William)
1932- . . . . . . **CLC 29; DAM NOV, POP**
See also BEST 89:4; CA 57-60; CANR 10, 43; DLBY 83; INT CANR-10; MTCW; SATA 62

James, Andrew
See Kirkup, James

James, C(yril) L(ionel) R(obert)
1901-1989 . . . . **CLC 33**
See also BW 2; CA 117; 125; 128; DLB 125; MTCW

James, Daniel (Lewis) 1911-1988
See Santiago, Danny
See also CA 125

James, Dynely
See Mayne, William (James Carter)

James, Henry Sr. 1811-1882 . . . . . **NCLC 53**

James, Henry
1843-1916 . . . . . . **TCLC 2, 11, 24, 40, 47, 64; DA; DAB; DAC; DAM MST, NOV; SSC 8; WLC**
See also CA 104; 132; CDALB 1865-1917; DLB 12, 71, 74; DLBD 13; MTCW

James, M. R.
See James, Montague (Rhodes)
See also DLB 156

James, Montague (Rhodes)
1862-1936 . . . . **TCLC 6; SSC 16**
See also CA 104

James, P. D. . . . . **CLC 18, 46**
See also White, Phyllis Dorothy James
See also BEST 90:2; CDBLB 1960 to Present; DLB 87

James, Philip
See Moorcock, Michael (John)

James, William 1842-1910 . . . . . **TCLC 15, 32**
See also CA 109

James I 1394-1437 . . . . **LC 20**

Jameson, Anna 1794-1860 . . . . **NCLC 43**
See also DLB 99, 166

Jami, Nur al-Din 'Abd al-Rahman
1414-1492 . . . . **LC 9**

Jandl, Ernst 1925- . . . . **CLC 34**

Janowitz, Tama
1957- . . . . **CLC 43; DAM POP**
See also CA 106; CANR 52

Japrisot, Sebastien 1931- . . . . **CLC 90**

Jarrell, Randall
1914-1965 . . . . **CLC 1, 2, 6, 9, 13, 49; DAM POET**
See also CA 5-8R; 25-28R; CABS 2; CANR 6, 34; CDALB 1941-1968; CLR 6; DLB 48, 52; MAICYA; MTCW; SATA 7

Jarry, Alfred
1873-1907 . . . . **TCLC 2, 14; DAM DRAM; SSC 20**
See also CA 104

Jarvis, E. K.
See Bloch, Robert (Albert); Ellison, Harlan (Jay); Silverberg, Robert

Jeake, Samuel, Jr.
See Aiken, Conrad (Potter)

Jonson, Ben(jamin) 1572(?)-1637 . . . . . . **LC 6, 33; DA; DAB; DAC; DAM DRAM, MST, POET; DC 4; WLC**
See also CDBLB Before 1660; DLB 62, 121

Jordan, June 1936- . . . . . **CLC 5, 11, 23; DAM MULT, POET**
See also AAYA 2; BW 2; CA 33-36R; CANR 25; CLR 10; DLB 38; MAICYA; MTCW; SATA 4

Jordan, Pat(rick M.) 1941- . . . . **CLC 37**
See also CA 33-36R

Jorgensen, Ivar
See Ellison, Harlan (Jay)

Jorgenson, Ivar
See Silverberg, Robert

Josephus, Flavius c. 37-100 . . . . . . **CMLC 13**

Josipovici, Gabriel 1940- . . . . **CLC 6, 43**
See also CA 37-40R; CAAS 8; CANR 47; DLB 14

Joubert, Joseph 1754-1824 . . . . **NCLC 9**

Jouve, Pierre Jean 1887-1976 . . . . . . **CLC 47**
See also CA 65-68

Joyce, James (Augustine Aloysius) 1882-1941 . . . . **TCLC 3, 8, 16, 35, 52; DA; DAB; DAC; DAM MST, NOV, POET; SSC 3; WLC**
See also CA 104; 126; CDBLB 1914-1945; DLB 10, 19, 36, 162; MTCW

Jozsef, Attila 1905-1937. . . . . **TCLC 22**
See also CA 116

Juana Ines de la Cruz 1651(?)-1695 . . . **LC 5**

Judd, Cyril
See Kornbluth, C(yril) M.; Pohl, Frederik

Julian of Norwich 1342(?)-1416(?) . . . . **LC 6**
See also DLB 146

Juniper, Alex
See Hospital, Janette Turner

Junius
See Luxemburg, Rosa

Just, Ward (Swift) 1935- . . . . **CLC 4, 27**
See also CA 25-28R; CANR 32; INT CANR-32

Justice, Donald (Rodney) 1925- . . . . **CLC 6, 19; DAM POET**
See also CA 5-8R; CANR 26; DLBY 83; INT CANR-26

Juvenal c. 55-c. 127 . . . . **CMLC 8**

Juvenis
See Bourne, Randolph S(illiman)

Kacew, Romain 1914-1980
See Gary, Romain
See also CA 108; 102

Kadare, Ismail 1936- . . . . **CLC 52**

Kadohata, Cynthia. . . . . **CLC 59**
See also CA 140

Kafka, Franz 1883-1924 . . . . **TCLC 2, 6, 13, 29, 47, 53; DA; DAB; DAC; DAM MST, NOV; SSC 5; WLC**
See also CA 105; 126; DLB 81; MTCW

Kahanovitsch, Pinkhes
See Der Nister

Kahn, Roger 1927- . . . . **CLC 30**
See also CA 25-28R; CANR 44; SATA 37

Kain, Saul
See Sassoon, Siegfried (Lorraine)

Kaiser, Georg 1878-1945 . . . . **TCLC 9**
See also CA 106; DLB 124

Kaletski, Alexander 1946- . . . . **CLC 39**
See also CA 118; 143

Kalidasa fl. c. 400- . . . . **CMLC 9**

Kallman, Chester (Simon) 1921-1975 . . . . **CLC 2**
See also CA 45-48; 53-56; CANR 3

Kaminsky, Melvin 1926-
See Brooks, Mel
See also CA 65-68; CANR 16

Kaminsky, Stuart M(elvin) 1934- . . . **CLC 59**
See also CA 73-76; CANR 29, 53

Kane, Paul
See Simon, Paul

Kane, Wilson
See Bloch, Robert (Albert)

Kanin, Garson 1912-. . . . . **CLC 22**
See also AITN 1; CA 5-8R; CANR 7; DLB 7

Kaniuk, Yoram 1930- . . . . **CLC 19**
See also CA 134

Kant, Immanuel 1724-1804 . . . . . . **NCLC 27**
See also DLB 94

Kantor, MacKinlay 1904-1977 . . . . . . **CLC 7**
See also CA 61-64; 73-76; DLB 9, 102

Kaplan, David Michael 1946- . . . . . . **CLC 50**

Kaplan, James 1951- . . . . **CLC 59**
See also CA 135

Karageorge, Michael
See Anderson, Poul (William)

Karamzin, Nikolai Mikhailovich 1766-1826 . . . . **NCLC 3**
See also DLB 150

Karapanou, Margarita 1946- . . . . **CLC 13**
See also CA 101

Karinthy, Frigyes 1887-1938 . . . . . . **TCLC 47**

Karl, Frederick R(obert) 1927- . . . . . **CLC 34**
See also CA 5-8R; CANR 3, 44

Kastel, Warren
See Silverberg, Robert

Kataev, Evgeny Petrovich 1903-1942
See Petrov, Evgeny
See also CA 120

Kataphusin
See Ruskin, John

Katz, Steve 1935- . . . . **CLC 47**
See also CA 25-28R; CAAS 14; CANR 12; DLBY 83

Kauffman, Janet 1945-. . . . . **CLC 42**
See also CA 117; CANR 43; DLBY 86

Kaufman, Bob (Garnell) 1925-1986 . . . . **CLC 49**
See also BW 1; CA 41-44R; 118; CANR 22; DLB 16, 41

Kaufman, George S. 1889-1961 . . . . . . **CLC 38; DAM DRAM**
See also CA 108; 93-96; DLB 7; INT 108

Kaufman, Sue . . . . **CLC 3, 8**
See also Barondess, Sue K(aufman)

Kavafis, Konstantinos Petrou 1863-1933
See Cavafy, C(onstantine) P(eter)
See also CA 104

Kavan, Anna 1901-1968 . . . . . . **CLC 5, 13, 82**
See also CA 5-8R; CANR 6; MTCW

Kavanagh, Dan
See Barnes, Julian

Kavanagh, Patrick (Joseph) 1904-1967 . . . . **CLC 22**
See also CA 123; 25-28R; DLB 15, 20; MTCW

Kawabata, Yasunari 1899-1972 . . . . **CLC 2, 5, 9, 18; DAM MULT; SSC 17**
See also CA 93-96; 33-36R

Kaye, M(ary) M(argaret) 1909-. . . . . **CLC 28**
See also CA 89-92; CANR 24; MTCW; SATA 62

Kaye, Mollie
See Kaye, M(ary) M(argaret)

Kaye-Smith, Sheila 1887-1956. . . . . **TCLC 20**
See also CA 118; DLB 36

Kaymor, Patrice Maguilene
See Senghor, Leopold Sedar

Kazan, Elia 1909- . . . . **CLC 6, 16, 63**
See also CA 21-24R; CANR 32

Kazantzakis, Nikos 1883(?)-1957 . . . . **TCLC 2, 5, 33**
See also CA 105; 132; MTCW

Kazin, Alfred 1915- . . . . **CLC 34, 38**
See also CA 1-4R; CAAS 7; CANR 1, 45; DLB 67

Keane, Mary Nesta (Skrine) 1904-1996
See Keane, Molly
See also CA 108; 114; 151

Keane, Molly. . . . . **CLC 31**
See also Keane, Mary Nesta (Skrine)
See also INT 114

Keates, Jonathan 19(?)- . . . . **CLC 34**

Keaton, Buster 1895-1966 . . . . **CLC 20**

Keats, John 1795-1821 . . . . **NCLC 8; DA; DAB; DAC; DAM MST, POET; PC 1; WLC**
See also CDBLB 1789-1832; DLB 96, 110

Keene, Donald 1922- . . . . **CLC 34**
See also CA 1-4R; CANR 5

Keillor, Garrison. . . . . **CLC 40**
See also Keillor, Gary (Edward)
See also AAYA 2; BEST 89:3; DLBY 87; SATA 58

Keillor, Gary (Edward) 1942-
See Keillor, Garrison
See also CA 111; 117; CANR 36; DAM POP; MTCW

Keith, Michael
See Hubbard, L(afayette) Ron(ald)

Keller, Gottfried 1819-1890. . . . . . . **NCLC 2**
See also DLB 129

Kellerman, Jonathan 1949- . . . . **CLC 44; DAM POP**
See also BEST 90:1; CA 106; CANR 29, 51; INT CANR-29

Kelley, William Melvin 1937- ...... **CLC 22**
See also BW 1; CA 77-80; CANR 27; DLB 33

Kellogg, Marjorie 1922- .... **CLC 2**
See also CA 81-84

Kellow, Kathleen
See Hibbert, Eleanor Alice Burford

Kelly, M(ilton) T(erry) 1947- .... **CLC 55**
See also CA 97-100; CAAS 22; CANR 19, 43

Kelman, James 1946- .... **CLC 58, 86**
See also CA 148

Kemal, Yashar 1923- .... **CLC 14, 29**
See also CA 89-92; CANR 44

Kemble, Fanny 1809-1893 .... **NCLC 18**
See also DLB 32

Kemelman, Harry 1908- .... **CLC 2**
See also AITN 1; CA 9-12R; CANR 6; DLB 28

Kempe, Margery 1373(?)-1440(?) ..... **LC 6**
See also DLB 146

Kempis, Thomas a 1380-1471 .... **LC 11**

Kendall, Henry 1839-1882 .... **NCLC 12**

Keneally, Thomas (Michael)
1935- ...... **CLC 5, 8, 10, 14, 19, 27, 43; DAM NOV**
See also CA 85-88; CANR 10, 50; MTCW

Kennedy, Adrienne (Lita)
1931- ..... **CLC 66; BLC; DAM MULT; DC 5**
See also BW 2; CA 103; CAAS 20; CABS 3; CANR 26, 53; DLB 38

Kennedy, John Pendleton
1795-1870 .... **NCLC 2**
See also DLB 3

Kennedy, Joseph Charles 1929-
See Kennedy, X. J.
See also CA 1-4R; CANR 4, 30, 40; SATA 14, 86

Kennedy, William
1928- ... **CLC 6, 28, 34, 53; DAM NOV**
See also AAYA 1; CA 85-88; CANR 14, 31; DLB 143; DLBY 85; INT CANR-31; MTCW; SATA 57

Kennedy, X. J. .... **CLC 8, 42**
See also Kennedy, Joseph Charles
See also CAAS 9; CLR 27; DLB 5; SAAS 22

Kenny, Maurice (Francis)
1929- .... **CLC 87; DAM MULT**
See also CA 144; CAAS 22; NNAL

Kent, Kelvin
See Kuttner, Henry

Kenton, Maxwell
See Southern, Terry

Kenyon, Robert O.
See Kuttner, Henry

Kerouac, Jack ..... **CLC 1, 2, 3, 5, 14, 29, 61**
See also Kerouac, Jean-Louis Lebris de
See also CDALB 1941-1968; DLB 2, 16; DLBD 3; DLBY 95

Kerouac, Jean-Louis Lebris de 1922-1969
See Kerouac, Jack
See also AITN 1; CA 5-8R; 25-28R; CANR 26; DA; DAB; DAC; DAM MST, NOV, POET, POP; MTCW; WLC

Kerr, Jean 1923- .... **CLC 22**
See also CA 5-8R; CANR 7; INT CANR-7

Kerr, M. E. .... **CLC 12, 35**
See also Meaker, Marijane (Agnes)
See also AAYA 2; CLR 29; SAAS 1

Kerr, Robert .... **CLC 55**

Kerrigan, (Thomas) Anthony
1918- .... **CLC 4, 6**
See also CA 49-52; CAAS 11; CANR 4

Kerry, Lois
See Duncan, Lois

Kesey, Ken (Elton)
1935- ...... **CLC 1, 3, 6, 11, 46, 64; DA; DAB; DAC; DAM MST, NOV, POP; WLC**
See also CA 1-4R; CANR 22, 38; CDALB 1968-1988; DLB 2, 16; MTCW; SATA 66

Kesselring, Joseph (Otto)
1902-1967 ..... **CLC 45; DAM DRAM, MST**
See also CA 150

Kessler, Jascha (Frederick) 1929- .... **CLC 4**
See also CA 17-20R; CANR 8, 48

Kettelkamp, Larry (Dale) 1933- .... **CLC 12**
See also CA 29-32R; CANR 16; SAAS 3; SATA 2

Key, Ellen 1849-1926 .... **TCLC 65**

Keyber, Conny
See Fielding, Henry

Keyes, Daniel
1927- .... **CLC 80; DA; DAC; DAM MST, NOV**
See also CA 17-20R; CANR 10, 26; SATA 37

Keynes, John Maynard
1883-1946 .... **TCLC 64**
See also CA 114; DLBD 10

Khanshendel, Chiron
See Rose, Wendy

Khayyam, Omar
1048-1131 .... **CMLC 11; DAM POET; PC 8**

Kherdian, David 1931- .... **CLC 6, 9**
See also CA 21-24R; CAAS 2; CANR 39; CLR 24; JRDA; MAICYA; SATA 16, 74

Khlebnikov, Velimir .... **TCLC 20**
See also Khlebnikov, Viktor Vladimirovich

Khlebnikov, Viktor Vladimirovich 1885-1922
See Khlebnikov, Velimir
See also CA 117

Khodasevich, Vladislav (Felitsianovich)
1886-1939 .... **TCLC 15**
See also CA 115

Kielland, Alexander Lange
1849-1906 .... **TCLC 5**
See also CA 104

Kiely, Benedict 1919- .... **CLC 23, 43**
See also CA 1-4R; CANR 2; DLB 15

Kienzle, William X(avier)
1928- .... **CLC 25; DAM POP**
See also CA 93-96; CAAS 1; CANR 9, 31; INT CANR-31; MTCW

Kierkegaard, Soren 1813-1855 .... **NCLC 34**

Killens, John Oliver 1916-1987 ..... **CLC 10**
See also BW 2; CA 77-80; 123; CAAS 2; CANR 26; DLB 33

Killigrew, Anne 1660-1685 .... **LC 4**
See also DLB 131

Kim
See Simenon, Georges (Jacques Christian)

Kincaid, Jamaica
1949- .... **CLC 43, 68; BLC; DAM MULT, NOV**
See also AAYA 13; BW 2; CA 125; CANR 47; DLB 157

King, Francis (Henry)
1923- .... **CLC 8, 53; DAM NOV**
See also CA 1-4R; CANR 1, 33; DLB 15, 139; MTCW

King, Martin Luther, Jr.
1929-1968 .... **CLC 83; BLC; DA; DAB; DAC; DAM MST, MULT**
See also BW 2; CA 25-28; CANR 27, 44; CAP 2; MTCW; SATA 14

King, Stephen (Edwin)
1947- .... **CLC 12, 26, 37, 61; DAM NOV, POP; SSC 17**
See also AAYA 1, 17; BEST 90:1; CA 61-64; CANR 1, 30, 52; DLB 143; DLBY 80; JRDA; MTCW; SATA 9, 55

King, Steve
See King, Stephen (Edwin)

King, Thomas
1943- ..... **CLC 89; DAC; DAM MULT**
See also CA 144; NNAL

Kingman, Lee .... **CLC 17**
See also Natti, (Mary) Lee
See also SAAS 3; SATA 1, 67

Kingsley, Charles 1819-1875 ..... **NCLC 35**
See also DLB 21, 32, 163; YABC 2

Kingsley, Sidney 1906-1995 .... **CLC 44**
See also CA 85-88; 147; DLB 7

Kingsolver, Barbara
1955- .... **CLC 55, 81; DAM POP**
See also AAYA 15; CA 129; 134; INT 134

Kingston, Maxine (Ting Ting) Hong
1940- .... **CLC 12, 19, 58; DAM MULT, NOV**
See also AAYA 8; CA 69-72; CANR 13, 38; DLBY 80; INT CANR-13; MTCW; SATA 53

Kinnell, Galway
1927- .... **CLC 1, 2, 3, 5, 13, 29**
See also CA 9-12R; CANR 10, 34; DLB 5; DLBY 87; INT CANR-34; MTCW

Kinsella, Thomas 1928- .... **CLC 4, 19**
See also CA 17-20R; CANR 15; DLB 27; MTCW

Kinsella, W(illiam) P(atrick)
1935- .... **CLC 27, 43; DAC; DAM NOV, POP**
See also AAYA 7; CA 97-100; CAAS 7; CANR 21, 35; INT CANR-21; MTCW

Kipling, (Joseph) Rudyard 1865-1936 ...... **TCLC 8, 17; DA; DAB; DAC; DAM MST, POET; PC 3; SSC 5; WLC**
See also CA 105; 120; CANR 33; CDBLB 1890-1914; CLR 39; DLB 19, 34, 141, 156; MAICYA; MTCW; YABC 2

Kirkup, James 1918- .... **CLC 1**
See also CA 1-4R; CAAS 4; CANR 2; DLB 27; SATA 12

Kirkwood, James 1930(?)-1989 ...... **CLC 9**
See also AITN 2; CA 1-4R; 128; CANR 6, 40

Kirshner, Sidney
See Kingsley, Sidney

Kis, Danilo 1935-1989 .... **CLC 57**
See also CA 109; 118; 129; MTCW

Kivi, Aleksis 1834-1872 .... **NCLC 30**

Kizer, Carolyn (Ashley) 1925- ..... **CLC 15, 39, 80; DAM POET**
See also CA 65-68; CAAS 5; CANR 24; DLB 5

Klabund 1890-1928.............. **TCLC 44**
See also DLB 66

Klappert, Peter 1942-............. **CLC 57**
See also CA 33-36R; DLB 5

Klein, A(braham) M(oses) 1909-1972 .... **CLC 19; DAB; DAC; DAM MST**
See also CA 101; 37-40R; DLB 68

Klein, Norma 1938-1989 .... **CLC 30**
See also AAYA 2; CA 41-44R; 128; CANR 15, 37; CLR 2, 19; INT CANR-15; JRDA; MAICYA; SAAS 1; SATA 7, 57

Klein, T(heodore) E(ibon) D(onald) 1947- .... **CLC 34**
See also CA 119; CANR 44

Kleist, Heinrich von 1777-1811 .... **NCLC 2, 37; DAM DRAM; SSC 22**
See also DLB 90

Klima, Ivan 1931-..... **CLC 56; DAM NOV**
See also CA 25-28R; CANR 17, 50

Klimentov, Andrei Platonovich 1899-1951
See Platonov, Andrei
See also CA 108

Klinger, Friedrich Maximilian von 1752-1831 .... **NCLC 1**
See also DLB 94

Klopstock, Friedrich Gottlieb 1724-1803 .... **NCLC 11**
See also DLB 97

Knebel, Fletcher 1911-1993 .... **CLC 14**
See also AITN 1; CA 1-4R; 140; CAAS 3; CANR 1, 36; SATA 36; SATA-Obit 75

Knickerbocker, Diedrich
See Irving, Washington

Knight, Etheridge 1931-1991 .... **CLC 40; BLC; DAM POET; PC 14**
See also BW 1; CA 21-24R; 133; CANR 23; DLB 41

Knight, Sarah Kemble 1666-1727 ..... **LC 7**
See also DLB 24

Knister, Raymond 1899-1932...... **TCLC 56**
See also DLB 68

Knowles, John 1926- ...... **CLC 1, 4, 10, 26; DA; DAC; DAM MST, NOV**
See also AAYA 10; CA 17-20R; CANR 40; CDALB 1968-1988; DLB 6; MTCW; SATA 8, 89

Knox, Calvin M.
See Silverberg, Robert

Knye, Cassandra
See Disch, Thomas M(ichael)

Koch, C(hristopher) J(ohn) 1932- ... **CLC 42**
See also CA 127

Koch, Christopher
See Koch, C(hristopher) J(ohn)

Koch, Kenneth 1925- .... **CLC 5, 8, 44; DAM POET**
See also CA 1-4R; CANR 6, 36; DLB 5; INT CANR-36; SATA 65

Kochanowski, Jan 1530-1584........ **LC 10**

Kock, Charles Paul de 1794-1871 .... **NCLC 16**

Koda Shigeyuki 1867-1947
See Rohan, Koda
See also CA 121

Koestler, Arthur 1905-1983 .... **CLC 1, 3, 6, 8, 15, 33**
See also CA 1-4R; 109; CANR 1, 33; CDBLB 1945-1960; DLBY 83; MTCW

Kogawa, Joy Nozomi 1935- ...... **CLC 78; DAC; DAM MST, MULT**
See also CA 101; CANR 19

Kohout, Pavel 1928-.............. **CLC 13**
See also CA 45-48; CANR 3

Koizumi, Yakumo
See Hearn, (Patricio) Lafcadio (Tessima Carlos)

Kolmar, Gertrud 1894-1943....... **TCLC 40**

Komunyakaa, Yusef 1947-...... **CLC 86, 94**
See also CA 147; DLB 120

Konrad, George
See Konrad, Gyoergy

Konrad, Gyoergy 1933- ...... **CLC 4, 10, 73**
See also CA 85-88

Konwicki, Tadeusz 1926-..... **CLC 8, 28, 54**
See also CA 101; CAAS 9; CANR 39; MTCW

Koontz, Dean R(ay) 1945- ...... **CLC 78; DAM NOV, POP**
See also AAYA 9; BEST 89:3, 90:2; CA 108; CANR 19, 36, 52; MTCW

Kopit, Arthur (Lee) 1937- ..... **CLC 1, 18, 33; DAM DRAM**
See also AITN 1; CA 81-84; CABS 3; DLB 7; MTCW

Kops, Bernard 1926-............... **CLC 4**
See also CA 5-8R; DLB 13

Kornbluth, C(yril) M. 1923-1958.... **TCLC 8**
See also CA 105; DLB 8

Korolenko, V. G.
See Korolenko, Vladimir Galaktionovich

Korolenko, Vladimir
See Korolenko, Vladimir Galaktionovich

Korolenko, Vladimir G.
See Korolenko, Vladimir Galaktionovich

Korolenko, Vladimir Galaktionovich 1853-1921 .... **TCLC 22**
See also CA 121

Korzybski, Alfred (Habdank Skarbek) 1879-1950 .... **TCLC 61**
See also CA 123

Kosinski, Jerzy (Nikodem) 1933-1991 .... **CLC 1, 2, 3, 6, 10, 15, 53, 70; DAM NOV**
See also CA 17-20R; 134; CANR 9, 46; DLB 2; DLBY 82; MTCW

Kostelanetz, Richard (Cory) 1940- .. **CLC 28**
See also CA 13-16R; CAAS 8; CANR 38

Kostrowitzki, Wilhelm Apollinaris de 1880-1918
See Apollinaire, Guillaume
See also CA 104

Kotlowitz, Robert 1924-............ **CLC 4**
See also CA 33-36R; CANR 36

Kotzebue, August (Friedrich Ferdinand) von 1761-1819 .... **NCLC 25**
See also DLB 94

Kotzwinkle, William 1938- ... **CLC 5, 14, 35**
See also CA 45-48; CANR 3, 44; CLR 6; MAICYA; SATA 24, 70

Kozol, Jonathan 1936-............ **CLC 17**
See also CA 61-64; CANR 16, 45

Kozoll, Michael 1940(?)- .... **CLC 35**

Kramer, Kathryn 19(?)- .... **CLC 34**

Kramer, Larry 1935- .. **CLC 42; DAM POP**
See also CA 124; 126

Krasicki, Ignacy 1735-1801....... **NCLC 8**

Krasinski, Zygmunt 1812-1859 .... **NCLC 4**

Kraus, Karl 1874-1936............ **TCLC 5**
See also CA 104; DLB 118

Kreve (Mickevicius), Vincas 1882-1954 .... **TCLC 27**

Kristeva, Julia 1941- .... **CLC 77**

Kristofferson, Kris 1936-.......... **CLC 26**
See also CA 104

Krizanc, John 1956-.............. **CLC 57**

Krleza, Miroslav 1893-1981......... **CLC 8**
See also CA 97-100; 105; CANR 50; DLB 147

Kroetsch, Robert 1927- .... **CLC 5, 23, 57; DAC; DAM POET**
See also CA 17-20R; CANR 8, 38; DLB 53; MTCW

Kroetz, Franz
See Kroetz, Franz Xaver

Kroetz, Franz Xaver 1946- .... **CLC 41**
See also CA 130

Kroker, Arthur 1945-............. **CLC 77**

Kropotkin, Peter (Aleksieevich) 1842-1921 .... **TCLC 36**
See also CA 119

Krotkov, Yuri 1917-.............. **CLC 19**
See also CA 102

Author Index

Lardner, Ring(gold) W(ilmer) 1885-1933 . . . . **TCLC 2, 14**
See also CA 104; 131; CDALB 1917-1929; DLB 11, 25, 86; MTCW

Laredo, Betty
See Codrescu, Andrei

Larkin, Maia
See Wojciechowska, Maia (Teresa)

Larkin, Philip (Arthur) 1922-1985 . . . . **CLC 3, 5, 8, 9, 13, 18, 33, 39, 64; DAB; DAM MST, POET**
See also CA 5-8R; 117; CANR 24; CDBLB 1960 to Present; DLB 27; MTCW

Larra (y Sanchez de Castro), Mariano Jose de 1809-1837 . . . . **NCLC 17**

Larsen, Eric 1941- . . . . **CLC 55**
See also CA 132

Larsen, Nella 1891-1964 . . . . **CLC 37; BLC; DAM MULT**
See also BW 1; CA 125; DLB 51

Larson, Charles R(aymond) 1938-. . . **CLC 31**
See also CA 53-56; CANR 4

Las Casas, Bartolome de 1474-1566 . . **LC 31**

Lasker-Schueler, Else 1869-1945 . . **TCLC 57**
See also DLB 66, 124

Latham, Jean Lee 1902-. . . . . **CLC 12**
See also AITN 1; CA 5-8R; CANR 7; MAICYA; SATA 2, 68

Latham, Mavis
See Clark, Mavis Thorpe

Lathen, Emma . . . . **CLC 2**
See also Hennissart, Martha; Latsis, Mary J(ane)

Lathrop, Francis
See Leiber, Fritz (Reuter, Jr.)

Latsis, Mary J(ane)
See Lathen, Emma
See also CA 85-88

Lattimore, Richmond (Alexander) 1906-1984 . . . . **CLC 3**
See also CA 1-4R; 112; CANR 1

Laughlin, James 1914- . . . . **CLC 49**
See also CA 21-24R; CAAS 22; CANR 9, 47; DLB 48

Laurence, (Jean) Margaret (Wemyss) 1926-1987 . . . . **CLC 3, 6, 13, 50, 62; DAC; DAM MST; SSC 7**
See also CA 5-8R; 121; CANR 33; DLB 53; MTCW; SATA-Obit 50

Laurent, Antoine 1952- . . . . **CLC 50**

Lauscher, Hermann
See Hesse, Hermann

Lautreamont, Comte de 1846-1870 . . . . **NCLC 12; SSC 14**

Laverty, Donald
See Blish, James (Benjamin)

Lavin, Mary 1912-1996 . . **CLC 4, 18; SSC 4**
See also CA 9-12R; 151; CANR 33; DLB 15; MTCW

Lavond, Paul Dennis
See Kornbluth, C(yril) M.; Pohl, Frederik

Lawler, Raymond Evenor 1922- . . . . **CLC 58**
See also CA 103

Lawrence, D(avid) H(erbert Richards) 1885-1930 . . . . **TCLC 2, 9, 16, 33, 48, 61; DA; DAB; DAC; DAM MST, NOV, POET; SSC 4, 19; WLC**
See also CA 104; 121; CDBLB 1914-1945; DLB 10, 19, 36, 98, 162; MTCW

Lawrence, T(homas) E(dward) 1888-1935 . . . . **TCLC 18**
See also Dale, Colin
See also CA 115

Lawrence of Arabia
See Lawrence, T(homas) E(dward)

Lawson, Henry (Archibald Hertzberg) 1867-1922 . . . . **TCLC 27; SSC 18**
See also CA 120

Lawton, Dennis
See Faust, Frederick (Schiller)

Laxness, Halldor . . . . **CLC 25**
See also Gudjonsson, Halldor Kiljan

Layamon fl. c. 1200- . . . . **CMLC 10**
See also DLB 146

Laye, Camara 1928-1980 . . . . **CLC 4, 38; BLC; DAM MULT**
See also BW 1; CA 85-88; 97-100; CANR 25; MTCW

Layton, Irving (Peter) 1912- . . . . **CLC 2, 15; DAC; DAM MST, POET**
See also CA 1-4R; CANR 2, 33, 43; DLB 88; MTCW

Lazarus, Emma 1849-1887. . . . . **NCLC 8**

Lazarus, Felix
See Cable, George Washington

Lazarus, Henry
See Slavitt, David R(ytman)

Lea, Joan
See Neufeld, John (Arthur)

Leacock, Stephen (Butler) 1869-1944 . . **TCLC 2; DAC; DAM MST**
See also CA 104; 141; DLB 92

Lear, Edward 1812-1888 . . . . **NCLC 3**
See also CLR 1; DLB 32, 163, 166; MAICYA; SATA 18

Lear, Norman (Milton) 1922- . . . . . . **CLC 12**
See also CA 73-76

Leavis, F(rank) R(aymond) 1895-1978 . . . . **CLC 24**
See also CA 21-24R; 77-80; CANR 44; MTCW

Leavitt, David 1961-. . . **CLC 34; DAM POP**
See also CA 116; 122; CANR 50; DLB 130; INT 122

Leblanc, Maurice (Marie Emile) 1864-1941 . . . . **TCLC 49**
See also CA 110

Lebowitz, Fran(ces Ann) 1951(?)- . . . . **CLC 11, 36**
See also CA 81-84; CANR 14; INT CANR-14; MTCW

Lebrecht, Peter
See Tieck, (Johann) Ludwig

le Carre, John . . . . **CLC 3, 5, 9, 15, 28**
See also Cornwell, David (John Moore)
See also BEST 89:4; CDBLB 1960 to Present; DLB 87

Le Clezio, J(ean) M(arie) G(ustave) 1940- . . . . **CLC 31**
See also CA 116; 128; DLB 83

Leconte de Lisle, Charles-Marie-Rene 1818-1894 . . . . **NCLC 29**

Le Coq, Monsieur
See Simenon, Georges (Jacques Christian)

Leduc, Violette 1907-1972 . . . . **CLC 22**
See also CA 13-14; 33-36R; CAP 1

Ledwidge, Francis 1887(?)-1917 . . . **TCLC 23**
See also CA 123; DLB 20

Lee, Andrea 1953- . . . . . **CLC 36; BLC; DAM MULT**
See also BW 1; CA 125

Lee, Andrew
See Auchincloss, Louis (Stanton)

Lee, Chang-rae 1965- . . . . **CLC 91**
See also CA 148

Lee, Don L. . . . . **CLC 2**
See also Madhubuti, Haki R.

Lee, George W(ashington) 1894-1976 . . . . **CLC 52; BLC; DAM MULT**
See also BW 1; CA 125; DLB 51

Lee, (Nelle) Harper 1926- . . . . **CLC 12, 60; DA; DAB; DAC; DAM MST, NOV; WLC**
See also AAYA 13; CA 13-16R; CANR 51; CDALB 1941-1968; DLB 6; MTCW; SATA 11

Lee, Helen Elaine 1959(?)- . . . . **CLC 86**
See also CA 148

Lee, Julian
See Latham, Jean Lee

Lee, Larry
See Lee, Lawrence

Lee, Laurie 1914- . . . . **CLC 90; DAB; DAM POP**
See also CA 77-80; CANR 33; DLB 27; MTCW

Lee, Lawrence 1941-1990. . . . . **CLC 34**
See also CA 131; CANR 43

Lee, Manfred B(ennington) 1905-1971 . . . . **CLC 11**
See also Queen, Ellery
See also CA 1-4R; 29-32R; CANR 2; DLB 137

Lee, Stan 1922-. . . . . **CLC 17**
See also AAYA 5; CA 108; 111; INT 111

Lee, Tanith 1947- . . . . **CLC 46**
See also AAYA 15; CA 37-40R; CANR 53; SATA 8, 88

Lee, Vernon . . . . **TCLC 5**
See also Paget, Violet
See also DLB 57, 153, 156

Lee, William
See Burroughs, William S(eward)

Lee, Willy
See Burroughs, William S(eward)

Lord, Bette Bao 1938- . . . . **CLC 23**
See also BEST 90:3; CA 107; CANR 41; INT 107; SATA 58

Lord Auch
See Bataille, Georges

Lord Byron
See Byron, George Gordon (Noel)

Lorde, Audre (Geraldine) 1934-1992 . . . . **CLC 18, 71; BLC; DAM MULT, POET; PC 12**
See also BW 1; CA 25-28R; 142; CANR 16, 26, 46; DLB 41; MTCW

Lord Jeffrey
See Jeffrey, Francis

Lorenzini, Carlo 1826-1890
See Collodi, Carlo
See also MAICYA; SATA 29

Lorenzo, Heberto Padilla
See Padilla (Lorenzo), Heberto

Loris
See Hofmannsthal, Hugo von

Loti, Pierre . . . . **TCLC 11**
See also Viaud, (Louis Marie) Julien
See also DLB 123

Louie, David Wong 1954- . . . . **CLC 70**
See also CA 139

Louis, Father M.
See Merton, Thomas

Lovecraft, H(oward) P(hillips) 1890-1937 . . . . **TCLC 4, 22; DAM POP; SSC 3**
See also AAYA 14; CA 104; 133; MTCW

Lovelace, Earl 1935-. . . . . **CLC 51**
See also BW 2; CA 77-80; CANR 41; DLB 125; MTCW

Lovelace, Richard 1618-1657. . . . . **LC 24**
See also DLB 131

Lowell, Amy 1874-1925 . . . . **TCLC 1, 8; DAM POET; PC 13**
See also CA 104; 151; DLB 54, 140

Lowell, James Russell 1819-1891 . . **NCLC 2**
See also CDALB 1640-1865; DLB 1, 11, 64, 79

Lowell, Robert (Traill Spence, Jr.) 1917-1977 . . . **CLC 1, 2, 3, 4, 5, 8, 9, 11, 15, 37; DA; DAB; DAC; DAM MST, NOV; PC 3; WLC**
See also CA 9-12R; 73-76; CABS 2; CANR 26; DLB 5; MTCW

Lowndes, Marie Adelaide (Belloc) 1868-1947 . . . . **TCLC 12**
See also CA 107; DLB 70

Lowry, (Clarence) Malcolm 1909-1957 . . . . **TCLC 6, 40**
See also CA 105; 131; CDBLB 1945-1960; DLB 15; MTCW

Lowry, Mina Gertrude 1882-1966
See Loy, Mina
See also CA 113

Loxsmith, John
See Brunner, John (Kilian Houston)

Loy, Mina . . . . **CLC 28; DAM POET; PC 16**
See also Lowry, Mina Gertrude
See also DLB 4, 54

Loyson-Bridet
See Schwob, (Mayer Andre) Marcel

Lucas, Craig 1951- . . . . **CLC 64**
See also CA 137

Lucas, George 1944-. . . . . **CLC 16**
See also AAYA 1; CA 77-80; CANR 30; SATA 56

Lucas, Hans
See Godard, Jean-Luc

Lucas, Victoria
See Plath, Sylvia

Ludlam, Charles 1943-1987 . . . . . **CLC 46, 50**
See also CA 85-88; 122

Ludlum, Robert 1927- . . . **CLC 22, 43; DAM NOV, POP**
See also AAYA 10; BEST 89:1, 90:3; CA 33-36R; CANR 25, 41; DLBY 82; MTCW

Ludwig, Ken. . . . . **CLC 60**

Ludwig, Otto 1813-1865. . . . . **NCLC 4**
See also DLB 129

Lugones, Leopoldo 1874-1938 . . . . . **TCLC 15**
See also CA 116; 131; HW

Lu Hsun 1881-1936 . . . . . . **TCLC 3; SSC 20**
See also Shu-Jen, Chou

Lukacs, George . . . . **CLC 24**
See also Lukacs, Gyorgy (Szegeny von)

Lukacs, Gyorgy (Szegeny von) 1885-1971
See Lukacs, George
See also CA 101; 29-32R

Luke, Peter (Ambrose Cyprian) 1919-1995 . . . . **CLC 38**
See also CA 81-84; 147; DLB 13

Lunar, Dennis
See Mungo, Raymond

Lurie, Alison 1926-. . . . . **CLC 4, 5, 18, 39**
See also CA 1-4R; CANR 2, 17, 50; DLB 2; MTCW; SATA 46

Lustig, Arnost 1926-. . . . . **CLC 56**
See also AAYA 3; CA 69-72; CANR 47; SATA 56

Luther, Martin 1483-1546 . . . . **LC 9**

Luxemburg, Rosa 1870(?)-1919. . . . **TCLC 63**
See also CA 118

Luzi, Mario 1914-. . . . . **CLC 13**
See also CA 61-64; CANR 9; DLB 128

L'Ymagier
See Gourmont, Remy (-Marie-Charles) de

Lynch, B. Suarez
See Bioy Casares, Adolfo; Borges, Jorge Luis

Lynch, David (K.) 1946-. . . . . **CLC 66**
See also CA 124; 129

Lynch, James
See Andreyev, Leonid (Nikolaevich)

Lynch Davis, B.
See Bioy Casares, Adolfo; Borges, Jorge Luis

Lyndsay, Sir David 1490-1555 . . . . . . **LC 20**

Lynn, Kenneth S(chuyler) 1923- . . . . **CLC 50**
See also CA 1-4R; CANR 3, 27

Lynx
See West, Rebecca

Lyons, Marcus
See Blish, James (Benjamin)

Lyre, Pinchbeck
See Sassoon, Siegfried (Lorraine)

Lytle, Andrew (Nelson) 1902-1995 . . **CLC 22**
See also CA 9-12R; 150; DLB 6; DLBY 95

Lyttelton, George 1709-1773 . . . . **LC 10**

Maas, Peter 1929- . . . . **CLC 29**
See also CA 93-96; INT 93-96

Macaulay, Rose 1881-1958 . . . . . **TCLC 7, 44**
See also CA 104; DLB 36

Macaulay, Thomas Babington 1800-1859 . . . . **NCLC 42**
See also CDBLB 1832-1890; DLB 32, 55

MacBeth, George (Mann) 1932-1992 . . . . **CLC 2, 5, 9**
See also CA 25-28R; 136; DLB 40; MTCW; SATA 4; SATA-Obit 70

MacCaig, Norman (Alexander) 1910- . . . . . **CLC 36; DAB; DAM POET**
See also CA 9-12R; CANR 3, 34; DLB 27

MacCarthy, (Sir Charles Otto) Desmond 1877-1952 . . . . **TCLC 36**

MacDiarmid, Hugh . . . . **CLC 2, 4, 11, 19, 63; PC 9**
See also Grieve, C(hristopher) M(urray)
See also CDBLB 1945-1960; DLB 20

MacDonald, Anson
See Heinlein, Robert A(nson)

Macdonald, Cynthia 1928-. . . . . . **CLC 13, 19**
See also CA 49-52; CANR 4, 44; DLB 105

MacDonald, George 1824-1905 . . . . . **TCLC 9**
See also CA 106; 137; DLB 18, 163; MAICYA; SATA 33

Macdonald, John
See Millar, Kenneth

MacDonald, John D(ann) 1916-1986 . . . . **CLC 3, 27, 44; DAM NOV, POP**
See also CA 1-4R; 121; CANR 1, 19; DLB 8; DLBY 86; MTCW

Macdonald, John Ross
See Millar, Kenneth

Macdonald, Ross. . . . . **CLC 1, 2, 3, 14, 34, 41**
See also Millar, Kenneth
See also DLBD 6

MacDougal, John
See Blish, James (Benjamin)

MacEwen, Gwendolyn (Margaret) 1941-1987 . . . . **CLC 13, 55**
See also CA 9-12R; 124; CANR 7, 22; DLB 53; SATA 50; SATA-Obit 55

Macha, Karel Hynek 1810-1846 . . **NCLC 46**

Machado (y Ruiz), Antonio 1875-1939 . . . . **TCLC 3**
See also CA 104; DLB 108

Machado de Assis, Joaquim Maria 1839-1908 . . . . **TCLC 10; BLC**
See also CA 107

Machen, Arthur. . . . . **TCLC 4; SSC 20**
See also Jones, Arthur Llewellyn
See also DLB 36, 156

Machiavelli, Niccolo 1469-1527 . . . . . . **LC 8; DA; DAB; DAC; DAM MST**

MacInnes, Colin 1914-1976 . . . . . . **CLC 4, 23**
See also CA 69-72; 65-68; CANR 21; DLB 14; MTCW

MacInnes, Helen (Clark) 1907-1985 . . . . . **CLC 27, 39; DAM POP**
See also CA 1-4R; 117; CANR 1, 28; DLB 87; MTCW; SATA 22; SATA-Obit 44

Mackay, Mary 1855-1924
See Corelli, Marie
See also CA 118

Mackenzie, Compton (Edward Montague) 1883-1972 . . . . **CLC 18**
See also CA 21-22; 37-40R; CAP 2; DLB 34, 100

Mackenzie, Henry 1745-1831 . . . . **NCLC 41**
See also DLB 39

Mackintosh, Elizabeth 1896(?)-1952
See Tey, Josephine
See also CA 110

MacLaren, James
See Grieve, C(hristopher) M(urray)

Mac Laverty, Bernard 1942- . . . . **CLC 31**
See also CA 116; 118; CANR 43; INT 118

MacLean, Alistair (Stuart) 1922-1987 . . . . **CLC 3, 13, 50, 63; DAM POP**
See also CA 57-60; 121; CANR 28; MTCW; SATA 23; SATA-Obit 50

Maclean, Norman (Fitzroy) 1902-1990 . . . . **CLC 78; DAM POP; SSC 13**
See also CA 102; 132; CANR 49

MacLeish, Archibald 1892-1982 . . . . **CLC 3, 8, 14, 68; DAM POET**
See also CA 9-12R; 106; CANR 33; DLB 4, 7, 45; DLBY 82; MTCW

MacLennan, (John) Hugh 1907-1990 . . . . **CLC 2, 14, 92; DAC; DAM MST**
See also CA 5-8R; 142; CANR 33; DLB 68; MTCW

MacLeod, Alistair 1936- . . . . . . **CLC 56; DAC; DAM MST**
See also CA 123; DLB 60

MacNeice, (Frederick) Louis 1907-1963 . . . . . . **CLC 1, 4, 10, 53; DAB; DAM POET**
See also CA 85-88; DLB 10, 20; MTCW

MacNeill, Dand
See Fraser, George MacDonald

Macpherson, James 1736-1796 . . . . . . **LC 29**
See also DLB 109

Macpherson, (Jean) Jay 1931- . . . . . . **CLC 14**
See also CA 5-8R; DLB 53

MacShane, Frank 1927- . . . . **CLC 39**
See also CA 9-12R; CANR 3, 33; DLB 111

Macumber, Mari
See Sandoz, Mari(e Susette)

Madach, Imre 1823-1864 . . . . **NCLC 19**

Madden, (Jerry) David 1933- . . . . **CLC 5, 15**
See also CA 1-4R; CAAS 3; CANR 4, 45; DLB 6; MTCW

Maddern, Al(an)
See Ellison, Harlan (Jay)

Madhubuti, Haki R. 1942- . . . . **CLC 6, 73; BLC; DAM MULT, POET; PC 5**
See also Lee, Don L.
See also BW 2; CA 73-76; CANR 24, 51; DLB 5, 41; DLBD 8

Maepenn, Hugh
See Kuttner, Henry

Maepenn, K. H.
See Kuttner, Henry

Maeterlinck, Maurice 1862-1949 . . . . . . **TCLC 3; DAM DRAM**
See also CA 104; 136; SATA 66

Maginn, William 1794-1842. . . . . . . **NCLC 8**
See also DLB 110, 159

Mahapatra, Jayanta 1928- . . . . **CLC 33; DAM MULT**
See also CA 73-76; CAAS 9; CANR 15, 33

Mahfouz, Naguib (Abdel Aziz Al-Sabilgi) 1911(?)-
See Mahfuz, Najib
See also BEST 89:2; CA 128; DAM NOV; MTCW

Mahfuz, Najib . . . . **CLC 52, 55**
See also Mahfouz, Naguib (Abdel Aziz Al-Sabilgi)
See also DLBY 88

Mahon, Derek 1941- . . . . **CLC 27**
See also CA 113; 128; DLB 40

Mailer, Norman 1923- . . . . . . **CLC 1, 2, 3, 4, 5, 8, 11, 14, 28, 39, 74; DA; DAB; DAC; DAM MST, NOV, POP**
See also AITN 2; CA 9-12R; CABS 1; CANR 28; CDALB 1968-1988; DLB 2, 16, 28; DLBD 3; DLBY 80, 83; MTCW

Maillet, Antonine 1929- . . . . . . **CLC 54; DAC**
See also CA 115; 120; CANR 46; DLB 60; INT 120

Mais, Roger 1905-1955 . . . . **TCLC 8**
See also BW 1; CA 105; 124; DLB 125; MTCW

Maistre, Joseph de 1753-1821 . . . . **NCLC 37**

Maitland, Frederic 1850-1906 . . . . . **TCLC 65**

Maitland, Sara (Louise) 1950- . . . . . . **CLC 49**
See also CA 69-72; CANR 13

Major, Clarence 1936- . . . . **CLC 3, 19, 48; BLC; DAM MULT**
See also BW 2; CA 21-24R; CAAS 6; CANR 13, 25, 53; DLB 33

Major, Kevin (Gerald) 1949- . . . . **CLC 26; DAC**
See also AAYA 16; CA 97-100; CANR 21, 38; CLR 11; DLB 60; INT CANR-21; JRDA; MAICYA; SATA 32, 82

Maki, James
See Ozu, Yasujiro

Malabaila, Damiano
See Levi, Primo

Malamud, Bernard 1914-1986 . . . . . . **CLC 1, 2, 3, 5, 8, 9, 11, 18, 27, 44, 78, 85; DA; DAB; DAC; DAM MST, NOV, POP; SSC 15; WLC**
See also AAYA 16; CA 5-8R; 118; CABS 1; CANR 28; CDALB 1941-1968; DLB 2, 28, 152; DLBY 80, 86; MTCW

Malaparte, Curzio 1898-1957 . . . . . **TCLC 52**

Malcolm, Dan
See Silverberg, Robert

Malcolm X . . . . **CLC 82; BLC**
See also Little, Malcolm

Malherbe, Francois de 1555-1628 . . . . . **LC 5**

Mallarme, Stephane 1842-1898 . . . . **NCLC 4, 41; DAM POET; PC 4**

Mallet-Joris, Francoise 1930- . . . . . . **CLC 11**
See also CA 65-68; CANR 17; DLB 83

Malley, Ern
See McAuley, James Phillip

Mallowan, Agatha Christie
See Christie, Agatha (Mary Clarissa)

Maloff, Saul 1922- . . . . **CLC 5**
See also CA 33-36R

Malone, Louis
See MacNeice, (Frederick) Louis

Malone, Michael (Christopher) 1942- . . . . **CLC 43**
See also CA 77-80; CANR 14, 32

Malory, (Sir) Thomas 1410(?)-1471(?) . . . . . . **LC 11; DA; DAB; DAC; DAM MST**
See also CDBLB Before 1660; DLB 146; SATA 59; SATA-Brief 33

Malouf, (George Joseph) David 1934- . . . . **CLC 28, 86**
See also CA 124; CANR 50

Malraux, (Georges-)Andre 1901-1976 . . . . . . **CLC 1, 4, 9, 13, 15, 57; DAM NOV**
See also CA 21-22; 69-72; CANR 34; CAP 2; DLB 72; MTCW

Malzberg, Barry N(athaniel) 1939- . . . **CLC 7**
See also CA 61-64; CAAS 4; CANR 16; DLB 8

Mamet, David (Alan) 1947- . . . . **CLC 9, 15, 34, 46, 91; DAM DRAM; DC 4**
See also AAYA 3; CA 81-84; CABS 3; CANR 15, 41; DLB 7; MTCW

Mamoulian, Rouben (Zachary) 1897-1987 . . . . **CLC 16**
See also CA 25-28R; 124

Mandelstam, Osip (Emilievich) 1891(?)-1938(?) . . . . . . **TCLC 2, 6; PC 14**
See also CA 104; 150

Mander, (Mary) Jane 1877-1949 . . . **TCLC 31**

Mandiargues, Andre Pieyre de . . . . **CLC 41**
See also Pieyre de Mandiargues, Andre
See also DLB 83

Mandrake, Ethel Belle
See Thurman, Wallace (Henry)

Mangan, James Clarence 1803-1849 . . . . **NCLC 27**

Maniere, J.-E.
See Giraudoux, (Hippolyte) Jean

Manley, (Mary) Delariviere 1672(?)-1724 .... **LC 1**
See also DLB 39, 80

Mann, Abel
See Creasey, John

Mann, (Luiz) Heinrich 1871-1950... **TCLC 9**
See also CA 106; DLB 66

Mann, (Paul) Thomas 1875-1955 .... **TCLC 2, 8, 14, 21, 35, 44, 60; DA; DAB; DAC; DAM MST, NOV; SSC 5; WLC**
See also CA 104; 128; DLB 66; MTCW

Mannheim, Karl 1893-1947....... **TCLC 65**

Manning, David
See Faust, Frederick (Schiller)

Manning, Frederic 1887(?)-1935... **TCLC 25**
See also CA 124

Manning, Olivia 1915-1980...... **CLC 5, 19**
See also CA 5-8R; 101; CANR 29; MTCW

Mano, D. Keith 1942- .... **CLC 2, 10**
See also CA 25-28R; CAAS 6; CANR 26; DLB 6

Mansfield, Katherine .. **TCLC 2, 8, 39; DAB; SSC 9, 23; WLC**
See also Beauchamp, Kathleen Mansfield
See also DLB 162

Manso, Peter 1940- .... **CLC 39**
See also CA 29-32R; CANR 44

Mantecon, Juan Jimenez
See Jimenez (Mantecon), Juan Ramon

Manton, Peter
See Creasey, John

Man Without a Spleen, A
See Chekhov, Anton (Pavlovich)

Manzoni, Alessandro 1785-1873.. **NCLC 29**

Mapu, Abraham (ben Jekutiel) 1808-1867 .... **NCLC 18**

Mara, Sally
See Queneau, Raymond

Marat, Jean Paul 1743-1793........ **LC 10**

Marcel, Gabriel Honore 1889-1973 .... **CLC 15**
See also CA 102; 45-48; MTCW

Marchbanks, Samuel
See Davies, (William) Robertson

Marchi, Giacomo
See Bassani, Giorgio

Margulies, Donald................. **CLC 76**

Marie de France c. 12th cent. -.... **CMLC 8**

Marie de l'Incarnation 1599-1672.... **LC 10**

Mariner, Scott
See Pohl, Frederik

Marinetti, Filippo Tommaso 1876-1944 .... **TCLC 10**
See also CA 107; DLB 114

Marivaux, Pierre Carlet de Chamblain de 1688-1763 .... **LC 4**

Markandaya, Kamala .... **CLC 8, 38**
See also Taylor, Kamala (Purnaiya)

Markfield, Wallace 1926-........... **CLC 8**
See also CA 69-72; CAAS 3; DLB 2, 28

Markham, Edwin 1852-1940...... **TCLC 47**
See also DLB 54

Markham, Robert
See Amis, Kingsley (William)

Marks, J
See Highwater, Jamake (Mamake)

Marks-Highwater, J
See Highwater, Jamake (Mamake)

Markson, David M(errill) 1927-.... **CLC 67**
See also CA 49-52; CANR 1

Marley, Bob...................... **CLC 17**
See also Marley, Robert Nesta

Marley, Robert Nesta 1945-1981
See Marley, Bob
See also CA 107; 103

Marlowe, Christopher 1564-1593 ..... **LC 22; DA; DAB; DAC; DAM DRAM, MST; DC 1; WLC**
See also CDBLB Before 1660; DLB 62

Marmontel, Jean-Francois 1723-1799 .... **LC 2**

Marquand, John P(hillips) 1893-1960 .... **CLC 2, 10**
See also CA 85-88; DLB 9, 102

Marques, Rene 1919-1979 ...... **CLC 96; DAM MULT; HLC**
See also CA 97-100; 85-88; DLB 113; HW

Marquez, Gabriel (Jose) Garcia
See Garcia Marquez, Gabriel (Jose)

Marquis, Don(ald Robert Perry) 1878-1937 .... **TCLC 7**
See also CA 104; DLB 11, 25

Marric, J. J.
See Creasey, John

Marrow, Bernard
See Moore, Brian

Marryat, Frederick 1792-1848 .... **NCLC 3**
See also DLB 21, 163

Marsden, James
See Creasey, John

Marsh, (Edith) Ngaio 1899-1982 ...... **CLC 7, 53; DAM POP**
See also CA 9-12R; CANR 6; DLB 77; MTCW

Marshall, Garry 1934-............ **CLC 17**
See also AAYA 3; CA 111; SATA 60

Marshall, Paule 1929- .... **CLC 27, 72; BLC; DAM MULT; SSC 3**
See also BW 2; CA 77-80; CANR 25; DLB 157; MTCW

Marsten, Richard
See Hunter, Evan

Marston, John 1576-1634 .... **LC 33; DAM DRAM**
See also DLB 58

Martha, Henry
See Harris, Mark

Martial c. 40-c. 104 .... **PC 10**

Martin, Ken
See Hubbard, L(afayette) Ron(ald)

Martin, Richard
See Creasey, John

Martin, Steve 1945-............... **CLC 30**
See also CA 97-100; CANR 30; MTCW

Martin, Valerie 1948-............. **CLC 89**
See also BEST 90:2; CA 85-88; CANR 49

Martin, Violet Florence 1862-1915 .... **TCLC 51**

Martin, Webber
See Silverberg, Robert

Martindale, Patrick Victor
See White, Patrick (Victor Martindale)

Martin du Gard, Roger 1881-1958 .... **TCLC 24**
See also CA 118; DLB 65

Martineau, Harriet 1802-1876.... **NCLC 26**
See also DLB 21, 55, 159, 163, 166; YABC 2

Martines, Julia
See O'Faolain, Julia

Martinez, Jacinto Benavente y
See Benavente (y Martinez), Jacinto

Martinez Ruiz, Jose 1873-1967
See Azorin; Ruiz, Jose Martinez
See also CA 93-96; HW

Martinez Sierra, Gregorio 1881-1947 .... **TCLC 6**
See also CA 115

Martinez Sierra, Maria (de la O'LeJarraga) 1874-1974 .... **TCLC 6**
See also CA 115

Martinsen, Martin
See Follett, Ken(neth Martin)

Martinson, Harry (Edmund) 1904-1978 .... **CLC 14**
See also CA 77-80; CANR 34

Marut, Ret
See Traven, B.

Marut, Robert
See Traven, B.

Marvell, Andrew 1621-1678 ...... **LC 4; DA; DAB; DAC; DAM MST, POET; PC 10; WLC**
See also CDBLB 1660-1789; DLB 131

Marx, Karl (Heinrich) 1818-1883 .... **NCLC 17**
See also DLB 129

Masaoka Shiki................... **TCLC 18**
See also Masaoka Tsunenori

Masaoka Tsunenori 1867-1902
See Masaoka Shiki
See also CA 117

Masefield, John (Edward) 1878-1967 .... **CLC 11, 47; DAM POET**
See also CA 19-20; 25-28R; CANR 33; CAP 2; CDBLB 1890-1914; DLB 10, 19, 153, 160; MTCW; SATA 19

Maso, Carole 19(?)- .... **CLC 44**

Mason, Bobbie Ann 1940- .... **CLC 28, 43, 82; SSC 4**
See also AAYA 5; CA 53-56; CANR 11, 31; DLBY 87; INT CANR-31; MTCW

Mason, Ernst
See Pohl, Frederik

Mason, Lee W.
See Malzberg, Barry N(athaniel)

Mason, Nick 1945- . . . . **CLC 35**

Mason, Tally
See Derleth, August (William)

Mass, William
See Gibson, William

Masters, Edgar Lee
1868-1950 . . . . . . **TCLC 2, 25; DA; DAC; DAM MST, POET; PC 1**
See also CA 104; 133; CDALB 1865-1917; DLB 54; MTCW

Masters, Hilary 1928- . . . . **CLC 48**
See also CA 25-28R; CANR 13, 47

Mastrosimone, William 19(?)- . . . . . . **CLC 36**

Mathe, Albert
See Camus, Albert

Matheson, Richard Burton 1926- . . . **CLC 37**
See also CA 97-100; DLB 8, 44; INT 97-100

Mathews, Harry 1930- . . . . **CLC 6, 52**
See also CA 21-24R; CAAS 6; CANR 18, 40

Mathews, John Joseph
1894-1979 . . . . . . **CLC 84; DAM MULT**
See also CA 19-20; 142; CANR 45; CAP 2; NNAL

Mathias, Roland (Glyn) 1915- . . . . . . **CLC 45**
See also CA 97-100; CANR 19, 41; DLB 27

Matsuo Basho 1644-1694 . . . . **PC 3**
See also DAM POET

Mattheson, Rodney
See Creasey, John

Matthews, Greg 1949- . . . . **CLC 45**
See also CA 135

Matthews, William 1942- . . . . **CLC 40**
See also CA 29-32R; CAAS 18; CANR 12; DLB 5

Matthias, John (Edward) 1941- . . . . . . **CLC 9**
See also CA 33-36R

Matthiessen, Peter
1927- . . . . **CLC 5, 7, 11, 32, 64; DAM NOV**
See also AAYA 6; BEST 90:4; CA 9-12R; CANR 21, 50; DLB 6; MTCW; SATA 27

Maturin, Charles Robert
1780(?)-1824 . . . . **NCLC 6**

Matute (Ausejo), Ana Maria
1925- . . . . **CLC 11**
See also CA 89-92; MTCW

Maugham, W. S.
See Maugham, W(illiam) Somerset

Maugham, W(illiam) Somerset
1874-1965 . . . . **CLC 1, 11, 15, 67, 93; DA; DAB; DAC; DAM DRAM, MST, NOV; SSC 8; WLC**
See also CA 5-8R; 25-28R; CANR 40; CDBLB 1914-1945; DLB 10, 36, 77, 100, 162; MTCW; SATA 54

Maugham, William Somerset
See Maugham, W(illiam) Somerset

Maupassant, (Henri Rene Albert) Guy de
1850-1893 . . . . . **NCLC 1, 42; DA; DAB; DAC; DAM MST; SSC 1; WLC**
See also DLB 123

Maupin, Armistead
1944- . . . . **CLC 95; DAM POP**
See also CA 125; 130; INT 130

Maurhut, Richard
See Traven, B.

Mauriac, Claude 1914-1996 . . . . **CLC 9**
See also CA 89-92; 152; DLB 83

Mauriac, Francois (Charles)
1885-1970 . . . . **CLC 4, 9, 56**
See also CA 25-28; CAP 2; DLB 65; MTCW

Mavor, Osborne Henry 1888-1951
See Bridie, James
See also CA 104

Maxwell, William (Keepers, Jr.)
1908- . . . . **CLC 19**
See also CA 93-96; DLBY 80; INT 93-96

May, Elaine 1932- . . . . **CLC 16**
See also CA 124; 142; DLB 44

Mayakovski, Vladimir (Vladimirovich)
1893-1930 . . . . **TCLC 4, 18**
See also CA 104

Mayhew, Henry 1812-1887 . . . . . . **NCLC 31**
See also DLB 18, 55

Mayle, Peter 1939(?)- . . . . **CLC 89**
See also CA 139

Maynard, Joyce 1953- . . . . **CLC 23**
See also CA 111; 129

Mayne, William (James Carter)
1928- . . . . **CLC 12**
See also CA 9-12R; CANR 37; CLR 25; JRDA; MAICYA; SAAS 11; SATA 6, 68

Mayo, Jim
See L'Amour, Louis (Dearborn)

Maysles, Albert 1926- . . . . **CLC 16**
See also CA 29-32R

Maysles, David 1932- . . . . **CLC 16**

Mazer, Norma Fox 1931- . . . . **CLC 26**
See also AAYA 5; CA 69-72; CANR 12, 32; CLR 23; JRDA; MAICYA; SAAS 1; SATA 24, 67

Mazzini, Guiseppe 1805-1872 . . . . **NCLC 34**

McAuley, James Phillip
1917-1976 . . . . **CLC 45**
See also CA 97-100

McBain, Ed
See Hunter, Evan

McBrien, William Augustine
1930- . . . . **CLC 44**
See also CA 107

McCaffrey, Anne (Inez)
1926- . . . . . . **CLC 17; DAM NOV, POP**
See also AAYA 6; AITN 2; BEST 89:2; CA 25-28R; CANR 15, 35; DLB 8; JRDA; MAICYA; MTCW; SAAS 11; SATA 8, 70

McCall, Nathan 1955(?)- . . . . **CLC 86**
See also CA 146

McCann, Arthur
See Campbell, John W(ood, Jr.)

McCann, Edson
See Pohl, Frederik

McCarthy, Charles, Jr. 1933-
See McCarthy, Cormac
See also CANR 42; DAM POP

McCarthy, Cormac 1933- . . . . . **CLC 4, 57, 59**
See also McCarthy, Charles, Jr.
See also DLB 6, 143

McCarthy, Mary (Therese)
1912-1989 . . . **CLC 1, 3, 5, 14, 24, 39, 59**
See also CA 5-8R; 129; CANR 16, 50; DLB 2; DLBY 81; INT CANR-16; MTCW

McCartney, (James) Paul
1942- . . . . **CLC 12, 35**
See also CA 146

McCauley, Stephen (D.) 1955- . . . . . **CLC 50**
See also CA 141

McClure, Michael (Thomas)
1932- . . . . **CLC 6, 10**
See also CA 21-24R; CANR 17, 46; DLB 16

McCorkle, Jill (Collins) 1958- . . . . . . **CLC 51**
See also CA 121; DLBY 87

McCourt, James 1941- . . . . **CLC 5**
See also CA 57-60

McCoy, Horace (Stanley)
1897-1955 . . . . **TCLC 28**
See also CA 108; DLB 9

McCrae, John 1872-1918 . . . . **TCLC 12**
See also CA 109; DLB 92

McCreigh, James
See Pohl, Frederik

McCullers, (Lula) Carson (Smith)
1917-1967 . . . . **CLC 1, 4, 10, 12, 48; DA; DAB; DAC; DAM MST, NOV; SSC 9; WLC**
See also CA 5-8R; 25-28R; CABS 1, 3; CANR 18; CDALB 1941-1968; DLB 2, 7; MTCW; SATA 27

McCulloch, John Tyler
See Burroughs, Edgar Rice

McCullough, Colleen
1938(?)- . . . . **CLC 27; DAM NOV, POP**
See also CA 81-84; CANR 17, 46; MTCW

McDermott, Alice 1953- . . . . **CLC 90**
See also CA 109; CANR 40

McElroy, Joseph 1930- . . . . **CLC 5, 47**
See also CA 17-20R

McEwan, Ian (Russell)
1948- . . . . **CLC 13, 66; DAM NOV**
See also BEST 90:4; CA 61-64; CANR 14, 41; DLB 14; MTCW

McFadden, David 1940- . . . . **CLC 48**
See also CA 104; DLB 60; INT 104

McFarland, Dennis 1950- . . . . **CLC 65**

McGahern, John
1934- . . . . **CLC 5, 9, 48; SSC 17**
See also CA 17-20R; CANR 29; DLB 14; MTCW

McGinley, Patrick (Anthony)
1937- . . . . **CLC 41**
See also CA 120; 127; INT 127

McGinley, Phyllis 1905-1978 . . . . . . **CLC 14**
See also CA 9-12R; 77-80; CANR 19; DLB 11, 48; SATA 2, 44; SATA-Obit 24

McGinniss, Joe 1942- . . . . **CLC 32**
See also AITN 2; BEST 89:2; CA 25-28R; CANR 26; INT CANR-26

McGivern, Maureen Daly
See Daly, Maureen

McGrath, Patrick 1950-........... **CLC 55**
See also CA 136

McGrath, Thomas (Matthew)
1916-1990 .... **CLC 28, 59; DAM POET**
See also CA 9-12R; 132; CANR 6, 33; MTCW; SATA 41; SATA-Obit 66

McGuane, Thomas (Francis III)
1939- .... **CLC 3, 7, 18, 45**
See also AITN 2; CA 49-52; CANR 5, 24, 49; DLB 2; DLBY 80; INT CANR-24; MTCW

McGuckian, Medbh
1950- .... **CLC 48; DAM POET**
See also CA 143; DLB 40

McHale, Tom 1942(?)-1982....... **CLC 3, 5**
See also AITN 1; CA 77-80; 106

McIlvanney, William 1936-........ **CLC 42**
See also CA 25-28R; DLB 14

McIlwraith, Maureen Mollie Hunter
See Hunter, Mollie
See also SATA 2

McInerney, Jay
1955- .... **CLC 34; DAM POP**
See also AAYA 18; CA 116; 123; CANR 45; INT 123

McIntyre, Vonda N(eel) 1948- ..... **CLC 18**
See also CA 81-84; CANR 17, 34; MTCW

McKay, Claude
.... **TCLC 7, 41; BLC; DAB; PC 2**
See also McKay, Festus Claudius
See also DLB 4, 45, 51, 117

McKay, Festus Claudius 1889-1948
See McKay, Claude
See also BW 1; CA 104; 124; DA; DAC; DAM MST, MULT, NOV, POET; MTCW; WLC

McKuen, Rod 1933-............. **CLC 1, 3**
See also AITN 1; CA 41-44R; CANR 40

McLoughlin, R. B.
See Mencken, H(enry) L(ouis)

McLuhan, (Herbert) Marshall
1911-1980 .... **CLC 37, 83**
See also CA 9-12R; 102; CANR 12, 34; DLB 88; INT CANR-12; MTCW

McMillan, Terry (L.)
1951- .... **CLC 50, 61; DAM MULT, NOV, POP**
See also BW 2; CA 140

McMurtry, Larry (Jeff)
1936- .... **CLC 2, 3, 7, 11, 27, 44; DAM NOV, POP**
See also AAYA 15; AITN 2; BEST 89:2; CA 5-8R; CANR 19, 43; CDALB 1968-1988; DLB 2, 143; DLBY 80, 87; MTCW

McNally, T. M. 1961- .... **CLC 82**

McNally, Terrence
1939- ... **CLC 4, 7, 41, 91; DAM DRAM**
See also CA 45-48; CANR 2; DLB 7

McNamer, Deirdre 1950-.......... **CLC 70**

McNeile, Herman Cyril 1888-1937
See Sapper
See also DLB 77

McNickle, (William) D'Arcy
1904-1977 ...... **CLC 89; DAM MULT**
See also CA 9-12R; 85-88; CANR 5, 45; NNAL; SATA-Obit 22

McPhee, John (Angus) 1931- ...... **CLC 36**
See also BEST 90:1; CA 65-68; CANR 20, 46; MTCW

McPherson, James Alan
1943- .... **CLC 19, 77**
See also BW 1; CA 25-28R; CAAS 17; CANR 24; DLB 38; MTCW

McPherson, William (Alexander)
1933- .... **CLC 34**
See also CA 69-72; CANR 28; INT CANR-28

Mead, Margaret 1901-1978........ **CLC 37**
See also AITN 1; CA 1-4R; 81-84; CANR 4; MTCW; SATA-Obit 20

Meaker, Marijane (Agnes) 1927-
See Kerr, M. E.
See also CA 107; CANR 37; INT 107; JRDA; MAICYA; MTCW; SATA 20, 61

Medoff, Mark (Howard)
1940- .... **CLC 6, 23; DAM DRAM**
See also AITN 1; CA 53-56; CANR 5; DLB 7; INT CANR-5

Medvedev, P. N.
See Bakhtin, Mikhail Mikhailovich

Meged, Aharon
See Megged, Aharon

Meged, Aron
See Megged, Aharon

Megged, Aharon 1920-............. **CLC 9**
See also CA 49-52; CAAS 13; CANR 1

Mehta, Ved (Parkash) 1934-....... **CLC 37**
See also CA 1-4R; CANR 2, 23; MTCW

Melanter
See Blackmore, R(ichard) D(oddridge)

Melikow, Loris
See Hofmannsthal, Hugo von

Melmoth, Sebastian
See Wilde, Oscar (Fingal O'Flahertie Wills)

Meltzer, Milton 1915-............ **CLC 26**
See also AAYA 8; CA 13-16R; CANR 38; CLR 13; DLB 61; JRDA; MAICYA; SAAS 1; SATA 1, 50, 80

Melville, Herman
1819-1891 ..... **NCLC 3, 12, 29, 45, 49; DA; DAB; DAC; DAM MST, NOV; SSC 1, 17; WLC**
See also CDALB 1640-1865; DLB 3, 74; SATA 59

Menander
c. 342B.C.-c. 292B.C......... **CMLC 9; DAM DRAM; DC 3**

Mencken, H(enry) L(ouis)
1880-1956 .... **TCLC 13**
See also CA 105; 125; CDALB 1917-1929; DLB 11, 29, 63, 137; MTCW

Mercer, David
1928-1980 .... **CLC 5; DAM DRAM**
See also CA 9-12R; 102; CANR 23; DLB 13; MTCW

Merchant, Paul
See Ellison, Harlan (Jay)

Meredith, George
1828-1909 .. **TCLC 17, 43; DAM POET**
See also CA 117; CDBLB 1832-1890; DLB 18, 35, 57, 159

Meredith, William (Morris)
1919- .. **CLC 4, 13, 22, 55; DAM POET**
See also CA 9-12R; CAAS 14; CANR 6, 40; DLB 5

Merezhkovsky, Dmitry Sergeyevich
1865-1941 .... **TCLC 29**

Merimee, Prosper
1803-1870 .... **NCLC 6; SSC 7**
See also DLB 119

Merkin, Daphne 1954-............ **CLC 44**
See also CA 123

Merlin, Arthur
See Blish, James (Benjamin)

Merrill, James (Ingram)
1926-1995 .... **CLC 2, 3, 6, 8, 13, 18, 34, 91; DAM POET**
See also CA 13-16R; 147; CANR 10, 49; DLB 5, 165; DLBY 85; INT CANR-10; MTCW

Merriman, Alex
See Silverberg, Robert

Merritt, E. B.
See Waddington, Miriam

Merton, Thomas
1915-1968 .. **CLC 1, 3, 11, 34, 83; PC 10**
See also CA 5-8R; 25-28R; CANR 22, 53; DLB 48; DLBY 81; MTCW

Merwin, W(illiam) S(tanley)
1927- ...... **CLC 1, 2, 3, 5, 8, 13, 18, 45, 88; DAM POET**
See also CA 13-16R; CANR 15, 51; DLB 5; INT CANR-15; MTCW

Metcalf, John 1938-.............. **CLC 37**
See also CA 113; DLB 60

Metcalf, Suzanne
See Baum, L(yman) Frank

Mew, Charlotte (Mary)
1870-1928 .... **TCLC 8**
See also CA 105; DLB 19, 135

Mewshaw, Michael 1943-........... **CLC 9**
See also CA 53-56; CANR 7, 47; DLBY 80

Meyer, June
See Jordan, June

Meyer, Lynn
See Slavitt, David R(ytman)

Meyer-Meyrink, Gustav 1868-1932
See Meyrink, Gustav
See also CA 117

Meyers, Jeffrey 1939- .... **CLC 39**
See also CA 73-76; DLB 111

Meynell, Alice (Christina Gertrude Thompson)
1847-1922 .... **TCLC 6**
See also CA 104; DLB 19, 98

Meyrink, Gustav................ **TCLC 21**
See also Meyer-Meyrink, Gustav
See also DLB 81

Michaels, Leonard
1933- .... **CLC 6, 25; SSC 16**
See also CA 61-64; CANR 21; DLB 130; MTCW

Montaigne, Michel (Eyquem) de 1533-1592 . . . . . . **LC 8; DA; DAB; DAC; DAM MST; WLC**

Montale, Eugenio 1896-1981 . . . . **CLC 7, 9, 18; PC 13**
See also CA 17-20R; 104; CANR 30; DLB 114; MTCW

Montesquieu, Charles-Louis de Secondat 1689-1755 . . . . **LC 7**

Montgomery, (Robert) Bruce 1921-1978
See Crispin, Edmund
See also CA 104

Montgomery, L(ucy) M(aud) 1874-1942 . . . . **TCLC 51; DAC; DAM MST**
See also AAYA 12; CA 108; 137; CLR 8; DLB 92; DLBD 14; JRDA; MAICYA; YABC 1

Montgomery, Marion H., Jr. 1925- . . **CLC 7**
See also AITN 1; CA 1-4R; CANR 3, 48; DLB 6

Montgomery, Max
See Davenport, Guy (Mattison, Jr.)

Montherlant, Henry (Milon) de 1896-1972 . . . . **CLC 8, 19; DAM DRAM**
See also CA 85-88; 37-40R; DLB 72; MTCW

Monty Python
See Chapman, Graham; Cleese, John (Marwood); Gilliam, Terry (Vance); Idle, Eric; Jones, Terence Graham Parry; Palin, Michael (Edward)
See also AAYA 7

Moodie, Susanna (Strickland) 1803-1885 . . . . **NCLC 14**
See also DLB 99

Mooney, Edward 1951-
See Mooney, Ted
See also CA 130

Mooney, Ted . . . . **CLC 25**
See also Mooney, Edward

Moorcock, Michael (John) 1939- . . . . **CLC 5, 27, 58**
See also CA 45-48; CAAS 5; CANR 2, 17, 38; DLB 14; MTCW

Moore, Brian 1921- . . . . . . **CLC 1, 3, 5, 7, 8, 19, 32, 90; DAB; DAC; DAM MST**
See also CA 1-4R; CANR 1, 25, 42; MTCW

Moore, Edward
See Muir, Edwin

Moore, George Augustus 1852-1933 . . . . **TCLC 7; SSC 19**
See also CA 104; DLB 10, 18, 57, 135

Moore, Lorrie . . . . **CLC 39, 45, 68**
See also Moore, Marie Lorena

Moore, Marianne (Craig) 1887-1972 . . . . **CLC 1, 2, 4, 8, 10, 13, 19, 47; DA; DAB; DAC; DAM MST, POET; PC 4**
See also CA 1-4R; 33-36R; CANR 3; CDALB 1929-1941; DLB 45; DLBD 7; MTCW; SATA 20

Moore, Marie Lorena 1957-
See Moore, Lorrie
See also CA 116; CANR 39

Moore, Thomas 1779-1852. . . . . **NCLC 6**
See also DLB 96, 144

Morand, Paul 1888-1976 . . **CLC 41; SSC 22**
See also CA 69-72; DLB 65

Morante, Elsa 1918-1985. . . . . **CLC 8, 47**
See also CA 85-88; 117; CANR 35; MTCW

Moravia, Alberto. . . . . . . **CLC 2, 7, 11, 27, 46**
See also Pincherle, Alberto

More, Hannah 1745-1833 . . . . **NCLC 27**
See also DLB 107, 109, 116, 158

More, Henry 1614-1687. . . . . **LC 9**
See also DLB 126

More, Sir Thomas 1478-1535 . . . . **LC 10, 32**

Moreas, Jean. **TCLC 18**
See also Papadiamantopoulos, Johannes

Morgan, Berry 1919- . . . . **CLC 6**
See also CA 49-52; DLB 6

Morgan, Claire
See Highsmith, (Mary) Patricia

Morgan, Edwin (George) 1920- . . . . . **CLC 31**
See also CA 5-8R; CANR 3, 43; DLB 27

Morgan, (George) Frederick 1922- . . . . **CLC 23**
See also CA 17-20R; CANR 21

Morgan, Harriet
See Mencken, H(enry) L(ouis)

Morgan, Jane
See Cooper, James Fenimore

Morgan, Janet 1945- . . . . **CLC 39**
See also CA 65-68

Morgan, Lady 1776(?)-1859. . . . . . **NCLC 29**
See also DLB 116, 158

Morgan, Robin 1941- . . . . **CLC 2**
See also CA 69-72; CANR 29; MTCW; SATA 80

Morgan, Scott
See Kuttner, Henry

Morgan, Seth 1949(?)-1990 . . . . **CLC 65**
See also CA 132

Morgenstern, Christian 1871-1914 . . . . **TCLC 8**
See also CA 105

Morgenstern, S.
See Goldman, William (W.)

Moricz, Zsigmond 1879-1942 . . . . . **TCLC 33**

Morike, Eduard (Friedrich) 1804-1875 . . . . **NCLC 10**
See also DLB 133

Mori Ogai . . . . **TCLC 14**
See also Mori Rintaro

Mori Rintaro 1862-1922
See Mori Ogai
See also CA 110

Moritz, Karl Philipp 1756-1793 . . . . . . **LC 2**
See also DLB 94

Morland, Peter Henry
See Faust, Frederick (Schiller)

Morren, Theophil
See Hofmannsthal, Hugo von

Morris, Bill 1952-. . . . . **CLC 76**

Morris, Julian
See West, Morris L(anglo)

Morris, Steveland Judkins 1950(?)-
See Wonder, Stevie
See also CA 111

Morris, William 1834-1896 . . . . **NCLC 4**
See also CDBLB 1832-1890; DLB 18, 35, 57, 156

Morris, Wright 1910- . . . **CLC 1, 3, 7, 18, 37**
See also CA 9-12R; CANR 21; DLB 2; DLBY 81; MTCW

Morrison, Chloe Anthony Wofford
See Morrison, Toni

Morrison, James Douglas 1943-1971
See Morrison, Jim
See also CA 73-76; CANR 40

Morrison, Jim . . . . **CLC 17**
See also Morrison, James Douglas

Morrison, Toni 1931- . . . . **CLC 4, 10, 22, 55, 81, 87; BLC; DA; DAB; DAC; DAM MST, MULT, NOV, POP**
See also AAYA 1; BW 2; CA 29-32R; CANR 27, 42; CDALB 1968-1988; DLB 6, 33, 143; DLBY 81; MTCW; SATA 57

Morrison, Van 1945- . . . . **CLC 21**
See also CA 116

Mortimer, John (Clifford) 1923- . . . . . . **CLC 28, 43; DAM DRAM, POP**
See also CA 13-16R; CANR 21; CDBLB 1960 to Present; DLB 13; INT CANR-21; MTCW

Mortimer, Penelope (Ruth) 1918- . . . . **CLC 5**
See also CA 57-60; CANR 45

Morton, Anthony
See Creasey, John

Mosher, Howard Frank 1943- . . . . . . **CLC 62**
See also CA 139

Mosley, Nicholas 1923- . . . . **CLC 43, 70**
See also CA 69-72; CANR 41; DLB 14

Moss, Howard 1922-1987 . . . . **CLC 7, 14, 45, 50; DAM POET**
See also CA 1-4R; 123; CANR 1, 44; DLB 5

Mossgiel, Rab
See Burns, Robert

Motion, Andrew (Peter) 1952- . . . . . . **CLC 47**
See also CA 146; DLB 40

Motley, Willard (Francis) 1909-1965 . . . . **CLC 18**
See also BW 1; CA 117; 106; DLB 76, 143

Motoori, Norinaga 1730-1801 . . . . **NCLC 45**

Mott, Michael (Charles Alston) 1930- . . . . **CLC 15, 34**
See also CA 5-8R; CAAS 7; CANR 7, 29

Mountain Wolf Woman 1884-1960 . . . . **CLC 92**
See also CA 144; NNAL

Moure, Erin 1955- . . . . **CLC 88**
See also CA 113; DLB 60

Mowat, Farley (McGill) 1921- ...... **CLC 26; DAC; DAM MST**
See also AAYA 1; CA 1-4R; CANR 4, 24, 42; CLR 20; DLB 68; INT CANAR-24; JRDA; MAICYA; MTCW; SATA 3, 55

Moyers, Bill 1934- .... **CLC 74**
See also AITN 2; CA 61-64; CANR 31, 52

Mphahlele, Es'kia
See Mphahlele, Ezekiel
See also DLB 125

Mphahlele, Ezekiel 1919- ..... **CLC 25; BLC; DAM MULT**
See also Mphahlele, Es'kia
See also BW 2; CA 81-84; CANR 26

Mqhayi, S(amuel) E(dward) K(rune Loliwe) 1875-1945 .... **TCLC 25; BLC; DAM MULT**

Mrozek, Slawomir 1930- .... **CLC 3, 13**
See also CA 13-16R; CAAS 10; CANR 29; MTCW

Mrs. Belloc-Lowndes
See Lowndes, Marie Adelaide (Belloc)

Mtwa, Percy (?)- .... **CLC 47**

Mueller, Lisel 1924- .... **CLC 13, 51**
See also CA 93-96; DLB 105

Muir, Edwin 1887-1959 .... **TCLC 2**
See also CA 104; DLB 20, 100

Muir, John 1838-1914 .... **TCLC 28**

Mujica Lainez, Manuel 1910-1984 .... **CLC 31**
See also Lainez, Manuel Mujica
See also CA 81-84; 112; CANR 32; HW

Mukherjee, Bharati 1940- .... **CLC 53; DAM NOV**
See also BEST 89:2; CA 107; CANR 45; DLB 60; MTCW

Muldoon, Paul 1951- .... **CLC 32, 72; DAM POET**
See also CA 113; 129; CANR 52; DLB 40; INT 129

Mulisch, Harry 1927- .... **CLC 42**
See also CA 9-12R; CANR 6, 26

Mull, Martin 1943- .... **CLC 17**
See also CA 105

Mulock, Dinah Maria
See Craik, Dinah Maria (Mulock)

Munford, Robert 1737(?)-1783 .... **LC 5**
See also DLB 31

Mungo, Raymond 1946- .... **CLC 72**
See also CA 49-52; CANR 2

Munro, Alice 1931- ...... **CLC 6, 10, 19, 50, 95; DAC; DAM MST, NOV; SSC 3**
See also AITN 2; CA 33-36R; CANR 33, 53; DLB 53; MTCW; SATA 29

Munro, H(ector) H(ugh) 1870-1916
See Saki
See also CA 104; 130; CDBLB 1890-1914; DA; DAB; DAC; DAM MST, NOV; DLB 34, 162; MTCW; WLC

Murasaki, Lady .... **CMLC 1**

Murdoch, (Jean) Iris 1919- ...... **CLC 1, 2, 3, 4, 6, 8, 11, 15, 22, 31, 51; DAB; DAC; DAM MST, NOV**
See also CA 13-16R; CANR 8, 43; CDBLB 1960 to Present; DLB 14; INT CANR-8; MTCW

Murfree, Mary Noailles 1850-1922 .... **SSC 22**
See also CA 122; DLB 12, 74

Murnau, Friedrich Wilhelm
See Plumpe, Friedrich Wilhelm

Murphy, Richard 1927- .... **CLC 41**
See also CA 29-32R; DLB 40

Murphy, Sylvia 1937- .... **CLC 34**
See also CA 121

Murphy, Thomas (Bernard) 1935- ... **CLC 51**
See also CA 101

Murray, Albert L. 1916- .... **CLC 73**
See also BW 2; CA 49-52; CANR 26, 52; DLB 38

Murray, Les(lie) A(llan) 1938- .... **CLC 40; DAM POET**
See also CA 21-24R; CANR 11, 27

Murry, J. Middleton
See Murry, John Middleton

Murry, John Middleton 1889-1957 .... **TCLC 16**
See also CA 118; DLB 149

Musgrave, Susan 1951- .... **CLC 13, 54**
See also CA 69-72; CANR 45

Musil, Robert (Edler von) 1880-1942 .... **TCLC 12; SSC 18**
See also CA 109; DLB 81, 124

Muske, Carol 1945- .... **CLC 90**
See also Muske-Dukes, Carol (Anne)

Muske-Dukes, Carol (Anne) 1945-
See Muske, Carol
See also CA 65-68; CANR 32

Musset, (Louis Charles) Alfred de 1810-1857 .... **NCLC 7**

My Brother's Brother
See Chekhov, Anton (Pavlovich)

Myers, L. H. 1881-1944 .... **TCLC 59**
See also DLB 15

Myers, Walter Dean 1937- ..... **CLC 35; BLC; DAM MULT, NOV**
See also AAYA 4; BW 2; CA 33-36R; CANR 20, 42; CLR 4, 16, 35; DLB 33; INT CANR-20; JRDA; MAICYA; SAAS 2; SATA 41, 71; SATA-Brief 27

Myers, Walter M.
See Myers, Walter Dean

Myles, Symon
See Follett, Ken(neth Martin)

Nabokov, Vladimir (Vladimirovich) 1899-1977 ..... **CLC 1, 2, 3, 6, 8, 11, 15, 23, 44, 46, 64; DA; DAB; DAC; DAM MST, NOV; SSC 11; WLC**
See also CA 5-8R; 69-72; CANR 20; CDALB 1941-1968; DLB 2; DLBD 3; DLBY 80, 91; MTCW

Nagai Kafu .... **TCLC 51**
See also Nagai Sokichi

Nagai Sokichi 1879-1959
See Nagai Kafu
See also CA 117

Nagy, Laszlo 1925-1978 .... **CLC 7**
See also CA 129; 112

Naipaul, Shiva(dhar Srinivasa) 1945-1985 ..... **CLC 32, 39; DAM NOV**
See also CA 110; 112; 116; CANR 33; DLB 157; DLBY 85; MTCW

Naipaul, V(idiadhar) S(urajprasad) 1932- .... **CLC 4, 7, 9, 13, 18, 37; DAB; DAC; DAM MST, NOV**
See also CA 1-4R; CANR 1, 33, 51; CDBLB 1960 to Present; DLB 125; DLBY 85; MTCW

Nakos, Lilika 1899(?)- .... **CLC 29**

Narayan, R(asipuram) K(rishnaswami) 1906- .... **CLC 7, 28, 47; DAM NOV**
See also CA 81-84; CANR 33; MTCW; SATA 62

Nash, (Frediric) Ogden 1902-1971 .... **CLC 23; DAM POET**
See also CA 13-14; 29-32R; CANR 34; CAP 1; DLB 11; MAICYA; MTCW; SATA 2, 46

Nathan, Daniel
See Dannay, Frederic

Nathan, George Jean 1882-1958 ... **TCLC 18**
See also Hatteras, Owen
See also CA 114; DLB 137

Natsume, Kinnosuke 1867-1916
See Natsume, Soseki
See also CA 104

Natsume, Soseki .... **TCLC 2, 10**
See also Natsume, Kinnosuke

Natti, (Mary) Lee 1919-
See Kingman, Lee
See also CA 5-8R; CANR 2

Naylor, Gloria 1950- ..... **CLC 28, 52; BLC; DA; DAC; DAM MST, MULT, NOV, POP**
See also AAYA 6; BW 2; CA 107; CANR 27, 51; MTCW

Neihardt, John Gneisenau 1881-1973 .... **CLC 32**
See also CA 13-14; CAP 1; DLB 9, 54

Nekrasov, Nikolai Alekseevich 1821-1878 .... **NCLC 11**

Nelligan, Emile 1879-1941 .... **TCLC 14**
See also CA 114; DLB 92

Nelson, Willie 1933- .... **CLC 17**
See also CA 107

Nemerov, Howard (Stanley) 1920-1991 .... **CLC 2, 6, 9, 36; DAM POET**
See also CA 1-4R; 134; CABS 2; CANR 1, 27, 53; DLB 5, 6; DLBY 83; INT CANR-27; MTCW

Neruda, Pablo 1904-1973 ..... **CLC 1, 2, 5, 7, 9, 28, 62; DA; DAB; DAC; DAM MST, MULT, POET; HLC; PC 4; WLC**
See also CA 19-20; 45-48; CAP 2; HW; MTCW

Nerval, Gerard de 1808-1855 ..... **NCLC 1; PC 13; SSC 18**

Author Index

Nervo, (Jose) Amado (Ruiz de) 1870-1919 .... **TCLC 11**
See also CA 109; 131; HW

Nessi, Pio Baroja y
See Baroja (y Nessi), Pio

Nestroy, Johann 1801-1862...... **NCLC 42**
See also DLB 133

Neufeld, John (Arthur) 1938- ...... **CLC 17**
See also AAYA 11; CA 25-28R; CANR 11, 37; MAICYA; SAAS 3; SATA 6, 81

Neville, Emily Cheney 1919-....... **CLC 12**
See also CA 5-8R; CANR 3, 37; JRDA; MAICYA; SAAS 2; SATA 1

Newbound, Bernard Slade 1930-
See Slade, Bernard
See also CA 81-84; CANR 49; DAM DRAM

Newby, P(ercy) H(oward) 1918- .... **CLC 2, 13; DAM NOV**
See also CA 5-8R; CANR 32; DLB 15; MTCW

Newlove, Donald 1928- .... **CLC 6**
See also CA 29-32R; CANR 25

Newlove, John (Herbert) 1938-..... **CLC 14**
See also CA 21-24R; CANR 9, 25

Newman, Charles 1938-.......... **CLC 2, 8**
See also CA 21-24R

Newman, Edwin (Harold) 1919- .... **CLC 14**
See also AITN 1; CA 69-72; CANR 5

Newman, John Henry 1801-1890 .... **NCLC 38**
See also DLB 18, 32, 55

Newton, Suzanne 1936- .... **CLC 35**
See also CA 41-44R; CANR 14; JRDA; SATA 5, 77

Nexo, Martin Andersen 1869-1954 .... **TCLC 43**

Nezval, Vitezslav 1900-1958 ...... **TCLC 44**
See also CA 123

Ng, Fae Myenne 1957(?)-.......... **CLC 81**
See also CA 146

Ngema, Mbongeni 1955- .... **CLC 57**
See also BW 2; CA 143

Ngugi, James T(hiong'o)........ **CLC 3, 7, 13**
See also Ngugi wa Thiong'o

Ngugi wa Thiong'o 1938- ..... **CLC 36; BLC; DAM MULT, NOV**
See also Ngugi, James T(hiong'o)
See also BW 2; CA 81-84; CANR 27; DLB 125; MTCW

Nichol, B(arrie) P(hillip) 1944-1988 .... **CLC 18**
See also CA 53-56; DLB 53; SATA 66

Nichols, John (Treadwell) 1940- .... **CLC 38**
See also CA 9-12R; CAAS 2; CANR 6; DLBY 82

Nichols, Leigh
See Koontz, Dean R(ay)

Nichols, Peter (Richard) 1927- .... **CLC 5, 36, 65**
See also CA 104; CANR 33; DLB 13; MTCW

Nicolas, F. R. E.
See Freeling, Nicolas

Niedecker, Lorine 1903-1970 .... **CLC 10, 42; DAM POET**
See also CA 25-28; CAP 2; DLB 48

Nietzsche, Friedrich (Wilhelm) 1844-1900 .... **TCLC 10, 18, 55**
See also CA 107; 121; DLB 129

Nievo, Ippolito 1831-1861 .... **NCLC 22**

Nightingale, Anne Redmon 1943-
See Redmon, Anne
See also CA 103

Nik. T. O.
See Annensky, Innokenty Fyodorovich

Nin, Anais 1903-1977 ...... **CLC 1, 4, 8, 11, 14, 60; DAM NOV, POP; SSC 10**
See also AITN 2; CA 13-16R; 69-72; CANR 22, 53; DLB 2, 4, 152; MTCW

Nishiwaki, Junzaburo 1894-1982 .... **PC 15**
See also CA 107

Nissenson, Hugh 1933-........... **CLC 4, 9**
See also CA 17-20R; CANR 27; DLB 28

Niven, Larry .... **CLC 8**
See also Niven, Laurence Van Cott
See also DLB 8

Niven, Laurence Van Cott 1938-
See Niven, Larry
See also CA 21-24R; CAAS 12; CANR 14, 44; DAM POP; MTCW

Nixon, Agnes Eckhardt 1927-...... **CLC 21**
See also CA 110

Nizan, Paul 1905-1940........... **TCLC 40**
See also DLB 72

Nkosi, Lewis 1936- ..... **CLC 45; BLC; DAM MULT**
See also BW 1; CA 65-68; CANR 27; DLB 157

Nodier, (Jean) Charles (Emmanuel) 1780-1844 .... **NCLC 19**
See also DLB 119

Nolan, Christopher 1965-.......... **CLC 58**
See also CA 111

Noon, Jeff 1957-................. **CLC 91**
See also CA 148

Norden, Charles
See Durrell, Lawrence (George)

Nordhoff, Charles (Bernard) 1887-1947 .... **TCLC 23**
See also CA 108; DLB 9; SATA 23

Norfolk, Lawrence 1963-.......... **CLC 76**
See also CA 144

Norman, Marsha 1947- .... **CLC 28; DAM DRAM**
See also CA 105; CABS 3; CANR 41; DLBY 84

Norris, Benjamin Franklin, Jr. 1870-1902 .... **TCLC 24**
See also Norris, Frank
See also CA 110

Norris, Frank
See Norris, Benjamin Franklin, Jr.
See also CDALB 1865-1917; DLB 12, 71

Norris, Leslie 1921- .... **CLC 14**
See also CA 11-12; CANR 14; CAP 1; DLB 27

North, Andrew
See Norton, Andre

North, Anthony
See Koontz, Dean R(ay)

North, Captain George
See Stevenson, Robert Louis (Balfour)

North, Milou
See Erdrich, Louise

Northrup, B. A.
See Hubbard, L(afayette) Ron(ald)

North Staffs
See Hulme, T(homas) E(rnest)

Norton, Alice Mary
See Norton, Andre
See also MAICYA; SATA 1, 43

Norton, Andre 1912- .... **CLC 12**
See also Norton, Alice Mary
See also AAYA 14; CA 1-4R; CANR 2, 31; DLB 8, 52; JRDA; MTCW

Norton, Caroline 1808-1877...... **NCLC 47**
See also DLB 21, 159

Norway, Nevil Shute 1899-1960
See Shute, Nevil
See also CA 102; 93-96

Norwid, Cyprian Kamil 1821-1883 .... **NCLC 17**

Nosille, Nabrah
See Ellison, Harlan (Jay)

Nossack, Hans Erich 1901-1978 ..... **CLC 6**
See also CA 93-96; 85-88; DLB 69

Nostradamus 1503-1566............ **LC 27**

Nosu, Chuji
See Ozu, Yasujiro

Notenburg, Eleanora (Genrikhovna) von
See Guro, Elena

Nova, Craig 1945-.............. **CLC 7, 31**
See also CA 45-48; CANR 2, 53

Novak, Joseph
See Kosinski, Jerzy (Nikodem)

Novalis 1772-1801 .... **NCLC 13**
See also DLB 90

Nowlan, Alden (Albert) 1933-1983 .. **CLC 15; DAC; DAM MST**
See also CA 9-12R; CANR 5; DLB 53

Noyes, Alfred 1880-1958 .... **TCLC 7**
See also CA 104; DLB 20

Nunn, Kem 19(?)-................ **CLC 34**

Nye, Robert 1939- .... **CLC 13, 42; DAM NOV**
See also CA 33-36R; CANR 29; DLB 14; MTCW; SATA 6

Nyro, Laura 1947- .... **CLC 17**

Oates, Joyce Carol 1938- ...... **CLC 1, 2, 3, 6, 9, 11, 15, 19, 33, 52; DA; DAB; DAC; DAM MST, NOV, POP; SSC 6; WLC**
See also AAYA 15; AITN 1; BEST 89:2; CA 5-8R; CANR 25, 45; CDALB 1968-1988; DLB 2, 5, 130; DLBY 81; INT CANR-25; MTCW

O'Brien, Darcy 1939-............. **CLC 11**
See also CA 21-24R; CANR 8

O'Brien, E. G.
See Clarke, Arthur C(harles)

O'Brien, Edna
1936- .... **CLC 3, 5, 8, 13, 36, 65; DAM NOV; SSC 10**
See also CA 1-4R; CANR 6, 41; CDBLB 1960 to Present; DLB 14; MTCW

O'Brien, Fitz-James 1828-1862... **NCLC 21**
See also DLB 74

O'Brien, Flann........ **CLC 1, 4, 5, 7, 10, 47**
See also O Nuallain, Brian

O'Brien, Richard 1942-........... **CLC 17**
See also CA 124

O'Brien, Tim
1946- .... **CLC 7, 19, 40; DAM POP**
See also AAYA 16; CA 85-88; CANR 40; DLB 152; DLBD 9; DLBY 80

Obstfelder, Sigbjoern 1866-1900... **TCLC 23**
See also CA 123

O'Casey, Sean
1880-1964 ...... **CLC 1, 5, 9, 11, 15, 88; DAB; DAC; DAM DRAM, MST**
See also CA 89-92; CDBLB 1914-1945; DLB 10; MTCW

O'Cathasaigh, Sean
See O'Casey, Sean

Ochs, Phil 1940-1976............. **CLC 17**
See also CA 65-68

O'Connor, Edwin (Greene)
1918-1968 .... **CLC 14**
See also CA 93-96; 25-28R

O'Connor, (Mary) Flannery
1925-1964 .... **CLC 1, 2, 3, 6, 10, 13, 15, 21, 66; DA; DAB; DAC; DAM MST, NOV; SSC 1, 23; WLC**
See also AAYA 7; CA 1-4R; CANR 3, 41; CDALB 1941-1968; DLB 2, 152; DLBD 12; DLBY 80; MTCW

O'Connor, Frank........... **CLC 23; SSC 5**
See also O'Donovan, Michael John
See also DLB 162

O'Dell, Scott 1898-1989........... **CLC 30**
See also AAYA 3; CA 61-64; 129; CANR 12, 30; CLR 1, 16; DLB 52; JRDA; MAICYA; SATA 12, 60

Odets, Clifford
1906-1963 ... **CLC 2, 28; DAM DRAM; DC 6**
See also CA 85-88; DLB 7, 26; MTCW

O'Doherty, Brian 1934-........... **CLC 76**
See also CA 105

O'Donnell, K. M.
See Malzberg, Barry N(athaniel)

O'Donnell, Lawrence
See Kuttner, Henry

O'Donovan, Michael John
1903-1966 .... **CLC 14**
See also O'Connor, Frank
See also CA 93-96

Oe, Kenzaburo
1935- ..... **CLC 10, 36, 86; DAM NOV; SSC 20**
See also CA 97-100; CANR 36, 50; DLBY 94; MTCW

O'Faolain, Julia 1932-....... **CLC 6, 19, 47**
See also CA 81-84; CAAS 2; CANR 12; DLB 14; MTCW

O'Faolain, Sean
1900-1991 .... **CLC 1, 7, 14, 32, 70; SSC 13**
See also CA 61-64; 134; CANR 12; DLB 15, 162; MTCW

O'Flaherty, Liam
1896-1984 .... **CLC 5, 34; SSC 6**
See also CA 101; 113; CANR 35; DLB 36, 162; DLBY 84; MTCW

Ogilvy, Gavin
See Barrie, J(ames) M(atthew)

O'Grady, Standish James
1846-1928 .... **TCLC 5**
See also CA 104

O'Grady, Timothy 1951-.......... **CLC 59**
See also CA 138

O'Hara, Frank
1926-1966 .... **CLC 2, 5, 13, 78; DAM POET**
See also CA 9-12R; 25-28R; CANR 33; DLB 5, 16; MTCW

O'Hara, John (Henry)
1905-1970 .... **CLC 1, 2, 3, 6, 11, 42; DAM NOV; SSC 15**
See also CA 5-8R; 25-28R; CANR 31; CDALB 1929-1941; DLB 9, 86; DLBD 2; MTCW

O Hehir, Diana 1922- .... **CLC 41**
See also CA 93-96

Okigbo, Christopher (Ifenayichukwu)
1932-1967 .... **CLC 25, 84; BLC; DAM MULT, POET; PC 7**
See also BW 1; CA 77-80; DLB 125; MTCW

Okri, Ben 1959- .... **CLC 87**
See also BW 2; CA 130; 138; DLB 157; INT 138

Olds, Sharon
1942- ..... **CLC 32, 39, 85; DAM POET**
See also CA 101; CANR 18, 41; DLB 120

Oldstyle, Jonathan
See Irving, Washington

Olesha, Yuri (Karlovich)
1899-1960 .... **CLC 8**
See also CA 85-88

Oliphant, Laurence
1829(?)-1888 .... **NCLC 47**
See also DLB 18, 166

Oliphant, Margaret (Oliphant Wilson)
1828-1897 .... **NCLC 11**
See also DLB 18, 159

Oliver, Mary 1935-........... **CLC 19, 34**
See also CA 21-24R; CANR 9, 43; DLB 5

Olivier, Laurence (Kerr)
1907-1989 .... **CLC 20**
See also CA 111; 150; 129

Olsen, Tillie
1913- ..... **CLC 4, 13; DA; DAB; DAC; DAM MST; SSC 11**
See also CA 1-4R; CANR 1, 43; DLB 28; DLBY 80; MTCW

Olson, Charles (John)
1910-1970 ..... **CLC 1, 2, 5, 6, 9, 11, 29; DAM POET**
See also CA 13-16; 25-28R; CABS 2; CANR 35; CAP 1; DLB 5, 16; MTCW

Olson, Toby 1937- .... **CLC 28**
See also CA 65-68; CANR 9, 31

Olyesha, Yuri
See Olesha, Yuri (Karlovich)

Ondaatje, (Philip) Michael
1943- .... **CLC 14, 29, 51, 76; DAB; DAC; DAM MST**
See also CA 77-80; CANR 42; DLB 60

Oneal, Elizabeth 1934-
See Oneal, Zibby
See also CA 106; CANR 28; MAICYA; SATA 30, 82

Oneal, Zibby .... **CLC 30**
See also Oneal, Elizabeth
See also AAYA 5; CLR 13; JRDA

O'Neill, Eugene (Gladstone)
1888-1953 ...... **TCLC 1, 6, 27, 49; DA; DAB; DAC; DAM DRAM, MST; WLC**
See also AITN 1; CA 110; 132; CDALB 1929-1941; DLB 7; MTCW

Onetti, Juan Carlos
1909-1994 .... **CLC 7, 10; DAM MULT, NOV; SSC 23**
See also CA 85-88; 145; CANR 32; DLB 113; HW; MTCW

O Nuallain, Brian 1911-1966
See O'Brien, Flann
See also CA 21-22; 25-28R; CAP 2

Oppen, George 1908-1984 .... **CLC 7, 13, 34**
See also CA 13-16R; 113; CANR 8; DLB 5, 165

Oppenheim, E(dward) Phillips
1866-1946 .... **TCLC 45**
See also CA 111; DLB 70

Orlovitz, Gil 1918-1973........... **CLC 22**
See also CA 77-80; 45-48; DLB 2, 5

Orris
See Ingelow, Jean

Ortega y Gasset, Jose
1883-1955 ..... **TCLC 9; DAM MULT; HLC**
See also CA 106; 130; HW; MTCW

Ortese, Anna Maria 1914-......... **CLC 89**

Ortiz, Simon J(oseph)
1941- .... **CLC 45; DAM MULT, POET**
See also CA 134; DLB 120; NNAL

Orton, Joe .... **CLC 4, 13, 43; DC 3**
See also Orton, John Kingsley
See also CDBLB 1960 to Present; DLB 13

Orton, John Kingsley 1933-1967
See Orton, Joe
See also CA 85-88; CANR 35; DAM DRAM; MTCW

Orwell, George
..... **TCLC 2, 6, 15, 31, 51; DAB; WLC**
See also Blair, Eric (Arthur)
See also CDBLB 1945-1960; DLB 15, 98

Osborne, David
See Silverberg, Robert

Osborne, George
See Silverberg, Robert

Osborne, John (James)
1929-1994 ..... **CLC 1, 2, 5, 11, 45; DA; DAB; DAC; DAM DRAM, MST; WLC**
See also CA 13-16R; 147; CANR 21; CDBLB 1945-1960; DLB 13; MTCW

Paulding, James Kirke 1778-1860. . **NCLC 2**
See also DLB 3, 59, 74

Paulin, Thomas Neilson 1949-
See Paulin, Tom
See also CA 123; 128

Paulin, Tom . . . . **CLC 37**
See also Paulin, Thomas Neilson
See also DLB 40

Paustovsky, Konstantin (Georgievich)
1892-1968 . . . . **CLC 40**
See also CA 93-96; 25-28R

Pavese, Cesare
1908-1950 . . . . . **TCLC 3; PC 13; SSC 19**
See also CA 104; DLB 128

Pavic, Milorad 1929- . . . . **CLC 60**
See also CA 136

Payne, Alan
See Jakes, John (William)

Paz, Gil
See Lugones, Leopoldo

Paz, Octavio
1914- . . . . **CLC 3, 4, 6, 10, 19, 51, 65; DA; DAB; DAC; DAM MST, MULT, POET; HLC; PC 1; WLC**
See also CA 73-76; CANR 32; DLBY 90; HW; MTCW

p'Bitek, Okot
1931-1982 . . . . **CLC 96; BLC; DAM MULT**
See also BW 2; CA 124; 107; DLB 125; MTCW

Peacock, Molly 1947- . . . . **CLC 60**
See also CA 103; CAAS 21; CANR 52; DLB 120

Peacock, Thomas Love
1785-1866 . . . . **NCLC 22**
See also DLB 96, 116

Peake, Mervyn 1911-1968 . . . . **CLC 7, 54**
See also CA 5-8R; 25-28R; CANR 3; DLB 15, 160; MTCW; SATA 23

Pearce, Philippa . . . . **CLC 21**
See also Christie, (Ann) Philippa
See also CLR 9; DLB 161; MAICYA; SATA 1, 67

Pearl, Eric
See Elman, Richard

Pearson, T(homas) R(eid) 1956- . . . . **CLC 39**
See also CA 120; 130; INT 130

Peck, Dale 1967- . . . . **CLC 81**
See also CA 146

Peck, John 1941- . . . . **CLC 3**
See also CA 49-52; CANR 3

Peck, Richard (Wayne) 1934- . . . . . . **CLC 21**
See also AAYA 1; CA 85-88; CANR 19, 38; CLR 15; INT CANR-19; JRDA; MAICYA; SAAS 2; SATA 18, 55

Peck, Robert Newton
1928- . . **CLC 17; DA; DAC; DAM MST**
See also AAYA 3; CA 81-84; CANR 31; JRDA; MAICYA; SAAS 1; SATA 21, 62

Peckinpah, (David) Sam(uel)
1925-1984 . . . . **CLC 20**
See also CA 109; 114

Pedersen, Knut 1859-1952
See Hamsun, Knut
See also CA 104; 119; MTCW

Peeslake, Gaffer
See Durrell, Lawrence (George)

Peguy, Charles Pierre
1873-1914 . . . . **TCLC 10**
See also CA 107

Pena, Ramon del Valle y
See Valle-Inclan, Ramon (Maria) del

Pendennis, Arthur Esquir
See Thackeray, William Makepeace

Penn, William 1644-1718 . . . . **LC 25**
See also DLB 24

Pepys, Samuel
1633-1703 . . . . . **LC 11; DA; DAB; DAC; DAM MST; WLC**
See also CDBLB 1660-1789; DLB 101

Percy, Walker
1916-1990 . . . . **CLC 2, 3, 6, 8, 14, 18, 47, 65; DAM NOV, POP**
See also CA 1-4R; 131; CANR 1, 23; DLB 2; DLBY 80, 90; MTCW

Perec, Georges 1936-1982 . . . . **CLC 56**
See also CA 141; DLB 83

Pereda (y Sanchez de Porrua), Jose Maria de
1833-1906 . . . . **TCLC 16**
See also CA 117

Pereda y Porrua, Jose Maria de
See Pereda (y Sanchez de Porrua), Jose Maria de

Peregoy, George Weems
See Mencken, H(enry) L(ouis)

Perelman, S(idney) J(oseph)
1904-1979 . . . . . . **CLC 3, 5, 9, 15, 23, 44, 49; DAM DRAM**
See also AITN 1, 2; CA 73-76; 89-92; CANR 18; DLB 11, 44; MTCW

Peret, Benjamin 1899-1959 . . . . **TCLC 20**
See also CA 117

Peretz, Isaac Loeb 1851(?)-1915 . . . **TCLC 16**
See also CA 109

Peretz, Yitzkhok Leibush
See Peretz, Isaac Loeb

Perez Galdos, Benito 1843-1920 . . . **TCLC 27**
See also CA 125; HW

Perrault, Charles 1628-1703 . . . . **LC 2**
See also MAICYA; SATA 25

Perry, Brighton
See Sherwood, Robert E(mmet)

Perse, St.-John . . . . **CLC 4, 11, 46**
See also Leger, (Marie-Rene Auguste) Alexis Saint-Leger

Perutz, Leo 1882-1957 . . . . **TCLC 60**
See also DLB 81

Peseenz, Tulio F.
See Lopez y Fuentes, Gregorio

Pesetsky, Bette 1932- . . . . **CLC 28**
See also CA 133; DLB 130

Peshkov, Alexei Maximovich 1868-1936
See Gorky, Maxim
See also CA 105; 141; DA; DAC; DAM DRAM, MST, NOV

Pessoa, Fernando (Antonio Nogueira)
1888-1935 . . . . **TCLC 27; HLC**
See also CA 125

Peterkin, Julia Mood 1880-1961 . . . . **CLC 31**
See also CA 102; DLB 9

Peters, Joan K. 1945- . . . . **CLC 39**

Peters, Robert L(ouis) 1924- . . . . **CLC 7**
See also CA 13-16R; CAAS 8; DLB 105

Petofi, Sandor 1823-1849 . . . . **NCLC 21**

Petrakis, Harry Mark 1923- . . . . **CLC 3**
See also CA 9-12R; CANR 4, 30

Petrarch 1304-1374 . . . . **PC 8**
See also DAM POET

Petrov, Evgeny . . . . **TCLC 21**
See also Kataev, Evgeny Petrovich

Petry, Ann (Lane) 1908- . . . . . . **CLC 1, 7, 18**
See also BW 1; CA 5-8R; CAAS 6; CANR 4, 46; CLR 12; DLB 76; JRDA; MAICYA; MTCW; SATA 5

Petursson, Halligrimur 1614-1674 . . . . **LC 8**

Philips, Katherine 1632-1664 . . . . **LC 30**
See also DLB 131

Philipson, Morris H. 1926- . . . . **CLC 53**
See also CA 1-4R; CANR 4

Phillips, Caryl
1958- . . . . **CLC 96; DAM MULT**
See also BW 2; CA 141; DLB 157

Phillips, David Graham
1867-1911 . . . . **TCLC 44**
See also CA 108; DLB 9, 12

Phillips, Jack
See Sandburg, Carl (August)

Phillips, Jayne Anne
1952- . . . . **CLC 15, 33; SSC 16**
See also CA 101; CANR 24, 50; DLBY 80; INT CANR-24; MTCW

Phillips, Richard
See Dick, Philip K(indred)

Phillips, Robert (Schaeffer) 1938- . . . **CLC 28**
See also CA 17-20R; CAAS 13; CANR 8; DLB 105

Phillips, Ward
See Lovecraft, H(oward) P(hillips)

Piccolo, Lucio 1901-1969 . . . . **CLC 13**
See also CA 97-100; DLB 114

Pickthall, Marjorie L(owry) C(hristie)
1883-1922 . . . . **TCLC 21**
See also CA 107; DLB 92

Pico della Mirandola, Giovanni
1463-1494 . . . . **LC 15**

Piercy, Marge
1936- . . . . **CLC 3, 6, 14, 18, 27, 62**
See also CA 21-24R; CAAS 1; CANR 13, 43; DLB 120; MTCW

Piers, Robert
See Anthony, Piers

Pieyre de Mandiargues, Andre 1909-1991
See Mandiargues, Andre Pieyre de
See also CA 103; 136; CANR 22

Pilnyak, Boris . . . . **TCLC 23**
See also Vogau, Boris Andreyevich

Potter, Dennis (Christopher George) 1935-1994 . . . . **CLC 58, 86**
See also CA 107; 145; CANR 33; MTCW

Pound, Ezra (Weston Loomis) 1885-1972 . . . . . . **CLC 1, 2, 3, 4, 5, 7, 10, 13, 18, 34, 48, 50; DA; DAB; DAC; DAM MST, POET; PC 4; WLC**
See also CA 5-8R; 37-40R; CANR 40; CDALB 1917-1929; DLB 4, 45, 63; MTCW

Povod, Reinaldo 1959-1994 . . . . **CLC 44**
See also CA 136; 146

Powell, Adam Clayton, Jr. 1908-1972 . . . . **CLC 89; BLC; DAM MULT**
See also BW 1; CA 102; 33-36R

Powell, Anthony (Dymoke) 1905- . . . . **CLC 1, 3, 7, 9, 10, 31**
See also CA 1-4R; CANR 1, 32; CDBLB 1945-1960; DLB 15; MTCW

Powell, Dawn 1897-1965 . . . . **CLC 66**
See also CA 5-8R

Powell, Padgett 1952-. . . . . **CLC 34**
See also CA 126

Power, Susan . . . . **CLC 91**

Powers, J(ames) F(arl) 1917- . . . . **CLC 1, 4, 8, 57; SSC 4**
See also CA 1-4R; CANR 2; DLB 130; MTCW

Powers, John J(ames) 1945-
See Powers, John R.
See also CA 69-72

Powers, John R. . . . . **CLC 66**
See also Powers, John J(ames)

Powers, Richard (S.) 1957- . . . . **CLC 93**
See also CA 148

Pownall, David 1938-. . . . . **CLC 10**
See also CA 89-92; CAAS 18; CANR 49; DLB 14

Powys, John Cowper 1872-1963 . . . . **CLC 7, 9, 15, 46**
See also CA 85-88; DLB 15; MTCW

Powys, T(heodore) F(rancis) 1875-1953 . . . . **TCLC 9**
See also CA 106; DLB 36, 162

Prager, Emily 1952-. . . . . **CLC 56**

Pratt, E(dwin) J(ohn) 1883(?)-1964 . . . . **CLC 19; DAC; DAM POET**
See also CA 141; 93-96; DLB 92

Premchand . . . . **TCLC 21**
See also Srivastava, Dhanpat Rai

Preussler, Otfried 1923-. . . . . **CLC 17**
See also CA 77-80; SATA 24

Prevert, Jacques (Henri Marie) 1900-1977 . . . . **CLC 15**
See also CA 77-80; 69-72; CANR 29; MTCW; SATA-Obit 30

Prevost, Abbe (Antoine Francois) 1697-1763 . . . . **LC 1**

Price, (Edward) Reynolds 1933- . . . . **CLC 3, 6, 13, 43, 50, 63; DAM NOV; SSC 22**
See also CA 1-4R; CANR 1, 37; DLB 2; INT CANR-37

Price, Richard 1949- . . . . **CLC 6, 12**
See also CA 49-52; CANR 3; DLBY 81

Prichard, Katharine Susannah 1883-1969 . . . . **CLC 46**
See also CA 11-12; CANR 33; CAP 1; MTCW; SATA 66

Priestley, J(ohn) B(oynton) 1894-1984 . . . . **CLC 2, 5, 9, 34; DAM DRAM, NOV**
See also CA 9-12R; 113; CANR 33; CDBLB 1914-1945; DLB 10, 34, 77, 100, 139; DLBY 84; MTCW

Prince 1958(?)- . . . . **CLC 35**

Prince, F(rank) T(empleton) 1912- . . **CLC 22**
See also CA 101; CANR 43; DLB 20

Prince Kropotkin
See Kropotkin, Peter (Aleksieevich)

Prior, Matthew 1664-1721. . . . . **LC 4**
See also DLB 95

Pritchard, William H(arrison) 1932- . . . . **CLC 34**
See also CA 65-68; CANR 23; DLB 111

Pritchett, V(ictor) S(awdon) 1900- . . . . **CLC 5, 13, 15, 41; DAM NOV; SSC 14**
See also CA 61-64; CANR 31; DLB 15, 139; MTCW

Private 19022
See Manning, Frederic

Probst, Mark 1925- . . . . **CLC 59**
See also CA 130

Prokosch, Frederic 1908-1989. . . . **CLC 4, 48**
See also CA 73-76; 128; DLB 48

Prophet, The
See Dreiser, Theodore (Herman Albert)

Prose, Francine 1947-. . . . . **CLC 45**
See also CA 109; 112; CANR 46

Proudhon
See Cunha, Euclides (Rodrigues Pimenta) da

Proulx, E. Annie 1935- . . . . **CLC 81**

Proust, (Valentin-Louis-George-Eugene-) Marcel 1871-1922 . . . . **TCLC 7, 13, 33; DA; DAB; DAC; DAM MST, NOV; WLC**
See also CA 104; 120; DLB 65; MTCW

Prowler, Harley
See Masters, Edgar Lee

Prus, Boleslaw 1845-1912 . . . . **TCLC 48**

Pryor, Richard (Franklin Lenox Thomas) 1940- . . . . **CLC 26**
See also CA 122

Przybyszewski, Stanislaw 1868-1927 . . . . **TCLC 36**
See also DLB 66

Pteleon
See Grieve, C(hristopher) M(urray)
See also DAM POET

Puckett, Lute
See Masters, Edgar Lee

Puig, Manuel 1932-1990 . . . . **CLC 3, 5, 10, 28, 65; DAM MULT; HLC**
See also CA 45-48; CANR 2, 32; DLB 113; HW; MTCW

Purdy, Al(fred Wellington) 1918- . . . . **CLC 3, 6, 14, 50; DAC; DAM MST, POET**
See also CA 81-84; CAAS 17; CANR 42; DLB 88

Purdy, James (Amos) 1923- . . . . **CLC 2, 4, 10, 28, 52**
See also CA 33-36R; CAAS 1; CANR 19, 51; DLB 2; INT CANR-19; MTCW

Pure, Simon
See Swinnerton, Frank Arthur

Pushkin, Alexander (Sergeyevich) 1799-1837 . . . . . **NCLC 3, 27; DA; DAB; DAC; DAM DRAM, MST, POET; PC 10; WLC**
See also SATA 61

P'u Sung-ling 1640-1715 . . . . **LC 3**

Putnam, Arthur Lee
See Alger, Horatio, Jr.

Puzo, Mario 1920- . . . . . **CLC 1, 2, 6, 36; DAM NOV, POP**
See also CA 65-68; CANR 4, 42; DLB 6; MTCW

Pym, Barbara (Mary Crampton) 1913-1980 . . . . **CLC 13, 19, 37**
See also CA 13-14; 97-100; CANR 13, 34; CAP 1; DLB 14; DLBY 87; MTCW

Pynchon, Thomas (Ruggles, Jr.) 1937- . . . . . **CLC 2, 3, 6, 9, 11, 18, 33, 62, 72; DA; DAB; DAC; DAM MST, NOV, POP; SSC 14; WLC**
See also BEST 90:2; CA 17-20R; CANR 22, 46; DLB 2; MTCW

Qian Zhongshu
See Ch'ien Chung-shu

Qroll
See Dagerman, Stig (Halvard)

Quarrington, Paul (Lewis) 1953-. . . . **CLC 65**
See also CA 129

Quasimodo, Salvatore 1901-1968 . . . **CLC 10**
See also CA 13-16; 25-28R; CAP 1; DLB 114; MTCW

Quay, Stephen 1947- . . . . **CLC 95**

Quay, The Brothers
See Quay, Stephen; Quay, Timothy

Quay, Timothy 1947-. . . . . **CLC 95**

Queen, Ellery. . . . . **CLC 3, 11**
See also Dannay, Frederic; Davidson, Avram; Lee, Manfred B(ennington); Sturgeon, Theodore (Hamilton); Vance, John Holbrook

Queen, Ellery, Jr.
See Dannay, Frederic; Lee, Manfred B(ennington)

Queneau, Raymond 1903-1976 . . . . **CLC 2, 5, 10, 42**
See also CA 77-80; 69-72; CANR 32; DLB 72; MTCW

Quevedo, Francisco de 1580-1645. . . . **LC 23**

Quiller-Couch, Arthur Thomas 1863-1944 . . . . **TCLC 53**
See also CA 118; DLB 135, 153

Quin, Ann (Marie) 1936-1973 . . . . **CLC 6**
See also CA 9-12R; 45-48; DLB 14

Quinn, Martin
See Smith, Martin Cruz

Quinn, Peter 1947- . . . . **CLC 91**

Quinn, Simon
See Smith, Martin Cruz

Quiroga, Horacio (Sylvestre)
1878-1937 . . . . . **TCLC 20; DAM MULT; HLC**
See also CA 117; 131; HW; MTCW

Quoirez, Francoise 1935- . . . . **CLC 9**
See also Sagan, Francoise
See also CA 49-52; CANR 6, 39; MTCW

Raabe, Wilhelm 1831-1910 . . . . **TCLC 45**
See also DLB 129

Rabe, David (William)
1940- . . . . . . **CLC 4, 8, 33; DAM DRAM**
See also CA 85-88; CABS 3; DLB 7

Rabelais, Francois
1483-1553 . . . . . . **LC 5; DA; DAB; DAC; DAM MST; WLC**

Rabinovitch, Sholem 1859-1916
See Aleichem, Sholom
See also CA 104

Racine, Jean
1639-1699 . . . . **LC 28; DAB; DAM MST**

Radcliffe, Ann (Ward)
1764-1823 . . . . **NCLC 6, 55**
See also DLB 39

Radiguet, Raymond 1903-1923 . . . . **TCLC 29**
See also DLB 65

Radnoti, Miklos 1909-1944 . . . . **TCLC 16**
See also CA 118

Rado, James 1939- . . . . **CLC 17**
See also CA 105

Radvanyi, Netty 1900-1983
See Seghers, Anna
See also CA 85-88; 110

Rae, Ben
See Griffiths, Trevor

Raeburn, John (Hay) 1941- . . . . **CLC 34**
See also CA 57-60

Ragni, Gerome 1942-1991 . . . . **CLC 17**
See also CA 105; 134

Rahv, Philip 1908-1973 . . . . **CLC 24**
See also Greenberg, Ivan
See also DLB 137

Raine, Craig 1944- . . . . **CLC 32**
See also CA 108; CANR 29, 51; DLB 40

Raine, Kathleen (Jessie) 1908- . . . **CLC 7, 45**
See also CA 85-88; CANR 46; DLB 20; MTCW

Rainis, Janis 1865-1929 . . . . **TCLC 29**

Rakosi, Carl . . . . **CLC 47**
See also Rawley, Callman
See also CAAS 5

Raleigh, Richard
See Lovecraft, H(oward) P(hillips)

Raleigh, Sir Walter 1554(?)-1618 . . . . **LC 31**
See also CDBLB Before 1660

Rallentando, H. P.
See Sayers, Dorothy L(eigh)

Ramal, Walter
See de la Mare, Walter (John)

Ramon, Juan
See Jimenez (Mantecon), Juan Ramon

Ramos, Graciliano 1892-1953 . . . . . **TCLC 32**

Rampersad, Arnold 1941- . . . . **CLC 44**
See also BW 2; CA 127; 133; DLB 111; INT 133

Rampling, Anne
See Rice, Anne

Ramsay, Allan 1684(?)-1758 . . . . **LC 29**
See also DLB 95

Ramuz, Charles-Ferdinand
1878-1947 . . . . **TCLC 33**

Rand, Ayn
1905-1982 . . . . . . **CLC 3, 30, 44, 79; DA; DAC; DAM MST, NOV, POP; WLC**
See also AAYA 10; CA 13-16R; 105; CANR 27; MTCW

Randall, Dudley (Felker)
1914- . . . . . . **CLC 1; BLC; DAM MULT**
See also BW 1; CA 25-28R; CANR 23; DLB 41

Randall, Robert
See Silverberg, Robert

Ranger, Ken
See Creasey, John

Ransom, John Crowe
1888-1974 . . . . **CLC 2, 4, 5, 11, 24; DAM POET**
See also CA 5-8R; 49-52; CANR 6, 34; DLB 45, 63; MTCW

Rao, Raja 1909- . . . **CLC 25, 56; DAM NOV**
See also CA 73-76; CANR 51; MTCW

Raphael, Frederic (Michael)
1931- . . . . **CLC 2, 14**
See also CA 1-4R; CANR 1; DLB 14

Ratcliffe, James P.
See Mencken, H(enry) L(ouis)

Rathbone, Julian 1935- . . . . **CLC 41**
See also CA 101; CANR 34

Rattigan, Terence (Mervyn)
1911-1977 . . . . **CLC 7; DAM DRAM**
See also CA 85-88; 73-76; CDBLB 1945-1960; DLB 13; MTCW

Ratushinskaya, Irina 1954- . . . . **CLC 54**
See also CA 129

Raven, Simon (Arthur Noel)
1927- . . . . **CLC 14**
See also CA 81-84

Rawley, Callman 1903-
See Rakosi, Carl
See also CA 21-24R; CANR 12, 32

Rawlings, Marjorie Kinnan
1896-1953 . . . . **TCLC 4**
See also CA 104; 137; DLB 9, 22, 102; JRDA; MAICYA; YABC 1

Ray, Satyajit
1921-1992 . . . **CLC 16, 76; DAM MULT**
See also CA 114; 137

Read, Herbert Edward 1893-1968 . . . . **CLC 4**
See also CA 85-88; 25-28R; DLB 20, 149

Read, Piers Paul 1941- . . . . . . **CLC 4, 10, 25**
See also CA 21-24R; CANR 38; DLB 14; SATA 21

Reade, Charles 1814-1884 . . . . **NCLC 2**
See also DLB 21

Reade, Hamish
See Gray, Simon (James Holliday)

Reading, Peter 1946- . . . . **CLC 47**
See also CA 103; CANR 46; DLB 40

Reaney, James
1926- . . . . . . **CLC 13; DAC; DAM MST**
See also CA 41-44R; CAAS 15; CANR 42; DLB 68; SATA 43

Rebreanu, Liviu 1885-1944 . . . . **TCLC 28**

Rechy, John (Francisco)
1934- . . . . **CLC 1, 7, 14, 18; DAM MULT; HLC**
See also CA 5-8R; CAAS 4; CANR 6, 32; DLB 122; DLBY 82; HW; INT CANR-6

Redcam, Tom 1870-1933 . . . . **TCLC 25**

Reddin, Keith . . . . **CLC 67**

Redgrove, Peter (William)
1932- . . . . **CLC 6, 41**
See also CA 1-4R; CANR 3, 39; DLB 40

Redmon, Anne . . . . **CLC 22**
See also Nightingale, Anne Redmon
See also DLBY 86

Reed, Eliot
See Ambler, Eric

Reed, Ishmael
1938- . . . . **CLC 2, 3, 5, 6, 13, 32, 60; BLC; DAM MULT**
See also BW 2; CA 21-24R; CANR 25, 48; DLB 2, 5, 33; DLBD 8; MTCW

Reed, John (Silas) 1887-1920 . . . . . . **TCLC 9**
See also CA 106

Reed, Lou . . . . **CLC 21**
See also Firbank, Louis

Reeve, Clara 1729-1807 . . . . **NCLC 19**
See also DLB 39

Reich, Wilhelm 1897-1957 . . . . **TCLC 57**

Reid, Christopher (John) 1949- . . . . . **CLC 33**
See also CA 140; DLB 40

Reid, Desmond
See Moorcock, Michael (John)

Reid Banks, Lynne 1929-
See Banks, Lynne Reid
See also CA 1-4R; CANR 6, 22, 38; CLR 24; JRDA; MAICYA; SATA 22, 75

Reilly, William K.
See Creasey, John

Reiner, Max
See Caldwell, (Janet Miriam) Taylor (Holland)

Reis, Ricardo
See Pessoa, Fernando (Antonio Nogueira)

Remarque, Erich Maria
1898-1970 . . . . **CLC 21; DA; DAB; DAC; DAM MST, NOV**
See also CA 77-80; 29-32R; DLB 56; MTCW

Remizov, A.
See Remizov, Aleksei (Mikhailovich)

Remizov, A. M.
See Remizov, Aleksei (Mikhailovich)

Remizov, Aleksei (Mikhailovich)
1877-1957 . . . . **TCLC 27**
See also CA 125; 133

Renan, Joseph Ernest 1823-1892 . . . . **NCLC 26**

Renard, Jules 1864-1910 . . . . **TCLC 17**
See also CA 117

Renault, Mary . . . . **CLC 3, 11, 17**
See also Challans, Mary
See also DLBY 83

Rendell, Ruth (Barbara) 1930- . . . . **CLC 28, 48; DAM POP**
See also Vine, Barbara
See also CA 109; CANR 32, 52; DLB 87; INT CANR-32; MTCW

Renoir, Jean 1894-1979 . . . . **CLC 20**
See also CA 129; 85-88

Resnais, Alain 1922-. . . . . **CLC 16**

Reverdy, Pierre 1889-1960 . . . . **CLC 53**
See also CA 97-100; 89-92

Rexroth, Kenneth 1905-1982 . . . . . . **CLC 1, 2, 6, 11, 22, 49; DAM POET**
See also CA 5-8R; 107; CANR 14, 34; CDALB 1941-1968; DLB 16, 48, 165; DLBY 82; INT CANR-14; MTCW

Reyes, Alfonso 1889-1959 . . . . **TCLC 33**
See also CA 131; HW

Reyes y Basoalto, Ricardo Eliecer Neftali
See Neruda, Pablo

Reymont, Wladyslaw (Stanislaw) 1868(?)-1925 . . . . **TCLC 5**
See also CA 104

Reynolds, Jonathan 1942- . . . . **CLC 6, 38**
See also CA 65-68; CANR 28

Reynolds, Joshua 1723-1792 . . . . **LC 15**
See also DLB 104

Reynolds, Michael Shane 1937- . . . . **CLC 44**
See also CA 65-68; CANR 9

Reznikoff, Charles 1894-1976 . . . . **CLC 9**
See also CA 33-36; 61-64; CAP 2; DLB 28, 45

Rezzori (d'Arezzo), Gregor von 1914- . . . . **CLC 25**
See also CA 122; 136

Rhine, Richard
See Silverstein, Alvin

Rhodes, Eugene Manlove 1869-1934 . . . . **TCLC 53**

R'hoone
See Balzac, Honore de

Rhys, Jean 1890(?)-1979 . . . . **CLC 2, 4, 6, 14, 19, 51; DAM NOV; SSC 21**
See also CA 25-28R; 85-88; CANR 35; CDBLB 1945-1960; DLB 36, 117, 162; MTCW

Ribeiro, Darcy 1922- . . . . **CLC 34**
See also CA 33-36R

Ribeiro, Joao Ubaldo (Osorio Pimentel) 1941- . . . . **CLC 10, 67**
See also CA 81-84

Ribman, Ronald (Burt) 1932- . . . . **CLC 7**
See also CA 21-24R; CANR 46

Ricci, Nino 1959- . . . . **CLC 70**
See also CA 137

Rice, Anne 1941- . . . . . **CLC 41; DAM POP**
See also AAYA 9; BEST 89:2; CA 65-68; CANR 12, 36, 53

Rice, Elmer (Leopold) 1892-1967 . . . . **CLC 7, 49; DAM DRAM**
See also CA 21-22; 25-28R; CAP 2; DLB 4, 7; MTCW

Rice, Tim(othy Miles Bindon) 1944- . . . . **CLC 21**
See also CA 103; CANR 46

Rich, Adrienne (Cecile) 1929- . . . . **CLC 3, 6, 7, 11, 18, 36, 73, 76; DAM POET; PC 5**
See also CA 9-12R; CANR 20, 53; DLB 5, 67; MTCW

Rich, Barbara
See Graves, Robert (von Ranke)

Rich, Robert
See Trumbo, Dalton

Richard, Keith . . . . **CLC 17**
See also Richards, Keith

Richards, David Adams 1950- . . . . **CLC 59; DAC**
See also CA 93-96; DLB 53

Richards, I(vor) A(rmstrong) 1893-1979 . . . . **CLC 14, 24**
See also CA 41-44R; 89-92; CANR 34; DLB 27

Richards, Keith 1943-
See Richard, Keith
See also CA 107

Richardson, Anne
See Roiphe, Anne (Richardson)

Richardson, Dorothy Miller 1873-1957 . . . . **TCLC 3**
See also CA 104; DLB 36

Richardson, Ethel Florence (Lindesay) 1870-1946
See Richardson, Henry Handel
See also CA 105

Richardson, Henry Handel . . . . **TCLC 4**
See also Richardson, Ethel Florence (Lindesay)

Richardson, John 1796-1852 . . . . **NCLC 55; DAC**
See also DLB 99

Richardson, Samuel 1689-1761 . . . . . . **LC 1; DA; DAB; DAC; DAM MST, NOV; WLC**
See also CDBLB 1660-1789; DLB 39

Richler, Mordecai 1931- . . . . **CLC 3, 5, 9, 13, 18, 46, 70; DAC; DAM MST, NOV**
See also AITN 1; CA 65-68; CANR 31; CLR 17; DLB 53; MAICYA; MTCW; SATA 44; SATA-Brief 27

Richter, Conrad (Michael) 1890-1968 . . . . **CLC 30**
See also CA 5-8R; 25-28R; CANR 23; DLB 9; MTCW; SATA 3

Ricostranza, Tom
See Ellis, Trey

Riddell, J. H. 1832-1906 . . . . **TCLC 40**

Riding, Laura . . . . **CLC 3, 7**
See also Jackson, Laura (Riding)

Riefenstahl, Berta Helene Amalia 1902-
See Riefenstahl, Leni
See also CA 108

Riefenstahl, Leni . . . . **CLC 16**
See also Riefenstahl, Berta Helene Amalia

Riffe, Ernest
See Bergman, (Ernst) Ingmar

Riggs, (Rolla) Lynn 1899-1954 . . . . . **TCLC 56; DAM MULT**
See also CA 144; NNAL

Riley, James Whitcomb 1849-1916 . . . . . . **TCLC 51; DAM POET**
See also CA 118; 137; MAICYA; SATA 17

Riley, Tex
See Creasey, John

Rilke, Rainer Maria 1875-1926 . . . . **TCLC 1, 6, 19; DAM POET; PC 2**
See also CA 104; 132; DLB 81; MTCW

Rimbaud, (Jean Nicolas) Arthur 1854-1891 . . . . . **NCLC 4, 35; DA; DAB; DAC; DAM MST, POET; PC 3; WLC**

Rinehart, Mary Roberts 1876-1958 . . . . **TCLC 52**
See also CA 108

Ringmaster, The
See Mencken, H(enry) L(ouis)

Ringwood, Gwen(dolyn Margaret) Pharis 1910-1984 . . . . **CLC 48**
See also CA 148; 112; DLB 88

Rio, Michel 19(?)- . . . . **CLC 43**

Ritsos, Giannes
See Ritsos, Yannis

Ritsos, Yannis 1909-1990. . . . . **CLC 6, 13, 31**
See also CA 77-80; 133; CANR 39; MTCW

Ritter, Erika 1948(?)-. . . . . **CLC 52**

Rivera, Jose Eustasio 1889-1928. . . **TCLC 35**
See also HW

Rivers, Conrad Kent 1933-1968. . . . . . **CLC 1**
See also BW 1; CA 85-88; DLB 41

Rivers, Elfrida
See Bradley, Marion Zimmer

Riverside, John
See Heinlein, Robert A(nson)

Rizal, Jose 1861-1896. . . . . **NCLC 27**

Roa Bastos, Augusto (Antonio) 1917- . . . . . **CLC 45; DAM MULT; HLC**
See also CA 131; DLB 113; HW

Robbe-Grillet, Alain 1922- . . . . . . **CLC 1, 2, 4, 6, 8, 10, 14, 43**
See also CA 9-12R; CANR 33; DLB 83; MTCW

Robbins, Harold 1916- . . . . **CLC 5; DAM NOV**
See also CA 73-76; CANR 26; MTCW

Robbins, Thomas Eugene 1936-
See Robbins, Tom
See also CA 81-84; CANR 29; DAM NOV, POP; MTCW

Robbins, Tom. . . . . **CLC 9, 32, 64**
See also Robbins, Thomas Eugene
See also BEST 90:3; DLBY 80

Robbins, Trina 1938- . . . . **CLC 21**
See also CA 128

Roberts, Charles G(eorge) D(ouglas) 1860-1943 . . . . **TCLC 8**
See also CA 105; CLR 33; DLB 92; SATA 88; SATA-Brief 29

Roberts, Kate 1891-1985 . . . . **CLC 15**
See also CA 107; 116

Roberts, Keith (John Kingston) 1935- . . . . **CLC 14**
See also CA 25-28R; CANR 46

Roberts, Kenneth (Lewis) 1885-1957 . . . . **TCLC 23**
See also CA 109; DLB 9

Roberts, Michele (B.) 1949- . . . . **CLC 48**
See also CA 115

Robertson, Ellis
See Ellison, Harlan (Jay); Silverberg, Robert

Robertson, Thomas William 1829-1871 . . . . **NCLC 35; DAM DRAM**

Robinson, Edwin Arlington 1869-1935 . . . . **TCLC 5; DA; DAC; DAM MST, POET; PC 1**
See also CA 104; 133; CDALB 1865-1917; DLB 54; MTCW

Robinson, Henry Crabb 1775-1867 . . . . **NCLC 15**
See also DLB 107

Robinson, Jill 1936- . . . . **CLC 10**
See also CA 102; INT 102

Robinson, Kim Stanley 1952- . . . . . . **CLC 34**
See also CA 126

Robinson, Lloyd
See Silverberg, Robert

Robinson, Marilynne 1944- . . . . **CLC 25**
See also CA 116

Robinson, Smokey . . . . **CLC 21**
See also Robinson, William, Jr.

Robinson, William, Jr. 1940-
See Robinson, Smokey
See also CA 116

Robison, Mary 1949- . . . . **CLC 42**
See also CA 113; 116; DLB 130; INT 116

Rod, Edouard 1857-1910 . . . . **TCLC 52**

Roddenberry, Eugene Wesley 1921-1991
See Roddenberry, Gene
See also CA 110; 135; CANR 37; SATA 45; SATA-Obit 69

Roddenberry, Gene . . . . **CLC 17**
See also Roddenberry, Eugene Wesley
See also AAYA 5; SATA-Obit 69

Rodgers, Mary 1931- . . . . **CLC 12**
See also CA 49-52; CANR 8; CLR 20; INT CANR-8; JRDA; MAICYA; SATA 8

Rodgers, W(illiam) R(obert) 1909-1969 . . . . **CLC 7**
See also CA 85-88; DLB 20

Rodman, Eric
See Silverberg, Robert

Rodman, Howard 1920(?)-1985 . . . . . **CLC 65**
See also CA 118

Rodman, Maia
See Wojciechowska, Maia (Teresa)

Rodriguez, Claudio 1934- . . . . **CLC 10**
See also DLB 134

Roelvaag, O(le) E(dvart) 1876-1931 . . . . **TCLC 17**
See also CA 117; DLB 9

Roethke, Theodore (Huebner) 1908-1963 . . . . . . **CLC 1, 3, 8, 11, 19, 46; DAM POET; PC 15**
See also CA 81-84; CABS 2; CDALB 1941-1968; DLB 5; MTCW

Rogers, Thomas Hunton 1927- . . . . . **CLC 57**
See also CA 89-92; INT 89-92

Rogers, Will(iam Penn Adair) 1879-1935 . . . . . . **TCLC 8; DAM MULT**
See also CA 105; 144; DLB 11; NNAL

Rogin, Gilbert 1929- . . . . **CLC 18**
See also CA 65-68; CANR 15

Rohan, Koda . . . . **TCLC 22**
See also Koda Shigeyuki

Rohmer, Eric . . . . **CLC 16**
See also Scherer, Jean-Marie Maurice

Rohmer, Sax . . . . **TCLC 28**
See also Ward, Arthur Henry Sarsfield
See also DLB 70

Roiphe, Anne (Richardson) 1935- . . . . **CLC 3, 9**
See also CA 89-92; CANR 45; DLBY 80; INT 89-92

Rojas, Fernando de 1465-1541 . . . . . . **LC 23**

Rolfe, Frederick (William Serafino Austin Lewis Mary) 1860-1913. . . . . . **TCLC 12**
See also CA 107; DLB 34, 156

Rolland, Romain 1866-1944. . . . . . . **TCLC 23**
See also CA 118; DLB 65

Rolvaag, O(le) E(dvart)
See Roelvaag, O(le) E(dvart)

Romain Arnaud, Saint
See Aragon, Louis

Romains, Jules 1885-1972 . . . . **CLC 7**
See also CA 85-88; CANR 34; DLB 65; MTCW

Romero, Jose Ruben 1890-1952 . . . **TCLC 14**
See also CA 114; 131; HW

Ronsard, Pierre de 1524-1585 . . . . **LC 6; PC 11**

Rooke, Leon 1934- . . . . **CLC 25, 34; DAM POP**
See also CA 25-28R; CANR 23, 53

Roper, William 1498-1578 . . . . **LC 10**

Roquelaure, A. N.
See Rice, Anne

Rosa, Joao Guimaraes 1908-1967 . . . **CLC 23**
See also CA 89-92; DLB 113

Rose, Wendy 1948- . . . . **CLC 85; DAM MULT; PC 13**
See also CA 53-56; CANR 5, 51; NNAL; SATA 12

Rosen, Richard (Dean) 1949- . . . . **CLC 39**
See also CA 77-80; INT CANR-30

Rosenberg, Isaac 1890-1918. . . . . . . **TCLC 12**
See also CA 107; DLB 20

Rosenblatt, Joe . . . . **CLC 15**
See also Rosenblatt, Joseph

Rosenblatt, Joseph 1933-
See Rosenblatt, Joe
See also CA 89-92; INT 89-92

Rosenfeld, Samuel 1896-1963
See Tzara, Tristan
See also CA 89-92

Rosenthal, M(acha) L(ouis) 1917-1996 . . . . **CLC 28**
See also CA 1-4R; 152; CAAS 6; CANR 4, 51; DLB 5; SATA 59

Ross, Barnaby
See Dannay, Frederic

Ross, Bernard L.
See Follett, Ken(neth Martin)

Ross, J. H.
See Lawrence, T(homas) E(dward)

Ross, Martin
See Martin, Violet Florence
See also DLB 135

Ross, (James) Sinclair 1908- . . . . . . **CLC 13; DAC; DAM MST**
See also CA 73-76; DLB 88

Rossetti, Christina (Georgina) 1830-1894 . . . . . **NCLC 2, 50; DA; DAB; DAC; DAM MST, POET; PC 7; WLC**
See also DLB 35, 163; MAICYA; SATA 20

Rossetti, Dante Gabriel 1828-1882 . . . . **NCLC 4; DA; DAB; DAC; DAM MST, POET; WLC**
See also CDBLB 1832-1890; DLB 35

Rossner, Judith (Perelman) 1935- . . . . **CLC 6, 9, 29**
See also AITN 2; BEST 90:3; CA 17-20R; CANR 18, 51; DLB 6; INT CANR-18; MTCW

Rostand, Edmond (Eugene Alexis) 1868-1918 . . . . . . **TCLC 6, 37; DA; DAB; DAC; DAM DRAM, MST**
See also CA 104; 126; MTCW

Roth, Henry 1906-1995 . . . . **CLC 2, 6, 11**
See also CA 11-12; 149; CANR 38; CAP 1; DLB 28; MTCW

Roth, Joseph 1894-1939. . . . . **TCLC 33**
See also DLB 85

Roth, Philip (Milton) 1933- . . . . . . **CLC 1, 2, 3, 4, 6, 9, 15, 22, 31, 47, 66, 86; DA; DAB; DAC; DAM MST, NOV, POP; WLC**
See also BEST 90:3; CA 1-4R; CANR 1, 22, 36; CDALB 1968-1988; DLB 2, 28; DLBY 82; MTCW

Rothenberg, Jerome 1931- . . . . **CLC 6, 57**
See also CA 45-48; CANR 1; DLB 5

Roumain, Jacques (Jean Baptiste) 1907-1944 . . . . **TCLC 19; BLC; DAM MULT**
See also BW 1; CA 117; 125

Rourke, Constance (Mayfield) 1885-1941 . . . . **TCLC 12**
See also CA 107; YABC 1

Rousseau, Jean-Baptiste 1671-1741 . . . **LC 9**

Rousseau, Jean-Jacques 1712-1778 . . . . . **LC 14; DA; DAB; DAC; DAM MST; WLC**

Roussel, Raymond 1877-1933 . . . . . **TCLC 20**
See also CA 117

Rovit, Earl (Herbert) 1927- . . . . **CLC 7**
See also CA 5-8R; CANR 12

Rowe, Nicholas 1674-1718........... **LC 8**
See also DLB 84

Rowley, Ames Dorrance
See Lovecraft, H(oward) P(hillips)

Rowson, Susanna Haswell
1762(?)-1824 .... **NCLC 5**
See also DLB 37

Roy, Gabrielle
1909-1983 .... **CLC 10, 14; DAB; DAC; DAM MST**
See also CA 53-56; 110; CANR 5; DLB 68; MTCW

Rozewicz, Tadeusz
1921- .... **CLC 9, 23; DAM POET**
See also CA 108; CANR 36; MTCW

Ruark, Gibbons 1941- .... **CLC 3**
See also CA 33-36R; CAAS 23; CANR 14, 31; DLB 120

Rubens, Bernice (Ruth) 1923- ... **CLC 19, 31**
See also CA 25-28R; CANR 33; DLB 14; MTCW

Rudkin, (James) David 1936- ...... **CLC 14**
See also CA 89-92; DLB 13

Rudnik, Raphael 1933-............. **CLC 7**
See also CA 29-32R

Ruffian, M.
See Hasek, Jaroslav (Matej Frantisek)

Ruiz, Jose Martinez .... **CLC 11**
See also Martinez Ruiz, Jose

Rukeyser, Muriel
1913-1980 .... **CLC 6, 10, 15, 27; DAM POET; PC 12**
See also CA 5-8R; 93-96; CANR 26; DLB 48; MTCW; SATA-Obit 22

Rule, Jane (Vance) 1931-.......... **CLC 27**
See also CA 25-28R; CAAS 18; CANR 12; DLB 60

Rulfo, Juan
1918-1986 .... **CLC 8, 80; DAM MULT; HLC**
See also CA 85-88; 118; CANR 26; DLB 113; HW; MTCW

Runeberg, Johan 1804-1877...... **NCLC 41**

Runyon, (Alfred) Damon
1884(?)-1946 .... **TCLC 10**
See also CA 107; DLB 11, 86

Rush, Norman 1933-.............. **CLC 44**
See also CA 121; 126; INT 126

Rushdie, (Ahmed) Salman
1947- ..... **CLC 23, 31, 55; DAB; DAC; DAM MST, NOV, POP**
See also BEST 89:3; CA 108; 111; CANR 33; INT 111; MTCW

Rushforth, Peter (Scott) 1945- ..... **CLC 19**
See also CA 101

Ruskin, John 1819-1900.......... **TCLC 63**
See also CA 114; 129; CDBLB 1832-1890; DLB 55, 163; SATA 24

Russ, Joanna 1937-.............. **CLC 15**
See also CA 25-28R; CANR 11, 31; DLB 8; MTCW

Russell, George William 1867-1935
See A. E.
See also CA 104; CDBLB 1890-1914; DAM POET

Russell, (Henry) Ken(neth Alfred)
1927- .... **CLC 16**
See also CA 105

Russell, Willy 1947-.............. **CLC 60**

Rutherford, Mark .... **TCLC 25**
See also White, William Hale
See also DLB 18

Ruyslinck, Ward 1929-............ **CLC 14**
See also Belser, Reimond Karel Maria de

Ryan, Cornelius (John) 1920-1974 ... **CLC 7**
See also CA 69-72; 53-56; CANR 38

Ryan, Michael 1946- .... **CLC 65**
See also CA 49-52; DLBY 82

Rybakov, Anatoli (Naumovich)
1911- .... **CLC 23, 53**
See also CA 126; 135; SATA 79

Ryder, Jonathan
See Ludlum, Robert

Ryga, George
1932-1987 .. **CLC 14; DAC; DAM MST**
See also CA 101; 124; CANR 43; DLB 60

S. S.
See Sassoon, Siegfried (Lorraine)

Saba, Umberto 1883-1957 .... **TCLC 33**
See also CA 144; DLB 114

Sabatini, Rafael 1875-1950 .... **TCLC 47**

Sabato, Ernesto (R.)
1911- .... **CLC 10, 23; DAM MULT; HLC**
See also CA 97-100; CANR 32; DLB 145; HW; MTCW

Sacastru, Martin
See Bioy Casares, Adolfo

Sacher-Masoch, Leopold von
1836(?)-1895 .... **NCLC 31**

Sachs, Marilyn (Stickle) 1927- ..... **CLC 35**
See also AAYA 2; CA 17-20R; CANR 13, 47; CLR 2; JRDA; MAICYA; SAAS 2; SATA 3, 68

Sachs, Nelly 1891-1970 .... **CLC 14**
See also CA 17-18; 25-28R; CAP 2

Sackler, Howard (Oliver)
1929-1982 .... **CLC 14**
See also CA 61-64; 108; CANR 30; DLB 7

Sacks, Oliver (Wolf) 1933- .... **CLC 67**
See also CA 53-56; CANR 28, 50; INT CANR-28; MTCW

Sade, Donatien Alphonse Francois Comte
1740-1814 .... **NCLC 47**

Sadoff, Ira 1945-.................. **CLC 9**
See also CA 53-56; CANR 5, 21; DLB 120

Saetone
See Camus, Albert

Safire, William 1929-............. **CLC 10**
See also CA 17-20R; CANR 31

Sagan, Carl (Edward) 1934-........ **CLC 30**
See also AAYA 2; CA 25-28R; CANR 11, 36; MTCW; SATA 58

Sagan, Francoise .... **CLC 3, 6, 9, 17, 36**
See also Quoirez, Francoise
See also DLB 83

Sahgal, Nayantara (Pandit) 1927-... **CLC 41**
See also CA 9-12R; CANR 11

Saint, H(arry) F. 1941- .... **CLC 50**
See also CA 127

St. Aubin de Teran, Lisa 1953-
See Teran, Lisa St. Aubin de
See also CA 118; 126; INT 126

Sainte-Beuve, Charles Augustin
1804-1869 .... **NCLC 5**

Saint-Exupery, Antoine (Jean Baptiste Marie Roger) de
1900-1944 .... **TCLC 2, 56; DAM NOV; WLC**
See also CA 108; 132; CLR 10; DLB 72; MAICYA; MTCW; SATA 20

St. John, David
See Hunt, E(verette) Howard, (Jr.)

Saint-John Perse
See Leger, (Marie-Rene Auguste) Alexis Saint-Leger

Saintsbury, George (Edward Bateman)
1845-1933 .... **TCLC 31**
See also DLB 57, 149

Sait Faik .... **TCLC 23**
See also Abasiyanik, Sait Faik

Saki .... **TCLC 3; SSC 12**
See also Munro, H(ector) H(ugh)

Sala, George Augustus .... **NCLC 46**

Salama, Hannu 1936-............. **CLC 18**

Salamanca, J(ack) R(ichard)
1922- .... **CLC 4, 15**
See also CA 25-28R

Sale, J. Kirkpatrick
See Sale, Kirkpatrick

Sale, Kirkpatrick 1937- .... **CLC 68**
See also CA 13-16R; CANR 10

Salinas, Luis Omar
1937- ..... **CLC 90; DAM MULT; HLC**
See also CA 131; DLB 82; HW

Salinas (y Serrano), Pedro
1891(?)-1951 .... **TCLC 17**
See also CA 117; DLB 134

Salinger, J(erome) D(avid)
1919- ...... **CLC 1, 3, 8, 12, 55, 56; DA; DAB; DAC; DAM MST, NOV, POP; SSC 2; WLC**
See also AAYA 2; CA 5-8R; CANR 39; CDALB 1941-1968; CLR 18; DLB 2, 102; MAICYA; MTCW; SATA 67

Salisbury, John
See Caute, David

Salter, James 1925- .... **CLC 7, 52, 59**
See also CA 73-76; DLB 130

Saltus, Edgar (Everton)
1855-1921 .... **TCLC 8**
See also CA 105

Saltykov, Mikhail Evgrafovich
1826-1889 .... **NCLC 16**

Samarakis, Antonis 1919- .... **CLC 5**
See also CA 25-28R; CAAS 16; CANR 36

Sanchez, Florencio 1875-1910..... **TCLC 37**
See also HW

Sanchez, Luis Rafael 1936-........ **CLC 23**
See also CA 128; DLB 145; HW

Schulberg, Budd (Wilson)
1914- . . . . . **CLC 7, 48**
See also CA 25-28R; CANR 19; DLB 6, 26, 28; DLBY 81

Schulz, Bruno
1892-1942 . . . . . **TCLC 5, 51; SSC 13**
See also CA 115; 123

Schulz, Charles M(onroe) 1922- . . . . **CLC 12**
See also CA 9-12R; CANR 6; INT CANR-6; SATA 10

Schumacher, E(rnst) F(riedrich)
1911-1977 . . . . . **CLC 80**
See also CA 81-84; 73-76; CANR 34

Schuyler, James Marcus
1923-1991 . . . . . **CLC 5, 23; DAM POET**
See also CA 101; 134; DLB 5; INT 101

Schwartz, Delmore (David)
1913-1966 . . . **CLC 2, 4, 10, 45, 87; PC 8**
See also CA 17-18; 25-28R; CANR 35; CAP 2; DLB 28, 48; MTCW

Schwartz, Ernst
See Ozu, Yasujiro

Schwartz, John Burnham 1965- . . . . **CLC 59**
See also CA 132

Schwartz, Lynne Sharon 1939- . . . . . **CLC 31**
See also CA 103; CANR 44

Schwartz, Muriel A.
See Eliot, T(homas) S(tearns)

Schwarz-Bart, Andre 1928- . . . . **CLC 2, 4**
See also CA 89-92

Schwarz-Bart, Simone 1938- . . . . **CLC 7**
See also BW 2; CA 97-100

Schwob, (Mayer Andre) Marcel
1867-1905 . . . . . **TCLC 20**
See also CA 117; DLB 123

Sciascia, Leonardo
1921-1989 . . . . . **CLC 8, 9, 41**
See also CA 85-88; 130; CANR 35; MTCW

Scoppettone, Sandra 1936- . . . . **CLC 26**
See also AAYA 11; CA 5-8R; CANR 41; SATA 9

Scorsese, Martin 1942- . . . . **CLC 20, 89**
See also CA 110; 114; CANR 46

Scotland, Jay
See Jakes, John (William)

Scott, Duncan Campbell
1862-1947 . . . . . **TCLC 6; DAC**
See also CA 104; DLB 92

Scott, Evelyn 1893-1963. . . . . **CLC 43**
See also CA 104; 112; DLB 9, 48

Scott, F(rancis) R(eginald)
1899-1985 . . . . . **CLC 22**
See also CA 101; 114; DLB 88; INT 101

Scott, Frank
See Scott, F(rancis) R(eginald)

Scott, Joanna 1960- . . . . . **CLC 50**
See also CA 126; CANR 53

Scott, Paul (Mark) 1920-1978. . . . **CLC 9, 60**
See also CA 81-84; 77-80; CANR 33; DLB 14; MTCW

Scott, Walter
1771-1832 . . . . **NCLC 15; DA; DAB; DAC; DAM MST, NOV, POET; PC 13; WLC**
See also CDBLB 1789-1832; DLB 93, 107, 116, 144, 159; YABC 2

Scribe, (Augustin) Eugene
1791-1861 . . . . **NCLC 16; DAM DRAM; DC 5**

Scrum, R.
See Crumb, R(obert)

Scudery, Madeleine de 1607-1701. . . . . **LC 2**

Scum
See Crumb, R(obert)

Scumbag, Little Bobby
See Crumb, R(obert)

Seabrook, John
See Hubbard, L(afayette) Ron(ald)

Sealy, I. Allan 1951- . . . . . **CLC 55**

Search, Alexander
See Pessoa, Fernando (Antonio Nogueira)

Sebastian, Lee
See Silverberg, Robert

Sebastian Owl
See Thompson, Hunter S(tockton)

Sebestyen, Ouida 1924- . . . . . **CLC 30**
See also AAYA 8; CA 107; CANR 40; CLR 17; JRDA; MAICYA; SAAS 10; SATA 39

Secundus, H. Scriblerus
See Fielding, Henry

Sedges, John
See Buck, Pearl S(ydenstricker)

Sedgwick, Catharine Maria
1789-1867 . . . . . **NCLC 19**
See also DLB 1, 74

Seelye, John 1931- . . . . . **CLC 7**

Seferiades, Giorgos Stylianou 1900-1971
See Seferis, George
See also CA 5-8R; 33-36R; CANR 5, 36; MTCW

Seferis, George . . . . . **CLC 5, 11**
See also Seferiades, Giorgos Stylianou

Segal, Erich (Wolf)
1937- . . . . **CLC 3, 10; DAM POP**
See also BEST 89:1; CA 25-28R; CANR 20, 36; DLBY 86; INT CANR-20; MTCW

Seger, Bob 1945-. . . . . **CLC 35**

Seghers, Anna . . . . . **CLC 7**
See also Radvanyi, Netty
See also DLB 69

Seidel, Frederick (Lewis) 1936-. . . . . **CLC 18**
See also CA 13-16R; CANR 8; DLBY 84

Seifert, Jaroslav
1901-1986 . . . . . **CLC 34, 44, 93**
See also CA 127; MTCW

Sei Shonagon c. 966-1017(?) . . . . . . **CMLC 6**

Selby, Hubert, Jr.
1928- . . . . **CLC 1, 2, 4, 8; SSC 20**
See also CA 13-16R; CANR 33; DLB 2

Selzer, Richard 1928-. . . . . **CLC 74**
See also CA 65-68; CANR 14

Sembene, Ousmane
See Ousmane, Sembene

Senancour, Etienne Pivert de
1770-1846 . . . . . **NCLC 16**
See also DLB 119

Sender, Ramon (Jose)
1902-1982 . . **CLC 8; DAM MULT; HLC**
See also CA 5-8R; 105; CANR 8; HW; MTCW

Seneca, Lucius Annaeus
4B.C.-65. . . . . . . **CMLC 6; DAM DRAM; DC 5**

Senghor, Leopold Sedar
1906- . . . . . **CLC 54; BLC; DAM MULT, POET**
See also BW 2; CA 116; 125; CANR 47; MTCW

Serling, (Edward) Rod(man)
1924-1975 . . . . . **CLC 30**
See also AAYA 14; AITN 1; CA 65-68; 57-60; DLB 26

Serna, Ramon Gomez de la
See Gomez de la Serna, Ramon

Serpieres
See Guillevic, (Eugene)

Service, Robert
See Service, Robert W(illiam)
See also DAB; DLB 92

Service, Robert W(illiam)
1874(?)-1958 . . . . . . **TCLC 15; DA; DAC; DAM MST, POET; WLC**
See also Service, Robert
See also CA 115; 140; SATA 20

Seth, Vikram
1952- . . . . **CLC 43, 90; DAM MULT**
See also CA 121; 127; CANR 50; DLB 120; INT 127

Seton, Cynthia Propper
1926-1982 . . . . . **CLC 27**
See also CA 5-8R; 108; CANR 7

Seton, Ernest (Evan) Thompson
1860-1946 . . . . . **TCLC 31**
See also CA 109; DLB 92; DLBD 13; JRDA; SATA 18

Seton-Thompson, Ernest
See Seton, Ernest (Evan) Thompson

Settle, Mary Lee 1918- . . . . **CLC 19, 61**
See also CA 89-92; CAAS 1; CANR 44; DLB 6; INT 89-92

Seuphor, Michel
See Arp, Jean

Sevigne, Marie (de Rabutin-Chantal) Marquise de 1626-1696 . . . . . **LC 11**

Sexton, Anne (Harvey)
1928-1974 . . . . **CLC 2, 4, 6, 8, 10, 15, 53; DA; DAB; DAC; DAM MST, POET; PC 2; WLC**
See also CA 1-4R; 53-56; CABS 2; CANR 3, 36; CDALB 1941-1968; DLB 5; MTCW; SATA 10

Shaara, Michael (Joseph, Jr.)
1929-1988 . . . . **CLC 15; DAM POP**
See also AITN 1; CA 102; 125; CANR 52; DLBY 83

Shackleton, C. C.
See Aldiss, Brian W(ilson)

Shacochis, Bob . . . . . **CLC 39**
See also Shacochis, Robert G.

Author Index

Shacochis, Robert G. 1951-
See Shacochis, Bob
See also CA 119; 124; INT 124

Shaffer, Anthony (Joshua) 1926- .... **CLC 19; DAM DRAM**
See also CA 110; 116; DLB 13

Shaffer, Peter (Levin) 1926- ...... **CLC 5, 14, 18, 37, 60; DAB; DAM DRAM, MST**
See also CA 25-28R; CANR 25, 47; CDBLB 1960 to Present; DLB 13; MTCW

Shakey, Bernard
See Young, Neil

Shalamov, Varlam (Tikhonovich) 1907(?)-1982 .... **CLC 18**
See also CA 129; 105

Shamlu, Ahmad 1925- .... **CLC 10**

Shammas, Anton 1951-........... **CLC 55**

Shange, Ntozake 1948- .... **CLC 8, 25, 38, 74; BLC; DAM DRAM, MULT; DC 3**
See also AAYA 9; BW 2; CA 85-88; CABS 3; CANR 27, 48; DLB 38; MTCW

Shanley, John Patrick 1950-....... **CLC 75**
See also CA 128; 133

Shapcott, Thomas W(illiam) 1935- .. **CLC 38**
See also CA 69-72; CANR 49

Shapiro, Jane..................... **CLC 76**

Shapiro, Karl (Jay) 1913- .. **CLC 4, 8, 15, 53**
See also CA 1-4R; CAAS 6; CANR 1, 36; DLB 48; MTCW

Sharp, William 1855-1905 .... **TCLC 39**
See also DLB 156

Sharpe, Thomas Ridley 1928-
See Sharpe, Tom
See also CA 114; 122; INT 122

Sharpe, Tom..................... **CLC 36**
See also Sharpe, Thomas Ridley
See also DLB 14

Shaw, Bernard................... **TCLC 45**
See also Shaw, George Bernard
See also BW 1

Shaw, G. Bernard
See Shaw, George Bernard

Shaw, George Bernard 1856-1950 ... **TCLC 3, 9, 21; DA; DAB; DAC; DAM DRAM, MST; WLC**
See also Shaw, Bernard
See also CA 104; 128; CDBLB 1914-1945; DLB 10, 57; MTCW

Shaw, Henry Wheeler 1818-1885 .... **NCLC 15**
See also DLB 11

Shaw, Irwin 1913-1984 .... **CLC 7, 23, 34; DAM DRAM, POP**
See also AITN 1; CA 13-16R; 112; CANR 21; CDALB 1941-1968; DLB 6, 102; DLBY 84; MTCW

Shaw, Robert 1927-1978 .... **CLC 5**
See also AITN 1; CA 1-4R; 81-84; CANR 4; DLB 13, 14

Shaw, T. E.
See Lawrence, T(homas) E(dward)

Shawn, Wallace 1943- .... **CLC 41**
See also CA 112

Shea, Lisa 1953-................. **CLC 86**
See also CA 147

Sheed, Wilfrid (John Joseph) 1930- .... **CLC 2, 4, 10, 53**
See also CA 65-68; CANR 30; DLB 6; MTCW

Sheldon, Alice Hastings Bradley 1915(?)-1987
See Tiptree, James, Jr.
See also CA 108; 122; CANR 34; INT 108; MTCW

Sheldon, John
See Bloch, Robert (Albert)

Shelley, Mary Wollstonecraft (Godwin) 1797-1851 .... **NCLC 14; DA; DAB; DAC; DAM MST, NOV; WLC**
See also CDBLB 1789-1832; DLB 110, 116, 159; SATA 29

Shelley, Percy Bysshe 1792-1822 .... **NCLC 18; DA; DAB; DAC; DAM MST, POET; PC 14; WLC**
See also CDBLB 1789-1832; DLB 96, 110, 158

Shepard, Jim 1956-.............. **CLC 36**
See also CA 137

Shepard, Lucius 1947- .... **CLC 34**
See also CA 128; 141

Shepard, Sam 1943- .... **CLC 4, 6, 17, 34, 41, 44; DAM DRAM; DC 5**
See also AAYA 1; CA 69-72; CABS 3; CANR 22; DLB 7; MTCW

Shepherd, Michael
See Ludlum, Robert

Sherburne, Zoa (Morin) 1912-...... **CLC 30**
See also AAYA 13; CA 1-4R; CANR 3, 37; MAICYA; SAAS 18; SATA 3

Sheridan, Frances 1724-1766......... **LC 7**
See also DLB 39, 84

Sheridan, Richard Brinsley 1751-1816 .... **NCLC 5; DA; DAB; DAC; DAM DRAM, MST; DC 1; WLC**
See also CDBLB 1660-1789; DLB 89

Sherman, Jonathan Marc........... **CLC 55**

Sherman, Martin 1941(?)- .... **CLC 19**
See also CA 116; 123

Sherwin, Judith Johnson 1936-... **CLC 7, 15**
See also CA 25-28R; CANR 34

Sherwood, Frances 1940-.......... **CLC 81**
See also CA 146

Sherwood, Robert E(mmet) 1896-1955 ...... **TCLC 3; DAM DRAM**
See also CA 104; DLB 7, 26

Shestov, Lev 1866-1938 .... **TCLC 56**

Shevchenko, Taras 1814-1861 .... **NCLC 54**

Shiel, M(atthew) P(hipps) 1865-1947 .... **TCLC 8**
See also CA 106; DLB 153

Shields, Carol 1935-......... **CLC 91; DAC**
See also CA 81-84; CANR 51

Shiga, Naoya 1883-1971... **CLC 33; SSC 23**
See also CA 101; 33-36R

Shilts, Randy 1951-1994 .... **CLC 85**
See also CA 115; 127; 144; CANR 45; INT 127

Shimazaki, Haruki 1872-1943
See Shimazaki Toson
See also CA 105; 134

Shimazaki Toson................. **TCLC 5**
See also Shimazaki, Haruki

Sholokhov, Mikhail (Aleksandrovich) 1905-1984 .... **CLC 7, 15**
See also CA 101; 112; MTCW; SATA-Obit 36

Shone, Patric
See Hanley, James

Shreve, Susan Richards 1939-...... **CLC 23**
See also CA 49-52; CAAS 5; CANR 5, 38; MAICYA; SATA 46; SATA-Brief 41

Shue, Larry 1946-1985 ...... **CLC 52; DAM DRAM**
See also CA 145; 117

Shu-Jen, Chou 1881-1936
See Lu Hsun
See also CA 104

Shulman, Alix Kates 1932- ...... **CLC 2, 10**
See also CA 29-32R; CANR 43; SATA 7

Shuster, Joe 1914- .... **CLC 21**

Shute, Nevil...................... **CLC 30**
See also Norway, Nevil Shute

Shuttle, Penelope (Diane) 1947- ..... **CLC 7**
See also CA 93-96; CANR 39; DLB 14, 40

Sidney, Mary 1561-1621 .... **LC 19**

Sidney, Sir Philip 1554-1586 ..... **LC 19; DA; DAB; DAC; DAM MST, POET**
See also CDBLB Before 1660; DLB 167

Siegel, Jerome 1914-1996 .... **CLC 21**
See also CA 116; 151

Siegel, Jerry
See Siegel, Jerome

Sienkiewicz, Henryk (Adam Alexander Pius) 1846-1916 .... **TCLC 3**
See also CA 104; 134

Sierra, Gregorio Martinez
See Martinez Sierra, Gregorio

Sierra, Maria (de la O'LeJarraga) Martinez
See Martinez Sierra, Maria (de la O'LeJarraga)

Sigal, Clancy 1926-............... **CLC 7**
See also CA 1-4R

Sigourney, Lydia Howard (Huntley) 1791-1865 .... **NCLC 21**
See also DLB 1, 42, 73

Siguenza y Gongora, Carlos de 1645-1700 .... **LC 8**

Sigurjonsson, Johann 1880-1919... **TCLC 27**

Sikelianos, Angelos 1884-1951 .... **TCLC 39**

Silkin, Jon 1930- .... **CLC 2, 6, 43**
See also CA 5-8R; CAAS 5; DLB 27

Silko, Leslie (Marmon) 1948- .... **CLC 23, 74; DA; DAC; DAM MST, MULT, POP**
See also AAYA 14; CA 115; 122; CANR 45; DLB 143; NNAL

Sillanpaa, Frans Eemil 1888-1964 . . . **CLC 19**
See also CA 129; 93-96; MTCW

Sillitoe, Alan
1928- . . . . **CLC 1, 3, 6, 10, 19, 57**
See also AITN 1; CA 9-12R; CAAS 2; CANR 8, 26; CDBLB 1960 to Present; DLB 14, 139; MTCW; SATA 61

Silone, Ignazio 1900-1978 . . . . **CLC 4**
See also CA 25-28; 81-84; CANR 34; CAP 2; MTCW

Silver, Joan Micklin 1935- . . . . **CLC 20**
See also CA 114; 121; INT 121

Silver, Nicholas
See Faust, Frederick (Schiller)

Silverberg, Robert
1935- . . . . **CLC 7; DAM POP**
See also CA 1-4R; CAAS 3; CANR 1, 20, 36; DLB 8; INT CANR-20; MAICYA; MTCW; SATA 13

Silverstein, Alvin 1933- . . . . **CLC 17**
See also CA 49-52; CANR 2; CLR 25; JRDA; MAICYA; SATA 8, 69

Silverstein, Virginia B(arbara Opshelor)
1937- . . . . **CLC 17**
See also CA 49-52; CANR 2; CLR 25; JRDA; MAICYA; SATA 8, 69

Sim, Georges
See Simenon, Georges (Jacques Christian)

Simak, Clifford D(onald)
1904-1988 . . . . **CLC 1, 55**
See also CA 1-4R; 125; CANR 1, 35; DLB 8; MTCW; SATA-Obit 56

Simenon, Georges (Jacques Christian)
1903-1989 . . . . **CLC 1, 2, 3, 8, 18, 47; DAM POP**
See also CA 85-88; 129; CANR 35; DLB 72; DLBY 89; MTCW

Simic, Charles
1938- . . . . **CLC 6, 9, 22, 49, 68; DAM POET**
See also CA 29-32R; CAAS 4; CANR 12, 33, 52; DLB 105

Simmel, Georg 1858-1918 . . . . **TCLC 64**

Simmons, Charles (Paul) 1924- . . . . . **CLC 57**
See also CA 89-92; INT 89-92

Simmons, Dan 1948- . . . **CLC 44; DAM POP**
See also AAYA 16; CA 138; CANR 53

Simmons, James (Stewart Alexander)
1933- . . . . **CLC 43**
See also CA 105; CAAS 21; DLB 40

Simms, William Gilmore
1806-1870 . . . . **NCLC 3**
See also DLB 3, 30, 59, 73

Simon, Carly 1945- . . . . **CLC 26**
See also CA 105

Simon, Claude
1913- . . . . **CLC 4, 9, 15, 39; DAM NOV**
See also CA 89-92; CANR 33; DLB 83; MTCW

Simon, (Marvin) Neil
1927- . . . . **CLC 6, 11, 31, 39, 70; DAM DRAM**
See also AITN 1; CA 21-24R; CANR 26; DLB 7; MTCW

Simon, Paul 1942(?)- . . . . **CLC 17**
See also CA 116

Simonon, Paul 1956(?)- . . . . **CLC 30**

Simpson, Harriette
See Arnow, Harriette (Louisa) Simpson

Simpson, Louis (Aston Marantz)
1923- . . . . **CLC 4, 7, 9, 32; DAM POET**
See also CA 1-4R; CAAS 4; CANR 1; DLB 5; MTCW

Simpson, Mona (Elizabeth) 1957- . . . **CLC 44**
See also CA 122; 135

Simpson, N(orman) F(rederick)
1919- . . . . **CLC 29**
See also CA 13-16R; DLB 13

Sinclair, Andrew (Annandale)
1935- . . . . **CLC 2, 14**
See also CA 9-12R; CAAS 5; CANR 14, 38; DLB 14; MTCW

Sinclair, Emil
See Hesse, Hermann

Sinclair, Iain 1943- . . . . **CLC 76**
See also CA 132

Sinclair, Iain MacGregor
See Sinclair, Iain

Sinclair, Mary Amelia St. Clair 1865(?)-1946
See Sinclair, May
See also CA 104

Sinclair, May . . . . **TCLC 3, 11**
See also Sinclair, Mary Amelia St. Clair
See also DLB 36, 135

Sinclair, Upton (Beall)
1878-1968 . . . . . . **CLC 1, 11, 15, 63; DA; DAB; DAC; DAM MST, NOV; WLC**
See also CA 5-8R; 25-28R; CANR 7; CDALB 1929-1941; DLB 9; INT CANR-7; MTCW; SATA 9

Singer, Isaac
See Singer, Isaac Bashevis

Singer, Isaac Bashevis
1904-1991 . . . . **CLC 1, 3, 6, 9, 11, 15, 23, 38, 69; DA; DAB; DAC; DAM MST, NOV; SSC 3; WLC**
See also AITN 1, 2; CA 1-4R; 134; CANR 1, 39; CDALB 1941-1968; CLR 1; DLB 6, 28, 52; DLBY 91; JRDA; MAICYA; MTCW; SATA 3, 27; SATA-Obit 68

Singer, Israel Joshua 1893-1944 . . . **TCLC 33**

Singh, Khushwant 1915- . . . . **CLC 11**
See also CA 9-12R; CAAS 9; CANR 6

Sinjohn, John
See Galsworthy, John

Sinyavsky, Andrei (Donatevich)
1925- . . . . **CLC 8**
See also CA 85-88

Sirin, V.
See Nabokov, Vladimir (Vladimirovich)

Sissman, L(ouis) E(dward)
1928-1976 . . . . **CLC 9, 18**
See also CA 21-24R; 65-68; CANR 13; DLB 5

Sisson, C(harles) H(ubert) 1914- . . . . . **CLC 8**
See also CA 1-4R; CAAS 3; CANR 3, 48; DLB 27

Sitwell, Dame Edith
1887-1964 . . . . **CLC 2, 9, 67; DAM POET; PC 3**
See also CA 9-12R; CANR 35; CDBLB 1945-1960; DLB 20; MTCW

Sjoewall, Maj 1935- . . . . **CLC 7**
See also CA 65-68

Sjowall, Maj
See Sjoewall, Maj

Skelton, Robin 1925- . . . . **CLC 13**
See also AITN 2; CA 5-8R; CAAS 5; CANR 28; DLB 27, 53

Skolimowski, Jerzy 1938- . . . . **CLC 20**
See also CA 128

Skram, Amalie (Bertha)
1847-1905 . . . . **TCLC 25**

Skvorecky, Josef (Vaclav)
1924- . . . . **CLC 15, 39, 69; DAC; DAM NOV**
See also CA 61-64; CAAS 1; CANR 10, 34; MTCW

Slade, Bernard . . . . **CLC 11, 46**
See also Newbound, Bernard Slade
See also CAAS 9; DLB 53

Slaughter, Carolyn 1946- . . . . **CLC 56**
See also CA 85-88

Slaughter, Frank G(ill) 1908- . . . . . . **CLC 29**
See also AITN 2; CA 5-8R; CANR 5; INT CANR-5

Slavitt, David R(ytman) 1935- . . . . **CLC 5, 14**
See also CA 21-24R; CAAS 3; CANR 41; DLB 5, 6

Slesinger, Tess 1905-1945 . . . . **TCLC 10**
See also CA 107; DLB 102

Slessor, Kenneth 1901-1971 . . . . **CLC 14**
See also CA 102; 89-92

Slowacki, Juliusz 1809-1849 . . . . . **NCLC 15**

Smart, Christopher
1722-1771 . . . **LC 3; DAM POET; PC 13**
See also DLB 109

Smart, Elizabeth 1913-1986 . . . . **CLC 54**
See also CA 81-84; 118; DLB 88

Smiley, Jane (Graves)
1949- . . . . **CLC 53, 76; DAM POP**
See also CA 104; CANR 30, 50; INT CANR-30

Smith, A(rthur) J(ames) M(arshall)
1902-1980 . . . . **CLC 15; DAC**
See also CA 1-4R; 102; CANR 4; DLB 88

Smith, Anna Deavere 1950- . . . . **CLC 86**
See also CA 133

Smith, Betty (Wehner) 1896-1972 . . . **CLC 19**
See also CA 5-8R; 33-36R; DLBY 82; SATA 6

Smith, Charlotte (Turner)
1749-1806 . . . . **NCLC 23**
See also DLB 39, 109

Smith, Clark Ashton 1893-1961 . . . . **CLC 43**
See also CA 143

Smith, Dave . . . . **CLC 22, 42**
See also Smith, David (Jeddie)
See also CAAS 7; DLB 5

Smith, David (Jeddie) 1942-
See Smith, Dave
See also CA 49-52; CANR 1; DAM POET

Smith, Florence Margaret 1902-1971
See Smith, Stevie
See also CA 17-18; 29-32R; CANR 35; CAP 2; DAM POET; MTCW

Smith, Iain Crichton 1928- .... **CLC 64**
See also CA 21-24R; DLB 40, 139

Smith, John 1580(?)-1631 .... **LC 9**

Smith, Johnston
See Crane, Stephen (Townley)

Smith, Joseph, Jr. 1805-1844 .... **NCLC 53**

Smith, Lee 1944-.............. **CLC 25, 73**
See also CA 114; 119; CANR 46; DLB 143; DLBY 83; INT 119

Smith, Martin
See Smith, Martin Cruz

Smith, Martin Cruz
1942- ..... **CLC 25; DAM MULT, POP**
See also BEST 89:4; CA 85-88; CANR 6, 23, 43; INT CANR-23; NNAL

Smith, Mary-Ann Tirone 1944-..... **CLC 39**
See also CA 118; 136

Smith, Patti 1946- .... **CLC 12**
See also CA 93-96

Smith, Pauline (Urmson)
1882-1959 .... **TCLC 25**

Smith, Rosamond
See Oates, Joyce Carol

Smith, Sheila Kaye
See Kaye-Smith, Sheila

Smith, Stevie .... **CLC 3, 8, 25, 44; PC 12**
See also Smith, Florence Margaret
See also DLB 20

Smith, Wilbur (Addison) 1933- ..... **CLC 33**
See also CA 13-16R; CANR 7, 46; MTCW

Smith, William Jay 1918- .... **CLC 6**
See also CA 5-8R; CANR 44; DLB 5; MAICYA; SAAS 22; SATA 2, 68

Smith, Woodrow Wilson
See Kuttner, Henry

Smolenskin, Peretz 1842-1885.... **NCLC 30**

Smollett, Tobias (George) 1721-1771 .. **LC 2**
See also CDBLB 1660-1789; DLB 39, 104

Snodgrass, W(illiam) D(e Witt)
1926- .... **CLC 2, 6, 10, 18, 68; DAM POET**
See also CA 1-4R; CANR 6, 36; DLB 5; MTCW

Snow, C(harles) P(ercy)
1905-1980 .... **CLC 1, 4, 6, 9, 13, 19; DAM NOV**
See also CA 5-8R; 101; CANR 28; CDBLB 1945-1960; DLB 15, 77; MTCW

Snow, Frances Compton
See Adams, Henry (Brooks)

Snyder, Gary (Sherman)
1930- .. **CLC 1, 2, 5, 9, 32; DAM POET**
See also CA 17-20R; CANR 30; DLB 5, 16, 165

Snyder, Zilpha Keatley 1927- ...... **CLC 17**
See also AAYA 15; CA 9-12R; CANR 38; CLR 31; JRDA; MAICYA; SAAS 2; SATA 1, 28, 75

Soares, Bernardo
See Pessoa, Fernando (Antonio Nogueira)

Sobh, A.
See Shamlu, Ahmad

Sobol, Joshua..................... **CLC 60**

Soderberg, Hjalmar 1869-1941 .... **TCLC 39**

Sodergran, Edith (Irene)
See Soedergran, Edith (Irene)

Soedergran, Edith (Irene)
1892-1923 .... **TCLC 31**

Softly, Edgar
See Lovecraft, H(oward) P(hillips)

Softly, Edward
See Lovecraft, H(oward) P(hillips)

Sokolov, Raymond 1941- .... **CLC 7**
See also CA 85-88

Solo, Jay
See Ellison, Harlan (Jay)

Sologub, Fyodor .... **TCLC 9**
See also Teternikov, Fyodor Kuzmich

Solomons, Ikey Esquir
See Thackeray, William Makepeace

Solomos, Dionysios 1798-1857 ... **NCLC 15**

Solwoska, Mara
See French, Marilyn

Solzhenitsyn, Aleksandr I(sayevich)
1918- ...... **CLC 1, 2, 4, 7, 9, 10, 18, 26, 34, 78; DA; DAB; DAC; DAM MST, NOV; WLC**
See also AITN 1; CA 69-72; CANR 40; MTCW

Somers, Jane
See Lessing, Doris (May)

Somerville, Edith 1858-1949 ...... **TCLC 51**
See also DLB 135

Somerville & Ross
See Martin, Violet Florence; Somerville, Edith

Sommer, Scott 1951- .... **CLC 25**
See also CA 106

Sondheim, Stephen (Joshua)
1930- .... **CLC 30, 39; DAM DRAM**
See also AAYA 11; CA 103; CANR 47

Sontag, Susan
1933- .... **CLC 1, 2, 10, 13, 31; DAM POP**
See also CA 17-20R; CANR 25, 51; DLB 2, 67; MTCW

Sophocles
496(?)B.C.-406(?)B.C..... **CMLC 2; DA; DAB; DAC; DAM DRAM, MST; DC 1**

Sordello 1189-1269............. **CMLC 15**

Sorel, Julia
See Drexler, Rosalyn

Sorrentino, Gilbert
1929- .... **CLC 3, 7, 14, 22, 40**
See also CA 77-80; CANR 14, 33; DLB 5; DLBY 80; INT CANR-14

Soto, Gary
1952- .... **CLC 32, 80; DAM MULT; HLC**
See also AAYA 10; CA 119; 125; CANR 50; CLR 38; DLB 82; HW; INT 125; JRDA; SATA 80

Soupault, Philippe 1897-1990 ...... **CLC 68**
See also CA 116; 147; 131

Souster, (Holmes) Raymond
1921- ... **CLC 5, 14; DAC; DAM POET**
See also CA 13-16R; CAAS 14; CANR 13, 29, 53; DLB 88; SATA 63

Southern, Terry 1924(?)-1995 .... **CLC 7**
See also CA 1-4R; 150; CANR 1; DLB 2

Southey, Robert 1774-1843 .... **NCLC 8**
See also DLB 93, 107, 142; SATA 54

Southworth, Emma Dorothy Eliza Nevitte
1819-1899 .... **NCLC 26**

Souza, Ernest
See Scott, Evelyn

Soyinka, Wole
1934- .... **CLC 3, 5, 14, 36, 44; BLC; DA; DAB; DAC; DAM DRAM, MST, MULT; DC 2; WLC**
See also BW 2; CA 13-16R; CANR 27, 39; DLB 125; MTCW

Spackman, W(illiam) M(ode)
1905-1990 .... **CLC 46**
See also CA 81-84; 132

Spacks, Barry 1931-.............. **CLC 14**
See also CA 29-32R; CANR 33; DLB 105

Spanidou, Irini 1946- .... **CLC 44**

Spark, Muriel (Sarah)
1918- ..... **CLC 2, 3, 5, 8, 13, 18, 40, 94; DAB; DAC; DAM MST, NOV; SSC 10**
See also CA 5-8R; CANR 12, 36; CDBLB 1945-1960; DLB 15, 139; INT CANR-12; MTCW

Spaulding, Douglas
See Bradbury, Ray (Douglas)

Spaulding, Leonard
See Bradbury, Ray (Douglas)

Spence, J. A. D.
See Eliot, T(homas) S(tearns)

Spencer, Elizabeth 1921- .... **CLC 22**
See also CA 13-16R; CANR 32; DLB 6; MTCW; SATA 14

Spencer, Leonard G.
See Silverberg, Robert

Spencer, Scott 1945-.............. **CLC 30**
See also CA 113; CANR 51; DLBY 86

Spender, Stephen (Harold)
1909-1995 ...... **CLC 1, 2, 5, 10, 41, 91; DAM POET**
See also CA 9-12R; 149; CANR 31; CDBLB 1945-1960; DLB 20; MTCW

Spengler, Oswald (Arnold Gottfried)
1880-1936 .... **TCLC 25**
See also CA 118

Spenser, Edmund
1552(?)-1599 .... **LC 5; DA; DAB; DAC; DAM MST, POET; PC 8; WLC**
See also CDBLB Before 1660; DLB 167

Spicer, Jack
1925-1965 .... **CLC 8, 18, 72; DAM POET**
See also CA 85-88; DLB 5, 16

Spiegelman, Art 1948- .... **CLC 76**
See also AAYA 10; CA 125; CANR 41

Spielberg, Peter 1929- .... **CLC 6**
See also CA 5-8R; CANR 4, 48; DLBY 81

Spielberg, Steven 1947- . . . . **CLC 20**
See also AAYA 8; CA 77-80; CANR 32; SATA 32

Spillane, Frank Morrison 1918-
See Spillane, Mickey
See also CA 25-28R; CANR 28; MTCW; SATA 66

Spillane, Mickey . . . . **CLC 3, 13**
See also Spillane, Frank Morrison

Spinoza, Benedictus de 1632-1677 . . . . **LC 9**

Spinrad, Norman (Richard) 1940- . . . **CLC 46**
See also CA 37-40R; CAAS 19; CANR 20; DLB 8; INT CANR-20

Spitteler, Carl (Friedrich Georg)
1845-1924 . . . . **TCLC 12**
See also CA 109; DLB 129

Spivack, Kathleen (Romola Drucker)
1938- . . . . **CLC 6**
See also CA 49-52

Spoto, Donald 1941- . . . . **CLC 39**
See also CA 65-68; CANR 11

Springsteen, Bruce (F.) 1949- . . . . . . **CLC 17**
See also CA 111

Spurling, Hilary 1940- . . . . **CLC 34**
See also CA 104; CANR 25, 52

Spyker, John Howland
See Elman, Richard

Squires, (James) Radcliffe
1917-1993 . . . . **CLC 51**
See also CA 1-4R; 140; CANR 6, 21

Srivastava, Dhanpat Rai 1880(?)-1936
See Premchand
See also CA 118

Stacy, Donald
See Pohl, Frederik

Stael, Germaine de
See Stael-Holstein, Anne Louise Germaine Necker Baronn
See also DLB 119

Stael-Holstein, Anne Louise Germaine Necker Baronn 1766-1817 . . . . **NCLC 3**
See also Stael, Germaine de

Stafford, Jean 1915-1979 . . . **CLC 4, 7, 19, 68**
See also CA 1-4R; 85-88; CANR 3; DLB 2; MTCW; SATA-Obit 22

Stafford, William (Edgar)
1914-1993 . . . **CLC 4, 7, 29; DAM POET**
See also CA 5-8R; 142; CAAS 3; CANR 5, 22; DLB 5; INT CANR-22

Staines, Trevor
See Brunner, John (Kilian Houston)

Stairs, Gordon
See Austin, Mary (Hunter)

Stannard, Martin 1947- . . . . **CLC 44**
See also CA 142; DLB 155

Stanton, Maura 1946- . . . . **CLC 9**
See also CA 89-92; CANR 15; DLB 120

Stanton, Schuyler
See Baum, L(yman) Frank

Stapledon, (William) Olaf
1886-1950 . . . . **TCLC 22**
See also CA 111; DLB 15

Starbuck, George (Edwin)
1931- . . . . **CLC 53; DAM POET**
See also CA 21-24R; CANR 23

Stark, Richard
See Westlake, Donald E(dwin)

Staunton, Schuyler
See Baum, L(yman) Frank

Stead, Christina (Ellen)
1902-1983 . . . . **CLC 2, 5, 8, 32, 80**
See also CA 13-16R; 109; CANR 33, 40; MTCW

Stead, William Thomas
1849-1912 . . . . **TCLC 48**

Steele, Richard 1672-1729 . . . . **LC 18**
See also CDBLB 1660-1789; DLB 84, 101

Steele, Timothy (Reid) 1948- . . . . **CLC 45**
See also CA 93-96; CANR 16, 50; DLB 120

Steffens, (Joseph) Lincoln
1866-1936 . . . . **TCLC 20**
See also CA 117

Stegner, Wallace (Earle)
1909-1993 . . . **CLC 9, 49, 81; DAM NOV**
See also AITN 1; BEST 90:3; CA 1-4R; 141; CAAS 9; CANR 1, 21, 46; DLB 9; DLBY 93; MTCW

Stein, Gertrude
1874-1946 . . . . . . **TCLC 1, 6, 28, 48; DA; DAB; DAC; DAM MST, NOV, POET; WLC**
See also CA 104; 132; CDALB 1917-1929; DLB 4, 54, 86; MTCW

Steinbeck, John (Ernst)
1902-1968 . . . . . . **CLC 1, 5, 9, 13, 21, 34, 45, 75; DA; DAB; DAC; DAM DRAM, MST, NOV; SSC 11; WLC**
See also AAYA 12; CA 1-4R; 25-28R; CANR 1, 35; CDALB 1929-1941; DLB 7, 9; DLBD 2; MTCW; SATA 9

Steinem, Gloria 1934- . . . . **CLC 63**
See also CA 53-56; CANR 28, 51; MTCW

Steiner, George
1929- . . . . **CLC 24; DAM NOV**
See also CA 73-76; CANR 31; DLB 67; MTCW; SATA 62

Steiner, K. Leslie
See Delany, Samuel R(ay, Jr.)

Steiner, Rudolf 1861-1925 . . . . **TCLC 13**
See also CA 107

Stendhal
1783-1842 . . . . **NCLC 23, 46; DA; DAB; DAC; DAM MST, NOV; WLC**
See also DLB 119

Stephen, Leslie 1832-1904 . . . . **TCLC 23**
See also CA 123; DLB 57, 144

Stephen, Sir Leslie
See Stephen, Leslie

Stephen, Virginia
See Woolf, (Adeline) Virginia

Stephens, James 1882(?)-1950 . . . . . . **TCLC 4**
See also CA 104; DLB 19, 153, 162

Stephens, Reed
See Donaldson, Stephen R.

Steptoe, Lydia
See Barnes, Djuna

Sterchi, Beat 1949- . . . . **CLC 65**

Sterling, Brett
See Bradbury, Ray (Douglas); Hamilton, Edmond

Sterling, Bruce 1954- . . . . **CLC 72**
See also CA 119; CANR 44

Sterling, George 1869-1926 . . . . **TCLC 20**
See also CA 117; DLB 54

Stern, Gerald 1925- . . . . **CLC 40**
See also CA 81-84; CANR 28; DLB 105

Stern, Richard (Gustave) 1928- . . . **CLC 4, 39**
See also CA 1-4R; CANR 1, 25, 52; DLBY 87; INT CANR-25

Sternberg, Josef von 1894-1969 . . . . . **CLC 20**
See also CA 81-84

Sterne, Laurence
1713-1768 . . . . . . **LC 2; DA; DAB; DAC; DAM MST, NOV; WLC**
See also CDBLB 1660-1789; DLB 39

Sternheim, (William Adolf) Carl
1878-1942 . . . . **TCLC 8**
See also CA 105; DLB 56, 118

Stevens, Mark 1951- . . . . **CLC 34**
See also CA 122

Stevens, Wallace
1879-1955 . . . . **TCLC 3, 12, 45; DA; DAB; DAC; DAM MST, POET; PC 6; WLC**
See also CA 104; 124; CDALB 1929-1941; DLB 54; MTCW

Stevenson, Anne (Katharine)
1933- . . . . **CLC 7, 33**
See also CA 17-20R; CAAS 9; CANR 9, 33; DLB 40; MTCW

Stevenson, Robert Louis (Balfour)
1850-1894 . . . . . **NCLC 5, 14; DA; DAB; DAC; DAM MST, NOV; SSC 11; WLC**
See also CDBLB 1890-1914; CLR 10, 11; DLB 18, 57, 141, 156; DLBD 13; JRDA; MAICYA; YABC 2

Stewart, J(ohn) I(nnes) M(ackintosh)
1906-1994 . . . . **CLC 7, 14, 32**
See also CA 85-88; 147; CAAS 3; CANR 47; MTCW

Stewart, Mary (Florence Elinor)
1916- . . . . **CLC 7, 35; DAB**
See also CA 1-4R; CANR 1; SATA 12

Stewart, Mary Rainbow
See Stewart, Mary (Florence Elinor)

Stifle, June
See Campbell, Maria

Stifter, Adalbert 1805-1868 . . . . . . **NCLC 41**
See also DLB 133

Still, James 1906- . . . . **CLC 49**
See also CA 65-68; CAAS 17; CANR 10, 26; DLB 9; SATA 29

Sting
See Sumner, Gordon Matthew

Stirling, Arthur
See Sinclair, Upton (Beall)

Stitt, Milan 1941- . . . . **CLC 29**
See also CA 69-72

Stockton, Francis Richard 1834-1902
See Stockton, Frank R.
See also CA 108; 137; MAICYA; SATA 44

Swenson, May
1919-1989 .... **CLC 4, 14, 61; DA; DAB; DAC; DAM MST, POET; PC 14**
See also CA 5-8R; 130; CANR 36; DLB 5; MTCW; SATA 15

Swift, Augustus
See Lovecraft, H(oward) P(hillips)

Swift, Graham (Colin) 1949- .... **CLC 41, 88**
See also CA 117; 122; CANR 46

Swift, Jonathan
1667-1745 ...... **LC 1; DA; DAB; DAC; DAM MST, NOV, POET; PC 9; WLC**
See also CDBLB 1660-1789; DLB 39, 95, 101; SATA 19

Swinburne, Algernon Charles
1837-1909 ...... **TCLC 8, 36; DA; DAB; DAC; DAM MST, POET; WLC**
See also CA 105; 140; CDBLB 1832-1890; DLB 35, 57

Swinfen, Ann .... **CLC 34**

Swinnerton, Frank Arthur
1884-1982 .... **CLC 31**
See also CA 108; DLB 34

Swithen, John
See King, Stephen (Edwin)

Sylvia
See Ashton-Warner, Sylvia (Constance)

Symmes, Robert Edward
See Duncan, Robert (Edward)

Symonds, John Addington
1840-1893 .... **NCLC 34**
See also DLB 57, 144

Symons, Arthur 1865-1945 .... **TCLC 11**
See also CA 107; DLB 19, 57, 149

Symons, Julian (Gustave)
1912-1994 .... **CLC 2, 14, 32**
See also CA 49-52; 147; CAAS 3; CANR 3, 33; DLB 87, 155; DLBY 92; MTCW

Synge, (Edmund) J(ohn) M(illington)
1871-1909 .... **TCLC 6, 37; DAM DRAM; DC 2**
See also CA 104; 141; CDBLB 1890-1914; DLB 10, 19

Syruc, J.
See Milosz, Czeslaw

Szirtes, George 1948- .... **CLC 46**
See also CA 109; CANR 27

Tabori, George 1914- .... **CLC 19**
See also CA 49-52; CANR 4

Tagore, Rabindranath
1861-1941 .... **TCLC 3, 53; DAM DRAM, POET; PC 8**
See also CA 104; 120; MTCW

Taine, Hippolyte Adolphe
1828-1893 .... **NCLC 15**

Talese, Gay 1932- .... **CLC 37**
See also AITN 1; CA 1-4R; CANR 9; INT CANR-9; MTCW

Tallent, Elizabeth (Ann) 1954- ..... **CLC 45**
See also CA 117; DLB 130

Tally, Ted 1952- .... **CLC 42**
See also CA 120; 124; INT 124

Tamayo y Baus, Manuel
1829-1898 .... **NCLC 1**

Tammsaare, A(nton) H(ansen)
1878-1940 .... **TCLC 27**

Tan, Amy
1952- .... **CLC 59; DAM MULT, NOV, POP**
See also AAYA 9; BEST 89:3; CA 136; SATA 75

Tandem, Felix
See Spitteler, Carl (Friedrich Georg)

Tanizaki, Jun'ichiro
1886-1965 ...... **CLC 8, 14, 28; SSC 21**
See also CA 93-96; 25-28R

Tanner, William
See Amis, Kingsley (William)

Tao Lao
See Storni, Alfonsina

Tarassoff, Lev
See Troyat, Henri

Tarbell, Ida M(inerva)
1857-1944 .... **TCLC 40**
See also CA 122; DLB 47

Tarkington, (Newton) Booth
1869-1946 .... **TCLC 9**
See also CA 110; 143; DLB 9, 102; SATA 17

Tarkovsky, Andrei (Arsenyevich)
1932-1986 .... **CLC 75**
See also CA 127

Tartt, Donna 1964(?)- .... **CLC 76**
See also CA 142

Tasso, Torquato 1544-1595 .... **LC 5**

Tate, (John Orley) Allen
1899-1979 .... **CLC 2, 4, 6, 9, 11, 14, 24**
See also CA 5-8R; 85-88; CANR 32; DLB 4, 45, 63; MTCW

Tate, Ellalice
See Hibbert, Eleanor Alice Burford

Tate, James (Vincent) 1943- ... **CLC 2, 6, 25**
See also CA 21-24R; CANR 29; DLB 5

Tavel, Ronald 1940- .... **CLC 6**
See also CA 21-24R; CANR 33

Taylor, C(ecil) P(hilip) 1929-1981 ... **CLC 27**
See also CA 25-28R; 105; CANR 47

Taylor, Edward
1642(?)-1729 .... **LC 11; DA; DAB; DAC; DAM MST, POET**
See also DLB 24

Taylor, Eleanor Ross 1920- .... **CLC 5**
See also CA 81-84

Taylor, Elizabeth 1912-1975 ... **CLC 2, 4, 29**
See also CA 13-16R; CANR 9; DLB 139; MTCW; SATA 13

Taylor, Henry (Splawn) 1942- ...... **CLC 44**
See also CA 33-36R; CAAS 7; CANR 31; DLB 5

Taylor, Kamala (Purnaiya) 1924-
See Markandaya, Kamala
See also CA 77-80

Taylor, Mildred D. .... **CLC 21**
See also AAYA 10; BW 1; CA 85-88; CANR 25; CLR 9; DLB 52; JRDA; MAICYA; SAAS 5; SATA 15, 70

Taylor, Peter (Hillsman)
1917-1994 ..... **CLC 1, 4, 18, 37, 44, 50, 71; SSC 10**
See also CA 13-16R; 147; CANR 9, 50; DLBY 81, 94; INT CANR-9; MTCW

Taylor, Robert Lewis 1912- .... **CLC 14**
See also CA 1-4R; CANR 3; SATA 10

Tchekhov, Anton
See Chekhov, Anton (Pavlovich)

Teasdale, Sara 1884-1933 .... **TCLC 4**
See also CA 104; DLB 45; SATA 32

Tegner, Esaias 1782-1846 .... **NCLC 2**

Teilhard de Chardin, (Marie Joseph) Pierre
1881-1955 .... **TCLC 9**
See also CA 105

Temple, Ann
See Mortimer, Penelope (Ruth)

Tennant, Emma (Christina)
1937- .... **CLC 13, 52**
See also CA 65-68; CAAS 9; CANR 10, 38; DLB 14

Tenneshaw, S. M.
See Silverberg, Robert

Tennyson, Alfred
1809-1892 .... **NCLC 30; DA; DAB; DAC; DAM MST, POET; PC 6; WLC**
See also CDBLB 1832-1890; DLB 32

Teran, Lisa St. Aubin de .... **CLC 36**
See also St. Aubin de Teran, Lisa

Terence 195(?)B.C.-159B.C. ...... **CMLC 14**

Teresa de Jesus, St. 1515-1582 ...... **LC 18**

Terkel, Louis 1912-
See Terkel, Studs
See also CA 57-60; CANR 18, 45; MTCW

Terkel, Studs .... **CLC 38**
See also Terkel, Louis
See also AITN 1

Terry, C. V.
See Slaughter, Frank G(ill)

Terry, Megan 1932- .... **CLC 19**
See also CA 77-80; CABS 3; CANR 43; DLB 7

Tertz, Abram
See Sinyavsky, Andrei (Donatevich)

Tesich, Steve 1943(?)-1996 ...... **CLC 40, 69**
See also CA 105; 152; DLBY 83

Teternikov, Fyodor Kuzmich 1863-1927
See Sologub, Fyodor
See also CA 104

Tevis, Walter 1928-1984 .... **CLC 42**
See also CA 113

Tey, Josephine .... **TCLC 14**
See also Mackintosh, Elizabeth
See also DLB 77

Thackeray, William Makepeace
1811-1863 .... **NCLC 5, 14, 22, 43; DA; DAB; DAC; DAM MST, NOV; WLC**
See also CDBLB 1832-1890; DLB 21, 55, 159, 163; SATA 23

Thakura, Ravindranatha
See Tagore, Rabindranath

Tharoor, Shashi 1956- .... **CLC 70**
See also CA 141

Thelwell, Michael Miles 1939- ..... **CLC 22**
See also BW 2; CA 101

Theobald, Lewis, Jr.
See Lovecraft, H(oward) P(hillips)

Theodorescu, Ion N. 1880-1967
See Arghezi, Tudor
See also CA 116

Theriault, Yves
1915-1983 .. **CLC 79; DAC; DAM MST**
See also CA 102; DLB 88

Theroux, Alexander (Louis)
1939- .... **CLC 2, 25**
See also CA 85-88; CANR 20

Theroux, Paul (Edward)
1941- .... **CLC 5, 8, 11, 15, 28, 46; DAM POP**
See also BEST 89:4; CA 33-36R; CANR 20, 45; DLB 2; MTCW; SATA 44

Thesen, Sharon 1946- .... **CLC 56**

Thevenin, Denis
See Duhamel, Georges

Thibault, Jacques Anatole Francois
1844-1924
See France, Anatole
See also CA 106; 127; DAM NOV; MTCW

Thiele, Colin (Milton) 1920- .... **CLC 17**
See also CA 29-32R; CANR 12, 28, 53; CLR 27; MAICYA; SAAS 2; SATA 14, 72

Thomas, Audrey (Callahan)
1935- .... **CLC 7, 13, 37; SSC 20**
See also AITN 2; CA 21-24R; CAAS 19; CANR 36; DLB 60; MTCW

Thomas, D(onald) M(ichael)
1935- .... **CLC 13, 22, 31**
See also CA 61-64; CAAS 11; CANR 17, 45; CDBLB 1960 to Present; DLB 40; INT CANR-17; MTCW

Thomas, Dylan (Marlais)
1914-1953 ... **TCLC 1, 8, 45; DA; DAB; DAC; DAM DRAM, MST, POET; PC 2; SSC 3; WLC**
See also CA 104; 120; CDBLB 1945-1960; DLB 13, 20, 139; MTCW; SATA 60

Thomas, (Philip) Edward
1878-1917 ...... **TCLC 10; DAM POET**
See also CA 106; DLB 19

Thomas, Joyce Carol 1938- .... **CLC 35**
See also AAYA 12; BW 2; CA 113; 116; CANR 48; CLR 19; DLB 33; INT 116; JRDA; MAICYA; MTCW; SAAS 7; SATA 40, 78

Thomas, Lewis 1913-1993 .... **CLC 35**
See also CA 85-88; 143; CANR 38; MTCW

Thomas, Paul
See Mann, (Paul) Thomas

Thomas, Piri 1928- .... **CLC 17**
See also CA 73-76; HW

Thomas, R(onald) S(tuart)
1913- .... **CLC 6, 13, 48; DAB; DAM POET**
See also CA 89-92; CAAS 4; CANR 30; CDBLB 1960 to Present; DLB 27; MTCW

Thomas, Ross (Elmore) 1926-1995 .. **CLC 39**
See also CA 33-36R; 150; CANR 22

Thompson, Francis Clegg
See Mencken, H(enry) L(ouis)

Thompson, Francis Joseph
1859-1907 .... **TCLC 4**
See also CA 104; CDBLB 1890-1914; DLB 19

Thompson, Hunter S(tockton)
1939- .... **CLC 9, 17, 40; DAM POP**
See also BEST 89:1; CA 17-20R; CANR 23, 46; MTCW

Thompson, James Myers
See Thompson, Jim (Myers)

Thompson, Jim (Myers)
1906-1977(?) .... **CLC 69**
See also CA 140

Thompson, Judith .... **CLC 39**

Thomson, James
1700-1748 ..... **LC 16, 29; DAM POET**
See also DLB 95

Thomson, James
1834-1882 ..... **NCLC 18; DAM POET**
See also DLB 35

Thoreau, Henry David
1817-1862 ..... **NCLC 7, 21; DA; DAB; DAC; DAM MST; WLC**
See also CDALB 1640-1865; DLB 1

Thornton, Hall
See Silverberg, Robert

Thucydides c. 455B.C.-399B.C. ... **CMLC 17**

Thurber, James (Grover)
1894-1961 .... **CLC 5, 11, 25; DA; DAB; DAC; DAM DRAM, MST, NOV; SSC 1**
See also CA 73-76; CANR 17, 39; CDALB 1929-1941; DLB 4, 11, 22, 102; MAICYA; MTCW; SATA 13

Thurman, Wallace (Henry)
1902-1934 .... **TCLC 6; BLC; DAM MULT**
See also BW 1; CA 104; 124; DLB 51

Ticheburn, Cheviot
See Ainsworth, William Harrison

Tieck, (Johann) Ludwig
1773-1853 .... **NCLC 5, 46**
See also DLB 90

Tiger, Derry
See Ellison, Harlan (Jay)

Tilghman, Christopher 1948(?)- ..... **CLC 65**

Tillinghast, Richard (Williford)
1940- .... **CLC 29**
See also CA 29-32R; CAAS 23; CANR 26, 51

Timrod, Henry 1828-1867 .... **NCLC 25**
See also DLB 3

Tindall, Gillian 1938- .... **CLC 7**
See also CA 21-24R; CANR 11

Tiptree, James, Jr. .... **CLC 48, 50**
See also Sheldon, Alice Hastings Bradley
See also DLB 8

Titmarsh, Michael Angelo
See Thackeray, William Makepeace

Tocqueville, Alexis (Charles Henri Maurice Clerel Comte) 1805-1859 ..... **NCLC 7**

Tolkien, J(ohn) R(onald) R(euel)
1892-1973 .... **CLC 1, 2, 3, 8, 12, 38; DA; DAB; DAC; DAM MST, NOV, POP; WLC**
See also AAYA 10; AITN 1; CA 17-18; 45-48; CANR 36; CAP 2; CDBLB 1914-1945; DLB 15, 160; JRDA; MAICYA; MTCW; SATA 2, 32; SATA-Obit 24

Toller, Ernst 1893-1939 .... **TCLC 10**
See also CA 107; DLB 124

Tolson, M. B.
See Tolson, Melvin B(eaunorus)

Tolson, Melvin B(eaunorus)
1898(?)-1966 .... **CLC 36; BLC; DAM MULT, POET**
See also BW 1; CA 124; 89-92; DLB 48, 76

Tolstoi, Aleksei Nikolaevich
See Tolstoy, Alexey Nikolaevich

Tolstoy, Alexey Nikolaevich
1882-1945 .... **TCLC 18**
See also CA 107

Tolstoy, Count Leo
See Tolstoy, Leo (Nikolaevich)

Tolstoy, Leo (Nikolaevich)
1828-1910 ...... **TCLC 4, 11, 17, 28, 44; DA; DAB; DAC; DAM MST, NOV; SSC 9; WLC**
See also CA 104; 123; SATA 26

Tomasi di Lampedusa, Giuseppe 1896-1957
See Lampedusa, Giuseppe (Tomasi) di
See also CA 111

Tomlin, Lily .... **CLC 17**
See also Tomlin, Mary Jean

Tomlin, Mary Jean 1939(?)-
See Tomlin, Lily
See also CA 117

Tomlinson, (Alfred) Charles
1927- .... **CLC 2, 4, 6, 13, 45; DAM POET**
See also CA 5-8R; CANR 33; DLB 40

Tonson, Jacob
See Bennett, (Enoch) Arnold

Toole, John Kennedy
1937-1969 .... **CLC 19, 64**
See also CA 104; DLBY 81

Toomer, Jean
1894-1967 ...... **CLC 1, 4, 13, 22; BLC; DAM MULT; PC 7; SSC 1**
See also BW 1; CA 85-88; CDALB 1917-1929; DLB 45, 51; MTCW

Torley, Luke
See Blish, James (Benjamin)

Tornimparte, Alessandra
See Ginzburg, Natalia

Torre, Raoul della
See Mencken, H(enry) L(ouis)

Torrey, E(dwin) Fuller 1937- .... **CLC 34**
See also CA 119

Torsvan, Ben Traven
See Traven, B.

Torsvan, Benno Traven
See Traven, B.

Torsvan, Berick Traven
See Traven, B.

Torsvan, Berwick Traven
See Traven, B.

Torsvan, Bruno Traven
See Traven, B.

Torsvan, Traven
See Traven, B.

Tournier, Michel (Edouard)
1924- . . . . **CLC 6, 23, 36, 95**
See also CA 49-52; CANR 3, 36; DLB 83; MTCW; SATA 23

Tournimparte, Alessandra
See Ginzburg, Natalia

Towers, Ivar
See Kornbluth, C(yril) M.

Towne, Robert (Burton) 1936(?)- . . . . **CLC 87**
See also CA 108; DLB 44

Townsend, Sue 1946- . . **CLC 61; DAB; DAC**
See also CA 119; 127; INT 127; MTCW; SATA 55; SATA-Brief 48

Townshend, Peter (Dennis Blandford)
1945- . . . . **CLC 17, 42**
See also CA 107

Tozzi, Federigo 1883-1920 . . . . **TCLC 31**

Traill, Catharine Parr
1802-1899 . . . . **NCLC 31**
See also DLB 99

Trakl, Georg 1887-1914 . . . . **TCLC 5**
See also CA 104

Transtroemer, Tomas (Goesta)
1931- . . . . **CLC 52, 65; DAM POET**
See also CA 117; 129; CAAS 17

Transtromer, Tomas Gosta
See Transtroemer, Tomas (Goesta)

Traven, B. (?)-1969 . . . . **CLC 8, 11**
See also CA 19-20; 25-28R; CAP 2; DLB 9, 56; MTCW

Treitel, Jonathan 1959- . . . . **CLC 70**

Tremain, Rose 1943- . . . . **CLC 42**
See also CA 97-100; CANR 44; DLB 14

Tremblay, Michel
1942- . . . . . . **CLC 29; DAC; DAM MST**
See also CA 116; 128; DLB 60; MTCW

Trevanian . . . . **CLC 29**
See also Whitaker, Rod(ney)

Trevor, Glen
See Hilton, James

Trevor, William
1928- . . . . . **CLC 7, 9, 14, 25, 71; SSC 21**
See also Cox, William Trevor
See also DLB 14, 139

Trifonov, Yuri (Valentinovich)
1925-1981 . . . . **CLC 45**
See also CA 126; 103; MTCW

Trilling, Lionel 1905-1975 . . . . **CLC 9, 11, 24**
See also CA 9-12R; 61-64; CANR 10; DLB 28, 63; INT CANR-10; MTCW

Trimball, W. H.
See Mencken, H(enry) L(ouis)

Tristan
See Gomez de la Serna, Ramon

Tristram
See Housman, A(lfred) E(dward)

Trogdon, William (Lewis) 1939-
See Heat-Moon, William Least
See also CA 115; 119; CANR 47; INT 119

Trollope, Anthony
1815-1882 . . . . . **NCLC 6, 33; DA; DAB; DAC; DAM MST, NOV; WLC**
See also CDBLB 1832-1890; DLB 21, 57, 159; SATA 22

Trollope, Frances 1779-1863 . . . . . **NCLC 30**
See also DLB 21, 166

Trotsky, Leon 1879-1940 . . . . **TCLC 22**
See also CA 118

Trotter (Cockburn), Catharine
1679-1749 . . . . **LC 8**
See also DLB 84

Trout, Kilgore
See Farmer, Philip Jose

Trow, George W. S. 1943- . . . . **CLC 52**
See also CA 126

Troyat, Henri 1911- . . . . **CLC 23**
See also CA 45-48; CANR 2, 33; MTCW

Trudeau, G(arretson) B(eekman) 1948-
See Trudeau, Garry B.
See also CA 81-84; CANR 31; SATA 35

Trudeau, Garry B. . . . . **CLC 12**
See also Trudeau, G(arretson) B(eekman)
See also AAYA 10; AITN 2

Truffaut, Francois 1932-1984 . . . . **CLC 20**
See also CA 81-84; 113; CANR 34

Trumbo, Dalton 1905-1976 . . . . **CLC 19**
See also CA 21-24R; 69-72; CANR 10; DLB 26

Trumbull, John 1750-1831 . . . . **NCLC 30**
See also DLB 31

Trundlett, Helen B.
See Eliot, T(homas) S(tearns)

Tryon, Thomas
1926-1991 . . . . . . **CLC 3, 11; DAM POP**
See also AITN 1; CA 29-32R; 135; CANR 32; MTCW

Tryon, Tom
See Tryon, Thomas

Ts'ao Hsueh-ch'in 1715(?)-1763 . . . . **LC 1**

Tsushima, Shuji 1909-1948
See Dazai, Osamu
See also CA 107

Tsvetaeva (Efron), Marina (Ivanovna)
1892-1941 . . . . **TCLC 7, 35; PC 14**
See also CA 104; 128; MTCW

Tuck, Lily 1938- . . . . **CLC 70**
See also CA 139

Tu Fu 712-770 . . . . **PC 9**
See also DAM MULT

Tunis, John R(oberts) 1889-1975 . . . **CLC 12**
See also CA 61-64; DLB 22; JRDA; MAICYA; SATA 37; SATA-Brief 30

Tuohy, Frank . . . . **CLC 37**
See also Tuohy, John Francis
See also DLB 14, 139

Tuohy, John Francis 1925-
See Tuohy, Frank
See also CA 5-8R; CANR 3, 47

Turco, Lewis (Putnam) 1934- . . . **CLC 11, 63**
See also CA 13-16R; CAAS 22; CANR 24, 51; DLBY 84

Turgenev, Ivan
1818-1883 . . . . **NCLC 21; DA; DAB; DAC; DAM MST, NOV; SSC 7; WLC**

Turgot, Anne-Robert-Jacques
1727-1781 . . . . **LC 26**

Turner, Frederick 1943- . . . . **CLC 48**
See also CA 73-76; CAAS 10; CANR 12, 30; DLB 40

Tutu, Desmond M(pilo)
1931- . . . . . **CLC 80; BLC; DAM MULT**
See also BW 1; CA 125

Tutuola, Amos
1920- . . . . **CLC 5, 14, 29; BLC; DAM MULT**
See also BW 2; CA 9-12R; CANR 27; DLB 125; MTCW

Twain, Mark
. . . . . **TCLC 6, 12, 19, 36, 48, 59; SSC 6; WLC**
See also Clemens, Samuel Langhorne
See also DLB 11, 12, 23, 64, 74

Tyler, Anne
1941- . . . . **CLC 7, 11, 18, 28, 44, 59; DAM NOV, POP**
See also AAYA 18; BEST 89:1; CA 9-12R; CANR 11, 33, 53; DLB 6, 143; DLBY 82; MTCW; SATA 7

Tyler, Royall 1757-1826 . . . . **NCLC 3**
See also DLB 37

Tynan, Katharine 1861-1931 . . . . **TCLC 3**
See also CA 104; DLB 153

Tyutchev, Fyodor 1803-1873 . . . . . **NCLC 34**

Tzara, Tristan . . . . **CLC 47; DAM POET**
See also Rosenfeld, Samuel

Uhry, Alfred
1936- . . . . . **CLC 55; DAM DRAM, POP**
See also CA 127; 133; INT 133

Ulf, Haerved
See Strindberg, (Johan) August

Ulf, Harved
See Strindberg, (Johan) August

Ulibarri, Sabine R(eyes)
1919- . . . . **CLC 83; DAM MULT**
See also CA 131; DLB 82; HW

Unamuno (y Jugo), Miguel de
1864-1936 . . . **TCLC 2, 9; DAM MULT, NOV; HLC; SSC 11**
See also CA 104; 131; DLB 108; HW; MTCW

Undercliffe, Errol
See Campbell, (John) Ramsey

Underwood, Miles
See Glassco, John

Undset, Sigrid
1882-1949 . . . . **TCLC 3; DA; DAB; DAC; DAM MST, NOV; WLC**
See also CA 104; 129; MTCW

Ungaretti, Giuseppe
1888-1970 . . . . **CLC 7, 11, 15**
See also CA 19-20; 25-28R; CAP 2; DLB 114

Villiers de l'Isle Adam, Jean Marie Mathias Philippe Auguste Comte 1838-1889 . . . . **NCLC 3; SSC 14**
See also DLB 123

Villon, Francois 1431-1463(?) . . . . **PC 13**

Vinci, Leonardo da 1452-1519 . . . . **LC 12**

Vine, Barbara . . . . **CLC 50**
See also Rendell, Ruth (Barbara)
See also BEST 90:4

Vinge, Joan D(ennison) 1948- . . . . . . **CLC 30**
See also CA 93-96; SATA 36

Violis, G.
See Simenon, Georges (Jacques Christian)

Visconti, Luchino 1906-1976 . . . . **CLC 16**
See also CA 81-84; 65-68; CANR 39

Vittorini, Elio 1908-1966 . . . . . . **CLC 6, 9, 14**
See also CA 133; 25-28R

Vizinczey, Stephen 1933- . . . . **CLC 40**
See also CA 128; INT 128

Vliet, R(ussell) G(ordon) 1929-1984 . . . . **CLC 22**
See also CA 37-40R; 112; CANR 18

Vogau, Boris Andreyevich 1894-1937(?)
See Pilnyak, Boris
See also CA 123

Vogel, Paula A(nne) 1951- . . . . **CLC 76**
See also CA 108

Voight, Ellen Bryant 1943- . . . . **CLC 54**
See also CA 69-72; CANR 11, 29; DLB 120

Voigt, Cynthia 1942- . . . . **CLC 30**
See also AAYA 3; CA 106; CANR 18, 37, 40; CLR 13; INT CANR-18; JRDA; MAICYA; SATA 48, 79; SATA-Brief 33

Voinovich, Vladimir (Nikolaevich) 1932- . . . . **CLC 10, 49**
See also CA 81-84; CAAS 12; CANR 33; MTCW

Vollmann, William T. 1959- . . . . . . **CLC 89; DAM NOV, POP**
See also CA 134

Voloshinov, V. N.
See Bakhtin, Mikhail Mikhailovich

Voltaire 1694-1778 . . . . . **LC 14; DA; DAB; DAC; DAM DRAM, MST; SSC 12; WLC**

von Daeniken, Erich 1935- . . . . **CLC 30**
See also AITN 1; CA 37-40R; CANR 17, 44

von Daniken, Erich
See von Daeniken, Erich

von Heidenstam, (Carl Gustaf) Verner
See Heidenstam, (Carl Gustaf) Verner von

von Heyse, Paul (Johann Ludwig)
See Heyse, Paul (Johann Ludwig von)

von Hofmannsthal, Hugo
See Hofmannsthal, Hugo von

von Horvath, Odon
See Horvath, Oedoen von

von Horvath, Oedoen
See Horvath, Oedoen von

von Liliencron, (Friedrich Adolf Axel) Detlev
See Liliencron, (Friedrich Adolf Axel) Detlev von

Vonnegut, Kurt, Jr. 1922- . . . . . . **CLC 1, 2, 3, 4, 5, 8, 12, 22, 40, 60; DA; DAB; DAC; DAM MST, NOV, POP; SSC 8; WLC**
See also AAYA 6; AITN 1; BEST 90:4; CA 1-4R; CANR 1, 25, 49; CDALB 1968-1988; DLB 2, 8, 152; DLBD 3; DLBY 80; MTCW

Von Rachen, Kurt
See Hubbard, L(afayette) Ron(ald)

von Rezzori (d'Arezzo), Gregor
See Rezzori (d'Arezzo), Gregor von

von Sternberg, Josef
See Sternberg, Josef von

Vorster, Gordon 1924- . . . . **CLC 34**
See also CA 133

Vosce, Trudie
See Ozick, Cynthia

Voznesensky, Andrei (Andreievich) 1933- . . . . . . **CLC 1, 15, 57; DAM POET**
See also CA 89-92; CANR 37; MTCW

Waddington, Miriam 1917- . . . . **CLC 28**
See also CA 21-24R; CANR 12, 30; DLB 68

Wagman, Fredrica 1937- . . . . **CLC 7**
See also CA 97-100; INT 97-100

Wagner, Richard 1813-1883. . . . . . . **NCLC 9**
See also DLB 129

Wagner-Martin, Linda 1936- . . . . **CLC 50**

Wagoner, David (Russell) 1926- . . . . **CLC 3, 5, 15**
See also CA 1-4R; CAAS 3; CANR 2; DLB 5; SATA 14

Wah, Fred(erick James) 1939- . . . . . . **CLC 44**
See also CA 107; 141; DLB 60

Wahloo, Per 1926-1975 . . . . **CLC 7**
See also CA 61-64

Wahloo, Peter
See Wahloo, Per

Wain, John (Barrington) 1925-1994 . . . . **CLC 2, 11, 15, 46**
See also CA 5-8R; 145; CAAS 4; CANR 23; CDBLB 1960 to Present; DLB 15, 27, 139, 155; MTCW

Wajda, Andrzej 1926- . . . . **CLC 16**
See also CA 102

Wakefield, Dan 1932- . . . . **CLC 7**
See also CA 21-24R; CAAS 7

Wakoski, Diane 1937- . . . . **CLC 2, 4, 7, 9, 11, 40; DAM POET; PC 15**
See also CA 13-16R; CAAS 1; CANR 9; DLB 5; INT CANR-9

Wakoski-Sherbell, Diane
See Wakoski, Diane

Walcott, Derek (Alton) 1930- . . . . **CLC 2, 4, 9, 14, 25, 42, 67, 76; BLC; DAB; DAC; DAM MST, MULT, POET**
See also BW 2; CA 89-92; CANR 26, 47; DLB 117; DLBY 81; MTCW

Waldman, Anne 1945- . . . . **CLC 7**
See also CA 37-40R; CAAS 17; CANR 34; DLB 16

Waldo, E. Hunter
See Sturgeon, Theodore (Hamilton)

Waldo, Edward Hamilton
See Sturgeon, Theodore (Hamilton)

Walker, Alice (Malsenior) 1944- . . . . **CLC 5, 6, 9, 19, 27, 46, 58; BLC; DA; DAB; DAC; DAM MST, MULT, NOV, POET, POP; SSC 5**
See also AAYA 3; BEST 89:4; BW 2; CA 37-40R; CANR 9, 27, 49; CDALB 1968-1988; DLB 6, 33, 143; INT CANR-27; MTCW; SATA 31

Walker, David Harry 1911-1992. . . . **CLC 14**
See also CA 1-4R; 137; CANR 1; SATA 8; SATA-Obit 71

Walker, Edward Joseph 1934-
See Walker, Ted
See also CA 21-24R; CANR 12, 28, 53

Walker, George F. 1947- . . . . **CLC 44, 61; DAB; DAC; DAM MST**
See also CA 103; CANR 21, 43; DLB 60

Walker, Joseph A. 1935- . . . . **CLC 19; DAM DRAM, MST**
See also BW 1; CA 89-92; CANR 26; DLB 38

Walker, Margaret (Abigail) 1915- . . . . **CLC 1, 6; BLC; DAM MULT**
See also BW 2; CA 73-76; CANR 26; DLB 76, 152; MTCW

Walker, Ted . . . . **CLC 13**
See also Walker, Edward Joseph
See also DLB 40

Wallace, David Foster 1962- . . . . **CLC 50**
See also CA 132

Wallace, Dexter
See Masters, Edgar Lee

Wallace, (Richard Horatio) Edgar 1875-1932 . . . . **TCLC 57**
See also CA 115; DLB 70

Wallace, Irving 1916-1990 . . . . . **CLC 7, 13; DAM NOV, POP**
See also AITN 1; CA 1-4R; 132; CAAS 1; CANR 1, 27; INT CANR-27; MTCW

Wallant, Edward Lewis 1926-1962 . . . . **CLC 5, 10**
See also CA 1-4R; CANR 22; DLB 2, 28, 143; MTCW

Walley, Byron
See Card, Orson Scott

Walpole, Horace 1717-1797. . . . . **LC 2**
See also DLB 39, 104

Walpole, Hugh (Seymour) 1884-1941 . . . . **TCLC 5**
See also CA 104; DLB 34

Walser, Martin 1927- . . . . **CLC 27**
See also CA 57-60; CANR 8, 46; DLB 75, 124

Walser, Robert 1878-1956 . . . . **TCLC 18; SSC 20**
See also CA 118; DLB 66

Walsh, Jill Paton. . . . . **CLC 35**
See also Paton Walsh, Gillian
See also AAYA 11; CLR 2; DLB 161; SAAS 3

Walter, Villiam Christian
See Andersen, Hans Christian

Wambaugh, Joseph (Aloysius, Jr.)
1937- .... **CLC 3, 18; DAM NOV, POP**
See also AITN 1; BEST 89:3; CA 33-36R; CANR 42; DLB 6; DLBY 83; MTCW

Ward, Arthur Henry Sarsfield 1883-1959
See Rohmer, Sax
See also CA 108

Ward, Douglas Turner 1930-....... **CLC 19**
See also BW 1; CA 81-84; CANR 27; DLB 7, 38

Ward, Mary Augusta
See Ward, Mrs. Humphry

Ward, Mrs. Humphry
1851-1920 .... **TCLC 55**
See also DLB 18

Ward, Peter
See Faust, Frederick (Schiller)

Warhol, Andy 1928(?)-1987........ **CLC 20**
See also AAYA 12; BEST 89:4; CA 89-92; 121; CANR 34

Warner, Francis (Robert le Plastrier)
1937- .... **CLC 14**
See also CA 53-56; CANR 11

Warner, Marina 1946-............ **CLC 59**
See also CA 65-68; CANR 21

Warner, Rex (Ernest) 1905-1986.... **CLC 45**
See also CA 89-92; 119; DLB 15

Warner, Susan (Bogert)
1819-1885 .... **NCLC 31**
See also DLB 3, 42

Warner, Sylvia (Constance) Ashton
See Ashton-Warner, Sylvia (Constance)

Warner, Sylvia Townsend
1893-1978 .... **CLC 7, 19; SSC 23**
See also CA 61-64; 77-80; CANR 16; DLB 34, 139; MTCW

Warren, Mercy Otis 1728-1814... **NCLC 13**
See also DLB 31

Warren, Robert Penn
1905-1989 .... **CLC 1, 4, 6, 8, 10, 13, 18, 39, 53, 59; DA; DAB; DAC; DAM MST, NOV, POET; SSC 4; WLC**
See also AITN 1; CA 13-16R; 129; CANR 10, 47; CDALB 1968-1988; DLB 2, 48, 152; DLBY 80, 89; INT CANR-10; MTCW; SATA 46; SATA-Obit 63

Warshofsky, Isaac
See Singer, Isaac Bashevis

Warton, Thomas
1728-1790 .... **LC 15; DAM POET**
See also DLB 104, 109

Waruk, Kona
See Harris, (Theodore) Wilson

Warung, Price 1855-1911......... **TCLC 45**

Warwick, Jarvis
See Garner, Hugh

Washington, Alex
See Harris, Mark

Washington, Booker T(aliaferro)
1856-1915 .... **TCLC 10; BLC; DAM MULT**
See also BW 1; CA 114; 125; SATA 28

Washington, George 1732-1799...... **LC 25**
See also DLB 31

Wassermann, (Karl) Jakob
1873-1934 .... **TCLC 6**
See also CA 104; DLB 66

Wasserstein, Wendy
1950- .... **CLC 32, 59, 90; DAM DRAM; DC 4**
See also CA 121; 129; CABS 3; CANR 53; INT 129

Waterhouse, Keith (Spencer)
1929- .... **CLC 47**
See also CA 5-8R; CANR 38; DLB 13, 15; MTCW

Waters, Frank (Joseph)
1902-1995 .... **CLC 88**
See also CA 5-8R; 149; CAAS 13; CANR 3, 18; DLBY 86

Waters, Roger 1944-.............. **CLC 35**

Watkins, Frances Ellen
See Harper, Frances Ellen Watkins

Watkins, Gerrold
See Malzberg, Barry N(athaniel)

Watkins, Gloria 1955(?)-
See hooks, bell
See also BW 2; CA 143

Watkins, Paul 1964-.............. **CLC 55**
See also CA 132

Watkins, Vernon Phillips
1906-1967 .... **CLC 43**
See also CA 9-10; 25-28R; CAP 1; DLB 20

Watson, Irving S.
See Mencken, H(enry) L(ouis)

Watson, John H.
See Farmer, Philip Jose

Watson, Richard F.
See Silverberg, Robert

Waugh, Auberon (Alexander) 1939- .. **CLC 7**
See also CA 45-48; CANR 6, 22; DLB 14

Waugh, Evelyn (Arthur St. John)
1903-1966 ...... **CLC 1, 3, 8, 13, 19, 27, 44; DA; DAB; DAC; DAM MST, NOV, POP; WLC**
See also CA 85-88; 25-28R; CANR 22; CDBLB 1914-1945; DLB 15, 162; MTCW

Waugh, Harriet 1944- .... **CLC 6**
See also CA 85-88; CANR 22

Ways, C. R.
See Blount, Roy (Alton), Jr.

Waystaff, Simon
See Swift, Jonathan

Webb, (Martha) Beatrice (Potter)
1858-1943 .... **TCLC 22**
See also Potter, Beatrice
See also CA 117

Webb, Charles (Richard) 1939-...... **CLC 7**
See also CA 25-28R

Webb, James H(enry), Jr. 1946-.... **CLC 22**
See also CA 81-84

Webb, Mary (Gladys Meredith)
1881-1927 .... **TCLC 24**
See also CA 123; DLB 34

Webb, Mrs. Sidney
See Webb, (Martha) Beatrice (Potter)

Webb, Phyllis 1927-.............. **CLC 18**
See also CA 104; CANR 23; DLB 53

Webb, Sidney (James)
1859-1947 .... **TCLC 22**
See also CA 117

Webber, Andrew Lloyd............. **CLC 21**
See also Lloyd Webber, Andrew

Weber, Lenora Mattingly
1895-1971 .... **CLC 12**
See also CA 19-20; 29-32R; CAP 1; SATA 2; SATA-Obit 26

Webster, John
1579(?)-1634(?) ...... **LC 33; DA; DAB; DAC; DAM DRAM, MST; DC 2; WLC**
See also CDBLB Before 1660; DLB 58

Webster, Noah 1758-1843 .... **NCLC 30**

Wedekind, (Benjamin) Frank(lin)
1864-1918 ...... **TCLC 7; DAM DRAM**
See also CA 104; DLB 118

Weidman, Jerome 1913-............ **CLC 7**
See also AITN 2; CA 1-4R; CANR 1; DLB 28

Weil, Simone (Adolphine)
1909-1943 .... **TCLC 23**
See also CA 117

Weinstein, Nathan
See West, Nathanael

Weinstein, Nathan von Wallenstein
See West, Nathanael

Weir, Peter (Lindsay) 1944- .... **CLC 20**
See also CA 113; 123

Weiss, Peter (Ulrich)
1916-1982 .... **CLC 3, 15, 51; DAM DRAM**
See also CA 45-48; 106; CANR 3; DLB 69, 124

Weiss, Theodore (Russell)
1916- .... **CLC 3, 8, 14**
See also CA 9-12R; CAAS 2; CANR 46; DLB 5

Welch, (Maurice) Denton
1915-1948 .... **TCLC 22**
See also CA 121; 148

Welch, James
1940- ..... **CLC 6, 14, 52; DAM MULT, POP**
See also CA 85-88; CANR 42; NNAL

Weldon, Fay
1933- .... **CLC 6, 9, 11, 19, 36, 59; DAM POP**
See also CA 21-24R; CANR 16, 46; CDBLB 1960 to Present; DLB 14; INT CANR-16; MTCW

Wellek, Rene 1903-1995........... **CLC 28**
See also CA 5-8R; 150; CAAS 7; CANR 8; DLB 63; INT CANR-8

Weller, Michael 1942-......... **CLC 10, 53**
See also CA 85-88

Weller, Paul 1958-............... **CLC 26**

Wellershoff, Dieter 1925-.......... **CLC 46**
See also CA 89-92; CANR 16, 37

Welles, (George) Orson
1915-1985 .... **CLC 20, 80**
See also CA 93-96; 117

Wellman, Mac 1945- .... **CLC 65**

Wellman, Manly Wade 1903-1986 . . **CLC 49**
See also CA 1-4R; 118; CANR 6, 16, 44; SATA 6; SATA-Obit 47

Wells, Carolyn 1869(?)-1942 . . . . . . **TCLC 35**
See also CA 113; DLB 11

Wells, H(erbert) G(eorge) 1866-1946 . . . . **TCLC 6, 12, 19; DA; DAB; DAC; DAM MST, NOV; SSC 6; WLC**
See also AAYA 18; CA 110; 121; CDBLB 1914-1945; DLB 34, 70, 156; MTCW; SATA 20

Wells, Rosemary 1943-. . . . . **CLC 12**
See also AAYA 13; CA 85-88; CANR 48; CLR 16; MAICYA; SAAS 1; SATA 18, 69

Welty, Eudora 1909- . . . . . . **CLC 1, 2, 5, 14, 22, 33; DA; DAB; DAC; DAM MST, NOV; SSC 1; WLC**
See also CA 9-12R; CABS 1; CANR 32; CDALB 1941-1968; DLB 2, 102, 143; DLBD 12; DLBY 87; MTCW

Wen I-to 1899-1946 . . . . **TCLC 28**

Wentworth, Robert
See Hamilton, Edmond

Werfel, Franz (V.) 1890-1945 . . . . . . **TCLC 8**
See also CA 104; DLB 81, 124

Wergeland, Henrik Arnold 1808-1845 . . . . **NCLC 5**

Wersba, Barbara 1932-. . . . . **CLC 30**
See also AAYA 2; CA 29-32R; CANR 16, 38; CLR 3; DLB 52; JRDA; MAICYA; SAAS 2; SATA 1, 58

Wertmueller, Lina 1928- . . . . **CLC 16**
See also CA 97-100; CANR 39

Wescott, Glenway 1901-1987. . . . . . . **CLC 13**
See also CA 13-16R; 121; CANR 23; DLB 4, 9, 102

Wesker, Arnold 1932- . . . . **CLC 3, 5, 42; DAB; DAM DRAM**
See also CA 1-4R; CAAS 7; CANR 1, 33; CDBLB 1960 to Present; DLB 13; MTCW

Wesley, Richard (Errol) 1945-. . . . . . . **CLC 7**
See also BW 1; CA 57-60; CANR 27; DLB 38

Wessel, Johan Herman 1742-1785 . . . . **LC 7**

West, Anthony (Panther) 1914-1987 . . . . **CLC 50**
See also CA 45-48; 124; CANR 3, 19; DLB 15

West, C. P.
See Wodehouse, P(elham) G(renville)

West, (Mary) Jessamyn 1902-1984 . . . . **CLC 7, 17**
See also CA 9-12R; 112; CANR 27; DLB 6; DLBY 84; MTCW; SATA-Obit 37

West, Morris L(anglo) 1916-. . . . . **CLC 6, 33**
See also CA 5-8R; CANR 24, 49; MTCW

West, Nathanael 1903-1940 . . . . . **TCLC 1, 14, 44; SSC 16**
See also CA 104; 125; CDALB 1929-1941; DLB 4, 9, 28; MTCW

West, Owen
See Koontz, Dean R(ay)

West, Paul 1930- . . . . **CLC 7, 14, 96**
See also CA 13-16R; CAAS 7; CANR 22, 53; DLB 14; INT CANR-22

West, Rebecca 1892-1983 . . **CLC 7, 9, 31, 50**
See also CA 5-8R; 109; CANR 19; DLB 36; DLBY 83; MTCW

Westall, Robert (Atkinson) 1929-1993 . . . . **CLC 17**
See also AAYA 12; CA 69-72; 141; CANR 18; CLR 13; JRDA; MAICYA; SAAS 2; SATA 23, 69; SATA-Obit 75

Westlake, Donald E(dwin) 1933- . . . . **CLC 7, 33; DAM POP**
See also CA 17-20R; CAAS 13; CANR 16, 44; INT CANR-16

Westmacott, Mary
See Christie, Agatha (Mary Clarissa)

Weston, Allen
See Norton, Andre

Wetcheek, J. L.
See Feuchtwanger, Lion

Wetering, Janwillem van de
See van de Wetering, Janwillem

Wetherell, Elizabeth
See Warner, Susan (Bogert)

Whale, James 1889-1957 . . . . **TCLC 63**

Whalen, Philip 1923- . . . . **CLC 6, 29**
See also CA 9-12R; CANR 5, 39; DLB 16

Wharton, Edith (Newbold Jones) 1862-1937 . . . . . . **TCLC 3, 9, 27, 53; DA; DAB; DAC; DAM MST, NOV; SSC 6; WLC**
See also CA 104; 132; CDALB 1865-1917; DLB 4, 9, 12, 78; DLBD 13; MTCW

Wharton, James
See Mencken, H(enry) L(ouis)

Wharton, William (a pseudonym) . . . . **CLC 18, 37**
See also CA 93-96; DLBY 80; INT 93-96

Wheatley (Peters), Phillis 1754(?)-1784 . . . . **LC 3; BLC; DA; DAC; DAM MST, MULT, POET; PC 3; WLC**
See also CDALB 1640-1865; DLB 31, 50

Wheelock, John Hall 1886-1978 . . . . **CLC 14**
See also CA 13-16R; 77-80; CANR 14; DLB 45

White, E(lwyn) B(rooks) 1899-1985 . . **CLC 10, 34, 39; DAM POP**
See also AITN 2; CA 13-16R; 116; CANR 16, 37; CLR 1, 21; DLB 11, 22; MAICYA; MTCW; SATA 2, 29; SATA-Obit 44

White, Edmund (Valentine III) 1940- . . . . **CLC 27; DAM POP**
See also AAYA 7; CA 45-48; CANR 3, 19, 36; MTCW

White, Patrick (Victor Martindale) 1912-1990 . . **CLC 3, 4, 5, 7, 9, 18, 65, 69**
See also CA 81-84; 132; CANR 43; MTCW

White, Phyllis Dorothy James 1920-
See James, P. D.
See also CA 21-24R; CANR 17, 43; DAM POP; MTCW

White, T(erence) H(anbury) 1906-1964 . . . . **CLC 30**
See also CA 73-76; CANR 37; DLB 160; JRDA; MAICYA; SATA 12

White, Terence de Vere 1912-1994 . . . . **CLC 49**
See also CA 49-52; 145; CANR 3

White, Walter F(rancis) 1893-1955 . . . . **TCLC 15**
See also White, Walter
See also BW 1; CA 115; 124; DLB 51

White, William Hale 1831-1913
See Rutherford, Mark
See also CA 121

Whitehead, E(dward) A(nthony) 1933- . . . . **CLC 5**
See also CA 65-68

Whitemore, Hugh (John) 1936-. . . . . **CLC 37**
See also CA 132; INT 132

Whitman, Sarah Helen (Power) 1803-1878 . . . . **NCLC 19**
See also DLB 1

Whitman, Walt(er) 1819-1892 . . . . . **NCLC 4, 31; DA; DAB; DAC; DAM MST, POET; PC 3; WLC**
See also CDALB 1640-1865; DLB 3, 64; SATA 20

Whitney, Phyllis A(yame) 1903- . . . . **CLC 42; DAM POP**
See also AITN 2; BEST 90:3; CA 1-4R; CANR 3, 25, 38; JRDA; MAICYA; SATA 1, 30

Whittemore, (Edward) Reed (Jr.) 1919- . . . . **CLC 4**
See also CA 9-12R; CAAS 8; CANR 4; DLB 5

Whittier, John Greenleaf 1807-1892 . . . . **NCLC 8**
See also DLB 1

Whittlebot, Hernia
See Coward, Noel (Peirce)

Wicker, Thomas Grey 1926-
See Wicker, Tom
See also CA 65-68; CANR 21, 46

Wicker, Tom . . . . **CLC 7**
See also Wicker, Thomas Grey

Wideman, John Edgar 1941- . . . . **CLC 5, 34, 36, 67; BLC; DAM MULT**
See also BW 2; CA 85-88; CANR 14, 42; DLB 33, 143

Wiebe, Rudy (Henry) 1934- . . . . **CLC 6, 11, 14; DAC; DAM MST**
See also CA 37-40R; CANR 42; DLB 60

Wieland, Christoph Martin 1733-1813 . . . . **NCLC 17**
See also DLB 97

Wiene, Robert 1881-1938. . . . . **TCLC 56**

Wieners, John 1934-. . . . . **CLC 7**
See also CA 13-16R; DLB 16

Wister, Owen 1860-1938 .... **TCLC 21**
See also CA 108; DLB 9, 78; SATA 62

Witkacy
See Witkiewicz, Stanislaw Ignacy

Witkiewicz, Stanislaw Ignacy
1885-1939 .... **TCLC 8**
See also CA 105

Wittgenstein, Ludwig (Josef Johann)
1889-1951 .... **TCLC 59**
See also CA 113

Wittig, Monique 1935(?)-.......... **CLC 22**
See also CA 116; 135; DLB 83

Wittlin, Jozef 1896-1976 .... **CLC 25**
See also CA 49-52; 65-68; CANR 3

Wodehouse, P(elham) G(renville)
1881-1975 ... **CLC 1, 2, 5, 10, 22; DAB; DAC; DAM NOV; SSC 2**
See also AITN 2; CA 45-48; 57-60; CANR 3, 33; CDBLB 1914-1945; DLB 34, 162; MTCW; SATA 22

Woiwode, L.
See Woiwode, Larry (Alfred)

Woiwode, Larry (Alfred) 1941-... **CLC 6, 10**
See also CA 73-76; CANR 16; DLB 6; INT CANR-16

Wojciechowska, Maia (Teresa)
1927- .... **CLC 26**
See also AAYA 8; CA 9-12R; CANR 4, 41; CLR 1; JRDA; MAICYA; SAAS 1; SATA 1, 28, 83

Wolf, Christa 1929- .... **CLC 14, 29, 58**
See also CA 85-88; CANR 45; DLB 75; MTCW

Wolfe, Gene (Rodman)
1931- .... **CLC 25; DAM POP**
See also CA 57-60; CAAS 9; CANR 6, 32; DLB 8

Wolfe, George C. 1954- .... **CLC 49**
See also CA 149

Wolfe, Thomas (Clayton)
1900-1938 ..... **TCLC 4, 13, 29, 61; DA; DAB; DAC; DAM MST, NOV; WLC**
See also CA 104; 132; CDALB 1929-1941; DLB 9, 102; DLBD 2; DLBY 85; MTCW

Wolfe, Thomas Kennerly, Jr. 1931-
See Wolfe, Tom
See also CA 13-16R; CANR 9, 33; DAM POP; INT CANR-9; MTCW

Wolfe, Tom .... **CLC 1, 2, 9, 15, 35, 51**
See also Wolfe, Thomas Kennerly, Jr.
See also AAYA 8; AITN 2; BEST 89:1; DLB 152

Wolff, Geoffrey (Ansell) 1937- ..... **CLC 41**
See also CA 29-32R; CANR 29, 43

Wolff, Sonia
See Levitin, Sonia (Wolff)

Wolff, Tobias (Jonathan Ansell)
1945- .... **CLC 39, 64**
See also AAYA 16; BEST 90:2; CA 114; 117; CAAS 22; DLB 130; INT 117

Wolfram von Eschenbach
c. 1170-c. 1220 .... **CMLC 5**
See also DLB 138

Wolitzer, Hilma 1930- .... **CLC 17**
See also CA 65-68; CANR 18, 40; INT CANR-18; SATA 31

Wollstonecraft, Mary 1759-1797...... **LC 5**
See also CDBLB 1789-1832; DLB 39, 104, 158

Wonder, Stevie .... **CLC 12**
See also Morris, Steveland Judkins

Wong, Jade Snow 1922-........... **CLC 17**
See also CA 109

Woodcott, Keith
See Brunner, John (Kilian Houston)

Woodruff, Robert W.
See Mencken, H(enry) L(ouis)

Woolf, (Adeline) Virginia
1882-1941 .... **TCLC 1, 5, 20, 43, 56; DA; DAB; DAC; DAM MST, NOV; SSC 7; WLC**
See also CA 104; 130; CDBLB 1914-1945; DLB 36, 100, 162; DLBD 10; MTCW

Woollcott, Alexander (Humphreys)
1887-1943 .... **TCLC 5**
See also CA 105; DLB 29

Woolrich, Cornell 1903-1968....... **CLC 77**
See also Hopley-Woolrich, Cornell George

Wordsworth, Dorothy
1771-1855 .... **NCLC 25**
See also DLB 107

Wordsworth, William
1770-1850 .... **NCLC 12, 38; DA; DAB; DAC; DAM MST, POET; PC 4; WLC**
See also CDBLB 1789-1832; DLB 93, 107

Wouk, Herman
1915- .. **CLC 1, 9, 38; DAM NOV, POP**
See also CA 5-8R; CANR 6, 33; DLBY 82; INT CANR-6; MTCW

Wright, Charles (Penzel, Jr.)
1935- .... **CLC 6, 13, 28**
See also CA 29-32R; CAAS 7; CANR 23, 36; DLB 165; DLBY 82; MTCW

Wright, Charles Stevenson
1932- .... **CLC 49; BLC 3; DAM MULT, POET**
See also BW 1; CA 9-12R; CANR 26; DLB 33

Wright, Jack R.
See Harris, Mark

Wright, James (Arlington)
1927-1980 .... **CLC 3, 5, 10, 28; DAM POET**
See also AITN 2; CA 49-52; 97-100; CANR 4, 34; DLB 5; MTCW

Wright, Judith (Arandell)
1915- .... **CLC 11, 53; PC 14**
See also CA 13-16R; CANR 31; MTCW; SATA 14

Wright, L(aurali) R. 1939-......... **CLC 44**
See also CA 138

Wright, Richard (Nathaniel)
1908-1960 .... **CLC 1, 3, 4, 9, 14, 21, 48, 74; BLC; DA; DAB; DAC; DAM MST, MULT, NOV; SSC 2; WLC**
See also AAYA 5; BW 1; CA 108; CDALB 1929-1941; DLB 76, 102; DLBD 2; MTCW

Wright, Richard B(ruce) 1937- ...... **CLC 6**
See also CA 85-88; DLB 53

Wright, Rick 1945-............... **CLC 35**

Wright, Rowland
See Wells, Carolyn

Wright, Stephen Caldwell 1946- .... **CLC 33**
See also BW 2

Wright, Willard Huntington 1888-1939
See Van Dine, S. S.
See also CA 115

Wright, William 1930- .... **CLC 44**
See also CA 53-56; CANR 7, 23

Wroth, LadyMary 1587-1653(?) ..... **LC 30**
See also DLB 121

Wu Ch'eng-en 1500(?)-1582(?)........ **LC 7**

Wu Ching-tzu 1701-1754 .... **LC 2**

Wurlitzer, Rudolph 1938(?)- ... **CLC 2, 4, 15**
See also CA 85-88

Wycherley, William
1641-1715 ..... **LC 8, 21; DAM DRAM**
See also CDBLB 1660-1789; DLB 80

Wylie, Elinor (Morton Hoyt)
1885-1928 .... **TCLC 8**
See also CA 105; DLB 9, 45

Wylie, Philip (Gordon) 1902-1971... **CLC 43**
See also CA 21-22; 33-36R; CAP 2; DLB 9

Wyndham, John.................. **CLC 19**
See also Harris, John (Wyndham Parkes Lucas) Beynon

Wyss, Johann David Von
1743-1818 .... **NCLC 10**
See also JRDA; MAICYA; SATA 29; SATA-Brief 27

Xenophon
c. 430B.C.-c. 354B.C......... **CMLC 17**

Yakumo Koizumi
See Hearn, (Patricio) Lafcadio (Tessima Carlos)

Yanez, Jose Donoso
See Donoso (Yanez), Jose

Yanovsky, Basile S.
See Yanovsky, V(assily) S(emenovich)

Yanovsky, V(assily) S(emenovich)
1906-1989 .... **CLC 2, 18**
See also CA 97-100; 129

Yates, Richard 1926-1992 ..... **CLC 7, 8, 23**
See also CA 5-8R; 139; CANR 10, 43; DLB 2; DLBY 81, 92; INT CANR-10

Yeats, W. B.
See Yeats, William Butler

Yeats, William Butler
1865-1939 ..... **TCLC 1, 11, 18, 31; DA; DAB; DAC; DAM DRAM, MST, POET; WLC**
See also CA 104; 127; CANR 45; CDBLB 1890-1914; DLB 10, 19, 98, 156; MTCW

Yehoshua, A(braham) B.
1936- .... **CLC 13, 31**
See also CA 33-36R; CANR 43

Yep, Laurence Michael 1948- ...... **CLC 35**
See also AAYA 5; CA 49-52; CANR 1, 46; CLR 3, 17; DLB 52; JRDA; MAICYA; SATA 7, 69

Yerby, Frank G(arvin) 1916-1991 . . . . **CLC 1, 7, 22; BLC; DAM MULT**
See also BW 1; CA 9-12R; 136; CANR 16, 52; DLB 76; INT CANR-16; MTCW

Yesenin, Sergei Alexandrovich
See Esenin, Sergei (Alexandrovich)

Yevtushenko, Yevgeny (Alexandrovich) 1933- . . . . **CLC 1, 3, 13, 26, 51; DAM POET**
See also CA 81-84; CANR 33; MTCW

Yezierska, Anzia 1885(?)-1970 . . . . . **CLC 46**
See also CA 126; 89-92; DLB 28; MTCW

Yglesias, Helen 1915- . . . . **CLC 7, 22**
See also CA 37-40R; CAAS 20; CANR 15; INT CANR-15; MTCW

Yokomitsu Riichi 1898-1947 . . . . . . **TCLC 47**

Yonge, Charlotte (Mary) 1823-1901 . . . . **TCLC 48**
See also CA 109; DLB 18, 163; SATA 17

York, Jeremy
See Creasey, John

York, Simon
See Heinlein, Robert A(nson)

Yorke, Henry Vincent 1905-1974 . . . **CLC 13**
See also Green, Henry
See also CA 85-88; 49-52

Yosano Akiko 1878-1942 . . **TCLC 59; PC 11**

Yoshimoto, Banana . . . . **CLC 84**
See also Yoshimoto, Mahoko

Yoshimoto, Mahoko 1964-
See Yoshimoto, Banana
See also CA 144

Young, Al(bert James) 1939- . . . . . **CLC 19; BLC; DAM MULT**
See also BW 2; CA 29-32R; CANR 26; DLB 33

Young, Andrew (John) 1885-1971 . . . . **CLC 5**
See also CA 5-8R; CANR 7, 29

Young, Collier
See Bloch, Robert (Albert)

Young, Edward 1683-1765 . . . . **LC 3**
See also DLB 95

Young, Marguerite (Vivian) 1909-1995 . . . . **CLC 82**
See also CA 13-16; 150; CAP 1

Young, Neil 1945- . . . . **CLC 17**
See also CA 110

Young Bear, Ray A. 1950- . . . . **CLC 94; DAM MULT**
See also CA 146; NNAL

Yourcenar, Marguerite 1903-1987 . . . . **CLC 19, 38, 50, 87; DAM NOV**
See also CA 69-72; CANR 23; DLB 72; DLBY 88; MTCW

Yurick, Sol 1925- . . . . **CLC 6**
See also CA 13-16R; CANR 25

Zabolotskii, Nikolai Alekseevich 1903-1958 . . . . **TCLC 52**
See also CA 116

Zamiatin, Yevgenii
See Zamyatin, Evgeny Ivanovich

Zamora, Bernice (B. Ortiz) 1938- . . . . . **CLC 89; DAM MULT; HLC**
See also CA 151; DLB 82; HW

Zamyatin, Evgeny Ivanovich 1884-1937 . . . . **TCLC 8, 37**
See also CA 105

Zangwill, Israel 1864-1926 . . . . **TCLC 16**
See also CA 109; DLB 10, 135

Zappa, Francis Vincent, Jr. 1940-1993
See Zappa, Frank
See also CA 108; 143

Zappa, Frank . . . . **CLC 17**
See also Zappa, Francis Vincent, Jr.

Zaturenska, Marya 1902-1982 . . . . **CLC 6, 11**
See also CA 13-16R; 105; CANR 22

Zelazny, Roger (Joseph) 1937-1995 . . . . **CLC 21**
See also AAYA 7; CA 21-24R; 148; CANR 26; DLB 8; MTCW; SATA 57; SATA-Brief 39

Zhdanov, Andrei A(lexandrovich) 1896-1948 . . . . **TCLC 18**
See also CA 117

Zhukovsky, Vasily 1783-1852 . . . . **NCLC 35**

Ziegenhagen, Eric . . . . **CLC 55**

Zimmer, Jill Schary
See Robinson, Jill

Zimmerman, Robert
See Dylan, Bob

Zindel, Paul 1936- . . . . . **CLC 6, 26; DA; DAB; DAC; DAM DRAM, MST, NOV; DC 5**
See also AAYA 2; CA 73-76; CANR 31; CLR 3; DLB 7, 52; JRDA; MAICYA; MTCW; SATA 16, 58

Zinov'Ev, A. A.
See Zinoviev, Alexander (Aleksandrovich)

Zinoviev, Alexander (Aleksandrovich) 1922- . . . . **CLC 19**
See also CA 116; 133; CAAS 10

Zoilus
See Lovecraft, H(oward) P(hillips)

Zola, Emile (Edouard Charles Antoine) 1840-1902 . . . . . . **TCLC 1, 6, 21, 41; DA; DAB; DAC; DAM MST, NOV; WLC**
See also CA 104; 138; DLB 123

Zoline, Pamela 1941- . . . . **CLC 62**

Zorrilla y Moral, Jose 1817-1893 . . **NCLC 6**

Zoshchenko, Mikhail (Mikhailovich) 1895-1958 . . . . **TCLC 15; SSC 15**
See also CA 115

Zuckmayer, Carl 1896-1977 . . . . **CLC 18**
See also CA 69-72; DLB 56, 124

Zuk, Georges
See Skelton, Robin

Zukofsky, Louis 1904-1978 . . . . **CLC 1, 2, 4, 7, 11, 18; DAM POET; PC 11**
See also CA 9-12R; 77-80; CANR 39; DLB 5, 165; MTCW

Zweig, Paul 1935-1984 . . . . **CLC 34, 42**
See also CA 85-88; 113

Zweig, Stefan 1881-1942 . . . . **TCLC 17**
See also CA 112; DLB 81, 118

Literary Criticism Series Cumulative Topic Index

This index lists all topic entries in Gale's *Classical and Medieval Literature Criticism, Contemporary Literary Criticism, Literature Criticism from 1400 to 1800, Nineteenth-Century Literature Criticism,* and *Twentieth-Century Literary Criticism.*

TCLC Cumulative Nationality Index

ESTONIAN

FINNISH

FRENCH

GERMAN

GHANIAN

GREEK

HAITIAN

HUNGARIAN

Zhdanov, Andrei A(lexandrovich) **18**
Zoshchenko, Mikhail (Mikhailovich) **15**

SCOTTISH
Barrie, J(ames) M(atthew) **2**
Bridie, James **3**
Brown, George Douglas **28**
Buchan, John **41**
Cunninghame Graham, R(obert) B(ontine) **19**
Davidson, John **24**
Frazer, J(ames) G(eorge) **32**
Gibbon, Lewis Grassic **4**
Lang, Andrew **16**
MacDonald, George **9**
Muir, Edwin **2**
Sharp, William **39**
Tey, Josephine **14**

SOUTH AFRICAN
Bosman, Herman Charles **49**
Campbell, (Ignatius) Roy (Dunnachie) **5**
Mqhayi, S(amuel) E(dward) K(rune Loliwe) **25**
Schreiner, Olive (Emilie Albertina) **9**
Smith, Pauline (Urmson) **25**
Vilakazi, Benedict Wallet **37**

SPANISH
Alas (y Urena), Leopoldo (Enrique Garcia) **29**
Barea, Arturo **14**
Baroja (y Nessi), Pio **8**
Benavente (y Martinez), Jacinto **3**
Blasco Ibanez, Vicente **12**
Echegaray (y Eizaguirre), Jose (Maria Waldo) **4**
Garcia Lorca, Federico **1, 7, 49**
Jimenez (Mantecon), Juan Ramon **4**
Machado (y Ruiz), Antonio **3**
Martinez Sierra, Gregorio **6**
Martinez Sierra, Maria (de la O'LeJarraga) **6**
Miro (Ferrer), Gabriel (Francisco Victor) **5**
Ortega y Gasset, Jose **9**
Pereda (y Sanchez de Porrua), Jose Maria de **16**
Perez Galdos, Benito **27**
Salinas (y Serrano), Pedro **17**
Unamuno (y Jugo), Miguel de **2, 9**
Valera y Alcala-Galiano, Juan **10**
Valle-Inclan, Ramon (Maria) del **5**

SWEDISH
Bengtsson, Frans (Gunnar) **48**
Dagerman, Stig (Halvard) **17**
Heidenstam, (Carl Gustaf) Verner von **5**
Key, Ellen **65**
Lagerloef, Selma (Ottiliana Lovisa) **4, 36**
Soderberg, Hjalmar **39**
Strindberg, (Johan) August **1, 8, 21, 47**

SWISS
Ramuz, Charles-Ferdinand **33**
Rod, Edouard **52**
Saussure, Ferdinand de **49**
Spitteler, Carl (Friedrich Georg) **12**
Walser, Robert **18**

SYRIAN
Gibran, Kahlil **1, 9**

TURKISH
Sait Faik **23**

UKRAINIAN
Aleichem, Sholom **1, 35**
Bialik, Chaim Nachman **25**

URUGUAYAN
Quiroga, Horacio (Sylvestre) **20**
Sanchez, Florencio **37**

WELSH
Davies, W(illiam) H(enry) **5**
Lewis, Alun **3**
Machen, Arthur **4**
Thomas, Dylan (Marlais) **1, 8, 45**

TCLC VOL 66

ISBN 0-7876-1164-6